Collins

Edexcel GCSE
Maths
4th Edition

Higher Student Book

Kevin Evans
Keith Gordon
Brian Speed
Michael Kent

William Collins' dream of knowledge for all began with the publication of his first book in 1819. A self-educated mill worker, he not only enriched millions of lives, but also founded a flourishing publishing house. Today, staying true to this spirit, Collins books are packed with inspiration, innovation and practical expertise. They place you at the centre of a world of possibility and give you exactly what you need to explore it.

Collins. Freedom to teach

Published by Collins
An imprint of HarperCollins*Publishers*
1 London Bridge Street
London SE1 9GF

1st Floor, Watermarque Building,
Ringsend Road, Dublin 4, Ireland

Browse the complete Collins catalogue at
www.collins.co.uk

© HarperCollins*Publishers* Limited 2015

10 9

ISBN 978-0-00-811381-0

A catalogue record for this book is available from the British Library

The authors Kevin Evans, Keith Gordon, Brian Speed and Michael Kent assert their moral rights to be identified as the authors of this work.

Commissioned by Lucy Rowland and Katie Sergeant
Project managed by Elektra Media Ltd and Hart McLeod Ltd
Development edited by Joan Miller and Joanna Shock
Copyedited by Marie Taylor
Proofread by Laura Booth, Rosie Parrish and Saskia Besier
Answers checked by Amanda Dickson
Edited by Jennifer Yong
Typeset by Jouve India Private Limited
Picture research by Hart McLeod Ltd
Illustrations by Ann Paganuzzi
Designed by Ken Vail Graphic Design
Cover design by We are Laura
Production by Rachel Weaver

Printed and bound by Grafica Veneta S.p.A. in Italy

Acknowledgements
The publishers gratefully acknowledge the permissions granted to reproduce copyright material in this book. Every effort has been made to contact the holders of copyright material, but if any have been inadvertently overlooked, the publisher will be pleased to make the necessary arrangements at the first opportunity.

The publishers would like to thank the following for permission to reproduce photographs in these pages:

Cover (bottom) Procy/Shutterstock, cover (top) joingate/Shutterstock, p 8 xtock/Shutterstock, p 18 megainarmy/Shutterstock, p 38 leungchopan/Shutterstock, p 45 Used with kind permission of Casio Electronics Co. Limited, p 58 leungchopan/Shutterstock, p 86 (main) apiguide/Shutterstock, p86 (inset) lrafael/Shutterstock p 116 David Madison/Getty, p 150 hxdbzxy/Shutterstock, p 178 chungking/Shutterstock p182 alkkdsg/Shutterstock, p 216 Lonely/Shutterstock, p 248 Ant Clausen/Shutterstock, p 274 Yellowj/Shutterstock, p 304 Lewis Tse Pui Lung/Shutterstock, p 344 ARCHITECTEUR/Shutterstock, p 362 GrandeDuc/Shutterstock, p 386 Maciej Sojka/Shutterstock, p 402 Humannet/Shutterstock, p 436 science photo/Shutterstock, p 470 300dpi/Shutterstock, p 508 Anton Balazh/Shutterstock, p 538 ronfromyork/Shutterstock, p 558 Digital Vision/Getty, p 580 Sethislav/Shutterstock, p 596 Dmitry Kalinovsky/Shutterstock, p 628 solarseven/Shutterstock, p 666 fongfong/Shutterstock, p 686 Celso Diniz/Shutterstock.

In order to ensure that this resource offers high quality support for the associated Edexcel qualification, it has been through a review process by the awarding body to confirm that it fully covers the teaching and learning content of the specification or part of a specification at which it is aimed, and demonstrates an appropriate balance between the development of subject skills, knowledge and understanding, in addition to preparation for assessment.
While the publishers have made every attempt to ensure that advice on the qualification and its assessment is accurate, the official specification and associated assessment guidance materials are the only authoritative source of information and should always be referred to for definitive guidance.
Edexcel examiners have not contributed to any sections in this resource relevant to examination papers for which they have responsibility.
No material from an endorsed textbook will be used verbatim in any assessment set by Edexcel.
Endorsement of a textbook does not mean that the textbook is required to achieve this Edexcel qualification, nor does it mean that it is the only suitable material available to support the qualification, and any resource lists produced by the awarding body shall include this and other appropriate resources.

Contents (Higher tier only material appears **bold**)

How to use this book

Welcome to Collins *Edexcel GCSE Maths 4th Edition Higher Student Book*. You will find a number of features in the book that will help you with your course of study.

Chapter overview

See what maths you will be doing, what skills you will learn and how you can build on what you already know.

About this chapter

Maths has numerous everyday uses. This section puts the chapter's mathematical skills and knowledge into context, historically and for the modern world.

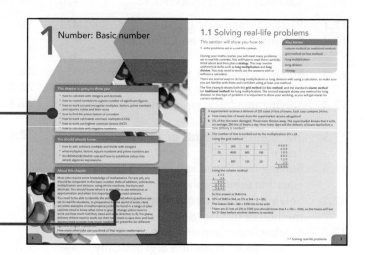

This section will show you …

Detailed learning objectives show you the skills you will learn in that section.

Key terms and glossary

Learn the important words you need to know. The explanations for the words in bold in the text can be found in the glossary at the back of the book.

Examples

Understand the topic before you start the exercise by reading the examples in blue boxes. These take you through questions step by step.

Exercises

Once you have worked through the examples you will be ready to tackle the exercises. There are plenty of questions, carefully designed to provide you with enough practice to become fluent.

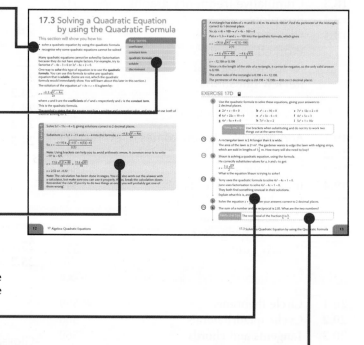

Hints and tips

These are provided where extra guidance can save you time or help you out.

Colour-coded questions

The questions in the exercises and the review questions are colour-coded, to show you how difficult they are. Most exercises start with more accessible questions and progress through intermediate to more challenging questions.

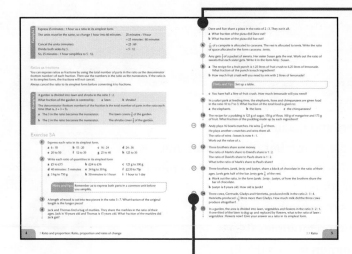

Mathematical skills

As you progress you will be expected to absorb new ways of thinking and working mathematically. Some questions are designed to help you develop a *specific* skill. Look for the icons:

(MR) Mathematical reasoning – you need to apply your skills and draw conclusions from mathematical information.

(CM) Communicate mathematically – you need to show how you have arrived at your answer by using mathematical arguments.

(PS) Problem solving and making connections – you need to devise a strategy to answer the question, based on the information you are given.

(EV) Evaluate and interpret – your answer needs to show that you have considered the information you are given and commented upon it.

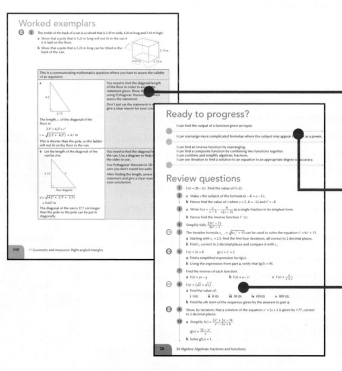

Worked exemplars

Develop your mathematical skills with detailed commentaries walking you through how to approach a range of questions.

Ready to progress?

Review what you have learnt from the chapter with this colour-coded summary to check you are on track throughout the course.

Review questions

Practise what you have learnt in all of the previous chapters and put your mathematical skills to the test. Questions range from accessible through to more challenging.

1 Number: Basic number

This chapter is going to show you:

- how to calculate with integers and decimals
- how to round numbers to a given number of significant figures
- how to work out and recognise multiples, factors, prime numbers and squares, cubes and their roots
- how to find the prime factors of a number
- how to work out lowest common multiples (LCM)
- how to work out highest common factors (HCF)
- how to calculate with negative numbers.

You should already know:

- how to add, subtract, multiply and divide with integers
- what multiples, factors, square numbers and prime numbers are
- the BIDMAS/BODMAS rule and how to substitute values into simple algebraic expressions.

About this chapter

Most jobs require some knowledge of mathematics. For any job, you should be competent in the basic number skills of addition, subtraction, multiplication and division, using whole numbers, fractions and decimals. You should know when it is sensible to use estimation or approximation and when it is important to have exact answers.

You need to be able to identify the skills required when questions are set in real-life situations, in preparation for the world of work. Here are some examples of mathematical problems faced in a range of jobs: cashiers need to know what coins to give in change; pilots need to work out how much fuel they need and what direction to fly the plane; delivery drivers need to work out their best route to save time and fuel; doctors need to know how much medicine to prescribe for different ages and weights of patients.

How many other jobs can you think of that require mathematics?

1.1 Solving real-life problems

This section will show you how to:

- solve problems set in a real-life context.

During your maths course, you will meet many problems set in *real-life* contexts. You will have to *read them carefully*, *think about* and then plan a **strategy**. This may involve arithmetical skills such as **long multiplication** and **long division**. You may need to work out the answers with or without a calculator.

There are several ways to do long multiplication or long division without using a calculator, so make sure you are familiar with them and confident in using at least one method.

The first example shows both the **grid method** (or **box method**) and the standard **column method** (or **traditional method**) for long multiplication. The second example shows one method for long division. In this type of problem it is important to show your working, as you will get marks for correct methods.

Example 1

A supermarket receives a delivery of 235 cases of tins of beans. Each case contains 24 tins.

a How many tins of beans does the supermarket receive altogether?

b 5% of the tins were damaged. These were thrown away. The supermarket knows that it sells, on average, 250 tins of beans a day. How many days will the delivery of beans last before a new delivery is needed?

a The number of tins is worked out by the multiplication 235×24.

Using the grid method

×	200	30	5
20	4000	600	100
4	800	120	20

```
  4 0 0 0
    6 0 0
    1 0 0
    8 0 0
    1 2 0
+    2 0
  5 6 4 0
```

Using the column method

```
    2 3 5
×    2 4
    9 4 0
  4 7 0 0
  5 6 4 0
```

So the answer is 5640 tins.

b 10% of 5640 is 564, so 5% is $564 \div 2 = 282$.

This leaves $5640 - 282 = 5358$ tins to be sold.

There are 21 lots of 250 in 5358 (you should know that $4 \times 250 = 1000$), so the beans will last for 21 days before another delivery is needed.

Example 2

A party of 613 children and 59 adults are going on a day out to a theme park.

a How many coaches, each holding 53 people, will be needed?

b One adult gets into the theme park free for every 15 children. How many adults will have to pay to get in?

a Altogether there are 613 + 59 = 672 people.

So the number of coaches needed is 672 ÷ 53 (number of seats on each coach).

The answer is 12 remainder 36. So, there will be 12 full coaches and one coach with 36 people on it. They would have to book 13 coaches.

```
      1 2
53 ) 6 7 2
     5 3 0
     1 4 2
     1 0 6
       3 6
```

b This is also a division, 613 ÷ 15. It is useful if you know the 15 times table. As 4 × 15 = 60, 40 × 15 = 600. This leaves a remainder of 13. So 40 adults get in free and 59 − 40 = 19 adults will have to pay.

Exercise 1A

1 There are 48 cans of soup in a crate. A supermarket had a delivery of 125 crates of soup.

  a How many cans of soup were in this delivery?

  b The supermarket is running a promotion on soup. If you buy five cans, you get one free. Each can costs 39p. How much will it cost to get 32 cans of soup?

2 Greystones Primary School has 12 classes, each of which has 24 students.

  a How many students are there at Greystones Primary School?

  b The teacher to student ratio at the school is 1 : 18. How many teachers are there at the school?

3 Exeter City Football Club is organising travel for an away game. 1300 adults and 500 juniors want to go. Each coach holds 48 people and costs £320 to hire. Tickets to the match cost £18 for adults and £10 for juniors.

  a How many coaches will be needed?

  b The club is charging adults £26 and juniors £14 for travel and a ticket. How much profit does the club make out of the trip?

4 Kirsty collects small models of animals. Last time she bought some, each one cost 45p. She saves enough to buy 23 models but, when she goes to the shop, she finds that the price has gone up to 55p. How many can she buy now?

5 The magazine *MTB Biker* comes out every month. In a newsagent the magazine costs £2.45. The annual (yearly) subscription for the magazine is £21. How much cheaper is each magazine when bought on subscription?

6 Paula buys a sofa. She pays a deposit of 10% of the cash price and then 36 monthly payments of £12.50. In total she pays £495. How much was the cash price of the sofa?

7 There are 125 people at a wedding. They need to get to the reception.

52 people are going by coach and the rest are travelling in cars. Each car can take up to five people.

What is the least number of cars needed to take everyone to the reception?

(PS) **8** A fish pond in a shop contains 240 fish.

Each week the manager has a delivery from one supplier of 45 new fish that he adds to the pond.

On average he sells 62 fish each week. When his stock falls below 200 fish, he buys in extra fish from a different supplier. After how many weeks will he need to buy in extra fish?

9 A baker supplies bread rolls to a catering company.

The bread rolls are sold in packs of 24 for £1.99 per pack. The catering company want 500 fresh rolls each day. How much will the bill be for one week, assuming they do not work on Sundays?

(MR) **10** Gavin's car does 8 miles to each litre of petrol. He does 12 600 miles a year, of which 4600 are on company business.

Petrol costs £1.35 per litre.

Insurance and servicing costs £800 a year.

Gavin's company gives him an allowance of 40p for each mile he drives on company business.

How much does Gavin pay towards running his car each year?

(EV) **11** Here are four students' methods for working out the calculation 32 × 51.

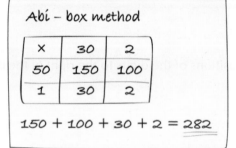

Abi – box method

×	30	2
50	150	100
1	30	2

150 + 100 + 30 + 2 = 282

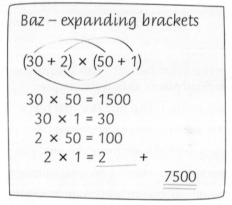

Baz – expanding brackets

(30 + 2) × (50 + 1)

30 × 50 = 1500
30 × 1 = 30
2 × 50 = 100
2 × 1 = 2   +

7500

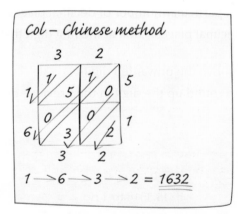

Col – Chinese method

1 → 6 → 3 → 2 = 1632

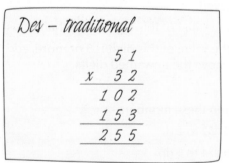

Des – traditional

```
      5 1
  x   3 2
    1 0 2
    1 5 3
    2 5 5
```

a Which student has worked out the correct answer?

b Three of the students have made mistakes. What are their mistakes?

1.2 Multiplication and division with decimals

Key terms

decimal place   decimal point

This section will show you how to:

- multiply a decimal number by another decimal number
- divide by a decimal by changing the calculation to division by an integer.

The number system is extended by using decimal numbers to represent fractions. The **decimal point** separates the decimal fraction from the whole-number part.

For example, the number 25.374 means:

Tens	Units		Tenths	Hundredths	Thousandths
10	1		$\frac{1}{10}$	$\frac{1}{100}$	$\frac{1}{1000}$
2	5	.	3	7	4

You can already use decimal notation to express amounts of money. For example:

$£32.67$ means $3 \times £10$

$2 \times £1$

$6 \times £0.10$ (10 pence)

$7 \times £0.01$ (1 penny)

Decimal places

When you write a number in decimal form, the positions of the digits to the right of the decimal point are called **decimal places** (dp). For example:

79.4 is written 'with one decimal place'

6.83 is written 'with two decimal places'

0.526 is written 'with three decimal places'.

These are the steps to round a decimal number to a particular number of decimal places.

- Start at the decimal point and count along the decimal places. Look at the first digit that needs to be removed.
- When the value of this digit is less than 5, just remove the unwanted digits.
- When the value of this digit is 5 or more, add 1 to round up the digit in the previous decimal place, then remove the unwanted digits.

Example 3

Round these numbers.

a 5.852 to 2 dp

b 7.156 to 2 dp

c 0.274 to 1 dp

d 15.3518 to 1 dp

a 5.852 rounds to 5.85 to 2 dp.

b 7.156 rounds to 7.16 to 2 dp.

c 0.274 rounds to 0.3 to 1 dp.

d 15.3518 rounds to 15.4 to 1 dp.

Multiplying two decimal numbers together

Follow these steps to multiply one decimal number by another decimal number.

Step 1: Multiply each decimal by a power of 10 to make it into a whole number.

Step 2: Multiply the two whole numbers.

Step 3: Multiply together the powers of 10 from step 1.

Step 4: Divide the product of the numbers from step 2 by the power of 10 from step 3.

Example 4

Work out this decimal multiplication. 3.42×2.7

Multiply each number by a power of 10 to make it into a whole number.

$3.42 \times 100 = 342$ and $2.7 \times 10 = 27$.

Multiply the whole numbers together.

```
      3 4 2
  ×     2 7
    2 3 9 4
    6 8 4 0
    9 2 3 4
```

Multiply the powers of 10 (100 and 10) together. $100 \times 10 = 1000$

Divide 9234 by this power of 10. $9234 \div 1000 = 9.234$

So, $3.42 \times 2.7 = 9.234$.

Dividing by a decimal

Look at the number you are dividing by. Decide what multiple of 10 (10, 100, 1000…) you would need to *multiply* it by, to make it a whole number or integer.

Then multiply both parts of the division by that multiple of 10.

Example 5

Work these out.   **a** $42 \div 0.2$ **b** $19.8 \div 0.55$

a   The calculation is $42 \div 0.2$, which can be rewritten as $420 \div 2$. In this case both values have been multiplied by 10 to make the divisor into a whole number. Then divide normally. The answer is 210.

Another way to view this is as a fraction problem.

$$\frac{42}{0.2} = \frac{42}{0.2} \times \frac{10}{10}$$

$$= \frac{420}{2}$$

$$= \frac{210}{1}$$

$$= 210$$

b $19.8 \div 0.55 = 198 \div 5.5$

$$= 1980 \div 55$$

This becomes a long division problem that can be solved using the method of repeated subtraction.

```
    1 9 8 0
  − 1 1 0 0    20 × 55
      8 8 0
  −   4 4 0    8 × 55
      4 4 0
  −   4 4 0    8 × 55
          0    36 × 55
```

So, $19.8 \div 0.55 = 36$.

Exercise 1B

1 Round each number to the number of decimal places (dp) indicated.

a 4.568 (1 dp)   **b** 0.0832 (2 dp)   **c** 45.715 93 (3 dp)   **d** 94.8531 (2 dp)

e 602.099 (1 dp)   **f** 671.7629 (2 dp)   **g** 7.1124 (1 dp)   **h** 6.903 54 (3 dp)

i 13.7809 (2 dp)   **j** 0.075 11 (1 dp)   **k** 4.001 84 (3 dp)   **l** 59.983 (1 dp)

2 Work these out.

a 0.14×0.2 **b** 0.3×0.3 **c** 5.6×9.1 **d** 9.12×5.1

3 For each part of this question:

  i estimate the answer by first rounding each number to the nearest whole number

  ii calculate the exact answer

  iii calculate the difference between your answers to parts **i** and **ii**.

a 4.8×7.3 **b** 2.4×7.6 **c** 15.3×3.9 **d** 19.8×7.1

4 Work these out.

a $3.6 \div 0.2$ **b** $56 \div 0.4$ **c** $0.42 \div 0.3$

d $8.4 \div 0.7$ **e** $3.45 \div 0.5$

5 Work these out.

a $67.2 \div 0.24$ **b** $6.36 \div 0.53$ **c** $132 \div 0.55$

d $162 \div 0.36$ **e** $2.17 \div 3.5$

(MR) 6   **a** Use any method to work out 26×22.

    b Use your answer to part **a** to work these out.

      i 2.6×2.2 **ii** 1.3×1.1 **iii** 2.6×8.8

(EV) 7 Lee and Tracey are trying to work out the answer to 8.6×4.7.

  a Lee says the answer is 40.24. Without working it out, can you tell whether his answer is correct?

  b Tracey says the answer is 46.42. Without working it out, can you tell whether her answer is correct?

  In each part, show how you decided.

8 Doris buys a big bag of safety pins. The bag weighs 180 g. Each safety pin weighs 0.6 g. How many safety pins are in the bag?

(MR) 9   **a** Use any method to work out: $81 \div 3$.

    b Use your answer to part **a** to work these out.

      i $8.1 \div 0.3$ **ii** $0.81 \div 30$ **iii** $0.081 \div 0.3$

(PS) 10 Mark went shopping. He went into three stores and bought one item from each store.

Music shop		Clothes shop		Book shop	
CDs	£5.98	Shirt	£12.50	Magazine	£2.25
DVDs	£7.99	Jeans	£32.00	Pen	£3.98

In total he spent £43.97. What did he buy?

The largest crowd to watch a match at Wembley was 89 874 for the Cup Final in 2008.

Here are three headlines from the newspapers the following day.

A: Wembley crowd a record – capacity of 90 000 almost reached.

B: A record crowd of 89 874 watch the Cup Final.

C: New Wembley record: 1345 more watched the Cup Final than the previous best attendance.

Comment on the usefulness of each headline.

1.3 Approximation of calculations

This section will show you how to:

- round to a given number of significant figures
- approximate the result before multiplying two numbers together
- approximate the result before dividing two numbers
- round a calculation, at the end of a problem, to give what is considered to be a sensible answer.

Key terms	
approximate	significant figure

Rounding to significant figures

You often use **significant figures** (sf) when you want to **approximate** a number with quite a few digits in it. You will use this technique in estimations.

Look at this table, which shows some numbers rounded to one, two and three significant figures.

One sf	8	50	200	90 000	0.000 07	0.003	0.4
Two sf	67	4.8	0.76	45 000	730	0.0067	0.40
Three sf	312	65.9	40.3	0.0761	7.05	0.003 01	0.400

The steps taken to round a number to a given number of significant figures are very similar to those used for rounding to a given number of decimal places.

- From the left, count the digits. If you are rounding to 2 sf, count two digits, for 3 sf count three digits, and so on. When the original number is less than 1, start counting from the first non-zero digit.

- Look at the next digit to the right. When the value of this next digit is less than 5, leave the digit you counted to the same. However, if the value of this next digit is equal to or greater than 5, add 1 to round up the digit you counted to.

- Ignore all the other digits, but put in enough zeros to keep the number the right size (value).

For example, this table shows some numbers rounded to 1, 2 and 3 significant figures, respectively.

Number	Rounded to 1 sf	Rounded to 2 sf	Rounded to 3 sf
45 281	50 000	45 000	45 300
568.54	600	570	569
7.3782	7	7.4	7.38
8054	8000	8100	8050
99.8721	100	100	99.9
0.7002	0.7	0.70	0.700

Exercise 1C

1 Round each number to 1 significant figure.

    a 46 313   **b** 85 299   **c** 30 569   **d** 199   **e** 0.5388

    f 0.00584   **g** 0.2823   **h** 9.9   **i** 0.047 85   **j** 999.99

2 Round each number to 2 significant figures.

    a 56 147   **b** 79 611   **c** 30 578   **d** 1.689   **e** 0.0658

    f 0.458   **g** 4.0854   **h** 8.0089   **i** 0.9996   **j** 0.8006

3 Round each number to the number of significant figures (sf) indicated.

    a 57 402 (1 sf)   **b** 5288 (2 sf)   **c** 89.67 (3 sf)   **d** 105.6 (2 sf)

    e 8.69 (1 sf)   **f** 1.087 (2 sf)   **g** 0.261 (1 sf)   **h** 0.732 (1 sf)

4 What are the least and the greatest numbers of sweets that can be found in these jars?

    a    **b**    **c**

    70 sweets (to 1sf)   100 sweets (to 1sf)   1000 sweets (to 1sf)

5 What are the least and the greatest numbers of people that live in these towns?

    Elsecar   population 800 (to 1 significant figure)

    Hoyland   population 1200 (to 2 significant figures)

    Barnsley   population 165 000 (to 3 significant figures)

(PS) **6** A joiner has from 15 to 25 (inclusive) pieces of skirting board in stock.

    He uses 8 pieces and now has between 10 and 15 (inclusive) left. How many pieces could he have had to start with? Work out all possible answers. Show your working.

(CM) **7** The number of fish in a pond is 500, to 1 significant figure. What is the least possible number of fish that could be taken from the pond so that the number of fish in the pond is 400, to 1 significant figure? Give a reason for your answer.

(CM) **8** Karen says that the population of Preston is 132 000 to the nearest thousand. Donte says that the population of Preston is 130 000. Explain why Donte could also be correct.

9 This is an aerial image of a penguin colony in Antarctica. Scientists use images like this to estimate the size of the penguin population. They use two methods.

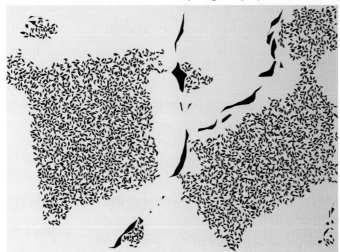

Method 1: Estimate the area of the whole colony and then assume there are three penguins per square metre.

Method 2: Draw a square, to scale, to represent 5 m by 5 m on the diagram. Count the penguins in the square, and then estimate the area of the whole colony and multiply the number of penguins in the sample square.

a Give one advantage and one disadvantage of using method 1.

b Give one advantage and one disadvantage of using method 2.

Multiplying and dividing by multiples of 10

Questions often involve multiplication of multiples of 10, 100, … This method is used in estimation. You should have the skill to do this mentally so that you can check that your answers to calculations are about right. (Approximation of calculations is covered in the next section.)

Use a calculator to work these out.

a $300 \times 200 =$ **b** $100 \times 40 =$ **c** $2000 \times 0.3 =$

d $0.2 \times 50 =$ **e** $0.2 \times 0.5 =$ **f** $0.3 \times 0.04 =$

Can you see a way of doing these without using a calculator or pencil and paper? You multiply the non-zero digits and then work out the number of zeros or the position of the decimal point by combining the zeros or decimal places in the original calculation.

The method for dividing is similar. Try doing these on your calculator.

a $400 \div 20 =$ **b** $200 \div 50 =$ **c** $1000 \div 0.2 =$

d $300 \div 0.3 =$ **e** $250 \div 0.05 =$ **f** $30\,000 \div 0.6 =$

Once again, there is a quick way of doing these 'in your head'. Look at these examples.

$300 \times 4000 = 1\,200\,000$ $5000 \div 200 = 25$ $20 \times 0.5 = 10$

$0.6 \times 5000 = 3000$ $400 \div 0.02 = 20\,000$ $800 \div 0.2 = 4000$

Can you see a connection between the digits, the number of zeros and the position of the decimal point, and the way in which these calculations are worked out?

For example:

$300 \times 4000 = 3 \times 4 \times 100 \times 1000$ $= 12 \times 100\,000$ $= 1\,200\,000$	$0.6 \times 5000 = 6 \times 500$ $= 3000$	$20 \times 0.5 = 2 \times 5$ $= 10$
$5000 \div 200 = 50\cancel{0}\cancel{0} \div 2\cancel{0}\cancel{0}$ $= 50 \div 2$ $= 25$	$400 \div 0.02 = 4000 \div 0.2$ $= 40\,000 \div 2$ $= 20\,000$	$800 \div 0.2 = 8000 \div 2$ $= 4000$

Exercise 1D

1 Write down the answers, without using a calculator.

a 200 × 300   **b** 30 × 4000   **c** 50 × 200   **d** 0.3 × 50

e 200 × 0.7   **f** 200 × 0.5   **g** 0.1 × 2000   **h** 0.4 × 0.2

i 0.3 × 0.3   **j** 0.3 × 150

2 Write down the answers, without using a calculator.

a 2000 ÷ 400   **b** 5000 ÷ 200   **c** 2100 ÷ 0.7

d 300 ÷ 0.5   **e** 400 ÷ 0.2   **f** 2000 ÷ 0.4

g 2000 × 40 ÷ 200   **h** 200 × 20 ÷ 0.5   **i** 200 × 6000 ÷ 0.3

3 Match each calculation to its answer and then write out the calculations in order, starting with the smallest answer.

5000 × 4000   600 × 8000   200 000 × 700   30 × 90 000

140 000 000   4 800 000   2 700 000   20 000 000

(MR) **4** You are given that 16 × 34 = 544.

Write down the value of each calculation.

a 160 × 340   **b** 544 000 ÷ 34

5 In 2009 there were £28 000 million worth of £20 notes in circulation.

How many notes is this?

(CM) **6** A teacher asks her class to work out sixty-thousand divided by two hundred. This is Matt's working.

$$600\cancel{000} \div 2\cancel{00} = 600 \div 2 = 300$$

When Matt read out his answer of 300, his teacher said he was correct. Is Matt correct? If not, what mistake has Matt made?

(PS) **7** There are 66 325 000 20p coins in circulation.
Each one weighs 5 g.

Bernie sees an advert for a yacht.

Bernie thinks that all of the 20p coins in circulation would weigh more than the yacht and would be worth enough in total to buy it. Is Bernie correct?

For sale

WHITE LIGHTNING
£13 000 000
WEIGHT 360 TONNES

(PS) **8** The National Debt of the United Kingdom is about £1420 billion. A billion is one thousand million. The population of the UK is about 64 million.

How much is the National Debt per head of population? Give your answer correct to 3 significant figures.

Approximation of calculations

How do you approximate the value of a calculation?

What do you actually do when you try to approximate an answer to a problem?

For example, what is the approximate answer to 35.1 × 6.58?

To approximate the answer in this and many other similar cases, you need to round each number to 1 significant figure, then work out the calculation.

So, in this case, the approximation is 35.1 × 6.58 ≈ 40 × 7 = 280.

Note that the ≈ symbol means 'approximately equal to'.

For the division 89.1 ÷ 2.98, the approximation is 90 ÷ 3 = 30.

If you are using a calculator, whenever you need to work out a fraction that has a calculation in the numerator and/or denominator, *always* put brackets around each calculation. This is to remind you to work out the numerator and denominator separately before completing the division. You can work out the numerator and denominator separately but most calculators will work out the answer straight away if you use brackets. Learning to use a calculator efficiently can save time and lead to you making fewer mistakes.

Example 6

a Find an approximate answer to each calculation.

   i $\dfrac{213 \times 69}{42}$ **ii** $\dfrac{78 \times 397}{0.38}$

b Use a calculator to work out each answer, correct to 3 significant figures.

a **i** Round each number to 1 significant figure. $\dfrac{200 \times 70}{40}$

    Work out the numerator. $= \dfrac{14\,000}{40}$

    Divide by the denominator. $= 350$

  ii Round each value to 1 significant figure. $\dfrac{80 \times 400}{0.4}$

    Work out the numerator. $= \dfrac{32000}{0.4}$

                                  $= \dfrac{320\,000}{4}$

    Divide by the denominator. $= 80\,000$

b To check your approximate answers, key in these sequences.

i (2 1 3 × 6 9) ÷ (4 2) =

    The display as a decimal should say 349.9285714, which rounds to 350. This agrees exactly with the estimate.

    Note that you do not have to put brackets around the 42 but it is a good habit to get into.

ii

(7 8 × 3 9 7) ÷ (0 • 3 8) =

    The display as a decimal should say 81489.47368, which rounds to 81 500. This agrees with the estimate.

Sensible rounding

Sensible rounding is simply writing or saying answers to questions with a real-life context, so that the answer makes sense and is the sort of thing someone may say in a normal conversation.

For example:

"The distance from Birmingham to Wolverhampton is 16 miles" is a sensible statement.

"The distance from Birmingham to Wolverhampton is 16.3247 miles" is not sensible.

"Painting a house takes 6 tins of paint" is sensible.

"Painting a house takes 5.91 tins of paint" is not sensible.

As a general rule, if it sounds sensible it will be acceptable.

When you need to give an answer to a sensible or appropriate degree of accuracy, express it to the same accuracy as the numbers in the question. So, for example, if the numbers in the question are given to 2 significant figures give your answer to 2 significant figures but remember, unless you are working out an approximation, do all the working to at least 4 significant figures or use the calculator display.

Exercise 1E

1 Find approximate answers.

    a 5435 × 7.31   **b** 5280 × 3.211   **c** 63.24 × 3.514 × 4.2

    d 354 ÷ 79.8   **e** 5974 ÷ 5.29   **f** 208 ÷ 0.378

2 Use a calculator to work out the answers to question **1**. Round your answers to 3 significant figures and compare them with the estimates you made.

3 Round each of the numbers in these statements to a suitable degree of accuracy.

    a I am 1.7359 m tall.

    b It took me 5 minutes 44.83 seconds to mend the television.

    c My kitten weighs 237.97 g.

    d The correct temperature at which to drink Earl Grey tea is 82.739 °C.

    e There were 34 827 people at the test match yesterday.

    f The distance from Winchester to Andover is 15.528 miles.

    g The area of the floor is 13.673 m².

4 By rounding, find approximate answers to each of these.

    a $\dfrac{783 - 572}{24}$ **b** $\dfrac{352 + 675}{999}$ **c** $\dfrac{3.82 \times 7.95}{9.9}$

5 Use a calculator to work out the answers to question **4**. Round your answers to 3 significant figures and compare them with the estimates you made.

6 Rewrite this blog, using sensible numbers.

DAILY NEWS
world - business - finance - lifestyle - travel - sport

It was a hot day; the temperature was 81.699 °F and still rising. I had now walked 5.3289 km in just over 113.98 minutes. But I didn't care since I knew that the 43 275 people watching the race were cheering me on. I won by clipping 6.2 seconds off the record time. This was the 67th time it had happened since records first began in 1788. Well, next year I will only have 15 practice walks beforehand as I strive to beat the record by at least another 4.9 seconds.

7 Find the approximate annual pay of each person.

    a Kevin: £270 a week   **b** Malcolm: £1528 a month   **c** David: £347 a week

8 Gold bars weigh 400 ounces (12.44 kg). On 6 October 2014, one gold bar was worth $413 080.

Approximately how much is 1 ounce of gold worth, in dollars?

9 It took me 6 hours 40 minutes to drive from Sheffield to Bude, a distance of 295 miles. My car uses petrol at the rate of about 32 miles per gallon. The petrol cost £3.51 per gallon.

    a Approximately how many miles did I travel each hour?

    b Approximately how many gallons of petrol did I use in driving from Sheffield to Bude?

    c What was the approximate cost of all the petrol I used in the journey to Bude and back again?

10 By rounding, find an approximate answer to each of these.

    a $\dfrac{462 \times 79}{0.42}$ **b** $\dfrac{583 - 213}{0.21}$ **c** $\dfrac{252 + 551}{0.78}$ **d** $\dfrac{296 \times 32}{0.325}$

    e $\dfrac{297 + 721}{0.578 - 0.321}$ **f** $\dfrac{12.31 \times 16.9}{0.394 \times 0.216}$ **g** $\dfrac{38.3 + 27.5}{0.776}$ **h** $\dfrac{29.7 + 12.6}{0.26}$

11 Use a calculator to work out the answers to question **10**. Round your answers to 3 significant figures and compare them with the estimates you made.

12 A sheet of paper is 0.012 cm thick. Approximately how many sheets will there be in a pile of paper that is 6.35 cm deep?

(MR) **13** A 5p coin weighs 4.2 g. How many 20-tonne lorries (lorries that can carry 20 tonnes) would be needed to transport a million pounds in 5p coins?

(EV) **14** The accurate temperature is 18.2 °C. David rounds the temperature to the nearest 5 °C. David says the temperature is about 20 °C.

How much would the temperature need to rise for David to say that the temperature is about 25 °C?

15 Use your calculator to complete these calculations. In each case:

    i write down the full calculator display of the answer

    ii round your answer to 3 significant figures.

    a $\dfrac{12.3 + 64.9}{6.9 - 4.1}$ **b** $\dfrac{13.8 \times 23.9}{3.2 \times 6.1}$ **c** $\dfrac{48.2 \times 58.9}{3.62 \times 0.042}$

(EV) **16** Here are three calculations.

    37.5×48.6 21.7×103.6 $985 \div 0.54$

    a Show that the estimated answer to each of them is the same.

    b Pete says that the largest actual answer must be to 21.7×103.6. Explain why Pete is correct.

    c He also says that it is not possible, without doing the full calculation, to say which of the other two has the larger answer. Is Pete correct? Use a calculator to work out which is larger.

17 The distance from the Sun to Earth is approximately 149 000 000 km. The speed of light is approximately 300 000 km per second.

 Use your calculator to work out how many seconds it takes for light to travel from the Sun to Earth. Give your answer to a sensible degree of accuracy.

18 **a** Explain why the estimated answer to 58.9 × 4.8 is 300.

 b Is the actual answer higher or lower than the estimate? Explain your answer.

 19 The population density of a country is measured by dividing the population by the area. For example, the population of the United Kingdom is about 64 000 000 and the area is 243 000 km², so the population density is approximately 260 people per square kilometre.

The most densely populated country is Macau with a population of 541 200 and an area of 29.2 km².

The least densely populated country is Greenland with a population of 57 000 and an area of 2 176 000 km².

How many times greater is the population density of Macau than the population density of Greenland?

Give your answer to a suitable degree of accuracy.

20 Which calculation will have the larger answer? Explain how you can tell.

26.8 ÷ 3.1   or   36.2 ÷ 3.9

1.4 Multiples, factors, prime numbers, powers and roots

This section will show you how to:

- find multiples and factors
- identify prime numbers
- identify square numbers and triangular numbers
- find square roots
- identify cubes and cube roots.

Multiple: Any number in the multiplication table. For example, the multiples of 7 are 7, 14, 21, 28, 35, …

Factor: Any whole number that divides exactly into another number. For example, factors of 24 are 1, 2, 3, 4, 6, 8, 12 and 24.

Prime number: Any number that only has two factors, 1 and itself. For example, 2, 3, 5, 7 and 11 are prime numbers. Note that 1 is not a prime number.

Square: A number that results from multiplying a number by itself. For example, 1, 4, 9, 16 and 25 are square numbers.

Triangular numbers: Numbers that can make triangular patterns. For example, 1, 3, 6, 10 and 15 are triangular numbers. Start with 1, add 2 to get 3, add 3 to 3 to get 6, add 4 to 6 to get 10, and so on.

Square root: The square root of a given number is a number that, when multiplied by itself, produces the given number. For example, the square root of 9 is 3, since 3 × 3 = 9.

A square root is represented by the symbol $\sqrt{\ }$. For example, $\sqrt{16} = 4$.

Note that $-4 \times -4 = 16$. Every positive number has two square roots.

So $\sqrt{16} = +4$ or -4. This can be written as $\sqrt{16} = \pm 4$ and you should read it as 'positive or negative four'.

Cube: The cube of a number is a number multiplied by itself and then by itself again. For example, the cube of 4 is $4 \times 4 \times 4 = 64$.

Cube root: The cube root of a number is the number that, when multiplied by itself and then multiplied by itself again, gives the number. For example, the cube root of 27 is 3 because $3 \times 3 \times 3 = 27$ and the cube root of -8 is -2 because $-2 \times -2 \times -2 = -8$. If the cube root of b is written as $\sqrt[3]{b}$ then $\sqrt[3]{b} \times \sqrt[3]{b} \times \sqrt[3]{b} = b$.

Powers: A square number may be written as 5^2. A cube may be written as 6^3. The small numbers are called powers and they tell you how many 'lots' of the number are multiplied together.

Exercise 1F

1 Choose the number from the box that fits each of these descriptions (one number per description).

   a a multiple of 3 and a multiple of 4
   b a square number and an odd number
   c a factor of 24 and a factor of 18
   d a prime number and a factor of 39
   e an odd factor of 30 and a multiple of 3
   f a number with four factors and a multiple of 2 and 7
   g a number with five factors exactly
   h a triangular number and a factor of 20
   i an even number and a factor of 36 and a multiple of 9
   j a prime number that is one more than a square number
   k a number with factors that, when written out in order, make a number pattern in which each number is twice the one before
   l an odd triangular number that is a multiple of 7

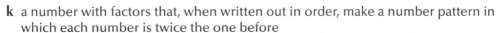

12   21
   8   15
13
      17
9   18
      10
            6
14   16

 2 Hot-dog sausages are sold in packs of 10 and hot-dog buns are sold in packs of 8. How many of each do you have to buy to have complete hot dogs with no wasted sausages or buns?

3 A bell chimes every 6 seconds. Another bell chimes every 5 seconds. If they both chime together, how many seconds will it be before they both chime together again?

4 Fred runs round a running track in 4 minutes. Debbie runs round in 3 minutes. If they both start together on the line at the end of the finishing straight, when will they both be on the same line together again? How many laps will Debbie have run? How many laps will Fred have run?

5 Copy these sums and write out the *next four* lines.

   $1 = 1$
   $1 + 3 = 4$
   $1 + 3 + 5 = 9$
   $1 + 3 + 5 + 7 = 16$

6 Write down the negative square root of each number.

a 4   **b** 49   **c** 144   **d** 1   **e** 900

7 Write down the cube root of each number.

a 1   **b** 27   **c** 64   **d** 8   **e** −64

8 Work out the value of each number.

a 20^2 **b** 30^2 **c** 50^2 **d** 0.5^2 **e** $(-4)^2$

9 The triangular numbers are 1, 3, 6, 10, 15, 21 …

a Investigate why they are called triangular numbers.

b Continue the sequence until the first triangular number that is greater than 100.

c Add up consecutive pairs of triangular numbers, starting with 1 + 3 = 4, 3 + 6 = 9. What do you notice?

(EV) **10** Here are four numbers.

8   28   49   64

Copy and complete the table by putting each of the numbers in the correct box.

	Square number	Factor of 56
Cube number		
Multiple of 7		

(CM) **11** John is writing out his 4 times table. Mary is writing out her 6 times table.

They notice that some answers are the same.

In which other times tables do these common answers also appear?

(EV) **12** **a** $36^3 = 46\,656$. Work out 1^3, 4^3, 9^3, 16^3, 25^3.

b $\sqrt{46\,656} = 216$. Use a calculator to find the square roots of the numbers you worked out in part **a**.

c $216 = 36 \times 6$. Can you find a similar connection between the answer to part **b** and the numbers cubed in part **a**?

d What type of numbers are 1, 4, 9, 16, 25 and 36?

13 Write down the values of these numbers.

a $\sqrt{0.04}$ **b** $\sqrt{0.25}$ **c** $\sqrt{0.36}$ **d** $\sqrt{0.81}$

e $\sqrt[3]{3.375}$ **f** $\sqrt[3]{9.261}$ **g** $\sqrt[3]{0.512}$ **h** $\sqrt[3]{0.343}$

14 Estimate the answers to these.

a $\dfrac{13.7 + 21.9}{\sqrt{0.239}}$ **b** $\dfrac{29.6 \times 11.9}{\sqrt{0.038}}$ **c** $\dfrac{87.5 - 32.6}{\sqrt{0.8} - \sqrt{0.38}}$

1.5 Prime factors, LCM and HCF

This section will show you how to:

- identify prime factors
- identify the lowest common multiple (LCM) of two numbers
- identify the highest common factor (HCF) of two numbers.

The unique factorisation theorem states that every integer greater than 1 is either a prime number or can be written as the product of prime numbers. This gives the prime factors of the number.

Consider 110. Find two numbers that, when multiplied together, give that number, for example, 2 × 55. Are they both prime? No, 55 isn't. So take 55 and repeat the operation, to get 5 × 11. Are these both prime? Yes, so:

$$110 = 2 \times 5 \times 11$$

The prime factors of 110 are 2, 5 and 11.

This method is not very logical and you need to know your multiplication tables well to use it. There are, however, two methods that you can use to make sure you do not miss any of the prime factors. The next two examples show you how to use the first of these methods.

Example 7

Find the prime factors of 24.

Divide 24 by any prime number that goes into it. (2 is an obvious choice.)

Divide the answer (12) by a prime number. Repeat this process until you have a prime number as the answer.

So the prime factors of 24 are 2 and 3.

$$24 = 2 \times 2 \times 2 \times 3$$

2	24
2	12
2	6
	3

When 24 is expressed as $2 \times 2 \times 2 \times 3$ it has been written as a product of its prime factors.

Another name for the product $2 \times 2 \times 2 \times 3$ or $2^3 \times 3$ is the prime factorisation of 24.

A quicker and neater way to write this answer is to use **index notation**, expressing the answer using powers.

In index notation, the prime factorisation of 24 is $2^3 \times 3$.

Example 8

Write 96 as a product of its prime factors. Give your answer in index form.

The prime factors of 96 are 2 and 3.

$$96 = 2 \times 2 \times 2 \times 2 \times 2 \times 3$$
$$= 2^5 \times 3$$

2	96
2	48
2	24
2	12
2	6
	3

The prime factorisation of 96 is $2 \times 2 \times 2 \times 2 \times 2 \times 3$ or $2^5 \times 3$, which is also the product of its prime factors.

The second method uses **prime factor trees**. You start by dividing the number into a pair of factors. Then you divide this, and carry on dividing until you get to prime numbers.

Example 9

Find the prime factors of 76.

Stop dividing the factors because 2, 2 and 19 are all prime numbers.

So, the prime factors of 76 are 2 and 19.

$76 = 2 \times 2 \times 19$

$\quad = 2^2 \times 19$

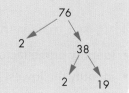

Example 10

Find the prime factors of 420.

The process can be done upside down to make an upright tree.

So, the prime factors of 420 are 2, 3, 5 and 7.

$420 = 2 \times 5 \times 2 \times 3 \times 7$

$\quad = 2^2 \times 3 \times 5 \times 7$

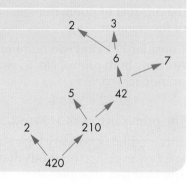

Exercise 1G

1 Copy and complete these prime factor trees.

a

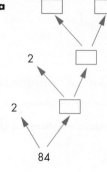

$84 = 2 \times 2 \ldots \ \ldots$

b

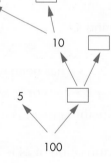

$100 = 5 \times 2 \ldots \ \ldots$

c

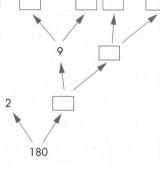

$180 = 2 \ \ldots \ \ldots \ \ldots \ \ldots$

d

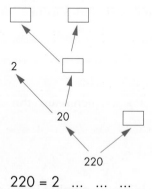

$220 = 2 \ \ldots \ \ldots \ \ldots$

e

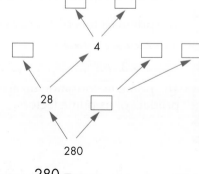

$280 = \ldots \ \ldots \ \ldots \ \ldots \ \ldots$

f

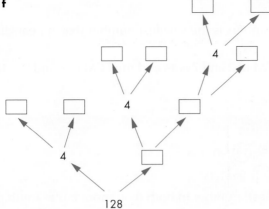

$128 = \ldots \quad \ldots \quad \ldots \quad \ldots \quad \ldots \quad \ldots \quad \ldots$

g

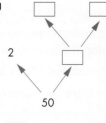

$50 = \ldots \quad \ldots \quad \ldots$

2 In index notation, 100 is written as $2^2 \times 5^2$ and 540 is written as $2^2 \times 3^3 \times 5$. Rewrite your answers to question **1** in index notation.

3 Write the numbers from 1 to 50 as products of their prime factors. Use index notation. For example:

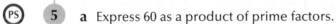

$1 = 1 \qquad 2 = 2 \qquad 3 = 3 \qquad 4 = 2^2 \qquad 5 = 5 \qquad 6 = 2 \times 3 \qquad \ldots$

4 **a** What is special about the numbers 2, 4, 8, 16, 32, …?

b What are the next two terms in this series?

c What are the next three terms in the series 3, 9, 27, …?

d Continue the series 4, 16, 64, … for three more terms.

e The series in part **a** can be written in index notation: $2^1, 2^2, 2^3, 2^4, 2^5, 2^6, 2^7, \ldots$

Rewrite the series in parts **a**–**d** in index notation.

(PS) **5** **a** Express 60 as a product of prime factors.

b Write your answer to part **a** in index form.

c Use your answer to part **b** to write 120, 240 and 480 as a product of prime factors in index form.

(PS) **6** $1001 = 7 \times 11 \times 13$

$1001^2 = 1\,002\,001$

$1001^3 = 1\,003\,003\,001$

a Write $1\,002\,001$ as a product of prime factors in index form.

b Write $1\,003\,003\,001$ as a product of prime factors in index form.

c Write 1001^{10} as a product of prime factors in index form.

7 Harriet wants to share £40 among three of her grandchildren. Explain why it is not possible for them to get equal shares.

(MR) **8** $98 = ab^2$, where a and b are prime numbers. Work out the value of a and b.

(MR) **9** A number x in prime factor form is 2^2a^3b where a and b are odd prime numbers.

a Which of the following are factors of x?

$\quad 8 \qquad 2ab \qquad a^4b \qquad a^2 \qquad 4b$

b Which of the following are multiples of x?

$\quad 8a^3b \qquad 2ab \qquad 4a^3b^2 \qquad a^3b \qquad 4ab$

Lowest common multiple

The **lowest common multiple** (LCM) of two numbers is the smallest number that appears in the multiplication tables of both numbers.

For example, the LCM of 3 and 5 is 15, the LCM of 2 and 7 is 14 and the LCM of 6 and 9 is 18.

There are two ways of working out the LCM.

Example 11

Find the LCM of 18 and 24.

Write out the 18 times table.   18, 36, 54, (72), 90, 108, …

Write out the 24 times table.   24, 48, (72), 96, 120, …

You can see that 72 is the smallest (lowest) number in both (common) tables (multiples).

Example 12

Find the LCM of 42 and 63.

Write 42 in prime factor form. $42 = 2 \times 3 \times 7$

Write 63 in prime factor form. $63 = 3^2 \times 7$

Now write down, in prime factor form, the smallest number that includes all the prime factors of 42 and of 63. $2 \times 3^2 \times 7$ (This includes $2 \times 3 \times 7$ and $3^2 \times 7$.)

Then work it out. $2 \times 3^2 \times 7 = 2 \times 9 \times 7$

$$= 18 \times 7$$

$$= 126$$

The LCM of 42 and 63 is 126.

Highest common factor

The **highest common factor** (HCF) of two numbers is the biggest number that divides exactly into both of them.

For example, the HCF of 24 and 18 is 6, the HCF of 45 and 36 is 9 and the HCF of 15 and 22 is 1.

There are two ways of working out the HCF.

Example 13

Find the HCF of 28 and 16.

Write out the factors of 28.   1, 2, (4), 7, 14, 28

Write out the factors of 16.   1, 2, (4), 8, 16

You can see that 4 is the biggest (highest) number in both (common) lists (factors).

Example 14

Find the HCF of 48 and 120.

Write 48 in prime factor form. $48 = 2^4 \times 3$

Write 120 in prime factor form. $120 = 2^3 \times 3 \times 5$

Write down the biggest number in prime factor form that is in the prime factors of 48 and 120.
            $2^3 \times 3$ (This is in both $2^4 \times 3$ and $2^3 \times 3 \times 5$.)

Then work it out. $2^3 \times 3 = 8 \times 3$

$$= 24$$

The HCF of 48 and 120 is 24.

Exercise 1H

1 Find the LCM of each pair of numbers.

    a 4 and 5   **b** 7 and 8   **c** 2 and 3   **d** 4 and 7

    e 2 and 5   **f** 3 and 5   **g** 3 and 8   **h** 5 and 6

2 What connection is there between the LCMs and the pairs of numbers in question **1**?

3 Find the LCM of each pair of numbers.

    a 4 and 8   **b** 6 and 9   **c** 4 and 6   **d** 10 and 15

4 Does the connection you found in question **2** still work for the numbers in question **3**? If not, explain why not.

5 Find the LCM of each pair of numbers.

    a 24 and 56   **b** 21 and 35   **c** 12 and 28   **d** 28 and 42

    e 12 and 32   **f** 18 and 27   **g** 15 and 25   **h** 16 and 36

6 Cheese slices are sold in packs of eight.

Bread rolls are sold in packs of six. What is the least number of each pack that needs to be bought to have the same number of cheese slices and bread rolls?

7 Find the HCF of each pair of numbers.

    a 24 and 56   **b** 21 and 35   **c** 16 and 36

    d 48 and 64   **e** 28 and 42   **f** 18 and 27

8 In prime factor form $1250 = 2 \times 5^4$ and $525 = 3 \times 5^2 \times 7$.

    a Which of these are common multiples of 1250 and 525?

        i $2 \times 3 \times 5^3 \times 7$ **ii** $2^3 \times 3 \times 5^4 \times 7^2$

        iii $2 \times 3 \times 5^4 \times 7$ **iv** $2 \times 3 \times 5 \times 7$

    b Which of these are common factors of 1250 and 525?

        i 2×3 **ii** 2×5

        iii 5^2 **iv** $2 \times 3 \times 5 \times 7$

9 The HCF of two numbers is 6. The LCM of the same two numbers is 72. What are the numbers?

10 $A = 2x^2y$ and $B = 3xy^2$.

    a Work out the LCM of A and B.

    b Work out the HCF of A and B.

1.6 Negative numbers

This section will show you how to:

- multiply and divide positive and negative numbers.

The number line

Look at the number line.

```
 -7  -6  -5  -4  -3  -2  -1   0   1   2   3   4   5   6   7
        negative                        positive
```

Notice that the negative numbers are to the left of 0 and the positive numbers are to the right of 0.

Numbers to the right of any number on the number line are always bigger than that number.

Numbers to the left of any number on the number line are always smaller than that number.

So, for example, you can see from a number line that:

- 2 is smaller than 5 because 2 is to the left of 5. You can write this as 2 < 5.
- −3 is smaller than 2 because −3 is to the left of 2. You can write this as −3 < 2.
- 7 is bigger than 3 because 7 is to the right of 3. You can write this as 7 > 3.
- −1 is bigger than −4 because −1 is to the right of −4. You can write this as −1 > −4.

Reminder: < means 'is less than'. > means 'is greater than' or 'is more than'.

Rules for adding and subtracting negative numbers

- To subtract a negative number, treat the − − as a +.
  For example: 4 − (−2) = 4 + 2 = 6
- To add a negative number, treat the + − as a −.
  For example: 3 + (−5) = 3 − 5 = −2

Rules for multiplying and dividing with negative numbers

- When the signs of the numbers are the same, the answer is positive.
  For example: 2 × 4 = 8, −12 ÷ −3 = 4
- When the signs of the numbers are different, the answer is negative.
  For example: 12 ÷ −3 = −4, −2 × 3 = −6

Negative numbers on a calculator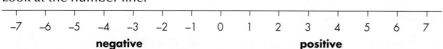

You can enter a negative number into your calculator and check the result.

Enter −5 by pressing the keys **5** and **(−)**. (The order in which you need to press these keys will depend on the type of calculator that you have.) You will see the calculator shows −5.

Here are two calculations with examples of key sequences. Try them and make sure you know how your calculator works.

−3 × 4 → **(−)** **3** **×** **4** **=** −12

−24 ÷ +4 → **(−)** **2** **4** **÷** **4** **=** −6

> **Hints and tips** Do not enter a plus sign for a positive number or your calculator will try to add it on.

Now try these calculations.

−8 − 7 → −15

6 − −3 → 9

Exercise 1I

1 Write down the answer to each calculation. Then use a calculator to check your answers.

   a $-2 + 9 =$ **b** $-6 + -2 =$ **c** $-1 + -4 =$ **d** $-8 + -3 =$

   e $5 - -6 =$ **f** $3 - -3 =$ **g** $6 - -2 =$ **h** $3 - -5 =$

   i $-5 - -3 =$ **j** $-2 - -1 =$ **k** $-4 - 5 =$ **l** $2 - 7 =$

   m $-3 + 8 =$ **n** $-4 + -5 =$ **o** $1 - -7 =$ **p** $-5 - -5 =$

2 Write down the answer to each calculation.

   a -3×5 **b** -2×7 **c** -4×6 **d** -2×-3

   e -7×-2 **f** $-12 \div -6$ **g** $-16 \div 8$ **h** $24 \div -3$

   i $16 \div -4$ **j** $-6 \div -2$ **k** 4×-6 **l** 5×-2

   m 6×-3 **n** -2×-8 **o** -9×-4

3 Write down the answers.

   a $-3 + -6$ **b** -2×-8 **c** $2 + -5$ **d** 8×-4

   e $-36 \div -2$ **f** -3×-6 **g** $-3 - -9$ **h** $48 \div -12$

   i -5×-4 **j** $7 - -9$ **k** $-40 \div -5$ **l** $-40 + -8$

   m $4 - -9$ **n** $5 - 18$ **o** $72 \div -9$

4 What number do you multiply -3 by to get each number?

   a 6 **b** -90 **c** -45

   d 81 **e** 21

5 Evaluate these.

   a $-6 + (4 - 7)$ **b** $-3 - (-9 - -3)$ **c** $8 + (2 - 9)$

6 Evaluate these.

   a $4 \times (-8 \div -2)$ **b** $-8 - (3 \times -2)$ **c** $-1 \times (8 - -4)$

 7 Write down six different multiplications that give the answer -12.

 8 Write down six different divisions that give the answer -4.

9 **a** Work out 12×-2.

   b The average temperature drops by 2 °C every day for 12 days. By how much has the temperature dropped altogether?

   c The temperature drops by 6 °C for each of the next three days. Write down the calculation to work out the total change in temperature over these three days.

10 Put these calculations in order from lowest result to highest.

   -15×4 $-72 \div 4$ $-56 \div -8$ 13×-6

11 The rule for converting degrees Celsius (°C) to degrees Fahrenheit (°F) is:

$$C = \frac{5}{9}(F - 32)$$

a Water freezes at 0 °C and boils at 100 °C. Work out the temperatures in degrees Fahrenheit that water freezes and boils at.

b Work out the temperature that is the same in °C and °F.

12 Absolute zero is the lowest temperature possible. It is −273.15 °C. Use the formula in question **11** to work out absolute zero in °F. Give your answer to the nearest degree.

Hierarchy of operations

Reminder: The order in which you *must* do mathematical operations should follow the BIDMAS/BODMAS rule.

B   Brackets

I/O   Indices (pOwers)

D   Division

M   Multiplication

A   Addition

S   Subtraction

Errors are often made because of negative signs or doing calculations in the wrong order.
For example:

$2 + 3 \times 4$ is equal to $2 + 12 = 14$ and *not* 5×4

-6^2 is *not* the same as $(-6)^2$

$$-6^2 = -(6 \times 6)$$
$$= -36$$

but $(-6)^2 = -6 \times -6$
$$= 36$$

Example 15

Work these out.

a $(8 - 3^2) \times 9 \div (-1 + 4)$ **b** $5 \times [6^2 + (5 - 8)^2]$

a Calculate the brackets first.

$$(8 - 3^2) \times 9 \div (-1 + 4) = (8 - 9) \times 9 \div 3$$
$$= -1 \times 9 \div 3$$
$$= -9 \div 3$$
$$= -3$$

b This has nested brackets. Complete the calculation in the inside (round) brackets first.

$$5 \times [6^2 + (5 - 8)^2] = 5 \times [6^2 + (-3)^2]$$
$$= 5 \times [36 + 9]$$
$$= 5 \times 45$$
$$= 225$$

Exercise 1J

1 Work these out. Remember to work out the brackets first.

   a $-2 \times (-3 + 5)$ **b** $6 \div (-2 + 1)$ **c** $(5 - 7) \times -2$

   d $-5 \times (-7 - 2)$ **e** $-3 \times (-4 \div 2)$ **f** $-3 \times (-4 + 2)$

2 Work these out.

   a $-6 \times -6 + 2$ **b** $-6 \times (-6 + 2)$ **c** $-6 \div 6 - 2$

   d $12 \div (-4 + 2)$ **e** $12 \div -4 + 2$ **f** $2 \times (-3 + 4)$

   g $-(5)^2$ **h** $(-5)^2$ **i** $(-1 + 3)^2 - 4$

   j $-(1 + 3)^2 - 4$ **k** $-1 + 3^2 - 4$ **l** $-1 + (3 - 4)^2$

3 Copy each of these and then put in brackets where necessary to make it true.

   a $3 \times -4 + 1 = -11$ **b** $-6 \div -2 + 1 = 6$ **c** $-6 \div -2 + 1 = 4$

   d $4 + -4 \div 4 = 3$ **e** $4 + -4 \div 4 = 0$ **f** $16 - -4 \div 2 = 10$

4 Work out the value of each expression when $a = -2$, $b = 3$ and $c = -5$.

   a $(a + c)^2$ **b** $-(a + b)^2$ **c** $(a + b)c$ **d** $a^2 + b^2 - c^2$

5 Work out the value of each expression.

   a $(6^2 - 4^2) \times 2$ **b** $9 \div (1 - 4)^2$

   c $2 \times [8^2 - (2 - 7)^2]$ **d** $[(3 + 2)^2 - (5 - 6)^2] \div 6$

6 Use each of the numbers 2, 3 and 4 and each of the symbols $-$, $\times$ and $\div$ to make a calculation with an answer -6.

7 Use any four different numbers to make a calculation with answer -8.

8 Explain the difference between $(-4)^2$ and $-(4)^2$.

9 Use the numbers 5, 6, 7, 8 and 9 in order, from smallest to largest, together with one of each of the symbols $+$, $-$, $\times$ and $\div$ and two pairs of brackets to make a calculation with an answer of $\frac{25}{8}$.

For example, to make a calculation with an answer of $\frac{43}{9}$: $(5 + 6) - (7 \times 8) \div 9 = \frac{43}{9}$.

10 Work out the value of x to make this equation true.

   $5 + 2 \times (x - 35) = (5 + 2) \times x - 35$

> **Hints and tips**   Make x the subject. The answer is negative.

Worked exemplars

  I earn £30 000 in 12 months.

20% of this is deducted for tax.

x% is deducted for National Insurance.

At the end of each month I have £1800 left.

Work out the value of x.

This is a problem-solving question. You will need to plan a strategy to solve it and, most importantly, communicate your method clearly.	

Method 1
 	
Yearly take home pay = £1800 × 12
          = £21 600
 	
Amount deducted = £30 000 − £21 600
          = £8400
 	
Tax deducted = £30 000 × 0.2
          = £6000
 	
NI deducted = £8400 − £6000
          = £2400
 	
NI as a percentage of earnings
          = 2400 ÷ 30 000 × 100
          = 0.08 × 100
          x = 8%
	There are two different methods that lead to the correct answer: method 1 works on yearly earnings and method 2 on monthly earnings. Use the one you find easier to explain.

Method 2 £30 000 ÷ 12 = £2500 £2500 − £1800 = £700 £2500 × 0.2 = £500 £700 − £500 = £200 £200 ÷ £2500 × £100 = 8%	*Do not* just write down numbers. Get used to writing, in words, what you are calculating. Copy these calculations and put some words at the start of each line to explain what is being worked out.

  Two numbers have been rounded.

The first number is 360 to two significant figures.

The second number is 500 to one significant figure.

What is the smallest possible sum of the two original numbers?

This question assesses your mathematical reasoning.	
The smallest that the first number could be is 355. The smallest that the second number could be is 450.	First work out the smallest possible value for each number.
Smallest sum = 355 + 450 = 805	Then work out the sum of these two numbers. Sometimes you may make a mistake, say working out the smallest value of the second number as 495, but as long as you have explained your working you can still get some credit. That is why it is essential to write down what you are working out.

3 a, b and c form a sequence with common difference 150.

$a = 3p^2q$ $b = 3^2p^3$ $c = 3p^2r$

p, q and r are prime numbers greater than 3.

Work out the values of p, q and r.

This is a problem-solving question. You will need to show your strategy clearly and make sure that for each line you write down it is clear what you are calculating	
Subtract the first two terms: $9p^3 - 3p^2q = 150$ Factorise: $3p^2(3p - q) = 150$ Divide by 3: $p^2(3p - q) = 50$	Use the information that you know. The difference between the first two terms is 150. Factorise and cancel as much as possible.
If p^2 is a factor of 50, $p = 5$. $\therefore 3p - q = 2 \Rightarrow q = 13$	The resulting equation shows that p^2 is a factor of 50 so it can only be 25, which means that $p = 5$. Then you can calculate the value of q.
$a = 975$ and $b = 1125$ $\therefore c = 1275$	Once you know p and q you can work out a, b and c.
$\therefore r = 1275 \div (3 \times 25)$ $= 17$	Once you know c you can work out r.
$\therefore p = 5$, $q = 13$ and $r = 17$	Write the final answers clearly.

 4 Two numbers, x and y, can be written in prime factor form as $x = 2^3 \times a \times b^2$ and $y = 2^2 \times a^3 \times b$, where a and b are prime numbers greater than 2.

a Which of these terms are factors of both x and y?

$2ab$ $\quad$ 4 $\quad$ $8a^2b$ $\quad$ $4a^2b^2$

b Which of these expressions is the LCM of x and y?

$2ab$ $\quad$ $8a^3b^2$ $\quad$ $4ab$ $\quad$ $32a^4b^3$

This is a mathematical reasoning question with a multi-choice answer, so there is no working to be shown.	
a $2ab$ and 4	Look at each expression and decide if it will divide into x and y. $2ab$ and 4 will divide into both but a^2 will not divide into x, and $8b^2$ will not divide into y.
b $8a^3b^2$	Take the number term and each letter term in turn. There must be at least 2^3, at least a^3 and at least b^2 in the LCM.

Ready to progress?

I can recognise and work out multiples, factors and primes.
I can multiply and divide with negative numbers.
I can round numbers to a given number of significant figures.
I can estimate the values of calculations involving positive numbers.
I can write a number as the product of its prime factors.
I can work out the LCM and HCF of pairs of numbers.
I can use a calculator efficiently and know how to give answers to an appropriate degree of accuracy.
I can work out the square roots of some decimal numbers.
I can estimate answers involving the square roots of decimals.

I can work out the HCF and the LCM of two numbers from their prime factors.
I can use numbers rounded to given accuracies to work out complex problems.

Review questions

1 Eric earns £14 per hour. He works for 38 hours per week. He saves $\frac{1}{4}$ of his earnings each week. How many weeks will it take him to save £1200?

2 A floor measures 5.25 m by 4.5 m. It is to be covered with square carpet tiles of side 25 cm. Tiles are sold in boxes of 24. How many boxes are needed?

3 Find the lowest common multiple (LCM) of 54 and 90.

4 **a** Express 315 as a product of its prime factors.

b Find the highest common factor (HCF) of 315 and 63.

5 Use a calculator to work out:

$$\sqrt{\frac{52.1 \times 10.5}{4.2}}$$

a Write down all the figures on your calculator display.

b Give your answer to part **a** to 3 significant figures.

6 **a** Use your calculator to work out the value of this expression.

$20.3^2 + \sqrt[3]{130} \div 9.87$

Write down your full calculator display.

b Use approximations to check your answer to **a**. Show your calculations clearly.

7 The Venn diagram shows the prime factors of two numbers, A and B.

a Which of the following describe the universal set ξ?

i Prime factors of A and B

ii Odd numbers less than 20

iii Prime numbers less than 20

iv HCF of A and B

b From the numbers in the box, write down:

i the value of A

ii the LCM of A and B

iii the HCF of A and B.

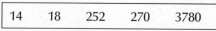

| 14 | 18 | 252 | 270 | 3780 |

8 Use your calculator to work out the value of $\sqrt{9.23^2 + 5.34^2}$.

   a Write down all the figures on your calculator display.

   b Write your answer to part **a** correct to 2 significant figures.

9 Work out an estimate for $\dfrac{6.13 \times 78.8}{0.405}$.

10 Mary set up her Christmas tree with two sets of twinkling lights.

Set A would twinkle every 4 seconds.

Set B would twinkle every 6 seconds.

How many times in a minute will both sets be twinkling at the same time?

11 **a** Use your calculator to work out $355 \div 113$. Give your answer as a decimal.

   b Part **a** is considered to be the best approximation to π as it is a simple calculation and easy to remember. The accurate value of π is 3.141 592 65 to 8 decimal places. Round your answer to **a** to 8 decimal places and calculate the percentage error in the approximation given by $355 \div 113$.

12 The Town Hall clock gains two minutes every hour. The clock at the library is accurate. They both chime on every quarter hour. Both clocks are set at 12:00 noon on Monday so they chime together.

   a At what time and day will they next chime together?

   b At what time and day will they next chime on the hour together?

13 In prime factor form, $240 = 2^4 \times 3 \times 5$ and $756 = 2^2 \times 3^3 \times 7$.

Work out, in prime factor form:

   a the LCM of 240 and 756   **b** the HCF of 240 and 756.

14 As a product of prime factors $60 = 2^2 \times 3 \times 5$.

   a What number is represented by $2 \times 3^2 \times 5$?

   b Find the lowest common multiple (LCM) of 60 and 48.

   c Find the highest common factor (HCF) of 60 and 78.

15 Jack thinks of two numbers.

He says, "The highest common factor (HCF) of my two numbers is 9.

The lowest common multiple (LCM) of my two numbers is 108."

Write down two numbers that Jack could be thinking of.

16 **a** Use approximations to estimate the value of $\dfrac{113 \times 8.08}{0.38}$.

   b Is the actual answer higher or lower than the estimate? Explain your answer.

17 **a** p, q and r are prime numbers such that $pqr^3 = 270$.

   Work out the values of p, q and r.

   b Work out the highest common factor of 270 and 105.

18 The number 864 can be written as $2^m \times 3^n$, where m and n are prime numbers. Find the value of m and the value of n.

2 Number: Fractions, ratio and proportion

This chapter is going to show you:

- how to work out one quantity as a fraction of another
- how to add, subtract, multiply and divide fractions with and without a calculator
- how to use a percentage multiplier
- how to work out percentage increase and decrease
- how to work out one quantity as a percentage of another.

You should already know:

- how to cancel fractions to their simplest form
- how to find equivalent fractions, decimals and percentages
- how to add and subtract fractions with the same denominator
- how to work out simple percentages, such as 10%, of quantities
- how to convert a mixed number to an improper fraction and vice versa.

About this chapter

Fractions and percentages are all around you, in your everyday life.

You will often see signs in shops or on the internet with messages such as 'Sale: Save $\frac{1}{4}$ off the marked price' or 'Special offer: 10% off'. When banks lend money they charge an annual percentage and when you save with them they give you a percentage in interest. For example, a bank might say, 'Loans interest rate $3\frac{1}{4}$%' or 'Savings interest rate $2\frac{1}{2}$%'. Salespeople often get a basic salary plus a percentage of the sales they make. The government uses fractions or percentages to set targets or make claims about changes. For example: 'Our aim is to cut carbon emissions by one-third by 2020', 'Unemployment has fallen by 1%', 'Inflation is 3.6%', 'Income tax is 20%' or 'Value-added tax is 20%'. Your school probably also uses fractions and percentages to tell parents about your progress. For example, 'Mandeep scored 67% in his mathematics test.'

Without a basic understanding of fractions and percentages, you will not be able to make sense of a lot of the figures you meet in day-to-day life.

2.1 One quantity as a fraction of another

This section will show you how to:

- find one quantity as a fraction of another.

Key terms

| fraction | quantity |

There are many situations when you may need to describe one amount or **quantity** as a **fraction** of another. For example, in one day you might find that about half the students in your school are boys, you spend about a third of your time in bed or your bus fares cost about a fifth of your money each week.

Sometimes you need to be more accurate and work with exact rather than approximate amounts. The next examples will show you how to do this.

Example 1

Write £5 as a fraction of £20.

£5 as a fraction of £20 is written as $\frac{5}{20}$.

Note that $\frac{5}{20} = \frac{1 \times 5}{4 \times 5}$ so you can cancel the fraction to $\frac{1}{4}$.

So £5 is one-quarter of £20.

Example 2

A book has 320 pages. 200 of the pages have illustrations. $\frac{3}{4}$ of these pages have colour illustrations.

How many of the pages of the whole book have colour illustrations? Express the answer as a fraction of the whole book.

200 pages have illustrations.

This is $\frac{200}{320} = \frac{10 \times 4 \times 5}{4 \times 10 \times 8}$

$= \frac{5}{8}$ of the book.

$\frac{3}{4}$ of the pages with illustrations are in colour. $\frac{3}{4} \times 200 = 150$

150 of the 320 pages have colour illustrations.

This is $\frac{150}{320}$ of the book. It cancels to $\frac{15}{32}$.

Exercise 2A

1   Write the first quantity as a fraction of the second.

   a 2 cm, 6 cm   **b** 4 kg, 20 kg   **c** £8, £20   **d** 5 hours, 24 hours

   e 12 days, 30 days   **f** 50p, £3   **g** 4 days, 2 weeks   **h** 40 minutes, 2 hours

2   During April, it rained on 12 days. For what fraction of the month did it rain?

3   In a class of 30 students, $\frac{3}{5}$ are boys. Of these boys $\frac{1}{3}$ are left-handed. What fraction of the whole class is made up of left-handed boys?

4   Reka wins £120 in a competition and puts £40 in a bank account. She gives $\frac{1}{4}$ of what is left to her sister and then spends the rest. What fraction of her winnings did she spend?

5   Jon earns £90 and saves £30 of it. Matt earns £100 and saves £35 of it. Who is saving the greater proportion of his earnings?

6   In two tests Harry gets 13 out of 20 and 16 out of 25. Which is the better mark? Explain your answer.

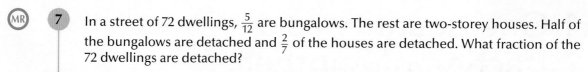

MR **7** In a street of 72 dwellings, $\frac{5}{12}$ are bungalows. The rest are two-storey houses. Half of the bungalows are detached and $\frac{2}{7}$ of the houses are detached. What fraction of the 72 dwellings are detached?

PS **8** I have 24 T-shirts. $\frac{1}{6}$ have logos on them; the rest are plain. $\frac{2}{5}$ of the plain T-shirts are long-sleeved. $\frac{3}{4}$ of the T-shirts with logos are long-sleeved. What fraction of all my T-shirts are long-sleeved?

PS **9** Three quantities are x, y and z. $\frac{x}{y} = \frac{3}{4}$ and $\frac{y}{z} = \frac{4}{7}$.
Work out the value of $\frac{x}{z}$.

PS **10** Three quantities are a, b and c. $\frac{a}{b} = \frac{3}{4}$ and $\frac{b}{c} = \frac{6}{11}$.
Work out the value of $\frac{a}{c}$.

2.2 Adding, subtracting and calculating with fractions

This section will show you how to:

- add and subtract fractions with different denominators.

You can only add or subtract fractions that have the same denominator. If necessary, change one or both to *equivalent fractions* with the same denominator. Then add or subtract the numerators.

Always look for the lowest common denominator of the fractions you are changing. This is the lowest common multiple (LCM) of both denominators.

Example 3

Work this out. $\frac{5}{6} - \frac{3}{4}$

The LCM of 4 and 6 is 12, so the problem becomes:

$$\frac{5}{6} - \frac{3}{4} = \frac{5}{6} \times \frac{2}{2} - \frac{3}{4} \times \frac{3}{3}$$

$$= \frac{10}{12} - \frac{9}{12}$$

$$= \frac{1}{12}$$

A fraction in which the numerator is bigger than the denominator is called an improper fraction. You know how to change improper fractions to mixed numbers, and mixed numbers to improper fractions.

You also know that a mixed number is made up of a whole number and a proper fraction, for example:

$\frac{14}{5} = 2\frac{4}{5}$ and $3\frac{2}{7} = \frac{23}{7}$

Example 4

Work these out. **a** $2\frac{1}{3} + 3\frac{5}{7}$ **b** $3\frac{1}{4} - 1\frac{3}{5}$

Separate the whole numbers from the fractions.

a $2\frac{1}{3} + 3\frac{5}{7} = 2 + 3 + \frac{1}{3} + \frac{5}{7}$

$= 5 + \frac{7}{21} + \frac{15}{21}$

$= 5 + \frac{22}{21}$

$= 5 + 1\frac{1}{21}$

$= 6\frac{1}{21}$

b $3\frac{1}{4} - 1\frac{3}{5} = 3 - 1 + \frac{1}{4} - \frac{3}{5}$

$= 2 + \frac{5}{20} - \frac{12}{20}$

$= 2 - \frac{7}{20}$

$= 1\frac{13}{20}$

Shop A sells a bicycle for £540 including VAT but has an offer of $\frac{1}{4}$ off the selling price.

Shop B sells the same model of bicycle for £350 (excluding VAT). VAT will add $\frac{1}{5}$ to the price.

In which shop is the bike cheaper? Show your working.

Shop A: $540 \div 4 \times 3 = 405$

Shop B: $350 \times \frac{1}{5} = 70$

$350 + 70 = 420$

So the bike is cheaper in shop A.

Exercise 2B

1 Work these out.

a $\frac{1}{3} + \frac{1}{5}$ b $\frac{1}{3} + \frac{1}{4}$ c $\frac{2}{3} + \frac{1}{4}$

d $\frac{1}{5} - \frac{1}{10}$ e $\frac{7}{8} - \frac{3}{4}$ f $\frac{5}{6} - \frac{3}{4}$

(MR) 2 Which is the biggest: half of 96, one-third of 141, two-fifths of 120 or three-quarters of 68?

3 Work these out.

a $3\frac{1}{3} + 1\frac{9}{20}$ b $1\frac{1}{8} - \frac{5}{9}$ c $\frac{7}{10} + \frac{3}{8} + \frac{5}{6}$ d $1\frac{1}{3} + \frac{7}{10} - \frac{4}{15}$

4 a In a class election, half of the students voted for Aminah, one-third voted for Jenet and the rest voted for Pieter. What fraction of the class voted for Pieter?

(EV) b One of the numbers in the box is the number of students in the class in part **a**.

| 25 | 28 | 30 | 32 |

How many students are there in the class?

(PS) 5 A one-litre bottle of milk is used to fill four glasses. Three glasses have a capacity of one-eighth of a litre. The fourth glass has a capacity of half a litre.

Priya likes milky coffee so she always has at least 10 cl of milk in her cup. Is there enough milk left in the bottle for Priya to have two cups of coffee?

(CM) 6 Mick has worked out this sum.

$1\frac{1}{3} + 2\frac{1}{4} = 3\frac{2}{7}$

His answer is incorrect. What mistake has he made? Work out the correct answer.

(CM) 7 Write down how you would explain to someone, in a telephone call, how to find the answer to this calculation.

$\frac{1}{4} + \frac{2}{5}$

(PS) 8 There are 900 students in a school. $\frac{11}{20}$ of the students are boys. Of the boys, $\frac{2}{11}$ are left-handed. Of the girls, $\frac{2}{9}$ are left-handed. What fraction of all the students are left-handed? Show your working.

9 There are 600 counters in a bag. Each counter is red, blue or yellow. $\frac{3}{8}$ of the counters are red. $\frac{1}{5}$ of the counters are blue.

a What fraction of the counters are yellow?

b How many yellow counters are there in the bag?

10 A small gym has 200 members. $\frac{27}{40}$ of the members are at least 40 years of age. $\frac{2}{5}$ of the members are women.

    a Use calculations to show that some of the women are at least 40 years of age.

    b $\frac{5}{8}$ of the women are at least 40 years old. How many of the men are aged less than 40?

11 This is how Jo works out the fraction at the mid-value of two other fractions.

- Write the two fractions with a common denominator.
- The numerator of the midpoint fraction is the sum of the numerators of the two fractions written with a common denominator.
- The denominator of the midpoint fraction is the sum of the denominators of the two fractions written with a common denominator.

For example, to find the midpoint fraction of $\frac{1}{5}$ and $\frac{3}{4}$:

$$\frac{1}{5} = \frac{4}{20} \qquad \frac{3}{4} = \frac{15}{20}$$

So the midpoint fraction is $\frac{4+15}{20+20} = \frac{19}{40}$.

    a Show that the calculation above does give the midpoint fraction of $\frac{1}{5}$ and $\frac{3}{4}$.

    b Does the method always work? Explain your answer.

2.3 Multiplying and dividing fractions

This section will show you how to:

- multiply proper fractions
- multiply mixed numbers
- divide by fractions.

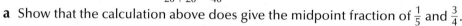

Key term

reciprocal

Multiplying fractions

To multiply fractions, follow these four steps.

Step 1: Convert any mixed numbers into improper fractions and rewrite the multiplication if necessary.

Step 2: Simplify the multiplication by cancelling by any common factors in the numerators and the denominators.

Step 3: Multiply the numerators to obtain the numerator of the answer and multiply the denominators to obtain the denominator of the answer.

Step 4: If the answer is an improper fraction, convert this into a mixed number.

Work these out. **a** $\frac{4}{9} \times \frac{3}{10}$ **b** $2\frac{2}{5} \times 1\frac{7}{8}$	
a $\dfrac{{}^2\cancel{4}}{{}_3\cancel{9}} \times \dfrac{\cancel{3}^{1}}{\cancel{10}_{5}} = \dfrac{2}{15}$	Identify any common factors in the numerators and denominators: 2 is a factor of 4 and 10; 3 is a factor of 3 and 9. Simplify the fractions, cancelling by 2 and 3, before multiplying.
b $2\frac{2}{5} \times 1\frac{7}{8} = \dfrac{12}{5} \times \dfrac{15}{8}$ $\dfrac{{}^3\cancel{12}}{{}_1\cancel{5}} \times \dfrac{\cancel{15}^{3}}{\cancel{8}_{2}} = \dfrac{9}{2} = 4\frac{1}{2}$	Convert the mixed numbers into improper fractions. Simplify the fractions, cancelling by 4 and 5.

Reciprocal of a fraction

The **reciprocal** of a number is simply the number divided into one. So the reciprocal of 2 is $1 \div 2 = \frac{1}{2}$.

The reciprocal of a fraction is simply the fraction turned upside down, so the reciprocal of $\frac{2}{5}$ is $\frac{5}{2}$.
Check on your calculator by keying in:

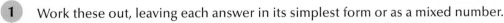

You will do more work on reciprocals in a later chapter.

For some topics in algebra, you will need to know about the negative reciprocal. This is exactly what it says: the negative reciprocal of $\frac{3}{4}$ is $-\frac{4}{3}$ and the negative reciprocal of $-\frac{2}{3}$ is $\frac{3}{2}$.

Dividing fractions

Dividing by a fraction is equivalent to multiplying by the reciprocal of the fraction. For example:

- dividing by $\frac{2}{3}$ is the same as multiplying by $\frac{3}{2}$
- dividing by $\frac{1}{4}$ is the same as multiplying by 4.

Follow these three steps to divide fractions.

Step 1: Convert any mixed numbers into improper fractions.

Step 2: Convert the division calculation into a multiplication calculation by writing the reciprocal of the divisor.

Step 3: Carry out the multiplication.

Example 7

Work these out.   **a** $\frac{5}{6} \div \frac{3}{4}$ **b** $2\frac{1}{2} \div 3\frac{1}{3}$

a $\frac{5}{6} \div \frac{3}{4} = \frac{5}{{}_3 6} \times \frac{4^2}{3}$ $= \frac{10}{9}$ $= 1\frac{1}{9}$	Convert the division calculation into a multiplication calculation by rewriting $\frac{5}{6} \div \frac{3}{4}$ as $\frac{5}{6} \times \frac{4}{3}$. Then cancel common factors, multiply and convert your answer to a mixed number.
b $2\frac{1}{2} \div 3\frac{1}{3} = \frac{5}{2} \div \frac{10}{3}$ $\frac{5}{2} \div \frac{10}{3} = \frac{5}{2} \times \frac{3}{10}$ $\frac{{}^1 5}{2} \times \frac{3}{10_2} = \frac{3}{4}$	Convert the mixed numbers into improper fractions. Convert the division into a multiplication calculation. Complete the multiplication.

Exercise 2C

1 Work these out, leaving each answer in its simplest form or as a mixed number.

a $\frac{1}{2} \times \frac{1}{3}$ **b** $\frac{3}{4} \times \frac{1}{2}$ **c** $\frac{14}{15} \times \frac{3}{8}$ **d** $\frac{6}{7} \times \frac{21}{30}$

e $1\frac{1}{4} \times \frac{1}{3}$ **f** $1\frac{3}{4} \times 1\frac{2}{3}$ **g** $3\frac{1}{4} \times 1\frac{1}{5}$ **h** $1\frac{1}{4} \times 2\frac{2}{3}$

2 Work these out, leaving your answer as a fraction or mixed number.

a $\frac{1}{4} \div \frac{1}{3}$ **b** $\frac{4}{5} \div \frac{3}{4}$ **c** $7\frac{1}{2} \div 1\frac{1}{2}$

d $1\frac{5}{12} \div 3\frac{3}{16}$ **e** $3\frac{3}{5} \div 2\frac{1}{4}$

3 Write down the reciprocal of each number.

    a 4   **b** $\frac{1}{5}$ **c** $\frac{3}{8}$ **d** $\frac{5}{4}$

4 Write down the negative reciprocal of each number.

    a 5   **b** $-\frac{1}{2}$ **c** $\frac{7}{9}$ **d** $-\frac{3}{5}$

5 Bilal eats one-quarter of a cake, and then half of what is left. How much cake is left uneaten?

6 You are given that 1 tonne = 1000 kilograms.

A dustbin lorry carries 12 tonnes of rubbish. Three-quarters of this is recycled.

Half of the remainder is sent for landfill and the rest is sent to an incinerator.

What fraction of the rubbish goes to landfill?

7 Zahar made $12\frac{1}{2}$ litres of lemonade for a party. His glasses could each hold $\frac{5}{16}$ of a litre. How many of the glasses could he fill from the $12\frac{1}{2}$ litres of lemonade?

8 Which is larger, $\frac{3}{4}$ of $2\frac{1}{2}$ or $\frac{2}{5}$ of $6\frac{1}{2}$?

(CM) 9 If £5.20 is two-thirds of three-quarters of a sum of money, what is the total amount of money?

10 Work these out.

    a $\frac{18}{25} \times \frac{15}{16} \div 2\frac{2}{5}$ **b** $\left(\frac{4}{5} \times \frac{4}{5}\right) \div \left(1\frac{1}{4} \times 1\frac{1}{4}\right)$

(CM) 11 During a heatwave a pond loses $\frac{1}{8}$ of the water it contains each day. Show that after two days it has $\frac{49}{64}$ of the original water left.

(PS) 12 A flour mill produces 120 kg of flour a day. The flour is packed into bags that weigh either $1\frac{1}{2}$ kg or $2\frac{1}{2}$ kg. One day they pack 50 of the $1\frac{1}{2}$ kg bags. How many $2\frac{1}{2}$ kg bags do they pack?

(CM) 13   **a** Show that you can use a fraction to estimate the answer to '77% of 243' as 180.

(EV)   **b** Will the answer to part **a** be higher or lower than the true value? Explain your answer.

2.4 Fractions on a calculator

This section will show you how to:

- use a calculator to add and subtract fractions
- use a calculator to multiply and divide fractions.

When you use a calculator for work on fractions, the method of working is different from when you work 'on paper'. For example, you will not need to change the denominators to add or subtract, and you may not need to change mixed numbers to improper fractions to multiply or divide. Your calculator should do this for you.

Some calculators may give answers as improper fractions. Make sure that you know which keys to use to convert them.

Hints and tips   Not all models of calculator work the same way, so make sure you know how yours works. The keystrokes in this section are based on a standard calculator.

Using a calculator to convert improper fractions to mixed numbers

Find the fraction key on your calculator. Remember, for some functions, you may need to use the **shift key**.

To key in a fraction, press [fraction key].

Input the fraction so that it looks like this: $\frac{9}{5}$ or 9⌟5

Now press the equals key [=] so that the fraction displays in the answer part of the screen.

Pressing shift and the key [S⇔D] will convert the fraction to a mixed number: 1⌟4⌟5

This is the mixed number $1\frac{4}{5}$.

Pressing the equals key [=] again will convert the mixed number back to an improper fraction.

- Try to think of a way of converting an improper fraction to a mixed number without using a calculator.
- Test your idea, and then use your calculator to check it.

Using a calculator to convert mixed numbers to improper fractions

To input a mixed number, press the shift key [shift] first and then the fraction key [fraction key].

Pressing the equals sign [=] will convert the mixed number to an improper fraction.

- Key in at least 10 improper fractions and convert them to mixed numbers.
- Remember to press the equals sign [=] to change the mixed numbers back to improper fractions.
- Input at least 10 mixed numbers and convert them to improper fractions.
- Look at your results. Try to think of a way of converting a mixed number to an improper fraction without using a calculator.
- Test your idea and then use your calculator to check it.

Using a calculator to add and subtract fractions

Practise adding and subtracting fractions until you are sure that you know how to do it. Then work through the next two examples.

Example 8

A water tank is half full. One-third of the full capacity of the tank is poured out.

What fraction of the tank is now full of water?

The calculation is $\frac{1}{2} - \frac{1}{3}$.

Keying in the calculation gives:

[fraction key] [1] [▼] [2] [▶] [−] [fraction key] [1] [▼] [3] [▶] [=]

The display should show $\frac{1}{6}$.

The tank is now one-sixth full of water.

Example 9

Work out the perimeter of a rectangle that is $1\frac{1}{2}$ cm long and $3\frac{2}{3}$ cm wide.

To work out the perimeter of this rectangle, use the formula:

$$P = 2l + 2w$$

where $l = 1\frac{1}{2}$ cm and $w = 3\frac{2}{3}$ cm.

$$P = 2 \times 1\frac{1}{2} + 2 \times 3\frac{2}{3}$$

Keying in the calculation gives:

2 × shift $\frac{\square}{\square}$ 1 ▶ 1 ▼ 2 ▶
\+ 2 × shift $\frac{\square}{\square}$ 3 ▶ 2 ▼ 3 ▶ =

The display should show $10\frac{1}{3}$.

So the perimeter is $10\frac{1}{3}$ cm.

Using a calculator to multiply and divide fractions

Example 10

Work out the area of a rectangle of length $3\frac{1}{2}$ m and width $2\frac{2}{3}$ m.

The formula for the area of a rectangle is area = length × width.

Keying in the calculation, where length = $3\frac{1}{2}$ and width = $2\frac{2}{3}$ gives:

shift $\frac{\square}{\square}$ 3 ▶ 1 ▼ 2 ▶ ×
shift $\frac{\square}{\square}$ 2 ▶ 2 ▼ 3 ▶ =

The display should show $9\frac{1}{3}$.

The area is $9\frac{1}{3}$ cm².

Example 11

Work out the average speed of a bus that travels $20\frac{1}{4}$ miles in $\frac{3}{4}$ hour.

The formula for the average speed is average speed = $\frac{\text{total distance travelled}}{\text{total time taken}}$.

The total distance is $20\frac{1}{4}$ miles and the total time is $\frac{3}{4}$ hour.

Keying in the calculation gives:

shift $\frac{\square}{\square}$ 2 0 ▶ 1 ▼ 4 ▶
÷ $\frac{\square}{\square}$ 3 ▼ 4 ▶ =

The display should show 27.

The average speed is 27 mph.

Exercise 2D

In this exercise, try to key in each calculation as one continuous set of operations, without writing down any intermediate values.

1 Use your calculator to work these out. Give your answers as fractions.

a $\frac{3}{4} + \frac{4}{5}$ **b** $\frac{4}{5} + \frac{9}{20}$ **c** $\frac{5}{8} + \frac{9}{16} + \frac{3}{5}$

d $\frac{9}{20} - \frac{1}{12}$ **e** $\frac{7}{16} + \frac{3}{8} - \frac{1}{20}$ **f** $\frac{4}{5} + \frac{9}{16} - \frac{2}{3}$

2

a What is the distance between Wickersley and Redbrook, using these roads?

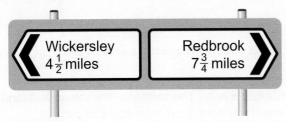

Wickersley
$4\frac{1}{2}$ miles

Redbrook
$7\frac{3}{4}$ miles

b How much further is it to Redbrook than to Wickersley?

3 Use your calculator to work these out. Give your answers as mixed numbers.

a $4\frac{3}{4} + 1\frac{4}{5}$ **b** $3\frac{5}{6} + 4\frac{7}{10}$ **c** $2\frac{5}{8} + 3\frac{9}{16} + 5\frac{3}{5}$

d $6\frac{9}{20} - 3\frac{1}{12}$ **e** $9\frac{7}{16} + 5\frac{3}{8} - 7\frac{1}{20}$ **f** $10\frac{3}{4} + 6\frac{2}{9} - 12\frac{3}{11}$

4 **a** Use your calculator to work out $\frac{18}{37} - \frac{23}{43}$.

b Explain how your answer tells you that $\frac{23}{43}$ is greater than $\frac{18}{37}$.

5 The formula for the perimeter, P, of a rectangle is:

$P = 2l + 2w$

where l is the length and w is the width.

Work out the perimeter when $l = 5\frac{1}{8}$ cm and $w = 4\frac{1}{3}$ cm.

6 A shape is rotated 90° clockwise and then a further 60° clockwise.

What fraction of a turn will return it to its original position?

Give both possible answers.

7 Use your calculator to work these out. Give your answers as fractions in their lowest terms.

a $\frac{3}{4} \times \frac{4}{5}$ **b** $\frac{5}{8} \times \frac{9}{16} \times \frac{3}{5}$ **c** $\frac{9}{20} \div \frac{1}{12}$

d $\frac{3}{4} \div \frac{7}{48}$ **e** $\frac{7}{16} \times \frac{3}{8} \div \frac{1}{20}$ **f** $\frac{3}{4} \times \frac{2}{9} \div \frac{3}{11}$

8 Use your calculator to work these out. Give your answers as mixed numbers.

a $4\frac{3}{4} \times 1\frac{4}{5}$ **b** $7\frac{4}{5} \times 8\frac{9}{20}$ **c** $2\frac{5}{8} \times 3\frac{9}{16} \times 5\frac{3}{5}$

d $6\frac{9}{20} \div 3\frac{1}{12}$ **e** $4\frac{3}{4} \div 2\frac{7}{48}$ **f** $9\frac{7}{16} \times 5\frac{3}{8} \div 7\frac{1}{20}$

9 The formula for the area of a rectangle is area = length × width.

Use this formula to work out the area of a rectangle of length $5\frac{2}{3}$ m and width $3\frac{1}{4}$ m.

10 The ribbon on a roll is $3\frac{1}{2}$ m long. Joe wants to cut pieces of ribbon that are each $\frac{1}{6}$ m long.

He needs 50 pieces.

How many rolls will he need?

(MR) **11** To work out the surface area, A, of a cube with edge length of x, square x and then multiply the result by 6.

    a Work out the surface area of a cube with an edge length of $1\frac{3}{4}$ cm.

    b Work out the edge length of a cube with a surface area of $34\frac{14}{25}$ cm². Give your answer as a mixed number.

(PS) **12** An approximation for the number π is $\frac{22}{7}$. The formulae for the area, A, and circumference, C, of a circle with radius r are $A = \pi r^2$ and $C = 2\pi r$.

    Work out the area of a circle with a circumference of 22 cm.

(PS) **13** An iron cuboid with length = $2\frac{1}{3}$ cm, width = $3\frac{1}{2}$ cm and height = $2\frac{3}{4}$ cm is melted down and formed into a sphere of radius r. The formula for the volume V_c of a cuboid is length × width × height. The formula for the volume V_s of a sphere is $V_s = \frac{4}{3}\pi \times r^3$.

    Work out the value of r. Take $\pi = \frac{22}{7}$.

(MR) **14** During a heatwave a pond loses $\frac{1}{8}$ of the water it contains each day. How much water is left after three days?

(PS) **15** A flour mill produces 120 kg of flour a day. It operates for $4\frac{1}{2}$ days a week. The flour is packed into bags with a mass of either $1\frac{1}{2}$ kg or $2\frac{1}{2}$ kg. One week they pack 175 of the $1\frac{1}{2}$ kg bags. How many $2\frac{1}{2}$ kg bags do they pack?

2.5 Increasing and decreasing quantities by a percentage

This section will show you how to:

- increase and decrease quantities by a percentage.

During sales, shops often state that they have reduced prices, and use a percentage to describe how much the prices have fallen. When newspapers describe increases in travel fares or wages, they will often use percentages to describe how much the prices have risen. This is useful because it allows you to compare the new price with the old.

Increasing by a percentage

There are two methods for increasing a quantity by a percentage. The first is to work out the increase and add it to the original amount.

Example 12

Work out the increase and add it to the original amount

Increase £6 by 5%.

Work out 5% of £6:   (5 ÷ 100) × 6 = £0.30

Add £0.30 to the original amount: £6 + £0.30 = £6.30

The second is to use a **multiplier**. For example, an increase of 6% is equivalent to the original 100% plus the extra 6%. This is a total of 106% ($\frac{106}{100}$) and is equivalent to the multiplier 1.06.

Decreasing by a percentage

There are also two methods for decreasing by a percentage. The first is to work out the decrease and subtract it from the original amount.

The second method is using a multiplier. For example, a 7% decrease is equivalent to 7% less than the original 100%, so it represents 100% – 7% = 93% of the original. This is a multiplier of 0.93.

Exercise 2E

1   Work out the multiplier you would use to increase a quantity by each percentage.

    a 10%   **b** 3%   **c** 20%

    d 7%   **e** 12%

2   Work out the multiplier you would use to decrease a quantity by each percentage.

    a 8%   **b** 15%   **c** 25%

    d 9%   **e** 12%

3   Increase each amount by the given percentage. Use any method you like.

    a 340 kg by 15%   **b** 670 cm by 23%   **c** 130 g by 95%

    d £82 by 75%   **e** 640 m by 15%   **f** £28 by 8%

4   Decrease each amount by the given percentage. Use any method you like.

    a 860 m by 15%   **b** 96 g by 13%   **c** 480 cm by 25%

    d 180 minutes by 35%   **e** 86 kg by 5%   **f** £65 by 42%

5   A large factory employed 640 people. It reduced the number of workers by 30%.
How many workers remain?

CM **6** Kerry wants to buy a sweatshirt (£19), a tracksuit (£26) and some running shoes (£56). If she joins the store's premium club, which costs £25, she can get 20% off the cost of the goods.

Should she join or not? Give calculations to support your answer.

CM **7** Kevin is on a salary of £27 500. He is offered a pay rise of 7% or an extra £150 per month. Which should he accept? Give calculations to support your answer.

8 In 2010 VAT was 17.5%. It was increased to 20% in January 2011.

a After the increase, how much more expensive was a TV that cost £245 without VAT?

EV **b** Which of these calculations would give the increase in cost of an item costing £x without VAT, after the rate increases from 17.5% to 20%?

$x \times 1.175 \div 1.2$ $x \times 1.2 \div 1.175$ $x \times 0.025$ $x \div 0.025$

EV **c** Which of these calculations would be the new cost of an item costing £y including 17.5% VAT, after the rate increases from 17.5% to 20%?

$y \div 1.175 \times 1.2$ $y \div 1.2 \times 1.175$ $y \times 0.025$ $y \div 0.025$

9 A cereal packet normally contains 300 g of cereal and costs £1.40.

There are two special offers.

Offer A: 20% more for the same price

Offer B: Same amount for 20% off the normal price

Which is the better offer?

a Offer A   **b** Offer B   **c** Both the same   **d** Cannot tell

Justify your choice.

CM **10** BookWorms increased its prices by 5%, and then increased them by 3%. Books Galore increased its prices by 3%, and then increased them by 5%.

Which shop's prices increased by the greater percentage?

a BookWorms   **b** Books Galore   **c** Both the same   **d** Cannot tell

Justify your choice.

CM **11** Shop A increased its prices by 4% and then by another 4%. Shop B increased its prices by 8%.

Which shop's prices increased by the greater percentage?

a Shop A   **b** Shop B   **c** Both the same   **d** Cannot tell

Give reasons for your answer.

12 A computer cost £450 at the start of 2013. At the start of 2014 the price was increased by 5%. At the start of 2015 the price was decreased by 10%. What did the computer cost at the start of 2015?

CM **13** Show that a 10% decrease followed by a 10% increase is equivalent to a 1% decrease overall.

| Hints and tips | Choose an amount to start with. |

PS **14** A circle has a radius of 8 cm. Its area increases by 60%. By what percentage does the radius increase? The formula for the area of a circle of radius r is $A = 3.14 \times r^2$.

(EV) **15** An approximate formula for the volume of a sphere of radius r is $V = 4r^3$.

    a The actual formula is $V = \frac{4}{3} \times \pi \times r^3$. Show that the approximate formula is accurate to within 5%.

> **Hints and tips**   Choose a value for r.

    b Is the value given by the approximate formula lower or higher than the actual value? Explain your answer.

2.6 Expressing one quantity as a percentage of another

This section will show you how to:

- express one quantity as a percentage of another
- work out percentage change.

Key terms

percentage change

percentage decrease

percentage increase

percentage loss

percentage profit

You can express one quantity as a percentage of another by setting up the first quantity as a fraction of the second, making sure that the units of each are the same. Then you convert the fraction into a percentage by multiplying by 100.

Example 16

Express £6 as a percentage of £40.

Set up the fraction and multiply by 100: $\frac{6}{40} \times 100 = 15\%$

Example 17

Express 75 cm as a percentage of 2.5 m.

First, change both quantities to a common unit: 2.5 m = 250 cm

Now you need to express 75 cm as a percentage of 250 cm.

Set up the fraction and multiply by 100: $\frac{75}{250} \times 100 = 30\%$

Percentage change

A **percentage change** may be a **percentage increase** or a **percentage decrease**.

$$\text{Percentage change} = \frac{\text{change}}{\text{original amount}} \times 100$$

You can use this to calculate **percentage profit** or **percentage loss** in a financial transaction.

Example 18

Jake buys a car for £1500 and sells it for £1800. What is Jake's percentage profit?

Jake's profit is £300, so his percentage profit is: $\dfrac{\text{profit}}{\text{original amount}} \times 100 = \dfrac{300}{1500} \times 100$

$$= 20\%$$

Using a multiplier (or decimal)

To use a multiplier, divide the increase by the original quantity and change the resulting decimal to a percentage.

Example 19

Express 5 as a percentage of 40.

Set up the fraction or decimal: $5 \div 40 = 0.125$

Convert the decimal to a percentage: $0.125 = 12.5\%$

Exercise 2F 🖩

1 Express each fraction as a percentage. Give suitably rounded figures where necessary.

  a £5 of £20   **b** £4 of £6.60   **c** 241 kg of 520 kg

  d 3 hours of 1 day   **e** 25 minutes of 1 hour **f** 12 m of 20 m

  g 125 g of 600 g   **h** 12 minutes of 2 hours **i** 1 week of a year

  j 1 month of 1 year   **k** 25 cm of 55 cm   **l** 105 g of 1 kg

2 Liam went to school with his pocket money of £2.50. He spent 80p at the tuck shop. What percentage of his pocket money did he spend?

3 In Greece, there are 3 654 000 acres of agricultural land. Olives are grown on 237 000 acres of this land. What percentage of the agricultural land is used for olives?

4 During the wet year of 1981, it rained in Manchester on 123 days of the year. What percentage of days were wet?

5 Find the percentage profit on each item. Give your answers to one decimal place.

	Item	Retail or selling price (£)	Wholesale price paid by the shop (£)
a	CD player	89.50	60
b	TV set	345.50	210
c	Computer	829.50	750

6 In 2012 Melchester County Council raised £14 870 000 in council tax. In 2013 it raised £15 597 000 in council tax. What was the percentage increase?

7 When Blackburn Rovers won the championship in 1995, they lost only four of their 42 league games. What percentage of games did they *not* lose?

8 These are the results from two tests taken by Calum and Stacey. Both tests are out of the same mark.

	Test A	Test B
Calum	12	17
Stacey	14	20

Whose result has the greater percentage increase from test A to test B?

Show your working.

CM **9** A supermarket advertises its cat food like this.

8 out of 10
cat owners choose
our cat food.

Trading standards are checking the claim.

They observe that over one hour, out of 46 people who buy cat food, 38 choose the store's own brand.

Based on these figures is the store's claim correct?

10 Three quantities are x, y and z. x is 60% of y. y is 75% of z. What percentage is x of z?

> Hints and tips | Choose a value for z.

11 Three quantities are x, y and z. x is 75% of y. x is 60% of z. What percentage is y of z?

12 In 2000 the population of a town was 4800. 30% of the population of the town owned a mobile phone. In 2015 the number of people in the town had increased by 20%. 70% of the population now owned a mobile phone. By what percentage has the number of people owning a mobile phone increased?

13 This letter appeared in a newspaper. Comment on the figures in the letter.

DAILY NEWS

world - business - finance - lifestyle - travel - sport

Dear Sir, in your last edition you said that the vote for Amir Patel was 5% greater than the vote for John Smith. The relevant percentages of the total vote were 31% and 26% respectively. A 31% share of the vote is in fact 19% greater than a 26% share. Did you mean that Amir Patel's vote was 5% more than John Smith's?

Worked exemplars

  Bob invests £1500 in some shares. After one month the shares have increased in value by 12%. Bob decides to buy another £3000 worth of the same shares. After another month the value of the shares has increased by 5%. Bob decides to sell the shares. How much profit does he make?

This is a problem-solving question so you will need to show your strategy.	
The multiplier is 1.12.	Write down the multiplier for an increase of 12%.
1500 × 1.12 = 1680	Work out the value after 1 month.
(3000 + 1680) × 1.05 = 4914	Add on the £3000 and work out the value after another month but, this time, use a multiplier of 1.05 as the increase has changed.
4914 − 4500 = 414	Subtract the original amount invested to get the profit.

a Work this out.

$$\frac{\left(\frac{2}{3}+\frac{4}{5}\right)}{1\frac{7}{9}}$$

b Decide whether $\frac{2}{3}+\frac{4}{5}$ is greater or less than $1\frac{7}{9}$.
Show clearly how you decide.

For part **a** you need to use basic mathematics skills. Then **b** is the 'communicating mathematics' part of the question. You need to make your method clear.	
a $\frac{2}{3}+\frac{4}{5}=\frac{10}{15}+\frac{12}{15}$ $\qquad =\frac{22}{15}$	First add the two fractions inside the brackets by writing them with a common denominator, that is, $\frac{10}{15}+\frac{12}{15}$.
$\frac{22}{15}\times\frac{9}{16}$	Change the mixed number $1\frac{7}{9}$ into an improper fraction, $\frac{16}{9}$, then find its reciprocal and multiply.
$\frac{^{11}\cancel{22}}{_{5}\cancel{15}}\times\frac{\cancel{9}^{3}}{\cancel{16}_{8}}=\frac{33}{40}$	Cancel the common factors. Then multiply the numerators and multiply the denominators.
b The answer to part **a** $\left(\frac{33}{40}\right)$ is less than 1. This means that the numerator $\left(\frac{2}{3}+\frac{4}{5}\right)$ must be smaller than the denominator $\left(1\frac{7}{9}\right)$.	This is a communicating mathematics question so you need to make sure your use your answer to part **a** to decide whether $\frac{2}{3}+\frac{4}{5}$ is greater or less than $1\frac{7}{9}$ and give a reason to support your answer.

Ready to progress?

I can write one quantity as a fraction of another.
I can add, subtract, multiply and divide fractions.
I can calculate percentage increases and decreases.

I can compare proportions using percentages.
I can use percentage multipliers to carry out percentage calculations.

I can calculate with mixed numbers.
I can solve complex problems involving percentage increases and percentage decreases.

Review questions

1. Mrs Patel earns £520 per week. She is awarded a pay rise of 10%. How much does she earn each week after the pay rise?

2. Five girls run a 200-metre race. Their times are shown in the table.

Name	Ali	Beth	Carol	Donna	Eve
Time (seconds)	28.0	32.0	36.0	36.0	27.0

   a Write down the modal time.

   b The five girls run another 200-metre race. They all reduce their times by 10%.

   i Calculate Ali's new time.

   ii Who won this race?

   iii Who improved her time by the least amount of time?

3. The bill for car repairs is £100 plus VAT. VAT is charged at 20%. What is the total bill?

4. The cost of a computer is the list price plus VAT at 20%.

   The list price of a computer is £480.

   Work out the cost of the computer.

5. A tin of cat food costs 45p.

   A shop has a special offer on the cat food.

   Julie wants 30 tins of cat food.

   a Work out how much she pays.

   The normal price of a dog collar and lead is £15.

   In a sale, the price of the collar and lead is reduced by 12%.

   b Work out the sale price of the collar and lead.

Special offer
Pay for 2 tins and
get 1 tin free

45p

Go Kitty

Go Kitty

Free

45p

6　**a** Change $\frac{7}{8}$ to a decimal.

　b Work out $\frac{3}{5} - \frac{2}{7}$.

　c Work out $3\frac{1}{4} \times 1\frac{3}{5}$.

7　A washing machine normally costs £350. It is reduced by 8% in a sale.

How much is the sale price of the washing machine?

8　Work out the value of $\frac{7}{8} - \frac{2}{5}$.

9　On Friday Bonnie the cat eats $1\frac{3}{4}$ sachets of cat food. On Saturday she eats $2\frac{1}{3}$ sachets of cat food.

Work out the total sachets of cat food that Bonnie eats on Friday and Saturday.

10　Arnold uses $\frac{3}{5}$ of a tin of paint to cover $1\frac{1}{2}$ m of fence. What is the smallest number of tins he needs to cover 12 m of fence?

11　$\dfrac{22}{7}$　　$\dfrac{54}{17}$　　$\dfrac{221}{71}$　　$\dfrac{312}{99}$

　a Put these numbers into order of size, largest on the left, smallest on the right.

　b Use your calculator to find which of the numbers is the closest approximation to π.

12　During 2014 the number of unemployed people in Truro fell from 1600 to 1152.

What was the percentage decrease?

13　A painter has 40 litres of paint. Each litre covers 3.5 m². The area to be painted is 108 m².

Estimate the percentage of paint used. Give your answer to the nearest one per cent.

14　There are 400 penguins in a zoo. $\frac{11}{20}$ of the penguins are male. $\frac{5}{9}$ of the females lay one egg each. All the chicks survive.

By what percentage has the number of penguins increased?

15　Bag A contains 48 balls, 9 of which are red. Bag B contains 59 balls, 11 of which are red. Tomas says: 'Bag B has the greater number of red balls so the probability of taking a red ball at random must be greater for bag B than for bag A.' Is Tomas correct? Show working to support your answer.

16　The cost of coffee increased by 15% one week but fell back to the original price the next week.

By what percentage did the cost of coffee fall in the second week? Give your answer to the nearest one per cent.

17　There are 250 men and women in a golf club.

There are 50% more men than women in the club.

　a How many men and women are in the golf club?

　b If 10% of the men and 15% of the women are left-handed, what percentage of the whole membership of the golf club is left-handed?

3 Statistics: Statistical diagrams and averages

This chapter is going to show you:

- how to draw and interpret pie charts
- how to draw and interpret line graphs
- how to solve problems that use averages
- how to calculate averages from frequency tables
- how to draw scatter diagrams and lines of best fit.

You should already know:

- how to calculate and use the mode, median and mean
- how to extract information from tables and diagrams.

About this chapter

William Playfair, a Scottish engineer, is thought to have originated the idea of representing statistics in a graphical way. He invented three types of diagram: the line graph and bar chart in 1786 and the pie chart in 1801.

Florence Nightingale was also a pioneer in presenting information visually. She was born in 1820 and was very good at mathematics from an early age. In 1859, she was elected the first female member of the Royal Statistical Society.

William Playfair pioneered charts and graphs such as this pie chart.

She developed a form of the pie chart now known as the 'polar area diagram' or the 'Nightingale rose diagram'. It illustrated monthly patient deaths in military field hospitals. She called these diagrams 'coxcombs' and used them a great deal to present reports on the conditions of medical care in the Crimean War to Parliament and to civil servants who may not have fully understood traditional statistical reports.

Florence Nightingale was a nurse and hospital reformer. She used charts and graphs in her work.

Since the latter part of the 20th century, statistical graphs have become an important way of analysing information. Computer-generated statistical graphs are seen every day on TV, in newspapers and in magazines. In this chapter, you will learn how to draw and interpret a range of these graphs.

3.1 Statistical representation

This section will show you how to:

- draw and interpret bar charts and pie charts
- draw and interpret line graphs.

Bar charts and pie charts

You are already familiar with bar charts in which the vertical axis represents frequency and the horizontal axis represents categorical data – the data you are considering.

The frequency table shows the average monthly rainfall over a six-month period.

Month	January	February	March	April	May	June
Rainfall (mm)	10	25	20	35	15	5

The diagrams below show three different ways the data can be represented.

As a pictogram:

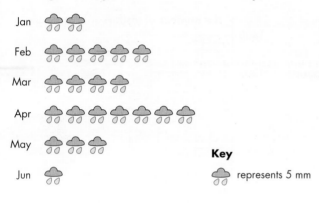

As a bar chart:

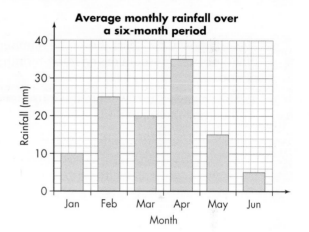

As a vertical line chart:

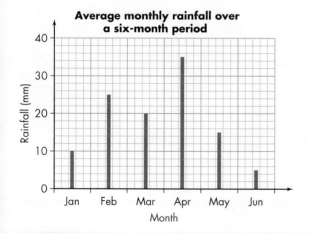

You should also be able to recognise and use multiple or dual bar charts and composite bar charts, which can be used to compare two sets of related data as shown in the next example.

Example 1

This dual bar chart shows the average daily maximum temperatures for England and Turkey over a five-month period.

In which month was the difference between temperatures in England and Turkey the greatest?

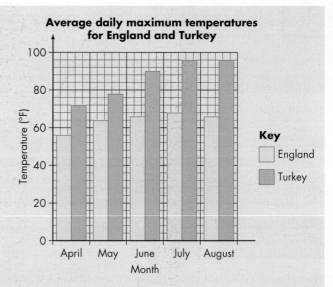

The largest difference can be seen in August.

Example 2

This composite bar chart shows the numbers of visitors to a museum over a three-month period.

a How many visitors went to the museum over the three-month period?

b How many visitors were children?

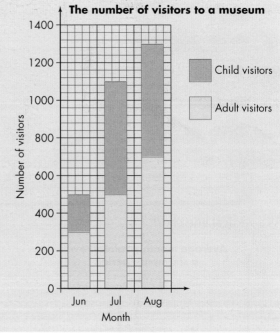

a Reading from the graph: 500 + 1100 + 1300 = 2900 visitors.

b Reading from the grey sections on the graph: 200 + 600 + 600 = 1400 children.

Pictograms, bar charts and vertical line charts are not always easy to interpret when there is a big difference between the frequencies or there are only a few categories. In these cases, it is often more convenient to illustrate the data on a pie chart.

In a pie chart, the whole of the data is represented by a circle (the 'pie') and each category of it is represented by a sector of the circle (a 'slice of the pie'). The angle of each sector is proportional to the frequency of the category it represents. So, unlike a bar chart, for example, a pie chart can only show proportions and not individual frequencies.

Example 3

In a survey, 120 people were asked to state which type of transport they used on their most recent holiday. This table shows the results of the survey.

Draw a pie chart to illustrate the data.

Type of transport	Train	Coach	Car	Ship	Aeroplane
Frequency	24	12	59	11	14

Method 1

Since 120 divides exactly into 360°, each person can be represented by 360° ÷ 120 = 3°.
So multiply all the frequencies by 3 to give the angles of all the sectors.

Type of transport	Frequency	Calculation	Angle
Train	24	24 × 3	72°
Coach	12	12 × 3	36°
Car	59	59 × 3	177°
Ship	11	11 × 3	33°
Aeroplane	14	14 × 3	42°
Totals	120		360°

This is referred to as the scaling method.

Method 2

Here you work out what fraction of the pie chart is for each type of transport by dividing each frequency by 120 and then multiplying this by 360°.

Type of transport	Frequency	Calculation	Angle
Train	24	$\frac{24}{120} \times 360°$	72°
Coach	12	$\frac{12}{120} \times 360°$	36°
Car	59	$\frac{59}{120} \times 360°$	177°
Ship	11	$\frac{11}{120} \times 360°$	33°
Aeroplane	14	$\frac{14}{120} \times 360°$	42°
Totals	120		360°

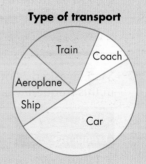

Type of transport

This is referred to as the proportional method.

Use the calculated angle for each sector to draw the pie chart.

Note

- Check that the sum of all the angles is 360°.
- Label each sector.
- You do not need to show the angles or frequencies on the pie chart.

Example 4

The pie charts show the favourite sports for two classes in a school.

James says that more students prefer football in class 2 than in class 1. Explain why he could be wrong.

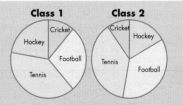

There could be a different number of students in each class. The pie charts only show proportions so there is no way of telling the numbers represented in each pie chart.

Exercise 3A 🖩

1 On a sports afternoon, students were asked to choose basketball, badminton or volleyball.

The table shows the sport they chose.

	Basketball	Badminton	Volleyball
Girls	16	12	10
Boys	22	22	20

  a Illustrate the data on a composite bar chart.

  b How many girls chose basketball?

  c How many boys chose either badminton or volleyball?

2 Draw a pie chart to represent each set of data.

> **Hints and tips** Remember to complete a table, as shown in the example, and check that the angles add up to 360°.

  a The numbers of children in 40 families

Number of children	0	1	2	3	4
Frequency	4	10	14	9	3

  b The favourite soap opera of 60 students

Programme	Home and Away	Neighbours	Coronation Street	EastEnders	Emmerdale
Frequency	15	18	10	13	4

  c How 90 students get to school

Journey to school	Walk	Car	Bus	Cycle
Frequency	42	13	25	10

3 Mariam asked 24 of her friends which sport they preferred to play. Her data is shown in this frequency table.

Sport	Rugby	Football	Tennis	Squash	Basketball
Frequency	4	11	3	1	5

  a Draw a pictogram to show the data.　　　**b** Draw a bar chart to show the data.

  c Draw a vertical line chart to show the data.　　**d** Draw a pie chart to show the data.

  e Which diagram best illustrates the data? Give a reason to support your answer.

4 Hassan wrote down the number of lessons he had per week in each subject on his school timetable.

Mathematics 5　English 5　Science 8　Languages 6　Humanities 6　Arts 4　Games 2

  a How many lessons did Hassan have on his timetable?

  b Draw a pie chart to show the data.

  c Draw a bar chart to show the data.

  d Which diagram better illustrates the data? Give a reason to support your answer.

5 In a poll during the run-up to an election, 720 people were asked which political party they would vote for. The results are given in the table.

Conservative	248
Labour	264
Liberal Democrat	152
Green Party	56

  a Draw a pie chart to illustrate the data.

(EV) **b** Why do you think pie charts are used to show this sort of information during elections?

6 This pie chart shows the proportions of the different shoe sizes worn by 144 students in Year 11 in a London school.

  a What is the angle of the sector representing shoe sizes 11 and 12?

  b How many students had a shoe size of 11 or 12?

  c What percentage of students wore the modal size?

Shoe sizes worn by 144 pupils in Year 11

7 The table shows the numbers of candidates, at each grade, gaining music examinations in Strings and Brass.

	Grades					Total number of candidates
	3	**4**	**5**	**6**	**7**	
Strings	300	980	1050	600	70	3000
Brass	250	360	300	120	70	1100

  a Draw a pie chart to represent each of the two instruments.

(MR) **b** Compare the pie charts to decide which group of candidates, Strings or Brass, are of a higher standard. Give reasons to justify your answer.

(PS) **8** In a survey, a rail company asked passengers whether their service had improved.

The results are shown in this pie chart.

Explain how you would work out the probability that a person picked at random from this survey answered *Don't know*.

Has the rail service improved?

Line graphs

Line graphs are usually used in statistics to show how data changes over a period of time. They can indicate **trends**: for example, line graphs can be used to show whether the Earth's temperature is increasing as the concentration of carbon dioxide builds up in the atmosphere, or whether a company's profit margin is falling year on year.

Line graphs are best drawn on graph paper.

Example 5

This line graph shows the outside temperature one day in November.

What does this graph show you and what are its limits?

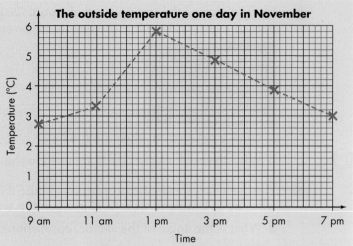

The outside temperature one day in November

On this graph, the values between the plotted points have no true meaning because only the temperatures at the plotted points are known. However, by joining the points with dashed lines, as shown, you can estimate the temperatures at points in between. Although the graph shows the temperature falling in the early evening, it would not be sensible to try to predict what will happen after 7 pm that night.

Exercise 3B

1 The table shows the estimated numbers of tourists worldwide.

Year	1975	1980	1985	1990	1995	2000	2005	2010
Number of tourists (millions)	100	150	220	280	290	320	340	345

a Draw a line graph for the data.

b Use your graph to estimate the number of tourists in 2002.

c In which five-year period did tourism increase the most?

d i Explain the trend in tourism.

  ii What reasons can you give to explain this trend?

2 The table shows the maximum and minimum daily temperatures for London over a week.

Day	Sunday	Monday	Tuesday	Wednesday	Thursday	Friday	Saturday
Maximum (°C)	12	14	16	15	16	14	10
Minimum (°C)	4	5	7	8	7	4	3

a Draw line graphs on the same axes to show the maximum and minimum temperatures.

b Work out the smallest and greatest differences between the maximum and minimum temperatures.

3 Maria opened a coffee shop. She was interested in how trade was picking up over the first few weeks. The table shows the numbers of coffees sold in these weeks.

Week	1	2	3	4	5
Coffees sold	46	71	89	103	113

a Draw a line graph for this data.

b From your graph, estimate the number of coffees Maria can hope to sell in week 6.

c Give a possible reason for the way in which the number of coffees sold increased.

4 A puppy is weighed at the end of each week, for five weeks after it is born.

Week	1	2	3	4	5
Mass (g)	850	920	940	980	1000

Is it possible to estimate how much the puppy will weigh after eight weeks?

Explain your answer.

 5 When plotting a graph to show the summer midday temperatures in Spain, Abbass decided to start his graph at the temperature 20 °C.

Explain why he might have made this decision.

3.2 Statistical measures

This section will show you how to:

- use averages to solve (more complex) problems
- identify the advantages and disadvantages of each type of average and learn which one to use in different situations
- work out and use the range of a set of data
- calculate the mode, the median and the mean from a frequency table
- identify the modal group
- estimate the mean from a grouped frequency table.

<table>
<tr><td colspan="1">Key terms</td></tr>
<tr><td>continuous data</td></tr>
<tr><td>discrete data</td></tr>
<tr><td>estimate of the mean</td></tr>
<tr><td>measure of location</td></tr>
<tr><td>modal group</td></tr>
<tr><td>stem-and-leaf diagram</td></tr>
</table>

Averages

You will often use the term 'average' when describing or comparing sets of data. The average is also known as a **measure of location**. For example, you may refer to the average rainfall in Britain, the average score of a batsman, an average weekly wage, the average mark in an examination. In each of these examples, you are representing the whole set of many values by just one single, typical value.

The idea of an average is extremely useful, because it enables you to compare one set of data with another set by comparing just two values – their averages.

There are several ways of expressing an average, but the most commonly used averages are the mode, the median and the mean.

An average must be truly representative of a set of data. So, when you need to find an average, it is crucial to choose the correct type of average for this particular set of data. If you use the wrong average, your results will be distorted and give misleading information.

This table, which compares the advantages and disadvantages of each type of average, will help you to make the correct decision.

	Mode	Median	Mean
Advantages	Very easy to find Not affected by extreme values Can be used for non-numerical data	Easy to find for ungrouped data Not affected by extreme values	Easy to find Uses all the values The total for a given number of values can be calculated from it
Disadvantages	Doesn't use all the values May not exist	Doesn't use all the values Often not understood	Extreme values can distort it Has to be calculated
Used for	Non-numerical data Finding the most likely value	Data with extreme values	Data with values that are spread in a balanced way

The range

You know that the range of a set of data is the difference between the highest value and the lowest values. The range is *not* an average. It shows the spread of the data. You can use it to compare two or more sets of similar data, for example, to comment on their consistency.

These are the ages of 20 people attending a conference.

23, 25, 26, 28, 28, 34, 34, 34, 37, 45, 47, 48, 52, 53, 56, 63, 67, 70, 73, 77

a Work out: **i** the mode **ii** the median **iii** the mean **iv** the range of the data.

b Which average best represents the age of the people at the conference?

a **i** The mode is 34. **ii** The median is 46.
iii The mean is $920 \div 20 = 46$. **iv** The range is 54.

b All three averages are similar (In this case the median and the mean are the same), but it is probably better to use the mean as it takes in all of the values.

Stem-and leaf diagrams

This is a list of the ages of 20 people in a queue for an ice rink.

23, 13, 34, 44, 26, 12, 41, 31, 20, 18, 19, 31, 48, 32, 45, 14, 12, 27, 31, 19

You already know how to work out the median and range for a set of **discrete data**, such as this one. Another method is to use a **stem-and-leaf diagram**.

First put the ages in order.

12, 12, 13, 14, 18, 19, 19, 20, 23, 26, 27, 31, 31, 31, 32, 34, 41, 44, 45, 48

Then the tens digits will be the 'stems' and the units digits will be the 'leaves'.

The completed stem-and-leaf diagram is on the right.

A stem-and-leaf diagram is useful because it gives you a visual display of how the data is distributed.

You should always include a key in a stem-and-leaf diagram.

```
1 | 2 2 3 4 8 9 9
2 | 0 3 6 7
3 | 1 1 1 2 4
4 | 1 4 5 8
```

Key 1 | 2 represents an age of 12

These are the exam marks for 15 students: 45, 62, 58, 58, 61, 49, 61, 47, 52, 58, 48, 56, 65, 46, 54

a Draw a stem-and-leaf diagram for the data.

b Work out the range of the marks.

c Work out the median mark.

a Write the marks, in order: 45, 46, 47, 48, 49, 52, 54, 56, 58, 58, 58, 61, 61, 62, 65

The stem-and-leaf diagram looks like this.

```
4 | 5 6 7 8 9
5 | 2 4 6 8 8 8
6 | 1 1 2 5
```

Key 4 | 5 represents 45 marks

b The range is $65 - 45 = 20$ marks.

c The median is the 8th value in the list, which is 56 marks.

Exercise 3C 🖩

1 These are the marks of 21 students in an English examination.

55, 63, 24, 47, 60, 45, 50, 89, 39, 47, 38, 43, 69, 73, 38, 47, 53, 64, 58, 71, 82

  a Work out the mode.   **b** Work out the median.

  c Work out the mean.   **d** Work out the range.

(MR) **2** Shopkeepers always want to keep the most popular items in stock.

Which average do you think is often known as 'the shopkeeper's average'?

3 A student records the number of text messages she receives each day for two weeks.

12, 18, 21, 9, 17, 25, 8, 12, 20, 13, 17, 22, 9, 9

  a Show the results on a stem-and-leaf diagram.

  b Work out the range.

  c Work out the median.

(PS) **4** A list comprises of seven even numbers. The largest number is 24. The smallest number is half the largest. The mode is 14 and the median is 16. Two of the numbers add up to 42.

  a What are the seven numbers?   **b** How many different answers can you find?

(MR) **5** Decide which average you would use for each statistic. Give reasons for your choices.

  a The average mark in an examination

  b The average pocket money for a group of 16-year-olds

  c The average shoe size for all the girls in Year 10

  d The average height for all the artistes on tour with a circus

  e The average hair colour for students in your school

  f The average mass of all newborn babies in a hospital's maternity ward

(MR) **6** This back-to-back stem-and-leaf diagram shows the marks for a group of boys and girls in a history test.

> **Hints and tips**   Read the boys' marks from right to left.

  a Write down the range of marks for the boys.

  b Write down the range of marks for the girls.

  c Work out the median mark for the boys.

  d Work out the median mark for the girls.

  e What overall conclusion can you draw from this data?

Boys						Girls					
9	6	6	5	**3**	0	5	7	9			
9	6	6	2	0	**4**	2	2	3	8	8	8
	5	4	4	3	**5**	1	1	5			

Key   Boys: 2 | 4   represents 42 marks

             Girls: 3 | 5   represents 35 marks

7 This table shows the annual salaries for a company's employees.

  a What is:

    i the modal salary

    ii the median salary

    iii the mean salary?

(EV) **b** The management has suggested a pay rise for all of 6%. The shopfloor workers want a pay rise for all of £1500. What difference to the mean salary would each suggestion make?

Chairman	£83 000
Managing director	£65 000
Floor manager	£34 000
Skilled worker 1	£28 000
Skilled worker 2	£28 000
Machinist	£20 000
Computer engineer	£20 000
Secretary	£20 000
Office junior	£8 000

8 Mr Brennan, a mathematics teacher, told each student their individual test mark. He told the whole class the modal mark, the median mark and the mean mark.

a Which average would tell a student whether they were in the top half or the bottom half of the class?

b Which average really tells the students nothing?

c Which average allows a student to gauge how well they have done, compared with everyone else?

9 Three players were hoping to be chosen for the basketball team.

The table shows their scores for the last few games they played.

The teacher said they would be selected by their best average score.

By which average would each boy choose to be selected?

Tom	16, 10, 12, 10, 13, 8, 10
David	16, 8, 15, 25, 8
Mohammed	15, 2, 15, 3, 5

 10 A list of nine numbers has a mean of 7.6. What number must be added to the list to give a new mean of 8?

 11 A dance group of 17 teenagers had a mean mass of 44.5 kg. To enter a competition, there needs to be 18 people in the group with an average mass of 44.4 kg or less. What is the maximum mass that the 18th person could be?

 12 The mean age of a group of eight walkers is 42. Joanne joins the group and the mean age changes to 40. How old is Joanne?

Frequency tables

When you have gathered a lot of information, it is often convenient to put it together in a frequency table. Then you can use your table to work out the values of the mode, median, mean and range of the data.

The results of a survey on the number of people in each car leaving the Meadowhall Shopping Centre, in Sheffield, are summarised in the table.

Number of people in each car	1	2	3	4	5	6
Frequency	45	198	121	76	52	13

Calculate:

a the mode **b** the median **c** the mean number of people in a car.

a The modal number of people in a car is easy to identify. It is the number with the largest frequency (198). Hence, the modal number of people in a car is 2.

b To find the median number of people in a car, you need to locate the middle value of the set of numbers. First, add up the frequencies to find the total number of cars surveyed. This comes to 505. Next, calculate the middle position.

$(505 + 1) \div 2 = 253$

You now need to find the group that contains the 253rd item. The 243rd item comes at the end of the group with 2 in a car. Therefore, the 253rd item must be in the group with 3 in a car. Hence, the median number of people in a car is 3.

c You can work out the mean number of people in a car by calculating the total number of people, and then dividing this total by the number of cars surveyed.

Hence, the mean number of people in a car is 1446 ÷ 505 = 2.9 (1 dp).

Number in car	Frequency	Number in these cars
1	45	1 × 45 = 45
2	198	2 × 198 = 396
3	121	3 × 121 = 363
4	76	4 × 76 = 304
5	52	5 × 52 = 260
6	13	6 × 13 = 78
Totals	505	1446

Using your calculator

You could also answer the previous example by using the statistical mode, which is available on some calculators. However, not all calculators are the same, so you will need either to read your instruction manual or to experiment with the statistical keys on your calculator.

You may find one labelled **DATA** or **M+** or **Σx** or **x̄**.

Try these keystrokes.

Exercise 3D

1 Work out: **i** the mode **ii** the median **iii** the mean from each frequency table.

a The results of a survey of the shoe sizes of all the Year 10 boys in a school

Shoe size	4	5	6	7	8	9	10
Number of students	12	30	34	35	23	8	3

b A record of the number of babies born each week over one year in a small maternity unit

Number of babies	0	1	2	3	4	5	6	7	8	9	10	11	12	13	14
Frequency	1	1	1	2	2	2	3	5	9	8	6	4	5	2	1

2 A survey of the number of children in each family of a school's intake gave these results.

Number of children	1	2	3	4	5
Frequency	214	328	97	26	3

a Assuming each child at the school is shown in the data, how many children are at the school?

b State the median number of children in a family.

c How many families have this mean number of children?

d How many families would consider themselves average from this survey?

3 A dentist kept records of how many teeth he extracted from his patients.

In 1989, he extracted 598 teeth from 271 patients.

In 1999, he extracted 332 teeth from 196 patients.

In 2009, he extracted 374 teeth from 288 patients.

a Calculate the mean number of teeth taken from each patient in each year.

b Explain why you think the mean number of teeth extracted falls each year.

4 The teachers in a school were asked to indicate the average number of hours they spent each day marking. The table summarises their replies.

Number of hours spent marking	1	2	3	4	5	6
Number of teachers	10	13	12	8	6	1

a How many teachers are there at the school?

b What is the modal number of hours spent marking?

c What is the mean number of hours spent marking?

5 Two friends often played golf together. They recorded their scores for each hole over five games to determine who was more consistent and who was the better player. The results are summarised in the table.

Number of shots to hole (score)	1	2	3	4	5	6	7	8	9
Roger	0	0	0	14	37	27	12	0	0
Brian	5	12	15	18	14	8	8	8	2

  a What is the modal score for each player?

  b What is the range of scores for each player?

  c What is the median score for each player?

  d What is the mean score for each player?

  e Which player is the more consistent? Explain why.

  f Who would you say is the better player? Explain why.

6 The table shows numbers of league goals scored by a football team over a season.

Number of goals scored	0	1	2	3	4	5	6	7
Number of matches	3	8	10	11	4	2	1	1

  a How many games were played that season?

  b What is the range of goals scored?

  c What is the modal number of goals scored?

  d What is the median number of goals scored?

  e What is the mean number of goals scored?

  f Which average do you think the team's supporters would say is the average number of goals scored by the team that season?

  g If the team also scored 20 goals in 10 cup matches that season, what was the mean number of goals the team scored throughout the whole season?

7 The table shows numbers of sweets in some tubes, but a coffee stain has deleted one of the figures.

The mean number of sweets in a tube is known to be 33.5.

Work out the missing number in the table.

Number of sweets	Frequency
32	4
33	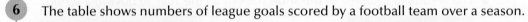
34	9
35	1
36	1

8 I have been given a frequency table by Corrin. She says: "I can calculate the mean to be an integer but not the median. Why is that?" Give a possible explanation.

9 The table shows the number of passengers in each of 100 taxis leaving London Heathrow Airport one day.

Number of passengers in a taxi	1	2	3	4
Number of taxis	x	40	y	26

  a Write down the value of $x + y$.

  b The mean number of passengers per taxi is known to be 2.66. Show that $x + 3y = 82$.

  c Work out the values of x and y by solving appropriate equations.

  d State the median of the number of passengers per taxi.

Grouped frequency tables

Sometimes the information may have too many values to represent easily so they are grouped in some way, as in the table in Example 9, which shows the range of weekly pocket money given to Year 10 students in a particular class. In this case, all values more than £1 up to £2 are counted as one group.

Example 9

From the data in the table:

a write down the **modal group** (the group with the greatest frequency)

b calculate an **estimate of the mean** weekly pocket money.

Pocket money, p (£)	$0 < p \leq 1$	$1 < p \leq 2$	$2 < p \leq 3$	$3 < p \leq 4$	$4 < p \leq 5$
Number of students	2	5	5	9	15

a The modal group is easy to pick out, since it is simply the one with the largest frequency. Here the modal group is £4 to £5 so you would write: $4 < p \leq 5$.

b The mean can only be estimated, since you do not have all the information. To estimate the mean, you simply assume that each person in each group has the midpoint amount, then you can proceed to build up the table as before.

To find the midpoint value, add the two end values and divide the total by two.

Pocket money, p (£)	Frequency (f)	Midpoint (m)	$f \times m$
$0 < p \leq 1$	2	0.50	1.00
$1 < p \leq 2$	5	1.50	7.50
$2 < p \leq 3$	5	2.50	12.50
$3 < p \leq 4$	9	3.50	31.50
$4 < p \leq 5$	15	4.50	67.50
Totals	36		120

The estimated mean is £120 ÷ 36 = £3.33 (correct to 2 decimal places).

Note the notation used for the groups.

$0 < p \leq 1$ means any amount above 0p up to and including £1.

$1 < p \leq 2$ means any amount above £1 up to and including £2.

If you had written 0.01–1.00, 1.01–2.00, … for the groups, the midpoint values would have been 0.505, 1.505, … Although technically correct, this makes the calculation of the mean harder and does not have a significant effect on the final answer, which is an estimate anyway.

This issue only arises because money is **discrete data**, which is data that consists of separate numbers. Other discrete data includes numbers of goals scored, marks in a test, numbers of children and shoe sizes. Normally, grouped tables use **continuous data**, which is data that can have an infinite number of different values, such as height, weight, time, area and capacity. It is always rounded information.

Whatever the type of data, remember to find the midpoint value by adding the two end values of the group and dividing by 2.

Exercise 3E 🖩

1. For each table of values, calculate: **i** the modal group   **ii** an estimate for the mean.

   a

x	$0 < x \leqslant 10$	$10 < x \leqslant 20$	$20 < x \leqslant 30$	$30 < x \leqslant 40$	$40 < x \leqslant 50$
Frequency	4	6	11	17	9

   b

y	$0 < y \leqslant 100$	$100 < y \leqslant 200$	$200 < y \leqslant 300$	$300 < y \leqslant 400$	$400 < y \leqslant 500$	$500 < y \leqslant 600$
Frequency	95	56	32	21	9	3

   c

z	$0 < z \leqslant 5$	$5 < z \leqslant 10$	$10 < z \leqslant 15$	$15 < z \leqslant 20$
Frequency	16	27	19	13

   d

Weeks	1–3	4–6	7–9	10–12	13–15
Frequency	5	8	14	10	7

   > **Hints and tips**   When you copy the tables, draw them vertically, as in Example 9.

2. Jason brought 100 pebbles back from the beach and weighed them all, to the nearest gram. His results are summarised in this table.

Mass, m (grams)	$40 < m \leqslant 60$	$60 < m \leqslant 80$	$80 < m \leqslant 100$	$100 < m \leqslant 120$	$120 < m \leqslant 140$	$140 < m \leqslant 160$
Frequency	5	9	22	27	26	11

   Work out:

   a the modal mass of the pebbles

   b an estimate for the total mass of the pebbles

   c an estimate for the mean mass of the pebbles.

3. One hundred light bulbs were tested by their manufacturer to see whether the average life span of the bulbs was over 200 hours. The table summarises the results.

Life span, h (hours)	$150 < h \leqslant 175$	$175 < h \leqslant 200$	$200 < h \leqslant 225$	$225 < h \leqslant 250$	$250 < h \leqslant 275$
Frequency	24	45	18	10	3

   a What is the modal length of time a bulb lasts?

   b What percentage of bulbs last longer than 200 hours?

   c Estimate the mean life span of the light bulbs.

   d Do you think the test shows that the average life span is over 200 hours? Explain your answer fully.

4. The owners of a boutique did a survey to find the average age of people using the boutique. The table summarises the results.

Age (years)	14–18	19–20	21–26	27–35	36–50
Frequency	26	24	19	16	11

   Calculate the average age of the people using the boutique.

5 The table shows the distances run by an athlete who is training for a marathon.

Distance, d (miles)	$0 < d \leq 5$	$5 < d \leq 10$	$10 < d \leq 15$	$15 < d \leq 20$	$20 < d \leq 25$
Frequency	3	8	13	5	2

   a It is recommended that an athlete's daily average mileage should be at least one-third of the distance of the race being trained for. A marathon is 26.2 miles. Is this athlete doing sufficient training?

   b The athlete records the times of some runs and calculates that her average pace for all runs is $6\frac{1}{2}$ minutes for a mile. Explain why she is wrong to expect a finishing time of $26.2 \times 6\frac{1}{2}$ minutes ≈ 170 minutes for the marathon.

   c The athlete claims that the difference between her shortest and longest run is 21 miles. Could this be correct? Explain your answer.

6 Three supermarkets each claimed to have the lowest average price increase over the year. The table summarises their average price increases.

Price increase (pence)	1–5	6–10	11–15	16–20	21–25	26–30	31–35
Soundbuy	4	10	14	23	19	8	2
Springfields	5	11	12	19	25	9	6
Setco	3	8	15	31	21	7	3

Using their average price increases, make a comparison of the supermarkets and write a report on which supermarket, in your opinion, has the lowest price increases over the year. Remember to justify your answers.

7 The table summarises the results of a survey about how quickly the AOne attended calls that were not on a motorway. The times are rounded to the nearest minute.

Time (minutes)	1–15	16–30	31–45	46–60	61–75	76–90	91–105
Frequency	2	23	48	31	27	18	11

   a How many calls were used in the survey?

   b Estimate the mean time taken per call.

   c Which average would the AOne use to advertise their average call-out time?

   d What percentage of calls do the AOne get to within the hour?

8 The table shows the numbers of runs scored by all the batsmen in a cricket competition.

Runs	0–9	10–19	20–29	30–39	40–49
Frequency	8	5	10	5	2

Helen noticed that two numbers were in the wrong part of the table and that this made a difference of 1.7 to the arithmetic mean.

Which two numbers were the wrong way round?

9 The table shows profit made each week by a charity shop, to the nearest pound (£).

Profit (£)	0–500	501–1000	1001–1500	1501–2000
Frequency	15	26	8	3

Explain how you would estimate the mean profit made each week.

10 The table shows the age of 100 members of a football club.

Age	20–29	30–39	40–49	50–59	60–69
Frequency	16	34	27	18	5

a Tebor claims that the median age of the members is 39.5.
   Is he correct? Explain your answer

b He also says that the range of the age of the members is 34.
   Could he be correct? Explain your answer.

3.3 Scatter diagrams

This section will show you how to:

- draw, interpret and use scatter diagrams
- draw and use a line of best fit.

Key terms

line of best fit

negative correlation

no correlation

outlier

positive correlation

scatter diagram

A **scatter diagram** (also called a scatter graph or scattergram)
is a method of comparing two variables by plotting their values
on a graph. The variables are treated just like a set of (x, y)
coordinates.

In this scatter diagram, the marks scored by students in an
English test are plotted against the marks they scored in a
mathematics test.

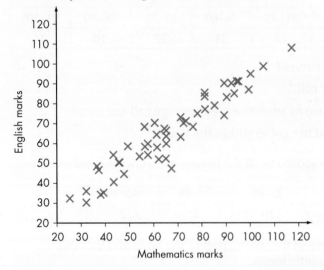

Comparison of English and mathematics marks

This graph shows that the students who got high marks in the mathematics test also tended to get
high marks in the English test.

Correlation

Here are three statements that may or may not be true.

- The taller people are, the wider their arm span is likely to be.
- The older a car is, the lower its value will be.
- The distance you live from your place of work will affect how much you earn.

These relationships could be tested by collecting data and plotting each set of data on a scatter diagram.

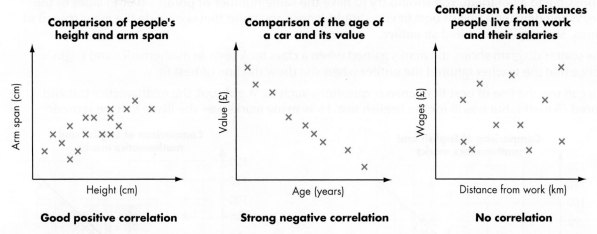

Comparison of people's height and arm span

Arm span (cm)

Height (cm)

Good positive correlation

Comparison of the age of a car and its value

Value (£)

Age (years)

Strong negative correlation

Comparison of the distances people live from work and their salaries

Wages (3)

Distance from work (km)

No correlation

The first statement may give a scatter diagram like the first one above. This diagram has **positive correlation** because as one quantity increases, so does the other. From such a scatter diagram you could say that the taller someone is, the wider the arm span.

Testing the second statement may give a scatter diagram like the second one. This diagram has strong **negative correlation** because as one quantity increases, the other quantity decreases. From such a scatter diagram you could say that as a car gets older, its value decreases.

Testing the third statement may give a scatter diagram like the third one. This scatter diagram has **no correlation**. There is no relationship between the distance a person lives from work and how much that person earns.

You can describe correlation as positive or negative, strong or weak. Always try to give a full description, rather than just saying there is positive, negative or no correlation.

Example 10

The two scatter diagrams show the relationship between the temperature and the amount of ice cream sold and people's age and the amount of ice cream they eat.

a Comment on the correlation of each graph.

b What does each graph tell you?

Amount of ice cream sold (£)

Temperature (°C)

Amount of ice cream eaten (g)

Age (years)

a The first diagram shows strong positive correlation.

The second diagram shows weak negative correlation.

b The first diagram tells you that as the temperature increases, the amount of ice cream sold increases.

The second diagram tells you that as people get older, they eat less ice cream.

Beware! Correlation does not give you any indication of the underlying causes or reasons for a trend. For example, you cannot make the assumption that older people do not like ice cream.

Remember: You can describe correlation as positive or negative, weak or strong. Try to give a full description, rather than just stating there is positive, negative or no correlation.

Line of best fit

A **line of best fit** is a straight line drawn between all the points on a scatter diagram, passing as close as possible to all of them. You should try to have the same number of points on both sides of the line. When drawing a line of best fit you should ignore any point that is outside the main spread of values. Such a point is called an **outlier**.

This scatter diagram shows the marks gained when a class took tests in mathematics and English. Notice that the teacher ignored the outlier when she drew the line of best fit.

You can use the line of best fit to answer questions such as: 'A girl took the mathematics test and scored 76 marks, but was ill for the English test. How many marks was she likely to have scored?'

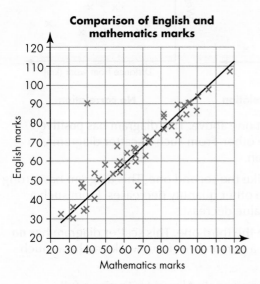

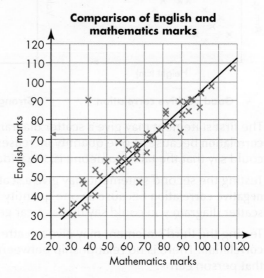

You can find the answer by drawing lines from 76 on the mathematics axis, up to the line of best fit and then across to the English axis. This gives 73, which is the mark she is likely to have scored in the English test.

Beware! When you are reading a value from a line of best fit (known as interpolation), remember that any point used is only an indication of what might happen; it is not an exact answer. Likewise, when predicting values beyond a line of best fit (known as extrapolation), you cannot assume the trend will continue.

Exercise 3F 🖩

1   Describe the correlation in each of these four scatter diagrams. Write down what each one tells you.

a

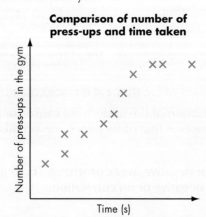

b

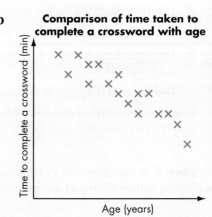

c

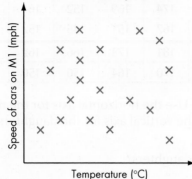

Comparison of speed of
cars and temperature

(vertical axis: Speed of cars on M1 (mph); horizontal axis: Temperature (°C))

d

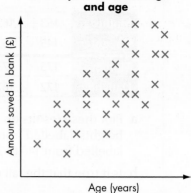

Comparison of savings
and age

(vertical axis: Amount saved in bank (£); horizontal axis: Age (years))

2 The table shows the results of a science experiment in which a ball is rolled along a desk top. The speed of the ball is measured at various points.

Distance from start (cm)	10	20	30	40	50	60	70	80
Speed (cm/s)	18	16	13	10	7	5	3	0

a Plot the data on a scatter diagram.

b Draw the line of best fit.

c If the ball's speed had been measured at 5 cm from the start, what is it likely to have been?

d Estimate how far from the start the ball was when its speed was 12 cm/s.

3 The table shows the marks for 10 students in their mathematics and geography examinations.

Student	Anna	Beryl	Cath	Dema	Ethel	Fatima	Greta	Hannah	Imogen	Joan
Maths	57	65	34	87	42	35	59	61	25	35
Geography	45	61	30	78	41	36	35	57	23	34

a Plot the data on a scatter diagram. Use the horizontal axis for the mathematics scores and mark it from 20 to 100. Use the vertical axis for the geography scores and mark it from 20 to 100.

b Draw a line of best fit.

c One of the students was ill when she took the geography examination. Which student was it most likely to be?

d Another student, Katya, was absent for the geography examination. She scored 75 in mathematics. What mark would you expect her to have scored in geography?

e If another student, Lynne, was absent for the mathematics examination but scored 65 in geography, what mark would you expect her to have got in mathematics?

4 These are the heights, in centimetres, of 20 mothers and their 15-year-old daughters.

Mother	153	162	147	183	174	169	152	164	186	178
Daughter	145	155	142	167	167	151	145	152	163	168
Mother	175	173	158	168	181	173	166	162	180	156
Daughter	172	167	160	154	170	164	156	150	160	152

a Plot these results on a scatter diagram. Use the horizontal axis for the mothers' heights, labelled from 140 to 200. Use the vertical axis for the daughters' heights, labelled from 140 to 200.

b Is it true that the tall mothers have tall daughters?

5 A teacher carried out a survey of his class. He asked students to say how many hours per week they spent playing sport and how many hours per week they spent watching TV. This table shows the results of the survey.

Student	1	2	3	4	5	6	7	8	9	10
Hours playing sport	12	3	5	15	11	0	9	7	6	12
Hours watching TV	18	26	24	16	19	27	12	13	17	14
Student	11	12	13	14	15	16	17	18	19	20
Hours playing sport	12	10	7	6	7	3	1	2	0	12
Hours watching TV	22	16	18	22	12	28	18	20	25	13

a Plot these results on a scatter diagram. Take the horizontal axis as the number of hours playing sport and the vertical axis as the number of hours watching TV.

(CM) **b** If you knew that another student from the class watched 8 hours of TV a week, would you be able to predict how long she or he spent playing sport? Explain why.

6 The table shows the time taken and distance travelled by a taxi driver for 10 journeys one day.

Distance (km)	1.6	8.3	5.2	6.6	4.8	7.2	3.9	5.8	8.8	5.4
Time (minutes)	3	17	11	13	9	15	8	11	16	10

a Draw a scatter diagram with time on the horizontal axis.

b Draw a line of best fit on your diagram.

c A taxi journey takes 5 minutes. How many kilometres would you expect the journey to have been?

d How long would you expect a journey of 4 km to take?

(CM) **e** Explain why you cannot give a time for a journey of 12 km.

(PS) **7** Oliver records the time taken, in hours, and the average speed, in mph, for several different journeys.

Time (h)	0.5	0.8	1.1	1.3	1.6	1.75	2	2.4	2.6
Speed (mph)	42	38	27	30	22	23	21	9	8

Estimate the average speed for a journey of 90 minutes.

(CM) **8** Describe what you would expect a scatter graph to look like if someone said that it showed negative correlation.

Worked exemplars

  The table shows the numbers of learners at each grade for two practice driving tests, Theory and Practical.

	Grades					
	Excellent	Very good	Good	Pass	Fail	Total number of learners
Theory	208	888	1032	696	56	2880
Practical	240	351	291	108	90	1080

a Represent each of the two practice tests in a pie chart.

b By comparing the pie charts, on which test (Theory or Practical) do you think learners did better overall? Give a reason to justify your answer.

This is a question that involves communicating mathematics. You will need to use the data in a form that can be compared, make that comparison, and then assess the validity of the statement made.

a Theory

Grade	Frequency	Calculation	Angle
Excellent	208	$\dfrac{208}{2880} \times 360°$	26°
Very good	888	$\dfrac{888}{2880} \times 360°$	111°
Good	1032	$\dfrac{1032}{2880} \times 360°$	129°
Pass	696	$\dfrac{696}{2880} \times 360°$	87°
Fail	56	$\dfrac{56}{2880} \times 360°$	7°
Total	2880		360°

Work out the angle for each grade.

Remember to check that all the angles add up to 360°.

Take care to interpret the information you are given accurately.

Grades for driving test: theory

Remember to label the pie chart. You do not need to show the angles.

Practical

Grade	Frequency	Calculation	Angle
Excellent	240	$\frac{240}{1080} \times 360°$	80°
Very good	351	$\frac{351}{1080} \times 360°$	117°
Good	291	$\frac{291}{1080} \times 360°$	97°
Pass	108	$\frac{108}{1080} \times 360°$	36°
Fail	90	$\frac{90}{1080} \times 360°$	30°
Total	1080		360°

Work out the angle for each grade.

Remember to check that all the angles add up to 360°.

Take care to interpret the information you are given accurately.

Grades for driving test: practical

Again, remember to label the pie chart. You do not need to show the angles.

b Overall the learners did better on the practical, as 55% obtained Excellent or Very good, whereas only 38% obtained Excellent or Very good on the theory.

You must justify your answer. This is for interpreting and communicating the information accurately.

2 Read these three statements.

- The older you are, the higher you score on a speed test.
- The higher the score on the speed test, the less TV you watch.
- The more TV you watch, the more hours you will sleep.

a Sketch a scatter diagram to illustrate the type of correlation you might see.

b Draw a line of best fit on each diagram and describe the relationship that it shows.

This is a problem-solving question. You need to think how you can show the relationship and then use the line of best fit to illustrate that trend.

a

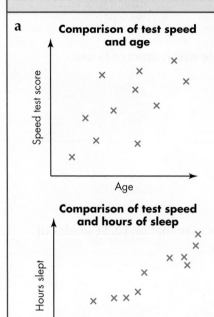

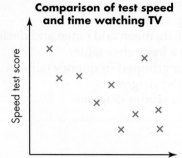

First you will need to decide on how to label the axes.

Then plot at least 10 points on the scatter diagram.

To show that you understand correlation, try to use a different type of correlation for each one where appropriate so that in part **b** you can use the terms: positive correlation, negative correlation, weak correlation and strong correlation.

This translates the problem into a mathematical context.

b

Weak positive correlation

Good negative correlation

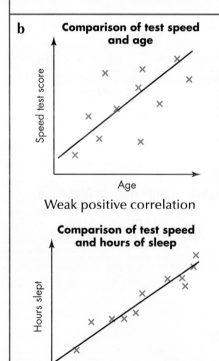

Strong positive correlation

Draw a line of best fit on each diagram and identify the correct relationship for each one. Remember to make sure you leave about equal numbers of points on either side of the line.

Ready to progress?

I can draw and interpret pie charts.
I can draw and interpret line graphs.
I can calculate the mode, median, mean and range and decide which average to use.
I can calculate the mean from a frequency table.
I can estimate the mean from a grouped frequency table.
I can draw and interpret a scatter diagram.
I can draw a line of best fit on a scatter diagram.

Review questions

1 The pie chart gives information about the mathematics examination GCSE grades of some students.

Mathematics examination grades

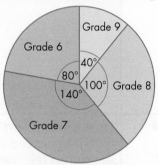

a What grade was the mode?

b What fraction of the students obtained a grade 8?

c 24 of the students got grade 9.

   i How many of the students got grade 6?

   ii How many of the students took the examination?

This accurate pie chart gives information about the English examination grades for a different set of students.

English examination grades

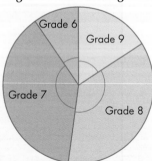

d Lizzy says: "More students got a grade 8 in English than in mathematics."

   Explain why Lizzy could be wrong.

2 The table lists the numbers of matches in 20 matchboxes.

Number of matches	Frequency
42	2
43	5
44	11
45	1
46	1

Calculate the mean number of matches in the 20 boxes.

3 Josh asked 30 students how many minutes they each took to get to school.

The table shows some information about his results.

Time taken, t (minutes)	Frequency
$0 < t \leqslant 10$	6
$10 < t \leqslant 20$	11
$20 < t \leqslant 30$	8
$30 < t \leqslant 40$	5

a Write down the modal group.

b Which class interval contains the median time?

c Calculate an estimate for the mean time.

4 The table shows the weekly pocket money of the students in one class. The values are rounded to the nearest pound.

Pocket money (£)	0–4	5–9	10–14	15–20
Frequency	4	6	12	8

a Sean says that he has estimated the mean amount of pocket money as £9.50.

Explain how you can tell Sean must be wrong without having to calculate the estimated mean.

b Calculate the correct estimate for the mean amount of pocket money.

5 The table shows the percentage sales for three products sold over a four-week period in a park kiosk.

	Ice cream	Chocolate bars	Crisps
Week 1	36%	36%	28%
Week 2	32%	28%	40%
Week 3	42%	26%	32%
Week 4	34%	32%	34%

Draw a composite bar chart to illustrate the data.

6 Tom and Margot grow tomatoes. One weekend they compared their tomatoes by each selecting 100 from their own plants. The group frequency table shows the masses of Tom's tomatoes.

Mass, m (grams)	Tom's tomatoes
$50 < m \leqslant 100$	21
$100 < m \leqslant 150$	28
$150 < m \leqslant 200$	26
$200 < m \leqslant 250$	14
$250 < m \leqslant 300$	9
$300 < m \leqslant 350$	2

a Write down the modal group.

b Which class interval contains the median mass for Tom's tomatoes?

c Calculate an estimate for the mean mass for Tom's tomatoes.

d This is the graph for Margot's tomatoes. Copy it on to graph paper. On the same grid draw the graph for Tom's tomatoes.

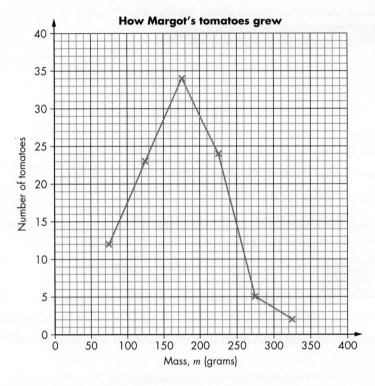

e Copy and complete the grouped frequency table for Margot's tomatoes.

Mass, m (grams)	Margot's tomatoes
$50 < m \leqslant 100$	
$100 < m \leqslant 150$	
$150 < m \leqslant 200$	
$200 < m \leqslant 250$	
$250 < m \leqslant 300$	
$300 < m \leqslant 350$	

f Calculate an estimate for the mean mass of Margot's tomatoes.

g Use the graph and the estimates for the mean to compare Tom and Margot's tomatoes.

7 The scatter diagrams show the results of a survey on the average number of hours of sunshine in a week during the summer in Eastbourne.

a

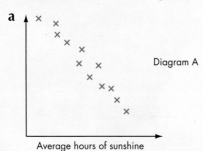

Diagram A

Average hours of sunshine

b

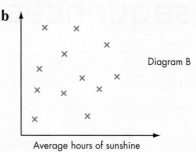

Diagram B

Average hours of sunshine

c

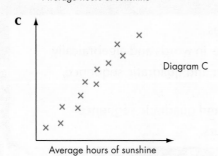

Diagram C

Average hours of sunshine

a Which scatter diagram do you think shows the average hours of sunshine plotted against:

   i the number of ice creams sold

   ii the number of umbrellas sold

   iii the number of births in the town?

b Describe the correlation shown in each diagram.

8 The table shows the time taken and distance travelled by a taxi driver for 10 journeys one day.

Time (minutes)	Distance (km)
3	1.7
17	8.3
11	5.1
13	6.7
9	4.7
15	7.3
8	3.8
11	5.7
16	8.7
10	5.3

a Plot a scatter diagram on a grid with time on the horizontal axis, from 0 to 20, and distance on the vertical axis, from 0 to 10.

b Draw a line of best fit on your diagram.

c A taxi journey takes 4 minutes. What distance is it likely to be?

d A taxi journey is 10 kilometres. How many minutes is it likely to take?

4 Algebra: Number and sequences

This chapter is going to show you:

- how to recognise rules for sequences
- how to express a rule for a sequence, in words and algebraically
- how to generate the terms of a linear and quadratic sequence, given a formula for the nth term
- how to find the nth term of a linear and quadratic sequence
- some common sequences of numbers.

You should already know:

- how to substitute numbers into an algebraic expression
- how to state a rule for a simple linear sequence in words
- how to factorise simple linear expressions
- how to expand a pair of linear brackets to get a quadratic expression.

About this chapter

Mathematicians enjoy finding patterns; you have already seen patterns in sequences such as square numbers and multiples. As well as being important in mathematics; number patterns can also help in the study of nature and geometric patterns.

Many mathematical patterns are found in nature. The most famous of these is probably the Fibonacci series, in which each term after the second is formed by adding the two previous terms.

1   1   2   3   5   8   13   21   ...

The sequence was discovered by the Italian, Leonardo Fibonacci, in 1202, when he was investigating the breeding patterns of rabbits! Since then, the pattern has been found in many other places in nature. The spirals found in a nautilus shell and in the seed heads of a sunflower plant also follow the Fibonacci series.

4.1 Patterns in number

This section will show you how to:

• recognise patterns in number sequences.

Key terms

pattern	sequence

Look at these number **patterns**.

$0 \times 9 + 1 = 1$	$1 \times 8 + 1 = 9$
$1 \times 9 + 2 = 11$	$12 \times 8 + 2 = 98$
$12 \times 9 + 3 = 111$	$123 \times 8 + 3 = 987$
$123 \times 9 + 4 = 1111$	$1234 \times 8 + 4 = 9876$
$1234 \times 9 + 5 = 11\,111$	$12345 \times 8 + 5 = 98\,765$

$1 \times 3 \times 37 = 111$	$7 \times 7 = 49$
$2 \times 3 \times 37 = 222$	$67 \times 67 = 4489$
$3 \times 3 \times 37 = 333$	$667 \times 667 = 444\,889$
$4 \times 3 \times 37 = 444$	$6667 \times 6667 = 44\,448\,889$

The numbers form a **sequence**. Check that the patterns you can see are correct, then try to continue each pattern without using a calculator. Check them with a calculator afterwards.

Spotting patterns is an important part of mathematics. It helps you to see rules for making calculations.

Exercise 4A

In questions **1** to **6**, look for the pattern and then write the next two lines. Check your answers with a calculator afterwards.

You might find that some of the answers are too big to fit in a calculator display. This is one of the reasons why spotting patterns is important.

> **Hints and tips** Look for symmetries in the number patterns.

1 **a**

$1 \times 1 = 1$
$11 \times 11 = 121$
$111 \times 111 = 12\,321$
$1111 \times 1111 = 1\,234\,321$

b

$9 \times 9 = 81$
$99 \times 99 = 9801$
$999 \times 999 = 998\,001$
$9999 \times 9999 = 99\,980\,001$

2 **a**

$3 \times 4 = 3^2 + 3$
$4 \times 5 = 4^2 + 4$
$5 \times 6 = 5^2 + 5$
$6 \times 7 = 6^2 + 6$

b $10 \times 11 = 110$
$20 \times 21 = 420$
$30 \times 31 = 930$
$40 \times 41 = 1640$

> **Hints and tips** Think of the answers to **2b** as 1 10, 4 20, 9 30, 16 40 …

3 **a**

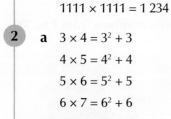

$1 = \quad 1 \Rightarrow 1^2$
$1 + 2 + 1 = \quad 4 \Rightarrow 2^2$
$1 + 2 + 3 + 2 + 1 = \quad 9 \Rightarrow 3^2$
$1 + 2 + 3 + 4 + 3 + 2 + 1 = 16 \Rightarrow 4^2$

b

$1 = \quad 1 \Rightarrow 1^3$
$3 + \quad 5 = \quad 8 \Rightarrow 2^3$
$7 + \quad 9 + 11 = 27 \Rightarrow 3^3$
$13 + 15 + 17 + 19 = 64 \Rightarrow 4^3$

4 **a**

$$1 = 1$$
$$1 + 1 = 2$$
$$1 + 2 + 1 = 4$$
$$1 + 3 + 3 + 1 = 8$$
$$1 + 4 + 6 + 4 + 1 = 16$$
$$1 + 5 + 10 + 10 + 5 + 1 = 32$$

b

$$12\ 345\ 679 \times 9 = 111\ 111\ 111$$
$$12\ 345\ 679 \times 18 = 222\ 222\ 222$$
$$12\ 345\ 679 \times 27 = 333\ 333\ 333$$
$$12\ 345\ 679 \times 36 = 444\ 444\ 444$$

(MR) **5** **a**

$$1^3 = 1^2 \qquad \Rightarrow 1$$
$$1^3 + 2^3 = (1 + 2)^2 \qquad \Rightarrow 9$$
$$1^3 + 2^3 + 3^3 = (1 + 2 + 3)^2 \Rightarrow 36$$

b

$$3^2 + 4^2 = 5^2$$
$$10^2 + 11^2 + 12^2 = 13^2 + 14^2$$
$$21^2 + 22^2 + 23^2 + 24^2 = 25^2 + 26^2 + 27^2$$

> **Hints and tips**
> $$4 + 5 = 9 \Rightarrow 3^2$$
> $$12 + 13 = 25 \Rightarrow 5^2$$
> $$24 + 25 = 49 \Rightarrow 7^2$$

Use your observations on the number patterns in questions **1** to **5** to answer question **6** without using a calculator.

(EV) **6** **a** $111\ 111\ 111 \times 111\ 111\ 111 =$

b $999\ 999\ 999 \times 999\ 999\ 999 =$

c $12 \times 13 =$

d $90 \times 91 =$

e $1 + 2 + 3 + 4 + 5 + 6 + 7 + 8 + 9 + 8 + 7 + 6 + 5 + 4 + 3 + 2 + 1 =$

f $57 + 59 + 61 + 63 + 65 + 67 + 69 + 71 =$

g $1 + 9 + 36 + 84 + 126 + 126 + 84 + 36 + 9 + 1 =$

h $12\ 345\ 679 \times 81 =$

i $1^3 + 2^3 + 3^3 + 4^3 + 5^3 + 6^3 + 7^3 + 8^3 + 9^3 =$

> **Hints and tips** Look for clues in the patterns from questions **1** to **5**, for example, $1111 \times 1111 = 1\ 234\ 321$. This is four 1s times four 1s, so what will it be for nine 1s times nine 1s?

(CM) **7** This is Gauss's method for working out the sum of all the numbers from 1 to 100.

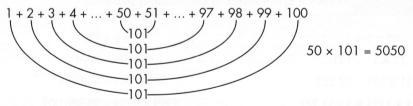

$$1 + 2 + 3 + 4 + \ldots + 50 + 51 + \ldots + 97 + 98 + 99 + 100$$

$$50 \times 101 = 5050$$

Use Gauss's method to work out the sum of all the whole numbers from 1 to 500.

4.2 Number sequences

This section will show you how to:
- recognise how number sequences are built up
- generate sequences, given the nth term.

You know that a number sequence is an ordered set of numbers based on a rule. The rule that takes you from one number to the next could be a simple addition or multiplication, but it may be a more complex rule. You always need to look very carefully at the pattern of a sequence.

Each number in a sequence is called a **term**. Each term has a specific position in the sequence. Terms that follow on, one from another, are called **consecutive** terms.

Look at these sequences and their rules.

3, 6, 12, 24, …	doubling the previous term each time	… 48, 96, …
2, 5, 8, 11, …	adding 3 to the previous term each time	… 14, 17, …
1, 10, 100, 1000, …	multiplying the previous term by 10 each time	… 10 000, 100 000, …
22, 15, 8, 1, …	subtracting 7 from the previous term each time	… −6, −13, …

The first thing to do is identify the link from one term to the next. A pattern in which each term (apart from the first) is derived from the term before it is a **term-to-term** sequence.

Differences

For some sequences you need to look at the **differences** between consecutive terms to determine the pattern.

Example 1

Find the next two terms of the sequence 1, 3, 6, 10, 15, …

Look at the differences between each pair of consecutive terms.

```
1   3   6   10   15
  ↑   ↑   ↑    ↑
  2   3   4    5
```

You can continue the sequence like this.

```
1   3   6   10   15   21   28
  ↑   ↑   ↑    ↑
  2   3   4    5  +6   +7
```

The differences usually form a number sequence of their own, so you need to work out the sequence of the differences before you can continue the original sequence.

Generalising to find the rule

Sometimes, you may need to know a specific term in a number sequence. To do this, you need to find the rule that produces the sequence and express it in a general form. To see how this works, look at the problem backwards: make up a rule and see how it produces a sequence.

Example 2

A sequence is formed by the rule $3n + 1$, where $n = 1, 2, 3, 4, 5, 6, …$ Write down the first five terms of the sequence.

Substituting $n = 1, 2, 3, 4, 5$ in turn:

$(3 \times 1 + 1)$	$(3 \times 2 + 1)$	$(3 \times 3 + 1)$	$(3 \times 4 + 1)$	$(3 \times 5 + 1)$	…
4	7	10	13	16	…

So the sequence is 4, 7, 10, 13, 16, …

In the last example, you used the expression $3n + 1$ for the rule that generates the sequence. This expression is called the **nth term** of the sequence and you can use it to find any term, by substituting the term number for n.

Notice that the difference between one term and the next is always 3, which is the **coefficient** of n (the number attached to n) in the rule. The constant term is the difference between the first term and the coefficient (in this case, $4 - 3 = 1$).

The nth term of a sequence is $4n - 3$. Write down the first five terms of the sequence.

Substituting $n = 1, 2, 3, 4, 5$ in turn:

$(4 \times 1 - 3)$	$(4 \times 2 - 3)$	$(4 \times 3 - 3)$	$(4 \times 4 - 3)$	$(4 \times 5 - 3)$	...
1	5	9	13	17	...

So the sequence is 1, 5, 9, 13, 17, …

Notice that the difference between each term and the next is always 4, which is the coefficient of n in the formula for the nth term. The constant term is the difference between the first term and the coefficient ($1 - 4 = -3$).

Exercise 4B

1 Look carefully at each number sequence below. Find the next two numbers in the sequence and explain the pattern.

a 1, 1, 2, 3, 5, 8, 13, …   **b** 1, 4, 9, 16, 25, 36, …   **c** 3, 4, 7, 11, 18, 29, …

> **Hints and tips** These patterns do not go up by the same value each time so you will need to find another connection between the terms.

2 The pattern shows how triangular numbers are formed.

1	3	6	10

Work out the next four triangular numbers.

3 The pattern shows how hexagonal numbers are formed.

 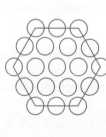 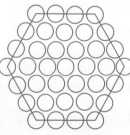

1	7	19	37

Work out the next three hexagonal numbers.

4 The first two terms of the sequence of fractions $\frac{n-1}{n+1}$ are:

$$n = 1: \frac{1-1}{1+1} = \frac{0}{2} = 0 \qquad n = 2: \frac{2-1}{2+1} = \frac{1}{3}$$

Work out the next five terms of the sequence.

5 A sequence is formed by the rule $\frac{1}{2} \times n \times (n+1)$ for $n = 1, 2, 3, 4, \ldots$

The first term is given by $n = 1$: $\qquad \frac{1}{2} \times 1 \times (1+1) = 1$

The second term is given by $n = 2$: $\qquad \frac{1}{2} \times 2 \times (2+1) = 3$

a Work out the next five terms of this sequence.

b This is a well-known sequence you have met before. What is it?

6 In mathematics, 5! means 'factorial 5', which is $5 \times 4 \times 3 \times 2 \times 1 = 120$.

In the same way 7! means $7 \times 6 \times 5 \times 4 \times 3 \times 2 \times 1 = 5040$.

a Calculate the values of 2!, 3!, 4! and 6!

b If your calculator has a factorial button, check that it gives the same answers as you get for part **a**. What is the largest factorial you can work out with your calculator before you get an error?

(PS) **7** On the first day of Christmas my true love sent to me:

> a partridge in a pear tree.

On the second day of Christmas my true love sent to me:

> two turtle doves
>
> and a partridge in a pear tree.

and so on until…

On the twelfth day of Christmas my true love sent to me:

> twelve drummers drumming
>
> eleven pipers piping
>
> ten lords a-leaping
>
> nine ladies dancing
>
> eight maids a-milking
>
> seven swans a-swimming
>
> six geese a-laying
>
> five golden rings
>
> four calling birds
>
> three French hens
>
> two turtle doves
>
> and a partridge in a pear tree.

How many presents were given, in total, during the 12 days of Christmas?

| Hints and tips | Work out the pattern for the number of presents each day. For example, on day 1 there was 1 present, on day 2 there were $2 + 1 = 3$ presents, and so on. Total the presents after each day, so after 1 day there was a total of 1 present, after 2 days a total of 4 presents, (remembering that the present for day 1 was repeated on day 2 and so on). Try to spot any patterns. |

(PS) **8** The letters of the alphabet are written as the pattern:

ABBCCCDDDDEEEEEFFFFFFGGGGGGG ...

so that the number of times each letter is written matches its place in the alphabet.

So, for example, as J is the 10th letter in the alphabet, there will be 10 Js in the list.

The pattern repeats when it gets to the 26th Z.

What letter will be the 1000th in the list?

Hints and tips	Work out how many letters there are in the sequence from ABB ... to ... ZZZ, then work out how many of these sequences you need to get past 1000 letters.

(CM) **9** Look at these two sequences.

8, 11, 14, 17, 20, ...

1, 5, 9, 13, 17, ...

The first term that they have in common is 17. What are the next two terms that the two sequences have in common?

(CM) **10** Look at these two sequences.

2, 5, 8, 11, 14, ...

3, 6, 9, 12, 15, ...

Will the two sequences ever have a term in common?

Give a reason for your answer.

(CM) **11** The nth term of a sequence is $3n + 7$.

The nth term of another sequence is $4n - 2$.

These two sequences have several terms in common but only one term that is common and has the same position in the sequence.

Without writing out the sequences, show how you can tell, using the expressions for the nth term, that it is the 9th term.

4.3 Finding the nth term of a linear sequence

This section will show you how to:

- find the nth term of a linear sequence.

A **linear** or **arithmetic sequence** has the same *difference* between each term and the next. For example, look at this sequence.

2, 5, 8, 11, 14, ...   difference of 3

The nth term of a sequence is a rule, written algebraically, that gives any term based on its position (n) in the sequence. The nth term of this sequence is given by $3n - 1$.

Here is another linear sequence.

5, 7, 9, 11, 13, ...   difference of 2

The nth term of this sequence is given by $2n + 3$.

The nth term of a linear sequence is *always* of the form $An \pm b$, where:

- A, the coefficient of n, is the difference between each term and the next term (consecutive terms)
- b is the difference between the first term and A.

Example 4

Find the nth term of each sequence.

a 5, 7, 9, 11, 13, …   **b** 95, 90, 85, 80, 75, …

a The difference between consecutive terms is +2. So the coefficient of n in the nth term is 2 and the nth term starts with $2n$.

Subtract A, 2, from the first term, 5, which gives $5 - 2 = 3$.

So the nth term is given by $2n + 3$.

(You can test it by substituting $n = 1, 2, 3, 4, …$)

b The difference between consecutive terms is –5. So the coefficient of n in the nth term is –5 and the nth term starts with $-5n$.

Subtract A, –5, from the first term, 95, which gives $95 - -5 = 100$.

So the nth term is given by $-5n + 100$.

(You can test it by substituting $n = 1, 2, 3, 4, …$)

Example 5

Find the nth term of the sequence 3, 7, 11, 15, 19, …

The difference between consecutive terms is 4. So the coefficient of n in the nth term is 4 and the nth term starts with $4n$.

Subtract A, 4, from the first term, 3, which gives $3 - 4 = -1$.

So the nth term is given by $4n - 1$.

Example 6

From the sequence 5, 12, 19, 26, 33, … work out:

a the nth term   **b** the 50th term   **c** the first term that is greater than 1000.

a The difference between consecutive terms is 7. So the coefficient of n in the nth term is 7 and the nth term starts with $7n$.

Subtract A, 7, from the first term, 5, which gives $5 - 7 = -2$.

So the nth term is given by $7n - 2$.

b Find the 50th term by substituting $n = 50$ into the rule, $7n - 2$.

Then the 50th term $= 7 \times 50 - 2 = 350 - 2 = 348$.

c The first term that is greater than 1000 is given by:

$7n - 2 > 1000$

$\Rightarrow 7n > 1000 + 2$

$\Rightarrow n > \dfrac{1002}{7}$

$n > 143.14$

So the first term (which has to be a whole number) that is over 1000 is the 144th term which is 1006.

Exercise 4C

1 Find the next two terms and the nth term in each linear sequence.

a 3, 5, 7, 9, 11, … **b** 5, 9, 13, 17, 21, … **c** 8, 13, 18, 23, 28, …

d 2, 8, 14, 20, 26, … **e** 5, 8, 11, 14, 17, … **f** 2, 9, 16, 23, 30, …

g 1, 5, 9, 13, 17, … **h** 3, 7, 11, 15, 19, … **i** 2, 5, 8, 11, 14, …

j 32, 22, 12, 2, … **k** 20, 16, 12, 8, … **l** 24, 19, 14, 9, 4, …

> **Hints and tips** Remember to look at the differences and the first term.

2 Find the nth term and the 50th term in each linear sequence.

a 4, 7, 10, 13, 16, … **b** 7, 9, 11, 13, 15, … **c** 3, 8, 13, 18, 23, …

d 1, 5, 9, 13, 17, … **e** 2, 10, 18, 26, … **f** 5, 6, 7, 8, 9, …

g 6, 11, 16, 21, 26, … **h** 3, 11, 19, 27, 35, … **i** 1, 4, 7, 10, 13, …

j 21, 24, 27, 30, 33, … **k** 40, 33, 26, 19, 12, … **l** 33, 25, 17, 9, 1, …

3 **a** Which term of the sequence 5, 8, 11, 14, 17, … is the first to be greater than 100?

b Which term of the sequence 1, 8, 15, 22, 29, … is the first one to be greater than 200?

c Which term of the sequence 4, 9, 14, 19, 24, … is the closest to 500?

4 For each sequence **a** to **j**, find:

i the nth term **ii** the 100th term **iii** the term closest to 100.

a 5, 9, 13, 17, 21, … **b** 3, 5, 7, 9, 11, 13, … **c** 4, 7, 10, 13, 16, …

d 8, 10, 12, 14, 16, … **e** 9, 13, 17, 21, … **f** 6, 11, 16, 21, …

g 0, 3, 6, 9, 12, … **h** 2, 8, 14, 20, 26, … **i** 197, 189, 181, 173, …

j 225, 223, 221, 219, …

5 A sequence of fractions is $\dfrac{3}{4}, \dfrac{5}{7}, \dfrac{7}{10}, \dfrac{9}{13}, \dfrac{11}{16}$ …

a Find the nth term in the sequence.

b Change each fraction to a decimal. What happens to the decimal values?

c What, as a decimal, will be the value of:

i the 100th term **ii** the 1000th term?

d Use your answers to part **c** to predict what the 10 000th term and the millionth term are. (Check these on your calculator.)

6 Repeat question **5** for the sequence $\dfrac{3}{6}, \dfrac{7}{11}, \dfrac{11}{16}, \dfrac{15}{21}, \dfrac{19}{26}$ …

7 A2B haulage uses this formula to calculate the cost of transporting n pallets.

For $n \leqslant 5$, the cost will be £($40n + 50$).

For $6 < n < 10$, the cost will be £($40n + 25$).

For $n \geqslant 11$, the cost will be £$40n$.

a How much will the company charge to transport 7 pallets?

b How much will the company charge to transport 15 pallets?

c A2B charged £170 for transporting pallets. How many pallets did they transport?

d Speedy haulage uses the formula £$50n$ to calculate the costs for transporting n pallets. At what value of n do the two companies charge the same amount?

(EV) **8** The formula for working out a series of fractions is $\dfrac{2n+1}{3n+1}$.

    a Work out the first three fractions in the series.

    b i Work out the value of the fraction as a decimal when $n = 1\,000\,000$.

      ii What fraction is equivalent to this decimal?

    c How can you tell this from the original formula?

(CM) **9** This chart is used by an online retailer for the charges for buying n T-shirts, including any postage and packing charges.

n	1	2	3	4	5	6	7	8	9	10	11	12	13	14	15
Charge (£)	10	18	26	34	42	49	57	65	73	81	88	96	104	112	120

    a Using the charges for one to five T-shirts, work out an expression for the nth term.

    b Using the charges for six to 10 T-shirts, work out an expression for the nth term.

    c Using the charges for 11 to 15 T-shirts, work out an expression for the nth term.

    d What is the basic charge for a T-shirt?

(CM) **10** Look at this series of fractions.

$\dfrac{31}{109}, \dfrac{33}{110}, \dfrac{35}{111}, \dfrac{37}{112}, \dfrac{39}{113}, \dots$

    a Show that the nth term of the sequence of the numerators is $2n + 29$.

    b Write down the nth term of the sequence of the denominators.

    c Show that the terms of the series will eventually get very close to 2.

(PS)   **d** Which term of the series has a value equal to 1?

> **Hints and tips** Use algebra to set up an equation.

(CM) **11** The nth term of the sequence of even numbers is $2n$. The nth term of the sequence of odd numbers is $2n - 1$.

    Explain why these expressions tell you that there can never be a number in both sequences.

(PS) **12** The nth term of a linear sequence is given by $An + b$, where A and b are integers.

    The 5th term is 10 and the 8th term is 19. Work out the values of A and b.

4.4 Special sequences

This section will show you how to:

- recognise and continue some special number sequences.

So far you have been working with arithmetic or linear sequences. In these sequences the difference between consecutive terms has a constant value. There are many other number sequences that you need to know about.

> **Key terms**
>
> geometric sequence
>
> powers of 2   powers of 10

- The even numbers are 2, 4, 6, 8, 10, 12, …   The nth term of this sequence is $2n$.
- The odd numbers are 1, 3, 5, 7, 9, 11, …   The nth term of this sequence is $2n - 1$.

- The square numbers are 1, 4, 9, 16, 25, 36, …   The nth term of this sequence is n^2.
- The cube numbers are 1, 8, 27, 64, 125, 216, …   The nth term of this sequence is n^3.
- The triangular numbers are 1, 3, 6, 10, 15, 21, …   The nth term of this sequence is $\frac{1}{2}n(n+1)$.
- The **powers of 2** are 2, 4, 8, 16, 32, 64, …   The nth term of this sequence is 2^n.
- The **powers of 10** are 10, 100, 1000, 10 000, 100 000, 1 000 000, …   The nth term of this sequence is 10^n.

Geometric sequences

A sequence in which you find each term by multiplying the previous term by a fixed value is a **geometric sequence**. The nth term of a geometric sequence is given by $a \times r^{n-1}$, where a is the first term and r is the multiplier. Note that any number raised to a power of 0 is 1.

For example: 2, 6, 18, 54, 162, …   The nth term for this sequence is $2 \times 3^{n-1}$.

  12, 48, 192, 768, 3072, …   The nth term for this sequence is $12 \times 4^{n-1}$.

Note that, as 12 has a factor of 4, the nth term of the last sequence could have been written as 3×4^n.

Fibonacci sequences

The sequence 1, 1, 2, 3, 5, 8, 13, 21, … was discovered by Leonardo Fibonacci in about 1200 AD. Starting with the third term, each term is the sum of the previous two terms:

  $1 + 1 = 2, 1 + 2 = 3, 2 + 3 = 5$ and so on.

There is no simple expression for the nth term.

Prime numbers

A prime number is a number that only has two factors, 1 and itself.

The first 20 prime numbers are 2, 3, 5, 7, 11, 13, 17, 19, 23, 29, 31, 37, 41, 43, 47, 53, 59, 61, 67, 71.

There is no pattern to the prime numbers so there is no formula for the nth term.

An important fact to remember is that 2 is the only even prime number.

Example 7

p is a prime number, q is an odd number and r is an even number.
Say if each expression is always odd (O), always even (E) or could be either odd or even (X).

a pq **b** $p + q + r$ **c** pqr **d** $q^2 + r^2$

a The easiest way to answer this question is to substitute numbers and see whether the outcome is odd or even.

For example, let $p = 2$ and $q = 3$. Then $pq = 6$ and is even; but p could also be 3 and q could be 5, which are both odd, so $pq = 3 \times 5 = 15$ which is odd.

So pq could be either (X).

b Let $p = 2$ or 3, $q = 5$ and $r = 4$; so $p + q + r = 2 + 5 + 4 = 11$, or $3 + 5 + 4 = 12$

So $p + q + r$ could be either (X).

c Let $p = 2$ or 3, $q = 5$ and $r = 4$; so $pqr = 2 \times 5 \times 4 = 40$ or $3 \times 5 \times 4 = 60$

Both are even, pqr is always even (E).

d Let $q = 5$ and $r = 4$; $q^2 + r^2 = 5^2 + 4^2 = 25 + 16 = 41$

This is odd, $q^2 + r^2$ is always odd (O).

Work out the first five terms of the sequences with these nth terms.

a $5 \times 3^{n-1}$ **b** 2×6^n

a Substitute $n = 1$ into the nth term expression, then multiply each term by the multiplier 3 to find the other terms.

$5 \times 3^0 = 5 \times 1 = 5, 5 \times 3 = 15, \ldots$ The sequence is 5, 15, 45, 135, 405, ...

b Substitute $n = 1$ into the nth term expression, then multiply each term by the multiplier 6 to find the other terms.

$2 \times 6^1 = 2 \times 6 = 12, 12 \times 6 = 72, \ldots$ The sequence is 12, 72, 432, 2592, 15 552, ...

Work out the nth term of each geometric sequence.

a 3, 15, 75, 375, 1875, ...   **b** 14, 28, 56, 112, 224, ...

a Each term is the result of multiplying the previous term by 5 so the number raised to a power will be 5.
The first term is 3, which is less than 5 so the power of 5 must be zero and the nth term is $3 \times 5^{n-1}$.

b Each term is the result of multiplying the previous term by 2 so the number raised to a power will be 2.
The first term is 14, which has a factor of 2 so the nth term can be written as 7×2^n.

Exercise 4D

1 **a** Pick any odd number. Pick another odd number. Add the two numbers together. Is the answer odd or even?

Copy and complete this table.

+	Odd	Even
Odd	Even	
Even		

b Pick any odd number. Pick another odd number. Multiply the two numbers together. Is the answer odd or even?

Copy and complete this table.

×	Odd	Even
Odd	Odd	
Even		

 2 **a** Write down the next two lines of this number pattern.

$1 = 1 = 1^2$

$1 + 3 = 4 = 2^2$

$1 + 3 + 5 = 9 = 3^2$

b Use the pattern in part **a** to write down the totals of these numbers.

   i $1 + 3 + 5 + 7 + 9 + 11 + 13 + 15 + 17 + 19$ **ii** $2 + 4 + 6 + 8 + 10 + 12 + 14$

3 **a** Work out the first 12 terms of the Fibonacci sequence 1, 1, 2, 3, 5, ...

 b Explain why the Fibonacci sequence always has a repeated pattern of two odd terms followed by one even term.

c The first three terms of a Fibonacci sequence are $a, b, a + b, \ldots$

   i Write out the next five terms.   **ii** Describe the pattern of the coefficients of a and b.

CM **4** p is an odd number, q is an even number. State if each expression is odd or even.

a $p + 1$ **b** $q + 1$ **c** $p + q$

d p^2 **e** $qp + 1$ **f** $(p + q)(p - q)$

g $q^2 + 4$ **h** $p^2 + q^2$ **i** p^3

CM **5** p is a prime number, q is an even number.

State if each expression is odd, even or could be either odd or even.

a $p + 1$ **b** $p + q$ **c** p^2

d $qp + 1$ **e** $(p + q)(p - q)$ **f** $2p + 3q$

CM **6** **a** p is an odd number, q is an even number and r is an odd number.

Is each expression odd or even?

i $pq + r$ **ii** pqr **iii** $(p + q)^2 + r$

b x is a prime number and both y and z are odd.

Write an expression using all of x, y and z, and no other numbers or letters, so that the answer is always even.

7 The powers of 2 are $2^1, 2^2, 2^3, 2^4, 2^5, \ldots$

This gives the sequence 2, 4, 8, 16, 32, …

The nth term is given by 2^n.

a Continue the sequence for another five terms.

b Give the nth term of these sequences.

     i 1, 3, 7, 15, 31, …   **ii** 3, 5, 9, 17, 33, …   **iii** 6, 12, 24, 48, 96, …

8 The powers of 10 are $10^1, 10^2, 10^3, 10^4, 10^5, \ldots$

This gives the sequence 10, 100, 1000, 10 000, 100 000, …

The nth term is given by 10^n.

a Describe the connection between the number of zeros in each term and the power of the term.

b If $10^n = 1\ 000\ 000$, what is the value of n?

c Give the nth term of these sequences.

     i 9, 99, 999, 9 999, 99 999, …   **ii** 20, 200, 2000, 20 000, 200 000, …

9 The first four cube numbers are 1, 8, 27 and 64.

a Write down the next two cube numbers.

b Add consecutive cube numbers together. For example:

1 + 8, 1 + 8 + 27, 1 + 8 + 27 + 64.

What do you notice about the answers?

10 The triangular numbers are 1, 3, 6, 10, 15, 21, …

a Continue the sequence for another five terms.

b The nth term of this sequence is given by $\frac{1}{2}n(n + 1)$.

Use the formula to find:

     i the 20th triangular number   **ii** the 100th triangular number.

c Add consecutive terms of the triangular number sequence.

For example, 1 + 3 = 4, 3 + 6 = 9, …

What do you notice?

CM **11** **a** n is a positive integer.

    i Explain why $n(n + 1)$ must be an even number.

    ii Explain why $2n + 1$ must be an odd number.

  b p is an odd number and q is an even number.

    Copy this table, then tick the correct box to show whether each expression is odd or even.

Expression	Odd	Even
p^2		
$p(q + 1)$		
$2p + 1 + 2q + 1$		
$3(q + 1) + 1$		
$(q - 1)^2$		

  c Show algebraically why, when you square an odd number, the answer is always odd and when you square an even number, the answer is always even.

CM **12** A palindromic number is one that reads the same forwards as backwards, such as 242 and 1001.

In the triangular number series 1, 3, 6, 10, 15, …, the first palindromic number is the 10th term, 55.

Find the next two palindromic triangular numbers.

MR **13** The square numbers are 1, 4, 9, 16, 25, …

The nth term of this sequence is n^2.

  a Continue the sequence for another five terms.

  b Give the nth term of each sequence.

    i 2, 5, 10, 17, 26, …   **ii** 2, 8, 18, 32, 50, …   **iii** 0, 3, 8, 15, 24, …

14 Work out the first five terms of the sequences with an nth term of:

  a $6 \times 4^{n-1}$ **b** 3×7^n **c** $2 \times 5^{n-1}$

  d $6 \times 10^{n-1}$ **e** 18×3^n

> **Hints and tips** Remember that any number raised to the power 0 is 1.

15 Work out the nth term of each geometric sequence.

  a 3, 6, 12, 24, 48, …   **b** 5, 20, 80, 320, 1280, …   **c** 20, 100, 500, 2500, 12 500, …

  d 21, 63, 189, 567, 1701, …   **e** 24, 192, 1536, 12 288, 98 304

PS **16** Mia adds two prime numbers. The result is another prime number. Write down the value of one of Mia's two prime numbers. Explain your answer.

PS **17** **a** Find two prime numbers that add together to give a square number greater than 30.

  b Find two square numbers with a difference that is a prime number.

4.5 General rules from given patterns

This section will show you how to:

- find the nth term from practical problems involving sequences.

Many problem-solving situations that you are likely to meet involve number sequences. So you need to be able to formulate general rules from given number patterns.

Example 10

The diagram shows how a pattern of squares builds up.

a How many squares will there be in the nth pattern?

b Which pattern has 99 squares in it?

a First, build up a table for the patterns.

Pattern number	1	2	3	4	5
Number of squares	1	3	5	7	9

Look at the differences between consecutive patterns.

It is always two squares, so use $2n$.

Subtract the difference 2 from the first number, which gives $1 - 2 = -1$.

So the number of squares in the nth pattern is $2n - 1$.

b Now find n when $2n - 1 = 99$.

$$2n - 1 = 99$$
$$2n = 99 + 1$$
$$= 100$$
$$n = 100 \div 2$$
$$= 50$$

The pattern with 99 squares is the 50th.

When you are trying to find a general rule from a sequence of diagrams, always set up a table to connect the pattern number with the number of items (such as squares, matches, seats) for which you are trying to find the rule. Once you have set up the table, you can find the nth term.

Exercise 4E

1 This pattern of squares is built up from matchsticks.

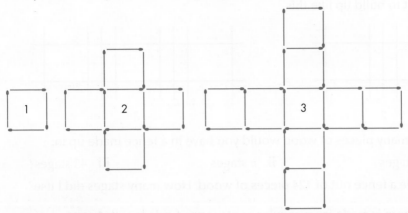

> **Hints and tips** Write out the number sequence to help you see the patterns.

a Draw the fourth diagram.

b How many squares are there in the *n*th diagram?

c How many squares are there in the 25th diagram?

d What is the biggest diagram that you could make with 200 squares?

2 This pattern of triangles is built up from matchsticks.

    1   2   3   4

a Draw the fifth set of triangles in this pattern.

b How many matchsticks would you need for the *n*th set of triangles?

c How many matchsticks would you need to make the 60th set of triangles?

d If you only have 100 matchsticks, what is the largest set of triangles you could make?

3 The tables at a conference centre can each take six people. When the tables are put together, people can sit as shown.

 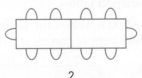 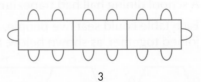

    1   2   3

a How many people could be seated at four tables put together in this way?

b How many people could be seated at *n* tables put together in this way?

c When 50 people attend a conference, they decide to use the tables in this way. How many tables do they need?

4 Prepacked fencing units come in the shape shown here.

Each is made up from four pieces of wood. When you put them together in stages to make a fence, you also need an extra joining piece, so the fence will start to build up like this.

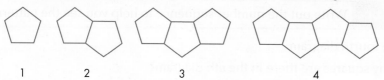

2   3

a How many pieces of wood would you have in a fence made up in:

  i 5 stages   **ii** n stages   **iii** 45 stages?

b I made a fence out of 124 pieces of wood. How many stages did I use?

5 This pattern is made from regular pentagons of side length 1 cm.

 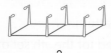 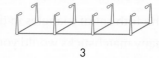

  1   2   3   4

a Write down the perimeter of each shape.

b What is the perimeter of patterns like this made from:

  i six pentagons   **ii** n pentagons   **iii** 50 pentagons?

c What is the largest number of pentagons that can be put together like this to have a perimeter less than 1000 cm?

6 Lamp-posts are put at the end of every 100 m stretch of a motorway.

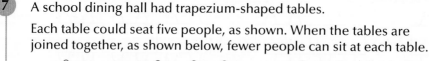

  1   2   3

a How many lamp-posts are needed for:

  i 900 m of this motorway   **ii** 8 km of this motorway?

b The contractor building the M99 motorway has ordered 1598 lamp-posts. How long is this motorway?

7 A school dining hall had trapezium-shaped tables.

Each table could seat five people, as shown. When the tables are joined together, as shown below, fewer people can sit at each table.

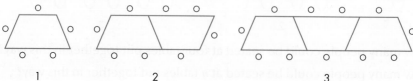

  1   2   3

a In this arrangement, how many could be seated if there were:

  i four tables   **ii** n tables   **iii** 13 tables?

b For an outside charity event, up to 200 people had to be seated. How many tables arranged like this did they need?

8 When setting out tins to make a display of a certain height, you need to know how many tins to start with at the bottom.

a How many tins are needed on the bottom if you wish the display to be:

  i five tins high   **ii** n tins high   **iii** 18 tins high?

b Albi started to build a display with 20 tins on the bottom. How high was the display when it was finished?

9 a The values of 2 raised to a positive whole-number power are 2, 4, 8, 16, 32, …

What is the nth term of this sequence?

b A supermarket sells four different-sized bottles of water: pocket size, 100 ml; standard size, 200 ml; family size, 400 ml; giant size, 800 ml.

  i Describe the number pattern that the contents form.

  ii The supermarket wants to sell a super-giant sized bottle, which is the next-sized bottle in the pattern. How much does this bottle hold?

c A litre of water weighs 1 kg. The supermarket estimates that the heaviest they could possibly make a bottle of water is 10 kg. Assuming that the plastic bottle has a negligible weight and that the pattern of bottles continues, what is the largest size of bottle the supermarket could have?

10 Draw an equilateral triangle.

Mark the midpoints of each side and draw and shade in the equilateral triangle formed by these points.

Repeat this with the three triangles that remain unshaded.

Keep on doing this with the unshaded triangles that are left.

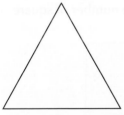 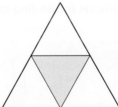 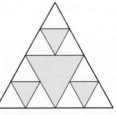 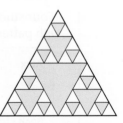

This is called a Sierpinski triangle. It is one of the earliest examples of a fractal pattern.

The shaded areas in each triangle are $\frac{1}{4}$, $\frac{7}{16}$, $\frac{37}{64}$, $\frac{175}{256}$, …

It is very difficult to work out an nth term for this series of fractions.

Use your calculator to work out the area left unshaded, for example, $\frac{3}{4}$, $\frac{9}{16}$, …

You should be able to write down a formula for the nth term of this pattern.

Pick a large value for n.

Will the shaded area ever cover all of the original triangle?

11 Thom is using matchsticks to build three different patterns. He builds the patterns in steps.

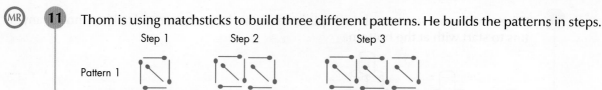

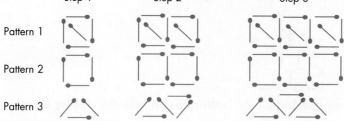

Thom has five boxes of matches, each labelled 'Average contents 42 matches'. Can Thom reach step 20 of each pattern? Show your working.

12 A supermarket manager wants to display grapefruit stacked in layers, each of which is a triangle. These are the first four layers.

a If the display is four layers deep, how many grapefruit will there be in the display?

b The manager tells her staff that there should not be any more than eight layers, as otherwise the fruit will get squashed. What is the most grapefruit that could be stacked?

13 Some students are making hollow patterns from small squares.

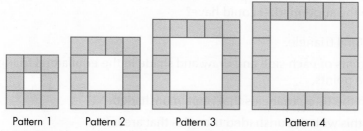

Pattern 1   Pattern 2   Pattern 3   Pattern 4

Four students write down their methods for finding the number of squares in the *n*th pattern.

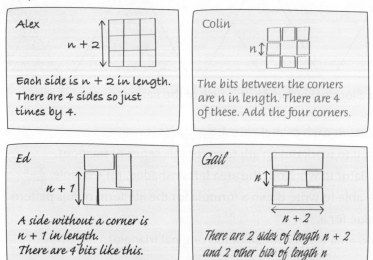

Alex

$n + 2$

Each side is $n + 2$ in length. There are 4 sides so just times by 4.

Colin

n

The bits between the corners are n in length. There are 4 of these. Add the four corners.

Ed

$n + 1$

A side without a corner is $n + 1$ in length. There are 4 bits like this.

Gail

n

$n + 2$

There are 2 sides of length $n + 2$ and 2 other bits of length n

Evaluate each student's method. Do they give the correct answer? Are any of their methods wrong? What mistake have they made? What should they do to correct it?

4.6 The nth term of a quadratic sequence

This section will show you how to:

- generate the terms of a quadratic sequence, given the nth term.

Some number sequences, called **quadratic sequences**, are governed by **quadratic rules**. Their nth term is a **quadratic expression**, such as $n^2 + 2n - 3$. This is also called the **position-to-term rule**.

With the term-to-term rule, the terms increase or decrease each time by an amount that follows a linear rule. These are called the **first differences**. The differences in the first differences are called the **second differences**. If the second differences of a sequence are constant, it is a quadratic sequence.

Key terms
first difference
position-to-term rule
quadratic expression
quadratic rule
quadratic sequence
second difference

The nth term of the sequence of triangular numbers is $\frac{1}{2}n(n + 1)$. Expanding this, to remove the brackets, gives $\frac{1}{2}n^2 + \frac{1}{2}n$. This has a 'squared' term so it is a quadratic expression.

The sequence of triangular numbers is a quadratic sequence. You can always test if a sequence is a quadratic sequence by working out the first differences and the second differences. If the sequence is quadratic then the second differences will always be constant.

You can use a diagram to show the differences for the sequence of triangular numbers.

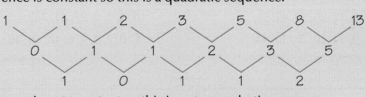

Example 11

Use the nth term to write down the first five terms of each sequence.

a $n^2 + 5$ **b** $n^2 + 2n$ **c** $n^2 + 3n - 4$

Substitute $n = 1, 2, 3, 4$ and 5 into the expressions to work out the first five terms.

a 6, 9, 14, 21, 30, … **b** 3, 8, 15, 24, 35, … **c** 0, 6, 14, 24, 36, …

Example 12

Work out the first and second differences for each sequence, then state if it is a quadratic sequence.

a 5, 7, 10, 14, 19, 25, 32, … **b** 1, 1, 2, 3, 5, 8, 13, …

a

The second difference is constant so this is a quadratic sequence.

b

The second difference is not constant so this is not a quadratic sequence.

Exercise 4F

1 In each sequence:

   i write down the next two terms   **ii** say how the sequence is building up.

a	1	4	8	13	19	26	... ...
b	3	4	6	9	13	18	... ...
c	9	14	20	27	35	44	... ...
d	102	92	83	75	68	62	... ...

2 Work out the first five terms of the sequence for which the nth term is given.

  a $n^2 + 3$ **b** $2n^2$ **c** $n^2 + n$

  d $n^2 + 2n + 1$ **e** $n^2 + 3n - 2$ **f** $2n^2 - 3n + 5$

3 **a** Write down the nth term of this linear sequence.

      3   5   7   9   11   13   ...

  b Write down the nth term of this linear sequence.

      1   2   3   4   5   6   ...

  c Hence write down the nth term of this sequence.

     $1 \times 3, 2 \times 5, 3 \times 7, 4 \times 9, 5 \times 11, 6 \times 13, ...$

  d Now write down the nth term of this sequence.

     4, 11, 22, 37, 56, 79, ...

4 This pattern of rectangles is made from squares.

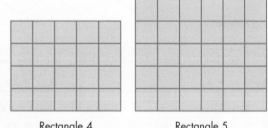

Rectangle 1   Rectangle 2   Rectangle 3   Rectangle 4   Rectangle 5

  a The heights of the rectangles give the sequence 1, 2, 3, ...

     Write down the nth term of this sequence of heights.

  b Write down the nth term of the sequence formed by the lengths of the rectangles.

  c Hence, write down the nth term of the sequence formed by the areas of the rectangles.

  d What is the area of the 99th rectangle in the pattern?

5 Find the first and second differences and decide whether each sequence is a quadratic sequence.

  a 6, 8, 11, 15, 20, 26, 33, 41, ...   **b** 1, 3, 5, 8, 11, 14, 18, 22, ...

  c 2, 6, 12, 20, 30, 42, 56, ...   **d** 1, 3, 9, 27, 81, 243, ...

  e 5, 9, 14, 20, 27, 35, 44, ...   **f** 0, 2, 2, 4, 6, 10, 16, 26, ...

6 This sequence of squares is made from smaller white and blue squares.

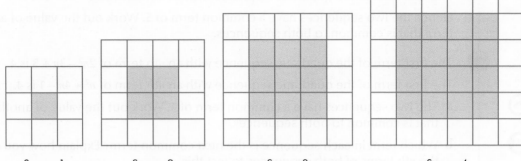

Square 1   Square 2   Square 3   Square 4

a The numbers of white squares form the sequence 8, 12, 16, 20, …

Write down the nth term of this sequence.

b The numbers of blue squares form the sequence 1, 4, 9, 16, …

Write down the nth term of this sequence.

c Hence write down the nth term of the sequence formed by the total number of smaller squares in each large square.

d Expand $(n + 2)^2$.

e Explain why the answers to parts **c** and **d** are the same.

7 The triangular numbers are 1, 3, 6, 10, 15, …

The square numbers are 1, 4, 9, 16, 25, …

Look at this pattern of shaded triangles.

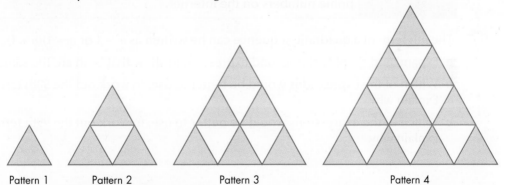

Pattern 1   Pattern 2   Pattern 3   Pattern 4

a Copy and complete this table.

Pattern	1	2	3	4	5	6
Number of shaded triangles	1	3	6			
Number of unshaded triangles	0	1	3			
Total number of triangles	1	4	9			

b One pattern in the sequence has 55 shaded triangles.

i How many unshaded triangles will there be in this pattern?

ii How many triangles will there be altogether in this pattern?

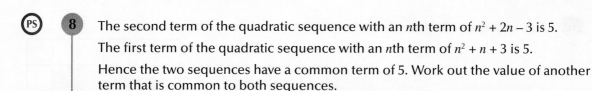

(PS) **8** The second term of the quadratic sequence with an nth term of $n^2 + 2n - 3$ is 5.

The first term of the quadratic sequence with an nth term of $n^2 + n + 3$ is 5.

Hence the two sequences have a common term of 5. Work out the value of another term that is common to both sequences.

9 The first term of the quadratic sequence with an nth term of $2n^2 - 3n + 5$ is 4.

The first term of the quadratic sequence with an nth term of $n^2 + 4n - 1$ is 4.

(PS) **a** The two sequences have a common term of 4. Work out the value of another term that is common to both sequences.

(CM) **b** Which term in each sequence is the next common term? Explain how you can use the nth terms of both sequences to test this.

(PS) **10** **a** The nth term of a quadratic sequence is given by $n^2 + an + b$, where a and b are positive or negative integers. Work out a possible pair of values for a and b so that the fourth term is 5.

b The nth term of a quadratic sequence is given by $n^2 + cn + d$, where c and d are positive or negative integers. Work out a possible pair of values for c and d so that the fourth term is 21 and the fifth term is 32.

(PS) **11** The nth term of a quadratic sequence is $n^2 + n + 41$.

Chas says: "All the terms of this sequence are prime numbers."

Chas is wrong as when $n = 41$, the value $41^2 + 41 + 41 = 43 \times 41$ which is not prime.

Is there another value for $n < 41$ for which $n^2 + n + 41$ is not prime?

> **Hints and tips** Set up a spreadsheet to work out the values and look up a list of prime numbers on the internet.

(CM) **12** The nth term of a quadratic sequence can be written as $n^2 - 1$ or $(n - 1)(n + 1)$.

a Expand and simplify the second expression to show that both are the same.

b Which of the expressions would be better to use, to work out the 50th term? Explain why.

c Which of the expressions would be better to use, to work out the 99th term? Explain why.

4.7 Finding the nth term for quadratic sequences

This section will show you how to:

- work out the nth term of a quadratic sequence.

There are several methods for finding the nth term of a quadratic sequence but they are all based on one simple rule:

If the second difference is constant then it is a quadratic sequence. The coefficient of n^2 is half the constant value of the second difference.

You can find the nth term in any of four ways, by:

- spotting a simple rule
- breaking into factors
- subtracting the squared term
- extending the differences backwards.

You need to be able to recognise the sequence of square numbers 1, 4, 9, 16, 25, 36, 49, … as 'simple rule' sequences are always based on n^2 alone. Look for a hint that it is based on the sequence of square numbers.

Example 13

Spotting a simple rule

State the nth terms of each sequence.

a 1, 4, 9, 16, 25, 36, 49, 64, …

b 4, 7, 12, 19, 28, 39, 52, 67, …

c 3, 12, 27, 48, 75, 108, 147, 192, …

a You should recognise this as the square numbers, so the nth term is simply n^2.

b Each term is 3 more than the corresponding square number in **a** so the nth term is $n^2 + 3$.

c Each term is 3 times as big as the corresponding square number in **a** so the nth term is $3n^2$.

Even if you do not recognise a simple sequence based on n^2, any of the other methods will always work.

Example 14

Breaking into factors

Find the nth term in the sequence 2, 6, 12, 20, 30, …

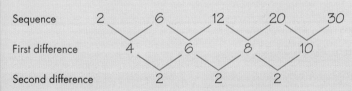

The second differences are constant (2) so the sequence is quadratic and the coefficient of n^2 is 1. So the nth term includes $1n^2$, which you just write as n^2.

Split each term into factors to try to find a pattern for how the numbers have been formed. Constructing a table like this can help to sort out which factors to use.

Term	2	6	12	20	30
Factors	1×2	2×3	3×4	4×5	5×6

Now break down the factors to obtain:

$1 \times (1 + 1)$ $2 \times (2 + 1)$ $3 \times (3 + 1)$ $4 \times (4 + 1)$ $5 \times (5 + 1)$

You can now see that the pattern is $n \times (n + 1)$.

So the nth term is $n(n + 1) = n^2 + n$.

It may not always be possible to spot how to break terms into factors but either of the next two methods will still always work.

Example 15

Subtracting the squared term

Find the nth term for the sequence of the triangular numbers 1, 3, 6, 10, 15, …

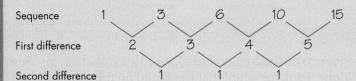

Sequence

First difference

Second difference

The second difference has a constant value of 1, so the coefficient of n^2 is $\frac{1}{2}$; hence the nth term includes $\frac{1}{2}n^2$.

Now subtract this term from each term of the original sequence. It can sometimes be easier to use a table.

n	1	2	3	4	5
Original	1	3	6	10	15
$\frac{1}{2}n^2$	$\frac{1}{2}$	2	$4\frac{1}{2}$	8	$12\frac{1}{2}$
Difference	$\frac{1}{2}$	1	$1\frac{1}{2}$	2	$2\frac{1}{2}$

The differences form a linear sequence $\frac{1}{2}$, 1, $1\frac{1}{2}$, 2, $2\frac{1}{2}$, … which has an nth term of $\frac{1}{2}n$.

Combining this with the squared term gives the nth term for the whole sequence of $\frac{1}{2}n^2 + \frac{1}{2}n$ and this can be written as $\frac{1}{2}n(n + 1)$, which is the usual formula for the nth triangular number.

The fourth method does not involve any difficult calculations. It works the sequence back to the term for $n = 0$, then the general quadratic $an^2 + bn + c$ when $n = 0$ gives the value of c. The first difference between the $n = 0$ and $n = 1$ terms eliminates c and is just $a \times 1^2 + b \times 1 = a + b$.

Example 16

Extending the differences backwards

Find the nth term of the sequence 5, 15, 31, 53, …

Set up a difference table.

n	1	2	3	4
nth term	5	15	31	53
First differences	10	16	22	
Second differences	6	6		

Now extend the table backwards to get the term for $n = 0$ and call the three lines of the table c, $a + b$ and $2a$.

n	0	1	2	3	4
c	1	5	15	31	53
$a + b$	4	10	16	22	
$2a$	6	6	6		

Starting with the last row: $2a = 6 \Rightarrow a = 3$ $a + b = 4 \Rightarrow b = 1$ $c = 1$

Thus the nth term is $3n^2 + n + 1$.

Exercise 4G

1 For each of the sequences **a** to **e**:

i write down the next two terms   **ii** find the nth term.

  a 1, 4, 9, 16, 25, …   **b** 0, 3, 8, 15, 24, …   **c** 3, 6, 11, 18, 27, …

  d 4, 7, 12, 19, 28, …   **e** –1, 2, 7, 14, 23, …   **f** 11, 14, 19, 26, …

2 For each of the sequences **a** to **e**:

i write down the next two terms   **ii** find the nth term.

  a 5, 10, 17, 26, …   **b** 3, 8, 15, 24, …   **c** 9, 14, 21, 30, …

  d 10, 17, 26, 37, …   **e** 8, 15, 24, 35, …

3 Look at each sequence to see whether the rule is linear, quadratic in n^2 alone or fully quadratic. Then write down:

i the nth term   **ii** the 50th term.

  a 5, 8, 13, 20, 29, …   **b** 5, 8, 11, 14, 17, …   **c** 3, 8, 15, 24, 35, …

  d 5, 12, 21, 32, 45, …   **e** 3, 6, 11, 18, 27, …   **f** 1, 6, 11, 16, 21, …

4 Find the nth term of each sequence, in the form $an^2 + bn + c$.

  a 1, 4, 11, 22, 37, …   **b** 2, 13, 30, 53, 82, …   **c** 4, 8, 13, 19, 26, …

  d 3, 9, 16, 24, 33, …   **e** 8, 11, 15, 20, 26, …   **f** 4, 7, 11, 16, 22, …

5 Work out a formula for the surface area of a large cube made up of smaller centimetre cubes with a side of n centimetres.

6 The diagram shows four houses of cards.

A one-level house of cards (L1) takes 2 cards.

A two-level house of cards (L2) takes 7 cards.

A three-level house of cards (L3) takes 15 cards.

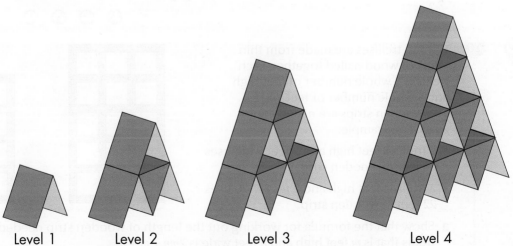

Level 1   Level 2   Level 3   Level 4

a How many cards are needed to make a four-level (L4) house of cards?

b Work out a formula for an n-level house of cards.

c The world record is a 75-level house of cards. How many cards were used to build this?

(PS) 7 A supermarket displays tins of beans by lining up n tins in a row and then putting $n - 1$ tins in a row on top of these, and then $n - 2$ tins in a row on top of these, and so on until there is just 1 tin on top. The diagram shows a display that starts with four tins on the bottom.

a A shop assistant lined up 9 tins as the bottom row. How many tins will there be in the display when it is finished?

b Health and safety regulations state that the display cannot be more than 15 rows high. The supermarket has 100 tins of beans in stock. Can they make a display that is 15 rows high?

(PS) 8 Tebor used centimetre cubes to make patterns of cuboids. Work out an expression for the surface area of cuboid n.

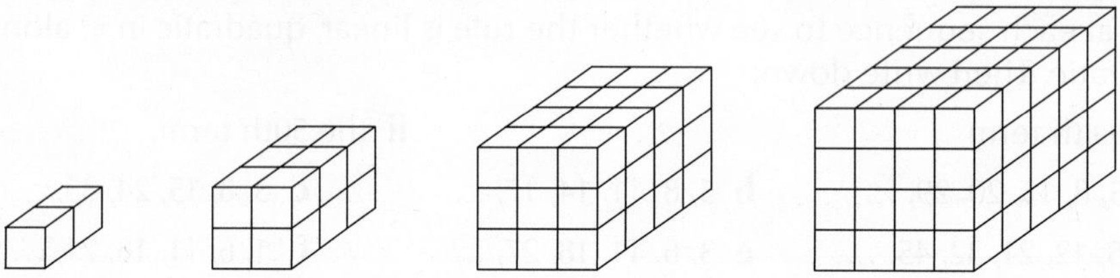

Cuboid 1   Cuboid 2   Cuboid 3   Cuboid 4

(PS) 9 The diagram shows the first four hexagonal numbers. Work out the 100th hexagonal number.

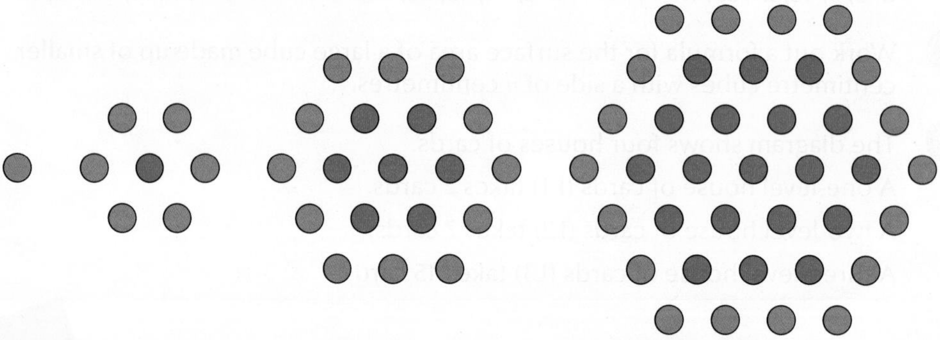

(EV) 10 Garden trellises are made from thin strips of wood nailed together. Each trellis is a whole number of feet high and a whole number of feet wide. The wooden strips are nailed a foot apart. For example:

- a trellis 5 feet high and 3 feet wide uses 38 feet of wooden strip

- a trellis 4 feet high and 2 feet wide uses 22 feet of wooden strip.

a Show that the formula for working out the length of wooden strip needed for a trellis that is m feet high and n feet wide is $2mn + m + n$.

b Two nails are used at every point where strips cross. Work out an expression for the number of nails that are used on a trellis that is m feet high and n feet wide.

Worked exemplars

 1 These are expressions for the nth terms of three sequences.

Sequence 1: $4n + 1$

Sequence 2: $5n - 2$

Sequence 3: $5n + 10$

Say if the sequences generated by the nth terms always give multiples of 5 (A), never give multiples of 5 (N) or sometimes give multiples of 5 (S).

This is a 'communicating mathematically' question so you must show how you arrive at your decisions.	
Sequence 1 → 5, 9, 13, 17, 21, 25, 29, … Sequence 2 → 3, 8, 13, 18, 23, 28, … Sequence 3 → 15, 20, 25, 30, 35, 40, …	Substitute $n = 1, 2, 3, …$ until you can be sure of the sequences. The sign → means 'gives'.
Sequence 1: Sometimes (S) Sequence 2: Never (N) Sequence 3: Always (A)	The series generated will show whether their terms are never, sometimes or always multiples of 5.

 2 A pattern made from squares builds up like this.

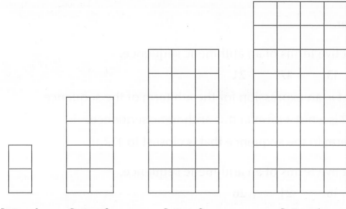

Pattern 1   Pattern 2   Pattern 3   Pattern 4

Work out the number of squares in the nth pattern.

For this 'problem solving' question, set up a table of pattern numbers and number of squares.	
<table><tr><td>**Pattern**</td><td>2</td><td>8</td><td>18</td><td>32</td></tr><tr><td>**Factors**</td><td>1×2</td><td>2×4</td><td>3×6</td><td>4×8</td></tr></table>	You could set up a difference table but there is a visual clue. Use the diagrams to spot the fact that the number of squares can be split into factors as in Example 14 and add another line to the table. Alternatively you can see that the width is n and the height is $2n$.
The nth term will be $n \times 2n = 2n^2$	The pattern is then the product of the two sides.
Check for $n = 3$: $2 \times 3^2 = 2 \times 9 = 18$ ✔	It is always worth checking with a known result that your formula works.

Ready to progress?

I can substitute numbers into an nth-term rule for a linear sequence.
I can understand how prime, odd and even numbers interact in addition, subtraction and multiplication problems.

I can give the nth term of a linear sequence.
I can give the nth term of a geometric sequence.
I can give the nth term of a sequence of powers of 2 or 10.
I can recognise special patterns, such as the Fibonacci sequence and geometric sequences.
I can generate the terms of a quadratic sequence, given the nth term.

I can find the nth term of a quadratic sequence.

Review questions

1 The nth term of a sequence is $3n + 4$.

Beth says: "Every odd term of this sequence is a prime number."

Is Beth correct?

Justify your answer.

2 These are the first five terms of an arithmetic sequence.

5   9   13   17   21

a Find, in terms of n, an expression for the nth term of the sequence.

b Explain why 112 is a not a term in this arithmetic sequence.

c Work out the term in the sequence that is closest to 112.

3 These are the first five terms of an arithmetic sequence.

6   11   16   21   26

Work out the 150th term in the sequence.

4 These are the first five terms of an arithmetic sequence.

9   15   21   27   33

a Find, in terms of n, an expression for the nth term of the sequence.

b Another arithmetic sequence has an nth term of $3n + 2$.

Will the two sequences ever have a term in common?

Show working to support your answer.

5 These are the first five terms of a geometric sequence.

2   6   18   54   162

a Find an expression, in terms of n, for the nth term of the sequence.

b Simon says that 1001 is a term in this sequence.

Explain why Simon is wrong.

6 These are the first four terms of a geometric sequence.

   5   30   180   1080

   a Find, in terms of n, an expression for the nth term of the sequence.

   b Which term in the sequence is the first that is greater than 1 million?

7 The nth term of a quadratic sequence is $2n^2 - 29$.

   a Are any of the first 5 terms of this sequence prime numbers?

   b Explain how you can tell, without working it out, that the 29th term will not be a prime number.

8 **a** Work out the first five terms of the sequence with an nth term of $2n^2 - n + 3$.

   b Work out the first five terms of the sequence with an nth term of $\frac{1}{2}n^2 - 1\frac{1}{2}n + 3$.

9 The nth term of a sequence is $\dfrac{2(n-1)(n-2)}{5}$.

Show that the third term is the first non-zero term and find its value.

10 Find the nth term of this quadratic sequence.

   3, 7, 15, 27, 43, 63, …

11 Mac is using small squares to make rectangle patterns.

   a Mac has 200 small squares. Can he make the 12th pattern?

   b How many squares will there be in the 40th pattern?

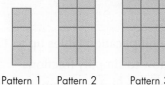

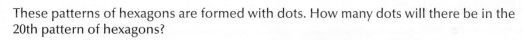

Pattern 1   Pattern 2   Pattern 3   Pattern 4

12 These patterns of hexagons are formed with dots. How many dots will there be in the 20th pattern of hexagons?

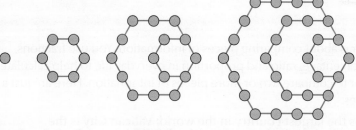

Pattern 1   Pattern 2   Pattern 3   Pattern 4

13 These patterns are made with pentagons with increasing numbers of dots along each side. The diagram shows the first four patterns.

How many dots will there be in the 50th pattern?

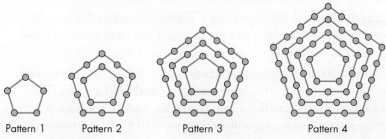

Pattern 1   Pattern 2   Pattern 3   Pattern 4

5 Ratio, proportion and rates of change: Ratio and proportion

This chapter is going to show you:

- what a ratio is
- how to divide an amount according to a given ratio
- how to solve problems involving direct proportion
- how to compare prices of products
- how to calculate compound measures (rates of pay, speed, density, pressure)
- how to calculate compound interest and repeated percentage change
- how to calculate a reverse percentage.

You should already know:

- multiplication tables up to 12×12
- how to simplify fractions
- how to find a fraction of a quantity
- how to multiply and divide, with and without a calculator.

About this chapter

This chapter is about comparing pieces of information. You use fractions, decimals, percentage, ratio and proportion in everyday life to help calculate quantities or to compare two or more pieces of information. Here are just a few examples.

- Russia is the largest country in the world; Vatican City is the smallest. The area of Russia is nearly 39 million times the area of Vatican City.
- Monaco has the most people per square mile, Mongolia has the fewest. The number of people per square mile in Monaco to the number of people in Mongolia is in the ratio 10 800 : 1.
- Japan has the highest life expectancy. Sierra Leone has the lowest life expectancy. On average, people in Japan live over twice as long as people in Sierra Leone.
- On 16 August 2009, Usain Bolt set a new world record of 9.58 seconds for the 100-metre sprint. This is an average speed of 23.3 mph. The fastest bird is the swift, which can travel at 106 mph. Can you work out approximately how long will it take a swift to travel 100 metres?

5.1 Ratio

This section will show you how to:

- simplify a ratio
- express a ratio as a fraction
- divide amounts into given ratios
- complete calculations from a given ratio and partial information.

A **ratio** is a way of comparing the sizes of two or more quantities.

A ratio can be expressed in a number of ways. For example, the ratio of the quantities when you mix 5 centilitres of cordial with 20 centilitres of water is shown below.

cordial	:	water	
5	:	20	
1	:	4	(Divide both sides by 5 to simplify.)

> **Hints and tips** When you say a ratio, you do not say '5 colon 20' or '1 colon 4', you say 'in the ratio 5 to 20' or 'in the ratio 1 to 4'.

When you are comparing ratios, you may find it helpful to use a table. So if the ratio is 5 : 20 (as above), you can summarise the quantities of cordial and water in a table like this one.

Cordial	5	1	2	4	10	25
Water	20	4	8	16	40	100

The value in each column is simply a multiplier or divisor of the value in a previous column.

This method is useful if you want to know how much cordial to mix with a litre (100 centilitres) of water. The last column shows that the answer is 25 centilitres.

How much water would you need if you only have 15 centilitres of cordial? You can find out by adding the numbers in the first and fifth columns, so the answer is 60 centilitres.

Common units

When working with a ratio involving different units, always convert them all to a **common unit**. You can only simplify or cancel a ratio when the units of each quantity are the same, because the ratio itself has no units.

For example, you must convert the ratio of 125 g to 2 kg to the ratio of 125 g to 2000 g, so that you can simplify it.

125	:	2000	
5	:	80	(Divide both sides by 25.)
1	:	16	(Divide both sides by 5.)

You can simplify the ratio 125 : 2000 to 1 : 16.

When a ratio has been simplified so that its parts do not have any common factors, it is in its simplest form.

Example 1

Express 25 minutes : 1 hour as a ratio in its simplest form.

The units must be the same, so change 1 hour into 60 minutes.	25 minutes : 1 hour
	= 25 minutes : 60 minutes
Cancel the units (minutes).	= 25 : 60
Divide both sides by 5.	= 5 : 12
So, 25 minutes : 1 hour simplifies to 5 : 12.	

Ratios as fractions

You can express ratios as fractions by using the total number of parts in the ratio as the denominator (bottom number) of each fraction. Then use the numbers in the ratio as the numerators. If the ratio is in its simplest form, the fractions will not cancel.

Always cancel the ratio to its simplest form before converting it to fractions.

Example 2

A garden is divided into lawn and shrubs in the ratio 3 : 2.

What fraction of the garden is covered by: **a** lawn   **b** shrubs?

The denominator (bottom number) of the fraction is the total number of parts in the ratio each time (that is, 2 + 3 = 5).

a The 3 in the ratio becomes the numerator.   The lawn covers $\frac{3}{5}$ of the garden.

b The 2 in the ratio becomes the numerator.   The shrubs cover $\frac{2}{5}$ of the garden.

Exercise 5A

1 Express each ratio in its simplest form.

a 6 : 18   **b** 15 : 20   **c** 16 : 24   **d** 24 : 36

e 20 to 50   **f** 12 to 30   **g** 25 to 40   **h** 125 to 30

2 Write each ratio of quantities in its simplest form.

a £5 to £15   **b** £24 to £16   **c** 125 g to 300 g

d 40 minutes : 5 minutes   **e** 34 kg to 30 kg   **f** £2.50 to 70p

g 3 kg to 750 g   **h** 50 minutes to 1 hour   **i** 1 hour to 1 day

Hints and tips	**Remember** to express both parts in a common unit before you simplify.

3 A length of wood is cut into two pieces in the ratio 3 : 7. What fraction of the original length is the longer piece?

4 Jack and Thomas find a bag of marbles. They share the marbles in the ratio of their ages. Jack is 10 years old and Thomas is 15 years old. What fraction of the marbles did Jack get?

5 Dave and Sue share a pizza in the ratio of 2 : 3. They eat it all.

    a What fraction of the pizza did Dave eat?

    b What fraction of the pizza did Sue eat?

6 $\frac{7}{10}$ of a campsite is allocated to caravans. The rest is allocated to tents. Write the ratio of space allocated in the form caravans : tents.

7 Amy gets $\frac{2}{3}$ of a packet of sweets. Her sister Susan gets the rest. Work out the ratio of sweets that each sister gets. Write it in the form Amy : Susan.

8   **a** The recipe for a fruit punch is 1.25 litres of fruit crush to 6.25 litres of lemonade. What fraction of the punch is each ingredient?

    b How much fruit crush will you need to mix with 2 litres of lemonade?

> **Hints and tips**   Set up a table.

    c You have half a litre of fruit crush. How much lemonade will you need?

9 In a safari park at feeding time, the elephants, lions and chimpanzees are given food in the ratio 10 to 7 to 3. What fraction of the total food is given to:

    a the elephants   **b** the lions   **c** the chimpanzees?

10 The recipe for a pudding is 125 g of sugar, 150 g of flour, 100 g of margarine and 175 g of fruit. What fraction of the pudding is made up by each ingredient?

(MR) **11** Andy plays 16 bowls matches. He wins $\frac{3}{4}$ of them.

    He plays another x matches and wins them all.

    The ratio of wins : losses is now 4 : 1.

    Work out the value of x.

(MR) **12** Three brothers share some money.

    The ratio of Mark's share to David's share is 1 : 2.

    The ratio of David's share to Paul's share is 1 : 2.

    What is the ratio of Mark's share to Paul's share?

(EV) **13** Three brothers, Jarek, Jerzy and Justyn, share a block of chocolate in the ratio of their ages. Jarek gets half of the bar. Jerzy gets $\frac{3}{5}$ of the rest.

    a Work out the ratio, in the form Jarek : Jerzy : Justyn, of how the brothers share the bar of chocolate.

    b Justyn is 8 years old. How old is Jarek?

(EV) **14** Three cows, Gertrude, Gladys and Henrietta, produced milk in the ratio 2 : 3 : 4. Henrietta produced $1\frac{1}{2}$ litres more than Gladys. How much milk did the three cows produce altogether?

(CM) **15** In a garden, the area is divided into lawn, vegetables and flowers in the ratio 3 : 2 : 1. If one-third of the lawn is dug up and replaced by flowers, what is the ratio of lawn : vegetables : flowers now? Give your answer as a ratio in its simplest form.

Dividing amounts in a given ratio

To divide an amount in a given ratio, you first look at the ratio to see how many parts there are altogether.

For example, 4 : 3 has 4 parts and 3 parts giving 7 parts altogether. The whole amount is 7 parts.

You can work out one part by dividing the whole amount by 7.

Then you can work out 3 parts and 4 parts from 1 part.

Example 3

Divide £28 in the ratio 4 : 3.

Method 1: Using a table

Set up the first column then continue the columns as multiples.

First part	4	8	12	16
Second part	3	6	9	12
Total	7	14	21	28

So £28 divided in the ratio 4 : 3 is £16 : £12.

Method 2: Dividing to find one part

4 + 3 = 7 parts altogether.

So 7 parts = £28.

Divide by 7 to find 1 part.	1 part = £4
Multiply by 4 to find 4 parts.	4 × £4 = £16
Multiply by 3 to find 3 parts.	3 × £4 = £12

So £28 divided in the ratio 4 : 3 is £16 : £12.

You can also use fractions to divide an amount in a given ratio. First, express the whole numbers in the ratio as fractions with the same common denominator. Then multiply the amount by each fraction.

Example 4

Divide £40 between Peter and Hitan in the ratio 2 : 3.

Method 1: Using a table

Set up the first column then work out what you need to multiply 5 by to get 40.

Do the same thing to the other rows.

Peter	2	2 × 8 = 16
Hitan	3	3 × 8 = 24
Total	5	5 × 8 = 40

So Peter receives £16 and Hitan receives £24.

Method 2: Using fractions

Change the ratio to fractions.

Peter's share $= \dfrac{2}{2+3} = \dfrac{2}{5}$

Hitan's share $= \dfrac{3}{2+3} = \dfrac{3}{5}$

So Peter receives £40 $\times \dfrac{2}{5} =$ £16 and Hitan receives £40 $\times \dfrac{3}{5} =$ £24.

Exercise 5B

1 Divide each amount according to the given ratio.

a 400 g in the ratio 2 : 3   **b** 280 kg in the ratio 2 : 5   **c** 500 in the ratio 3 : 7

d 1 km in the ratio 19 : 1   **e** 5 hours in the ratio 7 : 5   **f** £100 in the ratio 2 : 3 : 5

g £240 in the ratio 3 : 5 : 12   **h** 600 g in the ratio 1 : 5 : 6   **i** £5 in the ratio 7 : 10 : 8

j 200 kg in the ratio 15 : 9 : 1

2 The ratio of female to male members at Lakeside Gardening Club is 7 : 3. The total number of members of the group is 250.

 a How many members are female?

 b What percentage of members is male?

3 A supermarket aims to stock branded goods and their own goods in the ratio 2 : 3. They stock 500 kg of breakfast cereal.

 a What percentage of the cereal stock is branded?

 b How much of the cereal stock is their own?

4 Over the years 1981–1992, the Illinois Department of Health tested a total of 357 horses for rabies. They reported that the ratio of horses with rabies to those without was 1 : 16.

 How many of these horses had rabies?

5 Being overweight increases the chances of an adult suffering from heart disease. A test for whether an adult has an increased risk is based on comparing the waist measurement, W, with the hip measurement, H.

 For women, there is increased risk when $\dfrac{W}{H} > 0.8$.

 For men, there is increased risk when $\dfrac{W}{H} > 1.0$.

 a Find whether each of these people has an increased risk of heart disease.

 Miss Mott: waist 26 inches, hips 35 inches

 Mrs Wright: waist 32 inches, hips 37 inches

 Mr Brennan: waist 32 inches, hips 34 inches

 Ms Smith: waist 31 inches, hips 40 inches

 Mr Kaye: waist 34 inches, hips 33 inches

 b Give three examples of waist and hip measurements that would not suggest an increased risk of heart disease for a man, but would for a woman.

6 Rewrite each scale as a ratio in its simplest form.

 a 1 cm to 4 km   **b** 4 cm to 5 km   **c** 2 cm to 5 km

 d 4 cm to 1 km   **e** 5 cm to 1 km   **f** 2.5 cm to 1 km

 g 8 cm to 5 km   **h** 10 cm to 1 km   **i** 5 cm to 3 km

7 The most commonly used ordnance survey maps have a scale of 1 : 50 000.

 a How far is the actual distance represented by a distance of 1 cm on the map?

 b Ed plans a cycle ride. He estimates the distance on his ordnance survey map to be 78 cm. He plans to leave at 9:00 am and stop for about 30 minutes for a break. He will cycle at an average of 15 km/h. At about what time will he be back? Show your working.

| Hints and tips | 1 km = 1000 m = 100 000 cm |

8 Map A has a scale of 2 cm to 5 km. Map B, of the same area, has a scale of 1 cm to 10 km.

   a Rewrite these scales as ratios in their simplest form.

   b How long is a path that measures 0.8 cm on map A?

   c How long should a 12 km road be on map B?

   d A river is 1.2 cm long on map B. How long will it be on map A?

9 You can simplify a ratio by changing it into the form $1 : n$. For example, you can rewrite $5 : 7$ as $1 : 1.4$.

   Rewrite each ratio in the form $1 : n$.

   a $5 : 8$ **b** $4 : 13$ **c** $8 : 9$

   d $25 : 36$ **e** $5 : 27$ **f** $12 : 18$

   g 5 hours : 1 day   **h** 4 hours : 1 week   **i** £4 : £5

10 There are 150 cars in a car park. The ratio of diesel cars to petrol cars is $2 : 3$. $\frac{1}{5}$ of the diesel cars are red. $\frac{4}{9}$ of the petrol cars are red.

   Are more than one-third of all the cars in the car park red? Show your working.

11 A car is 240 miles from Manchester. A lorry is 180 miles from Manchester.

   a Work out the ratio of the distances, giving your answer in its simplest form.

      Two hours later the ratio of the distances is exactly the same.

      The car is 120 miles from Manchester.

   b How far is the lorry from Manchester at this time?

   c If the ratio of the distances stays the same for the entire journey to Manchester, which vehicle arrives first?

12 A piece of wood is 5 m long. It is cut into pieces.

   The lengths of the pieces are in the ratio $4 : 3 : 2 : 1$.

   The longest piece is then cut in the ratio $4 : 1$ so that there are now five pieces.

   How long is the smallest piece?

13 Look at this number line.

       A   B   C
       9   13

   The ratio AB : BC is $2 : 3$.

   Work out the number at B.

14 Athos has 24 more marbles than Zena. The ratio of the numbers of marbles that they have is $4 : 1$.

   How many marbles does Zena have?

Calculating with ratios when only part of the information is known

Example 5

Alisha makes a fruit drink by mixing orange squash with water in the ratio 2 : 3.

How much water does she need to add to 5 litres of orange squash to make the drink?

Method 1: Using a table

Squash	2	1	5
Water	3	1.5	7.5

Method 2: Comparing ratio and quantity

2 parts is 5 litres.

Divide by 2.   1 part is 2.5 litres.

Multiply by 3.   3 parts is 7.5 litres.

So, she needs 7.5 litres of water to make the drink.

Example 6

Two business partners, Lubna and Adama, divided their total profit in the ratio 3 : 5. Lubna received £2100. How much did Adama get?

Method 1: Using a table

Lubna	3	$3 \div 3 = 1$	$1 \times 2100 = 2100$
Adama	5	$5 \div 3 = 1\frac{2}{3}$	$1\frac{2}{3} \times 2100 = 3500$

Adama's share was £3500.

Method 2: Using fractions

Lubna's £2100 was $\frac{3}{8}$ of the total profit. (Check that you know why.)

$\frac{1}{8}$ of the total profit = £2100 ÷ 3

= £700

So Adama's share, which was $\frac{5}{8}$, was £700 × 5 = £3500.

Exercise 5C

 1 Derek, aged 15, and Ricki, aged 10, shared all the conkers they found in the woods in the same ratio as their ages. Derek had 48 conkers.

    a Write down and simplify the ratio of their ages.

    b How many conkers did Ricki have?

    c How many conkers did they find altogether?

 2 At a school party, the ratio of plain crisps to salt 'n' vinegar crisps was 5 : 3. The school bought 60 packets of salt 'n' vinegar crisps.

    a How many packets of plain crisps did they buy?

    b How many packets of crisps did they buy altogether?

3 Robin is making a drink from orange juice and lemon juice, mixed in the ratio 9 : 1. If Robin has only 3.6 litres of orange juice, how much lemon juice does he need to make the drink?

 4 An old recipe to make pancakes says: "For every four ounces of flour, add two eggs and half a pint milk. This is enough for 10 pancakes."

Jamie wants to make two pancakes each for 15 people. He has 1 litre of milk.

Does he have enough milk? Explain your decision.

5 The ratio of male to female spectators at ice hockey games is 5 : 4. At the Beavers' last match, 4500 men watched the match. What was the total attendance at the game?

MR **6** On an aeroplane the ratio of business to premium to economy seats is 1 : 6 : 30.

A family of 8 book all the business seats. How many seats are there on the aeroplane altogether?

7 Three business partners, Kevin, John and Margaret, put money into a business in the ratio 3 : 4 : 5. They shared any profits in the same ratio. Last year, Margaret received £3400 profit. How much did Kevin and John receive last year?

CM **8** The ratio of daffodils to tulips in a flowerbed is 3 : 7.

Decide whether each statement is true (**T**), false (**F**) or could be true (**C**). The first one has been done for you.

a There are 25 daffodils in the flowerbed.   **F**

b There are 140 flowers altogether in the flowerbed.

c The fraction of daffodils in the flowerbed is $\frac{3}{7}$.

d The percentage of tulips in the flowerbed is 70%.

e If half of the daffodils were dug up, the ratio of daffodils to tulips would be 3 : 14.

PS **9** In a factory, the ratio of female employees to male employees is 3 : 8. There are 85 more males than females.

How many females work in the factory?

PS **10** Some boys and girls are waiting for school buses. 25 girls get on the first bus. The ratio of boys to girls at the stop is now 3 : 2.

15 boys get on the second bus. There are now the same number of boys and girls at the bus stop.

How many students were originally at the bus stop?

PS **11** A jar contains 100 ml of a mixture of oil and water in the ratio 1 : 4. Enough oil is added to make the ratio of oil to water 1 : 2.

How much water must be added to make the ratio of oil to water 1 : 3?

12 For a school disco, the school bought Cola, Orange Fizz and Zesto in the ratio 10 : 5 : 3. The school bought 80 cans of Orange Fizz.

a How much Cola did they buy?   **b** How much Zesto did they buy?

13 **a** Iqra is making a drink from lemonade, orange juice and ginger ale in the ratio 40 : 9 : 1. If Iqra has only 4.5 litres of orange juice, how much of the other two ingredients does she need to make the drink?

b Another drink made from lemonade, orange juice and ginger ale uses the ratio 10 : 2 : 1.

Which drink has a larger proportion of ginger ale, Iqra's or this one? Show how you work out your answer.

14 A teacher asked her class to choose a number in the 10 times table then divide it into the ratio 1 : 3 : 5.

Zeke chose 10. Yoko chose 50. Will chose 90.

a Who made the most sensible choice and why?

b Zeke correctly worked out the values and wrote them down as 1.1 : 3.3 : 5.5.

Yoko correctly worked out the values and wrote them down as 5.56 : 16.67 : 27.78.

What mistake have they both made?

  15 The ratio of my sister's age to my age is 10 : 9.

The ratio of my brother's age to my age is 29 : 27.

I am over 40 years old but under 70 years old.

What is my age?

5.2 Direct proportion problems

This section will show you how to:

- recognise and solve problems that involve direct proportion.

Key terms
direct proportion
unit cost
unitary method

Suppose you buy 12 items that each cost the same. The total amount you spend is 12 times the cost of one item.

The total cost is in **direct proportion** to the number of items bought. The cost of a single item (the **unit cost**) is the constant factor that links the two quantities.

Direct proportion is not only concerned with costs. Any two related quantities can be in direct proportion to each other.

One way to solve any problem involving direct proportion is to start by finding the single unit value. This is called the **unitary method**. You can do this by using a table or just working out the single unit value. These methods are very similar, as you will see from Examples 7 and 8. The table can be useful if you have to do more complicated calculations.

Hints and tips	Before solving a direct proportion problem, think about it carefully to make sure that you know how to find the required single unit value.

Example 7

If eight pens cost £2.64, what is the cost of five pens?

Method 1: Using a table

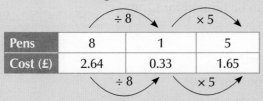

Pens	8	1	5
Cost (£)	2.64	0.33	1.65

The cost of five pens is £1.65.

Method 2: Unitary method

First, find the cost of 1 pen.
£2.64 ÷ 8 = £0.33

Then multiply to find the cost of 5 pens.
£0.33 × 5 = £1.65

So, the cost of five pens is £1.65.

Example 8

Emma uses eight loaves of bread to make packed lunches for 18 people.

a How many packed lunches can she make from 20 loaves?

b How many loaves will she need to make packed lunches for 60 people?

Method 1: Using a table

a

Loaves	8	1	20
Packed lunches	18	2.25	45

$\div 8$ $\times 20$

$\div 8$ $\times 20$

From 20 loaves she can make packed lunches for 45 people.

b

Loaves	8	$\frac{8}{18} = \frac{4}{9}$	$\frac{4}{9} \times 60 = 26\frac{2}{3}$
Packed lunches	18	1	60

$\div 18$ $\times 60$

$\div 18$ $\times 60$

To make packed lunches for 60 people she will require 27 loaves.

Hints and tips **Remember** that she will need to round up to a whole number of loaves.

Method 2: Unitary method

First, find how many lunches she can make from one loaf.

From one loaf she can make $18 \div 8 = 2.25$ lunches.

a So, with 20 loaves she can make $2.25 \times 20 = 45$ lunches.

b Work out how many loaves she needs for 1 packed lunch. $8 \div 18 = \frac{4}{9}$ or $0.444\ldots$

So for 60 packed lunches she will need $\frac{4}{9} \times 60 = 26\frac{2}{3}$ loaves, so she will need 27 loaves.

Exercise 5D 🖩

1 If 30 matches weigh 45 g, what do 40 matches weigh?

2 Five bars of chocolate cost £2.90. Find the cost of nine bars.

3 Eight men can chop down 18 trees in a day. How many trees can 20 men chop down in a day?

4 Find the cost of 48 eggs when 15 eggs can be bought for £2.10.

5 Seventy maths textbooks cost £875.

   a How much will 25 maths textbooks cost?

   b How many maths textbooks can you buy for £100?

Hints and tips **Remember** to work out the value of one unit each time. Always check that answers are sensible.

6 A lorry uses 80 litres of diesel fuel on a trip of 280 miles.

    a How much diesel would the same lorry use on a trip of 196 miles?

    b How far would the lorry get on a full tank of 100 litres of diesel?

7 During the winter, I find that 200 kg of coal keeps my open fire burning for 12 weeks.

    a If I want an open fire all through the winter (18 weeks), how much coal will I need to buy?

    b Last year I bought 150 kg of coal. For how many weeks did I have an open fire?

8 It takes a photocopier 16 seconds to produce 12 copies. How long will it take to produce 30 copies?

9 This is a recipe for 12 biscuits.

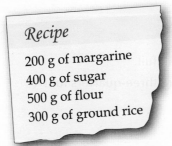

Recipe

200 g of margarine
400 g of sugar
500 g of flour
300 g of ground rice

    a What quantities are needed for:

      i 6 biscuits   **ii** 9 biscuits   **iii** 15 biscuits?

    b What is the maximum number of biscuits I could make if I had 1 kg of each ingredient?

(CM)

(MR) 10 Peter the butcher sells sausages in packs of 6 for £2.30.

    Paul the butcher sells sausages in packs of 10 for £3.50.

    I have £10 to spend on sausages.

    I want to buy as many sausages as possible from one shop. Which shop should I use? Show your working.

(EV) 11 Lorraine can make three loaves of bread with 1.8 kg of flour. She uses one loaf of bread to make 10 sandwiches. How much flour will she need to make enough bread for 400 sandwiches?

(PS) 12 Buns cost 40p each. Cakes cost 55p each. I spend exactly £4.35 on buns and cakes. How many of each did I buy?

(MR) 13 A shredding machine can shred 20 sheets of paper in 14 seconds. The bin has room for 1000 sheets of shredded paper.

    How long will it take to fill the bin if the machine has to stop for 3 minutes after every 200 sheets to prevent overheating?

14 This is a recipe for making Yorkshire pudding.

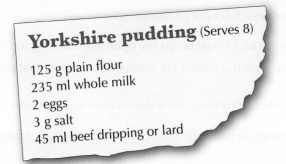

Yorkshire pudding (Serves 8)

125 g plain flour
235 ml whole milk
2 eggs
3 g salt
45 ml beef dripping or lard

Adjust this recipe to use it for two people. Justify any decision you make.

  15 An aircraft has two fuel tanks, one in each wing.

The tanks each hold 40 litres when full.

The left tank is quarter full. The right tank is half full.

How much fuel is needed so that both tanks are three-quarters full?

5.3 Best buys

This section will show you how to:

- find the cost per unit mass
- find the mass per unit cost
- use the above to find which product is the cheaper.

When you look around a supermarket and see all the different prices for the many different-sized packets, it is rarely obvious which are the **best buys**. However, with a calculator you can easily compare value for money by finding either the cost per unit **mass** or the mass per unit cost.

To find:

- cost per unit mass, divide cost by mass
- mass per unit cost, divide mass by cost.

The next two examples show you how to do this.

Note that people may say: "How much does this weigh?" or "I weigh 58 kg." They are actually talking about mass, which is measured in grams and kilograms.

Example 9

A 300 g tin of cocoa costs £1.20. Find the cost per unit mass and the mass per unit cost.

First change £1.20 to 120p, then divide using a calculator.

Cost per unit mass = 120 ÷ 300
                   = 0.4p per gram

Mass per unit cost = 300 ÷ 120
                   = 2.5 g per penny

Example 10

A supermarket sells Whito soap powder in two different-sized packets. The medium size contains 800 g and costs £1.60 and the large size contains 2.5 kg and costs £4.75. Which is the better buy?

Find the mass per unit cost for both packets.

Medium packet   800 ÷ 160 = 5 g per penny

Large packet   2500 ÷ 475 = 5.26 g per penny

From these it is clear that there is more mass per penny with the large size, which means that the large size is the better buy.

In some cases, it is easier to use a scaling method to compare prices and find **better value**.

Example 11

Which of these boxes of fish fingers is better value?

12 is a common factor of 24 and 36 so work out the cost of 12 fish fingers.

For the small box, 12 fish fingers cost £3.40 ÷ 2 = £1.70.

For the large box, 12 fish fingers cost £4.95 ÷ 3 = £1.65.

So the large box is better value.

In other examples, it is easier to use a table to compare the cost of one item in each case.

Example 12

Which of these packs of yoghurt is better value?

£1.45

£1.20

Set up a table for the six-pack.

Pots	6	1	5
Price (£)	1.45	0.241666…	1.208333…

÷ 6 → × 5 →
÷ 6 ↗ × 5 ↗

So five pots from the six-pack cost more than the five-pack.

(continued)

You could also do this the other way.

Set up a table for the five-pack.

Pots	5	1	6
Price (£)	1.20	0.24	1.44

÷5   ×6

÷5   ×6

So six pots from the five-pack cost less than the six-pack.

Either way, the five-pack is just better value!

Exercise 5E

1 Compare the prices of the products in each pair. State which, if either, is the better buy.

    a Chocolate bars: £2.50 for a 5-pack, £4.50 for a 10-pack

    b Eggs: £1.08 for 6, £2.25 for 12

    c Car shampoo: £4.99 for 2 litres, £2.45 for 1 litre

    d Dishwasher tablets: £7.80 for 24, £3.90 for 12

2 Compare the products in each pair. State which is the better buy. Explain your choice.

    a Coffee: a medium jar (140 g) for £1.10, a large jar (300 g) for £2.18

    b Toothpaste: a large tube (110 ml) for £1.79, a medium tube (75 ml) for £1.15

    c Frosted Flakes: a large box (750 g) for £1.64, a medium box (500 g) for £1.10

    d Hair shampoo: a medium bottle (400 ml) for £1.15, or a large bottle (550 ml) for £1.60

3 Julie wants to respray her car with yellow paint. In the local supermarket, she sees tins at these prices.

Small tin   350 ml for £1.79

Medium tin   500 ml for £2.40

Large tin   1.5 litres for £6.70

    a What is the cost per litre of paint in the small tin?

    b Which tin is offered at the lowest price per litre?

4 Tisco's sells bottled water in three sizes: 40 cl, 2 litres and 5 litres.

a Work out the cost per litre of the 40cl bottle.

b Which bottle is the best value for money?

CM

5 Mary and Jane are arguing about which of them is better at mathematics.

Mary scored 49 out of 80 on a test.

Jane scored 60 out of 100 on a test of the same standard.

Based on these results, who is better at mathematics?

PS

6 Paula and Kelly are comparing their running times.

Paula completed a 10-mile run in 65 minutes.

Kelly completed a 10-kilometre run in 40 minutes.

Given that 8 kilometres are equal to 5 miles, which girl has the greater average speed?

EV

7 Sachets of cat food cost 35p each. Aldo's supermarket sells them in packs of 12 or 40.

A pack of 12 costs £3.60. A pack of 40 costs £11.50. Today they have an offer.

> **Buy any 5 items and pay for 4!**
>
> Cheapest of 5 items free.
>
> **Offer only applies to individual items, not packs.**

Which is the better value: the 12-pack, the 40-pack or the '5 for 4' offer? Show your working.

8 Three people are comparing how much petrol their cars use.

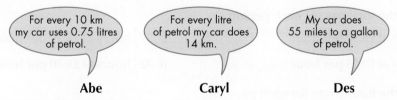

4.55 litres = 1 gallon

CM

a Whose car is the most economical?

CM

b Why is Abe's statement not very helpful when comparing his car's petrol consumption to those of Caryl and Des?

Hints and tips   Pick a distance and work out the amount of petrol they each use.

5.4 Compound measures

This section will show you how to:

- recognise and solve problems involving the compound measures or rates of pay, speed, density and pressure.

Key terms

average speed

compound measure

density

Compound measures always involve three variables. The three variables can be connected by a 'triangle' that shows the relationship between them. The triangle is shown in each section below.

Rates of pay

Many jobs are paid on an hourly rate. The amount earned is calculated by the rule:

Pay (P) = Hours worked (H) × hourly rate (R)

These three variables are connected by this triangle.

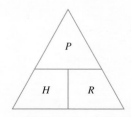

It shows the three relationships between the three variables.

$$P = H \times R \qquad H = \frac{P}{R} \qquad R = \frac{P}{H}$$

Example 13

Vikki works 42 hours one week. Her hourly rate of pay is £11.20.

From her weekly earnings, 20% is deducted as tax, 8% is deducted as National Insurance and £3.50 is deducted for union dues.

How much does Vikki take home after deductions?

Calculate her pay.	42 × 11.20 = £470.40
Calculate her tax.	0.2 × 470.40 = £94.08
Calculate her NI.	0.08 × 470.40 = £37.63
Find the sum of her deductions.	£94.08 + £37.63 + £3.50 = £135.21
Subtract to find her take-home pay.	£470.40 – £135.21 = £335.19

Exercise 5F

1 Work out the total pay for each person.

   a 40 hours at £6.50 per hour   **b** $37\frac{1}{2}$ hours at £8.20 per hour

   c 35 hours at £9.25 per hour   **d** $42\frac{1}{2}$ hours at £6.80 per hour

2 Work out the hourly rate for each payment.

   a £300 for 40 hours' work   **b** £380.10 for 42 hours' work

   c £217.50 for $37\frac{1}{2}$ hours' work   **d** £268.75 for 25 hours' work

3 Work out the number of hours worked for each job.

   a £321.10 at £8.45 per hour   **b** £390.10 at £9.40 per hour

   c £211.75 at £6.05 per hour   **d** £502 at £12.55 per hour

(CM) **4** Mary sees two job adverts for a cook.

> **The Loft Café**
> Cook wanted
> 35 hours per week.
> £8.40 per hour

> **Café Creme**
> Cook wanted
> 38 hours per week.
> £8.15 per hour

    a Give a reason why Mary might prefer the job at the Loft.

    b Give a reason why Mary might prefer the job at Café Crème.

5 Adele is a joiner. Her normal working week is from 8 to 5 Monday to Friday with a 1-hour lunch break. Her hourly rate is £13.50.

    If she works at weekends she is paid 'time and a half', which means she gets one and a half times the normal hourly rate.

    a How much does Adele earn for a normal working week?

    b One week she works for 8 hours at the weekend. How much does she earn that week?

6 Sasha works for 35 hours at her normal hourly rate and 6 hours at 'time and a half'. She earns a total of £303.60. What is her hourly rate of pay?

7 One week Bernice works her normal hours and 8 hours at 'time and a half'. She is paid £375. The next week she worked her normal hours and 4 hours at 'time and a half'. She is paid £330. How many hours is her normal week? Show your working

(PS) **8** Bill works 40 hours a week at an hourly rate of £x. Ben works 32 hours a week. They both get exactly the same weekly pay. What is Ben's hourly rate? Give your answer in terms of x.

(PS) **9** Steve works for $37\frac{1}{2}$ hours at an hourly rate of £11.80. He pays 20% of his pay in income tax. He also pays National Insurance at a rate of x%. After these deductions he is left with £327.45. What is the value of x? Show your working.

(PS) **10** Jeff works for a whole number of hours and is paid a whole number of pounds for each hour. He earns £407. He works more than one hour a week and the number of hours is higher than the hourly rate. Work out how many hours he works and his hourly rate.

Speed, time and distance

The relationship between speed (S), distance (D) and time (T) is:

$$\text{speed} = \frac{\text{distance}}{\text{time}}$$

This diagram will help you remember the relationships between distance, speed and time.

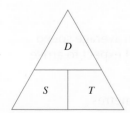

$$S = \frac{D}{T} \qquad \text{speed} = \frac{\text{distance}}{\text{time}}$$

$$D = S \times T \qquad \text{distance} = \text{speed} \times \text{time}$$

$$T = \frac{D}{S} \qquad \text{time} = \frac{\text{distance}}{\text{speed}}$$

In problems relating to speed, you usually mean **average speed**, as it would be unusual to maintain one exact speed for the whole of a journey. Speed is usually expressed in miles per hour (mph), kilometres per hour (kph) or metres per second (m/s).

Paula drove a distance of 270 miles in 5 hours. What was her average speed?

Paula's average speed = $\dfrac{\text{total distance she drove}}{\text{total time she took}}$

$$= \dfrac{270}{5}$$

$$= 54 \text{ miles per hour (mph)}$$

Sarah drove from Sheffield to Peebles in $3\frac{1}{2}$ hours at an average speed of 60 mph. How far is it from Sheffield to Peebles?

distance = speed × time

Change the time to a decimal number. $3\frac{1}{2}$ hours = 3.5 hours

Use this to find the distance from Sheffield to Peebles.   60 × 3.5 = 210 miles

Sean is going to drive from Newcastle upon Tyne to Nottingham, a distance of 190 miles. He estimates that he will drive at an average speed of 50 mph. How long will the journey take him?

Sean's time for the journey = $\dfrac{\text{total distance he drove}}{\text{his average speed}}$

$$= \dfrac{190}{50}$$

$$= 3.8 \text{ hours}$$

Change 0.8 hours into minutes.   0.8 × 60 = 48 minutes

So, Sean's journey will take 3 hours 48 minutes.

Remember When you calculate a time and get a decimal answer, as in Example 16, do not mistake the decimal part for minutes. You must either:

- leave the time as a decimal number and give the unit as hours, or
- change the decimal part to minutes by multiplying it by 60 (1 hour = 60 minutes) and give the answer in hours and minutes.

Exercise 5G

1 A cyclist travels a distance of 90 miles in 5 hours. What was her average speed?

2 How far along a motorway would you travel if you drove at 70 mph for 4 hours?

3 I drive to Bude in Cornwall from Sheffield in about 6 hours. The distance from Sheffield to Bude is 315 miles. What is my average speed?

4 The distance from Leeds to London is 210 miles. The train travels at an average speed of 90 mph. If I catch the 9:30 am train in London, at what time should I expect to arrive in Leeds?

5 How long will an athlete take to run 2000 m at an average speed of 4 metres per second?

6 Copy and complete this table.

	Distance travelled	Time taken	Average speed
a	150 miles	2 hours	
b	260 miles		40 mph
c		5 hours	35 mph
d		3 hours	80 km/h
e	544 km	8 hours 30 minutes	
f		3 hours 15 minutes	100 km/h
g	215 km		50 km/h

> **Hints and tips** **Remember** to convert time to a decimal if you are using a calculator, for example 8 hours 30 minutes is 8.5 hours.

7 Colin drives home from his son's house in 2 hours 15 minutes. He says that he drives at an average speed of 44 mph.

a Change 2 hours 15 minutes to a decimal.

b How far is it from Colin's home to his son's house?

8 The distance between Paris and Le Mans is 200 km. The express train between Paris and Le Mans travels at an average speed of 160 km/h.

a Calculate the time taken for the journey from Paris to Le Mans, giving your answer as a decimal number of hours.

b Change your answer to part **a** to hours and minutes.

CM **9** This timetable shows a train journey from Sheffield to London by the Midland mainline. The distance travelled is 150 miles.

Depart		Arrive		Travel by	Train company	Duration
11:29	Sheffield	13:30	London St Pancras Intl	Train	EAST MIDLANDS TRAINS	02h 01

This timetable shows a train journey from Sheffield to London by the East Coast mainline. The distance from Sheffield to Doncaster is 20 miles and from Doncaster to London is 160 miles.

Depart		Arrive		Travel by	Train company	Duration
11:10	Sheffield	11:35	Doncaster	Train	TRANSPENNINE EXPRESS	00h 25
11:46	Doncaster	13:28	London Kings Cross	Train	EAST COAST	01h 42

a Work out the average speed of each journey from Sheffield to London.

b Work out the average speed of the train journey from Doncaster to London.

MR **10** A train travels at 50 km/h for 2 hours, then slows down to do the last 30 minutes of its journey at 40 km/h.

a What is the total distance of this journey?

b What is the average speed of the train over the whole journey?

(MR) 11 Jade runs and walks the 3 miles from home to work each day. She runs the first 2 miles at a speed of 8 mph, then walks the next mile at a steady 4 mph.

What is her average speed for the whole journey?

12 Change the following speeds to metres per second.

a 36 km/h **b** 12 km/h **c** 60 km/h

> Hints and tips **Remember** that there are 3600 seconds in an hour and 1000 metres in a kilometre. So to change from km/h to m/s multiply by 1000 and divide by 3600.

13 Change the following speeds to kilometres per hour.

a 25 m/s **b** 12 m/s **c** 0.5 m/s

> Hints and tips To change from m/s to km/h multiply by 3600 and divide by 1000.

14 A train travels at an average speed of 18 m/s.

The train set off at 7:30 am on a 40-km journey.

At approximately what time will it reach its destination?

> Hints and tips To convert a decimal fraction of an hour to minutes, just multiply by 60.

(PS) 15 At 9:00 am Ajeet sets off on a cycle trail at an average speed of 16 km/h.

At 10:00 am Bijay sets off from the same place, in the same direction at an average speed of 24 km/h.

At approximately what time will Bijay catch up with Ajeet?

> Hints and tips Set up a table to show how far each cyclist has gone each 15 minutes after 10:00 am.

(CM) 16 Rebecca says: "If I travel for 10 minutes at 50 mph, then 10 minutes at 70 mph, then my average speed must be 60 mph."

Nick says: "If I travel for 10 miles at 40 mph, then 10 miles at 60 mph, then my average speed for the 20 miles will be 50 mph."

Are they both correct? Show your working.

(EV) 17 Josh and Nell need to travel from A to B.

Across town is 20 miles. By motorway it is 50 miles.

The speed limit in town is 30 mph and on the motorway it is 70 mph.

They work out the time it will take them to go via the town and via the motorway if they travel at the speed limit.

Josh decides to go via the town. Nell decides to go via the motorway.

Who is most likely to get there first? Use figures to back up your argument and explain any assumptions that you make.

Density

Density is the mass of a substance per unit of volume, usually expressed in grams per cm^3. The relationship between the three quantities is:

$$density = \frac{mass}{volume}$$

You can remember this with a triangle similar to that for distance, speed and time.

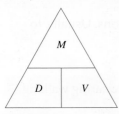

$M = DV$ mass = density × volume

$D = \dfrac{M}{V}$ density = mass ÷ volume

$V = \dfrac{M}{D}$ volume = mass ÷ density

Note: Density is defined in terms of mass. The common metric units for mass are grams and kilograms. Try not to mix up mass with weight. The common metric unit for weight is the newton (N). You may have learnt about the difference between mass and weight in science.

Example 17

A piece of metal has a mass of 30 g and a volume of 4 cm^3. What is the density of the metal?

$Density = \dfrac{mass}{volume}$

$= \dfrac{30}{4}$

$= 7.5$ g/cm^3

Example 18

What is the mass of a piece of rock that has a volume of 34 cm^3 and a density of 2.25 g/cm^3?

mass = density × volume

$= 2.25 \times 34$

$= 76.5$ g

Pressure

Pressure is the force per unit area and is expressed in newtons (N) per square metre (m^2). A force of 1 N applied to 1 m^2 is called 1 pascal (Pa). Other units to measure pressure are pounds per square inch and bars.

The relationship between pressure (P), force (F) and area (A) is pressure $= \dfrac{force}{area}$.

You can remember this with a triangle similar to that for distance, speed and time.

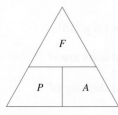

$P = \dfrac{F}{A}$ pressure = force ÷ area

$F = PA$ force = pressure × area

$A = \dfrac{F}{P}$ area = force ÷ pressure

As an example of pressure, think about pushing your thumb onto a piece of wood. Not much happens.

Now use your thumb to push a drawing pin onto the wood. The drawing pin will penetrate the wood.

The force is the same but the area it is applied to is much smaller so the pressure applied is much greater.

Note: If an object has a mass of x kg, then it exerts a downward force, due to gravity of xg newtons, where g is the acceleration due to gravity.

Under normal conditions, $g = 9.81$ m/s^2 so a mass of 1 kg exerts a force of 9.81 newtons. Usually, to make calculations easier, you take g as 10 m/s^2.

Example 19

a When does a woman exert the greater pressure on the floor: when she is wearing walking boots or high-heeled shoes?

Explain your answer.

b A woman has a mass of 50 kg. She is wearing a pair of high-heeled shoes. Each shoe has an area of 40 cm^2 for the sole and 1 cm^2 for the heel.

Take $g = 10$ m/s^2.

i When she is standing on both shoes with the heel down, what is the average pressure exerted on the ground?

ii She swivels round on the heel of one shoe only. How much pressure, in pascals, is exerted on the ground?

You are given that 1 cm^2 = 0.0001 m^2.

a A woman exerts more pressure on the floor when she is wearing high-heeled shoes as they have a much smaller contact area with the floor than walking boots.

b **i** Force is $50 \times 10 = 500$ N

Area is 82×0.0001 m^2 = 0.0082 m^2

pressure = force ÷ area

So average pressure is $500 \div 0.0082 \approx 61\ 000$ Pa.

ii On one heel, the pressure is $500 \div 0.0001 = 5\ 000\ 000$ Pa.

Exercise 5H

1 Find the density of a piece of wood with a mass of 6 g and a volume of 8 cm^3.

2 A force of 20 N acts over an area of 5 m^2. What is the pressure?

3 Calculate the density of a metal if 12 cm^3 of it has a mass of 100 g.

4 A pressure of 5 Pa acts on an area of $\frac{1}{2}$ m^2. What force is exerted?

5 Calculate the mass of a piece of plastic, 20 cm^3 in volume, if its density is 1.6 g/cm^3.

6 A crate weighs 200 N and exerts a pressure of 40 Pa on the ground. What is its area?

7 Calculate the volume of a piece of wood which has a mass of 102 g and a density of 0.85 g/cm^3.

8 Find the mass of a marble model, 56 cm^3 in volume, if the density of marble is 2.8 g/cm^3.

(CM) **9** A steel cuboid measures 30 cm by 20 cm by 10 cm. On which face should it be stood to exert least pressure?

10 Which of these will exert the greatest pressure: carrying a full shopping bag by the handles or carrying the same bag in your arms?

Explain your answer.

(PS) **11** Why do camels have large, wide feet?

12 A gold bar is in the shape of a cuboid with dimensions of 5 cm by 10 cm by 20 cm. The density of gold is 19.3 g/cm^3. The bar is placed on a weighing scale on its largest face.

    a What figure will show on the scale?

(CM)   **b** The bar is now placed on the scale on its smallest face. What figure will now show on the scale? Explain your answer.

    c Work out the pressure exerted on the scale in **a** and **b** above.

    Take $g = 10$ m/s^2.

(MR) **13** Two statues look identical and both appear to be made out of gold. One of them is a fake.

The density of gold is 19.3 g/cm^3.

The statues each have a volume of approximately 200 cm^3.

The first statue has a mass of 5.2 kg.

The second statue has a mass of 3.8 kg.

Which one is the fake?

14 A piece of metal has a mass of 345 g and a volume of 15 cm^3.

A different piece of metal has a mass of 400 g and a density of 25 g/cm^3.

Which piece of metal has the bigger volume and by how much?

(MR) **15** Two pieces of scrap metal are melted down to make a single piece of metal.

The first piece has a mass of 1.5 tonnes and a density of 7000 kg/m^3.

The second piece has a mass of 1 tonne and a density of 8000 kg/m^3.

Work out the total volume of the new piece of metal.

(PS) **16** A cuboid has a mass of 20 kg and a volume of 0.4 m^3.

When placed on each face the pressures exerted are 400 Pa, 250 Pa and 500 Pa.

Take $g = 10$ m/s^2. Work out the dimensions of the cuboid.

(CM) **17** The acceleration due to gravity on the Moon is about $\frac{1}{6}$ of what it is on Earth.

Say whether each one of these statements is true or false.

    a Buzz's mass is the same on the Earth and the Moon.

    b Buzz's weight is the same on the Earth and the Moon.

    c The pressure exerted by Buzz's feet when standing in his space suit is the same on the Earth as on the Moon.

    d When Buzz is standing in his space suit

$$\frac{\text{force on the Moon}}{\text{pressure on the Moon}} = \frac{\text{force on Earth}}{\text{pressure on Earth}}.$$

5.5 Compound interest and repeated percentage change

This section will show you how to:

- calculate simple interest
- calculate compound interest
- solve problems involving repeated percentage change.

Banks and building societies pay interest on savings accounts. **Simple interest** is when the same percentage of the original amount (**principal**) is paid each year. However, this is rarely used now and most banks pay **compound interest** on savings accounts.

For compound interest, the interest earned each year is added to the original amount and the new total then earns interest at the **annual rate** in the next year. This pattern is then repeated each year while the money is in the account.

The most efficient way to calculate the total amount in the account after one year or several years is to use a multiplier.

Example 20

Elizabeth invests £400 in a savings account. She can invest in an account that pays 6.5% simple interest if she leaves her money in for 3 years. Alternatively, she can put it in an account that pays 6% compound interest. Which account will give her more money after 3 years?

Simple interest pays the same interest each year.   6.5% of £400 = £26

3 × £26 = £78

After 3 years she will have £478 with the simple interest account.

With compound interest the amount in the account increases by 6% each year, so the multiplier is 1.06.

After 1 year she will have £400 × 1.06 = £424.

After 2 years she will have £424 × 1.06 = £449.44.

After 3 years she will have £449.44 × 1.06 = £476.41.

If you calculate the differences, you can see that the amount of interest increases each year (£24, £25.44 and £26.97).

So, the simple interest account gives the most money after 3 years.

You can see from this example that the amount in the account after three years could have been calculated as £400 × (1.06)^3. That is, you could have used the following formula for calculating the total amount due at any time:

total amount, $A = P + P \times$ multiplier raised to the power n

$$A = P\left(1 + \frac{r}{100}\right)^n$$

where P is the original amount invested, r is the percentage interest rate and n is the number of years for which the money is invested.

So, in Example 20, $P = £400$, $\frac{r}{100} = 0.06$, $n = 3$ and the total amount = £400 × (1.06)^3.

Using your calculator

You should see that you can do the above calculation on your calculator without having to write down all the intermediate steps.

To add on the 6% each time, just multiply by 1.06 each time. So you can do the calculation as:

or

or

$$4\ 0\ 0\ \times\ (\ 1\ 0\ 6\ \div\ 1\ 0\ 0\ )\ x^{\blacksquare}\ 3\ =$$

You need to find the method that you are comfortable with and that you understand.

The idea of compound interest does not only concern money. It also occurs, for example, in the growth in population, increases in salaries or increases in body weight or height.

The same idea can involve regular reduction by a fixed percentage: for example, car depreciation, population losses and even water losses. The next exercise shows the extent to which compound interest ideas are used.

Exercise 5I

1 Work out the interest on each account.

   a £2000 invested for 5 years at 4% simple interest

   b £1500 invested for 3 years at 2.5% simple interest

   c £200 invested for 2 years at 3.2% simple interest

   d £4000 invested for 3 years at 4% compound interest

2 Work out the number of years of investment for each return.

   a £3000 invested at 3% simple interest returns £3720

   b £5000 invested at 2.5% compound interest returns £6724, to the nearest pound (£)

3 A baby octopus increases its body weight by 5% each day for the first month of its life. In a safe ocean zoo, a baby octopus was born weighing 10 g.

   a What was its weight after:

      i 1 day   **ii** 2 days   **iii** 4 days   **iv** 1 week?

   b After how many days will the octopus first weigh over 15 g?

4 A certain type of conifer hedging increases in height by 17% each year for the first 20 years. When I bought some of this hedging, it was all about 50 cm tall. How long will it take to reach 3 m?

5 The manager of a small family business offered his staff an annual pay increase of 4% for every year they stayed with the firm.

   a Gareth started work at the business on a salary of £12 200. What salary will he be on after 4 years?

   b Julie started work at the business on a salary of £9350. How many years will it be until she is earning a salary of over £20 000?

6 Scientists have been studying the shores of Scotland and estimate that due to pollution the seal population of those shores will decline at the rate of 15% each year. In 2010 they counted about 3000 seals on those shores.

a If nothing is done about pollution, how many seals did they expect to be there in:

i 2011 **ii** 2012 **iii** 2015?

b How long will it take for the seal population to fall to less than 1000?

7 I am told that if I buy a new car its value will depreciate at the rate of 20% each year. If I bought a car in 2011 priced at £8500, what would be the value of the car in:

a 2012 **b** 2013 **c** 2015?

8 At the peak of a drought during the summer, a reservoir in Derbyshire was losing water at the rate of 8% each day. On 1 August this reservoir held 2.1 million litres of water.

a At this rate of losing water, how much would have been in the reservoir on the following days?

i 2 August **ii** 4 August **iii** 8 August

b The danger point is when the water drops below 1 million litres. When would this have been if things had continued as they were?

9 The population of a small country, Yebon, was only 46 000 in 2001, but it steadily increased by about 13% each year during the 2000s.

a Calculate the population in:

i 2002 **ii** 2006 **iii** 2010.

b If the population keeps growing at this rate, in what year will it reach half a million?

10 How long will it take to accumulate one million pounds in the following situations?

a An investment of £100 000 at a rate of 12% compound interest

b An investment of £50 000 at a rate of 16% compound interest

11 An oak tree is 60 cm tall. It grows at a rate of 8% per year. A conifer is 50 cm tall. It grows at a rate of 15% per year. How many years does it take before the conifer is taller than the oak?

12 A tree increases in height by 18% per year. When it is 1 year old, it is 8 cm tall. How long will it take the tree to grow to 10 m?

13 Show that a 10% increase followed by a 10% increase is equivalent to a 21% increase overall.

14 Here are two advertisements for savings accounts.

Bradley Bank

Invest £1000 for two years and earn 3.2% interest overall.

Monastery Building Society

Invest £1000.
Interest rate 1.3% compound per annum.
Bonus of 0.5% on balance after 2 years.

Which account is worth more after 2 years?

Show all your working.

15 A fish weighs 3 kg and increases in mass by 10% each month. A crab weighs 6 kg but decreases in mass by 10% each month. After how many months will the fish weigh more than the crab?

 16 There is a bread shortage.

Each week during the shortage, a shop increases its price of bread by 20% of the price the week before.

After how many weeks would the price of the bread have doubled?

5.6 Reverse percentage (working out the original amount)

This section will show you how to:

- calculate the original amount, given the final amount, after a known percentage increase or decrease.

Reverse percentage questions involve working backwards from the final amount to find the original amount when you know, or can work out, the final amount as a percentage of the original amount.

There are two methods: the unitary method and the multiplier method.

The unitary method

The unitary method has three steps.

Step 1 Equate the final percentage to the final value.

Step 2 Use this to calculate the value of 1%.

Step 3 Multiply by 100 to work out 100% (the original value).

Example 21

In a factory, 70 workers were given a pay rise. This was 20% of all the workers. How many workers are there altogether?

Step 1	Equate the values.	20% represents 70 workers.
Step 2	Calculate 1%.	70 ÷ 20 workers. (There is no need to work out this calculation yet.)
Step 3	Calculate 100% .	70 ÷ 20 × 100 = 350

So there are 350 workers altogether.

Example 22

The price of a car increased by 6% to £9116. Work out the price before the increase.

Step 1	Equate the values.	106% represents £9116.
Step 2	Calculate 1%.	£9116 ÷ 106
Step 3	Calculate 100% .	£9116 ÷ 106 × 100 = £8600

So the price before the increase was £8600.

The multiplier method

The multiplier method involves fewer steps.

Step 1 Write down the multiplier.

Step 2 Divide the final value by the multiplier to give the original value.

In a sale the price of a freezer is reduced by 12%. The sale price is £220. What was the price before the sale?

Step 1 Write down the multiplier. A decrease of 12% gives a multiplier of 0.88.

Step 2 Calculate the original amount. £220 ÷ 0.88 = £250

So the price before the sale was £250.

Exercise 5J

1. Find what 100% represents in each situation.

   a 40% represents 320 g   **b** 14% represents 35 m   **c** 45% represents 27 cm

   d 4% represents £123   **e** 2.5% represents £5   **f** 8.5% represents £34

2. On a gruelling army training session, only 28 youngsters survived the whole day. This represented 35% of the original group. How large was the original group?

3. VAT is a government tax added to goods and services. With VAT at 20%, what is the pre-VAT price of the following priced goods?

   T-shirt   £10.08   Tights   £1.44   Shorts   £6.24

   Sweater   £12.90   Trainers   £29.76   Boots   £38.88

4. Howard spends £200 a month on food. This represents 24% of his monthly take-home pay. How much is his monthly take-home pay?

5. Tina's weekly pay is increased by 5% to £315. What was Tina's pay before the increase?

6. The number of workers in a factory fell by 5% to 228. How many workers were there originally?

7. In a sale the price of a TV is reduced to £325.50. This is a 7% reduction on the original price. What was the original price?

8. If 38% of plastic bottles in a production line are blue and the remaining 7750 plastic bottles are brown, how many plastic bottles are blue?

9. I received £4.40 back from HM Revenue and Customs, which represented the 20% VAT on a piece of equipment. How much did I pay for this equipment in the first place?

10. A company is in financial trouble. The workers are asked to take a 10% pay cut for each of the next two years.

    a Rob works out that his pay in two years' time will be £1296 per month. How much is his pay now?

    b Instead he offers to take an immediate pay cut of 14% and have his pay frozen at that level for two years. Has he made the correct decision?

(CM) **11** The population in a village is 30% of the size of the population in a neighbouring town.

 a If both populations double, what is the population of the village as a percentage of the population of the town?

 b If the population of the village stays the same but the population of the town doubles, what is the population of the village as a percentage of the population of the town?

(CM) **12** A man's salary was increased by 5% in one year and reduced by 5% in the next year. Is his final salary greater or less than the original one and by how many per cent?

(MR) **13** A woman's salary increased by 5% in one year and then increased the following year by 5% again.

 Her new salary was £19 845.

 How much was the increase, in pounds, in the first year?

(CM) **14** When VAT was 17.5%, a quick way of estimating the pre-VAT price of an item with VAT added was to divide by 6 and then multiply by 5. For example, if an item costs £360 including VAT, it cost approximately $(360 \div 6) \times 5 = £300$ before VAT. Show that this gave an estimate to within £5 of the pre-VAT price for items costing up to £280.

(MR) **15** After a 6% increase followed by an 8% increase, the monthly salary of a chef was £1431. What was the original monthly salary?

(PS) **16** Cassie invests some money at 4% interest per annum for five years. After five years, she had £1520.82 in the bank. How much did she invest originally?

(PS) **17** In 2000, the population of a town was 5400. 28% of the population of the town owned a mobile phone. In 2015, the number of people in the town owning a mobile phone had increased by 150%. This represented 72% of the population. Has the population of the town increased or decreased between 2000 and 2015, and by how much?

(EV) **18** A teacher asked her class to work out the original price of a cooker for which, after a 12% increase, the price was £291.20.

 This is Baz's answer:

> *12% of 291.20 = £34.94*
>
> *Original price = 291.20 − 34.94 = 256.26 ≈ £260*

 When the teacher read out the answer, Baz ticked his work as correct.

 What errors has he made?

(PS) **19** In a survey, exactly 35% of the people surveyed wanted a new supermarket.

 What is the least number that could have been surveyed?

Worked exemplars

  Jonathan is comparing two ways to travel from his flat in London to his parents' house in Doncaster.

Tube, train and taxi

It takes 35 minutes to get to the railway station by tube in London. A train journey from London to Doncaster takes 1 hour 40 minutes. From Doncaster, it is 15 miles by taxi at an average speed of 20 mph.

Car

The car journey is 160 miles at an average speed of 50 mph.

a Which the journey takes longer: tube, train and taxi or car?

b How do any assumptions you have made affect your answer?

a This part of the question assesses 'communicating mathematically', so you must display your methods clearly and include words to explain what your calculations show. Imagine that you will pass your answer to a friend or relative and ask yourself whether or not they could understand it.	
For the taxi time = distance ÷ speed $= \dfrac{15}{20}$ = 0.75 hour (or 45 minutes)	First, work out the time taken by the taxi. It is not essential to show the formula 'time = distance ÷ speed' but it is useful to draw the triangle that shows the relationship. Be careful with time as a decimal: 0.75 hours = 45 minutes.
Total time for the journey by tube, rail and taxi: 35 minutes + 1 hour 40 minutes + 45 minutes = 3 hours	Next, work out the total time for tube, train and taxi.
For the car time = distance ÷ speed = 160 ÷ 50 = 3.2 hours (or 3 hours 12 minutes)	Now work out the time taken by the car. 0.1 hours = 6 minutes so 0.2 hours = 12 minutes
Travelling by car takes 12 minutes longer.	Finally, compare the times taken. It is essential to write a final conclusion: do not assume it is obvious from your working.

b This part asks you to evaluate your solution in light of any assumptions made, so think about the practicalities of both journeys.

No allowance is made for time between the different stages of the journey so the journey by tube, train and taxi will probably take longer.	The journey by tube train and taxi does not make any allowances for time between each part of the journey, for example, waiting to get a taxi at Doncaster station. In reality there will be several minutes between each stage. You do not need to write a detailed explanation, just make it clear what assumptions have been made and how this will affect the answer.

2 A, B, C and D are four points on a number line.

AB : BC = 7 : 3

BC : CD = 2 : 5

Work out the ratio AC : CD.

Give your answer in its simplest form.

This question requires you to 'interpret and communicate information', so you will need to extend the information beyond what is stated explicitly.	
A ——— B — C ——— D A ——— B — C ——— D	It may help to draw a diagram.
This table shows the given ratios. 	AB	7	
BC	3	2
CD		5		Set up a table and write in the information you are given.
BC has the same value in the first and second columns. 	AB	7		14
BC	3	2	6
CD		5	15		Now extend and complete the third column. Multiply AB and BC in the first column by 2 to give AB = 14 and BC = 6. Multiply BC and CD in the second column by 3 to give BC = 6 and CD = 15.
Add AB and BC to find AC. 	AB	7		14		
BC	3	2	6	20	4
CD		5	15	15	3		Now extend and complete a fourth column by combing AB and BC from the third column to get AC = 20 (column 4) and cancel AC and CD by a factor of 5 (column 5).
The ratio of AC : CD is 4 : 3.	Give your answer.

Ready to progress?

I can simplify a ratio.
I can calculate with ratios.
I can calculate distance from speed and time.
I can calculate time from speed and distance.
I can compare prices of products to find the 'best buy'.
I can solve problems involving density and pressure.
I can work out problems about simple interest.
I can work out compound interest problems.

I can use ratio to solve problems in appropriate situations.
I can solve reverse percentage problems.
I can solve more complex compound interest problems.

I can solve complex problems involving percentage increases and percentage decreases.

Review questions

1   Maura travelled 80 miles in 1 hour 40 minutes.

Work out Maura's average speed in miles per hour.

2   Ron drives 220 miles in 2 hours 45 minutes on French motorways.

The speed limit on French motorways is 120 km/h.

5 miles = 8 kilometres

Is it likely, unlikely or definite that Ron exceeds the speed limit?

(PS) 3   The ratio of the totals of the numbers in Box A and Box B is 2 : 3.

```
┌─────────────┐   ┌─────────────┐
│  4     5    │   │  6      7   │
│     9       │   │      13     │
│ 10    12    │   │  15     19  │
└─────────────┘   └─────────────┘
```

Swap two numbers, one from each box, so that the ratio of the totals of the numbers is now 9 : 11.

Show your working.

4   A farmer has three fields. The area of field A is 1.73 hectares, the area of field B is 2.64 hectares and the area of field C is 0.95 hectares. Cattle need 0.065 hectares of space each, horses need 0.04 hectares of space each and sheep need 0.01 hectares of space each.

   a Show that, if the farmer keeps horses in field A, cattle in field B and sheep in field C, she will be able to have a total of 178 animals.

(CM)   b Work out the combination of fields, cattle, horses and sheep that will allow the farmer to keep the maximum possible number of animals.

5   The interior angles of a triangle are in the ratio 1 : 3 : 5.

Calculate the size of the largest angle.

6 A company mixes two types of lawn seed.

EZgreen grass seed costs £18 per kilogram.

Evergreen grass seed costs £21 per kilogram.

The company mixes the seed in the ratio EZgreen : Evergreen = 2 : 3.

a How much Evergreen will the company need to mix with 15 kg of EZgreen?

b How much EZgreen will the company need to mix with 45 kg of Evergreen?

c How much will one kilogram of the mixture cost?

7 Mary invests £6000 for 12 years at 2.8% per annum compound interest.

Work out the value of the investment at the end of 12 years.

8 After a 12% increase, the cost of a washing machine is £420. How much did it cost before the increase?

9 Henry invested £4500 for 3 years in a savings account.

He was paid 3.2% per annum compound interest.

a How much did Henry have in his savings account after 3 years?

b Jake invested £1200 for n years in a savings account.

He was paid 2.5% per annum compound interest.

At the end of the n years, he told his sister he had £1360 in the savings account.

Work out the value of n.

Comment on what Jake told his sister.

10 The cost of petrol increased by 15% one week but fell back to the original price the next week.

By what percentage did the cost of petrol fall in the second week?

11 A group of 165 men and women visit a cinema.

There are 20% more men than women.

How many men are in the group?

12 Joe pays £41.40 for a meal which includes a £4.40 tip.

Lucy pays £41.40 for a meal which includes a 15% tip.

Whose meal cost more before the tip was added?

13 In 2014, Sally used 5400 units of electricity.

In 2015, the price of electricity increased by 8% but Sally reduced her usage to 4500 units.

Sally paid £680.40 for the units she used in 2015.

Did she pay more or less for the units she used in 2014? Show your working.

14 In a sale, the price of a jacket is reduced by 15%. On the last day of the sale, it is reduced by another 10% *of the sale price* and was priced at £50.50.

a How much was the original price of the jacket?

b What assumption can you make about the final price?

6 Geometry and measures: Angles

This chapter is going to show you:

- how to find angles on a line and around a point
- how to find angles in a triangle and in any polygon
- how to calculate angles in parallel lines
- how to calculate interior and exterior angles in polygons
- how to read scale maps and drawings
- how to use bearings.

You should already know:

- how to use a protractor to measure an angle
- the meaning of the terms 'acute', 'obtuse', 'reflex' and 'right' and how to use these terms to describe angles
- the names and angle properties of quadrilaterals
- what a polygon is and the names of polygons with up to ten sides
- that a diagonal is a line joining two non-adjacent vertices of a polygon
- the meaning of the terms 'parallel' and 'perpendicular' in relation to lines.

About this chapter

Ancient civilisations used right angles in surveying and constructing buildings, but not everything can be measured in right angles. They needed a smaller, more useful unit. The ancient Babylonians chose a unit angle that led to the development of the degree, which is what we still use now.

Historians think the ancient Babylonians believed the 'circle' of the year consisted of 360 days. The ancient Babylonians also knew that the side of a regular hexagon inscribed in a circle is equal to the radius of the circle. This may have led to the division of the full circle (360 'days') into six equal parts, each part consisting of 60 'days', and so giving a full circle 360 units. They divided one angle of an equilateral triangle into 60 equal parts, which we now call degrees.

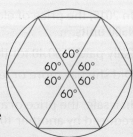

This chapter will show you the connections between various shapes and their angles. Angles help us construct many things, from tables to skyscrapers. It is essential that you understand them: they literally shape our world.

6.1 Angle facts

This section will show you how to:

- calculate angles on a straight line and angles around a point
- use vertically opposite angles.

Angles on a line

The **angles on a straight line** add up to 180°.

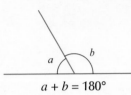 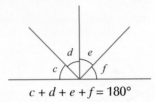

$$a + b = 180°$$ $$c + d + e + f = 180°$$

Draw an example for yourself (and measure a and b) to show that the statement is true.

Angles around a point

The sum of the **angles around a point** is 360°. For example:

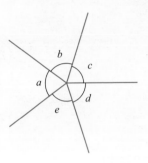

$$a + b + c + d + e = 360°$$

Again, check this for yourself by drawing an example and measuring the angles.

Sometimes you will need to use equations to solve angle problems, as shown in the next examples.

Example 1

Find the size of angle x in the diagram.

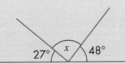

Angles on a straight line add up to 180°.

Therefore, $27° + x + 48° = 180°$

$$x = 180° - 75°$$

So $x = 105°$.

Example 2

Find the value of x in the diagram.

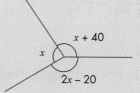

These angles are around a point, so they must add up to 360°.

Therefore, $x + x + 40° + 2x - 20° = 360°$

$$4x + 20° = 360°$$

$$4x = 340°$$

So $x = 85°$.

Vertically opposite angles

Vertically opposite angles are equal.

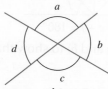

$a = c$ and $b = d$.

Example 3

Find the value of x in the diagram.

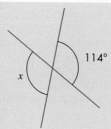

The two angles are vertically opposite, so $x = 114°$.

Exercise 6A

1 Calculate the size of the angle marked x in each of these examples.

a

b

c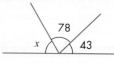

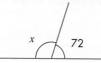

> **Hints and tips** Never measure angles in questions like these, as diagrams are not always drawn accurately. Always calculate angles unless you are told to measure them.

2 Write down the value of x in each of these diagrams.

a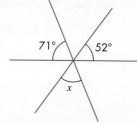

b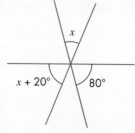

CM **3** In the diagram, angle ABD is 45° and angle CBD is 125°.

Decide whether ABC is a straight line. Write down how you decided.

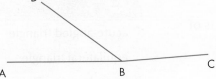

PS **4** Calculate the value of x in each of these examples.

a

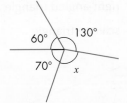

b

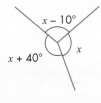

c

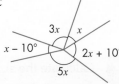

PS **5** Calculate the value of x in each of these examples.

a

b

c

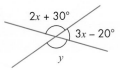

PS **6** Calculate the value of x and y in each of these examples. Calculate x first each time.

a

b

c

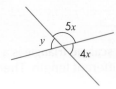

CM **7** Ella has a collection of tiles. They are all equilateral triangles and are all the same size.

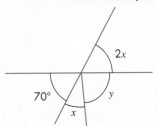

She says that six of the tiles will fit together and leave no gaps.

Explain why Ella is correct.

PS **8** Work out the value of y in the diagram.

6.2 Triangles

This section will show you how to:

- recognise and calculate the angles in different sorts of triangles.

Key terms

acute-angled triangle

equilateral triangle

isosceles triangle

obtuse-angled triangle

right-angled triangle

scalene triangle

Example 4

Calculate the size of angle a in this triangle.

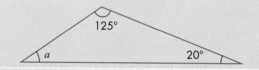

Angles in a triangle add up to 180°.

Therefore, $a + 20° + 125° = 180°$

$a + 145° = 180°$

So $a = 35°$.

Special triangles

Scalene triangle

A **scalene triangle** is a triangle where each side is a different length. Therefore, all 3 three angles are different.

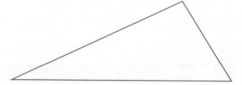

Equilateral triangle

An **equilateral triangle** is a triangle with all its sides equal. Therefore, all three angles are 60°.

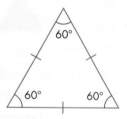

Isosceles triangle

An **isosceles triangle** is a triangle with two equal sides and, therefore, with two equal angles (at the foot of the equal sides).

Notice how to mark the equal sides and equal angles.

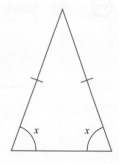

Right-angled triangle

A **right-angled triangle** has an angle of 90°.

$a + b = 90°$

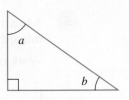

Obtuse-angled triangle

An **obtuse-angled triangle** is a triangle with an obtuse angle (more than 90°).

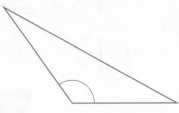

Acute-angled triangle

An **acute-angled triangle** is a triangle with *all* its angles less than 90°.

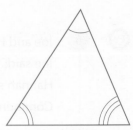

Exercise 6B

1 **a** Sketch a scalene obtuse-angled triangle.

b Sketch a scalene acute-angled triangle.

c Sketch a scalene right-angled triangle.

d Write down the angle sum of any triangle.

2 In the triangle on the right, all the angles are the same.

a What is the size of each angle?

b What is the name of a special triangle like this?

c What is special about the sides of this triangle?

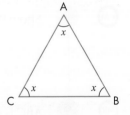

3 In the triangle on the right, two of the angles are the same.

a Work out the size of the lettered angles.

b What is the name of a special triangle like this?

c What is special about the sides AC and AB of this triangle?

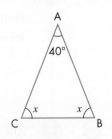

4 Find the size of the angle marked with a letter in each of these diagrams.

a   **b**   **c**

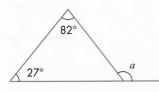
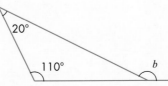
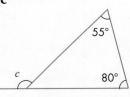

5 A town planner has drawn this diagram to show three paths in a park but they have missed out the angle marked x.

Work out the value of x.

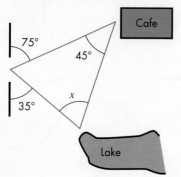

EV **6** Joe and Hannah looked at the triangle DEF.

Joe said: "It's a right-angled triangle."

Hannah said: "It's an isosceles triangle."

Comment on each of the statements.

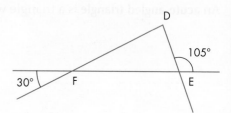

CM **7** The diagram shows three intersecting straight lines.

Work out the value of a.

Give reasons for your answers.

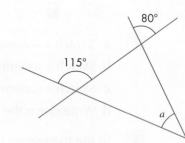

CM **8** Show that $x = a + b$.

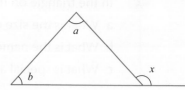

MR **9** ABC is a triangle.

Point D is on AC.

Work out the size of angle ABD.

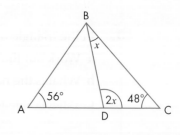

MR **10** ABC is a triangle.

Point D is on AC.

Work out the size of angle BDA.

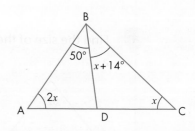

6.3 Angles in a polygon

This section will show you how to:

- calculate the sum of the interior angles in a polygon.

Key terms

interior angle   polygon

Angle sums from triangles

Working through Exercise 6C will show you how you can use triangles to help find the angle sum of polygons.

Exercise 6C

1   **a** Draw a quadrilateral (a four-sided shape).

b Draw in a diagonal to make it into two triangles.

c Copy and complete this statement:

The sum of the angles in a quadrilateral is equal to the sum of the angles in … triangles, which is … × 180° = …°.

2   **a** Draw a pentagon (a five-sided shape).

b Draw in two diagonals to make it into three triangles.

c Copy and complete this statement:

The sum of the angles in a pentagon is equal to the sum of the angles in … triangles, which is … × 180° = …°.

3   **a** Draw a hexagon (a six-sided shape).

b Draw in three diagonals to make it into four triangles.

c Copy and complete this statement:

The sum of the angles in a hexagon is equal to the sum of the angles in … triangles, which is … × 180° = …°.

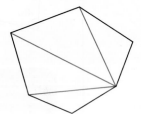

4   Complete the table below. Use the number pattern to carry on the angle sum up to a decagon (ten-sided shape).

Shape	Number of sides	Triangles	Angle sum
Triangle	3	1	180
Quadrilateral	4	2	
Pentagon	5	3	
Hexagon	6	4	
Heptagon	7		
Octagon	8		
Nonagon	9		
Decagon	10		

5   Using the number pattern, copy and complete this statement:

The number of triangles in a 20-sided shape is …, so the sum of the angles in a 20-sided shape is … × 180° = …°.

n-sided polygon

For an *n*-sided polygon, the sum of the **interior angles** is $180(n - 2)°$.

The interior angles are the angles inside the shape.

Calculate the size of angle *a* in this quadrilateral.

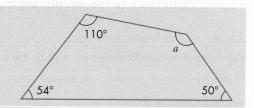

Angles in a quadrilateral add up to 360°.

Therefore, $a + 50° + 54° + 110° = 360°$

$$a + 214° = 360°$$

$$\text{So, } a = 146°.$$

Exercise 6D 🖩

1 Find the size of the angle marked with a letter in each of these quadrilaterals.

a

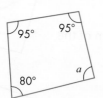

b

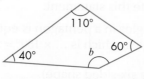

c

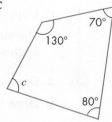

| Hints and tips | Remember, the sum of the interior angles of a quadrilateral is 360°. |

2 Do any of these sets of angles form the four interior angles of a quadrilateral? Explain your answer.

a 135°, 75°, 60°, 80° **b** 150°, 60°, 80°, 70° **c** 85°, 85°, 120°, 60°

d 80°, 90°, 90°, 110° **e** 95°, 95°, 60°, 110° **f** 102°, 138°, 90°, 30°

3 In this quadrilateral, all the angles are the same.

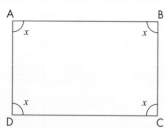

a What size is each angle?

b What is the name of a special quadrilateral like this?

c Is there another quadrilateral with four equal angles? If so, what is it called?

4 Work out the size of the angle marked with a letter in each of the polygons below.
You may find the table you completed in Exercise 6C useful.

a

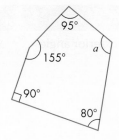

b

c

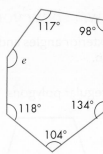

d

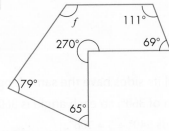

e

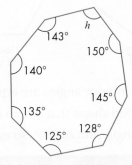

> **Hints and tips** Remember, the sum of the interior angles of an n-sided polygon is $180(n - 2)°$.

(PS) 5 Anna is drawing this logo for a school magazine.

It is made up of four equilateral triangles that are all the same size.

She needs to know the sizes of the six angles so that she can draw it accurately.

What are the sizes of the six angles?

> **Hints and tips** First mark the four equilateral triangles on a copy of the diagram.

(MR) 6 This quadrilateral is made from two isosceles triangles.
They are both the same size.

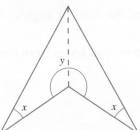

Find the value of y in terms of x.

(PS) 7 The four angles in a quadrilateral are $2x$, $x + 20$, $2x - 10$ and $3x + 30$.
What is the size of the smallest angle in the quadrilateral?

6.4 Regular polygons

This section will show you how to:

- calculate the exterior angles and the interior angles of a regular polygon.

Below are three regular polygons.

Square
4 sides

Pentagon
5 sides

Hexagon
6 sides

A polygon is regular if all its interior angles are equal and all its sides have the same length.

A square is a regular four-sided shape that has an angle sum of 360°, so each angle is 360° ÷ 4 = 90°.

A regular pentagon has an angle sum of 540°, so each angle is 540° ÷ 5 = 108°.

Shape	Number of sides	Angle sum	Each angle
Square	4	360°	90°
Pentagon	5	540°	108°
Hexagon	6	720°	720° ÷ 6 = 120°

Interior and exterior angles of regular shapes

Look again at these three regular polygons.

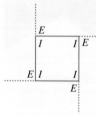
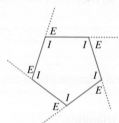
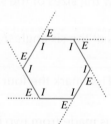

At each vertex, there is an interior angle, I, and an **exterior angle**, E. Notice that: $I + E = 180°$.

Clearly, the exterior angles of a square are each 90°. So, the sum of the exterior angles of a square is $4 \times 90° = 360°$.

You can calculate the exterior angle of a regular pentagon as follows. You know from the previous table that the interior angle of a regular pentagon is 108°.

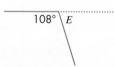

So the exterior angle is $180° - 108° = 72°$.

Therefore, the sum of the exterior angles is $5 \times 72° = 360°$.

From this table, you can see that the sum of the exterior angles is always 360°.

Regular polygon	Number of sides	Interior angle	Exterior angle	Sum of exterior angles
square	4	90°	90°	$4 \times 90° = 360°$
pentagon	5	108°	72°	$5 \times 72° = 360°$
hexagon	6	120°	60°	$6 \times 60° = 360°$

You can use this information to find the exterior angle and the interior angle for any regular polygon.

For an n-sided regular polygon, the exterior angle is given by $E = \frac{360°}{n}$ and the interior angle is given by $I = 180° - E$.

Example 6

Calculate the size of the exterior and interior angle of a regular 12-sided polygon (a regular dodecagon).

$E = \frac{360°}{12}$ $I = 180° - 30°$

$\quad = 30°$ $\quad = 150°$

Exercise 6E

1 Copy and complete the table below.

Regular polygon	Number of sides	Interior angle sum	Each interior angle
octagon	8		
nonagon	9		
decagon	10		

2 Copy and complete the table below for regular polygons.

Regular polygon	Number of sides	Interior angle	Exterior angle
square	4	90°	90°
pentagon	5	108°	72°
hexagon	6	120°	
octagon	8		
nonagon	9		
decagon	10		

3 Each diagram shows an interior angle of a regular polygon. For each polygon, work out:

i the exterior angle

ii the number of sides

iii the sum of the interior angles of the polygon.

a
135°

b
160°

c
165°

d
144°

4　Each diagram shows an exterior angle of a regular polygon. For each polygon, answer the following.

i　What is its interior angle?

ii　How many sides does it have?

iii　What is the sum of its interior angles?

a 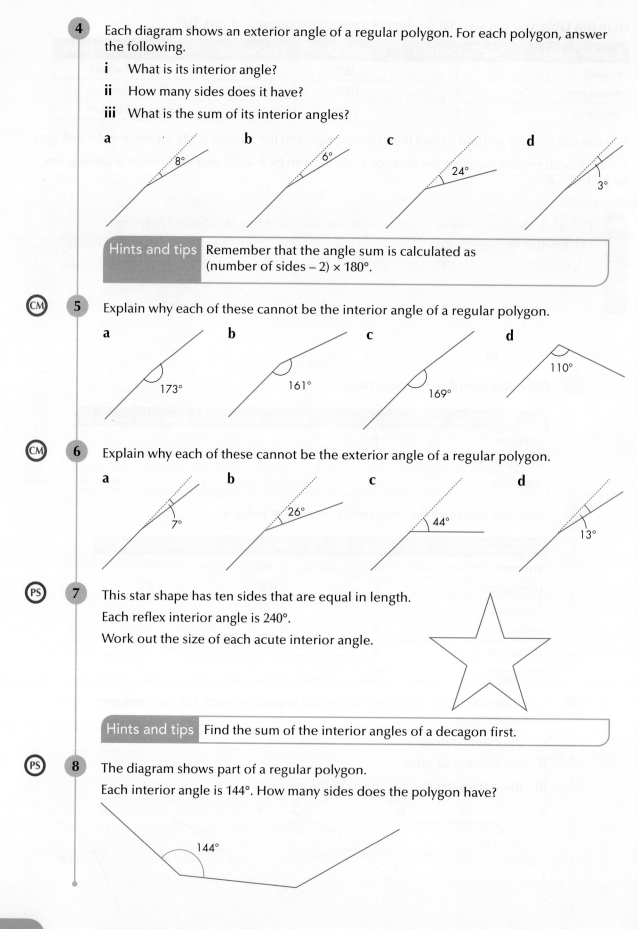 8°　　b 6°　　c 24°　　d 3°

> **Hints and tips** Remember that the angle sum is calculated as (number of sides − 2) × 180°.

CM

5　Explain why each of these cannot be the interior angle of a regular polygon.

a 173°　　b 161°　　c 169°　　d 110°

CM

6　Explain why each of these cannot be the exterior angle of a regular polygon.

a 7°　　b 26°　　c 44°　　d 13°

PS

7　This star shape has ten sides that are equal in length.

Each reflex interior angle is 240°.

Work out the size of each acute interior angle.

> **Hints and tips** Find the sum of the interior angles of a decagon first.

PS

8　The diagram shows part of a regular polygon.

Each interior angle is 144°. How many sides does the polygon have?

144°

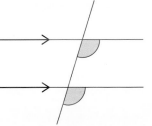

(MR) **9** Draw a sketch of a regular octagon and join each vertex to the centre.

Calculate the value of the angle at the centre.

What connection does this have with the exterior angle?

Is this true for all regular polygons?

(PS) **10** A joiner is making tables so that the shape of each one is half a regular octagon.

He needs to know the size of each angle on the table top.

What are the sizes of the angles?

(PS) **11** Find the sizes of the angles of a pentagon whose interior angles are in the ratio 2 : 2 : 3 : 4 : 4.

(MR) **12** Andrily measured all the angles in a polygon and got 987°, but he forgot to measure one angle. What was the size of the missing angle?

6.5 Angles in parallel lines

This section will show you how to:

- find angles in parallel lines.

By drawing a pair of parallel lines with a line through them, you can verify the following results for yourself.

Key terms	
allied angles	alternate angles
corresponding angles	

Angles like these	Angles like these	Angles like these
	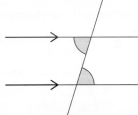	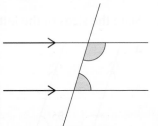
are called **corresponding angles**. Corresponding angles are equal.	are called **alternate angles**. Alternate angles are equal.	are called **allied angles** or co-interior angles. Allied angles add up to 180°.

Example 7

State the size of each lettered angle in the diagram and give a reason.

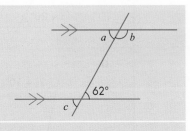

$a = 62°$ (alternate angle to 62°)

$b = 118°$ (allied angle to 62° or angles on a line with a)

$c = 62°$ (vertically opposite angle to 62° or corresponding angle to a)

Exercise 6F

1 Copy and complete these statements to make them true.

  a Angles h and ... are corresponding angles.

  b Angles d and ... are alternate angles.

  c Angles e and ... are allied angles.

  d Angles b and ... are corresponding angles.

  e Angles c and ... are allied angles.

  f Angles c and ... are alternate angles.

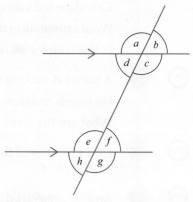

(CM) **2** State the sizes of the lettered angles in each diagram and give a reason.

a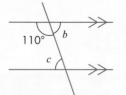

b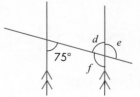

c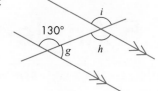

d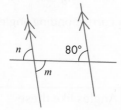

e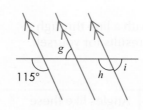

f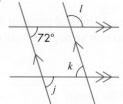

3 State the sizes of the lettered angles in these diagrams.

a

b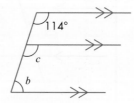

(PS) **4** Calculate the values of x and y in each diagram.

a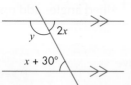

b

c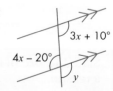

d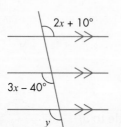

e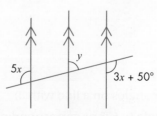

f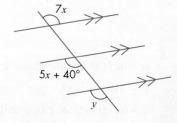

5 A company makes signs in the shape of a chevron.

This is one of their signs. It has one line of symmetry.

The designer for the company needs to know the size of the angle marked x on the diagram.

What is the size of angle x?

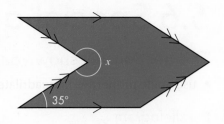

 6 In the diagram, AE is parallel to BD.

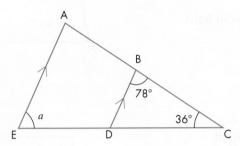

Work out the size of angle a.

Give a clear explanation of how you obtained your answer.

  7 In this diagram, the line XY crosses the parallel lines AB and CD at P and Q.

Lizzie is trying to find the size of angle DQY, giving reasons for her answer. This is her solution:

Angle PQD = 64° (corresponding angles).

So angle DQY = 124° (angles on a line = 190°).

Lizzie has made a number of errors in her solution. Identify her errors and write out a correct solution for the question.

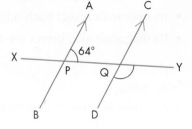

 8 Use this diagram to prove that the three angles in a triangle add up to 180°.

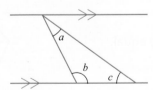

  9 Prove that $p + q + r = 180°$.

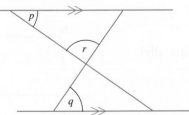

6.6 Special quadrilaterals

This section will show you how to:

- use angle properties in quadrilaterals.

Key term

bisect

Parallelogram

- A parallelogram has opposite sides parallel.
- Its opposite sides are equal.
- Its diagonals **bisect** each other (i.e. cut each other in half).
- Its opposite angles are equal. That is:

  angle BAD = angle BCD

  angle ABC = angle ADC

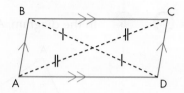

Rectangle

- A rectangle is a parallelogram with all its sides equal.
- All four angles are right angles.
- Its opposite sides are equal in length.

Rhombus

- A rhombus is a parallelogram with all its sides equal.
- Its diagonals bisect each other at right angles.
- Its diagonals also bisect the angles.

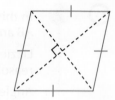

Square

- A square is a rhombus with all its angles equal (90°).

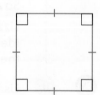

Kite

- A kite is a quadrilateral with two pairs of equal adjacent sides.
- Its longer diagonal bisects its shorter diagonal at right angles.
- The opposite angles between the sides of different lengths are equal.

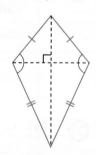

Trapezium

- A trapezium has two parallel sides.
- The sum of the interior angles at the ends of each non-parallel side is 180°. That is:

  angle BAD + angle ADC = 180°

  angle ABC + angle BCD = 180°

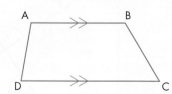

1 For each of these shapes calculate the sizes of the lettered angles.

a
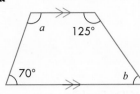

b
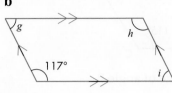

c
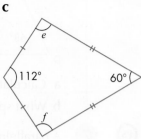

2 For each of these shapes calculate the sizes of the lettered angles.

a

b
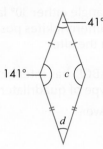

c
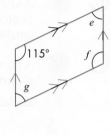

3 For each of these shapes calculate the value of x.

a
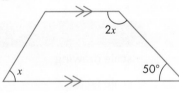

b
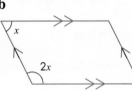

c
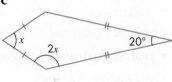

4 Dani is making a kite where angle C is half the size of angle A.

Work out the size of angles B and D.

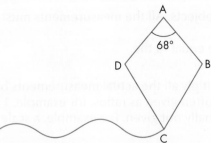

EV **5** David says that a parallelogram is a special type of rectangle.

Marie says that he is wrong and that a rectangle is a special type of parallelogram.

Who is correct? Give a reason for your answer.

6 The diagram shows a quadrilateral ABCD.

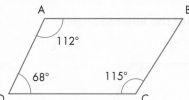

a Calculate the size of angle B.

b What special name is given to the quadrilateral ABCD? Explain your answer.

  7 A parallelogram has a pair of allied angles such that one is three times as large as the other. What is the size of that largest angle?

  8 A kite has every angle either 30° larger or 30° smaller than another one in the kite. Sketch the two different kites possible from this data and state the size of the smallest angle in the kite.

  9 A quadrilateral ABCD has interior angles of size x, $2x$, $3x$ and $4x$ respectively at A, B, C and D. What type of quadrilateral is this?

Explain your answer.

6.7 Scale drawings and bearings

This section will show you how to:

- read scale drawings and maps
- draw scale drawings
- use a bearing to specify a direction.

<table>
<tr><td>**Key terms**</td></tr>
<tr><td>scale drawing</td></tr>
<tr><td>scale factor</td></tr>
<tr><td>three-figure bearing</td></tr>
</table>

Scale drawings

A **scale drawing** is an accurate representation of a real object.

Scale drawings are usually smaller than the original objects. All the measurements must be in proportion to the corresponding
measurements of the original. All the angles must be equal to the
corresponding angles on the original.

To obtain the measurements for a scale drawing, multiply all the actual measurements by a common **scale factor**, usually referred to as a scale. Scales are often given as ratios, for example, 1 cm : 1 m. When the units in a ratio are the *same*, they are normally not given. For example, a scale of 1 cm : 1000 cm is written as 1 : 1000.

Note: When you are making a scale drawing, take care to express *all* measurements in the *same* unit.

Example 8

The diagram shows the front of a kennel.

It is drawn to a scale of 1 : 30. Find:

a the actual width of the front

b the actual height of the doorway.

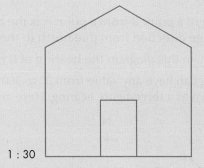

1 : 30

The scale of 1 : 30 means that a measurement of 1 cm on the diagram represents a measurement of 30 cm on the actual kennel.

a So the actual width of the front is: 4 cm × 30 = 120 cm

b The actual height of the doorway is: 1.5 cm × 30 = 45 cm

Map scales are often expressed as ratios, such as 1 : 50 000 or 1 : 200 000.

The first ratio means that 1 cm on the map represents 50 000 cm or 500 m in the real situation. The second ratio means that 1 cm represents 200 000 cm or 2 km.

Example 9

Find the actual distances between the following towns.

a Bran and Kelv   **b** Bran and Daid   **c** Daid and Malm

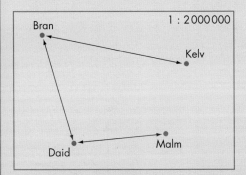

1 : 2 000 000

The map is drawn to a scale of 1 : 2 000 000.

2 000 000 cm = 20 000 m = 20 km so the scale means that a distance of 1 cm on the map represents a distance of 20 km on the land.

So, the actual distances are:

a Bran and Kelv: 4 × 20 km = 80 km

b Bran and Daid: 3 × 20 km = 60 km

c Daid and Malm: 2.5 × 20 km = 50 km

Bearings

The bearing of a point B from a point A is the angle through which you turn *clockwise* as you change direction from due north to the direction of B.

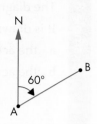

For example, in this diagram the bearing of B from A is 060°.

As a bearing can have any value from 0° to 360°, you give all bearings in three figures. This is known as a **three-figure bearing**. Here are three more examples of bearings.

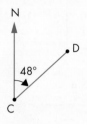

D is on a bearing of 048° from C

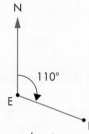

F is on a bearing of 110° from E

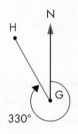

H is on a bearing of 330° from G

There are eight bearings you should be familiar with:

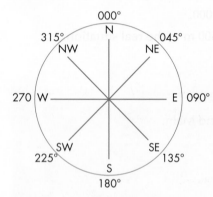

A, B and C are three towns.

a Write down the bearing of B from A and the bearing of C from A.

b Use the scale to work out the actual distances between:

   i A and B   **ii** A and C.

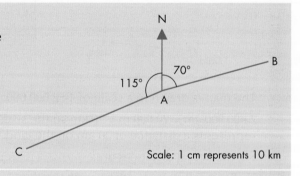

Scale: 1 cm represents 10 km

a The bearing of B from A is 070°.

The bearing of C from A is 360° − 115° = 245°.

Remember: A bearing is always measured clockwise from the north line.

b i On the diagram AB is 3 cm, so the actual distance between A and B is 30 km.

  ii On the diagram AC is 4 cm, so the actual distance between A and C is 40 km.

Exercise 6H

1 The diagram shows a sketch of a garden.

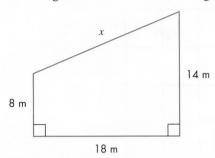

a Make an accurate scale drawing of the garden. Use a scale of 1 cm to represent 2 m.

b Marie wants to plant flowers along the side marked x on the diagram. The flowers need to be planted 0.5 m apart. Use your scale drawing to work out how many plants she needs.

2 This map is drawn to a scale of 1 : 4 000 000.

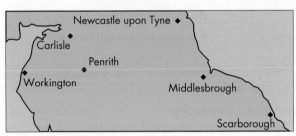

Give the approximate direct distances for each of the following.

a Penrith to:

   i Workington   **ii** Scarborough

   iii Newcastle upon Tyne   **iv** Carlisle

b Middlesbrough to:

   i Scarborough   **ii** Workington

   iii Carlisle   **iv** Penrith

3 This map is drawn to a scale of 1 : x.

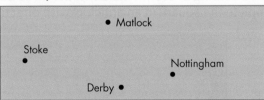

The distance from Stoke to Nottingham is 80 km.

a State the actual direct distance from Matlock to Derby.

b What is the value of x in the scale 1 : x?

4 Maps for walkers often give a scale of 1 inch represents 1 mile. Use these measurements to write this scale as a ratio.

12 inches = 1 foot   3 feet = 1 yard   1760 yards = 1 mile

5 This map is drawn on a centimetre-squared grid, to a scale of 1 cm to 2 km.

By measuring distances and angles, find the bearings and distances of each of the following.

N ↑

Greystones •

Abbey •

Ecclesall •

Dore •

Millhouses •

Totley •

a Totley from Dore

b Dore from Ecclesall

c Millhouses from Dore

d Greystones from Abbey

e Millhouses from Greystones

f Totley from Millhouses

6 Draw sketches to illustrate these situations.

a Castleton is on a bearing of 170° from Hope.

b Bude is on a bearing of 310° from Wadebridge.

(CM) **7** A is due north of C. B is due east of A. B is on a bearing of 045° from C.

a Sketch the layout of the three points, A, B and C.

b D is due south of B.

Al said that the bearing of A from D is 030°.

Explain how you know that Al must be wrong.

8 Captain Bird decided to sail his ship around the four sides of a square kilometre.

a Assuming he started sailing due north, write down the three bearings he should follow in order to complete the square in a clockwise direction.

b Assuming he started sailing on a bearing of 090°, write down the three bearings he should follow in order to complete the square in an anticlockwise direction.

(MR) **9** The diagram shows a port P and two harbours X and Y on the coast.

a A fishing boat sails to X from P.

What is the three-figure bearing of X from P?

b A yacht sails to Y from P.

What is the three-figure bearing of Y from P?

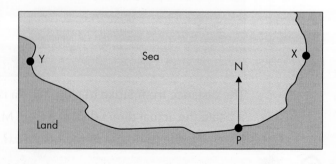

c Point X is 15 km away from point Y.

Show that it is 11.8 km from point Y to point P.

10 Draw diagrams to solve these problems.

   a The three-figure bearing of A from B is 070°. Work out the three-figure bearing of B from A.

   b The three-figure bearing of P from Q is 145°. Work out the three-figure bearing of Q from P.

   c The three-figure bearing of X from Y is 324°. Work out the three-figure bearing of Y from X.

11 The diagram shows the position of Kim's house (H) and the college (C).

   Scale: 1 cm represents 200 m

   a Use the diagram to work out the actual distance from Kim's house to the college.

   b Measure and write down the three-figure bearing of the college from Kim's house.

   c The supermarket (S) is 600 m from Kim's house on a bearing of 150°.

     Mark S on a copy of the diagram.

(PS) **12** Trevor is flying a plane on a bearing of 072°.

He is instructed by a control tower to turn and fly due south towards an airport.

Through what angle does he need to turn?

(PS) **13** Apple Bay (A), Broadside (B) and Caverly (C) are three villages in a bay.

The villages lie on the vertices of a square.

The bearing of B from A is 030°.

Work out the bearing of Apple Bay from Caverly.

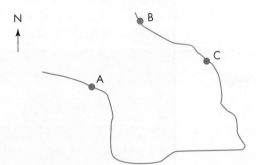

(PS) **14** Bryony set sail from Port Terry on a bearing of 036°. After sailing 5 km, she changed course on a bearing due east. After sailing a further 5 km, she changed course to sail due south. After sailing a further 10 km, Bryony sailed straight back to Port Terry. Find the length of the final part of Bryony's journey.

Worked exemplars

  1 ABC is a triangle. D is a point on AB such that BC = BD.

a Work out the value of x.

b Work out the value of y.

c Is it true that AD = DC? Give a reason for your answer.

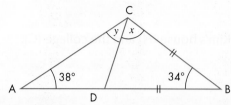

This is a question where you are required to communicate mathematically. You will need to clearly show how you have found the indicated angles and clearly explain your final response to part **c**.	
a Triangle BCD is isosceles, so angle BDC is equal to x. Angles in a triangle = 180° Therefore, $\quad 2x + 34° = 180°$ $\qquad\qquad 2x = 146°$ $\qquad\qquad x = 73°$	First, set up an equation in x from the knowledge that angles in a triangle add up to 180° and then solve.
b Method 1 Angle ADC = 180° − 73° $\qquad\qquad\quad = 107°$ (*angles on a line*) $y + 38° + 107° = 180°$ (*angles in a triangle*) $\quad y + 145° = 180°$ $\qquad\qquad y = 35°$ **Method 2** Angle ACB = 180° − (38° + 34°) $\qquad\qquad\quad = 108°$ (*angles in a triangle*) $y + x =$ Angle ACB $\qquad = 108°$ $\quad y = 108° − 73°$ $\qquad = 35°$	To find angle y, you need to show how you are using the given angles and the found angle x. You should show the mathematical reasoning used at each stage. There are two ways of finding y here. Both are acceptable.
c No, since triangle ACD is not an isosceles triangle, no two sides of the triangle are equal.	Clearly state your explanation about ACD not being isosceles. The answer 'No', alone, is not sufficient.

2 **a** Find the value of x.

b What can you deduce about lines AB and DC?

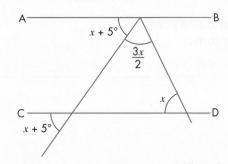

Part **a** is a problem-solving question, then part **b**, as an evaluation problem, requires you to to demonstrate your interpretive skills.

a Bottom left angle of the triangle is given by $x + 5$ as vertically opposite angles are equal. $x + x + 5 + \frac{3x}{2} = 180$ (*sum of angles in a triangle*) $\qquad x = 50°$	In this problem-solving question, you need to identify where there is a combination of angles with x included where you know the angle sum. There is another way of recognising that, with AB and CD being parallel, the top missing angle is x (*allied angle*). Then angles marked $(x + 5)$, $(\frac{3x}{2})$ and x add up to 180.
b Since there are two angles of $x + 5$, below the line AB and above the line DC, they are complementary angles and so imply that lines AB and DC are parallel.	This is an evaluation question where you need to demonstrate that you can interpret the results in a given situation. So you need to evaluate the scenario correctly and recognise that a pair of complementary angles implies parallel lines.

Ready to progress?

I can find angles on a line or at a point.
I can find angles in triangles, quadrilaterals and polygons.
I can find interior and exterior angles in polygons.
I can use scale drawings and bearings.

Review questions

(PS) **1** The diagram shows three angles on a straight line.

What is the value of x?

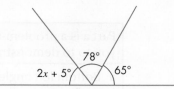

2 Look at the diagram.

a i Write down the value of x.

(CM) **ii** Give a reason for your answer.

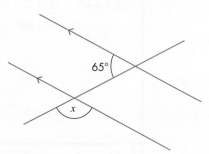

(EV) **b** Explain what is wrong with this diagram.

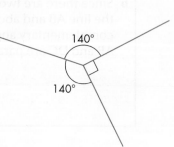

(PS) **3** Look at the triangle PQR.

a What is the size of the angle at P?

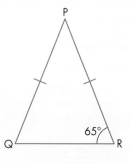

b The diagram has been extended to point T as shown.

What is the size of the acute angle at T?

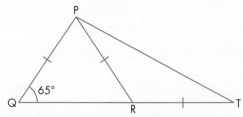

CM **4** Explain why the interior angles of a pentagon add up to 540°.

MR **5** A quadrilateral has three angles of x, $3x$, $5x$ and a right angle.

What is the size of the largest angle in the quadrilateral?

CM **6** Look at the diagram below and show that angle QTS is 66°.

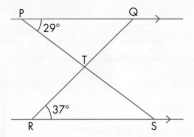

CM **7** Kwana sails from Port Kelly on a bearing of 153°. What bearing should he set to sail directly back?

CM **8** The diagram shows a regular octagon.

The exterior angle, x, is shown.

Explain how you know that angle x is 45°.

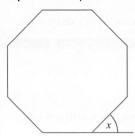

MR **9** This diagram shows a regular hexagon.

One of its interior angles is y.

Calculate the value of y.

EV **10** Selvi said that she had drawn a quadrilateral with opposite angles of 130°, so the shape must be a kite.

Explain whether Selvi must be correct or may be correct.

PS **11** A lighthouse is 35 km away from the lifeboat station on a bearing of 055°.

a Construct a diagram to show the positions of the lighthouse and the lifeboat station. Use a scale of 1 cm to represent 5 km.

b A lifeboat sails from the station on a bearing of 075° until it is due south of the lighthouse. How far away from the lighthouse is the lifeboat at this point?

7 Geometry and measures: Transformations, constructions and loci

This chapter is going to show you:

- how to show that two triangles are congruent
- how to find the order of rotational symmetry of a 2D shape
- what is meant by a transformation
- how to translate, reflect, rotate and enlarge 2D shapes
- how to bisect a line and an angle
- how to construct perpendiculars
- how to define a locus
- how to solve locus problems
- how to construct and interpret plans and elevations of 3D shapes.

You should already know:

- how to find the lines of symmetry of a 2D shape
- how to draw the lines with equations $x = \pm a$, $y = \pm b$, $y = x$ and $y = -x$
- how to measure lines and angles
- how to use scale drawings.

About this chapter

When a major new train line is planned, people often voice objections – from proximity to their village to avoiding areas of natural beauty – so the path traced out for a new rail route has to satisfy specific conditions, such as missing a village or a forest.

When a point moves according to certain specified conditions, the path traced out is called a *locus* (plural *loci*). This is a Latin word which means 'place'. Loci have a range of practical applications including helping to decide on suitable routes for a new train line.

This chapter is going to show you how to change the position of shapes to certain rules and how to construct loci from given criteria.

7.1 Congruent triangles

This section will show you how to:

- demonstrate that two triangles are congruent.

Two shapes are **congruent** if they are exactly the same size and shape.

For example, these triangles are all congruent.

Notice that the triangles can be differently oriented (reflected, translated or rotated).

Conditions for congruent triangles

Any one of the following four conditions is sufficient for two triangles to be congruent.

Condition 1

All three sides of one triangle are equal to the corresponding sides of the other triangle.

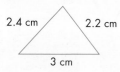

This condition is known as SSS (side, side, side).

Condition 2

Two sides and the angle between them of one triangle are equal to the corresponding sides and angle of the other triangle.

This condition is known as SAS (side, angle, side).

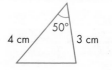

Condition 3

Two angles and a side of one triangle are equal to the corresponding angles and side of the other triangle.

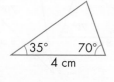 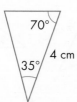 or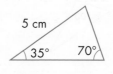

This condition is known as ASA (angle, side, angle) or AAS (angle, angle, side).

Condition 4

Both triangles have a right angle, an equal hypotenuse and another equal side.

This condition is known as RHS (right angle, hypotenuse, side).

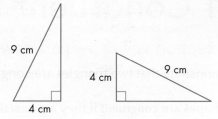

Notation

Once you have shown that triangle ABC is congruent to triangle PQR by one of the above conditions, it means that:

∠A = ∠P	AB = PQ
∠B = ∠Q	BC = QR
∠C = ∠R	AC = PR

In other words, the points ABC correspond exactly to the points PQR in that order. Triangle ABC is congruent to triangle PQR can be written as ΔABC ≡ ΔPQR.

Example 1

ABCD is a kite.

Show that triangle ABC is congruent to triangle ADC.

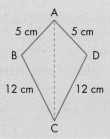

AB = AD

BC = CD

AC is common.

So ΔABC ≡ ΔADC (SSS).

Exercise 7A

1 The triangles in each pair are congruent. State the condition that shows that the triangles are congruent.

a

b

c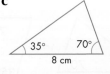

d

e

f

(MR) **2** The triangles in each pair are congruent. State the condition that shows that the triangles are congruent and write down the corresponding points.

a ABC where AB = 8 cm, BC = 9 cm, AC = 7.4 cm

   PQR where PQ = 9 cm, QR = 7.4 cm, PR = 8 cm

b ABC where AB = 5 cm, BC = 6 cm, ∠B = 35°

   PQR where PQ = 6 cm, QR = 50 mm, ∠Q = 35°

3 Triangle ABC is congruent to triangle PQR; ∠A = 60°, ∠B = 80° and AB = 5 cm. Find these.

a ∠P   **b** ∠Q   **c** ∠R   **d** PQ

4 ABCD is congruent to PQRS; ∠A = 110°, ∠B = 55°, ∠C = 85° and RS = 4 cm. Find these.

a ∠P   **b** ∠Q   **c** ∠R   **d** ∠S   **e** CD

(CM) **5** Draw a rectangle EFGH. Draw in the diagonal EG. Prove that triangle EFG is congruent to triangle EHG.

(CM) **6** Draw an isosceles triangle ABC where AB = AC. Draw the line from A to X, the midpoint of BC. Prove that triangle ABX is congruent to triangle ACX.

(MR) **7** In the diagram ABCD and DEFG are squares.

Use congruent triangles to prove that AE = CG.

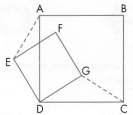

(EV) **8** Jez says that these two triangles are congruent because two angles and a side are the same.

Explain why he is wrong.

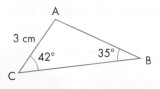
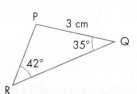

7.2 Rotational symmetry

This section will show you how to:

- find the order of rotational symmetry for a 2D shape
- recognise shapes with rotational symmetry.

Key terms

order of rotational symmetry

rotational symmetry

A 2D shape has **rotational symmetry** if it can be rotated about a point to look exactly the same in a new position.

The **order of rotational symmetry** is the number of different positions in which the shape looks the same when it is rotated about the point.

One way to find the order of rotational symmetry for any shape is to trace it and count the number of times that the shape stays the same as you turn the tracing paper through one complete turn.

Example 2

Find the order of rotational symmetry for this shape.

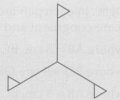

First, hold the tracing paper on top of the shape and trace the shape. Place the sharp end of a pencil on the centre of the shape and rotate the tracing paper, counting the number of times the tracing matches the original shape in one complete turn.

You will find three different positions.

So the order of rotational symmetry for the shape is 3.

Exercise 7B

1. Find the order of rotational symmetry for each of these shapes.

   a   b   c   d   e

2. The following are Greek capital letters. Write down the order of rotational symmetry for each one.

   a **Φ**   b **H**   c **Z**   d **Θ**   e **Ξ**

(PS) 3. The upright capital letter A fits exactly onto itself only once. So, its order of rotational symmetry is 1. This means that it has no rotational symmetry. Write down all the upright capital letters of the alphabet that have rotational symmetry of order 1.

(MR) 4. Here is an Islamic star pattern.

   Inside the star there are patterns that have rotational symmetry.

   a What is the order of rotational symmetry of the whole star?

   b There is a pattern inside the shape with an order of rotational symmetry 8. Identify where this pattern is found.

   c There is another pattern inside the star with an order of rotational symmetry higher than 8. What is it and where is it found?

(PS) 5. Copy the grid below. On your copy, shade in four squares so that the shape has rotational symmetry of order 2.

(MR) **6** Copy the table below. On your copy, write the letter for each shape in the correct box. The first one has been done for you.

		Number of lines of symmetry			
		0	1	2	3
Order of rotational symmetry	1		A		
	2				
	3				

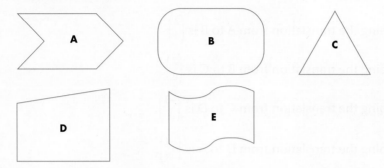

(EV) **7** A shape with three flagpoles has rotational symmetry of order 3.

Sue says, "The angle between each pole is 120°."

Evaluate Sue's comment.

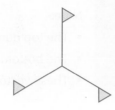

(EV) **8** Rachel looked at a triangle and said: "It has line symmetry but no rotational symmetry so it must be isosceles." Is Rachel correct? Explain your answer.

7.3 Transformations

This section will show you how to:

• translate, reflect, rotate and enlarge a 2D shape.

A **transformation** changes the position or the size of a shape.

The original shape is called the **object** and the transformed shape is called the **image**.

There are four basic ways of transforming 2D shapes: **translation**, **reflection**, **rotation** and **enlargement**.

Key terms	
angle of rotation	
centre of enlargement	
centre of rotation	
enlargement	
image	
invariant	mirror line
object	reflection
rotation	transformation
translation	vector

Translation

A translation is the 'movement' of a shape from one place to another without enlarging it, reflecting it or rotating it. It is sometimes called a glide, since the shape appears to glide from one place to another. Every point in the shape moves in the same direction and through the same distance.

You describe translations by using **vectors**. A vector is represented by the combination of a horizontal shift and a vertical shift.

The object and its image will always be congruent.

Example 3

Use vectors to describe the translations of the following triangles.

a A to B

b B to C

c C to D

d D to A

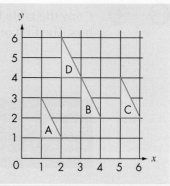

a The vector describing the translation from A to B is $\begin{pmatrix} 2 \\ 1 \end{pmatrix}$.

b The vector describing the translation from B to C is $\begin{pmatrix} 2 \\ 0 \end{pmatrix}$.

c The vector describing the translation from C to D is $\begin{pmatrix} -3 \\ 2 \end{pmatrix}$.

d The vector describing the translation from D to A is $\begin{pmatrix} -1 \\ -3 \end{pmatrix}$.

Note:

- The top number in the vector describes the horizontal movement. To the right +, to the left –.
- The bottom number in the vector describes the vertical movement. Upwards +, downwards –.
- These vectors are also called *direction vectors*.

Exercise 7C

1 Use vectors to describe the translations of the shapes on this grid.

a i A to B   **ii** A to C

   iii A to D   **iv** A to E

b i B to A   **ii** B to C

   iii B to F   **iv** B to G

c i C to D   **ii** C to E

   iii C to F   **iv** C to G

d i D to E   **ii** E to B

   iii F to C   **iv** G to D

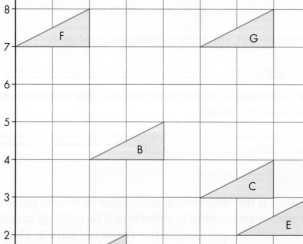

2 **a** Draw a set of coordinate axes, $-5 \leqslant x \leqslant 5$, $-5 \leqslant y \leqslant 5$. Draw the triangle with coordinates A(1, 1), B(2, 1) and C(1, 3).

    b Draw the image of ABC after a translation with vector $\begin{pmatrix} 2 \\ 3 \end{pmatrix}$. Label this triangle P.

    c Draw the image of ABC after a translation with vector $\begin{pmatrix} -1 \\ 2 \end{pmatrix}$. Label this triangle Q.

    d Draw the image of ABC after a translation with vector $\begin{pmatrix} 3 \\ -2 \end{pmatrix}$. Label this triangle R.

    e Draw the image of ABC after a translation with vector $\begin{pmatrix} -2 \\ -4 \end{pmatrix}$. Label this triangle S.

3 Using your diagram from question **2**, use vectors to describe the translation that will move:

    a P to Q   **b** Q to R   **c** R to S   **d** S to P

    e R to P   **f** S to Q   **g** R to Q   **h** P to S.

 4 Draw a set of coordinate axes, $-5 \leqslant x \leqslant 5$, $-5 \leqslant y \leqslant 5$. Draw the triangle with coordinates A(0, 0), B(1, 0) and C(0, 1). How many different translations are there that use integer values only and move the triangle ABC to somewhere in the grid?

 5 In a game of *Snakes and ladders*, each of the snakes and ladders can be described by a translation.

    Ladders $\begin{pmatrix} 1 \\ 2 \end{pmatrix}$, $\begin{pmatrix} 2 \\ 5 \end{pmatrix}$, $\begin{pmatrix} -3 \\ 4 \end{pmatrix}$, $\begin{pmatrix} -2 \\ 3 \end{pmatrix}$, $\begin{pmatrix} 3 \\ 2 \end{pmatrix}$

    Snakes $\begin{pmatrix} 1 \\ -3 \end{pmatrix}$, $\begin{pmatrix} 3 \\ -4 \end{pmatrix}$, $\begin{pmatrix} -2 \\ -2 \end{pmatrix}$, $\begin{pmatrix} -1 \\ -3 \end{pmatrix}$, $\begin{pmatrix} 2 \\ -5 \end{pmatrix}$

    a Put all five ladders and all five snakes described above onto a 10 by 10 coordinate grid in order to design a *Snakes and ladders* game board.

    b Explain why the bottom part of the vectors above are:

      i always positive for the ladders

      ii always negative for the snakes.

(MR) **6** If a translation is given by $\begin{pmatrix} x \\ y \end{pmatrix}$ describe the translation that would take the image back to the original position of the object.

(PS) **7** A plane flies between three cities: A, B and C. It uses direction vectors, with distances in kilometres.

    The direction vector for the flight from A to B is $\begin{pmatrix} 500 \\ 200 \end{pmatrix}$ and the direction vector for the flight from B to C is $\begin{pmatrix} -200 \\ 300 \end{pmatrix}$.

    a Using centimetre-squared paper, draw a diagram to show the three flights. Use a scale of 1 cm represents 100 km.

    b Work out the direction vector for the flight from C to A.

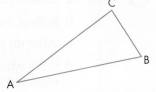

8 A pleasure launch travels between three jetties on a lake: X, Y and Z. It uses direction vectors, with distances in kilometres.

The direction vector from X to Y is $\begin{pmatrix} 3 \\ -1 \end{pmatrix}$ and the direction vector from Y to Z is $\begin{pmatrix} -2 \\ -3 \end{pmatrix}$.

a Using centimetre-squared paper, draw a diagram to show journeys between X, Y and Z. Use a scale of 1 cm to 1 km.

b Work out the direction vector for the journey from Z to X.

9 A triangle has been translated to a new position. Explain how you know the two triangles are congruent.

Reflections

A reflection transforms a shape so that it becomes a mirror image of itself.

Notice the reflection of each point in the object (original shape) is perpendicular to the **mirror line**. So if you 'fold' the whole diagram along the mirror line, the object will coincide with its image (reflection).

The object and image will always be congruent.

All transformations, except translations, have points that are **invariant** – they will not change. For example, in a reflection, any points on the line of reflection will be invariant.

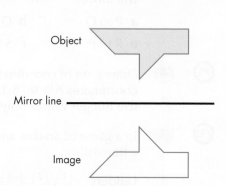

Object

Mirror line

Image

Exercise 7D

1 **a** Draw a pair of axes. Label the x-axis from –5 to 5 and the y-axis from –5 to 5.

b Draw the triangle with coordinates A(1, 1), B(3, 1) and C(4, 5).

c Reflect the triangle ABC in the x-axis. Label the image P.

d Reflect triangle P in the y-axis. Label the image Q.

e Reflect triangle Q in the x-axis. Label the image R.

f Describe the reflection that will move triangle ABC to triangle R.

2 **a** Draw a pair of axes. Label the x-axis from –5 to +5 and the y-axis from –5 to 5.

b Reflect the points A(2, 1), B(5, 0), C(–3, 3) and D(3, –2) in the x-axis.

c What do you notice about the values of the coordinates of the reflected points?

d What would the coordinates of the reflected point be if the point (a, b) were reflected in the x-axis?

3 **a** Draw a pair of axes. Label the x-axis from –5 to 5 and the y-axis from –5 to 5.

b Reflect the points A(2, 1), B(0, 5), C(3, –2) and D(–4, –3) in the y-axis.

c What do you notice about the values of the coordinates of the reflected points?

d What would the coordinates of the reflected point be if the point (a, b) were reflected in the y-axis?

e Write down three points that are invariant in a reflection in the y-axis.

(PS) 4 By using the middle square as the starting square ABCD, describe how to keep reflecting the square to obtain the final shape in the diagram.

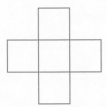

(MR) 5 Triangle A is drawn on a grid.

Triangle A is reflected to form a new triangle B.

The coordinates of B are (–4, 4), (–3, 1) and (–5, 1).

What is the equation of the mirror line?

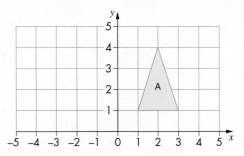

6 Draw each of these triangles on squared paper, leaving plenty of space on the opposite side of the given mirror line. Then draw the reflection of each triangle.

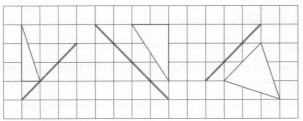

> **Hints and tips** Turn the page around so that the mirror lines are vertical or horizontal.

7 **a** Draw a pair of axes and the lines $y = x$ and $y = -x$, as shown.

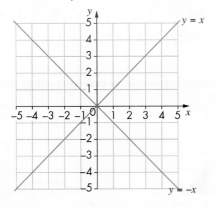

b Draw the triangle with coordinates A(2, 1), B(5, 1) and C(5, 3).

c Draw the reflection of triangle ABC in the x-axis and label the image P.

d Draw the reflection of triangle P in the line $y = -x$ and label the image Q.

e Draw the reflection of triangle Q in the y-axis and label the image R.

f Draw the reflection of triangle R in the line $y = x$ and label the image S.

g Draw the reflection of triangle S in the x-axis and label the image T.

h Draw the reflection of triangle T in the line $y = -x$ and label the image U.

i Draw the reflection of triangle U in the y-axis and label the image W.

j What single reflection will move triangle W to triangle ABC?

8 Copy the diagram and reflect the triangle in these lines.

    a $y = x$ **b** $x = 1$ **c** $y = -x$ **d** $y = -1$

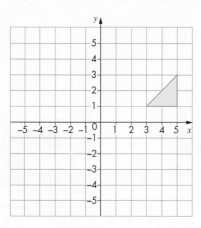

(EV) **9** **a** Draw a pair of axes. Label the x-axis from –5 to 5 and the y-axis from –5 to 5.

    b Draw the line $y = x$.

    c Reflect the points A(2, 1), B(5, 0), C(–3, 2) and D(–2, –4) in the line $y = x$.

    d What do you notice about the values of the coordinates of the reflected points?

    e What would the coordinates of the reflected point be if the point (a, b) were reflected in the line $y = x$?

    f Write down two points that are invariant in a reflection in the line $y = x$.

(EV) **10** **a** Draw a pair of axes. Label the x-axis from –5 to 5 and the y-axis from –5 to 5.

    b Draw the line $y = -x$.

    c Reflect the points A(2, 1), B(0, 5), C(3, –2) and D(–4, –3) in the line $y = -x$.

    d What do you notice about the values of the coordinates of the reflected points?

    e What would the coordinates of the reflected point be if the point (a, b) were reflected in the line $y = -x$?

(CM) **11** Triangle A has been reflected in a straight line. Explain how you know that the triangle A and its reflection are congruent.

Rotations

A rotation transforms a shape to a new position by turning it about a fixed point called the **centre of rotation**.

See how the shapes shown here are rotated around the points indicated.

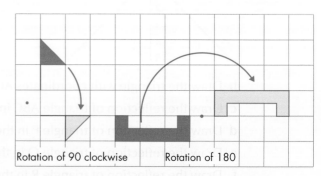

Rotation of 90 clockwise   Rotation of 180

Note:

- The direction of turn or the **angle of rotation** is expressed as clockwise or anticlockwise.

- The position of the centre of rotation is always specified.

- The rotations 180° clockwise and 180° anticlockwise are the same.

- When a shape is rotated, the rotated shape is congruent to the original shape.

- In a rotation, the point that is always invariant is the centre of rotation.

Exercise 7E

1 On squared paper, draw each of these shapes and its centre of rotation, leaving plenty of space all around the shape.

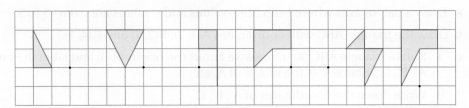

a Rotate each shape about its centre of rotation:

  i first by 90° clockwise (call the image A)

  ii then by 90° anticlockwise (call the image B).

b Describe, in each case, the rotation that would take:

  i A back to its original position   **ii** A to B.

2 A graphic designer came up with the following routine for creating a design.

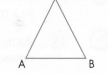

- Start with a triangle ABC.
- Reflect the triangle in the line AB.
- Rotate the whole shape about point C clockwise 90°, then a further clockwise 90°, then a further clockwise 90°.

a From any triangle of your choice, create a design using the above routine.

b Describe in detail how you could use the triangle above in a series of rotations to create a regular hexagon.

3 By using the middle square as a starting square ABCD, describe how to keep rotating the square to obtain the final shape in the diagram.

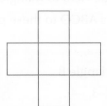

4 Copy the diagram and rotate the given triangle as described.

a 90° clockwise about (0, 0)

b 180° about (3, 3)

c 90° anticlockwise about (0, 2)

d 180° about (–1, 0)

e 90° clockwise about (–1, –1)

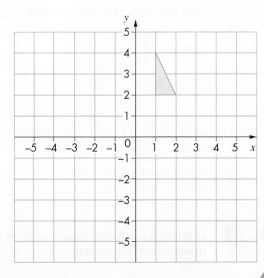

5 What other rotations are equivalent to these rotations?

    a 270° clockwise   **b** 90° clockwise   **c** 60° anticlockwise

    d 100° anticlockwise

(MR) 6   **a** Draw a pair of axes where both the *x*-values and *y*-values are from –5 to 5.

    b Draw the triangle ABC with coordinates A(1, 2), B(2, 4) and C(4, 1).

    c **i** Rotate triangle ABC 90° clockwise about the origin (0, 0) and label the image A′, B′, C′, where A′ is the image of A, etc.

      ii Write down the coordinates of A′, B′, C′.

      iii What connection is there between A, B, C and A′, B′, C′?

      iv Will this connection always be so for a 90° clockwise rotation about the origin?

(MR) 7 Repeat question **6**, but rotate triangle ABC through 180°.

(MR) 8 Repeat question **6**, but rotate triangle ABC 90° anticlockwise.

9 In a rotation of 90°, what point(s) will be invariant?

(CM) 10 Show that a reflection in the *x*-axis followed by a reflection in the *y*-axis is equivalent to a rotation of 180° about the origin.

(EV) 11 Raith said that a reflection in the line $y = x$ followed by a reflection in the line $y = -x$ is equivalent to a rotation of 180° about the origin.

    What can you say about Raith's comment?

12 **a** Draw a regular hexagon ABCDEF with centre O.

    b Using O as the centre of rotation, describe a transformation that will result in the following movements.

      i Triangle AOB to triangle BOC   **ii** Triangle AOB to triangle COD

      iii Triangle AOB to triangle DOE   **iv** Triangle AOB to triangle EOF

    c Describe the transformations that will move the rhombus ABCO to these positions.

      i Rhombus BCDO   **ii** Rhombus DEFO

13 Triangle A, as shown on the grid, is rotated to form a new triangle B.

The coordinates of the vertices of B are (0, –2), (–3, –2) and (–3, –4).

Describe fully the rotation that maps triangle A onto triangle B.

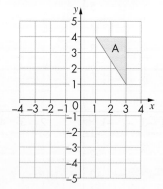

(CM) 14 Triangle B is rotated to form a new triangle C. Explain how you know that the two triangles are congruent.

Enlargements

An enlargement changes the size of a shape to give a similar image. It always has a **centre of enlargement** and a scale factor.

Every length of the enlarged shape will be original length × scale factor.

The distance of each image point on the enlargement from the centre of enlargement will be distance of original point from centre of enlargement × scale factor

The centre of enlargement is the only point in the enlargement that is invariant.

This diagram shows the enlargement of triangle ABC by scale factor 3 from the centre of enlargement X.

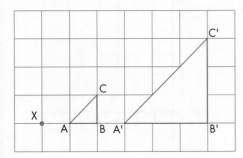

Note:

- Each length on the enlargement A′B′C′ is three times the corresponding length on the original shape. This means that the corresponding sides are in the same ratio:
  AB : A′B′ = AC : A′C′ = BC : B′C′ = 1 : 3

- The distance of any point on the enlargement from the centre of enlargement is three times the distance from the corresponding point on the original shape to the centre of enlargement.

- There are two distinct ways to enlarge a shape: the ray method and the coordinate, or counting squares, method.

Ray method

This is the *only* way to construct an enlargement when the diagram is not on a grid.

See how the triangle ABC has been enlarged by scale factor 3 from the centre of enlargement X.

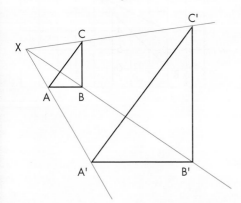

Notice that the rays have been drawn from the centre of enlargement to each vertex and beyond.

The distance from X to each vertex on triangle ABC is measured and multiplied by 3 to give the distance from X to each vertex A′, B′ and C′ for the enlarged triangle A′B′C′.

Once each image vertex has been found, the whole enlarged shape can then be drawn.

Check the measurements and see for yourself how the calculations have been done.

Notice again that the length of each side on the enlarged triangle is three times the length of the corresponding side on the original triangle.

Counting squares method

In this method, you use the coordinates of the vertices to 'count squares'.

See how the triangle ABC has been enlarged by scale factor 3 from the centre of enlargement (1, 2).

To find the coordinates of each image vertex, first work out the horizontal and vertical distances from each original vertex to the centre of enlargement.

Then multiply each of these distances by 3 to find the position of each image vertex.

For example, to find the coordinates of C' work out the distance from the centre of enlargement (1, 2) to the point C(3, 5).

horizontal distance = 2

vertical distance = 3

Make these 3 times longer to give:

new horizontal distance = 6

new vertical distance = 9

So the coordinates of C' are: (1 + 6, 2 + 9) = (7, 11)

Notice again that the length of each side is three times as long in the enlargement.

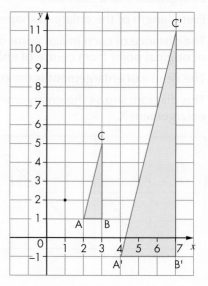

Negative enlargement

A negative enlargement produces an image shape on the opposite side of the centre of enlargement to the original shape.

See how triangle ABC has been enlarged by scale factor –2, with the centre of enlargement at (1, 0).

You can enlarge triangle ABC to give triangle A'B'C' by either the ray method or the coordinate method. You calculate the new lengths on the opposite side of the centre of enlargement to the original shape.

Notice how a negative scale factor also inverts the original shape.

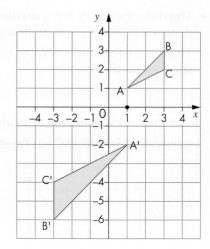

Fractional enlargement

You can have an enlargement in mathematics that is actually smaller than the original shape!

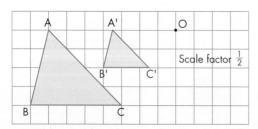

Scale factor $\frac{1}{2}$

See how triangle ABC has been enlarged by a scale factor of $\frac{1}{2}$ from the centre of enlargement O to give triangle A'B'C'.

Exercise 7F

1 Copy each of these shapes with its centre of enlargement. Use the ray method to enlarge it by the given scale factor.

a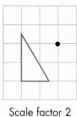

Scale factor 2

b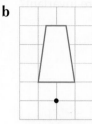

Scale factor 3

c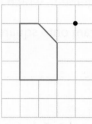

Scale factor 2

d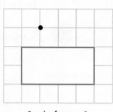

Scale factor 3

2 Copy each of these shapes and grids onto squared paper. Enlarge them by scale factor 2, using the given centre of enlargement.

a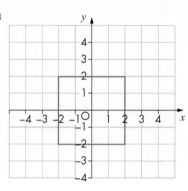

Centre of enlargement (–1, 1)

b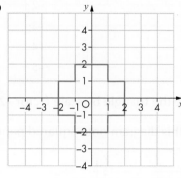

Centre of enlargement (–2, –3)

3 Enlarge each of these shapes by a scale factor of $\frac{1}{2}$ from the given centre of enlargement.

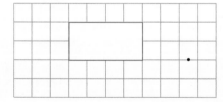 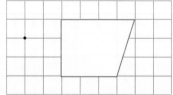

4 Copy this diagram onto squared paper.

a Enlarge the rectangle A by scale factor $\frac{1}{3}$ from the origin. Label the image B.

b Write down the ratio of the lengths of the sides of rectangle A to the lengths of the sides of rectangle B.

c Work out the ratio of the perimeter of rectangle A to the perimeter of rectangle B.

d Work out the ratio of the area of rectangle A to the area of rectangle B.

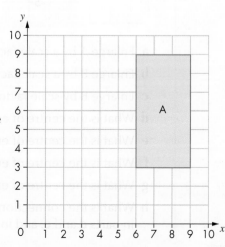

(MR) **5** A triangle ABC has vertices A(1, 1), B(2, –1), C(–2, –2). It is enlarged by scale factor 2, with a centre of enlargement (1, 1).

    a What are the coordinates of the vertices of the enlarged shape?

    b In this enlargement, which point(s) are invariant?

6 Copy this diagram onto squared paper.

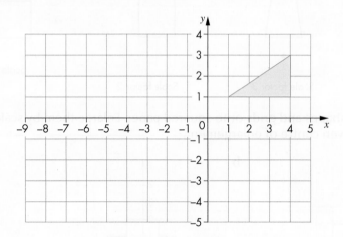

Enlarge the triangle by scale factor –2 from the origin.

(PS) **7** Copy this diagram onto squared paper.

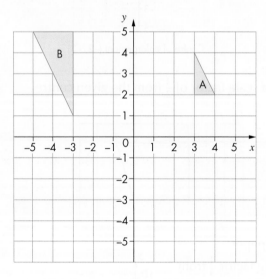

    a Enlarge A by a scale factor of 3 from a centre (4, 5). Label It C.

    b Enlarge B by a scale factor $\frac{1}{2}$ from a centre (–1, –3). Label it D.

    c Enlarge B by scale factor $-\frac{1}{2}$ from a centre (–3, –1). Label it E.

    d What is the centre of enlargement and scale factor which maps B onto A?

    e What is the centre of enlargement and scale factor which maps A onto B?

    f What is the centre of enlargement and scale factor which maps D onto E?

    g What is the centre of enlargement and scale factor which maps E onto D?

    h What is the connection between the scale factors and the centres of enlargement in parts **d** and **e**, and in parts **f** and **g**?

(PS) **8** Triangle A has vertices with coordinates (2, 1), (4, 1) and (4, 4).

Triangle B has vertices with coordinates (–5, 1), (–5, 7) and (–1, 7).

Describe fully the single transformation that maps triangle A onto triangle B.

(CM) **9** Triangle B has been enlarged by a scale factor of 1.5 to create triangle C. Explain how you know the two triangles are not congruent.

7.4 Combinations of transformations

This section will show you how to:

• combine transformations.

You often have to use more than one transformation in a question. In this exercise, you will practise combining the transformations you have met so far.

Remember:

• to describe a translation fully, you need to use a vector
• to describe a reflection fully, you need to use a mirror line
• to describe a rotation fully, you need a centre of rotation, an angle of rotation and the direction of turn
• to describe an enlargement fully, you need a centre of enlargement and a scale factor.

Exercise 7G

1 A point P(3, 4) is reflected in the *x*-axis, then rotated by 90° clockwise about the origin. What are the coordinates of the image of P?

(MR) **2** A point Q(5, 2) is rotated by 180°, then reflected in the *x*-axis.

a What are the coordinates of the image of point Q?

b What single transformation would have taken point Q directly to the image point?

(CM) **3** Describe fully the transformations that will map the shaded triangle onto each of the triangles A–F.

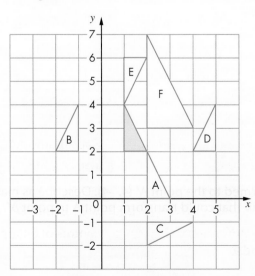

4 A designer is told to use the following routine.

- Start with a rectangle ABCD.
- Reflect ABCD in the line AC.
- Rotate the whole new shape about C through 180°.
- Enlarge the whole shape scale factor 2, centre of enlargement point A.

Start with any rectangle of your choice and create the design above.

CM 5 Describe fully the transformations that will result in the following movements.

a T₁ to T₂

b T₁ to T₆

c T₂ to T₃

d T₆ to T₂

e T₆ to T₅

f T₅ to T₄

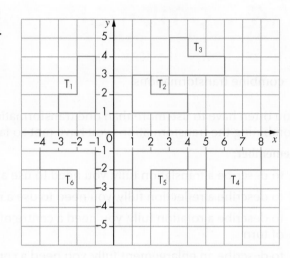

CM 6
a Plot a triangle T with vertices (1, 1), (2, 1) and (1, 3).

b Reflect triangle T in the y-axis and label the image T$_b$.

c Rotate triangle T$_b$ 90° anticlockwise about the origin and label the image T$_c$.

d Reflect triangle T$_c$ in the y-axis and label the image T$_d$.

e Describe fully the transformation that will move triangle T$_d$ back to triangle T.

7 Find the coordinates of the image of the point (3, 5) after a clockwise rotation of 90° about the point (1, 3).

CM 8 Describe fully at least three different transformations that could move the square labelled S to the square labelled T.

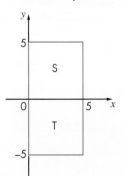

PS 9 The point A (4, 4) has been transformed to the point A′ (4, −4). Describe as many different transformations as you can that could transform point A to point A′.

CM **10** Copy the diagram onto squared paper.

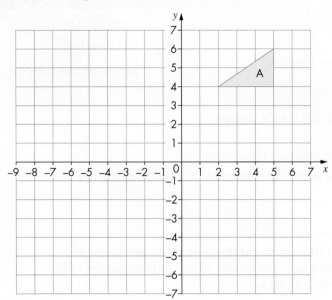

a Triangle A is translated by the vector $\begin{pmatrix} -1.5 \\ -3 \end{pmatrix}$ to give triangle B.

Triangle B is then enlarged by a scale factor -2 from the origin to give triangle C.

Draw triangles B and C on your diagram.

b Describe fully the single transformation that maps triangle C onto triangle A.

EV **11** Helen said that if you reflect a shape in line $y = A$ then reflect that image in a line $y = B$ (where A and B are any numbers), the final image is always a rotation from the original.

Is this is true?

12 Triangle ABC has vertices A(6, 0), B(6, 9), C(9, 3).

a Rotate triangle ABC through 180° about the point (2, 4). Label the image R.

b Enlarge triangle ABC by scale factor $\frac{1}{3}$ from the centre of enlargement (3, 0). Label the image E.

c Describe fully the single transformation which maps E onto R.

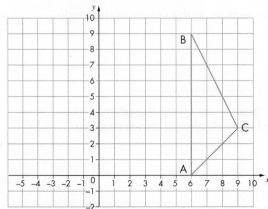

MR **13** Consider reflecting a shape in the line $y = x$ and then reflecting the shape in the line $x = 10$. Which is the only point of invariance in the combined transformation?

7.5 Bisectors

This section will show you how to:

- construct the bisectors of lines and angles
- construct angles of 60° and 90°.

To bisect means to divide in half. So a bisector divides something into two equal parts.

A **line bisector** divides a straight line into two equal lengths.

An **angle bisector** is the straight line that divides an angle into two equal angles.

To construct a line bisector

Step 1: Here is a line to bisect.

Step 2: Open your compasses to a radius of about three-quarters of the length of the line. Using each end of the line as a centre, and without changing the radius of your compasses, draw two intersecting arcs.

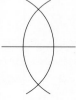

Step 3: Join the two points where the arcs intersect. This line is the **perpendicular bisector** of the original line.

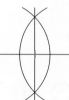

To construct an angle bisector

Step 1: Here is an angle to bisect.

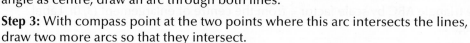

Step 2: Open your compasses to any reasonable radius that is less than the length of the lines forming the angle. If in doubt, go for about 3 cm. With the vertex of the angle as centre, draw an arc through both lines.

Step 3: With compass point at the two points where this arc intersects the lines, draw two more arcs so that they intersect.

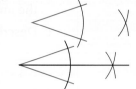

Step 4: Join the point where these two arcs intersect to the vertex of the angle. This line is the angle bisector.

To construct an angle of 60°

Step 1: Draw a line and mark a point on it.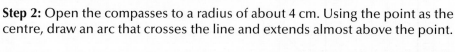

Step 2: Open the compasses to a radius of about 4 cm. Using the point as the centre, draw an arc that crosses the line and extends almost above the point.

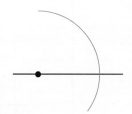

Step 3: Keep the compasses set to the same radius. Using the point where the first arc crosses the line as a centre, draw another arc that intersects the first one.

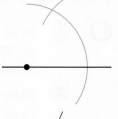

Step 4: Join the original point to the point where the two arcs intersect.

Step 5: Use a protractor to check that the angle is 60°.

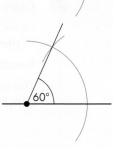

To construct a perpendicular from a point on a line (an angle of 90°)

Step 1: Draw a line and mark a point on it.

Step 2: Open your compasses to about 2 or 3 cm. With point A as the centre, draw two short arcs to intersect the line at each side of the point.

Step 3: Extend the radius of your compasses to about 4 cm. With centres at the two points where the arcs intersect the line, draw two arcs to intersect at X above the line.

Step 4: Join AX.

AX is perpendicular to the line.

Note that if you needed to construct a 90° angle at the end of a line, you would first have to extend the line.

You could be even more accurate by also drawing two arcs underneath the line, which would give three points in line.

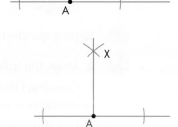

To construct a perpendicular from a point to a line

Note: this perpendicular distance from a point to a line is the shortest distance to the line.

Step 1: With point A as centre, draw an arc that intersects the line at two points.

Step 2: Using these two points of intersection as centres, draw two arcs to intersect each other both above and below the line.

Step 3: Join the two points where the arcs intersect.

The resulting line passes through point A and is perpendicular to the line.

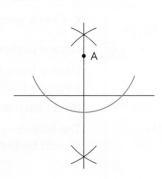

Note: When a question says *construct*, you must *only* use compasses, not a protractor. When it says *draw*, you may use whatever you can to produce an accurate diagram. But also note, when constructing you may use your protractor to check your accuracy.

Exercise 7H ▦

(EV) **1** Draw a line 7 cm long and bisect it. Check your accuracy by measuring each half.

> **Hints and tips** Remember to show your construction lines.

2 Draw a circle of about 4 cm radius.

Draw a triangle inside the circle so that the corners of the triangle touch the circle.

Bisect each side of the triangle.

The bisectors should all meet at the same point, which should be the centre of the circle.

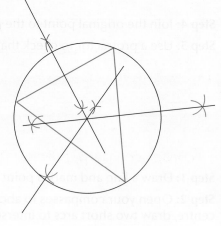

3 **a** Draw any triangle with sides that are between 5 cm and 10 cm.

b On each side construct the line bisector.

Your line bisectors should all intersect at the same point.

c Using this point as the centre, draw a circle that goes through every vertex of the triangle.

4 Repeat question **3** with a different triangle and check that you get a similar result.

5 **a** Draw the following quadrilateral.

b Construct the line bisector of each side. These all should intersect at the same point.

c Use this point as the centre of a circle that goes through the quadrilateral at each vertex. Draw this circle.

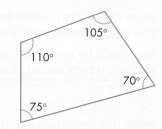

(EV) **6** **a** Draw an angle of 50°.

b Construct the angle bisector.

c Check your accuracy by measuring each half.

7 Draw a circle with a radius of about 3 cm.

Draw a triangle so that the sides of the triangle are tangents to the circle.

Bisect each angle of the triangle.

The bisectors should all meet at the same point, which should be the centre of the circle.

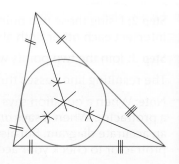

8 **a** Draw any triangle with sides that are between 5 cm and 10 cm.

b At each angle construct the angle bisector. All three bisectors should intersect at the same point.

c Use this point as the centre of a circle that just touches the sides of the triangle.

9 Repeat question **8** with a different triangle.

(PS) **10** Draw a circle with radius about 4 cm.

Draw a quadrilateral, *not* a rectangle, inside the circle so that each vertex is on the circumference.

Construct the bisector of each side of the quadrilateral.

Where is the point where these bisectors all meet?

(CM) **11** Briefly outline how you would construct a triangle with angles 90°, 60° and 30°.

12 **a** Draw a line AB, 6 cm long, and construct an angle of 90° at A.

b Bisect this angle to construct an angle of 45°.

13 **a** Draw a line AB, 6 cm long, and construct an angle of 60° at A.

b Bisect this angle to construct an angle of 30°.

14 Draw a line AB, 6 cm long, and mark a point C, 4 cm above the middle of the line.

Construct the perpendicular from the point C to the line AB.

7.6 Defining a locus

This section will show you how to:

- draw a locus for a given rule.

Key terms	
equidistant	locus (loci)

A **locus** (plural **loci**) is the movement of a point according to a given rule.

Example 4

What is the locus of a point that is always 5 cm away from a fixed point A?

The locus of the point (P) is such that AP = 5 cm. This will give a circle of radius 5 cm, centre A.

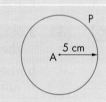

Example 5

What is the locus of a point that is always the same distance from two fixed points A and B?

The locus of the point P is such that AP = BP.

This will have a locus that is the perpendicular bisector of the line joining A and B.

Note that a point that is always the same distance from two points is **equidistant** from the two points.

.A

P

.B

Example 6

What is the locus of a point that is always 5 cm from a line AB?

A point that moves so that it is always 5 cm from a line AB will have a locus that is a racetrack shape around the line.

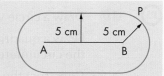

Questions will often ask about practical situations rather than abstract mathematical ones.

Example 7

Imagine a grassy, flat field in which a horse is tethered to a stake by a rope that is 10 m long. What is the shape of the area that the horse can graze?

In reality, the horse may not be able to reach the full 10 m if the rope is tied round its neck but ignore fine details like that. You 'model' the situation by saying that the horse can move around in a 10 m circle and graze all the grass within that circle.

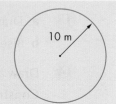

In this example, the locus is the whole of the area inside the circle.

You can express this mathematically as:

the locus of the point P is such that AP ⩽ 10 m.

Exercise 7I

1 A is a fixed point. Draw the locus of the point P in each of these situations.

   a AP = 2 cm   **b** AP = 4 cm   **c** AP = 5 cm

   > **Hints and tips**   Sketch the situation before doing an accurate drawing.

2 A and B are two fixed points 5 cm apart. Draw the locus of the point P for each of these situations.

   a AP = BP   **b** AP = 4 cm and BP = 4 cm

   c P is always within 2 cm of the line AB

(PS) **3** **a** A horse is tethered in a field on a rope 4 m long. Describe or sketch the area that the horse can graze.

   b The horse is still tethered by the same rope but there is now a long, straight fence running 2 m from the stake. Draw the area that the horse can now graze.

4 ABCD is a square of side 4 cm. In each of the following loci, the point P moves only inside the square. Sketch the locus in each case.

   a AP = BP   **b** AP < BP   **c** AP = CP

   d CP < 4 cm   **e** CP > 2 cm   **f** CP > 5 cm

(MR) **5** One of the following diagrams is the locus of a point on the rim of a bicycle wheel as it moves along a flat road. Which is it?

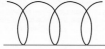   

6 Draw the locus of the centre of the wheel for the bicycle in question **5**.

(PS) 7 ABC is a triangle.

The region R is defined as the set of points inside the triangle such that:

- they are closer to the line AB than the line AC
- they are closer to the point A than the point C.

Using a ruler and compasses, construct the region R.

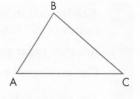

(PS) 8 ABCD is a rectangle.

Copy the diagram and draw the locus of all points that are 2 cm from the edges of the rectangle.

(CM) 9 Explain how you could construct an equilateral triangle with sides of 3 cm using only a ruler.

(EV) 10 Mark drew a triangle and asked Gary to draw the locus of all the points that were 1 cm away from the sides of the triangle.

Gary said: "That's easy, it'll be a triangle inside and a triangle outside the original triangle."

Comment on Gary's statement.

7.7 Loci problems

This section will show you how to:

- solve practical problems using loci.

Most loci problems you come across will be of a practical nature, as in the next example.

Example 8

A radio company wants to find a site for a transmitter. The transmitter must be the same distance from Doncaster and Leeds and within 20 miles of Sheffield.

In mathematical terms, this means they are concerned with the perpendicular bisector between Leeds and Doncaster and the area within a circle of radius 20 miles from Sheffield.

The diagram, drawn to a scale of 1 cm = 10 miles, illustrates the situation and shows that the transmitter can be built anywhere along the thick part of the blue line.

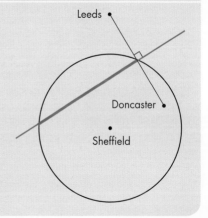

Example 9

A radar station in Birmingham has a range of 150 km (that is, it can pick up any aircraft within a radius of 150 km).

Another radar station in Norwich has a range of 100 km.

Can an aircraft be picked up by both radar stations at the same time?

The situation is represented by a circle of radius 150 km around Birmingham and another circle of radius 100 km around Norwich.

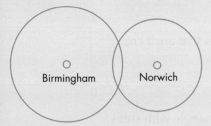

The two circles overlap, so an aircraft could be picked up by both radar stations when it is in the overlap.

Example 10

A dog is tethered by a rope, 3 m long, to the corner of a shed, 4 m by 2 m.

What is the area that the dog can guard effectively?

Draw the locus.

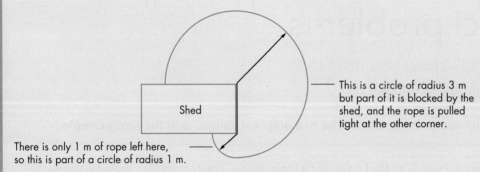

This is a circle of radius 3 m but part of it is blocked by the shed, and the rope is pulled tight at the other corner.

There is only 1 m of rope left here, so this is part of a circle of radius 1 m.

1 In a field, a horse is tethered to a stake by a rope 6 m long. Draw the locus of the area that the horse can graze. Use a scale of 1 cm to 2 m.

For questions **2** to **6**, you should start by sketching the picture given in each question before drawing the locus accurately. The scale for each question is given.

2 **a** A goat is tethered by a rope, 7 m long, in a corner of a field with a fence at each side. What is the locus of the area that the goat can graze? Use a scale of 1 cm to 2 m.

b A horse is tethered to a stake near a corner of a fenced field, at a point 4 m from each fence. The rope is 6 m long. Sketch the area that the horse can graze. Use a scale of 1 cm to 2 m.

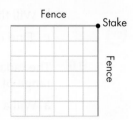

3 A cow is tethered to a rail at the top of a fence 6 m long. The rope is 3 m long. Sketch the area that the cow can graze. Use a scale of 1 cm to 2 m.

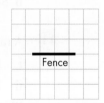

4 A horse is tethered to a corner of a shed, 2 m by 1 m. The rope is 2 m long. Sketch the area that the horse can graze. Use a scale of 1 cm to 1 m.

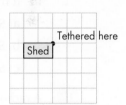

5 A goat is tethered by a 4 m rope to a stake at one corner of a pen, 4 m by 3 m. Sketch the area of the pen on which the goat cannot graze. Use a scale of 1 cm to 1 m.

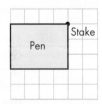

6 A puppy is tethered to a stake by a rope, 1.5 m long, on a flat lawn on which there are two raised brick flower beds. The stake is situated at one corner of a bed, as shown. Sketch the area that the puppy is free to roam in. Use a scale of 1 cm to 1 m.

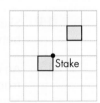

7 Wathsea Harbour is shown in the diagram. A boat sets off from point A and steers so that it stays the same distance from the sea wall and the West Pier. Another boat sets off from B and steers so that it stays the same distance from the East Pier and the sea wall. If each boat sailed at the same speed, would they hit each other?

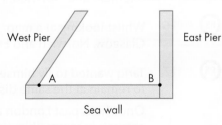

Explain your answer fully.

8 A distress call is heard by coastguards in both Newcastle and Bristol. The signal strength suggests that the call comes from a ship that is the same distance from both places.

Explain how the coastguards could find the area of sea to search.

For questions **9** to **17**, you should use a copy of the map opposite. For each question, trace the map and mark on those points that are relevant to that question.

9 A radio station broadcasts from London on a frequency of 1000 kHz with a range of 300 km. Another radio station broadcasts from Glasgow on the same frequency with a range of 200 km.

   a Sketch the area to which each station can broadcast.

   b Will they interfere with each other?

(EV)   **c** Find out what happens if the Glasgow station increases its range to 400 km.

10 The radar at Leeds airport has a range of 200 km. The radar at Exeter airport has a range of 200 km.

   a Will a plane flying over Birmingham be detected by the Leeds radar?

   b Sketch the area where a plane can be picked up by both radars at the same time.

11 A radio transmitter is to be built according to these rules.

   i   It has to be the same distance from York and Birmingham.

   ii It must be within 350 km of Glasgow.

   iii It must be within 250 km of London.

      a Sketch the line that is the same distance from York and Birmingham.

      b Sketch the area that is within 350 km of Glasgow and 250 km of London.

      c Show clearly the possible places where the transmitter could be built.

12 A radio transmitter centred at Birmingham is designed to give good reception in an area greater than 150 km and less than 250 km from the transmitter. Sketch the area of good reception.

13 Three radio stations pick up a distress call from a boat in the Irish Sea. The station at Glasgow can tell from the strength of the signal that the boat is within 300 km of the station. The station at York can tell that the boat is between 200 km and 300 km from York. The station at London can tell that it is less than 400 km from London. Sketch the area where the boat could be.

14 Sketch the area that is between 200 km and 300 km from Newcastle upon Tyne, and between 150 km and 250 km from Bristol.

15 An oil rig is situated in the North Sea in such a position that it is the same distance from Newcastle upon Tyne and Manchester. It is also the same distance from Sheffield and Norwich. Find out where the oil rig is located.

(PS) **16** Whilst looking at a map, Fred notices that his house is the same distance from Glasgow, Norwich and Exeter. Where is it?

(PS) **17** Tariq wanted to fly himself north, from the Isle of Wight, towards Scotland. He wanted to remain at the same distance from London as from Bristol as much as possible.

     Once he is past London and Bristol, which city should he aim toward to keep him, as accurately as possible, the same distance from London and Bristol? Use the map to help you.

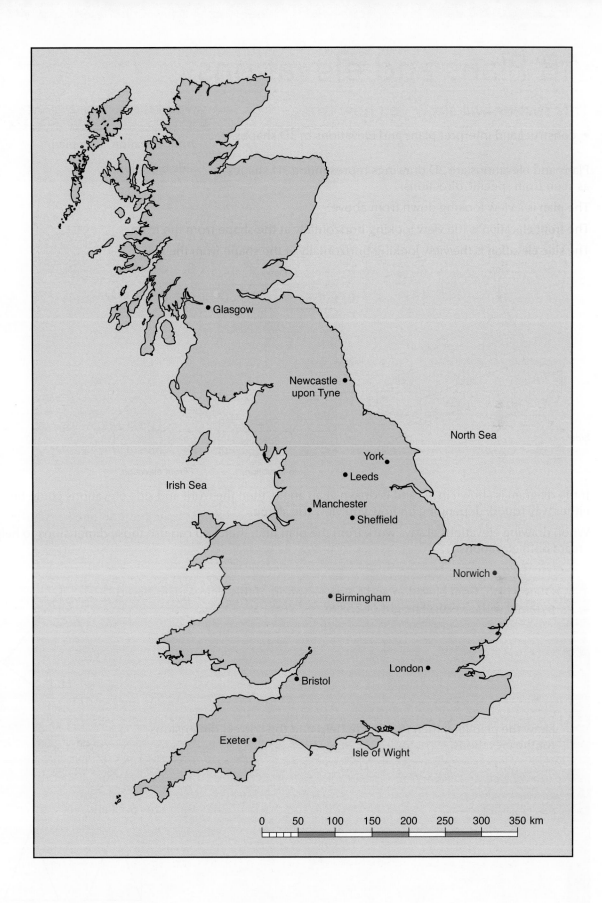

7.8 Plans and elevations

This section will show you how to:

- construct and interpret plans and elevations of 3D shapes.

Key terms

front elevation	plan
side elevation	

Plans and elevations are 2D drawings representing 3D shapes as seen from specific directions.

The **plan** is a view looking down from above.

The **front elevation** is the view looking horizontally at the shape from the front.

The **side elevation** is the view looking horizontally at the shape from the side.

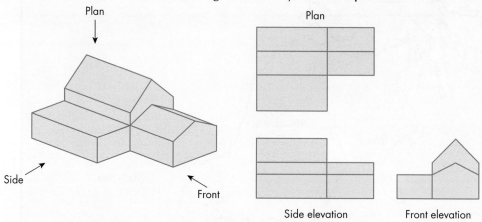

If the diagram is shown in 3D and is drawn at an angle, then the front and side elevations could be either way round, depending on how you view the shape.

When drawing elevations always work from the plan first, then you can use those dimensions to help create both elevations.

Example 11

Draw a plan, front elevation and a side elevation of this 2 cm square-based pyramid with a vertical height of 2.5 cm.

Draw the plan first, then use that to help find the correct dimensions for the elevations.

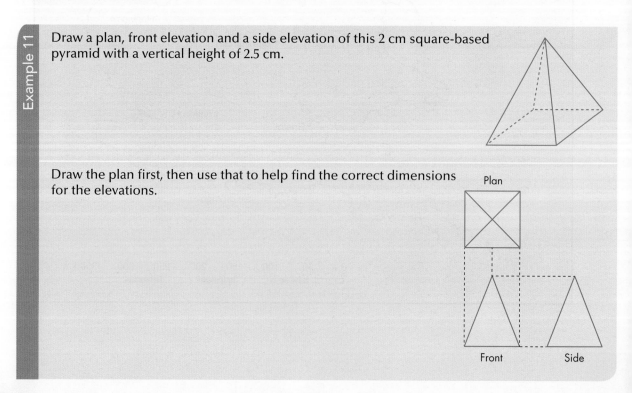

Example 12

Describe the 3D shape that has the following plan and elevations.

This is a cone with the top part cut off. The cone is slanting towards the back.

Plan

Front   Side

Example 13

Here is a plan and side elevation of a prism. The side elevation shows the regular cross section of the prism.

a Draw the front elevation.

b Sketch the 3D shape.

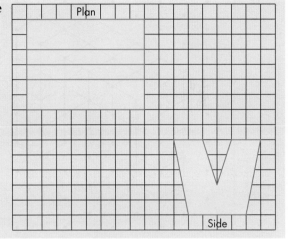

a Use the grid lines to help find the front elevation.

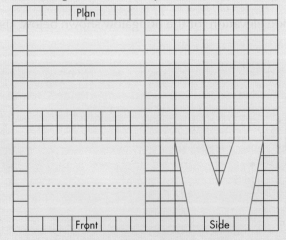

Note how the dotted line shows the hidden line that cannot be seen from the outside.

b The shape is a prism in the shape of a V.

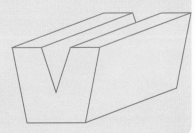

1 Draw the plan, front elevation and side elevation for each shape.

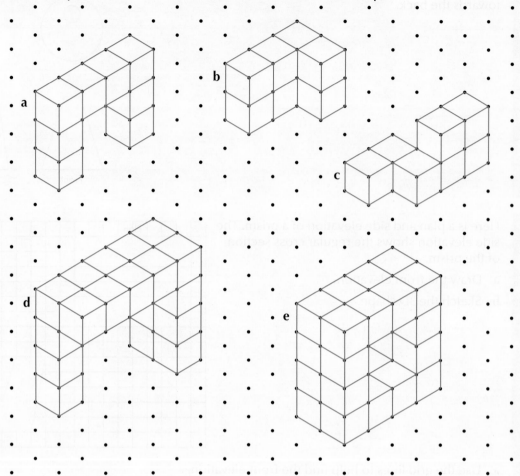

a

b

c

d

e

2 Draw a plan, front elevation and side elevation for the bungalow shown below. Use a scale of 1 cm to 2 m.

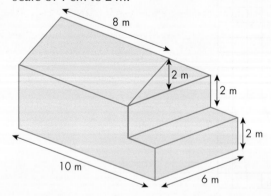

8 m

2 m

2 m

2 m

10 m

6 m

MR **3** Describe the shapes shown by each plan, front elevation and side elevation.

a

Plan

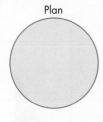

Front   Side

b

Plan

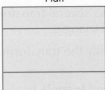

Front   Side

4 The diagram shows the side elevation of a garden shed, which is the same shape from end to end. The shed is 4 metres long.

Draw the plan and front elevation of the shed using a scale of 2 cm to 1 m.

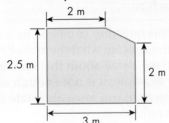

MR **5** Draw an accurate plan, front elevation and side elevation for a 8-cm-long regular octagonal prism with side length 3 cm.

EV **6** Chris, Hannah and Joe look at this diagram, which is a side view of a shape.

Chris says, "The shape is a cylinder with a circular hole through the middle."

Hannah says, "It could be a cuboid with a square hole through the middle."

Joe says, "The shape could be a sort of triangular shape standing on a short, flat side."

a Draw a sketch of each person's suggestion.

b Draw another possible shape with this plan.

Worked exemplars

1 The grid shows several transformations of the shaded triangle.

   a Describe fully the transformation that takes:

     i the shaded triangle to shape A

     ii the shaded triangle to shape E.

   b There are two reflections shown in the diagram that do not involve the shaded triangle. Fully describe each reflection and the triangles concerned.

   c Pete says that to transform shape C to shape D you need a translation and then a reflection. Kathy says you need a rotation and then a reflection.

   Comment on what each person says.

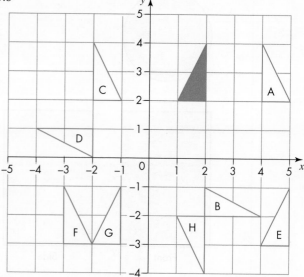

This is a communicating mathematics question, in which you need to communicate clearly and mathematically your responses to each part.	

1 a i Reflection in the line $x = 3$
 	
   ii Translation of $\begin{pmatrix} 3 \\ -5 \end{pmatrix}$
 	
 b F to G, reflection in line $x = -2$
 	
   H to B, reflection in the line between $(0, 0)$ and $(4, -4)$, which is $y = -x$
	In this question you need to accurately communicate what the transformation is and the detail about that transformation. For example, it is not enough to say *reflection*; you must also state the line of the reflection.

c They are both correct. For Pete's suggestion you would translate the shape by $\begin{pmatrix} 0 \\ -1 \end{pmatrix}$ then reflect in the line between $(-4, 3)$ and $(-1, 0)$. For Kathy's suggestion, rotate the shaded shape 90° anticlockwise about $(-2, 2)$ and then reflect in the line $y = 1.5$.	This part of the question assesses if you can evaluate each statement and make suitable mathematical comments. You need to work through both statements, state whether or not they are correct and show why.

2 Some wind turbines follow a design based on arcs within an equilateral triangle.

Construct this design, based on an equilateral triangle with sides of length 5 cm.

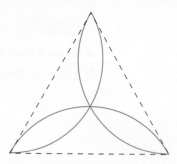

This is a problem-solving question. You must recognise that, to create this shape, you will first need the equilateral triangle and then recognise that the centre of each arc lies on the bisectors of each side of that triangle.

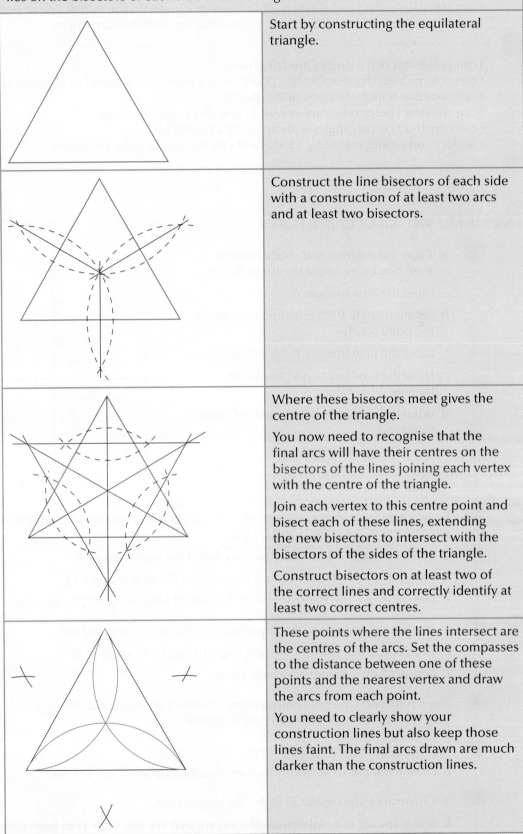

	Start by constructing the equilateral triangle.
	Construct the line bisectors of each side with a construction of at least two arcs and at least two bisectors.
	Where these bisectors meet gives the centre of the triangle. You now need to recognise that the final arcs will have their centres on the bisectors of the lines joining each vertex with the centre of the triangle. Join each vertex to this centre point and bisect each of these lines, extending the new bisectors to intersect with the bisectors of the sides of the triangle. Construct bisectors on at least two of the correct lines and correctly identify at least two correct centres.
	These points where the lines intersect are the centres of the arcs. Set the compasses to the distance between one of these points and the nearest vertex and draw the arcs from each point. You need to clearly show your construction lines but also keep those lines faint. The final arcs drawn are much darker than the construction lines.

Ready to progress?

I can translate, reflect and rotate a 2D shape with a given vector, mirror line or point and angle.
I can draw plans and elevations from a given diagram and interpret them.

I can prove that two triangles are congruent.
I can enlarge a 2D shape about any point using a positive, fractional or negative scale factor.
I can combine transformations of 2D shapes.
I can construct perpendiculars as well as line and angle bisectors.
I can construct certain angles without using a protractor.
I understand what is meant by a locus and can use loci to solve problems.

Review questions

1   **a** Copy the diagram and rotate triangle
P 90° clockwise about the point (–1, 1).

Label the new triangle A.

b Rotate triangle P 90° anticlockwise about
the point (–1, 1).

Label the new triangle B.

c Describe how you would transform
triangle A to triangle B.

d What is the only invariant point of these
rotations?

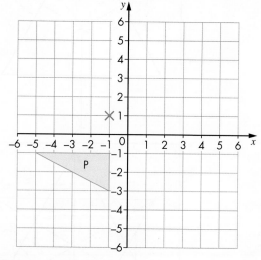

CM **2**   Draw a grid from $-5 \leqslant x \leqslant 5$ and $-5 \leqslant y \leqslant 5$. On the grid, draw a triangle with
coordinates A(2, 1), B(4, 1) and C (4, 2).

a Reflect triangle ABC in the line $y = x$. Label the new triangle T.

b Reflect triangle ABC in the line $y = -x$. Label the new triangle Q.

c Describe fully the transformation that would map triangle Q to triangle T.

EV **3**   **a** Use a ruler and a pair of compasses to construct an angle of 90°.

b Construct a bisector of this right angle to create an angle of 45°.

c Evaluate how accurate you have been.

4   Use a ruler and a pair of compasses to construct an equilateral triangle with sides of
length 5 cm. Show all your construction lines.

5   **a** Draw a line AB that is 6 cm long.

b Draw the locus of all points that are exactly 2 cm from the line AB.

6   **a** Construct a square ABCD with side length 4 cm.

b Shade the set of points inside the square that are less than 3 cm from either point
A or B and less than 1.5 cm from the line BC.

7

a Using ruler and compasses only, draw a line AB 8 cm long and construct its perpendicular bisector.

b Copy and complete this sentence.

The perpendicular bisector of the line AB is the locus of points that are …

PS

8

a With ruler and compasses only, construct a hexagon ABCDEF, with side length 3 cm.

b The region R is defined as the set of points inside the hexagon that are:

- closer to the side AB than the side BC and

- closer to the point C than the point F.

Accurately construct the region R.

9 The diagram shows an L shape, with one line 7 cm and the other 3 cm.

Draw the diagram and construct the locus of all points 2 cm from the L shape.

10 Two lifeboat stations P and Q receive a distress call from a boat.

The boat is within 5 kilometres of station P.

The boat is within 7 kilometres of station Q.

On a copy of the diagram, shade the possible locations of the boat.

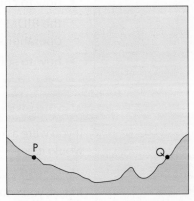

Scale: 1 cm represents 2 km

11 The triangle ABC has coordinates A(3, 1), B(5, –2) and C(–4, 0).

Triangle ABC is translated by the vector $\begin{pmatrix} 6 \\ -1 \end{pmatrix}$.

What are the new coordinates of triangle ABC?

12 Draw a plan and front and side elevations for a 5 cm cube with a 3 cm by 2 cm rectangular hole from top to bottom straight through its centre.

EV

13 Kieron said that if you rotate a shape by 90° then reflect that image in a line $y = A$ (where A is any number), the final image is always a reflection of the original shape.

Is this true?

CM

14 ABCD is a rhombus. Prove that triangle ACD is congruent to ACB.

8 Algebra: Algebraic manipulation

This chapter is going to show you:

- how to substitute numbers into expressions and formulae
- how to simplify expressions by collecting like terms
- how to expand and factorise expressions
- how to expand two or more binomials
- how to factorise quadratic expressions
- how to rearrange formulae.

You should already know:

- how to use letters to represent numbers
- the basic language of algebra
- how to collect together like terms
- the BIDMAS rule, which gives the order you must use the operations of arithmetic when they occur together
- how to solve basic linear equations.

About this chapter

If you were asked to circle one of these to describe mathematics, which would it be?

Art   Science   Sport   Language

In fact, you could circle them all.

But perhaps the most important description in the list above is mathematics as language. Mathematics is the only universal language. If you write the equation $3x = 9$, it will be understood by people in all countries.

Algebra is the way that the language of mathematics is expressed.

Algebra comes from the Arabic *al-jabr* which means something similar to 'completion'. It was used in a book written in AD820 by a Persian mathematician called al-Khwarizmi.

The use of symbols then developed until the middle of the 17th century, when René Descartes developed what is regarded as the basis of the algebra we use today.

8.1 Basic algebra

This section will show you how to:

- recognise expressions, equations, formulae and identities
- substitute into, manipulate and simplify algebraic expressions.

Key terms

equation	expand
expression	formula
identity	like terms
simplify	substitute
variable	

Here are some algebraic words that you need to know.

Variable Letters that are used to represent numbers are called **variables**. These letters can take on any value, so they are said to *vary*.

Expression An **expression** is any combination of letters and numbers.

For example, $2x + 4y$ and $\frac{p-6}{5}$ are expressions.

Equation An **equation** contains an 'equals' sign and at least one variable. The important fact is that a value can be found for the variable. This is called *solving the equation*.

Formula You may already have seen lots of formulae (the plural of **formula**). These are like equations in that they contain an 'equals' sign, but there is more than one variable and they are rules for working out things such as area or the cost of taxi fares.

For example, $V = x^3$, $A = \frac{1}{2} bh$ and $C = 3 + 4m$ are formulae.

Identity These look like formulae, but the important fact about an **identity** is that it is true for all values, whether numerical or algebraic.

For example, $5n \equiv 2n + 3n$ and $(x + 1)^2 \equiv x^2 + 2x + 1$ are identities. Note that the special sign $\equiv$ is sometimes used to show an identity.

Term Terms are the separate parts of expressions, equations, formulae and identities.

For example, in $3x + 2y - 7$, there are three terms: $3x$, $+2y$ and -7.

Example 1

State if each of the following is an expression, equation, formula or identity.

A: $x - 5 = 7$ B: $P = 4x$ C: $2x - 3y$ D: $3n - n = 2n$

A is an equation as it can be solved to give $x = 12$.

B is a formula. This is the formula for the perimeter of a square with a side of length x.

C is an expression with two terms.

D is an identity as it is true for all values of n.

Substitution

Substitution involves replacing one or more letters with numbers in an expression or formula.

Whenever you **substitute** a number for a variable in an expression, always put the value in brackets before working it out. This will help you to avoid calculation errors, especially with negative numbers.

To find the value of $3x^2 - 5$ when $x = 3$, write $3(3)^2 - 5 = 3 \times 9 - 5$

$$= 27 - 5$$
$$= 22$$

To find the value when $x = -4$, write $3(-4)^2 - 5 = 3 \times 16 - 5$

$$= 48 - 5$$
$$= 43$$

Find the value of $L = a^2 - 8b^2$ when $a = -6$ and $b = \frac{1}{2}$.

Substitute the values -6 and $\frac{1}{2}$ for the letters a and b.

$L = a^2 - 8b^2$

$\quad = (-6)^2 - 8(\frac{1}{2})^2$

$\quad = 36 - 8 \times \frac{1}{4}$

$\quad = 36 - 2$

$\quad = 34$

Note: If you do not use brackets and write -6^2, you could wrongly evaluate L as -36.

The formula for the electricity bill each quarter in a household is: total bill = £7.50 + £0.07 × number of units. A family uses 6720 units in a quarter.

a How much is their total bill?

b The family pays a direct debit of £120 per month towards their electricity costs.

By how much will they be in credit or debit after the quarter?

a Substituting 6720 into the formula   £7.50 + £0.07 × number of units = total bill

$\qquad\qquad\qquad\qquad\qquad\qquad\qquad\qquad 7.5 + 0.07 \times 6720 = 477.9$

$\qquad\qquad\qquad\qquad\qquad\qquad\qquad\qquad$ Total bill = £477.90

b A quarter is three months, so the family pays £360 through their direct debit.

£360 is less than £477.90, so they haven't paid enough, which means they are in debit.

$477.90 - 360 = 117.90$

The family are £117.90 in debit.

Exercise 8A

1 Find the value of $4b + 3$ when: **a** $b = 2.5$ **b** $b = -1.5$ **c** $b = \frac{1}{2}$.

2 Where $P = \dfrac{5w - 4y}{w + y}$, find the value of P when:

   a $w = 3$ and $y = 2$ **b** $w = 6$ and $y = 4$ **c** $w = 2$ and $y = 3$.

3 Where $A = b^2 + c^2$, find the value of A when:

   a $b = 2$ and $c = 3$ **b** $b = 5$ and $c = 7$ **c** $b = -1$ and $c = -4$.

4 Where $A = \dfrac{180(n - 2)}{n + 5}$, find the value of A when:

   a $n = 7$ **b** $n = 3$ **c** $n = -1$.

5 Where $Z = \dfrac{y^2 + 4}{4 + y}$, find the value of Z when:

   a $y = 4$ **b** $y = -6$ **c** $y = -1.5$.

6 A holiday cottage costs £150 per day to rent.

A group of friends decide to rent the cottage for seven days.

a Which of the following formulae would represent the cost per day if there are n people in the group and they share the cost equally?

$$\frac{150}{n} \qquad \frac{150}{7n} \qquad \frac{1050}{n} \qquad \frac{150n}{7}$$

b Eventually 10 people go on the holiday.

When they get the bill, they find that there is a discount for a seven-day rental. After the discount, they each find it costs them £12.50 less than they expected.

How much does a seven-day rental cost?

> **Hints and tips** To check your choice in part **a**, make up some numbers and try them in the formulae. For example, take $n = 5$.

 7 Kaz knows that x, y and z have the values 2, 8 and 11, but she does not know which variable has which value.

a What is the maximum value that the expression $2x + 6y - 3z$ could have?

b What is the minimum value that the expression $5x - 2y + 3z$ could have?

> **Hints and tips** You can just try all combinations but, if you think for a moment, the $6y$ term has to be the biggest, and this will give you a clue to the other terms.

 8 x and y are different positive whole numbers.

Work out a possible pair of values of x and y so that the value of the expression $5x + 3y$

a is odd **b** is prime.

> **Hints and tips** You need to remember the prime numbers, 2, 3, 5, 7, 11, 13, 17, 19, …

 9 **a** p is an odd number and q is an even number.

Say if the following expressions are odd or even.

i $p + q$ **ii** $p^2 + q$ **iii** $2p + q$ **iv** $p^2 + q^2$

b x, y and z are all odd numbers.

Write an expression using x, y and z so that the value of the expression is always even.

10 A formula for the cost of delivery, in pounds, of orders from a do-it-yourself warehouse is:

$$D = 2M - \frac{C}{5}$$

where D is the cost of the delivery, M is the distance in miles from the warehouse and C is the cost of the goods to be delivered.

a How much is the delivery cost when $M = 30$ and $C = 200$?

b Bob buys goods worth £300 and lives 10 miles from the warehouse.

i The formula gives a negative value for the cost of delivery. What is this value?

ii Explain why Bob will not get a rebate from the warehouse.

c Martha buys goods worth £400. She calculates that her cost of delivery will be zero.

What is the greatest distance Martha could live from the warehouse?

11 State if each of the following is an expression, equation, formula or identity.

A: $2x - 5$

B: $s = \sqrt{A}$

C: $2(x + 3) = 2x + 6$

D: $2x - 3 = 1$

EV **12** Marvin hires a car for the day for £40. He wants to know how much it costs him for each mile he drives.

Petrol is 98p per litre and the car does 10 miles per litre.

Marvin works out the following formula for the cost per mile, C in pounds, for M miles driven:

$$C = 0.098 + \frac{40}{M}$$

a Explain each term of the formula.

b How much will it cost per mile if Marvin drives 200 miles that day?

| Hints and tips | Use the information in the question in your explanation. |

Expansion

In mathematics, to '**expand**' usually means 'multiply out'. For example, expressions such as $3(y + 2)$ and $4y^2(2y + 3)$ can be expanded by multiplying them out.

Remember that there is an invisible multiplication sign between the outside number and the opening bracket. So $3(y + 2)$ is really $3 \times (y + 2)$ and $4y^2(2y + 3)$ is really $4y^2 \times (2y + 3)$.

You expand by multiplying *everything inside* the brackets by what is outside the brackets.

So in the case of the two examples above,

$$3(y + 2) = 3 \times (y + 2) = 3 \times y + 3 \times 2 = 3y + 6$$
$$4y^2(2y + 3) = 4y^2 \times (2y + 3) = 4y^2 \times 2y + 4y^2 \times 3 = 8y^3 + 12y^2$$

Look at these next examples of expansion, which show clearly how the term outside the brackets has been multiplied with the terms inside them.

$y(y^2 - 4x) = y^3 - 4xy$	$3(2t + 5) = 6t + 15$
$m(p + 7) = mp + 7m$	$-2x(3 - 4x) = -6x + 8x^2$
$4t(t^3 + 2) = 4t^4 + 8t$	$3t(2 + 5t - p) = 6t + 15t^2 - 3pt$

Remember:

the product of a negative and a positive is negative

the product of a negative and a negative is positive.

As a result, the signs change when a negative quantity is outside the brackets. For example,

$a(b + c) = ab + ac$	$a(b - c) = ab - ac$
$-a(b + c) = -ab - ac$	$-a(b - c) = -ab + ac$
$-(a - b) = -a + b$	$-(a + b - c) = -a - b + c$

Note: A minus sign on its own in front of the brackets is actually –1, so:

$$-(x + 2y - 3) = -1 \times (x + 2y - 3) = -1 \times x + -1 \times 2y + -1 \times -3 = -x - 2y + 3$$

Collecting like terms

Like terms are terms that have the same letter(s) raised to the same power but can have different numerical **coefficients** (numbers in front). For example,

m, $3m$, $4m$, $-m$ and $76m$ are all like terms in m

t^2, $4t^2$, $7t^2$, $-t^2$, $-3t^2$ and $98t^2$ are all like terms in t^2

pt, $5tp$, $-2pt$, $7pt$, $-3tp$ and $103pt$ are all like terms in pt.

Note: All the terms in tp are also like terms to all the terms in pt.

When you have an expression with like terms, you can **simplify** the expression by combining the like terms together. For example,

$3y + 4y + 3 = 7y + 3$ $\qquad$ $4h - h = 3h$ $\qquad$ $2t^2 + 5t^2 = 7t^2$

$2m + 6 + 3m = 5m + 6$ $\qquad$ $3ab + 2ba = 5ab$ $\qquad$ $10g - 4 - 3g = 7g - 4$

Expand and simplify

When two brackets are expanded there are often like terms that you can collect together. Always simplify algebraic expressions as much as possible.

Consider finding a simplified expression for the perimeter of a rectangle with sides of $(5x - 8)$ cm and $(2x + 11)$ cm.

It has two of each side so: $\quad 2(5x - 8) + 2(2x + 11) = 10x - 16 + 4x + 22$

$$= (14x + 6) \text{ cm}$$

Example 4

Expand and simplify $3t(5t + 4) - 2t(3t - 5)$.

$3t(5t + 4) - 2t(3t - 5) = 15t^2 + 12t - 6t^2 + 10t$

$\qquad\qquad\qquad\qquad\quad = 9t^2 + 22t$

Exercise 8B

1 Expand these expressions.

   a $2(3 + m)$ **b** $5(2 + l)$ **c** $3(4 - y)$ **d** $4(5 + 2k)$

   e $3(2 - 4f)$ **f** $2(5 - 3w)$ **g** $5(2k + 3m)$ **h** $4(3d - 2n)$

   i $t(t + 3)$ **j** $k(k - 3)$ **k** $4t(t - 1)$ **l** $2k(4 - k)$

   m $4g(2g + 5)$ **n** $5h(3h - 2)$ **o** $y(y^2 + 5)$ **p** $h(h^3 + 7)$

   q $k(k^2 - 5)$ **r** $3t(t^2 + 4)$ **s** $3d(5d^2 - d^3)$ **t** $3w(2w^2 + t)$

   u $5a(3a^2 - 2b)$ **v** $3p(4p^3 - 5m)$ **w** $4h^2(3h + 2g)$ **x** $2m^2(4m + m^2)$

2 The local supermarket is offering £1 off a large tin of biscuits. Morris wants five tins.

   a If the normal price of one tin is £t, which of the expressions below represents how much it will cost Morris to buy five tins?

     $5(t - 1)$ $\qquad$ $5t - 1$ $\qquad$ $t - 5$ $\qquad$ $5t - 5$

   b Morris has £20 to spend. If each tin is £4.50, will he have enough money for five tins? Show working to justify your answer.

EV **3** Dylan wrote the following.

$3(5x - 4) = 8x - 4$

Dylan has made two mistakes.

Explain the mistakes that Dylan has made.

Hints and tips It is not enough to give the right answer. You must try to explain why Dylan wrote 8 for 3×5 instead of 15.

MR **4** The expansion $2(x + 3) = 2x + 6$ can be shown by this diagram.

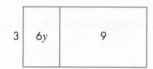

a What expansion is shown in this diagram?

b Write down an expansion that is shown in this diagram.

12z	8

5 Expand and simplify.

a $3(4 + t) + 2(5 + t)$ **b** $5(3 + 2k) + 3(2 + 3k)$

c $4(3 + 2f) + 2(5 - 3f)$ **d** $5(1 + 3g) + 3(3 - 4g)$

Hints and tips Be careful with minus signs. For example, $-2(5e - 4) = -10e + 8$

6 Expand and simplify.

a $4(3 + 2h) - 2(5 + 3h)$ **b** $5(3g + 4) - 3(2g + 5)$

c $5(5k + 2) - 2(4k - 3)$ **d** $4(4e + 3) - 2(5e - 4)$

7 Expand and simplify.

a $m(4 + p) + p(3 + m)$ **b** $k(3 + 2h) + h(4 + 3k)$

c $4r(3 + 4p) + 3p(8 - r)$ **d** $5k(3m + 4) - 2m(3 - 2k)$

8 Expand and simplify.

a $t(3t + 4) + 3t(3 + 2t)$ **b** $2y(3 + 4y) + y(5y - 1)$

c $4e(3e - 5) - 2e(e - 7)$ **d** $3k(2k + p) - 2k(3p - 4k)$

9 Expand and simplify.

a $4a(2b + 3c) + 3b(3a + 2c)$ **b** $3y(4w + 2t) + 2w(3y - 4t)$

c $5m(2n - 3p) - 2n(3p - 2m)$ **d** $2r(3r + r^2) - 3r^2(4 - 2r)$

10 A two-carriage train has f first-class seats and $2s$ standard-class seats.

A three-carriage train has $2f$ first-class seats and $3s$ standard-class seats.

On a weekday, 5 two-carriage trains and 2 three-carriage trains travel from Hull to Liverpool.

a Write down an expression for the total number of first-class and standard-class seats available during the day.

b On average in any day, half of the first-class seats are used at a cost of £60.

On average in any day, three-quarters of the standard-class seats are used at a cost of £40.

How much money does the rail company earn in an average day on this route? Give your answer in terms of f and s.

c $f = 15$ and $s = 80$. It costs the rail company £30 000 per day to operate this route. How much profit do they make on an average day?

11 Fill in whole-number values so that the following expansion is true.

$$3(\ldots x + \ldots y) + 2(\ldots x + \ldots y) = 11x + 17y$$

> **Hints and tips** There is more than one answer. You don't have to give them all.

12 A rectangle with sides 5 and $3x + 2$ has a smaller rectangle with sides 3 and $2x - 1$ cut from it.

Work out the remaining area.

```
        3x + 2
   ┌──────────────┐
   │   2x – 1     │
   │  ┌──────┐    │
 5 │ 3│      │    │
   │  └──────┘    │
   └──────────────┘
```

> **Hints and tips** Write out the expression for the difference between the two rectangles and then work it out.

8.2 Factorisation

This section will show you how to:

- factorise an algebraic expression.

Factorisation is the opposite of expansion. It puts an expression back into the brackets it may have come from.

In factorisation, you have to look for the **common factors** in *every* term of the expression.

To factorise the expression $6t + 9m$, first look at the numerical coefficients 6 and 9. These have a common factor of 3.

Then look at the letters, t and m. These do not have any common factors as they do not appear in both terms.

The expression can be thought of as $3 \times 2t + 3 \times 3m$, which gives the factorisation:

$$6t + 9m = 3(2t + 3m)$$

Note: You can always check a factorisation by expanding the answer.

Example 5

Factorise each expression.

a $6my + 4py$ **b** $5k^2 - 25k$ **c** $10a^2b - 15ab^2$

a First look at the numbers. These have a common factor of 2.

m and p do not occur in both terms but y does, and is a common factor, so the factorisation is:

$6my + 4py = 2y(3m + 2p)$

b 5 is a common factor of 5 and 25 and k is a common factor of k^2 and k.

$5k^2 - 25k = 5k(k - 5)$

c 5 is a common factor of 10 and 15, a is a common factor of a^2 and a, b is a common factor of b and b^2.

$10a^2b - 15ab^2 = 5ab(2a - 3b)$

Note: If you multiply out each answer, you will get the expressions you started with.

Exercise 8C

1 Factorise these expressions.

a $6m + 12t$ **b** $9t + 3p$ **c** $8m + 12k$

d $4r + 8t$ **e** $mn + 3m$ **f** $5g^2 + 3g$

g $4w - 6t$ **h** $3y^2 + 2y$ **i** $4t^2 - 3t$

j $3m^2 - 3mp$ **k** $6p^2 + 9pt$ **l** $8pt + 6mp$

m $8ab - 4bc$ **n** $5b^2c - 10bc$ **o** $8abc + 6bed$

p $4a^2 + 6a + 8$ **q** $6ab + 9bc + 3bd$ **r** $5t^2 + 4t + at$

s $6mt^2 - 3mt + 9m^2t$ **t** $8ab^2 + 2ab - 4a^2b$ **u** $10pt^2 + 15pt + 5p^2t$

2 Three friends have a meal together. They each have a main meal costing £6.75 and a dessert costing £3.25.

Chris says that the bill will be $3 \times 6.75 + 3 \times 3.25$.

Mary says that she has an easier way to work out the bill as $3 \times (6.75 + 3.25)$.

a Explain why Chris' and Mary's methods both give the correct answer.

b Explain why Mary's method is better. **c** What is the total bill?

3 Factorise these expressions where possible. List those that do not factorise.

a $7m - 6t$ **b** $5m + 2mp$ **c** $t^2 - 7t$

d $8pt + 5ab$ **e** $4m^2 - 6mp$ **f** $a^2 + b$

g $4a^2 - 5ab$ **h** $3ab + 4cd$ **i** $5ab - 3b^2c$

4 Three students are asked to factorise the expression $12m - 8$. These are their answers.

Aidan   Bernice   Craig

$2(6m - 4)$ $4(3m - 2)$ $4m(3 - \frac{2}{m})$

All the answers are accurately factorised, but only one is the normally accepted answer.

a Which student gave the correct answer?

b Explain why the other two students' answers are not acceptable as correct answers.

5 Explain why $5m + 6p$ cannot be factorised.

 6 Show that the perimeter of this shape can be written as $8(2x + 3)$.

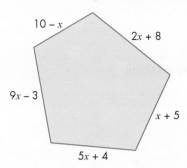

10 − x
2x + 8
9x − 3
x + 5
5x + 4

 7 Alvin has correctly factorised the top and bottom of an algebraic fraction and cancelled out the terms to give a final answer of $2x$. Unfortunately some of his work has had coffee spilt on it. What was the original fraction?

$$\frac{4x\blacksquare}{2} = \frac{4\blacksquare}{2(x - 3)} = 2x$$

8.3 Quadratic expansion

This section will show you how to:

- expand two binomials to obtain a quadratic expression.

A quadratic expression is one where the highest power of the variables is 2. For example

$$y^2 \qquad 3t^2 + 5t \qquad 5m^2 + 3m + 8$$

You can expand an expression such as $(3y + 2)(4y - 5)$ to give a quadratic expression.

$(3y + 2)$ and $(4y - 5)$ are examples of **binomials**. A binomial is the sum of two terms.

Multiplying out pairs of these brackets is usually called *quadratic expansion*.

The rule for expanding expressions such as $(t + 5)(3t - 4)$ is similar to the rule for expanding single brackets:

Multiply everything in one set of brackets by everything in the other set of brackets.

There are several methods for doing this. Examples 6 to 8 show the three main methods: expansion, FOIL and the box method.

Example 6

In the expansion method, split the terms in the first set of brackets, make each of them multiply both terms in the second set of brackets and then simplify the outcome.

Expand $(x + 3)(x + 4)$.

$(x + 3)(x + 4) = x(x + 4) + 3(x + 4)$

$\qquad\qquad = x^2 + 4x + 3x + 12$

$\qquad\qquad = x^2 + 7x + 12$

Exercise 8D

1 Use the expansion method to expand these expressions.

  a $(x + 3)(x + 2)$ **b** $(t + 4)(t + 3)$

  c $(w + 1)(w + 3)$ **d** $(m + 5)(m + 1)$

2 Use the expansion method to expand these expressions.

  a $(p + 10)(p - 7)$ **b** $(u - 8)(u - 4)$

  c $(k - 3)(k + 5)$ **d** $(z - 9)(z - 3)$

(EV) 3 Find the mistake in each expansion.

  a $(v + 5)(v + 7) = v^2 + 12v + 30$

  b $(w - 8)(w + 10) = w^2 + 2w + 80$

  c $(x - 6)(x - 4) = x^2 - 2x + 24$

  d $(y + 11)(y + 1) = y^2 + 11y + 11$

  e $(z - 7)(z - 2) = z^2 + 9z + 14$

FOIL stands for First, Outer, Inner and Last. This is the order of multiplying the terms from each set of brackets.

Example 7

Expand $(t + 5)(t - 2)$.

First terms give: $t \times t = t^2$

Outer terms give: $t \times -2 = -2t$

Inner terms give: $5 \times t = 5t$

Last terms give: $+5 \times -2 = -10$

$(t + 5)(t - 2) = t^2 - 2t + 5t - 10$

$\qquad\qquad\quad = t^2 + 3t - 10$

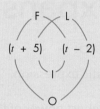

Exercise 8E

1 Use the FOIL method to expand these expressions.

  a $(k + 3)(k + 5)$ **b** $(a + 4)(a + 1)$

  c $(x + 4)(x - 2)$ **d** $(t + 5)(t - 3)$

  e $(w + 3)(w - 1)$ **f** $(f + 2)(f - 3)$

2 Use the FOIL method to expand these expressions.

  a $(r - 2)(r - 8)$ **b** $(s - 10)(s - 7)$

  c $(d - 1)(d - 16)$ **d** $(m - 6)(m - 3)$

  e $(q - 9)(q - 11)$ **f** $(y - 5)(y - 8)$

3 Complete the answer for each expansion.

  a $(a + 7)(a + 13) = a^2 + \ldots\ldots + 91$

  b $(b - 8)(b + 11) = b^2 + \ldots\ldots - 88$

  c $(c + 20)(c + 10) = c^2 + 30c + \ldots\ldots$

  d $(d - 7)(d - 4) = d^2 \ldots\ldots + 28$

  e $(e + 14)(e - 2) = e^2 + \ldots\ldots - \ldots\ldots$

The box method is similar to that used to do long multiplication.

Expand $(k - 3)(k - 2)$.

×	k	-3
k	k^2	$-3k$
-2	$-2k$	$+6$

$(k - 3)(k - 2) = k^2 - 2k - 3k + 6$

$\qquad\qquad\qquad = k^2 - 5k + 6$

Warning: Be careful with the signs. This is the main place where you can easily make mistakes in questions involving expanding brackets.

Note that whatever method you use, it is important to show that you know there are four terms in the expansion before it is simplified.

a Expand $(x + 3)(x + 5)$.

b Use your answer to **a** to find the value of 3.2×5.2.

a Expand the brackets using one of the methods in Examples 6 to 8: $\quad x^2 + 8x + 15$

b $(x + 3)(x + 5)$ is the same as 3.2×5.2 when $x = 0.2$.

Substitute $x = 0.2$ into $x^2 + 8x + 15$: $\quad 0.2^2 + 8 \times 0.2 + 15 = 0.04 + 1.6 + 15 = 16.64$

Exercise 8F

1 Use the box method to expand these expressions.

a $(g + 1)(g - 4)$ **b** $(y + 4)(y - 3)$

c $(x - 3)(x + 4)$ **d** $(p - 2)(p + 1)$

e $(k - 4)(k + 2)$ **f** $(y - 2)(y + 5)$

g $(a - 1)(a + 3)$

> **Hints and tips** A common error is to get minus signs wrong. $-2x - 3x = -5x$ and $-2 \times -3 = +6$

2 The expansions in this question follow a pattern. Work out the first few and try to spot the pattern that will allow you immediately to write down the answers to the rest.

a $(x + 3)(x - 3)$ **b** $(t + 5)(t - 5)$ **c** $(m + 4)(m - 4)$

d $(t + 2)(t - 2)$ **e** $(y + 8)(y - 8)$ **f** $(p + 1)(p - 1)$

g $(5 + x)(5 - x)$ **h** $(7 + g)(7 - g)$ **i** $(x - 6)(x + 6)$

3 This rectangle is made up of four parts with areas of x^2, $2x$, $3x$ and 6 square units.

Work out expressions for the sides of the rectangle, in terms of x.

x^2	$2x$
$3x$	6

4 This square has an area of x^2 square units.

It is split into four rectangles.

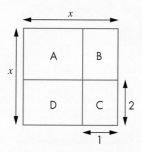

a Copy and fill in the table below to show the dimensions and area of each rectangle.

Rectangle	Length	Width	Area
A	$x - 1$	$x - 2$	$(x-1)(x-2)$
B			
C			
D			

b Add together the areas of rectangles B, C and D.

Expand any brackets and collect like terms together.

c Use the results to explain why $(x-1)(x-2) = x^2 - 3x + 2$.

5 **a** Expand $(x-3)(x+3)$.

b Use the result in **a** to write down the answers to these. (Do not use a calculator or do a long multiplication.)

i 97×103 **ii** 197×203

6 **a** Expand $(y+9)(y+5)$.

b Use the result in **a** to write down the answers to these. (Do not use a calculator or do a long multiplication.)

i 9.01×5.01 **ii** 9.03×5.03 **iii** 8.98×4.98 **iv** 109×105

7 Expand these expressions.

a $(x+1)(x+1)$

b $(x-1)(x-1)$

c $(x+1)(x-1)$

d Use the results in parts **a**, **b** and **c** to show that $(p+q)^2 \equiv p^2 + 2pq + q^2$ is an identity.

> **Hints and tips**   Take $p = x + 1$ and $q = x - 1$.

Quadratic expansion with non-unit coefficients

All the algebraic terms in x^2 in Exercise 8F have a coefficient of 1 or −1. The next two examples show what to do if you have to expand brackets containing terms in x^2 with coefficients that are not 1 or −1.

Example 10

Expand $(2t + 3)(3t + 1)$.

$(2t + 3)(3t + 1) = 6t^2 + 2t + 9t + 3$

$\qquad\qquad\qquad = 6t^2 + 11t + 3$

×	2t	+3
3t	$6t^2$	+9t
+1	+2t	+3

Example 11

Expand $(4x - 1)(3x - 5)$.

$(4x - 1)(3x - 5) = 4x(3x - 5) - (3x - 5)$ **Note:** $(3x - 5)$ is the same as $1(3x - 5)$.

$\qquad\qquad\qquad = 12x^2 - 20x - 3x + 5$

$\qquad\qquad\qquad = 12x^2 - 23x + 5$

Example 12

A triangle has a base of $(2x + 8)$ m and a perpendicular height of $(x - 5)$ m. Find an expression for its area.

The area of a triangle is given by $A = \frac{1}{2}bh$ $= \frac{1}{2}(2x + 8)(x - 5)$

$\qquad\qquad\qquad\qquad\qquad\qquad = \frac{1}{2}(2x^2 - 10x + 8x - 40)$

$\qquad\qquad\qquad\qquad\qquad\qquad = \frac{1}{2}(2x^2 - 2x - 40)$

$\qquad\qquad\qquad\qquad\qquad\qquad = x^2 - x - 20$

Exercise 8G

1 Expand these expressions.

a $(2x + 3)(3x + 1)$

b $(3y + 2)(4y + 3)$

c $(3t + 1)(2t + 5)$

d $(4t + 3)(2t - 1)$

e $(5m + 2)(2m - 3)$

f $(4k + 3)(3k - 5)$

g $(3p - 2)(2p + 5)$

h $(5w + 2)(2w + 3)$

i $(2a - 3)(3a + 1)$

j $(4r - 3)(2r - 1)$

k $(3g - 2)(5g - 2)$

l $(4d - 1)(3d + 2)$

m $(5 + 2p)(3 + 4p)$

n $(2 + 3t)(1 + 2t)$

o $(4 + 3p)(2p + 1)$

p $(6 + 5t)(1 - 2t)$

q $(4 + 3n)(3 - 2n)$

r $(2 + 3f)(2f - 3)$

s $(3 - 2q)(4 + 5q)$

t $(1 - 3p)(3 + 2p)$

u $(4 - 2t)(3t + 1)$

> **Hints and tips** Always give answers in the form $\pm ax^2 \pm bx \pm c$ even if the quadratic coefficient is negative.

2 **a** Without expanding the brackets, match each expression on the left with an expression on the right. One is done for you.

$(3x - 2)(2x + 1)$ $4x^2 - 4x + 1$

$(2x - 1)(2x - 1)$ $6x^2 - x - 2$

$(6x - 3)(x + 1)$ $6x^2 + 7x + 2$

$(4x + 1)(x - 1)$ $6x^2 + 3x - 3$

$(3x + 2)(2x + 1)$ $4x^2 - 3x - 1$

b Taking any expression on the left, explain how you can match it with an expression on the right without expanding the brackets.

3 Try to spot the pattern in each of the expressions in parts **a–o** so that you can immediately write down the expansion.

a $(2x + 1)(2x - 1)$ **b** $(3t + 2)(3t - 2)$ **c** $(5y + 3)(5y - 3)$

d $(4m + 3)(4m - 3)$ **e** $(2k - 3)(2k + 3)$ **f** $(4h - 1)(4h + 1)$

g $(2 + 3x)(2 - 3x)$ **h** $(5 + 2t)(5 - 2t)$ **i** $(6 - 5y)(6 + 5y)$

j $(a + b)(a - b)$ **k** $(3t + k)(3t - k)$ **l** $(2m - 3p)(2m + 3p)$

m $(5k + g)(5k - g)$ **n** $(ab + cd)(ab - cd)$ **o** $(a^2 + b^2)(a^2 - b^2)$

(PS) **4** Imagine a square of side a units with a square of side b units cut from one corner.

a What is the area remaining after the small square is cut away?

b The remaining area is cut into rectangles A, B and C, and rearranged as shown.

Write down the dimensions and area of the rectangle formed by A, B and C.

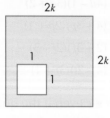

c Explain why $a^2 - b^2 = (a + b)(a - b)$.

(PS) **5** Explain why the areas of the shaded regions are the same.

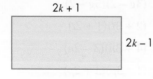

(MR) **6** **a** Expand $(3w + 4)(w + 6)$.

b Use the result in **a** to write down the answers to these. (Do not use a calculator or do a long multiplication.)

     i 304×106 **ii** 3.97×5.99 **iii** 4.00006×6.00002

(PS) **7** **a** Expand $(7a + b)(7a - b)$.

b Use the result in **a** to write down the answer to 72×68. (Do not use a calculator or do a long multiplication.)

8.4 Expanding squares

This section will show you how to:

- expand the square of a binomial.

Whenever you see a linear bracketed term squared, such as $(x - 2)^2$, write the brackets down twice and then use whichever method you prefer to expand.

Example 13

a Expand $(x + 3)^2$.

b Use the answer to find the value of 1003^2.

a $(x + 3)^2 = (x + 3)(x + 3)$

$\qquad = x(x + 3) + 3(x + 3)$

$\qquad = x^2 + 3x + 3x + 9$

$\qquad = x^2 + 6x + 9$

b $(x + 3)^2$ is the same as 1003^2 when $x = 1000$.

When $x = 1000$, $1000^2 + 6 \times 1000 + 9 = 1\,000\,000 + 6000 + 9 = 1\,006\,009$

Example 14

Expand $(3x - 2)^2$.

$(3x - 2)^2 = (3x - 2)(3x - 2)$

$\qquad = 9x^2 - 6x - 6x + 4$

$\qquad = 9x^2 - 12x + 4$

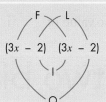

Exercise 8H

1 Expand the squares and simplify.

   a $(x + 5)^2$ **b** $(m + 4)^2$ **c** $(6 + t)^2$

   d $(3 + p)^2$ **e** $(m - 3)^2$ **f** $(t - 5)^2$

   g $(4 - m)^2$ **h** $(7 - k)^2$

> **Hints and tips**   Remember *always* write down the brackets twice. Do not try to take any short cuts.

2 Expand the squares and simplify.

   a $(3x + 1)^2$ **b** $(4t + 3)^2$ **c** $(2 + 5y)^2$ **d** $(3 + 2m)^2$

   e $(4t - 3)^2$ **f** $(3x - 2)^2$ **g** $(2 - 5t)^2$ **h** $(6 - 5r)^2$

   i $(x + y)^2$ **j** $(m - n)^2$ **k** $(2t + y)^2$ **l** $(m - 3n)^2$

   m $(x + 2)^2 - 4$ **n** $(x - 5)^2 - 25$ **o** $(x + 6)^2 - 36$ **p** $(x - 2)^2 - 4$

3 A teacher asks her class to expand $(3x + 1)^2$.

Bernice's answer is $9x^2 + 1$.

Pete's answer is $3x^2 + 6x + 1$.

a Explain the mistakes that Bernice has made.

b Explain the mistakes that Pete has made.

c Work out the correct answer.

 4 Use the diagram to show algebraically and diagrammatically that:

$(2x - 1)^2 = 4x^2 - 4x + 1$

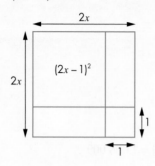

 5 Expand $(3p^3 + 7q^7)^2$.

 6 **a** Expand $(4 + 3k)^2$.

b Use the answer to find the value of   **i** 4.03^2 **ii** 304^2 **iii** 4.015^2

8.5 More than two binomials

This section will show you how to:

- expand more than two binomials.

When more than two binomials are multiplied together, you multiply one pair of binomials together, then multiply the result by another binomial, and so on. The expansion and the box method techniques you have met already can be extended, as shown in the examples, although FOIL would need extra letters for the middle term.

Note that the general rule is that you need to multiply everything in one pair of brackets by everything in the other pair of brackets, and then continue this for additional pairs of brackets.

Example 15

Show that $(x + 3)(x - 4)(x - 10) = x^3 - 11x^2 + ax + 120$, and find the value of a.

Using the expansion method for $(x + 3)(x - 4)$:

$(x + 3)(x - 4) = x(x - 4) + 3(x - 4)$

$\qquad\qquad\qquad = x^2 - 4x + 3x - 12$

$\qquad\qquad\qquad = x^2 - x - 12$

Now use the expansion method for $(x^2 - x - 12)(x - 10)$

$(x^2 - x - 12)(x - 10) = x^2(x - 10) - x(x - 10) - 12(x - 10)$

$\qquad\qquad\qquad\qquad\qquad = x^3 - 10x^2 - x^2 + 10x - 12x + 120$

$\qquad\qquad\qquad\qquad\qquad = x^3 - 11x^2 - 2x + 120$

This is the result you were asked for. $a = -2$.

Example 16

Find a simplified expression for the volume of a cuboid that has sides of $(2x - 1)$ metres, $(x + 4)$ metres and $(x + 7)$ metres.

The volume of a cuboid is the product of the lengths of its sides.

$V = (2x - 1)(x + 4)(x + 7)$.

Using the box method for $(2x - 1)(x + 4)$

×	$2x$	-1
x	$2x^2$	$-x$
4	$8x$	-4

$(2x - 1)(x + 4) = 2x^2 + 8x - x - 4$

$\qquad\qquad\qquad = 2x^2 + 7x - 4$

Using the box method for $(2x^2 + 7x - 4)(x + 7)$

×	$2x^2$	$7x$	-4
x	$2x^3$	$7x^2$	$-4x$
7	$14x^2$	$49x$	-28

$(2x^2 + 7x - 4)(x + 7) = 2x^3 + 14x^2 + 7x^2 + 49x - 4x - 28$

$\qquad\qquad\qquad\qquad\quad = 2x^3 + 21x^2 + 45x - 28$

The volume of the cuboid can be written as $(2x^3 + 21x^2 + 45x - 28)$ m^3.

Example 17

a Expand $(x + 2)^3$.

b Find the value of 2.01^3 without using a calculator.

a $(x + 2)^3$ is the same as $(x + 2)(x + 2)(x + 2)$.

Using the expansion method

$(x + 2)(x + 2) = x(x + 2) + 2(x + 2)$

$\qquad\qquad\qquad = x^2 + 2x + 2x + 4$

$\qquad\qquad\qquad = x^2 + 4x + 4$

$(x^2 + 4x + 4)(x + 2) = x^2(x + 2) + 4x(x + 2) + 4(x + 2)$

$\qquad\qquad\qquad\qquad = x^3 + 2x^2 + 4x^2 + 8x + 4x + 8$

$\qquad\qquad\qquad\qquad = x^3 + 6x^2 + 12x + 8$

So $(x + 2)^3 = x^3 + 6x^2 + 12x + 8$

b If $x = 0.01$, then $(x + 2)^3 = 2.01^3$.

Substitute $x = 0.01$ in the expression $x^3 + 6x^2 + 12x + 8$:

$2.01^3 = 0.01^3 + 6 \times 0.01^2 + 12 \times 0.01 + 8$

$\qquad = 0.000\,001 + 0.0006 + 0.12 + 8$

$\qquad = 8.120\,601$

1 Expand these expressions.

    a $(x + 1)(x + 2)(x + 3)$ **b** $(x + 5)(x + 3)(x - 8)$

    c $(x - 2)(x + 2)(x + 9)$

2 Expand these expressions.

    a $(x - 1)^2(x + 9)$ **b** $(x^2 + 3x + 5)(x - 2)$

3 Expand these expressions.

    a $(x + 4)^3$ **b** $(x - 6)^3$ **c** $(x + a)^3$

(EV) **4** **a** Find the expansion of $(x + 7)(x + 3)(x + 1)$. Start by multiplying $(x + 7)$ and $(x + 3)$.

    b Now find the expansion of $(x + 7)(x + 3)(x + 1)$, starting by multiplying $(x + 7)$ and $(x + 1)$.

    c Now find the expansion of $(x + 7)(x + 3)(x + 1)$, starting by multiplying $(x + 3)$ and $(x + 1)$.

    d What do your answers tell you about the order in which you expand the brackets?

(MR) **5** **a** Expand $(x + a)(x + b)(x + c)$.

    b If $(x + 3)(x - 5)(x + 2) = x^3 + px^2 + qx + r$, use your answer from **a** to find the values of p, q and r.

(PS) **6** A cuboid has edges of $(x + 1)$ cm, $(x + 3)$ cm and $(x - 19)$ cm.

    Find simplified expressions for

    a the volume of the cuboid

    b the surface area of the cuboid.

(CM) **7** **a** Expand these expressions.   **i** $(x + 1)^2$ **ii** $(x + 1)^3$ **iii** $(x + 1)^4$

    b By using a suitable substitution, use your answers to find the values of 11^2, 11^3 and 11^4.

    c How do your answers relate to the coefficients of the terms in the answers?

(MR) **8** **a** Expand $(x + 3)^3$.

    b Find the value of 3.001^3 without using a calculator.

9 Expand these expressions.

    a $(2x - 3)(x + 5)(x - 2)$

    b $(x + 2)^2(3x - 1)$

10 Expand these expressions.

    a $(3x - 5)(2x + 7)(4x - 3)$ **b** $(5x - 2)^2(2x - 11)$ **c** $(3x - 4)^3$

11 Simplify this expression. $(2x - 1)(x - 4)(x - 2) - (2x - 3)(x + 5)(x + 6)$

8.6 Quadratic factorisation

This section will show you how to:

- factorise a quadratic expression of the form $x^2 + ax + b$ into two linear brackets.

Key term

difference of two squares

Factorisation involves putting a quadratic expression back into its brackets (if possible).

You start by factorising quadratic expressions of the type:

$$x^2 + ax + b$$

where a and b are integers.

There are some rules that will help you to factorise.

- The expression inside each set of brackets will start with an x, and the signs in the quadratic expression show which signs to put after the xs.

- When the second sign in the expression is positive, the signs in both sets of brackets are the same as the first sign.

   $x^2 + ax + b = (x + ?)(x + ?)$ Since everything is positive.

   $x^2 - ax + b = (x - ?)(x - ?)$ Since $-ve \times -ve = +ve$

- When the *second* sign is *negative*, the signs in the brackets are *different*.

   $x^2 + ax - b = (x + ?)(x - ?)$ Since $+ve \times -ve = -ve$

   $x^2 - ax - b = (x + ?)(x - ?)$

- Next, look at the *last* number, b, in the expression. When multiplied together, the two numbers in the brackets must give b.

- Finally, look at the coefficient *of x*, a. The *sum* of the two *numbers* in the brackets will give a.

Example 18

Factorise $x^2 - x - 6$.

Because of the signs you know the brackets must be $(x + ?)(x - ?)$.

Two numbers that have a product of -6 and a sum of -1 are -3 and $+2$.

So, $x^2 - x - 6 = (x + 2)(x - 3)$.

Example 19

a   Factorise $x^2 - 9x + 20$.

b   Find the value of $x^2 - 9x + 20$ when $x = 24$ without using a calculator.

a   Because of the signs you know the brackets must be $(x - ?)(x - ?)$.

   Two numbers that have a product of $+20$ and a sum of -9 are -4 and -5.

   So, $x^2 - 9x + 20 = (x - 4)(x - 5)$.

b   You could calculate $24^2 - 9 \times 24 + 20$, but it is simpler to substitute $x = 24$ into the factorised expression.

   $(x - 4)(x - 5) = (24 - 4)(24 - 5)$

   $\qquad\qquad\qquad = 20 \times 19$

   $\qquad\qquad\qquad = 380$

1 Factorise these expressions.

a $x^2 + 5x + 6$ **b** $t^2 + 5t + 4$ **c** $m^2 + 7m + 10$ **d** $k^2 + 10k + 24$

e $p^2 + 14p + 24$ **f** $r^2 + 9r + 18$ **g** $w^2 + 11w + 18$ **h** $x^2 + 7x + 12$

i $a^2 + 8a + 12$ **j** $k^2 + 10k + 21$ **k** $f^2 + 22f + 21$ **l** $b^2 + 20b + 96$

m $t^2 - 5t + 6$ **n** $d^2 - 5d + 4$ **o** $g^2 - 7g + 10$ **p** $x^2 - 15x + 36$

q $c^2 - 18c + 32$ **r** $t^2 - 13t + 36$ **s** $y^2 - 16y + 48$ **t** $j^2 - 14j + 48$

2 Factorise these expressions.

a $p^2 - 8p + 15$ **b** $y^2 + 5y - 6$ **c** $t^2 + 2t - 8$ **d** $x^2 + 3x - 10$

e $m^2 - 4m - 12$ **f** $r^2 - 6r - 7$ **g** $n^2 - 3n - 18$ **h** $m^2 - 7m - 44$

i $w^2 - 2w - 24$ **j** $t^2 - t - 90$ **k** $h^2 - h - 72$ **l** $t^2 - 2t - 63$

m $d^2 + 2d + 1$ **n** $y^2 + 20y + 100$ **o** $t^2 - 8t + 16$ **p** $m^2 - 18m + 81$

q $x^2 - 24x + 144$ **r** $d^2 - d - 12$ **s** $t^2 - t - 20$ **t** $q^2 - q - 56$

> **Hints and tips**   First decide on the signs in the brackets, then look at the numbers.

(PS) 3 This rectangle is made up of four parts. Two of the parts have areas of x^2 and 6 square units.

The sides of the rectangle are of the form $x + a$ and $x + b$.

There are two possible answers for a and b.

Work out both answers and copy and complete the areas in the other parts of the rectangle.

(CM) 4 **a** Expand $(x + a)(x + b)$.

b If $x^2 + 7x + 10 = (x + p)(x + q)$, use your answer to part **a** to write down the values of:

    i $p + q$ **ii** pq

c Explain how you can tell that $x^2 + 12x + 7$ will not factorise.

(CM) 5 **a** Substitute $x = 19$ into the expression $x^2 + 4x + 3$.

b **i** Factorise $x^2 + 4x + 3$.

    ii Show that you get the same answer as **a** substituting $x = 19$ into your answer to **b i**.

(PS) 6 Factorise these expressions.

a $x^4 - 11x^2 + 24$ **b** $y^{10} - 100y^5 - 416$ **c** $z^{3456} - 862z^{1728} - 1728$

Difference of two squares

In Exercise 8G, you multiplied out, for example, $(a + b)(a - b)$ and obtained $a^2 - b^2$. This type of quadratic expression, with only two terms that are both perfect squares, separated by a minus sign, is called the **difference of two squares**.

Expand $(x - 7)(x + 7)$.

$(x - 7)(x + 7) = x^2 - 7x + 7x - 49$

$\qquad\qquad\qquad = x^2 - 49$

Note that when you collect the $-7x$ and $+7x$ terms, they add together to make zero.

This process will only work when the terms in the brackets are different signs, which is why the difference of two squares has a minus sign.

You can use this idea to factorise expressions written as the difference of two squares:

$\qquad x^2 - 9 = (x - 3)(x + 3)$

$\qquad x^2 - 25 = (x - 5)(x + 5)$

$\qquad 25x^2 - 4 = (5x - 2)(5x + 2)$

Three conditions must be met for the difference of two squares to work.

- There must be two terms.
- They must be separated by a negative sign.
- Each term must be a perfect square, say x^2 and n^2.

When these three conditions are met, the factorisation is: $\qquad x^2 - n^2 = (x + n)(x - n)$

Example 20

a Factorise $x^2 - 9$.

b Use your answer to find the two prime factors of 4891.

a Recognise the difference of two squares, x^2 and 9.

So it factorises to $(x + 3)(x - 3)$.

Expanding the brackets shows that they do come from the original expression.

b If $\qquad x^2 - 9 = 4891$

then $\qquad x^2 = 4900$

and $\qquad x = 70$

(x could also equal -70 but that answer will not give you prime factors.)

When $x = 70$, the factors are $70 + 3$ and $70 - 3$.

The prime factors are 73 and 67.

Example 21

Factorise $9x^2 - 169$.

Recognise the difference of two squares $(3x)^2$ and 13^2.

So it factorises to $(3x + 13)(3x - 13)$.

Exercise 8K

1 Each of the expressions is the difference of two squares. Factorise them.

a $x^2 - 9$ **b** $t^2 - 25$ **c** $m^2 - 16$

d $9 - x^2$ **e** $49 - t^2$ **f** $k^2 - 100$

g $4 - y^2$ **h** $x^2 - 64$ **i** $t^2 - 81$

> **Hints and tips** Learn how to spot the difference of two squares as you will come across them a lot.

2 **a** A square has a side of x units.

What is the area of the square?

b A rectangle, A, 2 units wide, is cut from the square and placed at the side of the remaining rectangle, B.

A square, C, is then cut from the bottom of rectangle A to leave a final rectangle, D.

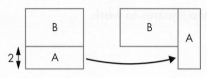

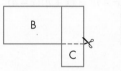

i What is the height of rectangle B?

ii What is the width of rectangle D?

iii What is the area of rectangle B plus rectangle A?

iv What is the area of square C?

c By working out the area of rectangle D, explain why $x^2 - 4 = (x + 2)(x - 2)$.

3 **a** Expand and simplify: $(x + 2)^2 - (x + 1)^2$

b Factorise: $a^2 - b^2$

c In your answer for part **b**, replace a with $(x + 2)$ and b with $(x + 1)$.

Expand and simplify the answer.

d What can you say about the answers to parts **a** and **c**?

e Simplify: $(x + 1)^2 - (x - 1)^2$

4 Factorise these expressions.

a $x^2 - y^2$ **b** $x^2 - 4y^2$ **c** $x^2 - 9y^2$ **d** $9x^2 - 1$

e $16x^2 - 9$ **f** $25x^2 - 64$ **g** $4x^2 - 9y^2$ **h** $9t^2 - 4w^2$

i $16y^2 - 25x^2$

5 Factorise the expressions.

a $121x^6 - 9y^6$ **b** $25m^{10} - 81n^{18}$ **c** $576p^{576} - 961q^{288}$

6 **a** Factorise the expression $9x^2 - 1$.

b Use your answer to find the prime factors of 899.

7 **a** Factorise the expression $4x^2 - 49$.

b Use your answer to find the three unique prime factors of 39 951.

8.7 Factorising $ax^2 + bx + c$

This section will show you how to:

- factorise a quadratic expression of the form $ax^2 + bx + c$ into two linear brackets.

You can adapt the method for factorising $x^2 + ax + b$ to take into account the factors of the coefficient of x^2.

Example 22

Factorise $3x^2 + 8x + 4$.

First, note that both signs are positive. So the signs in the brackets must be $(?x + ?)(?x + ?)$.

As 3 has only 3×1 as factors, the brackets must be $(3x + ?)(x + ?)$.

Next, note that the factors of 4 are 4×1 and 2×2.

Now find which pair of factors of 4 combine with 3 and 1 to give 8.

$$\begin{array}{c|cc} ③ & 4 & ② \\ ① & 1 & ② \end{array}$$

You can see that the combination 3×2 and 1×2 adds up to 8.

So, the complete factorisation becomes $(3x + 2)(x + 2)$.

Example 23

Factorise $6x^2 - 7x - 10$.

First, note that both signs are negative. So the signs in the brackets must be $(?x + ?)(?x - ?)$.

As 6 has 6×1 and 3×2 as factors, the brackets could be $(6x \pm ?)(x \pm ?)$ or $(3x \pm ?)(2x \pm ?)$.

Next, note that the factors of 10 are 5×2 and 1×10.

Now find which pair of factors of 10 combine with the factors of 6 to give -7.

$$\begin{array}{cc|cc} 3 & ⑥ & \pm 1 & ⑥{\pm2} \\ 2 & ① & \pm 10 & ⑤{\pm5} \end{array}$$

You can see that the combination 6×-2 and 1×5 adds up to -7.

So, the complete factorisation becomes $(6x + 5)(x - 2)$.

Example 24

Use the factorisation of $2x^2 - 17x + 35$ to find its value when $x = 15$.

Since the coefficient of the x-term is negative but the coefficient of the constant is positive, the signs in the brackets must be $(?x - ?)(?x - ?)$.

As 2 has only 2×1 as factors, the brackets must be $(2x - ?)(x - ?)$.

Next, note that the factors of 35 are 35×1 and 7×5.

Now find which pair of factors of 35 combine with 2 and 1 to give 17.

$$\begin{array}{c|cccc} ② & -35 & -7 & -1 & ⑤{-5} \\ ① & -1 & -5 & -35 & ⑦{-7} \end{array}$$

You can see that the combination 2×-5 and 1×-7 adds up to -17.

So, the complete factorisation becomes $(2x - 7)(x - 5)$.

Substitute $x = 15$ into $(2x - 7)(x - 5)$: $(2 \times 15 - 7)(15 - 5) = 23 \times 10 = 230$

1 Factorise these expressions.

  a $2x^2 + 5x + 2$ **b** $7x^2 + 8x + 1$ **c** $4x^2 + 3x - 7$

  d $24t^2 + 19t + 2$ **e** $15t^2 + 2t - 1$ **f** $16x^2 - 8x + 1$

  g $6y^2 + 33y - 63$ **h** $4y^2 + 8y - 96$ **i** $8x^2 + 10x - 3$

  j $6t^2 + 13t + 5$ **k** $3x^2 - 16x - 12$ **l** $7x^2 - 37x + 10$

(PS) **2** This rectangle is made up of four parts, with areas of $12x^2$, $3x$, $8x$ and 2 square units.

$12x^2$	$3x$
$8x$	2

Work out expressions for the sides of the rectangle, in terms of x.

(CM) **3** Three students are asked to factorise the expression $6x^2 + 30x + 36$.

These are their answers.

Adam Bertie Cara

$(6x + 12)(x + 3)$ $(3x + 6)(2x + 6)$ $(2x + 4)(3x + 9)$

All the answers are correctly factorised.

  a Explain why one quadratic expression can have three different factorisations.

  b Which of the following is the most complete factorisation?

   $2(3x + 6)(x + 3)$ $6(x + 2)(x + 3)$ $3(x + 2)(2x + 6)$

   Explain your choice.

4 Use the factorisation of $3x^2 + 47x - 16$ to find its value when $x = 14$.

5 **a** Factorise $33x^2 - 65x - 2$.

  b Use the factorisation to show that when $x = 3$, the value of $33x^2 - 65x - 2$ is 100.

(MR) **6** Given that $(5x + 9)$ is one factor of $15x^2 - 73x - 180$, find the other factor.

(PS) **7** The area of a rectangle is given by the expression $6x^2 + 7x - 20$.

Find both possible expressions for the perimeter of the rectangle.

8.8 Changing the subject of a formula

This section will show you how to:

- change the subject of a formula.

Key terms

inverse operations	rearrange
subject	transpose

The **subject** is the variable (letter) in a formula or equation which stands on its own, usually on the left-hand side of the equals sign. For example, x is the subject of each of the following equations.

$$x = 5t + 4 \qquad x = 4(2y - 7) \qquad x = \frac{1}{t}$$

To change the existing subject to a different variable, you have to **rearrange** (**transpose**) the formula to get that variable on the left-hand side. You do this by using **inverse operations**.

For example, if $2x + 7 = 13$, you subtract 7 from both sides, which gives you $2x = 6$. Subtracting 7 is the inverse operation of adding 7.

Next, you divide both sides by 2, which gives you $x = 3$. Dividing by 2 is the inverse operation of multiplying by 2.

The main difference between rearranging formulae and solving equations is that when you solve an equation each step gives a numerical value. When you rearrange a formula each step gives an algebraic expression.

Example 25

Make m the subject of this formula. $\qquad T = m - 3$

Add the 3 so that the m is on its own. $\quad T + 3 = m$

Reverse the formula. $\qquad m = T + 3$

Example 26

From the formula $P = 4t$, express t in terms of P.

(This is another common way of asking you to make t the subject.)

$$P = 4t$$

Divide both sides by 4: $\quad \dfrac{P}{4} = \dfrac{4t}{4}$

Reverse the formula: $\quad t = \dfrac{P}{4}$

Example 27

Make m the subject of the formula $C = 2m^2 + 3$.

Subtract the 3 so that the $2m^2$ is on its own: $\quad C - 3 = 2m^2$

Divide both sides by 2: $\qquad \dfrac{C - 3}{2} = \dfrac{2m^2}{2}$

Reverse the formula: $\qquad m^2 = \dfrac{C - 3}{2}$

Take the square root on both sides: $\qquad m = \sqrt{\dfrac{C - 3}{2}}$

Example 28

The formula $v^2 = u^2 + 2as$ relates the final velocity (v) of an object to the initial velocity (u), the acceleration (a) and the displacement (s).

a Make a the subject of the formula.

b Find the acceleration of a particle which has an initial velocity of 7 m/s, a final velocity of 11 m/s and a displacement of 6 m.

a
$$v^2 = u^2 + 2as$$

Subtract the u^2 so that the $2as$ is on its own $v^2 - u^2 = 2as$

Divide both sides by $2s$:
$$a = \frac{v^2 - u^2}{2s}$$

b Substitute $u = 7$, $v = 11$ and $s = 6$.
$$a = \frac{11^2 - 7^2}{2 \times 6}$$
$$= \frac{121 - 49}{12}$$
$$= \frac{72}{12}$$
$$= 6 \text{ m/s}^2$$

Exercise 8M

1 $T = 3k$ Make k the subject.

2 $X = y - 1$ Express y in terms of X.

3 $Q = \frac{p}{3}$ Express p in terms of Q.

4 $A = 4r + 9$ Make r the subject.

5 $p = m + t$ **a** Make m the subject.   **b** Make t the subject.

6 $g = \frac{m}{v}$ Make m the subject.

7 $t = m^2$ Make m the subject.

8 $P = 2l + 2w$ Make l the subject.

9 $m = p^2 + 2$ Make p the subject.

10 The formula for converting degrees Fahrenheit to degrees Celsius is $C = \frac{5}{9}(F - 32)$.

     a Show that when $F = -40$, C is also equal to -40.

     b Find the value of C when $F = 68$.

     c Use this flow diagram to establish the formula for converting degrees Celsius to degrees Fahrenheit.

11 Distance, speed and time are connected by the formula:

distance = speed × time.

A delivery driver drove 126 km in 1 hour and 45 minutes. On the return journey, he was held up at some road works so his average speed decreased by 9 km per hour.

How long was he held up at the road works?

> **Hints and tips**   Work out the average speed for the first journey, then work out the average speed for the return journey.

(CM) **12** Given that $C = 2\pi r$ and $A = \pi r^2$, show that $A = \dfrac{C^2}{4\pi}$

(EV) **13** Kieran notices that the price of five cream buns is 75p more than the price of nine mince pies.

Let the price of a cream bun be x pence and the price of a mince pie be y pence.

a Based upon Kieran's observation, express the cost of one mince pie, y, in terms of the price of a cream bun, x.

b The price of a cream bun is 60p and the price of a mince pie is 25p. Check your formula is correct.

Marlon states that the price of seven cream buns is 40p more than the price of ten mince pies.

c Based upon Marlon's statement, express the cost of one mince pie, y, in terms of the price of a cream bun, x.

d Given the prices of the cream bun and mince pie, evaluate whether or not Marlon's statement is correct.

> **Hints and tips** Set up a formula, using the first sentence of information, then rearrange it.

14 $v = u + at$ **a** Make a the subject.   **b** Make t the subject.

15 $A = \frac{1}{4}\pi d^2$ Make d the subject.

16 $x = 5y - w$ **a** Make y the subject.   **b** Express w in terms of x and y.

17 $k = 2p^2$ Make p the subject.

18 $v = u^2 - t$ **a** Make t the subject.   **b** Make u the subject.

19 $K = 5n^2 + w$ **a** Make w the subject.   **b** Make n the subject.

(MR) **20** **a** $U = K - \dfrac{P}{3D - Y}$ Make D the subject.

b Find the value of D when $U = -3$, $Y = 37$, $P = 77$ and $K = 4$.

Worked exemplars

  a Expand $(5x + 3y)(3x - 4y)$.

b Use your answer to find the value of 50.03×29.96 without using a calculator.

This is a question requiring mathematical reasoning. This means that once you have expanded the brackets for part **a**, you then need to find a link between parts **a** and **b** so that you can use your answer from **a** to help you with **b**.	
a $(5x + 3y)(3x - 4y) = 15x^2 - 20xy + 9xy - 12y^2$ $\qquad\qquad\qquad\qquad = 15x^2 - 11xy - 12y^2$	
b $x = 10$ $y = 0.01$	Comparing the algebra in **a** with the multiplication sum in **b**, you need to recognise that they are the same when $x = 10$ and $y = 0.01$
$15x^2 - 11xy - 12y^2$ $= 15 \times 10^2 - 11 \times 10 \times 0.01 - 12 \times 0.01^2$	Substitute $x = 10$ and $y = 0.01$ into the expansion.
$= 1500 - 1.1 - 0.0012$ $= 1498.8988$	

2   A rectangle has a length of $2x + 4$ and width of $x + 2$.

a   Show that the perimeter can be written as $6(x + 2)$.

b   Mark says that the perimeter must always be an even number.

Prove that Mark is wrong.

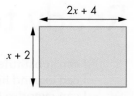

Part **a** is a problem solving question, which means that you need to find the connections between two topics, in this case collecting like terms and finding the perimeter.

For part **b**, this question requires you to assess the validity of an argument.

a Perimeter = $2 \times (2x + 4) + 2 \times (x + 2)$ $\qquad = 2 \times 2(x + 2) + 2(x + 2)$ $\qquad = 4(x + 2) + 2(x + 2)$ $\qquad = 6(x + 2)$ [Alternatively, Perimeter = $2x + 4 + 2x + 4 + x + 2 + x + 2$ $\qquad = 6x + 12$ $6x + 12 = 6(x + 2)$]	You need to show your method clearly. Write down a correct unsimplified expression for the perimeter. You have to write your answer of $6(x + 2)$ to show a complete accurate proof.
b Mark is wrong because although $6(x + 2)$ is always even when $(x + 2)$ is a whole number, there are values of x for which $(x + 2)$ is not a whole number. Example: $x = 2.5$, $6(x + 2) = 6 \times 4.5 = 27$ 27 is not even [Alternatively, $6(x + 2) = 15$ $\qquad x + 2 = 2.5$ $\qquad\quad x = 0.5$ It is possible for the perimeter to be a number which is not even.]	Either choose a value of x for which the perimeter is not even (such as 2.5) or choose a perimeter which is not even (such as 15) and find the corresponding value of x. Note that there are many answers. Any value that makes the value inside the brackets 'something and a half', such as $x = 1.5$ or $x = 2.5$ will work.

Ready to progress?

I can substitute numbers into expressions and formulae.
I can expand linear brackets and simplify expressions by collecting like terms.
I can factorise linear expressions.
I can rearrange simple formulae.

I can expand two or more binomials.
I can factorise quadratic expressions of the form $x^2 + ax + b$.
I can recognise the difference of two squares.

I can factorise quadratic expressions of the form $ax^2 + bx + c$.

Review questions ✗

1. **a** Find an expression for the sum of the expressions $(2x + 9)$, $(6x - 5)$, $(3x + 11)$ and $(9x + 1)$.

   b Find the mean of the expressions $(2x + 9)$, $(6x - 5)$, $(3x + 11)$ and $(9x + 1)$.

2. $R = 5c - 9 + 3d + 2(c + 7)$

   a Make c the subject of the formula.   **b** Find c when $R = 20$ and $d = -9$.

3. (PS) A formula for calculating a dose (D) of medicine (in ml) for a person of age a is given by
   $D = \dfrac{4(a + 7)}{a + 10}$.

   a Find the dose for a person aged:

   i 14   **ii** 30   **iii** 65.

   b Find the age of a person who would take a dose of:

   i 3.625 ml   **ii** 3.75 ml   **iii** 3.88 ml.

4. (PS) Find the area of a triangle with a base of $(5x - 11)$ metres and a height of $\dfrac{x^2 - 7}{x - 1}$ metres when $x = 4$.

5. (PS) The surface area, A, of a cylinder with a radius, r, and a height, h is given by the formula $A = 2\pi r^2 + 2\pi rh$.

   a Factorise $2\pi r^2 + 2\pi rh$.   **b** Make h the subject of the formula.

   c Find the height of a cylinder which has an area of 208π cm^2 and a radius of 8 cm.

6. The formula $A = y + 0.01xy$ calculates the size of an amount y after it has been increased by x%.

   a Make x the subject of the formula.   **b** Factorise $y + 0.01xy$.

   (PS) **c** Use the formula to find the mass after 28 g has been increased by 37%.

7. (PS) A right-angled triangle has a base of 30 m and a height of $(3x + 1)$ m. If the area of the right-angled triangle is 240 m^2, find the value of x.

(PS) 8 The formula $v^2 = u^2 + 2as$ relates the final velocity (v) of an object to the initial velocity (u), the acceleration (a) and the displacement (s). The formula $v = u + at$ relates the final velocity (v) to the initial velocity (u), the acceleration (a) and the time (t).

A ball rolls for 2 seconds, increasing its velocity from 8 m/s to 12 m/s. Find the displacement of the ball.

(PS) 9 A bag has ($7x + 3$) blue balls, ($2x - 4$) red balls and ($19 - 4x$) green balls.

a A ball is removed from the bag and discarded. Write down an expression for the probability that the ball is green.

b A second ball is removed from the bag. If the first ball was green, what is the probability that this ball is also green?

> **Hints and tips** Remember that the probability of taking a particular colour of ball (e.g. yellow) is $\dfrac{\text{Number of yellow balls}}{\text{Total number of balls}}$

10 **a** Factorise $2x - 16$. **b** Factorise $x^2 - 16x$.
    c Factorise $x^2 - 16$. **d** Factorise $x^2 - 16x + 63$.

11 $y = 3(2x - 5)(x - 6)$
    a Show that when $x = 10$, $y = 180$. **b** Expand the expression.

(PS) 12 A rectangle has a base of ($3x - 8$) cm and a height of ($5x + 7$) cm.

a Find simplified expressions for:
    i its area **ii** its perimeter.

b If the perimeter of the rectangle is 70 cm, find its area.

(MR) 13 **a** Expand $(2x + 1)^2$. **b** By substituting $x = 10$, find the value of 21^2.
    c Use the difference of two squares to find the value of 23×19.

(MR) 14 **a** Expand $(a + b)^3$. **b** Use your answer to expand $(2x + 3)^3$.
    c Hence find the value of 3.02^3 without a calculator.

(PS) 15 A cuboid has edges of ($x + 3$) cm, ($x + 4$) cm and ($x + 5$) cm.

a Find expressions for:
    i the total length of all the edges
    ii the surface area of the cuboid
    iii the volume of the cuboid.

b If the sum of the edges of the cuboid is 180 cm, find the surface area and volume.

16 **a** Expand the brackets: $(3x + 5y)(4x - 7y)$
    b Factorise: $6x^2 - xy - 35y^2$

(MR) 17 Given that $3x^2 + ax + 8$ can be factorised, state all the possible values that a can take.

(MR) 18 **a** Factorise $2x^2 + 7x + 6$.
    b Use your answer to find the value of:
    i 23×12 **ii** 203×102 **iii** 3.02×2.01.

9 Geometry and measures: Length, area and volume

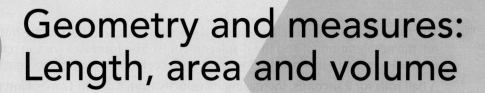

This chapter is going to show you:

- how to calculate the circumference and area of a circle
- how to calculate the area of a parallelogram and a trapezium
- how to calculate the length of an arc
- how to calculate the area and angle of a sector
- how to calculate the volume of a prism and a pyramid
- how to calculate the volume and surface area of a cylinder, a cone and a sphere.

You should already know:

- the formula for the area of a rectangle: area = length × width or $A = lw$
- the formula for the area of a triangle: area = $\frac{1}{2}$ × base × height or $A = \frac{1}{2}bh$
- the formula for the volume of a cuboid:
  volume = length × width × height *or* $V = lwh$
- the common metric units to measure area, volume and capacity shown in this table.

Area	Volume	Capacity
100 mm² = 1 cm²	1000 mm³ = 1 cm³	1000 cm³ = 1 litre
10 000 cm² = 1 m²	1 000 000 cm³ = 1 m³	1 m³ = 1000 litres

About this chapter

From earliest times, farmers have wanted to know the area of their fields to see how many crops they could grow or animals they could support. One of the oldest units of area used in England was the acre, which was the amount of land that a man could plough in a day. Even today, when land is bought and sold, the cost depends on the area. A considerable part of the cost of a new house is the cost of the land it stands on.

Volumes are important, too. They tell us how much space there is inside any structure. Whether it is a house, barn, aeroplane, car or office, the volume is important. Did you know, for example, that in England there is a regulation that governs the number of people that can use an office, based on the volume of the room?

So how can you measure areas and volumes? Some shapes and objects are easy. Others take more ingenuity and skill. In this chapter, you will learn formulae that can be used to calculate areas and volumes of different shapes, based on a few measurements. Many of these formulae were first worked out thousands of years ago. The fact that these formulae are still in use today shows how important they are.

9.1 Circumference and area of a circle

This section will show you how to:

- calculate the circumference and area of a circle.

Circumference of a circle

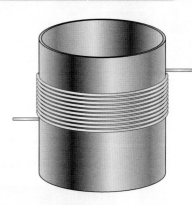

- Find a cylinder or tin and measure its diameter, d.
- Wrap a piece of string around the cylinder 10 times and measure the length, L; of the string.
- Divide L; by 10 to find the **circumference**, C; of the cylinder.
- Divide the circumference, C; by diameter, d; and check you get the result 3.1.

If you were able to do this accurately you would get the result as 3.141 592…, which is the number π, found on your calculator. π is a Greek letter; you pronounce it as 'pi'.

This result illustrates the relationship between the circumference, C, of a circle and its diameter, d.

$$C = \pi d$$

Example 1

Calculate the circumference of the circle. Give your answer to 3 significant figures.

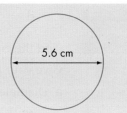
5.6 cm

$C = \pi d$

   $= \pi \times 5.6$ cm

   $= 17.6$ cm (3 sf)

Area of a circle

You could divide a circle into 32 sectors as shown.

These 32 sectors are then cut out and rearranged together as the new shape shown.

This shape is close to a rectangle.

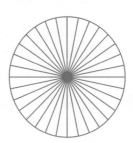

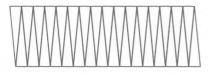

Notice that the length of the rectangle is half the circumference, that is $\frac{1}{2}\pi d =$ or πr as $d = 2r$.

Notice that the width of the rectangle is the radius, r, of the circle.

So the area of the circle = the area of rectangle = $\pi r \times r = \pi r^2$.

This result illustrates the relationship between the area, A, and the radius, r, of a circle.

$$A = \pi r^2$$

Example 2

Calculate the area of the circle. Give your answer in terms of π.

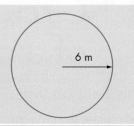

6 m

$A = \pi r^2$

$\quad = \pi \times 6^2 \text{ m}^2$

$\quad = 36\pi \text{ m}^2$

Exercise 9A

1 Copy and complete this table.

Give your answers to 3 significant figures.

Circle	Radius	Diameter	Circumference	Area
a	4.0 cm			
b	2.6 m			
c		12.0 cm		
d		3.2 m		

2 Find the circumference of each of the following circles.

Give your answers in terms of π.

a Diameter: 5 cm   **b** Radius: 4 cm   **c** Radius: 9 m   **d** Diameter: 12 cm

3 Find the area of each of the following circles.

Give your answers in terms of π.

a Radius: 5 cm   **b** Diameter: 12 cm   **c** Radius: 10 cm   **d** Diameter: 1 m

(PS) 4 A rope is wrapped eight times around a capstan (a cylindrical post), with a diameter of 35 cm.

How long is the rope?

(PS) 5 The roller used on a cricket pitch has a radius of 70 cm.

A cricket pitch has a length of 20 m.

How many complete revolutions does the roller make when rolling the pitch?

6 The diameter of each of these four coins is as follows.

1p: 2.0 cm   2p: 2.6 cm   5p: 1.7 cm   10p: 2.4 cm

Calculate the area of one face of each coin.

Give your answers to 1 decimal place.

7 The distance around the outside of a large pipe is 2.6 m.

What is the diameter of the pipe?

(PS) **8** What is the total perimeter of a semicircle of diameter 15 cm?

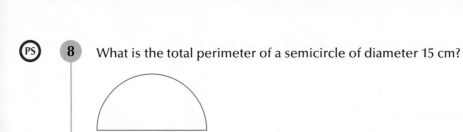

15 cm

(EV) **9** A restaurant sells two sizes of pizza. The diameters are 24 cm and 30 cm.

The restaurant claims that the larger size is 50% bigger.

Your friend disagrees and wants to complain. What would you advise? Give a reason for your answer.

10 Calculate the area of each of these shapes, giving your answers in terms of π.

a
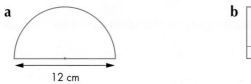

12 cm

b

4 cm

(MR) **11** Calculate the area of the shaded part of the diagram, giving your answer in terms of π.

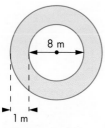

8 m

1 m

(EV) **12** A tree in Sequoia National Park in the USA is considered to be the largest in the world. It has a circumference at the base of 31.3 m. Would the base of the tree fit inside your classroom? Explain how you know.

(PS) **13** The wheel of a bicycle has a diameter of 70 cm.

The bicycle travels 100 m.

How many complete revolutions does the wheel make?

(MR) **14** The shape shown is made up of semicircles.

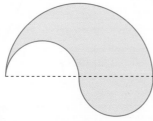

a If the radius of the small semicircle is 1 cm, find the area of the shaded shape in terms of π.

b Repeat part **a** if the small semicircle has a radius of:

i 2 cm **ii** 3 cm **iii** 4 cm.

c What link is there between the radius, r, of the small semicircle and the area, A, of the shaded shape?

9.2 Area of a parallelogram

This section will show you how to:

• calculate the area of a parallelogram.

The diagram shows that a parallelogram can be rearranged to form a rectangle with the same base and perpendicular height.

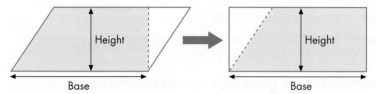

This means that the formula for the area of a parallelogram is the same as the formula for the area of a rectangle:

area = base × perpendicular height

$A = bh$

where b is the length of the base and h is the perpendicular height of the parallelogram.

Example 3

Work out the area of this parallelogram.

6 cm

8 cm

Area = 8 cm × 6 cm

= 48 cm^2

Exercise 9B

1 Calculate the area of each parallelogram.

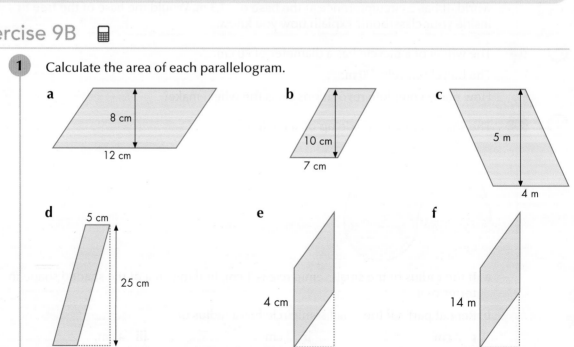

a
8 cm
12 cm

b
10 cm
7 cm

c
5 m
4 m

d
5 cm
25 cm

e
4 cm
$2\frac{1}{2}$ cm

f
14 m
8 m

2 Sandeep says that the area of this parallelogram is 30 cm².

Is she correct? Give a reason for your answer.

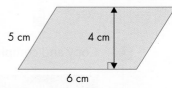

CM **3** This shape is made from four identical parallelograms. The total area of the shape is 120 cm².

Freya said the length marked x on the diagram is 20 cm.

Show that Freya is incorrect.

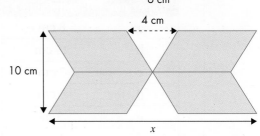

PS **4** This logo, made from two identical parallelograms, is cut from a sheet of card.

a Calculate the area of the logo.

b How many logos can be cut from a sheet of card that measures 1 m by 1 m?

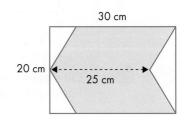

9.3 Area of a trapezium

This section will show you how to:

• calculate the area of a trapezium.

You can calculate the area of a trapezium by finding the average of the lengths of its parallel sides and multiplying this by the perpendicular distance between them.

$A = \frac{1}{2}(a + b)h$

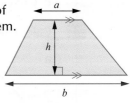

Example 4

Find the area of the trapezium ABCD.

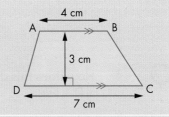

$A = \frac{1}{2}(4 + 7) \times 3 \text{ cm}^2$

$= 16.5 \text{ cm}^2$

1 Copy and complete this table.

Trapezium	Parallel side 1	Parallel side 2	Vertical height	Area
a	8 cm	4 cm	5 cm	
b	10 cm	12 cm	7 cm	
c	7 cm	5 cm	4 cm	
d	5 cm	9 cm	6 cm	
e	3 m	13 m	5 m	
f	4 cm	10 cm		42 cm²
g	7 cm	8 cm		22.5 cm²
h	6 cm		5 cm	40 cm²

2 **a** On squared paper, draw a trapezium similar to the one shown below. Using dotted lines, split your trapezium into two triangles and a rectangle.

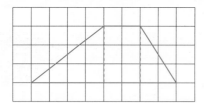

b Find the area of the whole shape by adding the areas of the triangles to the area of the rectangle.

c Check that you get the same result by using $\frac{1}{2}(a + b)h$.

3 Calculate the area of each of these trapeziums.

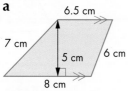

a 6.5 cm, 7 cm, 5 cm, 6 cm, 8 cm

b 12 cm, 7 cm, 6 cm, 8.4 cm

c 8 m, 9.1 m, 9 m, 9.4 m, 12 m

4 How does this diagram show that the area of a trapezium is $\frac{1}{2}(a + b)h$?

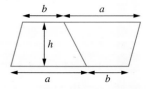

5 Find the area of each of the four shaded parts of this picture frame.

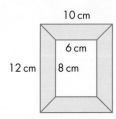

10 cm, 6 cm, 12 cm, 8 cm

6 Calculate the area of each of these compound shapes.

a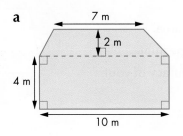

b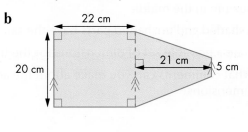

c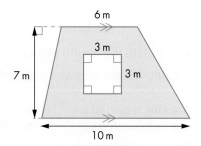

(MR) **7** Show that the area of the shaded part in this diagram is 47 m².

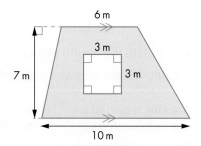

(PS) **8** This is a sketch of a shed with four walls and a sloping roof.

A one-litre can of wood-protection paint will cover 10 m².

How many one-litre cans would you need, to put two coats of preservative on each of the four walls?

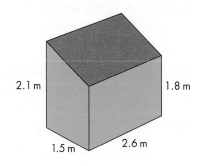

(PS) **9** What percentage of this shape has been shaded?

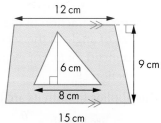

(MR) **10** The shape of most of Egypt roughly approximates to a trapezium. The north coast is about 900 km long, the south boundary is about 1100 km long and the distance from north to south is about 1100 km.

What is the approximate area of this part of Egypt?

(PS) **11** The diagram shows a trapezium.

Calculate its area.

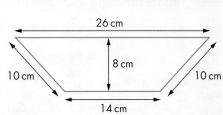

The diagram shows a circle of diameter 8 cm with an isosceles trapezium in the middle.

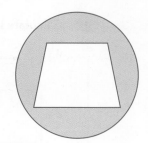

The shaded and unshaded parts have the same area.

a State a possible set of dimensions for the trapezium.

b What comments can you make about the accuracy of your dimensions?

9.4 Sectors

This section will show you how to:

- calculate the length of an arc
- calculate the area and angle of a sector.

Key terms	
arc	sector
subtend	

A **sector** is part of a circle, bounded by two radii and one of the **arcs** formed by the intersections of these radii with the circumference.

The angle **subtended** at the centre of the circle by the arc of a sector is known as the angle of the sector.

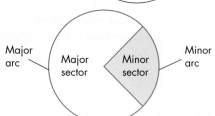

When you divide a circle into only two sectors, the larger one is called the major sector and the smaller one is called the minor sector. Their arcs are called the major arc and the minor arc, respectively.

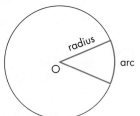

Length of an arc and area of a sector

A sector is a fraction of the whole circle. The size of the fraction is determined by the size of angle of the sector. The angle is often written as θ, a Greek letter pronounced *theta*. For example, the sector shown in the diagram represents the fraction $\frac{\theta}{360}$.

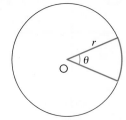

This applies to both its arc length and its area and gives us these results.

$$\text{arc length} = \frac{\theta}{360} \times 2\pi r \quad \text{or} \quad \frac{\theta}{360} \times \pi d$$

$$\text{sector area} = \frac{\theta}{360} \times \pi r^2$$

Example 5

Find the arc length AB and the area of the sector AOB in the diagram.

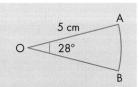

The sector angle is 28° and the radius is 5 cm. So:

arc length $= \dfrac{28}{360} \times \pi \times 2 \times 5$

$= 2.4$ cm (1 dp)

sector area $= \dfrac{28}{360} \times \pi \times 5^2$

$= 6.1$ cm^2 (1 dp)

Example 6

A sector has a radius of 8 cm and an arc length of 5 cm. What is the angle of the sector?

Arc length = $5 = \dfrac{\theta}{360} \times 2 \times \pi \times 8$

$\theta = \dfrac{5 \times 360}{2 \times \pi \times 8}$

$= 35.8°$ (3 sf)

Exercise 9D

1 For each of these sectors, calculate:

i the arc length **ii** the sector area.

a
40°
8 cm

b
95°
5 cm

c
78°
12 cm

d
130°
7 cm

2 Calculate the arc length and the area of a sector whose arc subtends an angle of 60° at the centre of a circle with a diameter of 12 cm. Give your answer in terms of π.

3 Calculate the total perimeter of each of these sectors.

a
11 cm

b
22°
8.5 cm

(MR) **4** Show that the area of the sector shown has the same area as a circle with diameter 8 cm.

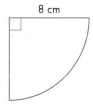
8 cm

5 Calculate the area of each of these sectors.

a
110°
7 cm

b
50°
8 cm

6 O is the centre of a circle of radius 12.5 cm.

Calculate the length of the arc ACB.

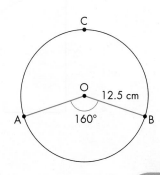
C
O
12.5 cm
A
160°
B

(CM) **7** **a** Calculate the angle of the minor sector of this circle. Give your answer in terms of π.

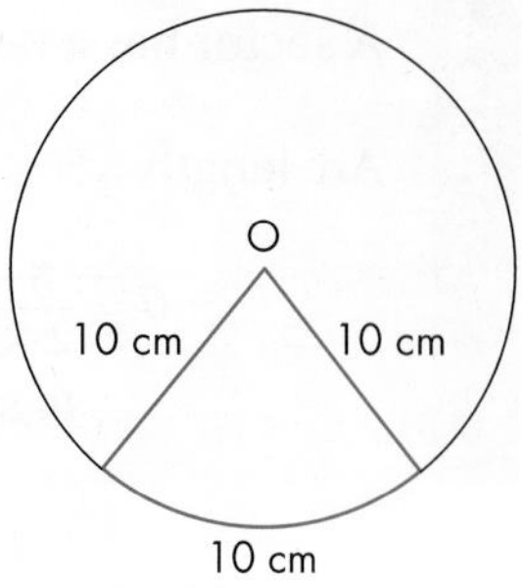

b Angles are sometimes measured in radians.

The angle you found in part **a** is equal to one radian.

By comparing the sector to an equilateral triangle of side 10 cm, explain why one radian must be a little less than 60°.

(PS) **8** **a** What is the angle of a sector with a radius of 6 cm and an arc length of 7 cm?

b What is the area of a sector with a radius of 5 cm and an arc length of 4 cm?

(CM) **9** Effie said: "The area of a sector can be found just by halving the product of the arc length and the radius."

Prove that Effie is correct.

(PS) **10** The diagram shows quarter of a circle. Calculate the area of the shaded shape, giving your answer in terms of π.

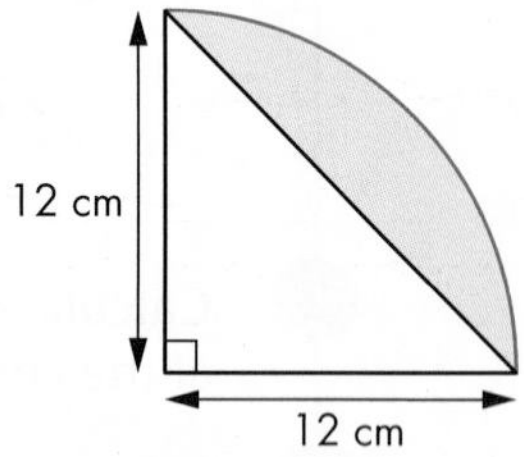

(PS) **11** ABCD is a square of side length 8 cm. APC and AQC are arcs of the circles with centres D and B. Calculate the area of the shaded part.

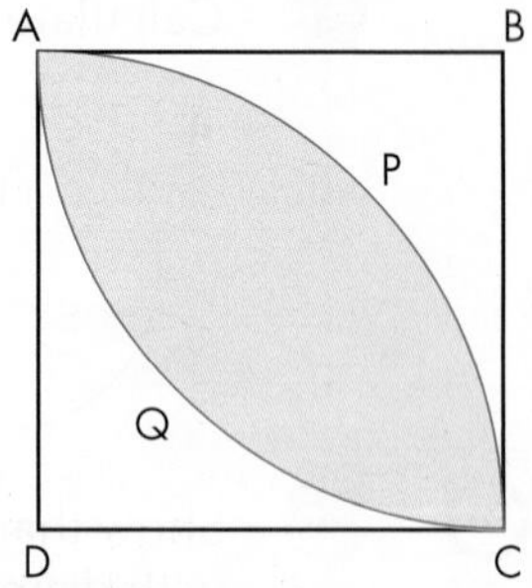

(PS) **12** Antique clocks are powered by a pendulum that swings from side to side.

The pendulum of an old clock is 90 cm long.

It swings from side to side through an angle of 10°.

How wide does the clock case need to be so that the pendulum can swing freely?

(CM) **13** Both squares shown have the same area.

Square X shows a quarter of a circle.

Square Y shows four identical quarter circles.

Show that the shaded shapes in the squares have equal areas.

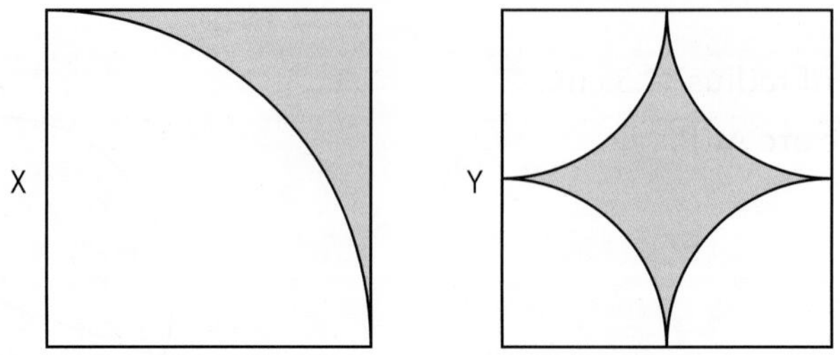

9.5 Volume of a prism

This section will show you how to:

• calculate the volume of a prism.

A **prism** is a 3D shape that has the same **cross-section** running all the way through it.

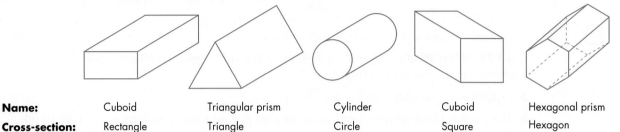

Name:	Cuboid	Triangular prism	Cylinder	Cuboid	Hexagonal prism
Cross-section:	Rectangle	Triangle	Circle	Square	Hexagon

You can find the volume of a prism by multiplying the area of its cross-section by the length of the prism (or height if the prism is standing on end).

That is, volume of prism $= V = Al$

where A is area of cross-section and l is the length of the prism.

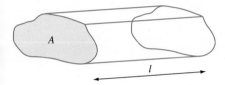

Example 7

Find the volume of the triangular prism.

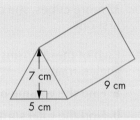

First find the area of the triangular cross-section. $A = \dfrac{5 \times 7}{2} = 17.5 \text{ cm}^2$

Use this to find the volume. $V = Al$

$$= 17.5 \times 9$$
$$= 157.5 \text{ cm}^3$$

Exercise 9E

1   For each prism calculate:

   i   the area of the cross-section   **ii**   the volume.

   a 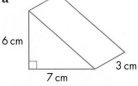   **b** 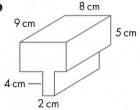   **c**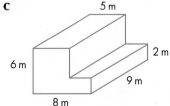

2 Calculate the volume of each of these prisms.

a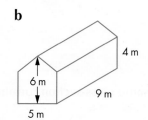
7 m, 4 m, 3 m, 3 m, 4 m, 6 m, 4 m

b
4 m, 6 m, 9 m, 5 m

c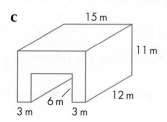
15 m, 11 m, 12 m, 6 m, 3 m, 3 m

(CM) **3** A swimming pool is 10 m wide and 25 m long.

It is 1.2 m deep at one end and 2.2 m deep at the other end. The floor slopes uniformly from one end to the other.

a Explain why the shape of the pool is a prism.

b The pool is filled with water at a rate of 2 m³ per minute. How long will it take to fill the pool?

(PS) **4** A conservatory is in the shape of a prism. Calculate the volume of air inside the conservatory in cubic centimetres.

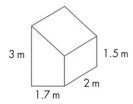
3 m, 1.5 m, 2 m, 1.7 m

(MR) **5** A girl builds 27 cubes, each of edge 2 cm, into a single large cube. Show that with 37 more cubes, she could build a larger cube with edge 2 cm longer than the first one.

6 Each of these prisms has a uniform cross-section in the shape of a right-angled triangle.

a Find the volume of each prism.

b Find the total surface area of each prism.

i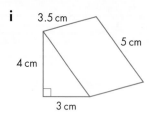
3.5 cm, 5 cm, 4 cm, 3 cm

ii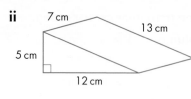
7 cm, 13 cm, 5 cm, 12 cm

(PS) **7** The top and bottom of the container shown here are the same size. They are made up of a rectangle, 4 cm by 9 cm, with a semicircle at each end. The container is 3 cm deep. Find the volume of the container.

(PS) **8** In 2009 the sculptor Anish Kapoor exhibited a work called *Svayambh* at the Royal Academy of Arts (RA) in London. It was a block of red wax in the shape of a prism that slowly travelled through the galleries on a track.

The cross-section was in the shape of an arched entrance.

It was 8 m long and weighed 30 tonnes.

Calculate the volume of wax used for the sculpture.

4.5 m

2.3 m

(PS) **9** A horse trough is in the shape of a semicircular prism as shown. What volume of water will the trough hold when it is filled to the top? Give your answer in litres.

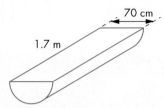

70 cm

1.7 m

(PS) **10** The dimensions of the cross-section of a girder (in the shape of a prism), 2 m in length, are shown on the diagram. The girder is made of iron. 1 cm³ of iron weighs 79 g. What is the mass of the girder?

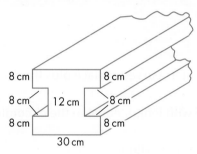

8 cm

8 cm

8 cm   12 cm   8 cm

8 cm   8 cm

30 cm

(EV) **11** Suzanna and her daughter, Maisy, were trying to work out the volume of this prism.

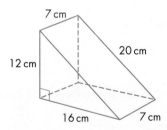

7 cm

20 cm

12 cm

16 cm   7 cm

Suzanna says it has volume 26 880 cm³. Maisy says: "Don't be silly, Mum!"

Explain why Maisy says this and calculate the actual volume of the prism.

9.6 Cylinders

This section will show you how to:

- calculate the volume and surface area of a cylinder.

Key terms

cylinder   surface area

Volume

Since a **cylinder** is an example of a prism, you can find its volume by multiplying the area of one of its circular ends by its height. That is

$$\text{volume} = \pi r^2 h$$

where r is the radius of the cylinder and h is its height or length.

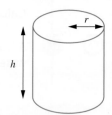

Example 8

What is the volume of a cylinder with a radius of 5 cm and a height of 12 cm?

Volume = area of circular base × height

$$= \pi r^2 h$$

$$= \pi \times 5^2 \times 12$$

$$= 942 \text{ cm}^3 \text{ (3 sf)}$$

Surface area

The total **surface area** of a cylinder is made up of the area of its curved surface plus the area of its two circular ends.

The curved surface area, when opened out, is a rectangle with length equal to the circumference of the circular end.

curved surface area = circumference of end × height of cylinder

$$= 2\pi r h \quad \text{or} \quad \pi d h$$

area of one end $= \pi r^2$

This gives total surface area $= 2\pi r h + 2\pi r^2$ or $\pi d h + 2\pi r^2$.

Example 9

What is the total surface area of a cylinder with a radius of 15 cm and a height of 2.5 m? Give your answer correct to 3 significant figures.

First, you must change the dimensions to a *common unit*. Use centimetres in this case.

Total surface area $= 2\pi r h + 2\pi r^2$

$$= 2 \times \pi \times 15 \times 250 + 2 \times \pi \times 15^2$$

$$= 23\,562 + 1414$$

$$= 24\,976$$

$$= 25\,000 \text{ cm}^2 \text{ (3 sf)}$$

1 For the cylinders below find: **i** the volume   **ii** the total surface area.

Give your answers to 3 significant figures.

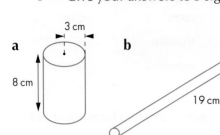
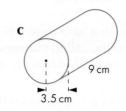
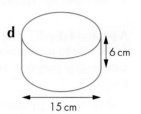

2 For each of these cylinder dimensions find:

   i   the volume   **ii** the curved surface area.

Give your answers in terms of π.

   a Base radius 3 cm, height 8 cm   **b** Base diameter 8 cm, height 7 cm

   c Base diameter 12 cm, height 5 cm   **d** Base radius 10 m, length 6 m

3 The diameter of a cylindrical marble column is 60 cm and its height is 4.2 m. The cost of making this column is quoted as £67.50 per cubic metre. Show that the estimated total cost of making the column is £80.

4 Find the mass of a solid iron cylinder 55 cm high with a base diameter of 60 cm. The density of iron is 7.9 g/cm³.

5 A cylindrical food can has a height of 10.5 cm and a diameter of 7.4 cm.

What can you say about the dimensions of the paper label around the can?

6 A cylindrical container is 65 cm in diameter. Water is poured into the container until it is 1 m deep. Show that there are approximately 332 litres of water in the container.

7 A drinks manufacturer wishes to market a new drink in a can. The quantity in each can must be 330 ml. Suggest a suitable height and diameter for the can.

You may like to look at the dimensions of a real drinks can.

8 A metal bar, 1 m long and with a diameter of 6 cm, has a mass of 22 kg. What is the density of the metal that the bar is made from?

9 Wire is commonly made by putting hot metal through a hole in a plate.

What length of wire, of diameter 1 mm, can be made from a 1 cm cube of metal?

10 The engine size of a car is measured in litres. This tells you the total capacity of the cylinders in which the pistons move up and down. For example, in a 1.6 litre engine with four cylinders, each cylinder will have a capacity of 0.4 litres.

Cylinders of a particular size can be long and thin or short and fat; they will give the engine different running characteristics.

In a racing car, the diameter can be approximately twice the length. This means the engine will run at very high revs.

Suggest possible dimensions for a 0.4 litre racing car cylinder.

9.7 Volume of a pyramid

This section will show you how to:

- calculate the volume of a pyramid.

Key terms

apex	edge
frustum	pyramid
vertex	vertices

A **pyramid** is a 3D shape with a base from which triangular faces rise to a common **vertex**, called the **apex**. The base can be any polygon, but is usually a triangle, a rectangle or a square.

The faces of a pyramid meet at **edges**. This is the name of the line where any two faces meet in a 3D shape. A pyramid has eight edges.

Note also that a vertex is the point where any two lines or two edges meet. The plural of vertex is **vertices**. The vertices of 2D shapes are the corners where the angles are found. The vertices of a 3D shape are the points where the edges meet. A square-based pyramid has five vertices.

The volume of a pyramid is:

$$\text{volume } (V) = \frac{1}{3}Ah$$

where A is the base area and h is the vertical height.

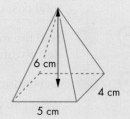

Example 10

Calculate the volume of this pyramid.

First find the base area. $5 \times 4 = 20 \text{ cm}^2$

Then use the formula to find the volume. $\frac{1}{3} \times 20 \times 6 = 40 \text{ cm}^3$

Example 11

A pyramid, with a square base of side 8 cm, has a volume of 320 cm³. What is the vertical height of the pyramid?

Let h be the vertical height of the pyramid. Then,

$$\text{volume} = \frac{1}{3} \times 64 \times h = 320$$

$$\frac{64h}{3} = 320$$

$$h = \frac{960}{64}$$

$$h = 15 \text{ cm}$$

1 Calculate the volume of each of these rectangular-based pyramids.

a

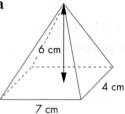

6 cm
4 cm
7 cm

b

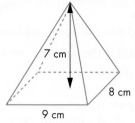

7 cm
8 cm
9 cm

c

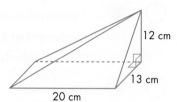

12 cm
13 cm
20 cm

d

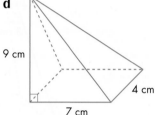

9 cm
4 cm
7 cm

e

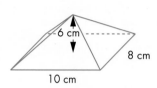

6 cm
8 cm
10 cm

(MR) 2 Show that the volume of a pyramid with a square base of side 9 cm and a vertical height of 10 cm is 270 cm³.

(CM) 3 Suppose you have six pyramids that each have a height that is half the side of the square base.

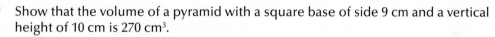

a Explain how they can fit together to make a cube.

b How does this show that the formula for the volume of a pyramid is correct?

(PS) 4 The glass pyramid outside the Louvre Museum in Paris was built in the 1980s. It is 20.6 m tall and the base is a square of side 35 m. The design was very controversial.

Suppose that, instead of a pyramid, the building was a conventional shape with the same square base, a flat roof and the same volume.

How high would it have been?

5 Calculate the volume of each of these shapes.

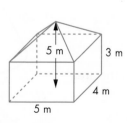

5 m
3 m
4 m
5 m

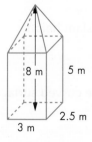

8 m
5 m
3 m
2.5 m

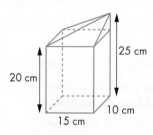

25 cm
20 cm
15 cm
10 cm

(PS) 6 What is the mass of a solid pyramid with a square base of side 4 cm, a height of 3 cm and a density of 13 g/cm³? (1 cm³ has a mass of 13 g.)

(MR) 7 A crystal is in the form of two square-based pyramids joined at their bases (see diagram).

The crystal has a mass of 31.5 g.

What is the mass of 1 cm³ of the substance?

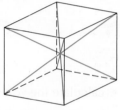

7 cm
3 cm

8 A pyramid has a square base of side 6.4 cm.

Its volume is 81.3 cm³.

Show that the height of the pyramid is 6.0 cm.

 9 A square-based pyramid has the same volume as a cube of side 10 cm.

The height of the pyramid is the same as the side of the square base.

Calculate the height of the pyramid.

 10 The pyramid in the diagram has its top 5 cm cut off as shown.
The shape that is left is called a **frustum**. Hannah said:
"The volume of the frustum is $\frac{26}{27}$ of the original pyramid."

Evaluate Hannah's comment.

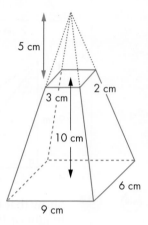

9.8 Cones

This section will show you how to:

- calculate the volume and surface area of a cone.

You can treat a cone as a pyramid with a circular base. So the formula for the volume of a cone is the same as the formula for a pyramid:

volume = $\frac{1}{3}$ × base area × vertical height

$$V = \frac{1}{3}\pi r^2 h$$

where r is the radius of the base and h is the **vertical height** of the cone.

The curved surface area of a cone is:

curved surface area = π × radius × slant height

$$S = \pi r l$$

where l is the **slant height** of the cone.

So the total surface area of a cone (A) is the curved surface area plus the area of its circular base.

$$A = \pi r l + \pi r^2$$

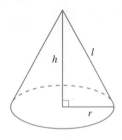

Example 12

For the cone in the diagram, calculate:
i its volume **ii** its total surface area.
Give your answers in terms of π.

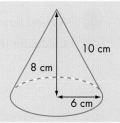

i The volume is $V = \frac{1}{3}\pi r^2 h$
$$= \frac{1}{3} \times \pi \times 36 \times 8$$
$$= 96\pi \text{ cm}^3$$

ii The total surface area is $A = \pi r l + \pi r^2$
$$= \pi \times 6 \times 10 + \pi \times 36$$
$$= 96\pi \text{ cm}^2$$

Exercise 9H

1 For each cone, calculate:

    i its volume   **ii** its total surface area.

    Give your answers to 3 significant figures.

a 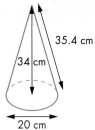   **b** 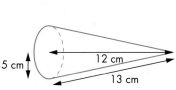   **c**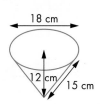

2 A solid cone, base radius 6 cm and vertical height 8 cm, is made of metal with a density of 3.1 g/cm³. Find the mass of the cone.

3 The total surface area of a cone with base radius 3 cm is 24π cm² . Show that its slant height is 5 cm.

4 Calculate the volume of each of these shapes. Give your answers in terms of π.

a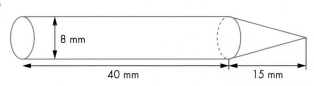

b

5 A cone has the dimensions shown in the diagram.

Calculate the total surface area, leaving your answer in terms of π.

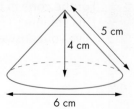

EV **6** A sector of a circle, as in the diagram, can be made into a cone (without a base) by sticking the two straight edges together.

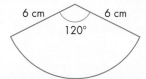

a What would be the diameter of the base of the cone in this case?

b What is the diameter if the angle is changed to 180°?

c Investigate other angles.

CM **7** If the slant height of a cone is equal to the base diameter, show that the area of the curved surface is twice the area of the base.

PS **8** The model shown on the right is made from aluminum.

The mass of the model is 140 g. What is the density of aluminum?

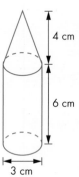

PS **9** A container in the shape of a cone, base radius 10 cm and vertical height 19 cm, is full of water. The water is poured into an empty cylinder of radius 15 cm. How high is the water in the cylinder?

PS **10** A cone of base radius 8 cm and height 12 cm has its top cut off to make a frustum. The frustum is 9 cm high and has a circular top of radius 2 cm. Find the volume of this frustum in terms of π.

9.9 Spheres

This section will show you how to:

• calculate the volume and surface area of a sphere.

The volume of a **sphere**, radius r, is:

$V = \frac{4}{3}\pi r^3$

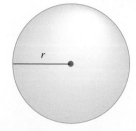

Its surface area is:

$A = 4\pi r^2$

Example 13

For a sphere of radius of 8 cm, calculate: **i** its volume   **ii** its surface area.

i The volume is given by $V = \frac{4}{3}\pi r^3$.

So, $\frac{4}{3} \times \pi \times 8^3 = \frac{2048}{3} \times \pi$

$= 2140 \text{ cm}^3 \text{ (3 sf)}$

ii The surface area is given by $A = 4\pi r^2$.

So, $4 \times \pi \times 8^2 = 256 \times \pi$

$= 804 \text{ cm}^3 \text{ (3 sf)}$

Exercise 9I

1 Calculate the volume of each of these spheres. Give your answers in terms of π.

    a Radius: 3 cm   **b** Radius: 6 cm   **c** Diameter: 20 cm

2 Calculate the surface area of each of these spheres. Give your answers in terms of π.

    a Radius: 3 cm   **b** Radius: 5 cm   **c** Diameter: 14 cm

3 Calculate the volume and surface area of a sphere with a diameter of 50 cm.

(PS) 4 A solid sphere fits exactly into an open cubical box of side 25 cm.

    a What is the surface area of the sphere?

    b How much water can be poured into the box, with the sphere in it, before it spills?

(MR) 5 A metal sphere of radius 15 cm is melted down and recast into a solid cylinder of radius 6 cm. Calculate the height of the cylinder.

(PS) 6 Lead has a density of 11.35 g/cm³. Calculate the maximum number of shot (spherical lead pellets) of radius 1.5 mm that can be made from 1 kg of lead.

(MR) 7 A sphere with a radius of 5.0 cm has the same volume as a cone with a base radius of 8.0 cm.

Calculate the height of the cone.

(EV) 8 The standard (size 5) football must be between 68 cm to 70 cm in circumference and weigh between 410 g to 450 g. They are usually made from 32 panels: 12 regular pentagons and 20 regular hexagons.

    a Will a football manufacturer be more interested in the surface area or the volume of the ball? Why?

    b What variation in the surface area of a football is allowed?

(PS) 9 A sphere of diameter 10 cm is carved out of a wooden block in the shape of a cube of side 10 cm.

What percentage of the wood is wasted?

(MR) 10 A manufacturer is making cylindrical packaging for a sphere as shown.

The curved surface of the cylinder is made from card.

Show that the area of the card is the same as the surface area of the sphere.

Worked exemplars

 1 Hari has a cylindrical glass and another glass in the shape of a cone connected to a stem.

They both hold the same amount of liquid.

The cylindrical glass has a diameter of 5 cm and is 6 cm high.

The other glass has an opening of diameter of 6.4 cm and a stem height of 3 cm.

How high is this glass?

This is a problem-solving question. You need to recognise that you must find the volume of one glass and then set up an equation to help find the height of the other glass.	
The cylindrical glass has a base radius of 2.5 cm. The volume is $\pi \times 2.5^2 \times 6 = 37.5\pi$ cm³.	First, find the volume of the cylindrical glass.
If the height of the cone in the second glass is h cm then: $\frac{1}{3} \times \pi \times 3.2^2 \times h = 37.5\pi$ $h = \frac{37.5 \times \pi \times 3}{\pi \times 3.2^2}$ $= 10.9863$ cm.	Then set up an equation and solve it to find the height of the other glass. Note you don't need to complete the calculations fully – you can leave them in terms of π, as π will cancel out.
The height of the glass is $11 + 3$ cm $= 14$ cm.	You need to round the final answer off appropriately.

 2 Three balls of diameter 8.2 cm just fit inside a cylindrical container.

Andrew said: "The volume of that container is 1300 cm³."

Sophia said: "No, it's not."

Explain the validity of each claim.

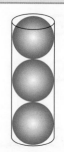

This is an evaluating question where you need to evaluate the results obtained.	
The diameter of the cylinder is 8.2 cm and the height is 24.6 cm. The internal volume $= \pi \times 4.1^2 \times 24.6$ $= 1299.13\ldots$ $= 1300$ cm³ (2 sf)	Before you can evaluate the comments, you first need to calculate the actual volume.
Andrew has correctly stated the volume to 2 (or 3) significant figures, which is 1300 cm². Sophia could also be correct as the volume is only 1300 cm³ as a rounded answer.	Once you have found the volume, you should evaluate each comment, seeing where they may have made an error or what makes their statement correct. Here, you need to make sure you state Andrew's accuracy is to 2 or 3 sf and also state a reason why Sophia is correct. You could also argue that since the original data was 2 sf, the accuracy of the answer could be given to 1 sf, which would be 1000 cm³.

3 The key hole shape shown is made up of a circle radius 1 cm and a sector of angle 30°.

Show that the area of this shape is $\frac{9\pi}{4}$.

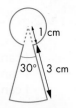

This is a communicating mathematics question where you need to construct and communicate chains of reasoning to achieve a given result.	
Area of sector $= \frac{\theta}{360} \times \pi \times r^2$ $= \frac{30}{360} \times \pi \times 4^2$ $= \frac{480}{360} \times \pi$ $= \frac{4}{3}\pi$	Plan your solution by considering how to find the total area of the shape. Remember that in this type of question you have the final result to work towards, so if your answer is not correct, you should be able to see what you have done wrong.
Area of major sector in circle $= \frac{\theta}{360} \times \pi \times r^2$ $= \frac{330}{360} \times \pi \times 1^2$ $= \frac{11}{12}\pi$	
Total area $= \frac{4}{3}\pi + \frac{11}{12}\pi$ $= \frac{(16+11)}{12}\pi$ $= \frac{27}{12}\pi$ $= \frac{9}{4}\pi$	

Ready to progress?

I can calculate the circumference and area of a circle.
I can calculate the area of a parallelogram and a trapezium.
I can calculate the volume and surface area of prisms and cylinders.

I can calculate the length of an arc and the area of a sector.
I can calculate the volume of pyramids, cones and spheres.
I can calculate the surface area of cones and spheres.

Review questions

1 The diagram shows a circle inside a trapezium.

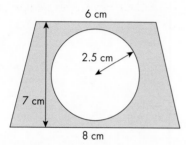

6 cm

2.5 cm

7 cm

8 cm

Calculate the shaded area of the shape.

2 The diagram shows a cylinder.

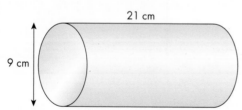

21 cm

9 cm

Calculate the total surface area of the cylinder.

(PS) **3** A solid cube of side 20 cm has a circular hole cut through.
The cylinder has a diameter of 12 cm.
Calculate the volume remaining.

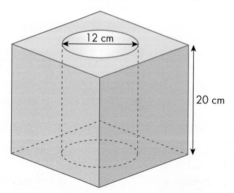

12 cm

20 cm

(PS) **4** A solid cylinder has a radius of 5 cm and a height of 12 cm.

The cylinder is made from wood with a density of 0.65 g/cm³.

Calculate the mass of the cylinder. Give your answer correct to a suitable degree of accuracy.

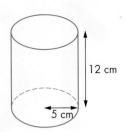

(PS) **5** The diagram shows a right-angled triangular prism.

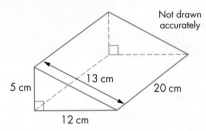

Not drawn accurately

5 cm · 13 cm · 20 cm · 12 cm

The surface area of the prism is the same as the curved surface area of a cone that has a base radius of 12 cm. What is the slant height of the cone?

(PS) **6** The diagram shows a solid prism.

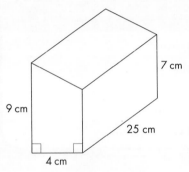

7 cm · 9 cm · 25 cm · 4 cm

The prism is made from plastic with a density of 0.45 g/cm³.

Calculate the mass of the prism.

(PS) **7** The diagram shows a sector of a circle, centre O.

The radius of the circle is 12 cm.

The angle of the sector is 155°.

Calculate the total perimeter of the sector, correct to 3 significant figures.

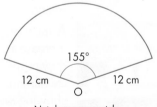

155°

12 cm · 12 cm · O

Not drawn accurately

(CM) **8** The diagram has rotational symmetry of order 4.

Show that the percentage of the shape that has been shaded is 57%.

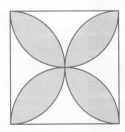

(PS) **9** A ball is packaged in a cylindrical box. The ball touches the sides of the box all the way round including the top and bottom. What fraction of the box is left empty?

10 Algebra: Linear graphs

This chapter is going to show you:

- how to draw a straight-line graph from its equation
- how to find the equation of a linear graph
- how to read information from a conversion graph
- how to use graphs to find formulae and solve simultaneous linear equations
- how to draw linear graphs parallel or perpendicular to other lines.

You should already know:

- how to plot coordinates in all four quadrants
- how to substitute numbers into a formula
- how to read and estimate from scales
- how to plot a graph from a given table of values
- how to plot equations of horizontal and vertical lines.

About this chapter

The saying: 'A picture is worth a thousand words' is definitely true in mathematics: graphs are worth many lines of algebra as they show the relationship between two variables in a visual way.

A linear graph (often called a straight-line graph) shows two variables that increase at a constant rate. You will meet linear graphs and the relationships they represent in various situations in daily life. For example, when exchanging money to travel abroad: $D = 1.68P$ is the equation of the graph showing the exchange rate when £1 = \$1.68. For every extra £1, there is an extra \$1.68 (the constant rate). When there is £0, there is \$0.

When hiring a van to move house: $C = 25T + 20$ is the equation of the graph used by a van hire company to calculate their fees. Every extra hour costs an extra £25 and there is also a fixed charge of £20 for hiring the van in the first place. When buying tins at the supermarket: $C = 40T$ is the equation of the graph showing the cost in pence, C, of T tin cans, where C is given in pence.

This sign from a supermarket, showing 40p cans sold as 5 for £2, shows that the supermarket chain understands how straight line graphs work!

5 for £2 black eye beans in water 410 g (235 g) **40p**

10.1 Drawing linear graphs from points

This section will show you how to:

- draw linear graphs by finding points.

Key term

linear graph

This section is about drawing straight-line graphs. These are usually referred to as **linear graphs**.

Here are some tips that will help you.

- You need to plot at least two points to draw a linear graph, but it is better to use three or more because that gives at least one point to act as a check.
- Use a sharp pencil and mark each point with an accurate cross.
- Position yourself so that your eyes are directly over the graph. If you look from the side, you will not be able to line up your ruler accurately.

Example 1

Draw the graph of $y = 4x - 5$ for values of x from 0 to 5.

Note that this is usually written as $0 \leqslant x \leqslant 5$.

Choose three values for x.

These should be the highest and lowest x-values and one in between. It is usually a good idea to choose 0 as one of the x-values.

Work out the y-values by substituting the x-values into the equation.

When $x = 0$, $y = 4(0) - 5 = -5$.   This gives the point $(0, -5)$.

When $x = 3$, $y = 4(3) - 5 = 7$.   This gives the point $(3, 7)$.

When $x = 5$, $y = 4(5) - 5 = 15$.   This gives the point $(5, 15)$.

Keep a record of your calculations in a table.

x	0	3	5
y	−5	7	15

You are given the extent (range) of the x-axis, but you need to decide on the extent for the y-axis. You can find this by looking at the coordinates that you have so far. The smallest y-value is −5, the largest is 15. Now draw the axes, plot the points and complete the graph.

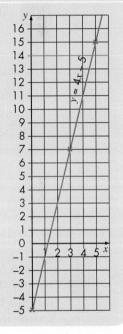

Read through these hints before drawing the linear graphs in Exercise 10A.

- Use the highest and lowest values of x given in the range.
- Don't pick x-values that are too close together, for example 1 and 2. Try to space them out so you can draw a more accurate graph.
- Always label your graph with its equation. This is particularly important when you are drawing two graphs on the same set of axes.
- Create a table of values.

Exercise 10A

Hints and tips Complete the table of values first, then you will know the extent of the *y*-axis.

1 Draw the graph of $y = 2x - 5$ for $0 \leqslant x \leqslant 5$.

2 Draw the graph of $y = \frac{x}{3} + 4$ for $-6 \leqslant x \leqslant 6$.

3
a On the same axes, draw the graphs of $y = 4x - 1$ and $y = 2x + 3$ for $0 \leqslant x \leqslant 5$.

b At which point do the two lines intersect?

CM **4**
a On the same axes, draw the graphs of $y = \frac{x}{3} - 1$ and $y = \frac{x}{2} - 2$ for $0 \leqslant x \leqslant 12$.

b On another set of axes, draw the graphs of $y = 3x + 1$ and $y = 3x - 2$ for $0 \leqslant x \leqslant 4$.

c Where possible, write down for parts **a** and **b** where the two lines intersect.
If it is not possible to write this down, explain why.

CM **5** Liam has completed a table for the equation $y = 2x + 1$ and drawn a graph.

x	−3	−2	−1	0	1	2	3
y	−7	−5	−3	1	3	5	7

a How can Liam tell that he has made a mistake?

b Correct Liam's working.

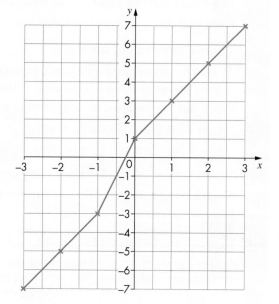

EV **6** Ian the electrician used this formula to work out how much to charge for a job:

$C = 25 + 30H$, where C is the charge (in £) and H is how long the job takes (in hours).

Joan the electrician uses this formula: $C = 35 + 27.5H$.

a On a copy of the grid, draw lines to represent these formulae.

b Who would you hire for a job that takes 2 hours? Explain your choice.

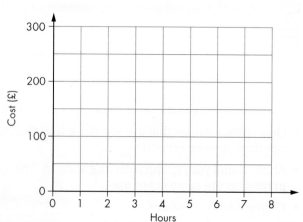

(EV) 7 Remi and Jada use different methods for finding points on the graph of $y = 4x + 2$.

Their methods are shown below.

Remi
$x = 0 \rightarrow y = 4 \times 0 + 2 = 2$
$x = 1 \rightarrow y = 4 \times 1 + 2 = 6$
$x = 2 \rightarrow y = 4 \times 2 + 2 = 10$
$x = 3 \rightarrow y = 4 \times 3 + 2 = 14$
$x = 4 \rightarrow y = 4 \times 4 + 2 = 18$

Jada
$x = 0 \rightarrow y = 2$ $) + 4$
$x = 1 \rightarrow y = 6$ $) + 4$
10 $) + 4$
14 $) + 4$
18

Whose method is more efficient?

(PS) 8 **a** Draw the graphs $y = 4$, $y = x$ and $x = 1$ on a copy of the grid shown on the right.

b What is the area of the triangle formed by the three lines?

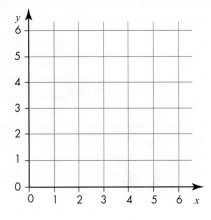

(PS) 9 The first two graphs show y against x and y against z.

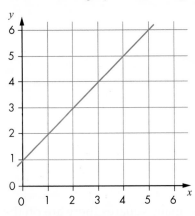

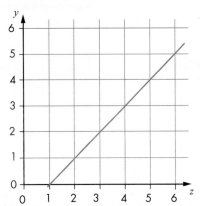

On a copy of the blank grid, show the graph of x against z.

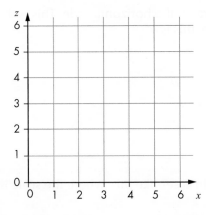

(PS) 10 Find the area (in square units) of the quadrilateral formed by these lines.

$x + y = 5$ $y = 3x + 5$ $y = 2$ $y = -1$

10.2 Gradient of a line

This section will show you how to:

- find the gradient of a straight line
- draw a line with a certain gradient.

Key term

gradient

The slope of a line is called its **gradient**. The steeper the slope of the line, the further the value of the gradient is from zero. So a gradient of 8 is steeper than a gradient of 3. Lines with gradients of 5 and –5 have the same steepness.

You can measure the gradient of the line by drawing a large right-angled triangle with part of the line as its hypotenuse (sloping side). The gradient is then given by:

$$\text{gradient} = \frac{\text{distance measured up}}{\text{distance measured along}}$$

$$= \frac{\text{difference on } y\text{-axis}}{\text{difference on } x\text{-axis}}$$

For example, to measure the steepness of the line in the next figure, you first draw a right-angled triangle where the hypotenuse is part of this line. The gradient will be the same wherever you draw the triangle as you are calculating the ratio of two sides of the triangle. However, it makes the calculations much easier if you choose a sensible place. This usually means using existing grid lines to avoid fractional values.

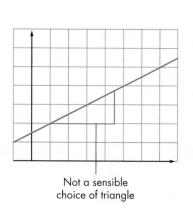

Not a sensible choice of triangle

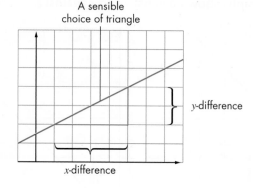

A sensible choice of triangle

y-difference

x-difference

After you have drawn the triangle, measure (or count) how many squares there are on the vertical side. This is the difference between your y-coordinates. In the line above, this is 2.

You then measure (or count) how many squares there are on the horizontal side. This is the difference between your x-coordinates. In the line above, this is 4.

Work out the gradient.

$$\text{gradient} = \frac{\text{difference of the } y\text{-coordinates}}{\text{difference of the } x\text{-coordinates}}$$

$$= \frac{2}{4}$$

$$= \frac{1}{2} \text{ or } 0.5$$

Note: You can only use the method of counting squares in cases like this, where the scale is one square to one unit.

Remember: When a line slopes down from left to right, the gradient is negative, so you must place a minus sign in front of the fraction.

Example 2

Find the gradient of each of these lines.

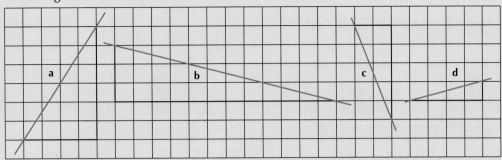

In each case, a sensible choice of triangle has already been made.

a y difference = 6, x difference = 4   Gradient = $6 \div 4 = \frac{3}{2} = 1.5$

b y difference = 3, x difference = 12   Line slopes down from left to right,
so gradient = $-(3 \div 12) = -\frac{1}{4} = -0.25$

c y difference = 5, x difference = 2   Line slopes down from left to right,
so gradient = $-(5 \div 2) = -\frac{5}{2} = -2.5$

d y difference = 1, x difference = 4   Gradient = $1 \div 4 = \frac{1}{4} = 0.25$

Drawing a line with a certain gradient

To draw a line with a certain gradient, you reverse the process described above. So use the given gradient to draw the right-angled triangle. For example, take a gradient of 2.

Start at a convenient point (A in the diagrams below). A gradient of 2 means that for an x-step of 1 the y-step must be 2 (because 2 is the fraction $\frac{2}{1}$). So, move one square across and two squares up, and mark a dot.

Repeat this as many times as you like and draw the line. You can also move one square back and two squares down, which gives the same gradient, as the third diagram shows.

Stage 1

Stage 2

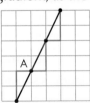

Stage 3

Example 3

Draw lines with these gradients.   **a** $\frac{1}{3}$ **b** -3 **c** $-\frac{1}{4}$

a This is a fractional gradient which has a y-step of 1 and an x-step of 3. Move three squares across and one square up every time.

b This is a negative gradient, so for every one square across, move three squares down.

c This is also a negative gradient and it is a fraction. So for every four squares across, move one square down.

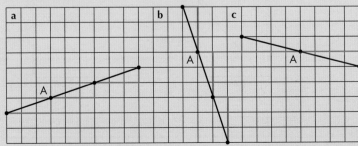

1 Find the gradient of lines **a** to **j**.

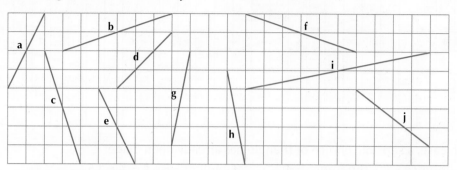

2 Draw lines with these gradients.

a 4 **b** $\frac{2}{3}$ **c** –2 **d** $-\frac{4}{5}$ **e** 6 **f** –6

(EV) 3 Arianwen and Brianna are working out the gradient of the same line.

Arianwen

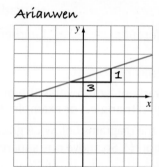

Brianna

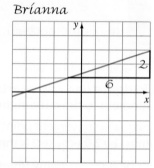

a Whose method is correct?

b Whose method is more likely to give correct results in general?

(EV) 4 Safety regulations stipulate that a ladder must be positioned with a gradient between 2 and 4.

a Why do you think the gradient has to be greater than 2?

b Why do you think the gradient has to be less than 4?

c Determine whether each of these ladders satisfies the safety regulations.

A

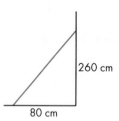

260 cm

80 cm

B

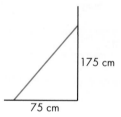

175 cm

75 cm

C

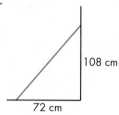

108 cm

72 cm

D

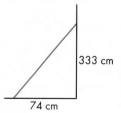

333 cm

74 cm

E

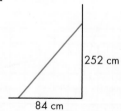

252 cm

84 cm

F

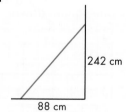

242 cm

88 cm

MR

5 The line on grid **e** is horizontal. The lines on grids **a** to **d** get nearer and nearer to the horizontal.

 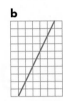

Find the gradient of each line in grids **a** to **d**. By looking at the values you obtain, what do you think the gradient of a horizontal line is?

MR

6 The line on grid **e** is vertical. The lines on grids **a** to **d** get nearer and nearer to the vertical.

Find the gradient of each line in grids **a** to **d**. By looking at the values you obtain, what do you think the gradient of a vertical line is?

CM

7 Raisa says the gradients of these two lines are the same.

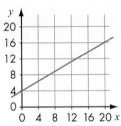 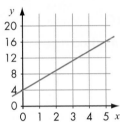

Why is Raisa wrong?

CM

8 This puzzle shows what appears to be a right-angled triangle with a base of 13 squares and a height of 5 squares consisting of four pieces. When the pieces are rearranged, they appear to make the same triangle but with a square hole.

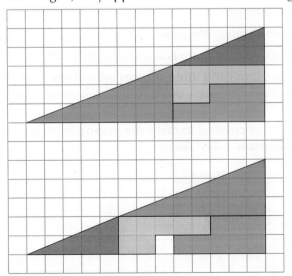

a Find the gradient of the hypotenuse of the red triangle.

b Find the gradient of the hypotenuse of the blue triangle.

c Explain where the square hole comes from.

9 Find the gradient of each side of this pentagon.

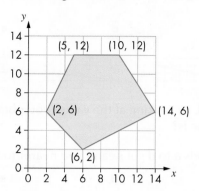

10.3 Drawing graphs by gradient-intercept and cover-up methods

This section will show you how to:

- draw graphs using the gradient-intercept method
- draw graphs using the cover-up method.

Key terms
constant term
cover-up method
gradient-intercept
intercept
$y = mx + c$

Gradient-intercept method

The equation of a straight line can be written in the form $y = mx + c$. The **constant term**, c, is the **intercept** on the y-axis and the number in front of x (called the coefficient of x), m, is the gradient of the line.

Consider drawing the graph of $y = 3x - 1$.

3 is the gradient of the line and -1 is the y-intercept.

Because the intercept, c, is -1, the graph goes through the y-axis at -1.

Because the gradient, m, is 3, for an x-step of one unit, there is a y-step of three units.

Starting at -1 on the y-axis, move one square across and three squares up and mark the point with a dot or a cross (diagram **i**). Then repeat this from every new point. You can also move one square back and three squares down.

When you have enough points, join the dots (or crosses) to make the graph (diagram **ii**). Note that if the points are not in a straight line, you have made a mistake.

i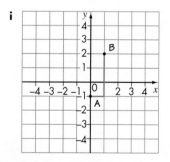

ii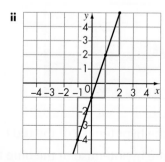

This method is called the **gradient-intercept** method.

Example 4

Use the gradient-intercept method to draw the graph of $y = 2x - 5$.

$c = -5$ Mark this point with a dot.

$m = 2$ Move one square across and two squares up.

Repeat at least twice and plot the line.

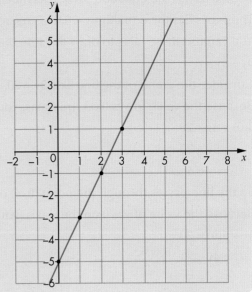

Exercise 10C

1 Draw these lines using the gradient-intercept method. Use the same grid, taking x from −10 to 10 and y from −10 to 10. If the grid gets too 'crowded', draw another one.

a $y = 2x + 6$ **b** $y = 3x - 4$ **c** $y = \frac{1}{2}x + 5$

d $y = x + 7$ **e** $y = 4x - 3$ **f** $y = 2x - 7$

g $y = \frac{1}{4}x + 3$ **h** $y = \frac{2}{3}x + 4$ **i** $y = 6x - 5$

j $y = x + 8$ **k** $y = \frac{4}{5}x - 2$ **l** $y = 3x - 9$

2 **a** Using the gradient-intercept method, draw the following lines on the same grid. Use axes with ranges $-14 \leqslant x \leqslant 4$ and $-2 \leqslant y \leqslant 6$.

i $y = \frac{x}{3} + 3$ **ii** $y = \frac{x}{4} + 2$

b Where do the lines cross?

(MR) 3 Here are the equations of three lines.

A: $y = 3x - 1$ B: $2y = 6x - 4$ C: $y = 2x - 2$

a State a mathematical property that lines A and B have in common.

b State a mathematical property that lines B and C have in common.

c Which of the following points is the intersection of lines A and C?

$(1, -4)$ $(-1, -4)$ $(1, 4)$

(PS) 4 **a** What is the gradient of line A?

b What is the gradient of line B?

c What angle is there between lines A and B?

d What relationship do the gradients of A and B have with each other?

e Another line C has a gradient of 3.

What is the gradient of a line perpendicular to C?

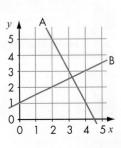

Cover-up method

The x-axis has the equation $y = 0$. This means that all points on the x-axis have a y-value of 0.

The y-axis has the equation $x = 0$. This means that all points on the y-axis have an x-value of 0.

You can use these facts to draw any line that has an equation of the form:

$$ax + by = c$$

Consider the graph of the line $4x + 5y = 20$.

Because the value of x is 0 on the y-axis, you can solve the equation for y:

$$4(0) + 5y = 20$$
$$5y = 20$$
$$\Rightarrow y = 4$$

So the line passes through the point (0, 4) on the y-axis (diagram **A**).

Because the value of y is 0 on the x-axis, you can also solve the equation for x:

$$4x + 5(0) = 20$$
$$4x = 20$$
$$\Rightarrow x = 5$$

So the line passes through the point (5, 0) on the x-axis (diagram **B**).

You only need two points to draw a line. (Normally, you would like a third point but, in this case, you can accept two.) Draw the graph by joining the points (0, 4) and (5, 0) (diagram **C**).

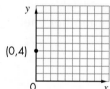 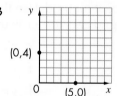 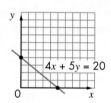

This type of equation can be drawn very easily, without much working at all, using the **cover-up method**.

Start with the equation:	$4x + 5y = 20$
Cover up the x-term:	$\bigcirc + 5y = 20$
Solve the equation (when $x = 0$):	$y = 4$
Now cover up the y-term:	$4x + \bigcirc = 20$
Solve the equation (when $y = 0$):	$x = 5$

This gives the points (0, 4) on the y-axis and (5, 0) on the x-axis.

Example 5

Draw the graph of $2x - 3y = 12$.

Solve the equation (when $x = 0$). $\quad -3y = 12$
$$y = -4$$

Solve the equation (when $y = 0$). $\quad 2x = 12$
$$x = 6$$

This gives the points (0, –4) on the y-axis and (6, 0) on the x-axis.

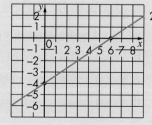

Exercise 10D

 1 Draw these lines using the cover-up method. Use the same grid, taking x from –10 to 10 and y from –10 to 10. If the grid gets too 'crowded', draw another.

a $3x + 2y = 6$ **b** $4x + 3y = 12$ **c** $4x - 5y = 20$

d $x + y = 10$ **e** $3x - 2y = 18$ **f** $x - y = 4$

g $5x - 2y = 15$ **h** $2x - 3y = 15$ **i** $6x + 5y = 30$

j $x + y = -5$ **k** $x + y = 3$ **l** $x - y = -4$

 2 **a** Using the cover-up method, draw the following lines on the same grid.
Use axes with ranges $-2 \leqslant x \leqslant 6$ and $-3 \leqslant y \leqslant 6$.

i $x + 2y = 6$ **ii** $2x - y = 2$

b Where do the lines cross?

  3 Here are the equations of three lines.

A: $2x + 6y = 12$ B: $x - 2y = 6$ C: $x + 3y = -9$

a State a mathematical property that lines A and B have in common.

b State a mathematical property that lines B and C have in common.

c State a mathematical property that lines A and C have in common.

d The line A crosses the y-axis at $(0, 2)$.

The line C crosses the x-axis at $(-9, 0)$.

Find values of a and b so that the line $ax + by = 18$ passes through $(0, 2)$ and $(-9, 0)$.

  4 Match the equations and the graphs.

i $y = 2x - 3$ **ii** $y = 1.5x$ **iii** $3y = x + 1$

iv $x + y = 2$ **v** $2x + y = 0$ **vi** $2x + 3y = -4$

a 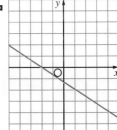 **b** 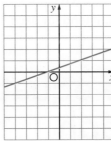 **c**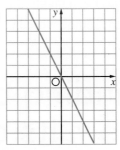

d 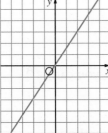 **e** 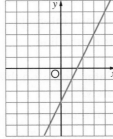 **f**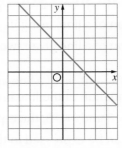

 5 Put these lines in order of steepness, from steepest to least steep.

$y = 3x + 4$ $2y - 5x = 10$ $2y - x = 7$ $y = -6x$ $y = 4$

(MR) **6** Which two lines cross at the same point on the y-axis?

$y = 6x - 3$ $\qquad$ $3x + 2y = 18$ $\qquad$ $y = 3x - 1$ $\qquad$ $2x + 5y = 15$ $\qquad$ $y = 9 - x$ $\qquad$ $4x + y = 6$

(PS) **7** The diagram shows an octagon ABCDEFGH.

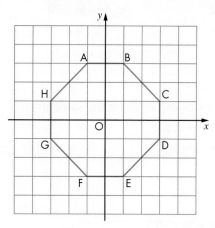

The equation of the line through A and B is $y = 3$.

The equation of the line through B and C is $x + y = 4$.

a Write down the equation of the lines through these vertices.

   i C and D $\qquad\qquad$ **ii** D and E $\qquad\qquad$ **iii** E and F

   iv F and G $\qquad\qquad$ **v** G and H $\qquad\qquad$ **vi** H and A

b The gradient of the line through F and B is 3.

   Write down the gradient of the lines through these vertices.

   i A and E $\qquad\qquad$ **ii** G and C $\qquad\qquad$ **iii** H and D

(EV) **8** Elsa has been asked to plot the lines $2x + y = 10$ and $y = 11 - 2x$.

She has been taught the gradient-intercept method and the cover-up method.

Which method would you recommend for each line? Explain your choices.

10.4 Finding the equation of a line from its graph

This section will show you how to:

- find the equation of a line, using its gradient and intercept
- find the equation of a line given two points on the line.

If you know the gradient, m, of a line and its intercept, c, on the y-axis, you can write down the equation of the line immediately.

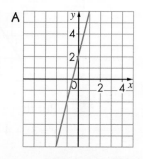

For example, if $m = 3$ and $c = -5$, the equation of the line is $y = 3x - 5$.

All linear graphs can be expressed in the form $y = mx + c$. This gives a method of finding the equation of any line drawn on a pair of coordinate axes.

Consider this line.

The graph crosses the y-axis at $(0, 2)$ so $c = 2$.

Draw a triangle to measure the gradient of the line.

y-step = 8

x-step = 2

gradient = $8 \div 2 = 4$

So $m = 4$

Hence the equation of the line is $y = 4x + 2$.

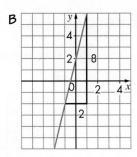

Example 6

Find the equation of the line that passes through the points (2, 7) and (10, 3).

Draw a sketch of the two points.

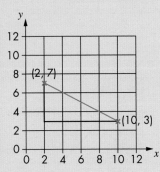

y difference = 4, x difference = 8   Line slopes down from left to right,

so gradient = $-(4 \div 8) = -\frac{1}{2}$.

Substitute $m = -\frac{1}{2}$ into $y = mx + c$. $y = -\frac{1}{2}x + c$

Substitute into $y = -\frac{1}{2}x + c$.   You could choose either point to substitute but (2, 7) has smaller numbers.

$7 = -\frac{1}{2} \times 2 + c$

$7 = -1 + c$

$c = 8$

So $y = -\frac{1}{2}x + 8$.

You can also work out the x and y differences without drawing a sketch, meaning you can find the equation of a graph directly from just two points.

To find the equation of the line that passes through the points (2, –1) and (6, 11), calculate the x and y differences:

y difference = $11 - -1 = 12$

x difference = $6 - 2 = 4$

So the gradient $\left(\dfrac{y\text{-difference}}{x\text{-difference}}\right)$ is $12 \div 4 = 3$.

Substitute $m = 3$ into $y = mx + c$ to get $y = 3x + c$.

Now choose one of the two points and substitute for x and y. (6, 11) is simpler to use because both x and y are positive.

$11 = 3 \times 6 + c$

$11 = 18 + c$

$c = -7$

So $y = 3x - 7$.

Exercise 10E

1 Give the equation of each of these lines, all of which have positive gradients.

a

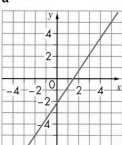

b

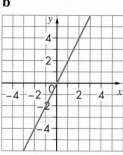

c

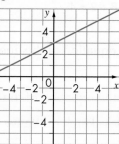

2 In each of these grids, there are two lines.

a

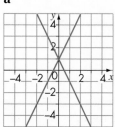

b

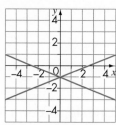

c

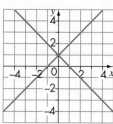

For each grid:

  i find the equation of each of the lines   **ii** describe any symmetries that you can see

  iii describe any connection between the gradients of each pair of lines.

3 A straight line passes through the points (1, 3) and (2, 5).

  a Explain how you can tell that the line also passes through (0, 1).

  b Explain how you can tell that the line has a gradient of 2.

  c Work out the equation of the line that passes through (1, 5) and (2, 8).

4 Give the equation of each of these lines. They all have negative gradients.

a

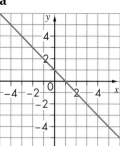

b

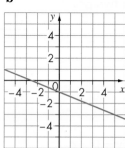

c

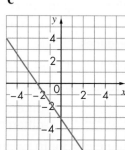

5 In each of these grids, there are three lines. One of them is $y = x$.

a 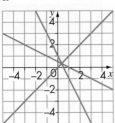   **b** 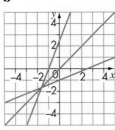   **c**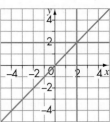

For each grid:

   i find the equation of each of the other two lines

   ii describe any symmetries that you can see

   iii describe any connection between the gradients of each group of lines.

6 On which of these lines does the point (12, 13) lie?

$x + y = 25$ $y = \frac{1}{2}x + 7$ $y = 37 - 2x$ $y = 19 - \frac{1}{2}x$

$y = 13$ $y = \frac{1}{4}x + 9$ $x = 12$ $y = \frac{2}{3}x + 5$

7 Use the clues to find the equation of each line in the form $y = mx + c$.

   a gradient is –3, y-intercept is 5

   b gradient is 2, line passes through the point (5, 6)

   c y-intercept is –3, line passes through the point (2, 13)

   d line passes through the points (3, 19) and (9, 7)

   e line passes through the points (–9, –7) and (18, 11)

8 Find the equation of the line that passes through the points (6, 0) and (0, 5), giving the equation in the form $ax + by = c$.

9 Ashleigh has drawn a straight-line graph.

Chris says that the point (12, 8) will lie on the graph.

Helen says that the point (12, 8) will not lie on the graph.

Who is correct? Explain your answer.

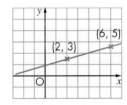

10 Here are four sets of four points.

   a (75, 25), (17, 83), (50, 50), (k, 99)   **b** (46, 5), (46, 10), (46, –3), (k, 26)

   c (13, 27), (48, 97), (32, 65), (k, 121)   **d** (–3, 16), (11, 30), (28, 47), (k, 2)

For each set:

   i find the equation of the line passing through the points

   ii find the value of k.

11 Line L_1 passes through the points (–2, 14) and (6, 10).

Line L_2 passes through the points (–1, –4) and (2, 5).

Find the coordinates of the point where the two lines intersect.

10.5 Real-life uses of graphs

This section will show you how to:

- convert from one unit to another unit by using a conversion graph
- use straight-line graphs to find formulae.

Key term

conversion graph

You need to be able to read **conversion graphs** by finding a value on one axis and following it through to the other axis. Make sure you understand the scales on the axes to help you estimate the answers.

Example 7

This is a conversion graph between litres and gallons.

a   How many litres are there in 5 gallons?

b   How many gallons are there in 15 litres?

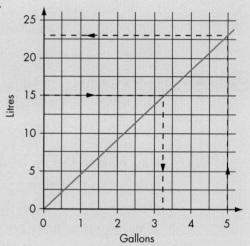

From the graph you can see that:

a   5 gallons are approximately equivalent to 23 litres.

b   15 litres are approximately equivalent to $3\frac{1}{4}$ gallons.

This graph illustrates taxi fares in one part of England, it tells you that a fare will cost more, the further you go.

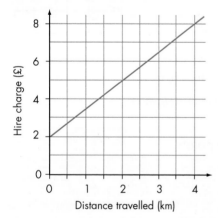

The taxi company charges a basic hire fee to start with of £2.00. This is shown on the graph as the point where the line cuts through the hire-charge axis (when distance travelled is 0).

The gradient of the line is:

$$\frac{8-2}{4} = \frac{6}{4} = 1.5$$

This represents the hire charge per kilometre travelled.

So the total hire charge is made up of two parts: a basic hire charge of £2.00 and an additional charge of £1.50 per kilometre travelled. This can be put in a formula as

hire charge = £2.00 + £1.50 per kilometre

In this example, £2.00 is the constant term in the formula (the equation of the graph).

Exercise 10F

 1 Two taxi companies use these rules for calculating fares.

- CabCo: £2.50 basic charge and £0.75 per kilometre
- YellaCabs: £2.00 basic charge and £0.80 per kilometre

This map shows the distances, in kilometres, that three friends, Anya (A), Bettina (B) and Calista (C) live from a restaurant (R) and from each other.

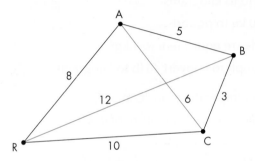

Not drawn to scale

You may find a copy of the grid below useful in answering this question.

a If they each take an individual cab home from the restaurant, which company should they each choose?

b Work out the cheapest way they can travel home from the restaurant if two, or all three, share a cab.

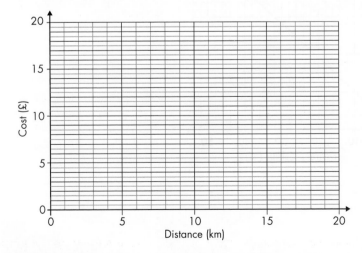

> **Hints and tips** Draw a graph for both companies on the grid. Use this to work out the costs of the journeys.

(MR) **2** This is a conversion graph between kilograms (kg) and pounds (lb).

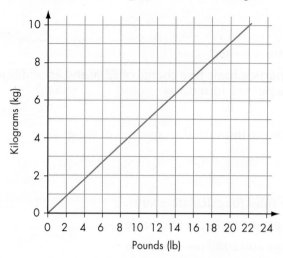

a Use the graph to make an approximate conversion of:

i 18 lb to kilograms   **ii** 5 lb to kilograms

iii 4 kg to pounds   **iv** 10 kg to pounds.

b Approximately how many pounds are equivalent to 1 kg?

c Explain how you could use the graph to convert 48 lb to kilograms.

3 This is a conversion graph between temperatures in °C and °F.

a What temperature in °F is equivalent to a temperature of 0 °C?

b What is the gradient of the line?

c From your answers to parts **a** and **b**, write down a rule that can be used to convert °C to °F.

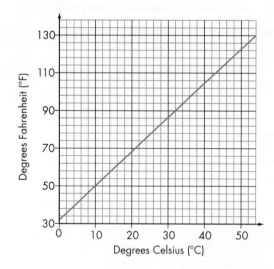

4 This graph illustrates charges for fuel.

   a What is the gradient of the line?

   b The standing charge is the basic charge before the cost per unit is added. What is the standing charge?

   c Write down the rule used to work out the total charge for different amounts of units used.

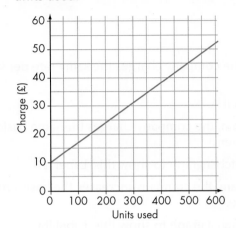

5 Over the course of a year, the exchange rate between the American dollar and the British pound changes.

   The graph shows the exchange rate for three different months of a year.

   a If Mr Errington changed £1000 into dollars in March and another £1000 into dollars in December, approximately how much less did he get in December than in March?

   b George went to America in March and stayed until July. In March, he changed £5000 into dollars. In July, he still had $2000 dollars left and he changed them back into pounds.

   i How much, in dollars, did George spend between March and July?

   ii How much, in pounds, did George actually spend between March and July?

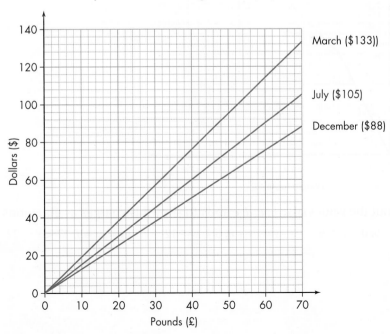

MR **6** This graph is a sketch of the rate charged for taxi journeys by a firm during weekdays from 6 am to 8 am.

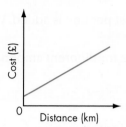

a At weekends from 6 am to 8 am, the company charges the same rate per kilometre but increases the basic charge.

Sketch a graph to show this. Label it A.

b During weekdays from 8 pm to 6 am, the company charges the same basic charge but an increased charge per kilometre.

On the same axes as in part **a**, sketch a graph to show this. Label it B.

c During weekends from 8 pm to 6 am, the company increases the basic charge and increases the charge per kilometre.

On the same axes as in part **a**, sketch a graph to show this. Label it C.

PS **7** A motorcycle courier will deliver packages, up to a weight of 22 pounds, within a city centre.

The courier has three charging bands: packages up to 5 pounds, packages from 5 to 12 pounds and packages over 12 pounds.

This graph shows how much he charges. y is the cost (in £) and x is the weight (in pounds).

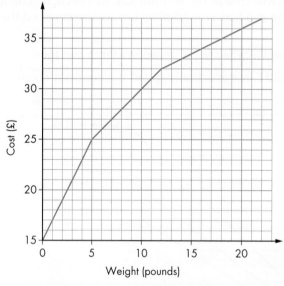

Work out the values of a, b, c, d, e and f to show his charges as equations.

$y = ax + b, 0 < x \leqslant 5$ $y = cx + d, 5 < x \leqslant 12$ $y = ex + f, 12 < x \leqslant 22$

10.6 Solving simultaneous equations using graphs

This section will show you how to:

- solve simultaneous linear equations using graphs.

Key term

simultaneous equation

Two different straight lines that are not parallel will intersect at one point. This point is the solution of the equations of the lines, or the **simultaneous equations**. You can solve simultaneous equations algebraically (as shown in Chapter 15) or graphically, as described below.

Consider finding the solution of the simultaneous equations $3x + y = 6$ and $y = 4x - 1$.

Draw the graph of $3x + y = 6$ using the cover-up method. It crosses the x-axis at $(2, 0)$ and the y-axis at $(0, 6)$.

Draw the graph of $y = 4x - 1$ by finding some points or by the gradient-intercept method. Using the gradient-intercept method, the graph crosses the y-axis at -1 and has a gradient of 4.

The point where the graphs intersect is $(1, 3)$. So the solution to the simultaneous equations is $x = 1$, $y = 3$.

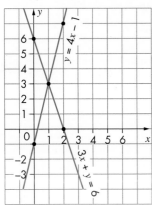

Example 8

Draw graphs to find the solution of the simultaneous equations $y = \frac{1}{2}x + 1$ and $x + y = 7$.

Plot both lines on the graph.

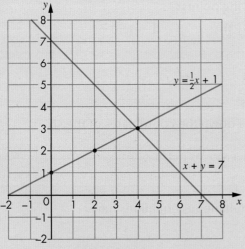

They intersect at $(4, 3)$ so $x = 4$ and $y = 3$.

Exercise 10G

In questions 1–9, draw the graphs to find the solution of each pair of simultaneous equations.

1 $x + 4y = 8$
$x - y = 3$

2 $y = 2x - 1$
$3x + 2y = 12$

3 $y = 2x + 4$
$y = x + 7$

4 $y = x + 8$
$x + y = 4$

5 $y - 3x = 9$
$y = x - 3$

6 $y = -x$
$y = 4x - 5$

7 $3x + 2y = 18$
$y = 3x$

8 $y = 3x + 2$
$y + x = 10$

9 $y = \dfrac{x}{3} + 1$
$x + y = 11$

(PS) 10 One cheesecake and two chocolate gateaux cost £9.50.

Two cheesecakes and one chocolate gateau cost £8.50.

Use x to represent the cost of a cheesecake and y to represent the cost of a gateau.

Use graphs to find the cost of a cheesecake and the cost of a gateau.

(PS) 11 The graph shows four lines.

P: $y = 4x + 1$ Q: $y = 2x + 2$ R: $y = x - 2$ S: $x + y + 1 = 0$

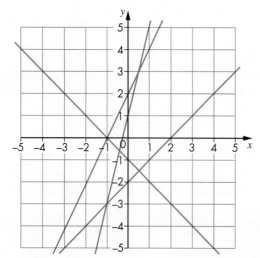

Which pairs of lines intersect at the following points?

a $(-1, -3)$ **b** $(\frac{1}{2}, -1\frac{1}{2})$ **c** $(\frac{1}{2}, 3)$ **d** $(-1, 0)$

(MR) 12 Four lines have the following equations.

A: $y = x$ B: $y = 2$ C: $x = -3$ D: $y = -x$

These lines intersect at six different points.

Without drawing the lines accurately, write down the coordinates of the six intersection points.

| Hints and tips | Sketch the lines. |

(CM) 13 How many solutions does each pair of simultaneous equations have?

Explain your answers geometrically.

a $3x + 5y = 15$
$3x + 5y = 10$

b $2x + y = 7$
$4x = 14 - 2y$

c $3x + 2y = 12$
$4x + y = 11$

10.7 Parallel and perpendicular lines

This section will show you how to:

- draw linear graphs parallel or perpendicular to other lines and passing through a specific point.

If two lines are parallel, then their gradients are equal.

If two lines are perpendicular, their gradients are **negative reciprocals** of each other.

Consider the line AB. Point A is at (2, –1) and point B is at (4, 5).

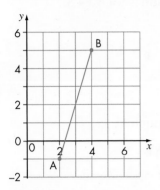

Finding the equation of a parallel line

The gradient of AB is 3, so any parallel line can be written in the form $y = 3x + c$.

To find the equation of the parallel line that passes through the point C at (2, 8), substitute $x = 2$ and $y = 8$ into the equation $y = 3x + c$.

$$8 = 3 \times 2 + c$$
$$\Rightarrow c = 2$$

So the parallel line that passes through (2, 8) is $y = 3x + 2$.

Finding the equation of a perpendicular line

The gradient of the perpendicular line is the negative reciprocal of 3, which is $-\frac{1}{3}$.

To find the equation of the perpendicular line that passes through the midpoint of AB, find the midpoint and substitute for x and y into the equation $y = -\frac{1}{3}x + c$, or sketch the perpendicular line on the grid.

To find the x-coordinate of the midpoint of a line between two points, you add the x-coordinates of the points and divide by 2. To find the y-coordinate, you add the y-coordinates of the points and divide by 2. This gives you a pair of coordinates.

The midpoint of AB is (3, 2).

The perpendicular line passes through (0, 3).

So the equation of the perpendicular line through the midpoint of AB is $y = -\frac{1}{3}x + 3$.

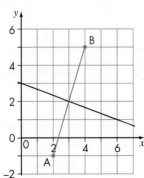

Example 9

Two points A and B are A(0, 1) and B (2, 4).

a Work out the equation of the line AB.

b Write down the equation of the line parallel to AB and passing through the point (0, 5).

c Write down the gradient of a line perpendicular to AB.

d Write down the equation of a line perpendicular to AB and passing through the point (0, 2).

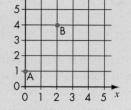

a The gradient of AB is $\frac{3}{2}$ and the intercept is (0, 1), so the equation is $y = \frac{3}{2}x + 1$.

b The gradient is the same ($\frac{3}{2}$) and the intercept is (0, 5), so the equation is $y = \frac{3}{2}x + 5$.

c The perpendicular gradient is the negative reciprocal $-\frac{2}{3}$.

d The gradient is $-\frac{2}{3}$ and the intercept is (0, 2), so the equation is $y = -\frac{2}{3}x + 2$.

Example 10

Find the line that is perpendicular to the line $y = \frac{1}{2}x - 3$ and passes through (0, 5).

The gradient of the new line will be the negative reciprocal of $\frac{1}{2}$ which is –2.

The point (0, 5) is the intercept on the y-axis so the equation of the line is $y = -2x + 5$.

Exercise 10H

1 Here are the equations of three lines.

A: $y = 3x - 2$ B: $y = 3x + 1$ C: $y = -\frac{1}{3}x + 1$

a Give a reason why line A is the odd one out of the three.

b Give a reason why line C is the odd one out of the three.

c Which of the following would be a reason why line B is the odd one out of the three?

i Line B is the only one that intersects the negative x-axis.

ii Line B is not parallel to either of the other two lines.

iii Line B does not pass through (0, –2).

2 Write down the negative reciprocals of the following numbers.

a 2   **b** –3   **c** $\frac{1}{2}$

d $-\frac{2}{3}$ **e** 1.5   **f** $\frac{4}{3}$

3 Four of these lines make a rectangle. Which four?

$y = 3x + 5$ $y = 5x + 3$ $3x + y = 6$ $x + 3y = 10$ $y = 8 - \frac{1}{3}x$ $y = 3(x + 2)$

4 Match the pairs of perpendicular lines.

$x = 6$ $x + y = 5$ $y = 8x - 9$ $2y = x + 4$

$2x + y = 9$ $y = -\frac{1}{8}x + 6$ $5y = 2x + 15$ $y = 0.1x + 2$

$y = 33 - 10x$ $y = -2$ $2y + 5x = 2$ $y = x + 4$

5 Write down the equations of these lines.

   a Parallel to $y = \frac{1}{2}x + 3$ and passes through $(0, -2)$

   b Parallel to $y = -x + 2$ and passes through $(0, 3)$

   c Perpendicular to $y = 3x + 2$ and passes through $(0, -1)$

   d Perpendicular to $y = -\frac{1}{3}x - 2$ and passes through $(0, 5)$

(CM) 6 The line segment AB joins A(10, 11) and B(12, 3).

   a Find the gradient of AB.

   b State the gradient of the line perpendicular to AB.

   c Find the midpoint of AB.

   d The line L is perpendicular to AB and passes through the midpoint of AB.

     Show that the equation of L is given by $4y - x = 17$.

7 Find the equation of the line perpendicular to $y = 4x - 3$, passing though $(-4, 3)$.

(PS) 8 Here are the coordinates of the vertices of three quadrilaterals

   i A(−2, 3)   B(3, 2)   C(4, 3)   D(−1, 4)

   ii A(3, 5)   B(9, 9)   C(7, 12)   D(1, 8)

   iii A(0, 3)   B(10, 7)   C(6, 6)   D(1, 4)

   a For each one, work out the gradients of AB, BC, CD and DA.

   b Determine which quadrilateral is a rectangle, which is a parallelogram and which is a trapezium, explaining your answers.

(PS) 9 Find the equation of the perpendicular bisector of the points A(1, 2) and B(3, 6).

(CM) 10 A is the point (0, 4), B is the point (4, 6) and C is the point (2, 0).

   a Find the equation of the line BC.

   b Show that the point of intersection of the perpendicular bisectors of AB and AC is (3, 3).

   c Show algebraically that this point lies on the line BC.

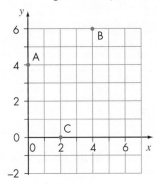

(PS) 11 The points A(1, 34), B(27, 12) and C(21, −6) lie on the circumference of a circle.

   Given that a radius perpendicular to a chord always bisects the chord, find the coordinates of the centre of the circle.

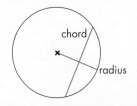

Worked exemplars

1 A triangle has vertices at A(–1, 3), B(7, 12) and C(9, 8).

Demonstrate that the triangle is right-angled and identify which of A, B and C is the right angle.

> This question requires you to communicate mathematically. You need to present a valid argument, showing each step in your solution and proving that the triangle is right-angled.

Method 1
 	
AB: y difference = 12 – 3 = 9
 	
    x difference = 7 – (–1) = 8
 	
    Gradient = 9 ÷ 8 = $\frac{9}{8}$
 	
AC: y difference = 8 – 3 = 5
 	
    x difference = 9 – (–1) = 10
 	
    Gradient = 5 ÷ 10 = $\frac{1}{2}$
 	
BC: y difference = 8 – 12 = –4
 	
    x difference = 9 – 7 = 2
 	
    Gradient = –4 ÷ 2 = –2
	There are two different methods. One is to work out the gradients of each of the lines (Method 1), the other is to work out the lengths of the lines using Pythagoras' theorem.
	
	In both cases, you need to use your calculations to justify why they are showing you that the triangle is right-angled.
	
	Each method is equally valid.

Since the gradients of AC and BC are negative reciprocals of each other, AC and BC are perpendicular. So ABC is a right-angled triangle.	
Since AC and BC are perpendicular, the right angle is at C.	

Method 2
 	
Using Pythagoras' theorem:
 	
    $AB = \sqrt{9^2 + 8^2} = \sqrt{145}$
 	
    $AC = \sqrt{5^2 + 10^2} = \sqrt{125}$
 	
    $BC = \sqrt{(-4)^2 + 2^2} = \sqrt{20}$	

Since $AC^2 + BC^2 = AB^2$, the sides of the triangle satisfy Pythagoras' theorem. So ABC is a right-angled triangle.	
Given that $AC^2 + BC^2 = AB^2$, AB is the hypotenuse and the right angle is at C.	

(PS) **2** A shop on a cross-channel ferry accepts both pounds and euros.

The exchange rate is £1 = €1.25.

George pays £2.25 for five apples and three bananas.

Pierre pays €1.00 for one apple and two bananas.

a Represent this information in a graph.

b Using the graph, work out the cost of buying three apples and one banana in pounds.

This is a problem-solving question. You need to plan a strategy to solve it and you should expect to use your knowledge of other areas of mathematics, in this case currency conversions.	
a €1.00 ÷ 1.25 = £0.80	Because the final answer will be in pounds, it makes sense to solve the whole question in pounds or pence.

The variables are:
 	
    x = the price of an apple
 	
    y = the price of a banana
 	
The equations are:
 	
    $5x + 3y = 225$
 	
    $x + 2y = 80$	

Using the cover-up method:
 	
    $5x + 3y = 225$
 	
when $x = 0$, $y = 75$
 	
when $y = 0$, $x = 45$
 	
    $x + 2y = 80$
 	
when $x = 0$, $y = 40$
 	
when $y = 0$, $x = 80$
 	
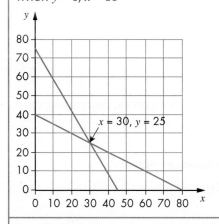
	You can use any method for plotting the lines, but the cover-up method is simplest here.

b The lines intersect when $x = 30$, $y = 25$. An apple costs 30p. A banana costs 25p.	
$3x + y = 3 \times 30 + 1 \times 25 = 115$ Three apples and one banana cost £1.15.	

Ready to progress?

I can read off values from a conversion graph.
I can draw a linear graph without being given a table of values.
I can find the gradient of a line.
I can draw straight lines using the gradient-intercept method.
I can draw straight lines using the cover-up method.

I can find the equation of a line.
I can use graphs to find formulae.

I can use graphs to solve simultaneous linear equations.
I can draw linear graphs parallel or perpendicular to other lines.

Review questions

1 Draw the graph of $y = 3x + 4$ for $0 \leqslant x \leqslant 5$.

2 Draw the graph of $y = \frac{x}{2} - 3$ for $0 \leqslant x \leqslant 10$.

3 On a copy of the grid, draw the graph of $x + y = 6$.

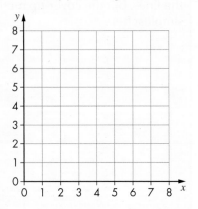

4 This graph shows the hire charge for a conference centre, depending on the number of people at the conference.

a Calculate the gradient of the line.

b What is the basic fee for hiring the conference centre?

c Write down the rule used to work out the total hire charge for the centre.

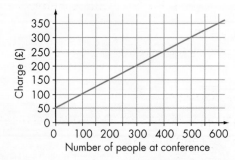

5 This graph shows the length of a spring when different weights are attached to it.

a Calculate the gradient of the line.

b How long is the spring when no weight is attached to it?

c By how much does the spring extend per kilogram?

d Write down the rule for finding the length of the spring for different weights.

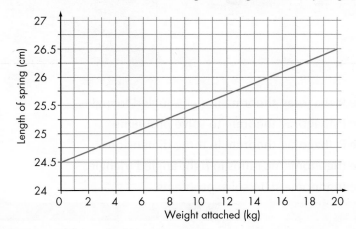

6 Draw the graphs to find the solution of each pair of simultaneous equations.

a $y = x$

$x + y = 10$

b $y = 2x + 3$

$5x + y = 10$

c $y = 5x + 1$

$y = 2x + 10$

7 A has coordinates (0, 2). B has coordinates (2, 6).

a Work out the gradient of the line that passes through A and B.

b Find the equation of the line that passes through A and B.

c Find the equation of the line perpendicular to AB that passes through B.

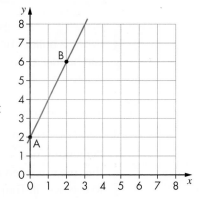

8 **a** The line $y = 1 + 2x$ is transformed to the line $y = 1 - 2x$.

Describe two possible transformations that could have been applied.

b The line $y = 3x + 1$ is transformed to the line $y = -\frac{1}{3}x + 1$.

Describe two possible transformations that could have been applied.

9 Find the area of the parallelogram bounded by the lines with equations $x = -2$, $y = \frac{1}{2}x + 3$, $x = 4$ and $y = \frac{1}{2}x - 2$.

10 Find the area of the trapezium bounded by the lines with equations $y = 2x + 8$, $y = 4$, $y = 2x - 4$ and $x + y = -4$.

11 The line segment AB has A at (−2, −2) and B at (10, −8).

Line L_1 is perpendicular to the line segment AB and passes through its midpoint.

Line L_2 passes through the points C(3, 17) and D(8, −3).

Find the coordinates of the point E where L_1 and L_2 intersect.

11 Geometry and measures: Right-angled triangles

This chapter is going to show you:

- how to use Pythagoras' theorem in right-angled triangles
- how to use Pythagoras' theorem to solve problems
- how to use Pythagoras' theorem in three dimensions
- how to use trigonometric ratios in right-angled triangles
- how to use trigonometry to solve problems.

You should already know:

- how to find the square and square root of a number
- how to round numbers to a suitable degree of accuracy.

About this chapter

When a builder needs to build two walls at right angles to each other, how can he make sure the angle between them is 90°? The chances are that he will use a 3–4–5 triangle. What the builder may not know is that exactly the same technique has been used by builders for thousands of years, as far back as the construction of the pyramids of Egypt and maybe even before that.

The 3–4–5 rule works because it is a special case of Pythagoras' theorem.

Pythagoras was a Greek who lived about 2600 years ago but, although the rule was been named after him, he was certainly not the first person to discover it. There is written evidence that the theorem was known in ancient Mesopotamia, China and India and it was probably discovered independently at different times in different parts of the world.

This chapter will show you how you can use Pythagoras' rule and trigonometric functions to solve a variety of problems involving right-angled triangles.

11.1 Pythagoras' theorem

This section will show you how to:

- calculate the length of the hypotenuse in a right-angled triangle.

Pythagoras, who was a philosopher as well as a mathematician, was born in 580 BC, on the Greek island of Samos. He later moved to Crotona (Italy), where he established the Pythagorean Brotherhood, which was a secret society devoted to politics, mathematics and astronomy. It is said that when he discovered his famous theorem he was so full of joy that he showed his gratitude to the gods by sacrificing one hundred oxen.

Consider drawing squares on each side of a right-angled triangle, with sides 3 cm, 4 cm and 5 cm.

The longest side is called the **hypotenuse** and is always opposite the right angle.

Pythagoras' theorem can then be stated as follows:

For any right-angled triangle, the area of the square drawn on the hypotenuse is equal to the sum of the areas of the squares drawn on the other two sides.

The form of the rule that most people remember is:

In any right-angled triangle, the square of the hypotenuse is equal to the sum of the squares of the other two sides.

Pythagoras' theorem is more usually written as a formula.

$c^2 = a^2 + b^2$

Remember that you can only use Pythagoras' theorem in right-angled triangles.

You can also use Pythagoras' theorem to test if a triangle is right-angled.

To see if the triangle with sides 7 cm, 12 cm and 13 cm is right-angled, square each side and see if the sum of the squares of the two shorter sides is the same as the square of the longest side.

Sum the squares of the two shorter sides. $\qquad 7^2 + 12^2 = 49 + 144$
$$= 193$$

Square the longest side. $\qquad\qquad\qquad 13^2 = 169$

These are not the same, so this triangle is not right-angled.

Finding the length of the hypotenuse

If you know the lengths of the two smaller sides of a triangle, you can use Pythagoras' theorem to find the length of the hypotenuse. You can square each of the smaller sides, add them together, and then find the square root. In some cases, you need to round the length of the hypotenuse to a suitable degree of accuracy.

Example 1

Find the length of the hypotenuse, marked x on the diagram.

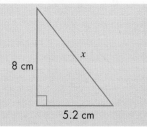

Using Pythagoras' theorem gives: $x^2 = 8^2 + 5.2^2$
$$= 64 + 27.04$$
$$= 91.04$$
$$\Rightarrow x = \sqrt{91.04}$$
$$= 9.5 \text{ cm (1 dp)}$$

MR 1 The diagram shows a right-angled triangle with sides of 3, 4 and 5 units.

a Check that this is a right-angled triangle.

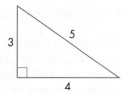

b If you enlarge this triangle by scale factor 2, you get this larger triangle. Check to see that this is also a right-angled triangle.

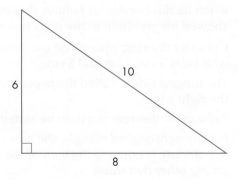

c Choose three more scale factors and sketch the enlargement of the 3, 4, 5 triangle with your scale factors. Check to see whether or not Pythagoras' theorem also holds for these triangles.

PS 2 The numbers 3, 4 and 5 are called a **Pythagorean triple** because $3^2 + 4^2 = 5^2$. Any three (positive) integers – a, b and c – are said to form a Pythagorean Triple if $a^2 + b^2 = c^2$.

Find as many Pythagorean triples as you can, using numbers of 100 or less.

3 Calculate the length of the hypotenuse, x, for each triangle. Give your answers correct to 1 decimal place.

a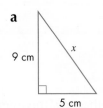

b

c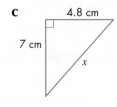

d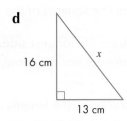

e

f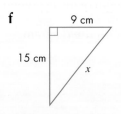

g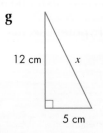

h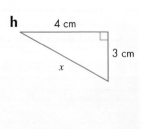

> **Hints and tips** You are finding the hypotenuse in all these examples so add the squares of the two short sides each time.

4 **a** Calculate the lengths of H_1, H_2 and H_3 in the diagram shown, leaving your answers in square-root form (for example, $\sqrt{x}$).

b Explain how you can write down the value of H_4 with little calculation.

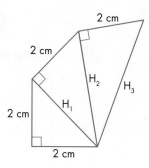

 5 How does this diagram show that Pythagoras' theorem is true?

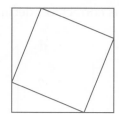 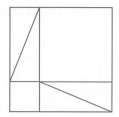

11.2 Finding the length of a shorter side

This section will show you how to:

- calculate the length of a shorter side in a right-angled triangle.

If you rearrange the formula for Pythagoras' theorem, you can use it to calculate the length of one of the shorter sides.

$$c^2 = a^2 + b^2$$
$$\Rightarrow a^2 = c^2 - b^2 \quad \text{and}$$
$$b^2 = c^2 - a^2$$

Calculate the value of x in this triangle.

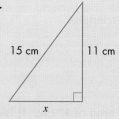

The side labelled x is one of the shorter sides.

Use Pythagoras' theorem.

$$x^2 = 15^2 - 11^2$$
$$= 225 - 121$$
$$= 104$$
$$\Rightarrow x = \sqrt{104}$$
$$= 10.2 \text{ cm (1 dp)}$$

Exercise 11B ▯

1 Calculate the value of x for each triangle. Give your answers correct to 1 decimal place.

a

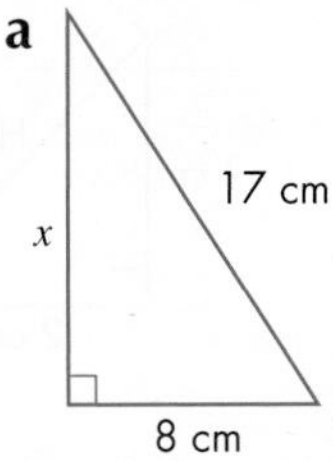

17 cm

x

8 cm

b

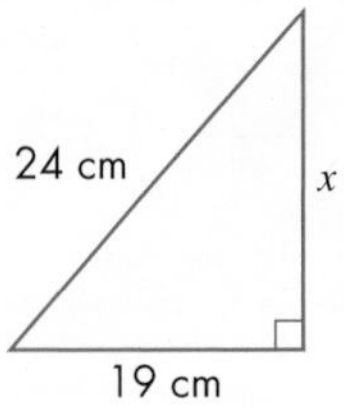

24 cm

x

19 cm

c

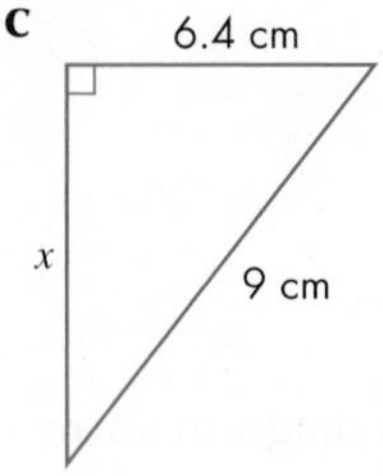

6.4 cm

x

9 cm

d

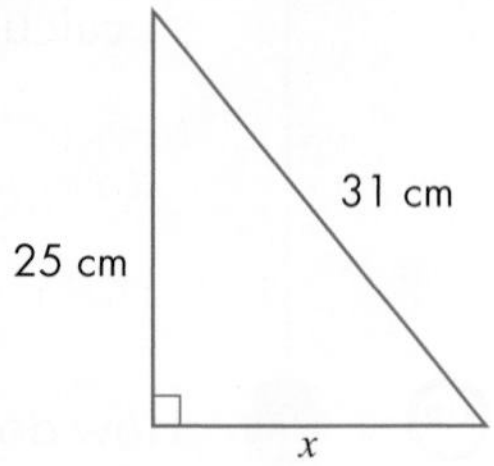

31 cm

25 cm

x

2 Calculate the value of x for each triangle. Give your answers correct to 1 decimal place.

a

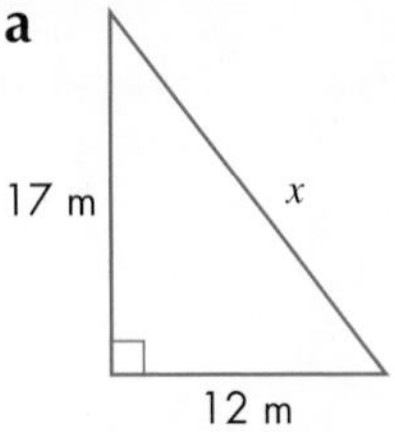

17 m

x

12 m

b

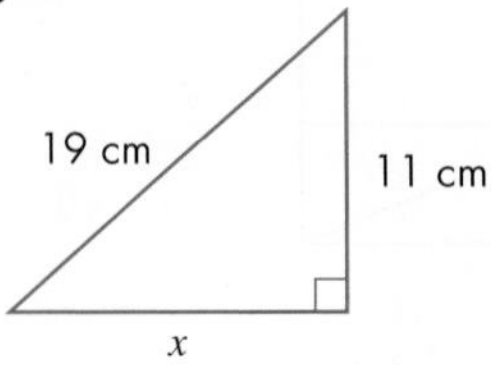

19 cm

11 cm

x

c

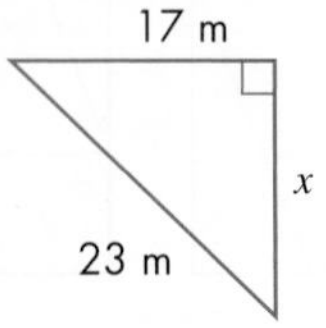

17 m

x

23 m

d

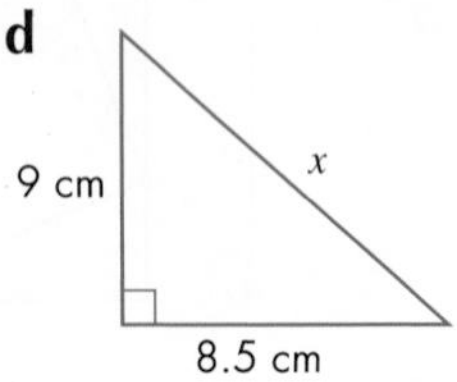

9 cm

x

8.5 cm

> **Hints and tips** These examples are a mixture. Make sure you combine the squares of the sides correctly.

3 Work out the length marked x for each triangle.

a

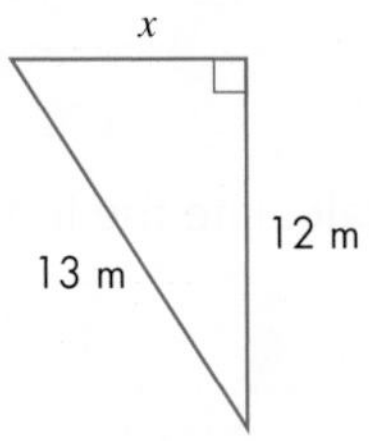

x

13 m

12 m

b

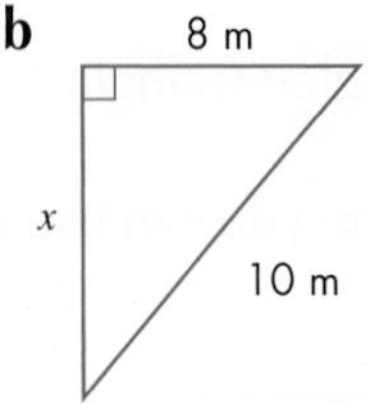

8 m

x

10 m

c

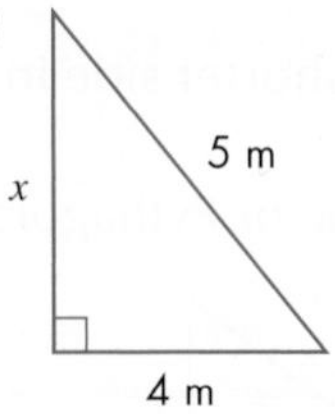

x

5 m

4 m

d

30 cm

x

40 cm

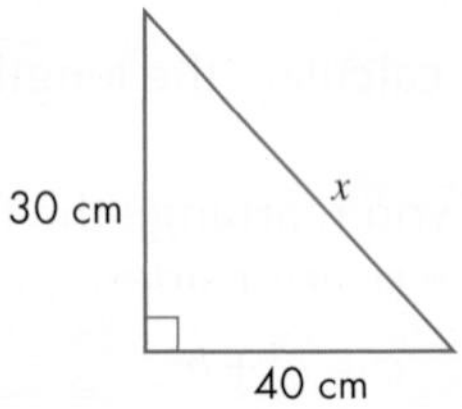

(PS) 4 In question **3** you found sets of three whole numbers that satisfy the rule $a^2 + b^2 = c^2$.
Find at least two more.

(PS) 5 Calculate the area of the triangle.

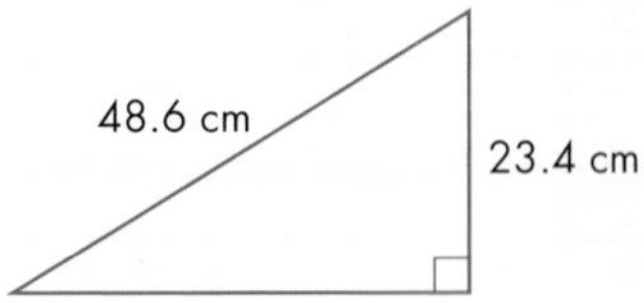

48.6 cm

23.4 cm

(PS) 6 The square ABCD has an area of 17 cm². It is drawn at an angle on a 1-cm coordinate grid where point A is (1, 4). Point B is on the intersection of two lines of the grid. What is a possible coordinate for point B?

(PS) 7 The diagonal length of a rectangle is 10 cm. Show that the maximum area of the rectangle is 50 cm².

8 This is a visual proof of Pythagoras' theorem.

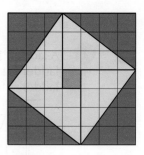

This is an explanation of how this diagram illustrates Pythagoras' rule.

The large square is 7 by 7, giving 49 square units.

The red and yellow triangles all have shorter lengths of 3 and 4, with an area of 6 square units.

The area of the inner square (green and yellow) must be $49 - 4 \times 6 = 25$, so the hypotenuse of the yellow triangles must be $\sqrt{25} = 5$.

You can see that $3^2 + 4^2 = 5^2$.

Complete a similar proof using a triangle with sides of length 5, 12 and 13.

11.3 Applying Pythagoras' theorem in real-life situations

This section will show you how to:

- use Pythagoras' theorem to solve problems.

You can use Pythagoras' theorem to solve certain practical problems. When a problem involves only two lengths, follow these steps.

- Draw a diagram that includes a right-angled triangle.
- Look at the diagram and decide which side you need to find: the hypotenuse or one of the shorter sides.
- Label the unknown side x.
- If it's the hypotenuse, then square both numbers, add the squares and take the square root of the sum. If it's one of the shorter sides, then square both numbers, subtract the smaller square from the larger and take the square root of the difference.
- Finally, round the answer to a suitable degree of accuracy.

Example 3

A plane leaves Manchester Airport and heads due east. It flies 160 km before turning due north. It then flies a further 280 km and lands. What is the distance of the return flight if the plane flies straight back to Manchester Airport?

First, sketch the situation.

Then use Pythagoras' theorem.

$$x^2 = 160^2 + 280^2$$
$$= 25\ 600 + 78\ 400$$
$$= 104\ 000$$
$$\Rightarrow x = \sqrt{104\ 000}$$
$$= 322 \text{ km (3 sf)}$$

The distance of the return flight is 322 km.

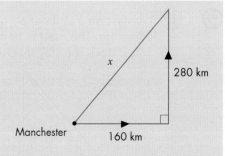

Hints and tips Always set out your solution as in Example 3. Avoid taking shortcuts, since they often cause errors.

Exercise 11C

(PS) **1** A ladder, 12 m long, leans against a wall. The ladder reaches 10 m up the wall. A ladder is safe if the foot of the ladder is about 2.5 m away from the wall. Is this ladder safe?

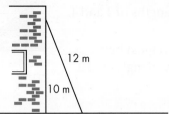

2 A model football pitch is 2 m long and 0.5 m wide. How long is the diagonal?

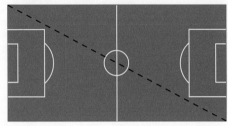

(PS) **3** How long is the diagonal of a square with a side of 8 m?

(PS) **4** A ship going from a port to a lighthouse steams 15 km east and 12 km north. The journey takes 1 hour. How much time would be saved by travelling (at the same speed) directly to the lighthouse in a straight line?

(PS) **5** Some pedestrians want to get from point X on one road to point Y on another. The two roads meet at right angles.

Instead of following the roads, they decide to follow a footpath that goes directly from X to Y.

How much shorter is this route?

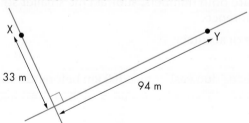

(PS) **6** A mast on a sailboat is strengthened by a wire (called a stay), as shown on the diagram. The mast is 10 m tall and the stay is 11 m long. How far from the base of the mast does the stay reach?

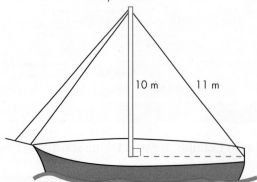

(PS) **7** A ladder, 4 m long, is put up against a wall.

   a How far up the wall will it reach when the foot of the ladder is 1 m away from the wall?

   b When it reaches 3.6 m up the wall, how far is the foot of the ladder away from the wall?

(PS) **8** A pole, 8 m high, is supported by metal wires, each 8.6 m long, attached to the top of the pole. How far from the foot of the pole are the wires fixed to the ground?

(CM) **9** A and B are two points on a coordinate grid. They have coordinates (13, 6) and (1, 1). Show that the line that joins them has length 13 units.

(PS) **10** The regulation for safe use of ladders states that the foot of a 5.00 m ladder must be placed at 1.20 – 1.30 m from the foot of the wall.

   a What is the maximum height the ladder can safely reach up the wall?

   b What is the minimum height the ladder can safely reach up the wall?

(CM) **11** Is the triangle with sides 7 cm, 24 cm and 25 cm a right-angled triangle? Give a reason for your answer.

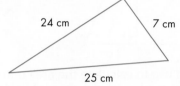

(PS) **12** A ladder 4 m long is leaning against a wall. The foot of the ladder is 1 m from the wall. The foot of the ladder is not securely held and slips 20 cm further away from the wall.

   How far does the top of the ladder move down the wall?

(EV) **13** The diagonal of a rectangle is 10 cm.

   Callum said: "The perimeter of that rectangle is between 20 and 30 cm."

   Comment on Callum's statement.

11.4 Pythagoras' theorem and isosceles triangles

This section will show you how to:

- use Pythagoras' theorem in isosceles triangles.

Every isosceles triangle has a line of symmetry that divides the triangle into two congruent right-angled triangles. So when you are faced with a problem involving an isosceles triangle, you may have to split that triangle down the middle to create a right-angled triangle to help solve the problem.

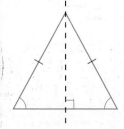

Example 4

Calculate the area of this triangle.

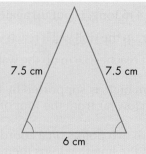

It is an isosceles triangle and you need to calculate its height to find its area.

First split the triangle into two right-angled triangles to find its height.

Let the height be x.

Then use Pythagoras' theorem.

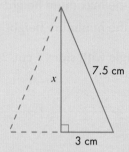

$$x^2 = 7.5^2 - 3^2$$
$$= 56.25 - 9$$
$$= 47.25$$
$$\Rightarrow x = \sqrt{47.25} \text{ cm}$$
$$= 6.873\,864 \text{ cm}$$

Keep the accurate figure in the calculator memory and use to calculate the area of the triangle.

$\frac{1}{2} \times 6 \times 6.873\,864$ cm² (from the calculator memory)

$= 20.6$ cm² (1 dp)

Exercise 11D

1 Calculate the areas of these isosceles triangles.

a

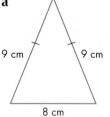

9 cm   9 cm

8 cm

b

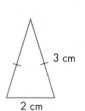

3 cm

2 cm

c

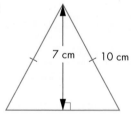

7 cm   10 cm

2 Calculate the area of an isosceles triangle with sides of 8 cm, 8 cm and 6 cm.

3 Calculate the area of an equilateral triangle of side 6 cm.

4 An isosceles triangle has sides of 5 cm and 6 cm.

   a Sketch the two different isosceles triangles that fit this data.

   b Which of the two triangles has the greater area?

5 **a** Sketch a regular hexagon, showing all its lines of symmetry.

   b Calculate the area of the hexagon if its side is 8 cm.

6 Calculate the area of a hexagon of side 10 cm.

7 These isosceles triangles have the same perimeter.

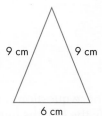 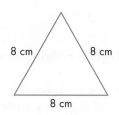 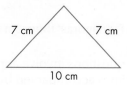

    a Do the three triangles have the same area?

    b Can you find an isosceles triangle with the same perimeter but a larger area?

    c Can you generalise your findings?

8 A piece of land is in the shape of an isosceles triangle with sides 6.5 m, 6.5 m and 7.4 m. Show that the area of the land is 19.8 m².

9 The diagram shows an isosceles triangle ABC.

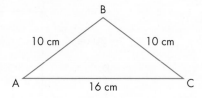

Calculate the area of triangle ABC.

10 Calculate the lengths marked x in these isosceles triangles.

 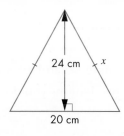 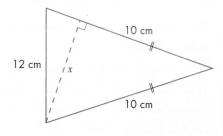

> **Hints and tips** Find the area first.

11 The area of an isosceles triangle with two sides of 5 cm, is 12 cm². Find the length of the base of the triangle.

12 A kite had two lengths of 8 cm and two lengths of 10 cm. One of the diagonals was 12 cm long.

Andrew and Olly both calculated the area of the kite. Andrew calculated the area to be 79.7 cm² and Olly calculated it to be 79.8 cm².

Evaluate the accuracy of each answer.

11.5 Pythagoras' theorem in three dimensions

This section will show you how to:

- use Pythagoras' theorem to solve problems involving three dimensions.

Some questions involve applying Pythagoras' theorem in 3D situations. These questions are sometimes accompanied by clearly labelled diagrams, to help you identify the lengths needed for your solutions.

You deal with these 3D problems in exactly the same way as 2D problems.

- Identify the right-angled triangle you need.

- Redraw this triangle and label it with the given lengths and the length to be found, usually x or y.

- From your diagram, decide whether you need to find the hypotenuse or one of the shorter sides.

- Solve the problem and round to a suitable degree of accuracy.

Example 5

What is the longest piece of straight wire that can be stored in this box measuring 30 cm by 15 cm by 20 cm?

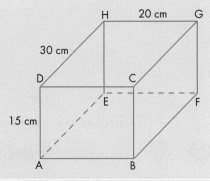

The longest distance across this box is any one of the diagonals AG, DF, CE or HB.

Consider AG.

First, identify a right-angled triangle containing AG and draw it.

This gives a triangle AFG, which contains two lengths you do not know, AG and AF.

Let $AG = x$ and $AF = y$.

Next identify a right-angled triangle that contains the side AF and draw it.

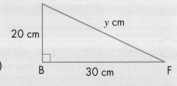

This gives a triangle ABF. You can now find the value of AF.

Use Pythagoras' theorem. $y^2 = 30^2 + 20^2$

$\qquad\qquad\qquad\qquad = 1300$ (There is no need to find y.)

Now find AG using Pythagoras' theorem and triangle AFG.

$x^2 = y^2 + 15^2$

$\quad = 1300 + 225$

$\quad = 1525$

$\Rightarrow x = 39.1$ cm (1 dp)

So, the longest straight wire that can be stored in the box is 39.1 cm.

Note that in any cuboid with sides a, b and c, the length of a diagonal is given by:

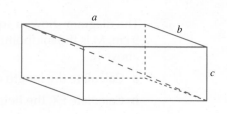

$$\sqrt{(a^2 + b^2 + c^2)}$$

So that in this example you could have gone straight to this.

Diagonal length $= \sqrt{(15^2 + 30^2 + 20^2)}$

$$= \sqrt{1525}$$

$$= 39.1 \text{ cm}$$

Exercise 11E

1 A box measures 8 cm by 12 cm by 5 cm.

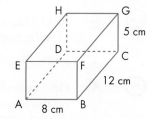

 a Calculate the following lengths.

  i AC **ii** BG **iii** BE

 b Calculate the diagonal distance BH.

(PS) **2** A garage is 5 m long, 3 m wide and 3 m high. Can a pole 7 m long be stored in it?

(PS) **3** Spike, a spider, is at the corner S of the wedge shown in the diagram. Fred, a fly, is at the corner F of the same wedge.

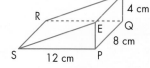

 a Calculate the shortest distance Spike would have to travel to get to Fred if she used only the edges of the wedge.

 b Calculate the shortest distance Spike would have to travel across the face of the wedge to get directly to Fred.

(PS) **4** A corridor is 3 m wide and turns through a right angle, as in the diagram.

 a What is the longest pole that can be carried along the corridor horizontally?

 b If the corridor is 3 m high, what is the longest pole that can be carried along in any direction?

(CM) **5** If each side of a cube is 10 cm long, show that it's 17.3 cm from one corner of the cube to the opposite corner.

(PS) **6** A pyramid has a square base of side 20 cm and each sloping edge is 25 cm long.

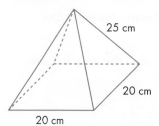

 How high is the pyramid?

7 The diagram shows a square-based pyramid with base length 8 cm and sloping edges 9 cm. M is the midpoint of the side AB, X is the midpoint of the base and E is directly above X.

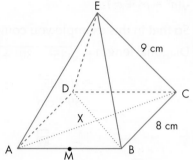

a Calculate the length of the diagonal AC.

b Calculate EX, the height of the pyramid.

c Using triangle ABE, calculate the length EM.

(CM) **8** ABCDEFGH is a cuboid where AB = EH = 22.5 cm, BC = GH = 30 cm and AF = CH = 40 cm. M is the midpoint of the side GH.

Show that the length of AM is 48.3 cm.

(PS) **9** On a cylindrical can, as shown, there is a straight line drawn from F, on the top to S, at the bottom, going around the can. Point F is directly above point S. Find the length of the line FS.

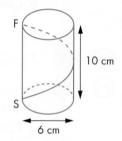

Hints and tips	Imagine the can opened out flat.

11.6 Trigonometric ratios

This section will show you how to:

- use the three trigonometric ratios.

Trigonometry is concerned with the calculation of sides and angles in triangles, and involves the use of three important ratios: **sine**, **cosine** and **tangent**. These ratios are defined in terms of the sides of a right-angled triangle and an angle. The angle is often described as theta, which is the Greek letter θ.

Key terms	
adjacent side	cosine
opposite side	sine
tangent	trigonometry

In a right-angled triangle:

- the side opposite the right angle is called the hypotenuse and is the longest side
- the side opposite the angle θ is called the **opposite side**
- the other side next to both the right angle and the angle θ is called the **adjacent side**.

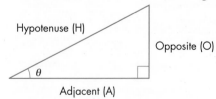

The sine, cosine and tangent ratios for θ are defined as:

$$\text{sine } \theta = \frac{\text{Opposite}}{\text{Hypotenuse}} \qquad \text{cosine } \theta = \frac{\text{Adjacent}}{\text{Hypotenuse}} \qquad \text{tangent } \theta = \frac{\text{Opposite}}{\text{Adjacent}}$$

These ratios are usually abbreviated as:

$$\sin \theta = \frac{O}{H} \qquad \cos \theta = \frac{A}{H} \qquad \tan \theta = \frac{O}{A}$$

These abbreviated forms are also used on calculator keys.

To memorise these formulae, you can use a mnemonic such as,

Some **O**ld **H**ens **C**ackle **A**ll **H**ours **T**il **O**ld **A**ge

in which the first letter of each word is taken in order to give:

$$S = \frac{O}{H} \quad C = \frac{A}{H} \quad T = \frac{O}{A}$$

Using your calculator

- You will need to use a calculator to find trigonometric ratios. Different calculators work in different ways, so make sure you know how to use your model.

- Angles can be measured in degrees, radians or grads. Calculators can be set to operate in any of these three units, so make sure your calculator is set up to work in degrees.

- To find the sine of 60 degrees you will probably press the keys  in that order, but it may be different on your calculator. The answer should be 0.8660... or $\frac{\sqrt{3}}{2}$. If your calculator gives answers in the form $\frac{\sqrt{3}}{2}$, make sure you can convert that to the decimal form.

- 3 cos 57° is a shorthand way of writing 3 × cos 57°. On some calculators you do not need to use the × button and you can just press the keys in the way it is written:

Check to see whether your calculator works this way. The answer should be 1.63.

Example 6

Find 5.6 sin 30°.

This means 5.6 × sine of 30 degrees.

5.6 sin 30° = 2.8

Exercise 11F 🖩

1. Find these values, rounding your answers to 3 significant figures (sf).

   a sin 43° **b** sin 56° **c** sin 67.2° **d** sin 90°

   e sin 45° **f** sin 20° **g** sin 22° **h** sin 0°

2. Find these values, rounding your answers to 3 significant figures.

   a cos 43° **b** cos 56° **c** cos 67.2° **d** cos 90°

   e cos 45° **f** cos 20° **g** cos 22° **h** cos 0°

(MR) **3** From your answers to questions **1** and **2**, what angle has the same value for sine and cosine?

(MR) **4**
a i What is sin 35°?   **ii** What is cos 55°?

b i What is sin 12°?   **ii** What is cos 78°?

c i What is cos 67°?   **ii** What is sin 23°?

d What connects the values in parts **a**, **b** and **c**?

e Copy and complete these sentences.

    i sin 15° is the same as cos …

    ii cos 82° is the same as sin …

    iii sin x is the same as cos …

5 Find these values.

  a tan 43°   **b** tan 56°   **c** tan 67.2°   **d** tan 90°

  e tan 45°   **f** tan 20°   **g** tan 22°   **h** tan 0°

6 Find these values.

  a sin 73°   **b** cos 26°   **c** tan 65.2°   **d** sin 88°

  e cos 35°   **f** tan 30°   **g** sin 28°   **h** cos 5°

(EV) **7** What is so different about tan compared with both sin and cos?

8 Work out these values.

  a 5 sin 65°   **b** 6 cos 42°   **c** 6 sin 90°   **d** 5 sin 0°

9 Work out these values.

  a 5 tan 65°   **b** 6 tan 42°   **c** 6 tan 85°   **d** 5 tan 0°

10 Work out these values.

  a 4 sin 63°   **b** 7 tan 52°   **c** 5 tan 80°   **d** 9 cos 8°

11 Calculate these values.

  a $\dfrac{5}{\sin 63°}$ **b** $\dfrac{6}{\sin 32°}$ **c** $\dfrac{6}{\sin 90°}$ **d** $\dfrac{5}{\sin 30°}$

12 Calculate these values.

  a $\dfrac{3}{\tan 64°}$ **b** $\dfrac{7}{\tan 42°}$ **c** $\dfrac{5}{\tan 89°}$ **d** $\dfrac{6}{\sin 40°}$

13 Calculate these values.

  a 8 sin 75°   **b** $\dfrac{19}{\sin 23°}$ **c** 7 cos 71°   **d** $\dfrac{15}{\sin 81°}$

14 Calculate these values.

  a 8 tan 75°   **b** $\dfrac{19}{\tan 23°}$ **c** 7 tan 71°   **d** $\dfrac{15}{\tan 81°}$

15 Calculate sin x, cos x and tan x for these triangles. Leave your answers as fractions.

a

b

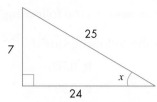

 16 You are told that $\tan x = \frac{5}{12}$.

Show how you can find sin x and cos x from this information without using a calculator.

11.7 Calculating angles

This section will show you how to:

• use the trigonometric ratios to calculate an angle.

What angle has a cosine of 0.6? You can use a calculator to find out.

You write 'the angle with a cosine of 0.6' as cos⁻¹ 0.6. This is called the '**inverse** cosine of 0.6'.

Find out where cos⁻¹ is on your calculator.

You will probably find it on the same key as cos, but you will need to press **shift** or **INV** or **2ndF** first. Look to see if cos⁻¹ is written above the cos key.

Check that cos⁻¹ 0.6 = 53.1301… = 53.1° (1 dp).

Check that cos 53.1° = 0.600 (3 dp).

Check that you can find the inverse sine and the inverse tangent in the same way.

Example 7

What angle has a sine of $\frac{3}{8}$?

You need to find sin⁻¹ $\frac{3}{8}$.

You could use the fraction button on your calculator or you could calculate sin⁻¹ (3 ÷ 8).

If you use the fraction key you may not need a bracket, or your calculator may put one in automatically.

Try to do it in both of these ways and then use whichever you prefer.

The answer is 22.0°.

Example 8

Find the angle with a tangent of 0.75.

tan⁻¹ 0.75 = 36.869 897…

= 36.9° (1 dp)

Exercise 11G 🖩

Use your calculator to find the answers to the following. Give your answers to 1 decimal place.

1 What angles have the following sines?

    a 0.5   **b** 0.785   **c** 0.64

    d 0.877   **e** 0.999   **f** 0.707

2 What angles have the following cosines?

    a 0.5   **b** 0.64   **c** 0.999

    d 0.707   **e** 0.2   **f** 0.7

3 What angles have the following tangents?

    a 0.6   **b** 0.38   **c** 0.895

    d 1.05   **e** 2.67   **f** 4.38

4 What angles have the following sines?

    a $4 \div 5$ **b** $2 \div 3$ **c** $7 \div 10$

    d $5 \div 6$ **e** $1 \div 24$ **f** $5 \div 13$

5 What angles have the following cosines?

    a $4 \div 5$ **b** $2 \div 3$ **c** $7 \div 10$

    d $5 \div 6$ **e** $1 \div 24$ **f** $5 \div 13$

6 What angles have the following tangents?

    a $3 \div 5$ **b** $7 \div 9$ **c** $2 \div 7$

    d $9 \div 5$ **e** $11 \div 7$ **f** $6 \div 5$

(CM) 7

    a What happens when you try to find the angle with a sine of 1.2?

    b What is the largest value of sine you can put into your calculator without getting an error when you ask for the inverse sine?

    c What is the smallest value of sine you can put into your calculator without getting an error when you ask for the inverse sine? (The correct answer is not 0.)

(EV) 8

    a i What angle has a sine of 0.3? (Keep the answer in your calculator memory.)

    ii What angle has a cosine of 0.3?

    iii Add the two accurate answers of parts **i** and **ii** together.

    b Will you always get the same answer to part a, whatever number you start with?

(CM) 9 You are told that $\cos 60° = \frac{1}{2}$.

    a Use this fact to show that the exact value of $\tan 30° = \frac{1}{\sqrt{3}}$.

    b Express $\tan 60°$ in square-root form.

    c Write down the exact value of $\sin 60°$.

    d Write down the exact value of $\cos 30°$.

    e Write down the exact value of $\sin 30°$.

(CM) 10 You are told that $\tan 45° = 1$.

    a Use this fact to show that the exact value of $\sin 45° = \frac{1}{\sqrt{2}}$.

    b Express $\cos 45°$ in square-root form.

11.8 Using the sine and cosine functions

This section will show you how to:

- find lengths of sides and angles in right-angled triangles using the sine and cosine functions.

Sine function

Remember sine $\theta = \dfrac{\text{Opposite}}{\text{Hypotenuse}}$

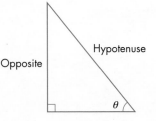

You can use the sine ratio to calculate the lengths of sides and angles in right-angled triangles.

To find the value of angle θ in this triangle:

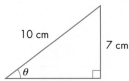

use the sine ratio as you have the opposite side (7 cm) and the hypotenuse (10 cm).

$$\sin \theta = \frac{O}{H}$$
$$= \frac{7}{10}$$
$$= 0.7$$

To find out what angle has a sine of 0.7, use the inverse sine function on your calculator.

$\sin^{-1} 0.7 = 44.4°$ (1 dp)

Example 9

Find the length of the side marked a in this triangle.

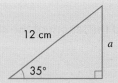

Side a is the opposite side, with 12 cm as the hypotenuse, so use the sine ratio.

$$\sin \theta = \frac{O}{H}$$

$$\sin 35° = \frac{a}{12}$$

$$\Rightarrow a = 12 \sin 35°$$

$$= 6.88 \text{ cm (3 sf)}$$

Example 10

Find the length of the hypotenuse, *h*, in this triangle.

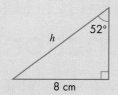

Note that although the angle is in the other corner, the opposite side is again given. So use the sine ratio.

$$\sin \theta = \frac{O}{H}$$

$$\sin 52° = \frac{8}{h}$$

$$\Rightarrow h = \frac{8}{\sin 52°}$$

$$= 10.2 \text{ cm (3 sf)}$$

Exercise 11H

1 Find the size of the angle marked *x* in each of these triangles.

a

b

c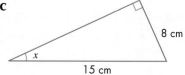

2 Find the length of the side marked *x* in each of these triangles.

a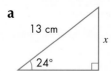

b

c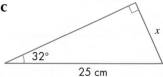

3 Find the length of the side marked *x* in each of these triangles.

a

b

c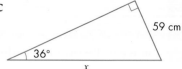

4 Find the length of the side marked *x* in each of these triangles.

a

b

c

d

5 Find the value of x in each of these triangles.

a
11 cm   15 cm x

b
9 cm x 37°

c
17° x 4 cm

d
x 8 cm   13 cm

6 Angle θ has a sine of $\frac{3}{5}$. Calculate the missing lengths in these triangles.

a
θ 10 x

b
θ x 9

c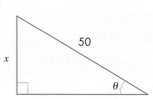
50   x θ

7 **a** Write down the exact value of sin 30°.

b Sketch a right-angled triangle with an angle of 30°.

c Label the hypotenuse with a length of 2 and then, without using a calculator, write down the lengths of the other two sides.

8 **a** Write down the exact value of sin 45° in square-root form.

b Sketch a right-angled triangle with an angle of 45°.

c Label the opposite side with a length of 1 and then, without using a calculator, write down the lengths of the other two sides.

Cosine function

Remember cosine $\theta = \dfrac{\text{Adjacent}}{\text{Hypotenuse}}$

You can use the cosine ratio to calculate the lengths of sides and angles in right-angled triangles.

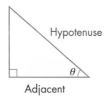

Hypotenuse θ Adjacent

To find the angle θ in this triangle:

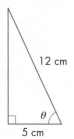

12 cm θ 5 cm

use the cosine ratio as you have the adjacent side (5 cm) and the hypotenuse (12 cm).

$\cos \theta = \dfrac{A}{H} = \dfrac{5}{12}$

To find out what angle has a cosine of $\frac{5}{12}$, use the inverse cosine function on your calculator.

$\cos^{-1} \dfrac{5}{12} = 65.4°$ (1 dp)

Example 11

Find the length of the side marked *a* in this triangle.

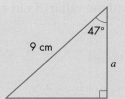

Side *a* is the adjacent side, with 9 cm as the hypotenuse, so use the cosine ratio.

$$\cos \theta = \frac{A}{H}$$

$$\cos 47° = \frac{a}{9}$$

$$\Rightarrow a = 9 \cos 47°$$

$$= 6.14 \text{ cm (3 sf)}$$

Example 12

Find the length of the hypotenuse, *h*, in this triangle.

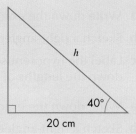

The adjacent side is given, so use the cosine ratio.

$$\cos \theta = \frac{A}{H}$$

$$\cos 40° = \frac{20}{h}$$

$$\Rightarrow h = \frac{20}{\cos 40°}$$

$$= 26.1 \text{ cm (3 sf)}$$

Exercise 11I

1 Find the angle marked *x* in each of these triangles.

a

b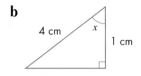

c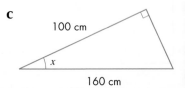

2 Find the side marked *x* in each of these triangles.

a

b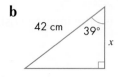

c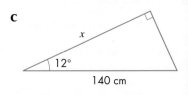

3 Find the side marked x in each of these triangles.

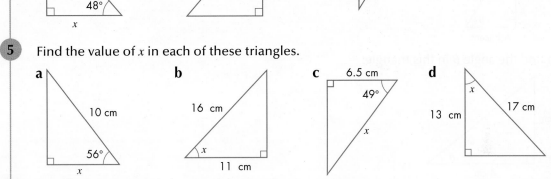

a

x 35° 6 cm

b

x 69° 14 cm

c

125 cm 22° x

4 Find the side marked x in each of these triangles.

a

8 cm 48° x

b

36° x 12 cm

c

11 cm 24° x

d

52° 14 cm x

5 Find the value of x in each of these triangles.

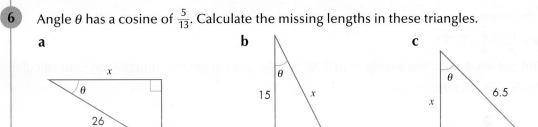

a

10 cm 56° x

b

16 cm x 11 cm

c

6.5 cm 49° x

d

x 13 cm 17 cm

6 Angle θ has a cosine of $\frac{5}{13}$. Calculate the missing lengths in these triangles.

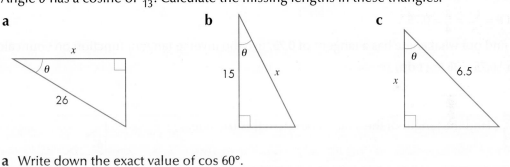

a

x θ 26

b

θ 15 x

c

θ x 6.5

7 **a** Write down the exact value of cos 60°.

   b Sketch a right-angled triangle with an angle of 60°.

   c Label the hypotenuse with a length of 2 and then, without using a calculator, write down the lengths of the other two sides.

8 **a** Write down the exact value of cos 45° in square-root form.

   b Sketch a right-angled triangle with an angle of 45°.

   c Label the opposite side with a length of 1 and then, without using a calculator, write down the lengths of the other two sides.

11.9 Using the tangent function

This section will show you how to:

- find lengths of sides and angles in right-angled triangles using the tangent function.

Remember tangent $\theta = \dfrac{\text{Opposite}}{\text{Adjacent}}$

You can use the tangent ratio to calculate the lengths of sides and angles in right-angled triangles.

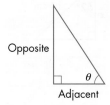

To find the angle θ in this triangle:

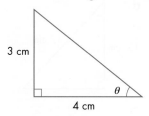

use the tangent ratio as you have the opposite side (3 cm) and the adjacent side (4 cm).

$\tan \theta = \dfrac{O}{A} = \dfrac{3}{4} = 0.75$

To find out what angle has a tangent of 0.75, use the inverse tangent function on your calculator.

$\tan^{-1} 0.75 = 36.9°$ (1 dp)

Example 13

Find the length of the side marked x in this triangle.

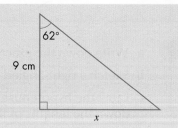

Side x is the opposite side, with 9 cm as the adjacent side, so use the tangent ratio.

$\tan \theta = \dfrac{O}{A}$

$\tan 62° = \dfrac{x}{9}$

$\Rightarrow x = 9 \tan 62°$

$\quad\quad = 16.9$ cm (3 sf)

Example 14

Find the length of the side marked *a* in this triangle.

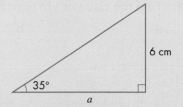

6 cm

35°

a

Side *a* is the adjacent side and the opposite side is given, so use the tangent ratio.

$$\tan \theta = \frac{O}{A}$$

$$\tan 35° = \frac{6}{a}$$

$$\Rightarrow a = \frac{6}{\tan 35°}$$

$$= 8.57 \text{ cm (3 sf)}$$

Exercise 11J 🖩

1 Find the angle marked *x* in each of these triangles.

a
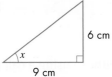
6 cm
x
9 cm

b
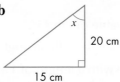
x
20 cm
15 cm

c

35 cm
45 cm
x

2 Find the side marked *x* in each of these triangles.

a
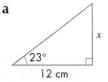
x
23°
12 cm

b
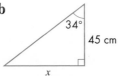
34°
45 cm
x

c
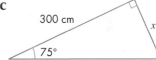
300 cm
x
75°

3 Find the side marked *x* in each of these triangles.

a
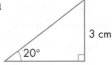
3 cm
20°
x

b

40°
x
52 cm

c
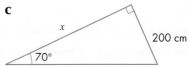
x
200 cm
70°

4 Find the side marked *x* in each of these triangles.

a

x
61°
5 cm

b
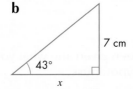
7 cm
43°
x

c
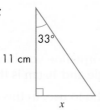
33°
11 cm
x

d
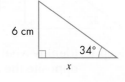
6 cm
34°
x

5 Find the value of x in each of these triangles.

a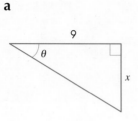

b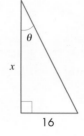

c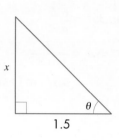

d

6 Angle θ has a tangent of $\frac{4}{3}$. Calculate the missing lengths in these triangles.

a

b

c

(MR) **7** **a** Write down the exact value of tan 60°.

b Sketch a right-angled triangle with an angle of 60°.

c Label the hypotenuse with a length of of 2 and then, without using a calculator, write down the lengths of the other two sides.

(MR) **8** **a** Write down the exact value of tan 45°.

b Sketch a right-angled triangle with an angle of 45°.

c Label the opposite side with a length of 1 and then, without using a calculator, write down the lengths of the other two sides.

11.10 Which ratio to use

This section will show you how to:

- decide which trigonometric ratio to use in a right-angled triangle.

The difficulty with any trigonometric problem is knowing which ratio to use to solve it.

To find the length of the side marked x in this triangle, follow the steps below.

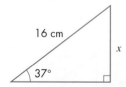

Step 1 Identify what information you have been given and what you need to find. In this case, x is opposite the angle and 16 cm is the hypotenuse.

Step 2 Decide which ratio to use. In this case, use the sine ratio as it uses the opposite and hypotenuse.

Step 3 Remember $\sin\theta = \dfrac{O}{H}$.

Step 4 Put in the numbers and letters. $\sin 37° = \dfrac{x}{16}$

Step 5 Rearrange the equation and work out the answer. $x = 16 \sin 37°$

$= 9.629\,040\,371$ cm

Step 6 Give the answer to an appropriate degree of accuracy. $x = 9.63$ cm (3 sf)

In reality, you may not need to write down every step. You can mark the triangle for step 1 and you can do steps 2 and 3 in your head. You should write down steps 4 to 6 to show your working.

The next examples are set out in a way that shows the *minimum* amount of working but gives the correct answers.

Example 15

Find the length of the side marked x in this triangle.

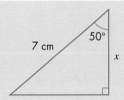

Mark on the triangle the side you know (H) and the side you want to find (A).

Recognise it is a cosine problem because you have A and H.

So, $\cos 50° = \dfrac{x}{7}$

$\Rightarrow x = 7 \cos 50°$

$= 4.50$ cm (3 sf)

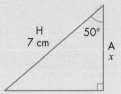

Example 16

Find the angle marked x in this triangle.

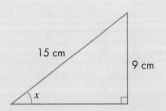

Mark on the triangle the sides you know.

Recognise it is a sine problem because you have O and H.

So, $\sin x = \dfrac{9}{15} = 0.6$

$\Rightarrow x = \sin^{-1} 0.6$

$= 36.9°$ (1 dp)

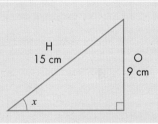

Example 17

Find the angle marked x in this triangle.

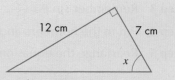

Mark on the triangle the sides you know.

Recognise it is a tangent problem because you have O and A.

So, $\tan x = \frac{12}{7}$

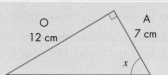

$\Rightarrow x = \tan^{-1} \frac{12}{7}$

$= 59.7°$ (1 dp)

Exercise 11K

1 Find the length marked x in each of these triangles.

a
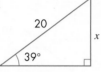

b
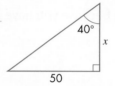

c

d

e
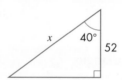

f
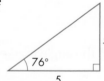

2 Find the angle marked x in each of these triangles.

a

b
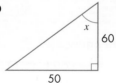

c

d
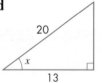

e
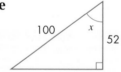

f
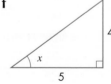

3 Find the angle or length marked x in each of these triangles.

a
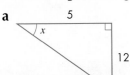

b
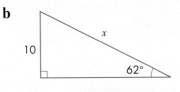

c
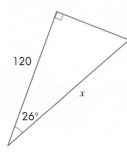

d

e

f
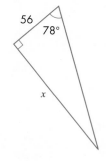

g
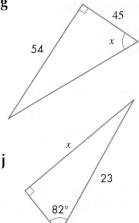

h
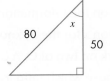

i
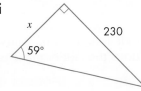

j
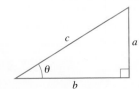

(CM) **4** **a** How does this diagram show that $\tan \theta = \dfrac{\sin \theta}{\cos \theta}$?

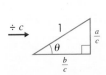

b How does the diagram show that $(\sin \theta)^2 + (\cos \theta)^2 = 1$?

c Choose a value for θ and check the two results in parts **a** and **b** are true.

(CM) **5** Complete this table, leaving your answers in square-root form.

	30°	45°	60°
Sine			
Cosine			
Tangent			

11.11 Solving problems using trigonometry

This section will show you how to:

- solve practical problems using trigonometry
- solve problems using an angle of elevation or an angle of depression.

Key terms

angle of depression

angle of elevation

Many trigonometry problems do not come as straightforward triangles. Sometimes, solving a triangle is part of solving a practical problem. You should follow these steps when solving a practical problem using trigonometry.

- Draw the triangle required.
- Put on the information given (angles and sides).
- Put on x for the unknown angle or side.
- Mark on two of O, A or H as appropriate.
- Choose which ratio to use.
- Write out the equation with the numbers in.
- Rearrange the equation, if necessary, and then work out the answer.
- Give your answer to a sensible degree of accuracy.

Example 18

A window cleaner has a ladder that is 7 m long. The window cleaner leans it against a wall so that the foot of the ladder is 3 m from the wall. What angle does the ladder make with the wall?

Draw the situation as a right-angled triangle.

Then mark the sides and angle.

Recognise it is a sine problem because you have O and H.

So, $\sin x = \frac{3}{7}$

$\Rightarrow x = \sin^{-1} \frac{3}{7}$

$= 25°$ (to the nearest degree)

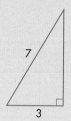

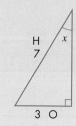

Exercise 11L

In these questions, give answers involving angles to the nearest degree.

1 A ladder, 6 m long, rests against a wall. The foot of the ladder is 2.5 m from the base of the wall. What angle does the ladder make with the ground?

PS **2** The ladder in question **1** has a 'safe angle' with the ground of 70°–80°. What are the safe limits for the distance of the foot of this ladder from the wall? How high up the wall does the ladder reach?

3 A ladder, of length 10 m, is placed so that it reaches 7 m up the wall. What angle does it make with the ground?

4 A ladder is placed so that it makes an angle of 76° with the ground. The foot of the ladder is 1.7 m from the foot of the wall. How high up the wall does the ladder reach?

(PS) **5** Calculate the angle that the diagonal makes with the long side of a rectangle that measures 10 cm by 6 cm.

(EV) **6** This diagram shows a frame for a bookcase.

   a What angle does the diagonal strut make with the long side?

   b Calculate the length of the strut.

   c Why may your answers be inaccurate in this case?

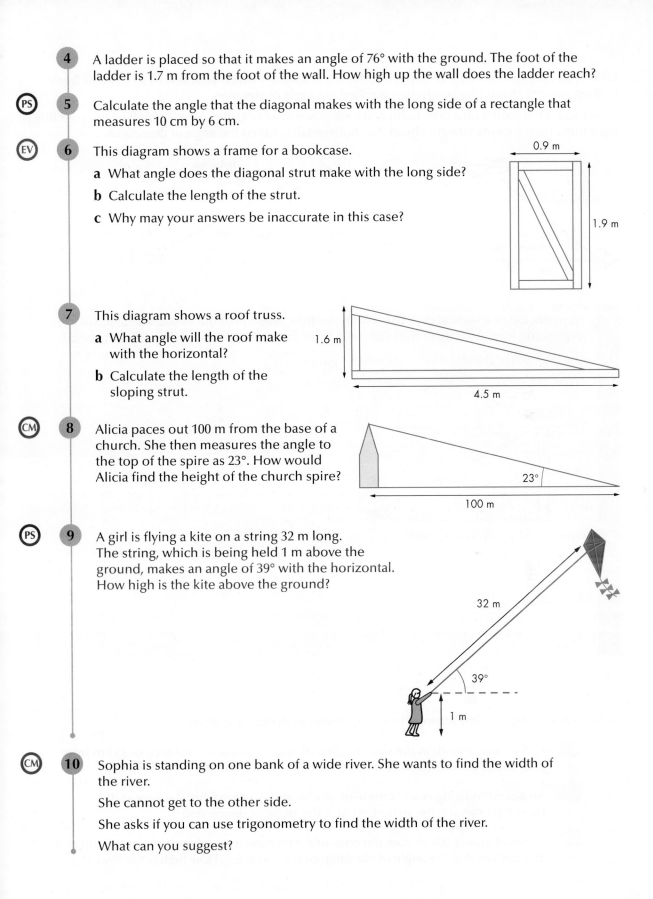

7 This diagram shows a roof truss.

   a What angle will the roof make with the horizontal?

   b Calculate the length of the sloping strut.

(CM) **8** Alicia paces out 100 m from the base of a church. She then measures the angle to the top of the spire as 23°. How would Alicia find the height of the church spire?

(PS) **9** A girl is flying a kite on a string 32 m long. The string, which is being held 1 m above the ground, makes an angle of 39° with the horizontal. How high is the kite above the ground?

(CM) **10** Sophia is standing on one bank of a wide river. She wants to find the width of the river.

   She cannot get to the other side.

   She asks if you can use trigonometry to find the width of the river.

   What can you suggest?

Angles of elevation and depression

When you look *up* at an aircraft in the sky, the angle through which your line of sight turns from looking straight ahead (the horizontal) is called the **angle of elevation**.

When you are standing on a high point and look *down* at a boat, the angle through which your line of sight turns from looking straight ahead (the horizontal) is called the **angle of depression**.

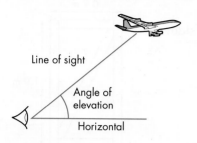

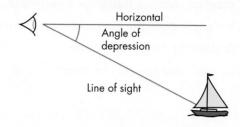

From the top of a vertical cliff, 100 m high, Andrew sees a boat out at sea. The angle of depression from Andrew to the boat is 42°. How far from the base of the cliff is the boat?

The diagram of the situation is shown in figure **i**.

From this, you get the triangle shown in figure **ii**.

i

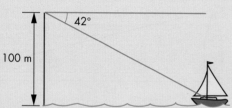

ii

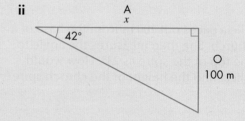

From figure **ii**, you see that this is a tangent problem.

So, $\tan 42° = \dfrac{100}{x}$

$\Rightarrow x = \dfrac{100}{\tan 42°}$

$= 111$ m (3 sf)

Exercise 11M

In these questions, give any answers involving angles to the nearest degree.

1 Eric sees an aircraft in the sky. The aircraft is at a horizontal distance of 25 km from Eric. The angle of elevation is 22°. How high is the aircraft?

2 An aircraft is flying at an altitude of 4000 m and is 10 km from the airport. If a passenger can see the airport, what is the angle of depression?

3 A man standing 200 m from the base of a television transmitter looks at the top of it and notices that the angle of elevation of the top is 65°. How high is the tower?

4 a From the top of a vertical cliff, 200 m high, a boat has an angle of depression of 52°. How far from the base of the cliff is the boat?

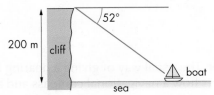

b The boat now sails away from the cliff so that the distance is doubled. Does that mean that the angle of depression is halved? Give a reason for your answer.

5 From a boat, the angle of elevation of the foot of a lighthouse on the edge of a cliff is 34°.

a If the cliff is 150 m high, how far from the base of the cliff is the boat?

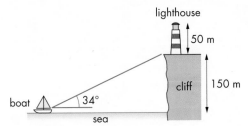

b If the lighthouse is 50 m high, what is the angle of elevation of the top of the lighthouse from the boat?

6 A bird flies from the top of a 12-m tall tree, at an angle of depression of 34°, to catch a worm on the ground.

a How far does the bird actually fly?

b How far was the worm from the base of the tree?

7 Sunil wants to find the height of a building. He stands about 50 m away from the building. The angle of elevation from Sunil to the top of the building is about 15°.

a How tall is the building?

b Evaluate your answer.

8 The top of a ski run is 100 m above the finishing line. The run is 300 m long. Show that the angle of depression of the ski run is 70.5°.

9 Nessie and Cara are standing on opposite sides of a tree.

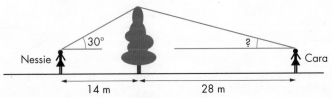

Nessie is 14 m away and the angle of elevation of the top of the tree is 30°.

Cara is 28 m away. She says the angle of elevation for her must be 15° because she is twice as far away.

Is Cara correct? If not, give the actual angle of elevation.

10 Isaac is in a boat on the sea and the angle of elevation to the top of the cliffs is 65°. His brother, William, is in another boat 30 m in front of him and directly in line with the same cliffs. For William, the angle of elevation of the cliffs is 70°.

How far from the foot of the cliffs are both boys?

11.12 Trigonometry and bearings

This section will show you how to:

- solve bearing problems using trigonometry.

A bearing is the direction to one place from another. The usual way of giving a bearing is as an angle measured from north in a clockwise direction. This is how a navigational compass and a surveyor's compass measure bearings.

A bearing is always written as a three-digit number, known as a three-figure bearing.

The diagram shows how this works, using the main compass points as examples.

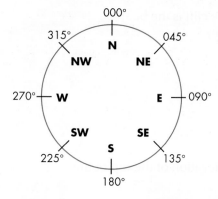

When working with bearings, remember:

- always work clockwise from North
- always give a bearing in degrees as a three-figure bearing.

Trigonometry problems with bearings can be difficult when there are angles greater than 90°. To avoid this, you have to find a right-angled triangle that you can easily use. Example 20 shows you how to deal with such a situation.

Example 20

A ship sails on a bearing of 120° for 50 km. How far east has it travelled?

The diagram of the situation is shown in figure **i**.

From this, you can get the acute-angled triangle shown in figure **ii**.

From figure **ii**, you see that this is a cosine problem.

So, $\cos 30° = \dfrac{x}{50}$

$\Rightarrow x = 50 \cos 30°$

$\qquad = 43.301$

The ship has sailed 43.3 km east (to 3 sf).

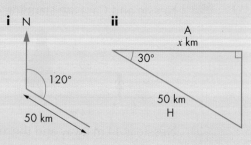

---

1 A ship sails for 75 km on a bearing of 078°.

  a How far east has it travelled?   **b** How far north has it travelled?

2 Lopham is 17 miles from Wath on a bearing of 210°.

  a How far south of Wath is Lopham?   **b** How far east of Lopham is Wath?

(CM) 3 A plane sets off from an airport and flies due east for 120 km, then turns to fly due south for 70 km before landing at Seddeth. Another pilot decides to fly the direct route from the airport to Seddeth.

  Show that he should fly on an approximate bearing of 120°.

4 A helicopter leaves an army base and flies 60 km on a bearing of 278°.

  a How far west has the helicopter flown?

  b How far north has the helicopter flown?

5 A ship sails from a port on a bearing of 117° for 35 km before heading due north for 40 km and docking at Angle Bay.

  a How far south had the ship sailed before turning?

  b How far north had the ship sailed from the port to Angle Bay?

  c How far east of the port is Angle Bay?

  d What is the bearing of Angle Bay from the port?

(PS) 6 Mountain A is due west of a walker. Mountain B is due north of the walker. The guidebook says that mountain B is 4.3 km from mountain A, on a bearing of 058°. How far is the walker from mountain B?

7 The shopping centre is 5.5 km east of my house and the supermarket is 3.8 km south. What is the bearing of the supermarket from the shopping mall?

8 The diagram shows the relative distances and bearings of three ships A, B and C.

  a How far north of A is B? (Distance x on diagram.)

  b How far north of B is C? (Distance y on diagram.)

  c How far west of A is C? (Distance z on diagram.)

  d What is the bearing of A from C? (Angle $w°$ on diagram.)

(PS) 9 A ship sails from port A for 42 km on a bearing of 130° to point B. It then changes course and sails for 24 km on a bearing of 040° to point C, where it breaks down and anchors. A helicopter flies directly from port A to the ship at C. What is its course?

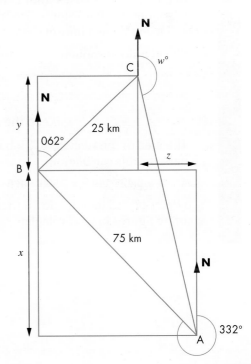

11.13 Trigonometry and isosceles triangles

This section will show you how to:

- use trigonometry to solve problems involving isosceles triangles.

Isosceles triangles often feature in trigonometry problems because they can be split into two right-angled triangles that are the same.

Example 21

a Find the length x in this isosceles triangle.

b Calculate the area of the triangle.

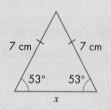

Draw a perpendicular from the apex of the triangle to its base, splitting the triangle into two the same, right-angled triangles.

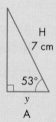

a To find the length y, which is half of x, use cosine.

So, $\cos 53° = \frac{y}{7}$

$\Rightarrow y = 7 \cos 53°$

$= 4.212\,705\,1$ cm

So $x = 2y = 8.43$ cm (3 sf).

b To calculate the area of the original triangle, you first need to find its vertical height, h.

You have two choices, both of which involve the right-angled triangle of part **a**. You can use either Pythagoras' theorem ($h^2 + y^2 = 7^2$) or trigonometry. It is safer to use trigonometry again, since you are then still using known information.

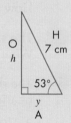

This is a sine problem. $\sin 53° = \frac{h}{7}$

$\Rightarrow h = 7 \sin 53°$

$= 5.590\,448\,6$ cm

(Keep the accurate figure in the calculator.)

The area of the triangle is $\frac{1}{2} \times$ base $\times$ height. You should use the most accurate figures you have for this calculation.

$A = \frac{1}{2} \times 8.425\,410\,3 \times 5.590\,448\,6 = 23.6$ cm^2 (3 sf)

You do not need to write down these eight-figure numbers, provided that you use the accurate figures in your calculator.

Exercise 11P

1 Find the value of the side or angle marked x.

a

b
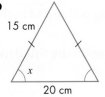

c

d
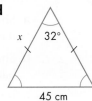

2 This diagram below shows a roof truss. How wide is the roof?

(PS) 3 Calculate the area of each of these triangles.

a

b
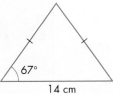

c
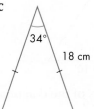

d
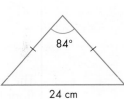

(PS) 4 An equilateral triangle has sides of length 10 cm.

A square is drawn on each side.

The corners of the squares are joined as shown.

What is the area of the resulting hexagon?

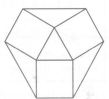

(PS) 5 The diagonals of a rectangle make an angle of 40° with each other. If each diagonal is 11 cm long, what is the area of the rectangle?

(CM) 6 Show that the volume of a cone with a vertical angle of 62° and a height of 8 cm is 194 cm³.

Worked exemplars

1 The inside of the back of a van is a cuboid that is 2.10 m wide, 4.20 m long and 3.10 m high.

a Show that a pole that is 5.25 m long will not fit in the van if it is laid on the floor.

b Show that a pole that is 5.25 m long can be fitted in the back of the van.

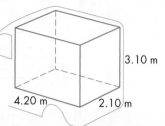

3.10 m

4.20 m   2.10 m

This is a communicating mathematics question where you have to assess the validity of an argument.

a 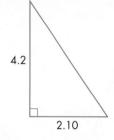 4.2 2.10 The length, c, of the diagonal of the floor is: $2.1^2 + 4.2^2 = c^2$ $c = \sqrt{(2.1^2 + 4.2^2)} = 4.7$ m This is shorter than the pole, so the ladder will not fit on the floor in the van.	You need to find the diagonal length of the floor in order to assess the statement given. Show the calculation using Pythagoras' theorem and then assess the statement. Don't just say the statement is wrong: give a clear reason for your conclusion.
b Let the length of the diagonal of the van be d m. 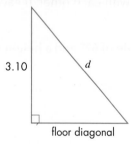 3.10 d floor diagonal $d = \sqrt{(4.2^2 + 2.1^2 + 3.1^2)}$ $= 5.627$ m The diagonal of the van is 37.7 cm longer than the pole so the pole can be put in diagonally.	You need to find the diagonal length of the van. Use a diagram to help identify the sides to use. Use Pythagoras' theorem in 3D to make sure you don't round too early. After finding the length, assess the statement and give a clear reason for your conclusion.

a Find the area of a regular hexagon of side 6 cm.

b Comment on the accuracy of your answer.

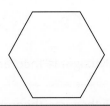

This is an evaluating question where you are required to evaluate a result.	
a 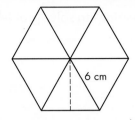 Area of one triangle = $\frac{1}{2} \times 6 \times$ height height = $\sqrt{(6^2 - 3^2)}$ Area of hexagon = 6 × area of triangle $= 6 \times \frac{1}{2} \times 6 \times \sqrt{(6^2 - 3^2)}$ $= 93.53\,0744$ $= 94 \text{ cm}^2$ (2 sf)	You need to show how you are accurately calculating the area of the shape without rounding too early. Then give a final answer with suitable rounding.
b The accuracy was kept by not rounding until the last stage. The initial data was assumed to be accurate, and so 2 sf gives an appropriate degree of accuracy.	You should make a suitable comment reflecting the accuracy, giving a clear reason why you selected the accuracy you did.

  A clock is designed to have a circular face on a triangular surround.
The triangle is equilateral.

The face extends to the edge of the triangle.

The diameter of the clock face is 18 cm.

Show that the perimeter of the triangle is 94 cm.

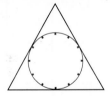

This is a communicating mathematics question where you have to construct a chain of reasoning to achieve a given result.	
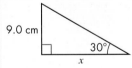 The radius is 9 cm. The angle is 30° because it is half the angle of an equilateral triangle. $\tan 30° = \dfrac{9}{x}$ $\Rightarrow x = \dfrac{9}{\tan 30°}$	You have to find the strategy of getting to the given result of 94 cm, clearly showing your method at each stage. You need to show a correct trigonometry ratio that can be used to calculate x, half the length of the side of the triangle. Use the lengths you are given, and what you can deduce, to draw a triangle.
Perimeter of triangle = $6 \times \dfrac{9}{\tan 30°}$ $= 93.53\ldots$ cm $= 94$ cm (2 sf)	Show the correct value of 93.53 and how you rounded to 2 sf in order to get the given solution of 94 cm.

Ready to progress?

I can use Pythagoras' theorem to solve problems in 2D.

I can use Pythagoras' theorem to solve problems in 3D.
I can use the trigonometric ratios for sine, cosine and tangent in right-angled triangles.
I can use trigonometry to solve problems.
I can use angles of elevation, angles of depression and bearings to solve problems.

Review questions

(PS) **1** ABC is a right-angled triangle.

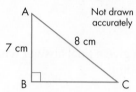

What is the area of the triangle?

(PS) **2** A lighthouse, L, is 15 km due west of a port, P.
A ship, S, is 8 km due north of the lighthouse, L.

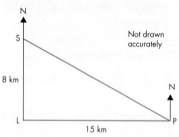

The ship leaves its position at 12 noon.
It sails directly to the port at a speed of 8.5 km/h.

What time will it reach the port?

(CM) **3** This cuboid is 3 cm wide, 4 cm long and 12 cm high.

Show that the diagonal of this cuboid is 13 cm.

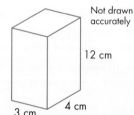

4 A lighthouse, L, is 4.3 km due east of a port, P. A ship, S, is 2.8 km due north of the lighthouse, L. Find the bearing of the port, P, from the ship, S.

5 The diagram is made up of two right-angled triangles ABC and BCD.

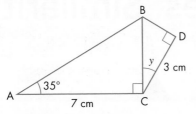

Calculate the value of y.

6 The circle with centre X has a radius of 7 cm.

The circle with centre Y has a radius of 2 cm.

The two circles touch each other and have a common tangent AB.

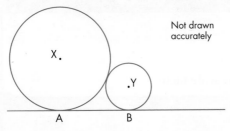

Not drawn accurately

a Explain why ABYX is a trapezium.

b Show that the area of ABYX is 33.7 cm².

7 Calculate the area of a pentagon with side length of 8 cm.

8 Leo only had a basic calculator with no trigonometrical functions. He needed to find the value of sin 60°.

Joy said he could calculate sin 60° by remembering how to express it in square-root form.

Chris said he could calculate it by using Pythagoras' theorem and an equilateral triangle of side length 10 cm.

Evaluate the accuracy of each method.

12 Geometry and measures: Similarity

This chapter is going to show you:

- how to work out the scale factor for two similar shapes
- how to work out lengths of sides in similar shapes
- how to work out areas and volumes of similar shapes.

You should already know:

- how to use and simplify ratios
- how to enlarge a shape by a given scale factor.

About this chapter

Thales of Miletus (c.624–c.547 BC) was a Greek philosopher and one of the Seven Sages of Greece. He is believed to have been the first person to use similar triangles to find the height of tall objects.

Thales discovered that, at a particular time of day, the height of an object and the length of its shadow were the same. He used this observation to calculate the height of the Egyptian pyramids. Later, he took this knowledge back to Greece. His observations are considered to be the forerunner of using similar triangles to solve such problems.

Astronomers use the geometry of triangles to measure the distance to nearby stars. They take advantage of Earth's journey in its orbit around the Sun to calculate the maximum distance between two measurements. They observe the star twice, from the same point on Earth and at the same time of day, but six months apart.

This chapter will show you what similar triangles and shapes are and how we can use the ratio of lengths to solve different sorts of problems.

12.1 Similar triangles

This section will show you how to:

- show two triangles are similar
- work out the scale factor between similar triangles.

Key terms

| similar | similar triangles |

Triangles are **similar** if their angles are equal. Their corresponding sides are then in the same ratio.

These two right-angled triangles are **similar triangles**.

The scale factor of the enlargement is 2.

The ratios of the lengths of corresponding sides can all be simplified to give the same ratio.

$3 : 6 = 4 : 8$
$ = 5 : 10$
$ = 1 : 2$

All corresponding angles are equal.

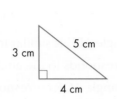
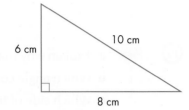

Example 1

The triangles ABC and PQR are similar.
Calculate the length of the side PR.

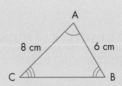
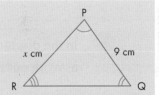

Take two pairs of corresponding sides, where one pair contains the unknown side. Form each pair into a fraction, so that x is on top. Since these fractions must be equal,

$$\frac{PR}{AC} = \frac{PQ}{AB}$$

$$\frac{x}{8} = \frac{9}{6}$$

To calculate x:

$$x = \frac{9 \times 8}{6} \text{ cm}$$

$$\Rightarrow \quad x = \frac{72}{6}$$

$$ = 12 \text{ cm}$$

Alternatively, you could use the scale factor method. The scale factor from ABC to PQR is $\frac{9}{6}$, which is 1.5. Hence PR is $8 \times 1.5 = 12$ cm

---

Exercise 12A

  1 Are these pairs of shapes similar? If so, give the scale factor. If not, give a reason.

a

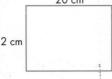

b

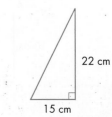

2 These triangles are similar.

a Give the ratio of the sides.

b Which angle corresponds to angle C?

c Which side corresponds to side QP?

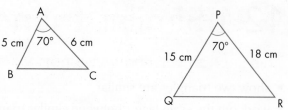

 3 These two triangles are similar.

a Which angle corresponds to angle A?

b Which side corresponds to side AC?

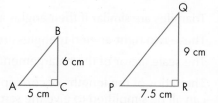

 4 a Explain why triangle ABC is similar to triangle AQR.

b Which angle corresponds to the angle at B?

c Which side of triangle AQR corresponds to side AC of triangle ABC? Your answers to question **3** may help you.

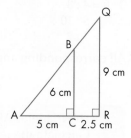

5 In the diagrams **a** to **f**, each pair of shapes are similar but not drawn to scale.

a Work out x.

b Work out PQ.

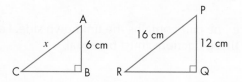

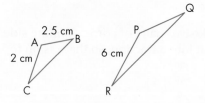

c Work out x and y.

d Work out x and y.

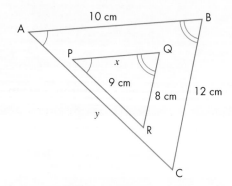

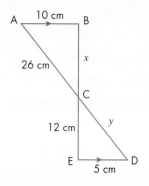

e Work out the lengths of AB and PQ.

f Work out the length of QR.

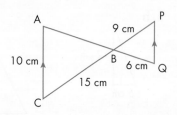

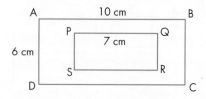

6 **a** Explain why these two triangles are similar.

b What is the ratio of their sides?

c Use Pythagoras' theorem to calculate the length of side AC of triangle ABC.

d Write down the length of the side PR of triangle PQR.

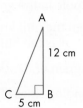

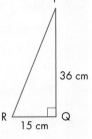

7 Sean is standing next to a tree.

His height is 1.6 m and he casts a shadow that has a length of 2.4 m.

The tree casts a shadow that has a length of 7.8 m.

Use what you know about similar triangles to work out the height of the tree, *h*.

8 Here are two rectangles.

Explain why the two rectangles are not similar.

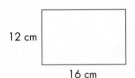

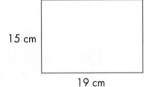

9 Triangle ABC is similar to triangle EDC.

Jay says that the length of DE is 14 cm.

Evaluate Jay's comment.

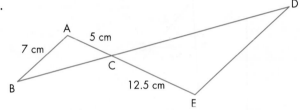

Further examples of similar triangles

Calculate the lengths marked *x* and *y* in the diagram (not drawn to scale).

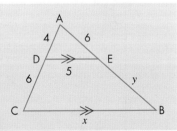

Using the properties of parallel lines, you can see that triangles AED and ABC are similar. So using the corresponding sides CB, DE with AC, AD gives,

$$\frac{x}{5} = \frac{10}{4}$$

$$\Rightarrow x = \frac{10 \times 5}{4}$$

$$= 12.5$$

Using the corresponding sides AE, AB with AD, AC gives,

$$\frac{y + 6}{6} = \frac{10}{4}$$

$$\Rightarrow y + 6 = \frac{10 \times 6}{4}$$

$$= 15$$

$$\Rightarrow y = 15 - 6$$

$$= 9$$

Example 3

Ahmed wants to work out the height of a tall building.

He sticks a 2 m pole in the ground at 100 paces from the building.

At 110 paces from the building he notices that the top of the pole and the top of the building are in line. How tall is the building?

First, draw a diagram of the situation and label it.

Using corresponding sides ED, CB with AD, AB gives:

$$\frac{x}{2} = \frac{110}{10}$$

$$\Rightarrow x = \frac{110 \times 2}{10}$$

$$= 22 \text{ m.}$$

So the building is 22 m high.

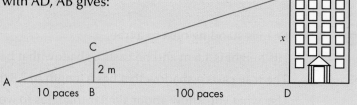

Exercise 12B

1   In each of the cases below, state a pair of similar triangles and calculate the length marked x. Separate the similar triangles if it makes it easier for you.

a

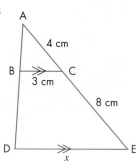

b

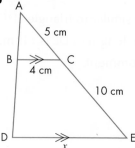

2   **a**   Work out the value of x.   **b**   Work out the length of CE.

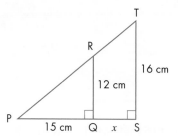

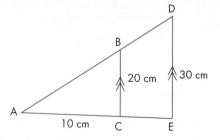

c   Work out the values of x and y.   **d**   Work out the lengths of DC and EB.

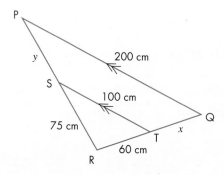

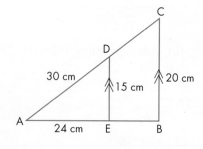

(PS) **3** This diagram shows a method of working out the height of a tower.

A stick, 2 m long, is placed vertically 120 m from the base of a tower so that the top of the tower and the top of the stick are in line with a point on the ground 3 m from the base of the stick. How high is the tower?

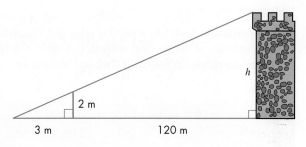

2 m

3 m   120 m

h

(CM) **4** It is known that a factory chimney is 330 feet high. Priya paces out distances as shown in the diagram, so that the top of the chimney and the top of the flag pole are in line with each other. Show that the flag pole is 220 feet tall.

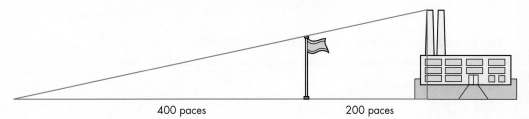

400 paces   200 paces

(PS) **5** The height of a golf flag is 1.5 m. Use the diagram to calculate the height of the tree.

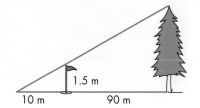

1.5 m

10 m   90 m

(PS) **6** Work out the height of a pole that casts a shadow of 1.5 m when at the same time a man of height 165 cm casts a shadow of 75 cm.

(PS) **7** Bob, a builder, is making this wooden frame for a roof.

In the diagram, triangle ABC is similar to triangle AXY.

AB = 1.5 m, BX = 3.5 m and XY = 6 m

What is the length of wood that Bob needs to make BC?

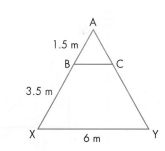

A

1.5 m

B   C

3.5 m

X

6 m   Y

(MR) **8** Triangle ABC is similar to triangle DAC.

AC = 9 cm and CD = 6 cm

Prove that BC is 13.5 cm.

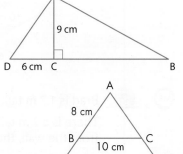

A

9 cm

D   6 cm   C   B

(EV) **9** In the diagram, triangle ABC is similar to triangle AXY.

Which of the following is the correct length of BX?

Explain how you decide.

a 2 cm   **b** 3 cm

c 4 cm   **d** 5 cm

A

8 cm

B   C

10 cm

X   Y

15 cm

More complicated problems

The information given in a similar triangle situation can be complicated, and you will need to have good algebraic skills to deal with it. Example 4 is typical of the more complicated problem you could be asked to solve, so follow it through carefully.

Example 4

Work out the value of x in this triangle.

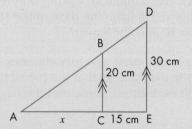

You know that triangle ABC is similar to triangle ADE.

Splitting up the triangles may help you to see what you will need.

So your equation will be:

$$\frac{x + 15}{x} = \frac{30}{20}$$

Multiplying both sides by x and both sides by 20 gives:

$$20x + 300 = 30x$$
$$\Rightarrow 300 = 10x$$
$$\Rightarrow x = 30 \text{ cm}$$

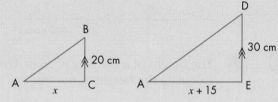

Exercise 12C

1 Calculate the lengths x or x and y in the diagrams **a** to **f**.

a

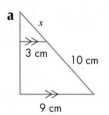

b

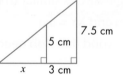

c

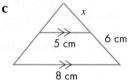

d

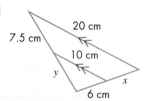

e

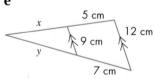

f

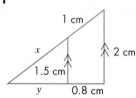

(MR) 2 Brad is 1.7 m tall. He is looking at a building that he knows is 180 m tall.

There is a 2 m tall wall between him and the building. When he is standing 12 m away from the wall, the top of the building is just hidden by the wall.

a Show that the building is just over 7 km from the other side of the wall.
b What assumptions have you made to calculate the distance?

12.2 Areas and volumes of similar shapes

This section will show you how to:

- solve problems involving the area and volume of similar shapes.

There are relationships between the lengths, areas and volumes of similar shapes.

You have already seen that when you enlarge a 2D shape by a given scale factor to form a new, similar shape, the corresponding lengths of the original shape and the new shape are all in the same ratio, which is equal to the scale factor. This scale factor of the lengths is called the length ratio or **linear scale factor**.

Two similar shapes also have an area ratio, which is equal to the ratio of the squares of their corresponding lengths. The area ratio, or **area scale factor**, is the square of the length ratio.

Likewise, two 3D shapes are similar if their corresponding lengths are in the same ratio. Their volume ratio is equal to the ratio of the cubes of their corresponding lengths. The volume ratio, or **volume scale factor**, is the cube of the length ratio.

You can verify this with the following investigation.

1. Draw or build one cube.

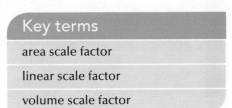

A

2. Draw or build another cube twice as long as the first.

3. Count how many faces of the small cube can fit in one face of the larger cube.

4. Count how many smaller cubes can fit in the larger cube.

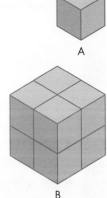

B

5. Draw or build another cube that is three times as long as the first one.

6. Count how many faces of the small cube can fit in one face of this new cube.

7. Count how many cubes can fit in this new cube.

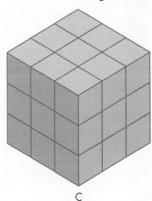

C

8. Comment on the following results.

Cubes	Length ratio	Area ratio	Volume ratio
A : B	1 : 2	1 : 4	1 : 8
A : C	1 : 3	1 : 9	1 : 27
B : C	2 : 3	4 : 9	8 : 27

You will notice that you can express the relationship between similar shapes as:

Length ratio: $x : y$ Area ratio: $x^2 : y^2$ Volume ratio: $x^3 : y^3$

Example 5

A model yacht is made to a scale of $\frac{1}{20}$ of the size of the real yacht. The area of the sail of the model is 150 cm². What is the area of the sail of the real yacht?

Linear scale factor	$= 1 : 20$
Area scale factor	$= 1^2 : 20^2$
	$= 1 : 400$ (square of the linear scale factor)
Area of real sail	$= 400 \times$ area of model sail
	$= 400 \times 150$ cm²
	$= 60\,000$ cm²
	$= 6$ m²

Example 6

A bottle has a base radius of 4 cm, a height of 15 cm and a capacity of 650 cm³. A similar bottle has a base radius of 3 cm.

a What is the length ratio?

b What is the volume ratio?

c What is the volume of the smaller bottle?

a The length ratio is given by the ratio of the two radii, that is, $4 : 3$.

b The volume ratio is therefore $4^3 : 3^3 = 64 : 27$.

c Let v be the volume of the smaller bottle. Then the volume ratio is:

$$\frac{\text{volume of smaller bottle}}{\text{volume of larger bottle}} = \frac{v}{650}$$

Therefore $\frac{v}{650} = \frac{27}{64}$

$$\Rightarrow v = \frac{27 \times 650}{64}$$

$$= 274 \text{ cm}^3 \text{ (3 significant figures)}$$

Example 7

The cost of a tin of paint, with height 12 cm, is £3.20 and its label has an area of 24 cm².

a If the cost is based on the amount of paint in the tin, what is the cost of a similar tin, 18 cm high?

b Assuming the labels are similar, what is the area of the label on the larger tin?

a The cost of the paint is proportional to the volume of the tin.

Length ratio $= 12 : 18$
$= 2 : 3$

Volume ratio $= 2^3 : 3^3$
$= 8 : 27$

Let P be the cost of the larger tin. Then the cost ratio is:

$$\frac{\text{cost of larger tin}}{\text{cost of smaller tin}} = \frac{P}{3.2}$$

Therefore:

$$\frac{P}{3.2} = \frac{27}{8}$$

$$\Rightarrow P = \frac{27 \times 3.2}{8}$$

$$= £10.80.$$

b Area ratio $= 2^2 : 3^2$
$= 4 : 9$

Let A be the area of the larger label. Then the area ratio is:

$$\frac{\text{larger label area}}{\text{smaller label area}} = \frac{A}{24}$$

Therefore:

$$\frac{A}{24} = \frac{9}{4}$$

$$\Rightarrow A = \frac{9 \times 24}{4}$$

$$= 54 \text{ cm}^2$$

Exercise 12D

1 **a** What is the area ratio between two solids whose length ratio is:

    i 1 : 3   **ii** 2 : 5   **iii** 4 : 7?

  b What is the volume ratio between two solids whose length ratio is:

    i 1 : 3   **ii** 2 : 5   **iii** 4 : 7?

2 Copy and complete this table.

Linear scale factor	Linear ratio	Linear fraction	Area scale factor	Volume scale factor
2	1 : 2	$\frac{2}{1}$		
3				
$\frac{1}{4}$	4 : 1	$\frac{1}{4}$		$\frac{1}{64}$
			25	
				$\frac{1}{1000}$

3 A shape has an area of 15 cm². What is the area of a similar shape with lengths that are three times the corresponding lengths of the first shape?

4 A toy brick has a surface area of 14 cm². What would be the surface area of a similar toy brick with lengths that are:

  a twice the corresponding lengths of the first brick

  b three times the corresponding lengths of the first brick?

5 A rug has an area of 12 m². What area would be covered by rugs with lengths that are:

  a twice the corresponding lengths of the first rug

  b half the corresponding lengths of the first rug?

6 A brick has a volume of 300 cm³. What would be the volume of a similar brick whose lengths are:

  a twice the corresponding lengths of the first brick

  b three times the corresponding lengths of the first brick?

7 A tin of paint, 6 cm high, holds half a litre of paint. Show that a similar tin 12 cm high would hold 4 litres of paint.

8 A model statue is 10 cm high and has a volume of 100 cm³. The real statue is 2.4 m high. What is the volume of the real statue? Give your answer in m³.

9 A small tin of paint costs 75p.

  a What is the cost of a larger similar tin with height twice that of the smaller tin?

  b What assumption have you had to make?

10 A small trinket box of width 2 cm has a volume of 10 cm³. What is the width of a similar trinket box with a volume of 80 cm³?

11 A cinema sells popcorn in two different-sized tubs that are similar in shape.

Show that it is true that the big tub is better value.

Popcorn

10 cm

20 cm

Small tub
60p

Large tub
£4.00

Better value if you buy the Big tub

12 The diameters of two ball bearings are as shown.

Work out the ratio of:

a their radii

b their surface areas

c their volumes.

6 mm   8 mm

13 Cuboid A is similar to cuboid B.

The length of cuboid A is 10 cm and the length of cuboid B is 5 cm.

The volume of cuboid A is 720 cm³.

Shona says that the volume of cuboid B must be 360 cm³.

Explain why she is wrong.

More complex problems using area and volume ratios

In some problems involving similar shapes, the length ratio is not given, so you have to start with the area ratio or the volume ratio. Then you may need to find the length ratio in order to find the solution.

Example 8

A manufacturer makes a range of clown hats that are all similar in shape. The smallest hat is 8 cm tall and uses 180 cm² of card. What will be the height of a hat made from 300 cm² of card?

The area ratio is 180 : 300.

Therefore, the length ratio is $\sqrt{180} : \sqrt{300}$ (do not calculate these yet).

Let the height of the larger hat be H; then:

$$\frac{H}{8} = \frac{\sqrt{300}}{\sqrt{180}}$$

$$\Rightarrow H = 8 \times \frac{\sqrt{300}}{\sqrt{180}}$$

$$= 10.3 \text{ cm (1 decimal place)}$$

Example 9

A supermarket stocks similar small and large tins of soup. The areas of their labels are 110 cm² and 190 cm² respectively. The mass of a small tin is 450 g. What is the mass of a large tin?

The area ratio is 110 : 190.

Therefore, the length ratio is $\sqrt{110} : \sqrt{190}$ (do not calculate these yet).

So the volume (mass) ratio is $(\sqrt{110})^3 : (\sqrt{190})^3$.

Let the mass of a large tin be M; then:

$$\frac{M}{450} = \frac{(\sqrt{190})^3}{(\sqrt{110})^3}$$

$$\Rightarrow M = 450 \times \frac{(\sqrt{190})^3}{(\sqrt{110})^3}$$

$$= 1020 \text{ g} \qquad \text{(3 significant figures)}$$

Two similar tins hold 1.5 litres and 2.5 litres of paint. The area of the label on the smaller tin is 85 cm². What is the area of the label on the larger tin?

The volume ratio is 1.5 : 2.5.

Therefore, the length ratio is $\sqrt[3]{1.5} : \sqrt[3]{2.5}$ (do not calculate these yet).

So the area ratio is $(\sqrt[3]{1.5})^2 : (\sqrt[3]{2.5})^2$.

Let the area of the label on the larger tin be A; then

$$\frac{A}{85} = \frac{(\sqrt[3]{2.5})^2}{(\sqrt[3]{1.5})^2}$$

$$\Rightarrow A = 85 \times \frac{(\sqrt[3]{2.5})^2}{(\sqrt[3]{1.5})^2}$$

$$= 119 \text{ cm}^2 \quad \text{(3 significant figures)}$$

Exercise 12E

(PS) **1** Look at these pairs of similar solids. Work out the missing volume in each pair. Give your answers correct to 3 sf.

a

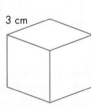

3 cm

5 cm

Volume = 24 cm³   Volume = V

b

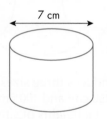

7 cm

10 cm

Volume = 220 cm³   Volume = V

c

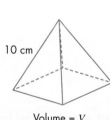

10 cm

15 cm

Volume = V   Volume = 900 cm³

d

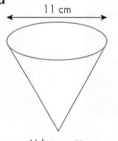

11 cm

5 cm

Volume = V   Volume = 40 cm³

2 Find the volumes and lengths as indicated. Give your answers to the nearest whole number.

Height	5 cm	
Surface area	22 cm²	32 cm²
Volume	14 cm³	

Height		11 cm
Surface area	160 cm²	300 cm²
Volume		130 cm³

a

b

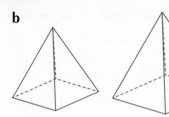

Height	3 cm	
Surface area	45 cm²	80 cm²
Mass		250 g

Height	2.5 cm	
Surface area	30 cm²	50 cm²
Volume		280 cm³

c

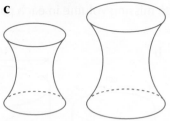

d

3 A firm produces three sizes of similar-shaped labels for its cans. Their areas are 150 cm², 250 cm² and 400 cm². The 250 cm² label just fits around a can of height 8 cm. Calculate the heights of similar cans which the other two labels would just fit around.

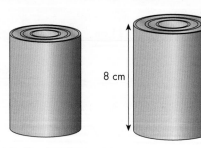

8 cm

4 A firm makes similar gift boxes in three different sizes: small, medium and large. The areas of their lids are as follows.

Small: 30 cm²   Medium: 50 cm²   Large: 75 cm²

The medium box is 5.5 cm high. Work out the heights of the other two sizes.

(MR) **5** A cone of height 8 cm can be made from a piece of card with an area of 140 cm². Show that the height of a similar cone made from a similar piece of card with an area of 200 cm² is 9.56 cm.

6 It takes 5.6 litres of paint to paint a chimney that is 3 m high. What is the tallest similar chimney that can be painted with 8 litres of paint?

7 A piece of card, 1200 cm² in area, will make a tube 13 cm long. How long is a similar tube made from a similar piece of card with an area of 500 cm²?

8 If a TV screen with area 220 cm² has a diagonal length of 21 cm, what will be the diagonal length of a similar TV screen with area 350 cm²?

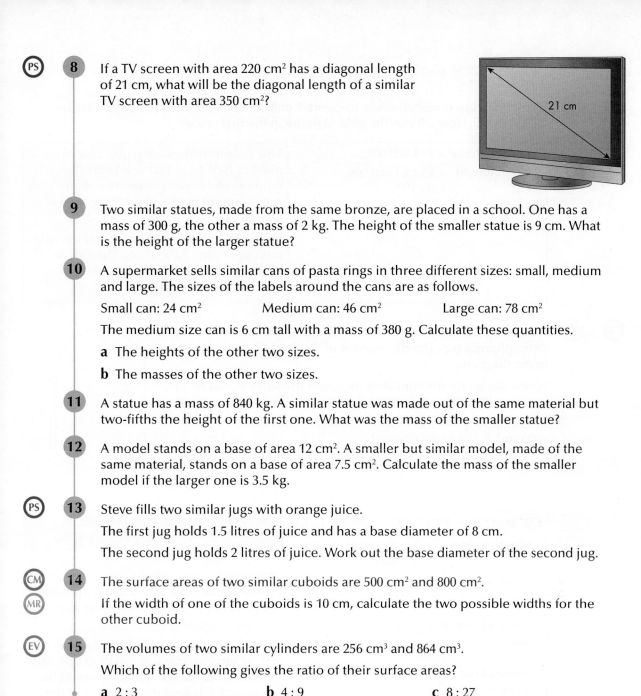

21 cm

9 Two similar statues, made from the same bronze, are placed in a school. One has a mass of 300 g, the other a mass of 2 kg. The height of the smaller statue is 9 cm. What is the height of the larger statue?

10 A supermarket sells similar cans of pasta rings in three different sizes: small, medium and large. The sizes of the labels around the cans are as follows.

Small can: 24 cm²   Medium can: 46 cm²   Large can: 78 cm²

The medium size can is 6 cm tall with a mass of 380 g. Calculate these quantities.

a The heights of the other two sizes.

b The masses of the other two sizes.

11 A statue has a mass of 840 kg. A similar statue was made out of the same material but two-fifths the height of the first one. What was the mass of the smaller statue?

12 A model stands on a base of area 12 cm². A smaller but similar model, made of the same material, stands on a base of area 7.5 cm². Calculate the mass of the smaller model if the larger one is 3.5 kg.

13 Steve fills two similar jugs with orange juice.

The first jug holds 1.5 litres of juice and has a base diameter of 8 cm.

The second jug holds 2 litres of juice. Work out the base diameter of the second jug.

14 The surface areas of two similar cuboids are 500 cm² and 800 cm².

If the width of one of the cuboids is 10 cm, calculate the two possible widths for the other cuboid.

15 The volumes of two similar cylinders are 256 cm³ and 864 cm³.

Which of the following gives the ratio of their surface areas?

a $2:3$ **b** $4:9$ **c** $8:27$

Worked exemplars

  1 A golden figure is melted down to create a million similar miniature figures that are all 3.5 cm tall. How tall was the golden figure in the first place?

Ratio of volume = 1 : 1 000 000 Ratio of length $= \sqrt[3]{1} : \sqrt[3]{1\,000\,000}$ $\qquad\qquad\quad = 1 : 100$ So original statue = 3.5 cm × 100 $\qquad\qquad\qquad = 350$ cm	This is a problem-solving question. You need to recognise that you know the ratio of volumes of similar shapes and can therefore work out what the ratio of lengths is. Show clearly how you work out the length ratio by finding cube roots. Then show how you use that ratio to calculate the original statue height.

  2 A camping gas container is in the shape of a cylinder with a hemispherical top. The dimensions of the container are shown in the diagram.

A new design for the container increases the surface area by 15%, keeping the new container mathematically similar to the old one.

It is suggested that this new design makes the container contain 1000 cm³. Is this claim correct?

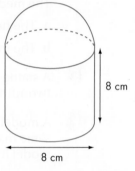

8 cm

8 cm

Old area : New area = 100% : 115% = 1 : 1.15 $\quad$ Length ratio = $\sqrt{1} : \sqrt{1.15}$ $\qquad\qquad\qquad = 1 : 1.0723805$ Volume ratio $= 1^3 : 1.0723805^3$ $\qquad\qquad\quad = 1 : 1.2332376$ Volume of $= \pi r^2 h + \frac{1}{2} \times \frac{4}{3} \pi r^3$ container Volume of old $= \pi \times 16 \times 8 + \frac{4}{6} \times \pi \times 64$ container $\qquad\qquad\quad = 536.16515$ cm³ Volume of new = $536.16515 \times 1.2332376$ container $\qquad\qquad\quad = 661$ cm³ (3 sf) This is much less than 1000 cm³. The claim would only be correct if rounded to the nearest thousand.	This is a communicating mathematics question where you are assessing the validity of a statement. You need to recognise that you have to use the area scale factor to get the length scale factor in order to work out the volume scale factor. You could calculate the new dimensions of the larger container and then calculate the volume, but the numbers would be awkward. It is simplest to work out the volume of the old container and then increase that volume by the found scale factor as here. You then have to evaluate the claim made. It is incorrect but it is good to recognise what could have made the claim correct.

3 A supermarket sold beans in similar tins: small, with a paper label of area 23 cm²; medium, with a paper label of area 45 cm²; large, with a paper label of area 75 cm². The medium tin is 7 cm tall with a mass of 350 g.

a Calculate the heights of the other two tins.

b Maisie suggested that the mass of the small tin will be 130 g and the mass of the larger tin will be 740 g. Comment on Maisie's suggestion.

Part **a** requires you to work with ratios but part **b** is an evaluating question in which you must explain how Maisie's suggestion ties in with the actual answers.

a Let the height of the small tin be h. Then the ratio of (lengths)² is the ratio of the areas. Hence: $$\left(\frac{h}{7}\right)^2 = \frac{23}{45}$$ $$\Rightarrow h^2 = 49 \times \frac{23}{45}$$ $$h = 5.004\ 442\ 5$$ $$= 5.0\text{ cm (2 sf)}$$	Using h and H to represent the respective heights makes the working clear. You need to show clearly where the ratios used have come from.
Let the height of the large tin be H. Again, the ratio of (lengths)² is the ratio of the areas. $$\left(\frac{H}{7}\right)^2 = \frac{75}{45}$$ $$\Rightarrow H^2 = 49 \times \frac{75}{45}$$ $$H = 9.036\ 961\ 1$$ $$= 9.0\text{ cm (2sf)}$$	You need to be able to use the accurate heights later in your solution to part **b**. so keep a note of them but round suitably for the heights in this part.

b Let the mass of the small tin be m.

Then the ratio of (lengths)^3 is the ratio of the volumes and the ratio of the masses is the same as the ratio of the volumes.

Hence:

$$\frac{m}{350} = \left(\frac{5.004\ 425}{7}\right)^3$$

$$\Rightarrow m = 350 \times \left(\frac{125.332\ 17}{343}\right)$$

$$= 127.889\ 97$$

$$= 130\text{ g (2 sf)}$$

Maisie is correct to 2 sf.

Let the mass of the large tin be M.

Then, as above:

$$\frac{M}{350} = \left(\frac{9.036\ 961}{7}\right)^3$$

$$\Rightarrow M = 350 \times \left(\frac{738.018\ 48}{343}\right)$$

$$= 753.080\ 08$$

$$= 750\text{ g (2 sf)}$$

Maisie has either rounded incorrectly or she used the rounded figure of 9.0 in the calculation.

Check: using 9.0 gives:

$$M = 350 \times \frac{729}{343}$$

$$= 743.877\ 55$$

$$= 740\text{g (2 sf)}$$

So It looks as though Maisie used the rounded earlier figures in this last calculation.

Again, using m and M to represent the respective mass's makes the working clear. You need to calculate the actual accurate answer in order to be able to evaluate Maisie's comments.

Use the most accurate data you can for the calculations. Note down the intermediary answers in case you need to check the answers later.

Show clearly where each ratio has come from and use the accurate figures from part **a** in order to be as accurate as possible in this last part.

Once you have found the accurate answers you can comment on Maisie's answers.

The small mass is a good answer but the large mass is incorrect. Try to suggest why the wrong answer was calculated. Here, it is likely that Maisie used the rounded figure of 9.0. Checking gives the same answer as Maisie had.

This is a reminder not to use rounded figures in the final calculation.

Ready to progress?

I can work out the ratios between two similar shapes.
I can work out unknown lengths, areas and volumes of similar 3D shapes.
I can solve practical problems using similar shapes.
I can solve problems using area and volume ratios.

Review questions

CM **1** SQT and RQP are straight lines.

Show that the vertical height of the larger triangle is 5 cm longer than the smaller triangle.

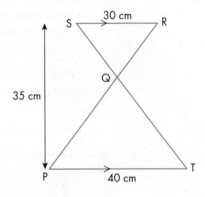

2 **a** Explain why the volume of a solid shape increases by a factor of 27 when the side lengths are tripled.

b When Alun bought a plant he was told that when it was watered, within 24 hours it would be 27 times larger than it was then! It was 4 cm tall when he brought it home.

After he watered it, within 24 hours it grew to a similarly shaped plant that was 12 cm tall.

Was the claim about the plant justified?

EV **3** Andrew calculated BE as 5.25 cm.

Eve said that ED is 8 cm.

Evaluate both statements.

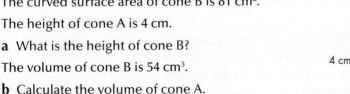

Not drawn accurately

PS **4** Two cones, A and B, are mathematically similar.

The curved surface area of cone A is 36 cm².

The curved surface area of cone B is 81 cm².

The height of cone A is 4 cm.

a What is the height of cone B?

The volume of cone B is 54 cm³.

b Calculate the volume of cone A.

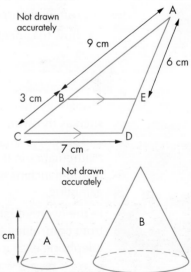

Not drawn accurately

MR **5** The cylinders A and B are mathematically similar.

The curved surface area of cylinder A is 100 cm².

The curved surface area of cylinder B is 324 cm².

The length of cylinder A is 5 cm.

a Show that the length of cylinder B is 9 cm.

The volume of cylinder A is 160 cm³.

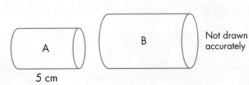

Not drawn accurately

b Work out the volume of cylinder B. Give your answer to 3 significant figures.

13 Probability: Exploring and applying probability

This chapter is going to show you:

- how to work out the probabilities of outcomes of events, using theoretical or experimental models
- how to recognise mutually exclusive, exhaustive and complementary outcomes
- how to predict the likely number of successful outcomes, given the number of trials and the probability of any one outcome
- how to use two-way tables to solve probability problems
- how to use Venn diagrams to solve probability problems.

You should already know:

- that the probability scale goes from 0 to 1
- how to use the probability scale to assess the likelihood of outcomes, depending on their position on the scale
- how to cancel, add and subtract fractions.

About this chapter

Probability theory originated from the study of games of chance, such as throwing a dice or spinning a roulette wheel, in the sixteenth and seventeenth centuries. Probability theory developed as a branch of mathematics in the seventeenth century when French gamblers asked mathematicians Blaise Pascal and Pierre de Fermat for help in their gambling.

In the twenty-first century, probability has many everyday applications from controlling the flow of traffic through road systems to running telephone exchanges and studying the spread of infections.

13.1 Experimental probability

This section will show you how to:

- calculate experimental probabilities and relative frequencies
- estimate probabilities from experiments
- use different methods to estimate probabilities.

Key terms
event
experimental probability
outcome
random
relative frequency
theoretical probability
trial

Terminology

The topic of probability has its own special vocabulary. For example, a **trial** is one attempt at performing something that may have one or more results, such as throwing a dice or tossing a coin. If you throw a dice 10 times, you perform 10 trials.

An **event** is an activity that may have several possible results.
An **outcome** is one of the results of an event. An event is also described as a set of outcomes. You will usually be interested in the probability of one or more outcomes occurring.

At **random** means 'without knowing what the outcome is in advance'.

Probability facts

Probability is defined as:

$$P(\text{outcome}) = \frac{\text{number of ways the outcome can happen}}{\text{total number of all possible outcomes}}.$$

This always leads to a fraction, which you should cancel to its simplest form. Make sure that you know how to cancel fractions, with or without a calculator. It is acceptable to give a probability as a decimal or a percentage, but fractions are most commonly used.

The probability of a certain outcome is 1 and the probability of an impossible outcome is 0.

Probability is never greater than 1 or less than 0.

Many probability trials involve coins, dice and packs of cards.

- Throwing a coin has two possible outcomes: head or tail.
- Throwing an ordinary six-sided dice has six possible outcomes: 1, 2, 3, 4, 5, 6.
- A pack of cards consists of 52 cards divided into four suits: hearts (red), spades (black), diamonds (red) and clubs (black). Each suit consists of 13 cards bearing the following values: 2, 3, 4, 5, 6, 7, 8, 9, 10, jack, queen, king and ace – the jack, queen and king being called 'picture cards'. So the total number of outcomes is 52.

Example 1

A card is drawn from a normal pack of cards. Count the value of an ace as 1. What is the probability that it is:

a   a red card

b   a spade

c   a seven

d   a picture card

e   a number less than 5

f   a red king?

a   There are 26 red cards, so P(red card) = $\frac{26}{52}$, which cancels to $\frac{1}{2}$.

b   There are 13 spades, so P(spade) = $\frac{13}{52}$, which cancels to $\frac{1}{4}$.

c   There are 4 sevens, so P(seven) = $\frac{4}{52}$, which cancels to $\frac{1}{13}$.

d   There are 12 picture cards, so P(picture card) = $\frac{12}{52}$, which cancels to $\frac{3}{13}$.

e   If you count the value of an ace as 1, there are 16 cards with a value less than 5. So, P(number less than 5) = $\frac{16}{52}$, which cancels to $\frac{4}{13}$.

f   There are 2 red kings, so P(red king) = $\frac{2}{52}$, which cancels to $\frac{1}{26}$.

The value calculated as $\dfrac{\text{number of successful outcomes}}{\text{number of trials}}$ is the **experimental probability** of the desired outcome. As the number of trials or experiments increases, the value of the experimental probability gets closer to the true or **theoretical probability**.

The experimental probability is also known as the **relative frequency** of an outcome. The relative frequency of an outcome is an estimate for the theoretical probability.

Relative frequency of an outcome = $\dfrac{\text{frequency of the desired outcome}}{\text{total number of trials}}$

Example 2

The frequency table shows the speeds of 160 vehicles that pass a radar speed check on a dual carriageway.

Speed (mph)	20–29	30–39	40–49	50–59	60–69	70+
Frequency	14	23	28	35	52	8

a What is the relative frequency that a vehicle is travelling faster than 70 mph?

b 500 vehicles pass the speed check. Estimate how many will be travelling faster than 70 mph.

a The relative frequency is $\frac{8}{160} = \frac{1}{20}$.

b The number of vehicles travelling faster than 70 mph will be $\frac{1}{20}$ of 500.

This is $500 \div 20 = 25$ vehicles.

Finding probabilities

You can find the probability of an outcome in one of three ways.

- If you can work out the theoretical probability of an outcome – for example, drawing a king from a pack of cards – you are using equally likely outcomes.

- Some events, such as people buying dog food, cannot be investigated by using equally likely outcomes. To find the probability of each possible outcome, you can perform an experiment or conduct a survey. This is called 'collecting experimental data'. The more data you collect, the better the estimate is.

- You cannot find the probability of an event such as an earthquake occurring in Japan by either of the above methods. However, you can look at data collected over a long period of time and make an estimate (sometimes called a 'best guess') at the chance of something happening. This is called 'looking at historical data'.

Example 3

Which method (A, B or C) would you use to estimate the probabilities for **a** to **e**?

A: Use equally likely outcomes.

B: Conduct a survey/Collect data.

C: Look at historical data.

a Someone in your class will go abroad for a holiday this year.

b You will score a head when you toss a coin.

c Your bus home will be late.

d It will snow on Christmas Day.

e You will pick a red 7 from a pack of cards.

a You would have to ask all the members of your class what they intended to do for their holidays this year. You would therefore conduct a survey – method B.

b There are two possibilities – head or tail – so P(head) = $\frac{1}{2}$. This is an equally likely outcome – so method A.

c If you catch the bus every day, you can collect data over several weeks. This would be method C.

d If you check whether it snowed on Christmas Day for the last few years, you would be able to make a good estimate of the probability. This would be method C.

e There are 2 red 7s out of 52 cards, so you can calculate the probability of picking one of them: P(red seven) = $\frac{2}{52}$, which cancels to $\frac{1}{26}$. This is method A.

Exercise 13A

1 Naseer throws a fair, six-sided dice and records the number of sixes that he gets after various numbers of throws. The table shows his results.

Number of throws	10	50	100	200	500	1000	2000
Number of sixes	2	4	10	21	74	163	329

a Calculate the experimental probability of throwing a six at each stage that Naseer recorded his results.

b How many ways can a normal dice land?

c How many of these ways give a six?

d What is the theoretical probability of throwing a six with a dice?

e If Naseer threw the dice a total of 6000 times, how many sixes would you expect him to get?

2 Marie made a five-sided spinner, like the one shown here.

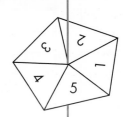

She used it to play a board game with her friend Sarah. The girls thought that the spinner wasn't very fair, as it seemed to land on some numbers more often than on others. They spun the spinner 200 times and recorded the results, as shown in the table.

Side spinner lands on	1	2	3	4	5
Number of times	19	27	32	53	69

a Work out the relative frequency of the spinner landing on each number.

b How many times would you expect each number to occur if the spinner is fair?

c Do you think that the spinner is fair? Give a reason for your answer.

3 Sarah thought that she could make a much more accurate spinner. After she had made it, she tested it and recorded how many times she scored a 5. Her results are shown in the table.

Number of spins	10	50	100	500
Number of 5s	3	12	32	107

a Sarah made a mistake in recording the number of 5s. Which number in the second row of her table is wrong? Give a reason for your answer.

b These are the full results for 500 spins.

Side spinner lands on	1	2	3	4	5
Number of times	96	112	87	98	107

Do you think Sarah's spinner is fair? Give a reason for your answer.

4 Which method, A, B or C, would you use to estimate or state the probabilities of **a** to **h**?

A: Use equally likely outcomes.

B: Conduct a survey or experiment.

C: Look at historical data.

a How people will vote in the next election.

b A drawing pin dropped on a desk will land point up.

c A premiership football team will win the FA Cup.

d You will win a school raffle.

e The next car to come down the road will be red.

f You will throw a double six with two dice.

g Someone in your class likes classical music.

h A person picked at random from your school will be a vegetarian.

5 A sampling bottle is a sealed bottle with a clear plastic tube at one end. When the bottle is tipped up, one of the balls inside will fall into the tube. Kenny's sampling bottle contains 200 balls, which are either black or white. Kenny conducts an experiment to see how many black balls there are in the bottle. He takes various numbers of samples and records how many of them revealed a black ball. The results are shown in the table.

Number of samples	Number of black balls	Experimental probability
10	2	
100	25	
200	76	
500	210	
1000	385	
5000	1987	

a Copy the table and calculate the experimental probability of getting a black ball at each stage.

b Using this information, how many black balls do you think there are in the bottle?

6 A four-sided dice has faces numbered 1, 2, 3 and 4. The score is the face on which it lands. Five students decide to throw the dice to see if it is biased. They each throw it a different number of times. Their results are shown in the table.

Student	Total number of throws	Score			
		1	2	3	4
Ayesha	20	7	6	3	4
Brian	50	19	16	8	7
Caryl	250	102	76	42	30
Deema	80	25	25	12	18
Evan	150	61	46	26	17

a Which student will have the most reliable set of results? Why?

b Add up all the score columns and work out the relative frequency of each score. Give your answers correct to 2 decimal places (2 dp).

c Is the dice biased? Explain your answer.

(CM) 7 At a computer factory, tests were carried out to see how many faulty computer chips were produced in one week.

	Monday	Tuesday	Wednesday	Thursday	Friday
Sample	850	630	1055	896	450
Number faulty	10	7	12	11	4

On which day was the number of faulty chips produced the highest? Use what you know about probability to explain your answer.

(PS) 8 Andrew made an eight-sided spinner. He tested it out to see if it was fair.

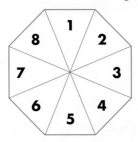

He spun the spinner and recorded the results.

He spilt coffee over his results table, so he could not see the middle part.

Number spinner lands on	1	2	3			6	7	8
Frequency	18	19	22			19	20	22

Copy and complete the table for Andrew. Assume the spinner was fair.

(EV) 9 Steve threw a coin 1000 times to see how many heads he scored.

He said: "If this is a fair coin, I should get exactly 500 heads."

Explain why he is wrong.

(MR) 10 Roxy has an eight-sided spinner, marked like this.

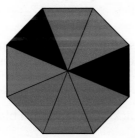

She tests it by spinning it 100 times and records the results, as shown in the table.

Colour	Red	Blue	Black	Green
Frequency	48	13	28	11

Roxy says the spinner is fair, as the frequencies are close to what may be expected.

Sam says the spinner is unfair, as there are far more reds than any other colour.

Who is correct? Give reasons for your answer.

13.2 Mutually exclusive and exhaustive outcomes

This section will show you how to:

- recognise mutually exclusive, exhaustive and complementary outcomes.

Key terms

complementary

exhaustive

mutually exclusive

Suppose a bag contains three black, two yellow and five white balls and only one ball is allowed to be taken at random from the bag. Then, by the basic definition of probability:

$$P(\text{black ball}) = \frac{3}{10}$$

$$P(\text{yellow ball}) = \frac{2}{10}, \text{ which cancels to } \frac{1}{5}$$

$$P(\text{white ball}) = \frac{5}{10}, \text{ which cancels to } \frac{1}{2}.$$

The probability of choosing a black ball or a yellow ball $= \frac{5}{10}$, which cancels to $\frac{1}{2}$.

When only one ball is taken out, the outcomes 'picking a yellow ball' and 'picking a black ball' can never happen at the same time: a ball can only be either black or yellow. Such outcomes are **mutually exclusive**. Other examples of mutually exclusive outcomes are 'throwing a head' and 'throwing a tail' with a coin and 'throwing an even number' and 'throwing an odd number' with a dice.

An example of outcomes that are not mutually exclusive would be 'drawing a red card' and 'drawing a king' from a pack of cards. There are two red kings, so both outcomes could occur at the same time.

Example 4

Trevor throws an ordinary dice.

a What is the probability that he throws: i   an even number   ii   an odd number?

b What is the total of the answers to part **a**?

c Is it possible to get a score on a dice that is both odd and even?

a   i $P(\text{even}) = \frac{1}{2}$ ii $P(\text{odd}) = \frac{1}{2}$ b $\frac{1}{2} + \frac{1}{2} = 1$ c   No

---

Outcomes such as those in Example 4 are mutually exclusive because they can never happen at the same time. Because there are no other possibilities, they are also exhaustive outcomes. The probabilities of **exhaustive** outcomes add up to 1.

Example 5

A bag contains only black and white balls. The probability of picking at random a black ball from the bag is $\frac{7}{10}$.

a What is the probability of picking a white ball from the bag?

b Can you say how many black balls and white balls there are in the bag?

a   As 'picking a white ball' and 'picking a black ball' are mutually exclusive and exhaustive then:

$$P(\text{white}) = 1 - P(\text{black})$$

$$= 1 - \frac{7}{10}$$

$$= \frac{3}{10}.$$

b   You cannot say precisely what the numbers of balls are, although you can say that there could be seven black and three white, fourteen black and six white, or any combination of black and white balls in the ratio 7 : 3.

Complementary outcomes

If there is an outcome A, the **complementary** outcome of A is outcome A *not* happening.

Any outcome is mutually exclusive and exhaustive to its complementary outcome.

P(outcome A not happening) = 1 – P(outcome A happening)

that can be stated as:

P(outcome) + P(complementary outcome) = 1

For example, the probability of getting a king from a pack of cards is $\frac{4}{52} = \frac{1}{13}$, so the probability of *not* getting a king is $1 - \frac{1}{13} = \frac{12}{13}$.

Exercise 13B

1 Say whether these pairs of outcomes are mutually exclusive.

   a Throwing a head with a coin *and* throwing a tail with a coin

   b Throwing a number less than 3 with a dice *and* throwing a number greater than 3 with a dice

   c Drawing a spade from a pack of cards *and* drawing an ace from a pack of cards

   d Drawing a heart from a pack of cards *and* drawing a picture card from a pack of cards

   e Choosing two girls *and* choosing two boys, when two people are to be chosen from three girls and two boys

   f Drawing a red card from a pack of cards *and* drawing a black card from the same pack of cards

2 Which of the pairs of mutually exclusive events in question **1** are also exhaustive?

3 Each morning I run to work or get a lift. The probability that I run to work is $\frac{2}{5}$. What is the probability that I get a lift?

4 A letter is to be chosen at random from this set of letter cards.

   S   T   A   T   I   S   T   I   C   S

   a What is the probability that the letter is:

   i an S   **ii** a T   **iii** a vowel

   v not an A   **v** not an I?

   b Which of these pairs of outcomes are mutually exclusive?

   i Picking an S *and* picking a T

   ii Picking an S *and* picking a vowel

   iii Picking an S *and* picking another consonant

   iv Picking a vowel *and* picking a consonant

   c Which pair of mutually exclusive outcomes in part **b** is also exhaustive?

5 Two of these five people are to be chosen for a job.

Jane   Dave   Anne   Jack   John

  a List all ten possible pairs.

  b What is the probability that the pair of people chosen will:

    i both be female   **ii** both be male

    iii both have the same initial   **iv** have different initials?

  c Which of these pairs of outcomes are mutually exclusive?

    i Picking two women *and* picking two men

    ii Picking two people of the same sex *and* picking two people of opposite sexes

    iii Picking two people with the same initial *and* picking two men

    iv Picking two people with the same initial *and* picking two women

  d Which pair of mutually exclusive outcomes in part **c** is also exhaustive?

6 A spinner consists of an outer ring of coloured sectors and an inner circle of numbered sectors, as shown.

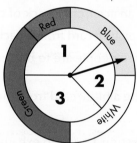

  a The probability of scoring 2 is $\frac{1}{4}$. The probabilities of scoring 1 or 3 are equal.

    What is the probability of scoring 3?

  b The probability of scoring blue is $\frac{1}{4}$. The probability of scoring white is $\frac{1}{4}$.

    The probability of scoring green is $\frac{3}{8}$. What is the probability of scoring red?

  c Which of these pairs of outcomes are mutually exclusive?

    i Scoring 3 *and* scoring 2   **ii** Scoring 3 *and* scoring green

    iii Scoring 3 *and* scoring blue   **iv** Scoring blue *and* scoring red

  d Explain why it is not possible to score a colour that is mutually exclusive to the outcome 'scoring an odd number'.

7 During morning break, I have the choice of coffee, tea or hot chocolate. The probability I choose coffee is $\frac{3}{5}$ and the probability I choose tea is $\frac{1}{4}$. What is the probability I choose hot chocolate?

(CM) **8** Four friends, Kath, Ann, Sandra and Padmini, regularly ran races against one another in the park. The chance of:

- Kath winning the race is 0.7
- Ann winning the race is $\frac{1}{6}$
- Sandra winning the race is 12%.

What is the chance of Padmini winning the race?

9 Assemblies at school are always taken by the head, the deputy head or the senior teacher. When the head takes the assembly, the probability that she goes over time is $\frac{1}{2}$. When the deputy head takes the assembly, the probability that he goes over time is $\frac{1}{4}$. Explain why it is not necessarily true to say that the probability that the senior teacher goes over time is $\frac{1}{4}$.

10 A hotelier conducted a survey of guests staying at her hotel. The table shows some of the results of her survey.

Type of guest	Probability
Man	0.7
Woman	0.3
American man	0.2
American woman	0.05
Vegetarian	0.3
Married	0.6

a A guest was chosen at random. From the table, work out these probabilities.

i The guest was American.   **ii** The guest was single.

iii The guest was not a vegetarian.

b Explain why it is not possible to work out from the table the probability of a guest being a married vegetarian.

c From the table, give two examples of pairs of types of guest that would form a mutually exclusive pair.

d From the table, give one example of a pair of types of guest that would form an exhaustive pair.

11 In a restaurant, the head waiter has worked out the probability of customers choosing certain dishes.

A starter	0.7
A dessert	0.4
Beef	0.3
Pork	0.2
Chicken	0.45
Vegetarian	0.08
Vegetables	0.8
Red wine	0.4
White wine	0.5

a What is the probability that the first person entering the restaurant:

i chooses a meat dish

ii chooses wine

iii does not have a starter?

b Explain why it is not possible to work out from the table the probability of someone having either a starter or a dessert.

c Give an example of a choice from the table that would form a mutually exclusive pair.

12 Ziq always walks, goes by bus or is given a lift by his dad to school.

If he walks, the probability that he is late for school is 0.3.

If he goes by bus, the probability that he is late for school is 0.1.

Explain why it is not necessarily true that if his dad gives him a lift, the chance of his being late for school is 0.6.

13.3 Expectation

This section will show you how to:

- predict the likely number of successful outcomes, given the number of trials and the probability of any one outcome.

When you know the probability of an outcome, you can predict how many times you would expect that outcome to occur in a certain number of trials. This is called **expectation**.

Note that this is what you *expect*. It is not what is going to happen. If what you expected always happened, life would be very dull and boring and playing computer games would be a waste of time.

Example 6

A bag contains 20 balls, nine of which are black, six are white and five are yellow. Petre draws a ball at random from the bag, notes its colour and then puts it back in the bag. He does this 500 times.

a   How many times would you expect him to draw a black ball?

b   How many times would you expect him to draw a yellow ball?

c   How many times would you expect him to draw a black ball or a yellow ball?

a   P(black ball) = $\frac{9}{20}$ So, expected number of black balls is $\frac{9}{20} \times 500 = 225$.

b   P(yellow ball) = $\frac{5}{20}$, which cancels to $\frac{1}{4}$ So, expected number of yellow balls is $\frac{1}{4} \times 500 = 125$.

c   The expected number of black or yellow balls is $225 + 125 = 350$.

Example 7

Four in ten cars sold in Britain are made by Japanese companies.

a   What is the probability that the next car to be driven down your road will be Japanese?

b   If there are 2000 cars in a multistorey car park, how many of them would you expect to be Japanese?

a   P(Japanese car) = $\frac{4}{10}$, which cancels to $\frac{2}{5}$

b   The expected number of Japanese cars in 2000 cars is $\frac{2}{5} \times 2000 = 800$ cars.

Exercise 13C

1   I throw an ordinary dice 150 times. How many times can I expect to score a 6?

2   I throw a coin 2000 times. How many times can I expect to score a head?

3   I draw a card from a pack of cards and replace it. I do this 520 times. How many times would I expect to get:

a a black card   b a king   c a heart   d the king of hearts?

4   The ball in a roulette wheel can land in 37 spaces, which are numbered from 0 to 36 inclusive. I always choose the same number, 13. If I play all evening and there are altogether 185 spins of the wheel in that time, how many times could I expect to win?

5   In a bag there are 30 balls, 15 of which are red, 5 yellow, 5 green and 5 blue. I take out a ball at random, note its colour and then replace it. I do this 300 times. How many times would I expect to get:

a a red ball   b a yellow or blue ball

c a ball that is not blue   d a pink ball?

6 A class does the experiment described in question **5** 1000 times. Approximately how many times would they expect to get:

    a a green ball   **b** a ball that is not blue?

7 A sampling bottle contains red and white balls. Jared knows that the probability of getting a red ball is 0.3. He takes 1500 samples. How many of them would he expect to give a white ball?

(MR) **8** Josie said: "When I throw a dice, I expect to get a score of 3.5."

"Impossible," said Paul, "you can't score 3.5 with a dice."

"Do this and I'll prove it," said Josie.

    a Josie throws an ordinary dice 60 times. Copy and complete the table for the expected number of times each score will occur.

Score						
Expected occurrences						

    b Now work out the average score that she can expect over 60 throws.

    c There is an easy way to get an answer of 3.5 for the expected average score. Can you see what it is?

9 The table shows the probabilities of some cloud types being seen on any day.

Cumulus	0.3
Stratocumulus	0.25
Stratus	0.15
Altocumulus	0.11
Cirrus	0.05
Cirrocumulus	0.02
Nimbostratus	0.005
Cumulonimbus	0.004

    a What is the probability of not seeing one of the above clouds in the sky?

    b On how many days of the year would you expect to see altocumulus clouds in the sky?

(PS) **10** Every evening Tamara and Chris cut a pack of cards to see who washes up.

If they cut a king or a jack, Chris washes up.

If they cut a queen, Tamara washes up.

Otherwise they wash up together.

In a year of 365 days, how many days would you expect them to wash up together?

(MR) **11** A market gardener is supplied with tomato plant seedlings. She knows that the probability that any plant will develop a disease is 0.003.

How will she calculate the number of tomato plants that are likely not to develop a disease?

(PS) **12** I have 20 tickets for a raffle and I know that the probability of my winning the prize is 0.05. How many tickets were sold altogether in the raffle?

13.4 Probability and two-way tables

This section will show you how to:

- read two-way tables and use them to work out probabilities.

Key term

two-way table

A **two-way table** is a table that links together two variables. This two-way table shows the colours and makes of cars in the school car park.

	Red	Blue	White
Ford	2	4	1
Vauxhall	0	1	2
Toyota	3	3	4
Peugeot	2	0	3

One variable is written in the rows of the table and the other variable is written in the columns of the table.

Example 8

This two-way table shows the numbers of boys and girls in a class and whether they are left-handed or right-handed.

	Boys	Girls
Left-handed	2	4
Right-handed	10	13

a If a student is selected at random, what is the probability that it will be a left-handed boy?

b It is known that a student selected at random is a girl. What is the probability that she is right-handed?

a The total number of students is 29.   So, P(left-handed boy) = $\frac{2}{29}$.

b The total number of girls is 17.   So, P(right-handed girl) = $\frac{13}{17}$.

Exercise 13D

  This two-way table shows the ages and genders of a sample of 50 students in a school.

	Age (years)					
	11	12	13	14	15	16
Number of boys	4	3	6	2	5	4
Number of girls	2	5	3	6	4	6

a How many students are aged 13 years or younger?

b What percentage of the students in the table are aged 16?

c A student from the table is selected at random. What is the probability that the student will be 14 years of age? Give your answer as a fraction in its simplest form.

d There are 1000 students in the school. Use the table to estimate how many boys there are in the school altogether.

2 This two-way table shows the numbers of adults and the numbers of cars they owned, in 50 houses in one street.

		Number of adults			
		1	2	3	4
Number of cars	0	2	1	0	0
	1	3	13	3	1
	2	0	10	6	4
	3	0	1	4	2

a How many houses have exactly two adults and two cars?

b How many houses altogether have three cars?

c What percentage of the houses have three cars?

d What percentage of the houses with just one car have three adults living in the house?

3 Jenna has two spinners. One has the numbers 1 to 4 on it and the other has the numbers 5 to 8. Jenna spins the arrows on both spinners at the same time.

Spinner A   Spinner B

This two-way table shows all the ways the two arrows can land.

Some of the total scores are filled in.

		Score on spinner A			
		1	2	3	4
Score on spinner B	5	6	7		
	6	7			
	7				
	8				

a Copy and complete the table to show all the possible total scores.

b How many of the total scores are 9?

c When the arrows on the two spinners are spun together, what is the probability that the total score will be:

 i 9   **ii** 8   **iii** a prime number?

4 This table gives information about the numbers of items in Granny's music collection.

		Type of music		
		Pop	Folk	Classical
Format	Tape	16	5	2
	CD	51	9	13
	Vinyl	9	2	0

a How many pop tapes does Granny have?

b How many items of folk music does Granny have?

c How many CDs does Granny have?

d If Granny chooses a CD at random from all her CDs, what is the probability that it will be a pop CD?

5 Zoe throws a fair coin and rolls a fair dice.

If the coin shows a head she records the score on the dice.

If the coin shows tails she doubles the number on the dice.

a Copy and complete the two-way table to show Zoe's possible scores.

		Number on dice					
		1	2	3	4	5	6
Coin	Head	1	2				
	Tail	2	4				

b How many of the scores are square numbers?

c What is the probability of getting a score that is a square number?

6 The two-way table shows the wages for the men and women in a factory.

Wage, per week (£w)	Men	Women
£100 < w ⩽ £150	3	4
£150 < w ⩽ £200	7	5
£200 < w ⩽ £250	23	12
£250 < w ⩽ £300	48	27
£300 < w ⩽ £350	32	11
More than £350	7	1

a Work out the probability that a person chosen at random will earn more than £350 per week.

b What percentage of the men earn from £250 to £300 per week?

c What percentage of the women earn from £250 to £300 per week?

d Is it possible to work out the mean wage of the men and women? Explain your answer.

7 Hassan has two hexagonal spinners.

Spinner A is numbered 3, 5, 7, 9, 11 and 13.

Spinner B is numbered 4, 5, 6, 7, 8 and 9.

What is the probability that when Hassan spins the two spinners, the product of the two numbers he scores will be a number greater than 40?

8 Jenica spins two fair spinners and adds the numbers scored together.

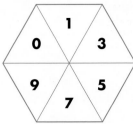 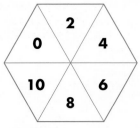

a Draw a two-way diagram showing all the possible totals.

b What is the most likely score?

c What is the probability of Jenica getting a total of 12?

d What is the probability of her getting a total of 11 or more?

e What is the probability of her getting a total that is an odd number?

13.5 Probability and Venn diagrams

This section will show you how to:

- use Venn diagrams to solve probability questions.

A **set** is a collection of objects or **elements**. Capital letters are often used to represent a set. For example, the set of odd numbers less than 10 could be represented by A.

$A = \{1, 3, 5, 7, 9\}$

You already know that the probability of outcome A occurring is written P(A).

Suppose outcome A does not happen. This is written as A'. This is the complement of A and you read it as 'A dash'.

The probability of A not happening is written P(A').

The **universal set** is a set that contains all elements used and is represented as ξ.

Example 9

Given that P(A) = 0.6, write down P(A').

$$P(A') = 1 - P(A)$$
$$= 1 - 0.6$$
$$= 0.4$$

Diagrams that represent connections between different sets are called **Venn diagrams**. They are named after John Venn who introduced them in about 1880.

All the elements of A are in the shaded area.

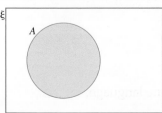

A is shaded.

All the elements that are in the complement of A, which means that they are not in A, are in the shaded area.

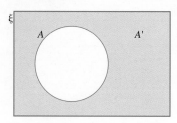

A' is shaded.

This is a Venn diagram for two sets A and B.

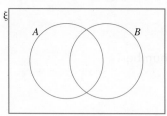

The region where the sets overlap represents the elements that are in both sets. It is called the **intersection** and is written as $A \cap B$.

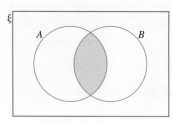

$A \cap B$ is shaded.

The combined set that contains all of A and all of B is called the **union** and is written $A \cup B$.

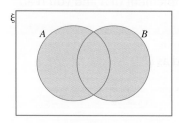

$A \cup B$ is shaded.

This Venn diagram shows the numbers of students who study French (F) and Spanish (S).

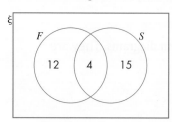

12 students study French only.

15 students study Spanish only.

4 students study both French and Spanish.

16 students study French.

19 students study Spanish.

All students study at least one language.

The Venn diagram shows the number of people with fair hair (A) and the number of people with blue eyes (B) at a party.

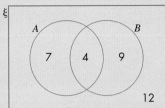

a   How many people are there altogether at the party?

b   What is the probability that a person chosen at random has blue eyes?

c   Work out $P(A')$.

d   Work out $P(A \cap B)$.

e   Work out $P(A \cup B)$.

f   Work out the probability that a person chosen at random has fair hair but does not have blue eyes.

a $7 + 4 + 9 + 12 = 32$

b   There are $4 + 9 = 13$, with blue eyes, so $P(B) = \frac{13}{32}$.

c A' means not in A or does not have fair hair.
    $9 + 12 = 21$ do not have fair hair, so $P(A') = \frac{21}{32}$.

d $A \cap B$ means has fair hair *and* has blue eyes. There are only four of these, so $P(A \cap B) = \frac{4}{32}$, which cancels to $\frac{1}{8}$.

e $A \cup B$ means has fair hair or blue eyes or both. There are 20 of these, so $P(A \cup B) = \frac{20}{32}$, which cancels to $\frac{5}{8}$.

f P(fair hair but *not* blue eyes) $= \frac{7}{32}$.

Exercise 13E

1 $P(A) = 0.1$ and $P(B) = 0.3$. Write down:

   a $P(A')$ b $P(B')$.

2 $P(A) = 0.25$ and $P(B) = 0.55$. Write down:

   a $P(A')$ b $P(B')$.

3 $\xi = \{1, 2, 3, 4, 5, 6, 7, 8, 9, 10\}$ $A = \{1, 2, 4, 8\}$ $B = \{1, 3, 4, 9, 10\}$

   a   Show this information in a Venn diagram.

   b   Use your Venn diagram to work out:

   i $P(A)$ ii $P(A')$ iii $P(B)$

   iv $P(B')$ v $P(A \cup B)$ vi $P(A \cap B)$.

4 In a survey, Polly asked 100 people if they liked cats (*C*) and dogs (*D*).

The results are shown in the Venn diagram.

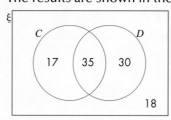

A person is chosen at random.

a Work out:

  i P(*C*)   **ii** P(*C*′)   **iii** P(*D*)

  iv P(*D*′)   **v** P(*C*∪*D*)   **vi** P(*C*∩*D*).

b Work out the probability that a person likes dogs but does not like cats.

5 The Venn diagram shows some probabilities.

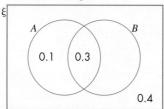

a Copy and complete the Venn diagram.

b Work out:

  i P(*B*)   **ii** P(*A*∪*B*)   **iii** P(*A*∩*B*).

6 A snack bar kept a record of the 100 sandwiches it sold one lunch-time.

20 had only meat in them.

25 had only cheese in them.

10 had neither meat nor cheese in them.

How many sandwiches had:

a some meat in them

b some cheese in them

c either meat or cheese in them?

(PS) **7** ξ = {1, 2, 3, 4, 5, 6, 7, 8, 9, 10}

A = {even numbers}   *B* = {numbers greater than 6}

Work out:

a P(*A*)   **b** P(*B*)   **c** P(*A*∪*B*)   **d** P(*A*∩*B*).

(MR) **8** The Venn diagram shows the numbers of students who walk to school (*S*) and the number of students who walk home from school (*H*).

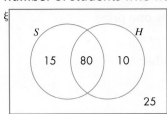

a How many students are there altogether?

b i Work out P(*S*∩*H*).   **ii** Describe in words what P(*S*∩*H*) represents.

c What is the probability that a student chosen at random only walks one way, either to or from school?

(PS) **9** P(*A*) = 0.7   P(*B*) = 0.6   P(*A*∪*B*) = 0.9

Work out P(*A*∩*B*).

(PS) **10** The probability of Tim selecting a blue bead Is 0.12.

The probability that he chooses a bead with a hole through it is 0.45.

The probability that he chooses a blue bead with a hole through it is 0.07.

What is the probability that he chooses a bead that is either blue or has a hole through it, (or both)?

(CM) **11** Use set notation to describe the shaded area in each Venn diagram.

a   **b**

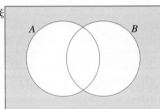   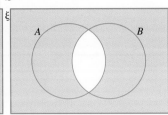

12 In a car park there are 80 cars.

24 are black and have traction control.

43 have traction control.

31 are black.

Work out the probability that the first car to leave the car park does not have traction control.

(CM) **13** For each part, copy the Venn diagram and shade the appropriate area.

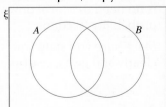

a *A*′∪*B*   **b** (*A*′∩*B*)′   **c** (*A*′∪*B*)′

Worked exemplars

 1 In a raffle 400 tickets have been sold. There is only one prize.

Mr Raza buys 5 tickets for himself and sells another 40.

Mrs Raza buys 10 tickets for herself and sells another 50.

Mrs Hewes just sells 52 tickets.

a What is the probability of:

  i Mr Raza winning the raffle

  ii Mr Raza selling the winning ticket?

b What is the probability of either Mr or Mrs Raza selling the winning ticket?

c What is the probability of Mrs Hewes not selling a winning ticket?

d Which person has the greatest chance of either winning the raffle or selling the winning ticket? Explain your answer.

Give your answers as fractions in their simplest form.

This is a problem-solving question and so you must communicate your method clearly. Do not just write down probabilities without some explanation.	
a i $\frac{5}{400} = \frac{1}{80}$ **ii** $\frac{40}{400} = \frac{1}{10}$	Remember to cancel the fractions and make sure you read the information given in the question.
b $\frac{40}{400} + \frac{50}{400} = \frac{90}{400}$ $\qquad\qquad\quad = \frac{9}{40}$	Remember to show how you obtain the answer. It is usual to give it in its lowest terms.
c $1 - \frac{52}{400} = \frac{348}{400}$ $\qquad\qquad = \frac{87}{100}$	Remember that these are complementary outcomes.
d P(Mr Raza either winning the raffle or selling the winning ticket) $= \frac{45}{400}$ P(Mrs Raza either winning the raffle or selling the winning ticket) $= \frac{60}{400}$ P(Mrs Hewes either winning the raffle or selling the winning ticket) $= \frac{52}{400}$ Mrs Raza has the greatest chance, as $\frac{60}{400}$ is the largest fraction.	As you will need to compare fractions to solve the problem, there is no need to cancel down the three probability fractions. Make sure you state your conclusion clearly and give a reason.

The Venn diagram shows the number of students who study geography (G) and the number who study history (H).

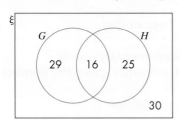

a Explain how you would work out P(a student chosen at random studies history).

b Describe in words what P(G∩H) represents.

c Describe in words what P(G∪H) represents.

This question assesses your skills in written communication.	
a There are 29 + 16 + 25 + 30 = 100 students altogether. 41 study history. So P(H) is $\dfrac{16 + 25}{100} = \dfrac{41}{100}$.	Do not just write down a probability. You must explain in words how you arrived at your answer.
b G∩H represents those students who study both geography and history. P(G∩H) is the probability that a student chosen at random studies both geography and history.	Make sure you interpret the questions carefully. You need to explain what each probability represents. It is important to remember that the students are chosen at random.
c G∪H represents those students who study geography, history or both. P(G∪H) is the probability that a student chosen at random studies geography, history or both.	

Ready to progress?

I can work out experimental probabilities and relative frequencies.
I can use different methods to estimate probabilities.
I can recognise mutually exclusive, exhaustive and complementary events.
I know how to predict the likely number of successful outcomes, given the number of trials and the probability of any one outcome.
I can read two-way tables and use them to work out probabilities.
I can understand set notation.

I can use Venn diagrams to work out probabilities.

Review questions

1 There are two red pens, three blue pens and five black pens in a box.

Harry takes a pen, at random, from the box.

a Write down the probability that he takes a black pen.

b Write down the probability that he takes a pen that is not blue.

(MR) **2** Rhodd spins a four-sided spinner 100 times.

His results are shown in the table.

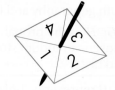

Number	1	2	3	4
Frequency	13	20	39	28

a What is the relative frequency of scoring a 4?

b How can you tell that the spinner is biased?

(MR) **3** **a** Joe has a bag containing 20 discs. Each disc is red, green or blue. He takes a disc at random from the bag and notes its colour. He then replaces the disc in the bag. He does the experiment 50 times. The table shows his results.

Colour	Red	Green	Blue
Frequency	25	15	10

i What is the relative frequency of picking a green disc?

ii How many of each coloured disc are there likely to be in the bag?

b Susie takes a disc at random from another bag and replaces it. She does this 10 times and gets six reds and four greens. She claims that there are no blue discs in the bag.

Explain why she could be wrong.

(PS) **4** Here is some information about a group of 50 teenagers.

• There are four more boys than girls.

• One-third of the boys walk to school.

Use this information to copy and complete this two-way table.

	Boys	Girls	Total
Walk to school			30
Do not walk to school			20
Total			50

5 This Venn diagram shows the number of students who like football (F) and the number who like hockey (H).

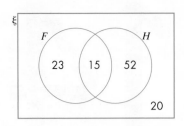

a How many students are there altogether?

b Work out P(F).

c Work out P($F \cap H$).

d What is the probability that a student chosen at random does not like football?

6 Henri has a five-sided spinner, with the numbers 1, 2, 3, 4 and 5 on it.

The table shows some of the probabilities of the spinner landing on the numbers.

The probability that the spinner lands on 3 is equal to the probability that it lands on 4.

a Calculate the probability that the spinner lands on 3.

b Calculate the probability that the spinner lands on either 1 or 2.

c Do you think that the spinner is biased? Give a reason for your answer.

Number	Probability
1	0.24
2	0.25
3	
4	
5	0.15

7 Sam and Tomas are playing a game with dice.

a Sam uses a biased dice. The probability that he throws a 6 is 0.2.

  i Write down the probability that he does not throw a 6.

  ii Sam throws this biased dice 60 times. Work out an estimate for the number of times he will throw a 6.

b Tomas uses a fair dice. He throws this fair dice 60 times. Is he likely to throw more 6s than Sam?

Give a reason for your answer.

8 A bag contains five discs numbered 1, 2, 3, 4 and 5.

Sanna is playing a game. She takes a disc at random from the bag, writes down the number and replaces the disc. She then takes another disc at random from the bag and writes down this number. She then adds the two numbers together to obtain a total score.

Sanna wins the game if her total score is greater than 6.

Is she more likely to win or lose this game?

Show your working to explain your answer.

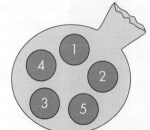

9 This Venn diagram shows some probabilities.

Work out:

a P(A)   **b** P(B')

c P($A \cup B$)   **d** P($A' \cap B$).

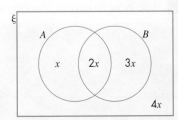

14 Number: Powers and standard form

This chapter is going to show you:

- how to calculate using powers (indices)
- how to write numbers in standard form
- how to calculate with standard form.

You should already know:

- how to multiply and divide by 10, 100, 1000, …
- the meaning of square root and cube root.

About this chapter

It can be very difficult to read – and understand – very large and very small numbers. Scientists use standard form as a short way of representing such numbers.

For example, the planets and the Sun are huge distances away from Earth. The furthest known galaxy is about 110 000 000 000 000 000 000 000 000 km from Earth. Writing this out every time you want to do a calculation takes time and, more than likely, you will miscount the zeros and be out by a factor of 10. Being out by a factor of 10 when sending astronauts to the Moon would be disastrous. Therefore, using standard form not only makes it easier to write large and small numbers, it also means you are less likely to make errors in calculations. The standard form version of the distance is 1.1×10^{26}, which is much neater.

Electrons, unlike the planets, are very small. The mass of an electron is about 0.000 000 000 000 000 000 000 000 000 000 91 kg. Again, this is not an easy number to work with. It can be written as 9.1×10^{-31} kg. This chapter will show you how to do calculations with numbers written in this notation.

14.1 Powers (indices)

This section will show you how to:

- use powers (also known as indices)
- multiply and divide by powers of 10.

Powers are a convenient way of writing repeated multiplications. Powers are also called **indices**, singular **index**.

The power tells you how many 'lots' of a number to multiply together. For example:

$4^6 = 4 \times 4 \times 4 \times 4 \times 4 \times 4$ six lots of 4 multiplied together

$6^4 = 6 \times 6 \times 6 \times 6$ four lots of 6 multiplied together

$7^3 = 7 \times 7 \times 7$

$12^2 = 12 \times 12$

You can write a million as $1\,000\,000 = 10^6$.

You need to know the square numbers (power 2) up to $15^2 = 225$.

You should also know the cubes of numbers (power 3).

$1^3 = 1$, $2^3 = 8$, $3^3 = 27$, $4^3 = 64$, $5^3 = 125$ and $10^3 = 1000$

Example 1

a What is the value of: i   7 squared   ii   5 cubed?

b Write each of these out in full.

   i 2^5 ii 8^4 iii 7^3 iv 12^2

c Use powers to write these multiplications.

   i $3 \times 3 \times 3 \times 3 \times 3 \times 3 \times 3 \times 3$ ii $13 \times 13 \times 13 \times 13 \times 13$

   iii $7 \times 7 \times 7 \times 7$ iv $5 \times 5 \times 5 \times 5 \times 5 \times 5 \times 5$

a i   7 squared $= 7^2 = 7 \times 7 = 49$ ii   5 cubed $= 5^3 = 5 \times 5 \times 5 = 125$

b i $2^5 = 2 \times 2 \times 2 \times 2 \times 2$ ii $8^4 = 8 \times 8 \times 8 \times 8$

   iii $7^3 = 7 \times 7 \times 7$ iv $12^2 = 12 \times 12$

c i $3 \times 3 \times 3 \times 3 \times 3 \times 3 \times 3 \times 3 = 3^8$ ii $13 \times 13 \times 13 \times 13 \times 13 = 13^5$

   iii $7 \times 7 \times 7 \times 7 = 7^4$ iv $5 \times 5 \times 5 \times 5 \times 5 \times 5 \times 5 = 5^7$

Working out powers on your calculator

The power button on your calculator will probably look like this $\boxed{x^{\square}}$. You can use the power button to work out 5^7 on your calculator.

$5^7 = 5 \;\boxed{x^{\square}}\; 7 = 78\,125$

Two special powers

Power 1	**Power 0 (zero)**
Any number to the power 1 is the same as the number itself. This is always true so normally you do not write the power 1.	Any number to the power 0 is equal to 1.
For example: $5^1 = 5$ $32^1 = 32$ $(-8)^1 = -8$	For example: $5^0 = 1$ $32^0 = 1$ $(-8)^0 = 1$

You can use your calculator to check these results.

Exercise 14A

1 Write these expressions in index notation. Do not work them out yet.

a $2 \times 2 \times 2 \times 2$ **b** $3 \times 3 \times 3 \times 3 \times 3$

c 7×7 **d** $5 \times 5 \times 5$

e $10 \times 10 \times 10 \times 10 \times 10 \times 10 \times 10$ **f** $6 \times 6 \times 6 \times 6$

g 4 **h** $1 \times 1 \times 1 \times 1 \times 1 \times 1 \times 1$

i $0.5 \times 0.5 \times 0.5 \times 0.5$ **j** $100 \times 100 \times 100$

2 Write each of these power terms out in full. Do not work them out yet.

a 3^4 **b** 9^3 **c** 6^2 **d** 10^5 **e** 2^{10}

f 8^1 **g** 0.1^3 **h** 2.5^2 **i** 0.7^3 **j** 1000^2

3 Use the power key on your calculator (or any method you prefer) to work out the value of each power term in question **1**.

4 Use the power key on your calculator (or any method you prefer) to work out the value of each power term in question **2**.

5 A storage container is in the shape of a cube. The length of the container is 5 m.

Work out the total storage space in the container. Use the formula for the volume of a cube.

volume = (length of edge)^3

6 Write each number as a power of a different number. The first one has been done for you.

a $32 = 2^5$ **b** 100 **c** 8 **d** 25

7 The powers of 2 are 2, 4, 8, 16, 32, 64, ... The units' digits form a pattern 2, 4, 8, 6, 2, 4, 8, ...

Write out the first six powers of 3, 4 and 5 and describe the patterns formed by their units' digits.

8 Work out the value of each power term. Do not use a calculator.

a 2^0 **b** 4^1 **c** 5^0 **d** 1^9 **e** 1^{235}

9 What do the answers to question **8 d** and **e** tell you about powers of 1?

10 Write the answer to question **1**, part **j** as a power of 10.

11 Write the answer to question **2**, part **j** as a power of 10.

12 Using your calculator, or otherwise, work out the value of each power term.

a $(-1)^0$ **b** $(-1)^1$ **c** $(-1)^2$ **d** $(-1)^4$ **e** $(-1)^5$

13 Using your answers to question **12**, write down the value of each power term.

a $(-1)^8$ **b** $(-1)^{11}$ **c** $(-1)^{99}$ **d** $(-1)^{80}$ **e** $(-1)^{126}$

14 The number 16 777 216 is a power of 2. It is also a power of 4, a power of 8 and a power of 16.

Write the number 16 777 216 in terms of each of the powers.

15 Solve this equation. $\quad 2^{x+3} = 512$

14.2 Rules for multiplying and dividing powers

This section will show you how to:

* use rules for multiplying and dividing powers.

What happens when you multiply numbers that are written as powers of the same number or variable (letter)?

$$3^3 \times 3^5 = (3 \times 3 \times 3) \times (3 \times 3 \times 3 \times 3 \times 3) \qquad a^2 \times a^3 = (a \times a) \times (a \times a \times a)$$
$$= 3^8 \qquad\qquad\qquad\qquad\qquad\qquad = a^5$$

Can you see the rule? You can find these products just by adding the powers.

$$2^3 \times 2^4 \times 2^5 = 2^{3+4+5} \qquad\qquad a^3 \times a^4 = a^{3+4}$$
$$= 2^{12} \qquad\qquad\qquad\qquad = a^7$$

What happens when you divide numbers that are written as powers of the same number or letter (variable)?

$$7^6 \div 7 = (7 \times 7 \times 7 \times 7 \times 7 \times 7) \div (7) \qquad a^5 \div a^2 = (a \times a \times a \times a \times a) \div (a \times a)$$
$$= 7 \times 7 \times 7 \times 7 \times 7 \qquad\qquad = a \times a \times a$$
$$= 7^5 \qquad\qquad\qquad\qquad\qquad = a^3$$

Can you see the rule? You can complete these divisions just by subtracting the powers.

$$a^4 \div a^3 = a^{4-3} \qquad\qquad\qquad b^7 \div b^4 = b^{7-1}$$
$$= a^1 \qquad\qquad\qquad\qquad\qquad = b^3$$
$$= a$$

What happens when you are dividing numbers that are written as powers, and the power of the second number is higher than the power of the first?

$$c^5 \div c^7 = \frac{c \times c \times c \times c \times c}{c \times c \times c \times c \times c \times c \times c}$$
$$= \frac{1}{c \times c}$$
$$= \frac{1}{c^2}$$

You can write $\frac{1}{c^2}$ as c^{-2}. The negative power is a short way of writing the reciprocal of the positive power.

When you multiply powers of the same number or variable, you *add* the indices, even if you are working with negative indices.

$$3^4 \times 3^5 = 3^{(4+5)} = 3^9 \qquad 2^3 \times 2^4 \times 2^5 = 2^{12} \qquad 10^4 \times 10^{-2} = 10^2 \qquad 10^{-3} \times 10^{-1} = 10^{-4} \qquad a^x \times a^y = a^{(x+y)}$$

When you divide powers of the same number or variable, you *subtract* the indices.

$$a^4 \div a^3 = a^{(4-3)} = a^1 = a \qquad b^4 \div b^7 = b^{-3} \qquad 10^4 \div 10^{-2} = 10^6 \qquad 10^{-2} \div 10^{-4} = 10^2 \qquad a^x \div a^y = a^{(x-y)}$$

When you raise a power to a further power, you *multiply* the indices.

$$(a^2)^3 = (a \times a)^3$$

$$(a \times a)^3 = (a \times a) \times (a \times a) \times (a \times a)$$

and $a \times a \times a \times a \times a \times a = a^6$

So $(a^2)^3 = a^{2 \times 3}$ or a^6

Similarly: $\qquad (a^{-2})^4 = a^{-8} \qquad (a^2)^6 = a^{12} \qquad (a^x)^y = a^{xy}$

Here are some examples of different kinds of expressions that include numbers and powers. To reduce the chance of making mistakes, separate the numbers and powers.

$2a^2 \times 3a^4 = (2 \times 3) \times (a^2 \times a^4)$ $\qquad = 6 \times a^6$ $\qquad = 6a^6$	$4a^2b^3 \times 2ab^2 = (4 \times 2) \times (a^2 \times a) \times (b^3 \times b^2)$ $\qquad = 8a^3b^5$
$12a^5 \div 3a^2 = (12 \div 3) \times (a^5 \div a^2)$ $\qquad = 4a^3$	$(2a^2)^3 = (2)^3 \times (a^2)^3$ $\qquad = 8 \times a^6$ $\qquad = 8a^6$

Exercise 14B

1 Write each of these as a single power of 5.

   a $5^2 \times 5^2$ **b** 5×5^2 **c** $5^{-2} \times 5^4$ **d** $5^6 \times 5^{-3}$ **e** $5^{-2} \times 5^{-3}$

2 Write each of these as a single power of 6.

   a $6^5 \div 6^2$ **b** $6^4 \div 6^4$ **c** $6^4 \div 6^{-2}$ **d** $6^{-3} \div 6^4$ **e** $6^{-3} \div 6^{-5}$

3 Simplify these and write each of them as a single power of a.

   a $a^2 \times a$ **b** $a^3 \times a^2$ **c** $a^4 \times a^3$

   d $a^6 \div a^2$ **e** $a^3 \div a$ **f** $a^5 \div a^4$

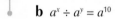

4 **a** $a^x \times a^y = a^{10}$ Write down a possible pair of values for x and y.

   b $a^x \div a^y = a^{10}$ Write down a possible pair of values for x and y.

5 Write each of these as a single power of 4.

   a $(4^2)^3$ **b** $(4^3)^5$ **c** $(4^1)^6$

   d $(4^3)^{-2}$ **e** $(4^{-2})^{-3}$ **f** $(4^7)^0$

6 Simplify each of these expressions.

   a $2a^2 \times 3a^3$ **b** $3a^4 \times 3a^{-2}$ **c** $(2a^2)^3$

   d $-2a^2 \times 3a^2$ **e** $-4a^3 \times -2a^5$ **f** $-2a^4 \times 5a^{-7}$

7 Simplify these expressions.

   a $6a^3 \div 2a^2$ **b** $12a^5 \div 3a^2$ **c** $15a^5 \div 5a$

   d $18a^{-2} \div 3a^{-1}$ **e** $24a^5 \div 6a^{-2}$ **f** $30a \div 6a^5$

> **Hints and tips** Deal with numbers and indices separately and do not confuse the rules. For example: $12a^5 \div 4a^2 = (12 \div 4) \times (a^5 \div a^2)$.

8 Simplify these expressions.

   a $2a^2b^3 \times 4a^3b$ **b** $5a^2b^4 \times 2ab^{-3}$ **c** $6a^2b^3 \times 5a^{-4}b^{-5}$

   d $12a^2b^4 \div 6ab$ **e** $24a^{-3}b^4 \div 3a^2b^{-3}$ **f** $16a^7b^{-2} \div 4a^2b^3$

9 Simplify these expressions.

   a $\dfrac{6a^4b^3}{2ab}$ **b** $\dfrac{2a^2bc^2 \times 6abc^3}{4ab^2c}$ **c** $\dfrac{3abc \times 4a^3b^2c \times 6c^2}{9a^2bc}$

(MR) **10** Write down **two** possible:

    a multiplication questions with an answer of $12x^2y^5$

    b division questions with an answer of $12x^2y^5$.

(PS) **11** a, b and c are three different positive integers.

    What is the smallest possible value of a^2b^3c?

12 Use the general rule for dividing powers of the same number, $\frac{a^x}{a^y} = a^{x-y}$, to prove that any number raised to the power zero is 1.

14.3 Standard form

This section will show you how to:

- change a number into standard form
- calculate using numbers in standard form.

Multiplying and dividing by powers of 10

When you write a million in figures, how many zeros does it have? What is a million as a power of 10? This table shows some of the pattern of the powers of 10.

Number	0.001	0.01	0.1	1	10	100	1000	10 000	100 000	1 000 000
Power of 10	10^{-3}	10^{-2}	10^{-1}	10^0	10^1	10^2	10^3	10^4	10^5	10^6

What is the pattern in the top row? What is the pattern in the powers in the bottom row?

Note that the negative indices give decimal values. A negative index means 'divide that power of 10 into 1'.

$10^{-1} = \frac{1}{10^1}$ and $10^{-2} = \frac{1}{10^2}$

$= \frac{1}{10}$ $= \frac{1}{100}$

$= 0.1$ $= 0.01$

Multiplication by powers of 10

Remember:

- multiplying any number by zero gives zero
- multiplying any number by one gives the original number.

Try these on your calculator.

a 7.34×10 **b** 0.678×10 **c** 0.007×10

Can you see the rule for multiplying by 10? You may have learned that when you multiply a number by 10, you 'add a zero' to the end of the number. This is only true when you start with a whole number. It is not true for a decimal. You need to know the rules.

When you multiply a number by 10, the place value of each digit is increased. For example, 0.07 becomes 0.7, 0.3 becomes 3, and so on. All the digits move one place to the left.

Now see what happens when you multiply by 100. Try these on your calculator.

a 7.34×100 **b** 0.678×100 **c** 0.007×100

This time you should find that the digits move two places to the left. When you multiply by 100 the place value of each digit increases by 2 places, so 0.07 becomes 7, and 0.3 becomes 30, and so on. Similar rules will apply to multiplying by 1000, 10 000 …, which you will see in the examples below.

You can write 100, 1000, 10 000 as powers of 10. For example:

$100 = 10 \times 10$ $1000 = 10 \times 10 \times 10$ $10\ 000 = 10 \times 10 \times 10 \times 10$

$= 10^2$ $= 10^3$ $= 10^4$

So to multiply by any power of 10, you must move the digits according to these two rules.

- When the index is positive, move the digits to the left by the same number of places as the value of the index.

- When the index is negative, move the digits to the right by the same number of places as the value of the index.

Example 2

Write these as ordinary numbers.

a 12.356×10^2 **b** 3.45×10^1 **c** 753.4×10^{-2} **d** 6789×10^{-1}

a $12.356 \times 10^2 = 1235.6$ **b** $3.45 \times 10^1 = 34.5$

c $753.4 \times 10^{-2} = 7.534$ **d** $6789 \times 10^{-1} = 678.9$

Sometimes, you have to insert zeros to make up the required number of digits.

Example 3

Write these as ordinary numbers.

a 75×10^4 **b** 2.04×10^5 **c** 6.78×10^{-3} **d** 0.897×10^{-4}

a $75 \times 10^4 = 750\,000$ **b** $2.04 \times 10^5 = 204\,000$

c $6.78 \times 10^{-3} = 0.006\,78$ **d** $0.897 \times 10^{-4} = 0.000\,089\,7$

Division by powers of 10

Try these on your calculator. Look for the connection between the calculation and the answer.

a $12.3 \div 10$ **b** $3.45 \div 1000$ **c** $3.45 \div 10^3$

d $0.075 \div 100$ **e** $2.045 \div 10^2$ **f** $6.78 \div 1000$

Working with multiples of powers of 10

You can use this principle to multiply multiples of 10, 100, … You also use this method in estimation. You should have the skill to do this mentally so that you can check that your answers to calculations are about right. Use a calculator to work out these multiplications.

a $200 \times 300 =$ **b** $100 \times 40 =$ **c** $2000 \times 3000 =$

Is there a way of doing them without using a calculator or pencil and paper?

Use a calculator to do these divisions.

a $400 \div 20 =$ **b** $250 \div 50 =$ **c** $30\,000 \div 600 =$

Once again, can you see an easy way of doing these 'in your head'? Look at these examples.

$$300 \times 4000 = 1\,200\,000 \qquad 5000 \div 200 = 25 \qquad 200 \times 50 = 10\,000$$

$$60 \times 5000 = 300\,000 \qquad 400 \div 20 = 20 \qquad 30\,000 \div 600 = 50$$

To multiply 200×3000, for example, you multiply the non-zero digits ($2 \times 3 = 6$) and then write the total number of zeros in both numbers at the end, to give 600 000.

$$200 \times 3000 = 2 \times 100 \times 3 \times 1000 = 6 \times 100\,000 = 600\,000$$

For division, you divide the non-zero digits and then cancel the zeros. For example:

$$400\,000 \div 80 = \frac{400\,000}{80}$$
$$= \frac{\overset{5}{\cancel{400}}\,000}{\cancel{80}_{\,1}}$$
$$= 5000$$

392   14 Number: Powers and standard form

Example 4

Write these as ordinary numbers.

a $712.35 \div 10^2$ **b** $38.45 \div 10^1$ **c** $3.463 \div 10^{-2}$ **d** $6.789 \div 10^{-1}$

- To divide by any power of 10, you must move the digits according to these two rules.
- When the index is positive, move the digits to the right by the same number of places as the value of the index. You are actually decreasing the place value of the digits.
- When the index is negative, move the digits to the left by the same number of places as the value of the index. You are actually increasing the place value of the digits.

a $712.35 \div 10^2 = 7.1235$ **b** $38.45 \div 10^1 = 3.845$

c $3.463 \div 10^{-2} = 346.3$ **d** $6.789 \div 10^{-1} = 67.89$

Sometimes, you have to insert zeros to make up the required number of digits.

Example 5

Write these as ordinary numbers.

a $75 \div 10^4$ **b** $2.04 \div 10^5$ **c** $6.78 \div 10^{-3}$ **d** $0.08 \div 10^{-4}$

a $75 \div 10^4 = 0.0075$ **b** $2.04 \div 10^5 = 0.000\,0204$

c $6.78 \div 10^{-3} = 6780$ **d** $0.08 \div 10^{-4} = 800$

When you work through the next exercise, remember:

$$10\,000 = 10 \times 10 \times 10 \times 10 = 10^4 \qquad 1 = 10^0$$
$$1000 = 10 \times 10 \times 10 \quad = 10^3 \qquad 0.1 = 1 \div 10 \quad = 10^{-1}$$
$$100 = 10 \times 10 \quad = 10^2 \qquad 0.01 = 1 \div 100 \quad = 10^{-2}$$
$$10 = 10 \quad = 10^1 \qquad 0.001 = 1 \div 1000 = 10^{-3}$$

Exercise 14C

1 Write down the answers without using a calculator.

a 200×300 **b** 30×4000 **c** 3×50 **d** 60×700

e 200×7 **f** 10×30 **g** $(20)^2$ **h** $(20)^3$

i $(400)^2$ **j** 30×150 **k** 40×200 **l** 50×5000

2 Write down the answers without using a calculator.

a $2000 \div 400$ **b** $3000 \div 60$ **c** $5000 \div 200$

d $6000 \div 200$ **e** $2100 \div 300$ **f** $9000 \div 30$

g $300 \div 50$ **h** $2100 \div 70$ **i** $5000 \div 5000$

j $30\,000 \div 2000$ **k** $2000 \times 40 \div 2000$ **l** $200 \times 20 \div 800$

m $200 \times 6000 \div 30\,000$ **n** $20 \times 80 \times 600 \div 3000$

3 You are given that $16 \times 34 = 544$.

a Write down the value of 160×340. **b** What is $544\,000 \div 34$?

4 Write these calculations in order, starting with the one that gives the smallest answer.

5000×4000 600×8000 $200\,000 \times 700$ $30 \times 90\,000$

5 One year there were £20 notes to the value of £28 000 million in circulation. How many £20 notes is this?

6 Write down the value of each expression.

a 3.1×10 **b** 3.1×100 **c** 3.1×1000 **d** $3.1 \times 10\,000$

7 Write down the value of each expression.

a 6.5×10 **b** 6.5×10^2 **c** 6.5×10^3 **d** 6.5×10^4

8 Write down the value of each expression.

a $3.1 \div 10$ **b** $3.1 \div 100$ **c** $3.1 \div 1000$ **d** $3.1 \div 10\,000$

9 Write down the value of each expression.

a $6.5 \div 10$ **b** $6.5 \div 10^2$ **c** $6.5 \div 10^3$ **d** $6.5 \div 10^4$

10 Evaluate each expression.

a 2.5×100 **b** 3.45×10 **c** 4.67×1000 **d** 34.6×10

e 20.789×10 **f** 56.78×1000 **g** 2.46×10^2 **h** 0.076×10

i 0.999×10^6 **j** 234.56×10^2 **k** 98.7654×10^3 **l** 43.23×10^6

m 0.0034578×10^5 **n** 0.0006×10^7 **o** $0.005\,67 \times 10^4$ **p** 56.0045×10^4

11 Evaluate each expression.

a $2.5 \div 100$ **b** $3.45 \div 10$ **c** $4.67 \div 1000$ **d** $34.6 \div 10$

e $20.789 \div 100$ **f** $56.78 \div 1000$ **g** $2.46 \div 10^2$ **h** $0.076 \div 10$

i $0.999 \div 10^6$ **j** $234.56 \div 10^2$ **k** $98.7654 \div 10^3$ **l** $43.23 \div 10^6$

m $0.003\,4578 \div 10^5$ **n** $0.0006 \div 10^7$ **o** $0.005\,67 \div 10^4$ **p** $56.0045 \div 10^4$

12 Work these out without using a calculator.

a 2.3×10^2 **b** 5.789×10^5 **c** 4.79×10^3 **d** 5.7×10^7

e 2.16×10^2 **f** 1.05×10^4 **g** 3.2×10^{-4} **h** 9.87×10^3

13 Which of these statements is true about the numbers in question 12?

a The first part is always a number from 1 to 10.

b There is always a multiplication sign in the middle of the expression.

c There is always a power of 10 at the end.

d Calculator displays sometimes show numbers in this form.

14 The mass of Mars is 6.4×10^{23} kg. The mass of Venus is 4.9×10^{24} kg.

Without working out the answers, explain how you can tell which planet is the heavier.

15 A number is between one million and 10 million. It is written in the form 4.7×10^n.

What is the value of n?

| Hints and tips | Even though you are really moving digits left or right, you may think of it as the decimal point moving right or left. |

Standard form

Standard form is also known as **standard index form**. It is a way of writing very large and very small numbers, using powers of 10. Any number can be written as a value from 1 to 10 multiplied by a power of 10. This is the definition of a number written in standard form.

$A \times 10^n$ where $1 \leqslant A < 10$, and n is a whole number.

In these examples, to see how to write numbers, the bold numbers are in standard form.

$$73 = 7.3 \times 10 \Rightarrow \mathbf{7.3 \times 10^1}$$
$$389 = 3.89 \times 100 \Rightarrow \mathbf{3.89 \times 10^2}$$
$$3147 = 3.147 \times 1000 \Rightarrow \mathbf{3.147 \times 10^3}$$

When you are writing a number in this way, you must always follow two rules.

• The first part must be a number between 1 and 10 (1 is allowed but 10 isn't).
• The second part must be a whole-number (negative or positive) power of 10. Note that you would *not normally* write the power 1.

Standard form on a calculator

It is difficult to key a number such as 123 000 000 000 into a calculator. Instead, you can enter it in standard form (assuming you are using a scientific calculator).

$$123\ 000\ 000\ 000 = 1.23 \times 10^{11}$$

These are the keystrokes to enter this number into a typical calculator.

| 1 | • | 2 | 3 | ×10ˣ | 1 | 1 |

Your calculator display will display the number either as an ordinary number, if there is enough space in the display, or in standard form if there is not.

Standard form for numbers less than 1

These numbers are written in standard form. Make sure that you understand how they are formed.

a $0.4 = 4 \times 10^{-1}$ **b** $0.05 = 5 \times 10^{-2}$ **c** $0.007 = 7 \times 10^{-3}$ **d** $0.123 = 1.23 \times 10^{-1}$

e $0.007\ 65 = 7.65 \times 10^{-3}$ **f** $0.9804 = 9.804 \times 10^{-1}$ **g** $0.0098 = 9.8 \times 10^{-3}$ **h** $0.000\ 0078 = 7.8 \times 10^{-6}$

On a typical calculator you would enter 1.23×10^{-6}, for example, as:

| 1 | • | 2 | 3 | ×10ˣ | (−) | 6 |

Exercise 14D

1 Write down the value of each expression.

     a 3.1×0.1 **b** 3.1×0.01 **c** 3.1×0.001 **d** 3.1×0.0001

2 Write down the value of each expression.

     a 6.5×10^{-1} **b** 6.5×10^{-2} **c** 6.5×10^{-3} **d** 6.5×10^{-4}

(PS) **3**   **a** What is the largest number you can enter into your calculator?

     b What is the smallest number you can enter into your calculator?

4 Work out the value of each expression.

     a $3.1 \div 0.1$ **b** $3.1 \div 0.01$ **c** $3.1 \div 0.001$ **d** $3.1 \div 0.0001$

5 Work out the value of each expression.

     a $6.5 \div 10^{-1}$ **b** $6.5 \div 10^{-2}$ **c** $6.5 \div 10^{-3}$ **d** $6.5 \div 10^{-4}$

6 Write these numbers out in full.

  a 2.5×10^2 **b** 3.45×10 **c** 4.67×10^{-3} **d** 3.46×10

  e 8.97×10^5 **f** 8.65×10^{-3} **g** 6×10^7 **h** 5.67×10^{-4}

7 Write these numbers in standard form.

  a 250   **b** 0.345   **c** 46 700

  d 3 400 000 000   **e** 20 780 000 000   **f** 0.000 567 8

  g 0.0006   **h** 0.005 67   **i** 56.0045

For questions **8** and **9**, write each of the given numbers in standard form.

(CM) **8** The largest number of dominoes ever toppled by one person is 281 581, although 30 people set up and toppled 1 382 101.

(CM) **9** The asteroid *Phaethon* comes within 12 980 000 miles of the Sun, whilst the asteroid *Pholus*, at its furthest point, is a distance of 2997 million miles from Earth. The closest an asteroid ever came to Earth was 93 000 miles from the planet.

(MR) **10** How many times bigger is 3.2×10^6 than 3.2×10^4?

Calculating with standard form

Calculations involving very large or very small numbers can be done more easily if you use standard form. These examples show you how to work out the area of a pixel on a computer screen, and how long it takes light to reach Earth from a distant star.

Example 6

Work out   **a** $2.3 \times 10^5 + 1.7 \times 10^6$ **b** $3.89 \times 10^{18} - 2.9 \times 10^{17}$

a You can change these to ordinary numbers but this is not easy if the powers are very big, so it is better to change the numbers so they have the same power of 10. Always change to the biggest power of 10.

So, $2.3 \times 10^5 = 0.23 \times 10^6$

$0.23 \times 10^6 + 1.7 \times 10^6 = 1.93 \times 10^6$

b $3.89 \times 10^{18} - 2.9 \times 10^{17} = 3.89 \times 10^{18} - 0.29 \times 10^{18}$

$3.89 \times 10^{18} - 0.29 \times 10^{18} = 3.6 \times 10^{18}$

Example 7

A pixel on a computer screen is 2×10^{-2} cm long by 7×10^{-3} cm wide.

What is the area of the pixel?

The area is given by 'length × width'.

$$\text{Area} = (2 \times 10^{-2}) \times (7 \times 10^{-3}) \text{ cm}^2$$
$$= (2 \times 7) \times (10^{-2} \times 10^{-3}) \text{ cm}^2$$
$$= 14 \times 10^{-5} \text{ cm}^2$$

Note that you multiply the numbers and add the powers of 10. (You should not need to use a calculator to do this calculation.) The answer is not in standard form as the first part is not between 1 and 10, so now you have to change it to standard form.

$$14 = 1.4 \times 10^1$$

So the area is 14×10^{-5} cm^2 = $1.4 \times 10^1 \times 10^{-5}$ cm^2

$$= 1.4 \times 10^{-4} \text{ cm}^2$$

Example 8

The star *Betelgeuse* is 1.8×10^{15} miles from Earth. Light travels at 1.86×10^5 miles per second.

a How many seconds does it take light to travel from *Betelgeuse* to Earth? Give your answer in standard form.

b How many years does it take light to travel from *Betelgeuse* to Earth?

a Time = distance ÷ speed

$$= (1.8 \times 10^{15} \text{ miles}) \div (1.86 \times 10^5 \text{ miles per second})$$

$$= (1.8 \div 1.86) \times (10^{15} \div 10^5) \text{ seconds}$$

$$= 0.967\,741\,935 \times 10^{10} \text{ seconds}$$

Note that you divide the numbers and subtract the powers of 10. To change the answer to standard form, first round it, which gives:

$$0.97 \times 10^{10} = 9.7 \times 10^9 \text{ seconds}$$

b To convert from seconds to years, you have to divide first by 3600 to change seconds to hours, then by 24 to change hours to days, and finally by 365 to change days to years.

$$9.7 \times 10^9 \div (3600 \times 24 \times 365) = 307.6 \text{ years}$$

Exercise 14E

1 These numbers are not in standard form. Write them in standard form.

a 56.7×10^2 **b** 0.06×10^4 **c** 34.6×10^{-2}

d $2 \times 10^2 \times 35$ **e** 160×10^{-2} **f** 23 million

g 0.0003×10^{-2} **h** 25.6×10^5 **i** $16 \times 10^2 \times 3 \times 10^{-1}$

j $2 \times 10^4 \times 56 \times 10^{-4}$ **k** $(18 \times 10^2) \div (3 \times 10^3)$ **l** $(56 \times 10^3) \div (2 \times 10^{-2})$

2 Work these out. Give your answers in standard form.

a $4.5 \times 10^8 + 3.1 \times 10^7$ **b** $9.3 \times 10^{12} - 1.5 \times 10^{11}$ **c** $5.65 \times 10^9 + 2 \times 10^7$

d $2 \times 10^{14} - 5.4 \times 10^{13}$ **e** $1.6 \times 10^{22} + 3 \times 10^{20}$ **f** $2 \times 10^4 \times 6 \times 10^4$

g $2 \times 10^{-4} \times 5.4 \times 10^3$ **h** $1.6 \times 10^{-2} \times 4 \times 10^4$ **i** $2 \times 10^4 \times 6 \times 10^{-4}$

j $7.2 \times 10^{-3} \times 4 \times 10^2$ **k** $(5 \times 10^3)^2$ **l** $(2 \times 10^{-2})^3$

3 Work these out. Give your answers in standard form, rounding to an appropriate degree of accuracy where necessary.

a $2.1 \times 10^{14} + 5.4 \times 10^{13}$ **b** $1.6 \times 10^8 - 3.8 \times 10^7$ **c** $2.4 \times 10^4 \times 6.6 \times 10^4$

d $7.3 \times 10^{-6} \times 5.4 \times 10^3$ **e** $(3.1 \times 10^4)^2$ **f** $(6.8 \times 10^{-4})^2$

g $5.7 \times 10 \times 3.7 \times 10$ **h** $1.9 \times 10^{-2} \times 1.9 \times 10^9$ **i** $5.9 \times 10^3 \times 2.5 \times 10^{-2}$

j $5.2 \times 10^3 \times 2.2 \times 10^2 \times 3.1 \times 10^3$ **k** $1.8 \times 10^2 \times 3.6 \times 10^3 \times 2.4 \times 10^{-2}$

l $3.4 \times 10^8 + 4.27 \times 10^7 - 1.7 \times 10^6$ **m** $7.8 \times 10^{12} - 6.35 \times 10^{11} + 1.5 \times 10^{10}$

4 Work these out. Give your answers in standard form.

a $(5.4 \times 10^4) \div (2 \times 10^3)$ **b** $(4.8 \times 10^2) \div (3 \times 10^4)$ **c** $(1.2 \times 10^4) \div (6 \times 10^4)$

d $(2 \times 10^{-4}) \div (5 \times 10^3)$ **e** $(1.8 \times 10^4) \div (9 \times 10^{-2})$ **f** $\sqrt{36 \times 10^{-4}}$

g $(5.4 \times 10^{-3}) \div (2.7 \times 10^2)$ **h** $(1.8 \times 10^6) \div (3.6 \times 10^3)$ **i** $(5.6 \times 10^3) \div (2.8 \times 10^2)$

5 Work these out. Give your answers in standard form, rounding to an appropriate degree of accuracy where necessary.

    a $(2.7 \times 10^4) \div (5 \times 10^2)$ **b** $(2.3 \times 10^4) \div (8 \times 10^6)$ **c** $(3.2 \times 10^{-1}) \div (2.8 \times 10^{-1})$

    d $(2.6 \times 10^{-6}) \div (4.1 \times 10^3)$ **e** $\sqrt{8 \times 10^4}$ **f** $\sqrt{30 \times 10^{-4}}$

    g $5.3 \times 10^3 \times 2.3 \times 10^2 \div (2.5 \times 10^3)$ **h** $1.8 \times 10^2 \times 3.1 \times 10^3 \div (6.5 \times 10^{-2})$

6 A typical adult has about 20 000 000 000 000 red corpuscles. Each red corpuscle has a mass of about 0.000 000 000 1 g. Write both of these numbers in standard form and work out the total mass of red corpuscles in a typical adult.

7 A man puts one grain of rice on the first square of a chess board, two on the second square, four on the third, eight on the fourth and so on.

    a How many grains of rice will he put on the 64th square of the board?

    b How many grains of rice will there be altogether?

Give your answers in standard form.

> **Hints and tips**   Compare powers of 2 with the running totals.
> By the fourth square you have 15 grains altogether, and $2^4 = 16$.

8 The surface area of the Earth is approximately 2×10^8 square miles. The area of Earth's surface that is covered by water is approximately 1.4×10^8 square miles.

    a Calculate the area of the Earth's surface not covered by water. Give your answer in standard form.

    b What percentage of the Earth's surface is not covered by water?

9 Evaluate the value of $\dfrac{E}{M}$ when $E = 1.5 \times 10^3$ and $M = 3 \times 10^{-2}$, giving your answer in standard form.

10 Work out the value of $\dfrac{3.2 \times 10^7}{1.4 \times 10^2}$, giving your answer in standard form, correct to 2 significant figures.

11 In one year, British Airways carried 33 million passengers. Of these, 70% passed through London Heathrow Airport. On average, each passenger carried 19.7 kg of luggage. Calculate the total mass of the luggage carried by these passengers. Give your answer in standard form.

12 These four numbers are written in standard form.

    1.6×10^4 4.8×10^6 3.2×10^2 6.4×10^3

    a Work out the smallest answer you can have by multiplying two of these numbers together.

    b Work out the largest answer you can have by adding two of these numbers together.

Give your answers in standard form.

13 Many people withdraw money from their banks by using 'hole-in-the-wall' machines. Each day there are eight million withdrawals from 32 000 machines. What is the average number of withdrawals per machine? Give your answer in standard form.

14 The mass of Saturn is 5.686×10^{26} tonnes. The mass of Earth is 6.04×10^{21} tonnes. How many times heavier is Saturn than Earth? Give your answer in standard form to a suitable degree of accuracy.

Worked exemplars

  1 This is a table of powers of 3.

3^1	3^2	3^3	3^4	3^5	3^6	3^7
3	9	27	81	243	729	2187

a Use your calculator to work out $27 \div 243$. Give the answer as a fraction.

b Use the rules of indices to write $3^3 \div 3^5$ as a single power of 3.

c Deduce the value, as a fraction, of 3^{-3}.

This is a mathematical reasoning question. The first two parts set up the information you will need.	
a $\dfrac{27}{243} = \dfrac{1}{9}$	Write $27 \div 243$ as a fraction, then cancel to the simplest form. Make sure you know how to change an answer into a fraction if the display shows a decimal, in this case 0.111…
b $3^3 \div 3^5 = 3^{3-5} = 3^{-2}$	Apply the rules of indices. When dividing powers with the same base, subtract them.
c (a) and (b) $\Rightarrow \dfrac{1}{9} = 3^{-2}$ $\therefore 3^{-3} = \dfrac{1}{27}$	This is where the mathematical reasoning comes in. Parts (a) and (b) are linked in that they are the same calculation in different forms, so the answers must be the same. So if $\frac{1}{9} = 3^{-2}$, then 3^{-3} must be $\frac{1}{27}$. Remember that the symbol $\Rightarrow$ means 'implies' and $\therefore$ means 'therefore'.

    2 The population of the world is approximately 7 billion.

One grain of sand has a mass of 0.0026 grams.

2.6 grams of sand have a total volume of 1 cm³.

Work out the size of a cube that would be big enough to hold as many grains of sand as the population of the world.

This problem-solving question requires you to translate a real-life problem into a series of mathematical processes.	
Number of grains of sand in 1 cm³ = $2.6 \div 0.0026 = 1000$ or 10^3	First work out how many grains of sand there are in 1 cm³. Don't forget to write down what you are working out.
Number of cubic centimetres that would hold 7 billion grains $= 7 \times 10^9 \div 10^3$ $= 7 \times 10^6$	Next work out how many cubic centimetres would hold 7 billion grains.
Side of cube = $\sqrt[3]{7 \times 10^6}$ $= 191 \text{ cm} \approx 2 \text{ m}$	Now work out the side of the cube by finding the cube root of the answer. You can leave the answer in centimetres or convert to metres. The answer is surprisingly small. Remember that $\approx$ means 'approximately'. Rounding the answer is acceptable, as long as you show working, as all values are approximations.

Ready to progress?

I can write and calculate with numbers written in index form.
I can multiply and divide numbers written in index form.

I can write ordinary numbers in standard form and vice versa.
I can use standard form to calculate in various problems.

Review questions

1 **a** Write these numbers as powers of 2.

    i 16   **ii** 256

    b Write these numbers as powers of 10.

    i 1000   **ii** a billion (one thousand million)

2 Work these out.

    a 300×5000 **b** 3 thousand $\times$ 2 million

3 **a** Write down the value of 14^2.

    b Explain how you know that 35^2 is not equal to 1220.

4 Simplify each expression.

    a $7^4 \times 7^5$ **b** $x^8 \div x^4$

    c Sammi writes: $3x^2 \times 5x^7 = 8x^{14}$

      Explain the mistakes he has made.

      Write down the correct answer to $3x^2 \times 5x^7$.

5 Simplify each expression.

    a $t^5 \times t^3$ **b** $\dfrac{m^8}{m^3}$ **c** $(3x^3)^2$ **d** $2a^2h \times 5a^5h^4$

6 Simplify each expression.

    a $x^5 \times x^6$ **b** $\dfrac{m}{m^6}$ **c** $(2k^3m^2) \times (4k^2m)$

7 **a** Write the number 75 000 in standard form.

    b Write 9×10^{-3} as an ordinary number.

8 Simplify each expression.   **a** $\dfrac{4x^3y^2 \times 3xy^2}{6x^4y^3}$ **b** $(2m^3p^4)^3$

9 $x = \dfrac{p - q}{pq}$

Given that $p = 5 \times 10^8$ and $q = 4 \times 10^6$, find the value of x. Give your answer in standard form.

10 There are approximately 5.3×10^{24} molecules of oxygen in a cubic metre of air.

A typical human takes in approximately $\frac{1}{2}$ litre of air with each breath.

How many molecules are taken in with each breath?

11 Is this triangle right-angled? All lengths are in centimetres.

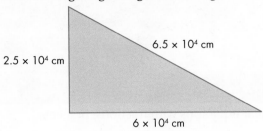

2.5 × 10⁴ cm

2.5×10^4 cm

6.5×10^4 cm

6×10^4 cm

12 The perimeter of this rectangle is 2.6×10^7 cm.

8×10^6 cm

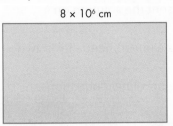

Work out the area of the rectangle.

13 The Moon is a sphere with a radius of 1.080×10^3 miles. Use the formula for the surface area of a sphere.

surface area = $4\pi r^2$

Calculate the surface area of the Moon.

14 In 1600 the world population was approximately 5.5×10^8. In 2000 it was approximately 6.1×10^9.

By how much did the population rise on average every year between 1600 and 2000?

15 Olivia writes down a number in standard form. It is greater than 100 million and less than 1000 million.

Write down a possible value of Olivia's number, in standard form.

16 The speed of sound (Mach 1) is 1236 kilometres per hour. 8 km is approximately 10 miles. An aircraft travelling at Mach 3 would be travelling at three times the speed of sound. How many miles would an aircraft travelling at Mach 3 cover in 1 minute?

17

1.2×10^7 cm

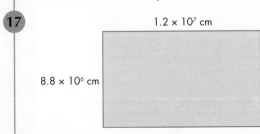

8.8×10^6 cm

a Work out the perimeter of the rectangle.

b Work out the area of the rectangle.

15 Algebra: Equations and inequalities

This chapter is going to show you:

- how to set up and solve linear equations with fractions, brackets and variables on both sides
- how to solve linear simultaneous equations
- how to solve a linear inequality and represent the solution on a number line
- how to find a region on a graph that obeys a linear inequality in two variables
- how to use trial and improvement to solve non-linear equations.

You should already know:

- the basic language of algebra
- how to collect together like terms
- how to solve basic linear equations.

About this chapter

The theory of linear programming, which uses inequalities in two dimensions, was developed at the start of the Second World War in 1939.

It was used to work out ways to get armaments as efficiently as possible and to increase the effectiveness of resources. It was such a powerful analytical tool that the Allies did not want the Germans to know about it, so it was not made public until 1947.

George Dantzig, one of the inventors of linear programming, came late to a lecture at university one day and saw two problems written on the blackboard. He copied them, thinking they were the homework assignment. He solved both problems, but had to apologise to the lecturer because, as he found them a little harder than usual, it took him a few days to solve them.

$2x + 3y = 9$

$x + 2y = 7$

$x > 2x$

The lecturer was astonished. The problems written on the board were not homework but examples of 'impossible problems'. Not after that!

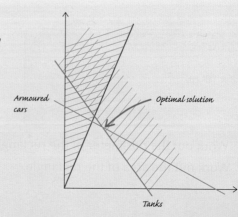

Armoured cars

Optimal solution

Tanks

15.1 Linear equations

This section will show you how to:

- solve equations in which the variable (the letter) appears as part of the numerator of a fraction
- solve equations where you have to expand brackets first
- solve equations where the variable appears on both sides of the equals sign
- set up equations from given information and then solve them.

Fractional equations

To solve equations with fractions you will need to multiply both sides of the equation by the denominator at some stage. It is important to do the inverse operations in the right order.

Sometimes you need to eliminate the constant term first before multiplying by the denominator of the fraction. However, if all of the left-hand side is part of the fraction, you need to multiply both sides by the denominator first. It is essential to check your answer in the original equation.

Solve the equation $\frac{x}{3} + 1 = 5$.

Subtract 1 from both sides: $\quad \frac{x}{3} = 4$

Now multiply both sides by 3: $\quad x = 12$

Check the answer is correct by substituting it into the equation: $\quad \frac{12}{3} + 1 = 4 + 1$
$$= 5$$

Example 1

Solve this equation and check your answer. $\quad \frac{3x}{4} - 3 = 1$

Add 3 to both sides: $\qquad \frac{3x}{4} = 4$

Now multiply both sides by 4: $\qquad 3x = 16$

Now divide both sides by 3: $\qquad x = \frac{16}{3}$
$$= 5\frac{1}{3}$$

Check: $\quad \dfrac{3 \times 5\frac{1}{3}}{4} - 3 = \dfrac{16}{4} - 3$
$$= 4 - 3$$
$$= 1$$

Example 2

Adam opened a packet of biscuits and ate two of them before sharing the rest with his four friends. As a result, they each received three biscuits.

How many biscuits were in the packet originally?

Set up the equation. If there were x biscuits, he took away 2 and then shared $(x - 2)$ biscuits among 5 people.

$$\frac{x - 2}{5} = 3$$

Multiply both sides by 5: $\qquad x - 2 = 15$

Now add 2 to both sides: $\qquad x = 17$

There were 17 biscuits in the packet originally.

Check: $\quad \dfrac{17 - 2}{5} = \dfrac{15}{5}$
$$= 3$$

Exercise 15A

1 Solve these equations.

a $\dfrac{f}{5} + 2 = 8$　　**b** $\dfrac{w}{3} - 5 = 2$　　**c** $\dfrac{x}{8} + 3 = 12$　　**d** $\dfrac{5t}{4} + 3 = 18$　　**e** $\dfrac{3y}{2} - 1 = 8$

f $\dfrac{2x}{3} + 5 = 12$　　**g** $\dfrac{t}{5} + 3 = 1$　　**h** $\dfrac{x+3}{2} = 5$　　**i** $\dfrac{t-5}{2} = 3$　　**j** $\dfrac{3x+10}{2} = 8$

k $\dfrac{2x+1}{3} = 5$　　**l** $\dfrac{5y-2}{4} = 3$　　**m** $\dfrac{6y+3}{9} = 1$　　**n** $\dfrac{2x-3}{5} = 4$　　**o** $\dfrac{5t+3}{4} = 1$

(MR) **2** The solution to the equation $\dfrac{2x-3}{5} = 3$ is $x = 9$.

Make up two more *different* equations of the form $\dfrac{ax \pm b}{c} = 3$ for which x is also 9, where a, b and c are positive whole numbers.

(EV) **3** A teacher asked her class to solve the equation $\dfrac{2x+4}{5} = 6$.

Amanda wrote:

$2x + 4 = 6 \times 5$

$2x + 4 - 4 = 30 - 4$

$2x = 26$

$2x \div 2 = 26 \div 2$

$x = 13$

Betsy wrote:

$\dfrac{2x}{5} = 6 + 4$

$2x = 6 + 4 + 5$

$2x = 15$

$2x - 2 = 15 - 2$

$x = 13$

The teacher gave the correct answer of 13. Both students ticked their work as correct.

a Which student used the correct method?

b Explain the mistakes the other student made.

(PS) **4** Five friends went for a meal in a cafeteria. The bill was £x. They decided to add a £10 tip and shared the bill equally between them. Each person paid £9.50.

a Set this problem up as an equation.

b Solve the equation and find the cost of the bill before the tip was added.

(PS) **5** The mean of the expressions $(3x + 7)$, $(x - 9)$, $(5x + 11)$ and $(6x - 5)$ is 11.

a Find the value of x.

b Check that your answer is correct. Show all your working.

Brackets

When you have an equation that contains brackets, multiply out the brackets and then solve the equation (as before).

Solve the equation $5(x + 3) = 25$.

First multiply out the brackets: $5x + 15 = 25$

Subtract 15 from both sides:　　　$5x = 25 - 15$

　　　　　　　　　　　　　　　　$= 10$

Divide by 5:　　　　　　　　　　$x = \dfrac{10}{5}$

　　　　　　　　　　　　　　　　$= 2$

Check your answer:　　$5(2 + 3) = 5 \times 5$

　　　　　　　　　　　　　　$= 25$

Example 3

A trapezium has parallel sides of $(x + 1)$ and $(2x - 9)$ cm and a perpendicular height of 6 cm. Its area is 21 cm². Find the value of x.

Write down the formula for the area of a trapezium:	$A = \frac{1}{2}(a + b)h$
Substitute the information:	$21 = \frac{1}{2}(x + 1 + 2x - 9) \times 6$
Simplify:	$21 = 3(3x - 8)$
Multiply out the brackets:	$21 = 9x - 24$
Add 24 to both sides:	$45 = 9x$
Divide both sides by 9:	$x = 5$

Exercise 15B

1 Solve each of these equations. Some of the answers may be decimals or negative numbers. Remember to check that each answer works for its original equation. Use your calculator if necessary.

a $6(3k + 5) = 39$ **b** $5(2x + 3) = 27$ **c** $9(3x - 5) = 9$

d $2(x + 5) = 6$ **e** $5(x - 4) = -25$ **f** $3(t + 7) = 15$

g $2(3x + 11) = 10$ **h** $4(5t + 8) = 12$

> **Hints and tips** When you expand brackets, remember to multiply everything inside the brackets by what is outside.

2 Fill in values for a, b and c so that the answer to this equation is $x = 4$.

$a(bx + 3) = c$

3 My son is x years old. In five years' time, I will be twice his age and both our ages will be multiples of 10. The sum of our ages will be between 50 and 100. How old am I now?

> **Hints and tips** Set up an equation and put it equal to 60, 70, 80, … Solve the equation and see if the answer fits the conditions.

4 The diagram shows a square.

Find x if the perimeter is 44 cm.

$(4x - 1)$

5 Max thought of a number. He then multiplied his number by 3. He added 4 to the answer. He then doubled that answer to get a final value of 38. What number did he start with?

6 Show that the answer to this equation is 6.

$8(x - 7) - 5(x + 4) - (19 - x) + 71 = 0$

7 A heptagon has two angles of $(3x - 17)°$ and one angle of $(4x - 36)°$. The remaining angles are all $(2x + 13)°$. Find the size of the largest angle in the heptagon.

> **Hints and tips** A heptagon has seven sides.

Equations with the variable on both sides

When a variable appears on both sides of an equation, it is best to use the 'do the same to both sides' method, and collect all the terms containing the variable on the left-hand side of the equation.

Solve the equation $5x + 4 = 3x + 10$.

There are more xs on the left-hand side, so don't turn the equation round.

Subtract $3x$ from both sides:	$2x + 4 = 10$
Subtract 4 from both sides:	$2x = 6$
Divide both sides by 2:	$x = 3$

Example 4

Solve the equation $3(2x + 5) + x = 2(2 - x) + 2$.

$$3(2x + 5) + x = 2(2 - x) + 2$$

Multiply out both brackets: $6x + 15 + x = 4 - 2x + 2$

Simplify both sides: $\qquad 7x + 15 = 6 - 2x$

There are more xs on the left-hand side, so don't turn the equation round.

Add $2x$ to both sides:	$9x + 15 = 6$
Subtract 15 from both sides:	$9x = -9$
Divide both sides by 9:	$x = -1$

Example 5

Alfie bought 2 multipacks of soap to add to the 3 bottles he already had at home. Jamie bought 6 identical multipacks of soap but then used 13 of the bottles for his art project. They found then that they each had exactly the same number of bottles of soap. How many bottles did each of them have?

Let x be the number of bottles of soap in a multipack.

Alfie ended up with $(2x + 3)$ bottles.

Jamie ended up with $(6x - 13)$ bottles.

Solve the equation: $\qquad\qquad 2x + 3 = 6x - 13$

There are more xs on the right-hand side, so turn the equation round:

$$6x - 13 = 2x + 3$$

Subtract $2x$ from both sides:	$4x - 13 = 3$
Add 13 to both sides:	$4x = 16$
Divide both sides by 4:	$x = 4$

So Alfie (and therefore Jamie) ended up with $2 \times 4 + 3 = 8 + 3 = 11$ bottles.

Check: Jamie ended up with $6 \times 4 - 13 = 24 - 13 = 11$ bottles.

Exercise 15C

1 Solve each of the following equations.

a $2x + 3 = x + 5$ **b** $5y + 4 = 3y + 6$ **c** $4a - 3 = 3a + 4$

d $5t + 3 = 2t + 15$ **e** $7p - 5 = 3p + 3$ **f** $6k + 5 = 2k + 1$

g $4m + 1 = m + 10$ **h** $8s - 1 = 6s - 5$

> **Hints and tips** Remember: 'Always do the same to both sides'. Show all your working. Rearrange before you simplify. If you try to do these at the same time you could get it wrong.

(PS) 2 Terry says: "I am thinking of a number. I multiply it by 3 and subtract 2."

June says: "I am thinking of a number. I multiply it by 2 and add 5."

Terry and June find that they both thought of the same number and both got the same final answer.

What number did they think of?

> **Hints and tips** Set up equations, make them equal and solve.

3 Solve each of the following equations.

a $2(d + 3) = d + 12$ **b** $5(x - 2) = 3(x + 4)$ **c** $3(2y + 3) = 5(2y + 1)$

d $3(h - 6) = 2(5 - 2h)$ **e** $4(3b - 1) + 6 = 5(2b + 4)$ **f** $2(5c + 2) - 2c = 3(2c + 3) + 7$

(CM) 4 **a** Explain why the equation $3(2x + 1) = 2(3x + 5)$ cannot be solved.

b Explain why there are an infinite number of solutions to the equation: $2(6x + 9) = 3(4x + 6)$.

(PS) 5 Wilson has eight coins of the same value and seven pennies.

Chloe has eleven coins of the same value as those that Wilson has and she also has five pennies.

Wilson says: "If you give me one of your coins and four pennies, we will have the same amount of money."

What is the value of the coins that Wilson and Chloe have?

> **Hints and tips** Call the value of the coin x and set up the equations, for example, Wilson has $8x + 7$, and then take one x and 4 from Chloe and add one x and 4 to Wilson. Then put the equations equal and solve.

(PS) 6 **a** Explain why $5x + 29 = x + 17$.

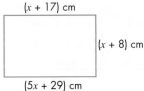
$(x + 17)$ cm

$(x + 8)$ cm

$(5x + 29)$ cm

b Find the area of the rectangle.

7 The diagram shows two number machines that perform the same operations.

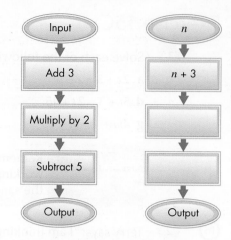

  a Starting with an input value of 7, work through the left-hand machine to get the output.

  b Find an input value that gives the same value for the output.

  c Write down the algebraic expressions in the right-hand machine for an input of n. (The first operation has been filled in for you.)

  d Set up an equation for the same input and output and show each step in solving the equation to get the answer in part **b**.

 8 Mary has a large and a small bottle of cola. The large bottle holds 50 cl more than the small bottle.

From the large bottle she fills four cups and has 18 cl left over.

From the small bottle she fills three cups and has 1 cl left over.

How much cola does each bottle hold?

> **Hints and tips** Set up equations for both, using x as the amount of cola in a cup. Make them equal but remember to add 50 to the small bottle equation to allow for the difference. Solve for x, and then work out how much is in each bottle.

  9 Solve the equation.

$(x - 1)(x + 4) = (x + 13)(x - 4)$

15.2 Elimination method for simultaneous equations

This section will show you how to:

- solve simultaneous linear equations in two variables using the elimination method.

Key term

eliminate

A pair of simultaneous equations is exactly that – two equations, usually linear, for which you want the same solution and must therefore solve together.

For example, $x + y = 10$ has many solutions: $x = 2, y = 8$ $x = 4, y = 6$ $x = 5, y = 5 \dots$

and $2x + y = 14$ has many solutions: $x = 2, y = 10$ $x = 3, y = 8$ $x = 4, y = 6 \dots$

But only one solution, $x = 4$ and $y = 6$, satisfies both equations at the same time.

Elimination method

One way to solve simultaneous equations is by the elimination method. There are six steps in this method.

Step 1: Balance the coefficients of one of the variables.

Step 2: Eliminate this variable by adding or subtracting the equations.

Step 3: Solve the resulting linear equation in the other variable.

Step 4: Substitute the value found back into one of the previous equations.

Step 5: Solve the resulting equation.

Step 6: Check that the two values found satisfy the original equations.

Example 6

Solve this pair of simultaneous equations. $\quad 6x + y = 15$ and $4x + y = 11$

First label the equations so that you can clearly explain the method:

$$6x + y = 15 \quad (1)$$
$$4x + y = 11 \quad (2)$$

Step 1: Since the y-term in both equations has the same coefficient there is no need to balance them. (You will learn how to do this later in the chapter.)

Step 2: Subtract one equation from the other. (Equation (1) minus equation (2) will give positive values.)

$$6x + y = 15 \quad (1)$$
$$4x + y = 11 \quad (2)$$

$$6x - 4x + y - y = 15 - 11 \quad (1) - (2)$$
$$2x = 4$$

Step 3: Solve this equation: $\quad x = 2$

Step 4: Substitute $x = 2$ into one of the original equations, usually the one with the smallest numbers involved.

Substitute $x = 2$ into: $\quad 4x + y = 11$

which gives: $\quad\quad\quad\quad 8 + y = 11$

Step 5: Solve this equation: $\quad\quad y = 3$

Step 6: Test the solution in the original equations. So substitute $x = 2$ and $y = 3$ into $6x + y$ which gives $12 + 3 = 15$, and into $4x + y$ which gives $8 + 3 = 11$. These are correct, so you can confidently say the solution is $x = 2$ and $y = 3$.

Example 7

Solve this pair of simultaneous equations. $\quad 3p + 2q = 29$ and $5p - 2q = 27$

Add the equations:

$$3p + 2q = 29 \quad (1)$$
$$5p - 2q = 27 \quad (2)$$
$$8p = 56 \quad (1) + (2)$$
$$p = 7$$

Substitute $p = 7$ into equation (1):

$$21 + 2q = 29$$
$$2q = 8$$
$$q = 4$$

1   Solve each pair of simultaneous equations by the elimination method.

     a $x + 3y = 9$ **b** $2x + 5y = 16$ **c** $3x - y = 9$

        $x + y = 6$ $2x + 3y = 8$ $5x + y = 11$

 2   Solve each pair of simultaneous equations by the elimination method.

     a $3a + b = 31$ **b** $7c + d = 39$ **c** $5e - 2f = 19$

        $3a + 5b = 71$ $7c - d = 17$ $e + 2f = 11$

 3   Solve this pair of simultaneous equations.

     $19x - 15y = 198$

      $8x - 15y = 66$

15.3 Substitution method for simultaneous equations

This section will show you how to:

- solve simultaneous linear equations in two variables using the substitution method.

This is an alternative method. The method you use depends on the coefficients of the variables and the way that the equations are written in the first place. There are five steps in the substitution method.

Step 1: Rearrange one of the equations into the form $y = \ldots$ or $x = \ldots$

Step 2: Substitute the right-hand side of this equation into the other equation in place of the variable on the left-hand side.

Step 3: Expand and solve this equation.

Step 4: Substitute the value into the $y = \ldots$ or $x = \ldots$ equation.

Step 5: Check that the values work in both original equations.

Example 8

Solve this pair of simultaneous equations. $y = 2x + 3$ and $3x + 4y = 1$

Because the first equation is in the form $y = \ldots$ it suggests that the substitution method should be used.

Again label the equations to help with explaining the method:

     $y = 2x + 3$ (1)

     $3x + 4y = 1$ (2)

Step 1: As equation (1) is in the form $y = \ldots$ there is no need to rearrange an equation.

Step 2: Substitute the right-hand side of equation (1) into equation (2) for the variable y:

                          $3x + 4(2x + 3) = 1$

Step 3: Expand and solve the equation: $3x + 8x + 12 = 1$

                                         $11x = -11$

                                           $x = -1$

Step 4: Substitute $x = -1$ into (1): $\qquad\qquad\qquad$ $y = -2 + 3$

$\qquad\qquad\qquad\qquad\qquad\qquad\qquad\qquad\qquad\qquad\qquad\qquad = 1$

Step 5: Test the solutions by substituting $x = -1$ and $x = -1$ into the original equations: (1) gives $1 = -2 + 3$ and (2) gives $-3 + 4 = 1$. These are correct so the solution is $x = -1$ and $y = 1$.

Exercise 15E

1   Solve each pair of simultaneous equations by the substitution method.

     a $3x + 7y = 13$ **b** $2x + y = 6$ **c** $4x - 3y = 18$

        $y = x - 11$ $y = 4x + 3$ $y = x - 7$

2   Solve each pair of simultaneous equations by the substitution method.

     a $2x + 5y = 37$ **b** $4x - 3y = 7$ **c** $4x - y = 17$

        $y = 11 - 2x$ $x = 13 - 3y$ $x = 2 + y$

3   Solve each pair of simultaneous equations by either elimination or substitution.

     a $3x + 11y = 36$ **b** $8x + y = 49$

        $y = 5 - 2x$ $8x - 3y = 13$

15.4 Balancing coefficients to solve simultaneous equations

This section will show you how to:

- solve simultaneous linear equations by balancing coefficients.

Balancing coefficients in one equation only

You were able to solve the pairs of equations in Examples 6, 7 and 8 simply by adding or subtracting the equations in each pair, or by substituting without rearranging. This does not always happen. The next examples show what to do when there are no identical terms to begin with, or when you need to rearrange.

Here, you solve simultaneous equations by balancing coefficients. You start by balancing the coefficients of one of the variables, then you use the elimination method as before.

Solve this pair of simultaneous equations.

$\qquad$ $5x + 2y = 24$ (1)

$\qquad$ $2x - y = 6$ (2)

Step 1: The equations have different y-coefficients, so they need to be balanced. Multiply the second equation by 2 and label it with a new equation number:

$\qquad$ $5x + 2y = 24$ (1)

$\qquad$ $4x - 2y = 12$ (3)

Step 2: As the signs in the equations are different, add the two equations to eliminate the y-terms.

$\qquad\qquad\qquad\qquad$ (1) + (3) $9x = 36$

Step 3: Solve this equation: $\qquad\qquad\qquad\qquad$ $x = 4$

Step 4: Substitute $x = 4$ into one of the original equations (1):

$$20 + 2y = 24$$

Step 5: Solve this equation: $\qquad\qquad\qquad y = 2$

Step 6: Test the solution by putting $x = 4$ and $y = 2$ into the original equations: (1) gives $20 + 4 = 24$ and (2) gives $8 - 2 = 6$. These are correct, so the solution is $x = 4$ and $y = 2$.

Balancing coefficients in both equations

There are also cases where both equations have to be changed to obtain identical terms. This is necessary when neither coefficient is a factor of the other. In this case, you find the lowest common multiple and multiply both equations. The next example shows you how to do this.

Note: The substitution method is not suitable for these types of equations as you end up with fractional terms.

Example 9

Solve this pair of simultaneous equations. $\qquad 4x + 3y = 27 \qquad$ (1)

$$5x + 2y = 25 \qquad \text{(2)}$$

Both equations have to be changed to obtain identical terms in either x or y.

You can make either the x- or y-coefficients the same. Since the y-coefficients are smaller, it will be easier to solve the equations if you make them the same.

Step 1: Multiply the first equation (1) by 2 (the y-coefficient of the other equation):

$\qquad$ (1) × 2 or 2 × (4x + 3y = 27) $\qquad \rightarrow \qquad 8x + 6y = 54 \qquad$ (3)

$\qquad$ Multiply the second equation (2) by 3 (the y-coefficient of the other equation):

$\qquad$ (2) × 3 or 3 × (5x + 2y = 25) $\qquad \rightarrow \qquad 15x + 6y = 75 \qquad$ (4)

$\qquad$ Label the new equations (3) and (4).

Step 2: Eliminate one of the variables: $\qquad$ (4) – (3) $\qquad\qquad 7x = 21$

Step 3: Solve the equation: $\qquad\qquad\qquad\qquad\qquad\qquad x = 3$

Step 4: Substitute into equation (1): $\qquad\qquad\qquad 12 + 3y = 27$

Step 5: Solve the equation: $\qquad\qquad\qquad\qquad\qquad\qquad y = 5$

Step 6: Check: $\qquad\qquad\qquad$ (1): $4 \times 3 + 3 \times 5 = 12 + 15 = 27$

$\qquad\qquad\qquad\qquad\qquad\qquad$ (2): $5 \times 3 + 2 \times 5 = 15 + 10 = 25$

These are correct so the solution is $x = 3$ and $y = 5$.

Exercise 15F

1 Solve each pair of simultaneous equations.

a $2x + 3y = 19$ $\qquad\qquad$ **b** $5x - 2y = 26$ $\qquad\qquad$ **c** $10x - y = 3$

$\quad 6x + 2y = 22$ $\qquad\qquad\qquad 3x - y = 15$ $\qquad\qquad\qquad 3x + 2y = 17$

d $5x - 2y = 4$ $\qquad\qquad$ **e** $2x + 3y = 13$ $\qquad\qquad$ **f** $3x - 2y = 3$

$\quad 3x - 6y = 6$ $\qquad\qquad\qquad 4x + 7y = 31$ $\qquad\qquad\qquad 5x + 6y = 12$

2 Solve each pair of simultaneous equations.

a $2x + 5y = 15$ $\qquad\qquad$ **b** $2x + 3y = 30$ $\qquad\qquad$ **c** $2x - 3y = 15$

$\quad 3x - 2y = 13$ $\qquad\qquad\qquad 5x + 7y = 71$ $\qquad\qquad\qquad 5x + 7y = 52$

d $3x - 2y = 15$ $\qquad\qquad$ **e** $5x - 3y = 14$ $\qquad\qquad$ **f** $3x + 2y = 28$

$\quad 2x - 3y = 5$ $\qquad\qquad\qquad 4x - 5y = 6$ $\qquad\qquad\qquad 2x + 7y = 47$

15.5 Using simultaneous equations to solve problems

This section will show you how to:

- solve problems using simultaneous linear equations.

You are now going to meet a type of problem that you need to express as a pair of simultaneous equations in order to solve it. The next example shows you how to tackle such a problem.

Example 10

Two families went to the theatre together but couldn't remember how much they paid for each adult ticket or each child ticket. They could, however, both remember what they had paid altogether.

Mr and Mrs Advani and their daughter Rupa paid £42.

Mrs Shaw and her two children, Len and Sue, paid £39.

How much would I have to pay for my wife, my four children and myself?

Write a pair of simultaneous equations from the information given:

Let x be the cost of an adult ticket, and y be the cost of a child ticket. Then:

$$2x + y = 42 \text{ for the Advani family}$$

and $x + 2y = 39$ for the Shaw family.

Now solve these equations just as you have done in the previous examples, to obtain:

$$x = £15 \text{ and } y = £12.$$

You can now find your cost, which will be $(2 \times £15) + (4 \times £12) = £78$.

Exercise 15G

  1 In this sequence, the next term is found by multiplying the previous term by a and then adding b, where a and b are positive whole numbers.

     3   14   47   …   …

a Explain why $3a + b = 14$.

b Set up another equation in a and b.

c Solve the equations to find a and b.

d Work out the next two terms in the sequence after 47.

 2 Amul and Kim have £10.70 between them. Amul has £3.70 more than Kim. Let x be the amount Amul has and y be the amount Kim has. Set up a pair of simultaneous equations. How much does each have?

3 In a tea shop it costs £8.10 for three teas and five buns.

In the same tea shop it costs £6.30 for three teas and three buns.

a Using t to represent the cost of a tea and b to represent the cost of a bun, write a pair of simultaneous equations to represent the above information.

b How much will I pay for four teas and six buns?

4 **a** Mary is solving the simultaneous equations $4x - 2y = 8$ and $2x - y = 4$.

She finds a solution of $x = 5$, $y = 6$ that works for both equations.

Explain why this is not a unique solution.

b Max is solving the simultaneous equations $6x + 2y = 9$ and $3x + y = 7$.

Why is it impossible to find a solution that works for both equations?

 5 Two people bought stamps at the Post Office. One person bought 10 second-class and 5 first-class stamps at a total cost of £8.40. The other bought 8 second-class and 10 first-class stamps at a total cost of £10.44.

a Let x be the cost of a second-class stamp and y be the cost of a first-class stamp. Set up two simultaneous equations to represent the information given.

b How much did I pay for three second-class and four first-class stamps?

6 The sum of my son's age and my age this year is 72.

Six years ago my age was double that of my son.

Let my age now be x and my son's age now be y.

a Explain why $x - 6 = 2(y - 6)$.

b Find the values of x and y.

7 Here are four equations.

A: $5x + 2y = 1$

B: $4x + y = 9$

C: $3x - y = 5$

D: $3x + 2y = 3$

Here are four sets of (x, y) values.

$(1, -2), (-1, 3), (2, 1), (3, -3)$

Match each pair of (x, y) values to a pair of equations.

> Hints and tips You could solve each possible set of pairs but there are six to work out. Alternatively, you can substitute values into the equations to see which work.

8 Three chews and four bubblies cost 72p. Five chews and two bubblies cost 64p. What would three chews and five bubblies cost?

9 On a nut-and-bolt production line, all the nuts had the same mass and all the bolts had the same mass. An order of 50 nuts and 60 bolts had a mass of 10.6 kg. An order of 40 nuts and 30 bolts had a mass of 6.5 kg. What should the mass of an order of 60 nuts and 50 bolts be?

10 My local taxi company charges a fixed amount plus a certain amount for each mile. When I took a six-mile journey the cost was £3.70. When I took a ten-mile journey the cost was £5.10. My next journey is going to be eight miles. How much will this cost?

11 Four sacks of potatoes and two sacks of carrots weigh 188 pounds.

Five sacks of potatoes and one sack of carrots weigh 202 pounds.

Baz buys seven sacks of potatoes and eight sacks of carrots.

Will he be able to carry them in his trailer, which has a safe working load of 450 pounds?

> Hints and tips | Set up two simultaneous equations using p and c for the weight of a sack of potatoes and carrots respectively.

12 Five bags of bark chipping and four trays of pansies cost £24.50.

Three bags of bark chippings and five trays of pansies cost £19.25.

Camilla wants six bags of bark chippings and eight trays of pansies.

She has £30. Will she have enough money?

13 **a** Find the area of the triangle enclosed by these three equations.

$$y - x = 2 \qquad x + y = 6 \qquad 3x + y = 6$$

b Find the area of the triangle enclosed by these three equations.

$$x - 2y = 6 \qquad x + 2y = 6 \qquad x + y = 3$$

> Hints and tips | Find the point of intersection of each pair of equations, plot the points on a grid and use any method to work out the area of the resulting triangle.

14 A teacher asks her class to solve this pair of simultaneous equations.

$$y = x + 4 \qquad (1)$$
$$2y - x = 10 \qquad (2)$$

Carmen says to Jeff, "To save time, you work out the x-value and I'll work out the y-value."

Jeff says: "Great idea."

This is Carmen's work.

	$y - x = 4$	(3)
	$2y - x = 10$	(2)
(2) − (3)	$3y = 6$	
	$y = 2$	

This is Jeff's work.

Substitute (1) into (2)

$$2(x + 4) - x = 10$$
$$2x + 8 - x = 10$$
$$3x = 18$$
$$x = 6$$

When the teacher reads out the answer as "two, six" the students mark their work as being correct.

Explain all the mistakes that Carmen and Jeff have made.

15.6 Linear inequalities

This section will show you how to:

- solve a simple linear inequality and represent it on a number line.

Key terms

inequality

inclusive inequality

strict inequality

Inequalities behave similarly to equations: you use the same rules to solve linear inequalities as you use to solve linear equations. There are four inequality signs:

- $<$ means 'less than'
- $>$ means 'greater than'
- $\leqslant$ means 'less than or equal to'
- $\geqslant$ means 'greater than or equal to'.

Be careful: never replace the inequality sign with an equals sign.

Solve the inequality $2x + 3 < 14$.

Subtract 3 from both sides: $\qquad 2x < 11$

Divide both sides by 2: $\qquad x < \dfrac{11}{2}$

$$\Rightarrow x < 5.5$$

This means that x can take any value below 5.5 but not the value 5.5.

$<$ and $>$ are called **strict inequalities**.

Note: Use the inequality sign given in the problem in the answer.

Example 11

Janet said: "If I were four years older than half my age, I'd still be at least 13 years old." How old must Janet be?

Write this information as an inequality, using x for Janet's current age: $\dfrac{x}{2} + 4 \geqslant 13$

Solve this inequality just like an equation but leave the inequality sign in place of the equals sign.

Subtract 4 from both sides: $\qquad \dfrac{x}{2} \geqslant 9$

Multiply both sides by 2: $\qquad x \geqslant 18$

This means that x can take any value above and including 18.

Janet is at least 18 years old but could be older.

$\leqslant$ and $\geqslant$ are called **inclusive inequalities**.

Example 12

Show that if $14 > \dfrac{3x + 7}{2}$, then x must be below 7.

Rewrite this as $\qquad \dfrac{3x + 7}{2} < 14$

Multiply both sides by 2: $\qquad 3x + 7 < 28$

Subtract 7 from both sides: $\qquad 3x < 21$

Divide both sides by 3: $\qquad x < 7$

Example 13

a Solve $-5 < 3x + 4 \leq 13$.

b State all the integers that solve the inequality.

a Divide the inequality into two parts, and treat each part separately.

$$-5 < 3x + 4 \qquad\qquad 3x + 4 \leq 13$$
$$\Rightarrow \quad -9 < 3x \qquad \Rightarrow \qquad 3x \leq 9$$
$$\Rightarrow \quad -3 < x \qquad \Rightarrow \qquad x \leq 3$$
$$\text{So} \quad -3 < x \leq 3$$

b x can be any integer between -3 and 3 but not -3 itself.
  You can write the answer in brackets using set notation: $\{-2, -1, 0, 1, 2, 3\}$

Exercise 15H

1 Solve the following linear inequalities.

a $4y + 5 \leq 17$ **b** $\dfrac{x}{2} + 4 < 7$ **c** $\dfrac{t}{3} - 2 \geq 4$

d $3(x - 2) < 15$ **e** $5(2x + 1) \leq 35$ **f** $2(4t - 3) \geq 34$

2 Write down the largest integer value of x that satisfies each of the following.

a $3x - 11 < 40$, where x is a square number

b $5x - 8 \leq 15$, where x is positive and odd

c $2x + 1 < 19$, where x is positive and prime

(PS) 3 Ahmed went to town with £20 to buy two CDs. His bus fare was £3. The CDs were both the same price. When he reached home he still had some money in his pocket. What was the most each CD could cost?

| Hints and tips | Set up an inequality and solve it. |

(CM) 4 **a** Explain why you cannot make a triangle with three sticks of length 3 cm, 4 cm and 8 cm.

b Three sides of a triangle are x, $x + 2$ and 10 cm.

x is a whole number.

What is the smallest value x can take?

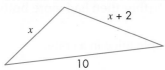

5 Five cards have inequalities and equations marked on them.

$x > 0$ $x < 3$ $x \geqslant 4$ $x = 2$ $x = 6$

The cards are shuffled and then turned over, one at a time.

If two consecutive cards have any numbers in common, then a point is scored.

If they do not have any numbers in common, then a point is deducted.

a The first two cards below score –1 because $x = 6$ and $x < 3$ have no numbers in common.

Explain why the total for this combination scores 0.

$x = 6$ $x < 3$ $x > 0$ $x = 2$ $x \geqslant 4$

b What does this combination score?

$x > 0$ $x = 6$ $x \geqslant 4$ $x = 2$ $x < 3$

c Arrange the cards to give a maximum score of 4.

6 Solve the following linear inequalities.

a $3y - 12 \leqslant y - 4$ **b** $2x + 3 \geqslant x + 1$ **c** $2(4x - 1) \leqslant 3(x + 4)$

d $\dfrac{x - 3}{5} > 7$ **e** $\dfrac{2x + 5}{3} < 6$ **f** $\dfrac{5y + 3}{5} \leqslant 2$

7 Solve the following linear inequalities.

a $7 < 2x + 1 < 13$ **b** $5 < 3x - 1 < 14$ **c** $-1 < 5x + 4 \leqslant 19$

d $1 \leqslant 4x - 3 < 13$ **e** $11 \leqslant 3x + 5 < 17$ **f** $-3 \leqslant 2x - 3 \leqslant 7$

8 Write the integers for each part of question **7** using set notation.

 9 Meg bought seven crates of pineapple juice and Arthur bought four crates of pineapple juice.

Each crate contained the same number of bottles of pineapple juice.

When Meg gave ten bottles of juice to Arthur, Arthur then had more bottles of juice than Meg.

Find the maximum number of bottles of pineapple juice in a crate.

The number line

You can show the solution to a linear inequality on a number line using the following conventions.

The solid circle means that the value is included.

The open circle means that the value is not included.

A strict inequality does not include the boundary point but an inclusive inequality does include the boundary point.

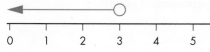

represents $x < 3$

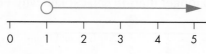

represents $x > 1$

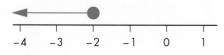

represents $x \leqslant -2$

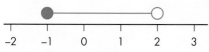

represents $x \geqslant 4$

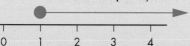

represents $-1 \leqslant x < 2$

The last example is a 'between' inequality. It can be written as $x \geqslant -1$ and $x < 2$, but the notation $-1 \leqslant x < 2$ is neater.

Example 14

a Write down the inequality shown by this diagram.

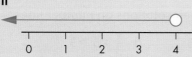

b i Solve the inequality $2x + 3 < 11$.

ii Mark the solution on a number line.

c Write down the integers that satisfy both the inequalities in **a** and **b**.

a The inequality shown is $x \geqslant 1$.

b i $2x + 3 < 11$

$\Rightarrow 2x < 8$

$\Rightarrow x < 4$

ii

c The integers that satisfy both inequalities are 1, 2 and 3.

Example 15

A rectangle has sides of x cm and $(x - 2)$ cm.

If its perimeter is no longer than 16 cm, explain why x can be represented like this:

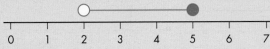

Set up an inequality: $\qquad x + x + x - 2 + x - 2 \leqslant 16$

Simplify: $\qquad\qquad\qquad\quad 4x - 4 \leqslant 16$

Add 4 to both sides: $\qquad\qquad 4x \leqslant 20$

Divide by 4: $\qquad\qquad\qquad\quad x \leqslant 5$

Also, since $(x - 2)$ cm is the length of one side of the rectangle, $x - 2 > 0$.

So $x > 2$.

Putting these inequalities together: $\qquad 2 < x \leqslant 5$

This is the inequality represented on the number line.

Exercise 15I

1 Write down the inequality that is represented by each diagram below.

a

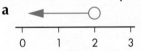

b

c

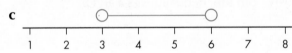

2 Draw diagrams to illustrate these inequalities.

a $x < 5$ **b** $x \geqslant -1$ **c** $2 < x \leqslant 5$ **d** $-1 \leqslant x \leqslant 3$

3 Solve the following inequalities and illustrate their solutions on number lines.

a $2(4x + 3) < 18$ **b** $\frac{x}{2} + 3 \leqslant 2$ **c** $\frac{x}{5} - 2 > 8$ **d** $\frac{x}{3} + 5 \geqslant 3$

(PS) **4** Max went to the supermarket with £1.20. He bought three apples costing x pence each and a chocolate bar costing 54p. When he got to the till, he found he didn't have enough money.

Max took one of the apples back and paid for two apples and the chocolate bar. He counted his change and found he had enough money to buy a 16p sweet.

a Explain why $3x + 54 > 120$ and solve the inequality.

b Explain why $2x + 54 \leqslant 104$ and solve the inequality.

c Show the solution to both of these inequalities on a number line.

d If the price is an integer, what possible prices could the apple be?

5 On copies of the number lines below, draw two inequalities so that only the integers {−1, 0, 1, 2} are common to both inequalities.

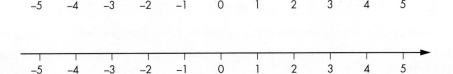

 6 What numbers are being described?

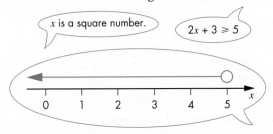

x is a square number.

$2x + 3 \geqslant 5$

 7 A square has sides of $(35 − 7x)$ cm. If its perimeter is at most 84 cm, show that x can be represented by the diagram below.

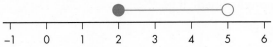

8 Solve the following inequalities and illustrate their solutions on number lines.

a $\dfrac{2x + 5}{3} > 3$ **b** $\dfrac{3x + 4}{2} \geqslant 11$ **c** $\dfrac{2x + 8}{3} \leqslant 2$ **d** $\dfrac{2x − 1}{3} \geqslant −3$

15.7 Graphical inequalities

This section will show you how to:

- show a graphical inequality
- find regions that satisfy more than one graphical inequality.

Key terms	
boundary	origin
region	

You can plot a linear inequality on a graph. The result is a region that lies on one side or the other of a straight line. You will recognise an inequality by the fact that it looks like an equation but instead of the equals sign it has an inequality sign: $<$, $>$, $\leqslant$ or $\geqslant$.

The following are examples of linear inequalities that can be represented on a graph.

$$y < 3 \qquad x > 7 \qquad −3 \leqslant y < 5 \qquad y \geqslant 2x + 3 \qquad 2x + 3y < 6 \qquad y \leqslant x$$

To draw the graph of an inequality, draw the **boundary** line that defines the inequality. To find this, replace the inequality sign with an equals sign.

When it is a strict inequality ($<$ or $>$), draw the boundary line as a *dashed line* to show that it *is not included* in the range of values. When $\leqslant$ or $\geqslant$ is used to state the inequality, draw the boundary line as a *solid line* to show that the boundary *is included*.

After drawing the boundary line, shade the required **region**.

To check which side of the line the region lies on, choose any point that is not on the boundary line and test it in the inequality. If it satisfies the inequality, that is the side required. If it doesn't, the other side is required.

Work through the six inequalities in the following example to see how to apply the procedure.

Example 16

Show each of the following inequalities on a graph.

a $y \leqslant 3$ **b** $x > 7$ **c** $-3 \leqslant y < 5$

d $y \leqslant 2x + 3$ **e** $2x + 3y < 6$ **f** $y \leqslant x$

a Draw the line $y = 3$. Since the inequality is stated as $\leqslant$, the line is solid.

Test a point that is not on the line. The **origin** is always a good choice if possible, as 0 is easiest to test.

Putting 0 into the inequality gives $0 \leqslant 3$. The inequality is satisfied and so the region containing the origin is the side you want. Shade it in.

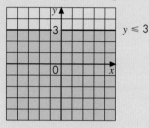

$y \leqslant 3$

b Since the inequality is stated as $>$, the line is *dashed*. Draw the line $x = 7$.

Test a point that is not on the line. Testing the origin gives $0 > 7$. This is not true, so you want the other side of the line from the origin. Shade it in.

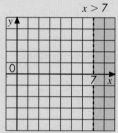

$x > 7$

c Draw the lines $y = -3$ (solid for $\leqslant$) and $y = 5$ (dashed for $<$).

Test a point that is not on either line, say $(0, 0)$. Zero is between -3 and 5, so the required region lies between the lines. Shade it in.

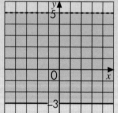

$-3 \leqslant y < 5$

d Draw the line $y = 2x + 3$. Since the inequality is stated as $\leqslant$, the line is solid.

Test a point that is not on the line, such as $(0, 0)$. Putting these x- and y-values in the inequality gives $0 \leqslant 2(0) + 3$, which is true. So the required region includes the origin. Shade it in.

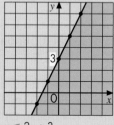

$y \leqslant 2x + 3$

e Draw the line $2x + 3y = 6$. Since the inequality is stated as $<$, the line is dashed.

Test a point that is not on the line, say $(0, 0)$. Is it true that $2(0) + 3(0) < 6$? The answer is yes, so the origin is in the region that you want. Shade it in.

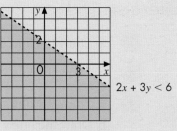

$2x + 3y < 6$

f Draw the line $y = x$. Since the inequality is stated as $\leqslant$, the line is solid.

This time the origin is on the line, so pick any other point, say $(1, 3)$. Putting $x = 1$ and $y = 3$ in the inequality gives $3 \leqslant 1$. This is not true, so the point $(1, 3)$ is not in the region you want.

Shade in the other side to $(1, 3)$.

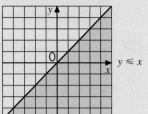

$y \leqslant x$

More than one inequality

Example 17

a On the same grid, shade the regions that represent the following inequalities.

   i $x > 2$ **ii** $y \geqslant x$ **iii** $x + y < 8$

b Are these points in the region that satisfies all three inequalities?

   i $(3, 4)$ **ii** $(2, 6)$ **iii** $(3, 3)$

a

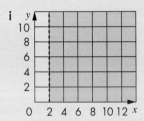

i The region $x > 2$ is shown in diagram **i**.

   The boundary line is $x = 2$ (dashed).

ii The region $y \geqslant x$ is shown in diagram **ii**.

   The boundary line is $y = x$ (solid).

iii The region $x + y < 8$ is shown in diagram **iii**.

   The boundary line is $x + y = 8$ (dashed). The regions have first been drawn separately so that each one is clear. This diagram shows all three regions on the same grid. The green triangular area defines the region that satisfies all three inequalities.

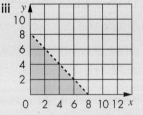

b i The point $(3, 4)$ is clearly within the region that satisfies all three inequalities.

ii The point $(2, 6)$ is on the boundary lines $x = 2$ and $x + y = 8$. As these are dashed lines, they are not included in the region defined by all three inequalities. So, the point $(2, 6)$ is not in this region.

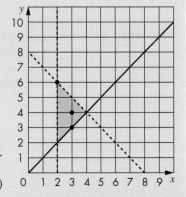

iii The point $(3, 3)$ is on the boundary line $y = x$. As this is a solid line, it is included in the region defined by all three inequalities. So, the point $(3, 3)$ is included in this region.

Exercise 15J

1 **a** Draw the line $x = 2$ (as a solid line). **b** Shade the region defined by $x \leqslant 2$.

2 **a** Draw the line $y = -3$ (as a dashed line). **b** Shade the region defined by $y > -3$.

3 **a** Draw the line $y = -1$ (as a dashed line).
   b Draw the line $y = 4$ (as a solid line) on the *same* grid.
   c Shade the region defined by $-1 < y \leqslant 4$.

4 **a** On the same grid, draw the regions defined by these inequalities.
   i $-3 \leqslant x \leqslant 6$ **ii** $-4 < y \leqslant 5$
   b Are the following points in the region defined by both inequalities?
   i $(2, 2)$ **ii** $(1, 5)$ **iii** $(-2, -4)$

> **Hints and tips** Always make it clear which region you are labelling or shading.

5 **a** Draw the line $y = 2x - 1$ (as a dashed line).
   b Shade the region defined by $y < 2x - 1$.

6 On separate axes, shade the region defined by each inequality.
   a $3x - 4y \leqslant 12$ **b** $y \geqslant \frac{1}{2}x + 3$ **c** $y < -3$

7 **a** Draw the line $y = 3x - 4$ (as a solid line).
   b Draw the line $x + y = 10$ (as a solid line) on the same diagram.
   c Shade the diagram to show the region defined by both $y \geqslant 3x - 4$ and $x + y \leqslant 10$.
   d Are the following points in the region defined by both inequalities?
   i $(2, 1)$ **ii** $(2, 2)$ **iii** $(2, 3)$

8 **a** Draw the line $y = x$ (as a solid line).
   b Draw the line $2x + 5y = 10$ (as a solid line) on the same diagram.
   c Draw the line $2x + y = 6$ (as a dashed line) on the same diagram.
   d Shade the diagram to show the region defined by $y \geqslant x$, $2x + 5y \geqslant 10$ and $2x + y < 6$.
   e Are the following points in the region defined by these inequalities?
   i $(1, 1)$ **ii** $(2, 2)$ **iii** $(1, 3)$

9 **a** On the same grid, draw the regions defined by the following inequalities.
   i $y > x - 3$ **ii** $3y + 4x \leqslant 24$ **iii** $x \geqslant 2$
   b Are the following points in the region defined by all three inequalities?
   i $(1, 1)$ **ii** $(2, 2)$ **iii** $(3, 3)$ **iv** $(4, 4)$

(MR) **10** The graph shows three points (1, 2), (1, 3) and (2, 3).

Write down three inequalities that between them surround these three grid intersection points and no others.

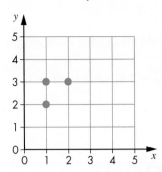

(MR) **11** If $x + y > 40$, which of the following may be true (M), must be false (F) or must be true (T)?

a $x > 40$ **b** $x + y \leqslant 20$ **c** $x - y = 10$

d $x \leqslant 5$ **e** $x + y = 40$ **f** $y > 40 - x$

g $y = 2x$ **h** $x + y \geqslant 39$

(CM) **12** Explain how you would find which side of the line represents the inequality $y < x + 2$.

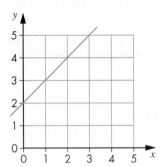

(PS) **13** The region marked R is the overlap of the inequalities:

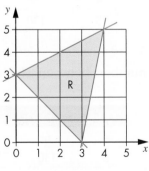

$x + y \geqslant 3$ $y \leqslant \frac{1}{2}x + 3$ $y \geqslant 5x - 15$

a For which point in the region R is the value of the expression $2x - y$ the greatest?

b For which point in the region R is the value of the expression $x - 3y$ the smallest?

14 Varsha is making cakes for a charity cake sale. She has 1800 g of flour and 22 eggs.

She has the recipes for lemon cakes and ginger cakes.

Each lemon cake requires 150 g of flour and 1 egg.

Each ginger cake requires 90 g of flour and 2 eggs.

The charity will receive £3.50 for each lemon cake sold and £5 for each ginger cake sold.

What is the maximum amount of money that Varsha will be able to raise for the charity?

15.8 Trial and improvement

This section will show you how to:

- estimate the answers to some questions that do not have exact solutions, using the method of trial and improvement.

Key term

trial and improvement

Certain equations cannot be solved exactly. However, you can find a close enough solution to these equations by the **trial-and-improvement** method. (Sometimes this is wrongly called the trial-and-error method.)

This method involves trying different values in the equation to take it closer and closer to the 'true' solution. Continue this step-by-step process until you find a value that gives a solution close enough to the accuracy required.

The trial-and-improvement method is used by computer programmes to solve equations.

Solve the equation $x^3 + x = 105$, giving the solution correct to one decimal place.

Step 1: To start, you must find the two consecutive whole numbers that x lies between. You do this by intelligent guessing.

Try $x = 4$: $64 + 4 = 68$ Too low – next trial needs to be larger

Try $x = 5$: $125 + 5 = 130$ Too high

Guess	$x^3 + x$	Comment
4	68	Too low
5	130	Too high

So now you know that the solution lies between $x = 4$ and $x = 5$.

Step 2: Next you must find the two consecutive 1-decimal-place numbers between which x lies. Try 4.5, which is halfway between 4 and 5.

$x = 4.5$ → $91.125 + 4.5 = 95.625$ Too small

Now attempt to improve this:

$x = 4.6$ → $97.336 + 4.6 = 101.936$ Still too small

$x = 4.7$ → 108.523 Too high

So the solution is between 4.6 and 4.7.

Guess	$x^3 + x$	Comment
4	68	Too low
5	130	Too high
4.5	95.625	Too low
4.6	101.936	Too low
4.7	108.523	Too high

It looks as though 4.7 is closer but there is a very important final step.

Step 3: Finally, test the value that is halfway between the two 1-decimal-place values.

$x = 4.65 \rightarrow 105.194\,625$

This means that 4.6 is nearer the actual solution than 4.7.

Never assume that the 1-decimal-place number that gives the closest value to the solution is the answer.

The approximate answer is $x = 4.6$ to 1 decimal place.

Guess	$x^3 + x$	Comment
4	68	Too low
5	130	Too high
4.5	95.625	Too low
4.6	101.936	Too low
4.7	108.523	Too high
4.65	105.194 625	Too high

In Chapter 24 you will meet iteration, which is another way of solving equations like these and does not require guesswork.

Example 18

Brendan says that one answer for the equation $5x^2 - x^3 = 14$ is 4.2 correct to 1 decimal place. Show that Brendan is correct.

x	$5x^2 - x^3$	Comment
4.2	$5 \times 4.2^2 - 4.2^3 = 14.112$	Too high
4.15	$5 \times 4.15^2 - 4.15^3 = 14.639125$	Too high
4.25	$5 \times 4.15^2 - 4.15^3 = 13.546875$	Too low

Since the answer lies between 4.2 and 4.25, it will round to 4.2 when rounded correct to 1 decimal place. So Brendan is correct.

Example 19

A cuboid has sides of x cm, $(x + 1)$ cm and $(x - 2)$ cm. Its volume is 300 cm³.

Find the value of x correct to 1 decimal place.

Set up an equation: $x(x + 1)(x - 2) = 300$

Expand the brackets: $x^3 - x^2 - 2x = 300$

Guess	$x^3 - x^2 - 2x$	Comment
7	280	Too low
8	432	Too high
7.5	350.625	Too high
7.2	307.008	Too high
7.1	293.301	Too low
7.15	300.103 375	Too high

This means that 7.1 is nearer the actual solution than 7.2.

The approximate answer is $x = 7.1$ to 1 decimal place.

1. Find the two consecutive whole numbers between which the solution to each of the following equations lies.

   a $x^2 + x = 24$ **b** $x^3 + 2x = 80$ **c** $x^3 - x = 20$

2. Copy and complete the table by using trial and improvement to find an approximate solution to this equation. $x^3 + 2x = 50$

   Give your answer correct to 1 decimal place.

Guess	$x^3 + 2x$	Comment
3	33	Too low
4	72	Too high

3. **a** Use trial and improvement to find an approximate solution to this equation. $x^3 - 3x = 40$

   Use a first guess of 4. Give your answer correct to 1 decimal place.

   b Find a solution to each of the following equations, correct to 1 decimal place.

      i $2x^3 + 3x = 35$ **ii** $3x^3 - 4x = 52$ **iii** $2x^3 + 5x = 79$

   c Use trial and improvement to find a solution to the equation $x^2 + x = 40$.

   > **Hints and tips**   Set up tables to show your working. This makes it easier for you to show the method and follow your process.

CM 4. Use trial and improvement to show that 2.53 is a solution of the equation $2x^3 + x = 35$ correct to 2 decimal places.

 5. Use trial and improvement to find an exact solution to $4x^2 + 2x = 12$.

6. Anisa is using trial and improvement to solve the equation $3x^3 + 2x = 900$, correct to 1 decimal place.

   Complete the gaps in the table.

Guess	$3x^3 + 2x$	Comment
	660	
	1043	
	836.875	
	956.896	
	915.689	
	875.688	
	895.538875	

PS 7. A rectangle has an area of 100 cm². Its length is 5 cm longer than its width.

   a Show that, if x represents the width, $x^2 + 5x = 100$.

   b Find, correct to 1 decimal place, the dimensions of the rectangle.

(PS) **8** Rob is designing a juice carton to hold $\frac{1}{2}$ litre (500 cm³).

He wants the sides of the base in the ratio 1 : 2.

He wants the height to be 8 cm more than the shorter side of the base.

Use trial and improvement to find the dimensions of the carton.

> **Hints and tips** Call the length of the side with 'ratio 1', x. Write down the other two sides in terms of x and then write down an equation for the volume = 500.

(EV) **9** Steph and Lilly are solving the equation $x^3 - 2x^2 = 251$ by trial and improvement.

Steph's solution finishes as follows:

Guess	$x^3 - 2x^2$	Comment
7.0	245	Too low
7.1	257.091	Too high
7.05	250.9976	Too low

Answer is 7.1 correct to 1 decimal place.

Lilly's solution finishes as follows:

Guess	$x^3 - 2x^2$	Comment
7.0	245	Too low
7.1	257.091	Too high

$251 - 245 = 6$

$257.091 - 251 = 6.091$

Since 245 is closer, answer is 7.0 correct to 1 decimal place.

a Who is correct? Explain your answer.

b Evaluate each student's approach.

(CM) **10** A cube of side x cm has a square hole of side $\frac{x}{2}$ and depth 8 cm cut from it.

The volume of the remaining solid is 1500 cm³.

a Explain why $x^3 - 2x^2 = 1500$.

b Use trial and improvement to find the value of x to 1 decimal place.

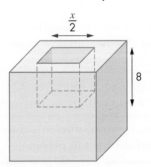

> **Hints and tips** Work out the volume of the cube and the hole and subtract them. The resulting expression is the volume of 1500.

(PS) **11** Two numbers a and b are such that $ab = 20$ and $a + b = 10$.

Use trial and improvement to find the two numbers to 2 decimal places.

Worked exemplars

 1 A bookshelf holds P paperback and H hardback books. The bookshelf can hold a total of 400 books. Explain which of the following may be true.

a $P + H < 300$

b $P \geqslant H$

c $P + H > 500$

This is a question on communicating mathematics so you need to make sure you communicate information accurately and articulately.	
a The first inequality ($P + H < 300$) could be true. The bookshelf doesn't have to be full.	Although it is important to state correctly whether or not a given statement is true, the emphasis is on the quality of your explanation.
b The second inequality ($P \geqslant H$) could be true. There could be more paperbacks than hardbacks.	
c The third inequality ($P + H > 500$) cannot be true. There can only be a maximum of 400 books.	

 2 Nicky did a 22 km hill race. She ran x km to the top of the hill at an average speed of 8 km/h. She then ran y km down the hill at an average speed of 15 km/h. She finished the race in 2 hours and 10 minutes.

Find out how long it took Nicky to get to the top of the hill.

This is a problem-solving question so you need to make connections between different part of mathematics (in this case speed, distance and time and simultaneous equations) and show your strategy clearly.	
$x + y = 22$ (1) $\frac{x}{8} + \frac{y}{15} = 2\frac{1}{6}$ (2)	First, set up two simultaneous equations using the information given.
$15x + 8y = 260$ (3)	Multiply equation (2) by 120 (the lowest common multiple of 15, 8 and 6).
$8x + 8y = 176$ (4) (3) – (4) $7x = 84$	Balance the coefficients (multiply (1) by 8) and subtract to eliminate y.
$x = 12$	Solve the equation.
Time = $12 \div 8$ = 1 hour 30 minutes	Work out the time taken, using distance ÷ speed.

3 Given that $3^{3x + 4y} = 9$ and $3^{4x + 5y} = 27$, show that $3^{x + 2y} = 1$.

This is a problem-solving question connecting two different parts of mathematics (in this case, indices and simultaneous equations) so you will need to show every step of your strategy.	
$3^{3x + 4y} = 3^2$ $3^{4x + 5y} = 3^3$	Deduce that 9 and 27 also need to be written as powers of 3.
$3x + 4y = 2$ $4x + 5y = 3$	Remove the base numbers and write the indices as simultaneous equations.
$12x + 16y = 8$ (1) $12x + 15y = 9$ (2) (1) − (2) $y = -1$	Balance coefficients (could balance x or y) and subtract to eliminate one variable.
$3x + 4(-1) = 2$ $3x - 4 = 2$ $3x = 6$ $x = 2$	Find x (or y) by substituting.
$3^{x + 2y} = 3^{2 + 2(-1)} = 3^{2 - 2} = 3^0$ $3^0 = 1$	Complete the proof by showing that $3^{x + 2y} = 1$.

Ready to progress?

I can solve linear equations containing brackets and fractions.

I can solve linear equations where the variable appears on both sides.
I can set up and solve linear equations from practical and real-life situations.
I can solve inequalities such as $3x + 2 < 5$ and represent the solution on a number line.
I can solve linear simultaneous equations by balancing, substituting and elimination.
I can use trial and improvement to solve non-linear equations.

I can represent a region that satisfies a linear inequality graphically, and solve more complex linear inequalities.
I can represent a region that simultaneously satisfies more than one linear inequality graphically.

Review questions

PS **1** A carpet costs £12.75 per square metre.

The shop charges £35 for fitting. The final bill was £137.

How many square metres of carpet were fitted?

PS **2** A boy is Y years old. His father is 25 years older than he is. The sum of their ages is 31. How old is the boy?

PS **3** A rectangular room is 3 m longer than it is wide. The perimeter is 16 m.

Carpet costs £9.00 per square metre.

Show that it will cost just under £125 to carpet the room.

PS **4** This diagram shows the traffic flow through a one-way system in a town centre.

Cars enter at A and at each junction the fractions show the proportion of cars that take each route.

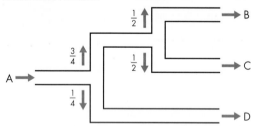

a x cars enter at A. How many come out of each of the exits, B, C and D?

b If 300 cars exit at B, set up and solve an equation to find how many cars entered at A.

c If 500 cars exit at D, set up and solve an equation to find how many exit at B.

CM **5** A teacher asked his class to find three angles of a triangle that were consecutive even numbers.

Tammy wrote: $x + x + 2 + x + 4 = 180$

$$3x + 6 = 180$$
$$3x = 174$$
$$x = 58$$

So the angles are 58°, 60° and 62°.

The teacher then asked the class to find four angles of a quadrilateral that are consecutive even numbers.

Can this be done? Explain your answer.

PS **6** My mother-in-law uses this formula to cook a turkey: $T = a + bW$

where T is the cooking time (minutes), W is the mass of the turkey (kg) and a and b are constants. She says it takes 4 hours 30 minutes to cook a 12 kg turkey, and 3 hours 10 minutes to cook an 8 kg turkey. How long will it take to cook a 5 kg turkey?

7 $-5 < x \leqslant 8$

x is an integer.

Write down all the possible values of x.

8 **a** Solve the equation $\dfrac{5x + 9}{4} = 18 - x$.

b Solve the inequality $\dfrac{5x + 9}{4} < 18 - x$ and represent the answer on a number line.

9 **a** Use trial and improvement to solve the equation $7(x - 2) = 30$, correct to 1 decimal place.

EV **b** Describe a more efficient method for solving this equation.

10 **a** Solve these inequalities.

 i $-11 < 2x - 5 < -3$ **ii** $-3 < \dfrac{x - 4}{2} < 0$ **iii** $21 < 3(x + 8) < 30$

 b Match two of your answers with the two representations shown below, then draw a number line to represent the other solution.

 a
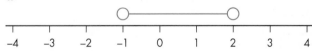

 b

11 Use trial and improvement to find the solution of the equation $x^3 + 2x = 27$, giving the answer correct to 2 decimal places. Show all your working.

PS **12** Two members of the same church went to the same shop to buy material to make Christingles. One bought 200 oranges and 220 candles at a cost of £65.60. The other bought 210 oranges and 200 candles at a cost of £63.30. They only needed 200 of each. How much should it have cost them?

13 When you book Bingham Hall for a conference you pay a fixed booking fee plus a charge for each delegate. Jathika booked a conference for 65 delegates and was charged £192.50. Jasmine booked a conference for 40 delegates and was charged £180. James wants to book for 70 delegates. How much will he be charged?

14 **a** Solve the simultaneous equations by balancing the coefficients of x and subtracting.

$992x + 8y = 3992$

$8x + 992y = 3008$

b i Add together the equations $992x + 8y = 3992$ and $8x + 992y = 3008$. Divide the resulting equation by its common factor.

ii Subtract the equation $8x + 992y = 3008$ from the equation $992x + 8y = 3992$. Divide the resulting equation by its common factor.

iii Show that the answers you get when you solve the simultaneous equations you obtained from parts **i** and **ii** are the same as those you obtained in **a**.

c Solve these simultaneous equations without using a calculator:

$4576a + 10\,848b = 95\,424$

$5424a + 9152b = 94\,576$

15 The racetrack shown is to be made with semicircles at each end, with an inner perimeter of 300 m and an outer perimeter of 320 m. How wide is the track?

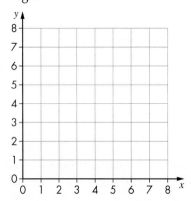

16 The region R satisfies the inequalities $x < 6$, $y \leqslant 5$, $x + y > 8$.

a On a copy of the grid below, draw straight lines and use shading to show the region R.

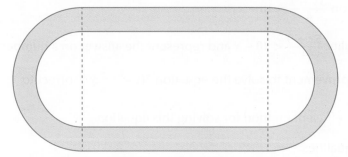

b Find the area of the region R.

c The region S satisfies the inequalities $x < 6$, $y < 5$ and $x + y < 8$.

Explain why you cannot find the area of the region S.

17 a is an integer that satisfies the inequality $\dfrac{50}{a^2} > 2$.

List all the possible values of a.

(PS) 18 Find the inequalities that define each of the shaded regions.

a

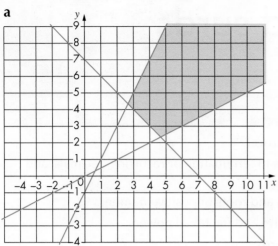

b

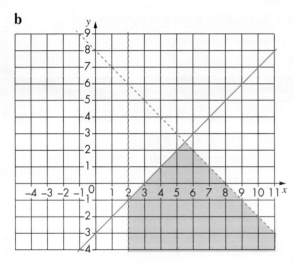

16 Number: Counting, accuracy, powers and surds

This chapter is going to show you:

- how to work out a reciprocal
- how to convert fractions to terminating or recurring decimals, and vice versa
- how to estimate powers and roots of positive numbers
- how to work with negative and fractional powers
- how to calculate with surds
- how to work out the error interval for rounded numbers
- how to use limits of accuracy in calculations
- how to use the product rule for counting.

You should already know:

- how to round numbers to the nearest 10, 100 or 1000
- how to round numbers to a given number of decimal places (dp)
- how to round numbers to a given number of significant figures (sf)
- squares of integers up to $15 \times 15 = 225$ and corresponding roots
- cubes of integers 1, 2, 3, 4, 5 and 10 and corresponding roots
- what indices, square roots and cube roots are
- how to divide by a fraction
- what terminating and recurring fractions are.

About this chapter

In everyday life most numbers that you use are whole numbers, simple fractions or decimal values written with, at most, three decimal places. Nobody could possibly cut a plank of wood to a length of 163.2647 cm. You may buy a 'quarter of a kilogram of potatoes', but you would never ask for 'five-elevenths of a kilogram of potatoes'. In daily life, you round numbers to something sensible.

However, engineers and scientists need to work to a much greater accuracy. That is why the area of a circle with a radius of 10 cm has an approximate area of 314 cm^2 but an accurate area of 100π cm^2. This chapter will show you some ways of writing numbers accurately and how to manipulate numbers written this way.

16.1 Rational numbers, reciprocals, terminating and recurring decimals

This section will show you how to:

- recognise rational numbers, reciprocals, terminating decimals and recurring decimals
- convert terminal decimals to fractions
- convert fractions to recurring decimals
- find reciprocals of numbers or fractions.

Key terms

rational number

recurring decimal

terminating decimal

Rational numbers

A **rational number** is a number that can be written as a fraction, for example, $\frac{1}{4}$ or $\frac{10}{3}$.

When a fraction is converted to a decimal it will either be:

- a **terminating decimal** or
- a **recurring decimal**.

A terminating decimal has a finite number of digits. For example, $\frac{1}{4} = 0.25$, $\frac{1}{8} = 0.125$.

A recurring decimal has a digit, or block of digits, that repeats. For example, $\frac{1}{3} = 0.3333...$, $\frac{2}{11} = 0.181\,818...$

You can write recurring digits by putting a dot over the first and last digit of the group that repeats.

0.3333... becomes $0.\dot{3}$ 0.181 818... becomes $0.\dot{1}\dot{8}$ 0.123 123 123... becomes $0.\dot{1}2\dot{3}$

0.583 33... becomes $0.58\dot{3}$ 0.618 181 8... becomes $0.6\dot{1}\dot{8}$ 0.412 312 312 3... becomes $0.4\dot{1}2\dot{3}$

Converting fractions into decimals

A fraction will convert to a terminating decimal or a recurring decimal. You may already know that $\frac{1}{3} = 0.333... = 0.\dot{3}$. This means that the 3s go on forever and the decimal never ends.

To convert a fraction, you divide the numerator by the denominator. If the denominator only has 2 and/or 5 in its prime factorisation, then the decimal will terminate; otherwise it will recur. You can use a calculator to divide the numerator by the denominator if you need to. Note that calculators round the last digit so it may not appear as a true recurring decimal in the display.

Use a calculator to check these terminating decimals.

$\frac{9}{16} = 0.5625$ $\frac{7}{40} = 0.175$ $\frac{96}{125} = 0.768$

Use a calculator to check these recurring decimals.

$\frac{2}{11} = 0.181\,818... = 0.\dot{1}\dot{8}$ $\frac{4}{15} = 0.2666... = 0.2\dot{6}$ $\frac{8}{13} = 0.615\,384\,615\,384\,6... = 0.\dot{6}15\,38\dot{4}$

Converting terminal decimals into fractions

To convert a terminating decimal to a fraction, take the decimal part of the number as the numerator. Then the denominator is 10, 100, 1000, … depending on the number of decimal places. Because a terminating decimal has a specific number of decimal places, you can use place value to work out exactly where the numerator and the denominator end. For example:

$$0.7 = \frac{7}{10} \qquad 0.23 = \frac{23}{100} \qquad\qquad 0.045 = \frac{45}{1000}$$

$$2.34 = \frac{234}{100} \qquad\qquad\qquad = \frac{9}{200}$$

$$= \frac{117}{50} \qquad\qquad 0.625 = \frac{625}{1000}$$

$$= 2\frac{17}{50} \qquad\qquad\qquad = \frac{5}{8}$$

Converting recurring decimals into fractions

You need to use an algebraic method to convert a recurring decimal to a fraction, as shown in the next two examples.

Example 1

Convert $0.\dot{7}$ to a fraction.

Let x be the fraction. Then:

$$x = 0.777\ 777\ 777\ldots \qquad (1)$$

Multiply (1) by 10: $\quad 10x = 7.777\ 777\ 777\ldots \qquad (2)$

Subtract (2) – (1): $\quad\ \ 9x = 7$

$$\Rightarrow x = \frac{7}{9}$$

Example 2

Convert $0.\dot{5}6\dot{4}$ to a fraction.

Let x be the fraction. Then:

$$x = 0.564\ 564\ 564\ldots \qquad (1)$$

Multiply (1) by 1000: $\quad 1000x = 564.564\ 564\ 564\ldots \qquad (2)$

Subtract (2) – (1): $\quad 999x = 564$

$$\Rightarrow x = \frac{564}{999} = \frac{188}{333}$$

As a general rule, multiply by 10 if one digit recurs, multiply by 100 if two digits recur, multiply by 1000 if three digits recur, and so on.

Finding reciprocals of numbers or fractions

You know that the reciprocal of any number is 1 divided by the number, so:

- the reciprocal of 2 is $1 \div 2 = \frac{1}{2} = 0.5$
- the reciprocal of 0.25 is $1 \div 0.25 = 4$.

You can find the reciprocal of a fraction by inverting it. For example:

- the reciprocal of $\frac{2}{3}$ is $\frac{3}{2}$
- the reciprocal of $\frac{7}{4}$ is $\frac{4}{7}$.

Exercise 16A

1 Work out each fraction as a terminating decimal or recurring decimal, as appropriate.

a $\frac{1}{2}$ **b** $\frac{1}{3}$ **c** $\frac{1}{4}$ **d** $\frac{1}{5}$ **e** $\frac{1}{6}$

f $\frac{1}{7}$ **g** $\frac{1}{8}$ **h** $\frac{1}{9}$ **i** $\frac{1}{10}$ **j** $\frac{1}{13}$

2 There are several patterns to be found in recurring decimals. For example:

$\frac{1}{7} = 0.142\,857\,142\,857\,142\,857\,142\,857\ldots$

$\frac{2}{7} = 0.285\,714\,285\,714\,285\,714\,285\,714\ldots$

$\frac{3}{7} = 0.428\,571\,428\,571\,428\,571\,428\,571\ldots$

a Write down the decimals for $\frac{4}{7}, \frac{5}{7}, \frac{6}{7}$ to 24 decimal places.

b What do you notice?

3 Work out the ninths, $\frac{1}{9}, \frac{2}{9}, \frac{3}{9}$ and so on, up to $\frac{8}{9}$, as recurring decimals.
Describe any patterns that you notice.

4 Work out the elevenths, $\frac{1}{11}, \frac{2}{11}, \frac{3}{11}$ and so on, up to $\frac{10}{11}$, as recurring decimals.
Describe any patterns that you notice.

5 Write each fraction as a decimal. Use your results to write the list in order of size, smallest first.

$\frac{4}{9}$ $\frac{5}{11}$ $\frac{3}{7}$ $\frac{9}{22}$ $\frac{16}{37}$ $\frac{6}{13}$

6 Convert each terminating decimal to a fraction.

a 0.125   **b** 0.34   **c** 0.725   **d** 0.3125

e 0.89   **f** 0.05   **g** 2.35   **h** 0.218 75

7 Use a calculator to work out the reciprocal of each number in decimal form.

a 12   **b** 16   **c** 20   **d** 25   **e** 50

8 Write down the reciprocal of each fraction.

a $\frac{3}{4}$ **b** $\frac{5}{6}$ **c** $\frac{2}{5}$

d $\frac{7}{10}$ **e** $\frac{11}{20}$ **f** $\frac{4}{15}$

9 **a** Write the fractions and their reciprocals from question **8** as terminating decimals or recurring decimals as appropriate.

b Is it always true that a terminating decimal has a reciprocal that is a recurring decimal?

10 Explain why zero has no reciprocal.

11 **a** Work out the reciprocal of the reciprocal of 10.

b Work out the reciprocal of the reciprocal of 2.

c What do you notice?

(EV) 12 x and y are two positive numbers. Given that x is less than y, which statement is true?

A: The reciprocal of x is less than the reciprocal of y.

B: The reciprocal of x is greater than the reciprocal of y.

C: It is impossible to tell.

Give an example to support your answer.

(EV) 13 Explain why a number multiplied by its reciprocal is equal to 1. Use examples to show that this is true for negative numbers.

14 $x = 0.242\ 424\ldots$

a What is $100x$?

b By subtracting the original value from your answer to part **a**, work out the value of $99x$.

c What is x as a fraction?

15 Convert each recurring decimal to a fraction.

a $0.\dot{8}$ **b** $0.\dot{3}\dot{4}$ **c** $0.\dot{4}\dot{5}$ **d** $0.5\dot{6}\dot{7}$ **e** $0.\dot{4}$ **f** $0.0\dot{4}$

g $0.1\dot{4}$ **h** $0.0\dot{4}\dot{5}$ **i** $2.\dot{7}$ **j** $7.6\dot{3}$ **k** $3.\dot{3}$ **l** $2.0\dot{6}$

(EV) 16 a $\frac{1}{7}$ is a recurring decimal. $(\frac{1}{7})^2 = \frac{1}{49}$ is also a recurring decimal.

Is it true that when you square any fraction that is a recurring decimal, the answer is another fraction that is also a recurring decimal? Try this with at least four numerical examples before you make a decision.

b $\frac{1}{4}$ is a terminating decimal. $(\frac{1}{4})^2 = \frac{1}{16}$ is also a terminating decimal.

Is it true that when you square any fraction that is a terminating decimal, you get another fraction that is also a terminating decimal? Try this with at least four numerical examples before you make a decision.

c What type of fraction do you get when you multiply a fraction that gives a recurring decimal by another fraction that gives a terminating decimal? Try this with at least four numerical examples before you make a decision.

(CM) 17 a Convert the recurring decimal $0.\dot{9}$ to a fraction.

b Prove that $0.4\dot{9}$ is equal to 0.5.

16.2 Estimating powers and roots

This section will show you:

- how to estimate powers and roots of any given positive number.

You know how to estimate the value of a calculation by rounding the numbers to one significant figure. For example:

$$\frac{112 \times 39}{78 - 57} \approx \frac{100 \times 40}{80 - 60}$$

$$= \frac{100 \times \overset{2}{\cancel{40}}}{\underset{1}{\cancel{20}}}$$

$$= 200$$

You can apply the same method to estimate powers and roots but, as powers above three usually lead to very large numbers, you may need to adjust your answer depending on whether the estimate is above or below the real answer.

You should know that the square root of 225 is 15, but what about the square root of 2250? A common error is to give the answer as 150, but it is actually about 47.4 – check on your calculator. The square root of 22 500 is 150, as 22 500 is 225 × 10 × 10, so the square root is 15 × 10.

You will never need to estimate a root very accurately but you should be able to find the integers between which a root lies.

These two number lines show some square roots and cube roots.

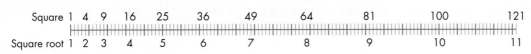

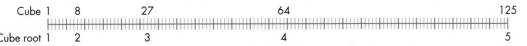

As you can see the gap between the cube roots increases rapidly.

Example 3

a Write these down. **i** $\sqrt{225}$ **ii** $\sqrt[3]{27}$

b Work these out. **i** 2^8 **ii** $\sqrt[3]{2^5 + 2^5}$

a **i** You should know the squares up to 15 × 15 and the corresponding roots.

$\sqrt{225} = 15$

ii You should know the cubes of 1, 2, 3, 4, 5 and 10 and the corresponding roots.

$\sqrt[3]{27} = 3$

b **i** To work out powers of 2, start with 2 and double each time: 2, 4, 8, 16, 32, 64, 128, 256. $2^8 = 256$

ii $2^5 = 32$, so $\sqrt[3]{2^5 + 2^5} = \sqrt[3]{32 + 32}$

$= \sqrt[3]{64}$

$= 4$

Example 4

a Estimate the value of $\sqrt{820\,000}$.

b Estimate the value of 8.2^4.

c Estimate the cube root of 3250.

a Split 820 000 into a product of a number and an even power of 10.

$820\,000 = 82 \times 10\,000$

Therefore $\sqrt{820\,000} = \sqrt{82} \times \sqrt{10\,000}$

$\approx 9.1 \times 100$

$= 910.$

(The actual answer is 905.5 to 4 sf.)

b $8.2^4 = 8.2 \times 8.2 \times 8.2 \times 8.2$

$\approx 8 \times 8 \times 8 \times 8$

$= 64 \times 64$

$\approx 60 \times 70$

$= 4200$

(The actual answer is 4521 to 4 sf.)

Hints and tips Note that one value of 64 was rounded down and the other was rounded up, which gave a better estimate. Sometimes you have to make sensible choices about rounding.

c Write 3250 as 3.25 × 1000. You should know that the cube root of 1000 is 10.

Sketch a number line showing the cube roots of 1 and 8. Estimate that the cube root of 3.25 is about 1.4.

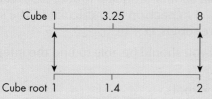

So the answer is 1.4 × 10 = 14. (The actual answer is 14.8 to 3 sf.)

Exercise 16B

1 Write down the answers to these.

    a $\sqrt{196}$ **b** $\sqrt[3]{1\,000\,000}$ **c** $\sqrt[3]{10^2 + 5^2}$ **d** $\sqrt{2 \times 5^3 - 9^2}$

(PS) **2** A square number and two cube numbers have a sum of 60. What are the numbers?

3 Between which two integers does the square root of 180 lie?

4 Between which two integers does the cube root of 200 lie?

5   **a** Estimate the value of each number.

    i $\sqrt{6600}$ **ii** $\sqrt{45}$ **iii** $\sqrt[3]{40}$

    iv 5.8^4 **v** $\sqrt[3]{45\,000}$

  b Use a calculator to check your answers.

16.3 Negative and fractional powers

This section will show you how to:

- apply the rules of powers to negative and fractional powers
- find and use the relationship between negative powers and roots.

You learned about positive powers and the rules of indices in an earlier chapter. How do these rules apply to negative and fractional powers?

A negative power is a convenient way of writing the reciprocal of a number or term.

The reciprocal of the integer 5 is $\frac{1}{5}$. You can write this as 5^{-1}.

In general, the reciprocal of $x^{-a} = \frac{1}{x^a}$.

Look at some more examples.

- $5^{-2} = \frac{1}{5^2}$

- $3^{-1} = \frac{1}{3}$

- $5x^{-2} = \frac{5}{x^2}$

Rewrite each number in the form 2^n.

a 8   **b** $\frac{1}{4}$ **c** -32 **d** $-\frac{1}{64}$

a $8 = 2 \times 2 \times 2 = 2^3$ **b** $\frac{1}{4} = \frac{1}{2^2}$

$= 2^{-2}$

c $-32 = -2^5$ **d** $-\frac{1}{64} = -\frac{1}{2^6}$

$= -2^{-6}$

Exercise 16C

1   Write down each number in fraction form.

    a 5^{-3} **b** 6^{-1} **c** 10^{-5} **d** 3^{-2} **e** 8^{-2}

    f 9^{-1} **g** w^{-2} **h** t^{-1} **i** x^{-m} **j** $4m^{-3}$

> **Hints and tips** One of the most common errors is to assume that a negative index means the answer must be negative. Do not make this mistake.

2   Write down each number in negative index form.

    a $\frac{1}{3^2}$ **b** $\frac{1}{5}$ **c** $\frac{1}{10^3}$ **d** $\frac{1}{m}$ **e** $\frac{1}{t^n}$

> **Hints and tips** If you move a power from top to bottom, or vice versa, the sign changes. Negative power means the reciprocal: it does not mean the answer is negative.

3   Change each expression into an index form of the type shown.

    a All of the form 2^n

      i 16   **ii** $\frac{1}{2}$ **iii** $\frac{1}{16}$ **iv** -8

    b All of the form 10^n

      i 1000   **ii** $\frac{1}{10}$ **iii** $\frac{1}{100}$ **iv** 1 million

    c All of the form 5^n

      i 125   **ii** $\frac{1}{5}$ **iii** $\frac{1}{25}$ **iv** $\frac{1}{625}$

    d All of the form 3^n

      i 9   **ii** $\frac{1}{27}$ **iii** $\frac{1}{81}$ **iv** -243

4 Rewrite each expression in fraction form.

a $5x^{-3}$ **b** $6t^{-1}$ **c** $7m^{-2}$ **d** $4q^{-4}$ **e** $10y^{-5}$

f $\frac{1}{2}x^{-3}$ **g** $\frac{1}{2}m^{-1}$ **h** $\frac{3}{4}t^{-4}$ **i** $\frac{4}{5}y^{-3}$ **j** $\frac{7}{8}x^{-5}$

5 Write each fraction in index form.

a $\frac{7}{x^3}$ **b** $\frac{10}{p}$ **c** $\frac{5}{t^2}$ **d** $\frac{8}{m^5}$ **e** $\frac{3}{y}$

6 Find the value of each number.

a $x = 5$ **i** x^2 **ii** x^{-3} **iii** $4x^{-1}$

b $t = 4$ **i** t^3 **ii** t^{-2} **iii** $5t^{-4}$

c $m = 2$ **i** m^3 **ii** m^{-5} **iii** $9m^{-1}$

d $w = 10$ **i** w^6 **ii** w^{-3} **iii** $25w^{-2}$

(PS) **7** Two different numbers can be written in the form 2^n.

The sum of the numbers is 40.

What is the difference between the numbers?

(MR) **8** x and y are integers.

$x^2 - y^3 = 0$

Work out possible values of x and y.

(MR) **9** You are given that $8^7 = 2\,097\,152$.

Write down the value of 8^{-7}.

(PS) **10** Put the numbers:

x^5 x^{-5} x^0

in order, from smallest to largest, when:

a x is greater than 1   **b** x is between 0 and 1   **c** $x = -10$.

Indices of the form $\frac{1}{n}$

Consider the problem $7^x \times 7^x = 7$. You can write this as:

$7^{(x+x)} = 7$

$7^{2x} = 7^1 \Rightarrow 2x = 1$

$\Rightarrow x = \frac{1}{2}$

If you now substitute $x = \frac{1}{2}$ in the original equation, you can see that:

$7^{\frac{1}{2}} \times 7^{\frac{1}{2}} = 7$

This makes $7^{\frac{1}{2}}$ the same as $\sqrt{7}$.

Similarly, you can show that $7^{\frac{1}{3}}$ is the same as $\sqrt[3]{7}$.

In general, $x^{\frac{1}{n}} = \sqrt[n]{x}$ (nth root of x).

So, in summary:

- the power $\frac{1}{2}$ is the same as the positive square root
- the power $\frac{1}{3}$ is the same as the cube root
- the power $\frac{1}{n}$ is the same as the nth root.

$$49^{\frac{1}{2}} = \sqrt{49} = 7 \qquad 8^{\frac{1}{3}} = \sqrt[3]{8} = 2 \qquad 10\,000^{\frac{1}{4}} = \sqrt[4]{10\,000} = 10 \qquad 36^{-\frac{1}{2}} = \frac{1}{\sqrt{36}} = \frac{1}{6}$$

Exercise 16D

1   Evaluate each number.

    a $25^{\frac{1}{2}}$ **b** $625^{\frac{1}{2}}$ **c** $27^{\frac{1}{3}}$ **d** $125^{\frac{1}{3}}$ **e** $400^{\frac{1}{2}}$

    f $625^{\frac{1}{4}}$ **g** $81^{\frac{1}{4}}$ **h** $100\,000^{\frac{1}{5}}$ **i** $729^{\frac{1}{6}}$ **j** $32^{\frac{1}{5}}$

    k $16^{-\frac{1}{2}}$ **l** $8^{-\frac{1}{3}}$ **m** $81^{-\frac{1}{4}}$ **n** $3125^{-\frac{1}{5}}$ **o** $1\,000\,000^{-\frac{1}{6}}$

2   Evaluate each number.

    a $\left(\dfrac{25}{36}\right)^{\frac{1}{2}}$ **b** $\left(\dfrac{100}{36}\right)^{\frac{1}{2}}$ **c** $\left(\dfrac{64}{81}\right)^{\frac{1}{2}}$ **d** $\left(\dfrac{81}{25}\right)^{\frac{1}{2}}$ **e** $\left(\dfrac{25}{64}\right)^{\frac{1}{2}}$

    f $\left(\dfrac{27}{125}\right)^{\frac{1}{3}}$ **g** $\left(\dfrac{8}{512}\right)^{\frac{1}{3}}$ **h** $\left(\dfrac{1000}{64}\right)^{\frac{1}{3}}$ **i** $\left(\dfrac{64}{125}\right)^{\frac{1}{3}}$ **j** $\left(\dfrac{512}{343}\right)^{\frac{1}{3}}$

3   Use the general rule for raising a power to another power to prove that $x^{\frac{1}{n}}$ is equivalent to $\sqrt[n]{x}$.

(MR)   **4**   Which of these is the odd one out?

    $16^{-\frac{1}{4}} \qquad 64^{-\frac{1}{2}} \qquad 8^{-\frac{1}{3}}$

    Show how you decided.

(CM)   **5**   Imagine that you are a teacher. Write down how you would teach the class that $27^{-\frac{1}{3}}$ is equal to $\frac{1}{3}$.

(PS)   **6**   Find values for x and y (greater than 1) that make this equation work.

    $x^{\frac{1}{2}} = y^{\frac{1}{3}}$

Indices of the form $\frac{a}{b}$

You know that a power that is a unit fraction represents the root equivalent to the denominator; for example, a power of $\frac{1}{4}$ is the fourth root.

$$x^{\frac{1}{n}} = \sqrt[n]{x}$$

What does a power that is not a unit fraction represent? Look carefully at these two examples.

$$t^{\frac{2}{3}} = t^{\frac{1}{3}} \times t^{\frac{1}{3}}$$
$$= (\sqrt[3]{t})^2$$
$$81^{\frac{3}{4}} = (\sqrt[4]{81})^3$$
$$= 3^3$$
$$= 27$$

Example 6

Evaluate each expression. **a** $27^{\frac{2}{3}}$ **b** $16^{-\frac{1}{4}}$ **c** $32^{-\frac{4}{5}}$

Work through problems like these one step at a time.

a $27^{\frac{1}{3}} = 3$ so $27^{\frac{2}{3}} = 3^2$ and $27^{\frac{2}{3}} = 9$.

When you are dealing with a negative index, remember that it represents a reciprocal.

Step 1: Rewrite the calculation as a fraction by dealing with the negative power.

Step 2: Take the root of the base number, given by the denominator of the fraction.

Step 3: Raise the result to the power given by the numerator of the fraction.

Step 4: Write out the answer as a fraction.

b Step 1: $16^{-\frac{1}{4}} = \left(\frac{1}{16}\right)^{\frac{1}{4}}$ Step 2: $16^{\frac{1}{4}} = \sqrt[4]{16} = 2$ Step 3: $2^1 = 2$ Step 4: $16^{-\frac{1}{4}} = \frac{1}{2}$

c Step 1: $32^{-\frac{4}{5}} = \left(\frac{1}{32}\right)^{\frac{4}{5}}$ Step 2: $32^{\frac{1}{5}} = \sqrt[5]{32} = 2$ Step 3: $2^4 = 16$ Step 4: $32^{-\frac{4}{5}} = \frac{1}{16}$

Exercise 16E

1 Evaluate each expression.

  a $32^{\frac{4}{5}}$ **b** $125^{\frac{2}{3}}$ **c** $1296^{\frac{3}{4}}$ **d** $243^{\frac{4}{5}}$

2 Rewrite each number in index form.

  a $\sqrt[3]{t^2}$ **b** $\sqrt[4]{m^3}$ **c** $\sqrt[5]{k^2}$ **d** $\sqrt{x^3}$

3 Evaluate each expression.

  a $8^{\frac{2}{3}}$ **b** $27^{\frac{2}{3}}$ **c** $16^{\frac{3}{2}}$ **d** $625^{\frac{5}{4}}$

4 Evaluate each expression.

  a $25^{-\frac{1}{2}}$ **b** $36^{-\frac{1}{2}}$ **c** $16^{-\frac{1}{4}}$ **d** $81^{-\frac{1}{4}}$

  e $16^{-\frac{1}{2}}$ **f** $8^{-\frac{1}{3}}$ **g** $32^{-\frac{1}{5}}$ **h** $27^{-\frac{1}{3}}$

5 Evaluate each expression.

  a $25^{-\frac{3}{2}}$ **b** $36^{-\frac{3}{2}}$ **c** $16^{-\frac{3}{4}}$ **d** $81^{-\frac{3}{4}}$

  e $64^{-\frac{4}{3}}$ **f** $8^{-\frac{2}{3}}$ **g** $32^{-\frac{2}{5}}$ **h** $27^{-\frac{2}{3}}$

6 Evaluate each expression.

  a $100^{-\frac{5}{2}}$ **b** $144^{-\frac{1}{2}}$ **c** $125^{-\frac{2}{3}}$ **d** $9^{-\frac{3}{2}}$

  e $4^{-\frac{5}{2}}$ **f** $64^{-\frac{5}{6}}$ **g** $27^{-\frac{4}{3}}$ **h** $169^{-\frac{1}{2}}$

(MR) **7** Which of these is the odd one out?

  $16^{-\frac{3}{4}}$ $64^{-\frac{1}{2}}$ $8^{-\frac{2}{3}}$

  Show how you decided.

(CM) **8** Imagine that you are a teacher. Write down how you would teach the class that $27^{-\frac{2}{3}}$ is equal to $\frac{1}{9}$.

(PS) **9** Solve this equation.

  $x^{-\frac{2}{3}} = 3x^{-1}$

16.4 Surds

This section will show you how to:

- simplify surds
- calculate and manipulate surds, including rationalising a denominator.

Key terms

exact value

surd

rationalise

Surds are roots of rational numbers. The square roots of 2, 3, 5, 10 and 15 are written like this.

$$\sqrt{2} \quad \sqrt{3} \quad \sqrt{5} \quad \sqrt{10} \quad \sqrt{15}$$

These are also referred to as **exact values**.

Here are four general rules for simplifying surds. Use numerical values to check that they work.

$$\sqrt{a} \times \sqrt{b} = \sqrt{ab} \qquad C\sqrt{a} \times D\sqrt{b} = CD\sqrt{ab} \qquad \sqrt{a} \div \sqrt{b} = \sqrt{\frac{a}{b}} \qquad C\sqrt{a} \div D\sqrt{b} = \frac{C}{D}\sqrt{\frac{a}{b}}$$

For example:	For example:	For example:	For example:
• $\sqrt{2} \times \sqrt{2} = \sqrt{4}$ $\quad = 2$ • $\sqrt{2} \times \sqrt{3} = \sqrt{6}$ • $\sqrt{2} \times \sqrt{8} = \sqrt{16}$ $\quad = 4$ • $\sqrt{2} \times \sqrt{10} = \sqrt{20}$ $\quad = \sqrt{4 \times 5}$ $\quad = \sqrt{4} \times \sqrt{5}$ $\quad = 2\sqrt{5}$ • $\sqrt{6} \times \sqrt{15} = \sqrt{90}$ $\quad = \sqrt{9} \times \sqrt{10}$ $\quad = 3\sqrt{10}$	• $3\sqrt{5} \times 4\sqrt{3} = 12\sqrt{15}$ • $9\sqrt{2} \times 7\sqrt{8} = 63$ $\quad = 63\sqrt{16}$ $\quad = 63 \times 4$ $\quad = 252$ • $3\sqrt{5} \times 4\sqrt{45} = 12\sqrt{225}$ $\quad = 12 \times 15$ $\quad = 180$	• $\sqrt{50} \div \sqrt{2}$ $\quad = \sqrt{\dfrac{50}{2}}$ $\quad = \sqrt{25}$ $\quad = 5$ • $\sqrt{96} \div \sqrt{4}$ $\quad = \sqrt{\dfrac{96}{4}}$ $\quad = \sqrt{24}$ $\quad = \sqrt{4} \times \sqrt{6}$ $\quad = 2\sqrt{6}$	• $36\sqrt{48} \div 9\sqrt{3} = \dfrac{36}{9}\sqrt{\dfrac{48}{3}}$ $\quad = 4\sqrt{16}$ $\quad = 4 \times 4$ $\quad = 16$ • $15\sqrt{27} \div 5\sqrt{75} = \dfrac{15}{3}\sqrt{\dfrac{27}{75}}$ $\quad = \dfrac{15 \times 3\sqrt{3}}{3 \times 5\sqrt{3}}$ $\quad = \dfrac{9}{5}$

Exercise 16F

1 Simplify each expression. Leave your answers in surd form if necessary.

a $\sqrt{2} \times \sqrt{3}$ b $\sqrt{5} \times \sqrt{3}$ c $\sqrt{2} \times \sqrt{2}$ d $\sqrt{2} \times \sqrt{8}$

e $\sqrt{5} \times \sqrt{8}$ f $\sqrt{3} \times \sqrt{3}$ g $\sqrt{6} \times \sqrt{2}$ h $\sqrt{7} \times \sqrt{3}$

i $\sqrt{2} \times \sqrt{7}$ j $\sqrt{2} \times \sqrt{18}$ k $\sqrt{6} \times \sqrt{6}$ l $\sqrt{5} \times \sqrt{6}$

2 Simplify each expression. Leave your answers in surd form if necessary.

a $\sqrt{12} \div \sqrt{3}$ b $\sqrt{15} \div \sqrt{3}$ c $\sqrt{12} \div \sqrt{2}$ d $\sqrt{24} \div \sqrt{8}$

e $\sqrt{40} \div \sqrt{8}$ f $\sqrt{3} \div \sqrt{3}$ g $\sqrt{6} \div \sqrt{2}$ h $\sqrt{21} \div \sqrt{3}$

i $\sqrt{28} \div \sqrt{7}$ j $\sqrt{48} \div \sqrt{8}$ k $\sqrt{6} \div \sqrt{6}$ l $\sqrt{54} \div \sqrt{6}$

3 Simplify each expression. Leave your answers in surd form if necessary.

a $\sqrt{2} \times \sqrt{3} \times \sqrt{2}$

b $\sqrt{5} \times \sqrt{3} \times \sqrt{15}$

c $\sqrt{2} \times \sqrt{2} \times \sqrt{8}$

d $\sqrt{2} \times \sqrt{8} \times \sqrt{3}$

e $\sqrt{5} \times \sqrt{8} \times \sqrt{8}$

f $\sqrt{3} \times \sqrt{3} \times \sqrt{3}$

g $\sqrt{6} \times \sqrt{2} \times \sqrt{48}$

h $\sqrt{7} \times \sqrt{3} \times \sqrt{3}$

i $\sqrt{2} \times \sqrt{7} \times \sqrt{2}$

j $\sqrt{2} \times \sqrt{18} \times \sqrt{5}$

k $\sqrt{6} \times \sqrt{6} \times \sqrt{3}$

l $\sqrt{5} \times \sqrt{6} \times \sqrt{30}$

4 Simplify each expression. Leave your answers in surd form.

a $\sqrt{2} \times \sqrt{3} \div \sqrt{2}$

b $\sqrt{5} \times \sqrt{3} \div \sqrt{15}$

c $\sqrt{32} \times \sqrt{2} \div \sqrt{8}$

d $\sqrt{2} \times \sqrt{8} \div \sqrt{8}$

e $\sqrt{5} \times \sqrt{8} \div \sqrt{8}$

f $\sqrt{3} \times \sqrt{3} \div \sqrt{3}$

g $\sqrt{8} \times \sqrt{12} \div \sqrt{48}$

h $\sqrt{7} \times \sqrt{3} \div \sqrt{3}$

i $\sqrt{2} \times \sqrt{7} \div \sqrt{2}$

j $\sqrt{2} \times \sqrt{18} \div \sqrt{3}$

k $\sqrt{6} \times \sqrt{6} \div \sqrt{3}$

l $\sqrt{5} \times \sqrt{6} \div \sqrt{30}$

5 Simplify each expression.

a $\sqrt{a} \times \sqrt{a}$

b $\sqrt{a} \div \sqrt{a}$

c $\sqrt{a} \times \sqrt{a} \div \sqrt{a}$

6 Simplify each surd into the form $a\sqrt{b}$.

a $\sqrt{18}$

b $\sqrt{24}$

c $\sqrt{12}$

d $\sqrt{50}$

e $\sqrt{8}$

f $\sqrt{27}$

g $\sqrt{48}$

h $\sqrt{75}$

i $\sqrt{45}$

j $\sqrt{63}$

k $\sqrt{32}$

l $\sqrt{200}$

m $\sqrt{1000}$

n $\sqrt{250}$

o $\sqrt{98}$

p $\sqrt{243}$

7 Simplify each expression.

a $2\sqrt{18} \times 3\sqrt{2}$

b $4\sqrt{24} \times 2\sqrt{5}$

c $3\sqrt{12} \times 3\sqrt{3}$

d $2\sqrt{8} \times 2\sqrt{8}$

e $2\sqrt{27} \times 4\sqrt{8}$

f $2\sqrt{27} \times 4\sqrt{8}$

g $2\sqrt{45} \times 3\sqrt{3}$

h $2\sqrt{63} \times 2\sqrt{7}$

i $2\sqrt{32} \times 4\sqrt{2}$

j $\sqrt{1000} \times \sqrt{10}$

k $\sqrt{250} \times \sqrt{10}$

l $2\sqrt{98} \times 2\sqrt{2}$

8 Simplify each expression.

a $4\sqrt{2} \times 5\sqrt{3}$

b $2\sqrt{5} \times 3\sqrt{3}$

c $4\sqrt{2} \times 3\sqrt{2}$

d $2\sqrt{2} \times 2\sqrt{8}$

e $2\sqrt{5} \times 3\sqrt{8}$

f $3\sqrt{3} \times 2\sqrt{3}$

g $2\sqrt{6} \times 5\sqrt{2}$

h $5\sqrt{7} \times 2\sqrt{3}$

i $2\sqrt{3} \times 3\sqrt{7}$

j $2\sqrt{2} \times 3\sqrt{18}$

k $2\sqrt{6} \times 2\sqrt{6}$

l $4\sqrt{5} \times 3\sqrt{6}$

9 Simplify each expression.

a $6\sqrt{12} \div 2\sqrt{3}$

b $3\sqrt{15} \div \sqrt{3}$

c $6\sqrt{12} \div \sqrt{2}$

d $4\sqrt{24} \div 2\sqrt{8}$

e $12\sqrt{40} \div 3\sqrt{8}$

f $5\sqrt{3} \div \sqrt{3}$

g $14\sqrt{6} \div 2\sqrt{2}$

h $4\sqrt{21} \div 2\sqrt{3}$

i $9\sqrt{28} \div 3\sqrt{7}$

j $12\sqrt{56} \div 6\sqrt{8}$

k $25\sqrt{6} \div 5\sqrt{6}$

l $4\sqrt{5} \div 3\sqrt{6}$

10 Simplify each expression.

a $4\sqrt{2} \times \sqrt{3} \div 2\sqrt{2}$

b $4\sqrt{5} \times \sqrt{3} \div \sqrt{15}$

c $2\sqrt{32} \times 3\sqrt{2} \div 2\sqrt{8}$

d $6\sqrt{2} \times 2\sqrt{8} \div 3\sqrt{8}$

e $3\sqrt{5} \times 4\sqrt{8} \div 2\sqrt{8}$

f $12\sqrt{3} \times 4\sqrt{3} \div 2\sqrt{3}$

g $3\sqrt{8} \times 3\sqrt{12} \div 3\sqrt{48}$

h $4\sqrt{7} \times 2\sqrt{3} \div 8\sqrt{3}$

i $15\sqrt{2} \times 2\sqrt{7} \div 3\sqrt{2}$

j $8\sqrt{2} \times 2\sqrt{18} \div 4\sqrt{3}$

k $5\sqrt{6} \times 5\sqrt{6} \div 5\sqrt{3}$

l $2\sqrt{5} \times 3\sqrt{6} \div \sqrt{30}$

11 Simplify each expression.

a $a\sqrt{b} \times c\sqrt{b}$

b $a\sqrt{b} \div c\sqrt{b}$

c $a\sqrt{b} \times c\sqrt{b} \div a\sqrt{b}$

(PS) **12** Find the value of a that makes each equation true.

     a $\sqrt{5} \times \sqrt{a} = 10$ **b** $\sqrt{6} \times \sqrt{a} = 12$ **c** $\sqrt{10} \times 2\sqrt{a} = 20$

     d $2\sqrt{6} \times 3\sqrt{a} = 72$ **e** $2\sqrt{a} \times \sqrt{a} = 6$ **f** $3\sqrt{a} \times 3\sqrt{a} = 54$

13 Simplify each expression.

     a $\left(\dfrac{\sqrt{3}}{2}\right)^2$ **b** $\left(\dfrac{5}{\sqrt{3}}\right)^2$ **c** $\left(\dfrac{\sqrt{5}}{4}\right)^2$ **d** $\left(\dfrac{6}{\sqrt{3}}\right)^2$ **e** $\left(\dfrac{\sqrt{8}}{2}\right)^2$

(EV) **14** Decide whether each statement is true or false.

     Show your working.

     a $\sqrt{a+b} = \sqrt{a} \times \sqrt{b}$ **b** $\sqrt{a-b} = \sqrt{a} - \sqrt{b}$

(PS) **15** Write down a product of two different surds that has an integer answer.

(PS) **16** By squaring both sides, prove that this statement is true only if the value of one or both of a or b is zero.

$$\sqrt{a} + \sqrt{b} = \sqrt{a+b}$$

Calculating with surds

You should be able to use surds in solving problems.

Example 7

In the right-angled triangle ABC, the length of BC is $\sqrt{6}$ cm and the length of AC is $\sqrt{18}$ cm.

Calculate the length of AB. Leave your answer in surd form.

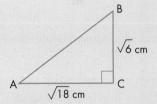

Use Pythagoras' theorem.

$$AC^2 + BC^2 = AB^2$$
$$(\sqrt{18})^2 + (\sqrt{6})^2 = 18 + 6$$
$$= 24$$
$$\Rightarrow AB = \sqrt{24} \text{ cm}$$
$$= 2\sqrt{6} \text{ cm}$$

Example 8

Calculate the area of a square with a side of length $2 + \sqrt{3}$ cm.

Give your answer in the form $a + b\sqrt{3}$.

Area $= (2 + \sqrt{3})^2$ cm^2

     $= (2 + \sqrt{3})(2 + \sqrt{3})$ cm^2

     $= 4 + 2\sqrt{3} + 2\sqrt{3} + 3$ cm^2

     $= 7 + 4\sqrt{3}$ cm^2

Hints and tips When you need to square a term in brackets, such as $(2 + \sqrt{3})^2$, always write it out in full, for example, as $(2 + \sqrt{3})(2 + \sqrt{3})$, and expand by your preferred method.

Rationalising a denominator

When you write a surd as a fraction in an answer, you should write it with a rational denominator, which means that the denominator should not include surds.

Multiplying the numerator and denominator by an appropriate square root will make the denominator into a whole number.

Example 9

Rationalise the denominator of each expression.   **a** $\frac{1}{\sqrt{3}}$ **b** $\frac{2\sqrt{3}}{\sqrt{8}}$

a Multiply the numerator and denominator by $\sqrt{3}$. $\frac{1\times\sqrt{3}}{\sqrt{3}\times\sqrt{3}}$

$$= \frac{\sqrt{3}}{3}$$

b Multiply the numerator and denominator by $\sqrt{8}$. $\frac{2\sqrt{3}\times\sqrt{8}}{\sqrt{8}\times\sqrt{8}}$

$$= \frac{2\sqrt{24}}{8}$$

$$= \frac{4\sqrt{6}}{8}$$

$$= \frac{\sqrt{6}}{2}$$

Alternatively, rewrite $\sqrt{8}$ as $2\sqrt{2}$. $\frac{2\sqrt{3}}{\sqrt{8}}$

$$= \frac{2\sqrt{3}}{2\sqrt{2}}$$

$$= \frac{\sqrt{3}}{\sqrt{2}}$$

Multiply the numerator and denominator by $\sqrt{2}$. $\frac{\sqrt{3}\times\sqrt{2}}{\sqrt{2}\times\sqrt{2}}$

$$= \frac{\sqrt{6}}{2}$$

Exercise 16G

  1   Show that each statement is true.

   a $(2+\sqrt{3})(1+\sqrt{3}) = 5+3\sqrt{3}$ **b** $(1+\sqrt{2})(2+\sqrt{3}) = 2+2\sqrt{2}+\sqrt{3}+\sqrt{6}$

   c $(4-\sqrt{3})(4+\sqrt{3}) = 13$

  2   Expand and simplify where possible.

   a $\sqrt{3}(2-\sqrt{3})$ **b** $\sqrt{2}(3-4\sqrt{2})$ **c** $\sqrt{5}(2\sqrt{5}+4)$

   d $3\sqrt{7}(4-2\sqrt{7})$ **e** $3\sqrt{2}(5-2\sqrt{8})$ **f** $\sqrt{3}(\sqrt{27}-1)$

3 Expand and simplify where possible.

a $(1 + \sqrt{3})(3 - \sqrt{3})$ **b** $(2 + \sqrt{5})(3 - \sqrt{5})$ **c** $(1 - \sqrt{2})(3 + 2\sqrt{2})$

d $(3 - 2\sqrt{7})(4 + 3\sqrt{7})$ **e** $(2 - 3\sqrt{5})(2 + 3\sqrt{5})$ **f** $(\sqrt{3} + \sqrt{2})(\sqrt{3} + \sqrt{8})$

g $(2 + \sqrt{5})^2$ **h** $(1 - \sqrt{2})^2$ **i** $(3 + \sqrt{2})^2$

4 Work out the missing lengths in each of these triangles, giving the answer in as simple a form as possible.

> **Hints and tips** Remember Pythagoras' theorem in Example 7.

a
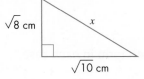

b
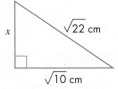

c
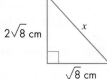

5 Calculate the area of each rectangle, simplifying your answers where possible. (The area of a rectangle with length l and width w is $A = l \times w$.)

a
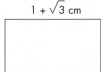

b
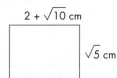

c
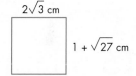

6 Rationalise the denominator of each expression.

a $\dfrac{1}{\sqrt{3}}$ **b** $\dfrac{1}{\sqrt{2}}$ **c** $\dfrac{1}{\sqrt{5}}$ **d** $\dfrac{1}{2\sqrt{3}}$ **e** $\dfrac{3}{\sqrt{3}}$

f $\dfrac{5}{\sqrt{2}}$ **g** $\dfrac{3\sqrt{2}}{\sqrt{8}}$ **h** $\dfrac{5\sqrt{3}}{\sqrt{6}}$ **i** $\dfrac{\sqrt{7}}{\sqrt{3}}$ **j** $\dfrac{1 + \sqrt{2}}{\sqrt{2}}$

k $\dfrac{2 - \sqrt{3}}{\sqrt{3}}$ **l** $\dfrac{5 + 2\sqrt{3}}{\sqrt{3}}$

7 **a** Expand and simplify each expression.

i $(2 + \sqrt{3})(2 - \sqrt{3})$ **ii** $(1 - \sqrt{5})(1 + \sqrt{5})$ **iii** $(\sqrt{3} - 1)(\sqrt{3} + 1)$

iv $(3\sqrt{2} + 1)(3\sqrt{2} - 1)$ **v** $(2 - 4\sqrt{3})(2 + 4\sqrt{3})$

b What happens in the answers to part **a**? Why?

 8 **a** Write down two surds that, when multiplied together, give a rational number.

b Write down two surds that, when multiplied together, do not give a rational number.

 9 **a** Write down two surds that, when divided, give a rational number.

b Write down two surds that, when divided, do not give a rational number.

10 An engineer uses a formula to work out the number of metres of cable she needs to complete a job. Her calculator displays the answer as $10\sqrt{70}$. The button for converting this to a decimal is not working.

She has 80 m of cable. Without using a calculator, decide whether she has enough cable. Show clearly how you decide.

11 Write $(3 + \sqrt{2})^2 - (1 - \sqrt{8})^2$ in the form $a + b\sqrt{c}$ where a, b and c are integers.

12 $x^2 - y^2 \equiv (x + y)(x - y)$ is an identity, which means it is true for any values of x and y whether they are numeric or algebraic.

Show that it is true for $x = 1 + \sqrt{2}$ and $y = 1 - \sqrt{8}$.

13 The perimeter of this rectangle is $8\sqrt{2}$ cm.

$\sqrt{2} - 1$ cm

Work out the area of the rectangle.

14   **a**   These are arithmetic sequences. Work out the nth term in each case.

     i $3 + \sqrt{2}, 3 + 2\sqrt{2}, 3 + 3\sqrt{2}, 3 + 4\sqrt{2}, ...$ **ii** $\dfrac{2}{\sqrt{3}}, \dfrac{3}{\sqrt{3}}, \dfrac{4}{\sqrt{3}}, \dfrac{5}{\sqrt{3}}, ...$

   b   These are geometric sequences. Work out the nth term in each case.

     i $\sqrt{5}, 5, 5\sqrt{5}, 25, ...$ **ii** $5 + \sqrt{2}, 5\sqrt{2} + 2, 10 + 2\sqrt{2}, 10\sqrt{2} + 4, ...$

16.5 Limits of accuracy

This section will show you how to:

- find the error interval or limits of accuracy of numbers that have been rounded to different degrees of accuracy.

Any recorded measurement has almost certainly been rounded. The true value will be somewhere between the **lower bound** and the **upper bound**. The lower and upper bounds are sometimes known as the **limits of accuracy** and the range between them is the **error interval**.

Key terms
continuous data
discrete data
error interval
limits of accuracy
lower bound
upper bound

Discrete data

Discrete data can only take certain values within a given range. Discrete data includes amounts of money and numbers of people.

Example 10

A coach is carrying 50 people, to the nearest 10.

What are the minimum and maximum numbers of people on the coach?

45 is the lowest whole number that rounds to 50 to the nearest 10.

54 is the highest whole number that rounds to 50 to the nearest 10.

So the minimum is 45 people and maximum is 54 people.

The limits are written like this.

     $45 \leqslant$ number of people $\leqslant 54$

Remember: You can only have a whole number of people.

Continuous data

Continuous data can take any value, within a given range. Continuous data includes length and mass.

A journey of 26 miles measured to the nearest mile could actually be as long as 26.499 999 9… miles or as short as 25.5 miles. It could not be 26.5 miles, as this would round up to 27 miles. However, 26.499 999 9… is virtually the same as 26.5.

You overcome this difficulty by saying that 26.5 is the upper bound of the measured value and 25.5 is its lower bound. You can therefore write:

25.5 miles $\leqslant$ actual distance < 26.5 miles

which states that the actual distance is *greater than or equal to* 25.5 miles but *less than* 26.5 miles.

When stating the upper bound, follow the accepted practice, as demonstrated here, which eliminates the difficulties of using recurring decimals.

A mathematical peculiarity

Let	$x = 0.999\,999\ldots$ (1)
Multiply by 10.	$10x = 9.999\,999\ldots$ (2)
Subtract (1) from (2).	$9x = 9$
Divide by 9.	$x = 1$
So,	$0.\dot{9} = 1.$

Hence, it is valid to give the upper bound without using recurring decimals.

Example 11

The length of a stick of wood is 32 cm, measured to the nearest centimetre.

What is the error interval of the actual length of the stick?

The lower limit is 31.5 cm, as this is the lowest value that rounds to 32 cm to the nearest centimetre.

The upper limit is 32.499 999 999… cm, as this is the highest value that rounds to 32 cm to the nearest centimetre, since 32.5 cm would round to 33 cm.

However, you say that 32.5 cm is the upper bound. So you write:

31.5 cm $\leqslant$ length of stick < 32.5 cm

Note the use of the strict inequality (<) for the upper bound.

Example 12

A time of 53.7 seconds is accurate to 1 decimal place. What is the error interval?

The smallest possible value is 53.65 seconds.

The largest possible value is 53.749 999 999… but 53.75 seconds is the upper bound.

So the error interval is 53.65 seconds $\leqslant$ time < 53.75 seconds.

Example 13

A skip has a mass of 220 kg measured to 3 significant figures. What are the limits of accuracy of the mass of the skip?

The smallest possible value is 219.5 kg.

The largest possible value is 220.499 999 99… kg but 220.5 kg is the upper bound.

So the limits of accuracy are 219.5 kg $\leqslant$ mass of skip < 220.5 kg.

1 Write down the error interval of each measurement.

   a 7 cm measured to the nearest centimetre

   b 120 g measured to the nearest 10 g

   c 3400 km measured to the nearest 100 km

   d 50 mph measured to the nearest mile per hour

   e £6 given to the nearest pound

   f 16.8 cm to the nearest tenth of a centimetre

   g 16 kg to the nearest kilogram

   h A football crowd of 14 500 given to the nearest 100

   i 55 miles given to the nearest mile

   j 55 miles given to the nearest 5 miles

2 Write down the limits of accuracy for each measurement. Each is rounded to the given degree of accuracy.

a 6 cm (1 significant figure)	**b** 17 kg (2 significant figures)
c 32 min (2 significant figures)	**d** 238 km (3 significant figures)
e 7.3 m (1 decimal place)	**f** 25.8 kg (1 decimal place)
g 3.4 h (1 decimal place)	**h** 87 g (2 significant figures)
i 4.23 mm (2 decimal places)	**j** 2.19 kg (2 decimal places)
k 12.67 min (2 decimal places)	**l** 25 m (2 significant figures)
m 40 cm (1 significant figure)	**n** 600 g (2 significant figures)
o 30 min (1 significant figure)	**p** 1000 m (2 significant figures)
q 4.0 m (1 decimal place)	**r** 7.04 kg (2 decimal places)
s 12.0 s (1 decimal place)	**t** 7.00 m (2 decimal places)

3 Write down the lower and upper bounds of each measurement, rounded to the accuracy stated.

a 8 m (1 significant figure)	**b** 26 kg (2 significant figures)
c 25 min (2 significant figures)	**d** 85 g (2 significant figures)
e 2.40 m (2 decimal places)	**f** 0.2 kg (1 decimal place)
g 0.06 s (2 decimal places)	**h** 300 g (1 significant figure)
i 0.7 m (1 decimal place)	**j** 366 g (3 significant figures)
k 170 weeks (2 significant figures)	**l** 210 g (2 significant figures)

(PS) **4** A bus has 53 seats, of which 37 are occupied.

The driver estimates that at the next bus stop 20 people, to the nearest 10, will get on and no one will get off.

If she is correct, is it possible they will all get a seat?

(EV) **5** A chain is 30 m long, measured to the nearest metre.

It is needed to fasten a boat to a harbour wall, a distance that is also 30 m, to the nearest metre.

Which statement is definitely true? Explain your decision.

A: The chain will be long enough.

B: The chain will not be long enough.

C: It is impossible to tell whether or not the chain is long enough.

6 A bag contains 2.5 kg of soil, to the nearest 100 g.

What is the least amount of soil in the bag?

Give your answer in kilograms and grams.

7 Billy has 40 identical marbles. Each marble has a mass of 65 g (to the nearest gram).

a What is the greatest possible mass of one marble?

b What is the least possible mass of one marble?

c What is the greatest possible mass of all the marbles?

d What is the least possible mass of all the marbles?

(PS) **8** A whole number, when rounded to 2 significant figures, is 350. When rounded to 1 significant figure it is 300. What is the range of values for the number?

(MR) **9** Three students are describing a number a. Abe says it is in the range $3 < a \leqslant 7$, Bee says it is in the range $2 \leqslant a < 5$ and Con says it is in the range $4 < a < 6$. Work out one possible value of the number a.

16.6 Problems involving limits of accuracy

This section will show you how to:

• combine limits of two or more variables to solve problems.

When rounded values are used for a calculation, the minimum and maximum possible exact values of the calculation can vary by large amounts. There are four operations that can be performed on limits of accuracy – addition, subtraction, multiplication and division.

Addition and subtraction

Suppose you have two bags, each with the mass given to the nearest kilogram.

The limits for bag A are 4.5 kg ≤ mass < 5.5 kg.

The limits for bag B are 8.5 kg ≤ mass < 9.5 kg.

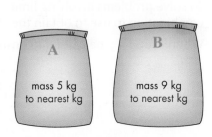

The minimum total mass of the two bags is 4.5 kg + 8.5 kg = 13 kg.

The maximum total mass of the two bags is 5.5 kg + 9.5 kg = 15 kg.

The minimum difference between the masses of the two bags is 8.5 kg – 5.5 kg = 3 kg.

The maximum difference between the masses of the two bags is 9.5 kg – 4.5 kg = 5 kg.

The table shows the combinations to give the minimum and maximum values for addition and subtraction of two numbers, a and b.

a and b lie within limits $a_{min} \leqslant a < a_{max}$ and $b_{min} \leqslant b < b_{max}$.

Operation	Minimum	Maximum
Addition ($a + b$)	$a_{min} + b_{min}$	$a_{max} + b_{max}$
Subtraction ($a - b$)	$a_{min} - b_{max}$	$a_{max} - b_{min}$

Multiplication and division

Suppose a car is travelling at an average speed of 30 mph, to the nearest 5 mph, for 2 hours, to the nearest 30 minutes.

The limits for the average speed are:

$\qquad$ 27.5 mph $\leqslant$ average speed $<$ 32.5 mph.

The limits for the time are:

$\qquad$ 1 hour 45 minutes (1.75 hours) $\leqslant$ time $<$ 2 hours 15 minutes (2.25 hours).

The minimum distance travelled = 27.5 × 1.75
$\qquad\qquad\qquad\qquad\qquad$ = 48.125 miles.

The maximum distance travelled = 32.5 × 2.25
$\qquad\qquad\qquad\qquad\qquad$ = 73.125 miles.

Suppose a lorry is travelling for 100 miles, to the nearest 10 miles, and takes 2 hours, to the nearest 30 minutes.

The limits for the distance are:

$\qquad$ 95 miles $\leqslant$ distance $<$ 105 miles.

The limits for the time are the same as for the car.

The minimum average speed is $\frac{95}{2.25} = 42$ mph.

The maximum average speed is $\frac{105}{1.75} = 60$ mph.

The table shows the combinations to give the minimum and maximum values for multiplication and division of two numbers a and b.

a and b lie within limits $a_{min} \leqslant a < a_{max}$ and $b_{min} \leqslant b < b_{max}$.

Operation	Minimum	Maximum
Multiplication ($a \times b$)	$a_{min} \times b_{min}$	$a_{max} \times b_{max}$
Division ($a \div b$)	$a_{min} \div b_{max}$	$a_{max} \div b_{min}$

To solve problems involving limits, write down all the limits for each value, and then decide which combination to use to obtain the required solution.

When rounding, be careful to ensure your answers are within the acceptable range of the limits.

A rectangle has sides given as 6 cm by 15 cm, to the nearest centimetre.

Calculate the limits of accuracy of the area of the rectangle.

Write down the limits: 5.5 cm $\leq$ width < 6.5 cm, 14.5 cm $\leq$ length < 15.5 cm

For maximum area, multiply maximum width by maximum length, and for minimum area, multiply minimum width by minimum length.

The upper bound of the width is 6.5 cm and of the length is 15.5 cm. So the upper bound of the area of the rectangle is:

6.5 cm × 15.5 cm = 100.75 cm².

The lower bound of the width is 5.5 cm and of the length is 14.5 cm. So the lower bound of the area of the rectangle is:

5.5 cm × 14.5 cm = 79.75 cm².

Therefore, the limits of accuracy for the area of the rectangle are:

79.75 cm² $\leq$ area < 100.75 cm².

The distance from Bristol to Bath is 15 miles, to the nearest mile. The time Jeff took to drive between Bristol and Bath was 40 minutes, to the nearest 10 minutes.

Calculate the upper limit of Jeff's average speed.

Write down the limits. 14.5 miles $\leq$ distance < 15.5 miles, 35 minutes $\leq$ time < 45 minutes

speed = distance ÷ time

To work out the maximum speed you need the maximum distance ÷ minimum time.

15.5 miles ÷ 35 minutes = 0.443 (3 significant figures) miles per minute

0.443 mph × 60 = 26.6 mph

The upper limit of Jeff's average speed = 26.6 mph.

Exercise 16I

1 Boxes have a mass of 7 kg, to the nearest kilogram.

What are the minimum and maximum masses of 10 of these boxes?

2 A machine cuts lengths of rope from a 50-m roll.

The lengths are 2.5 m long, to 1 decimal place.

What are the minimum and maximum numbers of pieces of rope that can be cut?

(MR) **3** Books each have a mass of 1200 g, to the nearest 100 g.

a What is the greatest possible mass of 10 books? Give your answer in kilograms.

b A trolley can safely hold up to 25 kg of books. How many books can safely be put on the trolley?

(PS) **4** Jack is five years old. Jill is eight years old.

What is the greatest difference between their ages? Show your working.

5 These are the dimensions of rectangles. In each case, find the limits of accuracy of the area. The measurements are shown to the level of accuracy indicated in brackets.

    a 5 cm × 9 cm (nearest centimetre)   **b** 4.5 cm × 8.4 cm (1 decimal place)

    c 7.8 cm × 18 cm (2 significant figures)

6 A rectangular garden has sides of 6 m and 4 m, measured to the nearest metre.

    a Write down the limits of accuracy for each length.

    b What is the maximum area of the garden?

    c What is the minimum perimeter of the garden?

7 A cinema screen is measured as 6 m by 15 m, to the nearest metre. Calculate the limits of accuracy for the area of the screen.

8 The measurements, to the nearest centimetre, of a box are given as 10 cm by 7 cm by 4 cm. Calculate the limits of accuracy for the volume of the box.

9 Mr Sparks is an electrician. He has a 50-m roll of cable, correct to the nearest metre.

He uses 10 m on each job, to the nearest metre.

If he does four jobs, what is the maximum amount of cable he will have left?

10 Jon and Matt are exactly 7 miles apart. They are walking towards each other.

Jon is walking at 4 mph and Matt is walking at 2 mph.

Both speeds are given to the nearest mile per hour.

Without doing any time calculations, decide whether it is possible for them to meet in 1 hour. Justify your answer.

11 The area of a rectangular field is given as 350 m², to the nearest 10 m². One length is given as 16 m, to the nearest metre. Find the limits of accuracy for the other length of the field.

12 In triangle ABC, AB = 9 cm, BC = 7 cm, and ∠ABC = 37°. All the measurements are given to the nearest unit. Calculate the limits of accuracy for the area of the triangle.

13 The price of pure gold is £18.25 per gram. The density of gold is 19.3 g/cm³. (Assume these figures are exact.) A solid gold bar in the shape of a cuboid has sides 4.6 cm, 2.2 cm and 6.6 cm. These measurements are made to the nearest 0.1 cm.

    a i What are the limits of accuracy for the volume of this gold bar?

      ii What are the upper and lower limits of the cost of this bar?

The gold bar was weighed and given a mass of 1296 g, to the nearest gram.

    b What are the upper and lower limits for the cost of the bar now?

    c Explain why the price ranges are so different.

14 A stopwatch records the time for the winner of a 100-m race as 14.7 seconds, measured to the nearest one-tenth of a second.

    a What are the greatest and least possible times for the winner?

    b The length of the 100-m track is correct to the nearest metre. What are the greatest and least possible lengths of the track?

    c What is the fastest possible average speed of the winner, with a time of 14.7 seconds in the 100-m race?

15 A cube has a side measured as 8 cm, to the nearest millimetre. What is the greatest percentage error of the following?

    a The calculated area of one face   **b** The calculated volume of the cube

16 A cube has a volume of 40 cm³, to the nearest cubic centimetre. Find the range of possible values of the side length of the cube.

17 A cube has a volume of 200 cm³, to the nearest 10 cm³. Find the limits of accuracy of the side length of the cube.

18 A model car travels 40 m, measured to one significant figure, at a speed of 2 m/s, measured to one significant figure. Between what limits does the time taken lie?

(PS) 19 The formula for calculating the tension, T newtons, in some coloured springs is:

$$T = \frac{20x}{l}$$

where x is the length that the spring is extended and l is the unstretched length of the spring.

If x and l are accurate to one decimal place, decide which colour of spring, if any, has the greater tension.

Red spring: $x = 3.4$ cm and $l = 5.3$ cm

Green spring: $x = 1.5$ cm and $l = 2.4$ cm

Blue spring: $x = 0.5$ cm and $l = 0.9$ cm

16.7 Choices and outcomes

This section will show you how to:

• work out the number of choices, arrangements or outcomes when choosing from lists or sets.

Key terms
combination
factorial
permutation
product rule for counting
systematic counting

Permutations

Look at these five letter cards.

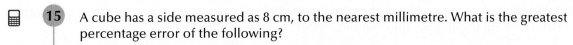

How many different ways can you rearrange them, still using all five? One example is ATHMS.

When you pick the first card, you have a choice of five. Then there are only four cards left, so for the second card you have a choice of four. Similarly, for the third card you have a choice of three, and so on. This gives a total of $5 \times 4 \times 3 \times 2 \times 1 = 120$ ways of ordering the cards. Each of these ways is a **permutation** of the cards. If we were only picking 3 cards there would be $5 \times 4 \times 3 = 60$ ways. These are examples of the **product rule for counting**.

You can write the calculation $5 \times 4 \times 3 \times 2 \times 1$ as 5!, which you say as 'five **factorial**'. Most calculators have a factorial button, which is often a 'SHIFT' function, and looks like this:

Note that 1! = 1 and, surprisingly, 0! = 1 as well. You can try these on your calculator. 1! = 1 may seem sensible but 0! = 1 seems a bit strange.

Imagine that you only want to choose three of the cards. How many different ways can you choose three cards from the five to give, for example, HAM?

For the first card you again have a choice of five, for the second you have a choice of four, and for the third a choice of three. This gives a total of 5 × 4 × 3 = 60 different ways of choosing three cards from five. You can write the calculation like this:

$$\frac{5!}{2!} = \frac{5 \times 4 \times 3 \times 2 \times 1}{2 \times 1}$$

$$= 60$$

In the previous examples, once you had chosen a card you could not choose it again. Now imagine you are asked how many three-digit numbers you can make with the digits 1, 2, 3, 4 and 5. In this case, you can repeat the digits: one possible three-digit number is 555.

You have a choice of five options for every digit. This means that you could make any of 5 × 5 × 5 = 5^3 = 125 different three-digit numbers.

So there are two different types of permutation.

Permutation with repetition

The formula for the number of ways (W) of picking r items from n when repetition is allowed is:

$$W = n^r.$$

Permutation without repetition

The formula for the number of ways (W) of picking r items from n when repetition is not allowed is:

$$W = \frac{n!}{(n - r)!}.$$

You can write 'picking r items from n' as $_nP_r$.

$$_nP_r = \frac{n!}{(n - r)!}$$

Your calculator may have an $\boxed{nPr}$ button. This is usually a SHIFT function.

Example 16

Work out:

a 10! Round your answer to 3 significant figures and write it in standard form.

b $_8P_3$

c the number of ways six different cups can be arranged in a line

d the number of ways four cups chosen from six different cups can be arranged in a line.

a 10! = 3 628 800

$\qquad$ = 3 630 000 (to 3 sf)

$\qquad$ 3 630 000 = 3.63 × 10^6 in standard form.

b $\dfrac{8!}{(8 - 3)!} = \dfrac{8!}{5!}$

$\qquad = \dfrac{8 \times 7 \times 6 \times 5 \times 4 \times 3 \times 2 \times 1}{5 \times 4 \times 3 \times 2 \times 1}$

$\qquad = 8 \times 7 \times 6$

$\qquad = 336$

c There are six options for the first cup, five for the second, and so on.

$\qquad 6 \times 5 \times 4 \times 3 \times 2 \times 1 = 6!$

$\qquad\qquad\qquad\qquad\qquad = 720$

d There are six options for the first cup, five for the second, four for the third and three for the fourth.

$\qquad 6 \times 5 \times 4 \times 3 = 360$

Example 17

In Mathsland, vehicle registration plates comprise one, two or three letters and one, two or three numbers. Given that the number cannot start with zero, how many possible vehicles can be registered?

Sometimes you have to be methodical and apply a **systematic counting** strategy.

Start with a single letter. There are 26 letters. Choosing two gives $26 \times 26 = 676$ options. Choosing three gives $26 \times 26 \times 26 = 17\,576$ options.

Now consider the numbers. For the first number there are nine options (1–9). The second number may be zero, so there are ten choices (0–9) and therefore, for two numbers, there are $9 \times 10 = 90$ options. Again, for the third number there are ten choices so for three numbers there are $9 \times 10 \times 10 = 900$ options.

Now combine all of the possible arrangements of letters and numbers: 1 letter 1 number, 1 letter, 2 numbers, … until you get to 3 letters and 3 numbers. You can write this in a table.

Numbers \ Letters	1 (26)	2 (676)	3 (17 576)
1 (9)	234	6084	158 184
2 (90)	2340	60 840	1 581 840
3 (900)	23 400	608 400	15 818 400

Adding up all of the options gives 18 259 722 different possibilities.

There are about 35 million vehicles on the road in Britain today!

Combinations

In a **combination** the order in which items are chosen does not matter. So if you just choose three cards from MATHS, then HAM counts as being the same as HMA, AMH, AHM, MHA or MAH.

This means that there are six ways ($3 \times 2 \times 1 = 3!$) in which you could pick the three letters H, A and M.

The formula for choosing three letters when the order matters is $\frac{5!}{2!} = 60$. This number will be reduced when the order doesn't matter. So, when choosing three items when the order doesn't matter, you have to divide the possible total (in this case 60) by $3! = 6$ to find the answer (10).

$$\frac{5!}{3!2!} = \frac{5 \times 4 \times 3 \times 2 \times 1}{(2 \times 1)(3 \times 2 \times 1)}$$

$$= 10$$

The formula for the number of ways (W) of picking r items from n when the order doesn't matter is:

$$W = \frac{n!}{r!(n-r)!}.$$

You can write the combination of r items from n items when the order does not matter as $_nC_r$.

$$_nC_r = \frac{n!}{r!(n-r)!}$$

Your calculator may have an **nCr** button. This is usually a SHIFT function.

Example 18

A basketball squad has 12 members. Only five players are allowed on court at a time, but substitutions are allowed at any time. How many different teams could play?

The order doesn't matter so this is a combination of 5 from 12.

Use the formula: $\dfrac{12!}{5!7!} = 792$

You can use a calculator to do this but there is a quick way of doing these calculations. Look for the smallest factorial on the bottom, in this case 5. Write down a numerator of $12 \times 11 \times 10 \times 9 \times 8$ (five values). The denominator will be 5!, so the calculation becomes:

$$\frac{12 \times 11 \times 10 \times 9 \times 8}{5 \times 4 \times 3 \times 2 \times 1}$$

which you can simplify, by cancelling, and then work out.

Example 19

You have five number cards.

How many odd numbers more than 30 000 can you make with these cards?

You need a systematic counting strategy. The number can only start with 3, 4 or 5 and must end in 1, 3 or 5. If it starts with 3 it cannot end in 3.

So, using ■ for any digit, the possibilities are 3■■■1, 3■■■5, 4■■■1, 4■■■3, 4■■■5, 5■■■1, 5■■■3, so there are seven possible options for the start and end digits.

The order of the three digits in the middle doesn't matter, so you can choose them in $3 \times 2 \times 1 = 6$ ways. So that is a total of $7 \times 6 = 42$ possible odd numbers more than 30 000.

Example 20

How many different five-letter arrangements of the letters in the word MINIM are there?

Note that there are two repeated letters, I and M. Ignoring the repeated letters there are 5! possible arrangements. As there are two Is, half of these will be duplicated, so divide by 2. Of the remaining arrangements as there are two Ms half of these will be duplicated so divide by 2 again.

$$5! \div 2 = 60, \; 60 \div 2 = 30$$

If the word had been SWISS, the answer would be $5! \div 3! = 20$ as there would be $3 \times 2 \times 1$ repetitions of the letter S.

Exercise 16J

(PS) 1 Two of these coins are chosen at random.

Work out the probability that the two coins will have a total value greater than £1.

(MR) 2 How many numbers between 0 and 200 have at least one digit of 6?

3 **a** Use your calculator to work out these numbers.

  i 7!   **ii** 20!

b $60! \approx 8.32 \times 10^{81}$, which is about the number of atoms in the whole universe.

What is the largest factorial that you can work out with your calculator?

(MR) 4 These keypads each require a four-key pass-code. How many possible codes are there for each keypad?

a

b

(MR) 5 The second keypad in question **4** has been reprogrammed. It still requires a four-key pass-code but now the first key pressed must be a letter. How many codes are possible?

6 Use your calculator to work these out.

a $_9P_3$ **b** $_{12}C_4$

7 Work these out without using a calculator.

a $_6P_2$ **b** $_8C_5$

8 A combination lock has three wheels. Each wheel has the digits 0 to 9 on it.

a How many different combinations are possible?

b Bill has forgotten his combination. He knows it uses the three digits of his house number, which is 432. How many possible combinations will Bill need to try to be certain he finds the correct one?

> **Hints and tips** In this case the word 'combination' has a different meaning. It is the arrangement of numbers to open the lock, so the order does matter.

9 Eight runners take part in a 100-m race. How many different ways can the first three places be filled?

10 **a** Two cards are taken from a regular 52-card pack, *with* replacement. What is the probability that an ace is drawn, followed by a king?

b Two cards are taken from a regular 52-card pack, *without* replacement. What is the probability that an ace is drawn, followed by a king?

11 This is Pascal's triangle. Each row starts and ends with 1 and each of the numbers in between is the sum of the numbers above it (to the left and right); for example,

$5 = 1 + 4$,
$10 = 6 + 4$.

```
            1
          1   1
        1   2   1
      1   3   3   1
    1   4   6   4   1
  1   5  10  10   5   1
```

a Copy the triangle and write down the next five rows.

b $_4C_2 = 6$. Work out:

   i $_5C_2$ **ii** $_6C_0$ **iii** $_8C_6$ **iv** $_7C_7$.

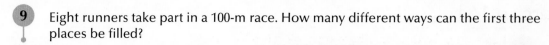

c How do these values relate to the rows and positions of the numbers in Pascal's triangle?

d Use Pascal's triangle to write down:

   i $_6C_3$ **ii** $_8C_1$ **iii** $_3C_2$ **iv** $_8C_4$.

e Write down the value of $_nC_n$.

12 In a noisy factory, a system of lights is used to summon workers to the office.

For example, using three lights gives eight possible options so that each employee has a unique code.

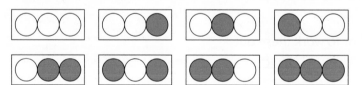

Note: 'All lights off' is not an option, since an employee with that code would be running to the office all the time.

a There are five lights and each one can be on or off. How many employees could there be? Do not include the situation where all lights are off.

b Another factory has 200 employees. How many lights will they need to make sure that every employee could have a unique light code?

13 **i** Read each scenario and identify whether it is:

A: a permutation where repetition is allowed

B: a permutation where no repetition is allowed

C: a combination where the order does not matter

D: a situation for which you need a systematic counting strategy.

ii Work out the answer to each scenario.

a Choose two students from a class of 30.

b A café offers a breakfast deal. How many different breakfast deals are possible?

> ### Breakfast Deal £2.99
> Choose 1 item from each list.
>
> | Breakfast sandwich | Extras | Drink |
> |---|---|---|
> | Ham and Egg | Beans | Tea |
> | Egg and Tomato | Mushrooms | Coffee |
> | Ham and Tomato | Pork sausage | Juice |
> | Egg and Cheese | | Beef extract |

c Naz is a vegetarian. How many breakfast deals could he have from the café above?

d Work out how many even three-digit numbers can be made from the digits 1, 2, 3 and 4.

e Chris has 15 identical balls in a bag. How many ways can she choose three balls from the 15 balls?

f Make a four-digit number from the digits 1, 2, 3, 4, 5 and 6.

g Seat five children in five chairs.

h Omar throws five regular dice. How many different ways could they land?

i An online retailer allocates codes to its products. The code consists of two letters followed by a two-digit number, which could start with zero. What is the maximum number of products the retailer could sell?

j How many two-digit numbers are odd, given that the first digit is not zero?

k An online assessment consists of 10 multiple-choice questions. The company sets the questions in a random order. How many different ways can the test be set?

l A team of three is to be chosen from five boys and four girls. There has to be at least one girl and one boy in the team. How many possibilities are there?

14 How many four-letter arrangements are there of the letters in the word MINI?

15 A three-digit number is formed from the digits 1, 2, 3, 4, 5 and 6. How many of these will be between 200 and 500?

16 A box contains three red balls, two blue balls and four yellow balls. How many different colour arrangements of three balls can be made from the box if at least one red ball must be included?

17 Eight friends go on a day out. They travel in two cars. One car can seat five people. The other car can seat four people. How many ways can they travel, given that the owners of the cars have to drive them?

(MR) 18 How many different symbols will be needed so that at least 1 million different three-symbol arrangements can be made?

(PS) 19 Four students are going to be chosen, from a group of 10, to represent their school at a conference. Only one of Aziz, Baz or Chris is to be included. In how many ways can the students be chosen?

(PS) 20 **a** In how many ways can the letters of the word READING be arranged so that the vowels always come together?

> **Hints and tips** Count the vowels as a single 'letter', and then work out how many ways they could be arranged.

b In how many ways can the letters of the word WEEDING be arranged so that the vowels always come together?

21 At the 2014 World Cup in Brazil, the England squad comprised:

Goalkeepers (3): Joe Hart, Ben Foster, Fraser Forster

Defenders (7): Glen Johnson, Leighton Baines, Gary Cahill, Phil Jagielka, Chris Smalling, Phil Jones, Luke Shaw

Midfield players (9): Steven Gerrard, Jack Wilshere, Frank Lampard, Jordan Henderson, Alex Oxlade-Chamberlain, James Milner, Raheem Sterling, Adam Lallana, Ross Barkley

Forwards (4): Daniel Sturridge, Wayne Rooney, Danny Welbeck, Rickie Lambert

There are 11 players in a football team. There is always one goalkeeper. The manager, Roy Hodgson, had various options for organising the 10 outfield players. For example, if he played 4–4–2 this means 4 defenders, 4 midfield players and 2 forwards.

a How many teams could he field if he chose the following systems?

i 4–4–2   **ii** 4–3–3   **iii** 4–5–1

(EV) b What assumptions have you made? How will this affect the answers?

22 A child's toy train set consists of an engine, a guard's van and eight wagons. The engine always has to be at the front of the train, with the guard's van at the back.

a If all 8 wagons are used how many different trains could there be?

(PS) b If at least one wagon is used, how many different trains could there be?

(CM) 23 A different factory from that in question **12** uses an array of lights that consists of 3 rows of 3 bulbs.

Ali says: "There are eight ways that any row could be lit up, so there are 8 × 8 × 8 ways minus the situation where all the lights are out, so this is $8^3 - 1$ ways."

Baz says: "That is wrong. Each light can be on or off, so the number of ways is $2^9 - 1$."

Who is correct? Explain your answer.

Worked exemplars

  1 Four-digit numbers are to be made using four of these five number cards.

Show clearly that the number of even four-digit numbers between 3000 and 5000 is 18.

This is a 'communicating mathematically' question so make it clear, using words, what you are doing.	
The even four-digit numbers between 3000 and 5000 will be 3■■2 or 3■■4 or 4■■2, where ■■ are any two of the remaining three digits. Picking 2 digits from 3 where the order matters is $_3P_2 = 3 \times 2 = 6$. As there are 3 possible sets and each set has 6 possible ways, this is $3 \times 6 = 18$.	Show that you understand where the numbers come from. Explain the number of ways of getting 2 digits from 3. Even though it is obvious that $3 \times 6 = 18$, explain the final step.

  2 The area of this rectangle is $(12 - 3\sqrt{2})$ cm².

Work out the perimeter of the rectangle. Give your answer in the form $a\sqrt{2} \pm b$, where a and b are integers.

$3\sqrt{2}$ cm

This is a problem-solving question so you will need to show your strategy. You need to establish the missing side first. There are two possible methods.	
Method 1 $\dfrac{12 - 3\sqrt{2}}{3\sqrt{2}} = \dfrac{\left(12 - 3\sqrt{2}\right) \times 3\sqrt{2}}{3\sqrt{2} \times 3\sqrt{2}}$ $= \dfrac{36\sqrt{2} - 18}{18}$ $= \dfrac{18\left(2\sqrt{2} - 1\right)}{18}$ $= 2\sqrt{2} - 1$	Divide the area by $3\sqrt{2}$, then rationalise the denominator. Simplify, then factorise. Divide top and bottom by 18.
Method 2 $12 = 6 \times \sqrt{2} \times \sqrt{2}$ $\quad = 2 \times 3 \times \sqrt{2} \times \sqrt{2}$ Hence $12 - 3\sqrt{2} = 3\sqrt{2}(2\sqrt{2} - 1)$	Factorise $3\sqrt{2}$ out of 12. Show the factorisation of 12 clearly.
Missing side is $2\sqrt{2} - 1$ so: $P = 2 \times 3\sqrt{2} + 2 \times (2\sqrt{2} - 1)$ $\quad = 6\sqrt{2} + 4\sqrt{2} - 2$ Perimeter $= 10\sqrt{2} - 2$	Once you have found the missing side show the calculation for getting the perimeter. Remember that the final answer is twice the total of both sides.

Ready to progress?

I can convert terminating decimals into fractions.

I can manipulate positive, negative and fractional indices.
I can find measures of accuracy for numbers given to whole-number, decimal-place and significant-figure accuracies.
I can use a systematic counting strategy to work out numbers of arrangements.
I can estimate powers and roots of any given positive number.

I can change a recurring decimal into a fraction.
I can work with surds and know how to manipulate them.
I can calculate the limits of compound measures.
I can use the product rule to work out choices, arrangements and outcomes.

Review questions

1. Write down the answers to these.

   a $\sqrt{169}$ **b** $\sqrt[4]{10\,000}$ **c** $\sqrt{5 \times 2^5 + 3^2}$

2. A school has 1850 students to the nearest 10.

   a What is the lowest number of students at the school?

   b What is the greatest number of students at the school?

3. (PS) A cube number and two square numbers have a sum of 60. What are the numbers?

4. (PS) Khalid writes down all the numbers from 100 to 200 inclusive. How many times does he write the digit 5?

5. Which is greater, $_{12}P_2$ or $_9C_4$?

6. A combination lock has four wheels. Each wheel has the digits 1 to 9 and the letters X, Y and Z on it.

   a How many different combinations are possible?

   b How many different combinations are possible if at least one letter must be included?

7. (PS) The letters of the word CODES are used to form five-letter codes.

   a Show that there are 120 possible codes.

   b All the possible codes are then arranged in alphabetical order. The first code is CDEOS; the 120th is SOEDC. What number in the list is the word CODES itself?

8. **a** Work out the value of $3^7 \div 3^3$.

   b Write down the value of $64^{\frac{1}{2}}$.

   c $4^n = \frac{1}{64}$. Find the value of n.

9. **a** Write down the exact value of 5^{-2}.

   b Simplify $\frac{6^3 \times 6^5}{6^4}$.

10 Express the recurring decimal 0.466 666 66… as a fraction. Give your answer in its simplest form.

11 Find values of a and b such that this statement is true.

$$(4 + \sqrt{5})(3 - \sqrt{5}) = a + b\sqrt{5}$$

(PS) 12 The area of this rectangle is 60 cm².

Find the value of x. Give your answer in the form $a\sqrt{b}$ where a and b are integers.

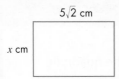

$5\sqrt{2}$ cm

x cm

13 **a** Prove that $0.5\overset{\bullet\bullet}{4} = \frac{6}{11}$.

b Hence, or otherwise, express $0.3\overset{\bullet}{5}\overset{\bullet}{4}$ as a fraction.

14 Express the recurring decimal $0.2\overset{\bullet}{4}$ as a fraction.

15 **a** Write down the value of $81^{\frac{1}{2}}$.

b Write $\sqrt{50}$ in the form $k\sqrt{2}$, where k is an integer.

16 **a** Rationalise the denominator of $\frac{1}{\sqrt{5}}$.

b Expand $(\sqrt{3} - 1)(\sqrt{3} + 1)$.

17 **a** **i** Show that $\sqrt{32} = 4\sqrt{2}$.

ii Expand and simplify $(\sqrt{2} + \sqrt{12})^2$.

(CM) **b** Show clearly that this triangle is right-angled. All lengths are in centimetres.

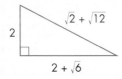

$\sqrt{2} + \sqrt{12}$

2

$2 + \sqrt{6}$

(PS) 18 **a** Calculate the length of the diagonal x in this cube of side 3 m.

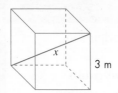

x

3 m

b A man is carrying a pole of length 5 m down a long corridor. The length of the pole is measured to the nearest centimetre. At the end of the corridor is a right-angled corner. The corridor is 3 m wide and 3 m high, both measurements correct to the nearest 10 cm. Will the man carrying the pole be certain to get round the corner?

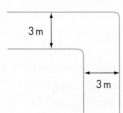

3 m

3 m

17 Algebra: Quadratic equations

This chapter is going to show you:

- how to draw quadratic graphs
- how to solve quadratic equations by factorisation, the quadratic formula and completing the square
- how to solve problems involving quadratic equations
- how to recognise and find the significant points of a quadratic graph
- how to use graphs to solve a pair of simultaneous equations, one linear and one non-linear
- how to use the method of intersection to solve one quadratic equation, using the graph of another quadratic equation and an appropriate straight line
- how to solve quadratic inequalities.

You should already know:

- how to substitute into simple algebraic functions
- how to plot a graph from a given table of values
- how to draw linear graphs
- how to find the equation of a graph
- how to collect together like terms
- how to multiply together two algebraic expressions
- how to solve simple linear equations and inequalities.

About this chapter

Like most mathematics, quadratic equations have their origins in ancient Egypt.

The Egyptians did not have a formal system of algebra but could solve problems that involved quadratics. This problem was written in hieroglyphics on the Berlin Papyrus, which was written some time around 2160–1700 BC:

The area of a square of 100 is equal to that of two smaller squares. The side of one is $\frac{1}{2} + \frac{1}{4}$ the side of the other.

Today we would express this as: $x^2 + y^2 = 100$

$$y = \frac{3}{4}x$$

In about 300 BC, Euclid developed a geometrical method for solving quadratics. This work was developed by Hindu mathematicians, but it was not until much later, in 1145 AD that the Arabic mathematician Abraham bar Hiyya Ha-Nasi, published the book *Liber embadorum*, which gave a complete solution of the quadratic equation.

17.1 Plotting quadratic graphs

This section will show you how to:

- draw and read values from quadratic graphs.

Key terms

| parabola | quadratic |

A **quadratic** graph has the form $y = ax^2 + bx + c$. All of the following are quadratic equations and each produces a quadratic graph, which is a smooth curve called a **parabola**:

$y = x^2$, $y = x^2 + 5$, $y = x^2 - 3x$, $y = x^2 + 5x + 6$, $y = 3x^2 - 5x + 4$

Draw the graph of $y = x^2 + 5x + 6$ for $-5 \leqslant x \leqslant 3$.

Make a table, as shown below. Work out the values in each row (x^2, $5x$, 6) separately, adding them together to obtain the values of y. Then plot the points from the table and join them with a smooth curve.

x	−5	−4	−3	−2	−1
x^2	25	16	9	4	1
$+5x$	−25	−20	−15	−10	−5
$+6$	6	6	6	6	6
y	6	2	0	0	2

x	0	1	2	3
x^2	0	1	4	9
$+5x$	0	5	10	15
$+6$	6	6	6	6
y	6	12	20	30

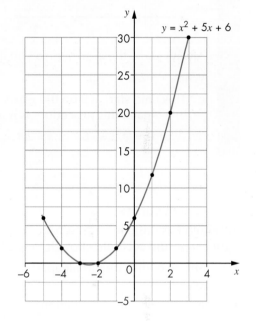

Example 1

a Complete the table for $y = 3x^2 - 5x + 4$ for $-1 \leqslant x \leqslant 3$, then draw the graph.

x	−1	−0.5	0	0.5	1	1.5	2	2.5	3
y	12		4	2.25	2			10.25	16

b Use your graph to find the value of y when $x = 2.2$.

c Use your graph to find the values of x that give a y-value of 9.

a The table only gives some values. So you either set up your own table with $3x^2$, $-5x$ and $+4$, or calculate each y-value on your calculator. For example, on the majority of scientific calculators, you would work out the value for -0.5 as:

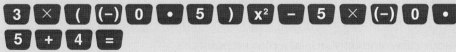

Make sure when you square a negative number that you put the negative number in brackets.

x	−1	−0.5	0	0.5	1	1.5	2	2.5	3
y	12	7.25	4	2.25	2	3.25	6	10.25	16

The graph is shown in the solution to part **b**.

(continued)

b To find the corresponding y-value for any value of x, you start on the x-axis at that x-value, go up to the curve, across to the y-axis and read off the y-value. This procedure is marked on the graph with arrows.

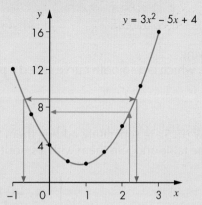

Always show these arrows so you can double check your readings.

When $x = 2.2$, $y = 7.5$.

c This time start at 9 on the y-axis and read off the two x-values that correspond to a y-value of 9. Again, this procedure is marked on the graph with arrows.

When $y = 9$, $x = -0.7$ or $x = 2.4$.

Drawing accurate graphs

Although it is difficult to draw accurate curves, you need to make sure that whatever you draw is the right shape and accurate enough to read off values. Try to avoid the following common errors:

- When the points are too far apart, a curve tends to 'wobble'.

- Drawing curves in small sections leads to 'feathering'.

- The place where a curve should turn smoothly is drawn 'flat'.

- A line is drawn through a point that, clearly, has been incorrectly plotted.

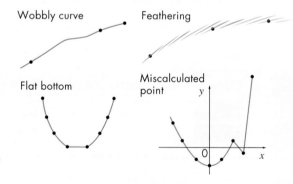

Here are some tips that will make it easier for you to draw smooth, curved lines.

- If you are *right-handed*, turn your paper or exercise book round so that you draw from left to right. Your hand is steadier this way than when you are trying to draw from right to left or away from your body. If you are *left-handed*, you should find drawing from right to left the more accurate way.

- Move your pencil over the points as a practice run without drawing the curve.

- Do one continuous curve and only stop at a plotted point.

- Use a *sharp* pencil and do not press too heavily, so that you may easily rub out mistakes.

You do not need to work out all values in a table, only the y-value. The other rows in the table are just working lines to break down the calculation. Learning how to calculate y-values with a calculator can make this process quicker.

Exercise 17A

In this exercise, suitable ranges are suggested for the axes. You can use any type of graph paper.

1 **a** Copy and complete the table or use a calculator to work out values for the graph of $y = x^2 - 2x - 8$ for values of x from -5 to 5. Plot the graph using $-5 \leqslant x \leqslant 5$ and $-10 \leqslant y \leqslant 30$ for your axes.

x	-5	-4	-3	-2	-1	0	1	2	3	4	5
x^2	25		9					4			
$-2x$	10							-4			
-8	-8							-8			
y	27							-8			

b Use your graph to find the value of y when $x = 0.5$.

c Use your graph to find the values of x that give a y-value of -3.

2 **a** Copy and complete the table or use a calculator to work out the values for the graph of $y = x^2 + 2x - 1$ for values of x from -3 to 3. Plot the graph using $-3 \leqslant x \leqslant 3$ and $-2 \leqslant y \leqslant 14$ for your axes.

x	-3	-2	-1	0	1	2	3
x^2	9				1	4	
$+2x$	-6		-2			4	
-1	-1	-1				-1	
y	2					7	

b Use your graph to find the y-value when $x = -2.5$.

c Use your graph to find the values of x that give a y-value of 1.

d On the same axes, draw the graph of $y = \frac{x}{2} + 2$.

e Where do the graphs $y = x^2 + 2x - 1$ and $y = \frac{x}{2} + 2$ cross?

3 **a** Copy and complete the table or use a calculator to work out values for the graph of $y = 2x^2 - 5x - 3$ for values of x from -2 to 4.

x	-2	-1.5	-1	-0.5	0	0.5	1	1.5	2	2.5	3	3.5	4
y	15	9			-3	-5				-3			9

b Where does the graph cross the x-axis?

(MR) **4** Shayla is writing out a table of values for the graph of $y = x^2 - 4x + 7$.

x	-3	-2	-1	0	1	2	3	4	5	6	7
y					4	3	4	7	12	19	28

a What do you notice about the value of y when $x = 1$ and when $x = 3$?

b Complete the table without substituting any values, explaining how it is possible to do so.

5 Copy the grid onto centimetre-squared paper.

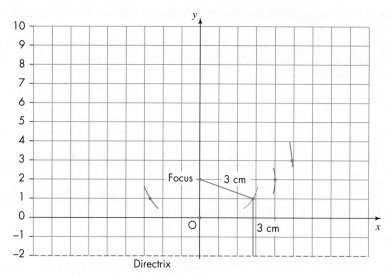

Mark a point at (0, 2). This is the focus.

Draw the line $y = -2$. This is the directrix.

All the points on a parabola are the same distance from the focus and the directrix.

The origin is 2 units away from both and this will be the lowest point of the parabola.

Set a pair of compasses to a radius of 3 cm. Using the focus as the centre, draw arcs on both sides to intersect with the line $y = 1$, which is 3 cm from the directrix.

Now set the compasses at 4 cm and draw arcs from the focus to intersect with $y = 2$.

Repeat with the compasses set to 5 cm, 6 cm, etc.

Once you have drawn all the points, join them with a smooth curve to show a parabola.

The parabola drawn has the equation $y = \frac{1}{8}x^2$.

CM **6** Here are three quadratic equations.

Parabola A: $y = 2x^2$

Parabola B: $y = -x^2$

Parabola C: $y = x^2 + 2$

Give a reason why each line may be the odd one out.

17.2 Solving quadratic equations by factorisation

This section will show you how to:

- solve a quadratic equation by factorisation
- rearrange a quadratic equation so that it can be factorised.

Solving the quadratic equation $x^2 + ax + b = 0$

To **solve** a quadratic equation such as $x^2 - 2x - 3 = 0$, you first have to be able to factorise it. You met factorising in Chapter 8.

To solve $x^2 + 6x + 5 = 0$, first factorise it to get $(x + 5)(x + 1) = 0$.

The only way this expression can ever equal 0 is if the value of one of the brackets is 0.
So either $(x + 5) = 0$ or $(x + 1) = 0$

$$\rightarrow \quad x + 5 = 0 \qquad \text{or} \qquad x + 1 = 0$$
$$\rightarrow \quad x = -5 \qquad \text{or} \qquad x = -1$$

So the solution is $x = -5$ or $x = -1$.

Example 2

Solve $x^2 + 9 = 6x$

Collect all terms to the left hand side.	$x^2 - 6x + 9 = 0$
Factorising gives:	$(x - 3)(x - 3) = 0$
Since $(x - 3)$ is repeated, you can rewrite this as:	$(x - 3)^2 = 0$
So there is only one solution:	$x = 3$

Example 3

A right-angled triangle has a hypotenuse of 13 cm.

The other two sides are $(x + 5)$ cm and $(x - 2)$ cm.

Calculate the perimeter of the triangle.

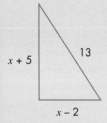

The sides of a right-angled triangle are connected by Pythagoras' theorem, which says that $c^2 = a^2 + b^2$.

$$(x + 5)^2 + (x - 2)^2 = 13^2$$
$$(x^2 + 10x + 25) + (x^2 - 4x + 4) = 169$$
$$2x^2 + 6x + 29 = 169$$
$$2x^2 + 6x - 140 = 0$$

Divide by a factor of 2: $\qquad x^2 + 3x - 70 = 0$

This factorises to: $\qquad (x + 10)(x - 7) = 0$

This gives: $\qquad x = -10$ or 7

You should reject the negative value as it would give negative lengths, so x must equal 7.

So the sides of the triangle are 5 cm, 12 cm and 13 cm and the perimeter is 30 cm.

Note: You may know the Pythagorean triple 5, 12, 13 and guess the answer, but this example demonstrates how you can solve a similar question when you do not know the Pythagorean triple.

Example 4

A coach driver travelled 300 km. Her actual average speed turned out to be 10 km/h less than expected. Therefore, the journey took 1 hour longer than expected. Find her actual average speed.

Let the actual average speed be x km/h.

So the expected speed would have been $(x + 10)$ km/h.

$$\text{Time taken} = \frac{\text{distance travelled}}{\text{speed}}$$

At x km/h, she took $\dfrac{300}{x}$ hours.

At $(x + 10)$ km/h, she took $\dfrac{300}{x + 10}$ hours.

Since the journey took 1 hour longer than expected, then:

$$\text{time taken} = \frac{300}{x + 10} + 1 = \frac{300}{x + 10} + \frac{x + 10}{x + 10} = \frac{300 + x + 10}{x + 10} = \frac{310 + x}{x + 10}$$

So $\dfrac{300}{x} = \dfrac{310 + x}{x + 10}$

Multiply both sides by x and by $(x + 10)$:

$$300(x + 10) = x(310 + x)$$
$$300x + 3000 = 310x + x^2$$

Rearranging into the form $x^2 + ax + b = 0$, gives: $\quad x^2 + 10x - 3000 = 0$

Factorising gives: $\qquad\qquad\qquad\qquad\qquad (x + 60)(x - 50) = 0$

$$\rightarrow x = -60 \text{ or } 50$$

The average speed could not be −60 km/h, so it has to be 50 km/h.

Exercise 17B

1 Solve the following equations.

   a $(x + 2)(x + 5) = 0$ **b** $(y - 9)(y - 4) = 0$ **c** $(z + 6)(z - 3) = 0$

2 First factorise, then solve each of the following.

   a $x^2 + 5x + 4 = 0$ **b** $x^2 - 6x + 8 = 0$ **c** $x^2 - 3x - 10 = 0$ **d** $x^2 - 2x - 15 = 0$

   e $t^2 + 3t - 18 = 0$ **f** $x^2 - x - 2 = 0$ **g** $m^2 + 10m + 25 = 0$ **h** $a^2 - 14a + 49 = 0$

(PS) **3** A rectangular field is 40 m longer than it is wide. The area is 48 000 square metres.

The farmer wants to place a fence all around the field.

How long will the fence be?

Hints and tips	If one solution to a real-life problem is negative, reject it and only give the positive answer.

Hints and tips	Let the width be x, set up a quadratic equation and solve it to find x.

4 Rearrange, then solve the following equations.

   a $t^2 + 7t = 30$ **b** $x^2 - 7x = 44$ **c** $t^2 - t = 72$ **d** $x^2 = 17x - 72$

   e $x^2 + 1 = 2x$ **f** $(x + 1)(x - 2) = 40$ **g** $(x + 1)(x - 2) = 4$

5 A teacher asks her class to solve $x^2 - 3x = 4$.

This is Mario's answer.

$$x^2 - 3x - 4 = 0$$
$$(x - 4)(x + 1) = 0$$
So $x - 4 = 0$ or $x + 1 = 0$
$$x = 4 \text{ or } -1$$

This is Sylvan's answer.

$$x(x - 3) = 4$$
So $x = 4$ or $x - 3 = 4 \rightarrow x = -3 + 4 = -1$

When the teacher reads out the answer of $x = 4$ or -1, both students mark their work as correct.

Who used the correct method and what mistakes did the other student make?

 6 Find the perimeter of a right-angled triangle with sides of $(x - 12)$ cm, $(x - 5)$ cm and $(x - 3)$ cm.

 7 On a journey of 400 km, the driver of a train calculates that if he were to increase his average speed by 2 km/h, he would take 20 minutes less. Work out his average speed.

 8 **a** Solve the equation $x^2 - 13x + 36 = 0$.

b Hence solve the following equations.

i $u^4 - 13u^2 + 36 = 0$ **ii** $v - 13v^{1/2} + 36 = 0$ **iii** $(w - 8)^4 + 36 = 13(w - 8)^2$

Solving the general quadratic equation by factorisation

The general quadratic equation is one of the form $ax^2 + bx + c = 0$ where a, b and c are positive or negative whole numbers. (It is easier to make sure that a is always positive.) Before you can solve any quadratic equation by factorisation, you must rearrange it into this form.

The factorisation method is then similar to the method used to solve equations of the form $x^2 + ax + b = 0$. That is, you have to find two **factors** of $ax^2 + bx + c$ with a product of 0.

Consider the quadratic equation $2x^2 - 11x + 15 = 0$.

This factorises to $(2x - 5)(x - 3) = 0$.

Since the product is equal to 0, one of the brackets must equal 0.

So either $2x - 5 = 0$ or $x - 3 = 0$
$$2x = 5$$
$$x = 2\frac{1}{2} \quad \text{or} \quad x = 3$$

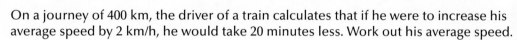

Solve these quadratic equations.   **a** $12x^2 - 28x = -15$ **b** $30x^2 - 5x - 5 = 0$

a First, rearrange the equation into the general form: $12x^2 - 28x + 15 = 0$

This factorises to: $(2x - 3)(6x - 5) = 0$

The only way this product can equal 0 is if the value of one of the brackets is 0.

So either $2x - 3 = 0$ or $6x - 5 = 0$
$\rightarrow$ $2x = 3$ or $6x = 5$
$\rightarrow$ $x = \dfrac{3}{2}$ or $x = \dfrac{5}{6}$

So the solution is $x = 1\frac{1}{2}$ or $x = \frac{5}{6}$

Note: It is better to leave the answer as a fraction so you can see which numbers were in the brackets. This makes it easier to check for a mistake than when you give the answer as a rounded decimal.

(continued)

b This equation is already in the general quadratic form and it will factorise to $(15x + 5)(2x - 1) = 0$ or $(3x + 1)(10x - 5) = 0$.

Look again at the equation. There is a common factor of 5 which you can take out to give:

$5(6x^2 - x - 1) = 0$

This is much easier to factorise to $5(3x + 1)(2x - 1) = 0$, which you can solve to give $x = -\frac{1}{3}$ or $x = \frac{1}{2}$.

Notice that you could divide the equation by 5 to get $(3x + 1)(2x - 1) = 0$ without changing the two solutions.

Solve this equation. $\quad 2x - \frac{3}{x} = 5$

Multiply through by x to give: $\qquad\qquad 2x^2 - 3 = 5x$

Rearrange into the general form: $\quad 2x^2 - 5x - 3 = 0$

This factorises to: $\qquad\qquad\quad (2x + 1)(x - 3) = 0$

So $x = -\frac{1}{2}$ or $x = 3$.

Special cases

Sometimes the values of b or c are zero. (Note that if a is zero the equation is no longer a quadratic equation but a linear equation.)

Solve these quadratic equations. $\qquad$ **a** $3x^2 - 4 = 0$ $\qquad$ **b** $4x^2 - 25 = 0$ $\qquad$ **c** $6x^2 - x = 0$

a Rearrange to get: $\qquad\qquad\qquad\qquad 3x^2 = 4$

Divide both sides by 3: $\qquad\qquad\qquad x^2 = \frac{4}{3}$

Take the square root on both sides: $\qquad x = \pm\sqrt{\frac{4}{3}}$

$$= \pm\frac{2}{\sqrt{3}}$$

Rationalise the denominator: $\qquad\qquad\quad = \pm\frac{2\sqrt{3}}{3}$

Note: A square root can be positive or negative. The answer is in *surd form* (see Chapter 16).

b You can use the method of part **a** or you should recognise this as the difference of two squares (see chapter 15). You can factorise this to $(2x - 5)(2x + 5) = 0$.

Each set of brackets can be put equal to zero.

$2x - 5 = 0 \quad \rightarrow \quad x = +\frac{5}{2}$

$2x + 5 = 0 \quad \rightarrow \quad x = -\frac{5}{2}$

So the solution is $x = \pm\frac{5}{2}$

c There is a common factor of x, so factorise as $x(6x - 1) = 0$.

There is only one set of brackets this time but each factor can be equal to zero, so $x = 0$ or $6x - 1 = 0$.

So $x = 0$ or $\frac{1}{6}$.

Exercise 17C

Give your answers either in rational form or as mixed numbers.

1 Solve these equations.

a $3x^2 + 8x - 3 = 0$ b $6x^2 - 5x - 4 = 0$ c $5x^2 - 9x - 2 = 0$

d $4t^2 - 4t - 35 = 0$ e $18t^2 + 9t + 1 = 0$ f $3t^2 - 14t + 8 = 0$

g $6x^2 + 15x - 9 = 0$ h $12x^2 - 16x - 35 = 0$ i $15t^2 + 4t - 35 = 0$

j $28x^2 - 85x + 63 = 0$ k $24x^2 - 19x + 2 = 0$ l $16t^2 - 1 = 0$

m $4x^2 + 9x = 0$ n $25t^2 - 49 = 0$ o $9m^2 - 24m - 9 = 0$

> 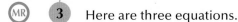 **Hints and tips** Look out for the special cases where b or c is zero.

2 Rearrange these equations into the general form and then solve them.

a $x^2 - x = 42$ b $8x(x + 1) = 30$

c $13x^2 = 11 - 2x$ d $10x^2 - x = 2$

e $8x^2 + 6x + 3 = 2x^2 + x + 2$ f $25x^2 = 10 - 45x$

g $8x - 16 - x^2 = 0$ h $(2x + 1)(5x + 2) = (2x - 2)(x - 2)$

i $5x + 5 = 30x^2 + 15x + 5$ j $2m^2 = 50$

k $6x^2 + 30 = 5 - 3x^2 - 30x$ l $4x^2 + 4x - 49 = 4x$

m $2t^2 - t = 15$

 3 Here are three equations.

A: $(x - 1)^2 = 0$ B: $3x + 2 = 5$ C: $x^2 - 4x = 5$

a Give a mathematical fact that equations A and B have in common.

b Give a mathematical reason why equation B is different from equations A and C.

4 Pythagoras' theorem states that the sum of the squares of the two short sides of a right-angled triangle equals the square of the long side (hypotenuse).

A right-angled triangle has a hypotenuse of $5x - 1$ and shorter sides of $2x + 3$ and $x + 1$ cm.

a Show that $20x^2 - 24x - 9 = 0$

b Find the area of the triangle.

5 a Show that $x = \frac{15}{8}$ is a solution to the equation $40x^2 + 117x = 360$.

b Find the other solution.

6 Solve the equation $2x + \frac{5}{x} = 11$.

7 A rectangular room is 3 m longer than it is wide.

It cost £364 to carpet the room. Carpet costs £16 per square metre.

How wide is the room?

17.3 Solving a quadratic equation by using the quadratic formula

This section will show you how to:

- solve a quadratic equation by using the quadratic formula
- recognise why some quadratic equations cannot be solved.

Many quadratic equations cannot be solved by factorisation because they do not have simple factors. For example, try to factorise $x^2 - 4x - 3 = 0$ or $3x^2 - 6x + 2 = 0$.

One way to solve this type of equation is to use the **quadratic formula**. You can use this formula to solve *any* quadratic equation that is **soluble**. (Some are not, which the quadratic formula would immediately show. You will learn about this later in this section.)

The solution of the equation $ax^2 + bx + c = 0$ is given by:

$$x = \frac{-b \pm \sqrt{b^2 - 4ac}}{2a}$$

where a and b are the coefficients of x^2 and x respectively and c is the constant term.

This is the quadratic formula.

The symbol $\pm$ states that the square root has a positive and a negative value, and you must use *both* of them in solving for x.

Example 8

Solve $5x^2 - 11x - 4 = 0$, giving solutions correct to 2 decimal places.

Substitute $a = 5$, $b = -11$ and $c = -4$ into the formula: $x = \dfrac{-b \pm \sqrt{b^2 - 4ac}}{2a}$

So $x = \dfrac{-(-11) \pm \sqrt{(-11)^2 - 4(5)(-4)}}{2(5)}$

Note: Using brackets can help you to avoid arithmetic errors. A common error is to write -11^2 is -121.

$x = \dfrac{11 \pm \sqrt{121 + 80}}{10} = \dfrac{11 \pm \sqrt{201}}{10}$

$x = 2.52$ or -0.32

Note: The calculation has been done in stages. You can also work out the answer with a calculator, but make sure you can use it properly. If not, break the calculation down. Remember the rule 'if you try to do two things at once, you will probably get one of them wrong'.

Example 9

A rectangle has sides of x m and $(x + 4)$ m. Its area is 100 m². Find the perimeter of the rectangle, correct to 1 decimal place.

So $x(x + 4) = 100 \rightarrow x^2 + 4x - 100 = 0$

Put $a = 1$, $b = 4$ and $c = -100$ into the quadratic formula, which gives

$$x = \frac{-(4) \pm \sqrt{(4)^2 - 4(1)(-100)}}{2(1)}$$

$$x = \frac{-4 \pm \sqrt{16 + 400}}{2} = \frac{-4 \pm \sqrt{416}}{2}$$

$x = -12.198$ or 8.198

Since x is the length of the side of a rectangle, it cannot be negative, so the only valid answer is 8.198.

The other side of the rectangle is $8.198 + 4 = 12.198$.

The perimeter of the rectangle is $2(8.198 + 12.198) = 40.8$ cm (1 decimal place).

Exercise 17D

1 Use the quadratic formula to solve these equations, giving your answers to 2 decimal places.

a $2x^2 + x - 8 = 0$ **b** $x^2 - x - 10 = 0$ **c** $7x^2 + 12x + 2 = 0$

d $6x^2 + 22x + 19 = 0$ **e** $x^2 + 3x - 6 = 0$ **f** $4x^2 + 5x = 3$

g $4x^2 - 9x + 4 = 0$ **h** $7x^2 + 3x = 2$ **i** $5x^2 + 1 = 10x$

> **Hints and tips** Use brackets when substituting and do not try to work two things out at the same time.

 2 A rectangular lawn is 2 m longer than it is wide.

The area of the lawn is 21 m². The gardener wants to edge the lawn with edging strips, which are sold in lengths of $1\frac{1}{2}$ m. How many will she need to buy?

 3 Shaun is solving a quadratic equation, using the formula.

He correctly substitutes values for a, b and c to get:

$$x = \frac{3 \pm \sqrt{37}}{2}$$

What is the equation Shaun is trying to solve?

 4 Terry uses the quadratic formula to solve $4x^2 - 4x + 1 = 0$.

June uses factorisation to solve $4x^2 - 4x + 1 = 0$.

They both find something unusual in their solutions.

Explain what this is, and why.

5 Solve the equation $x + \frac{3}{x} = 7$. Give your answers correct to 2 decimal places.

 6 The sum of a number and its reciprocal is 2.05. What are the two numbers?

> **Hints and tips** The reciprocal of the fraction $\frac{a}{b}$ is $\frac{b}{a}$.

7 **a** Solve these equations using the quadratic formula, giving all answers correct to 3 decimal places.

    i $x^2 + 3x + 1 = 0$ **ii** $x^2 - 10x + 23 = 0$ **iii** $x^2 = 7x + 4$ **iv** $x^2 + 6x = 8$

b Why do the two answers for each equation add up to $-b$?

Quadratic equations with no solution

The quantity $(b^2 - 4ac)$ in the quadratic formula is known as the **discriminant**.

All quadratic equations can be shown as parabolas.

Here are the graphs of the three types of quadratic equations:

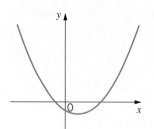 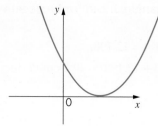 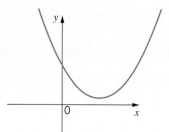

When the discriminant, $b^2 - 4ac$, is positive it means there are two solutions and the graph crosses the x-axis twice	When $b^2 - 4ac$ equals zero, it means there is only one solution and the graph just touches the x-axis	When $b^2 - 4ac$ is negative, you would have to find the square root of a negative number, so there are no solutions and the graph does not cross the x-axis

These rules are also true for negative parabolas.

Although it is possible to take the square root of a negative number and get something called an imaginary number, you won't learn about them at this level. So there are no solutions if the discriminant is negative.

Example 10

Find the discriminant $b^2 - 4ac$ of the equation $x^2 + 3x + 5 = 0$ and explain what the result tells you.

$b^2 - 4ac = (3)^2 - 4(1)(5)$

          $= 9 - 20$

          $= -11$

This means there are no solutions for x.

Example 11

How many times does the graph of $y = 13 - 2x - 3x^2$ meet the x-axis?

$b^2 - 4ac = (-2)^2 - 4(13)(-3)$

          $= 4 + 156$

          $= 160$

Since $b^2 - 4ac$ is positive, the graph meets the x-axis at two points.

Exercise 17E

1 Work out the discriminant $b^2 - 4ac$ of the equations. In each case say how many solutions the equation has.

    a $3x^2 + 2x - 4 = 0$ **b** $25x^2 - 30x + 9 = 0$ **c** $4x^2 + 3x + 2 = 0$

    d $2x^2 + x + 1 = 0$ **e** $x^2 - 2x - 16 = 0$ **f** $5x^2 + 5x + 3 = 0$

    g $6x - x^2 - 10 = 0$ **h** $48x - 9x^2 - 64 = 0$ **i** $45 - 7x - 2x^2 = 0$

 2 A quadratic equation has the solutions $x = 2 \pm 5\sqrt{3}$. Find the value of $b^2 - 4ac$.

 3 Bill works out the discriminant of the quadratic equation $x^2 + bx - c = 0$ as $b^2 - 4ac = 13$.

There are four possible equations that could lead to this discriminant. What are they?

 4 For which values of k does the equation $x^2 + (k + 2)x + (6 - k) = 0$ have only one answer?

 5 The ten quadratic equations below have been sorted into two categories, ones which can be factorised and ones which cannot be factorised. Evaluate $b^2 - 4ac$ for each one and determine what is special about the value of $b^2 - 4ac$ for equations that can be factorised.

Can be factorised	Cannot be factorised
$14x^2 + 27x - 20 = 0$	$8x^2 - 19x + 10 = 0$
$15x^2 + 11x + 2 = 0$	$3x^2 + 7x - 18 = 0$
$12x^2 - 25x + 12 = 0$	$30x^2 - 13x - 28 = 0$
$63 - 4x - 4x^2 = 0$	$9 - 6x - 5x^2 = 0$
$9x^2 + 18x - 16 = 0$	$10x^2 + 26x + 15 = 0$

17.4 Solving quadratic equations by completing the square

This section will show you how to:

- solve a quadratic equation by completing the square.

Another method for solving a quadratic equation is **completing the square**.

Consider the equation $x^2 - 8x + 16 = 25$

Factorise the expression on the left into $(x - 4)^2 = 25$

Take the square root of both sides. $\sqrt{(x - 4)^2} = \sqrt{25}$

Remember that 25 has two square roots (5 and −5) $x - 4 = \pm 5$

Add 4 to both sides $x = \pm 5 + 4$

Either $x = 5 + 4 = 9$ or $x = -5 + 4 = -1$.

Now consider the equation $x^2 + 6x = 7$

If you add 9 to both sides you make an expression on the left hand side that you can factorise as before.

$$x^2 + 6x + 9 = 16$$
$$(x + 3)^2 = 16$$

Take the square root as before. $x + 3 = \pm 4$

Subtract 3 from both sides. $x = \pm 4 - 3 = 1$ or -7

The process of rewriting $x^2 + 6x$ as $x^2 + 6x + 9$ is called completing the square.

This diagram shows you why.

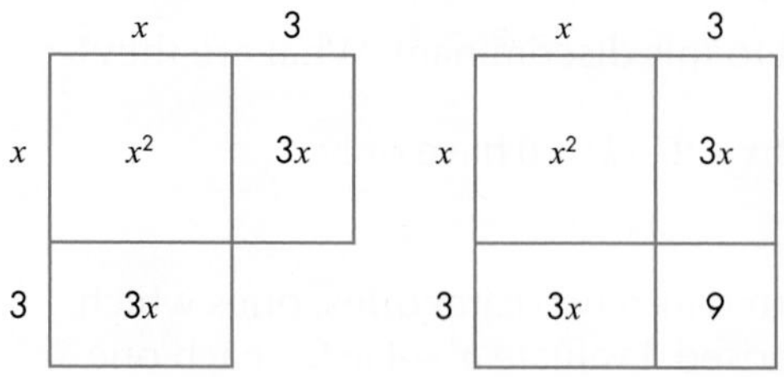

	x	3		x	3
x	x^2	$3x$	x	x^2	$3x$
3	$3x$		3	$3x$	9

In general, $x^2 + 2ax + a^2 = (x + a)^2$, which you can rearrange to give $x^2 + 2ax = (x + a)^2 - a^2$.

So $x^2 + 6x = (x + 3)^2 - 9$.

Example 12

Rewrite the following in the form $(x + a)^2 + b$ or $(x + a)^2 - b$.

a $x^2 + 10x$

b $x^2 + 6x - 13$

a $x^2 + 10x$ equals $x^2 + 2ax$ when $a = 5$.

Hence $x^2 + 10x = (x + 5)^2 - 25$.

b Ignore the -13 for the moment. $x^2 + 6x = (x + 3)^2 - 9$

Now bring the -13 back to get the final answer: $x^2 + 6x - 13 = (x + 3)^2 - 9 - 13$

$$= (x + 3)^2 - 22$$

Example 13

Rewrite $x^2 + 4x - 7$ in the form $(x + a)^2 - b$. Hence solve the equation $x^2 + 4x - 7 = 0$, giving your answers to 2 decimal places.

Start by ignoring the -7: $x^2 + 4x = (x + 2)^2 - 4$

Then adding the -7 back in gives: $x^2 + 4x - 7 = (x + 2)^2 - 4 - 7$

$$= (x + 2)^2 - 11$$

You can now rewrite $x^2 + 4x - 7 = 0$ by completing the square as: $(x + 2)^2 - 11 = 0$

Rearranging gives: $(x + 2)^2 = 11$

Taking the square root of both sides gives: $x + 2 = \pm\sqrt{11}$

$$x = -2 \pm \sqrt{11}$$

This answer is in surd form and you could leave it like this, but you are asked to evaluate it to 2 decimal places.

$x = 1.32$ or -5.32 (to 2 decimal places)

Example 14

Solve $x^2 - 6x - 1 = 0$ by completing the square. Leave your answer in the form $a \pm \sqrt{b}$.

$$x^2 - 6x = (x - 3)^2 - 9$$

So $x^2 - 6x - 1 = (x - 3)^2 - 9 - 1$

$$= (x - 3)^2 - 10$$

When $x^2 - 6x - 1 = 0$, then $(x - 3)^2 - 10 = 0$

$$\rightarrow (x - 3)^2 = 10$$

Taking the square root of both sides gives:

$$x - 3 = \pm\sqrt{10}$$

$$\rightarrow \quad x = 3 \pm\sqrt{10}$$

Exercise 17F

1 Write an equivalent expression in the form $(x \pm a)^2 - b$.

   a $x^2 + 4x$ **b** $x^2 + 14x$ **c** $x^2 - 6x$ **d** $x^2 + 6x$

   e $x^2 - 10x$ **f** $x^2 + 20x$ **g** $x^2 - 4x - 1$ **h** $x^2 + 6x + 3$

   i $x^2 + 8x - 6$ **j** $x^2 + 2x - 1$ **k** $x^2 - 2x - 7$ **l** $x^2 + 18x + 70$

 2 **a** Frankie writes the steps to solve $x^2 + 6x + 7 = 0$ by completing the square on sticky notes. Put the notes in the correct order.

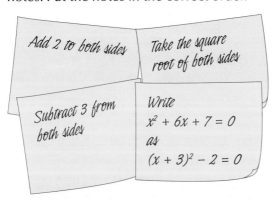

   b Write down the stages as in part **a** needed to solve the equation $x^2 - 4x - 3 = 0$.

   c Solve the equations below, giving the answers in surd form.

     i $x^2 + 6x + 7 = 0$ **ii** $x^2 - 4x - 3 = 0$

3 Solve the following equations by completing the square. Leave your answers in surd form where appropriate.

   a $x^2 + 4x - 1 = 0$ **b** $x^2 + 14x - 5 = 0$ **c** $x^2 - 6x + 3 = 0$

   d $x^2 - 10x - 5 = 0$ **e** $x^2 + 20x - 1 = 0$ **f** $x^2 + 8x - 6 = 0$

4 Solve by completing the square. Give your answers to 2 decimal places.

   a $x^2 + 2x - 5 = 0$ **b** $x^2 - 4x - 7 = 0$ **c** $x^2 + 2x - 9 = 0$

CM **5** Prove that the solutions to the equation $x^2 + bx + c = 0$ are:

$$-\frac{b}{2} \pm \sqrt{\left(\frac{b^2}{4} - c\right)}$$

(MR) **6** Dave rewrites the expression $x^2 + px + q$ by completing the square.

He correctly does this and gets $(x - 7)^2 - 52$.

What are the values of p and q?

(CM) **7** **a** Prove that the expression $x^2 - 12x + 40$ is positive for all values of x.

b What does this tell you about the graph of $y = x^2 - 12x + 40$?

(EV) **8** You have been asked to solve the equation $x^2 + 16x - 2436 = 0$.

You could factorise, use the quadratic formula or complete the square.

Evaluate all three methods, stating advantages and disadvantages where appropriate.

(PS) **9** The following statements are the steps in the method of completing the square to solve the equation $ax^2 + bx + c = 0$. Rearrange the steps to give the complete solution.

A $x = -\dfrac{b}{2a} \pm \sqrt{\dfrac{b^2}{4a^2} - \dfrac{c}{a}}$

B $\left(\left(x + \dfrac{b}{2a}\right)^2 - \dfrac{b^2}{4a^2}\right) + \dfrac{c}{a} = 0$

C $a\left(\left(x + \dfrac{b}{2a}\right)^2 - \dfrac{b^2}{4a^2}\right) + c = 0$

D $\left(x + \dfrac{b}{2a}\right)^2 = \dfrac{b^2}{4a^2} - \dfrac{c}{a}$

E $\left(x + \dfrac{b}{2a}\right)^2 - \dfrac{b^2}{4a^2} + \dfrac{c}{a} = 0$

F $x = -\dfrac{b}{2a} \pm \sqrt{\dfrac{b^2}{4a^2} - \dfrac{4ac}{4a^2}}$

G $x = -\dfrac{b}{2a} \pm \dfrac{1}{2a}\sqrt{b^2 - 4ac}$

H $a\left(x^2 + \dfrac{b}{a}x\right) + c = 0$

I $x = \dfrac{-b \pm \sqrt{b^2 - 4ac}}{2a}$

J $x + \dfrac{b}{2a} = \pm\sqrt{\dfrac{b^2}{4a^2} - \dfrac{c}{a}}$

17.5 The significant points of a quadratic curve

This section will show you how to:

- identify the significant points of a quadratic function graphically
- identify the roots of a quadratic function by solving a quadratic equation
- identify the turning point of a quadratic function by using symmetry or completing the square.

A quadratic curve has four interesting points for a mathematician. These are the points A, B, C and D on the diagram. The x-values at A and B are called the **roots**, and are where the curve crosses the x-axis. C is the point where the curve crosses the y-axis (the intercept) and D is the **turning point**, which is the lowest or highest point of the curve.

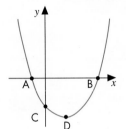
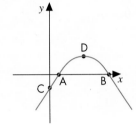

Exercise 17G

 1

    a Plot the graphs of
      i $y = x^2 - 4x - 5$ (use axes with $-2 \leqslant x \leqslant 6$ and $-10 \leqslant y \leqslant 7$)
      ii $y = x^2 + 6x + 8$ (use axes with $-7 \leqslant x \leqslant 1$ and $-1 \leqslant y \leqslant 15$) and
      iii $y = x^2 - 2x$ (use axes with $-2 \leqslant x \leqslant 4$ and $-1 \leqslant y \leqslant 8$).

    b State the coordinates of the points where each curve intersects the y-axis (the y-intercept). How does the y-intercept relate to the equation of the curve?

    c Solve each equation for $y = 0$.

    d Look at where each curve intersects the x-axis. Each curve should intersect the x-axis twice. How do these points relate to the equation of each curve?

    e Look at the turning point of each curve, the lowest point on each of these curves. Complete the square for each equation. What does this tell you about how the turning point relates to the equation of the curve?

The roots

You can find the roots of a quadratic curve by putting the expression equal to zero and solving the quadratic equation. Remember that you may have to use the formula or complete the square instead of factorising.

The y-intercept

The constant term of the equation $y = ax^2 + bx + c$ is where the curve crosses the y-axis, when $x = 0$. The intercept is at $(0, c)$.

The turning point

If the turning point is the highest point, it is called the **maximum**.

If the turning point is the lowest point, it is called the **minimum**.

Because a quadratic graph has a vertical line of symmetry passing through the turning point, the x-coordinate of the turning point is always half-way between the roots. You can then find the y-value by reading from the graph or by substituting the x-value into the original equation.

Alternatively, you can find the turning point by completing the square.

When a quadratic is written in the form $(x - p)^2 + q$ then the minimum point is (p, q). Note the sign change of p. You will learn how this can be used to transform a graph in Chapter 24.

Note: If the x^2 term is negative then the graph will be inverted and the turning point will be a maximum.

Example 15

a Find the y-intercept, roots and turning point of the graph $y = x^2 + 8x - 65$.

b Sketch the graph of $y = x^2 + 8x - 65$.

a The y-intercept is the point where $x = 0$. When $x = 0$, $y = -65$, so the y-intercept is at $(0, -65)$.

To find the roots, solve the equation $x^2 + 8x - 65 = 0$.

Factorise: $(x + 13)(x - 5) = 0$

$$\rightarrow x = -13 \text{ or } 5$$

The roots are at $(-13, 0)$ and $(5, 0)$.

To find the turning point, complete the square:

$$x^2 + 8x - 65 = (x + 4)^2 - 16 - 65$$
$$= (x + 4)^2 - 81$$

Hence the minimum value of $(x + 4)^2 - 81$ is -81 when $x = -4$.

The turning point is at $(-4, -81)$.

b Sketch the graph, using the coordinates of the roots, y-intercept and turning point.

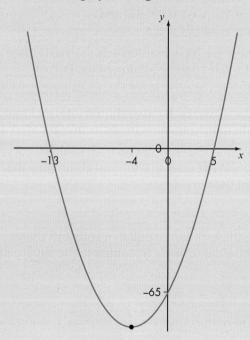

Example 16

a Find the y-intercept, roots and turning point of the graph $y = 1 + 4x - x^2$.

b Sketch the graph of $y = 1 + 4x - x^2$.

a The y-intercept is the point where $x = 0$, so the y-intercept is at $(0, 1)$.

To find the roots, solve the equation $1 + 4x - x^2 = 0$.

By multiplying both sides by -1, you can rewrite this equation as $x^2 - 4x - 1 = 0$.

This expression does not factorise ($b^2 - 4ac = 20$), but you can complete the square instead.

$$x^2 - 4x - 1 = 0$$
$$(x - 2)^2 - 4 - 1 = 0$$
$$(x - 2)^2 - 5 = 0$$
$$(x - 2)^2 = 5$$
$$x - 2 = \pm\sqrt{5}$$
$$\rightarrow x = 2 \pm \sqrt{5}$$

The roots are $(2 + \sqrt{5}, 0)$ and $(2 - \sqrt{5}, 0)$.

You can find the turning point by completing the square.

You found the roots by completing the square but on the expression $x^2 - 4x - 1$ rather than $1 + 4x - x^2$.

$$x^2 - 4x - 1 = (x - 2)^2 - 5$$

So multiplying both sides by -1 gives an equation we can use to find the turning point:
$$1 + 4x - x^2 = 5 - (x - 2)^2$$

$y = 5$ when $x = 2$ and the turning point is a maximum point $(2, 5)$.

b Sketch the graph, using the coordinates of the roots, y-intercept and turning point.

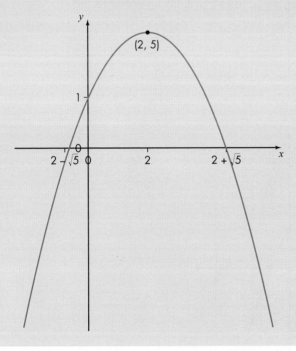

Exercise 17H

1 For each graph, write down

    i the coordinates of the *y*-intercept

    ii the coordinates of points where the curve intersects the *x*-axis

    iii the coordinates of the turning point.

a

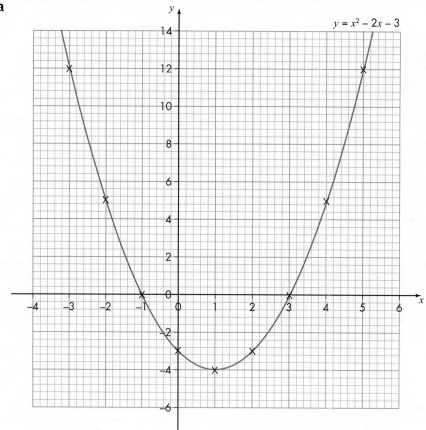

$y = x^2 - 2x - 3$

b

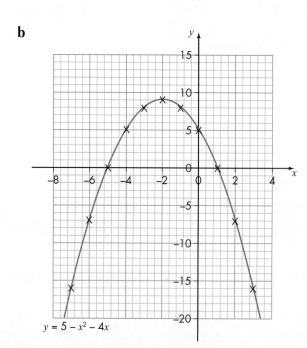

$y = 5 - x^2 - 4x$

2

a Plot the graph of $y = x^2 - 6x - 16$ for $-4 \leqslant x \leqslant 10$.

b Write down the coordinates of

   i the y-intercept

   ii the points where the curve intersects the x-axis

   iii the turning point.

3 Work out the roots and y-intercept of the graphs of:

   a $y = x^2 - 4$ **b** $y = x^2 - 6x$ **c** $y = x^2 - 2x - 3$ **d** $y = x^2 + 14x + 33$

4 Work out the coordinates of the turning point of the graph of $y = x^2 - 6x + 3$.

5 Work out the minimum value of the expression $x^2 - 8x + 2$.

6 Work out the maximum value of the expression $-x^2 + 2x - 6$.

(EV) **7**

a Work out the turning point of the graph of $y = x^2 - 4x + 4$.

b What does your answer tell you about the roots of $y = x^2 - 4x + 4$?

(PS) **8** Work out the roots, y-intercept and turning point of the graph of $y = 2x^2 - 9x - 5$.

9 Work out the roots and turning point of the graph of $y = 2x^2 - 25x + 73$, giving all values correct to 2 decimal places.

10 Sketch the graph of $y = x^2 - 10x - 39$. You should include the roots, y-intercept and turning point.

(MR) **11** Masood draws a quadratic graph that has a minimum point at $(3, -7)$ but forgets to label it.

He knows it is of the form $y = x^2 + px + q$.

Help Masood to find the values of p and q.

(MR) **12**

a The graph $y = x^2 + 4x + 2$ has a minimum point at $(-2, 2)$.

   Write down the minimum point of the graph $y = x^2 + 4x - 3$.

b The graph $y = x^2 - 2ax + b$ has a minimum point at $(a, b - a^2)$.

   Write down the minimum points of:

   i $y = x^2 - 2ax + 2b$

   ii $y = x^2 - 4ax + b$

(PS) **13** Find the equation of a quadratic graph from its significant points:

- its turning point is at $(-4, -18)$;
- its roots are at $(-7, 0)$ and $(-1, 0)$;
- its y-intercept is at $(0, 14)$.

(PS) **14** A ball is fired vertically upwards.

After t seconds, its height above the ground is given in metres by $h = 60 + 20t - 5t^2$.

a Write down its initial height above the ground.

b Work out the maximum height it reaches above the ground and the time at which this occurs.

c Work out the time at which the ball will hit the ground.

17.6 Solving one linear and one non-linear equation using graphs

This section will show you how to:

- solve a pair of simultaneous equations where one is linear and one is non-linear, using graphs.

Key terms

linear

non-linear

You will see how to use an algebraic method for solving a pair of simultaneous equations where one is **linear** (a straight line) and one is **non-linear** (a curve) in Section 17.8. In this section, you will learn how to do this graphically. The point where the graphs cross gives the solution. However, in most cases, there are two solutions, because the straight line will cross the curve twice.

Most of the non-linear graphs will be quadratic graphs, but there is one other type you can meet. This is an equation of the form $x^2 + y^2 = r^2$, which is a circle, with the centre as the origin and a radius of r.

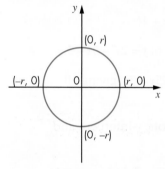

Consider finding the approximate solutions of the pair of equations $y = x^2 + x - 2$ and $y = 2x + 3$ by graphical means.

Set up a table for the quadratic equation.

x	−4	−3	−2	−1	0	1	2	3	4
y	10	4	0	−2	−2	0	4	10	18

Draw both graphs on the same set of axes.

From the graph, you can read the approximate solutions as (−1.8, −0.6) and (2.8, 8.6).

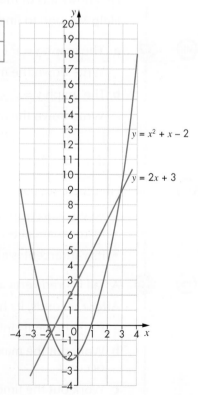

Example 17

Find the approximate solutions of the pair of equations $x^2 + y^2 = 25$ and $y = x + 2$ by graphical means.

The curve is a circle of radius 5 centred on the origin.

From the graph, you can read the approximate solutions as $(-4.4, -2.4)$, $(2.4, 4.4)$.

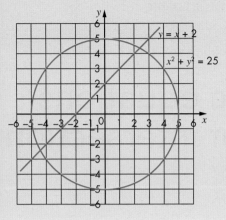

Exercise 17I

1 Use graphical methods to find the approximate or exact solutions to the following pairs of simultaneous equations. In this question, suitable ranges for the axes are given.

a $y = x^2 + 3x - 2$ and $y = x$ $(-5 \leqslant x \leqslant 5, -5 \leqslant y \leqslant 5)$

b $y = x^2 - 3x - 6$ and $y = 2x$ $(-4 \leqslant x \leqslant 8, -10 \leqslant y \leqslant 20)$

c $x^2 + y^2 = 25$ and $x + y = 1$ $(-6 \leqslant x \leqslant 6, -6 \leqslant y \leqslant 6)$

d $x^2 + y^2 = 4$ and $y = x + 1$ $(-5 \leqslant x \leqslant 5, -5 \leqslant y \leqslant 5)$

e $y = x^2 - 3x + 1$ and $y = 2x - 1$ $(0 \leqslant x \leqslant 6, -4 \leqslant y \leqslant 12)$

f $y = x^2 - 3$ and $y = x + 3$ $(-5 \leqslant x \leqslant 5, -4 \leqslant y \leqslant 8)$

g $y = x^2 - 3x - 2$ and $y = 2x - 3$ $(-5 \leqslant x \leqslant 5, -5 \leqslant y \leqslant 10)$

h $x^2 + y^2 = 9$ and $y = x - 1$ $(-5 \leqslant x \leqslant 5, -5 \leqslant y \leqslant 5)$

(CM) **2** **a** Solve the simultaneous equations $y = x^2 + 3x - 4$ and $y = 5x - 5$ $(-5 \leqslant x \leqslant 5, -8 \leqslant y \leqslant 8)$.

b What is special about the intersection of these two graphs?

c Show that $5x - 5 = x^2 + 3x - 4$ can be rearranged to $x^2 - 2x + 1 = 0$.

d Factorise and solve $x^2 - 2x + 1 = 0$.

e Explain how the solution in part **d** relates to the intersection of the graphs.

(CM) **3** **a** Solve the simultaneous equations $y = x^2 + 2x + 3$ and $y = x - 1$ $(-5 \leqslant x \leqslant 5, -5 \leqslant y \leqslant 8)$.

b What is special about the intersection of these two graphs?

c Rearrange $x - 1 = x^2 + 2x + 3$ into the general quadratic form $ax^2 + bx + c = 0$.

d Work out the discriminant $b^2 - 4ac$ for the quadratic in part **c**.

e Explain how the value of the discriminant relates to the intersection of the graphs.

(CM) **4** **a** Solve the simultaneous equations $y = 4x + 31 - x^2$ and $y = 12x - 1 - x^2$ $(-4 \leqslant x \leqslant 12, -5 \leqslant y \leqslant 40)$.

b Explain geometrically why these simultaneous equations have only one solution.

17.6 Solving one linear and one non-linear equation using graphs **493**

5 A pebble is projected vertically from the ground at 40 m/s. After t seconds, its height is $h = 40t - 5t^2$.

A second pebble is projected vertically from the ground one second later at 60 m/s. After t seconds, its height is $h = 60(t - 1) - 5(t - 1)^2$.

a Show that $60(t - 1) - 5(t - 1)^2$ can be rewritten as $5(13 - t)(t - 1)$.

b Plot both graphs on the same axes.

c Use the graph to find the time when both pebbles are at the same height.

17.7 Solving quadratic equations by the method of intersection

This section will show you how to:

- solve equations by the method of intersecting graphs.

You can solve many equations by drawing two intersecting graphs on the same axes and using the x-value(s) of their point(s) of intersection. Sometimes you can use the same graph to solve several equations.

To solve the equation $x^2 + 3x - 1 = 0$ using the graph of $y = x^2 + 3x - 2$ and its intersection with another graph, follow the steps below. This will give the equation of the other graph and the solution(s).

This method will give the required graph.

Step 1: Write down the original (given) equation. $y = x^2 + 3x - 2$

Step 2: Write down the (new) equation to be solved in reverse. $0 = x^2 + 3x - 1$

Step 3: Subtract these equations. $y = \qquad -1$

Step 4: Draw this line on the original graph to solve the new equation.

Draw the graphs of $y = x^2 + 3x - 2$ and $y = -1$ on the same axes.

The intersection of these two graphs is the solution of

$$x^2 + 3x - 1 = 0$$

The solutions, correct to 1 decimal place, are $x = -3.3$ and 0.3.

This works because you are drawing a straight line on the same axes as the original graph, and solving for x and y where they intersect.

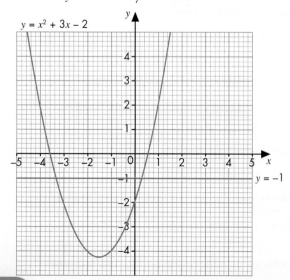

At the points of intersection the y-values will be the same and so will the x-values. This works because you can say:

$$\text{original equation} = \text{straight line}$$

Rearranging this gives: $\quad\quad\quad\quad$ (original equation) – (straight line) = 0

You have been asked to solve: $\quad\quad\quad\quad\quad$ (new equation) = 0

So $\quad\quad\quad\quad\quad\quad\quad$ (original equation) – (straight line) = (new equation)

Rearranging this again gives: $\quad\quad$ (original equation) – (new equation) = straight line

---

Example 18

Show how to solve the equation $x^2 + 2x - 3 = 0$ using the graph of $y = x^2 + 3x - 2$ and its intersection with another graph. Give the equation of the other graph and the solutions.

Write down the given graph: $\quad\quad$ $y = x^2 + 3x - 2$

Write down the new equation: $\quad$ $\underline{0 = x^2 + 2x - 3}$

Subtract: $\quad\quad\quad\quad\quad\quad\quad$ $y = \quad\quad x + 1$

Draw the graphs of $y = x^2 + 3x - 2$ and $y = x + 1$ on the same axes.

The intersection of the two graphs is the solution of $x^2 + 2x - 3 = 0$.

The solutions are $x = 1$ and -3.

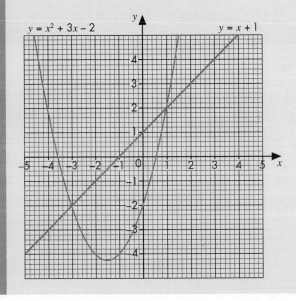

Exercise 17J

In questions **1** and **2**, use the graphs given here. Trace the graphs or place a ruler over them in the position of the line. You only need to give solution values to 1 decimal place. In later questions, draw the graphs yourself.

 1 Below is the graph of $y = x^2 - 3x - 6$.

   a Solve these equations.

      i $x^2 - 3x - 6 = 0$

      ii $x^2 - 3x - 6 = 4$

      iii $x^2 - 3x - 2 = 0$

   b By drawing a suitable straight line solve $2x^2 - 6x + 2 = 0$.

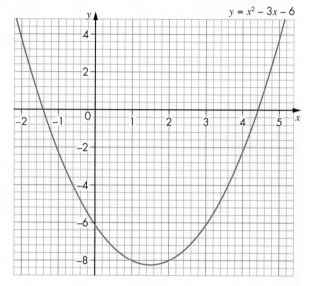

| Hints and tips | Cancel by 2 first. |

 2 Below are the graphs of $y = x^2 - 2$ and $y = x + 2$.

   a Solve these equations.

      i $x^2 - x - 4 = 0$

      ii $x^2 - 2 = 0$

   b By drawing suitable straight lines solve these equations.

      i $x^2 - 2 = 3$

      ii $x^2 - 4 = 0$

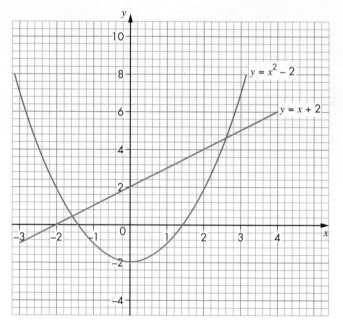

3 Draw the graphs of $y = x^2 - 3$ and $y = x + 2$ on the same axes. Use the graphs to solve these equations.

a $x^2 - 5 = 0$ **b** $x^2 - x - 5 = 0$

4 Draw the graph of $y = x^2 + 3x - 5$.

By drawing a suitable straight line, solve $x^2 + 2x - 7 = 0$.

(MR) **5** The graph shows the lines A: $y = x^2 + 3x - 2$; B: $y = x$; C: $y = x + 2$; D: $y + x = 3$ and E: $y + x + 1 = 0$.

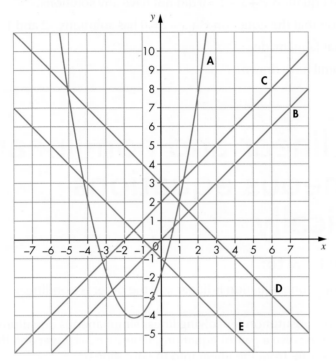

a Which pair of lines has a common solution of (0.5, 2.5)?

b Which pair of lines has the solutions of (1, 2) and (−5, 8)?

c What quadratic equation has an approximate solution of (−4.2, 3.2) and (0.2, −1.2)?

d The minimum point of the graph $y = x^2 + 3x - 2$ is at (−1.5, −4.25).

What is the minimum point of the graph $y = x^2 + 3x - 8$?

(MR) **6** Jack has already drawn a graph of $y = x^2 - 8x - 10$.

a Write down the straight line Jack would need to draw to use his graph to solve each of the following equations.

  i $x^2 - 8x - 10 = 5$ **ii** $x^2 - 8x - 10 = x + 3$ **iii** $x^2 - 8x = 0$

  iv $x^2 - 9x - 10 = 0$ **v** $x^2 - 11x - 1 = 0$ **vi** $x^2 - 7x - 12 = 0$

  vii $5x + 10 - x^2$

b What straight line could Jack draw to solve the equation $2x^2 = 17x + 26$?

(MR) **7** Jill has already drawn a graph of $y = 12 - 5x - x^2$.

a What equation is Jill trying to solve if she has plotted the line

  i $y = 7$ **ii** $y = x + 1$ **iii** $x + y = 3$ **iv** $3y = x + 6$?

  Write each answer with the right hand side equal to zero.

b Use the discriminant $b^2 - 4ac$ to show that $x + y = 17$ will not intersect $y = 12 - 5x - x^2$.

17.7 Solving quadratic equations by the method of intersection   **497**

(EV) 8 Jamil was given a sketch of the graph $y = x^2 + 3x + 5$ and asked to draw an appropriate straight line to solve $x^2 + x - 2 = 0$.

This is Jamil's working:

Original $\quad y = x^2 + 3x + 5$

New $\qquad \underline{0 = x^2 + x - 2}$

$\qquad\qquad y = \qquad 2x - 7$

When Jamil drew the line $y = 2x - 7$, it did not intersect with the parabola $y = x^2 + 3x + 5$.

He concluded that the equation $x^2 + x - 2 = 0$ did not have any solutions.

a Show by factorisation that the equation $x^2 + x - 2 = 0$ has solutions -2 and 1.

b Explain the error that Jamil made.

c What line should Jamil have drawn?

17.8 Solving linear and non-linear simultaneous equations algebraically

This section will show you how to:

- solve simultaneous equations where one equation is linear and the other is non-linear.

You have already seen the method of substitution for solving linear simultaneous equations. You can use a similar method when you need to solve a pair of equations, where one is linear and the other is non-linear, but you must always substitute from the linear into the non-linear.

Consider solving these simultaneous equations. Start by labelling them (1) and (2):

$$x^2 + y^2 = 5 \qquad (1)$$
$$x + y = 3 \qquad (2)$$

Rearrange equation (2) to obtain:

$$x = 3 - y$$

Substitute this into equation (1), which gives:

$$(3 - y)^2 + y^2 = 5$$

Expand and rearrange into the general form of the quadratic equation:

$$9 - 6y + y^2 + y^2 = 5$$
$$2y^2 - 6y + 4 = 0$$

Divide by 2:

$$y^2 - 3y + 2 = 0$$

Factorise:

$$(y - 1)(y - 2) = 0$$
$$\rightarrow y = 1 \text{ or } 2$$

Substitute for y in equation (2):

When $y = 1$, $x = 2$ and when $y = 2$, $x = 1$.

Note that you should always give answers as a pair of values in x and y.

Sometimes both equations will have y as the subject, in which case you can substitute for y.

Consider the simultaneous equations: $\qquad y = x^2 + x - 2$ and $y = 2x + 4$

Substituting for y gives: $\qquad\qquad\qquad 2x + 4 = x^2 + x - 2$

Rearranging into the general quadratic: $\qquad x^2 - x - 6 = 0$

Factorising and solving gives: $\qquad\qquad (x + 2)(x - 3) = 0$

$$x = -2 \text{ or } 3$$

Substituting back to find y: $\qquad\qquad$ When $x = -2$, $y = 0$.

$\qquad\qquad\qquad\qquad\qquad\qquad\qquad$ When $x = 3$, $y = 10$.

So the solutions are $(-2, 0)$ and $(3, 10)$.

Exercise 17K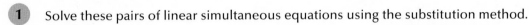

1. Solve these pairs of linear simultaneous equations using the substitution method.

   a $2x + y = 9$ $\qquad\qquad$ **b** $3x - 2y = 10$ $\qquad\qquad$ **c** $x - 2y = 10$
   $\quad\; x - 2y = 7$ $\qquad\qquad\qquad\;\; 4x + y = 17$ $\qquad\qquad\qquad\; 2x + 3y = 13$

2. Solve these pairs of simultaneous equations.

   a $y = x^2 + 2x - 3$ $\qquad$ **b** $y = x^2 - 2x - 5$ $\qquad$ **c** $y = x^2 - 2x$
   $\quad\; y = 2x + 1$ $\qquad\qquad\qquad\; y = x - 1$ $\qquad\qquad\qquad\;\; y = 2x - 3$

3. Solve these pairs of simultaneous equations.

   a $xy = 2$ $\qquad\qquad\qquad$ **b** $xy = -4$
   $\quad\; y = x + 1$ $\qquad\qquad\qquad\;\; 2y = x + 6$

4. Solve these pairs of simultaneous equations.

   a $x^2 + y^2 = 25$ $\qquad\qquad$ **b** $x^2 + y^2 = 9$
   $\quad\; x + y = 7$ $\qquad\qquad\qquad\;\; y = x + 3$

5. **a** FInd the coordinates of the points where the graphs of $x^2 + y^2 = 13$ and $5y + x = 13$ intersect.

   b Find the length of the chord joining the two points.

 6. **a** Given that $x^2 + y^2 = 74$ and that $y = 3x - 8$, show that $5x^2 - 24x - 5 = 0$.

   b Solve the simultaneous equations $x^2 + y^2 = 74$ and $y = 3x - 8$.

 7. **a** Given that $x^2 + y^2 = 185$ and that $y = 6x - 37$, show that $x^2 - 12x + 32 = 0$.

   b Solve the simultaneous equations $x^2 + y^2 = 185$ and $y = 6x - 37$.

8. Solve these pairs of simultaneous equations.

   a $x^2 + y^2 = 85$ $\quad$ **b** $x^2 + y^2 = 5$ $\quad$ **c** $x^2 + y^2 = 34$ $\quad$ **d** $x^2 + y^2 = 65$
   $\quad\; y = 2x - 5$ $\qquad\qquad\; y = 3x + 5$ $\qquad\qquad\; y = 4x - 17$ $\qquad\qquad\; y = 5x - 13$

9 **a** Solve the simultaneous equations: $y = x^2 + 3x - 4$ and $y = 5x - 5$.

b Which of the sketches below represents the graphs of the equations in part **a**?
Explain your choice.

i 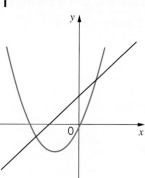 **ii** 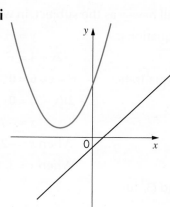 **iii**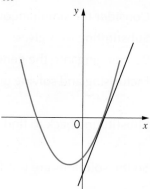

10 The simultaneous equations $x^2 + y^2 = 5$ and $y = 2x + 5$ only have one solution.

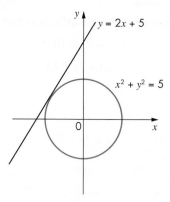

a Find the solution.

b Write down the intersection of each pair of graphs.

  i $x^2 + y^2 = 5$ and $y = -2x + 5$

  ii $x^2 + y^2 = 5$ and $y = -2x - 5$

  iii $x^2 + y^2 = 5$ and $y = 2x - 5$

11 Solve these pairs of simultaneous equations.

a $y = x^2 + x - 2$ **b** $y = x^2 + 2x - 3$

   $y = 5x - 6$ $y = 4x - 4$

c What is the geometrical significance of the answers to parts **a** and **b**?

12 A tennis court has an area of 224 m². If the length were decreased by 1 m and the width increased by 1 m, the area would be increased by 1 m². Find the dimensions of the court.

13 Helen worked out that she could save 30 minutes on a 45 km journey if she travelled at an average speed that was 15 km/h faster than her original intended speed. Find the speed at which Helen had originally planned to travel.

14 Claire intended to spend £3.20 on balloons for her party. But each balloon cost her 2p more than she expected, so she had to buy eight fewer balloons. Find the cost of each balloon.

17.9 Quadratic inequalities

This section will show you how to:

- solve quadratic inequalities.

In Chapter 15, you met linear inequalities, how to illustrate them on a number line and how to use set notation. In this section you will discover how to do the same for **quadratic inequalities**.

The expression '$x^2 - 4$' is greater than 0 when x is bigger than 2, but it is also greater than 0 when x is less than -2. For example, $5^2 - 4 = 21$, which is greater than zero, but $(-5)^2 - 4 = 21$ too.

So you would write that $x^2 - 4 > 0$ when $x < -2$ and $x > 2$.

Similarly, $x^2 - 4 < 0$ when $-2 < x < 2$.

Using set notation, the integer answers are $\{-1, 0, 1\}$.

Because of the shape of a quadratic graph, there may be one or two sets of values. Whether the quadratic expression is less than or greater than zero, you first need to find out when the quadratic expression is equal to zero, by solving a quadratic equation. These answers are called the **critical values**. You can then use these critical values to sketch the quadratic graph and you can then use the quadratic graph to determine the set(s) of values for x for which the quadratic inequality is true.

Example 19

Joseph has completed a table of values for $y = 2x^2 - 3x - 2$.

x	-2	-1.5	-1	-0.5	0	0.5	1	1.5	2	2.5	3	3.5
y	12	7	3	0	-2	-3	-3	-2	0	3	7	12

State the set of values for which

i $2x^2 - 3x - 2 = 0$ **ii** $2x^2 - 3x - 2 < 0$ **iii** $2x^2 - 3x - 2 \geqslant 0$.

i From the table, $y = 0$ when $x = -0.5$ and $x = 2$, so $2x^2 - 3x - 2 = 0$ when $x = -0.5$ and $x = 2$.

ii From the table, $y < 0$ for all values of x between -0.5 and 2. You would write $-0.5 < x < 2$. Note that this includes all the values between -0.5 and 2, not just the values in the table.

iii $y \geqslant 0$ for all values of x less than or equal to -0.5 and all values of x greater than or equal to 2. You would write this as $x \leqslant -0.5$ and $x \geqslant 2$.

Example 20

a Solve   **i** $x^2 + 2x - 15 \geqslant 0$ **ii** $x^2 + 2x - 15 < 0$

b Write the integer answers for part **ii** in set notation.

a i Factorise and solve $x^2 + 2x - 15 = 0$: $(x + 5)(x - 3) = 0$

The critical values are -5 and 3.

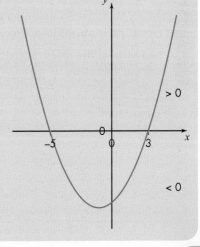

Sketch the quadratic graph, using the roots:

From the graph, $y \geqslant 0$ for $x \leqslant -5$ and $x \geqslant 3$.

a ii From the same graph, $y < 0$ for $-5 < x < 3$.

b The integer answers are $\{-4, -3, -2, -1, 0, 1, 2\}$

Example 21

A rectangle has sides of $(3x - 5)$ m and $(x - 2)$ m. If its area is less than 80 m² and its perimeter is at least 30 m, find the set of possible values for x.

Using the perimeter, you have a linear inequality:

$$2(3x - 5) + 2(x - 2) \geq 30$$
$$6x - 10 + 2x - 4 \geq 30$$
$$8x - 14 \geq 30$$
$$8x \geq 44$$
$$x \geq 5\frac{1}{2}$$

Using the area, you have a quadratic inequality:

$$(3x - 5)(x - 2) < 80$$
$$3x^2 - 11x + 10 < 80$$
$$3x^2 - 11x - 70 < 0$$

Solve the quadratic equation:

$$3x^2 - 11x - 70 = 0$$
$$(3x + 10)(x - 7) = 0$$

The critical values are $-\frac{10}{3}$ and 7.

Sketch the graph:

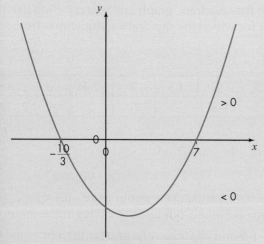

From the graph, $y < 0$ for $-\frac{10}{3} < x < 7$

Plot both answers on a number line.

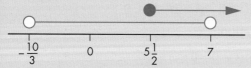

From the number line, the values of x that satisfy both inequalities are $5\frac{1}{2} \leq x < 7$.

Note that if the quadratic does not factorise but $b^2 - 4ac$ is still positive, you will need to find the critical values by using the quadratic formula or completing the square instead.

1 Solve

a $x^2 - 16 > 0$ **b** $x^2 - 100 \leqslant 0$ **c** $x^2 - x < 0$ **d** $x^2 + 5x \geqslant 0$

e $x^2 - 529 < 0$ **f** $4x^2 - 9 \geqslant 0$ **g** $3x^2 - 8x > 0$ **h** $2x^2 + 19x \leqslant 0$

2 State all the integers for which

a $x^2 - 9 \leqslant 0$ **b** $x^2 - 9x + 18 \leqslant 0$

Give the answers in set notation.

3 Solve

a $x^2 - 3x - 10 > 0$ **b** $x^2 + 12x + 35 < 0$ **c** $x^2 - 6x + 5 \geqslant 0$ **d** $x^2 \leqslant x + 72$

e $3x^2 - 10x + 3 \leqslant 0$ **f** $2x^2 + 13x + 11 > 0$ **g** $5x^2 + 6 \geqslant 13x$ **h** $6x^2 + 5x < 6$

4 Represent each solution on a number line:

a $x^2 + 10x - 24 < 0$ **b** $x^2 - 10x + 24 > 0$

5 **a** Find the set of values of x that satisfy both $4x - 23 \leqslant 2(x - 5)$ and $x^2 - 13x + 30 < 0$.

   b Find the set of values of x that satisfy both $5(x + 3) < 8x + 3$ and $3x^2 + 35 \leqslant 22x$.

6 Solve the inequality $12x < x^2 + 20$.

 7 For which values of x is the expression $x^2 - 4x + 6$ greater than the expression $21 + 3x - x^2$?

 8 A rectangle has sides of $(2x - 3)$ m and $(x + 1)$ m.

Its perimeter is at least 23 m and its area is at most 88 m².

Represent the possible values of x on a number line.

 9 **a** Solve $x^2 - 16x - 489\,936 < 0$.

   b Solve $x^2 + 8x + 11 > 0$, giving the critical values in surd form.

   c Solve $5x^2 \leqslant 3(x + 2)$, giving the critical values correct to 2 decimal places.

(PS) 10 A gardener has been asked to lay a patio 3 metres longer than its width.

Each slab is a square of side 0.5 m and costs £4.

The gardener has been asked to spend more than £220 but less than £448.

Find the two possible amounts he could spend.

(MR) 11 Solve the inequality $x^4 - 17x^2 + 16 > 0$

(MR) 12 **a** Verify that $\dfrac{30}{x - 3} > x + 4$ for $x = -10$ and $x = 5$.

   b Find the set(s) of all values of x for which $\dfrac{30}{x - 3} > x + 4$.

Worked exemplars

 1 A line segment is drawn between the points where the circle $x^2 + y^2 = 200$ and the line $y = x + 16$ intersect.

Show that the length of the line segment is $12\sqrt{2}$.

This is a question on communicating mathematically. You must demonstrate your method clearly, constructing a chain of reasoning that leads to a complete proof.	
$x^2 + y^2 = 200$ $x^2 + (x + 16)^2 = 200$ $x^2 + x^2 + 32x + 256 = 200$ $2x^2 + 32x + 56 = 0$ $x^2 + 16x + 28 = 0$ $(x + 2)(x + 14) = 0$ $x = -2, -14$ $y = 14, 2$ Lines intersect at $(-2, 14)$ and $(-14, 2)$	Start by finding the two points where the circle intersects the straight line.
Horizontal length: $-2 - (-14) = 12$ Vertical length: $14 - 2 = 12$ Length $= \sqrt{12^2 + 12^2}$ $= \sqrt{288}$ $= \sqrt{144} \times \sqrt{2}$ $= 12\sqrt{2}$	Finally, use Pythagoras' theorem to find the length of the line segment.

 2 The graph of $y = x^2 - 3x + 1$ has been plotted.

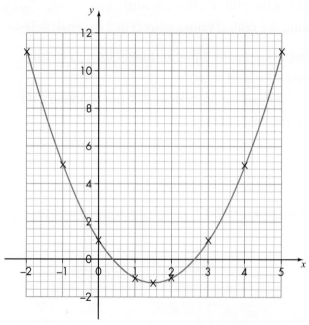

a By plotting an appropriate straight line on the same graph, solve the equation $x^2 - 4x - 2 = 0$.

b Comment on the accuracy of your answers.

This is an evaluation question, which means that you need to consider and analyse your results.

a $y = x^2 - 3x + 1$ $0 = x^2 - 4x - 2$ $\overline{y =\ \ \ \ \ \ \ \ x + 3}$	Start by determining the equation of the straight line that needs to be plotted.
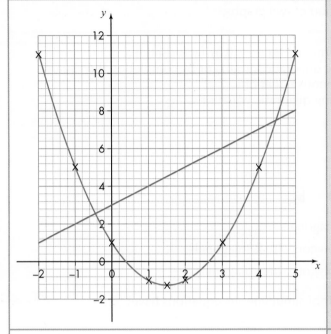	Plot $y = x + 3$.
$x = -0.4, 4.4$	Read off x values from intersection points correct to 1 decimal place.
b Quadratic Formula: $a = 1, b = -4, c = -2$ $x = \dfrac{-b \pm \sqrt{b^2 - 4ac}}{2a}$ $= \dfrac{-(-4) \pm \sqrt{(-4)^2 - 4(1)(-2)}}{2(1)}$ $= \dfrac{4 \pm \sqrt{24}}{2} = -0.4494897, 4.4494897 \text{ (7 dp)}$ Or: Completing the Square: $(x - 2)^2 - 4 - 2 = 0$ $\qquad\qquad\qquad\qquad (x - 2)^2 = 6$ $\qquad\qquad\qquad\qquad x - 2 = \pm\sqrt{6}$ $x = 2 \pm \sqrt{6} = -0.4494897, 4.4494897 \text{ (7 dp)}$	To check the accuracy of your results, use another method to solve the equation. Use the quadratic formula (or complete the square) to solve $x^2 - 4x - 2 = 0$. Write the answers to a greater accuracy than you found by the graphical method.
Answers found by method of intersection were accurate to 1 decimal place, but algebraic methods were more accurate.	Finally, evaluate the methods used and results obtained.

Ready to progress?

I can draw quadratic graphs from their tables of values.

I can solve a quadratic equation of the form $x^2 + ax + b = 0$
I can find the significant points of a quadratic graph.
I can solve equations, using the intersection of two graphs.

I can solve a quadratic equation of the form $ax^2 + bx + c = 0$ by factorisation.
I can solve a quadratic equation using the quadratic formula or by completing the square.
I can solve linear and non-linear simultaneous equations.
I can solve complicated problems involving quadratic equations.
I can solve quadratic inequalities.

Review questions

 1 An n-sided polygon has $\frac{1}{2}n(n-3)$ diagonals.

   a Find the number of sides of a polygon with 27 diagonals.

   b Find the number of sides of a polygon with n diagonals.

2 How many solutions does each pair of simultaneous equations have?

   a $x^2 + y^2 = 72$ and $x + y = 10$

   b $x^2 + y^2 = 72$ and $x + y = 12$

   c $x^2 + y^2 = 72$ and $x + y = 14$

3 **a** Show that the equation $\dfrac{6}{x+4} = \dfrac{8-5x}{x-2}$ can be rearranged to give $5x^2 + 18x - 44 = 0$.

   b Solve $\dfrac{6}{x+4} = \dfrac{8-5x}{x-2}$, giving your solutions correct to 3 significant figures.

> **Hints and tips** Multiply both sides by $(x+4)$ and $(x-2)$.

 4 The diagram shows a six-sided shape.

All the corners are right angles.

All the measurements are given in centimetres.

The area of the shape is 71 cm².

   a Show that $4x^2 + 9x - 69 = 0$.

   b Find the value of x, correct to 3 significant figures.

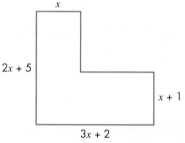

 5 The length of a rectangle is 5 m more than its width. Its area is 300 m². Find the actual dimensions of the rectangle.

6 **a** Plot the graph of $y = x^2 - 3x + 1$ for $-2 \leqslant x \leqslant 5$, $-1 \leqslant y \leqslant 11$.

   b By plotting appropriate straight lines, solve

     i $x^2 - 3x + 1 = 2$

     ii $x^2 - 4x + 2 = 0$

7 For the curve $y = x^2 - 20x + 36$, find

    a the coordinates of the y-intercept

    b the coordinates of the points where the curve intersects the x-axis

    c the coordinates of the turning point.

(MR) **8** A circle has the equation $x^2 + y^2 = 50$.

    Find algebraically where the line $x + y = 8$ intersects the circle.

9 Find the minimum possible value of:

    a $x^2 + 18x + 75$ **b** $x^2 - 8x + 19$

(PS) **10** A woman is x years old. Her husband is three years younger.

    The product of their ages is 550.

    a Set up a quadratic equation to represent this situation.

    b How old is the woman?

(MR) **11** Solve the inequalities:

    a $x^2 > 10x + 1575$

    b $x^2 < 4x + 89\,996$

    c $x^2 \geqslant 22x + 359\,879$

(PS) **12** The length of a carpet is 1 m more than its width. Its area is 9 m². Find the dimensions of the carpet to 2 decimal places.

(PS) **13** Find the area of a right-angled triangle with a hypotenuse of $(5x - 3)$ cm and shorter sides of $(x + 4)$ cm and $(4x + 3)$ cm.

14 Solve algebraically the simultaneous equations $x^2 + y^2 = 100$ and $y = 3x - 10$.

(MR) **15** **a** Factorise $p^2 - q^2$.

    b Hence show that $900 - 1 = 31 \times 29$

    c Given that $x^2 + 2x - 899$, find the value of $b^2 - 4ac$.

    d Hence solve $x^2 + 2x - 899 = 0$ by

        i factorisation   **ii** quadratic formula   **iii** completing the square.

(PS) **16** A rectangular garden measures 15 m by 11 m and is surrounded by a path of uniform width of area 41.25 m². Find the width of the path.

17 **a** Write $12 + 12x - x^2$ in the form $a - (x + b)^2$, where a and b are integers.

    b State the maximum possible value of $12 + 12x - x^2$.

(EV) **18** Sharon wants to solve the equation $a^2 + 26a = 9831$ but she does not have a calculator.

    Which method of solving quadratic equations would you recommend?

    Explain your answer and show the solution.

19 **a** Solve graphically the simultaneous equations $y = 16x - 10 - 2x^2$ and $y = 10x - 5 - x^2$.

    b Solve algebraically the simultaneous equations $y = 16x - 10 - 2x^2$ and $y = 10x - 5 - x^2$.

    c Solve $16x - 10 - 2x^2 \leqslant 10x - 5 - x^2$.

(CM) **20** Prove that $x^2 - 8x + 19$ is positive for all values of x.

18 Statistics: Sampling and more complex diagrams

This chapter is going to show you:

- how to collect data to obtain an unbiased sample
- how to draw and interpret frequency polygons
- how to draw and interpret cumulative frequency graphs
- how to draw and interpret box plots
- how to draw and interpret histograms.

You should already know:

- how to work out the mean, the median, the mode and the range from given data
- how to calculate an estimate for the mean from a grouped frequency table
- how to extract information from statistical diagrams
- the meaning of the terms 'discrete data' and 'continuous data'.

About this chapter

Statistical distributions can help you to understand your society and the world you live in. There are many different sorts of distribution, including population distribution and the normal distribution.

Population distribution asks or answers the question: "Where on Earth do people live?" Population density is a measure of the number of people living in a fixed area, such as a square mile or square kilometre. Calculating distributions over the whole planet shows that they are far from uniform.

Population density (people per km²) by country

The map shows areas of the world that are densely populated and areas where very few people live. In some areas it is easy to understand the distribution of the population. For example, central regions of Australia are so hot and so thickly covered in scrubland that very few people would want to live there, hence they are thinly populated. However, coastal regions that enjoy good climate are much more thickly populated.

The south-east of the UK is far more densely populated than the rest of the UK and much of Europe. In fact, the southern part of England has a very similar population density to India and Pakistan.

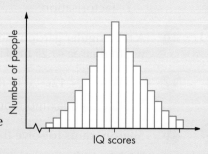

The normal distribution is a measure of the spread of data from a typical value. It is a very common distribution. For example, the bar chart shows the distribution of intelligence quotient (IQ) scores amongst a sample of the UK population. The curve follows the shape of the bar chart. It shows a typical normal distribution for a population, which you may meet in further studies of statistics.

18.1 Sampling

This section will show you how to:

- understand different methods of sampling
- collect unbiased reliable data for a sample.

Data collection

There is more than one way to collect data.

Data that you collect yourself is **primary data**. You control it, in terms of accuracy and amount.

Data collected by someone else is **secondary data**. There is a lot of this type of data available on the internet or in newspapers. It is useful because you can access a huge volume of data, but you do have to rely on its sources being accurate.

Statisticians often carry out surveys about a **population** for a wide variety of purposes. In statistics, the term 'population' can mean a group of objects or events as well as a group of people.

It is seldom possible to survey a whole population. There are some populations for which it would be physically impossible to survey every member. For example, suppose a marine biologist wanted to find the average length of eels in the North Sea. It would be impossible to find and measure every eel, so he would choose a small part of the population to survey and assume that the results for this **sample** are representative of the whole population. Even when it is physically possible, it would probably take too long and cost too much money.

To ensure the accuracy and reliability of a sample, you must address two questions.

- Will the sample be representative of the whole population and thereby eliminate **bias**?
- How large should the sample be, to give results that are valid for the whole population?

In statistics, you test hypotheses. A **hypothesis** is a statement based on a theory. Testing out a hypothesis involves a cycle of planning, collecting data, evaluating the significance of the data and then interpreting the results, which may or may not show that the hypothesis is true. This cycle often leads to a refinement of the problem, which starts the cycle all over again.

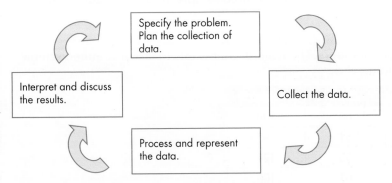

There are four parts to the data-handling cycle.

Part 1   State the hypothesis, outlining the problem and planning that needs to be done.

Part 2   Plan the data collection and collect the data. Record the data collected clearly.

Part 3   Choose the best way to process and represent the data. This will normally mean calculating averages (mean, median, mode) and measures of spread (range), then representing data in suitable diagrams.

Part 4   Interpret the data and make conclusions.

The hypothesis can then be refined or changes made to the data collected; for example, a different type of data may be collected or the same data may be collected in a different way. So the data-handling cycle helps to improve reliability in the collection and interpretation of data.

A gardener grows tomatoes, some in a greenhouse and some outside. He wants to investigate the following hypothesis.

'Tomato plants grown inside the greenhouse produce more tomatoes than those grown outside.'

Describe the data-handling cycle that may be applied to this problem.

Plan the data collection. Consider 30 tomato plants grown in the greenhouse and 30 plants grown outside. Count the tomatoes on each plant.

Collect the data. Record the numbers of tomatoes collected from the plants between June and September. Only count those that are 'fit for purpose'. This will avoid bias.

Choose the best way to process and represent the data. Calculate the mean number collected per plant, as well as the range. Draw a suitable diagram to show the data. This could be a pie chart or a bar chart.

Interpret the data and make conclusions. Look at the statistics. What do they show? Is there a clear conclusion or do you need to alter the hypothesis in any way? Discuss the results, refine the method and continue the cycle.

In describing the data-handling cycle, you must refer to each of the four parts.

Sampling methods

There are two main types of sample.

- In a **random sample**, every member of the population has an equal chance of being chosen. For example, it may be the first 100 people met in a survey, or 100 names picked from a hat or 100 names taken at random from the electoral register or a telephone directory.

- In a **stratified sample**, the population is first divided into categories and the number of members in each category is determined. The sample is then made up of members from these categories in the same proportions as they occur in the population. The required sample in each category is then chosen by random sampling.

The table shows a school's student numbers. The headteacher wants to take a stratified sample of 100 students for a survey on homework.

School year	Boys	Girls	Total
7	52	68	120
8	46	51	97
9	62	59	121
10	47	61	108
11	39	55	94
Total number in school			540

a Calculate the number of boys and girls in each year that should be interviewed.

b Explain how the students could then be chosen to give a random sample.

a First, work out the correct number in each category.

Boys in year 7: $\frac{52}{540} \times 100 = 9.6$ (1 dp)

Girls in year 7: $\frac{68}{540} \times 100 = 12.6$ (1 dp)

The table shows the results for all the years.

School year	Boys	Girls
7	9.6	12.6
8	8.5	9.4
9	11.5	10.9
10	8.7	11.3
11	7.2	10.2

Obviously you cannot have a decimal fraction of a student, so round all values and make sure that the total is 100. This gives the final table.

School year	Boys	Girls	Total
7	10	13	23
8	8	9	17
9	12	11	23
10	9	11	20
11	7	10	17
Total number in sample			100

b Within each category, choose students to survey at random. For example, you could put the names of all the Year 7 girls into a hat and draw out 13 names, or list them alphabetically and use the random number button on your calculator to pick out 13 names from 68.

Sample size

Before you start the sampling of a population you must determine how much data you need to collect, to ensure that the sample is representative of the population. This is called the **sample size**.

Sample size depends on:

- the desired precision with which the sample is to represent the population
- the amount of time or money available to meet the cost of collecting the sample data.

The greater the precision desired, the larger the sample size needs to be – but the larger the sample size, the greater the cost and the time taken. Therefore, you will always have to set the benefit of achieving high accuracy in a sample against the cost of achieving it.

The next example addresses some of the problems associated with obtaining an **unbiased** sample.

Example 3

You are going to conduct a survey among an audience of 30 000 people at a rock concert. How would you choose the sample?

You cannot question all of them, so you might settle for a sample size of 200 people.

Assuming that there will be as many men as women at the concert, you would need the sample to contain the same proportion of each: 100 men and 100 women.

Assuming that about 20% of the audience will be aged under 20, you would also need the sample to contain 40 people aged under 20 and 160 people aged 20 and over.

You would also need to select people from different parts of the audience, in equal proportions, to get a balanced view. So choose groups of people taken from the front, the back and the middle of the audience.

Exercise 18A

1 Decide whether you would use primary data or secondary data for each example.

   a Oliver wants to know which month of the year is the hottest.

   b Andrew wants to compare how good boys and girls are at estimating the size of an angle.

   c Joy thinks that more men than women go to football matches.

   d Sheehab wants to know if tennis is watched by more women than men.

   e A headteacher said that the more revision you do, the better your examination results.

   f A newspaper suggested that the older you are, the more likely you are to shop at a department store.

(CM) 2 Roxanne's maths teacher has asked her to find out if this hypothesis is true.

'In Year 11, the girls are better than the boys at spelling.'

Describe how she could use the data-handling cycle to test the hypothesis.

(CM) 3 Steve wants test this hypothesis.

'Students who play more sport watch less TV.'

Describe how he could use the data-handling cycle to test his hypothesis.

(MR) 4 Mr Charlton, the deputy head at High Storrs School, wanted to find out how often the upper-school students visited a fast-food outlet. The table shows the numbers of students in each upper-school year.

	Boys	Girls
Y9	119	85
Y10	107	118
Y11	104	110

   a Design a short questionnaire that Mr Charlton could use to sample the school.

   b Mr Charlton wanted to use a stratified sample using 60 students. To how many of each group of students should he give the questionnaire?

   c Explain how Mr Charlton could give out the questionnaires to each group of students.

(PS) 5 Naysha's school has 1860 students. She is in a class of 30 students. One day she noticed that that the headteacher was doing a survey over the whole school. Four boys and five girls in her class were involved in the survey.

Estimate the numbers of boys and girls in the whole school that were involved in the survey.

(CM) 6 You are asked to conduct a survey at a football match where the attendance is approximately 20 000. Explain how you could create a stratified sample of the crowd.

18 Statistics: Sampling and more complex diagrams

7 Claire makes a survey of the sixth-form students in her school. She wants to find out their opinions on the eating facilities in the school. The table shows the sizes of the two year groups in the sixth form.

Year group	Boys	Girls	Total
12	106	122	228
13	97	75	172
Total number in the sixth form			400

Claire decides to take a sample of 80 students.

a Explain why she should not sample equal numbers of boys and girls in the two years.

b Calculate the number of students she should sample in the sixth form.

  8 The manager of a company carries out a survey on wages for the employees using a 10% stratified sample. The table shows the numbers of staff in the sample.

	Male	Female	Total
Full time	13	7	20
Part time	4	6	10
Total number in the sample			30

Complete a similar table to show one possibility for the total number of employees in the company.

18.2 Frequency polygons

This section will show you how to:

- draw and interpret frequency polygons.

Key terms

frequency polygon

grouped data

mid-class value

Statistical information is often presented in pictorial or diagrammatic form to help people understand it. For example, you should have seen pictograms, pie charts, bar charts and vertical line charts.

You can also represent discrete or continuous **grouped data** in a **frequency polygon**. They show the shapes of distributions, and can be used to compare distributions. When you plot a frequency polygon for grouped data, you use the middle value of each group, just as in estimating the mean. This is called the **mid-class value**.

Example 4

The table shows the marks of 40 students in a spelling test.

Mark	0–4	5–9	10–14	15–19
Frequency	4	14	20	2

Show this grouped discrete data in a frequency polygon.

Write down the points to be plotted, based on the mid-class values.

(2, 4), (7, 14), (12, 20), (17, 2)

(continued)

Next, plot the frequencies and mid-class values.

(2, 4), (7, 14), (12, 20), (17, 2)

Complete the polygon by joining up the plotted points with straight lines.

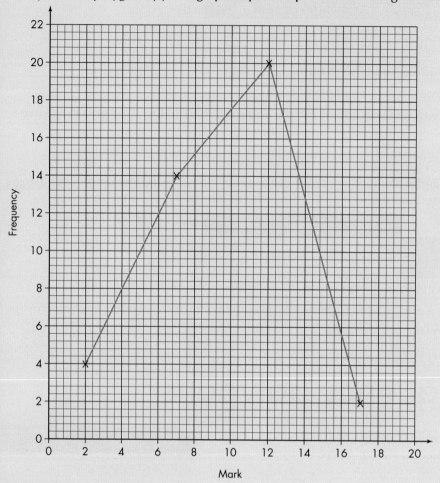

Example 5

The table shows the masses of 100 parcels.

Mass, m (kilograms)	$0 < m \leqslant 5$	$5 < m \leqslant 10$	$10 < m \leqslant 15$	$15 < m \leqslant 20$	$20 < m \leqslant 25$	$25 < m \leqslant 30$
Frequency	4	13	25	32	17	9

Show this grouped continuous data in a frequency polygon.

Plot the ordered pairs of mid-class values against the frequency.

(2.5, 4), (7.5, 13), (12.5, 25), (17.5, 32), (22.5, 17), (27.5, 9)

Complete the polygon by joining up the plotted points with straight lines.

You do not know what happens outside the range of the groups in the table, so do not draw lines before (2.5, 4) or after (27.5, 9).

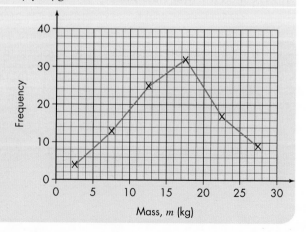

18 Statistics: Sampling and more complex diagrams

Exercise 18B

1 The table shows how many students were absent from one particular lesson during a term.

Number of students absent	1–3	4–6	7–9	10–12
Frequency	16	10	6	2

a Draw a frequency polygon to illustrate the data.

b Calculate an estimate for the mean number of absences for this lesson during the term.

(EV) 2 After a numeracy test, all the results were collated for girls and boys separately, as shown in the table.

Number of correct answers, n	$1 \leqslant n \leqslant 4$	$5 \leqslant n \leqslant 8$	$9 \leqslant n \leqslant 12$	$13 \leqslant n \leqslant 16$	$17 \leqslant n \leqslant 20$
Boys	3	7	21	26	15
Girls	4	8	17	23	20

a On the same diagram, draw frequency polygons to illustrate the boys' scores and the girls' scores.

b Estimate the mean scores for boys and girls separately.

c Comment on your results.

3 The table shows the heights of the girls in Year 11 at a London school.

Height, h (cm)	$120 < h \leqslant 130$	$130 < h \leqslant 140$	$140 < h \leqslant 150$	$150 < h \leqslant 160$	$160 < h \leqslant 170$
Frequency	15	37	25	13	5

a Draw a frequency polygon for the data.

b Estimate the mean height of the girls.

(EV) 4 The frequency polygon shows the amount of money spent in a corner shop by the first 40 customers one morning.

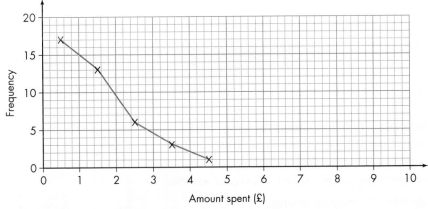

a i Use the frequency polygon to complete the table for the amounts spent by the first 40 customers.

Amount spent, m (£)	$0 < m \leqslant 1$	$1 < m \leqslant 2$	$2 < m \leqslant 3$	$3 < m \leqslant 4$	$4 < m \leqslant 5$
Frequency					

ii Calculate an estimate for the mean amount of money spent by these 40 customers.

b The shopkeeper records the amount spent by the first 40 customers in the afternoon. The table below shows the data.

Amount spent, m (£)	0 < m ≤ 2	2 < m ≤ 4	4 < m ≤ 6	6 < m ≤ 8	8 < m ≤ 10
Frequency	3	5	18	10	4

  i Copy the graph above and draw on it the frequency polygon to show this data.

  ii Calculate an estimate for the mean amount spent by the 40 afternoon customers.

c Comment on the differences between the frequency polygons and the average amounts spent by the different sets of customers.

5 A doctor was concerned at the length of time her patients had to wait to see her when they came to the morning surgery. The table shows the results of her three-day survey of waiting times.

Time, m (minutes)	0 < m < 10	10 < m ≤ 20	20 < m ≤ 30	30 < m ≤ 40	40 < m ≤ 50	50 < m ≤ 60
Monday	5	8	17	9	7	4
Tuesday	9	8	16	3	2	1
Wednesday	7	6	18	2	1	1

a On the same pair of axes, draw a frequency polygon for each day.

b What is the average amount of time spent waiting each day?

c Why might the average time for each day be different?

6 The frequency polygon shows the lengths of time that students spent on homework one weekend.

Calculate an estimate of the mean time spent on homework by the students.

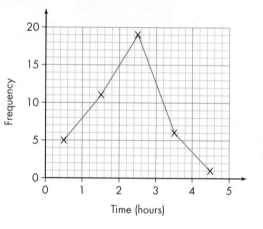

7 The frequency polygon shows the times that a number of people waited at a Post Office before being served one morning.

Julie said: "Most people spent 30 seconds waiting."

Explain why she may be wrong.

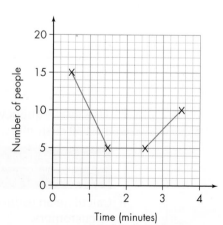

18.3 Cumulative frequency graphs

This section will show you how to:

• draw and interpret cumulative frequency graphs.

The marks of 50 students in a mathematics test have been put into this grouped table.

Mark	Frequency	Cumulative frequency
21 to 30	1	1
31 to 40	6	7
41 to 50	6	13
51 to 60	8	21
61 to 70	8	29
71 to 80	6	35
81 to 90	7	42
91 to 100	6	48
101 to 110	1	49
111 to 120	1	50

Key terms

cumulative frequency

cumulative frequency graph

cumulative frequency curve

dispersion	interquartile range
lower quartile	quartile
upper quartile	

The final column shows the cumulative frequency, which you can find by adding each frequency to the sum of all the preceding frequencies. For example, in the table, $1 + 6 = 7$, $7 + 6 = 13$, $13 + 8 = 21…$

You can use this data to plot a **cumulative frequency graph**. You would plot the points (30, 1), (40, 7), (50, 13), (60, 21), … to produce this graph. Notice that the points are plotted at the end of each group.

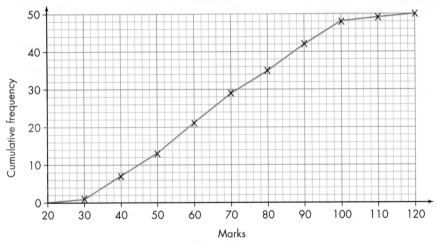

If the points are joined in a freehand curve, rather than as straight lines, the result is a **cumulative frequency curve**.

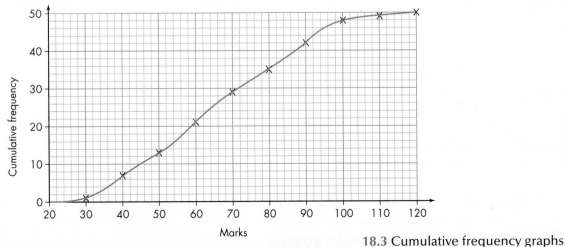

Note that the **cumulative frequency** is *always* shown on the vertical axis. The scales on both axes are labelled at each graduation mark, in the usual way.

Do not label the scales like this.

| 21–30 | 31–40 | 41–50 |

You can join the plotted points:

- by straight lines, to give a cumulative frequency polygon
- with a freehand curve, to give a **cumulative frequency curve**.

They are both called **cumulative frequency graphs**. If you need to draw a **cumulative frequency graph** you may use either form, but a cumulative frequency polygon is easier to draw.

The median

The median is the middle data value, when all the values are listed in order of size from lowest to highest. If you want to find the median from a simple list of discrete data, you *must* use the $\frac{1}{2}(n+1)$th value.

If n items of data values are plotted on a **cumulative frequency graph**, you can find the median from the middle value of the **cumulative frequency**, that is the $\frac{1}{2}n$th value. This is because the **cumulative frequency graph** treats the data as continuous, even for data such as examination marks, which are discrete. You can use the $\frac{1}{2}n$th value when working with cumulative frequency diagrams because you are only looking for an estimate of the median.

Since there are 50 values in the table above, the middle value is the 25th value. To find the median, you would draw a horizontal line from 25 on the cumulative frequency axis to meet the graph, then draw a vertical line down to the horizontal axis. This will give an estimate of the median. In this example, the median is about 65 marks.

The interquartile range

You can divide the cumulative frequency into four parts, to obtain the **quartiles** and the **interquartile range**.

The **lower quartile** is the value one-quarter of the way up the cumulative frequency axis and is given by the $\frac{1}{4}n$th value.

The **upper quartile** is the value three-quarters of the way up the cumulative frequency axis and is given by the $\frac{3}{4}n$th value.

The interquartile range is the difference between the lower and upper quartiles.

The interquartile range is a measure of the **dispersion** of a set of data. The advantage of the interquartile range is that it eliminates extreme values and bases the measure of spread on the middle 50% of the data.

Look again at the graph from the start of this section.

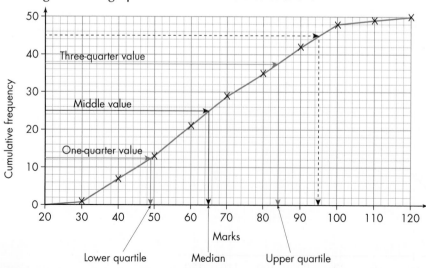

518   18 Statistics: Sampling and more complex diagrams

The quarter and three-quarter values out of 50 values are the 12.5th value and the 37.5th value. Drawing lines across to the cumulative frequency curve from these values and down to the horizontal axis gives the lower and upper quartiles. In this example, the lower quartile is 49 marks, the upper quartile is 84 marks and the interquartile range is 84 – 49 = 35 marks.

Consider this question. The headteacher gives an award to the top 10% of students. What is the minimum mark to earn the award?

The top 10% is the top five students (10% of 50 is 5). Drawing a line across from the 45th student to the graph and down to the horizontal axis gives a minimum mark of 95.

Example 6

The table shows the marks of 100 students in an English examination.

Mark	Number of students	Cumulative frequency
$21 \leqslant x \leqslant 30$	3	3
$31 \leqslant x \leqslant 40$	9	12
$41 \leqslant x \leqslant 50$	12	24
$51 \leqslant x \leqslant 60$	15	39
$61 \leqslant x \leqslant 70$	22	61
$71 \leqslant x \leqslant 80$	16	77
$81 \leqslant x \leqslant 90$	10	87
$91 \leqslant x \leqslant 100$	8	95
$101 \leqslant x \leqslant 110$	3	98
$111 \leqslant x \leqslant 120$	2	100

a Draw a cumulative frequency graph.

b Use your graph to find the median and the interquartile range.

c Students who score less than 44 have to resit the examination. Estimate the number of students who will have to resit the examination.

There are different ways of giving groups, depending whether the data is discrete or continuous, but the important thing to remember is to plot the highest value of each group against the corresponding cumulative frequency.

a Draw the graph.

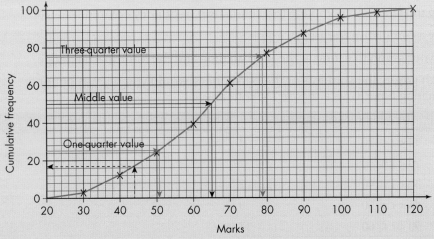

b Add the lines for the median (50th value), lower and upper quartiles (25th and 75th values).
Read the required answers from the graph.

Median = 65 marks   Lower quartile = 51 marks   Upper quartile = 79 marks

Interquartile range is 79 – 51 = 28 marks

(continued)

c Draw a perpendicular line up from 44 on the marks axis, to intersect the graph. At the point of intersection, draw a horizontal line across to the cumulative frequency axis, as shown.

The number of students who need to resit the examination is 17.

Hints and tips | The median is often abbreviated to m or Q_2, the lower quartile to Q_1, the upper quartile to Q_3 and the interquartile range to IQR.

Exercise 18C

1 A class of 30 students was asked to estimate a time of one minute. The teacher recorded the actual times when the students said one minute was over. The table shows the results.

a Copy the table and complete the cumulative frequency column.

b Draw a cumulative frequency graph.

c Use your graph to estimate the median time and the interquartile range.

Time, t (seconds)	Frequency	Cumulative frequency
$20 < t \leqslant 30$	1	
$30 < t \leqslant 40$	3	
$40 < t \leqslant 50$	6	
$50 < t \leqslant 60$	12	
$60 < t \leqslant 70$	3	
$70 < t \leqslant 80$	3	
$80 < t \leqslant 90$	2	

  2 A group of 50 pensioners was given the same task as the students in question **1**. The table shows the results.

a Copy the table and complete the cumulative frequency column.

b Draw a cumulative frequency graph.

c Use your graph to estimate the median time and the interquartile range.

d Which group, the students or the pensioners, would you say was better at estimating time? Give a reason for your answer.

Time, t (seconds)	Frequency	Cumulative frequency
$10 < t \leqslant 20$	1	
$20 < t \leqslant 30$	2	
$30 < t \leqslant 40$	2	
$40 < t \leqslant 50$	9	
$50 < t \leqslant 60$	17	
$60 < t \leqslant 70$	13	
$70 < t \leqslant 80$	3	
$80 < t \leqslant 90$	2	
$90 < t \leqslant 100$	1	

3 The table shows the numbers of students in 360 secondary schools in South Yorkshire.

a Copy the table and complete a cumulative frequency column.

b Draw a cumulative frequency graph.

c Use your graph to estimate the median number of students in the schools.

d Work out estimates for the lower and upper quartiles and write down the interquartile range.

e Schools with fewer than 350 students are threatened with closure. Estimate the percentage of schools that are threatened with closure.

Number of students	Frequency
101–200	12
201–300	18
301–400	33
401–500	50
501–600	63
601–700	74
701–800	64
801–900	35
901–1000	11

(MR) **4** The table shows the results when Sian recorded the midday temperature at 50 European resorts. Each temperature was recorded to the nearest degree.

a Copy the table and complete a cumulative frequency column.

b Explain why you must plot the temperature at the top ends of the groups at 7.5 °C, 10.5 °C, 13.5 °C, 16.5 °C, …

c Draw a cumulative frequency graph.

d Use your diagram to estimate the median temperature and the interquartile range.

Temperature, T (°C)	Frequency
5–7	2
8–10	3
11–13	5
14–16	6
17–19	6
20–22	9
23–25	8
26–28	6
29–31	5

5 At the school charity fête, a game consists of throwing three darts and recording the total score. The results of the first 80 people to throw are recorded in the table.

a Draw a cumulative frequency graph to show the data.

b Use your graph to estimate the median score and quartiles.

c People who score over 90 are given a prize. Estimate the percentage of the 80 people who receive a prize.

Total score, x	Frequency
$1 \leqslant x \leqslant 20$	9
$21 \leqslant x \leqslant 40$	13
$41 \leqslant x \leqslant 60$	23
$61 \leqslant x \leqslant 80$	15
$81 \leqslant x \leqslant 100$	11
$101 \leqslant x \leqslant 120$	7
$121 \leqslant x \leqslant 140$	2

6 Mrs James set her class an end-of-course test with two papers, A and B. She plotted cumulative frequency curves for the results.

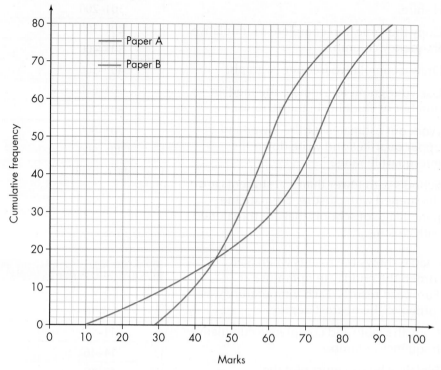

a What is the median score for each paper?

b What is the interquartile range for each paper?

c Which is the harder paper? Explain how you know.

d Mrs James wanted 80% of the students to pass each paper and 20% of the students to get a top grade in each paper.

What marks for each paper give:

   i a pass   **ii** the top grade?

7 Zara recorded the duration, in minutes, of 60 helpline telephone calls. She produced this cumulative frequency curve for the data.

Calculate an estimate for the mean length of the telephone calls.

8 The cumulative frequency table shows the ages of 200 people in a village.

Age, a (years)	Cumulative frequency
$0 < a \leqslant 20$	30
$20 < a \leqslant 40$	95
$40 < a \leqslant 60$	150
$60 < a \leqslant 80$	185
$80 < a \leqslant 100$	200

Calculate an estimate for the mean age of the people in the village.

18.4 Box plots

This section will show you how to:

- draw and interpret box plots.

Key terms

box-and-whisker plot

box plot

A **box plot** (sometimes called a **box-and-whisker plot**) is another way of displaying and comparing data. It requires five pieces of data: the lowest value, the lower quartile (Q_1), the median (Q_2), the upper quartile (Q_3) and the highest value.

Always place the data values against a scale so that you plot them accurately. This also means that anyone can interpret your box plot correctly.

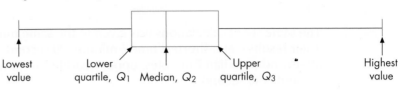

Lowest value   Lower quartile, Q_1 Median, Q_2 Upper quartile, Q_3 Highest value

Example 7

This is a box plot for the girls' marks in last year's end-of-year examination.

The boys' results for the same examination are: lowest mark 39, lower quartile 65, median 78, upper quartile 87 and highest mark 112.

a   On the same graph, draw the box plot for the boys' marks.

b   Comment on the differences between the two distributions of marks.

a

b   The girls and boys have the same median mark of 78. The interquartile range of 22 is also the same, but the range is smaller for the girls, showing that they are more consistent. Both the lower and upper quartiles for the girls are higher than those for the boys. This suggests that the girls did better than the boys overall, even though a boy got the highest mark.

Exercise 18D

(EV) 1 The box plot shows the times taken for a group of adults to do 10 long-multiplication calculations.

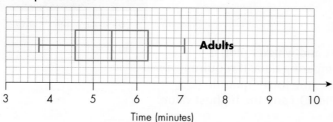

The same set of calculations was given to the same number of students in Year 11. Their results were: shortest time 3 minutes 20 seconds, lower quartile 6 minutes 10 seconds, median 7 minutes, upper quartile 7 minutes 50 seconds and longest time 9 minutes 40 seconds.

a Copy the diagram and draw a box plot for the students' times.

b Comment on the differences between the two distributions.

(EV) 2 The box plot shows the sizes of secondary schools in Dorset.

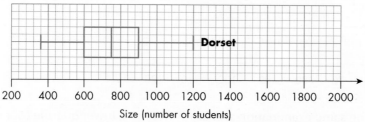

The data for schools in Lancashire is: smallest 280 students, lower quartile 1100 students, median 1400 students, upper quartile 1600 students and largest 1820 students.

a Copy the diagram and draw a box plot for the sizes of schools in Lancashire.

b Comment on the differences between the two distributions.

(EV) 3 The box plots for the noon temperature at two resorts, recorded over a year, are shown on the graph below.

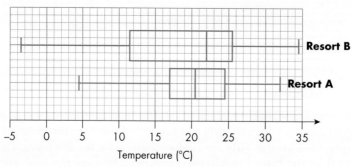

a Comment on the differences in the two distributions.

b Misha wants to go on holiday in July. Which resort would you recommend and why?

4 **EV** This table shows some data about the annual salaries for 100 men and 100 women.

	Lowest salary	Lower quartile	Median salary	Upper quartile	Highest salary
Men	£6500	£16 000	£20 000	£22 000	£44 500
Women	£7000	£14 000	£16 000	£21 500	£33 500

a Draw box plots to compare the sets of data.

b Comment on the differences between the distributions.

5 The table shows the monthly income of 100 families.

Monthly income (£)	Frequency
1451–1500	8
1501–1550	14
1551–1600	25
1601–1650	35
1651–1700	14
1701–1750	4

a Draw a cumulative frequency diagram to show the data.

b Estimate the median monthly income.

c Estimate the lower and upper quartiles.

d The lowest monthly income was £1480 and the highest was £1740.

Draw a box plot to show the distribution of incomes.

6 **MR** A health practice had two doctors, Dr Excel and Dr Collins.

The practice manager drew these box plots to illustrate the waiting times for their patients during October.

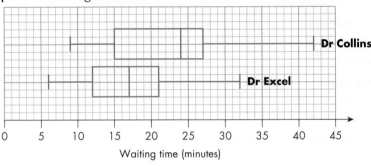

a For Dr Collins, what is:

i the median waiting time

ii the interquartile range for his waiting times

iii the longest waiting time for any patient in October?

b For Dr Excel, what is:

i the shortest waiting time for any patient in October

ii the median waiting time

iii the interquartile range for her waiting times?

c Anwar was deciding which doctor to try to see. Which one would you advise he chooses? Give reasons to support your answer.

7 **MR** Rodrigo was given a diagram showing box plots for the daily amounts of sunshine in the resorts of Bude and Torquay for August. No scale was shown.

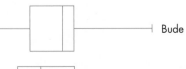

He was told to write a report about the differences between the amounts of sunshine in both resorts.

Write a report that he could possibly produce from these box plots.

These are the box plots for a school's end-of-year mathematics examination.

Estimate the difference between the means of the boys' and the girls' examination marks.

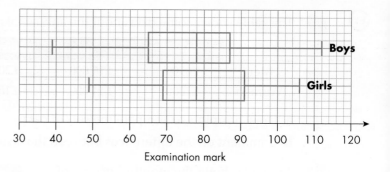

Examination mark

18.5 Histograms

This section will show you how to:

- draw and interpret histograms where the bars are of equal width
- draw and interpret histograms where the bars are of unequal width
- calculate the median, quartiles and interquartile range from a histogram.

Histograms with equal class intervals

A **histogram** looks similar to a bar chart, but there are four fundamental differences.

- There are no gaps between the bars.
- The horizontal axis has a continuous scale since it represents continuous data, such as time, mass or length and is divided into class intervals.
- The area of each bar represents the frequency of the bar.
- The vertical axis is labelled **frequency density**, where:
- frequency density = $\dfrac{\text{frequency of class interval}}{\text{width of class interval}}$.

The histogram below has been drawn from the table of times it takes people to walk to work.

Time, t (minutes)	$0 < t \leqslant 4$	$4 < t \leqslant 8$	$8 < t \leqslant 12$	$12 < t \leqslant 16$
Frequency	8	12	10	7
Frequency density	2	3	2.5	1.75

Each **class interval** has the same width of 4 minutes. You can work out the frequency density for each interval by dividing the frequency by 4.

Notice that each bar starts at the *least possible* time and finishes at the *greatest possible* time for each class interval.

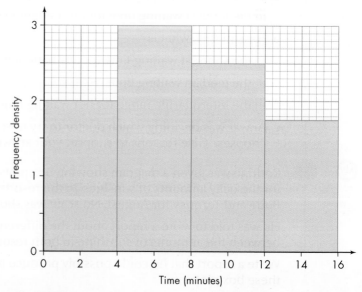

Histograms with unequal class intervals

Sometimes the data values in a frequency distribution are grouped into class intervals of different widths. In this case, the resulting histogram has bars of unequal width. It is important that you remember that the area of a bar in a histogram represents the class frequency of the bar.

In a histogram with bars of unequal width, you work out the height of each bar by dividing its class frequency by the width of its class interval (bar width), which is the difference between the lower and upper bounds for that interval. Conversely, given a histogram, you can find any of its class frequencies by multiplying the height of the corresponding bar by its width.

Example 8

The table gives the heights of a group of girls, classified as shown.

Height, h (cm)	$151 < h \leqslant 153$	$153 < h \leqslant 154$	$154 < h \leqslant 155$	$155 < h \leqslant 159$	$159 < h \leqslant 160$
Frequency	64	43	47	96	12

Draw a histogram to show this data.

It is convenient to write the table vertically and add two columns for class width and frequency density.

Work out the class width by subtracting the lower class boundary from the upper class boundary. Work out the frequency density by dividing the frequency by the class width.

Height, h (cm)	Frequency	Class width	Frequency density
$151 < h \leqslant 153$	64	2	32
$153 < h \leqslant 154$	43	1	43
$154 < h \leqslant 155$	47	1	47
$155 < h \leqslant 159$	96	4	24
$159 < h \leqslant 160$	12	1	12

Now draw the histogram. Mark the horizontal scale as normal, from a value below the lowest value in the table to a value above the largest value in the table. In this case, mark the scale from 150 cm to 160 cm. The vertical scale is always frequency density and is marked up to at least the largest frequency density in the table. In this case, 50 is a sensible value.

Draw each bar between the lower class boundary and the upper class boundary horizontally, and up to the frequency density vertically.

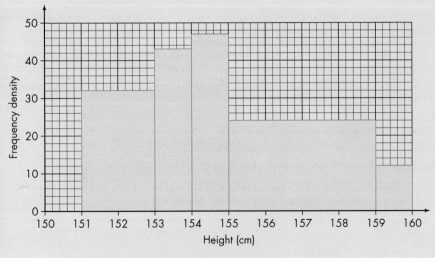

Example 9

This histogram shows the distribution of heights of 400 daffodils in a greenhouse.

a Complete a frequency table for the heights of the daffodils, and show the cumulative frequency.

b Calculate an estimate for the median height.

c Calculate an estimate for the interquartile range of the heights.

d Calculate an estimate for the mean of the distribution.

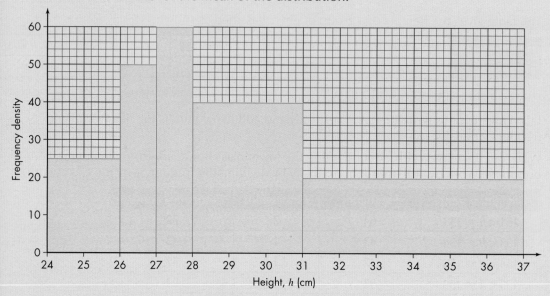

a The class intervals of the frequency table will be $24 < h \leq 26$, $26 < h \leq 27$, … Work out the frequencies by multiplying the width of each bar by the frequency density. Remember that the value on the vertical axis is not the frequency.

Height, h (cm)	$24 < h \leq 26$	$26 < h \leq 27$	$27 < h \leq 28$	$28 < h \leq 31$	$31 < h \leq 37$
Frequency	50	50	60	120	120
Cumulative frequency	50	100	160	280	400

b There are 400 values so the median will be the 200th value. Counting up the frequencies from the beginning, you reach the fourth column of the table above.

The median occurs in the interval $28 < h \leq 31$. There are 160 values before this group and 120 in it. To reach the 200th value you need to count 40 more values into this group. 40 out of 120 is one-third. One-third of the way through this group, which has a class interval of 3, is 29 cm. Hence the median is 29 cm.

This can be written as $28 + \dfrac{40}{120} \times 3 = 28 + 1 = 29$ cm.

c The interquartile range is the difference between the upper quartile and the lower quartile. In this case, the lower quartile is the 100th value and will be at the end of the $26 < h \leq 27$ interval. The upper quartile is the 300th value and will be in the $31 < h \leq 37$ interval. So, in the same way that you found the median, you can work out Q_1 and Q_3.

$Q_1 = 27$ cm

and $Q_3 = 31 + \dfrac{20}{120} \times 6 = 31 + 1 = 32$ cm.

So the interquartile range is 32 cm – 27 cm = 5 cm.

d To estimate the mean, use the table to get the midway values of the class intervals and multiply these by the corresponding frequencies. The sum of these divided by 400 will give the estimated mean. So, the mean is:

$$\frac{25 \times 50 + 26.5 \times 50 + 27.5 \times 60 + 29.5 \times 120 + 34 \times 120}{400}$$

$$= \frac{11\,845}{400}$$

$$= 29.6 \text{ cm (3 sf)}$$

Exercise 18E

1 Draw histograms, with equal class intervals, for these grouped frequency distributions.

a

Temperature, t (°C)	$8 < t \leqslant 10$	$10 < t \leqslant 12$	$12 < t \leqslant 14$	$14 < t \leqslant 16$	$16 < t \leqslant 18$
Frequency	5	13	18	4	3

b

Wage, w (£1000)	$6 < w \leqslant 10$	$10 < w \leqslant 14$	$14 < w \leqslant 18$	$18 < w \leqslant 22$
Frequency	12	24	40	18

2 Draw histograms, with unequal class intervals, for these grouped frequency distributions.

a

Age, a (years)	$11 < a \leqslant 14$	$14 < a \leqslant 16$	$16 < a \leqslant 17$	$17 < a \leqslant 21$
Frequency	21	24	10	20

b

Pressure, p (pascals)	$745 < p \leqslant 755$	$755 < p \leqslant 760$	$760 < p \leqslant 765$	$765 < p \leqslant 775$
Frequency	4	6	14	10

> **Hints and tips** The units for pressure are pascals (Pa).

c

Time, t (minutes)	$0 < t \leqslant 8$	$8 < t \leqslant 12$	$12 < t \leqslant 16$	$16 < t \leqslant 20$
Frequency	72	48	54	36

(PS) 3 The sales of a newspaper over 70 years are recorded in the table.

Years	1946–65	1966–85	1986–95	1996–2005	2006–10	2011–2015
Copies (nearest 1000)	62 000	68 000	71 000	75 000	63 000	52 000

Illustrate this information on a histogram.

(MR) **4** The London trains were always late, so one month a survey was undertaken to find how many trains were late, and by how many minutes (to the nearest minute).

The results are illustrated by this histogram.

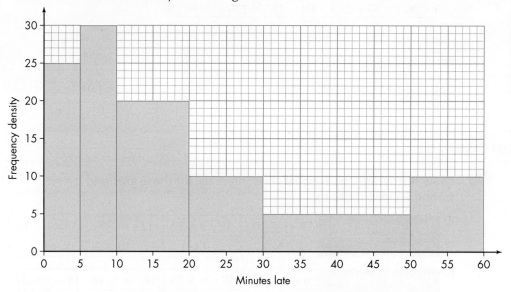

a i Explain how you work out the number of trains that were included in the survey.

ii Use your explanation to work out the number of trains in the survey.

b How many trains were delayed for longer than 15 minutes?

5 One summer, Monty monitored the mass of the tomatoes grown on each of his plants. His results are summarised in the table.

Mass, m (kg)	$6 \leqslant m < 10$	$10 \leqslant m < 12$	$12 \leqslant m < 16$	$16 \leqslant m < 20$	$20 \leqslant m < 25$
Frequency	8	18	28	16	10

a Draw a histogram for this distribution.

b Calculate an estimate for the median mass of tomatoes the plants produced.

c Calculate an estimate for the mean mass of tomatoes the plants produced.

d How many plants produced more than 15 kg of tomatoes?

6 The histogram illustrates the results of a survey to find the speeds of vehicles passing a particular point on the M1.

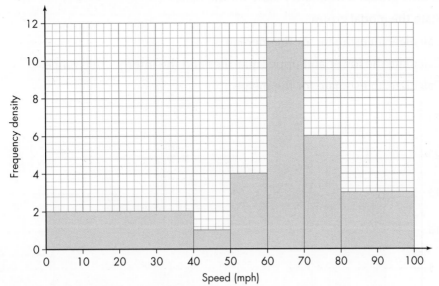

a Copy and complete the table.

Speed, v (mph)	$0 < v \leqslant 40$	$40 < v \leqslant 50$	$50 < v \leqslant 60$	$60 < v \leqslant 70$	$70 < v \leqslant 80$	$80 < v \leqslant 100$
Frequency						

b Work out the number of vehicles included in the survey.

c Calculate an estimate for the median speed of the vehicles passing this point on the M1.

d Calculate an estimate for the mean speed of the vehicles passing this point on the M1.

7 The histogram shows the test scores for 300 students in a school.

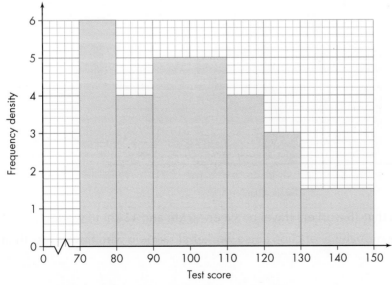

a Calculate an estimate for the median score.

b Calculate an estimate for the interquartile range of the scores.

c Calculate an estimate for the mean score.

d Given that 90% of the students passed this test, explain how to work out the pass mark.

8 The histogram shows the distribution of midday temperatures over a period of time.

   a Draw a grouped frequency table for the data.

   b State the modal group.

   c Calculate an estimate for the median.

   d Calculate the lower and upper quartiles and the interquartile range.

   e Calculate an estimate for the mean.

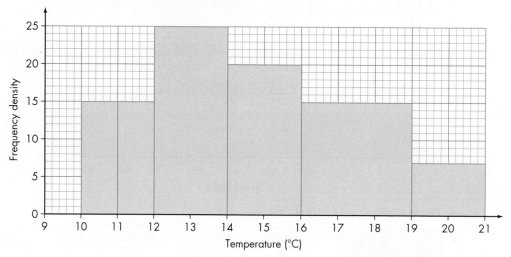

(PS) **9** The histogram shows the distances employees of a company travel to work.

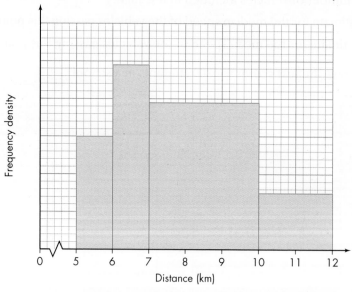

It is known that 18 workers travel between 10 km and 12 km to work.

What is the probability of choosing a worker at random who travels less than 7.5 km to work?

Worked exemplars

1 The mean speed of each member of a cycling club over a long-distance race was recorded and a frequency polygon was drawn.

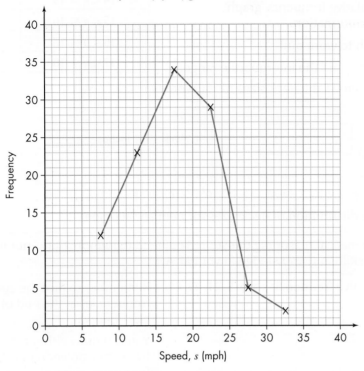

Use the frequency polygon to calculate an estimate for the mean speed.

This is a problem-solving question. You need to follow a series of processes to move the information from a graphical format into a tabular format.

	Create a grouped frequency table.			Remember that each plotted point is the mid-class value.

Speed, s (mph)	Frequency, f	Midpoint, m	$f \times m$
$5 < s \leqslant 10$	12	7.5	90
$10 < s \leqslant 15$	23	12.5	287.5
$15 < s \leqslant 20$	34	17.5	595
$20 < s \leqslant 25$	24	22.5	540
$25 < s \leqslant 30$	5	27.5	137.5
$30 < s \leqslant 35$	2	32.5	65
	100		1715

Estimate for the mean speed = 1715 ÷ 100	Use the information from your table to calculate an estimate for the mean speed to a suitable degree of accuracy.
= 17.15	
= 17.2 mph (1 dp)	

2 Simon makes men's and women's shirts. He needs to know the range of collar sizes so he measures 100 men's necks. The results are shown in the table.

Neck size, n (inches)	Frequency
$12 < n \leq 13$	5
$13 < n \leq 14$	16
$14 < n \leq 15$	28
$15 < n \leq 16$	37
$16 < n \leq 17$	10
$17 < n \leq 18$	4

a Draw a cumulative frequency graph to show this information.

b Use the graph to work out:

   i the median   **ii** the interquartile range.

c The box plot shows the neck sizes of 100 women.

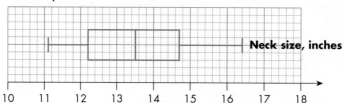

Compare the distribution of neck sizes for men and women.

This is a mathematical reasoning question. You need to demonstrate your use of mathematical skills and knowledge in your answer.

a The cumulative frequencies are: 5, 21, 49, 86, 96, 100

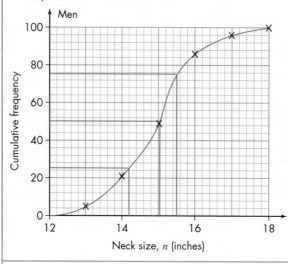

Remember to plot the cumulative frequencies at the end of each class interval.

You can draw either a cumulative frequency polygon or a cumulative frequency curve.

b **i** median = 15 inches

   ii lower quartile = 14.2 inches

      upper quartile = 15.5 inches

      So IQR = 15.5 – 14.2 = 1.3 inches

You need to read these values by drawing lines from the relevant places on the cumulative frequency axis: 50, 25 and 75.

c For women:

median = 13.5 inches

IQR = 14.7 – 12.2 = 2.5 inches

Comparing the medians shows that, on average, men have a larger neck size.

Comparing the IQRs show that the neck sizes of the women are more spread out.

You must carefully compare the medians and the IQRs and make a written conclusion.

Here you are making a deduction to draw a conclusion from mathematical information.

Ready to progress?

I know how to collect data to obtain an unbiased sample.
I can draw and interpret frequency polygons.

I can draw and interpret cumulative frequency diagrams.
I can work out the median, the quartiles and the interquartile ranges from cumulative frequency diagrams.
I can draw and interpret box plots.

I can use stratified sampling.
I can draw and interpret histograms where the class intervals are of equal and unequal widths.
I can calculate the mean, the median, the quartiles and the interquartile range from a histogram.

Review questions

CM **1** Explain how you can ensure that a sample is representative of a population.

EV **2** The frequency polygon shows the times taken by a group of 50 students to complete a mathematical puzzle.

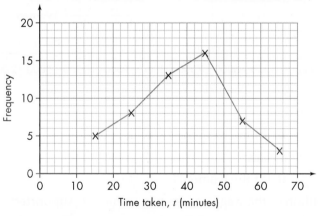

Time taken, t (minutes)

a The frequency table shows the times taken by a group of 50 adults to complete the same puzzle.

Time taken, t (minutes)	Frequency
$0 < t \leqslant 10$	4
$10 < t \leqslant 20$	11
$20 < t \leqslant 30$	19
$30 < t \leqslant 40$	10
$40 < t \leqslant 50$	6

On a copy of the diagram, draw a frequency polygon to show the times taken by the adults to complete the puzzle.

b Compare the times taken by each group to complete the puzzle. Make two comments supported by the data.

3 48 people went on a coach trip to the seaside.

The grouped frequency table shows information about their ages.

Age, a (years)	Frequency
$0 < a \leqslant 10$	4
$10 < a \leqslant 20$	6
$20 < a \leqslant 30$	10
$30 < a \leqslant 40$	22
$40 < a \leqslant 50$	4
$50 < a \leqslant 60$	2

a Copy the table and complete a cumulative frequency column.

b Draw a cumulative frequency graph.

c Use your graph to estimate the median age.

d Use your graph to estimate the lower quartile, the upper quartile and the interquartile range.

(MR) **4** The box plots show some information about the monthly wages of all the men and women who work for a large bank.

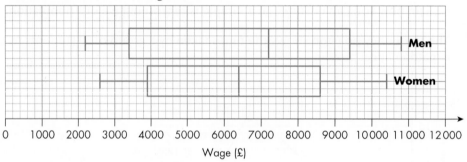

a Write down the median wage:

   i for the men   **ii** for the women.

b Work out the interquartile wage:

   i for the men   **ii** for the women.

c Compare the distribution of the wages. Make two comments supported by the data.

5 The table gives some information about the lengths of time some students took to run a cross country race.

Time taken, t (minutes)	Frequency
$40 < t \leqslant 50$	5
$50 < t \leqslant 55$	12
$55 < t \leqslant 60$	18
$60 < t \leqslant 70$	15
$70 < t \leqslant 90$	8

Draw a histogram to show the information in the table.

6 The histogram shows the distribution of ages.

a Draw the grouped frequency table for the data.

b State the modal group.

c Calculate an estimate for the median.

d Calculate the lower and upper quartiles and the interquartile range.

e Calculate an estimate for the mean.

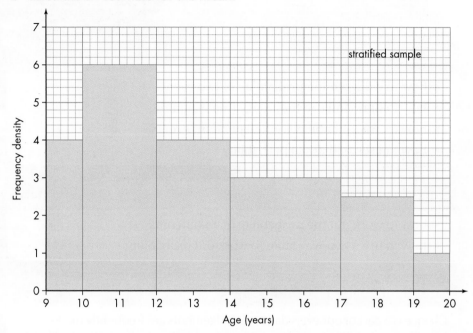

stratified sample

PS

7 Kelly has a cumulative frequency graph from a survey of 80 people about how much they spent at a local newspaper shop on one morning.

She knows that nobody spent less than 50p and nobody spent more than £6. The median amount was £3, the lower quartile was £2 and the upper quartile £4.

Explain how she could estimate the mean amount spent in the survey.

8 The table shows the number of students in each year group of a high school.

Year 7	Year 8	Year 9	Year 10	Year 11
214	205	242	266	273

There are 1200 students in the school.

The headteacher wants to carry out a survey on school uniform. She decides to take a stratified sample of 15% of all the students in the school.

How many students would she chose from each year group?

19 Probability: Combined events

This chapter is going to show you:

- how to work out the probability of two events
- how to draw and use frequency tree diagrams
- how to use probability for independent events
- how to use conditional probability.

You should already know:

- how to work out the probability of an outcome
- how to use a two-way table to work out probability.

About this chapter

Chance is a part of our everyday lives. Judgements are frequently made based on probability. A good example is the weather forecast. You are likely to hear, for example: "There is a 40 per cent chance of rain today."

How do they know that?

- Records of data that predict possibility of rainfall go back as far as 1854, when meteorologists regarded the presence of nimbus clouds as an indication that there was a good chance of rain.

- Barometers were used to predict the chance of rainfall. A sign of falling pressure on the barometer was taken as an indication of a good chance of rain.

- Finally, the direction of wind was used to determine the chances of rainfall. If the wind blew from a rainy part of the country, the chance of rain would be high.

The occurrence of all these three indicators would almost certainly mean that rain would come.

19.1 Addition rules for outcomes of events

This section will show you how to:

- work out the probability of different outcomes of combined events.

You have used the addition rule already but it has not yet been formally defined.

When two outcomes are mutually exclusive, you can work out the probability of either of them occurring by adding up the separate probabilities.

Example 1

A bag contains twelve red balls, eight green balls, five blue balls and fifteen black balls. A ball is drawn at random. What is the probability of it being:

a red	**b** black	**c** red or black
d not green	**e** neither green nor blue?	

a $P(\text{red}) = \frac{12}{40} = \frac{3}{10}$ **b** $P(\text{black}) = \frac{15}{40} = \frac{3}{8}$

c $P(\text{red or black}) = P(\text{red}) + P(\text{black}) = \frac{3}{10} + \frac{3}{8} = \frac{27}{40}$

d $P(\text{not green}) = \frac{32}{40} = \frac{4}{5}$

e $P(\text{neither green nor blue}) = P(\text{red or black}) = \frac{27}{40}$

Note: In part **e**, 'not green' and 'not blue' are not mutually exclusive as 'not green' includes 'blue' and 'not blue' includes 'green', so the addition rule does not work here.

So $P(\text{neither green nor blue}) \neq P(\text{not green}) + P(\text{not blue})$

Exercise 19A

1 Jenny picks a card from a standard pack. What is the probability that she picks:

a a heart   **b** a club   **c** a heart or a club?

2 Ben chooses a card at random from this set.

Work out:

a P(choosing a B)   **b** P(choosing a vowel)   **c** P(choosing a B or a vowel).

3 A bag contains 10 white balls, 12 black balls and 8 red balls. Keva picks a ball at random from the bag. Work out the probability that the ball she picks is:

a white   **b** black   **c** black or white

d not red   **e** neither red nor black.

4 At the School Fayre tombola stall you win a prize if you draw from the drum a ticket with a number that ends in 0 or 5. There are 300 tickets in the drum altogether, numbered 1 to 300.

a How many winning tickets are there in the drum?

b What is the probability of getting a losing ticket?

5 John needs his calculator for his mathematics lesson. It is always in his pocket, his school bag or his locker.

The probability it is in his pocket is 0.35 and the probability it is in his bag is 0.45. What is the probability that:

a he will have the calculator for the lesson   **b** his calculator is in his locker?

(MR) **6** A spinner is numbered and coloured as shown in the diagram. The probabilities of scoring the different colours are given in the table.

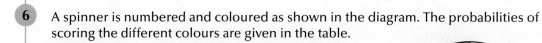

Colour	Probability	Number	Probability
Red	0.5	1	0.4
Green	0.25	2	0.35
Blue	0.25	3	0.25

Viv spins the arrow on the spinner.

a What is the probability of it stopping on:

   i red or green   **ii** 2 or 3   **iii** 3 or green   **iv** 2 or green?

b i Explain why P(1 or red) is not 0.9.

   ii Work out P(1 or red).

(PS) **7** A bag contains 200 coloured discs. Each disc is red, blue or green.

There are twice as many red discs as blue discs in the bag.

The probability of choosing a green disc is 0.31.

Work out the probability of choosing a red disc.

(CM) **8** The probability that it rains on Monday is 0.5. The probability that it rains on Tuesday is 0.3 and the probability that it rains on Wednesday is 0.2. Kelly argues that it is certain to rain on Monday, Tuesday or Wednesday because 0.5 + 0.3 + 0.2 = 1, which is the probability of a certainty. Explain why she is wrong.

9 Brian and Kathy want a selection of background music at their wedding reception. They upload 100 different tracks onto the MP3 player.

40 love songs   35 musical show songs

15 classical music tracks   10 rock tracks

They will set it to play the tracks continuously, at random.

a What is the probability that:

   i the first track played is a love song

   ii the last track of the evening is either a musical show song or a classical track

   iii the track when they start their meal is not a rock track?

b They want a love song or a classical track to be playing when they start cutting the cake. What is the probability that they will not get a track of their choice?

c The reception lasts for five and a half hours. For what amount of time, in hours and minutes, would you expect the MP3 player to be playing love song tracks?

10 James, John and Joe play the *Count Dracula* game together every Saturday. John is always the favourite to win, with a probability of 0.75.

In 2014 there were 52 Saturdays and James won eight times.

What was the probability of Joe winning?

19.2 Combined events

This section will show you how to:

- work out the probability of two outcomes or events occurring at the same time.

There are many situations where two events occur together. This is known as a **combined event**. Some examples are given below. Note that, in each case, all the possible outcomes of the combined events are shown in diagrams. These are called **theoretical probability space diagrams** or **sample space diagrams**.

Throwing two dice

Suppose you throw two fair dice, one red and one blue. The red dice can land with any one of six scores: 1, 2, 3, 4, 5 or 6. The blue dice can also land with any one of six scores. This gives a total of 36 possible combinations. These are shown in the left-hand diagram below, where each combination is given as a set of coordinates, such as (2, 3). The first number is the score on the blue dice and the second number is the score on the red dice.

The combination (2, 3) gives a total score of 5. The total scores for all the combinations are shown in the right-hand diagram.

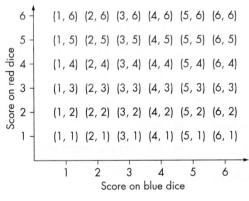 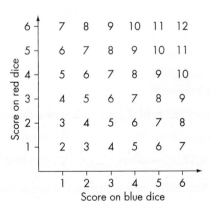

From the diagram on the right, you can see that there are two ways to get a score of 3. This gives a probability of:

$$P(3) = \frac{2}{36} = \frac{1}{18}$$

From the diagram on the left, you can see that there are six ways to get a 'double'. This gives a probability of:

$$P(\text{double}) = \frac{6}{36} = \frac{1}{36}$$

Coins and dice

Throwing one coin

There are two equally likely outcomes, head or tail.

$P(\text{head}) = P(\text{tail}) = \frac{1}{2}$

Throwing two coins together

There are four equally likely outcomes:

- two heads $\qquad\qquad$ P(2 heads) $= \frac{1}{4}$

- two tails $\qquad\qquad\quad$ P(2 tails) $= \frac{1}{4}$

- a head and a tail (two ways) $\quad$ P(head and tail) $= \frac{2}{4} = \frac{1}{2}$

Throwing a dice and a coin

There are 12 equally likely outcomes.

A head and an even number can be achieved in three ways.

$P(\text{head and an even number}) = \frac{3}{12} = \frac{1}{4}$

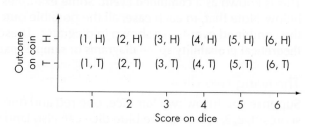

Exercise 19B

1 Sasha throws two fair dice, each numbered from 1 to 6.

a What is the most likely score?

b Which two scores are least likely?

c Copy and complete the table to show the probabilities of all scores from 2 to 12.

Score	2	3	4	5	6	7	8	9	10	11	12
Probability											

d What is the probability of a score that is:

  i bigger than 10   **ii** from 3 to 7 inclusive   **iii** even

  iv a square number   **v** a prime number   **vi** a triangular number?

2 When two fair dice are thrown, what is the probability that:

a the score is an even 'double'

b at least one of the dice shows a 2

c the score on one dice is twice the score on the other dice

d at least one of the dice shows a multiple of 3?

3 When two fair dice are thrown, what is the probability that:

a both dice show a 6

b at least one of the dice shows a 6

c exactly one dice shows a 6?

4 The sample space diagram shows the scores for the event 'the difference between the scores when two fair dice are thrown'.

a Copy and complete the diagram.

b What is the probability that the difference is:

   i 1   **ii** 0   **iii** 4

   iv 6   **v** an odd number?

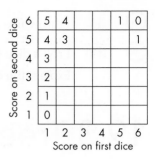

Score on second dice						
6	5	4			1	0
5	4	3				1
4	3					
3	2					
2	1					
1	0					
	1	2	3	4	5	6

Score on first dice

CM **5** Two fair coins are thrown together.

a What is the probability of scoring:

   i two heads   **ii** a head and a tail   **iii** at least one tail   **iv** no tails?

b Explain why the four events are exhaustive.

6 A dice and a coin are thrown together. What is the probability of scoring:

a a head on the coin and a 6 on the dice

b a tail on the coin and an even number on the dice

c a head on the coin and a square number on the dice?

7 Luka spins two fair five-sided spinners together. He records the total scores of the faces that they land on in a sample space diagram, like this.

a Copy and complete Luka's sample space diagram.

b What is the most likely score?

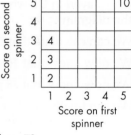

Score on second spinner					
5					10
4					
3	4				
2	3				
1	2				
	1	2	3	4	5

Score on first spinner

c When Luka spins two fair five-sided spinners together, what is the probability of his total score being:

   i 5   **ii** an even number   **iii** a 'double'   **iv** less than 7?

PS **8** **a** List all the possible outcomes when three fair coins are thrown together.

b Write down:

   i P(throwing three heads)   **ii** P(throwing two heads and one tail)

   iii P(throwing no heads)   **iv** P(throwing at least one tail).

MR **9** When one coin is thrown, there are two outcomes. When two coins are thrown, there are four outcomes. When three coins are thrown, there are eight outcomes.

a How many outcomes will there be when four coins are thrown?

b How many outcomes will there be when five coins are thrown?

c How many outcomes will there be when 10 coins are thrown?

d How many outcomes will there be when n coins are thrown?

PS **10** When Mel walked into her local shopping centre, she saw a competition taking place. Mel decided to have a go.

a Draw the sample space diagram for this event.

Roll 2 dice!

Score a total of 11 and win a prize!

b What is the probability of winning a prize?

c How many goes should she have in order to expect to win a prize at least once?

d If she had 40 goes, how many times could she expect to have won?

11 I throw five coins. What is the probability that I will get more heads than tails?

  12 I roll a dice three times and add the three numbers obtained.

Explain the difficulty in drawing a sample space to show all the possible events.

19.3 Tree diagrams

This section will show you how to:

- use tree diagrams to work out the probability of combined events.

In a survey of one hundred people about where they spent their main 2015 holiday, 80 people said they went abroad, the rest in the UK. Ninety one of them booked their holiday online, the rest at a travel agents. Four of the people who stayed in the UK for their main holiday booked at a travel agent.

We can show this information on a **frequency tree diagram**.

Start with 100 people in the left hand oval. Place the 80 people who went abroad and the 4 people who stayed in UK who booked at travel agents. (These are the numbers shown in black on the diagram).

We can calculate that 20 people stayed in the UK (100 – 80) shown on diagram in red.

We now know that 16 people who stayed in the UK booked on-line (20 – 4) shown in red.

We now know that 75 people who went abroad booked online (91 – 16) shown in red

We can finally say that 5 people who went abroad booked at a travel agents (80 – 75) shown in red.

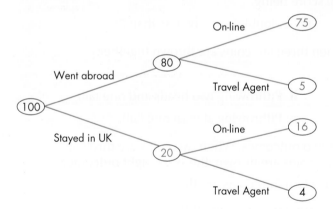

If one of these 100 people was chosen at random to win a free holiday, we can use this frequency tree diagram to help us to find the probability that this person went abroad after booking at a travel agents.

From the diagram we can see that 5 people went abroad after booking at a travel agents, giving the probability as 5/100 or 0.05.

Probability tree diagrams

Suppose you take two cards from this pack of six cards, but you replace the first card before you take the second card.

One way to show all the possible outcomes of this experiment is in a probability space diagram.

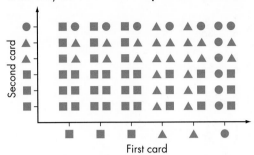

From the diagram, you can see immediately that the probability of taking, for example, two squares, is 9 out of 36 pairs of cards. So:

P(two squares) is $\frac{9}{36} = \frac{1}{4}$

Example 2

Look again at the probability space diagram above. What is the probability of taking:

a a square and a triangle (in any order)   **b** two circles   **c** two shapes that are the same?

a There are 6 combinations that give a square then a triangle and 6 that give a triangle then a square. So there are 12 combinations that give a square and a triangle altogether. So:

P(square and triangle, in any order) is $\frac{12}{36} = \frac{1}{3}$

b There is only 1 combination that gives two circles. So:

P(two circles) = $\frac{1}{36}$

c There are 9 combinations of two squares together, 4 combinations of two triangles together and 1 combination of two circles together. These give a total of 14 combinations with two shapes the same. So:

P(two shapes the same) is $\frac{14}{36} = \frac{7}{18}$

You can also use **probability tree diagrams** to solve problems involving combined events. Returning to the 'six-card' problem above, when you take the first card, there are three possible outcomes: a square, a triangle or a circle. For a single event:

P(square) = $\frac{3}{6}$ P(triangle) = $\frac{2}{6}$ P(circle) = $\frac{1}{6}$

You can show this by representing each outcome as a branch and writing its probability on that branch.

Then you can extend the diagram to show a second choice. Because the first card has been replaced, you can still take a square, a triangle or a circle, with the same probabilities. This is true no matter what you took the first time. You can demonstrate this by adding three more branches to each branch in the diagram.

Here is the complete probability tree diagram.

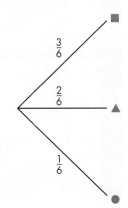

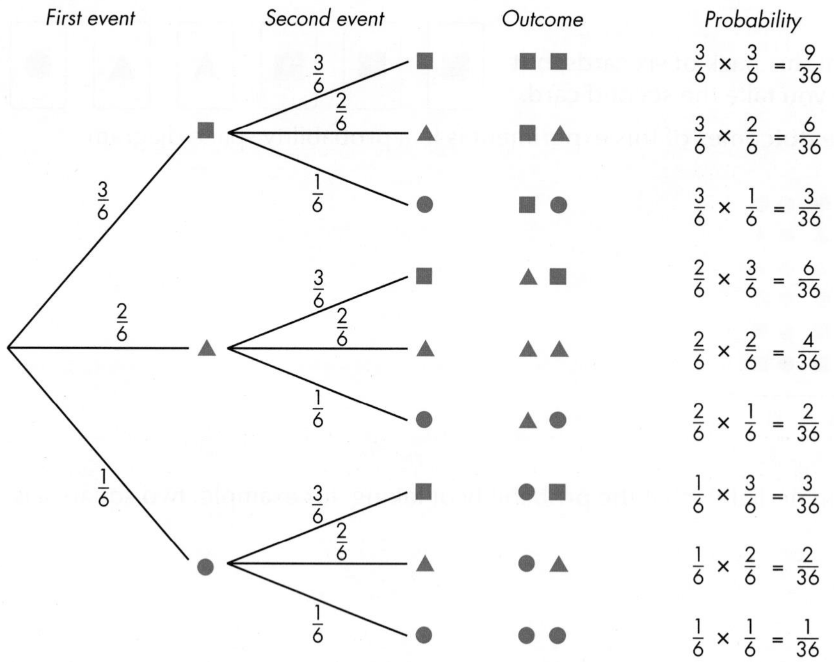

First event   Second event   Outcome   Probability

Probability tree diagram branches:

- First event square $\frac{3}{6}$:
  - $\frac{3}{6}$ → ■ ■ : $\frac{3}{6} \times \frac{3}{6} = \frac{9}{36}$
  - $\frac{2}{6}$ → ■ ▲ : $\frac{3}{6} \times \frac{2}{6} = \frac{6}{36}$
  - $\frac{1}{6}$ → ■ ● : $\frac{3}{6} \times \frac{1}{6} = \frac{3}{36}$
- First event triangle $\frac{2}{6}$:
  - $\frac{3}{6}$ → ▲ ■ : $\frac{2}{6} \times \frac{3}{6} = \frac{6}{36}$
  - $\frac{2}{6}$ → ▲ ▲ : $\frac{2}{6} \times \frac{2}{6} = \frac{4}{36}$
  - $\frac{1}{6}$ → ▲ ● : $\frac{2}{6} \times \frac{1}{6} = \frac{2}{36}$
- First event circle $\frac{1}{6}$:
  - $\frac{3}{6}$ → ● ■ : $\frac{1}{6} \times \frac{3}{6} = \frac{3}{36}$
  - $\frac{2}{6}$ → ● ▲ : $\frac{1}{6} \times \frac{2}{6} = \frac{2}{36}$
  - $\frac{1}{6}$ → ● ● : $\frac{1}{6} \times \frac{1}{6} = \frac{1}{36}$

Notice that the sum of all the probabilities is 1, as the outcomes are exhaustive.

You can calculate the probability of any final outcome by multiplying all the probabilities on its branches. For instance:

P(two squares) is $\frac{3}{6} \times \frac{3}{6} = \frac{9}{36}$ which cancels to $\frac{1}{4}$

P(triangle followed by circle) is $\frac{2}{6} \times \frac{1}{6} = \frac{2}{36}$ which cancels to $\frac{1}{18}$.

Example 3

Look again at the probability tree diagram above. What is the probability of taking:

a two triangles   **b** a circle followed by a triangle   **c** a square and a triangle, in any order

d two circles   **e** two shapes that are the same?

a P(two triangles) is $\frac{4}{36} = \frac{1}{9}$

b P(circle followed by triangle) is $\frac{2}{36} = \frac{1}{18}$

c There are 2 results in the outcome column that show a square and a triangle. These are in the second and fourth rows. The probability of each is $\frac{6}{36}$. Their combined probability is given by the addition rule.

P(square and triangle, in any order) is $\frac{6}{36} + \frac{6}{36} = \frac{12}{36}$
$$= \frac{1}{3}$$

d P(two circles) $= \frac{1}{36}$

e There are 3 final outcomes that have two shapes the same. These are on the first, fifth and last rows. The probabilities are respectively $\frac{9}{36}$, $\frac{4}{36}$ and $\frac{1}{36}$. Their combined probability is given by the addition rule.

P(two shapes the same) is $\frac{9}{36} + \frac{4}{36} + \frac{1}{36} = \frac{14}{36}$
$$= \frac{7}{18}$$

Note that the answers to parts **c**, **d** and **e** are the same as the answers found in Example 2.

Exercise 19C

1 80 students took a driving test.

Before the test each student predicted whether they would pass or fail.

50 students predicted they would pass.

After the test, 42 students who predicted they would pass did actually pass.

56 students passed the test.

Copy and complete the frequency tree diagram.

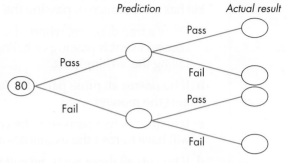

2 On my way to work, I drive through two sets of roadworks with traffic lights that only show green or red. I know that the probability of the first set being green is $\frac{1}{3}$ and the probability of the second set being green is $\frac{1}{2}$.

a What is the probability that the first set of lights will be red?

b What is the probability that the second set of lights will be red?

c Copy and complete the tree diagram, showing the possible outcomes when passing through both sets of lights.

d Use your tree diagram to work out the probability that:

   i I do not get held up at either set of lights.

   ii I get held up at exactly one set of lights.

   iii I get held up at least once.

e Over a school term I make 90 journeys to work. On how many days can I expect to get two green lights?

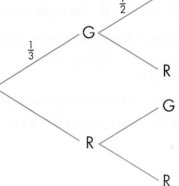

3 Six out of every 10 cars in Britain are made abroad.

a What is the probability that any car will be British made?

b Two cars can be seen approaching in the distance. Draw a tree diagram to work out the probability that:

   i both cars are British made   **ii** one car is British and the other was made abroad.

4 **a** Jack throws three fair coins. Copy and complete the tree diagram to show the possible outcomes.

First event	Second event	Third event	Outcome	Probability

$$\text{(H, H, H)} \quad \frac{1}{2} \times \frac{1}{2} \times \frac{1}{2} = \frac{1}{8}$$

b Use your tree diagram to work out the probability of throwing:

   i three tails   **ii** two heads and a tail   **iii** at least one tail.

5 Aziz takes a three-part language examination paper. He has a 0.4 chance of passing the first part, on 'speaking'. He has a 0.5 chance of passing the second, on 'listening'. He has a 0.7 chance of passing the third part, on 'writing'.

a Draw a tree diagram, where the first event is passing or failing the 'speaking' part, the second event is passing or failing the 'listening' part and the third event is passing or failing the 'writing' part.

b If he passes all three parts, his father will give him £50. What is the probability that he gets the money?

c If he passes two parts only, he can resit the other part. What is the probability that he will have to resit the examination?

d If he fails all three parts, he will be not be able to continue the course. What is the probability that he will not continue the course?

6 In a group of 10 girls, six like the pop group Smudge and four like the pop group Grudge. Two girls are to be chosen for a pop quiz.

a What is the probability that the first girl chosen will be a Smudge fan?

b Draw a tree diagram to show the outcomes when you choose, at random, two girls and ask which pop groups they like.

c Use your tree diagram to work out the probability that both girls will like:

  i Smudge   **ii** the same group   **iii** different groups.

(PS) **7** Look at all the tree diagrams that you have seen so far.

a What do the probabilities across any set of branches (outlined in the diagram below) always add up to?

b What do the final probabilities (outlined in the diagram below) always add up to?

c Now copy the diagram and fill in all of the missing values.

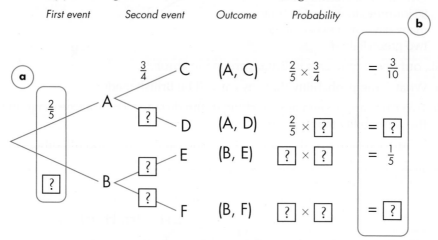

(PS) **8** When playing the game *Pontoon*, you are dealt two cards. If you get an ace and a king, queen or jack you have been dealt a 'Royal Pontoon'. What is the probability of being dealt a Royal Pontoon? Give your answer to 3 decimal places.

(MR) **9** I have a bag containing white, blue and green jelly babies. Explain how a tree diagram can help me find the probability of picking, at random, three sweets of different colours.

(MR) **10** **a** Suppose you throw a fair coin four times. Show how you could work out the probability of getting four heads without drawing a tree diagram.

b A fair coin is thrown n times. Write down the probability of scoring n heads.

19.4 Independent events

This section will show you how to:

- use the connectors 'and' and 'or' to work out the probabilities for combined events.

If the outcomes of an event A do not affect the outcomes of an event B, then events A and B are **independent events**. Most of the combined events you have studied so far have been independent events.

If A and B are independent, then P(A and B) = P(A) × P(B).

The next three examples show you how to work out problems about combined events without using tree diagrams. The method is similar to using a tree diagram but uses the words 'and' and 'or'.

Example 4

The chance that Ashley hits a target with an arrow is $\frac{1}{4}$. He has two shots at the target. What is the probability that he hits the target:

a both times   **b** once only?

a P(hits both times) = P(first shot hits and second shot hits)

$$= \frac{1}{4} \times \frac{1}{4} = \frac{1}{16}$$

b P(hits the target once only) = P(first hits and second misses or first misses and second hits)

$$= \left(\frac{1}{4} \times \frac{3}{4}\right) + \left(\frac{3}{4} \times \frac{1}{4}\right) = \frac{6}{16} = \frac{3}{8}$$

Note: The connections between the word 'and' and the operation 'times', and the word 'or' and the operation 'add'.

'At least' problems

When you are working with combined events, you may need to find the probability of at least one of the outcomes occurring. There are two ways to do this.

You can write out all the possibilities, which takes a long time.

Alternatively, you can use P(at least one) = 1 − P(none).

The second option is much quicker and there is less chance of making a mistake.

Example 5

A bag contains seven red balls and three black balls. Anton takes out a ball, notes the colour and replaces it. He does this three times. What is the probability that he takes out:

a no red balls   **b** at least one red ball?

a P(no reds) = P(black, black, black) = $\frac{3}{10} \times \frac{3}{10} \times \frac{3}{10} = \frac{27}{1000}$

b P(at least one red) = 1 − P(no reds)

Since P(no reds) = $\frac{27}{1000}$, P(at least one red) = $1 - \frac{27}{1000}$, which is $\frac{973}{1000}$.

Notice that the answer to part **b** is 1 minus the answer to part **a**.

Working in decimals, P(no reds) = 0.027 so P(at least one red) = 1 − 0.027, which is 0.973.

More advanced use of 'and' and 'or'

You have already seen how to solve some probability problems related to independent events by using tree diagrams or the *and/or* method. These methods are similar but the *and/or* method works better in the case of three events that occur one after another, or where the number of outcomes of one event is greater than two. This is because the tree diagram would be too large and involved.

Josh picks three cards from a normal pack. He replaces each card and shuffles the pack, before picking the next card. What is the probability that he draws:

a three kings   **b** exactly two kings and one other card

c no kings   **d** at least one king?

Let K be the outcome 'drawing a king'. Let N be the outcome 'not drawing a king'.

a $P(KKK) = \frac{1}{13} \times \frac{1}{13} \times \frac{1}{13} = \frac{1}{2197}$

b $P(\text{exactly two kings}) = P(KKN) \text{ or } P(KNK) \text{ or } P(NKK)$

$$= \left(\frac{1}{13} \times \frac{1}{13} \times \frac{12}{13}\right) + \left(\frac{1}{13} \times \frac{12}{13} \times \frac{1}{13}\right) + \left(\frac{12}{13} \times \frac{1}{13} \times \frac{1}{13}\right)$$

$$= \frac{36}{2197}$$

c $P(\text{no kings}) = P(NNN) = \frac{12}{13} \times \frac{12}{13} \times \frac{12}{13}$

$$= \frac{1728}{2197}$$

d $P(\text{at least one king}) = 1 - P(\text{no kings})$

$$= 1 - \frac{1728}{2197}$$

$$= \frac{469}{2197}$$

Note: The notation P(KKN) or P(KNK) or P(NKK) represents P(the first card is a king, the second is a king and the third is not a king) or P(the first is a king, the second is not a king and the third is a king) or P(the first is not a king, the second is a king and the third is a king).

Note also that the probability of each component of part **b** is exactly the same. So the calculation could be:

$3 \times \frac{1}{13} \times \frac{1}{13} \times \frac{12}{13} = \frac{36}{2197}$

Patterns of this kind often occur in probability.

Exercise 19D

 1   Jack throws a coin twice. The coin is biased so it has a probability of $\frac{2}{3}$ of landing on a head. What is the probability that Jack throws:

     a two heads   **b** a head and a tail?

 2   Bernie draws a card from a normal pack, replaces it, shuffles the pack and then draws another card. What is the probability that the cards he draws are:

     a both aces   **b** an ace and a king?

3 The probability that I am late for work on Monday is 0.4. The probability that I am late on Tuesday is 0.2. What is the probability that:

a I am late for work on Monday and Tuesday

b I am late for work on Monday and on time on Tuesday

c I am on time on both Monday and Tuesday.

(PS) **4** What is the probability of rolling the same number on a fair dice five times in a row?

5 A bag contains four red balls and six blue balls. Su takes out a ball, notes its colour and replaces it. Then she takes out another ball. Work out:

a P(both balls are red)   **b** P(both balls are blue)   **c** P(at least one ball is red).

6 The probability that Steve is late for work is $\frac{5}{6}$. The probability that Nigel is late for work is $\frac{9}{10}$. The probability that Gary is late for work is $\frac{1}{2}$. Work out:

a P(all three are late)   **b** P(none of them is late)   **c** P(at least one is late).

(MR) **7** **a** Sorcha throws a fair dice three times. What is the probability of scoring:

    i three sixes   **ii** no sixes   **iii** at least one six?

  b A fair dice is thrown n times. What is the probability of scoring:

    i n sixes   **ii** no sixes   **iii** at least one six?

8 The driving test is made up of a written test and a practical test. It is known that 90% of people who take the written test pass and 60% of people who take the practical test pass. A person who passes the written test does not have to take it again. A person who fails the practical test does have to take it again.

a What is the probability that someone passes both tests?

b What is the probability that someone passes the written test but takes two attempts to pass the practical test?

(CM) **9** Seven out of 10 cars in Britain are made by foreign manufacturers. Three cars can be seen approaching in the distance.

a What is the probability that all three cars are foreign?

b Explain why, if the first car is foreign, the probability of the second car being foreign is still 0.7.

c Explain why the probability that exactly two of the three cars are foreign is 0.441.

(PS) **10** The probability that an orchid planted in Cardasica will grow well is 0.6.

Kieron plants 10 orchids in Cardasica. What is the probability that at least nine of these orchids will grow well?

(PS) **11** Evie's mathematics teacher told her that the probability that she gets her mathematics homework correct is always the same. In four homeworks, the chance of her getting at least one incorrect is 0.5904.

What is the probability of Evie getting her mathematics homework correct on any one occasion?

(CM) **12** James has been dealt two cards and knows that if he is now dealt a 10, jack, queen or a king he will win.

James thinks that the chance of his winning is now $\frac{16}{50}$. Explain why he is wrong.

19.5 Conditional probability

This section will show you how to:

- work out the probability of combined events when the probabilities change after each event.

When the probability of one event is dependent on the outcome of another event, you are dealing with **conditional probability**. For instance, if you take a card from a pack and do not return it, then the probabilities for the next card drawn will be different. The next example illustrates this situation.

Example 7

A bag contains nine balls, of which five are white and four are black.

A ball is taken out and not replaced. Then another ball is taken out.

a If the first ball removed is black, what is the probability that:

   i the second ball will be black   **ii** both balls will be black?

b What is the probability that at least one black ball is taken out?

a When a black ball is removed, there are five white balls and three black balls left, reducing the total to eight.

You can either draw a tree diagram to show this information, or just write down the probabilities, remembering there is one fewer ball in the bag each time one is taken out.

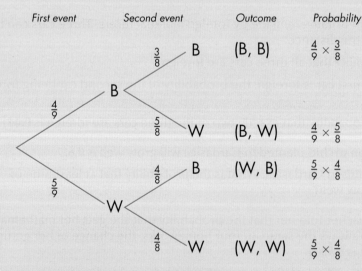

Hence, when the second ball is taken out:

i P(second ball black) = $\frac{3}{8}$

ii P(both balls black) = $\frac{4}{9} \times \frac{3}{8}$

                = $\frac{1}{6}$

(continued)

b P(at least one black ball) = 1 − P(none black)

$$= 1 - P(W, W)$$

$$= 1 - \frac{5}{9} \times \frac{4}{8}$$

$$= \frac{13}{18}$$

Exercise 19E

1 There are 10 calculators in a box. Three of them are faulty. What is the probability that:

   a Dave takes the first and it is a good one

   b Julie takes the second and it is a good one

   c Andrew takes the third and it is faulty?

2 65 men (M) and women (W) are asked if they are right (R) or left (L) handed.
The Venn Diagram shows the results.

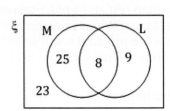 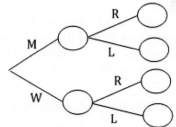

Copy and complete the frequency tree diagram.

3 A box contains 10 red balls and 15 yellow balls. One is taken out at random and not replaced. Another is then taken out.

   a If the first ball taken out is red, what is the probability that the second ball is:

     i red   **ii** yellow?

   b If the first ball taken out is yellow, what is the probability that the second ball is:

     i red   **ii** yellow?

   c Work out:

     i P(both balls are red)   **ii** P(both balls are yellow)

     iii P(the balls are different colours)

4 A fruit bowl contains six Granny Smith apples and four Golden Delicious apples.
Kevin takes two apples at random.

   a If the first apple is a Granny Smith, what is the probability that the second is:

     i a Granny Smith   **ii** a Golden Delicious?

   b If the first apple is a Golden Delicious, what is the probability that the second is:

     i a Granny Smith   **ii** a Golden Delicious?

   c Work out:

     i P(both are Granny Smiths)   **ii** P(both are Golden Delicious)

     iii P(the apples are different).

5 There are five white eggs and one brown egg in an egg box. Kate decides to use two of the eggs to make an omelette. She takes each egg from the box without looking at its colour.

  a What is the probability that the first egg taken is brown?

  b If the first egg taken is brown, what is the probability that the second egg taken will be brown?

  c What is the probability that Kate makes an omelette from:

   i two white eggs   **ii** one white and one brown egg   **iii** two brown eggs?

6 A bag contains three black balls and seven red balls. Aidan takes out a ball and does not replace it. He does this twice more.

  a Work out the probability for each event.

   i P(all three are black)   **ii** P(exactly two are black)

   iii P(exactly one is black)   **iv** P(none is black).

  b Explain why the four probabilities in **a** add up to 1.

7 A quarter of all cars on British roads are made in Britain. Jon sees a British-made car coming down the road. He says that the probability of the next car being British-made is $\frac{1}{3}$ because a British-made car has just gone past. Explain why he is wrong.

8 An engineering test is made up of two parts: a written test and a practical test. It is known that 90% of those who take the written test pass. When a person passes the written test, the probability that they will also pass the practical test is 60%. When a person fails the written test, the probability that they will pass the practical test is 20%.

  a What is the probability that someone passes both tests?

  b What is the probability that someone passes one test?

  c What is the probability that someone fails both tests?

  d Explain how you could check your answers to parts **a**, **b** and **c**.

9 A bag contains only blue discs and white discs, all the same size. Tony is asked to find the probability of taking out two discs of the same colour.

  Describe how Tony would do this, explaining carefully the point where he is most likely to go wrong.

10 What is the probability that the first four cards being dealt from a normal pack are all aces? Give your answer as a fraction in its simplest form.

11 In a survey of 140 students, 37 study music, 103 play a sport and 25 do neither.

  a Draw a Venn diagram to illustrate the data.

  b Use your diagram to calculate the probability that a student selected at random:

   i will study music and not play a sport

   ii will study music, given that they play a sport.

   Give your answers to 3 decimal places.

Worked exemplars

  Susie is rehearsing for a driving test. This test is made up of two parts, a practical and a theory. She is told that the probability of passing only one of these two tests is 0.44 and the probability of passing the practical is 0.8.

  a Draw a tree diagram to show this information.

  b Set up an equation to calculate the probability of passing the theory test.

This is a problem-solving question. You must process the problem into a series of algebraic steps.	
a	Here, you are solving the problem by making a decision to put it into an algebraic context. Let x = P(passing the theory test) and so P(failing the theory test) = $1 - x$.

b P(only pass one test) = P(PF) + P(FP)
                = $0.8(1 - x) + 0.2x$
So $0.8 - 0.8x + 0.2x = 0.44$
    $0.8 - 0.6x = 0.44 \Rightarrow 0.6x = 0.8 - 0.44$
          $x = \dfrac{0.8 - 0.44}{0.6} = 0.6$
	Use the tree diagram to work out P(only pass one test). Remember to add the two outcomes.
	This is the equation to solve.
	Rearrange the equation to calculate x.

The tree diagram for part **a**:

Practical — Pass 0.8 — Theory: Pass (x), Outcome PP, Probability $0.8x$; Fail ($1 - x$), Outcome PF, Probability $0.8(1 - x)$.

Practical — Fail 0.2 — Theory: Pass (x), Outcome FP, Probability $0.2x$; Fail ($1 - x$), Outcome FF, Probability $0.2(1 - x)$.

   a A bag contains 10 red discs, 10 white discs and 10 blue discs.

    Explain how to calculate P(3 red discs) if none are replaced.

  b Harry has a bag that contains a quantity of red discs, white discs and blue discs.

    He takes out ten discs at random, as a sample, and finds he has only blue discs and white discs. He says: "This shows that there are no red discs in the bag."

    Is he correct? Give a reason to support your answer.

This question assesses your mathematical reasoning. You need to draw conclusions from the given information and demonstrate your mathematical understanding.	

a P(first disc is red) = $\dfrac{10}{30}$
                  = $\dfrac{1}{3}$
P(second disc is red) = $\dfrac{9}{29}$
P(third disc is red) = $\dfrac{8}{28}$
                  = $\dfrac{2}{7}$
So P(3 red discs) = $\dfrac{1}{3} \times \dfrac{9}{29} \times \dfrac{2}{7}$
                = $\dfrac{6}{203}$
                = 0.0296 (3 sf)
	This is an example of conditional probability, as the discs are not replaced. You will need to show your working as part of the explanation. Your answer can be given as a fraction or a decimal.
	Here you are making a deduction to draw a conclusion from mathematical information.

b No, he is incorrect as there may be at least one red disc in the bag but he has not chosen them in the sample.	You need to say "No" and give a valid, specific reason from given information.

Ready to progress?

I can draw a tree diagram to work out the probability of combined events.
I can use *and/or* to work out probabilities of specific outcomes of combined events.

I can work out probabilities for independent events.
I can work out the probabilities of combined events when the probability of each event changes depending on the outcome of the previous event.
I can draw and use frequency tree diagrams to solve problems.

Review questions

1 Adel puts 8 red counters and 4 blue counters into a bag.

She takes, at random, a counter from the bag.

She writes down the colour of the counter.

She puts the counter in the bag again.

She then takes, at random, a second counter from the bag.

a Copy and complete the tree diagram.

b Work out the probability that Adel takes two counters that are the same colour.

c Work out the probability that Adel takes two counters that are different colours.

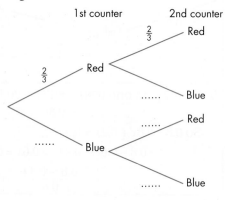

(MR) 2 Four hundred people take a two part test. In the first part of the test 80 people fail. In the second part of the test 160 people fail. There were 192 people who passed both tests.

a Use this information to complete the frequency tree diagram.

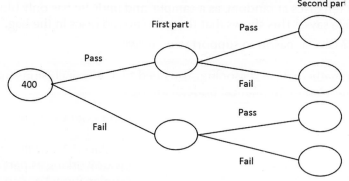

b One of these people is chosen at random. Work out the probability that this person failed both tests.

3 Mrs Smart drives to work. She passes through two sets of traffic lights.
The probability that she has to stop at the first set of traffic lights is $\frac{2}{5}$.

If she has to stop at the first set of traffic lights, the probability that she has to stop at the second is $\frac{5}{6}$.

If she does not have to stop at the first set of traffic lights, the probability that she has to stop at the second is $\frac{1}{3}$.

Work out the probability that she has to stop at only one set of traffic lights.

4 Tim has two bags of marbles.

Bag A contains 7 red marbles and 3 blue marbles.

Bag B contains 3 red marbles and 7 blue marbles.

Tim rolls a fair six-sided dice once.

If he rolls a 6 he takes a marble from bag A.

If he does not roll a 6 he takes a marble from bag B.

Calculate the probability that Tim chooses a red marble.

(CM) **5** Adam and Lara play in two different games of chess.

The probability that Adam and Lara both win their games is $\frac{5}{16}$.

The probability that Adam wins his game is $\frac{3}{8}$.

Explain how you would work out the probability that Lara wins her game.

(PS) **6** The two-way table shows the number of people watching a film at a cinema.

	Male	Female
Adult	21	14
Child	10	5

Two of these people are chosen at random to receive free cinema tickets.

Calculate the probability that the two people are children of the same gender.

Give your answer to 3 decimal places.

(PS) **7** Two outcomes A and B are independent.

The probability of B is double the probability of A.

The probability of both A and B occurring is $\frac{9}{32}$.

Work out the probability that outcome A occurs.

(MR) **8** A bag contains some red and some blue balls.

A ball is taken out at random and its colour is noted. The ball is then replaced in the bag. Another ball is then taken out at random and its colour is noted.

a Which of these **could not** be the probability of two red balls?

$\frac{9}{25}$ $\quad$ $\frac{1}{9}$ $\quad$ $\frac{13}{20}$

Give a reason for your choice.

b It is known that there are more blue balls than red balls in the bag.

Which of the probabilities in part **a** must be the probability of two red balls? Give a reason for your choice.

(PS) **9** In a sixth form of 260 students, 93 study Spanish, 95 study chemistry, 165 study mathematics, 18 study Spanish and chemistry, 75 study chemistry and mathematics, 20 study mathematics and Spanish and 15 study all three subjects.

a Draw a Venn diagram to illustrate the data.

b Use your diagram to calculate the probability that a student selected at random studies:

i only Spanish $\qquad$ **ii** mathematics and chemistry but not Spanish.

iii none of these subjects $\qquad$ **iv** Spanish, given that they study mathematics.

Give your answers to 3 significant figures.

20 Geometry and measures: Properties of circles

This chapter is going to show you:

- how to prove and use circle theorems to work out angles
- how to work out angles in cyclic quadrilaterals
- how to use tangents, chords and alternate segment theorem to work out angles in circles.

You should already know:

- that the three interior angles of a triangle add up to 180°
- that the four interior angles of a quadrilateral add up to 360°
- the properties of angles formed by a straight line (transversal) across parallel lines
- the correct terms for different parts of a circle.

About this chapter

Circles feature in all sorts of human activity, from making pottery and clocks to wheels. The most primitive wheels were probably logs rolled under the object to be moved. One of the largest wheels currently is the London Eye.

Engineers need to know about circles, since gears and pulleys rely on them. Circles are also used in what some see as an art form, others as vandalism – the formation of crop circles. In philosophy, circles are thought to represent a whole, as well as the completion of a cycle.

There is a famous story about the thirteenth-century Italian artist Giotto. Pope Boniface VIII wanted to find the best painter in Italy to work on some paintings for St Peter's Basilica in Rome. When Giotto was asked for a sample of his work, he took a brush and, in one even sweep, drew a perfect circle on a sheet of paper. The Pope's messenger was angry, but took the drawing and showed the Pope, explaining how Giotto had drawn it, freehand. Giotto got the commission.

Euclid, who lived in about 300 BC, is famous for his study of geometry, including many propositions or theorems based on circles. In this chapter, you will study some of those theorems.

20.1 Circle theorems

This section will show you how to:

- prove and use circle theorems to work out angles created in a circle from points on the circumference.

Key terms

prove   theorem

What can you remember about circles?

Work with a partner. Draw a diagram of a circle. Add a diameter and a radius.

Draw a chord on your diagram. Shade in a sector and a segment.

Draw a tangent to your circle.

Now colour the circumference. Use a different colour to shade an arc.

Mark the centre and shade a semicircle.

Exercise 20A

  1 **a** Draw a circle with radius about 5 cm. Mark clearly the centre, O.

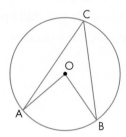

   b Choose any two points, A and B, on the circumference of the circle.

   c Mark a point C on the other side of the circle from AB.

   d Draw the lines OA, OB, AC and BC to produce a diagram like this.

   e Measure ∠AOB and ∠ACB.

   f Repeat parts **a–e** for three circles with a different radius.

   g Comment on your results.

  2 **a** Draw four circles with radii between 3 cm and 5 cm.

   b In each circle, draw a diameter and label it AB.

   c In each circle, mark any point on the circumference and label it C.

   d Measure ∠ABC.

   e Comment on what you have found out.

  3 **a** Draw any circle.

   b Mark any two points, A and B, on the circumference of the circle.

   c Label three points C, D and E on the circumference of the circle and opposite the arc AB, as shown in the diagram.

   d Draw the lines AC, BC, AD, BD, AE and BE.

   e Measure ∠ACB, ∠ADB and ∠AEB.

   f Comment on what you have found out.

   g Will this work for other circles?

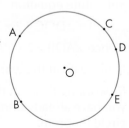

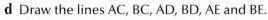

Now that you can identify the parts of a circle, and have discovered some important facts about them, you are ready to learn some circle **theorems**. Work through them carefully and try to follow the steps.

The diagram shows a circle, centre O, with an arc AB. The two radii, OA and OB, form an angle at O.

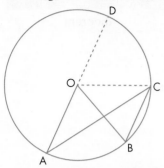

The two chords, AC and BC, join points A and B to point C on the circumference. You say that the arc AB subtends angles at the circumference, C, and at the centre, O.

OA = OB = OC = OD		All the radii in a circle are equal.
∠AOB + ∠COB + ∠DOC = 180°	(1)	AD is a straight line.
∠COB + ∠OCB + ∠CBO = 180°		Angles in a triangle add up to 180°.
OC = OB and ∠OCB = ∠CBO		Triangle OCB is isosceles.
Hence ∠COB + 2 × ∠OCB = 180°		
⇒ ∠COB = 180° − 2 × ∠OCB	(2)	

Substitute equation (2) into equation (1) to give:

∠AOB + (180° − 2 × ∠OCB) + ∠DOC = 180°

⇒ ∠AOB + 180° − 2 × ∠OCB + ∠DOC = 180°

⇒ ∠AOB − 2 × ∠OCB + ∠DOC = 180° − 180°

$$= 0$$

Hence ∠AOB = 2 × ∠OCB − ∠DOC   (3)

But ∠OCB = ∠OCA + ∠ACB   (4)

Substitute equation (4) into equation (3) to give:

∠AOB = 2 × (∠OCA + ∠ACB) − ∠DOC

Hence ∠AOB = 2 × ∠OCA + 2 × ∠ACB − ∠DOC   (5)

OA = OC and ∠OAC = ∠OCA		Triangle OAC is isosceles.
Hence ∠AOC + 2 × ∠OCA = 180°		Angles in a triangle add up to 180°.
But ∠AOC + ∠DOC = 180°		Angles on a straight line add up to 180°.
Hence ∠DOC = 2 × ∠OCA	(6)	

Substitute equation (6) into equation (5) to give:

∠AOB = ∠DOC + 2 × ∠ACB − ∠DOC

Hence ∠AOB = 2 × ∠ACB

Look again at the working above.

By working through the steps, making sure that you can justify each stage by referring to what you have already done, and giving reasons based on what you know, you have **proved** the first circle theorem.

Circle theorem 1

The angle at the centre of a circle is twice the angle at the circumference when they are both subtended by the same arc.

$\angle AOB = 2 \times \angle ACB$

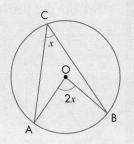

Look again at the diagram in circle theorem 1.

Imagine you move A and B apart, so that they become the endpoints of a diameter AB.

Then the angle at the centre becomes 180° and the angle at the circumference will be half of 180°, which is 90°.

This gives the second theorem.

Circle theorem 2

Every angle subtended at the circumference of a semicircle by the diameter is a right angle.

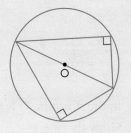

Theorem 1 tells you that any angle subtended from arc AB at a point C on the circumference is always half the angle subtended at the centre.

Therefore, every possible angle subtended from arc AB at the circumference will correspond to the same angle at the centre.

Hence all the angles subtended at the circumference will be equal.

Circle theorem 3

Angles subtended at the circumference in the same segment of a circle are equal.

Points C_1, C_2, C_3 and C_4 on the circumference are subtended by the same arc AB.

So $\angle AC_1B = \angle AC_2B = \angle AC_3B = \angle AC_4B$

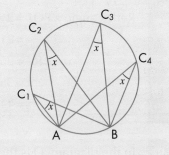

Hints and tips In circle theorem 3, the angles were described as 'in the same segment'.
Remember: A segment of a circle is the part cut off by a chord. So angles in the same segment are all on the same side of the chord AB.

Example 1

Work out the sizes of the angles marked a and b in each diagram. O is the centre of the circle.

a

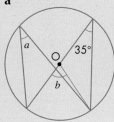

b

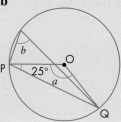

a	$a = 35°$	Angles in the same segment are equal.
	$b = 2 \times 35°$	The angle at the centre is twice the angle at the circumference.
	$= 70°$	

b	OP = OQ	Radii in a circle are equal.
	$\angle OPQ = \angle OQP$	Triangle OPQ is isosceles.
	$a + (2 \times 25°) = 180°$	The sum of the angles in triangle OPQ is 180°.
	$a = 180° - (2 \times 25°)$	
	$= 130°$	
	$b = 130° \div 2$	The angle at the centre is twice the angle at the circumference.
	$= 65°$	

Example 2

In the diagram, O is the centre of the circle. PQR is a straight line.

Show that $a = 144°$.

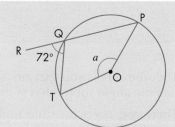

$\angle PQT = 180° - 72°$	
$= 108°$	Angles on a straight line add up to 180°.
Reflex angle $\angle POT = 2 \times 108°$	The angle at the centre is twice the angle at the circumference.
$= 216°$	
$a + 216° = 360°$	The sum of angles around a point add up to 360°.
$a = 360° - 216°$	
$= 144°$	

Example 3

In the diagram, O is the centre of the circle. POQ is parallel to TR.

a Work out the size of the angles labelled a and b.

b What size would you need to make $\angle ROQ$ for PTRO to become a parallelogram?

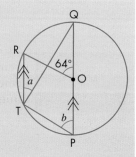

a $a = 64° \div 2$ The angle at the centre is twice the angle at the circumference.

    $a = 32°$

    $\angle TQP = a$ Alternate angles are equal.

       $= 32°$

    $\angle PTQ = 90°$ The angle at the circumference of a semicircle

    $b + 90° + 32° = 180°$ The sum of angles in $\triangle PQT$ is 180°.

          $b = 180° - 122°$

           $= 58°$

b Let $\angle RTQ = x$.

    $\angle ROQ = 2x$ The angle at the centre is twice the angle at the circumference.

  For PTRO to be a parallelogram:

    $\angle TPQ = 2x$ TPQ and ROQ are allied angles.

    $\angle QPT + \angle PTQ + \angle QTR = 180°$ Consecutive angles in a parallelogram add up to 180°.

    $2x + 90° + x = 180°$

      $3x + 90° = 180°$

    $x = 90° \div 3 = 30°$

  So, $\angle ROQ$ needs to be $2 \times 30° = 60°$ for PTRO to be a parallelogram.

Hints and tips	There are other acceptable methods for reaching this answer.

Exercise 20B

1 Work out the size of the angle marked x in each circle. O is the centre.

a   **b** 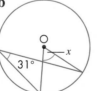   **c**   **d**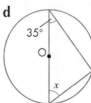

e   **f**   **g** 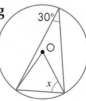   **h**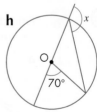

2 Find the size of the angle marked x in each diagram. O is the centre of the circle, where shown.

a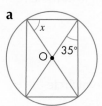

b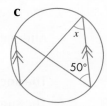

c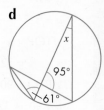

d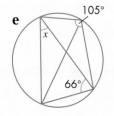

e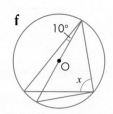

f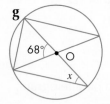

g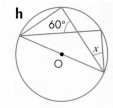

h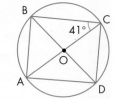

3 In the diagram, O is the centre of the circle.

Find the size of each of these angles.

a ∠ADB   **b** ∠DBA   **c** ∠CAD

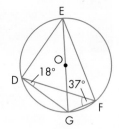

4 In the diagram, O is the centre of the circle.

Find the size of each of these angles.

a ∠EDF   **b** ∠DEG   **c** ∠EGF

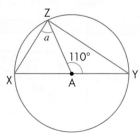

(CM) **5** In the diagram XY is a diameter of the circle, ∠AZX = a and A is the centre.

Show that the value of a is 55°.

(CM) **6** Find the values of x and y in each of these circles. O is the centre, where shown. Give reasons for your answers.

a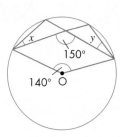

b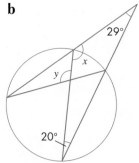

c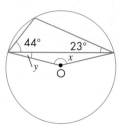

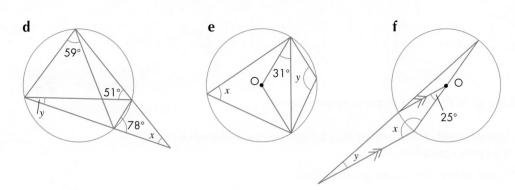

d 59° 51° 78° x y

e 31° x y

f 25° x y

MR **7** In the diagram, O is the centre and AD is a diameter of the circle.
Lana worked out that x was 68°. Lex worked out that x was 86°.
Evaluate both of the answers.

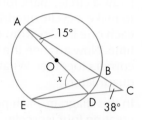

CM **8** In the diagram, O is the centre of the circle and
$\angle CBD = x$.
Prove that the reflex angle AOC is $2x$.

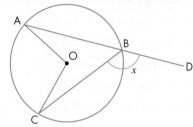

CM **9** A, B, C and D are points on the circumference of a circle, centre O.
Angle ABO is x and angle CBO is y.
a State the value of angle BAO.
b State the value of angle AOD.
c Prove that the angle subtended by the diameter of the circle at the circumference is a right angle.

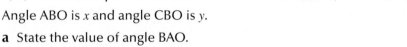
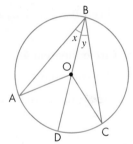

PS **10** A, B, C and D are four points on a circle, centre O.
$\angle OAB = 53°$ and $\angle OAD = 17°$
Work out the size of $\angle OBD$.

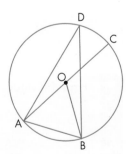

MR **11** Prove circle theorem 3: angles subtended at the circumference in the same segment of a circle are equal.

20.2 Cyclic quadrilaterals

This section will show you how to:

- find the sizes of angles in cyclic quadrilaterals.

Key term

cyclic quadrilateral

A quadrilateral with four vertices that lie on the circumference of a circle is a **cyclic quadrilateral**.

The diagram shows any cyclic quadrilateral.

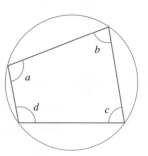

Draw a circle, mark four points on the circumference and join them, in order, to make a cyclic quadrilateral. Make two tracings of your quadrilateral and cut each one in two, from opposite corners. Cut along a different diagonal each time. Now arrange the two parts of each quadrilateral, putting opposite corners together. What do you notice? Try it again, with another cyclic quadrilateral.

In this diagram, each point on the circumference is joined to the centre, creating four isosceles triangles with base angles of x, y, w and t.

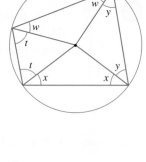

$x + x + y + y + w + w + t + t = 360°$ Angles of a quadrilateral add up to 360°.

So $2(x + y + w + t) = 360°$

and $x + y + w + t = 180°$ (1)

So $(x + y) + (w + t) = 180°$

But $(x + y)$ and $(w + t)$ are the opposite angles of the cyclic quadrilateral.

Also, $(x + t) + (y + w) = 180°$ (2)   Rearranging equation (1)

and $(x + t)$ and $(y + w)$ are the other opposite angles of the cyclic quadrilateral.

Circle theorem 4

The sum of the opposite angles of a cyclic quadrilateral is 180°.

$a + c = 180°$ and $b + d = 180°$

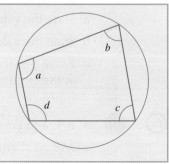

Example 4

Find the values of x and y in the diagram.

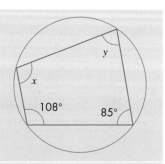

$x + 85° = 180°$ Opposite angles in a cyclic quadrilateral

So, $x = 95°$

$y + 108° = 180°$ Opposite angles in a cyclic quadrilateral

So, $y = 72°$

1 Work out the sizes of the lettered angles in each circle.

a
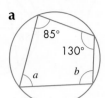

b
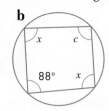

c
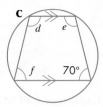

d
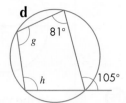

e
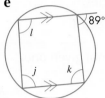

f
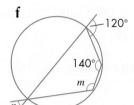

g
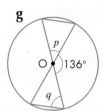

h
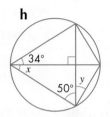

2 Find the values of x and y in each circle. O is the centre of the circle, where shown.

a
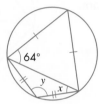

b

c
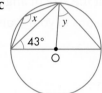

d

e
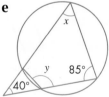

f
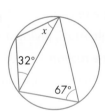

g

h
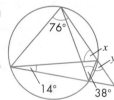

(PS) 3 **a** Judy said that every rectangle is cyclic. Prove that Judy is correct.

b Nathan said that every parallelogram is cyclic. How can you show this is incorrect without having to draw a parallelogram?

4 Find the values of x and y in each circle. O is the centre of the circle, where shown.

a
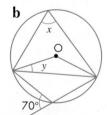

b

c
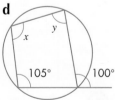

d

5 Find the values of x and y in each circle.

a
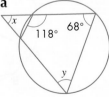

b
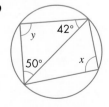

c
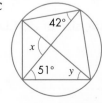

d
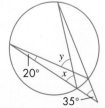

6 Find the values of x and y in each circle, centre O.

a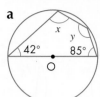

b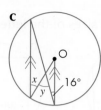

c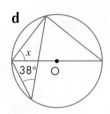

d

7 In the cyclic quadrilateral PQRT, O is the centre of the circle and angle ROQ = 38°.

POT is a diameter and is parallel to QR. Calculate these angles.

a ∠ORT **b** ∠QRT **c** ∠QPT

> **Hints and tips** It is helpful to draw a diagram, if you are not given one.

8 In the diagram, O is the centre of the circle.

a Explain why $3x - 30° = 180°$.

b Work out the size of angle CDO, marked y on the diagram.
Give reasons in your working.

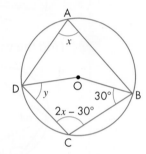

9 ABCD is a cyclic quadrilateral within a circle, centre O, and angle AOC = $2x$.

a State the value of ∠ABC, giving a reason.

b State the value of the reflex angle AOC, giving a reason.

c State the value of ∠ADC, giving a reason.

d Hence prove that the sum of any pair of opposite angles of a cyclic quadrilateral is 180°.

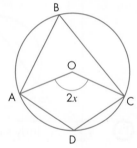

10 In the diagram, ABCE is a parallelogram.

Prove that ∠AED = ∠ADE.

Give reasons in your working.

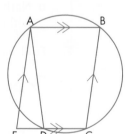

11 A, B, C and D are four points on a circle, centre O.

∠ABC = 139° and

∠OAD = 23°

Work out the size of ∠OCD.

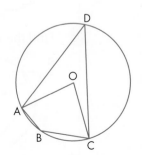

20.3 Tangents and chords

This section will show you how to:

- use tangents and chords to find the sizes of angles in circles.

A tangent is a straight line that touches a circle at only one point. This point is called the **point of contact.**

A chord is a line that joins two points on the circumference.

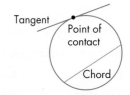

Circle theorem 5

A tangent to a circle is perpendicular to the radius drawn to the point of contact.

The radius OX is perpendicular to the tangent AB.

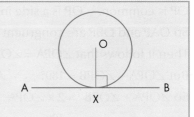

The diagram shows a circle with tangents drawn from point T to meet points A and B on the circumference.

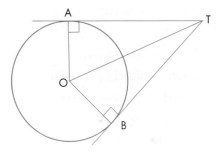

The radii OA and OB are perpendicular to the tangents.

In triangles OAT and OBT:

 OA = OB

OAT = OBT
   = 90°

OT is a common side.

Hence triangles OAT and OBT are congruent (RHS).

So AT = BT and ∠ATO = ∠BTO

From circle theorem 5

Radii in a circle are equal.

The radius is perpendicular to the tangent at the point of contact.

Circle theorem 6

Tangents to a circle from an external point to the points of contact are equal in length.

AX = AY

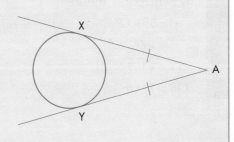

Circle theorem 7

The line joining an external point to the centre of the circle bisects the angle between the tangents.

∠OAX = ∠OAY

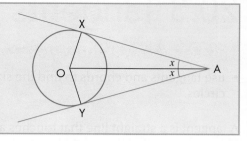

In this diagram, chord AB has been bisected at point P by another radius.

In the two triangles OAP and OBP:

OA = OB   Radii in a circle are equal.

AP = BP   P bisects AB.

OP is common.   OP is a side in both triangles.

So OAP and OBP are congruent (SSS).

Then it follows that ∠OPA = ∠OPB.

But ∠OPA + ∠OPB = 180°   Angles on a straight line.

So ∠OPA + ∠OPB = 2 × ∠OPA

$$= 180°$$

Hence ∠OPA = 180° ÷ 2

$$= 90°$$

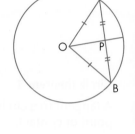

Circle theorem 8

A radius bisects a chord at 90°.

O is the centre of the circle.

∠BMO = 90° and

    BM = CM

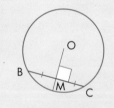

Example 5

OA is the radius of the circle and AB is a tangent.

OA = 5 cm and

AB = 12 cm

Show that the length of OB is 13 cm.

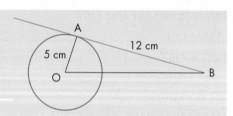

∠OAB = 90°   The radius is perpendicular to the tangent at the point of contact.

Let OB = x cm

By Pythagoras' theorem:

$$x^2 = 5^2 + 12^2$$

$$x^2 = 169$$

So $x = \sqrt{169}$

OB = 13 cm

1 TP and TQ are tangents to a circle with centre O. Find the value of x in each case.

a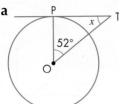

b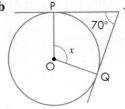

c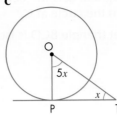

d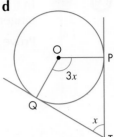

2 Each diagram shows tangents to a circle with centre O. Find the value of y in each case.

a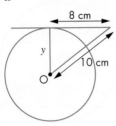

b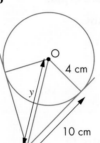

c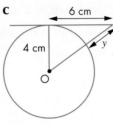

d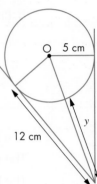

3 Each diagram shows a tangent to a circle with centre O. Find the values of x and y in each case.

a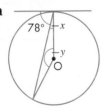

b

c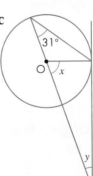

d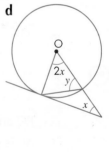

4 In each of the diagrams, TP and TQ are tangents to the circle with centre O. Find the value of x in each case.

a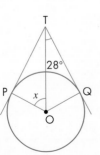

b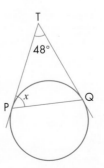

c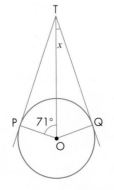

d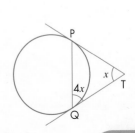

PS **5** Two circles with the same centre have radii of 7 cm and 12 cm respectively. A tangent to the inner circle cuts the outer circle at A and B. Find the length of AB.

CM **6** In the diagram, O is the centre of the circle and AB is a tangent to the circle at C.

Prove that triangle BCD is isosceles.

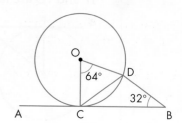

CM **7** BA and BC are tangents to the circle with centre O. OA and OC are radii.

a Prove that angles AOB and COB are equal.

b Prove that OB bisects the angle ABC.

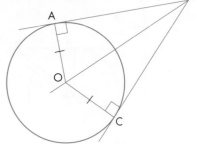

EV **8** The diagram shows a circle with centre O.

The circle fits exactly inside an equilateral triangle XYZ.

The lengths of the sides of the triangle are 20 cm.

Ling said that the radius of the circle is 5.8 cm.

Evaluate Ling's statement.

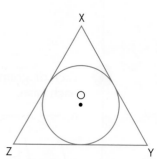

PS **9** The diagram shows a circle, centre O.

A, B, C and D are points on the circumference of the circle.

PQ and PR are tangents to the circle at B and D respectively.

AC is parallel to PR.

$\angle QPR = 52°$

What is the size of $\angle BOC$?

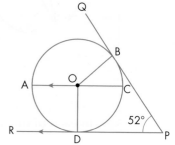

20.4 Alternate segment theorem

This section will show you:

- how to use the alternate segment theorem to find the sizes of angles in circles.

What is an **alternate segment**?

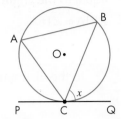

In the diagram, A, B and C are points on the circumference of the circle with centre O.

The segment containing the angle BAC is called the alternate segment of angle BCQ, because it is on the other side of the chord BC from the angle BCQ.

Exercise 20E

1   a Draw a circle with a radius of approximately 5 cm.

   b Draw a tangent, ATB, where T is the point of contact with the circle.

   c Draw a triangle RST in the circle, where S and R are two points on the circumference.

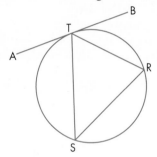

2   a Measure $\angle$ATS and $\angle$TRS on your diagram from question 1.

   b What do you notice?

3   a Measure $\angle$BTR and $\angle$RST on your diagram from question 1.

   b What do you notice?

You should have just found, experimentally, that the angle between a chord and the tangent at one of its endpoints is equal to the angle that the chord subtends at the circumference.

Now work through the proof.

The tangent PQ touches the circle at C.

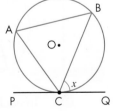

Angle BCQ $= x$

Then $\angle$OCB $= 90° - x$ OC is perpendicular to PQ.

$\quad \angle$OBC $= \angle$OCB   OBC is an isosceles triangle.

$\quad \angle$COB $= 180° - (90° - x) - (90° - x)$ The sum of the angles in a triangle is 180°.

$\qquad\qquad = 180 - 90 + x - 90 + x$

$\qquad\qquad = 2x$

$\angle$CAB is half $\angle$COB   The angle at the centre is twice the angle at the circumference.

So $\angle$CAB $= x$

$\qquad\quad = \angle$BCQ

Circle theorem 9

PTQ is the tangent to a circle at T.

The segment containing the angle TBA is the alternate segment of angle PTA.

The angle between a tangent and a chord through the point of contact is equal to the angle in the alternate segment.

∠PTA = ∠TBA

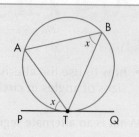

In the diagram, find the size of: **a** ∠ATS **b** ∠TSR.

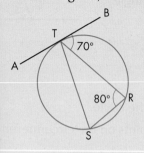

a ∠ATS = 80° Angle in the alternate segment

b ∠TSR = 70° Angle in the alternate segment

Exercise 20F

1 Find the size of the lettered angles in each diagram.

a 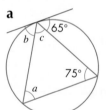 **b** 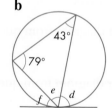 **c** 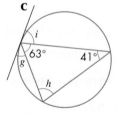 **d**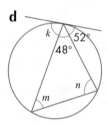

2 Find the size of the lettered angles in each diagram.

a 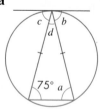 **b** 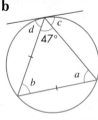 **c** 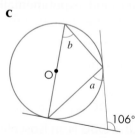 **d**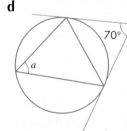

3 In each diagram, find the value of *x*.

a 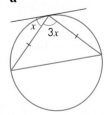 **b**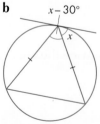

4 In each diagram, ATB is a tangent to the circle. O is the centre, where marked. Find the size of each lettered angle.

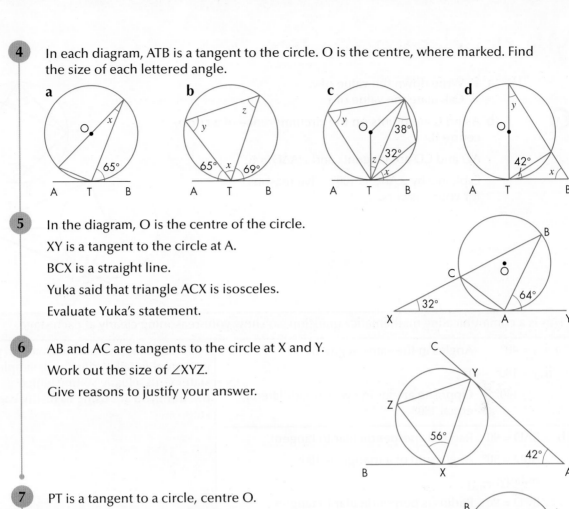

a

b

c

d

5 In the diagram, O is the centre of the circle.

XY is a tangent to the circle at A.

BCX is a straight line.

Yuka said that triangle ACX is isosceles.

Evaluate Yuka's statement.

6 AB and AC are tangents to the circle at X and Y.

Work out the size of ∠XYZ.

Give reasons to justify your answer.

7 PT is a tangent to a circle, centre O.

A and B are points on the circumference.

∠PBA = x

a Write down the value of ∠AOP.

b Calculate ∠OPA in terms of x.

c Prove that ∠APT = ∠PBA.

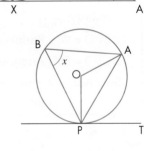

8 A circle has two tangents PQ and PT from a common point P.
Use the alternate segment theorem to prove that PQ = PT.

Worked exemplars

1 **a i** Write down the value of x.
    ii Calculate the value of y.

  b A and C are points on the circumference of a circle, centre B.

  AD and CD are tangents and $\angle A \triangle D = 40°$.

  Explain why $\angle ABC$ is 100°. Give reasons for your answers.

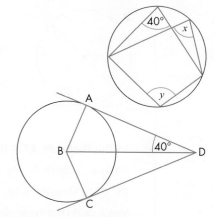

This is a communicating mathematics question, so show your reasoning clearly at each stage.	

a i $x = 40°$ Angles in the same segment
 	
  ii $y = 180° - 40°$
 	
     $= 140°$ Opposite angles in cyclic quadrilateral equal 180°
	Your explanation does not need to go into great detail. Write short, simple statements, clearly stating which theorem you are using to justify each step.

b $\angle BAD = 90°$ Radius is perpendicular to tangent. $\angle ABD = 50°$ Angle sum of a triangle is 180°. Similarly: $\angle BCD = 90°$ Radius is perpendicular to tangent. $\angle CBD = 50°$ Angle sum of a triangle is 180°. So $\angle ABC = 2 \times 50°$ $= 100°$	

2 In the diagram, XY is a tangent to the circle at A.

BCY is a straight line.

Work out the size of $\angle ABC$.

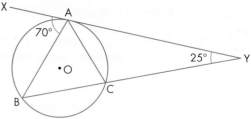

This is a problem-solving question where you need to plan your strategy to find the size of this angle.	
$\angle ACB = 70°$ Angle in alternate segment $\angle ACY = 110°$ Angles on a line = 180° $\angle CAY = 45°$ Angles in a triangle sum to 180° so $\angle ABC = 45°$ Angle in alternate segment	You need to combine your knowledge of angles in a triangle with angles in a circle to identify the unknown angles in the diagram until you are able to calculate the angle ABC.
	You need to show your reasoning at each stage: it's not sufficient to simply state the answer with no indication of how you found it.

3 In the diagram, ABCD is a cyclic quadrilateral.

AE is a tangent at A.

CDE is a straight line.

$\angle CAD = 32°$

$\angle ABD = 40°$

Chris worked out that $\angle AED$ is 68°.

Evaluate Chris's answer.

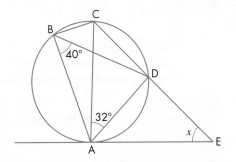

This is an evaluating question, so you need to look at an answer and see if it's correct. If it is not, say why you think the result has been given incorrectly.	

$\angle DAE = 40°$ Alternate segment theorem
 	
 $\angle ACD = 40°$ Angle subtended by the same chord
 	
 $\angle CAE = \angle CAD + \angle DAE$
       $= 40° + 32°$
       $= 72°$
 	
 $\angle AED = 180° - (\angle DAE + \angle ADE)$
 	
 $\angle ADE = 180° - \angle ADC$
       $= 180° - (180° - 32° - 40°)$
       $= 72°$
 	
 So $\angle AED = 180° - (72° + 40°)$ Angles in a triangle sum to 180°
 	
 so $\angle AED = 68°$
 	
 This shows that Chris was correct.
	Here you are able to show that Chris is correct, but you do need to show how this answer is found and indicate clearly the justification of each answer to each stage of the working.
	
	 There is more than one way to show this.

Ready to progress?

I can use tangents and chords to work out angles in circles.
I can calculate angles in cyclic quadrilaterals.
I can use the alternate segment theorem to calculate angles in circles.

I can prove circle theorems and use them to prove geometrical results.

Review questions

1 In each diagram, O is the centre of the circle.

a Write down the value of x.

b Write down the value of y.

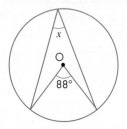

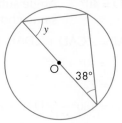

c Calculate the value of t, stating any assumptions you have made.

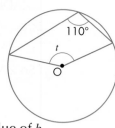

2 **a** Write down the value of a.

b Write down the value of b.

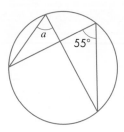

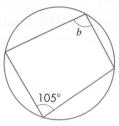

CM **3** A, B, C and D are all points on the circumference of a circle, centre O.

a Explain how you know that the value of x is 160°.

b Give a reason why y is 100°.

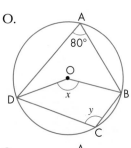

CM **4** A, B, C and D are all points on the circumference of a circle, centre O.

Show that OBCD could only be a rhombus if $x = 60°$.

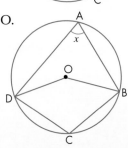

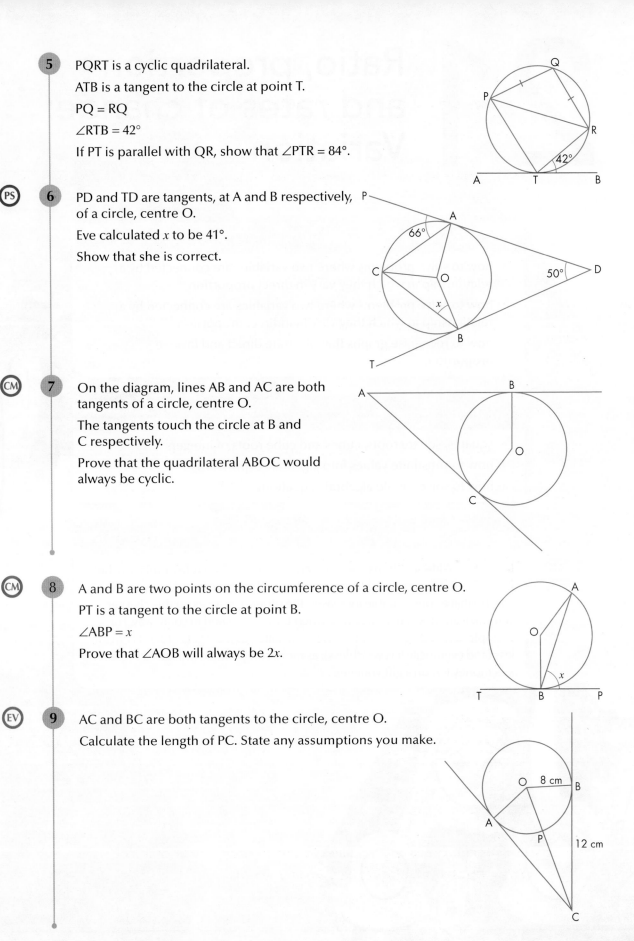

5. PQRT is a cyclic quadrilateral.

ATB is a tangent to the circle at point T.

PQ = RQ

∠RTB = 42°

If PT is parallel with QR, show that ∠PTR = 84°.

PS 6. PD and TD are tangents, at A and B respectively, of a circle, centre O.

Eve calculated x to be 41°.

Show that she is correct.

CM 7. On the diagram, lines AB and AC are both tangents of a circle, centre O.

The tangents touch the circle at B and C respectively.

Prove that the quadrilateral ABOC would always be cyclic.

CM 8. A and B are two points on the circumference of a circle, centre O.

PT is a tangent to the circle at point B.

∠ABP = x

Prove that ∠AOB will always be 2x.

EV 9. AC and BC are both tangents to the circle, centre O.

Calculate the length of PC. State any assumptions you make.

21 Ratio, proportion and rates of change: Variation

This chapter is going show you:

- how to solve problems where two variables are connected by a relationship in which they vary in direct proportion
- how to solve problems where two variables are connected by a relationship in which they vary in indirect proportion
- how to recognise graphs that illustrate direct and inverse proportion.

You should already know:

- squares, square roots, cubes and cube roots of integers
- how to substitute values into algebraic expressions
- how to solve simple algebraic equations.

About this chapter

In many real-life situations, variables are connected by a rule or relationship. It may be that as one variable increases, the other increases. Alternatively, it may be that as one variable increases, the other decreases. In this chapter you will learn how quantities vary when they are related in some way. For example, as plants get older they become taller; as a car gets older it is worth less (and eventually it is worthless); as more songs are downloaded there is less money left on a gift voucher.

21.1 Direct proportion

This section will show you how to:

- solve problems where two variables have a directly proportional relationship (direct variation)
- work out the constant of proportionality
- recognise graphs that show direct variation.

There is **direct variation** or direct proportion between two variables when one variable is a simple multiple of the other. That is, their ratio is a constant.

For example:

- 1 kilogram = 2.2 pounds

  There is a multiplying factor of 2.2 between kilograms and pounds.

- Area of a circle = πr^2

  There is a multiplying factor of π between the area of a circle and the square of its radius.

When you are working with direct variation, start by finding this multiplying factor or **constant of proportionality**. Then you can use it to solve the problem.

The symbol for variation or proportion is $\propto$.

You can write the statement 'pay is directly proportional to time' mathematically as:

pay $\propto$ time

This implies that:

pay = $k \times time$

where k is the constant of proportionality.

Follow these steps to solve proportionality problems.

Step 1: Set up the proportion statement, using the proportionality symbol, with letters or symbols to represent the variables.

Step 2: Set up the equation, using a constant of proportionality.

Step 3: Use the given information to work out the value of the constant of proportionality.

Step 4: Substitute the value of the constant of proportionality into the equation and use this equation to find unknown values.

Step 5: If you are asked to sketch (or identify) a graph, it will always be a straight line starting from the origin.

The gradient of the graph will depend on the value of the constant of proportionality.

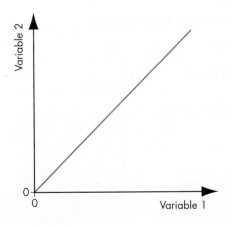

Example 1

The cost of repairing an article is directly proportional to the time spent working on it. A repair job that takes 6 hours to complete costs £180. Work out:

a the cost of a repair that takes 5 hours

b the length of time it takes to complete a repair costing £240.

Step 1: Let C be the cost of repairing an article and t the time it takes. Set up the proportion statement.

$$C \propto t$$

Step 2: Set up the equation.

$C = kt$ where k is the constant of proportionality

Note: You can replace the proportionality sign $\propto$ with '$= k$' to obtain the proportionality equation.

Step 3: Since $C = £180$ when $t = 6$ hours, then $180 = 6k$

$$\Rightarrow k = \frac{180}{6}$$
$$= 30$$

Step 4: So the formula is $C = 30t$.

a $t = 5$ hours, so:
$$C = 30 \times 5$$
$$= 150$$

The cost is £150.

b $C = £240$, so:
$$240 = 30 \times t$$
$$\Rightarrow t = \frac{240}{30}$$
$$= 8$$

The time spent completing the repair is 8 hours.

Exercise 21A

For questions **1** to **4**, first work out k, the constant of proportionality, and then the formula connecting the variables.

1 T is directly proportional to M. If $T = 20$ when $M = 4$, work out the value of:

    a T when $M = 3$ **b** M when $T = 10$.

2 W is directly proportional to F. If $W = 45$ when $F = 3$, work out the value of:

    a W when $F = 5$ **b** F when $W = 90$.

3 Q varies directly with P. If $Q = 100$ when $P = 2$, work out the value of:

    a Q when $P = 3$ **b** P when $Q = 300$.

4 You are given that x varies directly with y. This graph shows the relationship between x and y.

Find the value of: **a** x when $y = 9$ **b** y when $x = 30$.

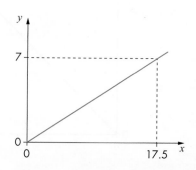

5 The distance a train travels is directly proportional to the time taken for the journey. The train travels 105 miles in 3 hours.

   a What distance will the train travel in 5 hours?

   b How much time will it take the train to travel 280 miles?

6 The cost of fuel delivery is directly proportional to its mass. The graph shows the relationship between cost and mass.

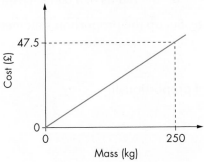

   a What is the delivery cost for 350 kg fuel?

   b How much fuel would be delivered if the cost were £33.25?

7 The number of children who can play safely in a playground is directly proportional to the area of the playground. A playground with an area of 210 m² is safe for 60 children.

   a How many children can safely play in a playground of area 154 m²?

   b A playgroup has 24 children. What is area of the smallest playground in which they could safely play?

8 The number of spaces in a car park is directly proportional to the area of the car park. A car park has 300 parking spaces in an area of 4500 m².

   a The area of the car park increases by 750 m². After the increase in area, how many extra spaces will there be, assuming that the constant of proportionality stays the same?

   b The car park is then redesigned to create 25 more spaces. Work out the new proportionality equation.

9 The number of passengers in a bus queue is directly proportional to the time that the person at the front of the queue has spent waiting.

   Karen is the first to arrive at a bus stop. When she has been waiting 5 minutes the queue has 20 passengers.

   A bus has room for 70 passengers.

   When an empty bus arrives, it fills up completely and takes all of the passengers in the queue. How long had Karen been waiting for the bus?

10 Hooke's Law for an elastic spring states that the distance a spring stretches varies directly as the force is applied. When a force of 160 N is applied the *total* length of the spring is 25 cm. When a force of 240 N is applied the *total* length of the spring is 26.25 cm. Work out the length of the spring when no force is applied.

Direct proportions involving squares, square roots, cubes and cube roots

The method for direct proportion involving squares, cubes, square roots and cube roots is the same as for linear direct variation.

The cost of a circular badge is directly proportional to the square of its radius. The cost of a badge with a radius of 2 cm is 68p. Work out:

a   the cost of a badge of radius 2.4 cm   **b**   the radius of a badge costing £1.53.

Step 1: Let C be the cost and r the radius of a badge. Set up the proportion statement.

$C \propto r^2$

Step 2: Set up the equation.

$C = kr^2$ where k is the constant of proportionality.

Step 3: Since $C = 68$p when $r = 2$ cm, then $68 = 4k$

$\Rightarrow k = \dfrac{68}{4}$

$= 17$

Step 4: So the formula is $C = 17r^2$.

a $r = 2.4$ cm, so $C = 17 \times 2.4^2 = 97.92$

The cost is 98p, as the value must be rounded.

b $C = 153$p, so $153 = 17r^2$

$\Rightarrow r^2 = \dfrac{153}{17} = 9$

$\Rightarrow r = 3$

The radius is 3 cm.

Recognising graphs showing direct proportion

Relationships for non-linear direct proportion have equations such as $y = kx^2$, $y = kx^3$, $y = k\sqrt{x}$ or $y = k\sqrt[3]{x}$. You need to be able to recognise graphs of this type.

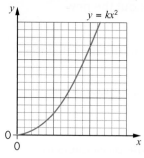

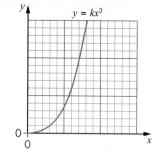

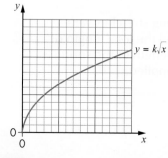

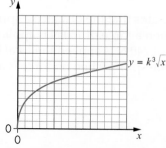

Example 3

The graph shows the relationship between y and x.

Work out:

a the value of y when $x = 3$

b the value of x when $y = 56$.

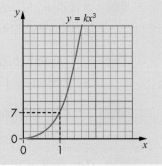

Use the values shown on the graph to set up the equation of proportionality.

$7 = k \times 1^3$

Hence the value of k is 7.

a When $x = 3$, $y = 7 \times 3^3$

$\qquad = 7 \times 27$

$\qquad = 189$

b When $y = 56$, $56 = 7 \times x^3$

$\qquad \Rightarrow x^3 = 56 \div 7$

$\qquad = 8$

$\qquad \Rightarrow x = \sqrt[3]{8}$

$\qquad x = 2$

Exercise 21B 🖩

For questions **1** to **6**, first work out k, the constant of proportionality, and then the formula connecting the variables.

1 T is directly proportional to x^2. If $T = 36$ when $x = 3$, find the value of:

    a T when $x = 5$ **b** x when $T = 400$.

2 W is directly proportional to M^2.

    The graph shows the relationship between W and M.

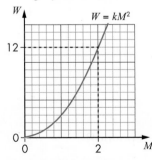

    Find the value of:

    a W when $M = 3$ **b** M when $W = 75$.

3 E varies directly with $\sqrt{C}$. If $E = 40$ when $C = 25$, find the value of:

    a E when $C = 49$ **b** C when $E = 10.4$.

4 X is directly proportional to $\sqrt{Y}$. If $X = 128$ when $Y = 16$, find the value of:

    a X when $Y = 36$ **b** Y when $X = 48$.

5 P is directly proportional to f^3. If $P = 400$ when $f = 10$, find the value of:

    a P when $f = 4$ **b** f when $P = 50$.

6 y is directly proportional to $\sqrt[3]{x}$. If $y = 100$ when $x = 125$, find the value of:

    a y when $x = 64$ **b** x when $y = 40$.

7 The cost of serving tea and biscuits varies directly with the square root of the number of people. It costs £25 to serve tea and biscuits to 100 people.

    a How much will it cost to serve tea and biscuits to 400 people?

    b I have a budget of £37.50. What is the maximum number of people that can be served tea and biscuits?

8 In an experiment, the temperature, in Celsius degrees (°C), varied directly with the square of the pressure, in atmospheres (atm). The temperature was 20 °C when the pressure was 5 atm.

    a What was the temperature at 2 atm?

    b What was the pressure at 80 °C?

9 The mass, in grams, of a ball bearing varies directly with the cube of the radius, measured in millimetres. A ball bearing of radius 4 mm has a mass of 115.2 g.

    a A ball bearing has a radius of 6 mm. What is its mass?

    b A ball bearing has a mass of 48.6 g. What is its radius?

10 The energy, in joules (J), of a particle varies directly with the square of its speed, in metres per second (m/s). A particle moving at 20 m/s has 50 J of energy.

    a How much energy has a particle moving at 4 m/s?

    b At what speed is a particle moving if it has 200 J of energy?

11 The cost, C, in pounds, of a trip varies directly with the square root of the distance travelled, M, in miles. The graph shows the relationship between C and M.

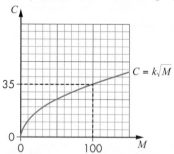

    a What is the cost of a 500-mile trip (to the nearest pound)?

    b What is the distance of a trip costing £70?

12 A sculptor is making statues.

The amount of clay used is directly proportional to the cube of the height of the statue.

The sculptor uses 500 cm³ of clay for a statue that is 10 cm in height.

How much clay will she use for a similar statue if it is twice as tall?

13 The cost of a machine is proportional to the time taken to build it.

A small machine costs £100 and takes 2 hours to build.

A large machine takes 5 hours to build. How much will it cost?

14 Match each proportion statement with the correct sketch graph.

a $y \propto x^2$ **b** $y \propto x$ **c** $y \propto \sqrt{x}$

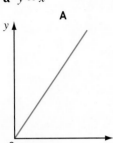 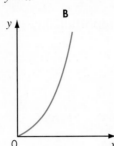 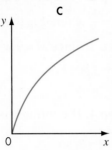

15 Match each table of values to one of the graphs in question **14**.

a

x	1	2	3
y	3	12	27

b

x	1	2	3
y	3	6	9

16 The surface area, S, of a cube is directly proportional to the *square* of the length of its side. The mass, M, of the cube is directly proportional to the *cube* of the length of its side. Work out an equation of proportionality that relates S to M.

21.2 Inverse proportion

This section will show you how to:

- solve problems in which two variables have an inversely proportional relationship (inverse variation)
- work out the constant of proportionality.

Key terms

inverse proportion

inverse variation

There is **inverse variation** or **inverse proportion** between two variables when one variable is directly proportional to the *reciprocal* of the other. That is, the product of the two variables is constant. As one variable increases, the other decreases.

For example, the faster you travel over a given distance, the less time it takes. So there is an inverse variation between speed and time. In other words, speed is inversely proportional to time.

$$S \propto \frac{1}{T} \text{ and so } S = \frac{k}{T}$$

which can be written as $ST = k$, where k is the constant of proportionality.

Example 4

M is inversely proportional to R. If $M = 9$ when $R = 4$, find the value of:

a M when $R = 2$ **b** R when $M = 3$.

Step 1: Set up the proportion statement.

$$M \propto \frac{1}{R}$$

Step 2: Set up the equation.

$M = \frac{k}{R}$ where k is the constant of proportionality.

Step 3: Since $M = 9$ when $R = 4$, $9 = \frac{k}{4}$

$\Rightarrow k = 9 \times 4$

$ = 36$

Step 4: The formula is $M = \frac{36}{R}$.

a $R = 2$, so: $\qquad\qquad\qquad M = \frac{36}{2} = 18$

b $M = 3$, so: $\qquad\qquad\qquad 3 = \frac{36}{R}$

$\qquad\qquad\qquad\qquad\qquad\quad \Rightarrow 3R = 36$

$\qquad\qquad\qquad\qquad\qquad\qquad\quad \Rightarrow R = 12$

Indirect proportions involving squares, square roots and cubes

The method for indirect proportion involving squares, cubes and square roots is the same as for standard indirect variation.

Recognising graphs showing indirect variation

Relationships for indirect variation have equations such as $y = \frac{k}{x}$, $y = \frac{k}{\sqrt{x}}$, $y = \frac{k}{x^2}$ or $y = \frac{k}{x^3}$. You need to be able to recognise graphs of this type.

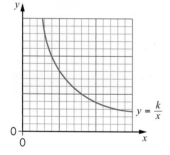

$y = \frac{k}{x}$

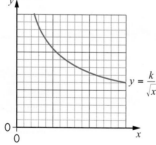

$y = \frac{k}{\sqrt{x}}$

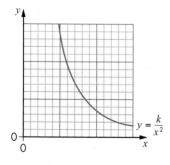

$y = \frac{k}{x^2}$

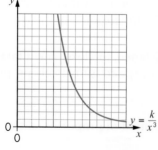

$y = \frac{k}{x^3}$

Example 5

The graph shows the relationship between y and x.

Work out:

a the value of y when $x = 4$ **b** the value of x when $y = 1.5$.

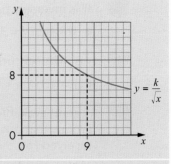

Use the values shown on the graph to set up the equation of proportionality.

$$8 = \frac{k}{\sqrt{9}}$$

Hence the value of k is 24.

a When $x = 4$, $y = 24 \div \sqrt{4}$

$$= 12$$

b When $y = 1.5$, $1.5 = 24 \div \sqrt{x}$

$$\Rightarrow \sqrt{x} = 24 \div 1.5$$

$$= 16$$

$$\Rightarrow x = 256$$

Exercise 21C

For questions **1** to **6**, first find the equation connecting the variables.

1 T is inversely proportional to m. If $T = 6$ when $m = 2$, find the value of:

    a T when $m = 4$ **b** m when $T = 4.8$.

2 W is inversely proportional to x. If $W = 5$ when $x = 12$, find the value of:

    a W when $x = 3$ **b** x when $W = 10$.

3 Q varies inversely with $(5 - t)$. If $Q = 8$ when $t = 3$, find the value of:

    a Q when $t = 10$ **b** t when $Q = 16$.

4 M varies inversely with t^2. The graph shows the relationship between M and t.

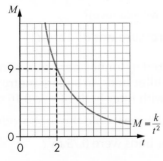

Find the value of:

    a M when $t = 3$ **b** t when $M = 1.44$.

5 W is inversely proportional to $\sqrt{T}$. If $W = 6$ when $T = 16$, find the value of:

    a W when $T = 25$ **b** T when $W = 2.4$.

6 y is inversely proportional to the cube of x. If $y = 4$ when $x = 2$, find the value of:

    a y when $x = 1$ **b** x when $y = \frac{1}{2}$.

7 A grant available to community groups was inversely proportional to the number of groups that qualified for the grant. When 30 groups qualified for the grant, they each received £60.

    a How much would each grant have been if 120 groups qualified for it?

    b If each grant had been £50, how many groups would have received it?

8 While doing underwater tests in one part of an ocean, a team of scientists noticed that the temperature, T, in Celsius degrees (°C), was inversely proportional to the depth, D, in kilometres (km). The graph shows the relationship between T and D.

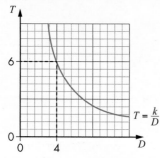

    a What was the temperature at a depth of 8 km?

    b At what depth was the temperature 2 °C?

9 In testing, it was found that a new car engine had serious problems. The distance it travelled, in kilometres (km), without breaking down was inversely proportional to the square of its speed in metres per second (m/s). When the speed was 12 m/s, the car broke down after 3 km.

    a Find the distance covered before a breakdown, when the speed was 15 m/s.

    b On one test, the engine broke down after 6.75 km. At what speed had it been travelling?

10 The pressure, in atmospheres (atm), in a balloon was inversely proportional to the square root of its height above sea level, in metres. When the balloon was at a height of 25 m, the pressure was 1.44 atm.

    a What was the pressure in the balloon at 9 m above sea level?

    b What was the height of the balloon when the pressure was 0.72 atm?

11 The amount of waste that a firm produces, measured in tonnes per hour, is inversely proportional to the square root of the area of the filter beds, in square metres (m²). The firm produces 1.25 tonnes of waste per hour with filter beds of size 0.16 m².

    a The filter beds used to be only 0.01 m². How much waste did the firm produce then?

    b How much waste could be produced if the filter beds were 0.75 m²?

12 Which statement does the graph represent? Give a reason for your answer.

A: $y \propto x$ B: $y \propto \dfrac{1}{x}$ C: $y \propto \sqrt{x}$

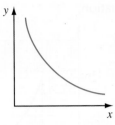

 13 In the table, y is inversely proportional to the cube root of x.

Copy and complete the table, leaving your answers as fractions.

x	8	27	
y	1		$\dfrac{1}{2}$

 14 The fuel consumption, in miles per gallon (mpg), of a car is inversely proportional to its speed, in miles per hour (mph). When the car is travelling at 30 mph, the fuel consumption is 60 mpg.

How much further would the car travel on 1 gallon of fuel by travelling at 60 mph instead of 70 mph?

 15 Newton's law states: 'The gravitational attraction force, F, between two point masses (m_1 and m_2) is directly proportional to the product of their masses and inversely proportional to the square of their separation distance, d. The force is always attractive and acts along the line joining them.' This is expressed as:

$$F = \frac{Gm_1m_2}{d^2}$$

A boy of mass 70 kg exerts a force of 70 N towards the centre of the Earth. The mass of the Earth is 5.98×10^{24} kg. The distance to the centre of the Earth is 6.38×10^6 metres.

The force exerted by the Moon on the Earth causes the rise and fall of the tides. Calculate this force, given that the mass of the Moon is 7.36×10^{22} kg and the distance from the Earth to the Moon is 3.85×10^8 metres.

Worked exemplars

1 **a** Match each graph with the correct proportionality equation.

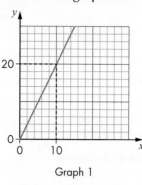 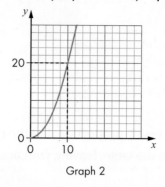 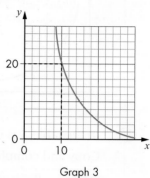

Graph 1   Graph 2   Graph 3

Equation A: $y = kx^2$ Equation B: $y = \dfrac{k}{x^2}$ Equation C: $y = kx$

CM

b In each case work out the value of y when $x = 20$.

This is a mathematical reasoning question, so you need to demonstrate that you can apply your mathematical skills and knowledge to answer it.	
a Graph 1 matches equation C. Graph 2 matches equation A. Graph 3 matches equation B.	Start with the graph with which you are most confident. This is the linear graph. When you have matched that one, look at the quadratic. This will leave only one graph and equation remaining.
b **Equation A** $20 = k \times 10^2$ $\Rightarrow k = \dfrac{1}{5}$ $y = \dfrac{1}{5} \times x^2$ $y = \dfrac{1}{5} \times 20^2$ $\quad = 80$	Set up the proportionality equation for each equation. Check that your graphs are correct in part **a** by substituting in values.
Equation B $20 = \dfrac{k}{10^2}$ $\Rightarrow k = 2000$ $y = \dfrac{2000}{x^2}$ $y = \dfrac{2000}{20^2}$ $\quad = 5$	
Equation C $20 = k \times 10$ $\Rightarrow k = 2$ $y = 2x$ $y = 2 \times 20 = 40$	

PS **2** The mass of a solid, M, is directly proportional to the cube of its height, h.

When $h = 10$, $M = 4000$.

The surface area, A, of the solid is directly proportional to the square of the height, h.

When $h = 10$, $A = 50$.

Find the value of A when $M = 32\,000$.

This is a problem-solving question that requires you to translate a non-mathematical problem into a series of mathematical processes.	
$M = kh^3$ $4000 = k \times 10^3$ $\Rightarrow k = 4$ $M = 4h^3$	Set up the proportionality statement for the mass and height, then use the given information to find the value of k.
$A = ph^2$ $50 = p \times 10^2$ $\Rightarrow p = \dfrac{1}{2}$ $A = \dfrac{1}{2}h^2$	Now set up the proportionality equation for the area and the height. Use a different letter for the constant of proportionality constant.
$32\,000 = 4h^3$ $h^3 = 8000$ $\Rightarrow h = 20$ $A = \dfrac{1}{2} \times 20^2$ $= 200$	Use $M = 32\,000$ to work out the corresponding value of h, then substitute this into the proportionality equation for A.

MR **3** Given that $y \propto x^2$ and that $y \propto \dfrac{1}{\sqrt{z}}$, which of these statements is true?

$x \propto z \qquad x \propto \dfrac{1}{z} \qquad x \propto \dfrac{1}{\sqrt{z}} \qquad x \propto \dfrac{1}{\sqrt[4]{z}}$

This question is about mathematical reasoning and is multi-choice.	
$y = kx^2$ and $y = \dfrac{K}{\sqrt{z}}$ $kx^2 = \dfrac{K}{\sqrt{z}}$	Set up the proportionality equations. Ignore the actual values of the proportionality constants as you do not need to work them out. Equate the two expressions for y.
$\sqrt{x^2} = \sqrt{\dfrac{K}{\sqrt{z}}} \Rightarrow x = \dfrac{\sqrt{K}}{\sqrt[4]{z}}$	Take the square root to get x as the subject. Because K just represents a constant, you can continue to use the same letter for the unknown value.
$x \propto \dfrac{1}{\sqrt[4]{z}}$	Choose the correct proportionality relationship.

Ready to progress?

I can recognise direct and inverse proportion.
I know what a constant of proportionality is, and how to find it.
I can find formulae describing inverse or direct proportion.
I can solve problems involving direct or inverse proportion.

Review questions

1 y is proportional to $\sqrt{x}$. Copy and complete the table.

x	25		400
y	10	20	

2 The energy, E, of an object moving horizontally is directly proportional to the speed, v, of the object. When the speed is 10 m/s the energy is 40 000 joules.

   a Find an equation connecting E and v.

   b Find the speed of the object when the energy is 14 400 joules.

3 y is inversely proportional to the cube root of x. When $y = 8$, $x = \frac{1}{8}$.

   a Find an expression for y in terms of x.

   b Calculate:

     i the value of y when $x = \frac{1}{125}$

     ii the value of x when $y = 2$.

4 The mass of a cube is directly proportional to the cube of its side. A cube with a side of 4 cm has a mass of 320 grams. Calculate the side length of a cube made of the same material with a mass of 36 450 grams.

5 y is directly proportional to the cube of x. When $y = 16$, $x = 3$. Find the value of y when $x = 6$.

6 D is directly proportional to the square of M. $D = 20$ when $M = 2$.

   a Express D in terms of M.

   b Work out the value of D when $M = 7$.

   c Work out the positive value of M when $D = 45$.

7 P is directly proportional to Q^3.

   When $Q = 3$, $P = 270$.

   Find the value of P when $Q = 2$.

8 Two variables, x and y, are known to be proportional to each other. When $x = 10$, $y = 25$.

   Find the constant of proportionality, k, if:

   a $y \propto x$ **b** $y \propto x^2$ **c** $y \propto \dfrac{1}{x}$ **d** $\sqrt{y} \propto \dfrac{1}{x}$.

9 y is directly proportional to the cube root of x. When $x = 27$, $y = 6$.

   a Find the value of y when $x = 125$.

   b Find the value of x when $y = 3$.

10 The surface area, A, of a solid is directly proportional to the square of the depth, d. When $d = 6$, $A = 12\pi$.

   a Find the value of A when $d = 12$. Give your answer in terms of π.

   b Find the value of d when $A = 27\pi$.

11 A is inversely proportional to the square of B.

   When $B = 2$, $A = 25$.

   a Find a formula for A in terms of B.

   b Calculate the value of A when $B = 5$.

12 The graph shows the relationship between y and x.

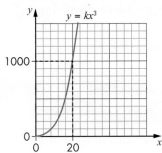

   Work out the value of y when $x = 10$.

13 The frequency, f, of sound is inversely proportional to the wavelength, w. A sound with a frequency of 36 hertz has a wavelength of 20.25 metres.

   a Calculate the frequency when the frequency and the wavelength have the same numerical value.

   b Explain why the wavelength could not be 0 metres.

14 y is proportional to x^2.

   When $x = 6$, $y = 324$.

   Work out the values of a and b on the graph.

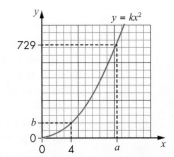

15 y and x are positive quantities. y is inversely proportional to x^2.
When $y = 160$, $x = 20$.

   y and z are both positive. y is directly proportional to z.
When $y = 50$, $z = 50$.

   The diagram shows both of these relationships.

   Find the value of x at the point of intersection.

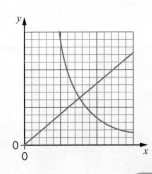

22 Geometry and measures: Triangles

This chapter is going to show you:

- how to use trigonometric ratios to solve more complex 2D problems and 3D problems
- how to calculate the sine, cosine and tangent of any angle from 0° to 360°
- how to use the sine and cosine rules to solve problems involving non right-angled triangles
- how to use the formula $A = \frac{1}{2}ab \sin C$ to calculate the area of a triangle.

You should already know:

- how to use Pythagoras' theorem to work out the sides of right-angled triangles
- how to use sine, cosine and tangent to work out angles and sides of right-angled triangles
- how to use bearings and calculate angles of elevation and depression
- how to use circle theorems.

About this chapter

In surveying, trigonometry is used extensively in the process of triangulation. Triangulation is used to work out the location of one point by measuring angles or bearings to it from two other known points, at either end of a fixed baseline. Triangulation can be used to calculate the position and distance to a ship from the shore. One observer measures the angle between the shore and the ship, and a second observer at a different point does the same. The sine rule is then applied to work out the position of the ship and its distance from shore.

The sine rule is one of a number of different trigonometrical rules you will explore in this chapter.

22.1 Further 2D problems

This section will show you how to:

- use trigonometric ratios and Pythagoras' theorem to solve more complex two-dimensional problems.

This section brings together previous work on Pythagoras' theorem, circle theorems and the trigonometric ratios – sine (sin), cosine (cos) and tangent (tan).

Example 1

In triangle ABC, AB = 6 cm, BC = 9 cm and angle ABC = 52°. Calculate:

a the length of the perpendicular from A to BC

b the area of the triangle.

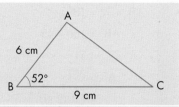

a Draw the perpendicular from A to BC to form the right-angled triangle ADB.

Let h be the length of the perpendicular AD.

$$\sin 52° = \frac{h}{6}$$

$h = 6 \sin 52°$ (Multiply both sides by 6)

$\quad = 4.73$ (3 sf)

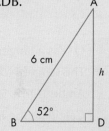

b The area of triangle ABC is $\frac{1}{2} \times$ base $\times$ height

$$= \frac{1}{2} \times 9 \times h$$

$$= 21.3 \text{ cm}^2 \text{ (3 sf)}$$

Example 2

SR is a diameter of a circle with radius 25 cm. PQ is a chord at right angles to SR. X is the midpoint of PQ. The length of XR is 1 cm. Calculate the length of the arc PQ.

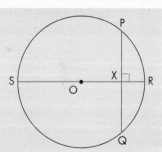

To calculate the length of the arc PQ, you need first to calculate the angle it subtends at the centre of the circle. So join P to the centre of the circle O to obtain the angle POX, which is equal to half the angle subtended by PQ at O.

In right-angled triangle POX:

OX = OR − XR

$\quad = 25 - 1$

$\quad = 24$ cm

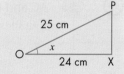

So, $\cos x = \dfrac{24}{25}$

$\quad \Rightarrow x = \cos^{-1} 0.96$

$\qquad = 16.26°$

So, the angle subtended at the centre by the arc PQ is $2 \times 16.26° = 32.52°$.

$\Rightarrow$ Arc length PQ is $\dfrac{\theta}{360} \times 2\pi r = \dfrac{32.52}{360} \times 2 \times \pi \times 25$

$\qquad\qquad = 14.2$ cm (3 sf)

AC is the diameter of a circle with radius 5 cm.

The length of BC is 7 cm.

Calculate the length of AB.

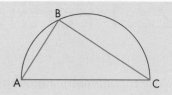

Angle ABC is a right angle (the angle at the circumference of a semicircle).

So use Pythagoras' theorem. $AB^2 + BC^2 = AC^2$

$AB^2 + 7^2 = 10^2$

$\quad AB^2 = 100 - 49$

$\qquad = 51$

$\quad AB = \sqrt{51}$

$\qquad = 7.1 \ (2 \ sf)$

QTP is a tangent to a circle, centre O, radius 4 cm.

The tangent touches the circle at T.

Angle TOP is 50°.

Calculate the length of OP.

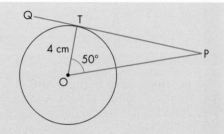

As QTP is a tangent to the circle, it is perpendicular to the radius, so OTP is a right angle.

$\qquad OT = 4 \ cm \ (radius)$

$\quad \cos 50° = \dfrac{4}{OP}$

$OP \times \cos 50° = 4 \qquad\qquad$ (Multiply both sides by OP)

$\qquad OP = \dfrac{4}{\cos 50°}$

$\qquad\quad = 6.2 \ cm \ (2 \ sf)$

Exercise 22A 🖩

 1 AC and BC are tangents to a circle of radius 7 cm.
Calculate the length of AB.

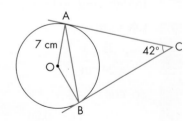

 2 CD, length 20 cm, is a diameter of a circle. AB, length 12 cm, is a chord at right angles to DC. Calculate the angle AOB.

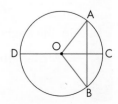

3 Calculate the length of AB in this diagram.

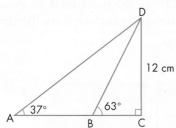

(PS) **4** A building has a ledge halfway up, as shown in the diagram. Asif measures the length AB as 100 m, the angle CAB as 31° and the angle EAB as 42°. Use this information to calculate the width of the ledge CD.

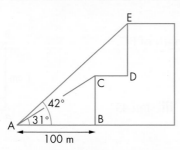

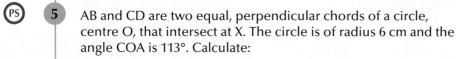
Hints and tips   Remember, the ledge is halfway up, so ED = CB.

(PS) **5** AB and CD are two equal, perpendicular chords of a circle, centre O, that intersect at X. The circle is of radius 6 cm and the angle COA is 113°. Calculate:

a the length AC

b the angle XAO

c the length XB.

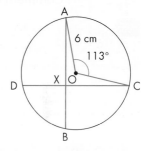

Hints and tips   AX = XC

(MR) **6** A vertical flagpole PQ is held by a wooden framework, as shown in the diagram. Show that the size of angle QRP is 38.0°.

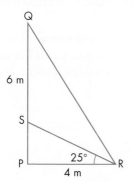

7 A mine descends from ground level for 500 m at an angle of 13° to the horizontal. It then continues for another 300 m at an angle of 17° to the horizontal, as shown in the diagram. There is also a vertical shaft, x metres along the surface from the opening.

Work out the distance between the two openings.

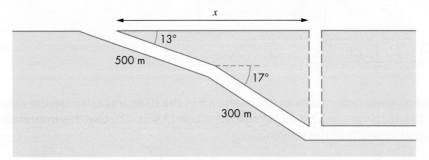

8 **a** Use Pythagoras' theorem to work out the length of BC.
   Leave your answer in surd form.

   b Write down the values of:

   i cos 45°   **ii** sin 45°   **iii** tan 45°

   leaving your answers in surd form.

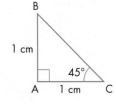

 9 In the diagram, AD = 5 cm, AC = 8 cm and AB = 12 cm.
   Eve says: "The angle CAB is 14°."
   Comment on Eve's statement.

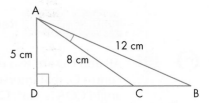

22.2 Further 3D problems

This section will show you how to:

- use trigonometric ratios and Pythagoras' theorem to solve more complex three-dimensional problems.

To solve a problem in three dimensions, you often need to identify a right-angled triangle that contains the required length or angle. This triangle will also need to contain two known measures that you can use to make the required calculation.

You should extract the triangle you are going to use from its 3D situation and redraw it as a separate right-angled triangle. Annotate the re-drawn triangle with the known quantities and the unknown quantity that you are going to calculate. Then use the trigonometric ratios (sine, cosine and tangent) and Pythagoras' theorem to solve the triangle.

Example 5

The diagram shows a cuboid 22.5 cm by 40 cm by 30 cm. M is the midpoint of FG.

Calculate these angles.

a ABE

b ECA

c EMH

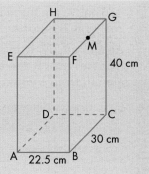

a The right-angled triangle containing the angle required is ABE.

Solving for α gives:

$$\tan \alpha = \frac{40}{22.5}$$

$$= 1.7777$$

$$\Rightarrow \alpha = \tan^{-1} 1.7777$$

$$= 60.6° \text{ (3 sf)}$$

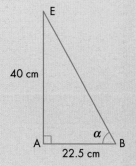

b The right-angled triangle containing the angle required is ACE, but you only know AE is so far. Therefore, you need to work out AC by applying Pythagoras' theorem to the right-angled triangle ABC.

$$x^2 = (22.5)^2 + (30)^2 \text{ cm}^2$$

$$\Rightarrow x = 37.5 \text{ cm}$$

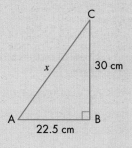

Returning to triangle ACE:

$$\tan \beta = \frac{40}{37.5}$$

$$= 1.0666$$

$$\Rightarrow \beta = \tan^{-1} 1.0666$$

$$= 46.8° \text{ (3 sf)}$$

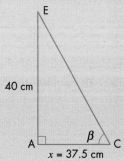

c EMH is an isosceles triangle.

Draw the perpendicular from M to N, the midpoint of HE, to form two right-angled triangles. Angle HMN equals angle EMN, and HN = NE = 15 cm.

Taking triangle MEN:

$$\tan \theta = \frac{15}{22.5}$$

$$= 0.666\,666$$

$$\Rightarrow \theta = \tan^{-1} 0.666\,666$$

$$= 33.7° \text{ (3 sf)}$$

Therefore, angle EHE is 2 × 33.7° = 67.4° (3 sf)

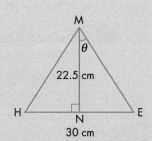

Example 6

A, B and C are three points at ground level. They are in the same horizontal plane. C is 50 km east of B. B is north of A. C is on a bearing of 050° from A.

An aircraft, flying in an easterly direction, passes over B and over C at the same height. When it passes over B, the angle of elevation from A is 12°. Work out the angle of elevation of the aircraft from A when it is over C.

First, draw a diagram containing all the known information.

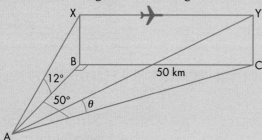

Next, use the right-angled triangle ABC to calculate AB and AC.

$$AB = \frac{50}{\tan 50°}$$

$$= 41.95 \text{ km (4 sf)}$$

$$AC = \frac{50}{\sin 50°}$$

$$= 65.27 \text{ km (4 sf)}$$

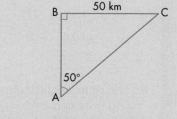

Then use the right-angled triangle ABX to calculate BX, and hence CY.

$$BX = 41.95 \tan 12°$$

$$= 8.917 \text{ km (4 sf)}$$

Finally, use the right-angled triangle ACY to calculate the required angle of elevation, θ.

$$\tan \theta = \frac{8.917}{65.27}$$

$$= 0.1366$$

$$\Rightarrow \theta = \tan^{-1} 0.1366$$

$$= 7.8° \text{ (1 dp)}$$

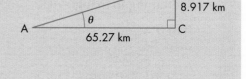

Always write down your intermediate working values to at least 4 significant figures, or use the answer on your calculator display to avoid inaccuracy in the final answer.

Exercise 22B

1 A vertical flagpole AP stands at the corner of a rectangular courtyard ABCD.

Calculate the angle of elevation of P from C.

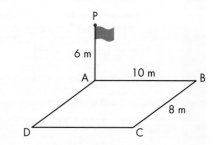

2 ABCD is a vertical rectangular plane. EDC is a horizontal triangular plane.

Angle CDE = 90°, AB = 10 cm, BC = 4 cm and ED = 9 cm. Calculate:

a angle AED

b angle DEC

c length EC

d angle BEC.

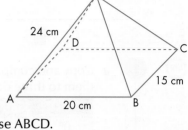

3 The diagram shows a pyramid. The base is a horizontal rectangle ABCD, 20 cm by 15 cm. The length of each sloping edge is 24 cm. The apex, V, is over the centre of the rectangular base. Calculate:

a the size of the angle VAC

b the height of the pyramid

c the volume of the pyramid

d the size of the angle between the face VAD and the base ABCD.

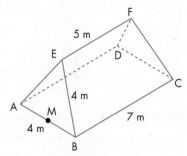

(PS) 4 The diagram shows the roof of a building. The base ABCD is a horizontal rectangle, 7 m by 4 m. The triangular ends are equilateral triangles. Each side of the roof is an isosceles trapezium. The length of the top of the roof, EF, is 5 m.

a Calculate the size of the angle between the face EAB and the base ABCD.

b A roofer charges £125 per square metre to tile a roof. How much would it cost to tile this roof?

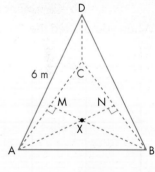

(PS) 5 The diagram shows a tetrahedron, where each face is an equilateral triangle of side 6 m. The lines AN and BM meet the sides CB and AC at right angles and intersect at X, which is directly below the vertex, D. Calculate:

a the distance AX

b the angle between the side DB and the base ABC.

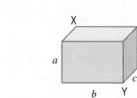

(CM) 6 The lengths of the sides of a cuboid are a, b and c.

Show that the length of the diagonal XY is $\sqrt{a^2 + b^2 + c^2}$.

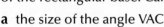

(EV) 7 In the diagram, XABCD is a right pyramid with a rectangular base.

Leo calculates the angle between the edge XD and the base ABCD to be 56.3°.

Explain why Leo's result might be wrong.

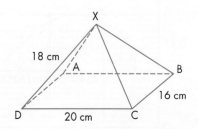

22.3 Trigonometric ratios of angles between 0° and 360°

This section will show you how to:

- calculate the sine, cosine and tangent of any angle from 0° to 360°.

The sine curve

Exercise 22C

1 **a** Copy and complete this table. Use your calculator to find the values, then round them to three decimal places.

x	sin x	x	sin x	x	sin x	x	sin x
0°		180°		180°		360°	
15°		165°		195°		345°	
30°		150°		210°		330°	
45°		135°		225°		315°	
60°		120°		240°		300°	
75°		105°		255°		285°	
90°		90°		270°		270°	

 b Comment on what you notice about the sine of each acute angle and its related non-acute angles.

2 **a** Draw a graph of sin x against x. Take x from 0° to 360° and sin x from –1 to 1.

 b Comment on any symmetries shown in your graph.

When you plotted the sine of angles between 0° and 360° in Exercise 22C, you produced the sine curve.

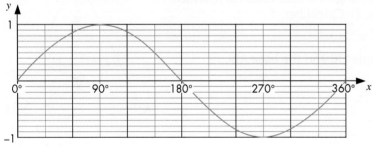

Sine x

Looking at the sine graph below, you can see that sin 27° = 0.45 (2 sf).

From the symmetry of the graph, 153° also has a sine of 0.45.   sin 153° = sin(180° – 153°) = sin 27°

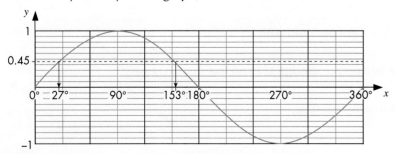

Sine x

So, when 90° < x < 180°, sin x = sin (180° – x).

Now look at this sine graph. Again, you can use the symmetry of the graph to see that the lines of $y = 0.56$ and $y = -0.56$ cut the graph at points that are symmetrical to each other.

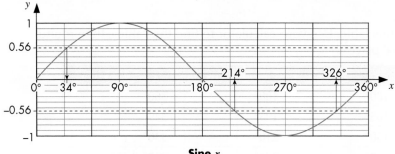

Sine x

You can see that:

- 0.56 is the sine of 34° and –0.56 is the sine of 214° and of 326°
- $\sin 214 = -\sin (214° - 180°) = -\sin 34° = -0.56$ (2 sf)
- $\sin 326 = -\sin (360° - 326°) = -\sin 34° = -0.56$ (2 sf)

So, when $180° < x < 270°$, $\sin x = -\sin (x - 180°)$

and when $270° < x < 360°$, $\sin x = -\sin (360° - x)$.

Note:

- Every value of sine between –1 and 1 gives *two* angles between 0° and 360°.
- When the value of sine is positive, both angles are between 0° and 180°.
- When the value of sine is negative, both angles are between 180° and 360°.
- You can use the sine graph from 0° to 360° to check approximate values.
- The graph is **periodic**. This means that it will keep on repeating the same shape as you go further down the horizontal axis. The period is 360° as this is the given shape that repeats.

Example 7

Calculate the angles between 0° and 360° with a sine of 0.56.

You know that both angles are between 0° and 180°.

Using your calculator to calculate $\sin^{-1} 0.56$, you get 34.1°.

The other angle is, therefore:

$180° - 34.1° = 145.9°$

So, the angles are 34.1° and 145.9°.

Example 8

Calculate the angles between 0° and 360° with a sine of –0.197.

You know that both angles are between 180° and 360°.

Using your calculator to calculate $\sin^{-1} 0.197$, you get 11.4°.

So the angles are:

$180° + 11.4°$ and $360° - 11.4°$

which gives 191.4° and 348.6°.

The cosine curve

Exercise 22D

 1 **a** Copy and complete this table. Use your calculator to find the values, then round them to three decimal places.

x	cos x	x	cos x	x	cos x	x	cos x
0°		180°		180°		360°	
15°		165°		195°		345°	
30°		150°		210°		330°	
45°		135°		225°		315°	
60°		120°		240°		300°	
75°		105°		255°		285°	
90°		90°		270°		270°	

b Comment on what you notice about the cosine of each acute angle and its related non-acute angles.

 2 **a** Draw a graph of cos x against x. Take x from 0° to 360° and cos x from –1 to 1.

b Describe any symmetries shown in your graph.

When you plotted the cosine of angles between 0° and 360° in Exercise 22D, you drew the cosine curve.

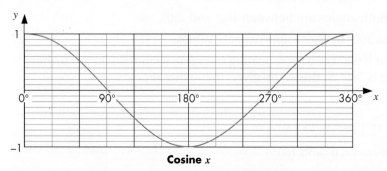

Cosine x

Using the symmetries of the graph and the lines $y = 0.77$ and $y = -0.77$, you can see that:

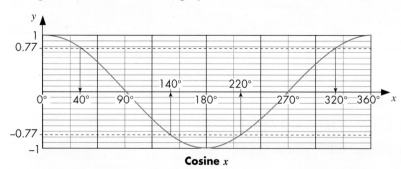

Cosine x

cos 40° = 0.77 and cos 320° = 0.77 so cos 320° = cos (360° – 40°)

cos 140° = –0.77 and cos 220° = –0.77 so cos 140° = –cos (180° – 140°) and cos 220° = –(220° – 180°)

- When 90° < x < 180°, cos x = –cos (180 – x)°.
- When 180° < x < 270°, cos x = –cos (x – 180°).
- When 270° < x < 360°, cos x = cos (360° – x).

Note:

- Every value of cosine between –1 and 1 gives *two* angles between 0° and 360°.
- When the value of cosine is positive, one angle is between 0° and 90° and the other is between 270° and 360°.
- When the value of cosine is negative, both angles are between 90° and 270°.
- You can use the cosine graph from 0° to 360° to check approximate values.
- The cosine curve is periodic, repeating every 360°.

Example 9

Calculate the angles between 0° and 360° with a cosine of 0.75.

You know that one angle is between 0° and 90° and the other is between 270° and 360°.

Using your calculator to calculate $\cos^{-1} 0.75$, you get 41.4°.

The other angle is, therefore

$360° - 41.4° = 318.6°$

So, the angles are 41.4° and 318.6°.

Example 10

Calculate the angles between 0° and 360° with a cosine of –0.285.

You know that both angles are between 90° and 270°.

Using your calculator to calculate $\cos^{-1} 0.285$, you get 73.4°.

So the angles are:

$180° - 73.4°$ and $180° + 73.4°$

which gives 106.6° and 253.4°.

You can use your calculator to check your answer, by keying in cosine.

Exercise 22E

1 State the two angles between 0° and 360° for each of these sine values.

a 0.6	**b** 0.8	**c** 0.75	**d** –0.7
e –0.25	**f** –0.32	**g** –0.175	**h** –0.814
i 0.471	**j** –0.097	**k** 0.553	**l** –0.5

 2 Which of these values is the odd one out? Give a reason for your answer.

  sin 36°   sin 144°   sin 234°   sin 324°

 3 The graph of sine x is periodic, which means that it repeats forever in each direction.

  a Write down one value of x greater than 360° for which the sine value is 0.978 147 6.

  b Write down one value of x less than 0° for which the sine value is 0.978 147 6.

  c Describe any symmetries of the graph of $y = \sin x$.

 4 Solve the equation $6(\sin x)^2 = 1 + \sin x$, giving all answers between 0° and 360°. Where appropriate, round answers to 1 decimal place.

  | Hints and tips | Replace sin x with y and solve the quadratic equation. |

5 State the two angles between 0° and 360° for each of these cosine values.

  a 0.6 **b** 0.58 **c** 0.458 **d** 0.575

  e 0.185 **f** −0.8 **g** −0.25 **h** −0.175

  i −0.361 **j** −0.974 **k** 0.196 **l** 0.714

(MR) **6** Which of these values is the odd one out? Give a reason for your answer.

  cos 58° cos 118° cos 238° cos 262°

(MR) **7** The graph of cosine x is periodic, which means that it repeats forever in each direction.

  a Write down one value of x greater than 360° for which the cosine value is −0.669 130 6.

  b Write down one value of x less than 0° for which the cosine value is −0.669 130 6.

  c Describe any symmetries of the graph of $y = \cos x$.

(EV) **8** The graph shows the heights of the tide one day in Bude over a 24-hour period.

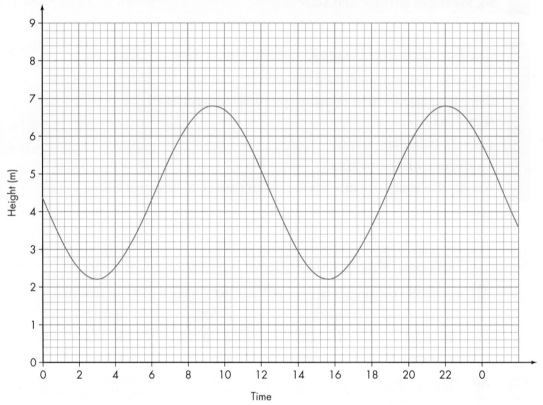

  a i What times are high tide and low tide? **ii** How long is it between each high tide?

  b Compare this graph with the sine curve.

   i What are the similarities? **ii** What are the differences?

Exercise 22F

1 Write down the sine of each of these angles.

  a 135° **b** 269° **c** 305° **d** 133°

2 Write down the cosine of each of these angles.

  a 129° **b** 209° **c** 95° **d** 357°

3 Write down the two possible values of x ($0° < x < 360°$) for each equation. Give your answers to 1 decimal place.

a $\sin x = 0.361$ **b** $\sin x = -0.486$ **c** $\cos x = 0.641$

d $\cos x = -0.866$ **e** $\sin x = 0.874$ **f** $\cos x = 0.874$

(MR) **4** Find two angles such that the sine of each is 0.5.

(MR) **5** Given that $\cos 41° = 0.755$, what is $\cos 139°$?

6 Write down the value of each of the following, correct to 3 significant figures.

a $\sin 50° + \cos 50°$ **b** $\cos 120° - \sin 120°$ **c** $\sin 136° + \cos 223°$

d $\sin 175° + \cos 257°$ **e** $\sin 114° - \sin 210°$ **f** $\cos 123° + \sin 177°$

(EV) **7** It is suggested that $(\sin x)^2 + (\cos x)^2 = 1$ is true for all values of x. Test out this suggestion to see if you agree.

(PS) **8** Suppose the sine key on your calculator is broken but the cosine key is working. Show how you could calculate these.

a $\sin 25°$ **b** $\sin 130°$

(PS) **9** Find a solution to each of these equations.

a $\sin (x + 20°) = 0.5$ **b** $\cos (5x) = 0.45$

(PS) **10** Use any suitable method to work out the solution to the equation $\sin x = (\cos x)^2$.

(EV) **11** Rose said that one angle with sine of 0.9659 could be 435°. Keiren said that was not quite correct. Evaluate each person's statement.

The tangent curve

Exercise 22G

(MR) **1** **a** Use your calculator to calculate $\tan 90°$. What do you notice?

b Which is the closest angle to 90° for which you can calculate the tangent on your calculator?

(MR) **2** What is the largest value for a tangent that you can get on your calculator?

(MR) **3** **a** Find values of $\tan x$ where $x = 0°, 15°, 30°, 45°, 60° \dots 360°$.

b Draw a graph of your results.

c State the tangents of 0°, 180° and 360°.

d Explain what appears to happen at $x = 90°$ and $x = 270°$.

(MR) **4** **a** State some rules for calculating both angles between 0° and 360° that have any given tangent.

b Do you think the tangent curve is periodic? If so, what is the period?

When you plotted the tangent of angles between 0° and 360° in Exercise 22G, then plotted them on a graph, you drew the tangent curve.

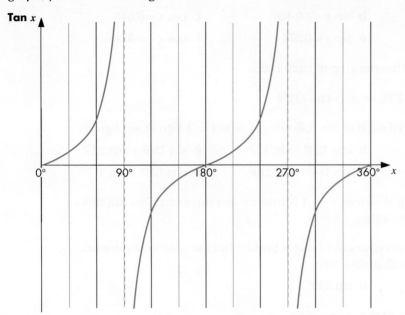

Using the symmetries of the graph and the lines $y = 1.2$ and $y = -1.2$, you can see that:

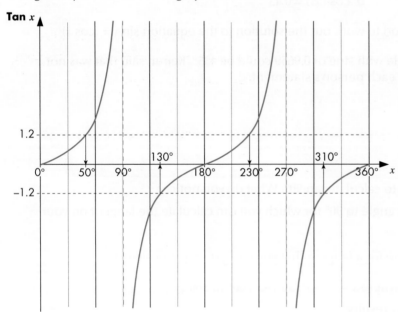

tan 50° = 1.2 and tan 230° = 1.2
so tan 230° = tan (230° − 180°) = tan 50°

tan 130° = tan 310° = −1.2°
so tan 130° = −tan (180° − 130°) = −tan 50°
and tan 310° = −tan (360° − 310°) = −tan 50°

- When 90° < x < 180°, tan x = −tan (180° − x)°.
- When 180° < x < 270°, tan x = tan (x − 180°).
- When 270° < x < 360°, tan x = −tan (360° − x)

Note

- Every value of tangent gives *two* angles between 0° and 360°.
- When the value of tangent is positive, one angle is between 0° and 90° and the other is between 180° and 270°.
- When the value of tangent is negative, one angle is between 90° and 180° and the other is between 270° and 360°.
- You can use the tangent graph from 0° to 360° to check approximate values.
- The tangent curve is periodic, repeating every 180°.

Exercise 22H

 1 Calculate the angles between 0° and 360° with a tangent of:

    a 0.875   **b** –1.5

2 State the angles between 0° and 360° for each of these tangent values.

    a 0.258   **b** 1.875   **c** 2.55   **d** –0.358

    e –0.634   **f** –3.68   **g** 1.397   **h** –1.153

    i –0.098   **j** 0.998

 3 Which of these values is the odd one out? Give a reason for your answer.

    tan 45°   tan 135°   tan 235°   tan 315°

4 The graph of tan x is periodic, which means that it repeats forever in each direction.

    a Write down one value of x greater than 360° for which the tangent value is 2.144 506 9.

    b Write down one value of x less than 0° for which the tangent value is 2.144 506 9.

    c Describe any symmetries of the graph of $y = \tan x$.

5 Mel said: "One angle with tangent of –0.4040 could be 158°." José said: "No, it's –22°." Evaluate each person's statement.

22.4 Solving any triangle

This section will show you how to:

- use the sine rule and the cosine rule to work out sides and angles in any triangle.

Key terms	
cosine rule	included angle
sine rule	

You know that every triangle has six measurements: three sides and three angles. To solve a triangle (that is, to work out any unknown angles or sides), you need to know at least three of these measurements. Any combination of three measurements, with the exception of three angles, is sufficient to work out the remaining measurements. In a right-angled triangle, one of the known measurements is, of course, the right angle.

When you solve a triangle with no right angle, you can use one of two rules, depending on what you know about the triangle. These are the **sine rule** and the **cosine rule**.

The sine rule

Take any triangle ABC and label the sides a, b and c, where a is opposite angle A, b is opposite angle B and c is opposite to angle C. Draw the perpendicular from A to the opposite side BC.

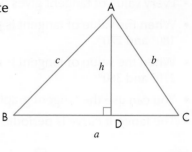

From right-angled triangle ADB, $h = c \sin B$

From right-angled triangle ADC, $h = b \sin C$

Therefore:

$c \sin B = b \sin C$

which you can rearrange to give:

$$\frac{c}{\sin C} = \frac{b}{\sin B}$$

By drawing a perpendicular from each of the other two vertices to the opposite side (or by algebraic symmetry), you can see that:

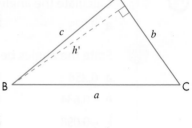

$$\frac{a}{\sin A} = \frac{c}{\sin C} \quad \text{and that} \quad \frac{a}{\sin A} = \frac{b}{\sin B}$$

These are usually combined in the form:

$$\frac{a}{\sin A} = \frac{b}{\sin B} = \frac{c}{\sin C}$$

which you can invert to give:

$$\frac{\sin A}{a} = \frac{\sin B}{b} = \frac{\sin C}{c}$$

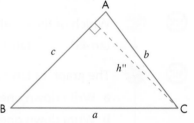

A triangle is not always conveniently labelled, as in these diagrams. So when using the sine rule, remember to take each side in turn, divide it by the sine of the angle opposite and then put the resulting fractions equal to each other.

Note

- When you are calculating a *side*, use the rule with the *sides on top*.

- When you are calculating an *angle*, use the rule with the *sines on top*.

Example 11

Work out the value of x.

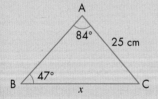

Use the sine rule with sides on top.

$$\frac{x}{\sin 84°} = \frac{25}{\sin 47°}$$

$$\Rightarrow x = \frac{25 \sin 84°}{\sin 47°} \qquad \text{(Multiply both sides by } \sin 84°\text{)}$$

$$= 34.0 \text{ cm (3 sf)}$$

Example 12

Work out the value of x.

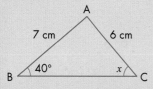

Use the sine rule with sines on top.

$$\frac{\sin x}{7} = \frac{\sin 40°}{6}$$

$$\Rightarrow \sin x = \frac{7 \sin 40°}{6} \qquad \text{(Multiply both sides by 7)}$$

$$= 0.7499$$

$$\Rightarrow x = \sin^{-1} 0.7499$$

$$= 48.6° \text{ (3 sf)}$$

The ambiguous case

It is possible to calculate the sine of an angle that is greater than 90° (see Section 22.3).

For example, $\sin 30° = \sin 150° = 0.5$.

(Notice that the two angles add up to 180°.)

So $\sin 25° = \sin 155°$ and $\sin 100° = \sin 80°$.

Example 13

In triangle ABC, AB = 9 cm, AC = 7 cm and angle ABC = 40°. Work out the angle ACB.

As you sketch triangle ABC, note that C can have two positions, giving two different configurations.

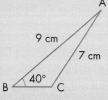 or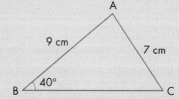

Proceed as in the normal sine rule situation.

$$\frac{\sin C}{9} = \frac{\sin 40°}{7}$$

$$\Rightarrow \sin C = \frac{9 \sin 40°}{7} \qquad \text{(Multiply both sides by 9)}$$

$$= 0.8264$$

Keying inverse sine on the calculator gives $C = 55.7°$.

However, there is another angle with a sine of 0.8264, given by $(180° - 55.7°) = 124.3°$.

These two values for C give the two different triangles shown above.

When you have an illustration of the triangle, it is clear whether the required angle is acute or obtuse. When you do not have an illustration, you have to consider the scenario carefully and decide which is the most logical.

1 Work out length x in each of these triangles.

a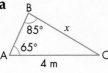

b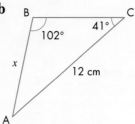

c

2 Work out angle x in each of these triangles.

a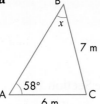

b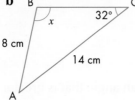

c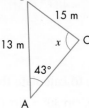

(MR) **3** In triangle ABC, angle A is 38°, side AB is 10 cm and side BC is 8 cm. Work out the two possible values of angle C.

(EV) **4** Abbey said: "The longest side in any triangle is opposite the largest angle."

Evaluate this statement.

(MR) **5** In triangle ABC, angle A is 42°, AB is 16 cm and BC is 14 cm. Work out the two possible lengths of AC.

(PS) **6** To calculate the height of a tower standing on a small hill, Mary made some measurements (see diagram).

From a point B, the angle of elevation of C is 20° and the angle of elevation of A is 50°. The distance BC is 25 m.

a Calculate these angles.

  i ABC

  ii BAC

b Using the sine rule and triangle ABC, calculate the height h of the tower.

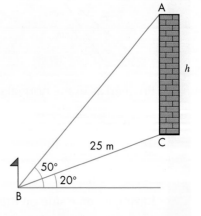

(PS) **7** Use the information on this sketch to calculate the width, w, of the river.

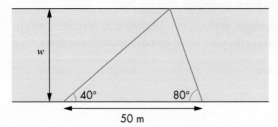

An old building is unsafe and is protected by a fence. A demolition company is going to demolish the building and has to work out the height BD, marked h on the diagram.

Use the measurements marked on the diagram to calculate the value of h.

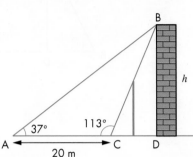

9 A light is hung from a horizontal beam using two strings. The shorter string is 2.5 m long and makes an angle of 71° with the horizontal. The longer string makes an angle of 43° with the horizontal. What is the length of the longer string?

10 An aircraft is found by two searchlights on the ground that are 3 km apart. The two beams of light meet on the aircraft at an angle of 125° vertically above the line joining the searchlights. One of the beams of light makes an angle of 31° with the horizontal.

Paul calculated the height of the aircraft as 676 m. Is Paul correct?

11 Two ships leave a port in directions that are 41° from each other. After half an hour, the ships are 11 km apart. If the speed of the slower ship is 7 km/h, what is the speed of the faster ship?

12 A rescue helicopter is based at an airfield at A.

The helicopter is sent out to rescue a man who has had an accident on a mountain at M, due north of A.

The helicopter then flies on a bearing of 145° to a hospital at H, as shown on the diagram.

Calculate the direct distance from the mountain to the hospital.

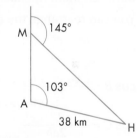

13 Choose four values of θ between 0 and 90 to show that $\sin \theta = \sin (180 - \theta)$.

14 Triangle ABC has an obtuse angle at B. Calculate the size of angle ABC.

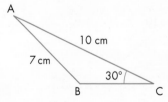

15 For any triangle ABC, prove the sine rule $\dfrac{a}{\sin A} = \dfrac{b}{\sin B} = \dfrac{c}{\sin C}$.

The cosine rule

Take the triangle, shown on the right, where D is the foot of the perpendicular to BC from A.

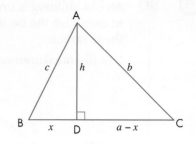

Using Pythagoras' theorem on triangle BDA:

$h^2 = c^2 - x^2$

Using Pythagoras' theorem on triangle ADC:

$h^2 = b^2 - (a - x)^2$

Therefore:

$c^2 - x^2 = b^2 - (a - x)^2$

$c^2 - x^2 = b^2 - a^2 + 2ax - x^2$

$\Rightarrow c^2 = b^2 - a^2 + 2ax$

From triangle BDA, $x = c \cos B$.

So:

$c^2 = b^2 - a^2 + 2ac \cos B$

which you can rearrange to give:

$b^2 = a^2 + c^2 - 2ac \cos B$

By algebraic symmetry:

$a^2 = b^2 + c^2 - 2bc \cos A$ and $c^2 = a^2 + b^2 - 2ab \cos C$

This is the cosine rule, which you can remember with the diagram on the right, where:

$a^2 = b^2 + c^2 - 2bc \cos A$

Note the symmetry of the rule and how the rule works using two adjacent sides and the angle between them (the **included angle**).

You can rearrange the formula to calculate any of the three angles.

$\cos A = \dfrac{b^2 + c^2 - a^2}{2bc}$

$\cos B = \dfrac{a^2 + c^2 - b^2}{2ac}$

$\cos C = \dfrac{a^2 + b^2 - c^2}{2ab}$

Work out the value of x in this triangle.

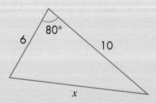

Use the cosine rule.

$x^2 = 6^2 + 10^2 - 2 \times 6 \times 10 \times \cos 80°$

$= 115.16$

$\Rightarrow x = 10.7 \qquad$ (3 sf)

Example 15

Work out the value of x in this triangle.

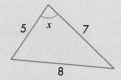

Use the cosine rule.

$$\cos x = \frac{5^2 + 7^2 - 8^2}{2 \times 5 \times 7} = 0.1428$$

$$\Rightarrow x = \cos^{-1} 0.1428$$

$$= 81.8° \quad (3 \text{ sf})$$

It is possible to calculate the cosine of an angle that is greater than 90° (see Section 22.3).
For example, $\cos 120° = -\cos 60° = -0.5$. (Notice the minus sign; the two angles add up to 18°.)

So $\cos 150° = -\cos 30° = -0.866$.

Example 16

A ship sails from a port on a bearing of 055° for 40 km. It then changes course to 123° for another 50 km. What bearing should the ship steer to go straight back to the port?

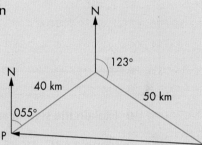

Previously, you have solved this type of problem using right-angled triangles. You could apply this method here but it would involve at least six separate calculations.

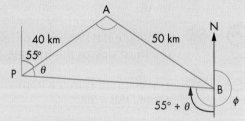

Using the cosine and sine rules, however, you can reduce the solution to two separate calculations, as follows.

The course diagram gives the triangle PAB, where you can use allied angles and angles round a point to work out angle PAB.

The allied angle with 055° is $180 - 55° = 125°$

So angle PAB $= 360° - (125° + 123°) = 112°$

Let φ be the bearing that the ship needs to steer. Then using alternate angles around P and B:

$$\varphi = \theta + 55° + 180°$$

To calculate θ, you first have to use the cosine rule to work out PB.

$$PB^2 = 40^2 + 50^2 - 2 \times 40 \times 50 \times \cos 112° \text{ km}^2 \qquad \text{(Remember the cosine of 112° is negative.)}$$

$$\Rightarrow PB^2 = 5598.43 \text{ km}^2$$

$$\Rightarrow PB = 74.82 \text{ km}$$

You can now calculate θ from the sine rule.

$$\frac{\sin \theta}{50} = \frac{\sin 112°}{74.82}$$

$$\Rightarrow \sin \theta = \frac{50 \times \sin 112°}{74.82} = 0.6196$$

$$\Rightarrow \theta = 38.3°$$

So the ship should steer on a bearing of $38.3° + 55° + 180° = 273.3°$.

1 Calculate the length x in each of these triangles.

a

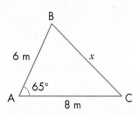

b

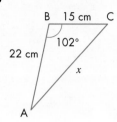

c

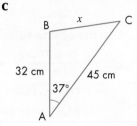

(EV) **2** Calculate the angle x in each of these triangles.

a

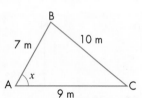

b

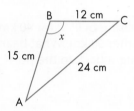

c

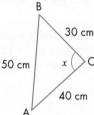

d Explain the significance of your answer to part **c**.

3 In triangle ABC, AB = 5 cm, BC = 6 cm and angle ABC = 55°. Work out the length of AC.

(PS) **4** A triangle has two sides of length 40 cm and an angle of 110°. Work out the length of the third side of the triangle.

(PS) **5** The diagram shows a trapezium ABCD. AB = 6.7 cm, AD = 7.2 cm, CB = 9.3 cm and angle DAB = 100°.

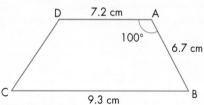

Calculate:

a the length DB
b angle DBA
c angle DBC
d the length DC
e the area of the trapezium.

6 A quadrilateral ABCD has AD = 6 cm, DC = 9 cm, AB = 10 cm and BC = 12 cm. Angle ADC = 120°. Calculate angle ABC.

(PS) **7** A triangle has two sides of length 30 cm and an angle of 50°. Unfortunately, the position of the angle is not known. Work out the two possible lengths of the third side of the triangle.

(PS) **8** A ship sails from a port on a bearing of 050° for 50 km then turns on a bearing of 150° for 40 km. A crewman is taken ill, so the ship drops anchor. What course and distance should a rescue helicopter fly from the port to reach the ship in the shortest possible time? Assume the shortest distance will take the shortest time.

9 The three sides of a triangle are $3a$, $5a$ and $7a$. Calculate the smallest angle in the triangle.

 10 ABCD is a trapezium where AB is parallel to CD. AB = 4 cm, BC = 5 cm, CD = 8 cm and DA = 6 cm. A line BX is parallel to AD and cuts DC at X. Calculate:

   a angle BCD **b** the length BD.

 11 Two ships, X and Y, leave a port at 9 am.

   Ship X travels at an average speed of 20 km/h on a bearing of 075° from the port.

   Ship Y travels at an average speed of 25 km/h on a bearing of 130° from the port.

   Calculate the distance between the two ships at 11 am.

 12 Choose four values of θ between 0° and 90° to show that $\cos \theta = -\cos (180° - \theta)$.

 13 Calculate the size of the largest angle in triangle ABC.

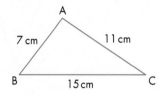

Choosing the correct rule

When solving triangles, there are only four situations that can occur.
You can solve each of them completely in three stages.

Two sides and the included angle

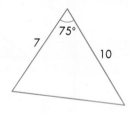

1 Use the cosine rule to work out the third side.

2 Use the sine rule to work out either of the other angles.

3 Use the sum of the angles in a triangle to work out the third angle.

Two angles and a side

1 Use the sum of the angles in a triangle to work out the third angle.

2, 3 Use the sine rule to work out the other two sides.

Three sides

1 Use the cosine rule to work out one angle.

2 Use the sine rule to work out another angle.

3 Use the sum of the angles in a triangle to work out the third angle.

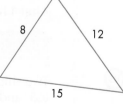

Two sides and a non-included angle

This is the ambiguous case already covered.

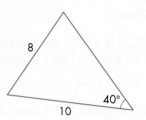

1 Use the sine rule to work out the two possible values of the appropriate angle.

2 Use the sum of the angles in a triangle to work out the two possible values of the third angle.

3 Use the sine rule to work out the two possible values for the length of the third side.

Exercise 22K 🔲

1 Calculate the value of x in each of these triangles.

a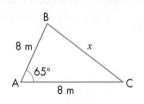

b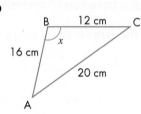

c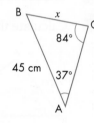

d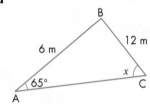

e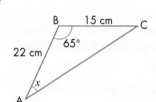

f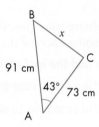

(PS) **2** The hands of a clock have lengths 3 cm and 5 cm. Work out the distance between the tips of the hands at 4 o'clock.

(PS) **3** A spacecraft is seen hovering in the same vertical plane as two towns, X and F. It is 8.5 km from X and 12 km from F. The angle of elevation of the spacecraft when observed from F is 43°. Calculate the distance between the two towns.

(PS) **4** Two boats, Mary Jo and Suzie, leave port at the same time.

Mary Jo sails at 10 knots on a bearing of 065°. Suzie sails on a bearing of 120°.

After 1 hour, Mary Jo is on a bearing of 330° from Suzie. What is Suzie's speed?

> **Hints and tips** A knot is a nautical mile per hour.

(PS) **5** Two ships leave port at the same time. Darling Dave sails at 12 knots on a bearing of 055° and Merry Mary sails at 18 knots on a bearing of 280°.

  a How far apart are the two ships after 1 hour?

  b What is the bearing of Merry Mary from Darling Dave after 1 hour?

6 Triangle ABC has sides with lengths a, b and c, as shown in the diagram.

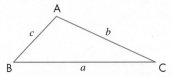

a What can you say about the angle BAC, if $b^2 + c^2 - a^2 = 0$?

b What can you say about the angle BAC, if $b^2 + c^2 - a^2 > 0$?

c What can you say about the angle BAC, if $b^2 + c^2 - a^2 < 0$?

 7 The diagram shows a sketch of a field ABCD.

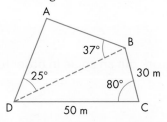

A farmer wants to put a new fence round the perimeter of the field.

William says the perimeter of the field is 142 m.

Evaluate on William's statement.

22.5 Using sine to calculate the area of a triangle

This section will show you how to:

- work out the area of a triangle if you know two sides and the included angle.

In triangle ABC, the vertical height is BD and the base is AC.

Let BD = h and AC = b, then the area of the triangle is given by:

$\frac{1}{2} \times$ AC $\times$ BD $= \frac{1}{2}bh$

However, in triangle BCD

h = BC sin $C = a$ sin C

where BC = a.

Substituting into bh gives:

$\frac{1}{2}b \times (a \sin C) = \frac{1}{2}ab \sin C$

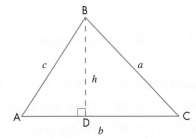

as the area of the triangle.

By taking the perpendicular from A to its opposite side BC, and the perpendicular from C to its opposite side AB, you can show that the area of the triangle is also given by:

$\frac{1}{2}ac \sin B$ and $\frac{1}{2}bc \sin A$

Note the pattern: the area is given by the product of two sides multiplied by the sine of the included angle. This is the **area rule**. Starting from any of the three forms, it is also possible to use the sine rule to establish the other two.

Example 17

Work out the area of triangle ABC.

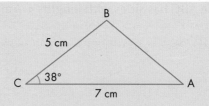

Area = $\frac{1}{2}ab \sin C$

Area = $\frac{1}{2} \times 5 \times 7 \times \sin 38°$

    = 10.8 cm² (3 sf)

Example 18

Work out the area of triangle ABC.

You have all three sides but no angle. So first you must work out an angle in order to apply the area rule.

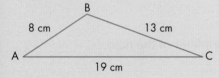

Calculate the value of angle C, using the cosine rule.

$\cos C = \dfrac{a^2 + b^2 - c^2}{2ab}$

$= \dfrac{13^2 + 19^2 - 8^2}{2 \times 13 \times 19}$

$= 0.9433$

$\Rightarrow C = \cos^{-1} 0.9433$

    $= 19.383\ldots°$ (Keep the exact value in your calculator memory.)

Now apply the area rule.

$\frac{1}{2}ab \sin C = \frac{1}{2} \times 13 \times 19 \times \sin 19.383\ldots°$

            $= 41.0$ cm²   (3 sf)

Exercise 22L

1 Work out the area of each of the following triangles.

   a Triangle ABC where BC = 7 cm, AC = 8 cm and angle ACB = 59°

   b Triangle ABC where angle BAC = 86°, AC = 6.7 cm and AB = 8 cm

   c Triangle PQR where QR = 27 cm, PR = 19 cm and angle QRP = 109°

   d Triangle XYZ where XY = 231 cm, XZ = 191 cm and angle YXZ = 73°

   e Triangle LMN where LN = 63 cm, LM = 39 cm and angle NLM = 85°

2 The area of triangle ABC is 27 cm². If BC = 14 cm and angle BCA = 115°, calculate AC.

3 The area of triangle LMN is 113 cm², LM = 16 cm and MN = 21 cm. Angle LMN is acute. Calculate these angles.

   a LMN   **b** MNL

(PS) 4 In a quadrilateral ABCD, DC = 4 cm, BD = 11 cm, angle BAD = 32°, angle ABD = 48° and angle BDC = 61°. Calculate the area of the quadrilateral.

5 A board is in the shape of a triangle with sides 60 cm, 70 cm and 80 cm. Work out the area of the board.

(PS) 6 Two circles, centres P and Q, have radii of 6 cm and 7 cm respectively. The circles intersect at X and Y. Given that PQ = 9 cm, work out the area of triangle PXQ.

(PS) 7 The points A, B and C are on the circumference of a circle, centre O and radius 7 cm. AB = 4 cm and BC = 3.5 cm. Calculate:

  a angle AOB   **b** the area of quadrilateral OABC.

(CM) 8 Prove that for any triangle ABC, area = $\frac{1}{2}ab \sin C$.

(PS) 9 Calculate the area of triangle PQR.

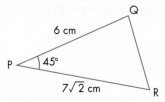

(PS) 10 Sanjay is making a kite.

The diagram shows a sketch of his kite.

Calculate the area of the material he will need to make the kite.

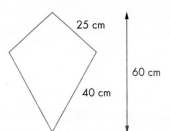

(PS) 11 An equilateral triangle has sides of length a.

Work out the area of the triangle, giving your answer in surd form.

(EV) 12 A pyramid has a square base of side length 10 cm.

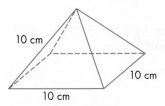

Which of these expressions gives the total surface area of the pyramid?

  a $100(1 + 2\sqrt{3})$ cm²   **b** $100(2 + \sqrt{3})$ cm²

  c $100(1 + \sqrt{3})$ cm²   **d** $100(1 + 2\sqrt{2})$ cm²

Worked exemplars

EV **1** The diagram shows a cuboid ABCDEFGH.

Ben said the size of angle AGE is 23°.

Evaluate Ben's statement.

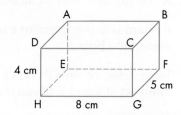

This is an evaluating question where you check the statement to see if it's correct. This means you need to calculate the given angle in order to check the validity of the statement. Identify a triangle from the given diagram with the required angle: AGE. You need to find length EG in order to have sufficient data in the triangle to work out the angle.	

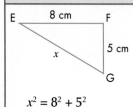 $x^2 = 8^2 + 5^2$ $\qquad = 89$ $\Rightarrow x = \sqrt{89}$ $\qquad = 9.434$ cm	Draw the right-angled triangle EFG and work out the length of EG using Pythagoras' theorem.
A triangle AGE with 4 cm, y, E, 9.434 cm, G $\tan y = \dfrac{O}{A}$ $\qquad = \dfrac{4}{9.434}$ $\qquad = 0.4240$ $\Rightarrow y = \tan^{-1} 0.420$ $\qquad = 23.0°$ (3 sf)	Draw the right-angled triangle AGE, label the required angle y and calculate its value.
So Ben is correct.	Once you have found the angle, say explicitly whether or not the statement is correct.

MR **2** A tetrahedron has one face that is an equilateral triangle of side 6 cm and three faces that are isosceles triangles with sides 6 cm, 9 cm and 9 cm.

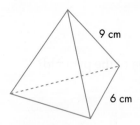

Show that the surface area of the tetrahedron is 92 cm².

This is a mathematical reasoning question where you have to construct a chain of reasoning to achieve a given result.

You need to plan a strategy to work out the area of each face, remembering that a tetrahedron is a triangular-based pyramid.

The base is an equilateral triangle with a side length 6 cm and angles of 60°: 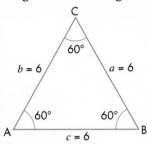 Area of base = $\frac{1}{2}ac$ sin B $= \frac{1}{2} \times 6 \times 6 \times$ sin 60° $= 15.588\,457\ldots$	You can work out the area of the base using the given information that it is an equilateral triangle.
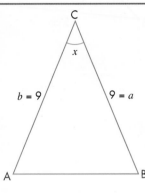 Angle C, in one of the isosceles triangles: $\cos C = \dfrac{a^2 + b^2 - c^2}{2ab}$ $= \dfrac{9^2 + 9^2 - 6^2}{2 \times 9 \times 9}$ $= 0.777\,777\ldots$ $\Rightarrow$ C $= 38.942\,448°$ Area of one of these faces: $\frac{1}{2}ab$ sin C $= \frac{1}{2} \times 9 \times 9 \times$ sin 38.942 448° $= 25.455\,848$ cm^2	The remaining three faces are identical. Draw one and use the cosine rule to work out an angle. Then use the area rule to work out the area of each face.
Total area = 3 × 25.455 848 + 15.588 457 $= 91.956\,001$ $= 92.0$ cm^2 (3 sf)	Finally, add the faces together. If you don't get the result given in the question, re-check both your strategy and your accuracy. Remember to keep the accurate intermediate answers to minimise rounding errors.

Ready to progress?

I can solve more complex 2D and 3D problems using Pythagoras' theorem and trigonometric ratios.

I can use the sine and cosine rules.

I can calculate the area of a triangle, using area = $\frac{1}{2}ab \sin C$.

I can calculate the trigonometric ratios for any angle up to 360°.

Review questions

EV **1** ABC is a triangle. AB = 12 cm, AC = 10 cm and BC = 15 cm.

Oliver calculated the size of angle A to be 85.4°.

Evaluate Oliver's result.

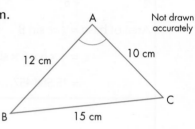

Not drawn accurately

MR **2** Show that the area of triangle ABC is 40.9 cm².

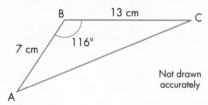

Not drawn accurately

CM **3** Show that angle C is the largest angle in triangle ABC.

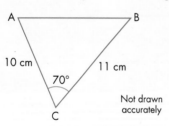

Not drawn accurately

MR **4** PQR is an equilateral triangle.

a i Show how you can use the diagram to work out the value of sin 30°.

   ii Use the diagram to work out the exact value of cos 30°, leaving your answer in surd form.

b Use the exact values of cos 30° and sin 30° to show that $(\cos 30°)^2 + (\sin 30°)^2 = 1$.

c Use the diagram to show that for all values of x between 0 and 90, $(\sin x)^2 + (\cos x)^2 = 1$.

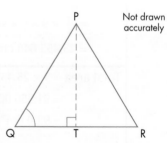

Not drawn accurately

5 The diagram shows a vertical chimney, QR, on horizontal ground, PTR.

Calculate the height of the chimney.

Give your answer to 3 significant figures.

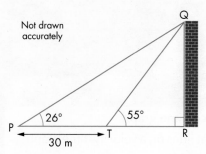

6 Solve the equation $6(\cos x)^2 = 1 + \cos x$, giving all answers between 0° and 360°. Round your answers, where appropriate, to 1 decimal place.

7 ABCD is the square base of a pyramid. The vertex V is directly above the centre of the square.

The length of AV is 30 cm and of AB is 22 cm.

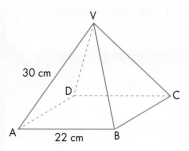

Calculate the angle AV makes with the base.

8 The cross-section of prism ABCDEF is a right-angled triangle.

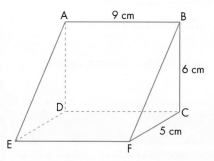

Show that the angle AFD is 30.2°.

9 The points A, B and C are on the circumference of a circle, centre O, and radius 5 cm.

The length of AB is 3 cm and of BC is 3.5 cm

Jamil said: "The area of quadrilateral OABC is 15.4 cm²."

Comment on Jamil's calculation.

23 Algebra: Graphs

This chapter is going to show you:

- how to work out speed from a distance–time graph
- how to interpret the gradients of straight lines on a velocity–time graph
- how to calculate and interpret the area under a velocity–time graph consisting of straight lines
- how to draw a graph of the depth of liquid as a container is filled
- how to estimate and interpret the area under a curve
- how to work out and interpret a gradient at a point on a curve
- how to find the equation of a tangent to a circle
- how to recognise and draw cubic, reciprocal and exponential graphs
- how to transform a graph.

You should already know:

- how speed, distance and time are related
- how to draw linear graphs and quadratic graphs
- how to find the gradient of a line
- how to find the equation of a graph using the gradient-intercept method
- how to find the equation of a perpendicular line
- that a tangent to a circle and a radius that meet at a point are perpendicular
- how to transform a shape by a translation (with a column vector) and a reflection (in a mirror line).

About this chapter

You will find graphs in newspapers, on the internet and in textbooks for most subjects you learn in school. They give a visual representation of the relationships between variables and can be used to compare data and give information in a way that simple lists of data cannot.

When you throw a ball in the air it is affected by gravity, wind and wind resistance. The height of the ball over time can be modelled by a quadratic graph, although the actual height at any time may be slightly different from the graph. Most real-life graphs are not smooth curves, but we use mathematical functions to model real-life situations.

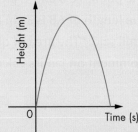

23.1 Distance–time graphs

This section will show you how to:

- interpret distance–time graphs
- draw a graph of the depth of liquid as a container is filled.

Key term

distance–time graph

As the name suggests, a **distance–time graph** gives information about how far someone or something has travelled over a given time period.

You can find the average speed from a distance–time graph, using the formula:

$$\text{average speed} = \frac{\text{total distance travelled}}{\text{total time taken}}.$$

This is the same as finding the gradient of the line.

$$\text{Gradient} = \frac{500 \text{ km}}{2 \text{ h}}$$

$$= 250 \text{ km/h}$$

The steeper the gradient, the faster the speed.

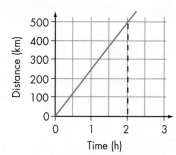

Example 1

Nottingham is 50 km from Barnsley. This distance–time graph represents a car journey from Barnsley Nottingham, and back again.

a What can you say about points B, C and D?

b What can you say about the journey between points D and F?

c Work out the average speed for each of the five stages of the journey.

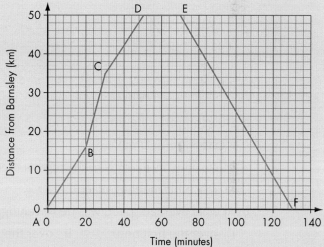

From the graph:

a B: After 20 minutes the car was 16 km away from Barnsley.

  C: After 30 minutes the car was 35 km away from Barnsley.

  D: After 50 minutes the car was 50 km away from Barnsley, so at Nottingham.

b D–F: The car stayed at Nottingham for 20 minutes, and then took 60 minutes for the return journey to Barnsley.

c Work out the average speeds over the five stages of the journey as follows.

  A to B represents 16 km in 20 minutes.

  Since 20 minutes = $\frac{1}{3}$ of an hour, you could use the formula:

  average speed = $16 \div \frac{1}{3} = 48$

  However, it is simpler to use a ratio.

(continued)

20 minutes is $\frac{1}{3}$ of an hour, so multiply by 3 to give distance per hour.

Multiplying both numbers by 3 gives 48 km in 60 minutes, which is 48 km/h.

B to C represents 19 km in 10 minutes.

Again, the most straightforward method is using a ratio.

Multiplying both numbers by 6 gives 114 km in 60 minutes, which is 114 km/h.

C to D represents 15 km in 20 minutes.

Multiplying both numbers by 3 gives 45 km in 60 minutes, which is 45 km/h.

D to E represents a stop, so the average speed is 0 km/h since no further distance was travelled.

E to F represents the return journey of 50 km in 60 minutes, which is 50 km/h.

Exercise 23A

1 This distance–time graph illustrates Paul's car journey to a meeting.

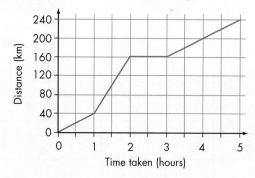

a How long after he set off did he:

   i stop for his break

   ii resume his journey following his break

   iii reach his meeting place?

b At what average speed was he travelling:

   i over the first hour   **ii** over the second hour

   iii for the last part of his journey?

> **Hints and tips**   If one part of a journey takes 30 minutes, double the distance to get the average speed per hour.

2 **a** Work out the speed for the first part of the journey shown in this distance–time graph.

   b For the second part of the journey, was the vehicle travelling faster or more slowly? Give a reason for your answer.

   c Work out the average speed for the whole journey.

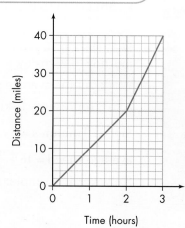

3 Calculate the average speed of the journey represented by each of these graphs.

a
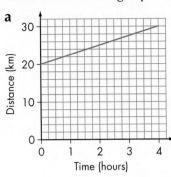

b
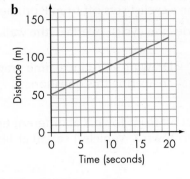

c
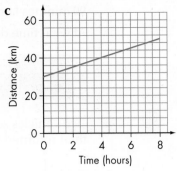

4 A small bus set off from Leeds to first pick up Mike, then his parents and grandparents. It then took them all to a hotel. The bus then went on a further 10 km to pick up another party and took them back to Leeds. This distance–time graph illustrates the journey.

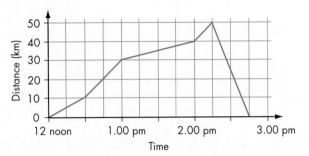

a How far from Leeds do Mike's parents and grandparents live?

b How far from Leeds is the hotel at which Mike and his family stayed?

c What was the average speed of the bus on its return journey to Leeds?

MR 5 Richard and Paul took part in a 5000-metre race. It is illustrated in this graph.

a Paul ran a steady race. What was his average speed in:

  i metres per minute

  ii kilometres per hour?

b Richard ran in spurts. What was his highest average speed?

c Who finished the race first and by how many minutes?

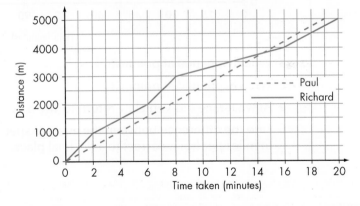

CM 6 Three friends, Patrick, Araf and Sean, ran a 1000-metre race. This distance–time graph illustrates their race.

a Describe the race.

b i What was Araf's average speed in metres per second?

  ii What is this speed in kilometres per hour?

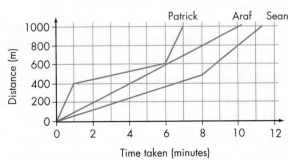

(PS) 7 A walker sets off at 9:00 am from point P to walk along a trail at a steady pace of 6 km/h.
90 minutes later, a cyclist sets off from P on the same trail at a steady pace of 15 km/h.
At what time does the cyclist overtake the walker?

| Hints and tips | Drawing a distance–time graph is a straightforward method of answering this question. |

(MR) 8 Two vehicles set off from Town X at different times. They both travelled to Town Y, then returned to Town X. Vehicle 1 set off at 14:30.

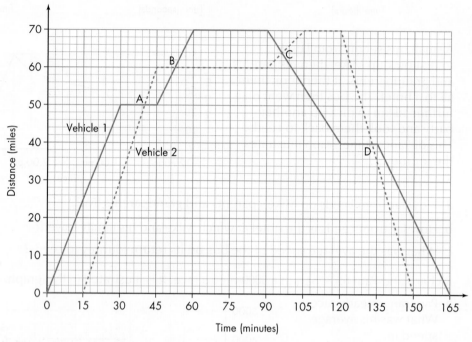

a What happened at point A?
c What happened at point C?

b What happened at point B?
d What happened at point D?

e At what time did Vehicle 1 return to Town X?

f Find the difference between the average speeds of the two vehicles. Give your answer in miles per hour, correct to 1 decimal place.

Filling containers

This graph shows the change in the depth of water in a flat-bottomed flask, as it is filled at a steady rate.

It shows that at first the depth of water increases quickly then slows down as the flask gets wider.

As the flask gets narrower again, the depth increases at a faster rate.

When the water reaches the neck, which has a constant cross-section, the depth increases at a constant rate up to the top of the neck.

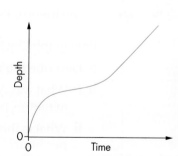

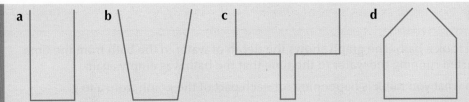

a   b   c   d

Draw a graph to show the change in depth of water in each flask as they are filled at a steady rate.

a The flask has the same diameter from bottom to top so the depth increases at a constant rate.

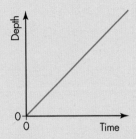

b The flask gets wider from bottom to top so at first the depth changes quickly, but it slows down as the flask gets wider.

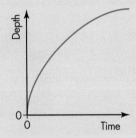

c The flask is made from two parts, both of a constant width, with the top half much wider than the bottom half. The depth increases at a constant fast rate at first, then at a constant much slower rate.

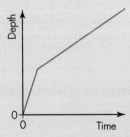

d The bottom of the flask is a constant diameter so fills at a constant rate. At the top of the flask, the flask gets narrower and the depth changes increasingly quickly.

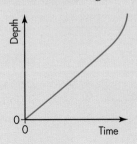

Exercise 23B

(MR) **1** Shejuti took a bath. The graph shows the depth of water in the bath from the time she started running the water to the time that the bath was empty again.

Explain what you think is happening for each part of the graph from **a** to **g**.

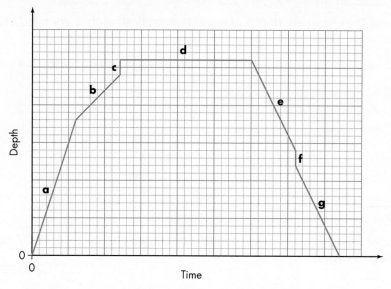

(MR) **2** **a** Liquid is poured at a steady rate into the bottle shown in the diagram.

As the bottle is filled, the depth, d, of the liquid in the bottle changes.

Which of the four graphs shows the change in depth?

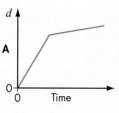 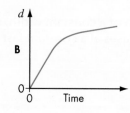 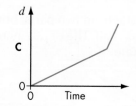 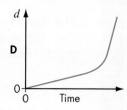

b Draw bottles for each of the other three graphs.

(MR) **3** Draw a graph of the depth of water in each of these containers as it is filled steadily.

a 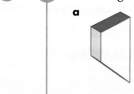 **b**  **c**   **d**

e   **f**   **g**

23.2 Velocity–time graphs

This section will show you how to:

- read information from a velocity–time graph
- work out the distance travelled from a velocity–time graph
- work out the acceleration from a velocity–time graph.

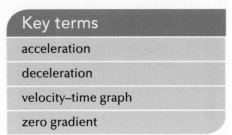

Key terms

acceleration

deceleration

velocity–time graph

zero gradient

You read a **velocity–time graph** in a similar way to a distance–time graph. A positive gradient means the velocity is increasing. A **zero gradient**, when the line is horizontal, indicates a steady or constant velocity. A negative gradient means the velocity is decreasing. Any line on the graph represents the average speed maintained over that section.

Look the journey represented by this graph.

A to B takes 2 hours and the speed increases from 0 km/h to 10 km/h.

B to C takes 1 hour and the speed increases from 10 km/h to 40 km/h.

C to D takes 2 hours and the speed is constant at 40 km/h.

D to E takes 1 hour and the speed decreases from 40 km/h to 0 km/h.

You can also work out the distance covered from a velocity–time graph. The distance covered is equal to the area under the graph. When the speed is constant, you can find this by multiplying speed by time.

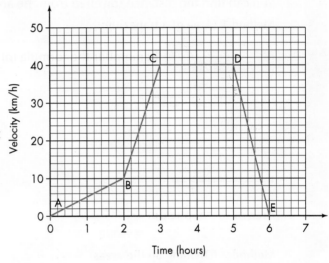

Example 3

The velocity–time graph represents a car journey.

What can you say about:

a the velocity

b the time taken

c the distance travelled?

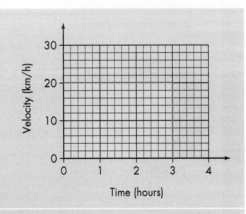

a As the line is horizontal, the velocity is constant (steady) at 20 km/h.

b The time taken is 3 hours.

c Use the formula:

distance travelled = average speed × time taken

The distance travelled is 20 × 3 = 60 km.

You can see that this is the same as working out the area of the rectangle shown on the graph (3 × 20 = 60 km/h).

Example 4

The velocity–time graph shows a train journey between two stations.

Work out:

a the distance travelled

b the average speed for the whole journey.

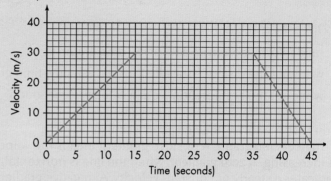

a You can find the distance travelled from the area under the graph.

Method 1 (Area of a trapezium)

| Hints and tips | Remember the formula for the area of a trapezium: $A = \frac{1}{2}(a + b)h$ |

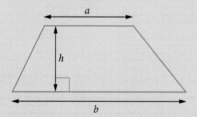

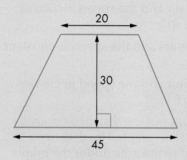

Area of the trapezium $= \frac{1}{2}(45 + 20) \times 30$
$= 975$ m

Method 2 (Dividing up the areas)

| Hints and tips | Remember the formula for the area of a triangle: area $= \frac{1}{2} \times$ base $\times$ perpendicular height |

Split the trapezium into triangles and rectangles to find the total area.

Area of first triangle: $\frac{1}{2} \times 15 \times 30 = 225$ m

Area of rectangle: $20 \times 30 = 600$ m

Area of second triangle:
$\frac{1}{2} \times 10 \times 30 = 150$ m

Total distance travelled:
$225 + 600 + 150 = 975$ m

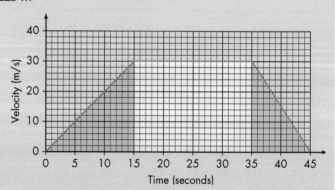

b Use the formula. average speed =

$$\frac{\text{total distance travelled}}{\text{total time taken}}$$

$$= \frac{975}{45}$$

$$= 21.7 \text{ m/s (1 dp)}$$

Exercise 23C

1 The diagram represents a car journey between two junctions of a bypass.

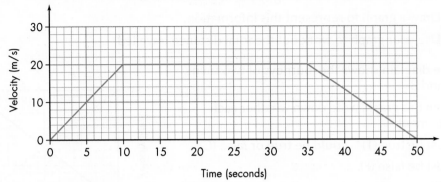

a What is the steady speed of the car?

b What distance does the car cover while speeding up?

c What distance does the car cover while slowing down?

d What is the distance between the junctions?

2 The diagram shows a velocity–time graph.

a Work out the total distance travelled.

b Work out the average speed for the whole journey.

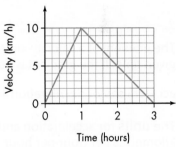

3 The graph shows four parts of a two-hour journey, AB, BC, CD and DE.

a Which part of the journey covers the greatest distance? Give a reason for your answer.

b Work out the distance covered travelling from C to E.

c Work out the total distance covered.

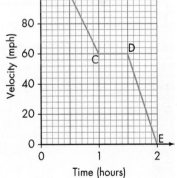

4 The graph shows 40 seconds of a car journey.

The maximum speed is v m/s.

The distance covered is 300 metres.

Work out the value of v.

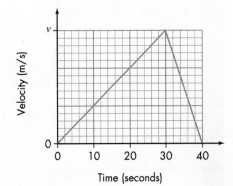

5 A cyclist increases her speed at a steady rate from rest (0 m/s) to 10 m/s in 15 seconds.

She then travels at a steady speed for 30 seconds before slowing down to rest over a further 20 seconds, decreasing speed at a steady rate.

a Draw a graph to represent this information.

b Use your graph to work out the total distance travelled.

6 The diagram shows the journeys of two trains, A and B.

From this graph, write down whether each statement:

must be true (T)   could be true or false (C)

must be false (F).

a The trains are travelling in opposite directions.

b The trains both cover the same distance.

c Train A is speeding up and train B is slowing down.

d Train A is travelling up a slope.

e Train A overtakes train B.

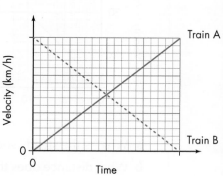

Acceleration

The gradient of a velocity–time graph gives the rate at which the velocity is increasing or decreasing in a given time. If the gradient is positive it is an **acceleration**. If the gradient is negative it is a **deceleration**.

$$\text{acceleration or deceleration} = \frac{\text{difference in velocity}}{\text{difference in time}}$$

The units for acceleration and deceleration are, for example, metres per second per second (m/s²) or kilometres per hour per hour (km/h²).

Example 5

In this velocity–time graph:

a find the initial velocity

b work out the acceleration.

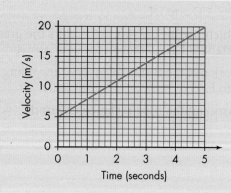

a Initial velocity is the velocity at the start of the journey and you read this from the y-intercept.

Initial velocity = 5 m/s

b Acceleration = $\dfrac{\text{difference in velocity}}{\text{difference in time}}$

$= \dfrac{20 - 5}{5}$ m/s²

$= \dfrac{15}{5}$ m/s²

$= 3$ m/s²

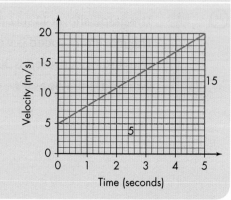

Exercise 23D

1 The graph shows the journey of a car travelling between two sets of traffic lights.

  a Find the initial acceleration of the car.

  b Find the final deceleration of the car.

  c For how long was the car not accelerating?

  d Find the distance travelled whilst the car was travelling at a steady speed.

  e Find the distance between the two sets of traffic lights.

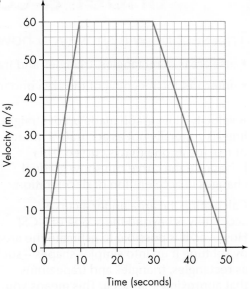

2 The graph shows the journey of a train travelling between two towns.

  a Work out the acceleration or deceleration for each section of the graph.

  b Find the total distance travelled.

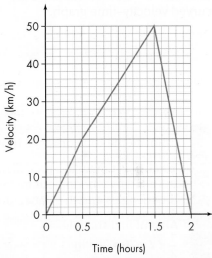

3 The graph shows the velocity of a car between two junctions.

  a Work out the acceleration in the first 10 seconds, in terms of v.

  b The distance travelled in the first 10 seconds is 75 metres. Work out the total distance travelled between the junctions.

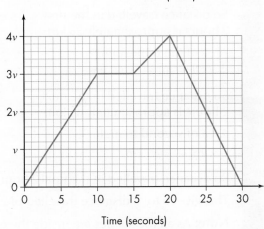

23.3 Estimating the area under a curve

This section will show you how to:

- use areas of rectangles, triangles and trapeziums to estimate the area under a curve
- interpret the meaning of the area under a curve.

A velocity–time graph made up of straight lines is generally not as accurate a model of real life as one that is curved. This is because the curve can show gradual changes in acceleration or deceleration.

Calculating the area under a curve accurately is beyond the scope of GCSE. However, it is possible to estimate the area by splitting it up into simpler shapes – such as rectangles, triangles and trapeziums – that approximate its area. This means you can estimate the distance travelled from a curved velocity–time graph.

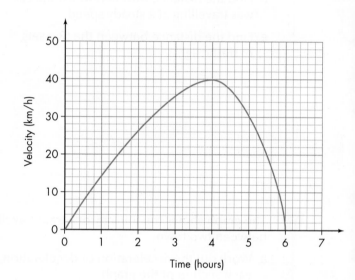

Example 6

Estimate the total distance travelled for the journey shown in the graph above.

You can estimate the total distance travelled by working out the areas of the triangles and the trapezium shown.

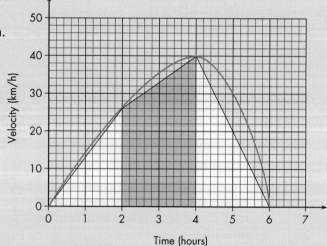

Area of first triangle:
$\frac{1}{2} \times 2 \times 26 = 26$ km

So distance travelled in the first 2 hours is approximately 26 km.

Area of the trapezium:
$\frac{1}{2} \times (26 + 40) \times 2 = 66$ km

So distance travelled in the next 2 hours is approximately 66 km.

Area of second triangle:
$\frac{1}{2} \times 2 \times 40 = 40$ km

So distance travelled in the final 2 hours is approximately 40 km.

This gives a total distance travelled of 26 + 66 + 40 = 132 km.

Note: As all the shapes are inside the curved area, this will be a slight under-estimation of the true distance covered.

Example 7

The velocity–time graph represents a journey.

a Estimate the distance travelled.

b State whether your estimate is an under-estimate or an over-estimate.

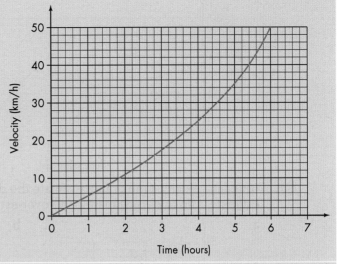

a Divide the area approximately into a triangle and trapezium.

Area of the triangle:

$\frac{1}{2} \times 4 \times 25 = 50$ km

Area of the trapezium:

$\frac{1}{2} \times (25 + 50) \times 2 = 75$ km

So the distance covered is approximately 50 km + 75 km = 125 km.

b This is an over-estimate as the areas found are greater than the area under the curve.

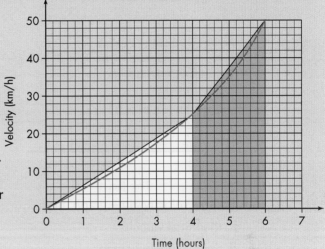

Exercise 23E

1   For each velocity–time graph, estimate the distance travelled and state whether your estimate is an under-estimate or an over-estimate.

a

b

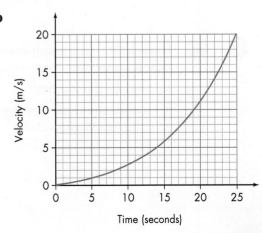

c

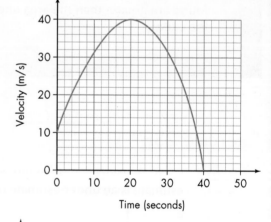

Graph c: Velocity (m/s) on vertical axis (0 to 30), Time (seconds) on horizontal axis (0 to 7). Curve rises to about 25 at t = 3 then falls to 0 at t = 6.

d

Graph d: Velocity (m/s) on vertical axis (0 to 30), Time (seconds) on horizontal axis (0 to 6+). Curve starts at 30, stays flat then curves down to about 11.

2 For each velocity–time graph, estimate the distance travelled and state whether your estimate is an under-estimate or an over-estimate.

a

Graph a: Velocity (mph) on vertical axis (0 to 5), Time (hours) on horizontal axis (0 to 2). Curve starts at 5, curves down to 3.

b

Graph b: Velocity (mph) on vertical axis (0 to 30), Time (hours) on horizontal axis (0 to 2). Curve rises from 20 to 30 at t = 1, then falls to 0 at t = 2.

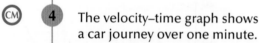

3 **a** For this velocity–time graph, find:

   i the initial velocity

   ii the maximum velocity.

  b Find an estimate for the total distance travelled using:

   i one trapezium and one triangle

   ii three trapezia and one triangle.

  c Which of your answers in part **b** is more accurate? Explain your answer.

Graph for Q3: Velocity (m/s) on vertical axis (0 to 40), Time (seconds) on horizontal axis (0 to 50). Curve starts at 10, rises to 40 at t = 20, then falls to 0 at t = 40.

4 The velocity–time graph shows a car journey over one minute.

  a Describe the journey.

  b Estimate the distance travelled in the first 20 seconds.

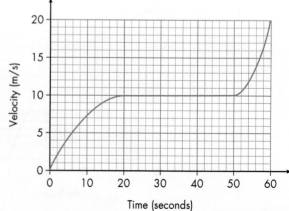

Graph for Q4: Velocity (m/s) on vertical axis (0 to 20), Time (seconds) on horizontal axis (0 to 60). Curve rises from 0 to 10 by t = 20, stays at 10 until about t = 50, then rises steeply to 20 at t = 60.

5 This velocity–time graph shows the same car journey as in question **4**. The dashed line also shows the journey of a lorry that sets off at the same time as the car.

a Compare the lorry journey with the car journey.

b Which travels further in one minute, the car or the lorry? Show how you decide.

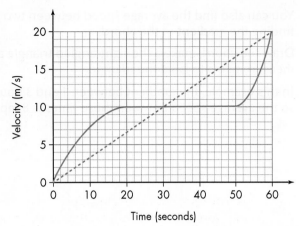

23.4 Rates of change

This section will show you how to:

- draw a tangent at a point on a curve and use it to work out the gradient at a point on a curve
- interpret the gradient at a point on a curve.

Key term

tangent

A **tangent** is a line that touches a curve at a point.

The **gradient** of a curve at a point is the same as the gradient of the tangent at that point.

Distance–time graphs

The gradient at any point on a distance–time graph gives the velocity at that point.

Follow these steps to calculate the velocity.

Step 1: Draw a tangent carefully at the point.

Step 2: Make a right-angled triangle as shown.

Step 3: Use measurements from the axes to label the lengths of the two shorter sides of the triangle.

Step 4: Use these measurements to calculate the gradient of the tangent and therefore the speed of the object.

In this example, the gradient of the tangent at T = 1.6 is $\frac{30}{3} = 10$, so the speed at this point is 10 mph.

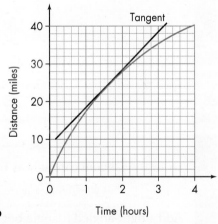

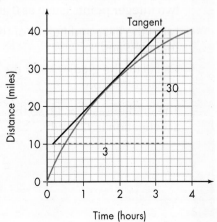

You can also find the average speed between two times by finding the gradient of the chord.

Draw the chord, make a the right-angled triangle and use the measurements to label the triangle.

In this example, the gradient between 1 and 3 hours is $\frac{16}{2} = 8$, so the average speed between these times is 8 mph.

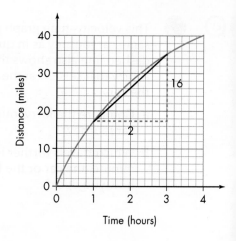

Velocity–time graphs

The gradient at any point on a velocity–time graph gives the acceleration at that point. Follow the same steps described above in relation to distance–time graphs.

Example 8

Estimate the acceleration in this journey at 1 hour.

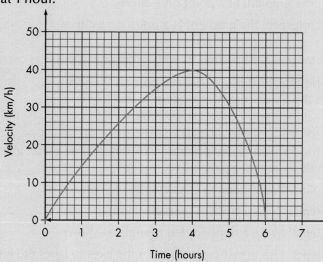

Draw the tangent carefully at 1 hour.

Add a right-angled triangle between two integer points (such as 0 and 3).

Label the base and height of the triangle 3 and 36.

Calculate the gradient and therefore the acceleration.

The gradient is $\frac{36}{3} = 12$, so the acceleration is 12 km/h².

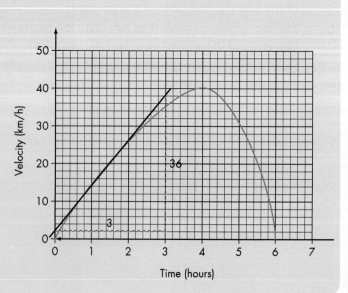

Exercise 23F

1 The graph shows the height of a ball as it is thrown into the air.

  a Draw a tangent at the point where $t = 1$.

  b Use your tangent to estimate the velocity of the ball after one second.

  c Write down the velocity of the ball after 2 seconds.

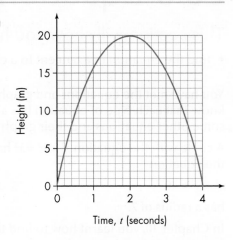

(MR) 2 Look at this distance–time graph.

  a Estimate the velocity when:

    i $t = 1$ **ii** $t = 4$.

  b At what time is the velocity zero?

  c Estimate average velocity from:

    i $t = 0$ to $t = 2$ **ii** $t = 3$ to $t = 5$.

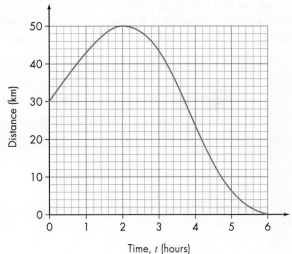

(CM) 3 Look at this velocity–time graph.

  a Estimate the acceleration when $t = 10$.

  b Estimate the acceleration when $t = 15$.

  c Estimate the deceleration when $t = 30$.

  d At what time is the acceleration zero? Explain how you know.

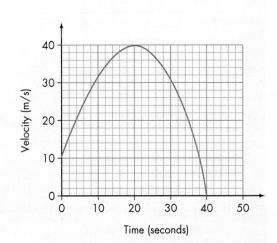

4 Look again at the graph in question **1**.

Find two times when the speeds are numerically equal but in opposite directions.

23.5 Equation of a circle

This section will show you how to:

- find the equation of a tangent to a circle.

You have met the equations and graphs of straight lines and quadratics in previous chapters and know that each type of equation has a different graph shape. In the next two sections you will look at some other equations and their graph shapes.

A circle with the equation $x^2 + y^2 = r^2$ has its centre at the origin and a radius of r. So a circle with the equation

$$x^2 + y^2 = 49$$

has a radius of 7.

In Chapter 10, you learnt how to find the gradient and equation of a line, and how to find the equation of a line perpendicular to it. In Chapter 20, you discovered a circle theorem, which stated that a tangent to a circle is perpendicular to a radius at the point of contact. You can put these two things together to find the equation of a tangent to a circle at a given point.

A circle has the equation $x^2 + y^2 = 52$.

a Find the diameter of the circle. Give your answer as a surd in its simplest form.

b Show that the equation of the tangent to the circle at the point $(4, -6)$ is given by $3y + 26 = 2x$.

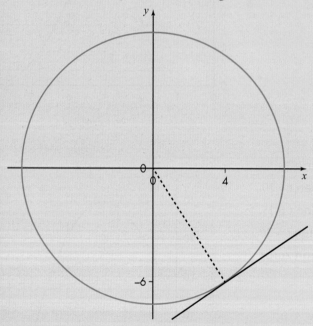

a $r^2 = 52$, so the radius, $r = \sqrt{52} = 2\sqrt{13}$. The diameter is twice as long as the radius, i.e. $4\sqrt{13}$.

b The gradient of the radius (the line segment from the origin to $(4, -6)$)

$$= \frac{\text{difference on } y\text{-axis}}{\text{difference on } x\text{-axis}}$$

$$= -\frac{6}{4}$$

$$= -\frac{3}{2}.$$

The tangent is perpendicular to the radius at this point so the gradient of the tangent is $\frac{2}{3}$.

(continued)

Substituting $x = 4$, $y = -6$ and $m = \frac{2}{3}$ into $y = mx + c$ gives: $\qquad -6 = \frac{2}{3} \times 4 + c$

which simplifies to; $\qquad\qquad\qquad\qquad\qquad\qquad\qquad -6 = \frac{8}{3} + c$

$$\Rightarrow \quad c = -6 - \frac{8}{3}$$

$$= -\frac{26}{3}$$

So, $y = \frac{2}{3}x - \frac{26}{3}$

Multiply both sides by 3. $\qquad\qquad\qquad\qquad\qquad 3y = 2x - 26$

Add 26 to both sides. $\qquad\qquad\qquad\qquad\qquad 3y + 26 = 2x$

Example 10

Find the equations of both tangents to the circle $x^2 + y^2 = 116$ with a gradient of $\frac{5}{2}$.

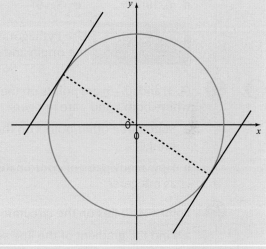

Since the tangents are parallel and have a gradient of $\frac{5}{2}$, the line between them (which is a diameter) will have a gradient of $-\frac{2}{5}$.

Since the diameter (and therefore radii) has a gradient of $-\frac{2}{5}$ and a y-intercept of 0, the equation of the radius that meets the tangent is:
$y = -\frac{2}{5}x$

Substitute $y = -\frac{2}{5}x$ into $x^2 + y^2 = 116$. $\qquad x^2 + (-\frac{2}{5}x)^2 = 116$

$$x^2 + \frac{4}{25}x^2 = 116$$

$$\frac{29}{25}x^2 = 116$$

$$29x^2 = 2900$$

$$x^2 = 100$$

$$x = \pm 10$$

From $y = -\frac{2}{5}x$:

When $x = 10$, $y = -\frac{2}{5} \times 10 = -4$

When $x = -10$, $y = -\frac{2}{5} \times -10 = 4$

So, one tangent has $x = 10$, $y = -4$ and $m = \frac{5}{2}$: $\quad -4 = \frac{5}{2} \times 10 + c \quad \Rightarrow c = -29$

So, $y = \frac{5}{2}x - 29$

The other tangent has $x = -10$, $y = 4$ and $m = \frac{5}{2}$: $\quad 4 = \frac{5}{2} \times -10 + c \quad \Rightarrow c = 29$

So, $y = \frac{5}{2}x + 29$

Exercise 23G

 1 State the radius of each circle. Give your answers as simplified surds, where appropriate.

    a $x^2 + y^2 = 36$ **b** $x^2 + y^2 = 12$ **c** $x^2 + y^2 = 75$ **d** $x^2 + y^2 = 576$

 2 State the diameter of each circle. Give your answers as simplified surds, where appropriate.

    a $x^2 + y^2 = 117$ **b** $x^2 + y^2 = 7744$ **c** $x^2 + y^2 = 3249$ **d** $x^2 + y^2 = \dfrac{9}{16}$

 3 A circle has equation $x^2 + y^2 = 100$. Determine whether each point lies inside the circle, outside the circle or on the circumference of the circle.

    a $(9, 4)$ **b** $(7, 8)$ **c** $(-8, 6)$

    d $(0, 10)$ **e** $(5, -9)$ **f** $(-7, 7)$

> **Hints and tips** Use Pythagoras' theorem to work out how far each point is from the origin and compare it with the radius.

 4 $(4, 3)$ and $(0, -5)$ are points on the circumference of the circle with equation $x^2 + y^2 = 25$, where both x and y are integers.

    a State three other points on the circumference of $x^2 + y^2 = 25$ where the coordinates are integers.

    b How many pairs of coordinates on the circumference of $x^2 + y^2 = 25$ have both values as integers?

5 Point A$(4, 2)$ lies on the circumference of the circle $x^2 + y^2 = 20$.

    a Find the gradient of the line segment joining A to the origin $(0, 0)$.

    b Find the gradient of the tangent to the circle at A.

    c Find the equation of the tangent to the circle at A in the form $y = mx + c$.

 6 Show that the tangent to the circle $x^2 + y^2 = 73$ at the point $(-8, 3)$ is given by the equation $3y = 8x + 73$.

7 Find the equation of the tangent in the form $y = mx + c$ for these situations.

    a Circle $x^2 + y^2 = 34$, tangent at $(3, -5)$

    b Circle $x^2 + y^2 = 40$, tangent at $(-2, -6)$

    c Circle $x^2 + y^2 = a^2$, tangent at (p, q)

8 Find the equations of both tangents to the circle $x^2 + y^2 = 45$ with a gradient of 2. Give your answers in the form $y = mx + c$.

9 A circle has the equation $x^2 + y^2 = 50$.

    Find the equations of the tangents to the circle that are parallel to $x + y = 8$.

10 A circle centred at the origin has a tangent with equation $y = -\dfrac{1}{3}x + c$ at the point $(3, 9)$.

    a Find the value of c.

    b Find the equation of the circle.

23.6 Other graphs

This section will show you how to:

- recognise and plot cubic, exponential and reciprocal graphs.

Key terms

asymptote	cubic
exponential function	reciprocal

Cubic graphs

A **cubic** function or graph is one that contains a term in x^3. These are examples of cubic functions.

$y = x^3$ $y = x^3 + 3x$ $y = x^3 + x^2 + x + 1$

The techniques you use to draw them are exactly the same as the ones you use for quadratic and linear graphs.

This is the graph of $y = x^3$.

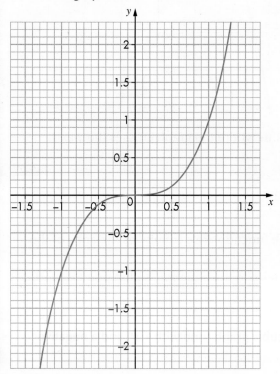

It has a characteristic shape that you should learn to recognise.

Example 11 shows you how to draw a cubic graph accurately.

You should use a calculator to work out the values of y and then round to 1 or 2 decimal places.

Example 11

a   Complete the table and draw the graph of $y = x^3 - x^2 - 4x + 4$ for $-3 \leqslant x \leqslant 3$.

x	–3	–2.5	–2	–1.5	–1	–0.5	0	0.5	1	1.5	2	2.5	3
y	–20.00		0.00		6.00		4.00	1.88				3.38	10.00

b   Use your graph to give the roots of the equation $x^3 - x^2 - 4x + 4 = 0$.

c   Write down the coordinates of:

   i   the minimum vertex   ii   the maximum vertex.

d   Write down the coordinates of the point where the graph intersects the y-axis.

a Complete the table of values.

x	–3	–2.5	–2	–1.5	–1	–0.5	0	0.5	1	1.5	2	2.5	3
y	–20.00	–7.88	0.00	4.38	6.00	5.63	4.00	1.88	0.00	–0.88	0.00	3.38	10.00

Use the table of values to complete the graph.

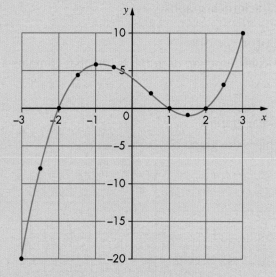

b Just as in quadratic graphs, the roots are the points where the graph crosses the x-axis. This is where $y = 0$.

So the roots are $x = -2$, 1 and 2.

c i The minimum vertex is at the point (1.5, –0.88).

ii The maximum vertex is at the point (–1, 6).

Note that the minimum and maximum values of the function are ± infinity, as the arms of the curve continue forever.

d Just as in a quadratic graph, this is the constant term in the equation, so the point is (0, 4).

Note the difference between the shape of a positive cubic graph (one with $+ x^3$) and a negative cubic graph (one with $-x^3$):

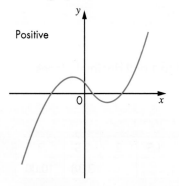

Positive

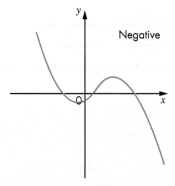

Negative

Reciprocal graphs

A **reciprocal** function has the form $y = \dfrac{a}{x}$.

These are examples of reciprocal functions.

$$y = \frac{1}{x} \qquad y = \frac{4}{x} \qquad y = -\frac{3}{x}$$

All reciprocal graphs have a similar shape and some symmetrical properties.

To draw the graph of $y = \dfrac{1}{x}$ for $-4 \leqslant x \leqslant 4$:

Start by finding the y-values for the integer x-values between -4 and 4 (except 0, since $\dfrac{1}{0}$ is infinity).

Round values to 2 decimal places, as it is difficult to plot a value more accurately than this.

x	-4	-3	-2	-1	1	2	3	4
y	-0.25	-0.33	-0.5	-1	1	0.5	0.33	0.25

The graph plotted from these values is shown in graph A. This does not show the properties of the reciprocal function.

Find the y-values for x-values between -0.8 to 0.8 in steps of 0.2.

x	-0.8	-0.6	-0.4	-0.2	0.2	0.4	0.6	0.8
y	-1.25	-1.67	-2.5	-5	5	2.5	1.67	1.25

Plotting these points as well gives graph B.

A
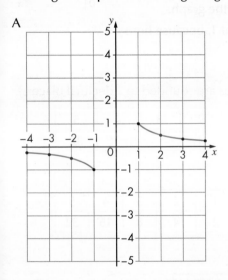

B
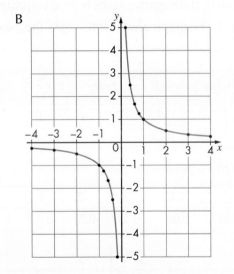

Graph B shows the characteristic properties of reciprocal graphs.

- The lines $y = x$ and $y = -x$ are lines of symmetry.

- The closer x gets to zero, the nearer the graph gets to the y-axis.

- As x increases, the graph gets closer to the x-axis.

The graph never actually touches the axes, it just gets closer and closer to them. When a graph gets closer to a line but never touches or crosses it, the line is called an **asymptote**.

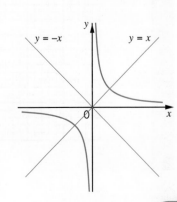

Note the difference between the shape of a positive reciprocal graph and a negative reciprocal graph:

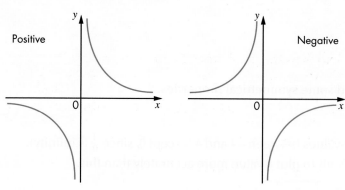

Exponential graphs

Equations that have the form $y = k^x$, where k is a positive number, are called **exponential functions**.

The graph of $y = k^x$ shows the properties of exponential functions.

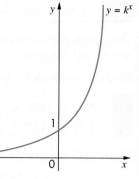

- When k is greater than 1, the value of y increases steeply as x increases, which you can see from the graph on the right.

- When k is greater than 1, as x takes on increasingly large negative values, y gets closer to zero. The graph gets nearer and nearer to the negative x-axis but y never actually becomes zero and so the graph never touches the negative x-axis. That is, the negative x-axis is an asymptote to the graph.

- Whatever the value of k, the graph always intercepts the y-axis at 1, because here $y = k^0$.

Example 12

a Complete the table below for $y = 2x$ for $-5 \leqslant x \leqslant 5$. (Values are rounded to 2 decimal places.)

x	−5	−4	−3	−2	−1	0	1	2	3	4	5
$y = 2^x$	0.03	0.06	0.13				1	2	4			32

b Plot the graph of $y = 2x$ for $-5 \leqslant x \leqslant 5$.

a

x	−5	−4	−3	−2	−1	0	1	2	3	4	5
$y = 2^x$	0.03	0.06	0.13	0.25	0.5	1	2	4	8	16	32

b

Exercise 23H

1 Sketch the graph of $y = -x^3$.

2 **a** Copy and complete the table and draw the graph of $y = 2x^3$ for $-3 \leqslant x \leqslant 3$.

x	−3	−2.5	−2	−1.5	−1	−0.5	0	0.5	1	1.5	2	2.5	3
y		−31.25		−6.75			0.00	0.25			16.00		

b Use your graph to find the y-value when $x = 2.7$.

3 **a** Draw the graph of $y = x^3 + 3$ for $-3 \leqslant x \leqslant 3$. Plot x-values in steps of 0.5.

b Use your graph to find the y-value when $x = 1.2$.

c Find the root of the equation $x^3 + 3 = 0$.

4 **a** Plot the graph of $y = x^3 - 2x + 5$ for $-3 \leqslant x \leqslant 3$.

b Use your graph to find:

   i the root of $x^3 - 2x + 5 = 0$

   ii the approximate value of the coordinate of the maximum vertex

   iii the approximate value of the coordinate of the minimum vertex

   iv the coordinates of the point where the graph crosses the y-axis.

5 Copy and complete the table and draw the graph of $y = -\dfrac{12}{x}$.

x	−12	−6	−4	−3	−2	−1	−0.5	0.5	1	2	3	4	6	12
y			−3									−3		

6 **a** Copy and complete the table and draw the graph of $y = \dfrac{5}{x}$ for $-20 \leqslant x \leqslant 20$.

x	−20	−15	−10	−5	−2	−1	−0.5	−0.4	−0.2	0.2	0.4	0.5	1	2	5	10	15	20
y										25		10						0.25

b Explain why there is no value when $x = 0$.

c On the same axes, draw the graph of $y = x + 10$.

d Use your graph to find the x-values of any points where the graphs intersect.

7 **a** Plot the graph of $y = 3^x$ for integer values of x from -4 to $+3$. Draw the y-axis from 0 to 30 and round y-values to 2 decimal places.

b Use your graph to estimate the value of y when $x = 2.5$.

c Use your graph to estimate the value of x when $y = 0.5$.

8 Identify each graph as linear, quadratic, reciprocal, cubic, exponential or none of these.

a
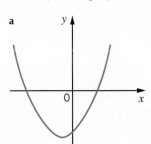

b
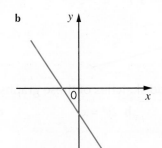

c
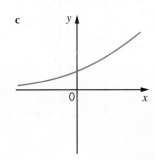

d
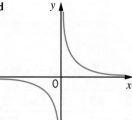

e
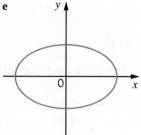

f
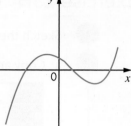

g
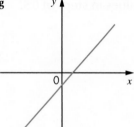

h
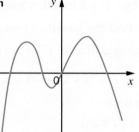

i
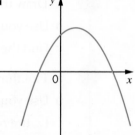

(PS) **9** One grain of rice is placed on the first square of a chess board. Two grains of rice are placed on the second square, four grains on the third square and so on.

a Explain why $y = 2^{(n-1)}$ gives the number of grains of rice on the nth square.

b How many grains of rice are there on the 64th square?

c If 1000 grains of rice are worth 5p, how much is the rice on the 64th square worth?

(PS) **10** An extremely large sheet of paper is 0.01 cm thick. It is torn in half and one piece placed on top of the other. These two pieces are then torn in half and one half is placed on top of the other half to give a pile four sheets thick. This happens 50 times.

a How many pieces will be in the pile after 50 tears?

b How thick is this pile?

(MR) **11** A curve of the form $y = ab^x$ passes through the points (0, 5) and (2, 45).

Work out the values of a and b.

(PS) **12** This is the graph of $y^2 = x$.

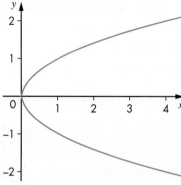

Copy this graph. Add sketches of these graphs to your sketch.

a $y^2 + 2 = x$ **b** $2y^2 = x$ **c** $(y - 2)^2 = x$

23.7 Transformations of the graph $y = f(x)$

This section will show you how to:

- transform a graph.

Changing the equation of a graph by adding or subtracting a value, or by changing the sign, transforms the graph in a certain way.

Exercise 23I

 1

  a Copy and complete the table for $y = x^2$, $y = x^2 + 3$ and $y = x^2 - 2$.

x	−4	−3	−2	−1	0	1	2	3	4
$y = x^2$									
$y = x^2 + 3$									
$y = x^2 - 2$									

  b Plot all three graphs on the same axes.

  c Describe the relationship between $y = x^2$ and $y = x^2 + 3$.

  d Describe the relationship between $y = x^2$ and $y = x^2 - 2$.

  e Using your answers to **c** and **d**, describe the relationship between:

    i $y = x^2$ and $y = x^2 + 6$

    ii $y = x^2$ and $y = x^2 - 6$.

 2

  a Copy and complete the table for $y = x^2$, $y = (x - 2)^2$ and $y = (x + 1)^2$.

x	−4	−3	−2	−1	0	1	2	3	4
$y = x^2$									
$y = (x - 2)^2$									
$y = (x + 1)^2$									

  b Plot all three graphs on the same axes.

  c Describe the relationship between $y = x^2$ and $y = (x - 2)^2$.

  d Describe the relationship between $y = x^2$ and $y = (x + 1)^2$.

  e Using your answers to **c** and **d**, describe the relationship between

    i $y = x^2$ and $y = (x - 3)^2$

    ii $y = x^2$ and $y = (x + 4)^2$.

The notation $f(x)$ is used to represent a **function** of x. A function of x is any algebraic expression in which x is the only variable. These are examples of functions of x.

$f(x) = x + 3$, $f(x) = 5x$, $f(x) = 2x - 7$, $f(x) = x^2$, $f(x) = x^3 + 2x - 1$, $f(x) = \sin x$ and $f(x) = \dfrac{1}{x}$.

In this section you will be introduced to four general statements or rules about **transforming** graphs.

Test these rules with a graphics calculator or a graph-drawing computer program to see them in action.

This sketch graph represents a function $y = f(x)$.

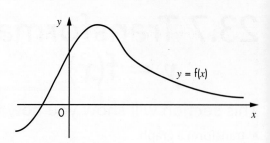

Rule 1 The graph of $y = f(x) + a$ is a translation of the graph of $y = f(x)$ by a vector $\begin{pmatrix} 0 \\ a \end{pmatrix}$.

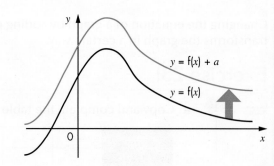

Rule 2 The graph of $y = f(x - a)$ is a translation of the graph of $y = f(x)$ by a vector $\begin{pmatrix} a \\ 0 \end{pmatrix}$.

Note The sign in front of a in the bracket is negative, but the translation is in the positive direction.

$f(x + a)$ would translate $f(x)$ by the vector $\begin{pmatrix} -a \\ 0 \end{pmatrix}$.

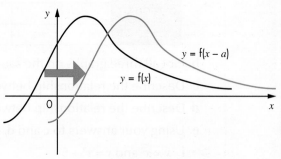

Rule 3 The graph of $y = -f(x)$ is the reflection of the graph $y = f(x)$ in the x-axis.

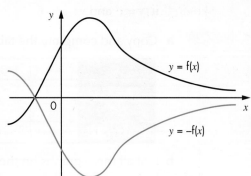

Rule 4 The graph of $y = f(-x)$ is the reflection of the graph $y = f(x)$ in the y-axis.

An invariant point is a point that does not change when a graph is transformed.

For Rule 3, the invariant points for $y = -f(x)$ lie on the x-axis.

For Rule 4, the invariant points for $y = f(-x)$ lie on the y-axis.

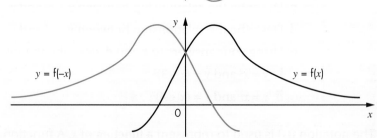

Example 13

i Sketch the following graphs.

a $y = x^2$ **b** $y = x^2 - 5$ **c** $y = -x^2$ **d** $y = (x - 5)^2$

ii Describe the transformation(s) that change(s) graph **a** to each of the other graphs.

a

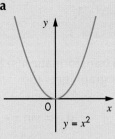

b

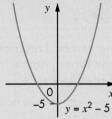

c

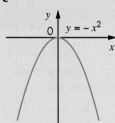

d

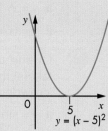

This is the basic graph to which you apply the rules to make the necessary transformations.

A translation of $\begin{pmatrix} 0 \\ -5 \end{pmatrix}$

A reflection in the x-axis

A translation of $\begin{pmatrix} 5 \\ 0 \end{pmatrix}$

The most common error with transformations concerns rule 2. **Remember:** $y = f(x + a)$

The translation is $\begin{pmatrix} -a \\ 0 \end{pmatrix}$, so the sign of the constant inside the bracket changes in the vector.

Example 14

This is the graph of $y = \sin x$.

Sketch the graph of:

a $y = \sin(x - 90°)$

b $y = 1 + \sin x$.

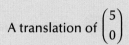

a The graph of $y = f(x - 90°)$ is a translation of the graph of $y = f(x)$ by a vector $\begin{pmatrix} 90 \\ 0 \end{pmatrix}$.

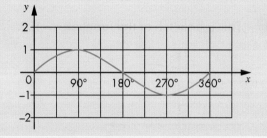

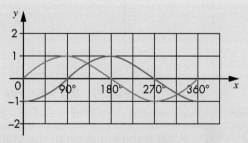

b The graph of $y = f(x) + 1$ is a translation of the graph of $y = f(x)$ by a vector $\begin{pmatrix} 0 \\ 1 \end{pmatrix}$.

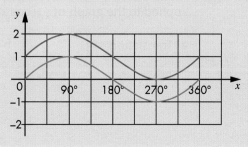

Exercise 23J

1 On the same axes, sketch the following graphs. Describe the transformation(s) that take(s) the graph in part **a** to each of the other graphs. If your graph gets too 'crowded', draw a new set of axes and re-draw part **a**.

    a $y = x^2$ **b** $y = x^2 + 3$ **c** $y = x^2 - 1$

    d $y = (x + 3)^2$ **e** $y = (x + 3)^2 - 1$ **f** $y = -x^2 + 3$

2 On the same axes, sketch the following graphs. Describe the transformation(s) that take(s) the graph in part **a** to each of the other graphs. If your graph gets too 'crowded', draw a new set of axes and re-draw part **a**.

    a $y = \sin x$ **b** $y = \sin (x + 90°)$ **c** $y = \sin (x - 45°)$ **d** $y = \sin x + 2$

    e $y = -\sin x$ **f** $y = \sin (-x)$ **g** $y = -\sin (-x)$

 3 Which equation represents this graph?

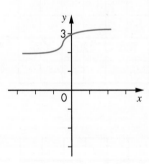

    A: $y = \sin x$ **B:** $y = \cos (x - 90°)$ **C:** $y = -\sin (-x)$

4 This is a sketch of the function $y = f(x)$.

Use this to sketch these functions.

    a $y = f(x) + 2$ **b** $y = f(x - 3)$

    c $y = -f(x)$ **d** $y = -f(x) - 2$

 5 What is the equation of the graph obtained when the following transformations are applied to the graph of $y = \cos x$?

    a Translation of $\begin{pmatrix} 0 \\ 3 \end{pmatrix}$ **b** Translation of $\begin{pmatrix} -30 \\ 0 \end{pmatrix}$ **c** Translation of $\begin{pmatrix} 45 \\ -2 \end{pmatrix}$

6 **a** Sketch the graph $y = x^3$.

   b Use your sketch in part **a** to draw the graphs obtained when $y = x^3$ is transformed as follows.

   i Reflection in the x-axis   **ii** Translation of $\begin{pmatrix} 0 \\ -2 \end{pmatrix}$ **iii** Translation of $\begin{pmatrix} -2 \\ 0 \end{pmatrix}$

   c Give the equation of each of the graphs you sketched in part **b**.

(EV) **7** A teacher asked her class to apply the following transformations to the function $f(x) = x^2$.

   a $f(-x)$ **b** $-f(x)$

   Martyn said that they must be the same because $-x^2 = x^2$.

   Is Martyn correct? Explain your answer.

(MR) **8** The graphs below are all transformations of $y = x^2$. The coordinates of two points are marked on each graph. Use this information to work out the equation of each graph.

a   **b**   **c**

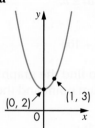   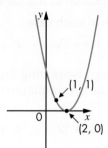   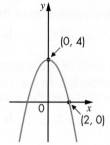

(PS) **9** Below are the graphs of $y = \sin x$ and $y = \cos x$.

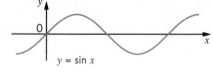   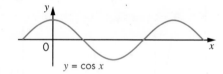

   a Describe a series of transformations that would take $y = \sin x$ to $y = \cos x$.

   b Which of these is equivalent to $y = \cos x$?

   i $y = \sin (x + 90°)$ **ii** $y = -\sin (x - 90°)$

Completing the square

In Chapter 17, you completed the square to solve an equation and to find the turning point of a quadratic graph. You can also relate completing the square to transforming a quadratic graph.

If $f(x) = x^2$, then $f(x \pm a) \pm b = (x \pm a)^2 \pm b$.

If $f(x) = -x^2$, then $f(x \pm a) \pm b = -[(x \pm a)^2 \pm b]$.

For example, you can rewrite $y = x^2 + 8x - 3$ as $y = (x + 4)^2 - 19$, which is equivalent to $y = f(x + 4) - 19$.

This is a translation of $\begin{pmatrix} -4 \\ -19 \end{pmatrix}$.

The minimum point of $y = x^2$ is $(0, 0)$ and is translated to $(-4, -19)$.

Exercise 23K

1 Given that $f(x) = x^2$, write each equation in the form $y = f(x \pm a) \pm b$.

State the translation of the graph in each case.

a $y = x^2 - 6x + 11$ **b** $y = x^2 + 14x + 35$ **c** $y = x^2 - 22x + 100$

2 Sketch each of these graphs, using completing the square to find the graph transformation. In each case, show the minimum or maximum point and the intersection with the y-axis.

a $y = x^2 + 2x + 3$ **b** $y = x^2 - 10x + 12$ **c** $y = 3 - x^2 - 16x$

 3 Each of these graphs can be written in the form $y = \pm x^2 \pm ax \pm b$.

State the equation of each graph.

a

(4, −9)

b

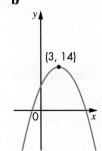

(3, 14)

c

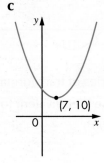

(7, 10)

Worked exemplars

1 Tracy and Les both drove to the airport. The distance–time graphs of their journeys are shown below.

Given that 5 miles is approximately 8 km, calculate who drove faster.

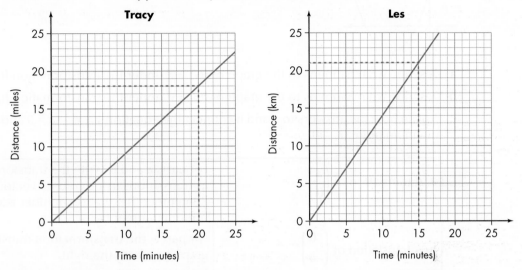

This is a problem-solving question, so you need to make connections between different parts of mathematics, in this case distance–time graphs and converting between units.	
Tracy travels 18 miles in 20 minutes, so is travelling at 54 mph. Les travels 21 km in 15 minutes, so is travelling at 84 km/h.	Start by converting the information from the graphs into speeds that can be used as a comparison. These speeds are normally given per hour.
$54 \times \dfrac{8}{5} = 86.4$ km/h or $84 \div \dfrac{8}{5} = 52.5$ mph	5 miles is equal to 8 km, so calculate Tracy's speed in km/h by multiplying her speed in miles per hour by $\dfrac{8}{5}$. Alternatively, divide Les' speed by $\dfrac{8}{5}$ to convert it into mph.
Hence: Tracy (86.4 km/h) is travelling faster than Les (84 km/h). or Tracy (54 mph) is travelling faster than Les (52.5 mph)	State your conclusion, comparing the two speeds.

2 The sketch shows the graph of $y = x^2 - 6x + 5$.

The minimum point of the graph is $(3, -4)$.

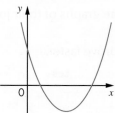

a Describe what happens to the graph of $f(x) = x^2$ under the transformation $f(x - 3)$.

b Describe what happens to the graph of $f(x) = x^2$ under the transformation $f(x) - 4$.

c Explain how the answers to **a** and **b** connect the equation $y = x^2 - 6x + 5$ and the minimum point $(3, -4)$.

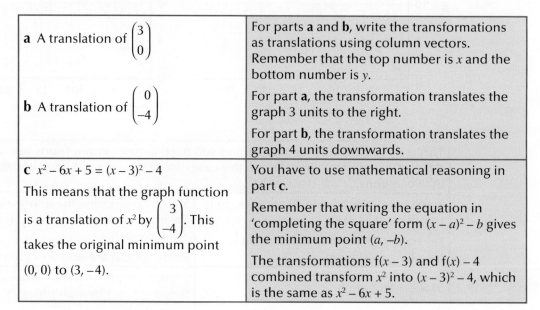

a A translation of $\begin{pmatrix} 3 \\ 0 \end{pmatrix}$	For parts **a** and **b**, write the transformations as translations using column vectors. Remember that the top number is x and the bottom number is y.
b A translation of $\begin{pmatrix} 0 \\ -4 \end{pmatrix}$	For part **a**, the transformation translates the graph 3 units to the right.
	For part **b**, the transformation translates the graph 4 units downwards.
c $x^2 - 6x + 5 = (x - 3)^2 - 4$ This means that the graph function is a translation of x^2 by $\begin{pmatrix} 3 \\ -4 \end{pmatrix}$. This takes the original minimum point $(0, 0)$ to $(3, -4)$.	You have to use mathematical reasoning in part **c**. Remember that writing the equation in 'completing the square' form $(x - a)^2 - b$ gives the minimum point $(a, -b)$. The transformations $f(x - 3)$ and $f(x) - 4$ combined transform x^2 into $(x - 3)^2 - 4$, which is the same as $x^2 - 6x + 5$.

Ready to progress?

I can draw and read information from a distance–time graph.
I can draw a graph of the depth of liquid as a container is filled.
I can calculate the gradient of a straight line and use this to find velocity from a distance–time graph.

I can calculate the area under a graph consisting of straight lines and can interpret the meaning of the area under a velocity–time graph.
I can interpret the gradients of the straight lines on a velocity–time graph.

I can draw and recognise the shapes of the graphs $y = x^3$, $y = \dfrac{1}{x}$ and $y = a^x$.

I can estimate and interpret the gradient and area under a velocity–time curve.
I can transform the graph of a given function and identify a transformation.
I can find the equation of a tangent to a circle.

Review questions

1 The depth–time graph shows how the depth changes as a flask is filled.

Sketch a possible flask that could be represented by the graph.

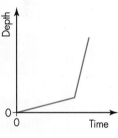

(PS) 2 A car accelerates from 5 m/s to V m/s at a constant rate over 20 seconds.

Given that it travels 240 m in that time, find:

a the value of V

b the acceleration of the car.

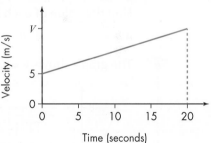

3 **a** On the same axes for $-4 \leqslant x \leqslant 5$, plot the graphs of:

   i $y = x^3 - 2x^2 - 9x + 18$ **ii** $y = 2^x$.

b Use your graph to find three solutions to the equation $x^3 - 2x^2 - 9x + 18 = 2^x$.
Give each solution correct to 1 decimal place.

(PS) 4 A motorcyclist is travelling along a road at 15 m/s when he passes a stationary police car.

The police officer sets off 10 seconds after she is passed by the motorcyclist, accelerating to 20 m/s in 5 seconds. She then maintains a steady speed until she catches the motorcyclist.

Given that they have travelled the same distance in the T seconds after the motorcyclist passes the police car, find the value of T.

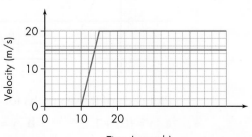

MR **5** Match each graph with the correct equation.

(1) $y = x^3 - 7x$ **(2)** $y = 8x^2 - x^3 - 15x - 20$ **(3)** $y = -x^3$

(4) $y = x^3 + 2$ **(5)** $y = x^3 - 3x^2 - 10x + 24$ **(6)** $y = 6 - 11x + 6x^2 - x^3$

a 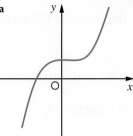   **b** 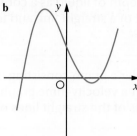   **c**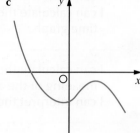

d 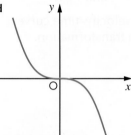   **e** 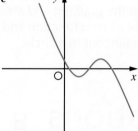   **f**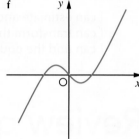

> **Hints and tips**   Notice that in this question the origin is labelled O. It is the point (0, 0).

6 A graph has the equation $y = ab^x$.

The graph passes through the points $(\frac{1}{2}, 10)$, $(\frac{3}{2}, 40)$ and $(3, k)$.

Find the value of each of these.

a a **b** b **c** k

7 The graph shows $y = f(x)$.

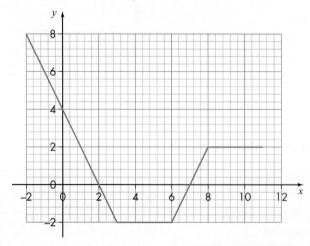

Plot each of these graphs for $-2 \leqslant x \leqslant 11$, on separate axes.

a $y = f(x) + 1$ **b** $y = f(x + 1)$

8 A circle has the equation $x^2 + y^2 = 50$.

a Find the coordinates of the two points, A and B, where the circle intersects the line with equation $2x + y = 15$.

The tangents of the circle at A and B intersect at point C.

b Find the coordinates of point C.

9 Look at this velocity–time graph.

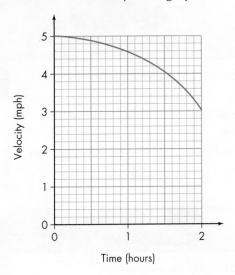

Time (hours)

a Estimate the acceleration when $t = 1$.

b Use two trapezia to estimate the total distance travelled.

(PS) 10 Sketch the graph of $y = \cos x$.

On the same axes, sketch each of these.

a $y = 1 + \cos x$ **b** $y = -\cos x$

c $y = \cos(-x)$ **d** $y = \cos(x + 90°)$

11 A ball is launched into the air from the ground at 40 m/s.

After t seconds, the ball is $(40t - 5t^2)$ m above the ground.

a Plot a graph of height against time for $0 \leqslant t \leqslant 8$.

b Find an estimate for the velocity of the ball after 3 seconds.

24 Algebra: Algebraic fractions and functions

This chapter is going to show you:

- how to combine fractions algebraically and solve equations with algebraic fractions
- how to rearrange and change the subject of a formula where the subject appears twice, or as a power
- how to find the inverse function and the composite of two functions
- how to find an approximate solution for an equation using the process of iteration.

You should already know:

- how to substitute numbers into an algebraic expression
- how to factorise linear and quadratic expressions
- how to expand a pair of linear brackets to get a quadratic equation.

About this chapter

Without algebra, humans would not have reached the Moon and aeroplanes would not fly. Defining numbers with letters allows mathematicians to use formulae and solve the very complicated equations that are needed for today's technologies. The ability to move from a special case to a generalisation is what makes algebra so useful.

Processes such as manipulating algebraic fractions, rearranging formulae, analysing functions and solving equations by iteration are used in a variety of professions in the areas of science, engineering and computing, as well as in the arts. For example, to use a spreadsheet competently, you need to understand how functions work.

Weather forecasting makes use of the iterative process where small changes in the initial conditions can lead to completely different results. This is known as chaos theory. When the forecaster on television or on the internet says that there is a 60% chance of rain, this probability has been determined by running hundreds of simulations through an iterative process.

24.1 Algebraic fractions

This section will show you how to:

- simplify algebraic fractions
- solve equations containing algebraic fractions.

Algebraic fractions can be added, subtracted, multiplied or divided using the same rules that apply to numbers.

To add and subtract, find a common denominator and then find equivalent fractions with that denominator.

Addition: For $\frac{a}{b} + \frac{c}{d}$, the common denominator is bd, so $\frac{a}{b} + \frac{c}{d} = \frac{ad}{bd} + \frac{bc}{bd}$

$$= \frac{ad + bc}{bd}$$

Subtraction: For $\frac{a}{b} - \frac{c}{d}$, the common denominator is bd, so $\frac{a}{b} - \frac{c}{d} = \frac{ad}{bd} - \frac{bc}{bd}$

$$= \frac{ad - bc}{bd}$$

This method works for more than two terms.

For example, for $\frac{a}{b} + \frac{c}{d} - \frac{e}{f}$, the common denominator is bdf, so

$$\frac{a}{b} + \frac{c}{d} - \frac{e}{f} = \frac{adf}{bdf} + \frac{bcf}{bdf} - \frac{bde}{bdf}$$

$$= \frac{adf + bcf - bde}{bdf}$$

To multiply, cancel any common factors, then multiply the numerators together and the denominators together.

Multiplication: $\frac{a}{b} \times \frac{c}{d} = \frac{ac}{bd}$

To divide, find the reciprocal of the fraction you are dividing by, and then multiply.

Division: $\frac{a}{b} \div \frac{c}{d} = \frac{a}{b} \times \frac{d}{c}$

$$= \frac{ad}{bc}$$

Note that a, b, c and d can be numbers, other letters or algebraic expressions. Remember to:

- use brackets, if necessary, to avoid problems with signs and help you expand expressions
- factorise if you can
- cancel if you can.

Example 1

Simplify these fractions. **a** $\frac{1}{x} + \frac{x}{2y}$ **b** $\frac{2}{b} - \frac{a}{2b}$

a The common denominator is $2xy$.

$$\frac{1}{x} + \frac{x}{2y} = \frac{(1)(2y) + (x)(x)}{(x)(2y)}$$

$$= \frac{2y + x^2}{2xy}$$

b The common denominator is $2b$.

$$\frac{2}{b} - \frac{a}{2b} = \frac{4}{2b} - \frac{a}{2b}$$

$$= \frac{4 - a}{2b}$$

Example 2

Simplify these fractions.

a $\dfrac{x}{3} \times \dfrac{x+2}{x-2}$ **b** $\dfrac{x}{3} \div \dfrac{2x}{7}$

a Multiplying: $\dfrac{x}{3} \times \dfrac{x+2}{x-2} = \dfrac{(x)(x+2)}{(3)(x-2)}$

$$= \dfrac{x^2 + 2x}{3x - 6}$$

Remember, the line that separates the top and bottom of an algebraic fraction acts as brackets as well as a division sign.

b Dividing: $\dfrac{x}{3} \div \dfrac{2x}{7} = \dfrac{(x)(7)}{(3)(2x)}$

$$= \dfrac{7}{6}$$

Example 3

Solve this equation.

$\dfrac{x+1}{3} - \dfrac{x-3}{2} = 1$

Subtract the fractions on the left-hand side. $\dfrac{(2)(x+1) - (3)(x-3)}{(2)(3)} = 1$

Multiply both sides by 6. $2(x+1) - 3(x-3) = 1(2)(3)$

Use brackets to avoid problems with signs and help you to expand to get a linear equation.

$2x + 2 - 3x + 9 = 6$

$-x = -5$

$x = 5$

Example 4

a Show that the equation

$\dfrac{3}{x-1} - \dfrac{2}{x+1} = 1$

can be rewritten as $x^2 - x - 6 = 0$.

b Hence solve the equation $\dfrac{3}{x-1} - \dfrac{2}{x+1} = 1$.

a Add the fractions.

$\dfrac{3(x+1) - 2(x-1)}{(x-1)(x+1)} = 1$

Multiply both sides by the denominator. $3(x+1) - 2(x-1) = (x-1)(x+1)$

(Use brackets to help with expanding and to avoid problems with minus signs.)

Expand the brackets. $3x + 3 - 2x + 2 = x^2 - 1$

(Note that the right-hand side is the difference of two squares.)

Rearrange into the general quadratic form. $x^2 - x - 6 = 0$

b Factorise and solve. $(x-3)(x+2) = 0$

$x = 3 \text{ or } -2$

Example 5

Simplify this fraction.

$$\frac{(x+6)(x+2)}{x+3} - \frac{(x+9)(x+1)}{x+5}$$

The common denominator is $(x+3)(x+5)$.

$$\frac{(x+6)(x+2)(x+5) - (x+9)(x+1)(x+3)}{(x+3)(x+5)}$$

Expand the brackets in the numerator and simplify.

$$\frac{(x^2+8x+12)(x+5) - (x^2+10x+9)(x+3)}{(x+3)(x+5)}$$

$$= \frac{(x^3+8x^2+12x+5x^2+40x+60) - (x^3+10x^2+9x+3x^2+30x+27)}{(x+3)(x+5)}$$

$$= \frac{x^3+13x^2+52x+60 - x^3-13x^2-39x-27}{(x+3)(x+5)}$$

$$= \frac{13x+33}{(x+3)(x+5)}$$

It is sometimes simpler to leave an algebraic fraction in a factorised form.

Example 6

Simplify this expression.

$$\frac{x+3}{x^2+5x+4} - \frac{x-1}{x^2+4x}$$

Factorise the denominators. $\quad \dfrac{x+3}{(x+4)(x+1)} - \dfrac{x-1}{x(x+4)}$

The common denominator is $x(x+1)(x+4)$. $\quad \dfrac{x(x+3) - (x-1)(x+1)}{x(x+1)(x+4)}$

Expand and simplify:

$$\frac{x^2+3x - (x^2-1)}{x(x+1)(x+4)} = \frac{x^2+3x-x^2+1}{x(x+1)(x+4)}$$

$$= \frac{3x+1}{x(x+1)(x+4)}$$

Example 7

Simplify this expression.

$$\frac{2x^2+x-3}{4x^2-9}$$

Factorise the numerator and denominator. $\dfrac{(2x+3)(x-1)}{(2x+3)(2x-3)}$ (Denominator is the difference of two squares.)

Cancel any common factors. $\quad \dfrac{\cancel{(2x+3)}(x-1)}{\cancel{(2x+3)}(2x-3)}$

If at this stage there isn't a common factor on the top and bottom, you should check your factorisations.

The remaining fraction is the answer. $\quad \dfrac{(x-1)}{(2x-3)}$

Example 8

Simplify this expression.

$$\frac{x+5}{\sqrt{x}-3} \times \frac{x^2-7x-18}{\sqrt{x}+3}$$

Factorise the quadratic expression.

$$\frac{x+5}{\sqrt{x}-3} \times \frac{(x-9)(x+2)}{\sqrt{x}+3}$$

Multiply.

$$\frac{(x+5)(x-9)(x+2)}{(\sqrt{x}-3)(\sqrt{x}+3)} = \frac{(x+5)(x-9)(x+2)}{x-3\sqrt{x}+3\sqrt{x}-9}$$

$$= \frac{(x+5)(x-9)(x+2)}{x-9}$$

$$= (x+5)(x+2)$$

$$= x^2+7x+10$$

Exercise 24A

1 Simplify each of these.

a $\dfrac{x}{2} + \dfrac{x}{3}$
  b $\dfrac{3x}{4} + \dfrac{2x}{5}$
  c $\dfrac{xy}{4} + \dfrac{2}{x}$

d $\dfrac{x+1}{2} + \dfrac{x+2}{3}$
  e $\dfrac{x}{5} + \dfrac{2x+1}{3}$
  f $\dfrac{x-4}{4} + \dfrac{2x-3}{2}$

2 Simplify each of these.

a $\dfrac{3x}{4} - \dfrac{x}{5}$
  b $\dfrac{x}{2} - \dfrac{y}{3}$
  c $\dfrac{xy}{4} - \dfrac{2}{y}$

d $\dfrac{2x+1}{2} - \dfrac{3x+1}{4}$
  e $\dfrac{x-2}{2} - \dfrac{x-3}{4}$
  f $\dfrac{x-4}{4} - \dfrac{2x-3}{2}$

3 Solve these equations.

a $\dfrac{x+1}{2} + \dfrac{x+2}{5} = 3$
  b $\dfrac{4x+1}{3} - \dfrac{x+2}{4} = 2$

c $\dfrac{2x+1}{2} - \dfrac{x+1}{7} = 1$
  d $\dfrac{3x+1}{5} - \dfrac{5x-1}{7} = 0$

4 Simplify each of these.

a $\dfrac{x}{2} \times \dfrac{x}{3}$
  b $\dfrac{4x}{3y} \times \dfrac{2y}{x}$
  c $\dfrac{x}{2} \times \dfrac{x-2}{5}$

d $\dfrac{x}{5} \times \dfrac{2x+1}{3}$
  e $\dfrac{x-5}{10} \times \dfrac{5}{x^2-5x}$

5 Simplify each of these.

a $\dfrac{2x}{7} \div \dfrac{4y}{14}$
  b $\dfrac{4y^2}{9x} \div \dfrac{2y}{3x^2}$
  c $\dfrac{x-3}{15} \div \dfrac{5}{2x-6}$

d $\dfrac{2x+1}{2} \div \dfrac{4x+2}{4}$
  e $\dfrac{x}{6} \div \dfrac{2x^2+x}{3}$
  f $\dfrac{x-2}{12} \div \dfrac{4}{x-3}$

g $\dfrac{x-5}{10} \div \dfrac{x^2-5x}{5}$

6 Simplify each of these. Factorise and cancel where appropriate.

a $\dfrac{3x}{4} + \dfrac{x}{4}$ **b** $\dfrac{3x}{4} - \dfrac{x}{4}$ **c** $\dfrac{3x}{4} \times \dfrac{x}{4}$

d $\dfrac{3x}{4} \div \dfrac{x}{4}$ **e** $\dfrac{3x+1}{2} + \dfrac{x-2}{5}$ **f** $\dfrac{3x+1}{2} - \dfrac{x-2}{5}$

g $\dfrac{3x+1}{2} \times \dfrac{x-2}{5}$ **h** $\dfrac{x^2-9}{10} \times \dfrac{5}{x-3}$ **i** $\dfrac{2x+3}{5} \div \dfrac{6x+9}{10}$

j $\dfrac{2x^2}{9} - \dfrac{2y^2}{3}$

7 Show that each algebraic fraction simplifies to the given expression.

a $\dfrac{2}{x+1} + \dfrac{5}{x+2} = 3$ simplifies to $3x^2 + 2x - 3 = 0$

b $\dfrac{3}{4x+1} - \dfrac{4}{x+2} = 2$ simplifies to $8x^2 + 31x + 2 = 0$

c $\dfrac{2}{2x-1} - \dfrac{6}{x+1} = 11$ simplifies to $22x^2 + 21x - 19 = 0$

8 **a** Simplify this expression. $\dfrac{x+2\sqrt{2}}{x+\sqrt{2}} \times \dfrac{x-2\sqrt{2}}{x-\sqrt{2}}$

b Use your answer to find the value of $\dfrac{x+2\sqrt{2}}{x+\sqrt{2}} \times \dfrac{x-2\sqrt{2}}{x-\sqrt{2}}$ when $x = 1$.

9 Write $\dfrac{2}{x+3} + \dfrac{3}{x+4} - \dfrac{4}{x+5}$ as a single fraction with an expanded denominator.

10 Simplify this expression. $\dfrac{x^2+5x+6}{x+2} \div \dfrac{x^2-x-30}{x+5}$

11 For homework a teacher asks his class to simplify the expression $\dfrac{x^2-x-2}{x^2+x-6}$.

This is Tom's answer: $\dfrac{x^{\cancel{2}} - x - \cancel{2}^{-1}}{x^{\cancel{2}} + x - \cancel{6}_{+3}} = \dfrac{-x-1}{x+3}$

$= \dfrac{x+1}{x+3}$

Tom has made several mistakes. What are they?

12 An expression of the form $\dfrac{ax^2 + bx - c}{dx^2 - 9}$ simplifies to $\dfrac{x-1}{2x-3}$.

What was the original expression?

13 Solve these equations.

a $\dfrac{4}{x+1} + \dfrac{5}{x+2} = 2$ **b** $\dfrac{18}{4x-1} - \dfrac{1}{x+1} = 1$ **c** $\dfrac{2x-1}{2} - \dfrac{6}{x+1} = 1$

d $\dfrac{3}{2x-1} - \dfrac{4}{3x-1} = 1$

14 Simplify these expressions.

a $\dfrac{x^2+2x-3}{2x^2+7x+3}$ **b** $\dfrac{4x^2-1}{2x^2+5x-3}$ **c** $\dfrac{6x^2+x-2}{9x^2-4}$

d $\dfrac{4x^2+x-3}{4x^2-7x+3}$ **e** $\dfrac{4x^2-25}{8x^2-22x+5}$

15 **a** Prove that the equation $\dfrac{7}{x+1} + \dfrac{4}{x+4} = 3$ simplifies to $3x^2 + 4x - 20 = 0$.

b Hence solve the equation $\dfrac{7}{x+1} + \dfrac{4}{x+4} = 3$.

 16 Emma swam 300 m at a speed of $(x-1)$ m/s, then a further 200 m at $(x-2)$ m/s. The total swim took Emma 10 minutes.

a Show that $6x^2 - 23x + 20 = 0$.

b Find the speed at which Emma swam the first 200 m.

> **Hints and tips** Remember how speed, distance and time are related.

17 **a** Expand and simplify $\left(x + \sqrt{2}\right)^3$.

b Hence show that $\left(1 + \sqrt{2}\right)^3 = 7 + 5\sqrt{2}$.

c Find the exact value of $\left(1 + \sqrt{2}\right)^6$.

18 Simplify these expressions.

a $\dfrac{x+4}{(x+3)^2} - \dfrac{x-4}{(x-3)^2}$ **b** $\dfrac{4}{x+1} + \dfrac{3}{x+2} - \dfrac{2}{x+3} - \dfrac{1}{x+4}$

19 Simplify this expression. $\dfrac{x^2 + x\sqrt{3} - 6}{x^2 - x\sqrt{3} - 18}$

24.2 Changing the subject of a formula

This section will show you how to:

• change the subject of a formula where the subject occurs more than once.

When studying algebraic manipulation, you considered how to change the subject of a formula where the subject only appears once. To rearrange formulae where the subject appears more than once, the principle is the same as rearranging a formula where the subject only appears once or solving an equation where the unknown appears on both sides.

Collect all the subject terms on the same side and everything else on the other side. Most often, you then need to factorise the subject out of the resulting expression.

Example 9	Make x the subject of this formula. $ax + b = cx + d$
	First, rearrange the formula to get all the x-terms on the left-hand side and all the other terms on the right-hand side:
	$ax - cx = d - b$
	Factorise x out of the left-hand side. $x(a - c) = d - b$
	Divide by the expression in brackets. $x = \dfrac{d - b}{a - c}$

Example 10

Make p the subject of this formula.

$$5 = \frac{ap + b}{cp + d}$$

First, multiply both sides by the denominator of the algebraic fraction: $\quad 5(cp + d) = ap + b$

Expand the brackets: $\hspace{7cm} 5cp + 5d = ap + b$

Now continue as in Example 9: $\hspace{6cm} 5cp - ap = b - 5d$

$$p(5c - a) = b - 5d$$

$$p = \frac{b - 5d}{5c - a}$$

Exercise 24B

1 Make c the subject of each formula.

    a $5(c - 3) = p$ **b** $5(c - 3) = cp$

2 Make G the subject of each formula.

    a $F = \dfrac{R}{G + 3}$ **b** $F = \dfrac{G + R}{G + 3}$

3 Make the letter in brackets the subject of the formula.

    a $p(a + b) = q(a - b)$ (a) **b** $p(a + b) = q(a - b)$ (b)

    c $5 = \dfrac{a + b}{a - c}$ (a) **d** $A = 2\pi rh + \pi rk$ (r)

    e $v^2 = u^2 + av^2$ (v) **f** $R = \dfrac{x - 3}{x - 2}$ (x)

4 **a** The perimeter of a shape is given by the formula $P = \pi r + 2kr$. Make r the subject of this formula.

    b The area of the same shape is given by $A = \frac{1}{2}[\pi r^2 + r^2\sqrt{(k^2 - 1)}]$. Make r the subject of this formula.

5 When £P is invested for Y years at a simple interest rate of R, the following formula gives the amount, A, at any time.

$$A = P + \frac{PRY}{100}$$

Make P the subject of this formula.

6 When two resistors with values a and b are connected in parallel, the total resistance is given by:

$$R = \frac{ab}{a + b}$$

    a Make b the subject of the formula.

    b Write the formula when a is the subject.

(EV) **7** **a** Make x the subject of this formula. $y = \dfrac{x + 2}{x - 2}$

    b Show that the formula $y = 1 + \dfrac{4}{x - 2}$ can be rearranged to give $x = 2 + \dfrac{4}{y - 1}$.

    c Combine the right-hand sides of each formula in part **b** into single fractions and simplify as much as possible.

    d What do you notice?

8 The volume of the solid shown is given by this formulae.

$$V = \tfrac{2}{3}\pi r^3 + \pi r^2 h$$

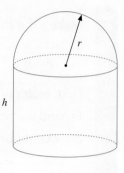

a Explain why it is not possible to make r the subject of this formula.

b Make π the subject.

c If $h = r$, can the formula be rearranged to make r the subject? If so, rearrange it to make r the subject.

9 Make x the subject of this formula. $\qquad W = \tfrac{1}{2}z(x + y) + \tfrac{1}{2}y(x + z)$

10 The following formulae in x can be rearranged to give the formulae in terms of y as shown.

$$y = \frac{x + 1}{x + 2} \text{ gives } x = \frac{1 - 2y}{y - 1} \qquad\qquad y = \frac{2x + 1}{x + 2} \text{ gives } x = \frac{1 - 2y}{y - 2}$$

$$y = \frac{3x + 2}{4x + 1} \text{ gives } x = \frac{2 - y}{4y - 3} \qquad\qquad y = \frac{x + 5}{3x + 2} \text{ gives } x = \frac{5 - 2y}{3y - 1}$$

Without rearranging the formula, write down $y = \dfrac{5x + 1}{2x + 3}$ as $x = \dots$ and explain how you can do this without any algebra.

11 Alice and Brian have been asked to make u the subject of the formula $\dfrac{1}{f} = \dfrac{1}{u} + \dfrac{1}{v}$.

Alice's answer is $u = \dfrac{fv}{v - f}$.

Brian's answer is $u = \dfrac{1}{\dfrac{1}{f} - \dfrac{1}{v}}$.

a Evaluate whether either or both of these answers are correct.

b Into which answer is it easier to substitute values?

24.3 Functions

This section will show you how to:

- find the output of a function
- find the inverse function.

This is a function machine.

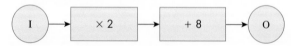

When you input a number into the function machine, it doubles the number and then adds 8 to produce an output. For example, if the input is 7, then the output is $7 \times 2 + 8 = 14 + 8 = 22$.

If you are told the output, then you can also find the input by applying the **inverse** operations in reverse order. For example, if the output is 30, then you subtract 8 and divide by 2.

$30 - 8 = 22 \qquad 22 \div 2 = 11$

So the input was 11.

Example 11

a Use this function machine to find the output for each input.

  i 6   **ii** −4

b Find both possible inputs if the output is 20.

a i $6^2 = 36$ $36 − 5 = 31$

  ii $(−4)^2 = 16$ $16 − 5 = 11$

b $20 + 5 = 25$ $\sqrt{25} = 5$ or $−5$

Another way of writing a function is to use the function notation f(x). The value of x that you substitute into a function f(x) is the input and the value of f(x) is the output of the function. For example, for the function f(x) = 3x + 10, when the input is 5, the output f(5) is $3 \times 5 + 10 = 25$.

Example 12

The function f(x) is defined as f(x) = 14 − 2x.

a Find: **i** f(3)   **ii** f(−5).   **b** Solve f(x) = 0.

a i f(3) = 14 − 2 × 3
      = 14 − 6
      = 8

  ii f(−5) = 14 − 2 × (−5)
        = 14 + 10
        = 24

b When f(x) = 0, 14 − 2x = 0,
    so x = 7.

Exercise 24C

1 **a** Use this function machine to find the output for each input.

  i 11   **ii** 26   **iii** −4   **iv** 1

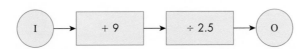

  b Find the input for each of these outputs.

  i 18   **ii** 0   **iii** 500   **iv** 3

2 **a** Use the function machine to find the output when the input is 29.

  b Find an algebraic expression for the output when the input is x.

  c Use your answer for **b** to find the input when the output is 10.

3 For this function machine, find the input for each of these outputs.

  a 30   **b** 60   **c** 18

4 For which input do these function machines also have the same output?

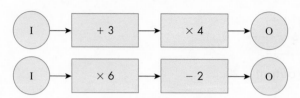

5 $f(x) = 2x^2 + 7$ Find the value of each of these.

a f(3)   **b** f(11)   **c** f(-2)

d f(30)   **e** f(-30)   **f** f($\sqrt{3}$)

g Given that f(k) = 57, find both values of k.

6 $g(x) = 25 - x^2$ Find the value of each of these.

a g(4)   **b** g(-8)   **c** g(9)

d g(-9)   **e** g($\sqrt{13}$)   **f** g(-0.4)

g Solve g(x) = 0.

(MR) **7** **a** Given that $f(x) = 2x^2 + 3x$, find the value of

i f(-6)   and   **ii** f(4).

$g(x) = x^2 + 8x + 6$

b Find the inputs for which f(x) and g(x) have the same outputs.

Inverse functions

An **inverse function** is a function that performs the opposite process of the original function, such as adding instead of subtracting or multiplying instead of dividing. If the original function turns an input of 3 into an output of 5, then the inverse function turns the output of 5 back into the input of 3, and it will do this for all inputs and outputs. The notation used for an inverse function is $f^{-1}(x)$.

For example, the inverse function of $f(x) = 2x + 1$ is $f^{-1}(x) = \dfrac{x-1}{2}$.

To find the inverse function, write f(x) as y; make x the subject of the function; replace x with $f^{-1}(x)$ and then replace y with x.

Consider $f(x) = 2x + 1$.

Writing f(x) as y gives $y = 2x + 1$.

Making x the subject of the function gives $x = \dfrac{y-1}{2}$.

Replacing x with $f^{-1}(x)$ and then y with x gives $f^{-1}(x) = \dfrac{x-1}{2}$.

Example 13

Find the inverse of the function $f(x) = x^3 + 10$.

Write f(x) as y.	$y = x^3 + 10$
Subtract 10 from both sides.	$y - 10 = x^3$
Cube root each side.	$\sqrt[3]{y - 10} = x$
Reverse the sides.	$x = \sqrt[3]{y - 10}$
Replace x with $f^{-1}(x)$ and then y with x.	$f^{-1}(x) = \sqrt[3]{x - 10}$

Exercise 24D

1 Find an expression for $f^{-1}(x)$ for:

a $f(x) = 4x - 5$ **b** $f(x) = x^3 + 2$ **c** $f(x) = \dfrac{10}{x+1}$

d $f(x) = 10 - 2x$ **e** $f(x) = \dfrac{x-7}{6}$ **f** $f(x) = \dfrac{3}{x} + 5$

2 **a** Given that $f(x) = \dfrac{x+2}{3x-5}$, find an expression for $f^{-1}(x)$.

     b Find the value of $f(1)$.

     c Substitute $f(1)$ into $f^{-1}(x)$ to verify that the answer is 1.

3 **a** Find the inverse functions of

       i $f(x) = 12 - x$ and   **ii** $g(x) = \dfrac{12}{x}$.

       What do you notice?

     b Find the inverse function of $f(x) = \dfrac{3x+8}{4x-3}$. What do you notice?

     c Prove that if $f(x) = \dfrac{ax+b}{cx-a}$, then $f^{-1}(x) = \dfrac{ax+b}{cx-a}$.

24.4 Composite functions

This section will show you how to:

- find the composite of two functions.

Key term

composite

A **composite** function is a combination of two functions to create a third function. For two functions $f(x)$ and $g(x)$, the function created by substituting $g(x)$ into $f(x)$ is called $fg(x)$. You work this out by finding $g(x)$ first and then substituting your answer into $f(x)$.

Example 14

The functions $f(x)$ and $g(x)$ are defined as $f(x) = 5x - 3$ and $g(x) = \frac{1}{2}x + 1$. Find the value of:

a $f(4)$ **b** $fg(4)$ **c** $ff(4)$.

a $f(4) = 5 \times 4 - 3$
       $= 20 - 3$
       $= 17$

b $g(4) = \frac{1}{2} \times 4 + 1$
       $= 2 + 1$
       $= 3$
     $f(3) = 5 \times 3 - 3$
       $= 15 - 3$
       $= 12$

c $f(4) = 17$
     $f(17) = 5 \times 17 - 3$
       $= 85 - 3$
       $= 82$

Example 15

The functions $f(x)$ and $g(x)$ are defined as $f(x) = 5x - 3$ and $g(x) = \frac{1}{2}x + 1$. Find the value of:

a $fg(x)$ **b** $gf(x)$ **c** $ff(x)$.

a Substitute $g(x)$ into $f(x)$.
    $f(x) = 5(\frac{1}{2}x + 1) - 3$
       $= 2\frac{1}{2}x + 5 - 3$
       $= 2\frac{1}{2}x + 2$

b Substitute $f(x)$ into $g(x)$.
    $g(x) = \frac{1}{2}(5x - 3) + 1$
       $= 2\frac{1}{2}x - 1\frac{1}{2} + 1$
       $= 2\frac{1}{2}x - \frac{1}{2}$

c Substitute $f(x)$ into $f(x)$.
    $f(x) = 5(5x - 3) - 3$
       $= 25x - 15 - 3$
       $= 25x - 18$

---

1 Given that $f(x) = 10 - 3x$ and $g(x) = \dfrac{x-3}{2}$, find the value of each of the following.

 a fg(4) **b** gf(–2) **c** ff(7) **d** gg(0) **e** fgfgfg(5.8)

> **Hints and tips** For fg(a), calculate g(a) and substitute this into f(x).

 2 Given that $f(x) = \dfrac{24}{x-1}$ and $g(x) = 5x - 11$, find the value of each of the following.

 a fg(2.5) **b** gf(1.5) **c** fgf(10) **d** gfg(3) **e** ff(–11) **f** gg(–3)

  3 $f(x) = x^3 - 6$ $g(x) = 4(x-2)$ $h(x) = 3 - x$

 a Find simplified expressions for each of the following.

  i gf(x) **ii** hg(x) **iii** fh(x) **iv** gg(x) **v** ff(x)

 b Prove that gh(x) can never equal hg(x) for any value of x.

> **Hints and tips** For gf(x), substitute f(x) into g(x).

  4 $f(x) = x^2 + a$ $g(x) = x - b$

 If fg(x) = gf(x), find x in terms of b.

24.5 Iteration

This section will show you how to:

- find an approximate solution for an equation using the process of iteration.

> **Key term**
>
> iteration

Many equations cannot be solved exactly using any of the techniques you have met already. You could use trial and improvement to solve an equation like this but there is a process called **iteration** that is more efficient and does not require you to make a new decision after each attempt. This involves solving the equation many times, using your result from the previous version each time to make the answer more accurate.

To perform iteration, first rearrange the equation so that x is the subject, although there will be x terms on the other side (the right-hand side) as well. The x that is the subject is called x_{n+1} and any x term on the right-hand side is called x_n.

For example, $x_{n+1} = \sqrt{2x_n + 6}$ can be used to solve the quadratic equation $x^2 - 2x - 6 = 0$.

Substitute an initial value, called x_1, into the right-hand side, and call the value obtained from this substitution x_2.

Example 16	Find the first four iterations of the iterative formula $x_{n+1} = 3x_n - 2$ with $x_1 = 2$.			
	$x_2 = 3x_1 - 2$	$x_3 = 3x_2 - 2$	$x_4 = 3x_3 - 2$	$x_5 = 3x_4 - 2$
	$= 3 \times 2 - 2$	$= 3 \times 4 - 2$	$= 3 \times 10 - 2$	$= 3 \times 28 - 2$
	$= 4$	$= 10$	$= 28$	$= 82$

Using a calculator makes iteration much easier.

To solve the quadratic equation $x^2 - 2x - 6 = 0$ using $x_{n+1} = \sqrt{2x_n + 6}$:

Let $x_1 = 4$.

On your calculator, type **4** **=**. This records the number 4 as the first 'answer'.

Next type **√** **2** **(** **×** **Ans** **+** **6** **)** **=**.

Note: Your calculator may work in a slightly different way, and require a different key press order. Check how this works on your calculator before starting any iteration questions.

$x_2 = \sqrt{2x_1 + 6} = \sqrt{14} = 3.7417$ (4 dp)

You then substitute this value back into the right hand side to generate the term x_3, and so on.

$x_3 = \sqrt{2x_2 + 6} = \sqrt{2 \times 3.7417 + 6} = 3.6720$ (4 dp)

$x_4 = \sqrt{2x_3 + 6} = \sqrt{2 \times 3.6720 + 6} = 3.6529$ (4 dp)

You can just keep pressing **=** on your calculator to generate further iterations.

Example 17

An approximate solution for the equation $x^3 - 16x + 9 = 0$ can be found using the iterative formula $x_{n+1} = \sqrt[3]{16x_n - 9}$ and an initial value of $x_1 = 4$.

a Find the first six iterations, correct to 5 decimal places.

b Verify that 3.68 is a solution of the equation, correct to 2 decimal places.

a Enter the initial value on the calculator: **4** **=**

Enter the iterative formula.

This substitutes $x_1 = 4$ into the formula. $x_2 = 3.80295$

Press **=** to substitute the value of x_2 into the formula: $x_3 = 3.72885$

Pressing **=** four more times gives: $x_4 = 3.70021$ $x_5 = 3.68902$ $x_6 = 3.68463$ $x_7 = 3.68290$

b Both x_6 and x_7 round to 3.68, correct to 2 decimal places.

Example 18

These steps can be used to find an approximate value for $x^3 = 6x + 8$.

Step 1: Start with $x = 3$.

Step 2: Find the value of $\sqrt[3]{6x + 8}$, correct to 4 decimal places.

Step 3: Compare your answer with the value of x you substituted. If it is the same, you have found the answer. If it is not the same, go back to step 2.

Find the solution of $x^3 = 6x + 8$ given by this process.

Enter the initial value on the calculator. **3** **=**

Enter the iterative formula.

First iteration $= \sqrt[3]{6 \times 3 + 8} = 2.9625$ (4 dp)	Not the same as 3 so return to step 2.
Second iteration $= 2.9539$ (4 dp)	Not the same as 2.9625 so return to step 2.
Third iteration $= 2.9520$ (4 dp)	Not the same as 2.9539 so return to step 2.
Fourth iteration $= 2.9515$ (4 dp)	Not the same as 2.9520 so return to step 2.
Fifth iteration $= 2.9514$ (4 dp)	Not the same as 2.9515 so return to step 2.
Sixth iteration $= 2.9514$ (4 dp)	The same as 2.9514 from the fifth iteration so this is the answer.

Example 19

For the iterative formula $x_{n+1} = \dfrac{3}{3 - x_n}$, find the value of x_{200} when $x_1 = 5$.

$x_2 = \dfrac{3}{3 - 5} = -\dfrac{3}{2}$ $\qquad\qquad$ $x_3 = \dfrac{3}{3 - \left(-\frac{3}{2}\right)} = \dfrac{3}{\frac{9}{2}} = \dfrac{2}{3}$

$x_4 = \dfrac{3}{3 - \left(\frac{2}{3}\right)} = \dfrac{3}{\frac{7}{3}} = \dfrac{9}{7}$ $\qquad$ $x_5 = \dfrac{3}{3 - \left(\frac{9}{7}\right)} = \dfrac{3}{\frac{12}{7}} = \dfrac{7}{4}$

$x_6 = \dfrac{3}{3 - \left(\frac{7}{4}\right)} = \dfrac{3}{\frac{5}{4}} = \dfrac{12}{5}$ $\qquad$ $x_7 = \dfrac{3}{3 - \left(\frac{12}{5}\right)} = \dfrac{3}{\frac{3}{5}} = 5$

Since you started with 5, this sequence will now cycle round 5, $-\frac{3}{2}$, $\frac{2}{3}$, $\frac{9}{7}$, $\frac{7}{4}$, $\frac{12}{5}$, returning to $\frac{12}{5}$ for every multiple of 6 (x_6, x_{12}, x_{18}, etc.).

The largest multiple of 6 below 200 is 198, which is 2 less than 200, so x_{200} (5) will be the same as x_2.

Hence $x_{200} = -\dfrac{3}{2}$.

Exercise 24F 🖩

1 Find the first four iterations using the iterative formula $x_{n+1} = 18 - 7x_n$ with $x_1 = 2$.

2 For the iterative formula $x_{n+1} = 5x_n - 12$, find x_5 for each initial value.

  a $x_1 = 6$ **b** $x_1 = -4$ **c** $x_1 = 1.2$ **d** $x_1 = 3$

3 These steps can be used to find an approximate value for $x^3 = 19x + 34$.

Step 1: Start with $x = 5$.

Step 2: Find the value of $\sqrt[3]{19x + 34}$, correct to 4 decimal places.

Step 3: Compare your answer with the value of x you substituted. If it is the same, you have found the answer. If it is not the same, go back to step 2.

Find the solution to $x^3 = 19x + 34$ given by this process.

Hints and tips | Type in the value of x_1, then use the **Ans** button to type in the iterative formula.

4 An approximate solution for the equation $x^3 - 7x - 10 = 0$ can be found using the iterative formula $x_{n+1} = \sqrt[3]{7x_n + 10}$ and an initial value of $x_1 = 3$.

Find the first five iterations, correct to 4 decimal places.

CM **5** The iterative formula $x_{n+1} = \sqrt[3]{x_n^2 + 5}$ can be used to find an approximate solution for the equation $x^3 - x^2 - 5 = 0$.

  a Using $x_1 = 2$, show that $x_5 = 2.12$, correct to 2 decimal places.

  b Verify that 2.12 is a solution, correct to 2 decimal places.

CM **6** Use the iterative formula $x_{n+1} = \sqrt[3]{5x_n + 2}$ to show that 2.4142 is an approximate solution for the equation $x^3 - 5x - 2 = 0$.

(EV) **7** **a** Solve, by factorisation, the equation $x^2 - 10x + 21 = 0$.

  b Use the iterative formula $x_{n+1} = \sqrt{10x_n - 21}$ with $x_1 = 5$ to determine which of the two answers is generated by the formula.

  c Investigate what happens with each of these initial values.

   i $x_1 = 3.001$ **ii** $x_1 = 2.999$ **iii** $x_1 = 100$ **iv** $x_1 = 3$

  d Generalise what happens for all values of x.

(CM) **8** You can use iterative formula $x_{n+1} = \sqrt[3]{x_n^2 + 5}$ to find an approximate solution for the equation $x^3 - x^2 - 5 = 0$.

  a Show that the equation $x = \dfrac{x + 4}{x - 1}$ can be rearranged as $x^2 - 2x - 4 = 0$ and hence

   $x_{n+1} = \dfrac{x_n + 4}{x_n - 1}$ is an iterative formula for the equation $x^2 - 2x - 4 = 0$.

  b When $x_1 = 3$, find the values of x_2, x_3 and x_4, writing the answers as fractions where appropriate.

  c When $x_1 = 3.25$, find the values of x_2, x_3 and x_4, writing the answers as fractions.

  d When $x_1 = 3.3$, find the values of x_2, x_3 and x_4, writing the answers as fractions.

  e When $x_1 = 1 + \sqrt{5}$, find the values of x_2, x_3 and x_4, writing the answers as surds.

  f Use the results from parts **b** to **e** to deduce a solution for the equation $x^2 - 2x - 4 = 0$.

(EV) **9** A square has sides of $(x^2 - 2)$ cm and $(x + 5)$ cm.

  a Show that $x^2 - x - 7 = 0$.

  b Use the iterative formula $x_{n+1} = \sqrt{x_n + 7}$ and an initial input of $x_1 = 3$ to find the area of the square, correct to the nearest integer.

  c How reliable is your answer for the area of the square?

(PS) **10** **a** For the iterative formula $x_{n+1} = x_n^2 - 3$, find the value of x_{36} when $x_1 = 2$.

  b For the iterative formula $x_{n+1} = \dfrac{1}{1 - x_n}$, find the value of x_{100} when $x_1 = 3$.

> **Hints and tips** Generate x_2, x_3, x_4 and so on, and look for a pattern.

(EV) **11** The equation $x^3 = 4x + 9$ is to be solved by an iterative formula with $x_1 = 3$.

  a Investigate what happens when the iterative formula used is given by

   $x_{n+1} = \dfrac{9}{x_n^2 - 4}$.

  b Investigate what happens when the iterative formula used is given by

   $x_{n+1} = \dfrac{x_n^3 - 9}{4}$.

  c Investigate what happens when the iterative formula used is given by

   $x_{n+1} = \sqrt{4 + \dfrac{9}{x_n}}$.

Worked exemplars

  The equation $x^3 - 19x + 9 = 0$ can be written as the iterative formula $x_{n+1} = \sqrt[3]{19x_n - 9}$.

a Using $x_1 = 4$, find the first two iterations, correct to 3 decimal places.

b Show that 4.10 is a solution to the equation, correct to 2 decimal places.

This is a question on communicating mathematics so you need to state your method clearly.	
a First iteration $x_2 = \sqrt[3]{19x_1 - 9}$ $\quad = \sqrt[3]{19 \times 4 - 9}$ $\quad = \sqrt[3]{67}$ $\quad = 4.062$ (3 dp)	Start by finding the first iteration. Although the method shown is correct, it is more efficient to register 4 as an answer in the calculator's memory and then to type in the iterative formula using Ans for x_n, especially if you need more than two iterations.
Second iteration $x_3 = \sqrt[3]{19x_2 - 9}$ $\quad = \sqrt[3]{19 \times \sqrt[3]{67} - 9}$ $\quad = 4.085$ (3 dp)	Then move on to the second iteration. Note that you should be using the exact answer from the first iteration rather than the rounded 4.062. (This would definitely happen if you were using the efficient calculator method.) In this example, 4.062 also gives a second iteration of 4.085, but this is not guaranteed.
b $x_4 = 4.094$ (3 dp) $x_5 = 4.097$ (3 dp) $x_6 = 4.099$ (3 dp) $x_7 = 4.099$ (3 dp)	Since you are asked to show that 4.1 is a solution, you are being asked to communicate information accurately. Continue to find iterations until two of them repeat.
Since x_6 and x_7 both equal 4.099 correct to 3 decimal places, 4.10 is a solution of the equation correct to 2 decimal places.	Include a conclusion.

(PS) **2** Given that $f(x) = \dfrac{x^2 + 3x - 10}{2x^2 - 9x + 10}$, prove that $f^{-1}(3) = 4$.

> This is a problem-solving question so you need to plan a strategy to solve it and, most importantly, communicate your method clearly. You need to show each step clearly.
>
> There are two different methods shown here.

Method 1 $f(x) = \dfrac{x^2 + 3x - 10}{2x^2 - 9x + 10}$ $= \dfrac{(x + 5)(x - 2)}{(2x - 5)(x - 2)}$ $f(x) = \dfrac{x + 5}{2x - 5}$	Factorise and cancel the numerator and denominator.
$y = \dfrac{x + 5}{2x - 5}$ $y(2x - 5) = x + 5$ $2xy - 5y = x + 5$ $2xy - x = 5y + 5$ $x(2y - 1) = 5y + 5$ $x = \dfrac{5y + 5}{2y - 1}$ $f^{-1}(x) = \dfrac{5x + 5}{2x - 1}$	Find the inverse function.
$f^{-1}(3) = \dfrac{5 \times 3 + 5}{2 \times 3 - 1} = \dfrac{20}{5} = 4$	Substitute $x = 3$.
Method 2 $3 = \dfrac{x^2 + 3x - 10}{2x^2 - 9x + 10}$	Put the function equal to 3.
$3(2x^2 - 9x + 10) = x^2 + 3x - 10$	Multiply by the denominator.
$6x^2 - 27x + 30 = x^2 + 3x - 10$ $5x^2 - 30x + 40 = 0$ $x^2 - 6x + 8 = 0$	Simplify.
$(x - 2)(x - 4) = 0$ $x = 2$ or 4	Factorise.
Not $x = 2$ because $f(x)$ is undefined for $x = 2$ in its original form, since both the numerator and denominator would equal zero, and division by zero is forbidden. $x = 4$, so $f^{-1}(3) = 4$	Explain why $x = 2$ would not be allowed.

Ready to progress?

I can find the output of a function given an input.

I can rearrange more complicated formulae where the subject may appear twice or as a power.

I can find an inverse function by rearranging.
I can find a composite function by combining two functions together.
I can combine and simplify algebraic fractions.
I can use iteration to find a solution to an equation to an appropriate degree of accuracy.

Review questions

1 $f(x) = 20 - 3x^2$. Find the value of $f(-2)$.

2 **a** Make x the subject of the formula $6x - K = a - Cx$.

   b Hence find the value of x when $a = 5$, $K = -12$ and $C = -8$.

3 **a** Write $f(x) = \dfrac{x}{x-3} - \dfrac{9}{x(x-3)}$ as a single fraction in its simplest form.

   b Hence find the inverse function $f^{-1}(x)$.

4 Simplify fully $\dfrac{21x^2 - 7x}{9x^2 - 1}$.

(EV) **5** The iterative formula $x_{n+1} = \sqrt[5]{6x_n^3 + 13}$ can be used to solve the equation $x^5 = 6x^3 + 13$.

   a Starting with $x_1 = 2.5$, find the first four iterations, all correct to 2 decimal places.

   b Find x_5 correct to 2 decimal places and compare it with x_4.

(CM) **6** $f(x) = 3x + 8$ $\qquad$ $g(x) = x^3 + 2$

   a Find a simplified expression for $fg(x)$.

   b Using the expression from part **a**, verify that $fg(3) = 95$.

7 Find the inverse of each function.

   a $f(x) = px - q$ $\qquad$ **b** $f(x) = a - x^3$ $\qquad$ **c** $f(x) = \dfrac{a}{x+c}$

(MR) **8** $f(x) = \left(\sqrt{2} + \sqrt{x}\right)^2$.

   a Find the value of:

   $\qquad$ **i** $f(0)$ $\qquad$ **ii** $ff(0)$ $\qquad$ **iii** $fff(0)$ $\qquad$ **iv** $ffff(0)$ $\qquad$ **v** $fffff(0)$.

   b Find the nth term of the sequence given by the answers to part **a**.

(CM) **9** Show, by iteration, that a solution of the equation $x^3 = 2x + 2$ is given by 1.77, correct to 2 decimal places.

10 **a** Simplify $f(x) = \dfrac{2x^2 + 3x - 14}{x^2 - 5x + 6}$.

   $g(x) = \dfrac{12 - x^2}{x}$

   b Solve $gf(x) = 1$.

(EV) **11** Alex was working out $f^{-1}(x)$ for the function $f(x) = \dfrac{4-x}{2-3x}$.

Find the mistakes in Alex's solution and write the correct solution.

$$y = \frac{4-x}{2-3x}$$

$$y(2-3x) = 4-x$$

$$2-3xy = 4-x$$

$$-3xy = 2-x$$

$$x - 3xy = 2$$

$$x(1-3y) = 2$$

$$x = \frac{1-3y}{2}$$

Hence $f^{-1}(x) = \dfrac{1-3x}{2}$.

(PS) **12** $x_{n+1} = \dfrac{2}{2-x_n}$

If $x_1 = 5$, find the value of each term.

  i x_{219} **ii** x_{238} **iii** x_{257} **iv** x_{276}

(PS) **13** Simplify fully $\dfrac{(x+2)(x+4)(x-6) - x^3}{7x^2 + 19x + 12}$.

(PS) **14** $f(x) = x^2 - 81$ $g(x) = 19 - x$

  a Solve $f(x) = g(x)$, giving both answers correct to 3 significant figures.

  b Solve $fg(x) \geqslant 0$.

  c Solve $gf(x) > 0$.

(PS) **15** A right-angled triangle has a base of $(x + 8)$ cm and a perpendicular height of $(x - 2)$ cm. The area of the triangle is 22 cm^2.

  a Show that $x^2 + 6x - 60 = 0$.

  The equation $x^2 + 6x - 60 = 0$ can be rewritten as the iterative formula
  $x_{n+1} = \sqrt{60 - 6x_n}$.

  b Find the value of x, correct to 3 significant figures.

(CM) **16** $f(x) = x^2 - 4x$ $g(x) = 2x + 3$

  a Find $fg(2)$.

  b Show that if $fg(x) = gf(x)$, then the answer can be written in the form $a \pm b\sqrt{3}$.

(PS) **17** Margaret has n beads in a bag, of which 5 are green. She removes two beads at random from the bag at the same time.

The probability that neither bead is green is $\frac{7}{22}$.

  a Show that $3n^2 - 47n + 132 = 0$.

  b How many beads were in the bag originally?

25 Geometry and measures: Vector geometry

This chapter is going to show you:

- how to add and subtract vectors
- the properties of vectors
- how to use vectors to solve geometrical problems
- how to prove geometric results.

You should already know:

- that vectors are used to describe translations.

About this chapter

When pilots are planning to land an aircraft, they must consider the speed and direction of the wind. In this situation, the wind may be represented as a vector. Vectors are an integral part of the computerised landing system.

Vectors are also used in the science of aerodynamics and, in particular, in the design of aircraft. They play a key role in the design of wings, where an upward force or lift is needed to enable the aircraft to fly.

Meteorologists or weather forecasters use vectors to map out weather patterns. They represent wind speeds by vectors of different lengths, to indicate the intensity of the wind.

Vectors are used extensively in computer graphics. Software designed to give the viewer the impression that an object or person is moving around a scene makes extensive use of the mathematics of vectors.

This chapter will give you a good understanding of how to use vectors in geometry.

25.1 Properties of vectors

This section will show you how to:

- add and subtract vectors.

A quantity that is completely described by its **magnitude**, and has no **direction** associated with it, is a **scalar**. The mass of a bus (10 tonnes) and the length of a line (25.4 mm) are scalars.

A **vector** is a quantity that has both magnitude and direction. It may be represented by a straight line, with an arrow to show its direction. The length of the line represents the magnitude of the vector.

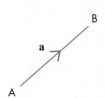

This vector **a** represents the translation or movement from A to B.

You used vectors in transformation geometry, where you described a translation in terms of horizontal and vertical shifts.

A translation was described as $\begin{pmatrix} x \\ y \end{pmatrix}$, where x is a movement parallel to the x-axis and y is a movement parallel to the y-axis. This means that $\begin{pmatrix} x \\ y \end{pmatrix}$ is a vector, since it has magnitude and direction.

The vector describing the translation from A to B is $\begin{pmatrix} 2 \\ 1 \end{pmatrix}$.

The vector describing the translation from B to C is $\begin{pmatrix} 2 \\ 0 \end{pmatrix}$.

The vector describing the translation from C to D is $\begin{pmatrix} -3 \\ 2 \end{pmatrix}$.

The vector describing the translation from D to A is $\begin{pmatrix} -1 \\ -3 \end{pmatrix}$.

You can express vectors in other ways.

- In textbooks, a vector may be shown as a small letter, such as **a**, printed in bold type. When you write the vector down, you underline it, like this: a̲.

- You may also write the vector **a** as $\overrightarrow{AB}$. The arrow above the letters shows the direction: here it is from A to B. The vector from B to A has the same magnitude but acts in the opposite direction, so you write it as $\overrightarrow{BA}$. The first letter is always the starting point and the second letter is the finishing point.

Multiplying a vector by a number (scalar) alters its magnitude (length) but not its direction. For example, the vector 2**a** is twice as long as the vector **a**, but acts in the same direction.

A negative vector, for example −**b**, has the same magnitude as the vector **b**, but acts in the opposite direction.

Addition and subtraction of vectors

Think about two non-parallel vectors, **a** and **b**.

Then **a** + **b** is the translation of **a** followed by the translation of **b**.

The vector **a** + **b** is the **resultant vector** as it is the result of adding them.

You can see this on a vector diagram.

Similarly, **a** – **b** is defined as the translation of **a** followed by the translation of **–b**.

This grid is made from congruent parallelograms.

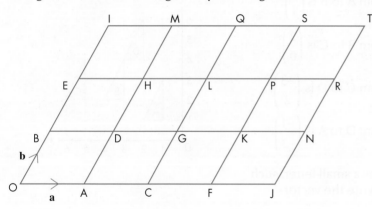

Each small parallelogram represents two independent vectors, **a** and **b**.

You can define the position of any point on this grid, with reference to O, as a vector expressed in terms of **a** and **b**. This is the **position vector** of the point, with respect to O.

- The position vector of K is $\overrightarrow{OK}$ or **k** = 3**a** + **b**.
- The position vector of E is $\overrightarrow{OE}$ or **e** = 2**b**.

You can also define the vector linking any two points, in terms of **a** and **b**.

$\overrightarrow{HT}$ = 3**a** + **b** $\overrightarrow{PN}$ = **a** – **b** $\overrightarrow{MK}$ = 2**a** – 2**b** $\overrightarrow{TP}$ = –**a** – **b**

Note:
- $\overrightarrow{OK}$ and $\overrightarrow{HT}$ are equal vectors because they have exactly the same length and act in the same direction
- $\overrightarrow{MK}$ and $\overrightarrow{PN}$ are parallel vectors but $\overrightarrow{MK}$ has twice the magnitude of $\overrightarrow{PN}$.

Example 1

a Refer to the grid on the previous page. Write down each of these vector in terms of **a** and **b**.

  i $\overrightarrow{BH}$ **ii** $\overrightarrow{HP}$ **iii** $\overrightarrow{GT}$

  iv $\overrightarrow{TI}$ **v** $\overrightarrow{FH}$ **vi** $\overrightarrow{BQ}$

b What is the relationship between the vectors in each pair?

  i $\overrightarrow{BH}$ and $\overrightarrow{GT}$ **ii** $\overrightarrow{BQ}$ and $\overrightarrow{GT}$ **iii** $\overrightarrow{HP}$ and $\overrightarrow{TI}$

c Show that B, H and Q lie on the same straight line.

a i $\mathbf{a} + \mathbf{b}$ **ii** $2\mathbf{a}$ **iii** $2\mathbf{a} + 2\mathbf{b}$

  iv $-4\mathbf{a}$ **v** $-2\mathbf{a} + 2\mathbf{b}$ **vi** $2\mathbf{a} + 2\mathbf{b}$

b i $\overrightarrow{BH}$ and $\overrightarrow{GT}$ are parallel and $\overrightarrow{GT}$ has twice the magnitude of $\overrightarrow{BH}$ because it is twice its length.

  ii $\overrightarrow{BQ}$ and $\overrightarrow{GT}$ are equal.

  iii $\overrightarrow{HP}$ and $\overrightarrow{TI}$ act in opposite directions and $\overrightarrow{TI}$ has twice the magnitude of $\overrightarrow{HP}$ because it is twice its length.

c $\overrightarrow{BH}$ and $\overrightarrow{BQ}$ are parallel and start at the same point B. Therefore, B, H and Q must lie on the same straight line.

Example 2

Tebor sees a pine tree, directly opposite him, across a river. He decides to swim across to pick up some cones. He swims with a velocity of 2 m/s, at right angles to the bank. The current of the river has a velocity of 4 m/s. The river is 40 metres wide.

a At what velocity will Tebor actually be travelling?

b How far along the bank from the tree will Tebor be when he reaches the other side?

As Tebor swims 2 m across the river, he is moved 4 m down the river by the current.

You can use a vector diagram to represent the velocity of Tebor swimming and the velocity of the current.

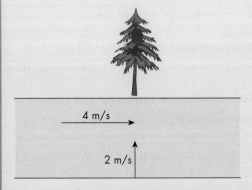
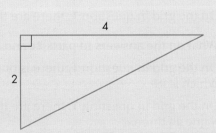

You can then add the two vectors to give the resultant velocity.

This force is represented by the hypotenuse in the right-angled triangle.

a Use Pythagoras' theorem to find the resultant.

  (Length of the hypotenuse)$^2 = 2^2 + 4^2$
  $$= 20$$

  Length of the hypotenuse $= \sqrt{20}$

  So Tebor's resultant velocity is 4.47 m/s.

(continued)

b Use similar triangles to find x, the distance travelled downstream.

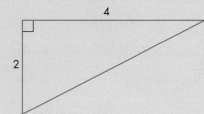 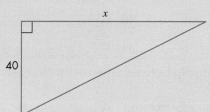

$$\frac{x}{4} = \frac{40}{2}$$

$$x = \frac{40 \times 4}{2}$$

$$= 80 \text{ m}$$

Tebor reaches the bank 80 m downstream from the tree.

Exercise 25A

1 On this grid, $\overrightarrow{OA}$ is **a** and $\overrightarrow{OB}$ is **b**.

  a Name three other vectors that are equivalent to **a**.

  b Name three other vectors that are equivalent to **b**.

  c Name three vectors that are equivalent to –**a**.

  d Name three vectors that are equivalent to –**b**.

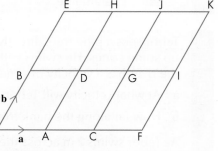

2 Look again at the grid in question **1**. Write each of these vectors in terms of **a** and **b**.

  a $\overrightarrow{OC}$ **b** $\overrightarrow{OE}$ **c** $\overrightarrow{OD}$ **d** $\overrightarrow{OG}$ **e** $\overrightarrow{OJ}$ **f** $\overrightarrow{OH}$

  g $\overrightarrow{AG}$ **h** $\overrightarrow{AK}$ **i** $\overrightarrow{BK}$ **j** $\overrightarrow{DI}$ **k** $\overrightarrow{GJ}$ **l** $\overrightarrow{DK}$

(MR) 3 **a** What do the answers to parts **2c** and **2g** tell you about the vectors $\overrightarrow{OD}$ and $\overrightarrow{AG}$?

  b On the grid in question **1**, there are three vectors equivalent to $\overrightarrow{OG}$. Name all three.

(MR) 4 **a** What do the answers to parts **2c** and **2e** tell you about vectors $\overrightarrow{OD}$ and $\overrightarrow{OJ}$?

  b On the grid in question **1**, there is one other vector that is twice the size of $\overrightarrow{OD}$. Which is it?

  c On the grid in question **1**, there are three vectors that are three times the size of $\overrightarrow{OA}$. Name all three.

5 Copy this grid. Use the information below to mark the points C to P on your grid.

  a $\overrightarrow{OC} = 2\mathbf{a} + 3\mathbf{b}$ **b** $\overrightarrow{OD} = 2\mathbf{a} + \mathbf{b}$

  c $\overrightarrow{OE} = \mathbf{a} + 2\mathbf{b}$ **d** $\overrightarrow{OF} = 3\mathbf{b}$

  e $\overrightarrow{OG} = 4\mathbf{a}$ **f** $\overrightarrow{OH} = 4\mathbf{a} + 2\mathbf{b}$

  g $\overrightarrow{OI} = 3\mathbf{a} + 3\mathbf{b}$ **h** $\overrightarrow{OJ} = \mathbf{a} + \mathbf{b}$

  i $\overrightarrow{OK} = 2\mathbf{a} + 2\mathbf{b}$ **j** $\overrightarrow{OM} = 2\mathbf{a} + \frac{3}{2}\mathbf{b}$

  k $\overrightarrow{ON} = \frac{1}{2}\mathbf{a} + 2\mathbf{b}$ **l** $\overrightarrow{OP} = \frac{5}{2}\mathbf{a} + \frac{3}{2}\mathbf{b}$

(CM) 6　**a** Look at the grid you completed in question **5**. What can you say about the points O, J, K and I?

b How could you tell this by looking at the vectors for parts **5g, 5h** and **5i**?

c There is another point on the same straight line as O and D. Which is it?

7　On this grid, $\vec{OA}$ is **a** and $\vec{OB}$ is **b**.

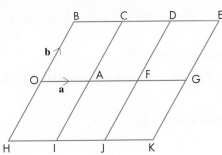

Write each of these vectors in terms of **a** and **b**.

a $\vec{OH}$　　　　**b** $\vec{OK}$　　　　**c** $\vec{OJ}$　　　　**d** $\vec{OI}$
e $\vec{OC}$　　　　**f** $\vec{CO}$　　　　**g** $\vec{AK}$　　　　**h** $\vec{DI}$
i $\vec{JE}$　　　　**j** $\vec{AB}$　　　　**k** $\vec{CK}$　　　　**l** $\vec{DK}$

(CM) 8　**a** What do your answers to parts **7e** and **7f** tell you about the vectors $\vec{OC}$ and $\vec{CO}$?

b On the grid in question **7**, there are five other vectors that are opposite to $\vec{OC}$. Name at least three.

(CM) 9　**a** What do your answers to parts **7j** and **7k** tell you about vectors $\vec{AB}$ and $\vec{CK}$?

b On the grid in question **7**, there are two vectors that are twice the size of $\vec{AB}$ and act in the opposite direction. Name both of them.

c On the grid in question **7**, there are three vectors that are three times the size of $\vec{OA}$ and act in the opposite direction. Name all three.

(PS) 10　An aircraft is flying at 500 mph through a wind of 80 mph blowing from the west. It is being steered due north. What is the actual bearing and speed of travel of the aircraft?

(PS) 11　A boat attempts to sail due east at 15 km/h, but is taken off course by a current of 5 km/h flowing in the south-west direction. Find the resultant speed of the boat and the bearing on which it sails.

(PS) 12　The diagram shows two sets of parallel lines.
$\vec{OA} = \mathbf{a}$ and $\vec{OB} = \mathbf{b}$
$\vec{OC} = 3\vec{OA}$ and $\vec{OD} = 2\vec{OB}$

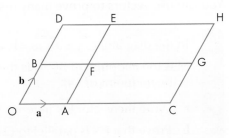

a Write each of these vectors in terms of **a** and **b**.
　i $\vec{OF}$　　　**ii** $\vec{OG}$
　iii $\vec{EG}$　　**iv** $\vec{CE}$

b Write down two vectors that can be written as $3\mathbf{a} - \mathbf{b}$.

(EV) **13** The points P, Q and R lie on a straight line. The vector $\overrightarrow{PQ}$ is $2\mathbf{a} + \mathbf{b}$, where $\mathbf{a}$ and $\mathbf{b}$ are vectors.

Work out which of these vectors could be the vector $\overrightarrow{PR}$ and which could not be the vector $\overrightarrow{PR}$. There are two of each.

a $2\mathbf{a} + 2\mathbf{b}$ **b** $4\mathbf{a} + 2\mathbf{b}$ **c** $2\mathbf{a} - \mathbf{b}$ **d** $-6\mathbf{a} - 3\mathbf{b}$

(EV) **14** The points P, Q and R lie on a straight line. The vector $\overrightarrow{PQ}$ is $3\mathbf{a} - \mathbf{b}$, where $\mathbf{a}$ and $\mathbf{b}$ are vectors.

a Write down any other vector that could represent $\overrightarrow{PR}$.

b How can you tell from another vector $\overrightarrow{PS}$ that S lies on the same straight line as P, Q and R?

(CM) **15** Use a vector diagram to prove that $\mathbf{a} + (\mathbf{b} + \mathbf{c}) = (\mathbf{a} + \mathbf{b}) + \mathbf{c}$.

(CM) **16** OABC is a quadrilateral.

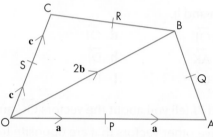

P, Q, R and S are the midpoints of OA, AB, BC and OC respectively.

$\overrightarrow{OA} = 2\mathbf{a}$, $\overrightarrow{OB} = 2\mathbf{b}$ and $\overrightarrow{OC} = 2\mathbf{c}$

a Work out these vectors in terms of $\mathbf{a}$, $\mathbf{b}$ and $\mathbf{c}$.

Give your answers in their simplest form.

  i $\overrightarrow{AB}$ **ii** $\overrightarrow{SP}$ **iii** $\overrightarrow{BC}$ **iv** $\overrightarrow{PR}$

b Use vectors to prove that PQRS is a parallelogram.

25.2 Vectors in geometry

This section will show you how to:

- use vectors to solve geometrical problems.

You can use vectors to prove many results in geometry. The next two examples will show you how.

Example 3

In the diagram, $\overrightarrow{OA} = \mathbf{a}$, $\overrightarrow{OB} = \mathbf{b}$, and $\overrightarrow{BC} = \frac{3}{2}\mathbf{a}$.

M is the midpoint of BC, N is the midpoint of AC and P is the midpoint of OB.

a Write the vector $\overrightarrow{BN}$ in terms of $\mathbf{a}$ and $\mathbf{b}$.

b Prove that PN is parallel to OA.

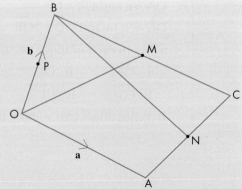

---

a $\overrightarrow{BN} = \overrightarrow{BC} + \overrightarrow{CN}$

$= \overrightarrow{BC} - \frac{1}{2}\overrightarrow{AC}$

$= \frac{3}{2}\mathbf{a} - \frac{1}{2}(-2\mathbf{a} + 2\mathbf{b} + \frac{3}{2}\mathbf{a})$

$= \frac{3}{2}\mathbf{a} - \frac{1}{4}\mathbf{a} - \frac{1}{2}\mathbf{b}$

$= \frac{5}{4}\mathbf{a} - \frac{1}{2}\mathbf{b}$

Check that if you started with
$\overrightarrow{BN} = \overrightarrow{BO} + \overrightarrow{OA} + \overrightarrow{AN}$,
you would get the same result.

b $\overrightarrow{AN} = \frac{1}{2}\overrightarrow{AC} = \frac{1}{2}(-\mathbf{a} + \mathbf{b} + \frac{3}{2}\mathbf{a}) = \frac{1}{2}(\frac{1}{2}\mathbf{a} + \mathbf{b})$

$\overrightarrow{PN} = \overrightarrow{PO} + \overrightarrow{OA} + \overrightarrow{AN}$

$= \frac{1}{2}(-\mathbf{b}) + \mathbf{a} + \frac{1}{2}(\frac{1}{2}\mathbf{a} + \mathbf{b})$

$= -\frac{1}{2}\mathbf{b} + \mathbf{a} + \frac{1}{4}\mathbf{a} + \frac{1}{2}\mathbf{b}$

$= \frac{5}{4}\mathbf{a}$

$\overrightarrow{PN}$ is a multiple of **a** only, so must be parallel to $\overrightarrow{OA}$.

Note: If three or more points lie on the same line, they are said to be **collinear**.

Example 4

OACB is a parallelogram.

$\overrightarrow{OA}$ is represented by the vector **a**.

$\overrightarrow{OB}$ is represented by the vector **b**.

P is the point that divides OC in the ratio 2 : 1.
M is the midpoint of AC.

Show that B, P and M are collinear.

$\overrightarrow{OC} = \overrightarrow{OA} + \overrightarrow{AC}$

$= \mathbf{a} + \mathbf{b}$

Since P divides OC in the ratio 2:1, then $\overrightarrow{OP} = \frac{2}{3}\overrightarrow{OC}$

$= \frac{2}{3}\mathbf{a} + \frac{2}{3}\mathbf{b}$

$\overrightarrow{OM} = \overrightarrow{OA} + \overrightarrow{AM}$

$= \overrightarrow{OA} + \frac{1}{2}\overrightarrow{AC}$

$= \mathbf{a} + \frac{1}{2}\mathbf{b}$

$\overrightarrow{BP} = \overrightarrow{BO} + \overrightarrow{OP}$

$= -\mathbf{b} + \frac{2}{3}\mathbf{a} + \frac{2}{3}\mathbf{b}$

$= \frac{2}{3}\mathbf{a} - \frac{1}{3}\mathbf{b}$

$= \frac{1}{3}(2\mathbf{a} - \mathbf{b})$

$\overrightarrow{BM} = \overrightarrow{BO} + \overrightarrow{OM}$

$= -\mathbf{b} + \mathbf{a} + \frac{1}{2}\mathbf{b}$

$= \mathbf{a} - \frac{1}{2}\mathbf{b}$

$= \frac{1}{2}(2\mathbf{a} - \mathbf{b})$

Therefore, $\overrightarrow{BM}$ is a multiple of $\overrightarrow{BP}$ ($\overrightarrow{BM} = \frac{3}{2}\overrightarrow{BP}$).

Therefore, $\overrightarrow{BP}$ and $\overrightarrow{BM}$ are parallel and, as they have a common point, B, they must lie on the same straight line.

Exercise 25B

1 In the diagram, $\overrightarrow{OA}$ = **a** and $\overrightarrow{OB}$ = **b**.

M is the midpoint of AB.

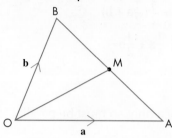

a i Work out the vector $\overrightarrow{AB}$.

  ii Work out the vector $\overrightarrow{AM}$.

  iii Explain why $\overrightarrow{OM}$ = $\overrightarrow{OA}$ + $\overrightarrow{AM}$.

  iv Use your answers to parts **ii** and **iii** to work out $\overrightarrow{OM}$ in terms of **a** and **b**.

b i Work out the vector $\overrightarrow{BA}$.

  ii Work out the vector $\overrightarrow{BM}$.

  iii Explain why $\overrightarrow{OM}$ = $\overrightarrow{OB}$ + $\overrightarrow{BM}$.

  iv Use your answers to parts **ii** and **iii** to work out $\overrightarrow{OM}$ in terms of **a** and **b**.

c Copy the diagram. Show the vector $\overrightarrow{OC}$ which is equal to **a** + **b**.

d Describe in geometrical terms the position of M in relation to O, A, B and C.

2 In the diagram, $\overrightarrow{OA}$ = **a** and $\overrightarrow{OC}$ = –**b**.

N is the midpoint of AC.

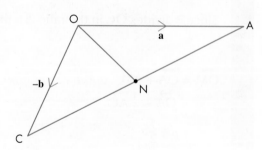

a i Work out the vector $\overrightarrow{AC}$.

  ii Work out the vector $\overrightarrow{AN}$.

  iii Explain why $\overrightarrow{ON}$ = $\overrightarrow{OA}$ + $\overrightarrow{AN}$.

  iv Using your answers to parts **ii** and **iii**, work out $\overrightarrow{ON}$ in terms of **a** and **b**.

b i Work out the vector $\overrightarrow{CA}$.

  ii Work out the vector $\overrightarrow{CN}$.

  iii Explain why $\overrightarrow{ON}$ = $\overrightarrow{OC}$ + $\overrightarrow{CN}$.

  iv Using your answers to parts **ii** and **iii**, work out $\overrightarrow{ON}$ in terms of **a** and **b**.

c Copy the diagram above and show on it the vector $\overrightarrow{OD}$ which is equal to **a** – **b**.

d Describe in geometrical terms the position of N in relation to O, A, C and D.

3 In the diagram, $\overrightarrow{OA} = \mathbf{a}$ and $\overrightarrow{OB} = \mathbf{b}$. The point C divides the line AB in the ratio 1 : 2.

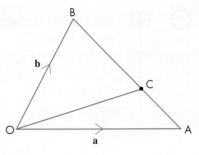

  a i Work out the vector $\overrightarrow{AB}$.
   ii Work out the vector $\overrightarrow{AC}$.
   iii Work out the vector $\overrightarrow{OC}$ in terms of **a** and **b**.

  b If point D now divides the line AB in the ratio 1 : 3, write down the vector that represents $\overrightarrow{OD}$.

4 The diagram shows the vectors $\overrightarrow{OA} = \mathbf{a}$ and $\overrightarrow{OB} = \mathbf{b}$.

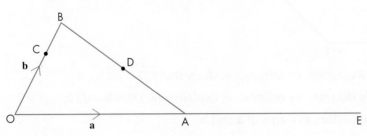

The point C divides OB in the ratio 2 : 1. The point E is such that $\overrightarrow{OE} = 2\overrightarrow{OA}$. D is the midpoint of AB.

  a Write down (or work out) these vectors in terms of **a** and **b**.
   i $\overrightarrow{OC}$ **ii** $\overrightarrow{OD}$ **iii** $\overrightarrow{CO}$

  b You can write vector $\overrightarrow{CD}$ as $\overrightarrow{CD} = \overrightarrow{CO} + \overrightarrow{OD}$. Use this fact to work out $\overrightarrow{CD}$ in terms of **a** and **b**.

  c Write down a similar rule to that in part **b** for the vector $\overrightarrow{DE}$. Use this rule to work out $\overrightarrow{DE}$ in terms of **a** and **b**.

  d Show how you know that C, D and E lie on the same straight line.

5 ABCDEF is a regular hexagon. $\overrightarrow{AB}$ is represented by the vector **a** and $\overrightarrow{BC}$ by the vector **b**.

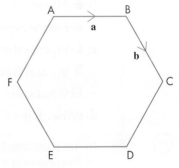

  a By means of a diagram, or otherwise, show that $\overrightarrow{CD} = \mathbf{b} - \mathbf{a}$.

  b Express these vectors in terms of **a** and **b**.
   i $\overrightarrow{DE}$ **ii** $\overrightarrow{EF}$ **iii** $\overrightarrow{FA}$

  c Work out the resultant vector of adding:
   $\overrightarrow{AB} + \overrightarrow{BC} + \overrightarrow{CD} + \overrightarrow{DE} + \overrightarrow{EF} + \overrightarrow{FA}$
   Explain your answer.

  d Express these vectors in terms of **a** and **b**.
   i $\overrightarrow{AD}$ **ii** $\overrightarrow{BE}$ **iii** $\overrightarrow{CF}$ **iv** $\overrightarrow{AE}$ **v** $\overrightarrow{DF}$

6 ABCDEFGH is a regular octagon. $\overrightarrow{AB}$ is represented by the vector **a** and $\overrightarrow{BC}$ by the vector **b**.

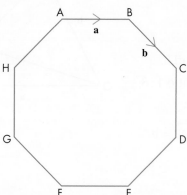

a By means of a diagram, or otherwise, show that $\overrightarrow{CD} = \sqrt{2}\,\mathbf{b} - \mathbf{a}$.

b By means of a diagram, or otherwise, explain why $\overrightarrow{DE} = \mathbf{b} - \sqrt{2}\,\mathbf{a}$.

c Express these vectors in terms of **a** and **b**.

   i $\overrightarrow{EF}$ **ii** $\overrightarrow{FG}$ **iii** $\overrightarrow{GH}$ **iv** $\overrightarrow{HA}$

   v $\overrightarrow{HC}$ **vi** $\overrightarrow{AD}$ **vii** $\overrightarrow{BE}$ **viii** $\overrightarrow{BF}$

7 In the quadrilateral OABC, M, N, P and Q are the midpoints of the sides as shown. $\overrightarrow{OA}$ is represented by the vector **a** and $\overrightarrow{OC}$ by the vector **c**. The diagonal $\overrightarrow{OB}$ is represented by the vector **b**.

a Express these vectors in terms of **a**, **b** and **c**.

   i $\overrightarrow{AB}$ **ii** $\overrightarrow{AP}$ **iii** $\overrightarrow{OP}$

   Give your answers as simply as possible.

b i Express the vector $\overrightarrow{ON}$ in terms of **b** and **c**.

   ii Hence express the vector $\overrightarrow{PN}$ in terms of **a** and **c**.

c i Express the vector $\overrightarrow{QM}$ in terms of **a** and **c**.

   ii What relationship is there between $\overrightarrow{PN}$ and $\overrightarrow{QM}$?

   iii What sort of quadrilateral is PNMQ?

d Prove that $\overrightarrow{AC} = 2\,\overrightarrow{QM}$.

8 In the diagram, L, M, N, P, Q, R are the midpoints of the line segments OA, OB, OC, BC, AC and AB, as shown.

$\overrightarrow{OA} = \mathbf{a}$, $\overrightarrow{OB} = \mathbf{b}$ and $\overrightarrow{OC} = \mathbf{c}$

a Express these vectors in terms of **a** and **c**.

   i $\overrightarrow{OL}$ **ii** $\overrightarrow{AC}$ **iii** $\overrightarrow{OQ}$ **iv** $\overrightarrow{LQ}$

b Express these vectors in terms of **a** and **b**.

   i $\overrightarrow{LM}$ **ii** $\overrightarrow{QP}$

c Prove that the quadrilateral LMPQ is a parallelogram.

d Find two other sets of four points that form parallelograms.

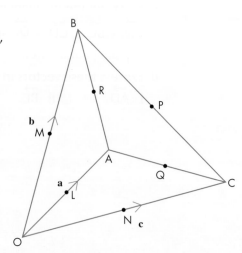

9 In the triangle OAB, M is the midpoint of AB.

$\vec{OA} = \mathbf{a}$ and $\vec{OB} = \mathbf{b}$

a Write $\vec{AM}$ in terms of **a** and **b**.

Give your answer in its simplest form.

b $\vec{OC} = \mathbf{a} + \mathbf{b}$

The length of OA is equal to the length of OB.

i Write down the name of the shape OACB.

ii Write down one fact about the points O, M and C.

Give a reason for your answer.

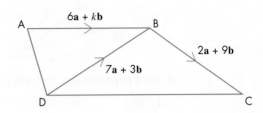

10 ABCD is a trapezium with AB parallel to DC.

$\vec{AB} = 6\mathbf{a} + k\mathbf{b}$, $\vec{BC} = 2\mathbf{a} + 9\mathbf{b}$ and $\vec{DB} = 7\mathbf{a} + 3\mathbf{b}$, where k is a number.

Work out the value of k.

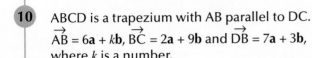

11 **a** and **b** are vectors.

$\vec{XY} = \mathbf{a} + \mathbf{b}$ $\vec{YZ} = 2\mathbf{a} + \mathbf{b}$ $\vec{ZW} = \mathbf{a} + 2\mathbf{b}$

a Show that $\vec{YW}$ is parallel to $\vec{XY}$.

b Write down the ratio YW : XY.

c What do your answers to **a** and **b** tell you about the points X, Y and W?

d O is the origin.

A, B and C are three points such that:

$$\vec{OA} = \begin{pmatrix} 6 \\ 2 \end{pmatrix} \qquad \vec{OB} = \begin{pmatrix} 1 \\ 1 \end{pmatrix} \qquad \vec{OC} = \begin{pmatrix} 2 \\ -4 \end{pmatrix}$$

Prove that angle ABC is a right angle.

12 Show, by using vectors that the diagonals of a parallelogram bisect each other.

Worked exemplars

1 The diagram shows triangle OAB. M is the midpoint of OA. P lies on BM and $BP = \frac{2}{3}BM$.
$\overrightarrow{OA} = 2\mathbf{a}$ and $\overrightarrow{OB} = 2\mathbf{b}$

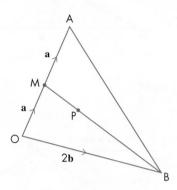

a Find expressions, in terms of **a** and **b**, for:

  i $\overrightarrow{BM}$ **ii** $\overrightarrow{OP}$.

  Write each answer in its simplest form.

b N is the midpoint of OB. Q lies on AN and $AQ = \frac{2}{3}AN$.

  i Find an expression for $\overrightarrow{OQ}$, in terms of **a** and **b**. Write your answer in its simplest form.

  ii What do your answers for $\overrightarrow{OP}$ and $\overrightarrow{OQ}$ tell you about the points P and Q?

This is an 'evaluating' question, so you need to interpret results in the context of the given problem.

1 a i $\overrightarrow{BM} = \mathbf{a} - 2\mathbf{b}$ **ii** $\overrightarrow{OP} = \overrightarrow{OB} + \frac{2}{3}\overrightarrow{BM}$ $= 2\mathbf{b} + \frac{2}{3}\mathbf{a} - \frac{4}{3}\mathbf{b}$ $= \frac{2}{3}\mathbf{a} + \frac{2}{3}\mathbf{b}$ **b i** $\overrightarrow{OQ} = \overrightarrow{OA} + \overrightarrow{AQ}$ $= \overrightarrow{OA} + \frac{2}{3}\overrightarrow{AN}$ But $\overrightarrow{AN} = \mathbf{b} - 2\mathbf{a}$ So $\overrightarrow{OQ} = 2\mathbf{a} + \frac{2}{3}(\mathbf{b} - 2\mathbf{a})$ $= 2\mathbf{a} + \frac{2}{3}\mathbf{b} - \frac{4}{3}\mathbf{a}$ $= \frac{2}{3}\mathbf{a} + \frac{2}{3}\mathbf{b}$ **ii** $\overrightarrow{OP} = \overrightarrow{OQ}$, so P and Q are the same point as both vectors share the same origin point O.	You are working towards finding a link between P and Q by being directed to finding $\overrightarrow{OP}$ and $\overrightarrow{OQ}$. Once you have found both $\overrightarrow{OP}$ and $\overrightarrow{OQ}$ in terms of **a** and **b**, then you are able to see what connection there is. Having found that $\overrightarrow{OP}$ and $\overrightarrow{OQ}$ are identical and both start from O, you can explain that this can only be true if points P and Q are the same. Alternatively you could point out that the position vectors of P and Q relative to O are the same and hence the same point.

(CM) (2) OABC is a parallelogram.

M is the midpoint of the diagonal OB.

$\overrightarrow{OA}$ = 2**a** and $\overrightarrow{OC}$ = 2**c**

a Express $\overrightarrow{OM}$ in terms of **a** and **c**.

b Use vectors to prove that M is also the midpoint of the diagonal AC.

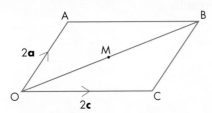

This is a communicating mathematics question where you are asked to present a proof of M being the midpoint of the other diagonal.	

a $\overrightarrow{OB}$ = 2**a** + 2**c** and $\overrightarrow{OM}$ = $\frac{1}{2}$ $\overrightarrow{OB}$
 	
so $\overrightarrow{OM}$ = **a** + **c**
b $\overrightarrow{AC}$ = 2**c** – 2**a**
 	
$\overrightarrow{AM}$ = $\overrightarrow{AO}$ + $\overrightarrow{OM}$
 	
    = –2**a** + **a** + **c**
 	
    = **c** – **a**
 	
So $\overrightarrow{AM}$ = $\frac{1}{2}$ $\overrightarrow{AC}$.
 	
Hence M is the midpoint of AC.
	You need to use vectors to demonstrate that AM is half of AC, this will show M is the midpoint of AC.
	
	You need to show clearly each stage of your working.

Ready to progress?

I can add and subtract vectors.
I know how to apply vector methods to solve geometrical problems.

I know how to use vectors to prove geometrical results.

Review questions

1 PQRS is a parallelogram.

M is the midpoint of QR.

N is a point on PS such that NS = 3PN

$\overrightarrow{PQ} = a$ $\overrightarrow{QM} = 2b$

Express these vectors as simply as possible,
in terms of **a** and **b**.

a $\overrightarrow{MS}$ **b** $\overrightarrow{SN}$ **c** $\overrightarrow{NM}$

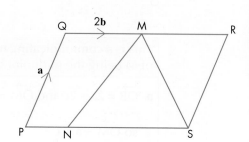

(EV) 2 OABC is a quadrilateral.

W, X, Y and Z are the midpoints of BC, OC, OA and AB.

$\overrightarrow{OX} = x$, $\overrightarrow{OY} = y$ and $\overrightarrow{OB} = 2b$.

a Write these vectors in terms of **b**, **x** and **y**.

  i $\overrightarrow{BA}$ **ii** $\overrightarrow{CB}$

b Show that $\overrightarrow{WZ} = y - x$

c Tim said: 'WXYZ is a parallelogram.' Evaluate
Tim's statement.

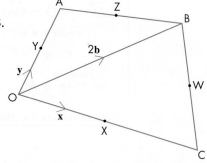

(CM) 3 ODEF is a parallelogram.

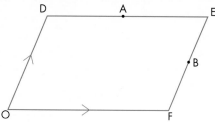

A is the midpoint of DE.

B is the midpoint of EF.

Show that AB is parallel to DF.

(CM) 4 OPQR is a parallelogram. Let $\overrightarrow{OP} = p$ and $\overrightarrow{OR} = r$.

a Express these vectors in terms of **p** and **r**.

  i $\overrightarrow{OQ}$ **ii** $\overrightarrow{PR}$

The point X is the midpoint of PR.

b Express $\overrightarrow{PX}$ in terms of **p** and **r**.

c Show that X is the midpoint of OQ.

5 In the triangle ABC, D is the midpoint of BC, E is the midpoint of AC and F is the midpoint of AB. G is a point on AD such that $AG = \frac{2}{3}AD$.

$\overrightarrow{AB} = \mathbf{x}$ $\overrightarrow{AC} = \mathbf{y}$

a Express each vector in terms of **x** and **y**.

    i $\overrightarrow{BC}$ **ii** $\overrightarrow{BD}$ **iii** $\overrightarrow{AD}$ **iv** $\overrightarrow{AG}$

    v $\overrightarrow{DG}$ **vi** $\overrightarrow{BG}$ **vii** $\overrightarrow{BE}$

b Show that B, G and E are collinear.

c Show that $\overrightarrow{BG} = \frac{2}{3}\overrightarrow{BE}$.

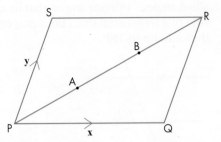

6 PQRS is a parallelogram. A and B are points on PR such that PA = AB = BR.

a State each of these vectors, in terms of **x** and **y**.

    i $\overrightarrow{PR}$ **ii** $\overrightarrow{PA}$ **iii** $\overrightarrow{PB}$

    iv $\overrightarrow{SA}$ **v** $\overrightarrow{BQ}$

b Show that SAQB is a parallelogram.

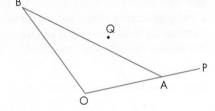

7 In the diagram, $\overrightarrow{OA} = 4\mathbf{a}$, $\overrightarrow{OB} = 2\mathbf{b}$, $\overrightarrow{AP} = 2\mathbf{a}$, $\overrightarrow{OQ} = 3\mathbf{a} + \mathbf{b}$.

a State each of these vectors, in terms of **a** and **b**.

    i $\overrightarrow{BP}$ **ii** $\overrightarrow{BQ}$

b Show that B, Q and P are collinear.

8 Prove that the line joining the midpoints of two sides of a triangle is parallel to the base and half its length.

9 OMNPQR is a regular hexagon.

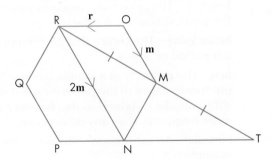

RM = MT

$\overrightarrow{OR} = \mathbf{r}$ $\overrightarrow{OM} = \mathbf{m}$ $\overrightarrow{RN} = 2\mathbf{m}$

a Work out the vector $\overrightarrow{RM}$ in terms of **r** and **m**.

b Prove that NT is parallel to OR.

Glossary

acceleration   The rate at which the velocity of a moving object increases.

acute-angled triangle   A triangle in which all the angles are acute.

adjacent side   The side that is between a given angle and the right angle, in a right-angled triangle.

algebraic fraction   A fraction that includes algebraic terms.

allied angles   Interior angles that lie on the same side of a transversal that cuts a pair of parallel lines; they add up to 180°.

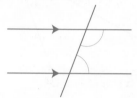

alternate angles   Angles that lie on either side of a transversal that cuts a pair of parallel lines; the transversal forms two pairs of alternate angles and the angles in each pair are equal.

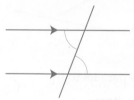

alternate segment   The segment in a circle that is based on the chord forming one side of an angle formed with a tangent at the point of contact, and is on the opposite side from the angle.

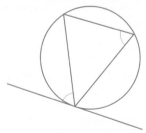

angle bisector   A line or line segment that divides an angle into two equal parts.

angle of depression   The angle between the horizontal line of sight of an observer and the direct line to an object that is viewed from above.

angle of elevation   The angle between the horizontal line of sight of an observer and the direct line to an object that is viewed from below.

angle of rotation   The angle through which an object is rotated, to form the image.

angles around a point   The angles formed at a point where two or more lines meet; their sum is 360°.

angles on a straight line   The angles formed at a point where one or more inclined (sloping) lines meet on one side of a straight line; their sum is 180°.

annual rate   A rate, such as interest, that is charged over a period of a year.

apex   The top point of a pyramid where all the edges of the sloping sides meet.

approximate   A value that is close but not exactly equal to another value, which can be used to give an idea of the size of the value; for example, a journey taking 58 minutes may be described as 'taking approximately an hour'; the ≈ sign means 'is approximately equal to'.

arc   Part of the circumference of a circle.

area rule   The rule for the area of triangle $A = \frac{1}{2} \times a \times b \times \sin C$, where a and b are two sides of the triangle and C is the included angle.

area scale factor   The ratio of the area of one shape to the area of another that is mathematically similar to it.

arithmetic sequence   A sequence of numbers in which the difference between one term and the next is constant.

asymptote   A line that a curve approaches but never quite meets.

average speed   The result of dividing the total distance travelled by the total time taken for a journey.

best buy   The price that gives best value for money, the greatest quantity for the least price.

better value   The choice that gives more product per pound or penny.

bias   The property of a sample being unrepresentative of the population; for example, a dice may be weighted so that it gives a score of 5 more frequently than any other score.

binomial   An expression with two terms; for example $(x + 3)$.

bisect   Cut exactly in half.

boundary   The line for an inequality shown on a graph, when the inequality symbol is replaced with =.

box plot   A diagram that shows the median, the quartiles and the range of a data set.

box-and-whisker plot   Another name for a *box plot*.

centre of enlargement   The point, inside or outside the object, on which an enlargement is centred; the point from which the enlargement of an object is measured.

centre of rotation   The point about which an object or shape is rotated.

circumference   The perimeter of a circle; every point on the circumference is the same distance from the centre, and this distance is the radius.

class interval   The range of a group of values in a set of grouped data.

coefficient   A number written in front of a variable in an algebraic term; for example, in $8x$, 8 is the coefficient of x.

collinear   Lying on the same straight line.

column method (or traditional method)   A method for multiplying large numbers, in which you multiply the units, tens and hundreds separately, then add the products together.

combination   A way of selecting members from a group, when the order of selection does not matter. For example, given three letters ABC, there are three ways of choosing two letters: AB, AC and BC. The mathematical formula for a combination of r items from a group of n is $\frac{n!}{r!(n-r)!}$, which may be written as $_nC_r$. See also 'permutations'.

combined event   Two or more events that occur together.

common factor   A factor that divides exactly into two or more numbers; 2 is a common factor of 6, 8 and 10.

common units   To enable you to compare quantities or simplify ratios, they must be expressed in the same or common units; for example, 2 m : 10 cm = 200 cm : 10 cm = 20 : 1.

complementary   Forming a whole, for example, the probability of an outcome happening and the probability of the same outcome not happening are complementary, their sum is 1.

completing the square   Rewriting the expression $x^2 - 2ax$ as $(x - a)^2 - a^2$.

composite   A function that is made from two or more separate functions.

compound interest   Interest that is paid on the amount in the account; after the first year interest is paid on interest earned in the previous years.

compound measure   A measure based on two units, such as kilometres per hour (speed) or mass per cubic centimetre (density).

conditional probability   The probability of one outcome occurring when it is known that another outcome has happened. For example, the probability of the colour of a second ball drawn from a bag is conditional on the colour of the first ball drawn from the bag – if the first ball is not replaced.

congruent   Exactly the same shape and size.

constant of proportionality   If two variables x and y are in direct proportion, you can write an equation, $y = kx$; if they are in inverse proportion, you can write $xy = k$. In either case, k is the constant of proportionality.

constant term   A term that has a fixed value; in the equation $y = 3x + 6$, the values of x and y may change, but 6 is a constant term.

continuous data   Data, such as mass, length or height, that can take any value; continuous data has no precise fixed value.

conversion graph   A graph that can be used to convert from one unit to another, constructed by drawing a line through two or more points where the equivalence is known; sometimes, but not always, a conversion graph passes through the origin.

corresponding angles   Angles that lie on the same side of a pair of parallel lines cut by a transversal; the transversal forms four pairs of corresponding angles, and the angles in each pair are equal.

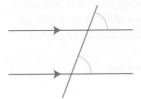

cosine   A trigonometric ratio related to an angle in a right-angled triangle, calculated as $\frac{\text{adjacent}}{\text{hypotenuse}}$.

cosine rule   A rule relating the cosine of one angle in a triangle to the lengths of all three sides.

$$a^2 = b^2 + c^2 - 2bc\cos A$$

$$\cos A = \frac{b^2 + c^2 - a^2}{2bc}$$

cover-up method   A method of solving equations by covering up one of the other terms.

critical values   The values of a quadratic inequality that make the expression equal to zero.

cross-section   A cut across a 3D shape, or the shape of the face that is exposed when a 3D shape is cut. For a prism, a cut across the shape, perpendicular to its length.

cubic   An expression where the highest power of the variable is 3.

cumulative frequency   The total frequency of all values up to the end of each class interval.

cumulative frequency curve   A cumulative frequency graph drawn as a curve.

cumulative frequency graph   A graph in which the cumulative frequency value is plotted at the end of each class interval. The points can be joined by lines or drawn as a curve.

cyclic quadrilateral   A quadrilateral with vertices that lie on the circumference of a circle; the sum of both pairs of opposite angles is 180°.

cylinder   A prism with a circular cross-section.

deceleration   The rate at which the velocity of a moving object decreases.

decimal place   The position, after the decimal point, of a digit in a decimal number; for example, in 0.025, 5 is in the third decimal place. Also, the number of digits to the right of the decimal point in a decimal number; for example, 3.142 is a number given correct to three decimal places (3 dp).

decimal point   A symbol, usually a small dot, written between the whole-number part and the fractional part in a decimal number.

density   The mass of a substance divided by its volume.

difference   The result of a subtraction.

difference of two squares   An expression of the form $x^2 - y^2$: the terms are squares and there is a minus sign between them.

direct proportion   A relationship in which one variable increases or decreases at the same rate as another; in the formula $y = 12x$, x and y are in direct proportion.

direct variation   Another name for *direct proportion*.

direction   The line along which a vector such as force, weight or velocity acts.

discrete data   Data that can only take certain values, such as a number of children; discrete data can only take fixed values.

discriminant   The expression $b^2 - 4ac$ based on the general equation $ax^2 + bx + c = 0$. If the discriminant of a quadratic equation is negative, then the equation is not soluble.

dispersion   A measure to show how a set of data is spread out.

distance–time graph   A graph that represents a journey, based on the distance travelled and the time taken.

edge   The line where two faces or surfaces of a 3D shape meet.

element   Any member of a set.

eliminate   Given a pair of simultaneous equations with two variables, you can manipulate one or both equations to remove or eliminate one of the variables by a process of substitution, addition or subtraction.

enlargement   A transformation in which the object is enlarged to form an image.

equation   A relation in which two expressions are separated by an equals sign with one or more variables. An equation can be solved to find one or more answers, but it may not be true for all values of x.

equidistant   At equal distances.

equilateral triangle   A triangle in which all the sides are equal and all the angles are 60°.

error interval   The interval within which a rounded value can lie. For example, if $x = 25$ to the nearest whole number, the error interval for x is $24.5 \leqslant x < 25.5$.

estimated mean   A mean that is estimated from grouped data, by multiplying the frequency by the mid-class value for each class, adding up the products and dividing by the total frequency.

event   Something that happens in a probability problem, such as tossing a coin or predicting the weather.

exact value   Numbers such as $\sqrt{2}$ and π cannot be calculated to give a terminating or recurring decimal, but can only be approximated to a number of decimal places or significant figures. The exact value is expressed in the form $\sqrt{x}$, which is also called a surd. π also represents an exact value.

exhaustive   All possible outcomes of an event; the sum of the probabilities of exhaustive outcomes equals 1.

expand   Multiply out (terms with brackets).

expectation   Predicting the number of times you would expect an outcome to occur.

experimental probability   An estimate for the theoretical probability.

exponential function   An expression that has an unknown such as x as an index; for example, 2^x.

expression   A collection of numbers, letters, symbols and operators representing a number or amount; for example, $x^2 - 3x + 4$.

exterior angle   The angle formed outside a 2D shape, when a side is extended beyond the vertex.

factorial   The product of the whole number n and all the whole numbers less than n down to 1. It is written as $x!$. For example $5! = 5 \times 4 \times 3 \times 2 \times 1 = 120$.

factorisation   The arrangement of a given number or expression into a product of its factors. (verb: factorise)

first difference   The numbers that are produced by subtracting each term of a sequence from the one before it, in turn.

formula   A mathematical rule, using numbers and letters, that shows a relationship between variables; for example, the conversion formula from temperatures in Fahrenheit to temperatures in Celsius is: $C = \frac{5}{9}(F - 32)$.

fraction   A part of a whole that has been divided into equal parts; a fraction describes how many parts you are talking about.

frequency density The frequency of a class interval divided by the width of the class interval, used when drawing histograms.

frequency polygon A graph in which the mid-points of the class intervals are joined, in turn, by straight lines.

front elevation The perpendicular view from the front of a solid shape.

frustum A 3D shape produced by removing the top from a pyramid or cone, by means of a cut parallel to the base.

function An algebraic expression in which there is only one variable, often x.

geometric sequence A sequence in which each term is multiplied or divided by the same number, to produce the next term; for example, 2, 4, 8, 16, ... is a geometric sequence.

gradient The slope of a line between two or more points, calculated as the vertical difference between the coordinates divided by the horizontal difference.

gradient-intercept A form for the equation of a line, written in terms of its gradient and the intercept on the vertical axis, $y = mx + c$ where m is the gradient and c is the y-intercept.

grid method (or box method) A method for multiplying numbers larger than 10, in which each number is split into its parts: for example, to calculate 158×67:

158 is 100, 50 and 8

67 is 60 and 7.

These numbers are arranged in a rectangle and each part is multiplied by the others.

×	100	50	8
60	6000	3000	480
7	700	350	56

```
    6000
    3000
     480
     700
     350
  +   56
   10586
```

grouped data Data arranged into smaller, non-overlapping sets, groups or classes, that can be treated as separate ranges or values, for example, 1–10, 11–20, 21–30, 31–40, 41–50; in this example there are equal class intervals.

highest common factor (HCF) The largest number that is a factor common to two or more other numbers.

histogram A diagram, similar to a bar chart, in which the area of each bar is proportional to the frequency of its class interval.

hypotenuse The longest side in a right-angled triangle, always opposite the right angle.

hypothesis A statement that has to be proved true or false.

identity Expressions either side of a $\equiv$ sign with one or more variables, which is true for all values; for example, $3(x + 2) \equiv 3x + 6$ is an identity.

image The result of a reflection or other transformation of an object.

included angle The angle between two given sides of a triangle.

inclusive inequality An inequality such as $\leqslant$ or $\geqslant$.

independent events Two or more events that have no effect on each other's outcomes.

index The power to which a base number is raised; in 3^4, 4 is the index and 3 is the base number.

index notation Expressing a number in terms of one or more of its factors, each expressed as a power.

inequality A statement that one expression is greater or less than another, written with the symbol > (greater than) or < (less than) instead of = (equals).

intercept The point where a line cuts or crosses the axis.

interior angle The inside angle between two adjacent sides of a 2D shape, at a vertex.

interquartile range A measure of dispersion calculated as the upper quartile minus the lower quartile, often abbreviated to IQR.

intersection The 'overlap', the set of elements that occur in two or more sets.

invariant A point that does not change.

inverse Going the other way.

inverse function Reverse or opposite; inverse operations cancel each other out or reverse the effect of each other.

inverse operations An operation that reverses the effect of another operation; for example, addition is the inverse of subtraction, division is the inverse of multiplication.

inverse proportion A relationship between two variables in which as one value increases, the other decreases; in the formula $xy = 12$, x and y are in inverse proportion.

inverse variation Another name for *inverse proportion*.

isosceles triangle A triangle in which two sides are equal and the angles opposite the equal sides are also equal.

iteration A process in which you repeatedly substitute an answer into an equation to generate an answer that is closer to the actual value.

like terms Terms in which the variables are identical, but the coefficients are different; for example, $2ax$ and $5ax$ are like terms but $5xy$ and $7y$ are not. Like terms can be combined by adding their numerical coefficients so $2ax + 5ax = 7ax$.

limits of accuracy   No measurement is entirely accurate. The accuracy depends on the tool used to measure it. The value of every measurement will be rounded to within certain limits. For example you can probably measure with a ruler to the nearest half-centimetre. Any measurement you take could be inaccurate by up to half a centimetre. This is your limit of accuracy. (See also *lower bound and upper bound*.)

line bisector   A line that divides another line exactly in half.

line graph   A graph to show how data changes, by means of points joined by straight lines.

line of best fit   A straight line drawn on a scatter diagram where there is correlation, so that there are equal numbers of points above and below it; the line shows the trend of the data.

linear   An expression (such as $5x + 2$) for which there is a term with an index of 1 and possibly a constant term.

linear graph   A straight-line graph that represents a linear function.

linear scale factor   The factor of increase between the lengths of two similar shapes.

linear sequence   A sequence or pattern of numbers in which the difference between consecutive terms is always the same.

loci   The plural of *locus*.

locus   The path of a point that moves obeying given conditions.

long division   A method of division showing all the working, used when dividing large numbers.

long multiplication   A method of multiplication showing all the working, used when multiplying large numbers.

lower bound   The lower limit of a measurement. (See also *limit of accuracy*.)

lower quartile   The lowest value of the three quartiles, often abbreviated to Q_1.

lowest common multiple (LCM)   The lowest number that is a multiple of two or more numbers; 12 is the lowest common multiple of 2, 3, 4 and 6.

magnitude   The size of a quantity.

mass   The amount of matter in an object.

maximum   A point on a graph where the gradient is zero, which is higher than the points either side of it.

measure of location   An average or typical value that represents a set of data.

mid-class value   The mid-point value of each class interval.

minimum   A point on a graph where the gradient is zero, which is lower than the points either side of it.

mirror line   Another name for a line of symmetry.

modal group   In grouped data, the class with the highest frequency.

multiplier   A number that is used to find the result of increasing or decreasing an amount by a percentage.

mutually exclusive   Outcomes that cannot occur at the same time.

negative correlation   A relationship between two sets of data, in which the values of one variable increase as the values of the other variable decrease.

negative reciprocal   The result of dividing a number into –1; the negative reciprocal of $\frac{a}{b}$ is $-\frac{b}{a}$.

no correlation   No relationship between two sets of data.

non-linear   An expression that is not linear, such as x^2.

nth term   An expression in terms of n; it allows you to find any term in a sequence, without having to use a term-to-term rule.

object   The original or starting shape, line or point before it is transformed to give an image.

obtuse-angled triangle   A triangle containing an obtuse angle.

opposite side   The side that is opposite a given angle, in a right-angled triangle.

order of rotational symmetry   The number of times a 2D shape looks the same as it did originally when it is rotated through 360° about a central point. If a shape has no rotational symmetry, its order of rotational symmetry is 1, because every shape looks the same at the end of a 360° rotation as it did originally.

origin   The point O(0, 0) on Cartesian coordinate axes.

outcome   A possible result of an event in a probability experiment, such as the different scores when throwing a dice.

outlier   In a data set, a value that is widely separated from the main cluster of values.

parabola   The shape of a quadratic curve.

pattern   Numbers or objects that are arranged to follow a rule.

percentage change   A change to a quantity, calculated as a percentage of the original quantity.

percentage decrease   A reduction or decrease to a quantity, calculated as a percentage of the original quantity.

percentage increase   An increase to a quantity, calculated as a percentage of the original quantity.

percentage loss   The loss on a financial transaction, calculated as the difference between the buying price and the selling price, calculated as a percentage of the original price.

percentage profit The profit on a financial transaction, calculated as the difference between the selling price and the buying price, calculated as a percentage of the original price.

periodic Repeating at regular periods or intervals.

permutation A way of selecting members from a group, when the order of selection matters. For example, given three letters ABC, there are six different ways of choosing two letters from this set, AB, BA, AC, CA, CB and BC. The mathematical formula for a combination of r items from a group of n is $nPr = \frac{n!}{r!}$. (See also 'combinations'.)

perpendicular bisector A line that divides a given line exactly in half, passing through its midpoint at right angles to it.

pi (π) The result of dividing the circumference of a circle by its diameter, represented by the Greek letter pi (π).

plan The view from directly above a solid shape.

point of contact The point where two lines or faces meet.

polygon A closed 2D shape with straight sides.

population The complete data set in a survey.

position vector The vector of a point in relation to an origin.

position-to-term rule A rule for generating a term in a sequence, depending on the position of the term within the sequence.

positive correlation A relationship between two sets of data, in which the values of one variable increase as the values of the other variable increase.

power The number of times you use a number or expression in a calculation; it is written as a small, raised number; for example, 2^2 is 2 multiplied by itself, $2^2 = 2 \times 2$ and $4^3 = 4 \times 4 \times 4$.

power of 10 A number that is produced by multiplying 10 by itself repeatedly.

power of 2 A number that is produced by multiplying 2 by itself repeatedly.

primary data Data you have collected yourself.

principal The amount invested or lent.

prism A 3D shape that has the same cross-section wherever it is cut perpendicular to its length.

product rule for counting A way of working out how many combinations there are for situations where choices can be made. Stated simply, if there are a ways of doing something and b ways of doing another thing, then there are $a \times b$ ways of performing both actions. For example, a pizza parlour offers two types of crust, three types of cheese and five types of toppings. Therefore $2 \times 3 \times 5 = 30$ different pizzas could be ordered.

prove To show without doubt, that something is true.

pyramid A 3D shape with a base and sides rising to form a single point.

Pythagoras' theorem The rule that, in any right-angled triangle, the square of the hypotenuse is equal to the sum of the squares of the other two sides.

Pythagorean triple Three numbers, a, b and c, that satisfy the Pythagorean rule $a^2 = b^2 + c^2$; {3, 4, 5} and {5, 12, 13} are examples.

quadratic Having terms involving one or two variables, and constants, such as $x^2 - 3$ or $y^2 + 2y + 4$ where the highest power of the variable is two.

quadratic expression An expression in which the highest power of any variable is 2, such as $2x^2 + 4$.

quadratic formula A formula used to solve quadratic equations of the form $ax^2 + bx + c = 0$, $x = \frac{-b \pm \sqrt{b^2 - 4ac}}{2a}$.

quadratic inequality Like a quadratic equation but with an inequality symbol such as <.

quadratic rule A rule for the generation of a quadratic sequence.

quadratic sequence A sequence in which the first differences are not constant, formed from a quadratic rule.

quantity A measurable amount of something that can be written as a number, or a number with appropriate units; for example, the capacity of a milk carton.

quartile One of three points that divides a set of data, in numerical order, into four equal parts.

random Chosen by chance, without looking; every item has an equal chance of being chosen.

random sample A sample in which every member of the population has an equal chance of being chosen.

ratio The ratio of A to B is a number found by dividing A by B. It is written as A : B. For example, the ratio of 1 m to 1 cm is written as 1 m : 1 cm = 100 : 1. Notice that the two quantities must both be in the same units if they are to be compared in this way.

rational number A number that can be written as a fraction, for example, $\frac{1}{4}$ or $\frac{10}{3}$.

rationalise Remove a surd from a denominator (by multiplying the numerator and denominator by that surd).

rearrange Put into a different order, to simplify.

reciprocal The result of dividing a number into 1, so 1 divided by the number is its reciprocal.

recurring decimal A decimal number in which a digit or pattern of digits repeats for ever.

reflection The image formed when a 2D shape is reflected in a mirror line or line of symmetry; the process of reflecting an object.

region An area bound by inequalities.

relative frequency An estimate for the theoretical probability.

resultant vector The result of combining two or more vectors.

right-angled triangle A triangle in which one angle is 90°.

roots The points on a graph where it crosses the x-axis.

rotation A turn about a central point, called the centre of rotation.

rotational symmetry A type of symmetry in which a 2D shape may be turned through 360° so that it looks the same as it did originally in two or more positions.

sample A selection taken from a larger data set, which can be researched to provide information about the whole population.

sample space diagram A diagram that shows all the outcomes of an experiment.

scalar A quantity such as mass that has quantity but does not act in a specific direction.

scale drawing A drawing that represents something much larger or much smaller, in which the lengths on the image are in direct proportion to the lengths on the object.

scale factor The ratio of the distance on the image to the distance it represents on the object; the number that tells you how much a shape is to be enlarged.

scalene triangle A triangle in which all sides are different lengths.

scatter diagram A graphical representation showing whether there is a relationship between two sets of data.

second difference The numbers that are produced by subtracting each first difference of a sequence from the one before it, in turn.

secondary data Data that has been collected by someone else.

sector A region of a circle, like a slice of a pie, enclosed by an arc and two radii.

sequence A pattern of numbers that are related by a rule.

set A collection of objects or elements.

shift key The key on a calculator that enables you to use the alternative functions associated with the main keys.

side elevation The perpendicular view from the end of a solid shape.

significant figure In the number 12 068, 1 is the first and most significant figure and 8 is the fifth and least significant figure. In 0.246 the first and most significant figure is 2. Zeros at the beginning or end of a number are not significant figures.

similar Two shapes are similar if one is an enlargement of the other; angles in the same position in both shapes are equal to each other.

similar triangles Two or more triangles where one is an enlargement of the other.

simple interest Money that a borrower pays a lender, for allowing them to borrow money.

simplify To make an equation or expression easier to work with or understand by combining like terms or cancelling; for example:
$4a - 2a + 5b + 2b = 2a + 7b$, $\frac{12}{18} = \frac{2}{3}$, $5 : 10 = 1 : 2$.

simultaneous equation Two equations that are both true for the same set of values for their variables.

sine A trigonometric ratio related to an angle in a right-angled triangle, calculated as $\frac{\text{opposite}}{\text{hypotenuse}}$.

sine rule A rule using sines of angles in any triangle showing that the ratio of the sine of an angle to the length of the side opposite it is always the same for any given triangle. $\frac{a}{\sin A} = \frac{b}{\sin B} = \frac{c}{\sin C}$.

slant height The length of the sloping side of a cone.

soluble Possible to solve.

sphere A 3D shape which is the locus of a point that moves a fixed distance from a given point, the centre; a 3D shape that has a circular cross-section whenever it is cut through its centre.

standard form A way of writing a number as $a \times 10^n$, where $1 \leq a \leq 10$ and n is a positive or negative integer.

standard index form See *standard form*.

stem-and-leaf diagram A diagram showing how discrete numerical data is distributed once the data is put in numerical order; the leaves are the units digits and the stems are the digits that occur before the units digits.

strategy A plan to solve a problem.

stratified sample A sample taken from each category of a population. The number in each category is in the same proportion as they occur in the population.

strict inequality An inequality such as < or >.

subject The variable on the left-hand side of the equals (=) sign in a formula or equation.

substitute Replace a variable in an expression with a number and evaluate it; for example, if you substitute 4 for t in $3t + 5$ the answer is 17 because $3 \times 4 + 5 = 17$.

subtend The joining of the lines from two points giving an angle.

surd An irrational number found by taking a root of a number such as the square root of 2 ($\sqrt{2}$) or the cube root of 5 ($\sqrt[3]{5}$).

surface area The total area of all of the surfaces of a 3D shape.

systematic counting If you wanted to work out how many times the digit 6 was written when writing down all the numbers from 200 to 300 you would use a systematic counting strategy; for example, 206, 216, … 296 is 10 times plus 260, 261, … 269 which is 10 times so the digit 6 will be written 20 times. Note that if the question was how many numbers between 200 and 300 contain the digit 6, the answer would be 19 as 266 would be counted only once. (See also 'product rule for counting'.)

tangent 1 A straight line that touches a circle just once.

2 A trigonometric ratio related to an angle in a right-angled triangle, calculated as $\frac{\text{opposite}}{\text{adjacent}}$.

term 1 A part of an expression, equation or formula. Terms are separated by + and − signs.

2 A number in a sequence or pattern.

terminating decimal A terminating decimal can be written down exactly. $\frac{33}{100}$ can be written as 0.33, but $\frac{1}{3}$ is 0.3333… with the 3s recurring forever.

term-to-term The rule that shows what to do to one term in a sequence, to work out the next term.

theorem A statement that is a result of a proof.

theoretical probability The exact or true probability of an event happening.

theoretical probability space diagram Another name for a sample space diagram.

three-figure bearing The angle from north clockwise, generally given as a three-digit figure.

transform Reflect, rotate, enlarge or translate.

transformation A change to a geometric 2D shape, such as a translation, rotation, reflection or enlargement.

translation A movement along, up or diagonally on a coordinate grid.

transpose Another word for rearrange.

tree diagram A diagram that is used to calculate the probability of combined events happening. All the probabilities of each single event are written on the branches of the diagram.

trend How data increases or decreases in a regular pattern.

trial A single experiment in a probability experiment.

trial and improvement A method for finding the solution to an equation by substituting values and using the results to get closer to the correct answer.

trigonometry The study of the relationship between angles and sides in triangles.

turning point Any point on a graph where the gradient is zero; could be a maximum or a minimum.

two-way table A table that records how two variables are linked.

unbiased The property of a sample being representative of the population, so that any member of the population may be chosen.

union The set of all the elements that occur in one or more sets.

unit cost The cost of one unit, such as a kilogram, litre or metre, of something.

unitary method A method of finding best value by finding the price per unit, or the quantity per pound or penny.

universal set The set that contains all possible elements, usually represented by the symbol ξ.

upper bound The higher limit of a measurement. (See also *limit of accuracy*.)

upper quartile The highest value of the three quartiles, often abbreviated to Q_3.

variable A letter that stands for a quantity that can take various values.

vector A quantity such as velocity that has magnitude and acts in a specific direction.

velocity–time graph A graph in which distance travelled is plotted against time taken.

Venn diagram A diagram that shows the relationships between different sets.

vertex The point at which two lines meet, in a 2D or 3D shape.

vertical height The height of the top vertex of a 3D shape, measured perpendicular to the base.

vertically opposite angles The angles on the opposite side of the point of intersection when two straight lines cross, forming four angles. The opposite angles are equal.

vertices The plural of vertex.

volume scale factor The factor of increase between the volumes of two similar shapes.

$y = mx + c$ The general equation of a straight line in which m is the gradient of the line and c is the intercept on the y-axis.

zero gradient A line that is parallel to the horizontal axis has zero gradient.

Index

H

I

Answers

Chapter 1 – Number: Basic number

Exercise 1A

1 a 6000
  b 5 cans cost £1.95, so 6 cans cost £1.95.
    32 = 5 × 6 + 2. Cost is £10.53.

2 a 288
  b 16

3 a 38
  b Coach price for adults = £8, coach price for juniors = £4, money for coaches raised by tickets = £12 400, cost of coaches = £12 160, profit = £240

4 (18.81...) Kirsty can buy 18 models.

5 £8.40 per year, 70p per copy

6 £450

7 15

8 3 weeks

9 £248.75

10 Gavin pays 2926.25 − 1840 = £1086.25

11 a Col is correct
  b Abi has multiplied 30 × 50 as 150 instead of 1500. Baz has lined up the columns wrongly when adding. Instead of lining up the units he has lined up the first digits. Des has forgotten to add a zero on the second line of the multiplication, it should be 1530.

Exercise 1B

1 a 4.6   **b** 0.08   **c** 45.716
  d 94.85   **e** 602.1   **f** 671.76
  g 7.1   **h** 6.904   **i** 13.78
  j 0.1   **k** 4.002   **l** 60.0

2 a 0.028 **b** 0.09   **c** 50.96   **d** 46.512

3 a 35, 35.04, 0.04   **b** 16, 18.24, 2.24
  c 60, 59.67, 0.33 **d** 140, 140.58, 0.58

4 a 18 **b** 140 **c** 1.4 **d** 12 **e** 6.9

5 a 280 **b** 12   **c** 240 **d** 450 **e** 0.62

6 a 572
  b i 5.72   **ii** 1.43   **iii** 22.88

7 a Incorrect as should end in the digit 2
  b Incorrect since 9 × 5 = 45, so answer must be less than 45

8 300

9 a 27
  b i 27   **ii** 0.027   **iii** 0.27

10 Mark bought a DVD, some jeans and a pen.

11 Headline A does not give the exact figure so does not convey any useful information. Headline B is accurate and records should be given accurately. Headline C may be correct but without the previous record does not convey any useful information.

Exercise 1C

1 a 50 000   **b** 90 000   **c** 30 000
  d 200   **e** 0.5   **f** 0.006
  g 0.3   **h** 10   **i** 0.05
  j 1000

2 a 56 000   **b** 80 000   **c** 31 000
  d 1.7   **e** 0.066   **f** 0.46
  g 4.1   **h** 8.0   **i** 1.0
  j 0.80

3 a 60 000   **b** 5300   **c** 89.7
  d 110   **e** 9   **f** 1.1
  g 0.3   **h** 0.7

4 a 65, 74   **b** 95, 149   **c** 950, 1499

5 Elsecar 750, 849; Hoyland 1150, 1249; Barnsley 164 500, 165 499

6 18 to 23 inclusive

7 1, because there could be 450 then 449

8 Donte has rounded to 2 significant figures or nearest 10 000

9 a Advantage – quick. Disadvantage – assumes 3 penguins a square metre which may not be accurate
  b Advantage. Quite accurate as 5 by 5 is a big enough area to give a reliable estimate. Disadvantage – takes a long time.

Exercise 1D

1 a 60 000   **b** 120 000 **c** 10 000
  d 15   **e** 140   **f** 100
  g 200   **h** 0.08   **i** 0.09
  j 45

2 a 5   **b** 25   **c** 3000
  d 600   **e** 2000   **f** 5000
  g 400   **h** 8000   **i** 4 000 000

3 30 × 90 000 = 2 700 000
  600 × 8000 = 4 800 000
  5000 × 4000 = 20 000 000
  200 000 × 700 = 140 000 000

4 a 54 400   **b** 16 000

5 1400 million

6 His answer is correct but he had one too many zeros on each value, which cancel each other out. Matt wrote 600,000 rather than 60,000 and 2000 rather than 200. The two mistakes cancelled themselves out due to the zeros involved.

7 a Value of the money is about 66 000 000 × 0.2 = £13 200 000, so it is enough to buy the yacht.
  b Weight is 66 000 000 × 5 = 330 000 000 grams = 330 tonnes, so they do not weigh as much as the yacht.

8 1420 000 000 000 ÷ 64 000 000 ≈ 22 200, so the National Debt per person is approximately £22 200.

Exercise 1E

1 a 35 000 **b** 15 000 **c** 960
d 5 **e** 1200 **f** 500

2 a 39 700 **b** 17 000 **c** 933
d 4.44 **e** 1130 **f** 550

3 a 1.74 m **b** 6 minutes **c** 240 g
d 83°C **e** 35 000 people **f** 15.5 miles
g 14 m^2

4 a 10 **b** 1 **c** 3

5 a 8.79 **b** 1.03 **c** 3.07

6 82°F, 5 km, 110 min, 43 000 people, 6.2 seconds, 67th, 1788, 15 practice walks, 5 seconds
The answers will depend on the approximations made. Your answers should be to the same order as these.

7 a £15 000 **b** £18 000 **c** £17 500

8 $1000

9 a 40 miles per hour **b** 10 gallons **c** £70

10 a 80 000 **b** 2000 **c** 1000 **d** 30 000
e 5000 **f** 2500 **g** 75 **h** 100

11 a 86 900 **b** 1760 **c** 1030 **d** 29 100
e 3960 **f** 2440 **g** 84.8 **h** 163

12 Approximately 500

13 £1 million pounds is 20 million 5p coins. 20 000 000 × 4.2 = 84 000 000 grams = 84 tonnes, so 5 lorries needed.

14 22.5° C − 18.2° C = 4.3 Celsius degrees

15 a i 27.571 428 57 **ii** 27.6
b i 16.896 516 39 **ii** 16.9
c i 18 672.586 16 **ii** 18 700

16 a 37.5 × 48.6 ≈ 40 × 50 = 2000 21.7 ×103.6 ≈ 20 × 100 = 2000   985 ÷ 0.54 ≈ 1000 ÷ 0.5 = 2000
b as both values are rounded down the actual answer must be bigger than 2000. The other two must be less than 2000.
c Pete is correct it is not possible to tell. 37.5 × 48.6 = 1822.5   985 ÷ 0.54 = 1824.074

17 149 000 000 ÷ 300 000 = 496.67 ≈ 500 seconds

18 a 58.9 × 4.8 ≈ 60 × 5 = 300
b Lower as both values are rounded up to get the estimate.

19 Macau's population density is approximately 710 000 times the population density of Greenland.

20 26.8 ÷ 3.1   ≈ 27 ÷ 3 = 9   36.2 ÷ 3.9 ≈ 36 ÷ 4 = 9. Second calculation must be biggest as first is smaller than 27 ÷ 3 and second is bigger than 36 ÷ 4.

Exercise 1F

1 a 12 **b** 9 **c** 6 **d** 13 **e** 15 **f** 14
g 16 **h** 10 **i** 18 **j** 17 **k** 8 or 16 **l** 21

2 4 packs of sausages and 5 packs of buns (or multiples of these)

3 30 seconds

4 12 minutes; Debbie will have run 4 laps; Fred will have run 3 laps.

5 1 + 3 + 5 + 7 + 9 = 25, 1 + 3 + 5 + 7 + 9 + 11 = 36, 1 + 3 + 5 + 7 + 9 + 11 + 13 = 49, 1 + 3 + 5 + 7 + 9 + 11 + 13 + 15 = 64

6 a −2 **b** −7 **c** −12 **d** −1 **e** −30

7 a 1 **b** 3 **c** 4 **d** 2 **e** −4

8 a 400 **b** 900 **c** 2500 **d** 0.25 **e** 16

9 a Student's own explanation
b 1, 3, 6, 10, 15, 21, 28, 36, 45, 55, 66, 78, 91, 105
c Adding consecutive pairs gives you square numbers.

10

	Square number	Factor of 56
Cube number	64	8
Multiple of 7	49	28

11 2, 3 and 12

12 a 1, 64, 729, 4096, 15 625
b 1, 8, 27, 64, 125
c $\sqrt{a^3} = a \times \sqrt{a}$
d Square numbers

13 a 0.2 **b** 0.5 **c** 0.6 **d** 0.9
e 1.5 **f** 2.1 **g** 0.8 **h** 0.7

14 The answers will depend on the approximations made. Your answers should be to the same order as these.
a 60 **b** 1500 **c** 150

Exercise 1G

1 a 84 = 2 × 2 × 3 × 7
b 100 = 2 × 2 × 5 × 5
c 180 = 2 × 2 × 3 × 3 × 5
d 220 = 2 × 2 × 5 × 11
e 280 = 2 × 2 × 2 × 5 × 7
f 128 = 2 × 2 × 2 × 2 × 2 × 2 × 2
g 50 = 2 × 5 × 5

2 a 84 = 2^2 × 3 × 7 **b** 100 = 2^2 × 5^2
c 180 = 2^2 × 3^2 × 5 **d** 220 = 2^2 × 5 × 11
e 280 = 2^3 × 5 × 7 **f** 128 = 2^7
g 50 = 2 × 5^2

3 1, 2, 3, 2^2, 5, 2 × 3, 7, 2^3, 3^2, 2 × 5, 11, 2^2 × 3, 13, 2 × 7, 3 × 5, 2^4, 17, 2 × 3^2, 19, 2^2 × 5, 3 × 7, 2 × 11, 2^3, 23 × 3, 5^2, 2 × 13, 3^3, 2^2 × 7, 29, 2 × 3 × 5, 31, 2^5, 3 × 11, 2 × 17, 5 × 7, 2^2 × 3^2, 37, 2 × 19, 3 × 13, 2^3 × 5, 41, 2 × 3 × 7, 43, 2^2 × 11, 3^2 × 5, 2 × 23, 47, 2^4 × 3, 7^2, 2 × 5^2

4 a 2 is always the only prime factor
b 64, 128 **c** 81, 243, 729
d 256, 1024, 4096
e 3, 3^2, 3^3, 3^4, 3^5, 3^6; 4, 4^2, 4^3, 4^4, 4^5, 4^6

5 a $2 \times 2 \times 3 \times 5$ **b** $2^2 \times 3 \times 5$
   c $120 = 2^3 \times 3 \times 5$, $240 = 2^4 \times 3 \times 5$,
     $480 = 2^5 \times 3 \times 5$

6 a $7^2 \times 11^2 \times 13^2$ **b** $7^3 \times 11^3 \times 13^3$
   c $7^{10} \times 11^{10} \times 13^{10}$

7 Because 3 is not a factor of 40 so it does not divide exactly.

8 $a = 2, b = 7$

9 a $2ab\ a^2\ 4b$ **b** $8a^3b\ 4a^3b^2$

Exercise 1H

1 a 20   **b** 56   **c** 6   **d** 28
   e 10   **f** 15   **g** 24   **h** 30

2 They are the two numbers multiplied together.

3 a 8   **b** 18   **c** 12   **d** 30

4 No. The numbers have a common factor. Multiplying them together would mean using this factor twice, thus increasing the size of the common multiple. It would not be the least common multiple.

5 a 168   **b** 105   **c** 84   **d** 84
   e 96   **f** 54   **g** 75   **h** 144

6 3 packs of cheese slices and 4 packs of bread rolls

7 a 8   **b** 7   **c** 4   **d** 16   **e** 14   **f** 9

8 a **ii** and **iii**   **b** **iii**

9 18 and 24

10 a $6x^2y^2$ **b** xy

Exercise 1I

1 a 7   **b** −8   **c** −5   **d** −11
   e 11   **f** 6   **g** 8   **h** 8
   l −2   **j** −1   **k** −9   **l** −5
   m 5   **n** −9   **o** 8   **p** 0

2 a −15   **b** −14   **c** −24   **d** 6
   e 14   **f** 2   **g** −2   **h** −8
   i −4   **j** 3   **k** −24   **l** −10
   m −18   **n** 16   **o** 36

3 a −9   **b** 16   **c** −3   **d** −32
   e 18   **f** 18   **g** 6   **h** −4
   i 20   **j** 16   **k** 8   **l** −48
   m 13   **n** −13   **o** −8

4 a −2   **b** 30   **c** 15   **d** −27   **e** −7

5 a −9   **b** 3   **c** 1

6 a 16   **b** −2   **c** −12

7 -1×12, 1×-12, -2×6, 2×-6, -3×4, 3×-4,

8 Any appropriate divisions

9 a −24   **b** 24 degrees   **c** 3×-6

10 13×-6, -15×4, $-72 \div 4$, $-56 \div -8$

11 a 32°F and 212°F   **b** −40°C = −40°F

12 −460°F

Exercise 1J

1 a −4   **b** −6   **c** 4   **d** 45   **e** 6   **f** 6

2 a 38   **b** 24   **c** −3   **d** −6   **e** −1   **f** 2
   g −25   **h** 25   **i** 0   **j** −20   **k** 4   **l** 0

3 a $(3 \times -4) + 1 = -11$ **b** $-6 \div (-2 + 1) = 6$
   c $(-6 \div -2) + 1 = 4$ **d** $4 + (-4 \div 4) = 3$
   e $(4 + -4) \div 4 = 0$ **f** $(16 - -4) \div 2 = 10$

4 a 49   **b** −1   **c** −5   **d** −12

5 a 40   **b** 1   **c** 78   **d** 4

6 Possible answer: $3 \times -4 \div 2$

7 Possible answer: $(2 - 4) \times (7 - 3)$

8 $(-4)^2 = -4 \times -4 = +16$, $-(4)^2 = -(4 \times 4) = -16$

9 $(5 + 6) - (7 \div 8) \times 9$

10 −6

Review questions

1 10 weeks

2 16

3 270

4 a $3^2 \times 5 \times 7$ **b** 63

5 a 11.412 712 21   **b** 11.4

6 a 412.603252   **b** 400.5

7 a **iii** Prime numbers less than 20
   b **i** 252   **ii** 3780   **iii** 18

8 a 10.663 418 78   **b** 11

9 1200

10 5

11 a 3.141 592 92   **b** 0.000 009%

12 a 7:30 pm (7:45pm on Town Hall clock)
   b 6:00 pm on Tuesday (7:00pm on Town Hall clock)

13 a 15 120   **b** 12

14 a 90   **b** 240   **c** 6

15 27 and 36

16 a 2000
   b Higher as top values rounded down and denominator rounded up.

17 a p and q are 2 and 5. r is 3   **b** 15

18 m = 5, n = 3

Chapter 2 – Number: Fractions, ratio and proportion

Exercise 2A

1 a $\frac{1}{3}$ **b** $\frac{1}{5}$ **c** $\frac{2}{5}$ **d** $\frac{5}{24}$

e $\frac{2}{5}$ **f** $\frac{1}{6}$ **g** $\frac{2}{7}$ **h** $\frac{1}{3}$

2 $\frac{12}{30} = \frac{2}{5}$

3 $\frac{1}{5}$

4 $\frac{1}{2}$

5 Jon saves $\frac{30}{90} = \frac{1}{3}$

Matt saves, $\frac{35}{100} = \frac{7}{20}$ which is greater than $\frac{1}{3}$, so Matt saves the greater proportion of his earnings.

6 $\frac{13}{20} = \frac{65}{100}$ and $\frac{16}{25} = \frac{64}{100}$ so 13 out of 20 is the better mark.

7 $\frac{3}{8}$

8 $\frac{11}{24}$

9 $\frac{3}{7}$

10 $\frac{9}{22}$

Exercise 2B

1 a $\frac{8}{15}$ **b** $\frac{7}{12}$ **c** $\frac{11}{12}$

d $\frac{1}{10}$ **e** $\frac{1}{8}$ **f** $\frac{1}{12}$

2 Three-quarters of 68

3 a $4\frac{47}{60}$ **b** $\frac{41}{72}$ **c** $1\frac{109}{120}$ **d** $1\frac{23}{30}$

4 a $\frac{1}{6}$ **b** 30

5 No, one eighth is left, which is 12.5 cl, so enough for one cup but not two cups.

6 He has added the numerators and added the denominators instead of using a common denominator. Correct answer is $3\frac{7}{12}$.

7 Possible answer: The denominators are 4 and 5. I first find a common denominator. The lowest common denominator is 20 because 4 and 5 are both factors of 20. So I am changing the fractions to twentieths. One-quarter is the same as five-twentieths (multiplying numerator and denominator by 5). Two-fifths is the same as eight-twentieths (multiplying numerator and denominator by 4). Five-twentieths plus eight-twentieths = thirteen-twentieths.

8 $\frac{11}{20}$ of 900 = 495, $\frac{2}{11}$ of 495 = 90 left-handed boys. 900 − 495 = 405 girls. $\frac{2}{9}$ of 405 = 90 left-handed

girls. 180 left-handed students altogether so 180 out of 900 = $\frac{1}{5}$.

9 $\frac{1}{5} + \frac{3}{8} = \frac{23}{40}$, so $\frac{17}{40}$ of the counters are yellow. $\frac{17}{40}$ of 600 = 255

10 a because $\frac{27}{40} + \frac{2}{5} = 1\frac{3}{40}$ which is greater than 1.

b $\frac{2}{5}$ of 200 = 80. $\frac{5}{8}$ of 80 = 50 women at least 40. $\frac{27}{40}$ of 200 = 135 members at least 40. 135 − 50 = 85 men at least 40. $\frac{3}{5}$ of 200 = 120, so 120 − 85 = 35 men under 40.

11 a $\frac{1}{5}$ is $\frac{8}{40}$. $\frac{3}{4}$ is $\frac{30}{40}$. Half-way between 8 and 30 is 19, so the mid-point fraction is $\frac{19}{40}$.

b Yes as the mid-point of any two numbers a and b is $(a + b) \div 2$ and adding the same denominator is the same thing as dividing by 2.

Exercise 2C

1 a $\frac{1}{6}$ **b** $\frac{3}{8}$ **c** $\frac{7}{20}$ **d** $\frac{3}{5}$

e $\frac{5}{12}$ **f** $2\frac{11}{12}$ **g** $3\frac{9}{10}$ **h** $3\frac{1}{3}$

2 a $\frac{3}{4}$ **b** $1\frac{1}{15}$ **c** 5 **d** $\frac{4}{9}$ **e** $1\frac{3}{5}$

3 a $\frac{1}{4}$ **b** 5 **c** $\frac{8}{3}$ **d** $\frac{4}{5}$

4 a $-\frac{1}{5}$ **b** 2 **c** $-\frac{9}{7}$ **d** $\frac{5}{3}$

5 $\frac{3}{8}$

6 $\frac{1}{8}$

7 40

8 $\frac{2}{5}$ of $6\frac{1}{2}$

9 £10.40

10 a $\frac{9}{32}$ **b** $\frac{256}{625}$

11 After 1 day $\frac{7}{8}$ of the water is left. On day 2, $\frac{1}{8} \times \frac{7}{8} = \frac{7}{64}$ is lost so total lost is $\frac{1}{8} + \frac{7}{64} = \frac{8}{64} + \frac{7}{64} = \frac{15}{64}$, so $1 - \frac{15}{64}$ is left = $\frac{49}{64}$

12 $50 \times 1\frac{1}{2} = 75$ kg. 120 − 75 = 45, $45 \div 2\frac{1}{2} = 18$, so 18 of the $2\frac{1}{2}$ kg bags are packed.

13 a 77% is about $\frac{3}{4}$. 243 is about 240, so $\frac{3}{4}$ of 240 = 180.

b Lower, as both estimates are lower than the original values.

Exercise 2D

1 **a** $1\frac{11}{20}$ **b** $1\frac{1}{4}$ **c** $1\frac{63}{80}$
   d $\frac{11}{30}$ **e** $\frac{61}{80}$ **f** $\frac{167}{240}$

2 **a** $12\frac{1}{4}$ miles **b** $3\frac{1}{4}$ miles

3 **a** $6\frac{11}{20}$ **b** $8\frac{8}{15}$ **c** $11\frac{63}{80}$
   d $3\frac{11}{30}$ **e** $7\frac{61}{80}$ **f** $4\frac{277}{396}$

4 **a** $-\frac{77}{1591}$ **b** Answer is negative

5 $18\frac{11}{12}$ cm

6 $\frac{5}{12}$ (anticlockwise) or $\frac{7}{12}$ (clockwise)

7 **a** $\frac{3}{5}$ **b** $\frac{27}{128}$ **c** $5\frac{2}{5}$
   d $5\frac{1}{7}$ **e** $3\frac{9}{32}$ **f** $\frac{11}{18}$

8 **a** $8\frac{11}{20}$ **b** $65\frac{91}{100}$ **c** $52\frac{59}{160}$
   d $2\frac{17}{185}$ **e** $2\frac{22}{103}$ **f** $7\frac{881}{4512}$

9 $18\frac{5}{12}$ m²

10 3

11 **a** $6 \times (1\frac{3}{4})^2 = 18\frac{3}{8}$ cm²
    b $34\frac{14}{25} \div 6 = \frac{144}{25}$, $\sqrt{\frac{144}{25}} = \frac{12}{5} = 2\frac{2}{5}$ cm

12 $22 \div (2 \times \frac{22}{7}) = \frac{7}{2}$, $\frac{22}{7} \times \frac{7}{2} \times \frac{7}{2} = 38\frac{1}{2}$ cm²

13 Volume cuboid $= 22\frac{11}{24}$ cm³, $22\frac{11}{24} \div (\frac{22}{7} \times \frac{4}{3}) =$
    $\frac{343}{64}$, $\sqrt[3]{\frac{343}{64}} = 1\frac{3}{4}$ cm

14 After 1 day $\frac{7}{8}$ is left, after two days $\frac{49}{64}$ and after
    three days $\frac{343}{512}$ is left

15 $120 \times 4\frac{1}{2} = 540$. $175 \times 1\frac{1}{2} = 262\frac{1}{2}$. $540 - 262\frac{1}{2}$
    $= 277\frac{1}{2}$. $277\frac{1}{2} \div 2\frac{1}{2} = 111$ bags.

Exercise 2E

1 **a** 1.1 **b** 1.03 **c** 1.2 **d** 1.07 **e** 1.12

2 **a** 0.92 **b** 0.85 **c** 0.75 **d** 0.91 **e** 0.88

3 **a** 391 kg **b** 824.1 cm **c** 253.5 g
   d £143.50 **e** 736 m **f** £30.24

4 **a** 731 m **b** 83.52 g **c** 360 cm
   d 117 min **e** 81.7 kg **f** £37.70

5 448

6 No, as the total is £101. She will save £20.20, which is less than the £25 it would cost to join the club.

7 7% pay rise is an increase of £1925 per year which is better than £150 × 12 = £1800

8 **a** £6.125 (£6.13)
   b $x \times 0.025$
   c $y \div 1.175 \times 1.2$

9 Offer A gives 360 grams for £1.40, i.e. 0.388 pence per gram.
   Offer B gives 300 grams for £1.12, i.e 0.373 pence per gram, so Offer B is the better offer.
   Or Offer A is 360 for 1.40 = 2.6 g/p, offer B is 300 for 1.12 = 2.7 g/p, so offer B is better.

10 **c** Both the same as 1.05 × 1.03 = 1.03 × 1.05

11 **a** Shop A as 1.04 × 1.04 = 1.0816, so an 8.16% increase.

12 £425.25

13 0.9 × 1.1 = 0.99 (99%)

14 Area of original circle = 200.96
    Enlarged area = 200.96 x 1.6 = 321.536
    Enlarged radius = $\sqrt{321.536 \div 3.14}$ =
    10.1192885125
    % increase = 2.11928/8 × 100 = 26.49%

15 **a** Let $r = 10$. Approx formula gives V = 4000, actual gives V = 4188.79, 188.79 ÷ 4188.79 = 0.045 which is 4.5%
    b The value is lower as $\frac{4}{3} \times \pi$ is greater than 4 as π is 3.14.

Exercise 2F

1 **a** 25% **b** 60.6% **c** 46.3% **d** 12.5%
   e 41.7% **f** 60% **g** 20.8% **h** 10%
   i 1.9% **j** 8.3% **k** 45.5% **l** 10.5%

2 32%

3 6.5%

4 33.7%

5 **a** 49.2% **b** 64.5% **c** 10.6%

6 4.9%

7 90.5%

8 Stacey had the greater percentage increase.
   Stacey: (20 − 14) × 100 ÷ 14 = 42.9%
   Calum: (17 − 12) × 100 ÷ 12 = 41.7%

9 Yes, as 38 out of 46 is over 80% (82.6%)

10 Let $z = 100$. $y = 75$, $x = 0.6 \times 75 = 45$, so x is 45% of z

11 Let z be 100, $x = 60$. If x is 75% of y, $y = 80$, so y is 80% of z.

12 30% of 4800 = 1440. 1.2 × 4800 = 5760. 70% of 5760 = 4032. (4032 − 1440) ÷ 1440 = 1.8, so the increase in numbers owning a mobile phone is 180%.

13 31 ÷ 26 = 1.19 which is a 19% increase. 31% is 5% more of the total votes cast than 26%

Review questions

1 £572

2 a 36 seconds
b i 25.2 seconds **ii** Eve **iii** Eve

3 £120

4 £576

5 a £9 **b** £13.20

6 a 0.875 **b** $\frac{11}{35}$ **c** $5\frac{1}{5}$

7 £322

8 $\frac{19}{40}$

9 $4\frac{1}{12}$

10 5

11 a $\frac{221}{71}$, $\frac{22}{7}$, $\frac{312}{99}$, $\frac{54}{17}$ **b** $\frac{22}{7}$

12 28%

13 77%

14 25%

15 For bag A P(red) = 0.1875 and for bag B P(red) = 0.186 so Tomas is wrong.

16 13%

17 a 150 men, 100 women **b** 12%

Chapter 3 – Statistics: Statistical diagrams and averages

Exercise 3A

1 a

Sports chosen by students

Number of students vs Sport chosen (Basketball, Badminton, Volleyball); Boys and Girls.

b 16 **c** 42

2 Pie charts with these angles:
a 36°, 90°, 126°, 81°, 27°
b 90°, 108°, 60°, 78°, 24°
c 168°, 52°, 100°, 40°

3 a Pictogram with suitable key
b Bar chart correctly labelled
c Vertical line chart correctly labelled
d Pie chart with these angles: 60°, 165°, 45°, 15°, 75° and correctly labelled
e Vertical line chart. It shows the frequencies, the easiest one to draw and comparisons can be made; or other chart with a valid supporting reason given.

4 a 36
b Pie charts with these angles: 50°, 50°, 80°, 60°, 60°, 40°, 20°
c Student's bar chart.
d Bar chart, because easier to make comparisons; or other chart stated with a valid supporting reason

5 a Pie charts with these angles: 124°, 132°, 76°, 28°
b Split of total data seen at a glance.

6 a 55° **b** 22 **c** $33\frac{1}{3}$ %

7 a Pie charts with these angles:
Strings: 36°, 118°, 126°, 72°, 8°
Brass: 82°, 118°, 98°, 39°, 23°
b Overall, the strings candidates did better, as a smaller proportion obtained lower grades. A higher proportion of Brass candidates scored very good grades.

8 Work out the angle for 'Don't know' = 40°, so
P(Don't know) = $\frac{40}{360}$ ° = $\frac{1}{9}$

Exercise 3B

1 a

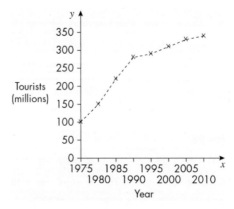

b About 328 million
c Between 1980 and 1985
d Rising steeply at first, but then leveling off. Rise in living standards, cheaper flights, more package holidays

2 a

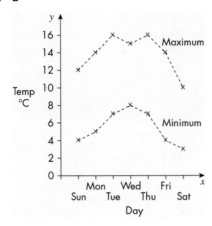

b Smallest difference Wednesday and Saturday (7°), greatest difference Friday (10°)

3 a

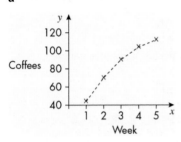

b about 120
c The same people keep coming back and tell others, but new customers each week become more difficult to find.

4 No, you cannot extrapolate the data or the data is likely to change after 5 weeks

5 All the temperatures were presumably higher than 20 °C.

Exercise 3C

1 **a** 47   **b** 53   **c** 55   **d** 65

2 Mode

3 a

0	8 9 9 9
1	2 2 3 7 7 8
2	0 1 2 5

Key   0 | 8   represents 8 text messages

b 17
c 15

4 Three possible answers: 12, 14, 14, 16, 18, 20, 24; or 12, 14, 14, 16, 18, 22, 24; or 12, 14, 14, 16, 20, 22, 24

5 a Median (mean could be unduly influenced by results of very able and/or very poor candidates)
b Median (mean could be unduly influenced by pocket money of students with very rich or generous parents)
c Mode (numerical value of shoe sizes irrelevant, just want most common size)
d Median (mean could be distorted by one or two extremely short or tall performers)
e Mode (the only way to get an 'average' of non-numerical values)
f Median (mean could be unduly influenced by very low weights of premature babies)

6 a 20   **b** 25   **c** 46   **d** 43
e The boys did better as they had a higher median and their marks were less spread out.

7 a i £20 000   **ii** £28 000   **iii** £34 000
b A 6% rise would increase the mean salary to £36 040, a £1500 pay increase would produce a mean of £35 500.

8 a Median   **b** Mode   **c** Mean

9 Tom – mean, David – median, Mohammed – mode

10 11.6

11 42.7 kg

12 24

Exercise 3D

1 **a i** 7   **ii** 6   **iii** 6.4
   b i 8   **ii** 8.5   **iii** 8.2

2 a 1280   **b** 1.9   **c** 0   **d** 328

3 a 2.2, 1.7, 1.3   **b** Better dental care

4 a 50   **b** 2   **c** 2.8

5 a Roger 5, Brian 4   **b** Roger 3, Brian 8
   c Roger 5, Brian 4   **d** Roger 5.4, Brian 4.5
   e Roger, smaller range   **f** Brian, better mean

6 a 40   **b** 7   **c** 3   **d** 2   **e** 2.5
   f the mode, 3   **g** 2.4

7 5

8 The total frequency could be an even number where the two middle numbers have an odd difference.

9 a 34
   b $x + 80 + 3y + 104 = 266$, so $x + 3y = 82$
   c $x = 10, y = 24$
   d 2.5

Exercise 3E

1 **a i** $30 < x \leq 40$ **ii** 29.5
   b i $0 < y \leq 100$ **ii** 158.3
   c i $5 < z \leq 10$ **ii** 9.43
   d i 7–9   **ii** 8.41

2 a $100 < m \le 120$ **b** 10.86 kg **c** 108.6 g

3 a $175 < h \le 200$ **b** 31% **c** 193.3 hours
   d No the mean was under 200 and so was the mode.

4 24

5 a Yes, average distance is 11.7 miles per day.
   b Because shorter runs will be run at a faster speed, which will affect the average.
   c Yes, for example: 22 miles − 1 mile = 21 miles

6 Soundbuy; average increases are Soundbuy 17.7p, Springfields 18.7p, Setco 18.2p

7 a 160 **b** 52.6 minutes
   c Modal group **d** 65%

8 The first 5 and the 10 are the wrong way round.

9 Find the midpoint of each group, multiply that by the frequency and add those products. Divide that total by the total frequency.

10 a Yes, as total in first two columns is 50, so median is between 39 and 40.
   b He could be correct, as the biggest possible range is 69 − 20 = 49, and the lowest is 60 − 29 = 31.

Exercise 3F

1 a Positive correlation, time taken increases with the number of press-ups
   b strong negative correlation, you complete a crossword more quickly as you get older
   c No correlation, speed of cars on M1 is not related to the temperature
   d weak positive correlation, older people generally have more money saved in the bank

2 a and b

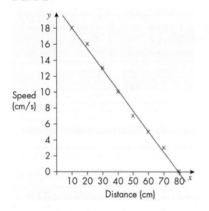

   c about 19 cm/s
   d about 34 cm

3 a and b

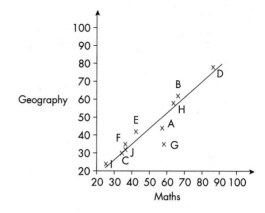

   c Greta
   d about 65
   e about 75

4 a

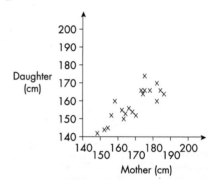

   b Yes, as positive correlation is observed.

5 a

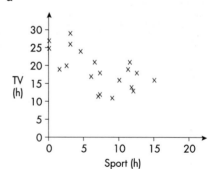

   b Very weak negative correlation, so cannot draw a line of best fit or predict the value

6 **a** and **b**

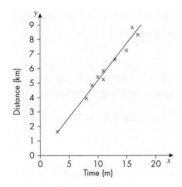

c about 2.4 km

d about 8 minutes

e You cannot extrapolate values from a scatter diagram or the data may change for longer journeys

7 About 23 mph

8 Points showing a line of best fit sloping down from top left to bottom right

Review questions

1 **a** Grade 7

  b $\frac{100}{360}$ or $\frac{5}{18}$

  c i 48   **iii** 216

  d e.g. pie charts show proportions or they are percentages, not actual numbers or do not know how many students, etc.

2 43.7 matches

3 **a** $10 < t \le 20$

  b $10 < t \le 20$

  c 19 minutes

4 **a** because over half the students have more than £10 pocket money, so the mean must be more than £10

  b £11.13

5

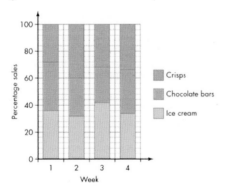

6 **a** $100 < m \le 150$

  b $150 < m \le 200$

  c 159 g

d

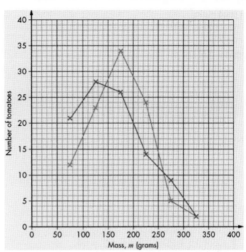

e

mass, m (grams)	Margot's tomatoes
$50 < m \le 100$	12
$100 < m \le 150$	23
$150 < m \le 200$	34
$200 < m \le 250$	24
$250 < m \le 300$	5
$300 < m \le 350$	2

f

mass, m (grams)	Margot's tomatoes	mid point x	$x \times m$
$50 < m \le 100$	12	75	900
$100 < m \le 150$	23	125	2875
$150 < m \le 200$	34	175	5950
$200 < m \le 250$	24	225	5400
$250 < m \le 300$	5	275	1375
$300 < m \le 350$	2	325	650
totals	100		17150

estimate for the mean = 171.5 g

g on average Tom's tomatoes had a smaller mass and were therefore probably smaller in size

7 **a i** Diagram C   **ii** Diagram A   **iii** Diagram B

  b Diagram A: strong negative correlation, diagram B: no correlation, diagram C: strong positive correlation

8 **a/b** Student's graph as follows: Time on horizontal axis from 0 to 20 and Distance (km) on vertical axis from 0 to 10 with the following points plotted: (3, 1.7) (17, 8.3) (11, 5.1) (13, 6.7) (9, 4.7) (15, 7.3) (8, 3.8) (11, 5.7) (16, 8.7) (10, 5.3) and with line of best fit drawn.

  c/d answers depend on student's line of best fit

Chapter 4 – Algebra: Number and sequences

Exercise 4A

1 a $11111 \times 11111 = 123\,454\,321$,
$111111 \times 111111 = 12\,345\,654\,321$
b $99999 \times 99999 = 9\,999\,800\,001$,
$999999 \times 999999 = 999\,998\,000\,001$

2 a $7 \times 8 = 7^2 + 7$, $8 \times 9 = 8^2 + 8$
b $50 \times 51 = 2550$, $60 \times 61 = 3660$

3 a $1 + 2 + 3 + 4 + 5 + 4 + 3 + 2 + 1 = 25 = 5^2$,
$1 + 2 + 3 + 4 + 5 + 6 + 5 + 4 + 3 + 2 + 1 = 36 = 6^2$
b $21 + 23 + 25 + 27 + 29 = 125 = 5^3$,
$31 + 33 + 35 + 37 + 39 + 41 = 216 = 6^3$

4 a $1 + 6 + 15 + 20 + 15 + 6 + 1 = 64$,
$1 + 7 + 21 + 35 + 35 + 21 + 7 + 1 = 128$
b $12\,345\,679 \times 45 = 555\,555\,555$,
$12\,345\,679 \times 54 = 666\,666\,666$

5 a $1^3 + 2^3 + 3^3 + 4^3 = (1 + 2 + 3 + 4)^2 = 100$,
$1^3 + 2^3 + 3^3 + 4^3 + 5^3 = (1 + 2 + 3 + 4 + 5)^2 = 225$
b $36^2 + 37^2 + 38^2 + 39^2 + 40^2 = 41^2 + 42^2 + 43^2 + 44^2$,
$55^2 + 56^2 + 57^2 + 58^2 + 59^2 + 60^2 = 61^2 + 62^2 + 63^2 + 64^2 + 65^2$

6 a $12\,345\,678\,987\,654\,321$
b $999\,999\,998\,000\,000\,001$
c $12^2 + 12$
d 8190
e $81 = 9^2$
f $512 = 8^3$
g 512
h $999\,999\,999$
i $(1 + 2 + 3 + 4 + 5 + 6 + 7 + 8 + 9)^2 = 2025$

7 $1 + 500 = 501$, $2 + 499 = 501$, ... $250 + 251 = 501$, $250 \times 501 = 125250$

Exercise 4B

1 a 21, 34: add previous 2 terms
b 49, 64: next square number
c 47, 76: add previous 2 terms

2 15, 21, 28, 36

3 61, 91, 127

4 $\frac{1}{2}, \frac{3}{5}, \frac{2}{3}, \frac{5}{7}, \frac{3}{4}$

5 a 6, 10, 15, 21, 28
b It is the sums of the natural numbers, or the numbers in Pascal's triangle or the triangular numbers.

6 a 2, 6, 24, 720   **b** 69!

7 364: Daily totals are 1, 3, 6, 10, 15, 21, 28, 36, 45, 55, 66, 78 (these are the triangular numbers). Cumulative totals are: 1, 4, 10, 20, 35, 56, 84, 120, 165, 220, 286, 364.

8 X. There are 351 $(1 + 2 + ... + 25 + 26)$ letters from A to Z. $3 \times 351 = 1053$. $1053 - 26 = 1027$, $1027 - 25 = 1002$, so, as Z and Y are eliminated, the 1000th letter must be X.

9 29 and 41

10 No, because in the first sequence, the terms are always one less than in the 2nd sequence

11 $4n - 2 = 3n + 7$ rearranges as $4n - 3n = 7 + 2$, so $n = 9$

Exercise 4C

1 a 13, 15, $2n + 1$ **b** 25, 29, $4n + 1$
c 33, 38, $5n + 3$ **d** 32, 38, $6n - 4$
e 20, 23, $3n + 2$ **f** 37, 44, $7n - 5$
g 21, 25, $4n - 3$ **h** 23, 27, $4n - 1$
i 17, 20, $3n - 1$ **j** $-8, -18, 42 - 10n$
k 4, 0, $24 - 4n$ **l** $-1, -6, 29 - 5n$

2 a $3n + 1$, 151   **b** $2n + 5$, 105   **c** $5n - 2$, 248
d $4n - 3$, 197   **e** $8n - 6$, 394   **f** $n + 4$, 54
g $5n + 1$, 251   **h** $8n - 5$, 395   **i** $3n - 2$, 148
j $3n + 18$, 168   **k** $47 - 7n$, -303 **l** $41 - 8n$, -359

3 a 33rd   **b** 30th   **c** 100th = 499

4 a i $4n + 1$ **ii** 401   **iii** 101, 25th
b i $2n + 1$ **ii** 201
   iii 99 or 101, 49th and 50th
c i $3n + 1$ **ii** 301   **iii** 100, 33rd
d i $2n + 6$ **ii** 206   **iii** 100, 47th
e i $4n + 5$ **ii** 405   **iii** 101, 24th
f i $5n + 1$ **ii** 501   **iii** 101, 20th
g i $3n - 3$ **ii** 297   **iii** 99, 34th
h i $6n - 4$ **ii** 596   **iii** 98, 17th
i i $205 - 8n$ **ii** -595 **iii** 101, 13th
j i $227 - 2n$ **ii** 27   **iii** 99 or 101, 64th and 63rd

5 a $\dfrac{2n + 1}{3n + 1}$

b Getting closer to $\frac{2}{3}$ $(0.\dot{6})$
c i 0.667 774 (6dp)   **ii** 0.666 778 (6dp)
d 0.666 678 (6dp), 0.666 667 (6dp)

6 a $\dfrac{4n - 1}{5n + 1}$

b Getting closer to $\frac{4}{5}$ (0.8)
c i 0.796 407 (6dp)   **ii** 0.799 640 (6dp)
d 0.799 964 (6dp), 0.799 9996 (7dp)

7 a £305   **b** £600   **c** 3   **d** 5

8 a $\frac{3}{4}, \frac{5}{7}, \frac{7}{10}$

b i 0.666 666 777 8   **ii** $\frac{2}{3}$

c For n, $\dfrac{2n + 1}{3n + 1} \approx \dfrac{2n}{3n} = \dfrac{2}{3}$

9 a $8n + 2$ **b** $8n + 1$ **c** $8n$ **d** £8

10 a Sequence goes up in 2s; first term is $2 + 29$
b $n + 108$
c Because it ends up as $2n \div n$
d 79th

11 If there was a common term then for some value of n the expressions would be equal i.e. $2n = 2n - 1$, Subtracting $2n$ from both sides gives $0 = -1$, which is impossible.

12 Difference is $19 - 10 = 9$. $9 \div 3 = 3$ so $A = 3$.
$3 \times 5 + b = 10$, $b = -5$

Exercise 4D

1 a Even,

+	Odd	Even
Odd	Even	Odd
Even	Odd	Even

b Odd,

×	Odd	Even
Odd	Odd	Even
Even	Even	Even

2 a $1 + 3 + 5 + 7 = 16 = 4^2$, $1 + 3 + 5 + 7 + 9 = 25 = 5^2$
b i 100 **ii** 56

3 a 1, 1, 2, 3, 5, 8, 13, 21, 34, 55, 89, 144
b because odd + odd = even, odd plus even = odd and even + odd = odd.
c i $a + 2b$, $2a + 3b$, $3a + 5b$, $5a + 8b$, $8a + 13b$
ii coefficient of a odd and b even, a even and b odd, both odd, etc.

4 a Even **b** Odd **c** Odd
d Odd **e** Odd **f** Odd
g Even **h** Odd **i** Odd

5 a Odd or even **b** Odd or even
c Odd or even **d** Odd
e Odd or even **f** Even

6 a i Odd **ii** Even **iii** Even
b Any valid answer, e.g. $x(y + z)$

7 a 64, 128, 256, 512, 1024
b i $2^n - 1$ **ii** $2^n + 1$ **iii** 3×2^n

8 a The number of zeros equals the power.
b 6
c i $10^n - 1$ **ii** 2×10^n

9 a 125, 216
b $1 + 8 = 9$, $1 + 8 + 27 = 36$, $1 + 8 + 27 + 64 = 100$… the answers are square numbers

10 a 28, 36, 45, 55, 66
b i 210 **ii** 5050
c You get the square numbers.

11 a i If n is odd, $n + 1$ is even.
If n is even, $n + 1$ is odd.
Even times odd is always even.
ii $2n$ must be even, since it has a factor of 2, so $2n + 1$ must be odd.
b Odd
Odd
Even
Even
Odd
c $(2n + 1)^2 = 4n^2 + 4n + 1$
or $(2n)^2 = 4n^2$

$4n^2 + 4n$ is even so adding 1 makes it odd
$4n^2$ is $2 \times 2n^2$ which is even

12 11th triangular number is 66, 18th triangular number is 171

13 a 36, 49, 64, 81, 100
b i $n^2 + 1$ **ii** $2n^2$ **iii** $n^2 - 1$

14 a 6, 24, 96, 384, 1536
b 21, 147, 1029, 7203, 50 421
c 2, 10, 50, 250, 1250
d 6, 60, 600, 6000, 60 000
e 54, 162, 486, 1458, 4374

15 a $3 \times 2^{n-1}$ **b** $5 \times 4^{n-1}$
c $20 \times 5^{n-1}$ or 4×5^n
d $21 \times 3^{n-1}$ or 7×3^n
e $24 \times 8^{n-1}$ or 3×8^n

16 2 as all other primes are odd, so the sum of two of them will be even, so could not be a prime.

17 a There are many answers, $5 + 31 = 36$, $7 + 29 = 36$, $2 + 47 = 49$ etc.
b There are many answers, $49 - 36 = 13$, $81 - 64 = 17$

Exercise 4E

1 a

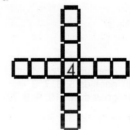

b $4n - 3$
c 97
d 50th diagram

2 a
b $2n + 1$
c 121 **d** 49th set

3 a 18 **b** $4n + 2$ **c** 12

4 a i 24 **ii** $5n - 1$ **iii** 224
b 25

5 a 5, 8, 11, 14
b i 20 cm **ii** $(3n + 2)$ cm **iii** 152 cm
c 332

6 a i 20 **ii** 162
b 79.8 km

7 a i 14 **ii** $3n + 2$ **iii** 41
b 66

8 a i 5 **ii** n **iii** 18
b 20 tins

9 a 2^n

   b i $100 \times 2^{n-1}$ ml   **ii** 1600 ml

   c Next sizes after super giant are 3.2l, 6.4l and 12.8l with weights of 3.2 kg, 6.4 kg and 12.8 kg, so the largest size is 6.4 litres.

10 The nth term is $\left(\dfrac{3}{4}\right)^n$, so as n gets very large, the unshaded area gets smaller and smaller and eventually it will be zero; so the shaded area will eventually cover the triangle.

11 Yes, as the number of matches is 12, 21, 30, 39, … which is $9n + 3$; so he will need $9 \times 20 + 3 = 183$ matches for the 20th step and he has $5 \times 42 = 210$ matches.

12 a 20   **b** 120

13 Alex's answer gives $4(n + 2) = 4n + 8$

   Colin's method gives $4n + 4$

   Ed's method gives $4(n + 1) = 4n + 4$

   Gail's method gives $2 \times n + 2(n + 2) = 2n + 2n + 4 = 4n + 4$

   Linear sequence is 8   12   16   20 …. Which has an nth term of $4n + 4$ so they are all valid methods except for Alex who forgot that the corners overlap and should have taken the 4 overlapping corners away to get $4n + 8 - 4 = 4n + 4$

Exercise 4F

1 a i 34, 43   **ii** goes up 3, 4, 5, 6, etc.

   b i 24, 31   **ii** goes up 1, 2, 3, 4, etc.

   c i 54, 65   **ii** goes up 5, 6, 7, 8, etc.

   d i 57, 53   **ii** goes down 10, 9, 8, 7, etc.

2 a 4, 7, 12, 19, 28   **b** 2, 8, 18, 32, 50

   c 2, 6, 12, 20, 30   **d** 4, 9, 16, 25, 36

   e 2, 8, 16, 26, 38   **f** 4, 7, 14, 25, 40

3 a $2n + 1$ **b** n

   c $n(2n + 1) = 2n^2 + n$

   d $2n^2 + n + 1$

4 a n **b** $n + 1$

   c $n(n + 1)$ **d** 9900 square units

5 a Yes, constant difference is 1   **b** No

   c Yes, constant difference is 2   **d** No

   e Yes, constant difference is 1   **f** No

6 a $4n + 4$ **b** n^2

   c $n^2 + 4n + 4$ **d** $n^2 + 4n + 4$

   e The sides of the large squares are of length $n + 2$ so the total number of squares is $(n + 2)^2$ which is the same answer as **c**.

7 a Table 10, 15, 21; 6, 10, 15; 16, 25, 36

   b i 45   **ii** 100

8 $n^2 + 2n - 3 = n^2 + n + 3$, gives $n = 6$. Substituting gives 45 for both expressions.

9 a Sequences are 4, 7, 14, 25, 40, 59, 82, … and 4, 11, 20, 31, 44, 59, 76, … so 59 is the next common term.

b 59 is the 6th term in each sequence so substitute 6 into each expression. This will give 59 in both cases.

10 a There are many answers, for example $a = -3$ and $b = 1$.

   b The only solution is $c = 2$ and $d = -3$

11 All values of n from 1 to 39 give a prime number. $n = 40$ gives 1681 which equals 41×41

12 a $(n + 1)(n - 1) = n^2 + n - n - 1 = n^2 - 1$

   b $n^2 - 1$ as $50 \times 50 - 1$ is easy to work out but 51×49 isn't

   c $(n + 1)(n - 1)$ as 100×98 is easy to work out but $99^2 - 1$ isn't.

Exercise 4G

1 a i 36, 49   **ii** n^2

   b i 35, 48   **ii** $n^2 - 1$

   c i 38, 51   **ii** $n^2 + 2$

   d i 39, 52   **ii** $n^2 + 3$

   e i 34, 47   **ii** $n^2 - 2$

   f i 35, 46   **ii** $n^2 + 10$

2 a i 37, 50   **ii** $(n + 1)^2 + 1$

   b i 35, 48   **ii** $(n + 1)^2 - 1$

   c i 41, 54   **ii** $(n + 1)^2 + 5$

   d i 50, 65   **ii** $(n + 2)^2 + 1$

   e i 48, 63   **ii** $(n + 2)^2 - 1$

3 a i $n^2 + 4$ **ii** 2504

   b i $3n + 2$ **ii** 152

   c i $(n + 1)^2 - 1$ **ii** 2600

   d i $n(n + 4)$ **ii** 2700

   e i $n^2 + 2$ **ii** 2502

   f i $5n - 4$ **ii** 246

4 a $2n^2 - 3n + 2$ **b** $3n^2 + 2n - 3$

   c $\frac{1}{2}n^2 + \frac{5}{2}n + 1$ **d** $\frac{1}{2}n^2 + 4\frac{1}{2}n - 2$

   e $\frac{1}{2}n^2 + 1\frac{1}{2}n + 6$ **f** $\frac{1}{2}n^2 + 1\frac{1}{2}n + 2$

5 $6n^2$

6 a 26   **b** $1\frac{1}{2}n^2 + \frac{1}{2}n$ **c** 8475

7 a 45

   b nth term is $\frac{1}{2}n^2 + \frac{1}{2}n$ so $\frac{1}{2} \times 15 \times 15 + \frac{1}{2} \times 15 = 120$, so no.

8 Front face is n^2, sides faces are $n \times (n + 1) = n^2 + n$ so total surface area is $2 \times n^2 + 4 \times (n^2 + n) = 6n^2 + 4n$.

9 Sequence is 1, 7, 19, 37. nth term is $3n^2 - 3n + 1$ so the 100th hexagonal number is 29 701.

10 a Taking the height first. There are $n + 1$ strips m feet long. That is $m(n + 1)$ in total.

   Taking the width. There are $m + 1$ strips n feet long. That is $n(m + 1)$ in total

   $m(n + 1) + n(m + 1) = mn + m + mn + n = 2mn + m + n$

   b Taking the nails across a width strip. There are $n + 1$ lots of 2 nails which is $2(n + 1)$.

   There are $m + 1$ width strips, so the total is $2(n + 1)(m + 1)$.

Review questions

1. No. Sequence is 7, 10, 13, 16, 19, 22, 25, 28, … so the first 3 odd terms are prime but 25 is not prime.

2. **a** $4n + 1$
   b Not odd
   c 28th term is 113

3. nth term is $5n + 1$. $5 \times 150 + 1 = 751$

4. **a** $6n + 3$
   b No, $3n + 2$ generates the sequence 5, 8, 11, 14, 17, 20, 23, … so the even terms of this sequence are always 1 less than the terms of the original sequence

5. **a** $2 \times 3^{n-1}$ **b** Not an even number

6. **a** $5 \times 6^{n-1}$ **b** 8th term is 1 399 680

7. **a** The first five terms in the sequence are –27, –21, –11, 3, 21. Of these terms, 3 is a prime number.
   b When $n = 29$ the expression can be factorised as $29(2 \times 29 - 1)$ so is not a prime number

8. **a** 4, 9, 18, 31, 48   **b** 2, 2, 3, 5, 8

9. $n = 1$ $(n - 1) = 0$, $n = 2$ $(n - 2) = 0$, $n = 3$ $2(3 - 1)(3 - 2) \div 5 = 2 \times 2 \times 1 \div 5 = 0.8$

10. $2n^2 - 2n + 3$

11. **a** nth term is $n^2 + 2n$, $12 \times 12 + 2 \times 12 = 168$, so yes he has enough squares
    b $40 \times 40 + 2 \times 40 = 1680$

12. $2n^2 - n$, $2 \times 20^2 - 20 = 780$

13. The sequence of dots is
    5, 15, 30, 50,…

n	0	1	2	3	4
c	0	5	15	30	50
$a + b$	5	10	15	20	
$2a$	5	5	5		

$a = 2\frac{1}{2}$, $b = 2\frac{1}{2}$ and $c = 0$,

so the nth term is $2\frac{1}{2} n^2 + 2\frac{1}{2} n$

$2\frac{1}{2} \times 50^2 + 2\frac{1}{2} \times 50 = 6375$

Chapter 5 – Ratio and proportion and rates of change: Ratio and proportion

Exercise 5A

1. **a** 1 : 3   **b** 3 : 4   **c** 2 : 3   **d** 2 : 3
   e 2 : 5   **f** 2 : 5   **g** 5 : 8   **h** 25 : 6

2. **a** 1 : 3   **b** 3 : 2   **c** 5 : 12
   d 8 : 1   **e** 17 : 15   **f** 25 : 7
   g 4 : 1   **h** 5 : 6   **i** 1 : 24

3. $\frac{7}{10}$

4. $\frac{2}{5}$

5. **a** $\frac{2}{5}$ **b** $\frac{3}{5}$

6. 7 : 3

7. 2 : 1

8. **a** Fruit crush $\frac{1}{6}$, lemonade $\frac{5}{6}$

Fruit Crush	1.25	1	0.2	0.4	0.5
Lemonade	6.25	5	1	2	2.5

   b 0.4 litres   **c** 2.5 litres

9. **a** $\frac{1}{2}$ **b** $\frac{7}{20}$ **c** $\frac{3}{20}$

10. Sugar $\frac{5}{22}$, flour $\frac{3}{11}$, margarine $\frac{2}{11}$, fruit $\frac{7}{22}$

11. 4

12. 1 : 4

13. **a** 5 : 3 : 2   **b** 20

14. $13\frac{1}{2}$ litres

15. 1 : 1 : 1

Exercise 5B

1. **a** 160 g, 240 g   **b** 80 kg, 200 kg
   c 150, 350   **d** 950 m, 50 m
   e 175 min, 125 min   **f** £20, £30, £50
   g £36, £60, £144   **h** 50 g, 250 g, 300 g
   i £1.40, £2, £1.60   **j** 120 kg, 72 kg, 8 kg

2. **a** 175   **b** 30%

3. **a** 40%   **b** 300 kg

4. 21

5. **a** Mott: no, Wright: yes, Brennan: no, Smith: no, Kaye: yes
   b For example: W26, H30; W31, H38; W33, H37

6. **a** 1 : 400 000   **b** 1 : 125 000   **c** 1 : 250 000
   d 1 : 25 000   **e** 1 : 20 000   **f** 1 : 40 000
   g 1 : 62 500   **h** 1 : 10 000   **i** 1 : 60 000

7. **a** $\frac{1}{2}$ km or 500m
   b 78 cm ≈ 39 km. 39 ÷ 15 ≈ 2.6. 2.6 hours = 2 h 36 m. Plus 30 mins is 3 h 06 m so he should be back at about 12.06 pm

8. **a** Map A 1 : 250 000,   Map B 1 : 1 000 000
   b 2 km
   c 1.2 cm
   d 4.8 cm

9. **a** 1 : 1.6   **b** 1 : 3.25   **c** 1 : 1.125
   d 1 : 1.44   **e** 1 : 5.4   **f** 1 : 1.5
   g 1 : 4.8   **h** 1 : 42   **i** 1 : 1.25

10 Diesel : Petrol = 60 : 90. $\frac{1}{5}$ of 60 = 12. $\frac{4}{9}$ of 90 = 40. Total red cars = 52 which is more than 150 ÷ 3 = 50 so Yes.

11 a 4 : 3   **b** 90 miles
   c Both arrive at the same time.

12 0.4 metres

13 13 − 9 = 4. 4 ÷ 5 = 0.8. 2 × 0.8 = 1.6, 9 + 1.6 = 10.6

14 Athos has 3 more parts than Zena. 24 ÷ 3 = 8, so 1 part is 8. Zena has 8 marbles.

Exercise 5C

1 a 3 : 2   **b** 32   **c** 80

2 a 100   **b** 160

3 0.4 litres

4 Jamie has 1.75 pints, so he has enough.

5 8100

6 296

7 Kevin £2040, John £2720

8 b C   **c** F   **d** T   **e** T

9 51

10 100

11 40 ml

12 a 160 cans   **b** 48 cans

13 a Lemonade 20 litres, ginger 0.5 litres
   b This one, in part a there are 50 parts in the ratio 40 : 9 : 1, so ginger is $\frac{1}{50}$ of total amount; in part b there are 13 parts in the ratio 10 : 2 : 1, so ginger is $\frac{1}{13}$ of total amount. $\frac{1}{13} > \frac{1}{50}$

14 a Will as his multiple of 10 is also a multiple of 9
   b Zeke has rounded off to 1 dp and and Yoko has rounded off to 2 dp. They have not used a recurring decimal notation.

15 54

Exercise 5D

1 60 g

2 £5.22

3 45

4 £6.72

5 a £312.50   **b** 8

6 a 56 litres   **b** 350 miles

7 a 300 kg   **b** 9 weeks

8 40 seconds

9 a i 100 g, 200 g, 250 g, 150 g
   ii 150 g, 300 g, 375 g, 225 g
   iii 250 g, 500 g, 625 g, 375 g
   b 24

10 I can buy four packs (24 sausages) from Peter (£9.20)
   I can only buy two packs (20 sausages) from Paul (£7)
   I should use Peter's shop to get the most sausages for £10.

11 400 ÷ 10 = 40 loaves needed. 1.8 kg ÷ 3 = 0.6 kg per loaf, so 40 × 0.6 = 24 kg of flour.

12 4 buns and 5 cakes

13 11 minutes 40 seconds + 12 minutes = 23 minutes 40 seconds

14 Possible answer:
   30 g plain flour (rounding to nearest 10 g)
   60 ml whole milk (rounding to nearest 10 ml)
   1 egg (need an egg)
   1 g salt (nearest whole number)
   10 ml beef dripping or lard (rounding to nearest 10 ml)

15 30 litres

Exercise 5E

1 a £4.50 for a 10-pack
   b £1.08 for 6
   c £2.45 for 1 litre
   d Same value

2 a Large jar as more g per £
   b 75 ml tube as more ml per £
   c Large box as more g per £
   d 400 ml bottle as more ml per £

3 a £5.11
   b Large tin (small £5.11/l, medium £4.80/l, large £4.47/l)

4 a 95p   **b** Family size

5 Mary

6 Kelly

7 12-pack 360 ÷ 12 = 30p per sachet. 40-pack 1150 ÷ 40 = 28.75p per sachet. 4 sachets cost 4 × 35 = £1.40 but you get 5, so 140 ÷ 5 = 28p per sachet, so the offer is the best value.

8 a Abe uses 10 × 0.75 = 7.5 litres to do 100 km. Caryl uses 100 ÷ 14 = 7.14 litres to do 100 km and Des uses 100 ÷ (55 × 1.6) × 4.55 = 5.17 litres to do 100 km, so Des's car is the most ecomonical.
   b It does not give a 'unit' value, ie miles per gallon or litres per mile.

Exercise 5F

1 a £260   **b** £307.50   **c** £323.75   **d** £289

2 a £7.50   **b** £9.05   **c** £5.80   **d** £10.75

3 a 38 h **b** $41\frac{1}{2}$ h **c** 35 h **d** 40 h

4 a Fewer hours **b** More pay

5 a £540 **b** £702

6 £6.90

7 375 − 330 = 45, 45 ÷ 6 = £7.50. (375 − 12 × 7.50) ÷ 7.50 = 38 hours

8 £$1\frac{1}{4}$ x

9 Pay is £442.50 tax is £88.50, NI is 442.50 − 88.50 − 327.45 = 26.55, 26.55 ÷ 442.5 = 0.06, so the NI rate is 6%

10 407 factorises to 1 × 407 or 11 × 37, so Jeff works 37 hours a week at £11 per hour.

Exercise 5G

1 18 mph

2 280 miles

3 52.5 mph

4 11:50 am

5 500 seconds

6 a 75 mph **b** 6.5 h
  c 175 miles **d** 240 km
  e 64 km/h **f** 325 km
  g 4.3 h (4 h 18 min)

7 a 2.25 h **b** 99 miles

8 a 1.25 h **b** 1 h 15 min

9 a Sheffield to London via Midland mainline 74.38 mph. Sheffield to London via East Coast mainline 78.26 mph, including the wait at Doncaster
  b Doncaster to London 94.12 mph, including the wait at Doncaster

10 a 120 km **b** 48 km/h

11 a 30 min **b** 6 mph

12 a 10 m/s **b** 3.3 m/s **c** 16.7 m/s

13 a 90 km/h **b** 43.2 km/h **c** 1.8 km/h

14 18 m/s is 64.8 km/h. 40 km at 64.8 km/h is 0.617 hours ≈ 37 minutes so train arrives at 8.07 am

15

Time	10	10.15	10.30	10.45	11
Ajeet	16	20	24	28	32
Bijay	0	6	12	18	24
Time	11.15	11.30	11.45	12	12.15
Ajeet	36	40	44	48	52
Bijay	30	36	42	48	54

Bijay catches Ajeet at 12 noon

6 Rebecca: 10 minutes at 50 mph covers 8.333 miles, 10 minutes at 70 mph covers 11.666 miles, so total distance is 20 miles in 20 minutes which is 60 mph, so Rebecca is correct.
Nick: 10 miles at 40 mph takes 15 minutes, 10 miles at 60 mph takes 10 minutes, so total distance is 20 miles in 25 minutes, which is 48 mph, so Nick is wrong.

17 Josh should take 40 minutes. Nell should take 50 ÷ 70 × 60 = 43 minutes, but Josh is likely to meet traffic through town so is unlikely to travel at anywhere near 30 mph. Nell is likely to be able to travel at 70 mph on the motorway.

Exercise 5H

1 a 0.75 g/cm^3

2 4 pa

3 $8\frac{1}{3}$ g/cm3

4 2 ½ N

5 32 g

6 5 m^2

7 120 cm^3

8 156.8 g

9 30 × 20

10 By the handle as smaller area

11 So they can walk on sand easier due to less pressure on the surface.

12 a 19.3 kg
  b 19.3 kg. Mass is same
  c On largest face 9560 Pa, On smallest face 38600 Pa

13 First statue is the fake as density is approximately 26 g/cm^3

14 Second piece by 1 cm^3

15 0.339 m^3

16 Areas are ½ m^2. 0.8 m^2. 0.4m^2. Sides are 1 m, $\frac{1}{2}$ m and 0.8 m

17 a T **b** F **c** F **d** T

Exercise 5I

1 a £400 **b** £112.50
  c £12.80 **d** £499.46

2 a 8 years **b** 12 years

3 a i 10.5 g **ii** 11.03 g
    iii 12.16 g **iv** 14.07 g
  b 9 days

4 12 years

5 a £14 272.27 **b** 20 years

6 a i 2550   **ii** 2168   **iii** 1331
  b 7 years

7 a £6800   **b** £5440   **c** £3481.60

8 a i 1.9 million litres
    ii 1.6 million litres
    iii 1.2 million litres
  b 10th August

9 a i 51 980
    ii 84 752
    iii 138 186
  b 2021

10 a 21 years   **b** 21 years

11 3 years

12 30 years

13 $1.1 \times 1.1 = 1.21$ (21% increase)

14 Bradley Bank account is worth £1032, Monastery Building Society account is worth £1031.30, so Bradley Bank by 70p.

15 4 months: fish weighs $3 \times 1.1^4 = 4.3923$ kg; crab weighs $6 \times 0.9^4 = 3.9366$ kg

16 4 weeks

Exercise 5J

1 a 800 g   **b** 250 m   **c** 60 cm
  d £3075   **e** £200   **f** £400

2 80

3 T-shirt £8.40, Tights £1.20, Shorts £5.20, Sweater £10.75, Trainers £24.80, Boots £32.40

4 £833.33

5 £300

6 240

7 £350

8 4750 blue bottles

9 £26.40

10 a £1600
  b With 10% cut each year he earns £1440 × 12 + £1296 × 12 = £17 280 + £15 552 = £32 832 With immediate 14% cut he earns £1376 × 24 = £33 024, so correct decision

11 a 30%   **b** 15%

12 Less by $\frac{1}{4}$%

13 £900

14 Calculate the pre-VAT price for certain amounts, and $\frac{5}{6}$ of that amount. Show the error grows as the amount increases. Up to £281 the error is less than £5.

15 £1250

16 £1250

17 $0.28 \times 5400 = 1512$. $1512 \times 2.5 = 3780$, $3780 \div 0.72 = 5250$, so population has declined by 150 people.

18 Baz has assumed that 291.2 is 100% instead of 112%. He rounded his wrong answer to the correct answer of £260.

19 $35\% = \frac{35}{100}$ which cancels to $\frac{7}{20}$, so the smallest number that could have been surveyed is 20.

Review questions

1 48 mph

2 Definite, as his average speed was 80 miles per hour which is 128 km/h

3 Totals are 40 and 60 giving 2 : 3 and a total of 100. 9 : 11 is a ratio of 45 : 55 so swap 10 and 15

4 a $1.73 \div 0.04 = 43.25$ so 43 horses, $2.64 \div 0.065 = 40.62$ so 40 cattle and $0.95 \div 0.01 = 95$. Total 43 + 40 + 95 = 178 animals.
  b Horses in field A = 43, Sheep in field B = $2.64 \div 0.01 = 264$, Cattle in field C, $0.95 \div 0.065 = 14.62$, so 14 cattle. Total 43 + 264 + 14 = 321 animals

5 100°

6 a 22.5 kg   **b** 30 kg   **c** £19.80

7 £8357.35

8 £375

9 a £4945.97
  b 5, yes he has £1357.68 in the account so he has rounded to the nearest £10

10 13.04%

11 90

12 Joe pays $41.4 - 4.4 = £37$, Lucy pays $41.4 \div 1.15 = £36$, so Joe's meal cost more.

13 $680.4 \div 4500 = £0.1512$ per units in 2015. $0.1512 \div 1.08 = £0.14$ pence per unit in 2014. $5400 \times £0.14 = £756$, so she paid more for the units in 2014.

14 $50.50 \div 0.9 \div 0.85 = 66.01$, so price was £66 and other prices are rounded off.

Chapter 6 – Geometry and measures: Angles

Exercise 6A

1 a 108°   **b** 52°   **c** 59°

2 a 57°   **b** 40°

3 No; 45° + 125° = 170° and for a straight line it should be 180°.

4 a $x = 100°$ **b** $x = 110°$ **c** $x = 30°$

5 a $x = 55°$ **b** $x = 45°$ **c** $x = 12.5°$

6 a $x = 34°, y = 98°$ **b** $x = 70°, y = 120°$
c $x = 20°, y = 80°$

7 6 × 60° = 360°; imagine six of the triangles meeting at a point

8 $x = 35°, y = 75°; 2x = 70°$ (opposite angles), so $x = 35°$ and $x + y = 110°$ (angles on a line), so $y = 75°$

Exercise 6B

1 a-c Students' own drawings **d** 180°

2 a 60° **b** Equilateral triangle
c Same length

3 a 70° each **b** Isosceles triangle
c Same length

4 a 109° **b** 130° **c** 135°

5 65°

6 Joe is not correct as DFE = 30, DEF = 75 hence angle D = 180 − 105 = 75 but Hannah is correct as FED = FDE = 75°

7 $a = 35°$ (angles in a triangle) because the other angles in the triangle are 65° (angles on a line) and 80° (opposite angles) giving a total of 145, this subtracted from the 180 degrees in a triangle leaves the answer of 35

8 Missing angle = y, $x + y = 180°$ and $a + b + y = 180°$ so $x = a + b$

9 32

10 72°

Exercise 6C

1 2, 2, 360°

2 3, 3, 540°

3 4, 4, 720°

4

Shape	Number of sides	Triangles	Angle sum
Triangle	3	1	180
Quadrilateral	4	2	360
Pentagon	5	3	540
Hexagon	6	4	720
Heptagon	7	5	900
Octagon	8	6	1080
Nonagon	9	7	1260
Decagon	10	8	1440

5 18, 18, 3240

Exercise 6D

1 a 90° **b** 150° **c** 80°

2 a No, total is 350° **b** Yes, total is 360°
c No, total is 350° **d** No, total is 370°
e Yes, total is 360° **f** Yes, total is 360°

3 a 90° **b** Rectangle **c** Square

4 a 120° **b** 136° **c** 149°
d 126° **e** 114°

5 60° + 60° + 120° + 120° + 120° + 240° = 720°

6 $y = 360° - 4x$; $2x + y + 2x = 360°$, $4x + y = 360°$, so $y = 360° - 4x$

7 $x = 40°$, so the smaller angle is 60°

Exercise 6E

1

Shape	Number of sides	Interior angle sum	Each interior angle
octagon	8	1080	135
nonagon	9	1260	140
decagon	10	1440	144

2

Regular polygon	Number of sides	Interior angle	Exterior angle
square	4	90	90
pentagon	5	108	72
hexagon	6	120	60
octagon	8	135	45
nonagon	9	140	40
decagon	10	144	36

3 a i 45° **ii** 8 **iii** 1080°
b i 20° **ii** 18 **iii** 2880°
c i 15° **ii** 24 **iii** 3960°
d i 36° **ii** 10 **iii** 1440°

4 a i 172° **ii** 45 **iii** 7740°
b i 174° **ii** 60 **iii** 10 440°
c i 156° **ii** 15 **iii** 2340°
d i 177° **ii** 120 **iii** 21 240°

5 a Exterior angle is 7°, which does not divide exactly into 360°
b Exterior angle is 19°, which does not divide exactly into 360°
c Exterior angle is 11°, which does divide exactly into 360°
d Exterior angle is 70°, which does not divide exactly into 360°

6 a 7° does not divide exactly into 360°
b 26° does not divide exactly into 360°
c 44° does not divide exactly into 360°
d 13° does not divide exactly into 360°

7 48°; $\dfrac{1440° - 5 \times 240°}{5}$

8 10

9 $x = 45°$, they are the same, true for all regular polygons

10 Three are 135° and two are 67.5°

11 72°, 72°, 108°, 144°, 144°

12 93° or 273°

Exercise 6F

1 a d **b** f **c** d **d** f **e** f **f** e

2 a $b = c = 70°$ **b** $d = 75°, e = f = 105°$
c $g = 50°, h = i = 130°$ **d** $n = m = 80°$
e $g = i = 65°, h = 115°$ **f** $j = k = 72°, l = 108°$

3 a $a = 95°$ **b** $b = 66°, c = 114°$

4 a $x = 30°, y = 120°$ **b** $x = 25°, y = 105°$
c $x = 30°, y = 100°$ **d** $x = 50°, y = 110°$
e $x = 25°, y = 55°$ **f** $x = 20°, y = 140°$

5 290°; x is double the angle allied to 35°, so is
$2 \times 145°$

6 angle BDC = 66° (angles in a triangle = 180°)
angle BDE = 114° (angles on a line = 180°) so
$a = 66°$ (corresponding angle or allied angle)

7 Angle PQD = 64° (alternate angles), so angle
DQY = 116° (angles on a line = 180°)

8 Use alternate angles to see b, a and c are all
angles on a straight line, and so total 180°

9 Third angle in triangle equals q (alternate angle),
angle sum of triangle is 180°.

Exercise 6G

1 a $a = 110°, b = 55°$ **b** $g = i = 63°, h = 117°$
c $e = f = 94°$

2 a $a = 58°, b = 47°$ **b** $c = 141°, d = 37°$
c $e = g = 65°, f = 115°$

3 a 65° **b** 60° **c** 68°

4 both 129°

5 Marie is correct, a rectangle is a parallelogram
with all angles equal to 90°

6 a 65°
b Trapezium, angle A + angle D = 180° and
angle B + angle C = 180°

7 135

8

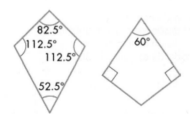

9 A trapezium; angles add up to 10x, two angles x
and 4x = 2x + 3x, the other pair of angles. Hence
each pair adds up to 180 (since 2 × 180 = 360).

Hence two pairs of allied angles, hence a
trapezium. Alternatively you could have found
that $x = 36$ which will give the same result.

Exercise 6H

1 a Student's scale drawing.
b About 19 m so about 38 plants

2 a i 65 km **ii** 212 km
iii 114 km **iv** 36 km
b i 83 km **ii** 196 km
iii 149 km **iv** 130 km

3 a 36 km **b** 2 000 000

4 1 : 63 360

5 a 110°, 12.6 km **b** 250°, 4.5 km
c 091°, 11.8 km **d** 270°, 8.4 km
e 130°, 7.2 km **f** 180°, 4.2 km

6 Students' Sketches

7 a Sketch
b D is due south of B and B is east of A, so A
must be west of D. A bearing to the west will
be greater than 180°

8 a 090°, 180°, 270° **b** 000°, 270°, 180°

9 a 045° **b** 286°
c measure the distance from X to Y and divide
15 by this to find the scale of the map. Then
measure the distance from Y to P and multiply
by the scale factor

10 a 250° **b** 325° **c** 144°

11 a 900 m **b** 280°
c angle NHS = 150° and HS = 3 cm

12 108°

13 255°

14 9.92 km

Review questions

1 16

2 a i 115°
ii Vertically opposite angles are equal and
co-interior angles add up to 180°
b the angles do not add up to 360°

3 a 50° **b** 32.5°

4 A five sided shape can be split into 3 triangles
hence 3 × 180
= 540°

5 150°

6 angle TQP = 37° (alternate angles), PTQ = 180 −
(29 + 37) = 114° (angles in a triangle), QTS = 180
− 114 (angles on a line) = 66°

7 333°

8 360 ÷ 8 = 45°; exterior angle formula is 360 ÷
number of sides, in this case 8

9 $180 - (360 \div 6) = 120°$ or $(180 \times 4) \div 6 = 120°$

10 Selvi might be correct. You will need to draw one example showing this is not a kite, and one example showing that this could be a kite

11 a Student's own sketch   **b** 12.4 km

Chapter 7 – Geometry and measures: Transformations, constructions and loci

Exercise 7A

1 a SAS   **b** SSS   **c** ASA
   d RHS   **e** SSS   **f** ASA

2 a SSS. A to R, B to P, C to Q
   b SAS. A to R, B to Q, C to P

3 a 60°   **b** 80°   **c** 40°   **d** 5 cm

4 a 110°   **b** 55°   **c** 85°   **d** 110°   **e** 4 cm

5 SSS or RHS

6 SSS or SAS or RHS

7 For example, use ∠ADE and ∠CDG. AD = CD (sides of large square), DE = DG (sides of small square), ∠ADE = ∠CDG (angles sum to 90° with ∠ADG), so ∆ADE ≡ ∆CDG (SAS), so AE = CG

8 AB and PQ are the corresponding sides to the 42° angle, but they are not equal in length.

Exercise 7B

1 a 4   **b** 5   **c** 6   **d** 4   **e** 6

2 a 2   **b** 2   **c** 2   **d** 2   **e** 2

3 A, B, C, D, E, F, G, J, K, L, M, P, Q, R, T, U, V, W, Y

4 a   1
   b the central white star or the large dark green star
   c order 16 – the light green star around the central white star, or order 9 – the light green shape between the outer petals and the inner stars

5 for example:

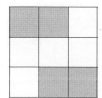

6

	Number of lines of symmetry			
Order of rotational symmetry	0	1	2	3
1	D	A		
2	E		B	
3				C

7 She is correct since the angle sum around the centre point is 360 and 360 ÷ 3 = 120

8 Yes she is correct. A triangle can only have 1 or 3 lines of symmetry. If a triangle has 3 lines of symmetry it also has rotational symmetry of order 3, so this triangle must only have 1 line of symmetry. This will mean it has two angles identical and two sides, and hence an isosceles triangle.

Exercise 7C

1 a i $\begin{pmatrix} 1 \\ 3 \end{pmatrix}$ **ii** $\begin{pmatrix} 4 \\ 2 \end{pmatrix}$ **iii** $\begin{pmatrix} 2 \\ -1 \end{pmatrix}$ **iv** $\begin{pmatrix} 5 \\ 1 \end{pmatrix}$

  b i $\begin{pmatrix} -1 \\ -3 \end{pmatrix}$ **ii** $\begin{pmatrix} 3 \\ -1 \end{pmatrix}$ **iii** $\begin{pmatrix} -2 \\ 3 \end{pmatrix}$ **iv** $\begin{pmatrix} 3 \\ 3 \end{pmatrix}$

  c i $\begin{pmatrix} -2 \\ -3 \end{pmatrix}$ **ii** $\begin{pmatrix} 1 \\ -1 \end{pmatrix}$ **iii** $\begin{pmatrix} -5 \\ 4 \end{pmatrix}$ **iv** $\begin{pmatrix} 0 \\ 4 \end{pmatrix}$

  d i $\begin{pmatrix} 3 \\ 2 \end{pmatrix}$ **ii** $\begin{pmatrix} -4 \\ 2 \end{pmatrix}$ **iii** $\begin{pmatrix} 5 \\ -4 \end{pmatrix}$ **iv** $\begin{pmatrix} -2 \\ -7 \end{pmatrix}$

2

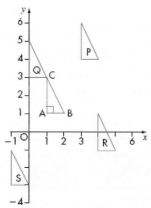

3 a $\begin{pmatrix} -3 \\ -1 \end{pmatrix}$ **b** $\begin{pmatrix} 4 \\ -4 \end{pmatrix}$ **c** $\begin{pmatrix} -5 \\ -2 \end{pmatrix}$ **d** $\begin{pmatrix} 4 \\ 7 \end{pmatrix}$

  e $\begin{pmatrix} -1 \\ 5 \end{pmatrix}$ **f** $\begin{pmatrix} 1 \\ 6 \end{pmatrix}$ **g** $\begin{pmatrix} -4 \\ 4 \end{pmatrix}$ **h** $\begin{pmatrix} -4 \\ -7 \end{pmatrix}$

4 $10 \times 10 = 100$ (including $\begin{pmatrix} 0 \\ 0 \end{pmatrix}$)

5 a Check students' designs for a Snakes and ladders board.
  b because the ladders always mean moving up the board
   ii the snakes always mean moving down the board

6 $\begin{pmatrix} -x \\ -y \end{pmatrix}$

7 a Check student's diagram

b $\begin{pmatrix} -300 \\ -500 \end{pmatrix}$

8 $\begin{pmatrix} -1 \\ 4 \end{pmatrix}$

9 Under a translation every points moves with the same vector, hence all the sides are the same length, so we can use the SSS rule of congruency.

Exercise 7D

1 a–e

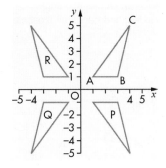

f Reflection in the y-axis

2 a–b

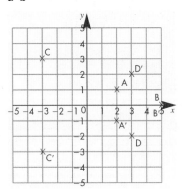

c y-value changes sign
d $(a, -b)$

3 a–b

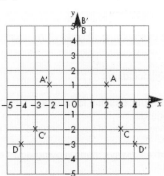

c x-value changes sign
d $(-a, b)$

e Any three points with x co-ordinate 0, e.g. (0, 1), (0, 2), (0, 3)

4 Possible answer: Take the centre square as ABCD then reflect this square each time in the line, AB, then BC, then CD and finally AD.

5 $x = -1$

6

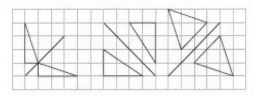

7 a–i

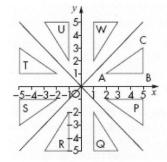

j A reflection in $y = x$

8

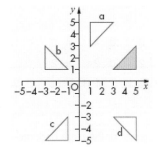

9 a–c

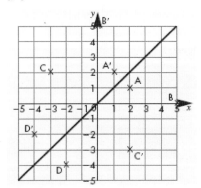

d Coordinates are reversed: x becomes y and y becomes x

e (b, a)

f Any point with x and y co-ordinates the same, e.g. (1, 1), (2, 2)

10 a–c

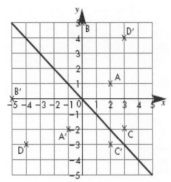

d Coordinates are reversed and change sign, x becomes $-y$ and y becomes $-x$

e $(-b, -a)$

11 Because a reflection is exactly the same shape as the original, just in a different orientation, hence we can use the rule SSS to show the two shapes are congruent.

Exercise 7E

1 a

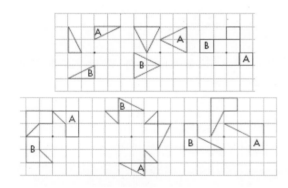

b i Rotation 90°anticlockwise
ii Rotation 180°

2 a

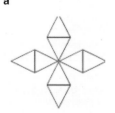

b rotate shape 60° around point B, then repeat another four times.

3 Possible answer: If ABCD is the centre square, rotate about A 90° anticlockwise, rotate about new B 180°, now rotate about new C 180°, and finally rotate about new D 180°.

4

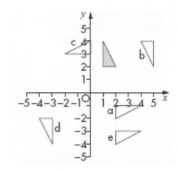

5 a 90° anticlockwise
b 270° anticlockwise
c 300° clockwise
d 260° clockwise

6 a b c i

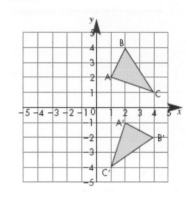

ii A' (2, −1), B' (4, −2), C' (1, −4)
iii Original coordinates (x, y) become $(y, -x)$
iv Yes

7 i

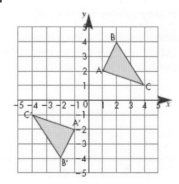

ii A' (−1, −2), B' (−2, −4), C' (−4, −1)
iii Original coordinates (x, y) become $(-x, -y)$
iv Yes

8 i

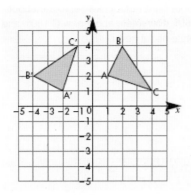

ii A' (–2, 1), B' (–4, 2), C' (–1, 4)
iii Original coordinates (x, y) become (–y, x)
iv Yes

9 The centre of rotation

10 Show by drawing a shape or use the fact that (a, b) becomes (a, –b) after reflection in the x-axis, and (a, –b) becomes (–a, –b) after reflection in the y-axis, which is equivalent to a single rotation of 180°.

11 she is correct

12 a

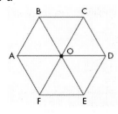

b i Rotation 60° clockwise about O
ii Rotation 120° clockwise about O
iii Rotation 180° about O
iv Rotation 240° clockwise about O
c i Rotation 60° clockwise about O
ii Rotation 180° about O

13 Rotation 90° anticlockwise about (3, –2)

14 Because under a rotation, the lengths of the original shape are preserved, so we can use the rule SSS to show they are congruent.

Exercise 7F

1

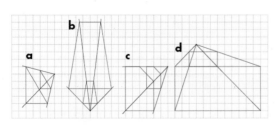

2 a

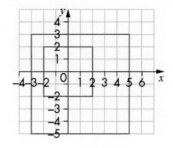

b

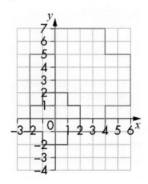

3

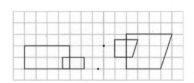

4 a

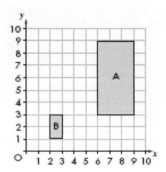

b 3 : 1
c 3 : 1
d 9 : 1

5 a (1, 1), (3, –3), (–5, –5)   **b** (1, 1)

6

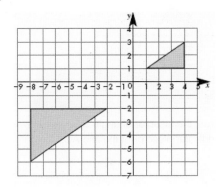

7 a–c

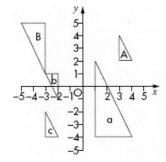

d Scale factor $-\frac{1}{2}$, centre (1, 3)
e Scale factor –2, centre (1, 3)
f Scale factor –1, centre (–2.5, –1.5)
g Scale factor –1, centre (–2.5, –1.5)
h Same centres, and the scale factors are reciprocals of each other

8 Enlargement, scale factor –2, about (1, 3)

9 Because the sides of triangle C are all larger than the original triangle B, and so the SSS rule will not apply.

Exercise 7G

1 (–4, –3)

2 a (–5, 2)
b Reflection in y-axis

3 A: translation $\begin{pmatrix} 1 \\ -2 \end{pmatrix}$, B: reflection in y-axis, C: rotation 90°clockwise about (0, 0), D: reflection in $x = 3$, E: reflection in $y = 4$, F: enlargement by scale factor 2, centre (0, 1)

4

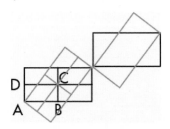

5. a T_1 to T_2: rotation 90°clockwise about (0, 0)
b T_1 to T_6: rotation 90°anticlockwise about (0, 0)
c T_2 to T_3: translation $\begin{pmatrix} 2 \\ 2 \end{pmatrix}$
d T_6 to T_2: rotation 180°about (0, 0)
e T_6 to T_5: reflection in y-axis
f T_5 to T_4: translation $\begin{pmatrix} 4 \\ 0 \end{pmatrix}$

6 a–d

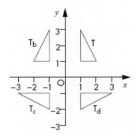

e T_d to T: rotation 90° anticlockwise about (0, 0)

7 (3, 1)

8 Reflection in x-axis, translation $\begin{pmatrix} 0 \\ -5 \end{pmatrix}$, rotation 90°clockwise about (0, 0)

9 Translation $\begin{pmatrix} 0 \\ -8 \end{pmatrix}$, reflection in x-axis, rotation 90°clockwise about (0, 0)

10 a

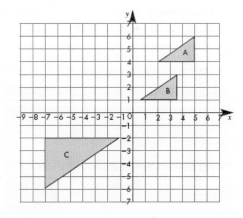

b enlargement of scale factor $-\frac{1}{2}$ about (1, 2)

11 No, this can be shown with an example.

12 a-b

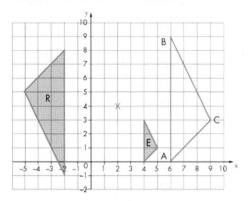

c An enlargement, scale factor –3, centre (2.5, 2)

13 (10, 10)

Exercise 7H

1–9 Practical work; check students' constructions

10 The centre of the circle

11 Start with a base line AB; then construct a perpendicular to the line from point A. At point B, construct an angle of 60°. Ensure that the line for this 60° angle crosses the perpendicular line; where they meet will be the final point C.

12–14 Practical work; check students' constructions

Exercise 7I

1 Circle with radius:
   a 2 cm   **b** 4 cm   **c** 5 cm

2 a   **b**   **c**

3 a Circle with radius 4 m   **b**

2 m

4 a   **b**   **c**

d   **e**   **f**

5

6

7 Construct the bisector of angle BAC and the perpendicular bisector of the line AC.

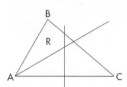

8

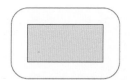

9. Start with a base line, AB, 3 cm long. At point A, draw a few points all 3 cm away from A towards the upper right side. Lightly join these dots with an arc. You can now find the point that is 3 cm away from point B and draw the equilateral triangle.

10. Gary is correct about the triangle inside, but not a triangle outside as there will be three straight lines, parallel to each side of the triangle, then these straight lines will be joined with arcs centred on the vertices of the original triangle.

Exercise 7J

1

2 a

b

3

4

5

6

7 No, if you accurately draw a diagram showing the path of each boat, you will find the boat leaving from point B meets the path of the other boat in a much shorter time as it's a smaller distance than fom A to the cross over point.)

8 On a map, draw a straight line from Newcastle to Bristol, construct the line bisector, then the search will be anywhere on the sea along that line.

9 a Sketch should show a circle of radius 6 cm around London and one of radius 4 cm around Glasgow.
   b No
   c Yes

10 a Yes
   b Sketch should show a circle of radius 4 cm around Leeds and one of radius 4 cm around Exeter. The area where they overlap should be shaded.

11 a This is the perpendicular bisector of the line from York to Birmingham. It should pass just below Manchester and just through the top of Norwich.

b Sketch should show a circle of radius 7 cm around Glasgow and one of radius 5 cm around London. The area where they overlap should be shaded.
   c The transmitter can be built anywhere on line constructed in part **a** that is within the area shown in part **b**.

12 Sketch should show two circles around Birmingham, one of radius 3 cm and one of radius 5 cm. The area of good reception is the area between the two circles.

13 Sketch should show a circle of radius 6 cm around Glasgow, two circles around York, one of radius 4 cm and one of radius 6 cm and a circle around London of radius 8 cm. The small area in the Irish Sea that is between the two circles around York and inside both the circle around Glasgow and the circle around London is where the boat can be.

14 Sketch should show two circles around Newcastle upon Tyne, one of radius 4 cm and one of radius 6 cm, and two circles around Bristol, one of radius 3 cm and one of radius 5 cm. The area that is between both pairs of circles is the area that should be shaded.

15 Sketch should show the perpendicular bisector of the line running from Newcastle upon Tyne to Manchester and that of the line running from Sheffield to Norwich. Where the lines cross is where the oil rig is located.

16 Sketch should show the perpendicular bisector of the line running from Glasgow to Norwich and that of the line running from Norwich to Exeter. Where the lines cross is where Fred's house is.

17 Leeds

Exercise 7K

1

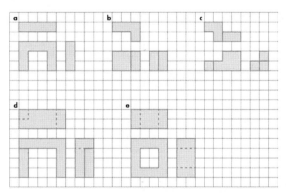

2

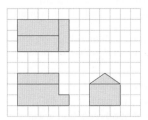

3 a A cylinder
   b A hexagonal prism

4

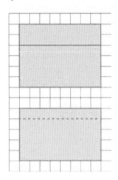

5

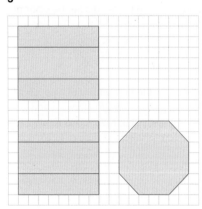

6

 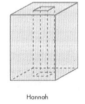 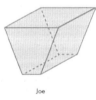

Chris   Hannah   Joe

Review questions

1 a-b

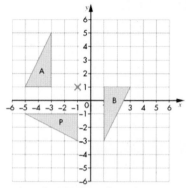

c rotation of 180° about (−1, 1)
d (−1, 1)

2 a-b

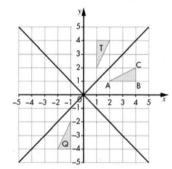

c rotation of 180° about O

3 You should have measured the error of the angle size and converted that to a percentage error.

4

5 cm

5

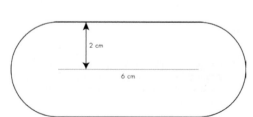

2 cm

6 cm

6

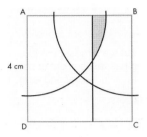

7 a

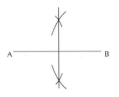

b … an equal distance from A and B

8

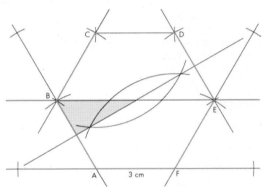

9

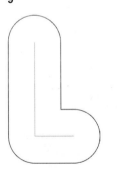

10

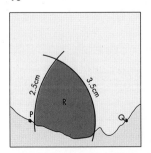

11 A (9, 0) B (11, −3) C (2, −1)

12

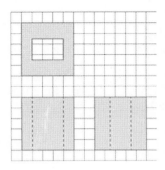

13 It is not always true

14 In a rhombus all sides are the same length, so
AB = BC = AD = DC, AC is a common length in
both triangles, so each triangle has the three
sides matching, SSS.

Chapter 8 – Algebra: Algebraic manipulation

Exercise 8A

1 a 13   **b** −3   **c** 5

2 a 1.4   **b** 1.4   **c** −0.4

3 a 13   **b** 74   **c** 17

4 a 75   **b** 22.5   **c** −135

5 a 2.5   **b** −20   **c** 2.5

6 a $\frac{150}{n}$ **b** £925

7 a $2 \times 8 + 6 \times 11 - 3 \times 2 = 76$
  b $5 \times 2 - 2 \times 11 + 3 \times 8 = 12$

8 a One odd one even value, different from each
other.
  b Any valid combination, e.g. $x = 1$, $y = 2$

9 a i Odd   **ii** Odd
   iii Even   **iv** Odd
  b Any valid expression such as $xy + z$

10 a £20
  b i −£40
    ii Delivery cost will be zero.
  c 40 miles

11 A expression, B formula, C identity, D equation

12 a First term is cost of petrol, each mile is a tenth
of £0.98. Second term is the hire cost divided
by the miles.
  b 29.8p per mile

Exercise 8B

1
a $6 + 2m$ **b** $10 + 5l$
c $12 - 3y$ **d** $20 + 8k$
e $6 - 12f$ **f** $10 - 6w$
g $10k + 15m$ **h** $12d - 8n$
i $t^2 + 3t$ **j** $k^2 - 3k$
k $4t^2 - 4t$ **l** $8k - 2k^2$
m $8g^2 + 20g$ **n** $15h^2 - 10h$
o $y^3 + 5y$ **p** $h^4 + 7h$
q $k^3 - 5k$ **r** $3t^3 + 12t$
s $15d^3 - 3d^4$ **t** $6w^3 + 3tw$
u $15a^3 - 10ab$ **v** $12p^4 - 15mp$
w $12h^3 + 8h^2g$ **x** $8m^3 + 2m^4$

2
a $5(t - 1)$ and $5t - 5$
b Yes, as $5(t - 1)$ when $t = 4.50$ is $5 \times 3.50 =$ £17.50

3 He has worked out 3×5 as 8 instead of 15 and he has not multiplied the second term by 3. Answer should be $15x - 12$.

4
a $3(2y + 3)$
b $2(6z + 4)$ or $4(3z + 2)$

5
a $22 + 5t$ **b** $21 + 19k$
c $22 + 2f$ **d** $14 + 3g$

6
a $2 + 2h$ **b** $9g + 5$
c $17k + 16$ **d** $6e + 20$

7
a $4m + 3p + 2mp$
b $3k + 4h + 5hk$
c $12r + 24p + 13pr$
d $19km + 20k - 6m$

8
a $9t^2 + 13t$ **b** $13y^2 + 5y$
c $10e^2 - 6e$ **d** $14k^2 - 3kp$

9
a $17ab + 12ac + 6bc$
b $18wy + 6ty - 8tw$
c $14mn - 15mp - 6np$
d $8r^3 - 6r^2$

10
a $5(f + 2s) + 2(2f + 3s) = 9f + 16s$
b £$(270f + 480s)$
c £42 450 − £30 000 = £12 450

11 For x-coefficients, 3 and 1 or 1 and 4; for y-coefficients, 5 and 1 or 3 and 4 or 1 and 7

12 $5(3x + 2) - 3(2x - 1) = 9x + 13$

Exercise 8C

1
a $6(m + 2t)$ **b** $3(3t + p)$
c $4(2m + 3k)$ **d** $4(r + 2t)$
e $m(n + 3)$ **f** $g(5g + 3)$
g $2(2w - 3t)$ **h** $y(3y + 2)$
i $t(4t - 3)$ **j** $3m(m - p)$
k $3p(2p + 3t)$ **l** $2p(4t + 3m)$
m $4b(2a - c)$ **n** $5bc(b - 2)$
o $2b(4ac + 3de)$ **p** $2(2a^2 + 3a + 4)$
q $3b(2a + 3c + d)$ **r** $t(5t + 4 + a)$
s $3mt(2t - 1 + 3m)$ **t** $2ab(4b + 1 - 2a)$
u $5pt(2t + 3 + p)$

2
a Mary has taken out a common factor.
b Because the bracket adds up to £10.
c £30

3 **a**, **d**, **f** and **h** do not factorise.
b $m(5 + 2p)$ **c** $t(t - 7)$ **e** $2m(2m - 3p)$
g $a(4a - 5b)$ **i** $b(5a - 3bc)$

4
a Bernice
b Aidan has not taken out the largest possible common factor. Craig has taken m out of both terms but there isn't an m in the second term.

5 There are no common factors.

6 Perimeter $= 2x + 8 + x + 5 + 5x + 4 + 9x - 3 + 10 - x = 16x + 24 = 8(2x + 3)$

7 $\dfrac{4x^2 - 12x}{2x - 6}$

Exercise 8D

1
a $x^2 + 5x + 6$ **b** $t^2 + 7t + 12$
c $w^2 + 4w + 3$ **d** $m^2 + 6m + 5$

2
a $p^2 + 3p - 70$ **b** $u^2 - 12u + 32$
c $k^2 + 2k - 15$ **d** $z^2 - 12z + 27$

3
a should be 35 on the end
b should be $- 80$
c should be $- 10x$
d should be $12y$
e should be $- 9z$

Exercise 8E

1
a $k^2 + 8k + 15$ **b** $a^2 + 5a + 4$
c $x^2 + 2x - 8$ **d** $t^2 + 2t - 15$
e $w^2 + 2w - 3$ **f** $f^2 - f - 6$

2
a $r^2 - 10r + 16$ **b** $s^2 - 17s + 70$
c $d^2 - 17d + 16$ **d** $m^2 - 9m + 18$
e $q^2 - 20q + 99$ **f** $y^2 - 13y + 40$

3
a $20a$ **b** $3b$ **c** 200
d $-11d$ **e** $12e, 28$

Exercise 8F

1
a $g^2 - 3g - 4$ **b** $y^2 + y - 12$
c $x^2 + x - 12$ **d** $p^2 - p - 2$
e $k^2 - 2k - 8$ **f** $y^2 + 3y - 10$
g $a^2 + 2a - 3$

2
a $x^2 - 9$ **b** $t^2 - 25$ **c** $m^2 - 16$
d $t^2 - 4$ **e** $y^2 - 64$ **f** $p^2 - 1$
g $25 - x^2$ **h** $49 - g^2$ **i** $x^2 - 36$

3 $(x + 2)$ and $(x + 3)$

4
a B: $1 \times (x - 2)$
     C: 1×2
     D: $2 \times (x - 1)$
b $(x - 2) + 2 + 2(x - 1) = 3x - 2$
c Area A $= (x - 1)(x - 2) =$ area of square minus areas (B + C + D) $= x^2 - (3x - 2) = x^2 - 3x + 2$

5
a $x^2 - 9$
b **i** 9991   **ii** 39 991

6 a $y^2 + 14y + 45$
  b i 45.1401 **ii** 45.4209
   iii 44.7204 **iv** 11 445

7 a $x^2 + 2x + 1$
  b $x^2 - 2x + 1$
  c $x^2 - 1$
  d Expand the expressions $[(x + 1) + (x - 1)]^2$ and
   $(x + 1)^2 + 2(x + 1)(x - 1) + (x - 1)^2$ to show that they are equal.

Exercise 8G

1 a $6x^2 + 11x + 3$ **b** $12y^2 + 17y + 6$
  c $6t^2 + 17t + 5$ **d** $8t^2 + 2t - 3$
  e $10m^2 - 11m - 6$ **f** $12k^2 - 11k - 15$
  g $6p^2 + 11p - 10$ **h** $10w^2 + 19w + 6$
  i $6a^2 - 7a - 3$ **j** $8r^2 - 10r + 3$
  k $15g^2 - 16g + 4$ **l** $12d^2 + 5d - 2$
  m $8p^2 + 26p + 15$ **n** $6t^2 + 7t + 2$
  o $6p^2 + 11p + 4$ **p** $-10t^2 - 7t + 6$
  q $-6n^2 + n + 12$ **r** $6f^2 - 5f - 6$
  s $-10q^2 + 7q + 12$ **t** $-6p^2 - 7p + 3$
  u $-6t^2 + 10t + 4$

2 a $(3x - 2)(2x + 1) = 6x^2 - x - 2$
   $(2x - 1)(2x - 1) = 4x^2 - 4x + 1$
   $(6x - 3)(x + 1) = 6x^2 + 3x - 3$
   $(4x + 1)(x - 1) = 4x^2 - 3x - 1$
   $(3x + 2)(2x + 1) = 6x^2 + 7x + 2$
  b Multiply the x terms to match the x^2 term and/or multiply the constant terms to get the constant term in the answer.

3 a $4x^2 - 1$ **b** $9t^2 - 4$ **c** $25y^2 - 9$
  d $16m^2 - 9$ **e** $4k^2 - 9$ **f** $16h^2 - 1$
  g $4 - 9x^2$ **h** $25 - 4t^2$ **i** $36 - 25y^2$
  j $a^2 - b^2$ **k** $9t^2 - k^2$ **l** $4m^2 - 9p^2$
  m $25k^2 - g^2$ **n** $a^2b^2 - c^2d^2$ **o** $a^4 - b^4$

4 a $a^2 - b^2$
  b Dimensions: $a + b$ by $a - b$; Area: $a^2 - b^2$
  c Areas are the same, so $a^2 - b^2 = (a + b) \times (a - b)$

5 First shaded area is $(2k)^2 - 1^2 = 4k^2 - 1$
   Second shaded area is $(2k + 1)(2k - 1) = 4k^2 - 1$

6 a $3w^2 + 22w + 24$
  b i 32 224 **ii** 23.7803
   iii 24.000 440 0012

7 a $49a^2 - b^2$ **b** 4896

Exercise 8H

1 a $x^2 + 10x + 25$ **b** $m^2 + 8m + 16$
  c $t^2 + 12t + 36$ **d** $p^2 + 6p + 9$
  e $m^2 - 6m + 9$ **f** $t^2 - 10t + 25$
  g $m^2 - 8m + 16$ **h** $k^2 - 14k + 49$

2 a $9x^2 + 6x + 1$ **b** $16t^2 + 24t + 9$
  c $25y^2 + 20y + 4$ **d** $4m^2 + 12m + 9$
  e $16t^2 - 24t + 9$ **f** $9x^2 - 12x + 4$
  g $25t^2 - 20t + 4$ **h** $25r^2 - 60r + 36$
  i $x^2 + 2xy + y^2$ **j** $m^2 - 2mn + n^2$
  k $4t^2 + 4ty + y^2$ **l** $m^2 - 6mn + 9n^2$
  m $x^2 + 4x$ **n** $x^2 - 10x$
  o $x^2 + 12x$ **p** $x^2 - 4x$

3 a Bernice has just squared the first term and the second term. She hasn't written down the brackets twice.
  b Pete has written down the brackets twice but has worked out $(3x)^2$ as $3x^2$ and not $9x^2$.
  c $9x^2 + 6x + 1$

4 Whole square is $(2x)^2 = 4x^2$.
   Three areas are $2x - 1$, $2x - 1$ and 1.
   $4x^2 - (2x - 1 + 2x - 1 + 1) = 4x^2 - (4x - 1)$
   $= 4x^2 - 4x + 1$

5 a $9p^6 + 42p^3q^7 + 49q^{14}$

6 a $9k^2 + 24k + 16$
  b i 16.2409 **ii** 92 416 **iii** 16.120 225

Exercise 8I

1 a $x^3 + 6x^2 + 11x + 6$
  b $x^3 - 49x - 120$
  c $x^3 + 9x^2 - 4x - 36$

2 a $x^3 + 7x^2 - 17x + 9$
  b $x^3 + x^2 - x - 10$

3 a $x^3 + 12x^2 + 48x + 64$
  b $x^3 - 18x^2 + 108x - 216$
  c $x^3 + 3ax^2 + 3a^2x + a^3$

4 abc $x^3 + 11x^2 + 31x + 21$
  d Can be performed in any order

5 a $x^3 + (a + b + c)x^2 + (ab + ac + bc)x + abc$
  b $p = 0$, $q = -19$, $r = -30$

6 a $x^3 - 15x^2 - 73x - 57$
  b $6x^2 - 60x - 146$

7 a i $x^2 + 2x + 1$ **ii** $x^3 + 3x^2 + 3x + 1$
   iii $x^4 + 4x^3 + 6x^2 + 4x + 1$
  b $11^2 = 121$, $11^3 = 1331$, $11^4 = 14\,641$
  c The digits are the same as the coefficients

8 a $x^3 + 9x^2 + 27x + 27$
  b 27.027 009 001

9 a $2x^3 + 3x^2 - 29x + 30$
  b $3x^3 + 11x^2 + 8x - 4$

10 a $24x^3 + 26x^2 - 173x + 105$
  b $50x^3 - 315x^2 + 228x - 44$
  c $27x^3 - 108x^2 + 144x - 64$

11 $82 - 5x - 32x^2$

Exercise 8J

1 a $(x + 2)(x + 3)$ **b** $(t + 1)(t + 4)$
  c $(m + 2)(m + 5)$ **d** $(k + 4)(k + 6)$
  e $(p + 2)(p + 12)$ **f** $(r + 3)(r + 6)$
  g $(w + 2)(w + 9)$ **h** $(x + 3)(x + 4)$
  i $(a + 2)(a + 6)$ **j** $(k + 3)(k + 7)$
  k $(f + 1)(f + 21)$ **l** $(b + 8)(b + 12)$
  m $(t - 2)(t - 3)$ **n** $(d - 4)(d - 1)$
  o $(g - 2)(g - 5)$ **p** $(x - 3)(x - 12)$
  q $(c - 2)(c - 16)$ **r** $(t - 4)(t - 9)$
  s $(y - 4)(y - 12)$ **t** $(j - 6)(j - 8)$

2 a $(p - 3)(p - 5)$ **b** $(y + 6)(y - 1)$
c $(t + 4)(t - 2)$ **d** $(x + 5)(x - 2)$
e $(m + 2)(m - 6)$ **f** $(r + 1)(r - 7)$
g $(n + 3)(n - 6)$ **h** $(m + 4)(m - 11)$
i $(w + 4)(w - 6)$ **j** $(t + 9)(t - 10)$
k $(h + 8)(h - 9)$ **l** $(t + 7)(t - 9)$
m $(d + 1)^2$ **n** $(y + 10)^2$
o $(t - 4)^2$ **p** $(m - 9)^2$
q $(x - 12)^2$ **r** $(d + 3)(d - 4)$
s $(t + 4)(t - 5)$ **t** $(q + 7)(q - 8)$

3 $(x + 2)(x + 3)$, giving areas of $2x$ and $3x$, or $(x + 1)(x + 6)$, giving areas of x and $6x$.

4 a $x^2 + (a + b)x + ab$
b i $p + q = 7$ **ii** $pq = 12$
c 7 can only be 1×7 and $1 + 7 \neq 12$

5 a 440
b i $(x + 3)(x + 1)$ **ii** $22 \times 20 = 440$

6 a $(x^2 - 3)(x^2 - 8)$ **b** $(y^5 - 104)(y^5 + 4)$
c $(z^{1728} - 864)(z^{1728} + 2)$

Exercise 8K

1 a $(x + 3)(x - 3)$ **b** $(t + 5)(t - 5)$
c $(m + 4)(m - 4)$ **d** $(3 + x)(3 - x)$
e $(7 + t)(7 - t)$ **f** $(k + 10)(k - 10)$
g $(2 + y)(2 - y)$ **h** $(x + 8)(x - 8)$
i $(t + 9)(t - 9)$

2 a x^2
b i $(x - 2)$ **ii** $(x + 2)$
  iii x^2 **iv** 4
c $A + B - C = x^2 - 4$, which is the area of D, which is $(x + 2)(x - 2)$.

3 a $x^2 + 4x + 4 - (x^2 + 2x + 1) = 2x + 3$
b $(a + b)(a - b)$
c $(x + 2 + x + 1)(x + 2 - x - 1) = (2x + 3)(1) = 2x + 3$
d The answers are the same.
e $4x$

4 a $(x + y)(x - y)$ **b** $(x + 2y)(x - 2y)$
c $(x + 3y)(x - 3y)$ **d** $(3x + 1)(3x - 1)$
e $(4x + 3)(4x - 3)$ **f** $(5x + 8)(5x - 8)$
g $(2x + 3y)(2x - 3y)$ **h** $(3t + 2w)(3t - 2w)$
i $(4y + 5x)(4y - 5x)$

5 a $(11x^3 - 3y^3)(11x^3 + 3y^3)$
b $(5m^5 - 9n^9)(5m^5 + 9n^9)$
c $(24p^{288} - 31q^{144})(24p^{288} + 31q^{144})$

6 a $(3x - 1)(3x + 1)$ **b** 29 and 31

7 a $(2x - 7)(2x + 7)$ **b** 3, 23 and 193

Exercise 8L

1 a $(2x + 1)(x + 2)$ **b** $(7x + 1)(x + 1)$
c $(4x + 7)(x - 1)$ **d** $(3t + 2)(8t + 1)$
e $(3t + 1)(5t - 1)$ **f** $(4x - 1)^2$
g $3(y + 7)(2y - 3)$ **h** $4(y + 6)(y - 4)$
i $(2x + 3)(4x - 1)$ **j** $(2t + 1)(3t + 5)$
k $(x - 6)(3x + 2)$ **l** $(x - 5)(7x - 2)$

2 $4x + 1$ and $3x + 2$

3 a All the terms in the quadratic have a common factor of 6.
b $6(x + 2)(x + 3)$. This has the highest common factor taken out.

4 $(3x - 1)(x + 16)$; 1230

5 a $(33x + 1)(x - 2)$ **b** $100 \times 1 = 100$

6 $(3x - 20)$

7 $12x^2 + 14x - 38$; $10x + 2$

Exercise 8M

1 $k = \dfrac{T}{3}$

2 $y = X + 1$

3 $p = 3Q$

4 $r = \dfrac{A - 9}{4}$

5 a $m = p - t$ **b** $t = p - m$

6 $m = gv$

7 $m = \sqrt{t}$

8 $l = \dfrac{P - 2w}{2}$

9 $p = \sqrt{m - 2}$

10 a $-40 - 32 = -72$, $-72 \div 9 = -8$, $5 \times -8 = -40$
b $68 - 32 = 36$, $36 \div 9 = 4$, $4 \times 5 = 20$
c $F = \dfrac{9}{5}C + 32$

11 Average speeds: outward journey = 72 kph, return journey = 63 kph, taking 2 hours. He was held up for 15 minutes.

12 $r = C/2\pi$, $A = \pi r^2 = \pi C^2/4\pi^2 = C^2/4\pi$

13 a $y = \dfrac{5x - 75}{9}$ **b** Pupil's own checks
c $y = \dfrac{7x - 40}{10}$ **d** Marlon is incorrect

14 a $a = \dfrac{v - u}{t}$ **b** $t = \dfrac{v - u}{a}$

15 $d = \sqrt{\dfrac{4A}{\pi}}$

16 a $y = \dfrac{x + w}{5}$ **b** $w = 5y - x$

17 $p = \sqrt{\dfrac{k}{2}}$

18 a $t = u^2 - v$ **b** $u = \sqrt{v + t}$

19 a $w = K - 5n^2$ **b** $n = \sqrt{\dfrac{K - w}{5}}$

20 a $D = \dfrac{P + Y(K - U)}{3(K - U)}$ or $\dfrac{\frac{P}{K-U} + Y}{3}$

b 16

Review questions

1 a $20x + 16$ **b** $5x + 4$

2 a $c = \dfrac{R - 3d - 5}{7}$ **b** 6

3 a i 3.5 ml   **ii** 3.7 ml   **iii** 3.84 ml
    b i 22   **ii** 38   **iii** 90

4 13.5 m²

5 a $2\pi r(r + h)$ **b** $h = \dfrac{A - 2\pi r^2}{2\pi r}$

   c 5 cm

6 a $x = \dfrac{A - y}{0.01y}$ **b** $y(1 + 0.01x)$

   c 38.36 g

7 $x = 5$

8 20 m

9 a $\dfrac{19 - 4x}{5x + 18}$ **b** $\dfrac{18 - 4x}{5x + 17}$

10 a $2(x - 8)$ **b** $x(x - 16)$
    c $(x - 4)(x + 4)$ **d** $(x - 7)(x - 9)$

11 a $3 \times 15 \times 4 = 180$ **b** $6x^2 - 51x + 90$

12 a i $15x^2 - 19x - 56$ **ii** $16x - 2$
    b 162.25 cm²

13 a $4x^2 + 4x + 1$ **b** 441   **c** 437

14 a $a^3 + 3a^2b + 3ab^2 + b^3$
    b $8x^3 + 36x^2 + 54x + 27$ **c** 27.543 608

15 a i $12x + 48$ **ii** $6x^2 + 48x + 94$
    iii $x^3 + 12x^2 + 47x + 60$
    b surface area = 1348 cm² and volume = 3360 cm³

16 a $12x^2 - xy - 35y^2$ **b** $(3x + 7y)(2x - 5y)$

17 ±10, ±11, ±14, ±25

18 a $(2x + 3)(x + 2)$
    b i 276   **ii** 20 706   **iii** 6.0702

Chapter 9 – Geometry and measures: Length, area and volume

Exercise 9A

1 a 8 cm, 25.1 cm, 50.3 cm²
   b 5.2 m, 16.3 m, 21.2 m²
   c 6 cm, 37.7 cm, 113 cm²
   d 1.6 m, 10.1 m, 8.04 m²

2 a 5π cm   **b** 8π cm
   c 18π m   **d** 12π cm

3 a 25π cm²   **b** 36π cm²
   c 100π cm²   **d** 0.25π m²

4 8.80 m

5 4 complete revolutions

6 1p : 3.1 cm², 2p : 5.3 cm², 5p : 2.3 cm², 10p : 4.5 cm²

7 0.83 m

8 38.6 cm

9 Claim is correct (ratio of the areas is just over 1.5 : 1)

10 a 18π cm²   **b** 4π cm²

11 9π cm²

12 Divide 31.3 by to get about 10 m. This is the diameter of the tree. Is your classroom smaller than 10 m × 10 m? It probably isn't, but you need to check.

13 45 complete revolutions

14 a 2π
   b I 8π **ii** 18π **iii** 32π

   c $A = 2 \times r^2 \times \pi$

Exercise 9B

1 a 96 cm²   **b** 70 cm²   **c** 20 m²
   d 125 cm²   **e** 10 cm²   **f** 112 m²

2 No, she has used the sloping side instead of the perpendicular height. It should be 6 × 4 = 24 cm²

3 Each parallelogram has an area of 30 cm². The height of each is 5 cm so the length of each must be 6 cm. x = 6 + 4 + 6 = 16 cm so Freya is incorrect.

4 a 500 cm²   **b** 3 × 5 = 15

Exercise 9C

1 a 30 cm²   **b** 77 cm²   **c** 24 cm²
   d 42 cm²   **e** 40 m²   **f** 6 cm
   g 3 cm   **h** 10 cm

2 Area = 15 cm²

3 a 36.25 cm²
   b 61.2 cm²
   c 90 m²

4 The area of the parallelogram is $\dfrac{(a + b)}{h}$. This is the same as two trapezia.

5 Two of 20 cm² and two of 16 cm²

6 a 57 m²   **b** 702.5 cm²   **c** 84 m²

7 trapezium area = 56, square area = 9, shaded area = 56 − 9 = 47 m²

8 4, because the total area doubled is about 32 m²

9 80.2%

10 1 100 000 km²

11 160 cm²

12 a many possible correct answers, e.g. base 6 cm, top 4 cm, height 5 cm. Shaded area is 8 π trapezium must be the same

   b the dimensions cannot be exact due to the value of π in the area of the circle

Exercise 9D

1 a i 5.59 cm   **ii** 22.3 cm²
  b i 8.29 cm   **ii** 20.7 cm²
  c i 16.3 cm   **ii** 98.0 cm²
  d i 15.9 cm   **ii** 55.6 cm²

2 2π cm, 6π cm²

3 a 73.8 cm   **b** 20.3 cm

4 area of sector = $\frac{1}{4} \times \pi \times 8^2 = 16\pi$,

  area of circle = $\pi \times 4^2 = 16\pi$

5 a 107 cm²
  b 173 cm²

6 43.6 cm

7 a $\frac{180}{\pi}$

  b If arc length is 10 cm, distance along chord joining the two points of the sector on the circumference will be less than 10 cm, so angle at centre will be less than 60°

8 a 66.8°   **b** 10 cm²

9 Let sector have radius R and arc length C, the angle of the sector is found by

$\theta = \frac{360 \times C}{2 \times \pi \times R}$

and so the area will be $\frac{360 \times C \times \pi \times R^2}{2 \times \pi \times R \times 360}$

$= \frac{CR}{2}$

10 (36π − 72) cm²

11 36.5 cm²

12 16 cm (15.7)

13 Each square has side length of r

Shaded part of square $X = r^2 - \frac{1}{4}r^2$

$= r^2 \left(1 - \frac{1}{4} \right)$

In square Y, the four quarter circles will join together to give an area of radius $\frac{1}{2}$ r, so shaded area

in Y = $r^2 - \left(\frac{r}{2}\right)\pi^2 = r^2 - \frac{1}{4}r^2 = r^2(1 - \frac{1}{4}\pi)$,

which is the same as square X.

Exercise 9E

1 a i 21 cm²   **ii** 63 cm³
  b i 48 cm²   **ii** 432 cm³
  c i 36 m²   **ii** 324 m³

2 a 432 m³   **b** 225 m³   **c** 1332 m³

3 a A cross-section parallel to the side of the pool always has the same shape.

  b About $3\frac{1}{2}$ hours

4 $V = \frac{1}{2}$ (1.5 + 3) × 1.7 × 2 = 7.65 m³

5 27 = 3 × 3 × 3, 27 + 37 = 64 = 4³, 4 − 3 = 1. Hence the side length is 1 small cube longer, hence 2 cm longer

6 a i 21 cm³   **ii** 210 cm³
  b i 54 cm²   **ii** 270 cm²

7 146 cm³

8 78 m³ (78.3 m³)

9 327 litres

10 10.2 tonnes

11 She was silly because 188160 is simply all the numbers multiplied together. The volume is 672 cm³

Exercise 9F

1 a i 226 cm³   **ii** 207 cm²
  b i 14.9 cm³   **ii** 61.3 cm²
  c i 346 cm³   **ii** 275 cm²
  d i 1060 cm³   **ii** 636 cm²

2 a i 72π cm³   **ii** 48π cm²
  b i 112π cm³   **ii** 56π cm²
  c i 180π cm³   **ii** 60π cm²
  d i 600π m³   **ii** 120π m²

3 Volume = $\pi \times (0.3)^2 \times 4.2 = 0.378\pi$

Cost = 0.378 × π × £67.50 = £80.16 which is £80 to 2sf

4 1.23 tonnes

5 Label should be less than 10.5 cm wide so that it fits the can and does not overlap the rim and more than 23.3 cm long to allow an overlap.

6 Volume = $\pi \times 32.5^2 \times 100 = 331830.7$ cm³
    1 litre = 1000 cm³
    volume = 331830.7 ÷ 1000 = 331.8307 litres = 332 litres (3 sf)

7 There is no right answer. Students could start with the dimensions of a real can. Often drinks cans are not exactly cylindrical. One possible answer is height of 6.6 cm and diameter of 8 cm.

8 7.78 g/cm³

9 About 127 cm

10 A diameter of 10 cm and a length of 5 cm give a volume close to 400 cm³ (0.4 litres).

Exercise 9G

1 a 56 cm³   **b** 168 cm³   **c** 1040 cm³
  d 84 cm³   **e** 160 cm³

2 $\frac{1}{3}$ base area × h = $\frac{1}{3}$ × 9 × 9 × 10 = 270 cm³

3 a Put the apexes of the pyramids together. The 6 square bases will then form a cube.

b If the side of the base is a then the height will be $\frac{1}{2}a$.

Total volume of the 6 pyramids is a^3.

Volume of one pyramid is $\frac{1}{6}a^3 =$

$\frac{1}{3} \times \frac{1}{2} \times a \times a^2 = \frac{1}{3} \times$ height $\times$ base area

4 6.9 m ($\frac{1}{3}$ height of pyramid)

5 a 73.3 m³   **b** 45 m³   **c** 3250 cm³

6 208 g

7 1.5 g

8 $\frac{1}{3} \times 6.4 \times 6.4 \times H = 81.3$

So $H = \frac{3 \times 81.3}{6.4 \times 6.4} = 5.954 = 6.0$ (2sf)

9 14.4 cm

10 Volume of pyramid $= \frac{1}{3} \times 6 \times 9 \times 15 = 270$ cm³

Volume of part cut off top $= \frac{1}{3} \times 3 \times 2 \times 5$
$= 10$ cm³

So frustum $= 270 - 10 = 260$ cm³

Hence $\frac{\text{volume of frustrum}}{\text{volume of pyramid}} = \frac{260}{270} = \frac{26}{27}$

therefore, Hannah is correct.

Exercise 9H

1 a i 3560 cm³   **ii** 1430 cm²
   b i 314 cm³   **ii** 283 cm²
   c i 1020 cm³   **ii** 679 cm²

2 935 g

3 Total area $= \pi rl + \pi r^2 = \pi \times 3 \times l + \pi \times 3^2$
$= (3l + 9)\pi = 24\pi$
So $3l + 9 = 24$, so $3l = 24 - 9 = 15$
$l = \frac{15}{3} = 5$

4 a 816π cm³   **b** 720π mm³

5 24π cm²

6 a 4 cm   **b** 6 cm
   c Various answers, e.g. 60° gives 2 cm, 240° gives 8 cm

7 If radius of base is r, slant height is $2r$.
Area of curved surface $= r \times 2\pi r = 2r^2\pi$, area of base $= \pi r^2$

8 2.7 g/cm³

9 2.81 cm

10 252π cm²

Exercise 9I

1 a 36π cm³   **b** 288π cm³   **c** 1330π cm³ (3 sf)

2 a 36π cm²   **b** 100π cm²   **c** 196π cm²

3 65 400 cm³, 7850 cm²

4 a 1960 cm² (to 3sf)   **b** 7444 cm³ (to nearest unit)

5 125 cm

6 6232

7 7.8 cm

8 a The surface area, because this is the amount of material (leather or plastic) needed to make the ball
   b Surface area can vary from about 1470 cm² to 1560 cm², difference of about 90 cm². This seems surprisingly large.

9 48%

10 Radius of sphere = base radius of cylinder = r, height of cylinder = $2r$ Curved surface area of cylinder = circumference × height = $2\pi r \times 2r = 4\pi r^2$ = surface area of sphere

Review questions

1 29.4 cm²

2 721 cm²

3 5740 cm³(to 3sf)

4 610 g (2sf)

5 17.5 cm

6 360 g

7 56.5 cm

8 Call length of square $2x$, so that radius of arcs is x.
Then area of square $= 4x^2$
Area of each semicircle $= \frac{1}{2}\pi x^2$ so area of 4 semi circles is $2x^2$
Area of shaded part is: area of 4 semicircles − area of square $= (2\pi - 4)x^2$

So percentage shaded $= \frac{2\pi - 4}{4x^2}x^2 \times 100 =$

$\frac{2\pi - 4}{4} \times 100 = 57\%$

9 $\frac{1}{3}$

Chapter 10 – Algebra: Linear graphs

Exercise 10A

1

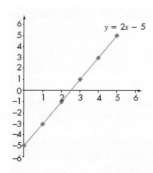

2

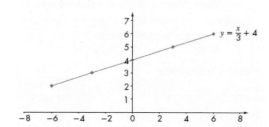

3 a

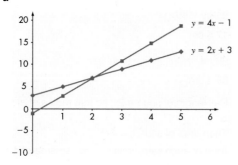

b (2, 7)

4 a

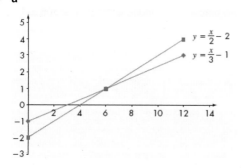

b

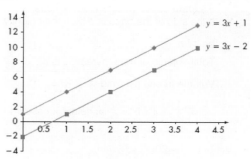

4 c lines in part **a** intersect at (6, 1), lines in part **b** don't intersect because they are parallel

5 a Line isn't straight

b

x	−3	−2	−1	0	1	2	3
y	−5	−3	−1	1	3	5	7

Correct line drawn

6 a

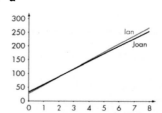

b Ian, Ian only charges £85, whilst Joan charges £90 for a 2-hour job.

7 a Jada's method

8 a

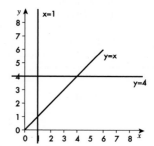

b 4.5 units squared

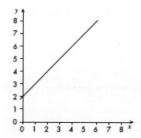

9

10 18 units squared

Exercise 10B

1 a 2 **b** $\frac{1}{3}$ **c** −3 **d** 1 **e** −2

  f $-\frac{1}{3}$ **g** 5 **h** −5 **i** $\frac{1}{5}$ **j** $-\frac{3}{4}$

2

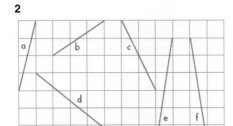

3 a Both answers are correct
  b Generally the bigger the triangle the more accurate the answer, so Brianna

4 a ladder might slip
  b ladder might topple
  c A, B, E and F satisfy the safety regulations; C and D do not

5 a 0.5 **b** 0.4 **c** 0.2 **d** 0.1 **e** 0

6 a $1\frac{2}{3}$ **b** 2 **c** $3\frac{1}{3}$ **d** 10 **e** ∞

7 Raisa has misread the scales. The second line has four times the gradient (2.4) of the first (0.6)

8 a $\frac{3}{8}$

  b $\frac{2}{5}$

  c Although the puzzle appears to be a right-angled triangle, because the gradients of the smaller triangles are different there is actually a bend in the large hypotenuse, so it is actually a quadrilateral. In the first diagram it has a concave angle and in the second diagram the equivalent angle is convex, and the area of the square hole is spread out between them.

9 0, 2, −1, $\frac{1}{2}$, $-\frac{3}{2}$

Exercise 10C

1 a, b, c, d

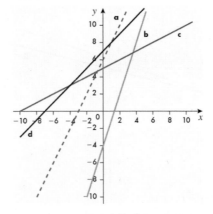

e, f, g, h

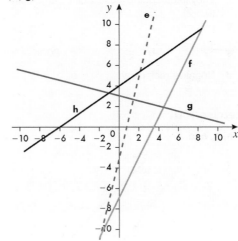

i, j, k, l

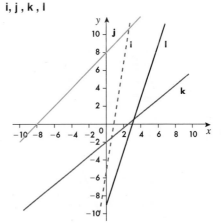

2 a

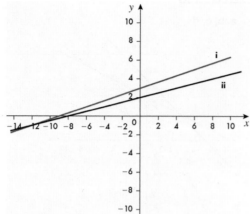

b (−12, −1)

3 a They have the same gradient (3).
b They intercept the y-axis at the same point (0, −2).
c (−1, −4)

4 a −2   **b** $\frac{1}{2}$ **c** 90°

d Negative reciprocal   **e** $-\frac{1}{3}$

Exercise 10D

1 a, b, c, d

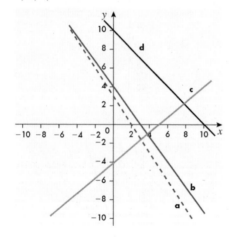

e, f, g, h

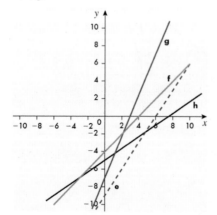

i, j, k, l

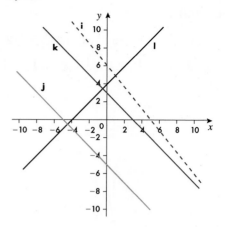

2 a

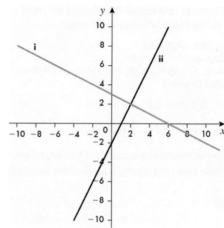

b (2, 2)

3 a Intersect at (6, 0)
b Intersect at (0, −3)
c Parallel
d $-2x + 9y = 18$

4 a vi   **b** iii   **c** v   **d** ii   **e** i   **f** iv

5 $y = -6x$; $y = 3x + 4$; $2y - 5x = 10$; $2y - x = 7$; $y = 4$

6 $3x + 2y = 18$ and $y = 9 - x$

7 a i $x = 3$ **ii** $x - y = 4$ **iii** $y = -3$
iv $x + y = -4$ **v** $x = -3$ **vi** $y = x + 4$
b i −3   **ii** $\frac{1}{3}$ **iii** $-\frac{1}{3}$

8 Cover-up method for $2x + y = 10$ and gradient-intercept method for $y = 11 - 2x$

Exercise 10E

1 a $y = \frac{7}{5}x - 2$ or $5y = 7x - 10$
b $y = 2x$ **c** $2y = x + 6$

2 a i $y = 2x + 1$, $y = -2x + 1$
ii Reflection in y-axis (and $y = 1$)
iii Different sign
b i $5y = 2x - 5$, $5y = -2x - 5$
ii Reflection in y-axis (and $y = -1$)
iii Different sign

c i $y = x + 1$, $y = -x + 1$
ii Reflection in y-axis (and $y = 1$)
iii Different sign

3 a x-coordinates go from $2 \to 1 \to 0$ and y-coordinates go from $5 \to 3 \to 1$.
b x-step between the points is 1 and y-step is **2.**
c $y = 3x + 2$

4 a $y = -x + 1$
b $5y = -2x - 5$
c $y = -\frac{3}{2}x - 3$ or $2y = -3x - 6$

5 a i $2y = -x + 1$, $y = -2x + 1$
ii Reflection in $x = y$
iii Reciprocal of each other
b i $2y = 5x + 5$, $5y = 2x - 5$
ii Reflection in $x = y$
iii Reciprocal of each other
c i $y = 2$, $x = 2$
ii Reflection in $x = y$
iii Reciprocal of each other (reciprocal of zero is infinity)

6 All of the lines except $y = \frac{1}{4}x + 9$

7 a $y = -3x + 5$ **b** $y = 2x - 4$
c $y = 8x - 3$ **d** $y = 25 - 2x$
e $y = \frac{2}{3}x - 1$

8 $5x + 6y = 30$

9 Chris is correct. The equation of the line is $y = \frac{1}{2}x + 2$ and (12, 8) satisfies the equation

10 a i $x + y = 100$ **ii** $k = 1$
b i $x = 46$ **ii** $k = 46$
c i $y = 2x + 1$ **ii** $k = 60$
d i $y = x + 19$ **ii** $k = -17$

11 (4, 11)

Exercise 10F

1 a Anya: CabCo £8.50, YellaCabs £8.40, so YellaCabs is best; Bettina: CabCo £11.50, YellaCabs £11.60, so CabCo is best; Calista: CabCo £10, YellaCabs £10, so either
b If they shared a cab, the shortest distance is 16 km, which would cost £14.50 with CabCo and £14.80 with Yellacabs.

2 a i $8\frac{1}{4}$ kg   **ii** $2\frac{1}{4}$ kg
iii 9 lb   **iv** 22 lb
b 2.2 lb
c Read off the value for 12 lb (5.4 kg) and multiply this by 4 (21.6 kg)

3 a 32° F
b $\frac{9}{5}$ (Take gradient at $C = 10°$ and $30°$)
c $F = \frac{9}{5}C + 32$

4 a 0.07 (Take gradient at $U = 0$ and 500)
b £10
c $C = £(10 + 0.07U)$ or Charge = £10 + 7p/unit

5 a \$1900 − \$1260 = \$640
b i \$7500   **ii** £3680

6

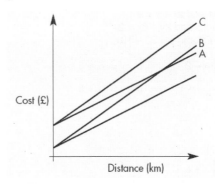

7 $y = 2x + 15$ $0 < x \le 5$
$y = x + 20$ $5 < x \le 12$
$y = \frac{1}{2}x + 26$ $12 < x \le 22$

Exercise 10G

1 (4, 1)

2 (2, 3)

3 (3, 10)

4 (−2, 6)

5 (−6, −9)

6 (1, −1)

7 (2, 6)

8 (2, 8)

9 $(7\frac{1}{2}, 3\frac{1}{2})$

10 $x + 2y = 9.5$, $2x + y = 8.5$
Graphs intersect at (2.5, 3.5), so a cheesecake costs £2.50 and a gâteau costs £3.50.

11 a P and R   **b** R and S
c P and Q   **d** Q and S

12 (0, 0), (−3, 3), (−3, −3), (−3, 2), (−2, 2), (2, 2)

13 a No solutions, lines are parallel
b Infinite solutions, lines are same
c One solution, lines intersect once

Exercise 10H

1 a Line A does not pass through (0, 1).
b Line C is perpendicular to the other two.
c (i)

2 a $-\frac{1}{2}$ **b** $\frac{1}{3}$ **c** -2 **d** $\frac{3}{2}$ **e** $-\frac{2}{3}$ **f** $-\frac{3}{4}$

3 $y = 3x + 5$, $x + 3y = 10$, $y = 8 - \frac{1}{3}x$, $y = 3(x + 2)$

4 $x = 6$ and $y = -2$

$x + y = 5$ and $y = x + 4$

$y = 8x - 9$ and $y = -\frac{1}{8}x + 6$

$2y = x + 4$ and $2x + y = 9$

$5y = 2x + 15$ and $2y + 5x = 2$

$y = 0.1x + 2$ and $y = 33 - 10x$

5 **a** $y = \frac{1}{2}x - 2$ **b** $y = -x + 3$

   c $y = -\frac{1}{3}x - 1$ **d** $y = 3x + 5$

6 **a** -4

   b $\frac{1}{4}$

   c $(11, 7)$

   d $y = \frac{1}{4}x + c$

   Substitute in $(11, 7)$ and solve to get $c = \frac{17}{4}$,
   so $4y - x = 17$

7 $y = -\frac{1}{4}x + 2$

8 **i** **a** AB: $-\frac{1}{5}$, BC: 1, CD: $-\frac{1}{5}$, DA: 1

      b Parallelogram (two pairs of parallel sides)

   ii **a** AB: $\frac{2}{3}$, BC: $-\frac{3}{2}$, CD: $\frac{2}{3}$, DA: $-\frac{3}{2}$

      b Rectangle (two pairs of perpendicular sides)

   iii **a** AB: $\frac{2}{5}$, BC: $\frac{1}{4}$, CD: $\frac{2}{5}$, DA: 1

      b Trapezium (one pair of parallel sides)

9 $y = -\frac{1}{2}x + 5$

10 **a** $y = 3x - 6$

   b Bisector of AB is $y = -2x + 9$, bisector of AC is
   $y = \frac{1}{2}x + \frac{3}{2}$, solving these equations shows
   the lines intersect at $(3, 3)$.

   c $(3, 3)$ lies on $y = 3x - 6$ because $(3 \times 3) - 6 = 3$

11 $(3, 10)$

Review questions

1

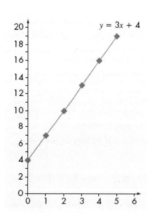

2

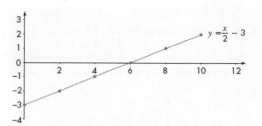

3

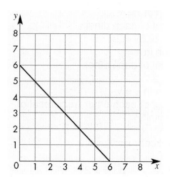

4 **a** $\frac{1}{2}$ (Take gradient at $N = 0$ and 500)

   b £50

   c $C = £(50 + \frac{N}{2})$ or £50 + 50p/person

5 **a** $\frac{1}{10}$

   b 24.5 cm

   c 0.1 cm or 1 mm

   d $L = 24.5 + \frac{W}{10}$ or Length = 24.5 + 1 mm/kg

6 **a** $(5, 5)$ **b** $(1, 5)$ **c** $(3, 16)$

7 **a** 2   **b** $y = 2x + 2$ **c** $y = -\frac{1}{2}x + 7$

8 **a** Reflection in y-axis ($x = 0$); reflection in $y = 1$
      (rotations also possible)

   b Rotation 90° clockwise; rotation 90°
      anticlockwise about the point $(0, 1)$
      (reflections also possible)

9 30 square units

10 36 square units

11 $(7, 1)$

Chapter 11 – Geometry: Right-angled triangles

Exercise 11A

1 Students' own diagrams

2 Possible answers include multiples of 3, 4, 5;
   multiples of 5, 12, 13; multiples of 7, 24, 25;
   multiples of 8, 15, 17

3 **a** 10.3 cm   **b** 5.9 cm   **c** 8.5 cm
    d 20.6 cm   **e** 18.6 cm   **f** 17.5 cm
    g 13 cm   **h** 5 cm

4 **a** $\sqrt{8}$, $\sqrt{12}$, $\sqrt{16}$
    b Add 4 to 16 to give H_4 as $\sqrt{20}$

5 The square in the first diagram and the sum of the two squares in the second have the same area.

Exercise 11B

1 **a** 15 cm   **b** 14.7 cm
    c 6.3 cm   **d** 18.3 cm

2 **a** 20.8 m   **b** 15.5 cm
    c 15.5 m   **d** 12.4 cm

3 **a** 5 m   **b** 6 m
    c 3 m   **d** 50 cm

4 There are infinite possibilities, e.g. any multiple of 3, 4, 5 such as 6, 8, 10; 9, 12, 15; 12, 16, 20; multiples of 5, 12, 13; multiples of 7, 24, 25 and of 8, 15, 17.

5 498.4 cm²

6 Any of (0, 0) , (5, 5), (2, 0), (5, 3), (2, 8), (0, 8), (–3, 3), (–3, 5) are the most likely points

7 Use Pythagoras' theorem to find a few possible dimensions of the rectangle, then plot a graph of one side length against the area. You will see that 50 is the highest the area will ever get to.

8 The large square is 17 by 17 giving 289 square units.
The red and yellow triangles all have shorter lengths of 5 and 12, with an area of 30 square units.
The area of the inner square (green and yellow) must be 289 − 4 × 30 = 169, so the hypotenuse of the yellow triangles must be $\sqrt{169}$ = 13
You can see that $5^2 + 12^2 = 13^2$

Exercise 11C

1 No. The foot of the ladder is about 6.6 m from the wall.

2 2.06 m

3 11.3 m

4 About 17 minutes, assuming it travels at the same speed.

5 127 m − 99.6 m = 27.4 m

6 4.58 m

7 **a** 3.87 m   **b** 1.74 m

8 3.16 m

9 This creates a right-angled triangle with two short sides of 5 and 12. Use Pythagoras' theorem to show length of line = $\sqrt{(5^2 + 12^2)}$ = 13

10 a 4.85 m
    b 4.83 m (There is only a small difference.)

11 Yes, because $24^2 + 7^2 = 25^2$

12 6 cm

13 He is partly correct. The perimeter must be larger than 20 cm or the rectangle has no width, and the area is largest when it's a square, giving a perimeter of 28.3 cm (3 sf). So he should have said the perimeter is between 20 and 28.3 cm.

Exercise 11D

1 **a** 32.2 cm²   **b** 2.83 cm²   **c** 50.0 cm²

2 22.2 cm²

3 15.6 cm²

4 **a**

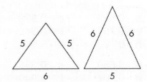

    b The areas are 12 cm² and 13.6 cm² respectively, so triangle with 6 cm, 6 cm, 5 cm sides has the greater area.

5 **a**   **b** 166.3 cm²

6 259.8 cm²

7 **a** No, areas vary from 24.5 cm² to 27.7 cm²
    b No, equilateral triangle gives the largest area.
    c The closer the isosceles triangle gets to an equilateral triangle the larger its area becomes.

8 Show the right-angled triangle made with hypotenuse 6.5 m and base 7.4 ÷ 2 = 3.7, giving the height of the triangle as 5.344 cm. Use area = ½ × 7.4 × 5.344 to give 19.7733 which rounds to 19.8 m² (3 sf)

9 48 cm²

10 a 10 cm   **b** 26 cm   **c** 9.6 cm

11 6 or 8 cm

12 Andrew didn't round off any answers until the last calculation, and Olly used a rounded off value to find an intermediate result.

Exercise 11E

1 a i 14.4 cm **ii** 13 cm   **iii** 9.4 cm
  b 15.2 cm

2 No, 6.6 m is longest length

3 a 20.6 cm   **b** 15.0 cm

4 a 8.49 m   **b** 9 m

5 $10^2 + 10^2 + 10^2 = 300$, $\sqrt{300} = 17.3$ cm (3sf)

6 20.6 cm

7 a 11.3 cm   **b** 7 cm   **c** 8.06 cm

8 AM = $\sqrt{(22.5^2 + 15^2 + 40^2)}$ = 48.283 = 48.3 cm (3 sf)

9 21.3 cm

Exercise 11F

1 a 0.682   **b** 0.829   **c** 0.922
  d 1   **e** 0.707   **f** 0.342
  g 0.375   **h** 0

2 a 0.731   **b** 0.559   **c** 0.388
  d 0   **e** 0.707   **f** 0.940
  g 0.927   **h** 1

3 45°

4 a i 0.574   **ii** 0.574
  b i 0.208   **ii** 0.208
  c i 0.391   **ii** 0.391
  d Same
  e i sin 15° is the same as cos 75°
    ii cos 82° is the same as sin 8°
    iii $\sin x$ is the same as $\cos (90° - x)$

5 a 0.933   **b** 1.48   **c** 2.38
  d Infinite (calculator will give a maths error)
  e 1   **f** 0.364   **g** 0.404
  h 0

6 a 0.956   **b** 0.899   **c** 2.16
  d 0.999   **e** 0.819   **f** 0.577
  g 0.469   **h** 0.996

7 Has values > 1

8 a 4.53 **b** 4.46 **c** 6   **d** 0

9 a 10.7   **b** 5.40
  c 68.58   **d** 0

10 a 3.56 **b** 8.96 **c** 28.4 **d** 8.91

11 a 5.61 **b** 11.3 **c** 6   **d** 10

12 a 1.46 **b** 7.77 **c** 0.087 **d** 9.33

13 a 7.73 **b** 48.6 **c** 2.28 **d** 15.2

14 a 29.9 **b** 44.8 **c** 20.3 **d** 2.38

15 a $\frac{4}{5}$, $\frac{3}{5}$, $\frac{4}{3}$

  b $\frac{7}{25}$, $\frac{24}{25}$, $\frac{7}{24}$

16 You should have drawn a right angled triangle as here. $H = 13$ since this is a 5, 12, 13 Pythagorean triple. See that opposite = 5 and adjacent = 12. Hence $\sin x = \frac{O}{H} = \frac{5}{13}$ and $\cos x = \frac{12}{13}$

Exercise 11G

1 a 30°   **b** 51.7°   **c** 39.8°
  d 61.3°   **e** 87.4°   **f** 45.0°

2 a 60°   **b** 50.2°   **c** 2.6°
  d 45.0   **e** 78.5°   **f** 45.6°

3 a 31.0°   **b** 20.8°   **c** 41.8°
  d 46.4°   **e** 69.5°   **f** 77.1°

4 a 53.1°   **b** 41.8°   **c** 44.4°
  d 56.4°   **e** 2.4°   **f** 22.6°

5 a 36.9°   **b** 48.2°   **c** 45.6°
  d 33.6°   **e** 87.6°   **f** 67.4°

6 a 31.0°   **b** 37.9°   **c** 15.9°
  d 60.9°   **e** 57.5°   **f** 50.2°

7 a Error message   **b** Largest value 1
  c Smallest value −1

8 a i 17.5°   **ii** 72.5°   **iii** 90°
  b Yes

9

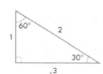

Adj = 1, Hyp = 2, hence Opp = $\sqrt{(2^2 - 1^2)} = \sqrt{3}$

  a 30 is the other acute angle in the triangle and so for 30, opp = 1 and adj = $\sqrt{3}$, hence tan 30 = $\frac{1}{\sqrt{3}}$

  b tan 60 = $\sqrt{3}$

  c sin 60 = $\frac{\sqrt{3}}{2}$

  d cos 30 = $\frac{\sqrt{3}}{2}$

  e sin 30 = $\frac{1}{2}$

10 Adj = 1, Opp = 1, hence Hyp = $\sqrt{(1^2 + 1^2)} = \sqrt{2}$

  a sin 45 = $\frac{1}{\sqrt{2}}$

  b cos 45 = $\frac{1}{\sqrt{2}}$

Exercise 11H

1 a 17.5° **b** 22.0° **c** 32.2°

2 a 5.29 cm **b** 5.75 cm **c** 13.2 cm

3 a 4.57 cm **b** 6.86 cm **c** 100 cm

4 a 5.12 cm **b** 9.77 cm
c 11.7 cm **d** 15.5 cm

5 a 47.2° **b** 5.42 cm
c 13.7 cm **d** 38.0°

6 a 6 **b** 15 **c** 30

7 a $\frac{1}{2}$
b and c

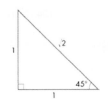

8 a $\frac{1}{\sqrt{2}}$

b

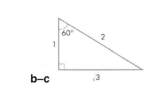

Exercise 11I

1 a 51.3° **b** 75.5° **c** 51.3°

2 a 6.47 cm **b** 32.6 cm **c** 137 cm

3 a 7.32 cm **b** 39.1 cm **c** 135 cm

4 a 5.35 cm **b** 14.8 cm
c 12.0 cm **d** 8.62 cm

5 a 5.59 cm **b** 46.6°
c 9.91 cm **d** 40.1°

6 a 10 **b** 39 **c** 2.5

7 a $\frac{1}{2}$

b–c

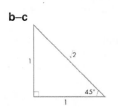

8a $\frac{1}{\sqrt{2}}$

b–c

Exercise 11J

1 a 33.7° **b** 36.9° **c** 52.1°

2 a 5.09 cm **b** 30.4 cm **c** 1120 cm

3 a 8.24 cm **b** 62.0 cm **c** 72.8 cm

4 a 9.02 cm **b** 7.51 cm
c 7.14 cm **d** 8.90 cm

5 a 13.7 cm **b** 48.4°
c 7.03 cm **d** 41.2°

6 a 12 **b** 12 **c** 2

7 a $\sqrt{3}$
b

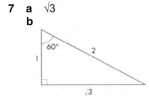

8 a 1

b

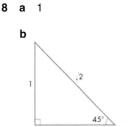

Exercise 11K

1 a 12.6 **b** 59.6 **c** 74.7
d 16.0 **e** 67.9 **f** 20.1

2 a 44.4° **b** 39.8° **c** 44.4°
d 49.5° **e** 58.7° **f** 38.7°

3 a 67.4° **b** 11.3 **c** 134
d 28.1° **e** 39.7 **f** 263
g 50.2° **h** 51.3° **i** 138
j 22.8

4 a Sides of right-hand triangle are sine and cosine
b Pythagoras' theorem
c Students should check the formulae

5

	30°	45°	60°
Sine	$\frac{1}{2}$	$\frac{1}{\sqrt{2}}$	$\frac{\sqrt{3}}{2}$
Cosine	$\frac{\sqrt{3}}{2}$	$\frac{1}{\sqrt{2}}$	$\frac{1}{2}$
Tangent	$\frac{1}{\sqrt{3}}$	1	$\sqrt{3}$

Exercise 11L

1 65°

2 The safe limits are between 1.04 m and 2.05 m. The ladder will reach between 5.63 m and 5.90 m up the wall.

3 44°

4 6.82 m

5 31°

6 a 25° **b** 2.10 m
  c Thickness of wood has been ignored

7 a 20° **b** 4.78 m

8 She would calculate 100 tan 23°. The answer is about 42.4 m

9 21.1 m

10 One way is stand opposite a feature, such as a tree, on the opposite bank, move a measured distance, x, along your bank and measure the angle, θ, between your bank and the feature. Width of river is $x \tan \theta$. This of course requires measuring equipment! An alternative is to walk along the bank until the angle is 45° (if that is possible). This angle is easily found by folding a sheet of paper. This way an angle measurer is not required.

Exercise 11M

1 10.1 km

2 22°

3 429 m

4 a 156 m
  b No. the new angle of depression is $\tan^{-1} \left(\frac{200}{312} \right) = 33°$ and half of 52° is 26°

5 a 222 m **b** 42°

6 a 21.5 m **b** 17.8 m

7 a 13.4 m
  b We don't know if the angle of elevation is from Sunil's feet or head. This would make a difference to the answer as we would need to add Sunil's height if the angle was from his head.

8 Cos $\theta = \frac{1}{3}$ so $\cos^{-1} 0.3333 = 70.5°$ (3 sf)

9 The angle is 16° so Cara is not quite correct.

10 William is 137 m away, Isaac is 107 m away.

Exercise 11N

1 a 73.4 km **b** 15.6 km

2 a 14.7 miles **b** 8.5 miles

3 Draw a diagram representing the relative places. Your diagram will show the angle of the bearing to fly the direct route as 90° + $\tan^{-1}$ (70/120) = 120°. So the bearing for the direct route is 120°.

4 a 59.4 km **b** 8.4 km

5 a 15.9 km **b** 24.1 km
  c 31.2 km **d** 052°

6 2.28 km

7 235°

8 a 66.2 km **b** 11.7 km
  c 13.1 km **d** 170°

9 48.4 km on a bearing of 100°

Exercise 11P

1 a 5.79 cm **b** 48.2°
  c 7.42 cm **d** 81.6 cm

2 9.86 m

3 a 36.4 cm² **b** 115 cm²
  c 90.6 cm² **d** 160 cm²

4 473 cm²

5 39.0 cm²

6 Base radius given by 8 tan 31°, so volume = $\frac{8}{3} \times$ $\pi(8 \tan 31)^2 = 193.57357 = 194$ (3 sf)

Review questions

1 13.6 cm²

2 2 pm

3 diagonal = $\sqrt{(3^2 + 4^2 + 12^2)} = \sqrt{169} = 13$

4 237°

5 52.3°

6 a AX and BY are both radii to the tangents at A and B and so perpendicular to AB, hence parallel. So ABYX is a trapezium.
  b Draw in a line, YT, parallel to the base AB, so that T lies on AX. This gives a right-angled triangle with height (7 − 2) cm = 5 cm. The hypotenuse is (7 + 2) cm = 9 cm, hence the line YT, which is the same length as AB = $\sqrt{(9^2 - 5^2)} = \sqrt{56} = 7.4833…$ The area of the trapezium = AB × (7 + 2)/2 = 7.4833 × 4.5 = 33.6749 = 33.7 cm² (3 sf)

7 110 cm²

8 Using square roots is dependent on remembering that sin 60° = $\frac{\sqrt{3}}{2}$, then calculating this as 0.866 (3 sf).
Using the equilateral triangle will give sin 60° as Height of triangle/10. The height found by Pythagoras as $\sqrt{(10^2 - 5^2)} = \sqrt{75} = 8.660254$, so sin 60° = 0.866 (3 sf).
Both answers are the same.

Chapter 12 – Geometry and measures: Similarity

Exercise 12A

1 a Yes, 4
b No, corresponding sides have different ratios.

2 a 1 : 3
b Angle R
c BA

3 a Angle P **b** PR

4 a Same angles
b Angle Q
c AR

5 a 8 cm
b 7.5 cm
c $x = 6.67$ cm, $y = 13.5$ cm
d $x = 24$ cm, $y = 13$ cm
e AB = 10 cm, PQ = 6 cm
f 4.2 cm

6 a Sides in same ratio **b** 1 : 3
c 13 cm **d** 39 cm

7 5.2 m

8 Corresponding sides are not in the same ratio, 12 : 15 ≠ 16 : 19.

9 Jay is wrong: DE = 17.5 cm; AC : EC = BA : DE, 5 : 12.5 = 7 : DE, DE = 7 × 12.5 ÷ 5 = 17.5 cm

Exercise 12B

1 a ABC and ADE; 9 cm
b ABC and ADE; 12 cm

2 a 5 cm
b 5 cm
c $x = 60$ cm, $y = 75$ cm
d DC = 10 cm, EB = 8 cm

3 82 m

4 $\frac{pole}{330} = \frac{400}{600}$, pole = $330 \times \frac{4}{6} = 220$

5 15 m

6 3.3 m

7 1.8 m

8 $\frac{BC}{9} = \frac{9}{6}$, hence BC = $9 \times \frac{9}{6} = 13.5$ cm

9 c

Exercise 12C

1 a 5 cm
b 6 cm
c 10 cm
d $x = 6$ cm, $y = 7.5$ cm
e $x = 15$ cm, $y = 21$ cm
f $x = 3$ cm, $y = 2.4$ cm

2 a $\frac{x+12}{12} = \frac{180-1.7}{2-1.7}$, $x = \frac{2136}{0.3} = 7120$ m, just over 7 km.
b The assumption is that the building, the brick wall and Brad are all standing on the same level.

Exercise 12D

1 a i 1 : 9 **ii** 4 : 25 **iii** 16 : 49
b i 1 : 27 **ii** 8 : 125 **iii** 64 : 343

2

Linear scale factor	Linear ratio	Linear fraction	Area scale factor	Volume scale factor
2	1 : 2	$\frac{2}{1}$	4	8
3	1 : 3	$\frac{3}{1}$	9	27
$\frac{1}{4}$	4 : 1	$\frac{1}{4}$	$\frac{1}{16}$	$\frac{1}{64}$
5	1 : 5	$\frac{5}{1}$	25	125
$\frac{1}{10}$	10 : 1	$\frac{1}{10}$	$\frac{1}{100}$	$\frac{1}{1000}$

3 135 cm^2

4 a 56 cm^2
b 126 cm^2

5 a 48 m^2
b 3 m^2

6 a 2400 cm^3
b 8100 cm^3

7 Length ratio = 1 : 2, so volume ratio = 1 : 8. So large tin volume = 0.5 × 8 = 4 litres

8 1.38 m^3

9 a £6
b Assume that the cost is only based on the volume of paint in the tin.

10 4 cm

11 8 × 60p = £4.80 so it is better value to buy the large tub

12 a 3 : 4
b 9 : 16
c 27 : 64

13 720 ÷ 8 = 90 cm^3

Exercise 12E

1 a 111 cm^3 **b** 641 cm^3
c 267 cm^3 **d** 426 cm^3

2 a Height = 6 cm, Volume = 25 cm^3
b Height = 8 cm, Volume = 51 cm^3
c Height = 4 cm, Mass = 105 g
d Height = 3 cm, Volume = 130 cm^3

3 6.2 cm, 10.1 cm

4 4.26 cm, 6.74 cm

5 $\frac{H^2}{8^2} = \frac{200}{140}$

$H^2 = 64 \times \frac{200}{140} = 91.428571$

$H = \sqrt{91.428571} = 9.56$ (3 sf)

6 3.38 m

7 8.39 cm

8 26.5 cm

9 16.9 cm

10 a 4.33 cm, 7.81 cm   **b** 143 g, 839 g

11 53.8 kg

12 1.73 kg

13 8.8 cm

14 7.9 cm and 12.6 cm

15 b

Review questions

1 Let height of larger triangle = h.

Using similar triangles: $\frac{h}{35-h} = \frac{40}{30}$

Rearrange to $30h = 1400 - 40h$
which gives $70h = 1400$
$\quad\quad h = 20$ cm
So small triangle is 35 – 20 = 15 cm tall.
Thus the difference between the heights is 20 cm – 15 cm = 5 cm

2 a For similar shapes, if the ratio of lengths is 1 : x, then the ratio of volumes will be 1 : x^3, so if ratio of lengths is 1 : 3, the ratio of volumes will be 1 : 3^3 = 1 : 27

b Yes, because if the size (volume) of the plant increases by a factor of 27, the lengths have increased by a factor of 3. Hence the new height should be 4 cm × 3 = 12 cm, which it is.

3 Andrew is correct, Eve has calculated the length of AD (8 cm) so ED should be 2 cm.

4 a 6 cm   **b** 16 cm³

5 a Area scale factor = $\frac{324}{100}$ = 3.24, length scale factor = $\sqrt{3.24}$ = 1.8, length of cylinder B = 5 × 1.8 = 9

b 933 cm³

Chapter 13 – Probability: Exploring and applying probability

Exercise 13A

1 a $\frac{1}{5}$, $\frac{2}{25}$, $\frac{1}{10}$, $\frac{21}{200}$, $\frac{37}{250}$, $\frac{163}{1000}$, $\frac{329}{2000}$

b 6   **c** 1   **d** $\frac{1}{6}$ **e** 1000

2 a $\frac{19}{200}$, $\frac{27}{200}$, $\frac{4}{25}$, $\frac{53}{200}$, $\frac{69}{200}$

b 40

c No, it is weighted towards the side with numbers 4 and 5

3 a 32 is too high, unlikely that 20 of the 50 throws between 50 and 100 were 5

b Yes, all frequencies fairly close to 100

4 a B   **b** B   **c** C   **d** A
e B   **f** A   **g** B   **h** B

5 a 0.2, 0.25, 0.38, 0.42, 0.385, 0.397
b 80

6 a Caryl, most throws   **b** 0.39. 0.31, 0.17, 0.14
c Yes, it is more likely to give a 1 or 2

7 Thursday as it had the highest proportion

8 The missing top numbers are 4 and 5; the two bottom numbers are likely to be close to 20.

9 Although you would expect the probability to be close to $\frac{1}{2}$, hence 500 heads, it is more likely that the number of heads is close to 500 rather than actually 500.

10 Roxy is correct, as the expected numbers are: 50, 12.5, 25, 12.5. Sam has not taken into account the fact that there are four red sectors.

Exercise 13B

1 a Yes   **b** Yes   **c** No
d No   **e** Yes   **f** Yes

2 Events **a** and **f**

3 $\frac{3}{5}$

4 a i $\frac{3}{10}$ **ii** $\frac{3}{10}$ **iii** $\frac{3}{10}$
   iv $\frac{9}{10}$ **v** $\frac{4}{5}$
b All except **iii**
c Event **iv**

5 a Jane/John, Jane/Jack, Jane/Anne, Jane/Dave, Dave/John, Dave/Jack, Dave/Anne, Anne/John, Anne/Jack, Jack/John

b i $\frac{1}{10}$ **ii** $\frac{3}{10}$
   iii $\frac{3}{10}$ **iv** $\frac{7}{10}$
c All except **iii**
d Event **ii**

6 a $\frac{3}{8}$ **b** $\frac{1}{8}$

   c All except **ii**
   d Outcomes overlap

7 $\frac{3}{20}$

8 $\frac{1}{75}$

9 Not mutually exclusive events

10 a i 0.25   **ii** 0.4   **iii** 0.7
   b Events not mutually exclusive
   c Man/woman, American man/American woman
   d Man/woman

11 a i 0.95
     ii 0.9 (assuming person chooses one or other)
     iii 0.3
   b Events not mutually exclusive
   c Possible answer: pork and vegetarian

12 These are not mutually exclusive events.

Exercise 13C

1 25

2 1000

3 a 260   **b** 40   **c** 130   **d** 10

4 5

5 a 150   **b** 100   **c** 250   **d** 0

6 a 167   **b** 833

7 1050

8 a

Score	1	2	3	4	5	6
Expected occurrences	10	10	10	10	10	10

   b $1 \times 10 + 2 \times 10 + 3 \times 10 + 4 \times 10 + 5 \times 10 + 6 \times 10 = 210 = 3.5$
   c Find the average of the scores, which is $\frac{21}{6} = 3.5$

9 a 0.111   **b** 40

10 281 days

11 Multiply the number of tomato plants by 0.997

12 400

Exercise 13D

1 a 23   **b** 20%   **c** $\frac{4}{25}$ **d** 480

2 a 10   **b** 7   **c** 14%   **d** 15%

3 a

	1	2	3	4
	5	6	7	8	9
	6	7	8	9	10
	7	8	9	10	11
	8	9	10	11	12

b 4

c i $\frac{1}{4}$ **ii** $\frac{3}{16}$ **iii** $\frac{1}{4}$

4 a 16   **b** 16   **c** 73   **d** $\frac{51}{73}$

5 a

1	2	3	4	5	6
1	2	3	4	5	6
2	4	6	8	10	12

   b 3   **c** $\frac{1}{4}$

6 a $\frac{2}{45}$ **b** 40%   **c** 45%
   d No, as you don't know how much the people who get over £350 actually earn

7 $\frac{22}{36} = \frac{11}{18}$

8 a

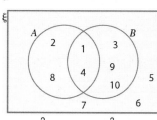

Score of second spinner						
10	10	11	13	15	17	19
8	8	9	11	13	15	17
6	6	7	9	11	13	15
4	4	5	7	9	11	13
2	2	3	5	7	9	11
0	0	1	3	5	7	9
	0	**1**	**3**	**5**	**7**	**9**
	Score of first spinner					

   b 9 or 11   **c** 0
   d $\frac{15}{36} = \frac{5}{12}$ **e** $\frac{30}{36} = \frac{5}{6}$

Exercise 13E

1 a 0.9   **b** 0.7

2 a 0.75   **b** 0.45

3 a

```
 ξ
   A ──────    ────── B
    ( 2   ( 1 )   3  )
    (     ( 4 )  9   )
    ( 8   (   ) 10  )   5
         7           6
```

   b i $\frac{2}{5}$ **ii** $\frac{3}{5}$ **iii** $\frac{1}{2}$
     iv $\frac{1}{2}$ **v** $\frac{7}{10}$ **vi** $\frac{1}{5}$

4 a i 0.52   **ii** 0.48   **iii** 0.65
     iv 0.35   **v** 0.82   **vi** 0.35
   b 0.3

5 a

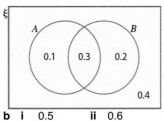

b i 0.5   **ii** 0.6   **iii** 0.3

6 a 65   **b** 70   **c** 90

7

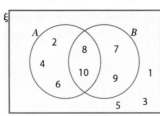

a $\frac{1}{2}$ **b** $\frac{2}{5}$

c $\frac{7}{10}$ **d** $\frac{1}{5}$

8 a 130

  b i $\frac{8}{13}$

    ii The probability that a student chosen at random walks to and from school

  c $\frac{5}{26}$

9 0.4

10 0.5

11 a $(A \cup B)'$ **b** $(A \cap B)'$

12 $\frac{37}{80}$

13 a

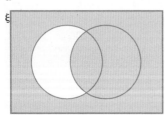

b

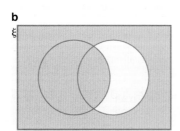

c

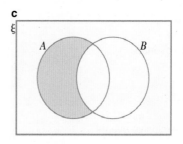

Review questions

1 a $\frac{1}{2}$ **b** $\frac{7}{10}$

2 a 0.28

  b the frequencies should all be close to 25

3 a i $\frac{3}{10}$ **ii** 10 red, 6 green, 4 blue

  b She may not have taken one in the 10 trials

4

	Boys	Girls	Total
Walk to school	9	21	30
Do not walk to school	18	2	20
Total	27	23	50

5 a 110   **b** $\frac{19}{55}$ **c** $\frac{3}{22}$ **d** $\frac{36}{55}$

6 a 0.18   **b** 0.49

  c No as the probabilities are close to 0.2

7 a i 0.8   **ii** 12

  b No as P(six) = $\frac{1}{6}$, so Tom is likely to throw 10 sixes

8 Draw a two-way table to show the outcomes

+	1	2	3	4	5
1	2	3	4	5	6
2	3	4	5	6	7
3	4	5	6	7	8
4	5	6	7	8	9
5	6	7	8	9	10

P(score greater than 6) = $\frac{10}{25}$, as $\frac{10}{25} < \frac{1}{2}$, she is likely to lose the game

9 a 0.3   **b** 0.5   **c** 0.6   **d** 0.3

Chapter 14 – Number: Powers and standard form

Exercise 14A

1 a 2^4 **b** 3^5 **c** 7^2 **d** 5^3
  e 10^7 **f** 6^4 **g** 4^1 **h** 1^7
  i 0.5^4 **j** 100^3

2 a $3 \times 3 \times 3 \times 3$

  b $9 \times 9 \times 9$

  c 6×6

  d $10 \times 10 \times 10 \times 10 \times 10$

e $2 \times 2 \times 2 \times 2 \times 2 \times 2 \times 2 \times 2 \times 2 \times 2$

f 8

g $0.1 \times 0.1 \times 0.1$

h 2.5×2.5

i $0.7 \times 0.7 \times 0.7$

j 1000×1000

3 a 16   **b** 243   **c** 49
d 125   **e** 10 000 000   **f** 1296
g 4   **h** 1   **i** 0.0625
j 1 000 000

4 a 81   **b** 729   **c** 36
d 100 000   **e** 1024   **f** 8
g 0.001   **h** 6.25   **i** 0.343
j 1 000 000

5 125 m^3

6 b 10^2 **c** 2^3 **d** 5^2

7 3: 3, 9, 27, 81, 243, 729 – pattern is 3, 9, 7, 1

4: 4, 16, 64, 256, 1024, 4096 – pattern is 4, 6

5: 5, 125, 625, 3125, 15 625, 78 125 – all 5

8 a 1   **b** 4   **c** 1
d 1   **e** 1

9 Any power of 1 is equal to 1.

10 10^6

11 10^6

12 a 1   **b** −1   **c** 1   **d** 1   **e** −1
13 a 1   **b** −1   **c** −1   **d** 1   **e** 1

14 2^{24}, 4^{12}, 8^8, 16^6

15 $x = 6$

Exercise 14B

1 a 5^4 **b** 5^3 **c** 5^2 **d** 5^3 **e** 5^{-5}

2 a 6^3 **b** 6^0 **c** 6^6 **d** 6^{-7} **e** 6^2

3 a a^3 **b** a^5 **c** a^7
d a^4 **e** a^2 **f** a^1

4 a Any two values such that $x + y = 10$
b Any two values such that $x - y = 10$

5 a 4^6 **b** 4^{15} **c** 4^6
d 4^{-6} **e** 4^6 **f** 4^0

6 a $6a^5$ **b** $9a^2$ **c** $8a^6$
d $-6a^4$ **e** $8a^8$ **f** $-10a^{-3}$

7 a $3a$ **b** $4a^3$ **c** $3a^4$
d $6a^{-1}$ **e** $4a^7$ **f** $5a^{-4}$

8 a $8a^5b^4$ **b** $10a^3b$ **c** $30a^{-2}b^{-2}$
d $2ab^3$ **e** $8a^{-5}b^7$ **f** $4a^5b^{-5}$

9 a $3a^3b^2$ **b** $3a^2c^4$ **c** $8a^2b^2c^3$

10 a Possible answer: $6x^2 \times 2y^5$ and $3xy \times 4xy^4$
b Possible answer: $24x^2y^7 \div 2y^2$ and $12x^6y^8 \div x^4y^3$

11 12 ($a = 2$, $b = 1$, $c = 3$)

12 $1 = a^x \div a^x = a^{x-x} = a^0$

Exercise 14C

1 a 60 000   **b** 120 000   **c** 150
d 42 000   **e** 1400   **f** 300
g 400   **h** 8000   **i** 160 000
j 4500   **k** 8000   **l** 250 000

2 a 5   **b** 50   **c** 25   **d** 30   **e** 7
f 300   **g** 6   **h** 30   **i** 1   **j** 15
k 40   **l** 5   **m** 40   **n** 320

3 a 54 400   **b** 16 000

4 $30 \times 90\ 000 = 2\ 700\ 000$
$600 \times 8000 = 4\ 800\ 000$
$5000 \times 4000 = 20\ 000\ 000$
$200\ 000 \times 700 = 140\ 000\ 000$

5 1400 million

6 a 31   **b** 310   **c** 3100   **d** 31 000

7 a 65   **b** 650   **c** 6500   **d** 65 000

8 a 0.31   **b** 0.031   **c** 0.0031   **d** 0.000 31

9 a 0.65   **b** 0.065   **c** 0.0065   **d** 0.000 65

10 a 250   **b** 34.5   **c** 4670
d 346   **e** 207.89   **f** 56 780
g 246   **h** 0.76   **i** 999 000
j 23 456   **k** 98 765.4   **l** 43 230 000
m 345.78   **n** 6000   **o** 56.7
p 560 045

11 a 0.025   **b** 0.345
c 0.004 67   **d** 3.46
e 0.207 89   **f** 0.056 78
g 0.0246   **h** 0.0076
i 0.000 000 999   **j** 2.3456
k 0.098 7654   **l** 0.000 043 23
m 0.000000034578   **n** 0.000 000 000 06
o 0.000 0005 67   **p** 0.005 600 45

12 a 230   **b** 578 900
c 4790   **d** 57 000 000
e 216   **f** 10 500
g 0.000 32   **h** 9870

13 a, **b** and **c**

14 Power 24 means more digits in the answer, so Venus is heavier.

15 6

Exercise 14D

1 a 0.31   **b** 0.031   **c** 0.0031   **d** 0.000 31

2 a 0.65   **b** 0.065   **c** 0.0065   **d** 0.000 65

3 a $9999999999 \times 10^{99}$
b $0.000000001 \times 10^{-99}$ (depending on number of digits displayed)

4 a 31   **b** 310   **c** 3100   **d** 31 000

5 a 65   **b** 650   **c** 6500   **d** 65 000

6 **a** 250 **b** 34.5 **c** 0.004 67
  d 34.6 **e** 897 000 **f** 0.00865
  g 60 000 000 **h** 0.000 567

7 **a** 2.5×10^2 **b** 3.45×10^{-1}
  c 4.67×10^4 **d** 3.4×10^9
  e 2.078×10^{10} **f** 5.678×10^{-4}
  g 6×10^{-4} **h** 5.67×10^{-3}
  i 5.60045×10^1

8 2.81581×10^5, 3×10^1, 1.382101×10^6

9 1.298×10^7, 2.997×10^9, 9.3×10^4

10 100

Exercise 14E

1 **a** 5.67×10^3 **b** 6×10^2
  c 3.46×10^{-1} **d** 7×10^3
  e 1.6 **f** 2.3×10^7
  g 3×10^{-6} **h** 2.56×10^6
  i 4.8×10^2 **j** 1.12×10^2
  k 6×10^{-1} **l** 2.8×10^6

2 **a** 4.81×10^8 **b** 9.15×10^{12}
  c 5.67×10^9 **d** 1.46×10^{14}
  e 1.63×10^{22} **f** 1.2×10^9
  g 1.08 **h** 6.4×10^2
  i 1.2×10^1 **j** 2.88
  k 2.5×10^7 **l** 8×10^{-6}

3 **a** 2.64×10^{14} **b** 1.22×10^8
  c 1.6×10^9 **d** 3.9×10^{-2}
  e 9.6×10^8 **f** 4.6×10^{-7}
  g 2.1×10^3 **h** 3.6×10^7
  i 1.5×10^2 **j** 3.5×10^9
  k 1.6×10^4 **l** 3.81×10^8
  k 7.18×10^{12}

4 **a** 2.7×10 **b** 1.6×10^{-2}
  c 2×10^{-1} **d** 4×10^{-8}
  e 2×10^5 **f** 6×10^{-2}
  g 2×10^{-5} **h** 5×10^2
  i 2×10

5 **a** 5.4×10 **b** 2.9×10^{-3}
  c 1.1 **d** 6.3×10^{-10}
  e 2.8×10^2 **f** 5.5×10^{-2}
  g 4.9×10^2 **h** 8.6×10^6

6 2×10^{13}, 1×10^{-10}, mass = 2×10^3 g (2 kg)

7 **a** (2^{63}) 9.2×10^{18} grains
  b $2^{64} - 1 = 1.8 \times 10^{19}$

8 **a** 6×10^7 sq miles **b** 30%

9 5×10^4

10 2.3×10^5

11 4.55×10^8 kg.

12 a 2.048×10^6 **b** 4.816×10^6

13 2.5×10^2

14 9.41×10^4

Review questions

1 **a i** 2^4 **ii** 2^8
  b i 10^3 **iii** 10^9

2 **a** 1 500 000 **b** 6 000 000 000

3 **a** 196
  b Units digits is $5 \times 5 = 25$ so it should end in 5

4 **a** 7^9 **b** x^4
  c Adds numbers and multiplies powers, but should be the other way round. $15x^9$

5 **a** t^8 **b** m^5 **c** $9x^6$ **d** $10a^7h^5$

6 **a** x^{11} **b** m^{-5} **c** $8k^5m^3$

7 **a** 7.5×10^4 **b** 0.009

8 **a** $2y$ **b** $8m^9p^{12}$

9 2.48×10^{-7}

10 1000 litres in a cubic metre, $5.3 \times 10^{24} \div 2000 = 2.65 \times 10^{21}$

11 Yes: $(6.5 \times 10^4)^2 = 4.225 \times 10^9$
  $(6 \times 10^4)^2 = 3.6 \times 10^9$
  $(2.5 \times 10^4)^2 = 6.25 \times 10^8 = 0.625 \times 10^9$
  $3.6 \times 10^9 + 0.625 \times 10^9 = 4.225 \times 10^9$

12 $2.6 \times 10^7 \div 2 = 1.3 \times 10^7$,
  short side = $1.3 \times 10^7 - 8 \times 10^6 = 13 \times 10^6 - 8 \times 10^6 = 5 \times 10^6$
  Area = $5 \times 10^6 \times 8 \times 10^6 = 40 \times 10^{12} = 4 \times 10^{13}$

13 1.5×10^7 sq miles

14 13 875 000

15 Any value from 1×10^8 to 1×10^9 (excluding 1×10^8 and 1×10^9), i.e. any value of the form $a \times 10^8$ where $1 < a < 10$

16 38.625

17 a 4.16×10^7 cm **b** 1.056×10^{14} cm^2

Chapter 15 – Algebra: Equations and inequalities

Exercise 15A

1 **a** 30 **b** 21 **c** 72 **d** 12
  e 6 **f** $10\frac{1}{2}$ **g** −10 **h** 7
  i 11 **j** 2 **k** 7 **l** $2\frac{4}{5}$
  m 1 **n** $11\frac{1}{2}$ **o** $\frac{1}{5}$

2 Any valid equations

3 **a** Amanda
  b First line: Betsy adds 4 instead of multiplying by 5.
    Second line: Betsy adds 5 instead of multiplying by 5.
    Fourth line: Betsy subtracts 2 instead of dividing by 2.

4 **a** $\frac{x+10}{5} = 9.50$
  b £37.50

5 a $\frac{8}{3}$ **b** Student's own checks

Exercise 15B

1 a $\frac{1}{2}$ **b** $1\frac{1}{5}$ **c** 2   **d** −2
   e −1   **f** −2   **g** −2   **h** −1

2 Any values that work, e.g. $a = 2$, $b = 3$ and $c = 30$.

3 55

4 3 cm

5 5

6 Multiplying out the brackets and simplifying gives $4x − 24 = 0$ which has the solution $x = 6$

7 168°

Exercise 15C

1 a $x = 2$ **b** $y = 1$ **c** $a = 7$ **d** $t = 4$
   e $p = 2$ **f** $k = −1$ **g** $m = 3$ **h** $s = −2$

2 $3x − 2 = 2x + 5$, $x = 7$

3 a $d = 6$ **b** $x = 11$ **c** $y = 1$ **d** $h = 4$
   e $b = 9$ **f** $c = 6$

4 a $6x + 3 = 6x + 10$; $6x − 6x = 10 − 3$; $0 = 7$, which is obviously false. Both sides have $6x$, which cancels out.
   b Multiplying out the brackets gives $12x + 18 = 12x + 18$, which is true for all values of x

5 $8x + 7 + x + 4 = 11x + 5 − x − 4$, $x = 10$

6 a They are both equal to the length of the rectangle
   b 70 cm²

7 a 15
   b −1
   c $2(n + 3)$, $2(n + 3) − 5$
   d $2(n + 3) − 5 = n$, $2n + 6 − 5 = n$, $2n + 1 = n$, $n = −1$

8 $4x + 18 = 3x + 1 + 50$, $x = 33$. Large bottle 1.5 litres, small bottle 1 litre

9 8

Exercise 15D

1 a $x = 4\frac{1}{2}$, $y = 1\frac{1}{2}$ **b** $x = −2$, $y = 4$
   c $x = 2\frac{1}{2}$, $y = −1\frac{1}{2}$

2 a $a = 7$, $b = 10$ **b** $c = 4$, $d = 11$
   c $e = 5$, $f = 3$

3 $x = 12$, $y = 2$

Exercise 15E

1 a $x = 9$, $y = −2$
   b $x = \frac{1}{2}$, $y = 5$ **c** $x = −3$, $y = −10$

2 a $x = 2\frac{1}{4}$, $y = 6\frac{1}{2}$
   b $x = 4$, $y = 3$ **c** $x = 5$, $y = 3$

3 a $x = 1$, $y = 3$ **b** $x = 5$, $y = 9$

Exercise 15F

1 a $x = 2$, $y = 5$ **b** $x = 4$, $y = −3$
   c $x = 1$, $y = 7$ **d** $x = \frac{1}{2}$, $y = −\frac{3}{4}$
   e $x = −1$, $y = 5$ **f** $x = 1\frac{1}{2}$, $y = \frac{3}{4}$

2 a $x = 5$, $y = 1$ **b** $x = 3$, $y = 8$
   c $x = 9$, $y = 1$ **d** $x = 7$, $y = 3$
   e $x = 4$, $y = 2$ **f** $x = 6$, $y = 5$

Exercise 15G

1 a 3 is the first term. The next term is $3 \times a + b$, which equals 14.
   b $14a + b = 47$ **c** $a = 3$, $b = 5$
   d 146, 443

2 Amul £7.20, Kim £3.50

3 a $3t + 5b = 810$, $3t + 3b = 630$
   b £10.20

4 a They are the same equation. Divide the first by 2 and it is the second, so they have an infinite number of solutions.
   b Double the second equation to get $6x + 2y = 14$ and subtract to get $9 = 14$. The left-hand sides are the same if the second is doubled so they cannot have different values.

5 a $10x + 5y = 840$, $8x + 10y = 1044$
   b £4.07

6 a My age minus 6 equals $2 \times$ (my son's age minus 6)
   b $x = 46$ and $y = 26$

7 (1, −2) is the solution to equations A and C; (−1, 3) is the solution to equations A and D; (2, 1) is the solution to B and C; (3, −3) is the solution to B and D.

8 84p

9 10.3 kg

10 £4.40

11 $p = 36$, $c = 22$. Total weight for Baz is 428 pounds so he can carry the load safely on his trailer.

12 $b = £3.50$, $p = £1.75$. Camilla needs £35 so she will not have enough money.

13 a Intersections points are (0, 6), (1, 3) and (2, 4). Area is 2 cm².
   b Intersection points are (0, 3), (6, 0) and (4, −1). Area is 6 cm².

14 When Carmen worked out (2) – (3), she should have got $y = 6$

When Jeff rearranged $2x + 8 - x = 10$, he should have got $x = 2$

They also misunderstood 'two, six' as this means $x = 2$ and $y = 6$, not the other way round.

Exercise 15H

1 a $y \le 3$ **b** $x < 6$ **c** $t \ge 18$
  d $x < 7$ **e** $x \le 3$ **f** $t \ge 5$

2 a 16 **b** 3 **c** 7

3 $2x + 3 < 20$, $x < 8.50$, so the most each could cost is £8.49

4 a Because $3 + 4 = 7$, which is less than the third side of length 8
  b $x + x + 2 > 10$, $2x + 2 > 10$, $2x > 8$, $x > 4$, so smallest value of x is 5

5 a $x = 6$ and $x < 3$ scores −1 (nothing in common), $x < 3$ and $x > 0$ scores +1 (1 in common for example), $x > 0$ and $x = 2$ scores +1 (2 in common), $x = 2$ and $x \ge 4$ scores −1 (nothing in common), so we get − 1 + 1 + 1 − 1 = 0
  b $x > 0$ and $x = 6$ scores +1 (6 in common), $x = 6$ and $x \ge 4$ scores +1 (6 in common), $x \ge 4$ and $x = 2$ scores −1 (nothing in common), $x = 2$ and $x < 3$ scores +1 (2 in common). + 1 + 1 − 1 + 1 = 2
  c Any acceptable combination, e.g. $x = 2$, $x < 3$, $x > 0$, $x \ge 4$, $x = 6$

6 a $y \le 4$ **b** $x \ge -2$ **c** $x \le \frac{14}{5}$
  d $x > 38$ **e** $x < 6\frac{1}{2}$ **f** $y \le \frac{7}{5}$

7 a $3 < x < 6$ **b** $2 < x < 5$ **c** $-1 < x \le 3$
  d $1 \le x < 4$ **e** $2 \le x < 4$ **f** $0 \le x \le 5$

8 a {4, 5} **b** {3, 4} **c** {0, 1, 2, 3}
  d {1, 2, 3} **e** {2, 3} **f** {0, 1, 2, 3, 4, 5}

9 6

Exercise 15I

1 a $x < 2$ **b** $x \ge -1$ **c** $3 < x < 6$

2

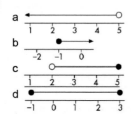

3

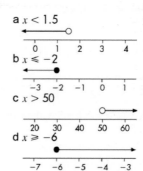

a $x < 1.5$

b $x \le -2$

c $x > 50$

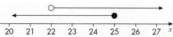

d $x \ge -6$

4 a Because 3 apples plus the chocolate bar cost more that £1.20: $x > 22$
  b Because 2 apples plus the chocolate bar left Max with at least 16p change: $x \le 25$
  c

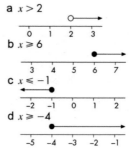

  d Apples could cost 23p, 24p or 25p.

5 Any two inequalities that overlap only on the integers −1, 0, 1 and 2 – for example, $x \ge -1$ and $x < 3$

6 1 and 4

7 $4(35 - 7x) \le 84$
$35 - 7x \le 21$
$7x \ge 14$
$x \ge 2$
Also $35 - 7x > 0$
$x < 5$
So the diagram represents this.

8

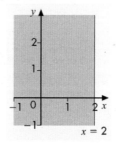

a $x > 2$

b $x \ge 6$

c $x \le -1$

d $x \ge -4$

Exercise 15J

1

2

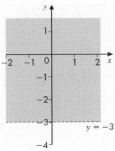

3

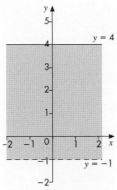

4 a

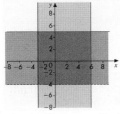

b i Yes **ii** Yes **iii** No

5

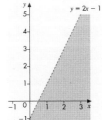

6 a

b

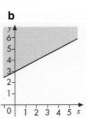

c

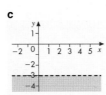

7 a–d

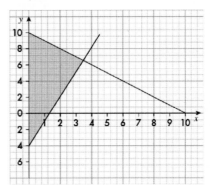

e i No **ii** Yes **iii** Yes

8 a–f

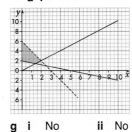

g i No **ii** No **iii** Yes

9 a

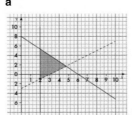

b i No **ii** Yes
 iii Yes **iv** No

10 For example, $x \geq 1$, $y \leq 3$ and $y \geq x + 1$. There are
many other valid answers.

11 May be true: a, c, d, g, h
Must be false: b, e
Must be true: f

12 Test a point such as the origin (0, 0), so 0 < 0 + 2, which is true. So the side that includes the origin is the required side.

13 a (3, 0)   **b** (4, 5)

14 £59.50

Exercise 15K

1 a 4 and 5   **b** 4 and 5   **c** 2 and 3

2 $x = 3.5$

3 a $x = 3.7$
  b i $x = 2.4$ **ii** $x = 2.8$ **iii** $x = 3.2$
  c $x = 5.8$

4 Student's own working

5 $x = 1.50$

6

Guess	$3x^3 + 2x$	Comment
6	660	Too low
7	1043	Too high
6.5	836.875	Too low
6.8	956.896	Too high
6.7	915.689	Too high
6.6	875.688	Too low
6.65	895.538875	Too low

7 a Area = $x(x + 5) = 100$
  b Width = 7.8 cm, length = 12.8 cm

8 Volume = $x \times 2x(x + 8) = 500$, $x^3 + 8x^2 = 250$, 4 ⇒ 192, 5 ⇒ 325, 4.4 ⇒ 240.064, 4.5 ⇒ 253.125, 4.45 ⇒ 246.541125, so dimensions are 4.5 cm, 9 cm and 12.5 cm

9 Steph is correct because if 7.05 is too low then the answer will round up to 7.1

10 a Cube is x^3, hole is $\frac{x}{2} \times \frac{x}{2} \times 8 = 2x^2$.
  Cube minus hole is 1500
  b 12 ⇒ 1440, 13 ⇒ 1859, 12.1 ⇒ 1478.741, 12.2 ⇒ 1518.168, 12.15 ⇒ 1498.368 375 so the value of $x = 12.2$ (to 1 dp)

11 2.76 and 7.24

Review questions

1 8

2 3 years

3 Length is 5.5 m, width is 2.5 m and area is 13.75 m². Carpet costs £123.75

4 a B: $\frac{3}{8}x$, C: $\frac{3}{8}x$, D: $\frac{1}{4}x$
  b $\frac{3}{8}x = 300$, 800 cars
  c : $\frac{1}{4}x = 500$, 750 cars

5 No, as $x + x + 2 + x + 4 + x + 6 = 360$ gives $x = 87°$ so the consecutive numbers (87, 89, 91, 93) are not even but odd

6 2 hr 10 min

7 −4, −3, −2, −1, 0, 1, 2, 3, 4, 5, 6, 7, 8

8 a $x = 7$,   **b** $x < 7$

9 a 6.3   **b** Solve as a linear equation

10 i $−3 < x < 1$, number line b;
  ii $−2 < x < 4$, number line below;
  iii $−1 < x < 2$, number line a

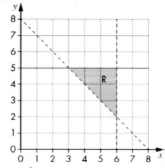

11 2.78

12 £62

13 £195

14 a $x = 4$, $y = 3$
  b i $1000x + 1000y = 7000 \rightarrow x + y = 7$
  ii $984x − 984y = 984 \rightarrow x − y = 1$
  c $a = 9$, $b = 5$

15 Let straight part of track = D, inner radius of end = r, outer radius = $r + x$
x being the width of the track
Length of inner track = $2D + 2\pi r = 300$ **(i)**
Length of outer track = $2D + 2\pi(r + x) = 320$ **(ii)**
Subtract equation **i** from **ii** to give
$2\pi(r + x) − 2\pi r = 20$
$2\pi r + 2\pi x − 2\pi r = 20$
$2\pi x = 20$
$x = 3.2$ (2 s.f.)

16 a

(graph with region R, axes labelled x and y)

  b $4\frac{1}{2}$ square units
  c It's infinite

17 −4, −3, −2, −1, 0, 1, 2, 3, 4

18 a $x + y \geq 7$, $y \leq 2x − 1$, $y \geq \frac{1}{2}x$
  b $y \leq x − 3$, $x > 2$, $x + y < 8$

Chapter 16 – Number: Counting, accuracy, powers and surds

Exercise 16A

1 a 0.5   **b** 0.$\dot{3}$ **c** 0.25
d 0.2   **e** 0.1$\dot{6}$ **f** 0.$\dot{1}$4285$\dot{7}$
g 0.125   **h** 0.$\dot{1}$ **i** 0.1
j 0.$\dot{0}$7692$\dot{3}$

2 a $\frac{4}{7}$ = 0.5714285...

     $\frac{5}{7}$ = 0.714 285 7...

     $\frac{6}{7}$ = 0.8571428...

b They all contain the same pattern of digits, starting at a different point in the pattern.

3 0.$\dot{1}$, 0.$\dot{2}$, 0.$\dot{3}$, etc. Digit in decimal fraction same as numerator.

4 0.$\dot{0}$$\dot{9}$, 0.$\dot{1}$$\dot{8}$, 0.$\dot{2}$$\dot{7}$, etc. Sum of digits in recurring pattern = 9. First digit is one less than numerator.

5 0.444 ..., 0.454 ..., 0.428 ..., 0.409 ..., 0.432 ..., 0.461 ...;

     $\frac{9}{22}$, $\frac{3}{7}$, $\frac{16}{37}$, $\frac{4}{9}$, $\frac{5}{11}$, $\frac{6}{13}$

6 a $\frac{1}{8}$ **b** $\frac{17}{50}$ **c** $\frac{29}{40}$ **d** $\frac{5}{16}$

   e $\frac{89}{100}$ **f** $\frac{1}{20}$ **g** $2\frac{7}{20}$ **h** $\frac{7}{32}$

7 a 0.08$\dot{3}$ **b** 0.0625   **c** 0.05
d 0.04   **e** 0.02

8 a $\frac{4}{3}$ **b** $\frac{6}{5}$ **c** $\frac{5}{2}$

   d $\frac{10}{7}$ **e** $\frac{20}{11}$ **f** $\frac{15}{4}$

9 a 0.75, 1.$\dot{3}$; 0.8$\dot{3}$, 1.2; 0.4, 2.5; 0.7, 1.$\dot{4}$2857$\dot{1}$;

     0.55, 1.$\dot{8}$$\dot{1}$; 0.2$\dot{6}$, 3.75

b Not always true, e.g. reciprocal of 0.4 ($\frac{2}{5}$) is

     $\frac{5}{2}$ = 2.5

10 1 ÷ 0 is infinite, so there is no finite answer.

11 a 10   **b** 2
c The reciprocal of a reciprocal is always the original number.

12 The reciprocal of x is greater than the reciprocal of y. For example, 2, 10, reciprocal of 2 is 0.5, reciprocal of 10 is 0.1, and 0.5 > 0.1

13 Possible answer: $-\frac{1}{2} \times -2 = 1$, $-\frac{1}{3} \times -3 = 1$

14 a 24.24242 ...   **b** 24

   c $\frac{24}{99} = \frac{8}{33}$

15 a $\frac{8}{9}$ **b** $\frac{34}{99}$ **c** $\frac{5}{11}$ **d** $\frac{21}{37}$

   e $\frac{4}{9}$ **f** $\frac{2}{45}$ **g** $\frac{13}{90}$ **h** $\frac{1}{22}$

i $2\frac{7}{9}$ **j** $7\frac{7}{11}$ **k** $3\frac{1}{3}$ **l** $2\frac{2}{33}$

16 a true   **b** true   **c** recurring

17 a $\frac{9}{9}$ **b** $\frac{45}{90} = \frac{1}{2} = 0.5$

Exercise 16B

1 a 14   **b** 100   **c** 5   **d** 13

2 8, 27 and 25

3 13 and 14

4 5 and 6

5 Answers can be about the same as these
   a i $\sqrt{(66 \times 100)} \approx 8.1 \times 10 = 81$
     ii $\sqrt{49} = 7$, so $\sqrt{45} \approx 6.7$
     iii $^3\sqrt{64} = 4$, $^3\sqrt{27} = 3$, so $^3\sqrt{40} \approx 3.4$
     iv $5.8^4 = 6^4 = 36 \times 36 \approx 30 \times 40 = 1200$
     v $^3\sqrt{45\,000} = {}^3\sqrt{45} \times 10 \approx 35$
   b i 81.24   **ii** 6.708   **iii** 3.42
     iv 1132   **v** 35.57

Exercise 16C

1 a $\frac{1}{5^3}$ **b** $\frac{1}{6}$ **c** $\frac{1}{10^5}$ **d** $\frac{1}{3^2}$

   e $\frac{1}{8^2}$ **f** $\frac{1}{9}$ **g** $\frac{1}{w^2}$ **h** $\frac{1}{t}$

   i $\frac{1}{x^m}$ **j** $\frac{4}{m^3}$

2 a 3^{-2} **b** 5^{-1} **c** 10^{-3} **d** m^{-1} **e** t^{-n}

3 a i 2^4 **ii** 2^{-1} **iii** 2^{-4} **iv** -2^3
   b i 10^3 **ii** 10^{-1} **iii** 10^{-2} **iv** 10^6
   c i 5^3 **ii** 5^{-1} **iii** 5^{-2} **iv** 5^{-4}
   d i 3^2 **ii** 3^{-3} **iii** 3^{-4} **iv** -3^5

4 a $\frac{5}{x^3}$ **b** $\frac{6}{t}$ **c** $\frac{7}{m^2}$ **d** $\frac{4}{q^4}$

   e $\frac{10}{y^5}$ **f** $\frac{1}{2x^3}$ **g** $\frac{1}{2m}$ **h** $\frac{3}{4t^4}$

   i $\frac{4}{5y^3}$ **j** $\frac{7}{8x^5}$

5 a $7x^{-3}$ **b** $10p^{-1}$ **c** $5t^{-2}$
   d $8m^{-5}$ **e** $3y^{-1}$

6 a i 25   **ii** $\frac{1}{125}$ **iii** $\frac{4}{5}$

   b i 64   **ii** $\frac{1}{16}$ **iii** $\frac{5}{256}$

   c i 8

     ii $\frac{1}{32}$

     iii $\frac{9}{2}$ or $4\frac{1}{2}$

   d i 1 000 000

     ii $\frac{1}{1000}$

     iii $\frac{1}{4}$

7 24 (32 − 8)

8 $x = 8$ and $y = 4$ (or $x = y = 1$)

9 $\frac{1}{2097152}$

10 a x^{-5}, x^0, x^5 **b** x^5, x^0, x^{-5} **c** x^5, x^{-5}, x^0

Exercise 16D

1 **a** 5 **b** 25 **c** 3 **d** 5
e 20 **f** 5 **g** 3 **h** 10
i 3 **j** 2 **k** $\frac{1}{4}$ **l** $\frac{1}{2}$
m $\frac{1}{3}$ **n** $\frac{1}{5}$ **o** $\frac{1}{10}$

2 **a** $\frac{5}{6}$ **b** $1\frac{2}{3}$ **c** $\frac{8}{9}$ **d** $1\frac{4}{5}$
e $\frac{5}{8}$ **f** $\frac{3}{5}$ **g** $\frac{1}{4}$ **h** $2\frac{1}{2}$
i $\frac{4}{5}$ **j** $1\frac{1}{7}$

3 $\left(x^{\frac{1}{n}}\right)^n = x^{\frac{1}{n} \times n} = x^1 = x$, but

$\left(\sqrt[n]{x}\right)^n = \sqrt[n]{x} \times \sqrt[n]{x} \ldots n$ times $= x$, so

$x^{\frac{1}{n}} = \sqrt[n]{x}$

4 $64^{-\frac{1}{2}} = \frac{1}{8}$, others are both $\frac{1}{2}$

5 Possible answer: The negative power gives the reciprocal, so $27^{-\frac{1}{3}} = \frac{1}{27^{\frac{1}{3}}}$

The power one-third means cube root, so you need the cube root of 27 which is 3, so $27^{\frac{1}{3}} = 3$ and $\frac{1}{27^{\frac{1}{3}}} = \frac{1}{3}$

6 Possible answers include $x = 16$ and $y = 64$, $x = 25$ and $y = 125$

Exercise 16E

1 **a** 16 **b** 25 **c** 216 **d** 81

2 **a** $t^{\frac{2}{3}}$ **b** $m^{\frac{3}{4}}$ **c** $k^{\frac{2}{5}}$ **d** $x^{\frac{3}{2}}$

3 **a** 4 **b** 9 **c** 64 **d** 3125

4 **a** $\frac{1}{5}$ **b** $\frac{1}{6}$ **c** $\frac{1}{2}$ **d** $\frac{1}{3}$
e $\frac{1}{4}$ **f** $\frac{1}{2}$ **g** $\frac{1}{2}$ **h** $\frac{1}{3}$

5 **a** $\frac{1}{125}$ **b** $\frac{1}{216}$ **c** $\frac{1}{8}$ **d** $\frac{1}{27}$
e $\frac{1}{256}$ **f** $\frac{1}{4}$ **g** $\frac{1}{4}$ **h** $\frac{1}{9}$

6 **a** $\frac{1}{100000}$ **b** $\frac{1}{12}$ **c** $\frac{1}{25}$ **d** $\frac{1}{27}$
e $\frac{1}{32}$ **f** $\frac{1}{32}$ **g** $\frac{1}{81}$ **h** $\frac{1}{13}$

7 $8^{-\frac{2}{3}} = \frac{1}{4}$, others are both $\frac{1}{8}$

8 Possible answer: The negative power gives the reciprocal, so $27^{-\frac{2}{3}} = \frac{1}{27^{\frac{2}{3}}}$

The power one-third means cube root, so we need the cube root of 27 which is 3 and the power 2 means square, so $3^2 = 9$, so $27^{\frac{2}{3}} = 9$ and $\frac{1}{27^{\frac{2}{3}}} = \frac{1}{9}$

9 $3 = x^{-\frac{2}{3}} \div x^{-1}$, $3 = x^{\frac{1}{3}}$, $x = 27$

Exercise 16F

1 **a** $\sqrt{6}$ **b** $\sqrt{15}$ **c** 2 **d** 4
e $2\sqrt{10}$ **f** 3 **g** $2\sqrt{3}$ **h** $\sqrt{21}$
i $\sqrt{14}$ **j** 6 **k** 6 **l** $\sqrt{30}$

2 **a** 2 **b** $\sqrt{5}$ **c** $\sqrt{6}$ **d** $\sqrt{3}$
e $\sqrt{5}$ **f** 1 **g** $\sqrt{3}$ **h** $\sqrt{7}$
i 2 **j** $\sqrt{6}$ **k** 1 **l** 3

3 **a** $2\sqrt{3}$ **b** 15 **c** $4\sqrt{2}$ **d** $4\sqrt{3}$
e $8\sqrt{5}$ **f** $3\sqrt{3}$ **g** 24 **h** $3\sqrt{7}$
i $2\sqrt{7}$ **j** $6\sqrt{5}$ **k** $6\sqrt{3}$ **l** 30

4 **a** $\sqrt{3}$ **b** 1 **c** $2\sqrt{2}$ **d** $\sqrt{2}$
e $\sqrt{5}$ **f** $\sqrt{3}$ **g** $\sqrt{2}$ **h** $\sqrt{7}$
i $\sqrt{7}$ **j** $2\sqrt{3}$ **k** $2\sqrt{3}$ **l** 1

5 **a** a **b** 1 **c** $\sqrt{a}$

6 **a** $3\sqrt{2}$ **b** $2\sqrt{6}$ **c** $2\sqrt{3}$ **d** $5\sqrt{2}$
e $2\sqrt{2}$ **f** $3\sqrt{3}$ **g** $4\sqrt{3}$ **h** $5\sqrt{3}$
i $3\sqrt{5}$ **j** $3\sqrt{7}$ **k** $4\sqrt{2}$ **l** $10\sqrt{2}$
m $10\sqrt{10}$ **n** $5\sqrt{10}$ **o** $7\sqrt{2}$ **p** $9\sqrt{3}$

7 **a** 36 **b** $16\sqrt{30}$ **c** 54 **d** 32
e $48\sqrt{6}$ **f** $48\sqrt{6}$ **g** $18\sqrt{15}$ **h** 84
i 64 **j** 100 **k** 50 **l** 56

8 **a** $20\sqrt{6}$ **b** $6\sqrt{15}$ **c** 24 **d** 16
e $12\sqrt{10}$ **f** 18 **g** $20\sqrt{3}$ **h** $10\sqrt{21}$
i $6\sqrt{21}$ **j** 36 **k** 24 **l** $12\sqrt{30}$

9 **a** 6 **b** $3\sqrt{5}$ **c** $6\sqrt{6}$ **d** $2\sqrt{3}$
e $4\sqrt{5}$ **f** 5 **g** $7\sqrt{3}$ **h** $2\sqrt{7}$
i 6 **j** $2\sqrt{7}$ **k** 5
l Does not simplify

10 **a** $2\sqrt{3}$ **b** 4 **c** $6\sqrt{2}$ **d** $4\sqrt{2}$
e $6\sqrt{5}$ **f** $24\sqrt{3}$ **g** $3\sqrt{2}$ **h** $\sqrt{7}$
i $10\sqrt{7}$ **j** $8\sqrt{3}$ **k** $10\sqrt{3}$ **l** 6

11 **a** abc **b** $\frac{a}{c}$ **c** $c\sqrt{b}$

12 **a** 20 **b** 24 **c** 10
d 24 **e** 3 **f** 6

13 **a** $\frac{3}{4}$ **b** $8\frac{1}{3}$ **c** $\frac{5}{16}$ **d** 12 **e** 2

14 **a** False **b** False

15 Possible answer: $\sqrt{3} \times 2\sqrt{3}$ $(= 6)$

16 $(\sqrt{a} + \sqrt{b})^2 = (\sqrt{a+b})^2$, $a + 2\sqrt{ab} + b = a + b$, Cancel a and b, $2\sqrt{ab} = 0$, so $a = 0$ and/or $b = 0$.

Exercise 16G

1 Expand the brackets each time.

2 **a** $2\sqrt{3} - 3$ **b** $3\sqrt{2} - 8$ **c** $10 + 4\sqrt{5}$
   d $12\sqrt{7} - 42$ **e** $15\sqrt{2} - 24$ **f** $9 - \sqrt{3}$

3 **a** $2\sqrt{3}$ **b** $1 + \sqrt{5}$ **c** $-1 - \sqrt{2}$
   d $\sqrt{7} - 30$ **e** -41 **f** $7 + 3\sqrt{6}$
   g $9 + 4\sqrt{5}$ **h** $3 - 2\sqrt{2}$ **i** $11 + 6\sqrt{2}$

4 **a** $3\sqrt{2}$ cm **b** $2\sqrt{3}$ cm **c** $2\sqrt{10}$ cm

5 **a** $\sqrt{3} - 1$ cm^2 **b** $2\sqrt{5} + 5\sqrt{2}$ cm^2
   c $2\sqrt{3} + 18$ cm^2

6 **a** $\frac{\sqrt{3}}{3}$ **b** $\frac{\sqrt{2}}{2}$ **c** $\frac{\sqrt{5}}{5}$ **d** $\frac{\sqrt{3}}{6}$
   e $\sqrt{3}$ **f** $\frac{5\sqrt{2}}{2}$ **g** $\frac{3}{2}$ **h** $\frac{5\sqrt{2}}{2}$
   i $\frac{\sqrt{21}}{3}$ **j** $\frac{\sqrt{2}+2}{2}$ **k** $\frac{2\sqrt{3}-3}{3}$ **l** $\frac{5\sqrt{3}+6}{3}$

7 **a** **i** 1 **ii** -4 **iii** 2
   iv 17 **v** -44
   b They become whole numbers. Difference of two squares makes the 'middle terms' (and surds) disappear.

8 **a** Possible answer: $\sqrt{2}$ and $\sqrt{2}$ or $\sqrt{2}$ and $\sqrt{8}$
   b Possible answer: $\sqrt{2}$ and $\sqrt{3}$

9 **a** Possible answer: $\sqrt{2}$ and $\sqrt{2}$ or $\sqrt{8}$ and $\sqrt{2}$
   b Possible answer: $\sqrt{3}$ and $\sqrt{2}$

10 Possible answer: $80^2 = 6400$, so $80 = \sqrt{6400}$ and $10\sqrt{70} = \sqrt{7000}$
    Since $6400 < 7000$, there is not enough cable.

11 $9 + 6\sqrt{2} + 2 - (1 - 2\sqrt{8} + 8) = 11 - 9 + 6\sqrt{2} + 4\sqrt{2} = 2 + 10\sqrt{2}$

12 $x^2 - y^2 = (1 + \sqrt{2})^2 - (1 - \sqrt{8})^2 = 1 + 2\sqrt{2} + 2 - (1 - 2\sqrt{8} + 8) = 3 - 9 + 2\sqrt{2} + 4\sqrt{2} = -6 + 6\sqrt{2}$
    $(x + y)(x - y) = (2 - \sqrt{2})(3\sqrt{2}) = 6\sqrt{2} - 6$

13 $4\sqrt{2} - (\sqrt{2} - 1) = 3\sqrt{2} + 1.$ $(\sqrt{2} - 1)(3\sqrt{2} + 1) = 5 - 2\sqrt{2}$

14 **a** **i** $3 + n\sqrt{2}$ **ii** $\frac{n+1}{\sqrt{3}}$
    b **i** $\left(\sqrt{5}\right)^n$ **ii** $\left(5 + \sqrt{2}\right) \times \left(\sqrt{2}\right)^{n-1}$

Exercise 16H

1 **a** 6.5 cm ≤ 7 cm < 7.5 cm
   b 115 g ≤ 120 g < 125 g
   c 3350 km ≤ 3400 km < 3450 km
   d 49.5 mph ≤ 50 mph < 50.5 mph
   e £$5.50 \leq$ £$6 <$ £6.50
   f 16.75 cm ≤ 16.8 cm < 16.85 cm
   g 15.5 kg ≤ 16 kg < 16.5 kg
   h $14\,450$ people $\leq 14\,500$ people $< 14\,550$ people
   i 54.5 miles ≤ 55 miles < 55.5 miles
   j 52.5 miles ≤ 55 miles < 57.5 miles

2 **a** 5.5 cm ≤ 6 cm < 6.5 cm
   b 16.5 kg ≤ 17 kg < 17.5 kg
   c 31.5 min ≤ 32 min < 32.5 min
   d 237.5 km ≤ 238 km < 238.5 km
   e 7.25 m ≤ 7.3 m < 7.35 m
   f 25.75 kg ≤ 25.8 kg < 25.85 kg
   g 3.35 h ≤ 3.4 h < 3.45 h
   h 86.5 g ≤ 87 g < 87.5 g
   i 4.225 mm ≤ 4.23 mm < 4.235 mm
   j 2.185 kg ≤ 2.19 kg < 2.195 kg
   k 12.665 min ≤ 12.67 min < 12.675 min
   l 24.5 m ≤ 25 m < 25.5 m
   m 35 cm ≤ 40 cm < 45 cm
   n 595 g ≤ 600 g < 605 g
   o 25 min ≤ 30 min < 35 min
   p 995 m ≤ 1000 m < 1050 m
   q 3.95 m ≤ 4.0 m < 4.05 m
   r 7.035 kg ≤ 7.04 kg < 7.045 kg
   s 11.95 s ≤ 12.0 s < 12.05 s
   t 6.995 m ≤ 7.00 m < 7.005 m

3 **a** 7.5 m, 8.5 m **b** 25.5 kg, 26.5 kg
   c 24.5 min, 25.5 min **d** 84.5 g, 85.5 g
   e 2.395 m, 2.405 m **f** 0.15 kg, 0.25 kg
   g 0.055 s, 0.065 s **h** 250 g, 350 g
   i 0.65 m, 0.75 m **j** 365.5 g, 366.5 g
   k 165 weeks, 175 weeks **l** 205 g, 215 g

4 There are 16 empty seats and the number getting on the bus is from 15 to 24 so it is possible if 15 or 16 get on.

5 C: The chain and distance are both any value between 29.5 and 30.5 metres, so there is no way of knowing if the chain is longer or shorter than the distance.

6 2 kg 450 grams

7 **a** < 65.5 g **b** 64.5 g
   c < 2620 g **d** 2580 g

8 345, 346, 347, 348, 349

9 Any number in range $4 < a < 5$, e.g. 4.5

Exercise 16I

1 Minimum 65 kg, maximum 75 kg

2 Minimum is 19, maximum is 20

3 **a** 12.5 kg **b** 20

4 3 years 364 days (Jack is on his fifth birthday; Jill is 9 years old tomorrow)

5 **a** 38.25 cm$^2 \leq$ area < 52.25 cm^2
   b 37.1575 cm$^2 \leq$ area < 38.4475 cm^2
   c 135.625 cm$^2 \leq$ area < 145.225 cm^2

6 **a** 5.5 m $\leq$ length < 6.5 m, 3.5 m $\leq$ width < 4.5 m
   b 29.25 m^2
   c 18 m

7 79.75 m$^2 \leq$ area < 100.75 m^2

8 216.125 cm$^3 \leq$ volume < 354.375 cm^3

9 12.5 metres

10 Yes, because they could be walking at 4.5 mph and 2.5 mph meaning that they would cover 4.5 miles + 2.5 miles = 7 miles in 1 hour

11 20.9 m ≤ length < 22.9 m (3 sf)

12 16.4 cm² ≤ area < 21.7 cm² (3 sf)

13 a i 64.1 cm³ ≤ volume < 69.6 cm³ (3 sf)
  ii £22 578 ≤ price < £24 515 (nearest £)
 b 23 643 ≤ price < £23 661 (nearest £)
 c Errors in length compounded by being used 3 times in **a**, but errors in weight only used once in **b**

14 a 14.65 s ≤ time < 14.75 s
 b 99.5 m ≤ length < 100.5 m
 c 6.86 m/s (3 sf)

15 a 1.25% (3 sf)
 b 1.89% (3 sf)

16 3.41 cm ≤ length < 3.43 cm (3 sf)

17 5.80 cm ≤ length < 5.90 cm (3 sf)

18 14 s ≤ time < 30 s

19 Cannot be certain as limits of accuracy for all three springs overlap:
 Red: 12.5 newtons to 13.1 newtons
 Green: 11.8 newtons to 13.2 newtons
 Blue: 9.5 newtons to 12.9 newtons
 For example, all tensions could be 12 newtons

Exercise 16J

1 Number of possible permutations is 7! ÷ 2!5! = 21. Of these any pair of the first 5 coins will be less than a £1, which is 5! ÷ 3! 2! = 10. Hence 11 pairs will have a value greater than £1.

2 6, 16, etc. up to 196, which is 19 plus 60 up to 69, which is 9 (66 already counted) plus 160 up to 169 which is 9 (166 already counted) giving a total of 37

3 a i 5040 **ii** 2.43 × 10¹⁸ (3 sf)
 b This depends on your calculator but 69! = 1.71 × 10⁹⁸, which is about the number of atoms in QUINTILLION (look it up) universes.

4 a 10⁴ = 10 000 **b** 13⁴ = 28 561

5 3 × 13³ = 6591

6 a 504 **b** 495

7 a 30 **b** 56

8 a 10³ = 1000 **b** 6

9 8 × 7 × 6 = 336

10 a 16 ways of choosing an Ace followed by a King out of 52 × 52 ways of picking 2 cards with replacement, so $\frac{16}{2704} = \frac{1}{169}$
 b Still 16 ways of taking an ace followed by a King but out of 52 × 51 so $\frac{16}{2652} = \frac{4}{663}$

11 a 1 6 15 20 15 6 1, 1 7 21 35 35 21 7 1, 1 8 28 56 70 56 28 8 1, 1 9 36 84 126 126 84 36 9 1, 1 10 45 120 210 252 210 120 45 10 1
 b i 10 **ii** 1 **iii** 28 **iv** 1
 c $_5C_2$ is the 3rd value in the 6th row, $_8C_6$ is the 7th value in the 9th row

d i 20 **ii** 8 **iii** 3 **iv** 70
e 1

12 a 31 **b** 8 (2⁸ = 256)

13 a C 435 **b** B 48 **c** B 12 **d** D 12
 e C 455 **f** A 64 = 1296
 g B 5! = 120
 h A 6⁵ = 7776
 i A 26² × 10² = 67 600
 j B 9 × 5 = 45
 k A 10! = 3 628 800
 l Mixture of D and C 60

14 12

15 144

16 6 (RBB, RBY, RYY, RRB, RRY, RRR)

17 Assume 5 seat car is full. Driver is fixed, other 4 seats can be filled by 6×5×4×3 arrangements = 360. In the 4 seat car driver is fixed but the 2 people left can sit in 3 × 2 = 6 arrangements. Total 6 × 360 = 2160. Now assume 4 seat car is full. That is 6 × 5 × 4 arrangements = 120 and in the 5 seat car the 3 people left can sit in 4 × 3 × 2 arrangements = 24, 24 × 120 = 2880. That is a total of 5040 different seating arrangements.

18 1000

19 105

20 a 5! × 3! = 720 **b** 5! × 3 = 360

21 a i 79 380 **ii** 35 280
  iii 52 920

 b Players could only be assigned to their own group. If not, then the number of possible teams would increase.

22 a 40 320
 b 109 600

23 They are both correct and give the answer 511.

Review questions

1 a 13 **b** 10 **c** 13

2 a 1845 **b** 1854

3 8, 16 and 36

4 19

5 $_{12}P_2$ = 132, $_9C_4$ = 126 so $_{12}P_2$ is greater

6 a 12⁴ = 20 736 **b** 3 × 12³ = 5184

7 a 5 × 4 × 3 × 2 × 1 = 5! = 120
 b There will be 24 starting with each letter and CODES will be the first CO word so 13th in the list

8 a 3⁴ = 81 **b** 8 **c** −3

9 a $\frac{1}{25}$ **b** 6⁴ = 1296

10 $\frac{7}{15}$

11 $a = 7$, $b = -1$

12 $6\sqrt{2}$

13 a $x = 0.5454..$, $100x = 54.5454..$, $99x = 54$

$x = \frac{54}{99}$, cancel by 9

b $0.35454.. = 0.3 + 0.05454.. = \frac{3}{10} + \frac{6}{110} =$

$\frac{33}{110} + \frac{6}{110} = \frac{39}{110}$

14 $\frac{11}{45}$

15 a 9   **b** $5\sqrt{2}$

16 a $\frac{\sqrt{5}}{5}$ **b** 2

17 a **i** $\sqrt{32} = \sqrt{16 \times 2} = \sqrt{16} \times \sqrt{2} = 4\sqrt{2}$
     ii $14 + 4\sqrt{6}$
   b $2^2 + (2 + \sqrt{6})^2 = 4 + 4 + 6 + 4\sqrt{6} = 14 + 4\sqrt{6} =$
     $(\sqrt{2} + \sqrt{12})^2$ so the sides obey Pythagoras'
     theorem

18 a $\sqrt{27} = 5.20$ m
   b Cube side 2.95 m has diagonal 5.07 m. Max
     length pole is 5.005 m so it will fit round the
     corner.

Chapter 17 – Algebra: Quadratic Equations

Exercise 17A

1 a Values of y: 27, 16, 7, 0, −5, −8, −9, −8, −5, 0, 7
   b −8.8   **c** 3.4 or −1.4

2 a Values of y: 2, −1, −2, −1, 2, 7, 14
   b 0.25   **c** 0.7 or −2.7
   d

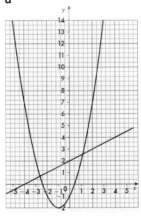

   e (1.1, 2.6) and (−2.6, 0.7)

3 a Values of y: 15, 9, 4, 0, −3, −5, −6, −6, −5, −3, 0, 4, 9
   b −0.5 and 3

4 a Same answer
   b

x	−3	−2	−1	0	1	2	3	4	5	6	7
y	28	19	12	7	4	3	4	7	12	19	28

Since the quadratic graph has a vertical line of symmetry and the y-values for $x = 1$ and $x = 3$ are the same, this means that the y-values will be symmetric about $x = 2$. Hence the y-values will be the same for $x = 0$ and $x = 4$, and so on.

5 Points plotted and joined should give a parabola.

6 Line A has a constant in front, so is 'thinner' than the rest.
Line B has a negative in front, so is 'upside down'.
Line C does not pass through the origin.

Exercise 17B

1 a −2, −5   **b** 4, 9   **c** −6, 3

2 a −4, −1   **b** 2, 4   **c** −2, 5
   d −3, 5   **e** −6, 3   **f** −1, 2
   g −5   **h** 7

3 $x(x + 40) = 48\,000$, $x^2 + 40x − 48\,000 = 0$,
$(x + 240)(x − 200) = 0$
Fence is $2 \times 200 + 2 \times 240 = 880$ m

4 a −10, 3   **b** −4, 11   **c** −8, 9
   d 8, 9   **e** 1   **f** −6, 7
   g −2, 3

5 Mario was correct.
Sylvan did not make it into a standard quadratic and only factorised the x terms. She also incorrectly solved the equation $x − 3 = 4$.

6 40 cm

7 48 km/h

8 a 4, 9
   b **i** 2, −2, 3, −3   **ii** 16, 81
     iii 5, 6, 10, 11

Exercise 17C

1 a $\frac{1}{3}$, −3   **b** $1\frac{1}{3}$, $-\frac{1}{2}$ **c** $-\frac{1}{5}$, 2
   d $-2\frac{1}{2}$, $3\frac{1}{2}$ **e** $-\frac{1}{6}$, $-\frac{1}{3}$ **f** $\frac{2}{3}$, 4
   g $\frac{1}{2}$, −3   **h** $\frac{5}{2}$, $-\frac{7}{6}$ **i** $-1\frac{2}{3}$, $1\frac{2}{5}$
   j $1\frac{3}{4}$, $1\frac{2}{7}$ **k** $\frac{2}{3}$, $\frac{1}{8}$ **l** $\pm\frac{1}{4}$
   m $-2\frac{1}{4}$, 0   **n** $\pm 1\frac{2}{5}$ **o** $-\frac{1}{3}$, 3

2 a 7, −6   **b** $-2\frac{1}{2}$, $1\frac{1}{2}$ **c** −1, $\frac{11}{13}$
   d $-\frac{2}{5}$, $\frac{1}{2}$ **e** $-\frac{1}{3}$, $-\frac{1}{2}$ **f** $\frac{1}{5}$, −2
   g 4   **h** −2, $\frac{1}{8}$ **i** $-\frac{1}{3}$, 0
   j ± 5 **k** $-1\frac{2}{3}$ **l** $\pm 3\frac{1}{2}$
   m $-2\frac{1}{2}$, 3

3 a Both only have one solution: $x = 1$.
   b B is a linear equation, but A and C are quadratic equations.

4 a $(5x − 1)^2 = (2x + 3)^2 + (x + 1)^2$, when expanded and collected into the general quadratic, gives the required equation.
   b $(10x + 3)(2x − 3)$, $x = 1.5$; area = 7.5 cm^2.

5 **a** Show by substituting into the equation

    b $-\frac{24}{5}$

6 5, 0.5

7 Area = 22.75, width = 3.5 m

Exercise 17D

1 **a** 1.77, −2.27   **b** 3.70, −2.70
   c −0.19, −1.53   **d** −1.39, −2.27
   e 1.37, −4.37   **f** 0.44, −1.69
   g 1.64, 0.61   **h** 0.36, −0.79
   i 1.89, 0.11

2 13

3 $x^2 - 3x - 7 = 0$

4 Terry gets $x = \frac{4+\sqrt{0}}{8}$ and June gets
   $(2x - 1)^2 = 0$, which only give one
   solution $x = \frac{1}{2}$

5 6.54, 0.46

6 1.25, 0.8

7 **a** **i** −0.382, −2.618 **ii** 6.414, 3.586
    iii 7.531, −0.531 **iv** 1.123, −7.123

   b Since $a = 1$, answers are $\dfrac{-b+\sqrt{b^2-4c}}{2}$ and

   $\dfrac{-b-\sqrt{b^2-4c}}{2}$. When added,

   $\dfrac{-b+\sqrt{b^2-4c}-b-\sqrt{b^2-4c}}{2} = \dfrac{-b-b}{2} = \dfrac{-2b}{2} = -b$

Exercise 17E

1 **a** 52 (TWO)   **b** 0 (ONE)
   c −23 (NONE)   **d** −7 (NONE)
   e 68 (TWO)   **f** −35 (NONE)
   g −4 (NONE)   **h** 0 (ONE)
   i 409 (TWO)

2 300

3 $x^2 + 3x - 1 = 0$; $x^2 - 3x - 1 = 0$; $x^2 + x - 3 = 0$; $x^2 - x - 3 = 0$

4 2 or −10

5 Can be factorised: $b^2 - 4ac = 1849, 1, 49, 1024,$
   900
   Cannot be factorised: $b^2 - 4ac = 41, 265, 3529,$
   216, 76
   For those that can be factorised, $b^2 - 4ac$ is a
   square number

Exercise 17F

1 **a** $(x - 2)^2 - 4$ **b** $(x + 7)^2 - 49$
   c $(x - 3)^2 - 9$ **d** $(x + 3)^2 - 9$
   e $(x - 5)^2 - 25$ **f** $(x + 10)^2 - 100$
   g $(x - 2)^2 - 5$ **h** $(x + 3)^2 - 6$
   i $(x + 4)^2 - 22$ **j** $(x + 1)^2 - 2$
   k $(x - 1)^2 - 8$ **l** $(x + 9)^2 - 11$

2 **a** 4th, 1st, 2nd and 3rd – in that order
   b Write $x^2 - 4x - 3 = 0$ as $(x - 2)^2 - 7 = 0$, Add 7
   to both sides, square root both sides, Add 2 to
   both sides
   c **i** $x = -3 \pm \sqrt{2}$ **ii** $x = 2 \pm \sqrt{7}$

3 **a** $-2 \pm \sqrt{5}$ **b** $-7 \pm 3\sqrt{6}$
   c $3 \pm \sqrt{6}$ **d** $5 \pm \sqrt{30}$
   e $-10 \pm \sqrt{101}$ **f** $-4 \pm \sqrt{22}$

4 **a** 1.45, −3.45   **b** 5.32, −1.32
   c −4.16, 2.16

5 Check for correct proof.

6 $p = -14, q = -3$

7 **a** $x^2 - 12x + 40 = (x - 6)^2 + 4 \geq 4$ for all x
   b Doesn't intersect the x-axis

8 The answers are 42, − 58. The equation can be
   factorised as $(x - 42)(x + 58) = 0$ but it would be
   hard to find the factors of 2436. Completing the
   square works well because $x^2 + 16x - 2436 = (x + 8)^2 - 2500$ and you can find the square root of
   2500 without a calculator. Completing the square
   is therefore the better of the two non-calculator
   methods. The formula could also be used without
   a calculator because $b^2 - 4ac = 10\,000$ so the
   square root can be taken, but you would have to
   work out $16^2 + 4 \times 2436$ in order to get there.

9 H, C, B, E, D, J, A, F, G, I

Exercise 17G

a **i**

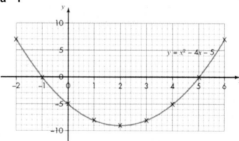

   ii

iii

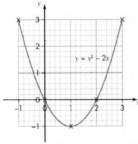

b Each equation is written in the form $x^2 + ax + b$. You should find that the y-intercept is the value of b. Graph (i) has its y-intercept at (0, −5), graph (ii) has its y-intercept at (0, 8) and graph (iii) has its y-intercept at (0, 0). Note that the graph (iii)'s equation has no value for b, so $b = 0$.

c **i** $x = 5$ or −1   **ii** $x = -2$ or −4
   iii $x = 0$ or 2

d The two x-intercepts have a product of b and add up to −a. This works because the x-intercepts are the answers of the quadratic equations when $y = 0$.

e The value of x for the turning point is exactly halfway between the values of x for the x-intercepts. By completing the square, you should also be able to see that the x co-ordinate is the value that makes the brackets zero and the y co-ordinate is the value at the end.

Exercise 17H

1 **a** **i** (0, −3)   **ii** (−1, 0) and (3, 0)
     iii (1, −4)
  b **i** (0, 5)   **ii** (−5, 0) and (1, 0)
     iii (−2, 9)

2
  a

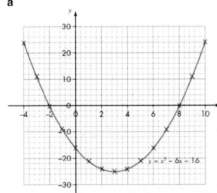

  b **i** (0, −16)   **ii** (−2, 0) and (8, 0)
     iii (3, −25)

3 **a** roots: (−2, 0) and (2, 0); y-intercept (0, −4)
  b roots: (0, 0) and (6, 0); y-intercept (0, 0)
  c roots: (−1, 0) and (3, 0); y-intercept (0, −3)
  d roots: (−11, 0) and (−3, 0); y-intercept (0, 33)

4 (3, −6)

5 −14

6 −5

7 **a** (2, 0)   **b** 2 is the only root

8 roots: (−0.5, 0) and (5, 0); y-intercept (0, −5); turning point: (2.25, −15.125)

9 roots: (4.65, 0) and (7.85, 0); turning point: (6.25, −5.13)

10

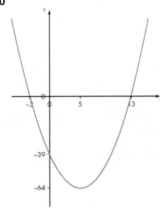

11 $y = (x - 3)^2 - 7$, $y = x^2 - 6x + 9 - 7$, $y = x^2 - 6x + 2$

12 **a** (−2, −7)
    b **i** $(a, 2b - a^2)$ **ii** $(2a, b - 4a^2)$

13 $y = 2x^2 + 16x + 14$

14 **a** 60 m   **b** 80 m, 2 s   **c** 6 s

Exercise 17I

1 **a** (0.7, 0.7), (−2.7, −2.7)
  b (6, 12), (−1, −2)
  c (4, −3), (−3, 4)
  d (0.8, 1.8), (−1.8, −0.8)
  e (4.6, 8.2), (0.4, −0.2)
  f (3, 6), (−2, 1)
  g (4.8, 6.6), (0.2, −2.6)
  h (2.6, 1.6), (−1.6, −2.6)

2 **a** (1, 0)
  b Only one intersection point
  c $x^2 + x(3 - 5) + (-4 + 5) = 0$
  d $(x - 1)^2 = 0 \Rightarrow x = 1$
  e Only one solution as line is a tangent to curve.

3 **a** There is no solution.
  b The graphs do not intersect.
  c $x^2 + x + 4 = 0$
  d $b^2 - 4ac = -15$
  e No solution as the discriminant is negative and there is no square root of a negative number.

4 **a** $x = 4$, $y = 31$
  b There is only one solution because the graphs have the same shape and are at a constant distance apart.

5 a Proof

b

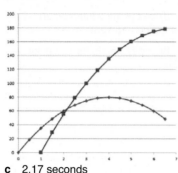

c 2.17 seconds

Exercise 17J

1 a i −1.4, 4.4   **ii** −2, 5   **iii** −0.6, 3.6
  b 2.6, 0.4

2 a i −1.6, 2.6   **ii** 1.4, −1.4
  b i 2.3, −2.3   **ii** 2, −2

3

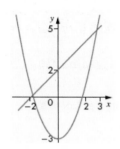

  a 2.2, −2.2   **b** −1.8, 2.8

4 −3.8, 1.8

5 a C and D   **b** A and D
  c $x^2 + 4x − 1 = 0$ **d** (−1.5, −10.25)

6 a i $y = 5$ **ii** $y = x + 3$
    iii $y = −10$ **iv** $y = x$
    v $y = 3x − 9$ **vi** $y = 2 − x$
    vii $y = −3x$
  b $y = \frac{1}{2}x + 3$

7 a i $5 − 5x − x^2 = 0$ **ii** $11 − 6x − x^2 = 0$
    iii $9 − 4x − x^2 = 0$ **iv** $30 − 16x − 3x^2 = 0$
  b Equation would be $−5 − 4x − x^2 = 0$. $b^2 − 4ac$
    $= −4$. Negative $b^2 − 4ac$ has no solutions.

8 a $(x + 2)(x − 1) = 0$ **b** $5 − −2 = +7$, not −7
  c $y = 2x + 7$

Exercise 17K

1 a (5, −1)   **b** (4, 1)   **c** (8, −1)

2 a (2, 5) and (−2, −3)   **b** (−1, −2) and (4, 3)
  c (3, 3) and (1, −1)

3 a (1, 2) and (−2, −1)
  b (−4, 1) and (−2, 2)

4 a (3, 4) and (4, 3)
  b (0, 3) and (−3, 0)

5 a (3, 2) and (−2, 3)   **b** $\sqrt{26}$

6 a Proof
  b $x = −\frac{1}{5}$, $y = −\frac{43}{5}$ or $x = 5$, $y = 7$

7 a Proof
  b $x = 4$, $y = −13$ or $x = 8$, $y = 11$

8 a $x = 6$, $y = 7$ or $x = −2$, $y = −9$
  b $x = −1$, $y = 2$ or $x = −2$, $y = −1$
  c $x = 3$, $y = −5$ or $x = 5$, $y = 3$
  d $x = 1$, $y = −8$ or $x = 4$, $y = 7$

9 a (1, 0)
  b iii as the straight line just touches the curve

10 a (−2, 1)
  b i (2, 1)   **ii** (−2, −1)   **iii** (2, −1)

11 a (2, 4)   **b** (1, 0)
  c The line is a tangent to the curve.

12 16 m by 14 m

13 30 km/h

14 10p

Exercise 17L

1 a $x < −4$, $x > 4$ **b** $−10 ≤ x ≤ 10$
  c $0 < x < 1$ **d** $x ≤ −5$, $x ≥ 0$
  e $−23 < x < 23$ **f** $x ≤ −\frac{3}{2}$, $x ≥ \frac{3}{2}$
  g $x < 0$, $x > \frac{8}{3}$ **h** $−\frac{19}{2} ≤ x ≤ 0$

2 a {−3, −2, −1, 0, 1, 2, 3}
  b {3, 4, 5, 6}

3 a $x < −2$, $x > 5$ **b** $−7 < x < −5$
  c $x ≤ 1$, $x ≥ 5$ **d** $−8 ≤ x ≤ 9$
  e $\frac{1}{3} ≤ x ≤ 3$ **f** $x < −\frac{11}{2}$, $x > −1$
  g $x ≤ \frac{3}{5}$, $x ≥ 2$ **h** $−\frac{3}{2} < x < \frac{2}{3}$

4 a

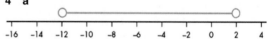

  b

5 a $3 < x ≤ 6\frac{1}{2}$ **b** $4 < x ≤ 5$

6 $x < 2$, $x > 10$

7 $x < −\frac{3}{2}$, $x > 5$

8

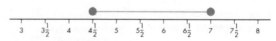

9 a $−692 < x < 708$
  b $x < −4 − \sqrt{5}$, $x > −4 + \sqrt{5}$
  c $−0.84 ≤ x ≤ 1.44$

10 £288, £364

11 $x < -4$, $-1 < x < 1$, $x > 4$

12 a $\frac{30}{-13} = -2.31 > -6$ and $\frac{30}{2} = 15 > 9$
   b $x < -7$, $3 < x < 6$

Review questions

1 a 9   **b** 5

2 a Two   **b** One   **c** None

3 b −5.27, 1.67

4 b 3.18

5 15 m, 20 m

6 b i −0.3, 3.3   **ii** 0.6, 3.4

7 a (0, 36)   **b** (2, 0), (18, 0)
   c (10, −64)

8 (1, 7), (7, 1)

9 a −6   **b** 3

10 a $x^2 - 3x - 550 = 0$ **b** 25

11 a $x < -35$, $x > 45$ **b** $-298 < x < 302$
   c $x \le -589$, $x \ge 611$

12 2.54 m, 3.54 m

13 210 cm²

14 (6, 8), (0, −10)

15 a $(p + q)(p - q)$
   b $30^2 - 1^2 = (30 + 1)(30 - 1)$
   c 3600
   d −31, 29

16 0.75 m

17 a $48 - (x - 6)^2$ **b** 48

18 Complete the square −113, 87

19 a, b (1, 4), (5, 20)   **c** $x \le 1$, $x \ge 5$

20 $x^2 - 8x + 19 = (x - 4)^2 + 3$
   Because $(x - 4)^2$ is a squared term, the smallest possible value it can have is zero.
   Hence 3 is the smallest possible value of $(x - 4)^2 + 3$, so $x^2 - 8x + 19$ is always positive.

Chapter 18 – Statistics: Sampling and more complex diagrams

Exercise 18A

1 a Secondary data
   b Primary data
   c Primary or secondary data
   d Primary or secondary data
   e Primary data
   f Primary or secondary data

2 *Plan the data collection.* Choose a random sample of 30 boys and 30 girls from Year 11. *Collect the data.* Ask each student to spell the same 10 words. This will avoid bias. Pick words that are often misspelt, e.g. accommodation, necessary
Choose the best way to process and represent the data. Calculate the mean number and range for the number of correct spellings for the boys and for the girls. Draw a dual bar chart to illustrate the data.
Interpret the data and make conclusions. Compare the mean and range to arrive at a conclusion. Is there a clear conclusion or do you need to change any of the 10 words or take a larger sample?

3 *Plan the data collection.* Choose a random sample of 20 boys and 20 girls from Year 11. *Collect the data.* Ask each student, on average, how many hours of sport they play and how many hours of TV they watch each week. *Choose the best way to process and represent the data.* Calculate the mean number of hours for the number of hours playing sport and the number of hours watching TV. Draw a scatter diagram to illustrate the data. *Interpret the data and make conclusions.* Compare the means and write down the type and strength of correlation for the scatter diagram to arrive at a conclusion. Is there a clear conclusion or do you need to take a larger sample?

4 a e.g.

> Tick the boxes to answer these questions.
>
> **1** What is your gender?
> ☐ Male ☐ Female
>
> **2** What year group are you in?
> ☐ Y9 ☐ Y10 ☐ Y11
>
> **3** How many times, on average, do you visit a fast food outlet in a week?
> ☐ Never ☐ 1 or 2 times
> ☐ 3 or 4 times ☐ More than 4 times

b e.g.

	Boys	Girls
Y9	20	20
Y10	20	20
Y11	20	20

c e.g. Get a list of the names of the students in alphabetical order for each group. Then choose a random sample for each one by picking every 10th student or use random digits on a calculator.

5 248 boys and 310 girls

6 Find the approximate number of men, women, boys and girls in the crowd and then decide on a sample size. A suitable sample size here is 100. Work out the proportion of men in the whole group and work out same proportion in the sample size to give the number of men in the sample. Similarly work out the proportion of women, boys and girls.

7 a There are more students in Year 12 and a different number of boys and girls in both years.

b e.g.

Year group	Boys	Girls	Total
12	21	24	45
13	20	15	35
			80

8 e.g.

	Male	Female	Total
Full time	130	70	200
Part time	40	60	100
			300

Exercise 18B

1 a–b 4

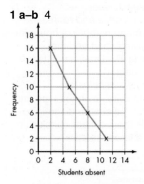

2 a–b Boys 12.9, girls 13.1
   c The girls did slightly better than the boys

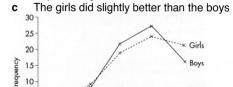

3 a–b 140.4 cm

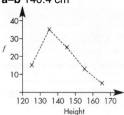

4 a i 17, 13, 6, 3,1   **ii** £1.45
   b i

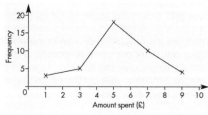

   ii £5.35

c Much higher mean. Early morning, people just want a paper or a few sweets. Later people are buying food for the day.

5 a

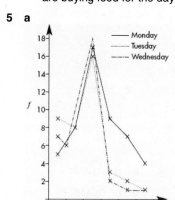

b Monday 28.4 min, Tuesday 20.9 min, Wednesday 21.3 min
c There are more patients on a Monday, and so longer waiting times, as the surgery is closed during the weekend.

6 2.19 hours

7 That is the middle value of the time group 0 to 1 minute. It would be very unusual for most of them to be exactly in the middle at 30 seconds.

Exercise 18C

1 a Cumulative frequencies 1, 4, 10, 22, 25, 28, 30
   b

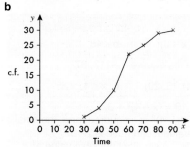

   c $m = 54$ s and IQR $= 16$ s

2 a Cumulative frequencies 1, 3, 5, 14, 31, 44, 47 49, 50
   b

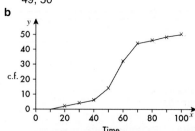

   c $m = 56$ s and IQR $= 17$ s
   d Pensioners as the median is closer to 1 minute and the IQRs are almost the same

3　**a**　Cumulative frequencies 12, 30, 63, 113, 176, 250, 314, 349, 360

b

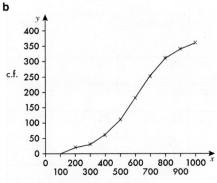

Number of students

c　$m = 606$ students

d　$Q_1 = 455$, $Q_3 = 732$ and IQR = 277

e　Approximately 13%

4　**a**　Cumulative frequency 2, 5, 10, 16, 22, 31, 39, 45, 50

b　Because the temperature was recorded to the nearest degree, so for example the highest temperature in the first group could have been 7.5°

c

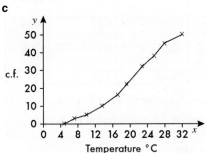

Temperature °C

d　$m = 20.5\ °C$ and IQR = 10 °C

5　**a**

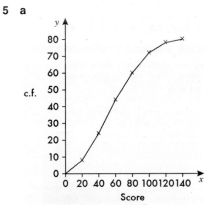

Score

b　$m = 56$, $Q_1 = 37$ and $Q_3 = 100$

c　Approximately 18%

6　**a**　Paper A $m = 66$, Paper B $m = 56$

b　Paper A IQR = 25, Paper B IQR = 18

c　Paper B is the harder paper, it has a lower median and a lower upper quartile.

d　**i**　Paper A 43, Paper B 45

　　ii　Paper A 78, Paper B 67

7　Create a grouped frequency table:

Time, t, (minutes)	Cumulative frequency	Frequency, f	Mid-point, x	$x \times f$
$0 < t \le 5$	6	6	2.5	15
$5 < t \le 10$	34	28	7.5	210
$10 < t \le 15$	56	22	12.5	275
$15 < t \le 20$	60	4	17.5	70
Total		60		570

$$\text{mean} = \frac{570}{60} = 9.5 \text{ minutes}$$

8　Create a grouped frequency table:

Age, a, (years)	Cumulative frequency	Frequency, f	Mid-point, x	$x \times f$
$0 < a \le 20$	30	30	10	300
$20 < a \le 40$	95	65	30	1950
$40 < a \le 60$	150	55	50	2750
$60 < a \le 80$	185	35	70	2450
$80 < a \le 100$	200	15	90	1350
Total		200		8800

$$\text{mean} = \frac{8800}{200} = 44 \text{ years}$$

Exercise 18D

1　**a**

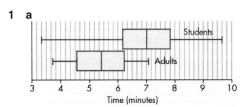

Time (minutes)

b　The adults are much quicker than the students. Both distributions have the same interquartile range, but the range is smaller for the adults showing that they are more consistent. The students' median and upper quartiles are 1 minute, 35 seconds higher. The fastest person to complete the calculations was a student, but so was the slowest.

2　**a**

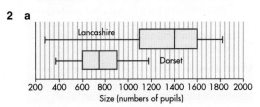

Size (numbers of pupils)

b Schools are much larger in Lancashire than in Dorset since it has a greater median. The interquartile range in Dorset is smaller, showing that they have a more consistent size.

3 a The resorts have similar median temperatures, but Resort A has a smaller interquartile range, showing that the temperatures are more consistent. Resort B has a much wider temperature range, where the greatest extremes of temperature are recorded.

b Resort A is probably a better choice as the weather seems more consistent.

4 a

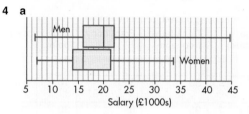

b Both distributions have a similar interquartile range, and there is little difference between the upper quartile values. Men have a wider range of salaries and the men have a higher median. This indicates that the men are better paid than the women.

5 a

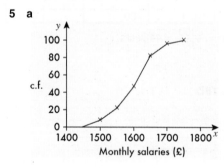

b $m = £1605$

c $Q_1 = £1550$ and $Q_3 = £1640$

d

6 a i 24 min   **ii** 12 min   **iii** 42 min
  b i 6 min   **ii** 17 min   **iii** 9 min
  c Either doctor with a plausible reason, e.g. Dr Excel because on average, her waiting times are always shorter or Dr Collins because he takes more time with each patient as the interquartile range is more spread out.

7 Many possible answers but not including any numerical values: eg Bude had a higher median amount of sunshine. Bude had a smaller interquartile range, showing more consistent sunshine in Bude. So overall this indicates that Bude had more sunshine on any one day.

8 Create a grouped frequency table using the quartiles:

For the boys

Mark, m	Cumulative frequency	Frequency, f	Mid-point, x	$x \times f$
$39 < m \leq 65$	25	25	52	1300
$65 < m \leq 78$	50	25	71.5	1787.5
$78 < m \leq 87$	75	25	82.5	2062.5
$87 < m \leq 112$	100	25	99.5	2487.5
Total		100		7637.5

mean = $\dfrac{7637.5}{100}$ = 76.4 marks (1 dp)

For the girls

Mark, m	Cumulative frequency	Frequency, f	Mid-point, x	$x \times f$
$49 < m \leq 69$	25	25	59	1475
$69 < m \leq 78$	50	25	73.5	1837.5
$78 < m \leq 91$	75	25	84.5	2112.5
$91 < m \leq 106$	100	25	98.5	2462.5
Total		100		7887.5

mean = $\dfrac{7887.5}{100}$ = 78.9 marks (1 dp)

The mean is 2.5 marks higher for the girls

Exercise 18E

1 The respective frequency densities on which each histogram should be based are:
  a 2.5, 6.5, 9, 2, 1.5   **b** 3, 6, 10, 4.5

2 The respective frequency densities on which each histogram should be based are:
  a 7, 12, 10, 5   **b** 0.4, 1.2, 2.8, 1
  c 9, 12, 13.5, 9

3

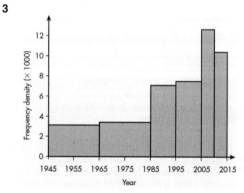

4 a i Work out the class width × frequency density for each bar and add these together, i.e. $5 \times 25 + 5 \times 30 + 10 \times 20 + 10 \times 10 + 20 \times 5 + 10 \times 10$
ii 775
b 400

5 a–b 14 kg **c** 14.6 kg **d** 33 plants

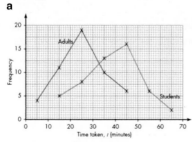

6 a

Speed, v (mph)	$0 < v \le 40$	$40 < v \le 50$	$50 < v \le 60$	$60 < v \le 70$	$70 < v \le 80$	$80 < v \le 100$
Frequency	80	10	40	110	60	60

b 360 **c** 64.5 mph **d** 59.2 mph

7 a 100 **b** 32.5 **c** 101.5
d 10% of 300 = 30, so the pass mark will be in the 70–80 interval. There are 60 students in this interval and 30 is half of 60. So the pass mark is half way between 70 and 80 = 75

8 a

Temperature, t (°C)	$10 < t \le 11$	$11 < t \le 12$	$12 < t \le 14$	$14 < t \le 16$	$16 < t \le 19$	$19 < t \le 21$
Frequency	15	15	50	40	45	15

b 12–14 °C **c** 14.5 °C
d 12.6 °C, 17 °C, 4.4 °C **e** 14.8 °C

9 0.45

Review questions

1 Choose a suitable sample size and decide whether to use a random sample or a stratified sample. Make sure that the sample is reliable and unbiased.
Remember that the greater the accuracy required, the larger the sample size needs to be. But the larger the sample size, the higher the cost will be and the time taken. Therefore, the benefit of achieving high accuracy in a sample will always have to be set against the cost of achieving it.

2 a

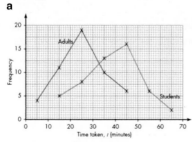

b The adults completed the puzzle quicker as their average time was better. Also their range was smaller which makes them more consistent.

3 a Cumulative frequencies: 4, 10, 20, 42, 46, 48
b

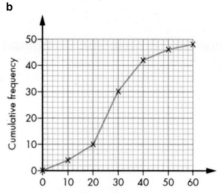

c 32 **d** $Q_1 = 22$, $Q_3 = 37$ and IQR = 15

4 a i £7200 **ii** £6400
b i £6000 **ii** £4700
c On average the men's wages are higher as their median is greater. The women's wages are more consistent as their interquartile range is smaller.

5

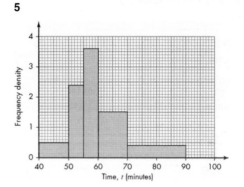

6 a

Age, t (years)	$9 < t \le 10$	$10 < t \le 12$	$12 < t \le 14$	$14 < t \le 17$	$17 < t \le 19$	$19 < t \le 20$
Frequency	4	12	8	9	5	1

b 10–12 **c** 13
d 11, 16, 5 **e** 13.4

7 Create a grouped frequency table using the quartiles:

Amount, m (£)	Cumulative frequency	Frequency, f	Mid-point, x	$x \times f$
$0.50 < m \le 2.00$	20	20	1.25	25
$2.00 < m \le 3.00$	40	20	2.50	50
$3.00 < m \le 4.00$	60	20	3.50	70
$4.00 < m \le 6.00$	80	20	5.00	100
	Total	80		245

mean = $\frac{245}{80}$ = £3.06

8 e.g.

Year 7	Year 8	Year 9	Year 10	Year 11
32	31	36	40	41

Chapter 19 – Probability: Combined events

Exercise 19A

1 a $\frac{1}{4}$ **b** $\frac{1}{4}$ **c** $\frac{1}{2}$

2 a $\frac{2}{11}$ **b** $\frac{4}{11}$ **c** $\frac{6}{11}$

3 a $\frac{1}{3}$ **b** $\frac{2}{5}$ **c** $\frac{11}{15}$ **d** $\frac{11}{15}$ **e** $\frac{1}{3}$

4 a 60 **b** $\frac{4}{5}$

5 a 0.8 **b** 0.2

6 a i 0.75 **ii** 0.6 **iii** 0.5 **iv** 0.6
  b i Cannot add P(red) and P(1) as events are not mutually exclusive
    ii 0.75 (= 1 – P(blue))

7 0.46

8 Probabilities cannot be summed in this way as events are not mutually exclusive.

9 a i 0.4 **ii** 0.5 **iii** 0.9
  b 0.45
  c 2 hours 12 minutes

10 $\frac{5}{52}$ or 0.096 to 3 decimal places

Exercise 19B

1 a 7
  b 2, 12
  c

Score	2	3	4	5	6	7	8	9	10	11	12
Probability	$\frac{1}{36}$	$\frac{1}{18}$	$\frac{1}{12}$	$\frac{1}{9}$	$\frac{5}{36}$	$\frac{1}{6}$	$\frac{5}{36}$	$\frac{1}{9}$	$\frac{1}{12}$	$\frac{1}{18}$	$\frac{1}{36}$

  d i $\frac{1}{12}$ **ii** $\frac{5}{9}$ **iii** $\frac{1}{2}$
    iv $\frac{7}{36}$ **v** $\frac{5}{12}$ **vi** $\frac{5}{18}$

2 a $\frac{1}{12}$ **b** $\frac{11}{36}$ **c** $\frac{1}{6}$ **d** $\frac{5}{9}$

3 a $\frac{1}{36}$ **b** $\frac{11}{36}$ **c** $\frac{5}{18}$

4 a

  b i $\frac{5}{18}$ **ii** $\frac{1}{6}$ **iii** $\frac{1}{9}$
    iv 0 **v** $\frac{1}{2}$

5 a i $\frac{1}{4}$ **ii** $\frac{1}{2}$ **iii** $\frac{3}{4}$ **iv** $\frac{1}{4}$
  b All possibilities are included

6 a $\frac{1}{12}$ **b** $\frac{1}{4}$ **c** $\frac{1}{6}$

7 a

  b 6
  c i $\frac{4}{25}$ **ii** $\frac{13}{25}$ **iii** $\frac{1}{5}$ **iv** $\frac{3}{5}$

8 a HHH, HHT, HTH, THH, HTT, THT, TTH, TTT
  b i $\frac{1}{8}$ **ii** $\frac{3}{8}$ **iii** $\frac{1}{8}$ **iv** $\frac{7}{8}$

9 a 16 **b** 32 **c** 1024 **d** 2^n

10 a

	1	2	3	4	5	6
1	2	3	4	5	6	7
2	3	4	5	6	7	8
3	4	5	6	7	8	9
4	5	6	7	8	9	10
5	6	7	8	9	10	11
6	7	8	9	10	11	12

  b $\frac{1}{18}$ **c** 18 **d** Twice

11 $\frac{1}{2}$

12 You would need a 3D diagram or there would be too many different events to list.

Exercise 19C

1 a

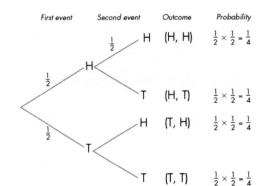

	First event	Second event	Outcome	Probability
		H	(H, H)	$\frac{1}{2} \times \frac{1}{2} = \frac{1}{4}$
		T	(H, T)	$\frac{1}{2} \times \frac{1}{2} = \frac{1}{4}$
		H	(T, H)	$\frac{1}{2} \times \frac{1}{2} = \frac{1}{4}$
		T	(T, T)	$\frac{1}{2} \times \frac{1}{2} = \frac{1}{4}$

b i $\frac{1}{4}$ **ii** $\frac{1}{2}$ **iii** $\frac{3}{4}$

2 a $\frac{2}{13}$ **b** $\frac{11}{13}$

c i $\frac{1}{169}$ **ii** $\frac{25}{169}$

3 a $\frac{2}{3}$ **b** $\frac{1}{2}$

c

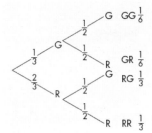

d i $\frac{1}{6}$ **ii** $\frac{1}{2}$ **iii** $\frac{5}{6}$

e 15 days

4 a $\frac{2}{5}$

b i $\frac{4}{25}$ **ii** $\frac{12}{25}$

5 a

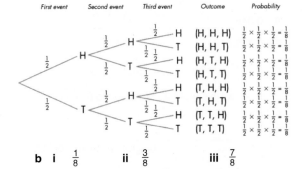

b i $\frac{1}{8}$ **ii** $\frac{3}{8}$ **iii** $\frac{7}{8}$

6 a

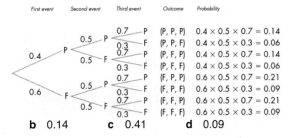

b 0.14 **c** 0.41 **d** 0.09

7 a $\frac{3}{5}$

b

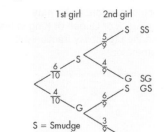

S = Smudge
G = Grudge

c i $\frac{1}{3}$ **ii** $\frac{7}{15}$ **iii** $\frac{8}{15}$

8 a 1 **b** 1

c

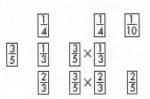

9 0.036

10 It will help to show all the 27 different possible events and which ones give the three different coloured sweets, then the branches will help you to work out the chance of each.

11 a $\frac{1}{2} \times \frac{1}{2} \times \frac{1}{2} \times \frac{1}{2} = \frac{1}{16}$ **b** $\left(\frac{1}{2}\right)^n$

Exercise 19D

1 a $\frac{4}{9}$ **b** $\frac{4}{9}$

2 a $\frac{1}{169}$ **b** $\frac{2}{169}$

3 a 0.08 **b** 0.32 **c** 0.48

4 $\left(\frac{1}{6}\right)^5 \times 6 = 0.000\,77$

5 a $\frac{4}{25}$ **b** $\frac{9}{25}$ **c** $\frac{16}{25}$

6 a $\frac{3}{8}$ **b** $\frac{1}{120}$ **c** $\frac{119}{120}$

7 a i $\frac{1}{216} = 0.005$ **ii** $\frac{125}{216} = 0.579$

iii $\frac{91}{216} = 0.421$

b i $(\frac{1}{6})^n$ **ii** $(\frac{5}{6})^n$ **iii** $1 - (\frac{5}{6})^n$

8 a 0.54 **b** 0.216

9 a 0.343 **b** Independent events
c P(exactly two of the three cars are foreign) =
P(FFB) + P(FBF) + P(BFF) = 3 × 0.7 × 0.7 ×
0.3 = 0.441

10 $10 \times 0.6^9 \times 0.4 + 0.6^{10} = 0.046$

11 0.8

12 The events are not independent as he may
already have a 10 or Jack or Queen or King in his
hand, in which case the probability fraction will
have a different numerator.

Exercise 19E

1 a $\frac{7}{10}$ **b** $\frac{2}{3}$ **c** $\frac{3}{8}$

2 a i $\frac{3}{8}$ **ii** $\frac{5}{8}$

b i $\frac{5}{12}$ **ii** $\frac{7}{12}$

c i $\frac{3}{20}$ **ii** $\frac{7}{20}$ **iii** $\frac{1}{2}$

3 a i $\frac{5}{9}$ **ii** $\frac{4}{9}$

b i $\frac{2}{3}$ **ii** $\frac{1}{3}$

c i $\frac{1}{3}$ **ii** $\frac{2}{15}$ **iii** $\frac{8}{15}$

4 a $\frac{1}{6}$ **b** 0

c i $\frac{2}{3}$ **ii** $\frac{1}{3}$ **iii** 0

5 a i $\frac{1}{120}$ **ii** $\frac{7}{40}$ **iii** $\frac{21}{40}$ **iv** $\frac{7}{24}$
b They are mutually exclusive and exhaustive
events

6 Both events are independent, the probability of
seeing a British made car is always ¼

7 a 0.54 **b** 0.38 **c** 0.08
d They should add up to 1

8 First work out P(first blue) and P(second blue)
remembering that the numerator and the
denominator will each be one less than for P(first
blue). Now work out P(first blue) × P(second
blue). Then work out P(first white) and P(second
white) remembering that the numerator and the
denominator will each be one less than for P(first
white). Now work out P(first white) × P(second
white). Finally add together the two probabilities.

9 $\frac{1}{270\,725}$

10 a

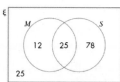

b i $\frac{12}{140} = 0.086$ **ii** $\frac{25}{103} = 0.243$

Review questions

1 a

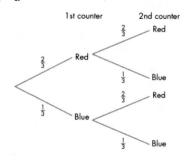

b $\frac{5}{9}$ **c** $\frac{4}{9}$

2 a

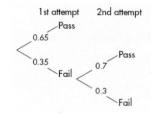

b i 0.895 **ii** 0.105
c Calculate 0.895^2

3 $\frac{4}{15}$

4 $\frac{11}{30}$

5 Work out $\frac{5}{16} \div \frac{3}{8}$ $(= \frac{5}{6})$

6 0.045

7 0.375

8 a $\frac{13}{20}$ as it cannot be square rooted

b $\frac{1}{9}$ as this gives a ratio of red to blue of 1 : 2

9 a

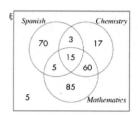

b **i** $\frac{70}{260} = 0.269$ **ii** $\frac{60}{260} = 0.231$

  iii $\frac{5}{260} = 0.0192$ **iv** $\frac{20}{165} = 0.121$

Chapter 20 – Geometry and Measures: Properties of circles

Exercise 20A

Students' own work.

Exercise 20B

1 a 56° **b** 62° **c** 105° **d** 55° **e** 45°
  f 30° **g** 60° **h** 145°

2 a 55° **b** 52° **c** 50° **d** 24° **e** 39°
  f 80° **g** 34° **h** 30°

3 a 41° **b** 49° **c** 41°

4 a 72° **b** 37° **c** 72°

5 $\angle AZY = 35°$ (angles in a triangle), $a = 55°$ (angle in a semicircle = 90°)

6 a $x = y = 40°$ **b** $x = 131°$, $y = 111°$
  c $x = 134°$, $y = 23°$ **d** $x = 32°$, $y = 19°$
  e $x = 59°$, $y = 121°$ **f** $x = 155°$, $y = 12.5°$

7 $\angle BED = 15°$ (angles at circumference from chord BD are equal); $\angle EBC = 180° - (15° + 38°) = 127°$ (angles in a triangle): $\angle ADC = 180° - (15° + 38°) = 127°$ (angles in a triangle); $x =$ its vertically opposite angle which equals $360° - (127° + 127° + 38°) = 68°$ (angles in a quadrilateral). So Lana is correct, but Lex probably misread his calculator answer.

8 $\angle ABC = 180° - x$ (angles on a line), $\angle AOC = 360° - 2x$ (angle at centre is twice angle at circumference), reflex $\angle AOC = 360° - (360° - 2x) = 2x$ (angles at a point)

9 a x **b** $2x$
  c Circle theorem 1 states from an arc AB, any point subtended from the arc on the circumference is half the angle subtended at the centre. So where this arc AB is the diameter, the angle subtended at the centre is 1 straight line and so 180°, the angle at the circumference then is half of 180 which is 90°, a right angle.

10 20°

11 It follows from theorem 1 that wherever point C is on the circumference, the angle subtended from arc AB at the circumference is always half the angle subtended at the centre. So every possible angle subtended at the circumference from arc AB will have the same angle at the centre and hence the same angle at the circumference. This proves circle theorem 3.

Exercise 20C

1 a $a = 50°$, $b = 95°$
  b $c = 92°$, $x = 90°$
  c $d = 110°$, $e = 110°$, $f = 70°$
  d $g = 105°$, $h = 99°$
  e $j = 89°$, $k = 89°$, $l = 91°$
  f $m = 120°$, $n = 40°$
  g $p = 44°$, $q = 68°$
  h $x = 40°$, $y = 34°$

2 a $x = 26°$, $y = 128°$ **b** $x = 48°$, $y = 78°$
  c $x = 133°$, $y = 47°$ **d** $x = 36°$, $y = 72°$
  e $x = 55°$, $y = 125°$ **f** $x = 35°$
  g $x = 48°$, $y = 45°$ **h** $x = 66°$, $y = 52°$

3 a Each angle is 90° and so opposite angles add up to 180° and hence a cyclic quadrilateral.
  b One pair of opposite angles are obtuse, i.e. more than 90°, hence their sum will be more than 180°.

4 a $x = 49°$, $y = 49°$ **b** $x = 70°$, $y = 20°$
  c $x = 80°$, $y = 100°$ **d** $x = 100°$, $y = 75°$

5 a $x = 50°$, $y = 62°$ **b** $x = 92°$, $y = 88°$
  c $x = 93°$, $y = 42°$ **d** $x = 55°$, $y = 75°$

6 a $x = 95°$, $y = 138°$ **b** $x = 14°$, $y = 62°$
  c $x = 32°$, $y = 48°$ **d** $x = 52°$

7 a 54.5° **b** 125.5° **c** 54.5°

8 a $x + 2x - 30° = 180°$ (opposite angles in a cyclic quadrilateral), so $3x - 30° = 180°$
  b $x = 70°$, so $2x - 30° = 110°$ $\angle DOB = 140°$ (angle at centre equals twice angle at circumference), $y = 80°$ (angles in a quadrilateral)

9 a x
  b $360° - 2x$
  c,d $\angle ADC = \frac{1}{2}$ reflex $\angle AOC = 180° - x$, so $\angle ADC + \angle ABC = 180°$

10 Let $\angle AED = x$, then $\angle ABC = x$ (opposite angles are equal in a parallelogram), $\angle ADC = 180° - x$ (opposite angles in a cyclic quadrilateral), so $\angle ADE = x$ (angles on a line)

11 18°

Exercise 20D

1 a 38° **b** 110° **c** 15° **d** 45°

2 a 6 cm **b** 10.8 cm **c** 3.21 cm **d** 8 cm

3 a $x = 12°$, $y = 156°$ **b** $x = 100°$, $y = 50°$
  c $x = 62°$, $y = 28°$ **d** $x = 30°$, $y = 60°$

4 a 62° **b** 66° **c** 19° **d** 20°

5 19.5 cm

6 $\angle OCD = 58°$ (triangle OCD is isosceles), $\angle OCB = 90°$ (tangent/radius theorem), so $\angle DCB = 32°$, hence triangle BCD is isosceles (2 equal angles)

7 **a** $\angle AOB = \cos^{-1} \dfrac{OA}{OB} = \cos^{-1} \dfrac{OC}{OB} = \angle COB$

    b As $\angle AOB = \angle COB$, so $\angle ABO = \angle CBO$, so OB bisects $\angle ABC$

8 If the tangent XY touches the circle at C, then CY = 10 cm. $\angle$ OYC = 30° (theorem 7). Hence where r is the radius of the circle, then $r/10 = \tan 30°$, hence $r = 10 \times \tan 30° = 5.7735$, So Ling is correct to one decimal place.

9 38°

Exercise 20E

Students' own work.

Exercise 20F

1 **a** $a = 65°$, $b = 75°$, $c = 40°$
    b $d = 79°$, $e = 58°$, $f = 43°$
    c $g = 41°$, $h = 76°$, $i = 76°$
    d $k = 80°$, $m = 52°$, $n = 80°$

2 **a** $a = 75°$, $b = 75°$, $c = 75°$, $d = 30°$
    b $a = 47°$, $b = 86°$, $c = 86°$, $d = 47°$
    c $a = 53°$, $b = 53°$
    d $a = 55°$

3 **a** 36° **b** 70°

4 **a** $x = 25°$
    b $x = 46°$, $y = 69°$, $z = 65°$
    c $x = 38°$, $y = 70°$, $z = 20°$
    d $x = 48°$, $y = 42°$

5 $\angle ACB = 64°$ (angle in alternate segment), $\angle ACX = 116°$ (angles on a line), $\angle CAX = 32°$ (angles in a triangle), so triangle ACX is isosceles (two equal angles)

6 $\angle AXY = 69°$ (tangents equal and so triangle AXY is isosceles), $\angle XZY = 69°$ (alternate segment), $\angle XYZ = 55°$ (angles in a triangle)

7 **a** $2x$ **b** $90° - x$
    c OPT = 90°, so APT = x

8 Mark any point R on the circumference of the circle so that angle QRT is in the alternate segment to angle PTQ. Draw triangle QRT. Then:
Angle PTQ = angle QRT (alternate segment theorem)
Angle PQT = angle QRT (alternate segment theorem)
Therefore angle PTQ = angle PQT and triangle PQT is isosceles.
Hence PQ = PT.
Other proofs may be possible.

Review questions

1 **a** 44°, both angles subtended from the same chord
    b 52°, each vertex touches the circumference
    c 140°, the three points not the centre are touching the circumference

2 **a** 55° **b** 75°

3 **a** DOB is double DAB
    b DAB and DCB add up to 180° since ABCD is a cyclic quadrilateral

4 To be a rhombus, DOB must equal DCB, you know that DOB = $2x$ (double DAB), you know that DCB = $180° - x$ (as ABCD is a cyclic quadrilateral), so $2x = 180° - x$, hence $3x = 180°$ → $x = 60°$

5 TPR = 42°, alternate segment; PRQ = 42°, alternate angles in parallel lines; RPQ = 42°, isosceles triangle; PQR = $180° - 2 \times 42° = 96°$, angles in a triangle; PTR = $180° - 96° = 84°$, opposite angles in a cyclic quadrilateral.

6 CAO = $90° - 66° = 24°$; ACO = 24°, isosceles triangle; AOB = $360° - (2 \times 90° + 50°) = 130°$, angles in quadrilateral; ACB = $130° \div 2 = 65°$, angles at centre double angle at circumference; OCB = $65° - 24° = 41°$; x = OCB, isosceles triangle hence $x = 41°$.

7 OCA = 90° and OBA = 90° as AB and AC are both tangents to the circle, centre O. This is a pair of opposite angles having the sum of 180°. Since the sum of the angles is 360°, the other pair of angles BC and BOC will add up to $360° - 180° = 180°$, so both pairs of opposite angles sum to 180°, hence it is a cyclic quadrilateral.

8 OBA = $90° - x$; OAB = $90° - x$, angles in an isosceles triangle. BOA = $180° - (90° - x + 90° - x) = 180° - (180° - 2x) = 180° - 180° + 2x = 2x$

9 Using Pythagoras' theorem, OC = $\sqrt{8^2 + 12^2}$ = 14.4 (3sf); PC = $14.4 - 8 = 6.4$ (2 sf); the answer is given to 2 sf with the assumption that the 12 is 2 sf.

Chapter 21 – Ratio, proportion and rates of change: Variation

Exercise 21A

1 **a** 15 **b** 2
2 **a** 75 **b** 6
3 **a** 150 **b** 6
4 **a** 22.5 **b** 12
5 **a** 175 miles **b** 8 hours
6 **a** £66.50 **b** 175 kg
7 **a** 44 **b** 84 m²
8 **a** 50 **b** Spaces = $\frac{1}{14}$ area
9 17 minutes 30 seconds
10 22.5 cm

Exercise 21B

1 **a** 100 **b** 10
2 **a** 27 **b** 5

3 a 56   **b** 1.69

4 a 192   **b** 2.25

5 a 25.6   **b** 5

6 a 80   **b** 8

7 a £50   **b** 225

8 a 3.2 °C   **b** 10 atm

9 a 388.8 g   **b** 3 mm

10 a 2 J   **b** 40 m/s

11 a £78   **b** 400 miles

12 4000 cm³

13 £250

14 a B   **b** A   **c** C

15 a B   **b** A

16 $S = kM^{\frac{2}{3}}$

Exercise 21C

1 $Tm = 12$ **a** 3   **b** 2.5

2 $Wx = 60$ **a** 20   **b** 6

3 $Q(5 - t) = 16$ **a** −3.2   **b** 4

4 $Mt^2 = 36$ **a** 4   **b** 5

5 $W\sqrt{T} = 24$ **a** 4.8   **b** 100

6 $x^3y = 32$ **a** 32   **b** 4

7 $gp = 1800$ **a** £15   **b** 36

8 $tD = 24$ **a** 3 °C   **b** 12 km

9 $ds^2 = 432$ **a** 1.92 km   **b** 8 m/s

10 $p\sqrt{h} = 7.2$ **a** 2.4 atm   **b** 100 m

11 $W\sqrt{F} = 0.5$ **a** 5 t/h   **b** 0.58 t/h

12 B – This is inverse proportion, as x increases y decreases.

13

x	8	27	64
y	1	$\frac{2}{3}$	$\frac{1}{2}$

14 4.3 miles

15 $F = 2.02 \times 10^{19}$ N

Review questions

1

x	25	100	400
y	10	20	40

2 a $E = 4000v$ **b** 3.6 m/s

3 a $y = 4x^{-\frac{1}{3}}$ or $y = \dfrac{4}{\sqrt[3]{x}}$

   b i 20   **ii** 8

4 19.4 cm

5 128

6 a $D = 5M^2$ **b** 245   **c** 3

7 80

8 a 2.5   **b** 0.25   **c** 250   **d** 50, −50

9 a 10   **b** 3.375

10 a 48π   **b** 9

11 a $A = \dfrac{100}{B^2}$ or $AB^2 = 100$ **b** 4

12 125

13 a 27 hertz   **b** Cannot divide by 0

14 $a = 9, b = 144$

15 40

Chapter 22 – Geometry and measures: Triangles

Exercise 22A

1 13.1 cm

2 73.7°

3 9.81 cm

4 33.5 m

5 a 10.0 cm   **b** 11.5°   **c** 4.69 cm

6 PS = 4 tan 25 = 1.865 230 6, angle QRP = tan⁻¹ $\dfrac{7.8652306}{4}$ = 63.0, angle QRP = 63.0 − 25 = 38.0

7 774 m

8 a $\sqrt{2}$ cm

   b i $\dfrac{\sqrt{2}}{2}$ (an answer of $\dfrac{1}{\sqrt{2}}$ would also be accepted)

     ii $\dfrac{\sqrt{2}}{2}$ **iii** 1

9 The calculated answer is 14.057 869, so Eve is correct to give 14° as her answer. She could also have been correct to round off to 14.1°

Exercise 22B

1 25.1°

2 a 24.0°   **b** 48.0°   **c** 13.5 cm   **d** 16.6°

3 a 58.6°   **b** 20.5 cm   **c** 2049 cm³   **d** 64.0°

4 a 73.2°   **b** £1508.31

5 a 3.46 m   **b** 70.5°

6 For example, the length of the diagonal of the base is $\sqrt{b^2 + c^2}$ and taking this as the base of the triangle with the height of the edge, then the hypotenuse is

$$\sqrt{(a^2 + (\sqrt{b^2 + c^2})^2)} = \sqrt{a^2 + b^2 + c^2}$$

7 It is 44.6°; use triangle XDM where M is the midpoint of BD; triangle DXB is isosceles, as X is over the point where the diagonals of the base cross; the length of DB is $\sqrt{656}$, the cosine of the required angle is $0.5 \sqrt{656} \div 18$.

Exercise 22C

1a

x	sin x	x	sin x	x	sin x	x	sin x
0°	0	180°	0	180°	0	360°	0
15°	0.259	165°	0.259	195°	−0.259	345°	−0.259
30°	0.5	150°	0.5	210°	−0.5	330°	−0.5
45°	0.707	135°	0.707	225°	−0.707	315°	−0.707
60°	0.866	120°	0.866	240°	−0.866	300°	−0.866
75°	0.966	105°	0.966	255°	−0.966	285°	−0.966
90°	1	90°	1	270°	−1	270°	−1

b They are the same for values between 90° and 180°. They have the opposite sign for values between 180° and 360°

2 a Sine graph
b Line symmetry about $x = 90, 270$ and rotational symmetry about (180, 0)

Exercise 22D

1a

x	cos x	x	cos x	x	cos x	x	cos x
0°	1	180°	−1	180°	−1	360°	1
15°	0.966	165°	−0.966	195°	−0.966	345°	0.966
30°	0.866	150°	−0.866	210°	−0.866	330°	0.866
45°	0.707	135°	−0.707	225°	−0.707	315°	0.707
60°	0.5	120°	−0.5	240°	−0.5	300°	0.5
75°	0.259	105°	−0.259	255°	−0.259	285°	0.259
90°	0	90°	0	270°	0	270°	0

b Negative cosines are between 90 and 270, the rest are positive,

2 a Cosine graph
b Line symmetry about $x = 180°$, rotational symmetry about (90°, 0) , (270°, 0)

Exercise 22E

1 a 36.9°, 143.1°   **b** 53.1°, 126.9°
   c 48.6°, 131.4°   **d** 224.4°, 315.6°
   e 194.5°, 345.5°   **f** 198.7°, 341.3°
   g 190.1°, 349.9°   **h** 234.5°, 305.5°
   i 28.1°, 151.9°   **j** 185.6°, 354.4°
   k 33.6°, 146.4°   **l** 210°, 330°

2 sin 234°, as the others all have the same numerical value.

3 a 438° or 78° + 360n°
   b −282° or 78° − 360n°
   c Line symmetry about ±90n° where n is an odd integer.
   Rotational symmetry about ±180n° where n is an integer.

4 30°, 150°, 199.5°, 340.5°

5 a 53.1°, 306.9°   **b** 54.5°, 305.5°
   c 62.7°, 297.3°   **d** 54.9°, 305.1°
   e 79.3°, 280.7°   **f** 143.1°, 216.9°
   g 104.5°, 255.5°   **h** 100.1°, 259.9°
   i 111.2°, 248.8°   **j** 166.9°, 193.1°
   k 78.7°, 281.3°   **l** 44.4°, 315.6°

6 cos 58°, as the others are negative.

7 a 492° or 132° + 360n°
   b −228° or 132° − 360n°
   c Line symmetry about ±180n° where n is an integer.
   Rotational symmetry about ±90n° where n is an odd integer.

8 a i High tides 0940, 2200, low tides 0300, 1520
   ii 12hrs 20min
   b i Same periodic shape
   ii The period of the cycle is in time not degrees, no negative values on the y axis

Exercise 22F

1 a 0.707   **b** −1 (−0.9998)
   c −0.819   **d** 0.731

2 a −0.629   **b** −0.875
   c −0.087   **d** 0.999

3 a 21.2°, 158.8°   **b** 209.1°, 330.9°
   c 50.1°, 309.9°   **d** 150.0°, 210.0°
   e 60.9°, 119.1°   **f** 29.1°, 330.9°

4 30°, 150°

5 −0.755

6 a 1.41   **b** −1.37   **c** −0.0367 **d** −0.138
   e 1.41   **f** −0.492

7 True

8 a cos 65°   **b** cos 40°

9 a 10°, 130°   **b** 12.7°, 59.3°

10 38.2°, 141.8°

11 $\sin^{-1} 0.9659 = 74.994\,28$, which is 75 to 2 sf. 435 = 75 + 360. From the sine curve extended, sine 75 = sine 435.
Rose is therefore correct as she has rounded her solution.
Keiren could also be correct as the answer could also be given more accurately as 434.9942838

Exercise 22G

1 a Maths error   **b** 89.999 999

2 5 729 577 951

3 **a–b** Graph of tan x **c** All 0

  d Students' own explanations

4 **a** Tan is positive for angles between 0–90° and 180–270°
  b Yes, 180°

Exercise 22H

1 **a** 41.2°, 221.2° **b** 123.7° and 303.7°

2 **a** 14.5°, 194.5° **b** 61.9°, 241.9°
  c 68.6°, 248.6° **d** 160.3°, 340.3°
  e 147.6°, 327.6° **f** 105.2°, 285.2°
  g 54.4°, 234.4° **h** 130.9°, 310.9°
  i 174.4°, 354.4° **j** 44.9°, 224.9°

2 tan 235°, as the others have a numerical value of 1

3 **a** 425° or 65° + 180n°, $n > 2$
  b −115° or 65° − 180n°
  c No line symmetry
    Rotational symmetry about ±180n° where n is an integer.

5 $\tan^{-1} 0.4040 = 21.9987$ which is 22 to 2 sf, so $\tan^{-1}(−0.4040)$ is same as tan 180 − 22 = 158. If you calculate $\tan^{-1}(−0.4040)$ on your calculator it will give −21.9987 = −22 (2 sf).
    Mel is therefore correct as he has rounded his solution. Jose is also correct.

Exercise 22I

1 **a** 3.64 m **b** 8.05 cm **c** 19.4 cm

2 **a** 46.6° **b** 112.0° **c** 36.2°

3 50.3°, 129.7°

4 This statement can be shown to be true by using $\dfrac{a}{\sin A} = \dfrac{b}{\sin B}$. As $a = b \times \dfrac{\sin A}{\sin B}$,

  if $a > b$ then $\sin A > \sin B$ and so $\dfrac{\sin A}{\sin B} > 1$,

  hence $b \times \dfrac{\sin A}{\sin B} > b$.

5 2.88 cm, 20.9 cm

6 **a i** 30° **ii** 40°
  b 19.4 m

7 36.5 m

8 22.2 m

9 3.47 m

10 The correct height is 767 m. Paul has mixed the digits up and placed them in the wrong order.

11 26.8 km/h

12 64.6 km

13 Check students' answers.

14 134°

15 Check that proof is valid.

Exercise 22J

1 **a** 7.71 m **b** 29.1 cm **c** 27.4 cm

2 **a** 76.2° **b** 125.1° **c** 90°
  d Right-angled triangle

3 5.16 cm

4 65.5 cm

5 **a** 10.7 cm **b** 41.7° **c** 38.3°
  d 6.69 cm
  e 54.4 cm^2

6 72.3°

7 25.4 cm, 38.6 cm

8 58.4 km at 092.5°

9 21.8°

10 **a** 82.8° **b** 8.89 cm

11 42.5 km

12 Check students' answers.

13 111°; the largest angle is opposite the longest side

Exercise 22K

1 **a** 8.60 m **b** 90° **c** 27.2 cm
  d 26.9° **e** 41.0° **f** 62.4 cm

2 7 cm

3 11.1 km

4 19.9 knots

5 **a** 27.8 miles
  b 262°

6 **a** $A = 90°$; this is Pythagoras' theorem
  b A is acute
  c A is obtuse

7 The answer is correct to 3 sf but the answer could be slightly less accurate (as 140 m to 2 sf) since the question data is given to 2 sf

Exercise 22L

1 **a** 24.0 cm^2 **b** 26.7 cm^2 **c** 243 cm^2
  d 21 097 cm^2 **e** 1224 cm^2

2 4.26 cm

3 **a** 42.3° **b** 49.6°

4 103 cm^2

5 2033 cm^2

6 21.0 cm^2

7 **a** 33.2° **b** 25.3 cm^2

8 Check that proof is valid.

9 21 cm^2

10 726 cm^2

11 $\dfrac{a^2\sqrt{3}}{4}$

12 c

Review questions

1 $\cos A = \dfrac{12^2 + 10^2 - 15^2}{2 \times 12 \times 10} = 0.079\,166,\ \cos^{-1}$

0.079 166 = 85.459 371 = 85.5° (3 sf), so Oliver is incorrect, he has truncated the final answer to 3 figures instead of rounding off.

2 area = $\dfrac{1}{2} \times 7 \times 13 \times \sin 116 = 40.895129 = 40.9$ (3 sf)

3 $AB^2 = 10^2 + 11^2 - 2 \times 10 \times 11 \times \cos 70$
$= 145.755\,57$, AB = 12.1 (3 sf). The longest side of a triangle is opposite the largest angle, so as AB is the longest side, then angle C must be the largest angle

4 a i Let QP = 1, then QT = $\dfrac{1}{2}$, angle QPT =

30°, $\sin 30 = \dfrac{\frac{1}{2}}{1} = \dfrac{1}{2}$

ii $PT^2 = 1^2 - (\frac{1}{2})^2 = \dfrac{3}{4}$, so PT = $-\dfrac{\sqrt{3}}{2}$, hence

$\cos 30 = \dfrac{\frac{\sqrt{3}}{2}}{1} = \dfrac{\sqrt{3}}{2}$

b $(\frac{\sqrt{3}}{2})^2 + (\frac{1}{2})^2 = \dfrac{3}{4} + \dfrac{1}{4} = 1$

c Assume QPT is any right-angled triangle with angle PQT as θ and PQ = 1. Then QT = cos θ, PT = sin θ, so using Pythagoras, where $QT^2 + PT^2 = PQ^2$, $(\sin x)^2 + (\cos x)^2 = 1$

5 22.2 m

6 60°, 109.5°, 250.5°, 300°

7 58.8°

8 FB = $\sqrt{5^2 + 6^2}$ = 7.81 cm

AF = $\sqrt{9^2 + 7.81^2}$ = 11.92 cm

So $\angle$AFD = $\sin^{-1}(\frac{6}{11.92})$ = 30.2°

9 Jamil is correct to 1 dp

Chapter 23 – Algebra: Graphs

Exercise 23A

1 a i 2 h **ii** 3 h **iii** 5 h
b i 40 km/h **ii** 120 km/h **iii** 40 km/h

2 a 10 mph
b Faster. The graph is steeper.
c $13\frac{1}{3}$ mph

3 a $2\frac{1}{2}$ km/h **b** 3.75 m/s **c** $2\frac{1}{2}$ km/h

4 a 30 km **b** 40 km **c** 100 km/h

5 a i 263 m/min (3 sf) **ii** 15.8 km/h (3 sf)
b i 500 m/min
c Paul by 1 minute

6 a Patrick ran quickly at first, then had a slow middle section but he won the race with a final sprint. Araf ran steadily all the way and came second. Sean set off the slowest, speeded up towards the end but still came third.
b i 1.67 m/s **ii** 6 km/h

7 There are three methods for doing this question. This table shows the first, which is writing down the distances covered each hour.

Time	9am	9:30	10:00	10:30	11:00	11:30	12:00	12:30
Walker	0	3	6	9	12	15	18	21
Cyclist	0	0	0	0	7.5	15	22.5	30

The second method is algebra:

Walker takes T hours until overtaken, so $T = \dfrac{D}{6}$;

Cyclist takes $T - 1.5$ to overtake, so

$T - 1.5 = \dfrac{D}{15}$.

Rearranging gives $15T - 22.5 = 6T$, $9T = 22.5$, $T = 2.5$.
The third method is a graph:

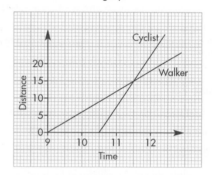

All methods give the same answer of 11:30 when the cyclist overtakes the walker.

8 a Vehicle 2 overtook Vehicle 1
b Vehicle 1 overtook Vehicle 2
c Vehicles travelling in different directions
d Vehicle 2 overtook Vehicle 1
e 17:15
f 32.0 mph if you only count travelling time, or 11.3 mph if you count total time.

Exercise 23B

1 a Two taps on **b** One tap on
c Shejuti gets in the bath
d Shejuti has a bath
e Shejuti takes the plug out, water leaves the bath
f Shejuti gets out of the bath
g Water continues to leave the bath until the bath is empty

2 a Graph C
b

3

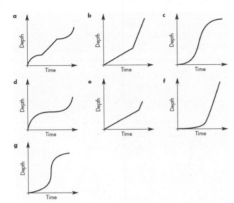

Exercise 23C

1 **a** 20 m/s   **b** 100 metres
   c 150 metres   **d** 750 metres

2 **a** 15 km   **b** 5 km/h

3 **a** AB, greatest area   **b** 45 miles   **c** 135 miles

4 15 m/s

5 **a**

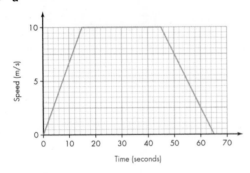

b 475 metres

6 **a** Could be true or false
   b Must be true
   c Must be true
   d Could be true or false
   e Could be true or false

Exercise 23D

1 **a** 6 m/s^2 **b** 3 m/s^2 **c** 20 s
   d 1200 m   **e** 2100 m

2 40 km/h^2, 30 km/h^2, 100 km/h^2 **b** 52.5 km

3 **a** $\frac{3v}{10}$ m/s^2 **b** 337.5 m

Exercise 23E

1 **a** 80 miles, underestimate
   b 250 metres, overestimate
   c 75 metres, underestimate
   d 180 metres, underestimate

2 **a** 8 miles, underestimate
   b 40 miles, overestimate

3 **a** **i** 10 m/s   **ii** 40 m/s
   b **i** 900 m
        ii Around 1070 m, depending on student's
             division of the shape
   c **ii** is more accurate because the shapes are
             closer to the curve

4 **a** Car starts from rest and speeds up to 10 m/s
        after 20 seconds. It then travels at a constant
        speed of 10 m/s for 30 seconds, and then
        speeds up again to reach 20 m/s in the next
        10 seconds.
   b 120 metres

5 **a** The lorry increases speed at a steady rate
        whereas the car speeds up quickly at first but
        then levels off to a constant speed and then
        speeds up at an increasing rate to reach 20
        m/s.
   b Lorry travels further (600 metres as against
        car, approximately 550 metres) as area under
        graph is greater.

Exercise 23F

1 **a** Tangent drawn   **b** 10 m/s   **c** 0 m/s

2 **a** **i** 10–12 km/h   **ii** 20–22 km/h
   b 2 hours
   c **i** 10 km/h   **ii** 19 km/h

3 **a** About 1.8 m/s^2
   b About 0.9 m/s^2
   c About 1.8 m/s^2
   d 20 s, gradient is zero because this is a
        maximum point

4 Any two points where the gradient of one is the
   negative of the other, e.g. at 1 s and 3 s.

Exercise 23G

1 **a** 6   **b** $2\sqrt{3}$ **c** $5\sqrt{3}$ **d** 24

2 **a** $6\sqrt{13}$ **b** 176   **c** 114   **d** $\frac{3}{2}$

3 **a** Inside   **b** Outside   **c** On circumference
   d On circumference
   e Outside   **f** Inside

4 **a** Any three points such that $x^2 + y^2 = 25$
   b 12

5 **a** $\frac{1}{2}$ **b** −2
   c $y = -2x + 10$

6 Check proof is valid.

7 **a** $y = \frac{3}{5}x - \frac{34}{5}$ **b** $y = -\frac{1}{3}x - \frac{20}{3}$
   c $y = -\frac{p}{q}x + \frac{p^2 + q^2}{q}$ (or $\frac{a^2}{q}$)

8 $y = 2x - 15$, $y = 2x + 15$

9 **b** $x + y = 10$, $x + y = -10$

10 **a** 10
   b $x^2 + y^2 = 90$

Exercise 23H

1

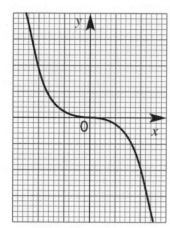

2 a Values of y: −54, −31.25, −16, −6.75, −2, −0.25, 0, 0.25, 2, 6.75, 16, 31.25, 54
b 39.4

3 a Values of y: −24, −12.63, −5, −0.38, 2, 2.9, 3, 3.13, 4, 6.38, 11, 18.63, 30
b 4.7 **c** −1.4 to −1.5

4 a Values of y: −16, −5.63, 1, 4.63, 6, 5.88, 5, 4.13, 4, 5.38, 9, 15.63, 26
b i −2.1 **ii** (−0.8, 6)
iii (0.7, 3.9) **iv** (0, 5)

5 Values of y: 1, 2, 3, 4, 6, 12, 24, −24, −12, −6, −4, −3, −2, −1

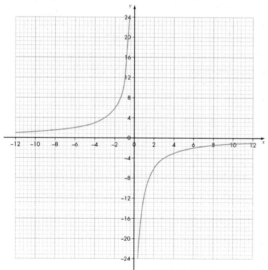

6 a Values of y: −0.25, −0.33, −0.5, −1, −2.5, −5, −10, −12.5, −25, 25, 12.5, 10, 5, 2.5, 1, 0.5, 0.33, 0.25

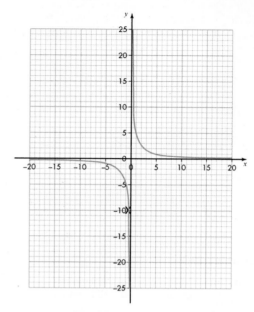

b Can't divide by 0
c

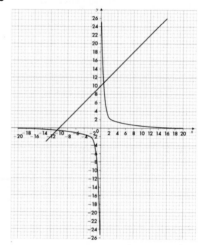

d 0.48 and −10.48

7 a Values of y: 0.01, 0.04, 0.11, 0.33, 1, 3, 9, 27
b 15.6 **c** −0.63

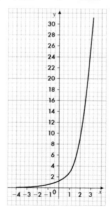

8 a Quadratic **b** Linear **c** Exponential
d Reciprocal **e** None **f** Cubic
g Linear **h** None **i** Quadratic

9 a The numbers go 1, 2, 4, … which is equivalent to 2^0, 2^1, 2^2, … so the formula is $2^{(n-1)}$

   b $2^{63} = 9.22 \times 10^{18}$ **c** £4.61×10^{14}

10 a Number of pieces = 2^n so $2^{50} = 1.1 \times 10^{15}$ pieces

   b 1.13×10^8 km

11 $a = 5$, $b = 3$

12

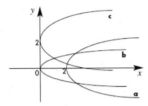

Exercise 23I

1 a, b

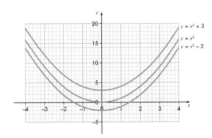

  c $y = x^2 + 3$ is 3 units higher than $y = x^2$

  d $y = x^2 - 2$ is 2 units lower than $y = x^2$

  e i $y = x^2 + 6$ is 6 units higher than $y = x^2$

    ii $y = x^2 - 6$ is 6 units lower than $y = x^2$

2 a, b

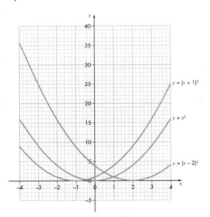

  c $y = (x - 2)^2$ is 2 units to the right of $y = x^2$

  d $y = (x + 1)^2$ is 1 unit to the left of $y = x^2$

  e i $y = (x - 3)^2$ is 3 units to the right of $y = x^2$

    ii $y = (x + 4)^2$ is 4 units to the left of $y = x^2$

Exercise 23J

1 a

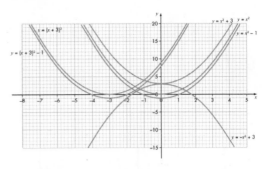

  b Up 3   **c** Down 1   **d** 3 to the left

  e 3 to the left and down 1

  f Reflect in the x-axis and move up 3

2 a

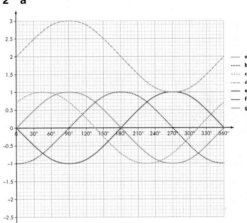

  b 90° to the left   **c** 45° to the right

  d Up 2   **e** Reflect in the x-axis

  f Reflect in the y-axis

  g Reflect in both axes

3 All of them.

4

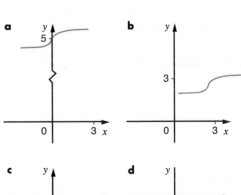

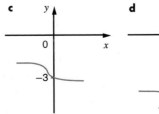

5 a $y = \cos x + 3$ **b** $y = \cos (x + 30°)$
   c $y = \cos (x - 45°) - 2$

6 a

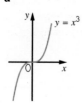

b

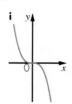

c i $y = -x^3$ **ii** $y = x^3 - 2$
   iii $y = (x + 2)^3$

7 No, as $f(-x) = (-x)^2 = x^2$, and $-f(x) = -(x)^2 = -x^2$

8 a $y = x^2 + 2$ **b** $y = (x - 2)^2$
   c $y = -x^2 + 4$

9 a Translation
   b i Equivalent   **ii** Equivalent

Exercise 23K

1 a $y = f(x - 3) + 2$; 3 right and 2 up
   b $y = f(x + 7) - 14$; 7 left and 14 down
   c $y = f(x - 11) - 21$; 11 right and 21 down

2

 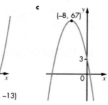

3 a $y = x^2 - 8x + 7$ **b** $y = -x^2 + 6x + 5$
   c $y = x^2 - 14x + 59$

Review questions

1

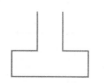

2 a 19   **b** 0.7 m/s²

3 a

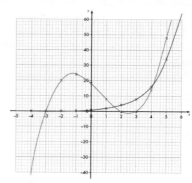

b −3.0, 1.6, 4.2

4 50

5 1F, 2C, 3D, 4A, 5B, 6E

6 a 5   **b** 4   **c** 320

7

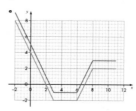 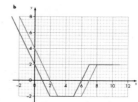

8 a (5, 5) and (7, 1)
   b $\left(\frac{20}{3} , \frac{10}{3} \right)$

9 a −(0.8–0.9) m/h²
   b 8.6 miles

10

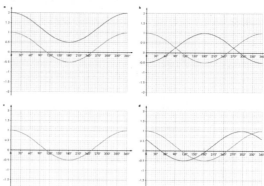

11 a

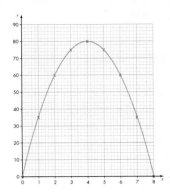

b 10 m/s

Chapter 24 – Algebra: Algebraic fractions and functions

Exercise 24A

1 a $\dfrac{5x}{6}$ **b** $\dfrac{23x}{20}$ **c** $\dfrac{x^2y + 8}{4x}$

d $\dfrac{5x + 7}{6}$ **e** $\dfrac{13x + 5}{15}$ **f** $\dfrac{5x - 10}{4}$

2 a $\dfrac{11x}{20}$ **b** $\dfrac{3x - 2y}{6}$ **c** $\dfrac{xy^2 - 8}{4y}$

d $\dfrac{x + 1}{4}$ **e** $\dfrac{x - 1}{4}$ **f** $\dfrac{2 - 3x}{4}$

3 a $x = 3$ **b** $x = 2$ **c** $x = 0.75$ **d** $x = 3$

4 a $\dfrac{x^2}{6}$ **b** $\dfrac{8}{3}$ **c** $\dfrac{x^2 - 2x}{10}$

d $\dfrac{2x^2 + x}{15}$ **e** $\dfrac{1}{2x}$

5 a $\dfrac{x}{y}$ **b** $\dfrac{2xy}{3}$ **c** $\dfrac{2x^2 - 12x + 18}{75}$

d 1 **e** $\dfrac{1}{4x + 2}$ **f** $\dfrac{x^2 - 5x + 6}{48}$

g $\dfrac{1}{2x}$

6 a x **b** $\dfrac{x}{2}$ **c** $\dfrac{3x^2}{16}$ **d** 3

e $\dfrac{17x + 1}{10}$ **f** $\dfrac{13x + 9}{10}$ **g** $\dfrac{3x^2 - 5x - 2}{10}$

h $\dfrac{x + 3}{2}$ **i** $\dfrac{2}{3}$ **j** $\dfrac{2x^2 - 6y^2}{9}$

7 All parts: students' own working

8 a $\dfrac{x^2 - 8}{x^2 - 2}$ **b** 7

9 $\dfrac{x^2 + 14x + 37}{x^3 + 12x^2 + 47x + 60}$

10 $\dfrac{x + 3}{x - 6}$

11 First, he did not factorise and just cancelled the x^2s. Then he cancelled 2 and 6 with the wrong signs. Then he said two minuses make a plus when adding, which is not true.

12 $\dfrac{2x^2 + x - 3}{4x^2 - 9}$

13 a 3, −1.5 **b** 4, −1.25 **c** 3, −2.5 **d** 0, 1

14 a $\dfrac{x - 1}{2x + 1}$ **b** $\dfrac{2x + 1}{x + 3}$ **c** $\dfrac{2x - 1}{3x - 2}$

d $\dfrac{x + 1}{x - 1}$ **e** $\dfrac{2x + 5}{4x - 1}$

15 a Proof **b** 2 or $\dfrac{-10}{3}$

16 a Proof **b** 2 m/s

17 a $x^3 + 3\sqrt{2}\, x^2 + 6x + 2\sqrt{2}$
b Proof **c** $99 + 70\sqrt{2}$

18 a $\dfrac{72 - 4x^2}{(x + 3)^2 (x - 3)^2}$

b $\dfrac{4x^3 + 40x^2 + 122x + 110}{(x + 1)(x + 2)(x + 3)(x + 4)}$

19 $\dfrac{x - \sqrt{3}}{x - 3\sqrt{3}}$

Exercise 24B

1 a $c = \dfrac{p}{5} + 3$ or $\dfrac{p + 15}{5}$ **b** $c = \dfrac{15}{5 - p}$

2 a $G = \dfrac{R}{F} - 3$ or $\dfrac{R - 3F}{F}$

b $G = \dfrac{R - 3F}{F - 1}$ or $\dfrac{3F - R}{1 - F}$

3 a $a = \dfrac{b(q + p)}{q - p}$ **b** $b = \dfrac{a(q - p)}{q + p}$

c $a = \dfrac{b + 5c}{4}$ **d** $r = \dfrac{A}{\pi(2h + k)}$

e $v = \dfrac{u}{\sqrt{(1 - a)}}$ **f** $x = \dfrac{2R - 3}{R - 1}$

4 a $r = \dfrac{P}{\pi + 2k}$ **b** $r = \sqrt{\dfrac{2A}{\pi + \sqrt{(k^2 - 1)}}}$

5 $P = \dfrac{100A}{100 + RY}$

6 a $b = \dfrac{Ra}{a - R}$ **b** $a = \dfrac{Rb}{b - R}$

7 a $x = \dfrac{2 + 2y}{y - 1}$

b $y - 1 = \dfrac{4}{x-2}$, $(x-2)(y-1) = 4$, $x - 2 =$

  $\dfrac{4}{y-1}$, $x = 2 + \dfrac{4}{y-1}$

c $y = 1 + \dfrac{4}{x-2} = \dfrac{x-2+4}{x-2} = \dfrac{x+2}{x-2}$ and

  $x = \dfrac{2+2y}{y-1}$

d Same formulae as in **a**

8 a Cannot take r as a common factor

 b $\pi = \dfrac{3V}{r^2(2r+3h)}$

 c Yes, $r = \sqrt[3]{\dfrac{3V}{5\pi}}$

9 $x = \dfrac{2W - 2zy}{z + y}$

10 $x = \dfrac{1 - 3y}{2y - 5}$

The first number at the top of the answer is the constant term on the top of the original.
The coefficient of y at the top of the answer is the negative constant term on the bottom of the original.
The coefficient of y at the bottom of the answer is the coefficient of x on the bottom of the original.
The constant term on the bottom is negative the coefficient of x on the top of the original.

11 a Both are correct
 b Alice's answer is easier to substitute into

Exercise 24C

1 a i 8 **ii** 14 **iii** 2 **iv** 4
 b i 36 **ii** −9 **iii** 1241 **iv** −1.5

2 a 6 **b** $\dfrac{x+7}{4} - 3$ **c** 45

3 a 29 **b** 218 **c** 7.832

4 7

5 a 25 **b** 249 **c** 15 **d** 1807
 e 1807 **f** 13 **g** ±5

6 a 9 **b** −39 **c** −56 **d** −56
 e 12 **f** 24.84 **g** ±5

7 a i 54 **ii** 44 **b** 6 and −1

Exercise 24D

1 a $f^{-1}(x) = \dfrac{x+5}{4}$ **b** $f^{-1}(x) = \sqrt[3]{x-2}$

 c $f^{-1}(x) = \dfrac{10}{x} - 1$ **d** $f^{-1}(x) = \dfrac{10-x}{2}$

 e $f^{-1}(x) = 6x + 7$ **f** $f^{-1}(x) = \dfrac{3}{x-5}$

2 a $f^{-1}(x) = \dfrac{5x+2}{3x-1}$ **b** $-\dfrac{3}{2}$ **c** $f^{-1}(-\tfrac{3}{2}) = 1$

3 a Both inverse functions are the same as the original function.

b The inverse function is the same as the original function.
c Proof

Exercise 24E

1 a $8\tfrac{1}{2}$ **b** $6\tfrac{1}{2}$ **c** 43 **d** −2.25 **e** 5.8

2 a 48 **b** 229 **c** 18
 d 29 **e** −8 **f** −141

3 a i $4x^3 - 32$ **ii** $11 - 4x$
  iii $21 - 27x + 9x^2 - x^3$
  iv $16x - 40$
  v $x^9 - 18x^6 + 108x^3 - 222$
 b $gh(x) = 4 - 4x$, $hg(x) = 11 - 4x$, $4 - 4x \neq 11 - 4x$

4 $\tfrac{1}{2}(b+1)$

Exercise 24F

1 $x_2 = 4$ $x_3 = -10$ $x_4 = 88$ $x_5 = -598$

2 a 1878 **b** −4372 **c** −54.048 **d** 3

3 5.0701

4 $x_2 = 3.1414$ $x_3 = 3.1745$ $x_4 = 3.1821$
  $x_5 = 3.1839$ $x_6 = 3.1843$

5 a $2.115 = 2.12$ (2 dp)
 b $f(2.12) = 0.03$ (2 dp)

6 Proof

7 a 3 and 7
 b 7
 c i Converges on 7
  ii Diverges, towards square root of a negative
  iii Converges on 7 **iv** stays on 3
 d $x < 3$: diverges, towards square root of a negative
  $x = 3$: stays on 3
  $x > 7$: converges on 7

8 a Proof
 b $x_2 = \tfrac{7}{2}$, $x_3 = 3$, $x_4 = \tfrac{7}{2}$
 c $x_2 = \tfrac{29}{9}$, $x_3 = \tfrac{13}{4}$, $x_4 = \tfrac{29}{9}$
 d $x_2 = \tfrac{73}{23}$, $x_3 = \tfrac{33}{10}$, $x_4 = \tfrac{73}{23}$
 e $x_2 = 1 + \sqrt{5}$, $x_3 = 1 + \sqrt{5}$, $x_4 = 1 + \sqrt{5}$
 f $x = 1 + \sqrt{5}$

9 a Proof **b** 67 cm²
 c This will depend upon how accurate the final value of x_{n+1} is

10 a 1 **b** 3

11 a Oscillates between 8.046, 0.148 and −2.262
 b Diverges
 c Converges on 2.707

Review questions

1 8

2 **a** $x = \dfrac{a + K}{C + 6}$ **b** 3.5

3 **a** $\dfrac{x + 3}{x}$ **b** $f^{-1}(x) = \dfrac{3}{x - 1}$

4 $\dfrac{7x}{3x + 1}$

5 **a** $x_1 = 2.54$, $x_2 = 2.57$, $x_3 = 2.58$, $x_4 = 2.59$
   b 2.59 – it's the same

6 **a** $fg(x) = 3x^3 + 14$ **b** $3 \times 3^3 + 14 = 95$

7 **a** $f^{-1}(x) = \dfrac{x + q}{p}$ **b** $f^{-1}(x) = \sqrt[3]{a - x}$

   c $f^{-1}(x) = \dfrac{a}{x} - c$

8 **a** **i** 2   **ii** 8   **iii** 18
   iv 32   **v** 50
   b $2n^2$

9 Proof

10 **a** $\dfrac{2x + 7}{x - 3}$ **b** $\dfrac{5}{6}$ or 16

11 $2 - 3xy = 4 - x$
   mistake here expanding the brackets
   $x = \dfrac{1 - 3y}{2}$ should be 2 divided by $(1 - 3y)$
   corrected: $y = \dfrac{4 - x}{2 - 3x}$
   $y(2 - 3x) = 4 - x$
   $2y - 3xy = 4 - x$
   $x - 3xy = 4 - 2y$
   $x(1 - 3y) = 4 - 2y$
   $x = \dfrac{4 - 2y}{1 - 3y}$
   Hence $f^{-1}(x) = \dfrac{4 - 2x}{1 - 3x}$

12 **i** $\dfrac{3}{4}$ **ii** $-\dfrac{2}{3}$ **iii** 5   **iv** $\dfrac{8}{5}$

13 $-\dfrac{4}{x + 1}$

14 **a** 9.51, –10.5
   b $x \le 10$, $x \ge 28$
   c $-10 < x < 10$

15 **a** Proof   **b** 5.31

16 **a** 21   **b** $a = -3$, $b = 2$

17 **a** Proof   **b** 12

Chapter 25 – Geometry and measures: Vector geometry

Exercise 25A

1 **a** Any three of: $\overrightarrow{AC}$, $\overrightarrow{CF}$, $\overrightarrow{BD}$, $\overrightarrow{DG}$, $\overrightarrow{GI}$, $\overrightarrow{EH}$, $\overrightarrow{HJ}$, $\overrightarrow{JK}$
   b Any three of: $\overrightarrow{BE}$, $\overrightarrow{AD}$, $\overrightarrow{DH}$, $\overrightarrow{CG}$, $\overrightarrow{GJ}$, $\overrightarrow{FI}$, $\overrightarrow{IK}$

   c Any three of: $\overrightarrow{AO}$, $\overrightarrow{CA}$, $\overrightarrow{FC}$, $\overrightarrow{IG}$, $\overrightarrow{GD}$, $\overrightarrow{DB}$, $\overrightarrow{KJ}$, $\overrightarrow{JH}$, $\overrightarrow{HE}$
   d Any three of: $\overrightarrow{BO}$, $\overrightarrow{EB}$, $\overrightarrow{HD}$, $\overrightarrow{DA}$, $\overrightarrow{JG}$, $\overrightarrow{GC}$, $\overrightarrow{KI}$, $\overrightarrow{IF}$

2 **a** 2**a**   **b** 2**b**   **c** **a** + **b**
   d 2**a** + **b**   **e** 2**a** + 2**b**   **f** **a** + 2**b**
   g **a** + **b**   **h** 2**a** + 2**b**   **i** 3**a** + **b**
   j 2**a**   **k** **b**   **l** 2**a** + **b**

3 **a** Equal   **b** $\overrightarrow{AI}$, $\overrightarrow{BJ}$, $\overrightarrow{DK}$

4 **a** $\overrightarrow{OJ} = 2\overrightarrow{OD}$ and parallel
   b $\overrightarrow{AK}$ **c** $\overrightarrow{OF}$, $\overrightarrow{BI}$, $\overrightarrow{EK}$

5

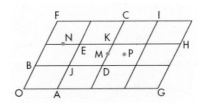

6 **a** Lie on same straight line
   b All multiples of **a** + **b** and start at O
   c H

7 **a** –**b**   **b** 3**a** – **b**   **c** 2**a** – **b**
   d **a** – **b**   **e** **a** + **b**   **f** –**a** – **b**
   g 2**a** – **b**   **h** –**a** – 2**b**   **i** **a** + 2**b**
   j –**a** + **b**   **k** 2**a** – 2**b**   **l** **a** – 2**b**

8 **a** Equal but in opposite directions
   b Any three of: $\overrightarrow{DA}$, $\overrightarrow{EF}$, $\overrightarrow{GJ}$, $\overrightarrow{FI}$, $\overrightarrow{AH}$

9 **a** Opposite direction and $\overrightarrow{AB} = -\frac{1}{2}\overrightarrow{CK}$
   b $\overrightarrow{BJ}$, $\overrightarrow{CK}$
   c $\overrightarrow{EB}$, $\overrightarrow{GO}$, $\overrightarrow{KH}$

10 506 mph on a bearing of 009°

11 12 km/h on a bearing of 107°

12 **a i** **a** + **b**   **ii** 3**a** + **b**
   iii 2**a** – **b**   **iv** 2**b** – 2**a**
   b $\overrightarrow{DG}$ and $\overrightarrow{BC}$

13 Parts **b** and **d** could be, parts **a** and **c** could not be

14 **a** Any multiple (positive or negative) of 3**a** – **b**
   b Will be a multiple of 3**a** – **b**

15 For example, let ABCD be a quadrilateral as shown.

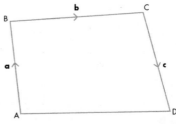

Then $\overrightarrow{AD} = \overrightarrow{AB} + \overrightarrow{BD} = \mathbf{a} + (\mathbf{b} + \mathbf{c})$.

But $\overrightarrow{AD} = \overrightarrow{AC} + \overrightarrow{CD} = (\mathbf{a} + \mathbf{b}) + \mathbf{c}$.
Hence $\mathbf{a} + (\mathbf{b} + \mathbf{c}) = (\mathbf{a} + \mathbf{b}) + \mathbf{c}$.

16 a i $2\mathbf{b} - 2\mathbf{a}$ **ii** $\mathbf{a} - \mathbf{c}$
      iii $2\mathbf{c} - 2\mathbf{b}$ **iv** $\mathbf{b} + \mathbf{c} - \mathbf{a}$

   b $\overrightarrow{RQ} = \mathbf{a} - \mathbf{c} = \overrightarrow{SP}$, similarly $\overrightarrow{PQ} = b = \overrightarrow{SR}$, so opposite sides are equal and parallel, hence PQRS is a parallelogram

Exercise 25B

1 a i $-\mathbf{a} + \mathbf{b}$ **ii** $\frac{1}{2}(-\mathbf{a} + \mathbf{b})$
      iii

      iv $\frac{1}{2}\mathbf{a} + \frac{1}{2}\mathbf{b}$

   b i $\mathbf{a} - \mathbf{b}$ **ii** $\frac{1}{2}\mathbf{a} - \frac{1}{2}\mathbf{b}$
      iii

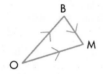

      iv $\frac{1}{2}\mathbf{a} + \frac{1}{2}\mathbf{b}$

   c

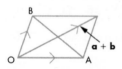

   d M is midpoint of parallelogram of which OA and OB are two sides.

2 a i $-\mathbf{a} - \mathbf{b}$ **ii** $-\frac{1}{2}\mathbf{a} - \frac{1}{2}\mathbf{b}$
      iii

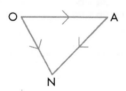

      iv $\frac{1}{2}\mathbf{a} - \frac{1}{2}\mathbf{b}$

   b i $\mathbf{b} + \mathbf{a}$ **ii** $\frac{1}{2}\mathbf{b} + \frac{1}{2}\mathbf{a}$
      iii

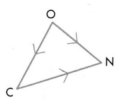

      iv $\frac{1}{2}\mathbf{a} - \frac{1}{2}\mathbf{b}$

c

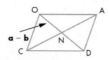

   d N is midpoint of parallelogram of which OA and OC are two sides

3 a i $-\mathbf{a} + \mathbf{b}$ **ii** $\frac{1}{3}(-\mathbf{a} + \mathbf{b})$ **iii** $\frac{2}{3}\mathbf{a} + \frac{1}{3}\mathbf{b}$

   b $\frac{3}{4}\mathbf{a} + \frac{1}{4}\mathbf{b}$

4 a i $\frac{2}{3}\mathbf{b}$ **ii** $\frac{1}{2}\mathbf{a} + \frac{1}{2}\mathbf{b}$ **iii** $-\frac{2}{3}\mathbf{b}$

   b $\frac{1}{2}\mathbf{a} - \frac{1}{6}\mathbf{b}$

   c $\overrightarrow{DE} = \overrightarrow{DO} + \overrightarrow{OE}$
          $= \frac{3}{2}\mathbf{a} - \frac{1}{2}\mathbf{b}$

   d $\overrightarrow{DE}$ parallel to $\overrightarrow{CD}$ (multiple of $\overrightarrow{CD}$) and D is a common point

5 a

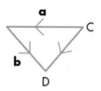

   $\overrightarrow{CD} = -\mathbf{a} + \mathbf{b} = \mathbf{b} - \mathbf{a}$
   b i $-\mathbf{a}$ **ii** $-\mathbf{b}$ **iii** $\mathbf{a} - \mathbf{b}$
   c 0, vectors return to starting point
   d i $2\mathbf{b}$ **ii** $2\mathbf{b} - 2\mathbf{a}$ **iii** $-2\mathbf{a}$
      iv $2\mathbf{b} - \mathbf{a}$ **v** $-\mathbf{a} - \mathbf{b}$

6 a

   $\overrightarrow{CX} = \sqrt{1^2 + 1^2}\ \mathbf{b} = \sqrt{2}\ \mathbf{b}$
   $\overrightarrow{CD} = \overrightarrow{CX} + \overrightarrow{XD} = \sqrt{2}\ \mathbf{b} - \mathbf{a}$
   b

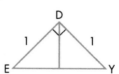

   $\overrightarrow{YE} = \sqrt{1^2 + 1^2}\ \mathbf{a} = \sqrt{2}\ \mathbf{a}$
   $\overrightarrow{DE} = \overrightarrow{DY} + \overrightarrow{YE} = \mathbf{b} - \sqrt{2}\ \mathbf{a}$
   c i $-\mathbf{a}$ **ii** $-\mathbf{b}$
      iii $\mathbf{a} - \sqrt{2}\ \mathbf{b}$ **iv** $\sqrt{2}\ \mathbf{a} - \mathbf{b}$
      v $\sqrt{2}\ \mathbf{a} + \mathbf{a}$ **vi** $\sqrt{2}\ \mathbf{b} + \mathbf{b}$
      vii $2\mathbf{b} + \sqrt{2}\ \mathbf{b} - \mathbf{a} - \sqrt{2}\ \mathbf{a}$
      viii $2\mathbf{b} + \sqrt{2}\ \mathbf{b} - 2\mathbf{a} - \sqrt{2}\ \mathbf{a}$

7 a i $-\mathbf{a} + \mathbf{b}$ **ii** $\frac{1}{2}(-\mathbf{a} + \mathbf{b}) = -\frac{1}{2}\mathbf{a} + \frac{1}{2}\mathbf{b}$

iii $\frac{1}{2}\mathbf{a} + \frac{1}{2}\mathbf{b}$

b i $\frac{1}{2}\mathbf{b} + \frac{1}{2}\mathbf{c}$ **ii** $-\frac{1}{2}\mathbf{a} + \frac{1}{2}\mathbf{c}$

c i $-\frac{1}{2}\mathbf{a} + \frac{1}{2}\mathbf{c}$ **ii** Equal

iii Parallelogram

d $\overrightarrow{AC} = -\mathbf{a} + \mathbf{c} = 2(-\frac{1}{2}\mathbf{a} + \frac{1}{2}\mathbf{c}) = 2\,\overrightarrow{QM}$

8 a i $\frac{1}{2}\mathbf{a}$ **ii** $\mathbf{c} - \mathbf{a}$

iii $\frac{1}{2}\mathbf{a} + \frac{1}{2}\mathbf{c}$ **iv** $\frac{1}{2}\mathbf{c}$

b i $-\frac{1}{2}\mathbf{a} + \frac{1}{2}\mathbf{b}$ **ii** $-\frac{1}{2}\mathbf{a} + \frac{1}{2}\mathbf{b}$

c Opposite sides are equal and parallel

d NMRQ and PNLR

9 a $-\frac{1}{2}\mathbf{a} + \frac{1}{2}\mathbf{b}$

b i Rhombus

ii They lie on a straight line, $\overrightarrow{OM} = \frac{1}{2}\overrightarrow{OC}$

10 $k = 8$

11 a $\overrightarrow{YW} = \overrightarrow{YZ} + \overrightarrow{ZW} = 2\mathbf{a} + \mathbf{b} + \mathbf{a} + 2\mathbf{b}$
$= 3\mathbf{a} + 3\mathbf{b} = 3(\mathbf{a} + \mathbf{b}) = 3\overrightarrow{XY}$

b $3 : 1$

c They lie on a straight line.

d Points are A(6, 2), B(1, 1) and C(2, 24). Using Pythagoras' theorem, $AB^2 = 26$, $BC^2 = 26$ and $AC^2 = 52$ so $AB^2 + BC^2 = AC^2$ hence $\angle ABC$ must be a right angle.

12 In parallelogram ABCD, $\overrightarrow{AB} = \overrightarrow{DC} = \mathbf{a}$, $\overrightarrow{BC} = \overrightarrow{AD}$ $= \mathbf{b}$. Let X be the midpoint of diagonal AC. Then
$\overrightarrow{DX} = -\mathbf{b} + \frac{1}{2}(\mathbf{a} + \mathbf{b}) = \frac{1}{2}(\mathbf{a} - \mathbf{b}) = \frac{1}{2}\overrightarrow{DB}$ which
is $\mathbf{a} - \mathbf{b}$, hence the midpoint of one diagonal is the same as the midpoint of the other diagonal, hence they bisect each other.

Review questions

1 a $2\mathbf{b} - \mathbf{a}$ **b** $-3\mathbf{b}$ **c** $\mathbf{a} + \mathbf{b}$

2 a i $2\mathbf{y} - 2\mathbf{b}$ **ii** $2\mathbf{b} - 2\mathbf{x}$

b $\overrightarrow{WZ} = \overrightarrow{WB} + \overrightarrow{BZ} = \frac{1}{2}(2\mathbf{b} - 2\mathbf{x}) + \frac{1}{2}(2\mathbf{y} - 2\mathbf{b})$
$= \mathbf{b} - \mathbf{x} + \mathbf{y} - \mathbf{b} = \mathbf{y} - \mathbf{x}$

c $\overrightarrow{XY} = \mathbf{y} - \mathbf{x}$, so parallel and equal in length to WZ, so Tim must be correct.

3 Let $\overrightarrow{OF} = \mathbf{x} = \overrightarrow{DE}$ and $\overrightarrow{OD} = \mathbf{y} = \overrightarrow{FE}$, then
$\overrightarrow{DF} = \mathbf{x} - \mathbf{y}$ and $\overrightarrow{AB} = \frac{1}{2}\mathbf{x} - \frac{1}{2}\mathbf{y} = \frac{1}{2}(\mathbf{x} - \mathbf{y})$

4 a i $\mathbf{p} + \mathbf{r}$ **ii** $\mathbf{r} - \mathbf{p}$

b $\frac{1}{2}(\mathbf{r} - \mathbf{p})$

c $\overrightarrow{OX} = \mathbf{p} + \frac{1}{2}(\mathbf{r} - \mathbf{p}) = \frac{1}{2}(\mathbf{p} + \mathbf{r}) = \frac{1}{2}\overrightarrow{OQ}$

5 a i $\mathbf{y} - \mathbf{x}$ **ii** $\frac{1}{2}(\mathbf{y} - \mathbf{x})$ **iii** $\frac{1}{2}(\mathbf{x} + \mathbf{y})$

iv $\frac{1}{3}(\mathbf{x} + \mathbf{y})$ **v** $-\frac{1}{6}(\mathbf{x} + \mathbf{y})$ **vi** $\frac{1}{3}(\mathbf{y} - 2\mathbf{x})$

vii $\frac{1}{2}\mathbf{y} - \mathbf{x}$

b $\overrightarrow{BG} = \frac{1}{3}(\mathbf{y} - 2\mathbf{x})$ and $\overrightarrow{BE} = \frac{1}{2}\mathbf{y} - \mathbf{x}$
$= \frac{1}{2}(\mathbf{y} - 2\mathbf{x})$, both are multiples of $(\mathbf{y} - 2\mathbf{x})$ so are parallel, and with a common point, they must all be collinear.

c $\frac{2}{3}\overrightarrow{BE} = \frac{2}{3} \times \frac{1}{2}(\mathbf{y} - 2\mathbf{x}) = \frac{1}{3}(\mathbf{y} - 2\mathbf{x}) = \overrightarrow{BG}$

6 a i $\mathbf{x} + \mathbf{y}$ **ii** $\frac{1}{3}(\mathbf{x} + \mathbf{y})$ **iii** $\frac{2}{3}(\mathbf{x} + \mathbf{y})$

iv $\frac{1}{3}(\mathbf{x} - 2\mathbf{y})$ **v** $\frac{1}{3}(\mathbf{x} - 2\mathbf{y})$

b $\overrightarrow{SA} = \frac{1}{3}(\mathbf{x} - 2\mathbf{y}) = \overrightarrow{BQ}$, $\overrightarrow{SB} = \overrightarrow{SA} + \overrightarrow{AB}$, $\overrightarrow{AQ}$
$= \overrightarrow{AB} + \overrightarrow{BQ} = \overrightarrow{AB} + \overrightarrow{SA}$, hence $\overrightarrow{SB} = \overrightarrow{AQ}$, hence SAQB has opposite sides equal and parallel, so a parallelogram.

7 a i $6\mathbf{a} - 2\mathbf{b}$ **ii** $3\mathbf{a} - \mathbf{b}$

b $\overrightarrow{BP} = 2(3\mathbf{a} - \mathbf{b})$ hence it is parallel to BQ with a common point Q, so the points B, Q and P are collinear.

8 In triangle ABC the midpoint of AB is M and the midpoint of AC is N
Let $\overrightarrow{AM} = \mathbf{x}$ and $\overrightarrow{AN} = \mathbf{y}$, then $\overrightarrow{MN} = \mathbf{y} - \mathbf{x}$, AB = $2\mathbf{x}$ and AC = $2\mathbf{y}$, so $\overrightarrow{BC} = 2\mathbf{y} - 2\mathbf{x} = 2(\mathbf{y} - \mathbf{x})$. $\overrightarrow{BC}$
is a multiple of $\overrightarrow{MN}$ and so parallel, $\overrightarrow{MN} = \frac{1}{2}\overrightarrow{BC}$
and so half its length.

9 a $\mathbf{m} - \mathbf{r}$

b $\overrightarrow{RT} = 2\overrightarrow{RM} = 2(\mathbf{m} - \mathbf{r})$, so $\overrightarrow{NT} = -2\mathbf{m} + 2\mathbf{m} -$ $2\mathbf{r} = -2\mathbf{r}$, parallel to $\mathbf{r}$, hence NT is parallel to OR.